SUPPLEMENT XIV
Cleanth Brooks to Logan Pearsall Smith

American Writers
A Collection of Literary Biographies

JAY PARINI
Editor in Chief

SUPPLEMENT XIV
Cleanth Brooks to Logan Pearsall Smith

CHARLES SCRIBNER'S SONS

An imprint of Thomson Gale, a part of The Thomson Corporation

THOMSON

GALE

Detroit • New York • San Francisco • San Diego • New Haven, Conn. • Waterville, Maine • London • Munich

American Writers, Supplement XIV
Jay Parini, Editor in Chief

LIBRARY OF CONGRESS CATALOGING-IN-PUBLICATION DATA

American writers : a collection of literary biographies / Leonard Unger, editor in chief.
    p. cm.
    The 4-vol. main set consists of 97 of the pamphlets originally published as the University of Minnesota pamphlets on American writers; some have been rev. and updated. The supplements cover writers not included in the original series.
    Supplement 2, has editor in chief, A. Walton Litz; Retrospective suppl. 1, c1998, was edited by A. Walton Litz & Molly Weigel; Suppl. 5 has editor-in-chief, Jay Parini.
    Includes bibliographies and index.
    Contents: v. 1. Henry Adams to T.S. Eliot — v. 2. Ralph Waldo Emerson to Carson McCullers — v. 3. Archibald MacLeish to George Santayana — v. 4. Isaac Bashevis Singer to Richard Wright — Supplement[s]: 1, pt. 1. Jane Addams to Sidney Lanier. 1, pt. 2. Vachel Lindsay to Elinor Wylie. 2, pt. 1. W.H. Auden to O. Henry. 2, pt. 2. Robinson Jeffers to Yvor Winters. — 4, pt. 1. Maya Angelou to Linda Hogan. 4, pt. 2. Susan Howe to Gore Vidal — Suppl. 5. Russell Banks to Charles Wright
.   ISBN 0-684-19785-5 (set) — ISBN 0-684-13662-7
    1. American literature—History and criticism. 2. American literature—Bio-bibliography. 3. Authors, American—Biography. I. Unger, Leonard. II. Litz, A. Walton. III. Weigel, Molly. IV. Parini, Jay. V. University of Minnesota pamphlets on American writers.

PS129 .A55
810'.9
[B]
        73-001759

ISBN: 0-684-31234-4

Printed in the United States of America
10 9 8 7 6 5 4 3 2 1

Editorial and Production Staff

Project Editor
JULIE KEPPEN
LARRY TRUDEAU

Copyeditors
LISA DIXON
JEFF HILL
ROBERT JONES
JANET PATTERSON
LINDA SANDERS

Proofreader
PATRICIA ONORATO

Permission Researchers
LORI HINES
EMMA HULL
JULIE VAN PELT

Indexer
KATHARYN DUNHAM

Compositor
GARY LEACH

Publisher
FRANK MENCHACA

Acknowledgments

Acknowledgment is gratefully made to those publishers and individuals who have permitted the use of the following material in copyright. Every effort has been made to secure permission to reprint copyrighted material.

CLEANTH BROOKS Excerpts from *The Well Wrought Urn: Studies in the Structure of Poetry*. Harvest Book, 1947. Copyright © 1947, renewed 1975 by Cleanth Brooks. Reproduced by permission of Harcourt, Inc.

JAMES LEE BURKE Excerpts from *Epoch*, v. 43, 1994 for "Water People" by James Lee Burke. Copyright © 1994 by Cornell University. Reproduced by permission of the author.

JOHN JAY CHAPMAN Excerpts from "Excerpts from Letters," in *John Jay Chapman and His Letters*. Edited By Mark Anthony DeWolfe Howe. Houghton Mifflin, 1937. Copyright © 1937 by M. A. DeWolfe Howe. Renewed 1964 by Quincy Howe, Helen Howe Allen and Mark Dew Howe. Reproduced by permission.

EVAN S. CONNELL Excerpts from *Los Angeles Times Magazine*, June 9, 1991. Copyright 1991 by Los Angeles Times. Reproduced by permission. Reproduced by permission. Connell, Evan S. From "Evan S. Connell," in *Contemporary Authors Autobiography Series, Vol. 2*. Edited by Adele Sarkissian. Gale Research Company, 1985. Copyright © 1985 by Gale Research Company. Reproduced by permission of The Gale Group. Connell, Evan S. From *Mrs. Bridge*. The Viking Press, 1958. Copyright © 1958, 1959 by Evan S. Connell, Jr. All rights reserved. Reproduced by permission of Don Congdon Associates, Inc. Connell, Evan. S. From *The Anatomy Lesson and Other Stories*. Viking, 1957. © 1957. Renewed 1985 by Evan S. Connell, Jr. Reprinted by permission of Don Congdon Associates. Inc. Hass, Robert. From *Twentieth Century Pleasure: Prose on Poetry*. The Ecco Press, 1984. Copyright © 1984 by Robert Hass. All rights reserved. Reproduced by permission of HarperCollins Publishers, Inc.

JOSEPH EPSTEIN Excerpts from *The American Scholar*, v. 44, autumn, 1975; v. 60, summer, 1991. Copyright © 1975, 1991 by Joseph Epstein. Reproduced by permission of the publisher. *Book World*, 1971, for "The Minnesota Fats of American Prose: A. J. Liebling" by Joseph Epstein. Copyright © 1971 by Washington Post Book World Service/Washington Post Writers Group. Reproduced by permission of the author. *Hudson Review*, v. 44, 1991 for "The Academic Zoo— In Theory and Practice" by Joseph Epstein. Copyright © 1991 by The Hudson Review, Inc. Reproduced by permission of the author. Epstein, Joseph. From *Narcissus Leaves the Pool: Familiar Essays*. Houghton Mifflin,

1999. Copyright © 1999 by Joseph Epstein. All rights reserved. Reproduced by permission of Georges Borchardt, Inc., for the author. Epstein, Joseph. From *Snobbery, the American Version*. Houghton Mifflin, 2002. Copyright © 2002 by Joseph Epstein. Reproduced by permission of Houghton Mifflin Company and Georges Borchardt, Inc., for the author.

SARA HENDERSON HAY Excerpts from *A Footing on This Earth*. Doubleday & Company, Inc. 1966. Copyright © 1966 by Sara Henderson Hay. All rights reserved. Reproduced by permission of Carnegie Mellon University.

HERBERT HUNCKE Excerpts from "Elsie John," in *The Herbert Huncke Reader.*. Edited by Benjamin G. Schafter. William Morrow and Company, Inc. 1997. Copyright © 1997 by the Estate of Herbert E. Huncke, Jerome Poynton, Executor. All rights reserved. Reproduced by permission. Foye, Raymond. From "Excerpts from Guilty of Everything," in *The Herbert Huncke Reader*. Edited by Benjamin G. Schafter. William Morrow and Company, Inc. 1997. Copyright © 1997 by the Estate of Herbert E. Huncke, Jerome Poynton, Executor. All rights reserved. Reproduced by permission. Foye, Raymond. From "Hallowe'en," in *The Herbert Huncke Reader*. Edited by Benjamin G. Schafter. William Morrow and Company, Inc. 1997. Copyright © 1997 by the Estate of Herbert E. Huncke, Jerome Poynton, Executor. All rights reserved. Reproduced by permission. Foye, Raymond. From "In the Park," in *The Herbert Huncke Reader*. Edited by Benjamin G. Schafter. William Morrow and Company, Inc. 1997. Copyright © 1997 by the Estate of Herbert E. Huncke, Jerome Poynton, Executor. All rights reserved. Reproduced by permission. Foye, Raymond. From "Introduction," in *The Herbert Huncke Reader*. Edited by Benjamin G. Schafter. William Morrow and Company, Inc. 1997. Copyright © 1997 by Raymond Foye. All rights reserved. Reproduced by permission of the author. Foye, Raymond. From "Joseph Martinez," in *The Herbert Huncke Reader*. Edited by Benjamin G. Schafter. William Morrow and Company, Inc. 1997. Copyright © 1997 by the Estate of Herbert E. Huncke, Jerome Poynton, Executor. All rights reserved. Reproduced by permission. Foye, Raymond. From "Kerouac," in *The Herbert Huncke Reader*. Edited by Benjamin G. Schafter. William Morrow and Company, Inc. 1997. Copyright © 1997 by the Estate of Herbert E. Huncke, Jerome Poynton, Executor. All rights reserved. Reproduced by permission. Foye, Raymond. From "Ponderosa Pine," in *The Herbert Huncke Reader*. Edited by Benjamin G. Schafter. William Morrow and Company, Inc. 1997. Copyright © 1997 by the Estate of Herbert E. Huncke, Jerome Poynton, Executor. All rights reserved. Reproduced by permission. Foye, Raymond. From "Sea Voyage," in *The Herbert*

Press, 1976. Copyright © 1976 by Charles Reznikoff. Reproduced by permission of Black Sparrow Books, an imprint of David R. Godine, Publisher. Reznikoff, Charles. From Poem 19, in I "Rhythms, 1918," from *Poems 1918—1936: Volume 1 of the Complete Poems of Charles Reznikoff.* Edited by Seamus Cooney. Black Sparrow Press, 1976. Copyright © 1976 by Charles Reznikoff. Reproduced by permission of Black Sparrow Books, an imprint of David R. Godine, Publisher. Reznikoff, Charles. From Poem 22 in III "Poems 1920," in *Poems 1918—1936: Volume I of the Complete Poems of Charles Reznikoff.* Edited by Seamus Cooney. Black Sparrow Press, 1976. Copyright © 1976 by Charles Reznikoff. Reproduced by permission of Black Sparrow Press, an imprint of David R. Godine, Publisher. Reznikoff, Charles. From Poem 39 in VII "Jerusalem the Golden, 1934," in *Poems 1918—1939: Volume I of the Complete Poems of Charles Reznikoff.* Edited by Seamus Cooney. Black Sparrow Press, 1976. Copyright © 1976 by Charles Reznikoff. Reproduced by permission of Black Sparrow Books, an imprint of David R. Godine, Publisher. Reznikoff, Charles. From Poem 6, in II "Rhythms II, 1919," in *Poems 1918—1936: Volume I of the Complete Poems of Charles Reznikoff.* Edited by Seamus Cooney. Black Sparrow Press, 1976. Copyright © 1976 by Charles Reznikoff. Reproduced by permission of Black Sparrow Books, an imprint of David R. Godine, Publisher. Reznikoff, Charles. From *Testimony: The United States: 1885—1890.* New Directions—San Francisco Review, 1965. Copyright © 1965 by Charles Reznikoff. Reproduced by permission of New Directions Publishing Corp. Reznikoff, Charles. From *Testimony: Volume I, The United States 1885—1915 Recitative.* Black Sparrow Press, 1978. Copyright © 1965, 1968 by Charles Reznikoff. Copyright © 1978 by Marie Syrkin. Reproduced by permission of Black Sparrow Books, an imprint of David R. Godine, Publisher. Reznikoff, Charles. From "Twilight," in II "Rhythms II, 1919," in *Poems 1918—1936: Volume I of the Complete Poems of Charles Reznikoff.* Edited by

Seamus Cooney. Black Sparrow Press, 1976. Copyright © 1976 by Charles Reznikoff. Reproduced by permission of Black Sparrow Books, an imprint of David R. Godine, Publisher. Syrkin, Marie. From "Charles: A Memoir," in *Charles Reznikoff: Man and Poet.* Edited by Milton Hindus. National Poetry Foundation, 1984. Reproduced by permission of the author.

RICHARD RODRIGUEZ Excerpts from *Insight and Outlook,* 1997 for "A View from the Melting Pot: An Interview with Richard Rodriguez," by Scott London. Copyright © 1997 by Scott London. Reproduced by permission of Scott London and Georges Borchardt, Inc. for Richard Rodriguez. *Reason Magazine,* 2000 for "The New, New World" interviewed by Virginia Postrel and Nick Gillespie. Copyright 2000 by Reason Foundation, 3415 S. Sepulveda Blvd., Suite 400, Los Angeles, CA 90034, www.reason.com. Reproduced with permission. *World Literature Today,* v. 68, 1994. Copyright 1994 by the University of Oklahoma Press. Reproduced by permission of the publisher. Rodriguez, Richard. From *Brown: The Last Discovery of America.* Viking, 2002. Copyright © 2002 by Richard Rodriguez. All rights reserved. Reproduced by permission of "Viking," a division of Penguin Group (USA) Inc. Rodriguez, Richard. From *Days of Obligation: An Argument with My Mexican Father.* Viking, 1992. Copyright © 1992 by Richard Rodriguez. All rights reserved. Reproduced by permission of "Viking," a division of Penguin Group (USA) Inc.

JOHN PATRICK SHANLEY Excerpts from *Moonstruck, Joe Versus the Volcano, and Five Corners, Screenplays.* Grove Press, 1996. Copyright © 1996 by Publishers Group West. Reproduced by permission.

LOGAN PEARSALL SMITH Excerpts from "Excerpts from Letters," in *A Chime of Words: The Letters of Logan Pearsall Smith.* Ticknor and Fields, 1984. Copyright © 1984 by John Russell. Reproduced by permission of Houghton Mifflin Company.

List of Subjects

Introduction   *xiii*

List of Contributors   *xvii*

CLEANTH BROOKS   1
Mark Royden Winchell

JAMES LEE BURKE   21
Patrick A. Smith

JOHN JAY CHAPMAN   39
Mark Richardson

CHARLES W. CHESNUTT   57
Mark Richardson

EVAN S. CONNELL   79
Donovan Hohn

JOSEPH EPSTEIN   101
Sanford Pinsker

SARA HENDERSON HAY   119
Ellen McGrath Smith

HERBERT HUNCKE   137
Hilary Holladay

CHRISTOPHER ISHERWOOD   155
John Walen-Bridge

ALDO LEOPOLD   177
James Barilla

ALAIN LOCKE   195
Christopher Buck

NORMAN MACLEAN   221
Judith Kitchen

DAVID MAMET   239
Philip Parry

LINDA McCARRISTON   259
Zack Rogow

CHARLES REZNIKOFF   277
Dave Gunton

RICHARD RODRIGUEZ   297
Judith Kitchen

JOHN PATRICK SHANLEY   315
Daniel Vilmure

LOGAN PEARSALL SMITH   333
Benjamin Ivry

Cumulative Index   *353*

Introduction

Francis Bacon once famously wrote: "Some books are to be tasted, others to be swallowed, some few to be chewed and digested." To a degree, Bacon was simply acknowledging a truth that most serious readers eventually come to understand, which is that not every book must be read from cover to cover. Only a few books, in the end, deserve careful reading and, then, rereading. In this volume of *American Writers,* we offer eighteen articles on American writers of fiction, drama, poetry, and nonfiction; they are all distinguished, yet none of them has yet been featured in this series. My hope is that these articles will prove useful to readers who want to go deeper into the work of these writers, helping them to decide which can simply be tasted and which must be swallowed or fully digested.

This series had its origin in a remarkable series of critical and biographical monographs that appeared between 1959 and 1972. *The Minnesota Pamphlets on American Writers* were incisively written and informative, treating ninety-seven American writers in a format and style that attracted a devoted following of readers. The series proved invaluable to a generation of students and teachers, who could depend on these reliable and interesting critiques of major figures. The idea of reprinting these essays occurred to Charles Scribner, Jr. (1921–1995). The series appeared in four volumes entitled *American Writers: A Collection of Literary Biographies* (1974).

Since then, thirteen supplements have appeared, treating well over two hundred American writers: poets, novelists, playwrights, essayists and autobiographers. The idea has been consistent with the original series: to provide clear, informative essays aimed at the general reader and intelligent student. These essays often rise to a high level of craft and critical vision, but they are meant to introduce a writer of some importance in the history of American literature, and to provide a sense of the scope and nature of the career under review. A certain amount of biographical and historical context is also offered, giving a context for the work itself.

The authors of these critical articles are mostly teachers, scholars, and writers. Most have published books and articles in their field, and several are well-known writers of poetry or fiction as well as critics. As anyone glancing through this volume will see, they are held to the highest standards of good writing and sound scholarship. The essays each conclude with a select bibliography intended to direct the reading of those should want to pursue the subject further.

Volume Fourteen treats a wide range of authors from the past and present. Among them are several interesting but neglected authors from the nineteenth century, including Charles W. Chesnutt, the black novelist, Logan Pearsall Smith, the essayist and critic, and Alain Locke, the black critic, historian, and editor. Each of these men lived into the early half of the twentieth century, and each was influential in his time. The work of these authors has only recently attracted the attention of contemporary critics, and these essays go a considerable distance toward making their careers accessible.

Three poets considered in this collection are Charles Reznikoff (who died in 1976), Sara Henderson Hay (who died in 1987), and Linda

McCarriston. They are poets of considerable achievement, yet their work has not yet received the kind of sustained critical attention that it deserves. These essays go some distance toward making amends here, giving a sense of the full range and quality of their work. In the case of McCarriston — who is still in mid-career — that work continues to unfold.

Among the lesser known but fascinating figures treated in this supplement is Herbert Huncke, a founding father of the Beat Movement, who wrote striking autobiographical essays and is credited with giving the movement its name. He has been called "the lost Beat" because his friends and colleagues, Allen Ginsberg and Jack Kerouac, were much better known. His reputation seems to be growing year by year.

One of the critics considered in this volume is Cleanth Brooks, a founder of the so-called New Criticism. With his friend, Robert Penn Warren, he edited an influential textbook in 1938 called *Understanding Poetry.* That book trained several generations of college students in the art of close reading. Brooks himself wrote many seminal works of criticism and literary history, including some important and early works on William Faulkner. He was also a major scholar in the field of modern poetry studies.

Four contemporary writers of nonfiction considered in this volume are Aldo Leopold, Norman Maclean, Joseph Epstein, and Richard Rodriguez. Leopold, who died in 1948, was a pioneer in the area of nature writing and conservation, the author of *A Sand County Almanac.* Maclean, who died in 1990 at the age of 87, was a well-known figure, the author of *A River Runs Through It,* which was made into a film. He wrote very little, but each of his books found a wide audience. Epstein and Rodriguez are mainly essayists, and each has forged a unique career in the small world of essay-writing. Their work has had a strong impact on the culture, too. Epstein, whose wry and un-flinching eye surveys the world with dismay and humor, has published numerous collections of entertaining essays. He was, for many years, editor of *The American Scholar.* Rodgriguez — a Mexican-American author — has been a

prolific essayist on a wide range of cultural (and multicultural) topics. He is also a popular figure on American television, contributing "essays" to the PBS *Newshour with Jim Lehrer.*

Perhaps the most widely known figure considered in this volume is Christopher Isherwood, the Anglo-American novelist who was born in Britain but spent much of his adult life in California, where he died in 1986. Isherwood, like his good friend W.H. Auden, left Britain on the brink of the Second World War, having established his reputation with a volume of stories set in Berlin (these were the basis of *Cabaret,* the popular musical). He made a home on the West Coast, where he wrote for the stage and screen and, of course, continued working on his own splendid fiction and autobiographical works, such as *Christopher and His Kind* — a popular memoir written in the third person. Isherwood was hugely admired in this country, and his work continues to attract readers and critics.

Four well-known contemporary authors of novels and plays are discussed in these pages. James Lee Burke is a writer of intensely literary crime fiction. Evan S. Connell is the novelist who wrote, among many other books, *Mr. Bridge and Mrs. Bridge* (turned into a film by Paul Newman and Joanne Woodward). David Mamet, whom many critics regard as the premier American playwright of today, is also a screenwriter and director. John Patrick Shanley is a playwright and screenwriter, author of *Moonstruck*— for which he won an Academy Award in screenwriting. The lengthy and various careers of these writers are discussed at length, in the context of their evolving lives. Like most authors of genre fiction, Burke has largely been ignored by serious critics. This article makes a good start in trying to come to terms with his work, which is quite serious in its overall intentions and effects. Connell has been written about less than Mamet, but both of them have already attracted the attention of critics, and they will continue to do so. Mamet has been the subject of many books and hundreds of articles; the study of his career included here attempts to take into account the whole of his massively complex, ongoing career. John Patrick Shanley has been, like Mamet, prolific and successful on the stage and screen, but his critical reputation has never quite reached the same level. Shanely is nevertheless a superb writer, and this full-length treatment of his work should bring needed attention his way.

The critics who contributed to this collection represent a catholic range of backgrounds and critical approaches, although the baseline for inclusion was that each essay should be accessible to the non-specialist reader or beginning student. The creation of culture involves the continuous reassessment of major texts produced by its writers, and my belief is that this supplement performs a useful service here, providing substantial introductions to American writers who matter, and it will assist readers in the difficult but rewarding work of eager reading.

—JAY PARINI

Contributors

James Barilla. Completing his doctoral degree in English at the University of California in Davis, where he has helped to manage a sixty-five-acre tract of the university campus called the Experimental Ecosystem. His research focuses on the intersections between ecological restoration and literature. He has published essays in *You Are Here: The Journal of Creative Geography* and the forthcoming book *Men and Nature* (University of Virginia Press). ALDO LEOPOLD

Christopher Buck. Teaches at Michigan State University. He has written widely on literature and religion. His essay on the African American poet, Robert Hayden, appeared recently in the *Oxford Encyclopedia of American Literature.* Among his books is *Paradise and Paradigm: Key Symbols in Persian Christianity and the Baha'i Faith* (1999). ALAIN LOCKE

Dave Gunton. Independent scholar living in New York City. He has published articles on modern poetry, with a special interest in Objectivist poets, including Charles Reznikoff, Louis Zukofsky, and George Oppen. CHARLES REZNIKOFF

Donovan Hohn. English teacher at Friends Seminary in New York City and a former senior editor of *Harper's Magazine,* to which he has contributed criticism, journalism, and translations. EVAN S. CONNELL

Hilary Holladay. Professor of English at the University of Massachusetts at Lowell, where she directs the biennial Jack Kerouac Conference on Beat Literature. She is the author of *Ann Petry* (1996) and *Wild Blessings: The Poetry of Lucille Clifton* (2004) and co-editor of *The Critical Response to Ann Petry's Short Fiction* (2004). HERBERT HUNCKE

Benjamin Ivry. Author of biographies of *Arthur Rimbaud* (Absolute Press), *Francis Poulenc* (Phaidon), and *Maurice Ravel* (Welcome Rain), as well a poetry collection, *Paradise for the Portuguese Queen* (Orchises). He has translated many books from French, by such authors as Andre Gide, Jules Verne, and Balthus. LOGAN PEARSALL SMITH

Judith Kitchen. Teaches at the Rainier Writing Workshop, MFA Program in Writing at Pacific Lutheran University in Tacoma, WA. She is the author of a novel, *The House on Eccles Road,* two books of personal essays, and a critical study of the work of William Stafford. She has co-edited two anthologies of short nonfiction pieces for W. W. Norton and is the poetry reviewer for *The Georgia Review.* NORMAN MACLEAN, RICHARD RODRIGUEZ

Philip Parry. Dr. Parry is Lecturer in English at the University of St. Andrews in Scotland. He is a well-known authority on American and British drama of the twentieth century. DAVID MAMET

Sanford Pinsker. Shadek Professor of Humanities at Franklin and Marshall College. He is the author of numerous books, articles, and reviews, including *The Schlemiel as Metaphor* and *Bearing the Bad News.* He has recently been named the U. S. literature editor for a revised version of the Encyclopedia Judaica. JOSEPH EPSTEIN

Mark Richardson. Assistant Professor of English, Doshisha University, Kyoto, Japan. He is the author of *The Ordeal of Robert Frost: the Poet and the Poetics* (1997), and coeditor (with Richard Poirier) of Robert Frost, *Collected Poems, Prose & Plays* (1995). JOHN JAY CHAPMAN, CHARLES W. CHESNUTT

Zack Rogow. Coordinates the Lunch Poems Reading Series at the University of California, Berkeley. He also teaches in the MFA in Writing Program at the California College of the Arts. His books of poetry include *Greatest Hits: 1979—2001* and *The Selfsame Planet.* LINDA McCARRISTON

Ellen McGrath Smith. Teaches writing and literature at the University of Pittsburgh. Her criticism has appeared in *Sagetrieb,* the *Denver Quarterly,* and the *American Book Review.* SARA HENDERSON HAY

Patrick A. Smith. Faculty member in the Department of English, Bainbridge College, Georgia. Author of *"The True Bones of My Life": Essays on the Fiction of Jim Harrison* and *Thematic Guide to Popular Short Stories.* His essays have appeared in *Studies in Short Fiction, Aethlon: The Journal of Sport Literature* and previous *American Writers* volumes, among others. JAMES LEE BURKE

Daniel Vilmure. Twice published novelist (*Life in the Land of the Living,* Knopf, Faber & Faber, 1987) and *Toby's Lie* (Simon & Schuster, Bloomsbury, 1995.) Graduate of Harvard and Stanford Universities, a former Fulbright Lecturer at the University of Jordan in Amman, Jordan, and Director of the Villanova University Literary Festival which has included such guests as Jonathan Franzen, Michael Cunningham, and Robert Creeley. Currently Assistant Professor of English and Creative Writing at Villanova University. JOHN PATRICK SHANLEY

John Walen-Bridge. Associate professor of English at the National University of Singapore and is the author of *Political Fiction and the American Self* (1998). He has recently published articles on Charles Johnson, Norman Mailer, Richard Rorty, and Edward Said. CHRISTOPHER ISHERWOOD

Mark Royden Winchell. Author of over 120 essays and reviews and fourteen books, including *Too Good to be True: The Life and Work of Leslie Fiedler* (2002). Winchell's book *Cleanth Brooks and the Rise of Modern Criticism* (1996) won the Robert Penn Warren/Cleanth Brooks Award for distinguished achievement in literary criticism. CLEANTH BROOKS

SUPPLEMENT XIV
Cleanth Brooks to Logan Pearsall Smith

Cleanth Brooks

1906–1994

*T*HE APPROACH TO literary criticism that probably was most important and showed the most staying power during the twentieth century was a form of close reading that challenged the historical and philological scholarship dominant in the universities of the Western World. Although literary historians can trace its roots all the way back to Aristotle, this brand of aesthetic formalism seemed so revolutionary that it came to be known as the "New Criticism." Its most influential practitioner was Cleanth Brooks. The generation of critics before Brooks consisted of such pioneers as T. S. Eliot, I. A. Richards, and John Crowe Ransom. These men helped fashion a criticism sophisticated enough to explain and evaluate the radical innovations being wrought in poetry and fiction by early modernism. Brooks extended the range of the New Criticism (which derived its innocuous name from the title of a book that Ransom published in 1941) by eventually applying it to the entire canon of English poetry from John Donne to William Butler Yeats. In his many critical works, especially *The Well Wrought Urn: Studies in the Structure of Poetry* (1947), and a series of influential textbooks he edited with Robert Penn Warren and others, Brooks taught several generations of students how to read literature as literature. He also helped invent the modern literary quarterly and wrote perhaps the best book ever on the works of William Faulkner.

THE ROAD TO BATON ROUGE

The son of Cleanth Brooks Sr. and Bessie Lee Witherspoon Brooks, Cleanth Brooks Jr. was born in Murray, Kentucky, on October 16, 1906. Because the elder Brooks was a Methodist minister who was reassigned to different churches every few years, the family moved eight times during young Brooks's childhood and early adolescence. After receiving his initial education in the public schools of southern Kentucky and western Tennessee, Brooks was enrolled in the privately run McTyeire School in McKenzie, Tennessee, in the fall of 1920. The curriculum consisted of four years each of English, mathematics, and Latin; three of Greek; and one of U.S. history. The students also were expected to attend chapel and to participate in sports. By the time he left McTyeire for Vanderbilt University in 1924, Brooks had what he regarded as the equivalent of a British "public school" education.

At the time that he enrolled as a freshman at Vanderbilt, a group of local poets were beginning careers that would alter the course of twentieth-century literature and profoundly shape the direction of Brooks's own life. As early as 1914 the group had begun meeting on alternate Saturday nights for philosophical discussions at the home of a Nashville businessman named James M. Frank. The original leader of the group, Frank's brother-in-law the eccentric autodidact Sidney Hirsch, eventually was supplanted by John Crowe Ransom (then a young English professor at Vanderbilt) when the focus of the discussions shifted to poetry. Long before creative writing workshops became fixtures of academic life, the members of the Hirsch circle exchanged drafts of poems they were writing and offered detailed critical analyses of one another's work. When they reformed after a hiatus during World War I, several younger members were added—including the undergraduates Allen Tate and Robert Penn Warren. In April 1922 the group began publishing a magazine of verse they called the *Fugitive* (perhaps in honor of the Wandering Jew who had been their original leader). By the time the magazine ceased publication in 1925, it had attracted an international reputation and several distinguished outside contributors.

To the young Cleanth Brooks, however, all this literary activity seemed like "a campfire still glowing in the distance" (quoted in Rob Roy Purdy, *Fugitives Reunion,* 1959). Although he took a course in advanced composition from Ransom, Brooks does not recall deriving anything of value from the class. During his senior year, however, he remembers a very different experience upon opening a volume of Ransom's poetry in a friend's dormitory room. "Suddenly, the scales fell from my eyes," he wrote years later (as quoted in *Community, Religion, and Literature,* 1995). "The code was broken, the poems became 'readable.' ... A serious blockage had suddenly disappeared. I was now a true convert." Brooks also encountered the indirect influence of another Fugitive when he heard a now forgotten graduate student reading a paper that Donald Davidson had written on a story by Rudyard Kipling. It was then that Brooks first realized that close reading could be applied to fiction as well as to poetry.

After earning his bachelor of arts degree from Vanderbilt in the spring of 1928, Brooks entered graduate school at Tulane University in New Orleans, where he roomed briefly with the future journalist Hodding Carter. Despite the proximity of a bohemian literary community, there was less creative activity at Tulane than there had been at Vanderbilt and almost no interest in what Brooks called in *Community, Religion, and Literature* "the interior life of the poem." Nevertheless, Brooks continued to write verse and to ask the sorts of critical questions that the old historical scholarship was ill equipped to answer. (His master's thesis dealt with varieties of metaphor in the Elizabethan sonnet sequences.) In addition to finishing his master's degree in 1929, Brooks successfully applied for a Rhodes Scholarship at Oxford University during his year at Tulane.

Upon his arrival at Oxford, Brooks was reunited with his fellow Vanderbilt alumnus Robert Penn Warren, who was in the final year of his own Rhodes Scholarship. (Although he was only a year older than his friend, the precocious Warren had been a junior and an established member of the Fugitives during Brooks's freshman year at Vanderbilt.) If Tulane had been relatively unventuresome in its approach to literary study, Oxford proved an even stodgier bastion of traditional scholarship. Under the direction of the eighteenth-century specialist David Nichol Smith, Brooks began editing the correspondence of the antiquarian scholar Bishop Thomas Percy and his friend Richard Farmer, head of a college at the University of Cambridge. Although he undertook this assignment as a B.Litt. project, Brooks did such a commendable job that he later joined Smith as coeditor of the entire corpus of Percy's letters. The first five volumes of this series appeared between 1944 and 1961. Then, after a seventeen-year lull occasioned by Smith's death in 1964, Brooks edited three more volumes with A. F. Falconer. What had begun as a student exercise for a young man of twenty-five turned into a labor of sixty years' duration.

As Brooks was establishing his credentials as a philological scholar at Oxford, he continued to write poetry while becoming increasingly interested in a literary revolution that was taking place down the road at the University of Cambridge. In 1921 the young Cambridge graduate Ivor Armstrong Richards joined the faculty of his alma mater as a lecturer in English and moral science. Eventually, his lectures proved so popular that some of them had to be held in the streets—the first time that had happened at Cambridge since the Middle Ages. Also, by the end of the decade, Richards was making seminal contributions to literary criticism. In 1924 he published a groundbreaking work called *Principles of Literary Criticism.* This was followed in 1929 by the even more influential *Practical Criticism: A Study of Literary Judgment.* When Brooks heard Richards lecture a few months after the publication of that book, he discovered not only that he agreed with the Cambridge critic but also that he was the only one among his circle of Oxford friends who could even understand what the man was saying.

THE LEFT BANK OF THE MISSISSIPPI

When Brooks completed his B.Litt. degree at Oxford in 1932 (which is roughly equivalent to an American doctorate), the United States was in the depth of an economic depression, and academic jobs were particularly scarce. Nevertheless, Huey Long (who was political dictator of Louisiana) was pouring vast sums of money into Louisiana State University. Also, Charles W. Pipkin, chairman of the committee that awarded Brooks his Rhodes Scholarship, was dean of the graduate school at LSU. In 1932 Brooks was hired as a lecturer in the LSU English department. Then, on September 12, 1934, he finally married his longtime fiancée, Edith Amy Blanchard (who was always called "Tinkum" after a comic strip character named Tinkum Tidy). Although the couple never had children, they were soon responsible for the care of Brooks's father, who had suffered a paralytic stroke and was living with his son. With a modest annual salary, the younger Brooks was the sole support of a wife, two aging parents, and a cousin who had been adopted into the family years earlier.

By the mid-1930s, Brooks was teaching a full load of courses and writing his first book—*The*

Relation of the Alabama-Georgia Dialect to the Provincial Dialects of Great Britain. (Four years after its publication in 1935, this book would be used by the dialect coach for the film version of Margaret Mitchell's *Gone with the Wind.*) Moreover, Brooks and his old friend Robert Penn Warren, who had been hired by the English department in the fall of 1934, were helping to edit the *Southwest Review,* a joint venture of LSU and Southern Methodist University. In 1935 LSU relinquished its role in publishing the *Southwest Review* to launch its own literary quarterly, which it called the *Southern Review.* During its seven years of existence, this magazine set such a standard for excellence that, in 1940, a writer for *Time* magazine declared that the center of literary criticism in the Western World had moved "from the left bank of the Seine to the left bank of the Mississippi."

More than any other single phenomenon, the *Southern Review* brought southern literature to the attention of a national and even international audience. It also brought national and international writers to the attention of southern readers. In addition to writings by Eudora Welty, Peter Taylor, Katherine Anne Porter, and various Fugitive poets, the *Southern Review* published work by Ford Madox Ford, Aldous Huxley, Kenneth Burke, Sidney Hook, Delmore Schwartz, I. F. Stone, F. O. Matthiessen, Mary McCarthy, Nelson Algren, James T. Farrell, John Dewey, Philip Rahv, and scores of other luminaries whom one would never think to associate with southern culture.

If Brooks arrived at Vanderbilt too late to be part of the Fugitive movement, he also missed participating in *I'll Take My Stand,* a collection of essays published in 1930 by Twelve Southerners, who defended the agrarian tradition of the Old South against the threats of industrialism and cultural assimilation. (Because Ransom, Tate, Warren, and Davidson were among the contributors to *I'll Take My Stand,* literary historians have tended to link the Fugitive and Agrarian movements.) Although Brooks was not one of the original twelve writers, he had become part of the larger Agrarian fraternity by the mid-1930s. Consequently, in 1936, he contributed to *Who Owns America?* a symposium of social and economic thought compiled by an assortment of cultural traditionalists and economic decentralists—principally the southern Agrarians and British Distributists, a largely Roman Catholic group of land reformers.

In his contribution to *Who Owns America?* Brooks dealt not with politics or economics but with religion. Titled "A Plea to the Protestant Churches," his essay warned that liberal Protestantism was abandoning a transcendent and supernatural faith for a rather tepid brand of secular humanism. In an attempt to be relevant to the modern world, the mainstream Protestant churches had made the fatal mistake of choosing science as their epistemological model. Brooks believed that, properly understood, religion had more in common with art—in that both art and religion involved a description of experience that was concrete, many faceted, and affective. Science, in contrast, was abstract, one-sided, and purely intellectual. Religion, of course, went beyond art in purporting to affirm eternal truths rather than merely asking for a willing suspension of disbelief. Liberal Protestantism had not even reached the level of aestheticism, much less passed beyond it.

At the same time that they were editing the *Southern Review* and pursuing their own writing projects, Brooks and Warren were trying to teach the intricacies of literature to students who often were too poorly prepared to understand even the paraphrased prose meaning of a poem. Here, they encountered a more extreme instance of a situation Richards had faced at Cambridge a decade earlier. In a series of classroom experiments, Richards had given his students thirteen unidentified poems and asked for critical responses. Confronting the text

without the benefit of history or biography, they fell prey to every conceivable form of misreading. Although it would have been easy enough for Richards to have given his students the "right" answers, he was more concerned with nurturing the sort of critical intelligence that would enable them to come up with those answers on their own. The end result of his labors was *Practical Criticism.*

In trying to teach students who lacked the elite background of those at Cambridge, Brooks and Warren faced an even more formidable challenge. Because they found the available textbooks of little help, their department head, William A. Read, urged them to prepare a thirty-page mimeographed booklet on metrics and imagery, which they used for the first time in the spring semester of 1935. Then, in the fall of 1936, Brooks, Warren, and a graduate student named John T. Purser published a critical anthology of poetry, fiction, drama, and expository prose under the title *An Approach to Literature: A Collection of Prose and Verse with Analyses and Discussions.* (Detractors began referring to it as "The *Reproach* to Literature.") In 1975, nearly forty years after its original publication, the book went into its fifth edition.

In 1938 Brooks and Warren published an even more influential textbook called *Understanding Poetry: An Anthology for College Students.* Although they would have preferred the more modest title "Reading Poems," the phrase "understanding poetry" is a perfect statement of the book's purpose. Its end is critical understanding rather than vague appreciation. And the object of that understanding is poetry, not literary history or biography. After a ten-page "Letter to the Teacher" and a twenty-five page introduction, the text is divided into seven sections of poems, each preceded by an editorial foreword. (There is also an afterword following the second section as well as three "notes" of several pages each in section four.) The distinctive feature of this approach is that the divisions are made according to literary rather than historical or geographical considerations. The main body of the book contains critical discussions of thirty-seven poems and the texts of more than two hundred others (many of which are accompanied by exercises). This is followed by a twenty-three-page glossary, heavily emphasizing matters of technique.

In their introduction Brooks and Warren try to define poetry by contrasting it with other kinds of discourse that students (and, indeed, all human beings) habitually use. Unlike technical language, poetry does not give an objective description of facts but expresses an attitude toward experience. Thus, in its function it resembles ordinary human speech far more than technical discourse does. One might easily come away from this definition thinking of poetry as nothing more than rhetoric, which is to say language used skillfully. In a sense, Brooks and Warren do see poetry as a kind of rhetoric—but one based on dramatic tension rather than didactic assertion or appeals to pathos (although both the latter elements appear in many good poems). As Brooks would do often in his subsequent writing, he and Warren make the analogy between a poem and a drama. "Every poem," they write, "implies a speaker of the poem, either the poet writing in his own person or someone into whose mouth the poem is put, and … the poem represents the reaction of such a person to a situation, a scene, or an idea."

Brooks's first important book of criticism, *Modern Poetry and the Tradition* (1939), exemplifies his propensity for putting flesh on the theories of others. In his seminal essay on the metaphysical poets, T. S. Eliot had spoken of a dissociation of sensibility that entered English poetry at the end of the seventeenth century. According to this view, John Milton and John Dryden separated emotion from intellect in poetry. Throughout the eighteenth and nineteenth centuries, there was considerable thought and feeling in English verse but very

few instances where the two were fused in a common image or metaphor. Presumably, the high modernist poets—under the influence of the French symbolists—were helping to restore the status quo ante. Not only does Brooks accept Eliot's thesis, but he also attempts to demonstrate its validity by writing a revisionist history of English poetry.

Brooks argues that the English poets of the eighteenth and nineteenth centuries developed certain aesthetic assumptions that the metaphysical poets did not hold and that the modern poets have rejected. Perhaps the most baneful of these is the existence of an inherently poetic subject matter. He traces this belief back to the seventeenth-century English philosopher Thomas Hobbes's view that the poet is a mere copyist, not a maker. If it is the poet's function simply to hold the mirror up to nature, he can please his audience most by holding his mirror up to pleasant objects. Closely related to this view is the notion that intellect is somehow inimical to the poetic faculty. Despite superficial differences between the neoclassical and the Romantic critics, both saw metaphysical wit as a trivialization of the deep emotion and high seriousness of poetry. Better to whisper sweet nothings into the ear of one's beloved than to tax her mind with ingenious metaphors and conceits. Better to worship God in utter simplicity than to write religious poems with puns in them.

Like Richards, Brooks rejects this essentially puritan notion of poetry. The New Critics and high modernists believed in a poetry that could accommodate a wide range of human experience—a poetry of inclusion, not of exclusion. For this reason, they refused to reduce poetry to mere sentiment or propaganda. Despite their obvious differences, both the sentimentalist and the propagandist are reluctant to subject their assertions to the disciplines of irony. For both the lover and the ideologue, action is more important than contemplation. In contrast, the truly imaginative poet agrees with Auden that "poetry makes nothing happen." He does not seek to change the world and is not disillusioned when he fails to do so.

From a technical standpoint, Brooks regards metaphor not as another figure of speech designed to dress up verse but as the very essence of poetry. Above all others, Brooks contends in *Modern Poetry and the Tradition,* "the metaphysical poets reveal the essentially functional character of all metaphor. We cannot remove the comparisons from their poems, as we might remove ornaments or illustrations attached to a statement, without demolishing the poems. The comparison *is* the poem in a structural sense." What makes the metaphysical conceit different from the sentimental metaphor (other than its superior inclusiveness) is its effect on the reader. The sentimental metaphor may seem apt on first reading; however, closer acquaintance reveals the disparities that the poet has been unwilling to acknowledge, Hence, it does not wear well. Because the metaphysical poet has acknowledged the disparities from the outset, has actually built his poem around them, his metaphor usually seems more apt with successive readings. Or, as Brooks puts the matter, "if it does not explode with a first reading, it is extremely durable."

The common view of literary history at the time that Brooks wrote *Modern Poetry and the Tradition* was that the Romantics had effected a literary revolution by breaking with the neoclassical concept of decorum prevalent in the eighteenth century and that the modernist poets of the early twentieth century had taken that revolution several steps further. Following Eliot's lead, Brooks disputes this view. For one thing, he sees the Romantic revolt as being a bogus revolution. "The Romantic poets, in attacking the neoclassic conception of the poetic, tended to offer new poetic objects rather than to discard altogether the conception of a special poetic material." In their failure to be suf-

ficiently revolutionary, the Romantics simply perpetuated the dissociation of sensibility that Eliot believes infected most English verse from the late seventeenth century on. At its worst, this leads to the twin sins of didacticism and sentimentality, both of which were carried to ridiculous extremes during the Victorian era. The modern poets revered by Brooks and Eliot were not extending the Romantic revolution so much as reversing the dissociation of sensibility, to which the Romantics were just as prone as their neoclassical predecessors and Victorian heirs.

Although some of Brooks's judgments ultimately would seem dated, one chapter of *Modern Poetry and the Tradition* that has clearly stood the test of time concerns Eliot's *The Waste Land.* So much has been written about that poem since 1939 that it is easy to forget how incompletely it had been understood before Brooks came along. His extensive and detailed explication of the text is as lucid as any beginning student could possibly want. The final pages of the chapter, however, are of immeasurably greater importance because of Brooks's startlingly revisionist interpretation of the poem. To read *The Waste Land* as a statement of despair or unbelief, Brooks contends, is to stay far too close to the surface of this supremely ironic text. Instead, *The Waste Land* is at least an inchoate affirmation of the same Christian faith that Eliot would later embrace.

Brooks contrasts the situation Eliot faced with that of Dante in fourteenth-century Italy and Edmund Spenser in sixteenth-century England. When Dante wrote his *Divine Comedy,* he was addressing an audience that shared his Catholic faith and agreed upon central points of dogma. As a Protestant, Spenser was writing *The Faerie Queene* for a generically Christian audience searching for a new structure of belief. Eliot, however, was writing for a post-Christian audience, which found the traditional symbols and terminology of Christianity to be, what Brooks called in *Modern Poetry and the Tradition,* "a mass of clichés." His task was to find a new vocabulary and new imagery capable of rehabilitating the discarded truths of Christianity for a skeptical age. When Brooks originally wrote his account of *The Waste Land* for the *Southern Review,* he sent a copy to Eliot, who responded in a letter dated March 15, 1937. "It seems to me on the whole excellent," Eliot wrote. "I think that this kind of analysis is perfectly justified so long as it does not profess to be a reconstruction of the author's method of writing. Reading your essay made me feel … that I had been much more ingenious than I had been aware of." (quoted in Mark Royden Winchell's *Cleanth Brooks and the Rise of Modern Criticism*).

Brooks's discussion of Eliot in *Modern Poetry and the Tradition* is followed by one on Yeats as mythmaker. Here again, Brooks makes the work of a difficult modern poet understandable without compromising its complexity. Because of his aversion to the modern industrial world, Yeats is a kindred spirit of the Agrarians. And like the southern formalists, he believes that the poetic imagination can divine truths inaccessible to science:

> "I am," Yeats tells us, "very religious, and deprived by Huxley and Tindall … of the simple-minded religion of my childhood, I had made a new religion, almost an infallible church of poetic tradition, of a fardel of stories, and of personages, and of emotions, inseparable from their first expression, passed on from generation to generation by poets and painters with some help from philosophers and theologians."

Brooks concludes his book by returning to the dissociation of sensibility as the key issue in English literary history. He argues that Hobbes is responsible not only for the wrong turn that poetry took at the end of the seventeenth century but also for the death of tragedy on the English stage. By emphasizing paradigmatic simplicity, the scientific worldview robbed poetry of the dialectical tension that made metaphysical verse

so rich. That same tension, Brooks argues, is essential to tragedy. To appreciate tragedy, we must be able simultaneously to admire and judge the tragic hero. The Elizabethans could do this (just as they could admire and judge dashing rogues). The heroic drama of the Restoration more nearly resembles melodrama. When character is purged of ambiguity, pathos is still possible, but tragedy is not.

If tragedy fared so badly after the Elizabethan era, one might ask why comedy remained so healthy well into the eighteenth century. More to the point, could wit really have been purged from literature when the appeal of the great Restoration comedies lay in little else? Brooks responds to this objection by distinguishing between the ironic wit that is characteristic of tragedy and the satiric wit that sustains comedy. Tragedy "represents something of a tension between unsympathetic laughter and sympathetic pity—between the impulse to condemn the protagonist and the impulse to feel pity for him." Perhaps the last significant character in seventeenth-century literature to exhibit tragic tension was John Milton's Satan. The Puritan in Milton condemned the Prince of Darkness, while the rebel secretly admired him. Although such an attitude raises both logical and theological problems, it is the very essence of the tragic imagination. The epistemological simplification introduced by Hobbes could accommodate a criticism of others but not the criticism of self authored by a truly introspective wit. Yeats said that we make rhetoric out of our arguments with others and poetry out of our arguments with ourselves. By this definition, the writing of true poetry became much more difficult after the dissociation of sensibility.

Even as Brooks was earning recognition in the larger academic world, he found his position at LSU to be increasingly embattled. After the assassination of Huey Long and the imprisonment of several of his subordinates for graft and corruption, power in both the state government and the university changed hands. The new president of LSU, General Campbell B. Hodges, was a former commandant at West Point who brought an authoritarian approach to his new position. While he was scrupulously honest, Hodges also suppressed much of the creative and intellectual activity at LSU. In what was ostensibly a wartime austerity measure, he suspended the *Southern Review* in 1942. (Many observers believed that the action was, at least in part, an attempt to punish Brooks for his role as a faculty dissident.) Shortly after the disappearance of the review, Warren left LSU for a position at the University of Minnesota. Over the next five years, Brooks himself was wooed by some of the most prestigious schools in the nation. Then, in 1947, he accepted an offer from Yale University.

SOUTH OF BOSTON

In March 1947, while he was preparing to make the transition to Yale, Brooks published the book on which his reputation as a critic probably rests. If *Modern Poetry and the Tradition* was an extended gloss on Eliot's view of English literary history, *The Well Wrought Urn* is an attempt to reread some of the most highly respected poems of the eighteenth and nineteenth centuries according to the same principles that one would use to read Donne or Yeats. Brooks hoped to do nothing less than identify those qualities shared by the great poetry of all ages, including that which seemed on the surface much different from metaphysical and modernist verse. For the most part, Brooks's theorizing is confined to a final chapter and two appendices. The heart of his book consists of close discussions of ten of the most admired poems in English literature—Donne's "The Canonization," Shakespeare's verse play *Macbeth*, Milton's "L'Allegro" and "Il Penseroso," Robert Herrick's "Corinna's Going a-Maying," Alexander Pope's "The Rape of the Lock,"

Thomas Gray's "Elegy Written in a Country Churchyard," William Wordsworth's "Ode: Intimations of Immortality," John Keats's "Ode on a Grecian Urn," Alfred Lord Tennyson's "Tears, Idle Tears," and Yeats's "Among School Children." A look at three representative chapters of this book should indicate Brooks's method and achievement.

One of the qualities that has allowed *The Well Wrought Urn* to endure when other seasonal classics have fallen by the wayside is the ease with which it moves between general theory and specific practice. Brooks's critical principles inform his readings, and his readings illuminate his principles. This symbiosis is evident as early as the first chapter, where Brooks illustrates his concept of poetic language by referring to important poems by Wordsworth, Pope, and Gray before reaching back in time to Donne. Brooks's basic assumption (boldly announced in the title of his first chapter) is that poetic language is "The Language of Paradox." He tells us that "it is a language in which the connotations play as great a part as the deno-tations. … The poet does not use a notation at all—as the scientist may properly be said to do so. The poet, within limits, has to make up his language as he goes." Whereas the scientist (really the technologist) is constantly purging his language of ambiguity, the poet thrives on ambiguity because it allows him to approximate more closely the rich texture of actual experience.

The title *The Well Wrought Urn* is itself remarkably suggestive and ambiguous. Brooks's reference is to the penultimate stanza of "The Canonization," where the speaker argues that the love he shares with his woman, although it be of no great moment in worldly terms, can serve as an example and inspiration to future lovers (just as the humble lives of saints can be a source of religious inspiration):

We'll build in sonnets pretty roomes;
As well a well-wrought urn becomes
The greatest ashes, as half-acre tombes.

As Brooks writes:

> The poem is an instance of the doctrine which it asserts; it is both the assertion and the realization of the assertion. The poet has actually built within the song the "pretty room" with which he says the lovers can be content. The poem itself is the well-wrought urn which can hold the lovers' ashes and which will not suffer in comparison with the prince's "half-acre tomb."

To demonstrate that paradox is the universal language of poetry, Brooks must discuss a representative selection of poems that are widely admired but generally thought to be free of paradox. The first of his texts to fall clearly into this category is Herrick's "Corinna's Going a-Maying." By examining the complex attitude that the speaker of this poem takes toward the carpe diem theme (whether or not this was the biographically known attitude of Parson Herrick), Brooks questions whether any true poem can ever be reduced to its paraphrasable prose content.

Brooks titles his chapter discussing this poem "What Does Poetry Communicate?" He answers that question by asserting, "The poem communicates so much and communicates it so richly and with such delicate qualifications that the thing communicated is mauled and distorted if we attempt to convey it by any vehicle less subtle than that of the poem itself." Taken too literally, that statement could mean that criticism is virtually impossible. If any critical analysis less subtle than the poem itself is inadequate, only the most discriminating minds are capable of criticism. And that criticism necessarily will be expressed in a prose that is different from the language of poetry. Faced with such a challenge, the prospective critic might well throw up his hands, read the poem verbatim, and say, "*That* is what it communicates." Brooks does not go that far, but he realizes that any critical theory that would reduce a poem to its prose paraphrase is incapable of answering the exasperated sopho-

more who asks, "Then, why didn't the poet just come out and say what he meant?"

Brooks's best-known and most-admired essay in *The Well Wrought Urn* probably is his discussion of Keats's "Ode on a Grecian Urn." Keats might not be as witty as Donne or as densely allusive as Eliot, but his originality of metaphor and sensuousness of imagery set him apart from all other Romantics. And "Ode on a Grecian Urn" generally is regarded as one of his best poems. But this wonderfully concrete artifact ends with an apparently sententious bit of philosophizing that even Keats's greatest admirers have found hard to defend. If the concluding equation of beauty and truth is inconsistent with the rest of Keats's poem, then it is an affront to logic. If it is not inconsistent, one suspects that it is probably superfluous. Brooks manages to resolve this dilemma by taking seriously Keats's metaphor of the urn as dramatic speaker. He asks if we might not read "Ode on a Grecian Urn" in such a way that the statement "Beauty is truth, truth beauty" rises as naturally from the dramatic context of the poem as King Lear's statement "Ripeness is all" does from the conflicts of Shakespeare's play.

Perhaps a more fundamental problem with the last two lines of the poem is determining what they might mean on a prose level. If the idea itself is merely gibberish, then its appropriateness to the poem becomes irrelevant—unless, of course, one wants to argue that Keats was deliberately writing nonsense verse (inviting not a comparison to *King Lear* but to Edward Lear). Brooks indicates the dilemma as follows:

> One can emphasize *beauty* is truth and throw Keats into the pure-art camp, the usual procedure. But it is only fair to point out that one could stress *truth* is beauty, and argue with the Marxist critics of the 'thirties for a propaganda art. The very ambiguity of the statement, "Beauty is truth, truth beauty" ought to warn us against insisting very much on the statement in isolation, and to drive

us back to a consideration of the context in which the statement is set.

Not surprisingly, Brooks discovers that rather than forcing us to accept either conflicting reading of the poem, this procedure allows us to synthesize both readings at a higher level of ambiguity.

The "message" that one gleans from examining the urn is riddled with paradox. Keats calls the urn a "sylvan historian," but Brooks reminds us in the title of his essay that the history in question is "without footnotes." The specificity of conventional historical accounts is absent from the scenes depicted on the urn. What we have is no facsimile representation of actual events but an unchanging paradigm of the richness of life—what Keats calls a "cold pastoral." "The sylvan historian," Brooks notes, "takes a few details and so orders them that we have not only beauty but insight into essential truth. Its 'history' … has the validity of myth—not myth as a pretty but irrelevant make-belief, an idle fancy, but myth as a valid perception into reality."

Truth for Keats is something far more general and far more beautiful than mere facts. Or, to put the matter differently, myth is all the history that we know or need to know. If we are sensitive to what the entire poem has been saying (largely in terms of paradox) "we shall be prepared for the enigmatic, final paradox which the 'silent form' utters." Thus, our response to those closing lines is a way of testing whether we have been reading the poem correctly. Had Keats simply meant that beauty is truth and written his "Ode" as a declaration of pure aestheticism, the poem would have been much less complex and its concluding statement of theme clearly beside the point. (The fact that theme so often is simplistically misread indicates how a reader's preconceptions can distort his or her understanding.) By stating the theme as a paradox that cannot be adequately understood except in terms of the entire poem,

however, Keats refuses to allow the careful reader an overly facile understanding of that theme.

Despite the great influence that the New Criticism enjoyed among students and scholars alike, it did not meet with universal approbation. Brooks and company encountered considerable resistance from old historicists, who argued that the New Critics paid too little attention to external evidence in their pursuit of exegetical ingenuity. A case in point is Douglas Bush's attack on Brooks's reading of Andrew Marvell's "Horatian Ode upon Cromwell's Return from Ireland." The poem in question was written by Marvell as a celebration of Oliver Cromwell's rise to power and his triumphant return from Ireland. In his essay (originally published in the *Sewanee Review* and reprinted in William R. Keast's *Seventeenth-Century English Poetry*), Brooks attempts to determine what Marvell's poem actually says about Cromwell, as opposed to what purely historical evidence might indicate the poet personally thought about the British Lord Protector. Providing a characteristically close reading of Marvell's poem, Brooks tries to indicate the ambiguity and complexity of the poetic speaker's point of view.

Unconvinced by his analysis, Bush questions Brooks on his interpretation of several specific lines. Bush believes that Marvell's opinion of Cromwell was one of unambiguous admiration. The purpose of Brooks's elaborate discriminations, he argues, is simply to educe a needlessly complex reading from a relatively straightforward poetic statement, in effect "to turn a seventeenth-century liberal into a modern one." Bush concludes that "this is one reason why historical conditioning has a corrective as well as a positive value."

The problem with Bush's position is that Brooks clearly did do his historical homework before approaching the text of the "Horatian Ode." He simply came to different conclusions from the same evidence. With his continuing work on the Percy letters and his immense scholarly curiosity, Brooks was never simplistically anti-historical. He merely wanted to go beyond what history can tell us about the meaning and merit of a work of literature. As his old friend and colleague Robert Bechtold Heilman put it, "For such a person [as Brooks] to say that history is not all is a rather different thing from an ignorant B.A.'s thinking that history is nothing." It is perhaps significant that the last book Brooks published in his life was titled *Historical Evidence and the Reading of Seventeenth-Century Poetry* (1991). Among the essays contained in that volume is a revised version of his discussion of Marvell's "Horatian Ode."

Another line of attack on the New Criticism came from such democratic nativists as Archibald MacLeish, Van Wyck Brooks, Alfred Kazin, and Howard Mumford Jones. With varying degrees of sophistication, these socially engaged men of letters accused the New Critics of a precious aestheticism. MacLeish regarded their disinterested view of literature as morally irresponsible when democracy was fighting for its very survival during World War II. Van Wyck Brooks believed that all of literary modernism represented a break with the vital and progressive spirit of the late nineteenth century. Kazin saw southern formalism (no less than militant Stalinism) as an attack on the liberal democratic ethos of American culture, while Jones urged his fellow countrymen to reject the anglophile Eliot and the gothic Faulkner in favor of the native optimism of Henry Wadsworth Longfellow and Louisa May Alcott.

Perhaps the most strident attack on the politics of the New Criticism occurred when the Fellows of the Library of Congress, a group heavily stacked with aesthetic formalists, bestowed the Bollingen Prize for Poetry on Ezra Pound's *The Pisan Cantos* (1948). In articles published in two successive issues of the *Saturday Review of Literature*, Robert Hillyer questioned whether an agency of the U.S. government should honor a Fascist collaborator such as Pound and a scurrilously antidemocratic poem such as *The Pisan Cantos*. Not content to attack Pound alone, Hillyer strongly implied that all literary modernists and their New Critical allies were traitors to democratic culture.

Just as he had defended his position against the attacks of historical scholars such as Bush, Brooks rose to the challenge posed by the democratic nativists. In a lecture delivered at the Jewish Theological Seminary in the winter of 1949, he argued that his opponents were begging an important question when they divided the literary world between the moralistic and the amoral. Many of the New Critics (Brooks and Eliot among them) still subscribed to an orthodox religious faith. Having weathered the assaults on religion made by Charles Darwin, Karl Marx, and Sigmund Freud, they saw no need to transform literature into a secular faith. (In the 1950s Brooks would argue that such archetypal critics as Leslie Fiedler and Northrop Frye came close to doing precisely that.) Behind the impulse to make literature into something more than religion (or less than politics) was the well-intentioned, but misguided figure of Matthew Arnold. To adopt the Arnoldian position, Brooks argued in "A Note on the Limits of 'History' and the Limits of 'Criticism,'" was to do a disservice to both God and art. "Though poetry has a very important role in any culture," he writes, "to ask that poetry save us is to impose a burden upon poetry that it cannot sustain. The danger is that we shall merely get an ersatz religion and an ersatz poetry."

Although Brooks and Warren were separated for a third time in their careers when Warren left LSU for the University of Minnesota in 1942, their friendship and collaboration continued. In 1943 they published *Understanding Fiction,* a companion volume to *Understanding Poetry,* and in 1949 a composition textbook titled *Modern Rhetoric, with Readings.* (In 1945

Brooks and Heilman had published *Understanding Drama.*) In addition to earning substantial royalties, these books helped establish the New Criticism as the dominant pedagogical method in college classrooms for more than a generation. The team of Brooks and Warren was united once again when Warren joined the Yale faculty in 1950.

By the time Brooks came to Yale in 1947, the English department had long been a bastion of historical scholarship. (The legendary eighteenth-century specialist Chauncey Brewster Tinker had brought James Boswell's papers to campus and had determined the direction of the English program for half a century.) Nevertheless, younger professors, such as Maynard Mack and Louis Martz, were far more sympathetic to the innovations of Brooks and Warren. Another strong advocate of the New Criticism was the European scholar René Wellek, who had come to Yale to start a program in comparative literature. Finally, Brooks's younger colleague William K. Wimsatt became one of the most articulate theoreticians of the new movement. In 1957 he and Brooks published their monumental study *Literary Criticism: A Short History.*

At a time when the close reading of poetry was falling out of favor with literary trendsetters, Brooks's critical interests focused increasingly on the South's greatest novelist. *William Faulkner: The Yoknapatawpha Country* (1963) was an attempt to emphasize the traditional and communitarian aspects of Faulkner's vision. Although detractors have accused Brooks of a Procrustean attempt to turn Faulkner into an honorary Agrarian, the thesis of his book is supported by astute readings of individual novels— particularly Brooks's frequently anthologized discussion of *Light in August.* Commenting on what he regards as the most significant unifying theme in that novel, Brooks writes:

> One way in which to gauge the importance of the community in this novel is by imagining the ac-

tion to have taken place in Chicago or on Manhattan Island, where the community—at least in Faulkner's sense—does not exist. ... The plight of the isolated individual cut off from any community of values is of course a dominant theme of contemporary literature. But by developing this theme in a rural setting in which a powerful sense of community still exists, Faulkner has given us a kind of pastoral—that is he has let us see our modern and complex problems mirrored in a simpler and more primitive world. *Light in August* is, in some respects, a bloody and violent pastoral. The plight of the lost sheep and of the black sheep can be given special point and meaning because there is still visible in the background a recognizable flock with its shepherds, its watchdogs, sometimes fierce and cruel, and its bellwethers.

Making a similar argument in his chapter on Faulkner's first great novel *The Sound and the Fury,* Brooks contends that

> the breakdown of a family can be exhibited more poignantly and significantly in a society which is old-fashioned and in which the family is still at the center. ... What happens to the Compsons might make less noise and cause less comment, and even bring less pain to the individuals concerned, if the Compsons lived in a more progressive and liberal environment.

If Faulkner's conservative social vision is most often comic, he was capable in his greatest novels of creating truly modern tragedies. Such is the case with *Absalom, Absalom!* Brooks warns, however, that we misconstrue Faulkner's meaning if we read this book specifically as a tragedy of the South. Thomas Sutpen is a completely self-made man, whose character has been neither formed nor constrained by any organic community. Admittedly, he is not a rebel against the community in the same sense as Joe Christmas in *Light in August.* He simply tries to establish his identity (which includes his role in society) according to his own private obsessions. In so doing, Thomas Sutpen becomes a victim of his own innocence. According to Brooks:

It is par excellence the innocence of modern man, though it has not, to be sure, been confined to modern times. One can find more than a trace of it in Sophocles' Oedipus, and it has its analogies with the rather brittle rationalism of Macbeth, though Macbeth tried to learn this innocence by an act of the will and proved to be a less than satisfactory pupil. But innocence of this sort can properly be claimed as a special characteristic of modern man, and one can claim further that it flourishes particularly in a secularized society.

Perhaps because Sutpen lives in a nonsecularized society, his innocence does not flourish but becomes the cause of his downfall.

The year after *William Faulkner: The Yoknapatawpha Country* was published, Brooks was appointed cultural attaché to the American embassy in London. Surely, his most memorable assignment there was to represent the U.S. government at the memorial service for T. S. Eliot in Westminster Abbey in February 1965. During his two years in England, Brooks delivered more than 140 lectures throughout Great Britain and the European continent. Several of them later were published in his collection of essays *A Shaping Joy: Studies in the Writer's Craft* (1971). The experience in England enabled Brooks to renew contacts with friends from his days at Oxford. In fact, his old tutor Nevill Coghill invited him to deliver a lecture at a performance of *Dr. Faustus,* which was to star Coghill's former student the actor Richard Burton and Burton's new wife, Elizabeth Taylor. This production was delayed when the Burtons were summoned to Hollywood for the filming of *Who's Afraid of Virginia Woolf?* By the time they returned to Oxford, Brooks was already back at Yale.

During the time that Brooks served at the embassy in London, profound changes had occurred in American society. Within the university old-fashioned humanists frequently were vilified as reactionaries. If the New Criticism had once been a radical innovation in literary theory, it was now an embattled orthodoxy in

the literary salons of the Northeast. Nevertheless, Brooks's stature remained high in his native South. During his final years at Yale and for a decade after his retirement in 1975, he was guest professor at several southern universities. From 1969 to 1984, he taught on two separate occasions at LSU, the University of Tennessee, and the University of North Carolina and once each at Tulane University and Millsaps College in Jackson, Mississippi. He held research fellowships at the University of South Carolina and at the Humanities Center in Research Triangle Park, North Carolina. He also continued to be a regular contributor to southern magazines, such as the *Sewanee Review* and the *Southern Review,* the latter of which had been resurrected by LSU in 1965. Although the Brookses never moved back to the South, they regularly attended the annual meeting of the South Atlantic Modern Language Association and formed many close friendships with Southern writers and scholars.

Although *William Faulkner: The Yoknapatawpha Country* is Brooks's best-known and most distinguished work on southern literature, it represented only the beginning of a renewed engagement with the writing of his native region. In 1978 he published *William Faulkner: Toward Yoknapatawpha and Beyond,* a study of Faulkner's writings set outside his mythic postage stamp of soil. This volume was followed in 1983 by *William Faulkner: First Encounters,* a collection of introductory essays designed for the beginning student. Finally, in 1987, Brooks published a miscellaneous selection of lectures and discussions titled *On the Prejudices, Predilections, and Firm Beliefs of William Faulkner.* Brooks's bibliography also includes a sizable number of uncollected essays on other southern writers.

In April 1984 Cleanth Brooks became the twenty-eighth distinguished scholar to deliver the Dorothy Blount Lamar lectures in southern culture at Mercer University in Macon, Georgia. For his subject, he returned to the topic of his first book, the British origins of the southern language. Less technical than that earlier dialect study, these discussions were addressed to a general audience. Nevertheless, Brooks's conclusions had the professional imprimatur of the highly respected linguist Raven McDavid. In 1985 the Lamar lectures were published as *The Language of the American South,* exactly fifty years after Brooks's first book on the southern dialect.

Among the highlights of Brooks's career in the 1980s were two other significant speaking engagements—the Paul Anthony Brick lectures at the University of Missouri in April 1982 and the Jefferson lecture in Washington, D.C., in May 1985. In the Brick lectures Brooks defended his approach to criticism against some of the recent attacks to which it had been subjected. Specifically, he reasserted his belief in the primacy of the text against those approaches that would privilege the author, the reader, or the linguistic medium. (Harold Bloom, Stanley Fish, and Susan Sontag were among the contemporary theorists he challenged.) Not since the appendices to *The Well Wrought Urn* had Brooks so ably validated René Wellek's description of him as a "critic of critics." In contrast, Brooks's Jefferson address was a more general defense of the humanities in an age of technology. This annual lecture program had been initiated by the National Endowment for the Humanities in the early 1970s. The thirteen lecturers given before Brooks' had been delivered by Sidney Hook, Barbara Tuchman, Edward Shils, C. Vann Woodward, Saul Bellow, John Hope Franklin, Erik Erikson, Lionel Trilling, and Robert Penn Warren.

In the fall of 1985 Brooks and Warren were invited back to LSU for a program commemorating the fiftieth anniversary of the founding of the *Southern Review.* For three days in October, a host of prominent writers and critics discussed the role of Southern letters within the larger modernist movement. The young filmmaker Ken Burns helped recreate the ambiance of 1935 by screening his cinematic documentary on Huey Long. The university and the surrounding community celebrated twenty years of the new *Southern Review.* The real purpose of the conference, however, was to honor the two men who, in launching the original series of the magazine, had brought the South into modern literature and modern literature into the South. Two years later Brooks made his last significant contribution to southern culture by helping found the Fellowship of Southern Writers. Since 1987 this organization has enabled a select group of creative writers (along with a few editors and historians) to assert their identity as southerners, while encouraging new literary talent in the region. Brooks was the group's first chancellor.

Although Brooks maintained his professional activities until he was practically on his deathbed, advancing age brought changes to his personal life. In 1981 he and his wife sold their remote country home in Northford, Connecticut, and moved back into New Haven. Then, in May 1986, Tinkum Brooks was diagnosed with terminal lung cancer. She passed away in New Haven on the first of October and was buried in Roselawn Cemetery in Baton Rouge. Despite intense grief for his wife of fifty-two years, Brooks proved himself to be a stoic and resourceful survivor. Although he was nearly blind, he continued to write and lecture and travel to various parts of the world. When a cataract operation in the late 1980s restored much of his vision, he picked up the pace of his professional activities and seemed to be more spirited and vigorous than ever. At the same time, many of his contemporaries were gone. After a four-year bout with cancer, Brooks's lifelong friend and collaborator Robert Penn Warren died in September 1989.

The end came for Brooks himself in the spring of 1994. The previous year, he had made a large bequest to Yale University. He was at work on several projects, including a collection of essays for the University of Missouri Press. Throughout academia a backlash seemed to be forming against the fashionable critical theories and tendentious moralizing that recently had dominated literary studies. If Brooks had not actually been vindicated, he at least had lived long enough to see the tide moving back in his direction. Then, in late 1993, he learned that he had cancer of the esophagus. (Not long after that, cancer was discovered in his liver as well.) Over the next few months, Brooks fought valiantly to maintain his life and his career even as his health was deteriorating. In a remarkable display of will, he made one final trip to England to deliver a lecture at the University of London in March 1994. Not long after he returned, it became apparent that he had only weeks to live. After suffering a fall some time during the early morning of May 6, he began to fail even more rapidly. He died in the early morning of May 10. The burial, which was scheduled for the following week in Baton Rouge, had to be postponed because of torrential rains. Finally, on Saturday morning, May 21, 1994, Cleanth Brooks was laid to rest in a family plot near his parents and next to his wife.

A BLOSSOMING LABOR

Like so many public figures, Cleanth Brooks may well have been a victim of his own success. By his early forties, he had become so closely identified with the New Criticism that he was rightly credited with the many virtues of that approach and unfairly blamed for its perceived shortcomings. As long as the New Criticism was the dominant movement in literary studies, Brooks benefited from this equation. By the late 1950s, however, every facet of high modernism (the New Criticism included)

was under attack. The publication of Allen Ginsberg's *Howl* in 1956, Robert Penn Warren's *Promises* in 1957, and Robert Lowell's *Life Studies* in 1959 all signaled the return of the personal voice and overt emotion to poetry. The New Criticism, with its emphasis on irony, paradox, and allusion was ill equipped to deal with these new developments.

If the supremacy of the New Criticism seemed to have been assured by the publication of *The Well Wrought Urn* in 1947, the appearance of Northrop Frye's *Anatomy of Criticism* exactly ten years later indicated that readers and scholars alike were once again eager to look for literary meaning beyond the narrow confines of the text. Then, after another decade had passed, the intentionalist E. D. Hirsch reasserted the primacy of the author in *Validity in Interpretation,* while Stanley Fish championed the primacy of the audience in *Surprised by Sin: The Reader in Paradise Lost.* (Both of these men had studied with the New Critics at Yale, Fish having served as a grader for Brooks.) Just a year earlier, Susan Sontag had questioned the very possibility of literary criticism in *Against Interpretation* (1966). Finally, throughout the 1970s and well into the 1980s, all forms of traditional literary study were attacked from two very different sources.

Despite heated disputes over methodology and emphasis, critics of previous generations had agreed on two propositions—that literature was an art with its own internal dynamics and that the world of literature was connected intimately with the rest of human life. By the final third of the twentieth century, too many political activists were bent on destroying the integrity of literature by reducing it to its ideological content. At the other end of the epistemological spectrum, deconstructionists were treating literary texts as if they were simply elaborate cryptograms with no necessary connection to life at all. The only thing that all of these newer criticisms seemed to have in common was disdain for the approach to literature exemplified by Cleanth Brooks and company.

Brooks had the good fortune to live long enough to see the beginnings of a counterreformation in literary studies. By the mid-to late 1980s, both political correctness and deconstruction were being challenged aggressively. Brooks's own participation in the culture wars that raged during the final decade of his life did much to refute the cartoon image of the New Critic "trapped in a cell without windows or doors, staring through a reading glass at his literary text, effectually cut off from all the activities of the world outside—from history and science, from the other arts, and from nature and humanity itself" (from *A Shaping Joy*). Of course, anyone who was genuinely familiar with his work knows that there was never a time when such a caricature could accurately be applied to Brooks. He is probably best described as a cultural critic and public intellectual, who found close reading to be a remarkably effective way of getting at larger issues. Even in his most purely exegetical work, *The Well Wrought Urn*, we find an inchoate moral sensibility. When he examines individual poems, he looks for instances of wit, irony, and paradox. When he steps back and speaks of poetry in general, however, he talks of "coherence, sensitivity, depth, richness, and tough-mindedness." These are terms that reflect an attitude not just toward art but toward life itself.

Although Brooks was not a charter Fugitive or Agrarian, no one did more to incorporate the values of those two movements into our literary tradition. If very few contemporary poets write verse in the manner of the Fugitives, many poets and critics reflect the attention to craft evident in the long-ago meetings of that group. Literary creation may be a solitary act, but persons who are genuinely interested in how a poem works often feel compelled to converse with other likeminded individuals. The New Criticism, especially as it was practiced by Brooks and others of the extended Fugitive family, was largely a conversation of working poets. (Even those with no public reputation as imaginative writers possessed the technical interest that made New Criticism possible.) Because so many of the New Critics were also teachers, that conversation finally was extended beyond the inner circle of practitioners to include the countless students who have used New Critical textbooks or have been taught by people who did. Beginning with the classroom experiments that formed the basis for Richards's *Practical Criticism* in the 1920s, the New Criticism has often been a practical response to a pedagogical necessity.

The notion of Brooks as cultural critic challenges powerful stereotypes of both Brooks and cultural criticism. As we have seen, the view of Brooks engaging in exegesis for its own sake does not even account for the full range of his activities as a close reader. It fails utterly to explain what he has accomplished in a book such as *William Faulkner: The Yoknapatawpha Country,* which is New Critical only in the most tangential sense of the term. What Brooks does in that book—and in most of what he wrote during the last forty years of his life—is to show how culture informs literature and how literature in turn illuminates culture. Unfortunately, our image of cultural criticism (so indelibly identified with the contributors to *Partisan Review*) tends to be urban, Jewish, and Trotskyite or ex-Trotskyite. In contrast, Brooks's orientation was Agrarian, Christian, and socially conservative. (Perhaps a circle of sorts was closed in 1991, when Brooks, after participating in *Partisan Review's* symposium on "The Changing Culture of the University," commented only half in jest that the old Trotskyites were now to his right.) Brooks's cultural vision has had an immense influence not only on Faulkner studies but also on the substantial body of conservative literary criticism that has appeared since the mid-1980s. To paraphrase Yeats's "Among School Children," his achievement has proved to be a blossoming labor.

Selected Bibliography

WORKS OF CLEANTH BROOKS

CRITICAL STUDIES

The Relation of the Alabama-Georgia Dialect to the Provincial Dialects of Great Britain. Baton Rouge: Louisiana State University Press, 1935.

Modern Poetry and the Tradition. Chapel Hill: University of North Carolina Press, 1939.

The Well Wrought Urn: Studies in the Structure of Poetry. New York: Reynal and Hitchcock, 1947.

Literary Criticism: A Short History. With William K. Wimsatt. New York: Knopf, 1957.

The Hidden God: Studies in Hemingway, Faulkner, Yeats, Eliot, and Warren. New Haven: Yale University Press, 1963.

William Faulkner: The Yoknapatawpha Country. New Haven: Yale University Press, 1963.

A Shaping Joy: Studies in the Writer's Craft. New York: Harcourt Brace Jovanovich, 1971.

William Faulkner: Toward Yoknapatawpha and Beyond. New Haven: Yale University Press, 1978.

The Rich Manifold: The Author, the Reader, the Linguistic Medium. Edited with an interview by Joseph M. Ditta and Ronald S. Librach. Columbia: *Missouri Review*, 1983.

William Faulkner: First Encounters. New Haven: Yale University Press, 1983.

The Language of the American South. Athens: University of Georgia Press, 1985.

On the Prejudices, Predilections, and Firm Beliefs of William Faulkner: Essays. Baton Rouge: Louisiana State University Press, 1987.

Historical Evidence and the Reading of Seventeenth-Century Poetry. Columbia: University of Missouri Press, 1991.

Community, Religion, and Literature. Columbia: University of Missouri Press, 1995.

BOOKS EDITED BY CLEANTH BROOKS

An Approach to Literature: A Collection of Prose and Verse with Analyses and Discussions. With Robert Penn Warren and John Thibaut Purser. Baton Rouge: Louisiana State University Press, 1936. Rev. ed., Englewood Cliffs, N.J.: Prentice-Hall, 1975.

Understanding Poetry: An Anthology for College Students. With Robert Penn Warren. New York: Henry Holt, 1938. Rev. ed., New York: Holt, Rinehart and Winston, 1976.

Understanding Fiction. With Robert Penn Warren. New York: F. S. Crofts, 1943. Rev. ed., Englewood Cliffs, N.J.: Prentice-Hall, 1979.

The Percy Letters. Baton Rouge: Louisiana State University Press, 1944–1961 (vols. 1–5); New Haven: Yale University Press, 1962–1988 (vols. 6–9). (Volumes 1–6 edited with David Nichol Smith and volumes 7–9 with A. F. Falconer.)

Understanding Drama: Twelve Plays. With Robert B. Heilman. New York: Henry Holt, 1945. Rev. ed., 1948.

Modern Rhetroic, with Readings. With Robert Penn Warren. New York: Harcourt Brace Jovanovich, 1949. Rev. ed., New York: Harcourt Brace Jovanovich, 1979.

Fundamentals of Good Writing: A Handbook of Modern Rhetoric. With Robert Penn Warren. New York: Harcourt Brace Jovanovich, 1950.

Poems of Mr. John Milton: The 1645 Edition with Essays in Analysis. With John Edward Hardy. New York: Harcourt Brace Jovanovich, 1951.

An Anthology of Stories from the Southern Review. With Robert Penn Warren. Baton Rouge: Louisiana State University Press, 1953.

Tragic Themes in Western Literature. New Haven: Yale University Press, 1955.

American Literature: The Makers and the Making. With R. W. B. Lewis and Robert Penn Warren. 2 vols. New York: St. Martin's Press, 1973.

COLLECTED CORRESPONDENCE

Cleanth Brooks and Allen Tate: Collected Letters, 1933–1976. Columbia: University of Missouri Press, 1998.

Cleanth Brooks and Robert Penn Warren: A Literary Correspondence. Columbia: University of Missouri Press, 1998.

UNCOLLECTED ESSAYS AND REVIEWS

"A Plea to the Protestant Churches." In *Who Owns America? A New Declaration of Independence.*

18 / AMERICAN WRITERS

Edited by Herbert Agar and Allen Tate. Boston: Houghton Mifflin, 1936. Pp. 323–333. Rev. ed., Wilmington, Delaware: ISI Books, 1999.

"The Poem as Organism: Modern Critical Procedure." In *English Institute Annual, 1940.* New York: Columbia University Press, 1941. Pp. 20–41.

"Metaphor and the Function of Criticism." In *Spiritual Problems in Contemporary Literature: A Series of Addresses and Discussions.* Edited by Stanley Romaine Hopper. New York: Institute of Religious and Social Studies, 1952. Pp. 127–137.

"Irony as a Principle of Structure." In *Literary Opinion in America: Essays Illustrating the Status, Methods, and Problems of Criticism in the United States in the Twentieth Century.* Edited by Morton D. Zabel. New York: Harper and Brothers, 1937. Rev. ed., New York: Harper & Row, 1962. Pp. 729–741.

"Marvell's 'Horatian Ode.'" In *Seventeenth-Century English Poetry: Modern Essays in Criticism.* Edited by William R. Keast. New York: Oxford University Press, 1962. Pp. 321–340. (Reprinted from *Sewanee Review* 55:199–222 [winter 1947].)

"A Note on the Limits of 'History' and the Limits of 'Criticism.'" *Seventeenth-Century English Poetry: Modern Essays in Criticism.* Edited by William R. Keast. New York: Oxford University Press, 1962. Pp. 352–358. (Reprinted from *Sewanee Review* 61:129–135 [winter 1953].)

"I. A. Richards and *Practical Criticism.*" In *The Critics Who Made Us: Essays from the Sewanee Review.* Edited by George Core. Columbia: University of Missouri Press, 1993. Pp. 35–46. (Reprinted from the *Sewanee Review* 89:586–595 [fall 1981].)

PERSONAL PAPERS

The bulk of Cleanth Brooks's papers are collected in the Beinecke Rare Book and Manuscript Library at Yale University. Other papers are held at the University of Kentucky, the Newberry Library of the University of Chicago, and the Joint University Libraries of the University of Tennessee.

BIBLIOGRAPHY

Walsh, John Michael. *Cleanth Brooks: An Annotated Bibliography.* New York: Garland, 1990. (An annotated primary and secondary bibliography. With the exception of Brooks's poetry, this is comprehensive up through the late 1980s.)

CRITICAL AND BIOGRAPHICAL STUDIES

Bush, Douglas. "The New Criticism: Some Old-Fashioned Queries." *PMLA* 64, supplement, part 2:13–21 (March 1949). (Dismisses the New Criticism as "an advanced course in remedial reading." Particularly critical of both *Modern Poetry and the Tradition* and *The Well Wrought Urn.*)

———. "Marvell's 'Horatian Ode.'" In *Seventeenth-Century English Poetry: Modern Essays in Criticism.* Edited by William R. Keast. New York: Oxford University Press, 1962. Pp. 341–351. (Reprinted from *Sewanee Review* 60:363–376 [fall 1952]. In his role as historical critic, Bush takes exception to Brooks's reading of Marvell's poem.)

Crane, Ronald S. "The Critical Monism of Cleanth Brooks." In *Critics and Criticism: Ancient and Modern.* Edited by Ronald S. Crane. Chicago: University of Chicago Press, 1952. Pp. 83–107. (A neo-Aristotelian attack on Brooks's critical method.)

Culler, Jonathan D. *On Deconstruction: Theory and Criticism after Structuralism.* Ithaca, N.Y.: Cornell University Press, 1982. (Contains an extensive deconstructive critique of Brooks's reading of Donne's "Canonization.")

Cutrer, Thomas W. *Parnassus on the Mississippi: The Southern Review and the Baton Rouge Literary Community, 1935–1942.* Baton Rouge: Louisiana State University Press, 1984. (This detailed history of the original series of the *Southern Review* contains much useful information on Brooks's early years at LSU.)

Fish, Stanley. "Why Literary Criticism Is Like Virtue." *London Review of Books,* June 10, 1993, pp. 11–16. (Champions Brooks's position in his debate with Bush over the meaning of Marvell's "Horatian Ode.")

Hardy, John Edward. "The Achievement of Cleanth Brooks." *Hopkins Review* 6:148–161 (spring 1953). (Defends Brooks against both his attackers and his more inept imitators.)

Heilman, Robert Bechtold. *The Southern Connection: Essays.* Baton Rouge: Louisiana State

University Press, 1991. (This book on southern culture contains six essays that provide insight into Brooks's life and work.)

Hirsch, E. D., Jr. *Validity in Interpretation.* New Haven: Yale University Press, 1967. (Using Brooks's reading of Wordsworth's "A slumber did my spirit seal," Hirsch faults the New Criticism for its indifference to authorial intention.)

Krieger, Murray. *The New Apologists for Poetry.* Minneapolis: University of Minnesota Press, 1956. (Critiques the aesthetic assumptions underlying the New Criticism, as practiced by Brooks and others.)

McHaney, Thomas L. "Brooks on Faulkner: The End of the Long View." *Review* 1:29–45 (1979). (Believes that Brooks's view of Faulkner is both too academic and too Southern.)

Purdy, Rob Roy, ed. *Fugitives Reunion: Conversations at Vanderbilt, May 3–5, 1956.* Nashville, Tenn.: Vanderbilt University Press, 1959.

Rubin, Louis D., Jr. "Cleanth Brooks: A Memory." *Sewanee Review* 103:265–280 (spring 1995). (An affectionate assessment of Brooks's life and work published shortly after his death.)

Shankar, D. A. *Cleanth Brooks: An Assessment.* Bangalore: G. K. Ananthram, IBH Prakashana, 1981. (A mostly negative discussion of Brooks's criticism.)

Simpson, Lewis P., ed. *The Possibilities of Order: Cleanth Brooks and His Works.* Baton Rouge: Louisiana State University Press, 1976. (A festschrift published at the time of Brooks's retirement from Yale. Includes a conversation between Brooks and Warren and essays by Allen Tate, Robert B. Heilman, Walter J. Ong, Thomas Daniel Young, and Monroe K. Spears.)

———. "A Certain Continuity." In *The Southern Review and Modern Literature, 1935–1985.* Edited by Lewis S. Simpson, James Olney, and Jo Gulledge. Baton Rouge: Louisiana State University Press, 1987. (A discussion of the relationship between the original series and the new series of the *Southern Review.*)

Spears, Monroe K. "'Kipper of de Vineyards.'" *New York Review of Books,* May 7, 1987, pp. 38–41. (An extremely favorable and discerning review of Brooks's *Language of the American South.*)

Tassin, Anthony G. "The Phoenix and the Urn: The

Literary Theory and Criticism of Cleanth Brooks." Ph.D. dissertation, Louisiana State University, Baton Rouge, 1966. (A comprehensive account of Brooks's contributions to the New Criticism through the 1950s. Particularly thorough in its consideration of objections to Brooks's methodology.)

Wellek, René. "Cleanth Brooks." In his *History of Modern Criticism, 1750–1950.* Volume 6, *American Criticism 1900–1950.* New Haven: Yale University Press, 1986. Pp. 188–213. (A discussion of Brooks's place in twentieth-century criticism. A shorter version of this essay had appeared in Simpson's *The Possibilities of Order.*)

Winchell, Mark Royden. "Cleanth Brooks as Fugitive Poet." *South Carolina Review* 27:13–20 (fall 1994/spring 1995). (A discussion of Brooks's poetry. Includes the texts of five poems.)

———. *Cleanth Brooks and the Rise of Modern Criticism.* Charlottesville: University Press of Virginia, 1996. (The definitive account of Brooks's life and work.)

Wortman, Marc. "Shattering the Urn." *Yale Alumni Magazine,* December 1990, pp. 32, 34–35, 38–39. (An account of the battle between the deconstructionists and New Critics at Yale.)

INTERVIEWS

Blanken, Linda. "Cleanth Brooks: The Fourteenth Jefferson Lecturer in the Humanities." *Humanities,* April 1985, pp. 4–6. (A general discussion of Brooks's life and work and the famous people he knew.)

Buckley, Reid. "A *Partisan* Conversation: Cleanth Brooks." *Southern Partisan* 3:22–26 (spring 1983). (Deals largely with Brooks's relationship to the South. Also touches on his disapproval of changes in the Episcopal liturgy.)

Ditta, Joseph M., and Ronald S. Librach. "Sounding the Past: A Discussion with Cleanth Brooks." *Missouri Review* 6:139–160 (fall 1982). (Interviewed at the time of the Brick lectures, Brooks comments on the shortcomings of some of the newer critical theories.)

Leggett, B. J. "Notes for a Revised History of the New Criticism: An Interview with Cleanth Brooks." *Tennessee Studies in Literature* 24:1–35

(1979). (An extended discussion of the state of criticism in the academy.)

Warren, Robert Penn. "A Conversation with Cleanth Brooks." In *The Possibilities of Order: Cleanth Brooks and His Works.* Edited by Lewis P. Simpson. Baton Rouge: Louisiana State University Press, 1976. Pp. 1–124. (A long discursive colloquy dealing with a wide range of topics.)

—*MARK ROYDEN WINCHELL*

James Lee Burke

1936–

"*I* HAVE NEVER thought of my vocation as work," James Lee Burke writes in the *New York Times* essay "Seeking a Vision of Truth, Guided by a Higher Power." "A real writer is driven both by obsession and a secret vanity, namely that he has a perfect vision of the truth. ... If the writer does not convey that vision to someone else, his talent turns to a self-consuming bitterness." Given the trials that Burke faced early in his career to become one of the most recognized crime writers working today—and arguably the most "literary" on his statement illustrates the writer's passion, determination, and respect for the creative impulse.

Burke was born December 5, 1936, in Houston, Texas, the only child of James Lee Burke Sr., a natural gas engineer, and Frances Benbow Burke, a secretary. Although he was raised in Houston (and he would make good use of his knowledge of Texas in the Billy Bob Holland novels), Burke spent much of his time in the bayous of Louisiana, particularly New Iberia, the place that would take on nearly mythic qualities in the highly successful Dave Robicheaux series. Those Gulf Coast landscapes were crucial in defining Burke's sensibility, his characters drawn from the people he knew growing up in oil country and his later work on a drilling rig in the Gulf of Mexico. An experience recounted in the short story "Water People" portrays the landscape as a character as strong as any of the men who make their living on the rig:

> Our drill barge was moored out in the middle of this long flat bay, like a big rectangle of gray iron welded onto a cookie sheet, I mean it was so hot anything you touched scalded your hand, and the sun was a red ball when it rose up out of the water, and you could smell dead things on the wind out in the marsh, amongst all those flooded willows and cypress and gum trees. That was right before Hurricane Audrey hit the Louisiana coast in 1957. The thundershowers we got in the afternoon weren't anything more than hot steam, and when lightning hit on the sandbars you could see it dancing under the chop, flickering, like yellow snakes flipping around in a barrel full of dark water.

Burke's ability to weave images of nature seamlessly into his fiction is a result of having been influenced by the work of the naturalists, especially the American novelists Stephen Crane and John Steinbeck. Fittingly, many of Burke's characters struggle against an environment that, for all its strength and beauty, seems to be utterly indifferent to their suffering.

Burke—whose later work would be compared with southern and hard-boiled crime writers as disparate as Jayne Anne Phillips, Walker Percy, John Kennedy Toole, Dashiell Hammett, and Raymond Chandler—had a penchant, even as a child, for recording his experiences. He became infatuated with the life of the writer while he was still a student at the Southwestern Louisiana Institute (later the University of Southwestern Louisiana) in Lafayette in the mid-1950s. His cousin, the noted writer Andre Dubus, encouraged Burke's own writing by winning a college writing contest; it was through Dubus that Burke later made connections with a New York agent, Philip Spitzer. While enrolled in college, Burke studied the classic storytellers and thinkers, including Homer, William Faulkner, Samuel Taylor Coleridge, Francis Bacon, and John Stuart Mill. He credits Lyle Williams, a freshman English professor, with being a profound influence on his writing and his attitude toward the craft. Williams cajoled her overly confident and undisciplined student into becoming a better writer by focusing on Burke's "heart" and fine-tuning the young writer's style.

After completing his bachelor's degree at the University of Missouri in 1959 and a master's in teaching a year later, Burke returned to teach at the University of Southwestern Louisiana. In 1965 his first novel, *Half of Paradise,* was published to positive reviews. Restless with his life, Burke and his wife, Pearl Pai Chu, a Chinese émigré who had come to the United States in 1949 and whom Burke had married in 1960, spent the next decade crossing the country in search of viable employment. Burke worked on many odd jobs, but the one most conducive to his writing was as a surveyor in Texas and Colorado. Burke also worked during those years as a truck driver for the U.S. Forest Service, a teacher in the Job Corps, a reporter, and a social worker in Los Angeles—varied experiences that would inform his fiction. Burke and his wife have four children, a fact that explains the strong family life of his protagonist Dave Robicheaux. Burke also immerses himself in the landscapes that he describes in his novels, dividing his time between Louisiana and Montana since receiving a Guggenheim Fellowship in 1989 and becoming a regular fixture on the *New York Times* best-seller list.

After early success, Burke was confident he had found his niche as a writer. In 1970 he published *To the Bright and Shining Sun,* the book that would be the high point of his career for more than a decade. He signed with the William Morris Agency, his representation when *Lay Down My Sword and Shield* (1971) was published the following year. The critical reception of Burke's third novel was lukewarm, and the relationship with Morris did little to further the author's career. While shopping the manuscript for his next novel, *The Lost Get-Back Boogie,* (1986) Burke received more than one hundred rejection slips—a record of futility that, as New York publishing lore has it, still stands. He was cut loose by the agency after his work languished for another six years without being published.

Despite a frustrating—and prolonged—lack of success after an encouraging start to his career, Burke spent the next decade writing short stories and completing manuscripts that he could not place. When Louisiana State University Press published *The Lost Get-Back Boogie* in 1986, the book was nominated for a Pulitzer Prize. In the *New York Times,* Regina Weinreich echoes what readers and critics alike admire about Burke's work when she deems Burke's writing in that book "exceptionally poetic: a muscular prose enlivened by lyric descriptions of the landscape and the lingo of the roughnecks Paret [the protagonist] encounters in the American hinterland."

The novel was important for both Burke's professional career and his personal life. The author's struggle with alcohol has been well documented, and Burke has been forthcoming in interviews about his descent, his dedication to a twelve-step program, and his faith in a higher power.

The Lost Get-Back Boogie was a fitting prelude to *The Neon Rain* (1987), the first in the best-selling Robicheaux series, which had reached a dozen installments by 2002. Burke wrote *The Neon Rain* at the suggestion of a writer and friend, Rick DeMarinis, as the two fished on Montana's Bitterroot River. In *Cimarron Rose* (1997), he introduced a new series protagonist, Billy Bob Holland, a Texas Ranger-cum-lawyer who has provided Burke's audience with a more contemplative complement to the hard-charging Robicheaux. *White Doves at Morning* (2002), a departure for Burke from both series, shifts the author's focus to a narrative that examines the root causes of racism and societal discord in the Civil War South.

MATTERS OF CHARACTER

Burke professes not to know the genesis of the characters and the plots for his novels, writing in "Seeking a Vision of Truth" that "the material for the stories is everywhere. The whole human family becomes your cast of characters. You can give voice to those who have none and expose those who would turn the earth into a sludge pit." Those characters suggest amalgams of Burke's memories and myth, the characters that have come down to him through experience and the oral tradition in the South.

Burke has a knack for humanizing even minor characters, whose names evoke a uniquely southern milieu: Bubba Rocque, Tee Beau Latiolais, Dixie Lee Pugh, Julie "Baby Feet" Balboni, Garland T. Moon, Vachel Carmouche, and myriad other similarly eclectic pimps, prostitutes, Mafiosi, and miscreants populate the novels. Burke draws those characters from the background into the fore of his novels at will and creates a thick context within which—and against which—Robicheaux, Holland, and his other protagonists live out their complex lives.

One recurring character who plays that role is Batist, the black man who works for Robicheaux in his bait shop in New Iberia. Like Robicheaux, Batist's greatest concern is the ordering of his life. Unlike Robicheaux, he is able to compartmentalize his experiences and place them in a context that allows him a peace of mind that often eludes Robicheaux. As Burke describes him in *Heaven's Prisoners* (1988):

> Batist was absolutely obsessive about understanding any information that was foreign to his world, but as a rule he would have to hack and hew it into pieces until it would assimilate into that strange Afro-Creole-Acadian frame of reference that was as natural to him as wearing a dime on a string around his ankle to ward off the gris-gris.

For that reason, as Richard B. Schwartz writes in *Nice and Noir,*

> Batist counsels prudence and serves as a form of conscience, like an intervening god in classical epic, grasping a hero's arm in a moment of rash action. As such, his portrayal is somewhat Faulknerian, a black figure holding society together, though he may not be sufficiently rewarded or appreciated for his actions.

Robicheaux's relationship with Batist is perhaps the most symbolic of any in the novels: though he is the man's friend, Robicheaux understands the contradictions inherent in the relationship, much as he understands that he is always one misstep away from destroying what he has so scrupulously cultivated over the years. The further Robicheaux retreats from his dissipative days, the more he has to lose; behind the scenes Batist provides a largely unspoken, and for the most part unacknowledged, bulwark against which Robicheaux leans in hard times.

The "southernness" of Burke's novels is articulated not only in the mannerisms of his many characters and the roles that they play but also in the way those characters lives are affected by their collective past, an earmark of the literature of the South, particularly in terms of race relations and genealogy. The encroachment of the past (read "history," in all the connotations of that word) on the present becomes more pronounced as the series continue. This is a reflection of the possibilities that arise after the characters have been initially developed and their lives have taken on the veneer of stability, a stability that is markedly absent in Robicheaux's life as he faces his demons and finally finds solace—tenuous as it is—in the landscapes of his childhood. Robicheaux is cognizant of the fact that history hangs like a shroud on the people who surround him, and he asserts:

> We all have an extended family, people whom we recognize as our own as soon as we see them. The

people closest to me have always been marked by a peculiar difference in their makeup. They're the walking wounded, the ones to whom a psychological injury was done that they will never be able to define.

The unspoken experiential choreography between the characters is as important as the plots themselves. Depth of character, more than any other aspect of Burke's fiction, is what blurs the line between crime fiction and more "literary" work.

EARLY WORK

The novels that Burke would write beginning with *The Neon Rain,* the first novel in the Robicheaux series, overshadow the work that came before. Those five novels and a collection of short stories are crucial, however, in establishing the later direction of Burke's writing. Before his thirtieth birthday, Burke published *Half of Paradise,* a novel (a loose accretion, really, of three novellas) that tells the stories of three men whose lives are connected by failure. Burke's descriptions of nature come to the fore, the first lines suggesting nature's passive complicity in their fates: "After the spring rains when the first hot days of summer begin, the inland waters of the Gulf of Mexico turn smoky-green from the floating seaweed, fading to dark blue beyond the sandbars where the great white pelicans dive for fish." Such openings would become one of the trademarks of Burke's fiction.

Each of the three "books" that make up the narrative is told in voices reminiscent of those in Faulkner's *As I Lay Dying,* one for each of the protagonists—Avery Broussard, J. P. Winfield, and Toussaint Boudreaux. Burke intertwines those scattershot images and events in a strategy mirroring the complex plotlines that came to characterize the Robicheaux and Holland series, focusing on characterization without sacrificing his eye for the pungent detail. For instance, in the third and final book, "When the Sun Begins to Shine," Toussaint Boudreaux

> smelled the clean odor of the earth. He rubbed some dirt between his hands. This was good land. The corn was high and green, and there was a field of strawberries across the road .... There had been his time in prison, and before that the city where he saw nothing except concrete buildings and the faces of people he didn't understand, nor who understood him. He could have lain in the field without ever getting up.

Boudreaux, a black New Orleans longshoreman and journeyman boxer, finds himself unwittingly used by a theft ring. After being sentenced to ten years in prison, he is killed during an attempted escape. Broussard, a white scion of a family that once held sway in the South, and Winfield, a poor white musician, meet similar ends; despite some otherwise saving qualities, the three are part of a larger cautionary tale.

Boudreaux's inability to function in a society from which he is profoundly alienated is evident here and is at the heart of much of Burke's fiction. Perhaps even more significant is his protagonist's connection with the earth, and Burke would build on these early statements of the fundamental goodness of man's cohabitation with nature in later narratives that decry big business and faceless corporations for the dissipation of our natural resources.

Burke's first fiction was lauded in a *New York Times* review in which Wirt Williams compared the book to John Dos Passo's *U.S.A.* trilogy. Williams also emphatically compared Burke's writing to that of Marcel Proust, André Gide, Faulkner, Ernest Hemingway, Thomas Hardy, and Jean-Paul Sartre, asserting that the author's narrative framework

> offers [him] a chance to create remarkably diverse areas of experience. He renders [scenes] vividly ...: shabby-genteel plantation houses, poor-white small towns and pool halls and brothels, the small-time prize ring, "country music" promoters, low-

level Louisiana politics, the pseudo artists of the French Quarter and an undiluted love affair.

The characters and contexts of Burke's first fiction are translated to the coalfields of Kentucky and the plains of Texas, respectively, in *To the Bright and Shining Sun* and *Lay Down My Sword and Shield*. The novels focus on the class warfare that would become an important issue in Burke's later work. Burke's protagonist in *To the Bright and Shining Sun* is Perry Woodson Hatfield James (a descendent of both the Hatfields of feud fame and Frank James, famed outlaw Jessie's brother), a seventeen-year-old, third-generation coal miner with a young man's capacity for indignation and a determination to survive in a world that cares little for him or what he does. When his father is injured and later dies in an explosion set by antiunion forces, James is forced to make the transition from impetuous young man to head of the family.

Physical confrontation permeates Burke's novels, and Burke establishes the rift here between the colliding factions in terms of violence: "Woodson James lost all his fingers on one hand except the thumb, his face was badly burned, and a sliver of board was driven through his back into the lung." Likewise, Burke articulates the visceral power of place and uses those descriptions to give even more depth to his material. The narrative hints at the explorations of history and its impact on the present that are at the core of Burke's later work. The novel ends much as it began—with an invocation of the landscape:

> The purple silhouette of the hills stood out against the sky when lightning crashed into a hollow, and he could smell the sweet odor of wet earth in the tobacco fields and meadows. Part of the moon shone from behind a cloud, and the rain in his hair reflected like drops of crystal.

In *Lay Down My Sword and Shield,* Hack Holland, a Texas lawyer, runs for Congress as a Democrat, an unpopular decision with the prevailing powers in government. The saga of the Holland family would be revisited in *Two for Texas* (1982), in which Son Holland, grandfather of Hack Holland, escapes from a prison camp and joins Sam Houston as he readies to battle the Mexican general Santa Anna in the fight for Texas independence. As with so much of Burke's fiction, there is a historic precedent in the story of Son Holland: Burke's great-great-grandfather actually fought with Sam Houston in 1835 and moved to New Iberia to become a sugar farmer in 1836. The book was a paperback original, as important to Burke's career for getting his name recognized in the publishing business as for the modest critical reception that the book garnered. Burke would not be published in hardcover again until Louisiana State University Press took on *The Convict: Stories* (1985), a collection of short stories through which the author kept his skills sharp while seeking a publisher, and the breakthrough *The Lost Get-Back Boogie.*

Although much of what Burke had written before the introduction of Robicheaux is deemed by critics to be a rehearsal for the author's most popular series, the character who most resembles Robicheaux is the protagonist of *The Lost Get-Back Boogie,* Iry Paret. Both Robicheaux and Paret gain voice through the first-person narrative; both men have been acculturated to (and have difficulty getting accustomed to) the New South; both view their society's inhabitants with a thoroughgoing ambivalence that underpins the narratives; both have a problem with alcohol; like Robicheaux later, Paret evokes the memory of his dead father; and Paret was wounded twice in Korea while Robicheaux carries physical and psychic scars from the war in Vietnam. In a flashback to Korea, Paret recalls that "I believed truly for the first time that I was all right, because I realized that insanity was not a matter of individual illness; it was abroad in all men, and its definition was a very relative matter."

The scenes would be revisited in more than one Robicheaux novel with the death of the protagonist's own father.

Perhaps the most important characteristic that the two protagonists share, however, is their righteous indignation over society's lack of concern for justice—in Paret's case, the denigration of America's natural resources. Paret moves to Montana upon his release from Angola Penitentiary, where he has been incarcerated for the accidental killing of a man in a barroom, a wanton act that still haunts him. Though he finds respite on the ranch of Frank Riordan—and with Riordan's estranged daughter-in-law—he realizes that he has landed in the midst of an Edenic landscape on the verge of destruction. That destruction is a metaphor for many of the problems society faces in Burke's later novels: poverty (and class warfare); a crumbling family structure; and the disintegration of a recognizable personal ethics. Paret manages to gain some peace in his life—namely, through marriage to a woman and the acquisition of a small plot of land that "has a small stream and apple trees on it, and at night the deer come down to feed in the grass under an ivory moon." Still, Burke has planted the seed for the confrontations that would follow. In the novel's epilogue, the blues piano that is central in Paret's life beats in rhythm with his own heart. While, on the surface, the image is a picture-perfect ending to the narrative, it belies a tension never fully dissipated in this novel or in the subsequent Robicheaux novels.

THE FALL AND RISE OF DAVE ROBICHEAUX

Five years after the first appearance of his most popular character, Burke received high praise from the author Joyce Carol Oates for his talent as a writer. She also singled him out for expanding the genre of the crime novel and creating a "complex and convincing protagonist, a deeply moral, but troubled and self-divided man who strikes us as the antithesis of the stereotypical macho detective of popular culture." Oates compares Burke favorably to such contemporary crime writers as James Ellroy, David Lindsey, Elmore Leonard, Sara Paretsky, Colin Harrison, and Thomas Harris, and she credits the author with revitalizing the crime-writing genre by exploring "issues of ecology, politics, gender, race, public vs. private morality, among others," and "blur[ring] the boundaries between such work and the literary mainstream."

The Neon Rain, the series' first novel, introduces the character that Burke's readers have come to admire over the space of a dozen novels. Robicheaux begins as an expansive archetype of the rough, alcoholic detective in the noir mold before establishing his own voice in later novels. And Burke's narrative focuses as much on Robicheaux's character—his weaknesses, his passion for justice, his growing and changing understanding of mortality—as it does on the crimes that play out in his sphere of influence, the fecund landscapes of Louisiana that Robicheaux compares in *Jolie Blon's Bounce* (2002) to a relationship with the "biblical whore of Babylon." In fact, Burke tells W. C. Stroby, the books are primarily "mysteries about the psychology of Dave Robicheaux."

Robicheaux's intimate knowledge of the characters that inhabit his landscape both facilitates and hinders his ability to solve crimes. Invariably, Robicheaux sides with the underdogs in these novels, though he cannot always trust his own instincts. Critical interest for the character has been fueled by the stark, at times disarming ambivalence with which Burke treats his protagonist and his actions. Robicheaux, a Vietnam veteran whose past randomly encroaches upon his psyche, lives in a dark world, only some of it of his enemies' making. In much hard-boiled fiction the good guys and the bad guys are clearly delineated; Robicheaux has no such luxury. His world could not be more nebulous, and he is often the root cause of the problems that arise in the course of the narratives. Not surprisingly, as Robicheaux is fully a product of the South (and Burke repeatedly attempts to discover the shifting locus of the concept of the "South" and to define that loaded word), he is, at least in part, determined by the cultural context within which he has been raised.

The first-person narrative, which some critics question for the artificiality of the omniscient narrator, allows Burke to combine elements of the "traditional" crime novel with a more focused exploration of the protagonist's professional and personal lives, which are rarely unrelated. Robicheaux's code of ethics—a combination of the gentility and decorum of the Old South and a liberal attitude toward nature and others (distinctly different from the "New South" that Robicheaux observes with disdain)—underpins the narratives. Although Robicheaux seldom wavers in his commitment to that code, he is occasionally so conflicted by the events of his past—his alcoholism, flashbacks to Vietnam, the fates of his parents and other loved ones, a general malaise that borders on clinical depression—that part of his character's appeal for a wide audience is that of the flawed common man who battles his demons to perform extraordinary acts. As Richard Schwartz asserts in reference to Robicheaux's neo-chivalric attitudes, "Such simple but high-minded ideals come very close to melodramatic or formulaic pieties. They are possible only within a narrative that is both morally compelling and highly textured. In order to make you feel, Burke first makes you see and taste, touch, hear, and smell."

Notions of place, so important in the early novels, take on added importance in the Robicheaux series: the detective's status as a recovering alcoholic makes him especially vulnerable to the decadence of New Orleans, and the external world he inhabits mirrors the contradictions that he faces daily within himself.

As Ralph Willett points out in his analysis of New Orleans as a hotbed for crime fiction, the binaries that exist in the city are an integral part of the negotiation and contradiction that defines Robicheaux's complex character:

> Poverty and decay surround the romantic, classy Garden District which clings to its French and Spanish origins; Desire, also the name of a street, runs parallel with Piety in the Fourth Ward. Such contrasts are typical. Elegant and decadent, New Orleans is a site of contradictions, of luxury and decline, of beauty and brutality, of Christianity and paganism.

LeRoy Panek, in his study *New Hard-Boiled Writers,* also asserts:

> In addition to the way in which Dave responds to the disparity between the Louisiana of his childhood and the Louisiana of the present, being brought up in the state brings with it other problems than those of the twentieth century .... Burke's books are southern novels, and one doesn't need to reread Faulkner to know about the ways in which being southern can make one miserable."

In his concern for the disenfranchised, Burke's protagonist often faces crises of confidence so severe that he lives always one arrest (or shooting or beating) from becoming what he so vehemently despises. That rage for order is a substitute for his drinking, and, not coincidentally, Robicheaux's references to "dry drunks"— feelings of intoxication and loss of control even while sober—come either immediately before or after gratuitous and ultimately cathartic acts of violence. In fact, the shifting line between Robicheaux and the "bad guys" is the gray area that Burke mines so effectively.

Those acts of violence are part of the litany of contradictions that define New Orleans and the Louisiana bayou. Despite his desire to the contrary, Robicheaux repeatedly proves capable of such violence, calling into question the stability that he so passionately seeks in his personal life. As in previous novels, *The Neon Rain* opens with a jarring image, the bayou described in terms both impressionistic and ominous:

> The evening sky was streaked with purple, the color of torn plums, and a light rain had started to fall when I came to the end of the blacktop road that cut through twenty miles of thick, almost impenetrable scrub oak and pine and stopped at the front gate of Angola penitentiary.

Robicheaux describes the scene on his way to visit the murderer Johnny Massina, who is about to be executed. Massina unburdens his soul to his unlikely confessor, making reference to the detective's sordid past and his tenuous connections to the New Orleans criminal underworld and surprising Robicheaux with news of a contract on his head. Racism, a central theme in the series, is fueled by Robicheaux's interest in the death of a young black girl, which draws attention from the mob, federal agents, and weapons smugglers.

The book marks the introduction of the recurring character Clete Purcel, Robicheaux's sometimes partner and longtime friend. Clete, whom Burke has compared to Don Quixote's companion Sancho Panza, has very little of the sense of right and wrong that generally guides Robicheaux's actions. He is a rough man with a "face [that] looked like it was made from boiled pigskin, except there were stitch scars across the bridge of his nose and through one eyebrow, where he'd been bashed by a pipe when he was a kid in the Irish Channel." In the novel *A Stained White Radiance* (1992), Robicheaux describes his friend as a "happy zoo animal." Nonetheless, the man's loyalty, which is questioned by Robicheaux on more than one occasion because of his absolute amorality and mercenary attitudes, keeps Robicheaux alive.

The first-person narrative is filtered through Robicheaux's own experiences, and Robicheaux offers frequent and candid admissions of his state of mind as signposts to further action. The reader can never be sure how reliable Robicheaux's perceptions are. In fact, even after four years of sobriety, Robicheaux concludes, "The darkness of my own meditation disturbed me. My years of drinking had taught me not to trust my unconscious, because it planned things for me in a cunning fashion that was usually a disaster for me, or for the people around me, or for all of us." At the same time, Robicheaux revisits and takes perverse solace in the myths he has heard since his boyhood—most of them predicated upon profoundly racist attitudes. He decides that, "like all myth, it was a more or less accurate metaphorical reflection of what was actually going on inside us, namely our dark fascination with man's iniquity." In short, the notion of what it means to be southern is merely a simulacrum, and the characters that inhabit Robicheaux's world do not understand that the past they profess to remember never existed. "No matter how educated a southerner is, or how liberal or intellectual … I don't believe you will meet many of my generation who do not still revere … all the old southern myths that we've supposedly put aside as members of the New South," Robicheaux rhapsodizes later in *A Stained White Radiance*, "You cannot grow up in a place where the tractor's plow can crack minie balls and grape-shot loose from the soil, even rake across a cannon wheel, and remain impervious to the past."

The Neon Rain also establishes a connection between Robicheaux and Central America—incongruous, given the milieu in which Robicheaux operates, though it is just one of many important social issues Burke tackles in the series. Jerome Gaylan Abshire, a patriot, a veteran of World War II, a two-star general, and a scion of the True South, lives in a palatial home in the upscale Garden District of New Orleans. Abshire perpetrates crimes against the citizens of Nicaragua with his involvement in weapons deals with the Contras. To drive home his point, Burke describes the fates of the

Contras' victims, including their having been thrown out of helicopters, a reference to the same acts against Argentina's people in that country's "Dirty War" in the late 1970s, a decade before the novel was published.

Such scenes are interspersed with references to Robicheaux's personal life, for instance, a meeting with Annie Ballard, a social worker and classical cellist, with whom Robicheaux falls in love. When Robicheaux declines an invitation from Annie to stay with her, he justifies his need to be alone by thinking to himself:

> After four years of sobriety I once again wanted to fill my mind with spiders and crawling slugs and snakes that grew corpulent off the pieces of my life that I would slay daily. ... I decided my temptation for alcohol and self-destruction was maybe even an indication that my humanity was still intact.

When he is later drugged against his will, the intoxication brings back vivid memories of his time in Vietnam and his wounding by a Claymore mine. The parallel between the self-destructiveness of his drinking and the ravages of war is clear, and that connection is strengthened through the first-person narrative and the brutality of the images. None of Robicheaux's relationships will be any less painful for him.

While Robicheaux understands the dissipative consequences of violence, he only fitfully hides his violent streak or his disdain for criminal behavior. Along with Clete, Robicheaux has been drunk on the job, reveled in the visceral rush of violence and the atavistic release it provides, and walked the fine line between keeping the peace and becoming a criminal himself. While Purcel leaves his wife and the country at the end of the novel, Robicheaux chooses another path—not altogether on his own—by retreating to the relative calm and safety of his boyhood haunts, where he will remain, unless called away, throughout the series. Implicit in the book's epilogue is

Robicheaux's acceptance of the power of place and the haunting echoes of the past, as he describes a brief moment of serenity:

> Annie and I went to Key West, walked along the ficus-shaded streets by the bay where Ernest Hemingway and James Audubon had once lived, scuba-dived on Seven Mile Reef, where the water was so clear and green at thirty feet that you could count the grains of sand like fragments of diamond in your palm.

When Robicheaux and Annie return to New Iberia—not to New Orleans, a place that clearly would have destroyed him—and open a bait shop and boat-rental business, he gives in not only to the power of the past (the two "watched yesterday steal upon us") but also to the attraction of home. Robicheaux's return to the place with which he is familiar and where he is comfortable is the surest sign of his returning strength and self-will.

The themes that would appear repeatedly in all of Burke's novels are articulated in *The Neon Rain*. The context of the novel when it was published in the late 1980s—America's involvement in Central America, the Iran-Contra scandal, arms smuggling—has continued relevance today, for both the ways in which Americans perceive the actions of their government and the role of the media in keeping the American public fully informed. The stark violence of Burke's narrative opened him to criticism, though Burke responded to the charges with typical candor.

In *Heaven's Prisoners,* Robicheaux rescues a Salvadoran girl named Alafair, the sole survivor of a plane crash in which her mother dies, and protects her from drug dealers and the Immigration and Naturalization Service. Alafair becomes Robicheaux's mirror image, a reflection of the issues that daily affect how the protagonist deals with and now, of necessity, must live with—literally and figuratively—racism, neglect, and class privilege.

As the events of *The Neon Rain* suggest, Robicheaux is given to intense psychological self-analysis in reaction to external stimuli, and his involvement in Alafair's rescue and protection—and subsequent run-ins with those who would destroy her (and, by extension, Robicheaux himself) compels him to assess his motivation:

> I had quit the New Orleans police department, the bourbon-scented knight-errant who said he couldn't abide any longer the political hypocrisy and the addictive, brutal ugliness of metropolitan law enforcement, but the truth was that I enjoyed it, that I got high on my knowledge of man's iniquity, that I disdained the boredom and predictability of the normal world as much as my strange alcoholic metabolism loved the adrenaline rush of danger and my feeling of power over an evil world that in many ways was mirrored in my own soul.

Robicheaux pieces together the memories of his past, the events of his childhood that would develop into the "code" that he follows on the street. He recalls:

> I had learned most of my lessons for dealing with problems from hunting and fishing and competitive sports. No book could have taught me what I had learned from my father in the marsh, and as a boxer in high school I had discovered that it was as important to swallow your blood and hide your injury as it was to hurt your opponent.

When Annie is murdered, Robicheaux begins working for the New Iberia Police Department—"hiding his injury," as it were. He realizes that he is powerless to act without the sanction of the state to redress the actions against him.

Black Cherry Blues (1989), the first of Burke's two Edgar Award–winning novels, takes Robicheaux to Montana to clear himself of a murder charge and to settle a debt with an oil company fronting mob activity. Robicheaux believes that the company is ultimately responsible for the death of his father in an oil-rig explosion years earlier. Aside from his obvious interest in discovering the circumstance surrounding his father's death, Robicheaux also is concerned with the environment (not unlike Paret in *The Lost Get-Back Boogie*), which is being compromised and destroyed for profit by the company. For Robicheaux, the venality of big business and the damage that corporations do to the environment in the name of profit are symptoms of a larger problem in society, namely, the privileging of new values over the more genteel attitudes of the past. (Hence his disdain for what he sees in the New South.)

The novel marks Robicheaux's mystical awakening; his dreams are haunted by visions of his murdered wife, Annie, and his dead father. Fittingly, the two appear together at the end of the novel while Robicheaux wanders a marsh near his home, neatly connecting the vision (and, implicitly, the power of memory) with the environment in which Robicheaux feels so much at home. Such mysticism would become commonplace, if not routine, in the series' later titles. Among other such elements are the juju woman Gros Mama Goula's prophecies in *A Morning for Flamingos* (1990); Alafair's discovery in *In the Electric Mist with Confederate Dead* (1993) of a Civil War photograph with Robicheaux's likeness on it; the appearance in the same book of John Bell Hood, a Confederate general, who visits Robicheaux and offers him council; and the appearance in *Burning Angel* (1995) of the dead Sonny Boy Marsallus, a local hood connected to an old plantation.

Also in *Black Cherry Blues,* Clete, Robicheaux's erstwhile partner, makes his first appearance since *The Neon Rain.* The reunion balances Robicheaux's mystic experiences with a dose of reality. Clete has been working for a mobster named Sally Dee, a man whom Robicheaux despises, but after Clete saves Robicheaux's life and Clete's Native American girlfriend, Darlene, is murdered, Robicheaux and Clete reconcile. Significantly, Robicheaux prays for Darlene and for his dead wife, Annie, at Darlene's funeral:

> I believe that God is not limited by time and space as we are, I believe perhaps that He can influence the past even though it has already happened. So sometimes when I'm alone, especially at night, in the dark, and I begin to dwell on the unbearable suffering that people probably experienced before their deaths, I ask God to retroactively relieve their pain.

The prayer applies equally to the pain that the women must have felt and to Robicheaux's own pain. The mysticism of the novels, intermingled here with a catch-all spirituality, is a lens through which Burke examines Robicheaux's psyche.

In *A Morning for Flamingos,* Robicheaux, seemingly at peace with himself after the cathartic appearance of Annie and his father in the previous novel, returns to police work, this time as a deputy in New Iberia. His tranquility does not last. Robicheaux is wounded and his partner killed when Jimmie Lee Boggs escapes during a prison transfer. Tee Beau Latiolais, another prisoner enlisted in the escape by Boggs, spares Robicheaux's life. Robicheaux, shamed by the escape and by having to beg for his life, swears to repay the debt. To recapture Boggs, Robicheaux returns to New Orleans to work for the Drug Enforcement Agency. Although he is intent upon not allowing the city to recapture him in its gravity, he is forced to risk losing himself to complete the job.

In the middle novels of the series, Burke expands on the primary issues and continues to develop Robicheaux's character. In *A Stained White Radiance,* Weldon Sonnier, a corrupt televangelist, has been serially molesting his children, one of whom Robicheaux dated many years before. Clete has established his own private investigation agency, and Robicheaux begins to better understand his ambivalent relationship with his old partner, who needs the action of the street as much as Robicheaux does.

In a revealing analysis of the people with whom Robicheaux daily comes in contact, the ones he calls the Members of the Pool, he describes the people who "leave behind warehouses of official paperwork as evidence that they have occupied the planet for a certain period of time." Later Robicheaux draws a connection between the Members of the Pool and the psychic and physical destruction that is their only legacy:

> Over the years I had seen all the dark players get to southern Louisiana in one form or another: the oil and chemical companies who drained and polluted the wetlands; the developers who could turn sugarcane acreage and pecan orchards into miles of tract homes and shopping malls that had the aesthetic qualities of a sewer works; and the Mafia, who operated out of New Orleans and brought us prostitution, slot machines, control of at least two big labor unions, and finally narcotics.

Robicheaux's attitude toward his professional life is not ameliorated by the fact that Bootsie, an old flame with whom he is finally reunited, has been diagnosed with lupus (a balancing of the karmic ledger, Burke suggests, the proviso on Robicheaux's happiness). Because of the turmoil in his personal and professional lives, Robicheaux is inclined to see corruption and crime—including rampant prejudice, which manifests itself here in the form of a racist politician, an analogue to Mississippi's David Duke—as not only inexorable but also necessary.

Still, relative to the turmoil of his previous life—his dissipative lifestyle, Annie's death, memories of Vietnam, and a list of killers and thugs too numerous to mention—Robicheaux's life has stabilized. Burke begins to focus on ways that the external events affect both his protagonist and society at large. In *In the Electric Mist with Confederate Dead,* Burke thoroughly examines the myths of southern history and a society's collective memory. Early in the novel Robicheaux recalls having seen the execution of a black prisoner in 1957, though no one in the present is interested in solving the crime. When a movie crew comes to town to shoot a film on the Civil War, the intrusion of the present upon the gentility of New Iberia causes, Burke implies, an upheaval of the past into the present, a hint of magical realism in a genre that traditionally relies on stark realism for its effect. Burke also uses the intrusion of Hollywood (an image revisited later, in *Sunset Limited,* 1998) on the relative serenity of New Iberia as a metaphor for the destruction of the traditional values to which Robicheaux clings.

Similarly, *Dixie City Jam* (1994) is a book more important for its analysis of Robicheaux's psyche than for its story line, which involves the search for a Nazi submarine in the Gulf of Mexico. The book is one of the few Burke novels taken to task for its plotting. Characterization does not falter, however, and the author examines the genesis of many of Robicheaux's neuroses, including having as a young boy seen his adulterous mother in bed with a lover. The infidelity of Robicheaux's mother and her inauspicious death would be revealed in *Sunset Limited* and *Purple Cane Road* (2000).

In *Dixie City Jam,* Robicheaux is back in New Orleans, where interracial relationships threaten to explode into violence. Will Buchalter, a neo-Nazi instigator, is one of Burke's most hateful villains, a man who has driven a cop to commit suicide through psychological manipulation and who sneaks into Robicheaux's house and watches him and Bootsie sleep. The scene echoes the sparing of Robicheaux's life in *A Morning for Flamingos* and once again calls into question the value of Robicheaux's efforts to battle consummate evil—and ultimately, his reason for needing to face that conflict. Buchalter's attention to Robicheaux threatens to ruin his personal life when Bootsie begins drinking and Robicheaux warns her of the consequences.

With the exception of the later historical novel *White Doves at Morning, Burning Angel* is the novel most concerned with race relations, and its structure has been compared to that of Faulkner's story "The Bear." Burke's vision, however, is on the whole more mystical than metaphysical. The novel's epigraph is taken from Solomon Northup's 1853 autobiography *Twelve Years a Slave,* and the opening of the novel describes the disenfranchisement of blacks who had lived on the land for generations.

Moleen Bertrand, a plantation owner descended from a well-to-do southern family, has struck a deal with a Mafia front company to build an incinerator where the families currently live. Moleen is symbolic of the "New Southerner," the kind of man whom Robicheaux is sworn to fight. Still, Robicheaux is surprised when he discovers that Moleen has for years been in love with a black woman, Ruthie Jean Fontenot, and that they had, in Robicheaux's words, "reenacted that old Southern black-white confession of need and dependence that, in its peculiar way, was a recognition of the simple biological fact of our brotherhood." The relationship does not negate in Robicheaux's mind, however, the issue of slavery, which acts as a current that moves the narrative's plot along. Nonetheless, he concludes that "if I learned anything from my association with Moleen and Ruthie Jean and Sonny Boy, it's the fact that we seldom know each other and can only guess at the lives that wait to be lived in every human being."

The theme of race relations is reprised in *Cadillac Jukebox* (1996), in which the murder of a civil-rights leader three decades earlier has been "solved" by Buford LaRose, a prominent politician and the state's next governor. LaRose implicates Aaron Crown, a noted miscreant, in the killing. (The primary plotline is a retelling of the murder of Medgar Evers in 1963.) The plot is complicated by Robicheaux's having had a brief affair many years before with the governor's wife.

The title of the novel comes from a reference to the songs on the jukebox in Robicheaux's bait shop. The albums are all "Cadillacs," classic songs from the 1950s that evoke for Robicheaux a sense of the past that haunts him to the point that he cuts the cord on the jukebox, a symbolic act in which he attempts to separate himself from the past. Despite Crown's essential lack of character, Robicheaux is touched by the man's devotion for his daughter—a spark of humanity in the man's otherwise dark soul—and agrees to look into the case. The novel also presents an interesting comparison between Robicheaux and LaRose: the governor, an arrogant and self-assured man who little respects the law, has in common with Robicheaux his ambition and an obsessive drive that allows him to succeed at all cost. Once again, Robicheaux has been held to the mirror and forced to look at his alter ego, though he again confronts that image with courage, if not with absolute self-assuredness.

As Robicheaux ages, his moments of introspection become fraught with an unspoken urgency that belies the serenity for which he strives. For that reason, critics have suggested that the brooding nature of *Sunset Limited* and Burke's ability to sustain interest in this novel for the relationship between Robicheaux and his mother is a defining moment in the series. The novel centers on the return of Megan Flynn, a Pulitzer Prize–winning photojournalist, to New Iberia. Flynn's father, Jack, a union activist who was dedicated to the plight of the poor, was murdered forty years earlier. Robicheaux focuses his investigation on the Terrebonne family, who have been in the area long enough to have made a fortune in the slave trade a century and a half ago, and their myriad connections to the past. Within Robicheaux's realization of the importance of history on the present is the equally poignant understanding, finally, of his own insignificance. The metaphysical smallness that manifests in Robicheaux's psyche is a direct result of the connection between his mother's desertion of the family and the worldview that her son has built for himself with her desertion as the central event.

The contemplation of his relationship with his mother carries over into *Purple Cane Road*, in which Robicheaux confronts the possibility that his mother was a prostitute at the time she died, having been drowned in a ditch by corrupt New Orleans police for witnessing a crime. Focusing Robicheaux's efforts on solving his mother's death is Letty Labiche, a former prostitute who is on death row for killing Vachel Carmouche, a man who had abused her for years when they were neighbors. Robicheaux's life is complicated by the appearance of Johnny Rameta, a killer who takes a liking to Alafair as a way to torment Robicheaux. Hampering the efforts is a stable of corrupt government officials and police. Everyone, it seems, is a suspect. Burke's plotting and action have reached their carrying capacity here. As Richard Bernstein writes in a *New York Times* review, "He provides a tingle here and there and a luscious sense of deep South iniquity, but his book's psychedelic straining for ever more stylized killings perversely robs it of that sense of plausibility and unexpectedness necessary for genuine suspense."

Burke seems to have sensed that conflict between characterization and plot, and in the novel that follows *Purple Cane Road*, he strips down the complex plotting of his previous novels to examine the aging Robicheaux's response to a personal attack. The defining image of *Jolie Blon's Bounce* is the beating of Robicheaux by the seventy-four-year-old Legion Guidry, who humiliates Robicheaux by exhibiting his physical control over the protagonist (a role reversal of sorts, since that dominance is most often reserved for Robicheaux). Guidry is another of Burke's exceptional psychotic criminals, dangerous for their randomness and their relentlessness. The people who have come in contact with Guidry—Ladice Hulin, for one, who was raped by Guidry and describes to Robicheaux the hold the man has on people—only polarize Robicheaux's notion of good and evil.

The title of the novel comes from a blues song by Tee Bobby Hulin, a black man accused of the rape and murder of Amanda Boudreau, a white teenager. The title is significant for its ironic description of the innocence of the young and the way that worldviews change. Robicheaux seems to be summing up his own evolution through the twelve novels at the same time that his memories come to rest on a particularly unsettling notion that he recalls from his first encounter with Guidry:

> Growing up during the 1940s in New Iberia, down on the Gulf Coast, I never doubted how the world worked …. I came to learn early on that no venal or meretricious enterprise existed without the community's consent. I thought I understood the nature of evil. I learned at age twelve that I did not.

Robicheaux is charged with investigating the murder of two women from much different backgrounds. In the process of hunting down the killer, he meets yet more Members of the Pool—the dregs of society who have both threatened him and allowed him a second chance at life. Ironically, Robicheaux is dependent upon the killers and pimps and drug dealers for his own psychological freedom. Later, Clete, who helps Robicheaux through a flirtation with sobriety that would surely threaten his career and family life, reminds his friend, "'This is Louisiana, Dave. Guatemala North. Quit pretending it's the United States. Life will make a lot more sense.'" Significantly, the attack on Robicheaux, is as much a psychic affront as a physical debilitation, though Robicheaux again exhibits his resilience.

Burke's greatest accomplishment in writing the Robicheaux series lies in his ability to keep the character fresh through the many machinations—some of which require a formulaic rendering of one or more aspects of the narrative—of both plot and minor characters. One advantage that Burke has in creating a protagonist with enough depth to carry the day is the breadth of the experiences that he draws on to describe Robicheaux's professional life—the narratives' plots—and his personal life, neither of which lend themselves to closure. As Fred Pfeil asks rhetorically:

> If Robicheaux ever were to transcend his internal divisions and resolve his wounded ambivalence towards the viciousness and beauty of the Old South so that he could take up battle with the New, what alternative fuel source would have to charge the novels up, what new interests would propel us to read on?

LATE WORK

Dave Robicheaux is not the only of Burke's protagonists to be featured in a series. Billy Bob Holland, a lawyer in Deaf Smith, Texas, is the great-grandson of Sam Morgan Holland, whose family populates two of Burke's earlier novels, *Lay Down My Sword and Shield* and *Two for Texas*. The setting that figures prominently in this series has moved from the Louisiana bayous to the Texas Hill Country. (Burke also set *Bitterroot* [2001] in Montana. A later Holland novel is set in Missoula and the Swan Valley.)

Much as Robicheaux wrestles with his past, Holland blames himself for the death of his partner, L. Q. Navarro, when the two were members of the Texas Rangers on patrol in Mexico. The dead Navarro acts similarly to the ghosts who visit Robicheaux, the southern Greek chorus—to give him advice, to warn him of his hubris, to encourage him. Navarro also acts as a spur to action for Holland, in the same way as Robicheaux's alcoholism and later mystical appearances by various figures from his past do.

Cimarron Rose, the first installment of the series and the book that Burke deems in a *Book Page* interview with Alden Mudge to be "the most biographical… I've ever written," won a second Edgar award for the author and met with generally positive reviews. In the novel Holland defends his illegitimate son, Lucas Smothers, on charges that he murdered and raped his girlfriend, crimes that the boy did not commit. Holland and his son battle the "East Enders," the country-club set and their children, who detest Lucas. Holland also confronts nemeses who could have come from one of the Robicheaux novels: Garland T. Moon, a murderer cut from the mold of Jimmie Lee Boggs; Felix Ringo, a trained assassin; and federal authorities who fight the same war on drugs that cost Holland his conscience and L. Q. Navarro his life.

The characters of Robicheaux's society are transplanted to Texas, and the past is alive there as well. Holland makes a habit of reading his great-grandfather's journal, a link to the history of the area and a metaphor for the relentless influence of the dead on the living. Sam Morgan Holland (a character based on Burke's own great-grandfather of the same name) details his search for the Rose of Cimarron, a beautiful woman who rode with the Dalton gang. Holland, like his great-grandson, is conflicted about his actions: previously a gunfighter on the Chisholm Trail, Holland has become an ordained minister. An entry penned on July 27, 1891, echoes through the century and calls to mind the lives of both Holland and Robicheaux: "I am fifty-six years old and fear I do not know who I am."

Billy Bob Holland returns in *Heartwood* (1999) and *Bitterroot,* the latter the protagonist's first foray into Montana. In *Heartwood,* Wilbur Pickett, a rodeo rider who has fallen on hard times, is a suspect in the robbery of a valuable watch and $300,000 in bonds. Holland confronts Earl Dietrich, the husband of his former girl-friend, Peggy Jean Murphy, and the plot becomes complicated when Pickett's wife, a blind woman, kills a man in self-defense.

The most apparent connection between the Holland and Robicheaux novels is the author's use of characterization and landscape. The Holland novels, however, have a more "Western" feel, the code of the South, as Robicheaux knows it, transmuted into a more cerebral and stylized (though often no less violent) brand of justice. The titles of both books come, fittingly, from nature: the one from heartwood, a tree that grows in layers from the inside out (a metaphor that Holland's father used to describe the human spirit) and the other from the Bitterroot Mountains of Montana, which similarly suggest the serenity and a stability that all of Burke's protagonists seek and that will remain implacable long after the participants in the rape of Doc Voss's daughter, the central event in *Bitterroot,* have disappeared.

The past that figures so prominently in both the Robicheaux series and the later Holland series is explored in depth in Burke's *White Doves at Morning,* the author's first historical novel. Although the setting has not changed— New Iberia and its environs is the backdrop for the action—the time period is the Civil War and Reconstruction. Willie Burke and two of his friends join the Confederate Army, though they have some misgivings as to their commitment to the "Cause." In fact, Burke (drawn in part from another of the author's ancestors) joins only to avenge the death of his good friend in the Battle of Shiloh. Willie meets and becomes infatuated with Abigail Dowling, an abolitionist nurse who works in the Underground Railroad. Abigail befriends Flower Jamison, a young slave whom Willie has secretly taught to read, and thus angers Ira Jamison, Flower's owner and biological father, and Rufus Atkins, the plantation's overseer and Willie's superior officer in the army.

The narrative revisits several important issues from Burke's previous novels—race relations first among them—and argues eloquently the characters' tragic sense of powerlessness and the ultimate victory of the human spirit over the tyranny of hate. Willie Burke, despite having fought for the Confederacy, is portrayed as a character not unlike Robicheaux, a moral man who struggles to remain on the right side of moral issues. Because of her mixed blood, Flower comes across as one of Burke's most engaging characters, as she transcends the boundaries of her birth, her station in life, and the attitudes of her society:

> Flower Jamison had always thought the beginning and end of the war would be marked by definite dates and events, that great changes would be effected by the battles and the thousands of men she had seen march through New Iberia, and the historical period in which she was living would survive only as a compartmentalized and aberrant experience that fitted between bookends for people to study in a happier time.

The novel's epilogue confirms the characters' fortunes, as Willie Burke and Flower Jamison both became educators, and Burke becomes known "for his bravery as a soldier, his refusal to discuss the war, his prescience about human events and his irreverence toward all those who seek authority and power over others."

The narrative is written in the third person omniscient, a departure for Burke that allows, ironically, for a more honest voice from the author and a more convincing portrayal of the totality of the characters' world. That voice is especially effective in conveying a sense of history that cannot help but enrich multiple readings of the earlier novels. The critical response of the book was positive, and reviewers focused on the connections between *White Doves at Morning* and Burke's series, particularly the author's ability to develop characters whose actions transcend societal boundaries. History, place, class, and race meet in the book in which,

as *Houston Chronicle* reviewer Mike Snyder writes, "Burke explores the possibilities for human nobility amid the moral abhorrence of slavery. It is perhaps his greatest literary achievement … [and] should afford him the critical respect that can be difficult for a genre writer to attain."

The scant critical attention given Burke's work is undoubtedly a result of the academy's perception of the author's fiction as too mainstream for serious academic consideration. After a writing apprenticeship that lasted two decades and nearly relegated Burke to the literary dustbin, the author became the crime genre's latest "overnight sensation." In the past decade the academy has followed the example of the mainstream in accepting Burke's work at face value: literary writing that, for the purposes of classification, has been deemed "crime fiction." Such a narrow categorization gives short shrift to the innovations that Burke has brought to a genre that many critics have denigrated as overwrought and overpublished.

Because he came late to crime fiction, Burke was able to avoid preconceived notions of what the crime novel should be and focus instead on drawing complex, flawed characters in addition to the background characters and settings that rarely play as important a part in the genre as they do in Burke's novels. That breadth of vision, writes Fred Pfeil, is what separates Burke from the masters of crime fiction and most of his peers, "the greater degree of connection and interrelation the new generation of detectives has with other characters and, in most cases, the social worlds they inhabit." Whether set in the bayous of Louisiana, in the mountains of Montana, or on the plains of Texas, Burke's vision appeals to readers of both mainstream crime fiction and those whose tastes run to more "literary" fiction.

Burke is modest about his reputation as a stylist. His humility and a long memory for the disappointments of his earlier career—both expressed poignantly in his *New York Times* essay—come across as a cautionary epigraph celebrating the deep ambivalence of a writer who knows success and failure in equal measure: "I believe creativity is a votive gift …. Those who become grandiose and vain about its presence in their lives usually see it taken from them and given to someone else. At least that has been my experience."

Selected Bibliography

WORKS OF JAMES LEE BURKE

NOVELS AND SHORT STORIES

Half of Paradise. Boston: Houghton Mifflin, 1965.

To the Bright and Shining Sun. New York: Scribners, 1970.

Lay Down My Sword and Shield. New York: Crowell, 1971.

Two for Texas. New York: Pocket Books, 1982.

The Convict: Stories. Baton Rouge: Louisiana State University Press, 1985.

The Lost Get-Back Boogie. Baton Rouge: Louisiana State University Press, 1986.

The Neon Rain. New York: Holt, 1987.

Heaven's Prisoners. New York: Holt, 1988.

Black Cherry Blues. Boston: Little, Brown, 1989.

A Morning for Flamingos. Boston: Little, Brown, 1990.

A Stained White Radiance. New York: Hyperion Press, 1992.

In the Electric Mist with Confederate Dead. New York: Hyperion Press, 1993.

Dixie City Jam. New York: Hyperion Press, 1994.

Burning Angel. New York: Hyperion Press, 1995.

Cadillac Jukebox. New York: Hyperion Press, 1996.

Cimarron Rose. New York: Hyperion Press, 1997.

Sunset Limited. New York: Doubleday, 1998.

Heartwood. New York: Doubleday, 1999.

Purple Cane Road. New York: Doubleday, 2000.

Bitterroot. New York: Simon & Schuster, 2001.

Jolie Blon's Bounce. New York: Simon & Schuster, 2002.

White Doves at Morning. New York: Simon & Schuster, 2002.

STORIES

"Water People." In *Best of the South: From Ten Years of New Stories from the South.* Edited by Shannon Ravenel. Selected and introduction by Anne Tyler. Chapel Hill, N.C.: Algonquin Books of Chapel Hill, 1996.

ESSAYS

"Seeking a Vision of Truth, Guided by a Higher Power." *New York Times,* December 2, 2002, p. E1.

CRITICAL AND BIOGRAPHICAL STUDIES

Folks, Jeffrey J., and Nancy Summers Folks. *The World Is Our Home: Society and Culture in Contemporary Southern Writing.* Lexington: University Press of Kentucky, 2000. (References to Burke are interspersed throughout the text.)

McCay, Mary A. "The Whore of Babylon: Louisiana and James Lee Burke." *New Orleans Review* 28, no.1: 176–184 (summer 2002). (General analysis of the Robicheaux series, written shortly after the publication of *Jolie Blon's Bounce.*)

Panek, LeRoy. "James Lee Burke." In *New Hard-Boiled Writers, 1970s–1990s.* Bowling Green, Ohio: Bowling Green University Popular Press, 2000. Pp. 159–184. (Close reading of Burke's work and a comprehensive examination of the Robicheaux series; one chapter in a book that also includes solid analyses of other contemporary crime writers.)

Pepper, Andrew. *The Contemporary American Crime Novel: Race, Ethnicity, Gender, Class.* Chicago: Fitzroy Dearborn Publishers, 2000. (General analysis suggested by the book's title, along with a chapter-length, theory-driven examination of Burke's work within the context of race, ethnicity, gender, and class.)

Pfeil, Fred. *White Guys: Studies in Postmodern Domination and Difference.* London: Verso, 1995. (As the title implies, a theory-based examination of Burke's work in the context of the "hard-boiled" crime novel; compares Burke's work to that of his contemporaries Robert Parker, Jonathan Kellerman, and K. C. Constantine.)

Schwartz, Richard B. *Nice and Noir: Contemporary American Crime Fiction.* Columbia: University of Missouri Press, 2002. (Survey of noir fiction and its contexts, including a chapter-length analysis of Burke's work up to and including *Purple Cane Road.*)

Shelton, Frank W. "James Lee Burke's Dave Robicheaux Novels." In *The World Is Our Home: Society and Culture in Contemporary Southern Writing.* Edited by Jeffrey J. Folks and Nancy Summers Folks. Lexington: University Press of Kentucky, 2000. Pp. 232–243. (Close reading of several of Burke's novels, up to and including *Sunset Limited.*)

Willett, Ralph. *The Naked City: Urban Crime Fiction in the USA.* Manchester, U.K.: Manchester University Press, 1996. (Study of New Orleans as a setting for contemporary crime fiction, with a brief discussion of the contexts for Burke's Robicheaux novels.)

BOOK REVIEWS

Bernstein, Richard. "Born on the Bayou; Dying There, Too." *New York Times Book Review,* August 21, 2000, p. 6. (Review of *Purple Cane Road.*)

Oates, Joyce Carol. "Some Time in the Sun." *Washington Post Book World,* April 5, 1992, p. 5. (Review of *A Stained White Radiance.*)

Snyder, Mike. "Burke Spreads Wings: Crime Novelist Ably Tries Historical Fiction." *Houston Chronicle,* December 13–15, 2002, p. 21. (Review of *White Doves at Morning.*)

Weinreich, Regina. Review of *The Lost Get-Back Boogie. New York Times Book Review,* January 11, 1987, p. 18.

Williams, Wirt. "On the Tracks to Doom." *New York Times Book Review,* March 14, 1965, p. 46. (Review of *Half of Paradise.*)

INTERVIEWS

Brainard, Dulcy, and Sybil Steinberg. "*PW* Interviews: James Lee Burke." *Publishers Weekly,* April 20, 1992, pp. 33–34.

Fuller, R. Reese. "The Man behind Dave Robicheaux." *Times of Acadiana,* June 5, 2002, pp. 17–20, 22–24.

Mudge, Alden. "A New Character Leaves Cajun Country Behind." *Book Page,* August 1997. (http://www.bookpage.com/9708bp/firstperson2.html).

Stroby, W. C. "Hanging Tough with James Lee Burke." *Writer's Digest* 73, no. 1: 38–40 (January 1, 1993).

FILM BASED ON THE WORK OF JAMES LEE BURKE

Heaven's Prisoners. Screenplay by Scott A. Frank and Harley Peyton. Directed by Phil Joanou. New Line Cinema, 1996.

—PATRICK A. SMITH

John Jay Chapman

1862–1933

AMONG THE ANECDOTES that come down to us from men who knew John Jay Chapman in his youth are two peculiarly telling ones. A classmate of his at the Saint Paul's School in Concord, New Hampshire, recalls Chapman's habit of passing his hands over their Latin textbook as if warming them at a fire; his idea was that "the language would enter his system through the pores." Owen Wister recalls from the same epoch Chapman's strange distraction while at the game of cricket. Chapman would stand sublimely oblivious of the ball that flew toward the wicket he guarded. Why? He was lost in prayer.

Captured here is Chapman's strange unworldliness—an abstraction that became with him a principle by which to live, though it was accompanied always by the conviction that duty to the other world is fulfilled only by intervention into the imperfect, fallen, games-playing world we actually inhabit during our three score years and ten. This way of taking hold of the present world, as from a position of ideality, was, in fact, Chapman's great inheritance from his abolitionist forebears, among whom, most notably, was his grandmother Maria Weston Chapman, the associate of William Lloyd Garrison.

Chapman writes in a memoir that lay unpublished at his death: "In Boston, antislavery continued to be taboo. Friendly relations were never re-established between the Garrisonians and the social life of Boston. The breach which began in 1829 lasted for a generation after the war." The reason was, he says, that the abolitionists "broke with ritual, with ceremony, with all the conventional pieties of religion, and they

never thereafter had time to improvise substitutes of their own." This latter omission was, in Chapman's view, a great fortune, for he developed early on a contempt for convention and ceremony and above all for institutions. In his later years this echt Protestant contempt for institutional authority led him into a series of bitter attacks on the Roman Catholic Church. He was "an inward creature," as he put it, "wandering about in worlds unrealized." And as for "institutions of all kinds," he has this to say: "A jail, a lunatic asylum, a summer school—community life of any sort, is a sanitarium. It says to me, 'Good morning; have you used Pear's soap? Now you may take ten minutes on the treadmill. It is such wholesome exercise.' I cannot bear to pass a town high school." The rather general and innocuous—in fact, conventionally eulogistic—word "community" is allowed here to take on absolutely sinister connotations.

Chapman admired the Garrisonian abolitionists, then, for their utter indifference to respectable society, with its treadmills and wholesome exercises; he carried Emersonian "self-reliance" to its ultimate degree. Chapman likely regretted that the breach between the abolitionists and Boston society was ever healed at all. He wanted the breach there; it was forever an index of the agitating disparity between the Ideal and the Actual, between the Real and the Apparent, between the Eternal and the merely Temporal. After all, "society" has everything to do with ritual, convention, piety, and ceremony—everything to do with form. And in the abolitionists Chapman found men and women who had the antinomian informality, and also the perfect conviction, of Henry David Thoreau.

Chapman's singular achievement was to have carried the high-strung temper of Garrisonian abolitionism into the 1890s and beyond, an era during which it struck most Americans as quaint and embarrassing and seemed to many an evil absolutely to be shunned. Louis Menand has argued, in his book *The Metaphysical Club* (2001) and elsewhere, that one of the great—and, to his mind, fortunate—casualties of the American Civil War was precisely the utopian absolutism that made men willing to kill and die for an idea. What replaced that absolutism was the more worldly, contingent, and compromising philosophy of pragmatism. Men no longer wandered about "in worlds unrealized" to which they demanded the "realized" world must somehow be made to correspond. Although Chapman went through Harvard precisely when this new way of thinking was consolidating itself and was a friend and correspondent of the philosopher William James, who as much as anyone is the architect of pragmatism, he could never be at ease in a world without "Truth with a big T," as James put it in his essay "Pragmatism's Conception of Truth." That is why Chapman remains, in this contemporary era of the uncertainty principle, a bracing admonition. "It's an accident when I *do* right," he once wrote to his second wife, "but I *am* right."

THE LIFE

John Jay Chapman was born on March 2, 1862, in New York City, the son of Henry Grafton Chapman, a Wall Street stockbroker, and Eleanor Jay Chapman. On his mother's side he was descended from the U.S. Supreme Court Chief Justice John Jay and on his father's side from Maria Weston Chapman, the distinguished abolitionist. A habit of political agitation, an almost fanatical devotion to the ideal of liberty, and a scorching conscience were among his

great inheritances from his ancestors. In 1876 Chapman entered the Saint Paul's School, though illness forced him to leave after only a year. Over the next few years he prepared himself privately to enter Harvard College, which he did in 1880. After graduating four years later, he toured Europe for a while and met, among other notables, Alfred, Lord Tennyson; Henry James; and Robert Louis Stevenson. On his return to the United States he entered Harvard Law School in 1885, and during his time there the incident that most vividly marks him took place.

Chapman had fallen in love with Minna Timmins, an Italian-American woman of great charm, and at a party in Cambridge he assaulted a man, Percival Lowell, whom he imagined—mistakenly, it turned out—to be his rival for her hand. His conscience so tormented him that, on returning to his rooms, he thrust his left hand into the coal-burning stove and held it there, searing it so badly as to leave the knuckles exposed. ("This will not do," he remembers having said as he backed away from the fire.) The hand had to be amputated, but after an enforced separation—on which the Timmins family had insisted—he did, in fact, marry Minna in 1889. Something of his depth of feeling for her may be discerned in the following portrait, which he set down in an introduction to a volume of letters by his son Victor:

> She had the man-minded seriousness of women in classic myths, the regular brown, heavy dark hair, free gait of the temperament that lives in heroic thought and finds the world full of chimeras, of religious mysteries, sacrifice, purgation. This part of her nature was her home and true refuge. Here dwelt the impersonal power that was never far from her. There have been few women like her; and most of them have existed only in the imagination of Aeschylus and the poets.

Chapman had been admitted to the New York bar in 1888, the year before his marriage to Minna, but he never practiced law seriously;

given that his father had left him financially independent, he did not have to. Later he described his flirtation with the law in a memoir that has never been published in full:

> As I worked in the office, I writhed in pain—the entire length and breadth of my physical system .... I got up and clutched the desk and prayed .... I had my head bound with a cap of iron, and when I used to stop working the suspended agony came down like a cataract, and I went uptown trembling, crying.

His real aspirations were political and literary, and he soon became deeply involved in the City Reform Club of New York, agitating against, among other things, the corruption of Tammany Hall. Out of his work there came two books, *Causes and Consequences* (1898), an engaging study of politics, education, and government, and *Practical Agitation* (1900), a sort of handbook for reformers.

During the same years he wrote some of the best literary and cultural criticism he was ever to publish, and he edited a highly eccentric journal of commentary called the *Political Nursery*. Thirty-six numbers of the journal were issued between March 1897 and January 1901. Above its masthead was the slogan: "The object of the *Nursery* is to tell the truth. There is no publication at present which seems to cover this exact field." The journal, which carried editorials, poetry, book reviews, and essays, ranged widely in topic; Chapman never limited himself to the vagaries of New York City machine politics. As Melvin Bernstein says, "The politics of his native city had grown to include the politics of his country, of England, of France, and, indeed, of the world. The corrupt politician merged in his Abolition-haunted mind with the lyncher of Negroes" and also with the colonial bureaucrats who administered the lives of Filipinos or Indians or Congolese. "Chapman's conscience," Bernstein concludes, "had caught the cosmos in which justice and love, the head and the heart, were locked in a gigantic, painful

embrace; and its pain Chapman felt in the marrow of his bones." Doubtless he did feel it, and the years of political work told on his tightly wound constitution; he suffered a total nervous collapse in 1900, from which he did not fully recover for ten years.

Minna died in 1897, shortly after the birth of their third son, and the next year Chapman married Elizabeth Chanler, with whom he would remain for the rest of his life and who gave birth in 1900 to his fourth son and last child. (Two sons did not survive him: one died by drowning in 1903, and another was killed in action during World War I.) Although he traveled with some regularity in Europe, Chapman remained based in New York throughout his life. He was awarded honorary doctorates by Hobart College (in 1900) and Yale University (in 1916), and he wrote and delivered the Phi Beta Kappa poem at Harvard in 1912. Chapman died with Elizabeth at his side on November 4, 1933, at Vassar Hospital in Poughkeepsie.

THE LITERARY CRITICISM

Chapman's literary essays bear little resemblance to what now passes for literary criticism, at least as IT is practiced in the academy. And yet we read his critical essays now as if on the date of their first publication. Nothing about them is dated. Chapman's essay on Ralph Waldo Emerson, for example—published first in two installments in the *Atlantic Monthly* and later collected in *Emerson, and Other Essays* (1898)—answers all the necessities of good criticism. Chapman is acutely sensitive to the effect on the reader of Emerson's remarkable style. As he writes in a paragraph that might well describe his own writing:

> There is no question that the power to throw your sitter into a receptive mood by a pass or two which shall give you his virgin attention is necessary to any artist. Nobody has the knack of this more strongly than Emerson in his prose writings. By a

phrase or a common remark he creates an ideal atmosphere in which his thought has the directness of great poetry.

Any good reader will recognize in this his or her own experience of, say, the following passage in Emerson's essay "Experience," which begins in platitude and ends in provocation: "Let us be poised, and wise, and our own, today. Let us treat men and women well: treat them as if they were real: perhaps they are." Or take this passage from "Fate," the glamour of which is by no means distinct from its cruelty:

> How shall a man escape from his ancestors, or draw off from his veins the black drop which he drew from his father's or his mother's life? It often appears in a family, as if all the qualities of the progenitors were potted in several jars,—some ruling quality in each son or daughter of the house,—and sometimes the unmixed temperament, the rank unmitigated elixir, the family vice, is drawn off in a separate individual, and the others are proportionally relieved.

Chapman lays his finger precisely on the thing that connects the style to the thought, the medium to the message. He puts us in touch not merely with Emerson but with Emerson thinking. Chapman explains:

> It is noticeable that in some of Emerson's important lectures the logical scheme is more perfect than in his essays. The truth seems to be that in the process of working up and perfecting his writings, in revising and filing his sentences, the logical scheme became more and more obliterated. Another circumstance helped make his style fragmentary. He was by nature a man of inspirations and exalted moods. He was subject to ecstasies during which his mind worked with phenomenal brilliancy. Throughout his works and in his diary we find constant reference to these moods, and to his own inability to control or recover them.

Surely Chapman is correct in finding the key to Emerson's famously saltatory style in this peculiar feature of his temperament. Strong criticism, of which this a signal example, always shows us how style emanates from character— or, to borrow a phrase from Robert Frost, from the way a man generally "carries himself" in the world.

Chapman is also a first-rate reader of Emerson's poetry, which fact alone sets him in elect company. Emerson, he points out, is "never merely conventional, and his poetry, like his prose, is homespun and sound." He "writes our domestic dialect," Chapman suggests in a letter composed while he was at work on the essay; all other American writers are "Britannia ware and French kid." And yet Emerson's ear, Chapman points out, "was defective: his rhymes are crude, and his verse is often lame and unmusical, a fault which can be countervailed by nothing but force, and force he lacks." Chapman continues with a devastating quotation:

> To say that his ear was defective is hardly strong enough. Passages are not uncommon which hurt the reader and unfit him to proceed; as, for example:—
>
> "Thorough a thousand voices
>   Spoke the universal dame:
> 'Who telleth one of my meanings
>   Is master of all I am.'"

He himself has very well described the impression his verse is apt to make on a new reader when he says,—

> "Poetry must not freeze, but flow."

The voice hardly knows what to do with this quatrain; four three-stress lines were never more uncertainly joined.

But even were his sensibility not so nuanced and receptive as to be "hurt" by a halting meter, and even were he not gifted with an astonishing knack for apt quotation, Chapman's essay on Emerson would be indispensable if only because it so tellingly links both the style and the thought of that great writer to the history of the period in which he wrote. "Let us remember the world upon which the young Emerson's eyes opened," Chapman explains:

> The South was a plantation. The North crooked the hinges of the knee where thrift might follow fawning…. This time of humiliation, when there was no free speech, no literature, little manliness, no reality, no simplicity, no accomplishment, was the era of American brag. We flattered the foreigner and we boasted of ourselves. We were oversensitive, insolent, and cringing…. Underneath everything lay a feeling of unrest, an instinct,— "this country cannot permanently endure half slave and half free,"—which was the truth, but which could not be uttered.

Such was the temper of the nation from the date of the Missouri Compromise in 1820 until 1861, when war offered its terrible release. In this context Emerson's mercurial, experimental style was itself a revolution. "Open his works at a hazard," says Chapman. "You hear a man talking." Chapman's Emerson is insurgent—a hater of tyranny of all kinds but a hater most of what Chapman calls "the tyranny of democracy." "The merit of Emerson was that he felt the atmospheric pressure" of all the timidity and cowardice and temporizing of the antebellum years without ever quite knowing its reason: "He felt he was a cabined, cribbed, confined creature, although every man about him was celebrating Liberty and Democracy, and every day was Fourth of July. He taxes language to its limits in order to express his revolt." In short, Emerson teaches us "that every man will write well in proportion as he has contempt for the public."

Something of Chapman's own situation in the 1890s, when he wrote the essay, enters into this, because, as he suggests, "much of what Emerson wrote about the United States in 1850 is true of the United States to-day. It would be hard to find a civilized people who are more timid, more cowed in spirit, more illiberal, than we." The great advances toward real liberty made, if only awkwardly, between 1863 and 1876, had been in full retreat since the collapse of Reconstruction. Chapman's essay on Emerson is, among many other things, an effort to evoke a radical clarifying spirit that seemed to have passed utterly from the American scene.

So much for Emerson's strengths. Chapman apprehends so perfectly his weaknesses as to disconcert (and also preempt) the most adversarial of contemporary literary critics. Nothing escapes him, as when he speaks tellingly of "a certain lack of the historic sense" in all that Emerson wrote: "The ethical assumption that all men are exactly alike permeates his work," says Chapman. "In his mind, Socrates, Marco Polo, and General Jackson stand surrounded by the same atmosphere, or rather stand as mere naked characters surrounded by no atmosphere at all. He is probably the last great writer who will fling about classic anecdotes as if they were club gossip." As for the habit of abstraction that mitigated Emerson's commitment to abolition, Chapman has this to say: "Not pity for the slave, but indignation at the violation of the Moral Law by Daniel Webster, was at the bottom of Emerson's anger. His abolitionism was secondary to his main mission, his main enthusiasm."

Many readers of Emerson have noted a strangely inhuman chill at the heart of his writings; none has expressed the problem so well as Chapman:

> Human sentiment was known to Emerson mainly in the form of pain. His nature shunned it; he cast it off as quickly as possible. There is a word or two in the essay on Love which seems to show that the inner and diaphanous core of this seraph had once, but not for long, been shot with blood: he recalls only the pain of it.

Emerson, he concludes, "makes us clutch about us to catch hold, if we somehow may, of the hand of a man." The problem appears to have been that "the sensuous and ready contact with nature which more carnal people enjoy was unknown" to Emerson. "His eyes saw nothing; his ears heard nothing. He believed that men traveled for distraction and to kill time. The most vulgar plutocrat could not be blinder to beauty nor bring home less from Athens than this cultivated saint." Even more devastating is Chapman's assertion:

> If an inhabitant of another planet should visit the earth, he would receive, on the whole, a truer notion of human life by attending an Italian opera than he would by reading Emerson's volumes. He would learn from the Italian opera that there were two sexes; and this, after all, is probably the fact with which the education of such a stranger ought to begin.
>
> In a review of Emerson's personal character and opinions, we are thus led to see that his philosophy, which finds no room for the emotions, is a faithful exponent of his own and of the New England temperament, which distrusts and dreads the emotions. Regarded as a sole guide to life for a young person of strong conscience and undeveloped affections, his works might conceivably be even harmful because of their unexampled power of purely intellectual stimulation.

Criticism seldom has the courage to say, at least to the purposes Chapman has in view here, that a great writer's works might possibly be harmful. To say so credits literary writing with real power, and it does this in such a way as always to indicate that the critic himself is susceptible to that power. By comparison to what Chapman gives us, the cynicism of so much literary criticism in the 1980s and 1990s—criticism that never tires of showing the reader that the monumental writers of the past had feet of clay—seems to proceed almost from weakness, if not from insensibility. The wary condescension many contemporary critics display toward literature has more to do with an abiding suspicion that great writing might have real power over *someone* than with the conviction that it has had power over *them*. In an essay on *Hamlet* in his book *A Glance toward Shakespeare* (1922), Chapman writes, "I scarcely know

what it is that puts the critic above the author, and provides him with his historic and invulnerable complacency; but I think it is due to leisure and the cheapness of writing materials."

A fitting coda to this review of Chapman's literary criticism may be found in an 1891 letter to Mrs. James T. Fields, wife of the Boston publisher:

> I hate sonnets because they are the most literary of all the forms of verse—even our best English poets are on their best literary behavior in the sonnet—their best foreign manner gloved and scented.
>
> Shakespeare's sonnets stand by themselves. They have the charm of his poetry, his songs and madrigals—and it is his own. They don't pretend to be sonnets. They don't follow the traditions of sonnets and they don't smell like sonnets. Michael Angelo being an Italian was at home, so to speak, in the sonnet and wasn't obliged to imitate anyone in particular—(for an Englishman to write a sonnet is as if he should try to say his prayers in French) and Michael Angelo was constantly taken up only with the endeavor to say the thing—he was not giving sops to literary tradition. He was like a powerful man packing a carpet bag—when he has too many things to go in. You can see the veins swell on his forehead as he grips the edges and tries to make it close. Half the time he takes everything out again on the floor and makes a new arrangement—with the shaving brush at the bottom—and then he is so uncertain which is best that he allows both readings to stand.
>
> But they have thought in 'em. There is not a fraud nor a paper stuffing nor a filigree ornament in the volume—and O, how can we ever be grateful enough for this! Here is a man that writes poetry which is as good as prose.
>
> [The language of his sonnets] is colloquial and simple—anything but literary.

Into this short passage Chapman condenses a highly suggestive history of the short poem in English in the age of Shakespeare. Astutely, if impatiently, Chapman scouts what would later be called the Petrarchan or—somewhat more grandly—the "golden" style in English verse, as we find it, say, in the sonnets of Edmund Spenser and Philip Sidney. He understands how utterly "secondary" that poetry can often be, even at its best, with its continental and Latinate affectations and with its often stultifying conventionality. This was at precisely the time when English lyric poetry was, in its other phases, attaining an astonishing colloquial vigor (in John Donne), a purity and simplicity of diction (in George Herbert and Ben Jonson), a brilliantly expressive facility with structure (again in Herbert), an unrivaled grace and poise (in Jonson again), and a complexity in thought and argument (in Shakespeare, Sir Fulke Greville, Donne, and Herbert) that was never to be matched. And if that were not enough, Chapman whimsically outlines just how difficult it can be, even for a poet native to the form, to "pack" a sonnet; it is a very tight valise. One cannot mistake the easy familiarity of Chapman's account of Michelangelo at work (the swelling of the veins in the forehead, the shaving brush). He came by this naturally, having himself translated the sonnets—or, to take up his metaphor, having himself unpacked and repacked them for a transatlantic journey into his own American English. This intimacy with the sonnet in its native context probably accounts for Chapman's feeling that the form wears so badly in English. In fact, sonnets in English seem to have struck his ear like a phony accent.

But the best of this remarkable letter is still to come:

> Do you know I really believe that there's a great deal of humbug talked about workmanship and form in poetry. These things are results—the shimmer and gleam that come from saying things well. They are not entities. They are no more things in themselves than the relation between two lights is a thing in itself, and anyone who sets to work to put good form on his poetry is like the man in the story who wanted good architecture put on to his house.

> These Aldriches who think style is the *means* of saying things well! How false is a philosophy of composition which admits that there is such a thing as beauty—as an end to be reached—and yet this simple proposition seems like a paradox—what better proof could we have of how thoroughly the plagiarists have overcrawled the world? "Use beauty-wash!" they cry—patent Italian sonnet-varnish—the only thing that has stood the test of time. Use the celebrated "Milton finish" for odes, epics and epitaphs—cures lame feet and rhymatism. Use the Petrarch burnisher—porcelain-lined, it secures fame. Use Shakespolio, Wordsworthene, and Racine—they never vary and are *Reliable*—Is it a wonder a man will not arrive anywhere if he spends all his life getting forward and backward over his style?

Seldom has the folly of abstracting form from meaning, or beauty from truth, been so forcefully expressed. The topic occasions a wicked satire of the off-the-shelf gentility and the superficial polish of American verse in the years between the end of Reconstruction and the turn of the century—a gentility that Chapman rightly associates with the editor of the *Atlantic Monthly*, Thomas Bailey Aldrich. The parody of American advertising jargon with which the letter concludes is used to make a definite point: American poetry, by the end of the nineteenth century, had been assimilated to the culture of commerce and business with the result that it took on something of the timidity and unacknowledged dishonesty of that culture. It was indeed a Rotarian sort of poetry, poetry written to please and above all never to startle or offend. And that poetry was the characteristic expression of an era that hardly knew what to do with the "lame feet and rhymatism" of so unkempt and original a poet as Emily Dickinson (she always "varied" and was never "reliable").

In a revealing essay titled "The Man of Letters as a Man of Business" from his book *Literature and Life* (1902), William Dean Howells writes: "At present business is the only human solidarity; we are all bound together with that chain, whatever interests and tastes and principles separate us." Human solidarity is all well and good, but what if it is the solidarity of being bound by a chain? The metaphor is not especially appealing, suggesting, as it does, constraint and bondage rather than the affectionate attractions of community. And what of those separate "interests and tastes and principles" that promise to undermine this solidarity? Howells does not clarify these differences; he leaves the reader to wonder how comfortably they are accommodated within the larger solidarity of commerce. The artist, Howells says later in the essay, must

> have a low rank among practical people; and he will be regarded by the great mass of Americans as perhaps a little off, a little funny, a little soft! Perhaps not; and yet I would rather not have a consensus of public opinion on the question; I think I am more comfortable without it.

Howells is not really aggrieved. But an uneasiness is nonetheless evident when he concedes:

> I feel quite sure that in writing of the Man of Letters as a Man of Business, I shall attract far more readers than I should in writing of him as an Artist. Besides, as an artist he has been done a great deal already; and a commercial state like ours has really more concern in him as a business man.

What better commentary on these developments could there be than Chapman's letter to Mrs. Fields, which in a few sentences suggests so much of what we need to know about the status of the artist "in a commercial state like ours"? In any case, Chapman's letters are full of literary criticism of the sort we find here—brilliant, provocative, inspired, and altogether unamenable to the conventions of the published essay.

WILLIAM LLOYD GARRISON

By all accounts the best of Chapman's books is *William Lloyd Garrison* (1913). "The idea of the book," he wrote to his mother on Christmas Day, 1911, as he began work on it, "is to put something into the hands of the young person which will be an introduction to the whole subject. I intend the volume not as the end and summary, but as the opening up of a field of historical research." The book appeared first in 1913 and then in a second edition in 1921, by which time the events of World War I had thrown its subject into a new light, so far as Chapman was concerned. "The flames of the Great War," he explained in the preface to the 1921 edition, have "passed through us," with the result that we have a "keener, more religious, and more dramatic understanding of our Antislavery period than we possessed prior to 1914." The "tidal revulsion" of war had swept over all Europe and America, leaving "the tin cans and dead dogs of humanity" exposed to view. In the light of this awful revelation, he believed, Americans could look again at the epoch in their own history most marked, as Melvin Bernstein suggests in his study of Chapman, by the "superiority of money over people"—the epoch during which the "Slave Power," as Chapman calls it, reached its apogee. Along the same line Emerson says in his "Ode Inscribed to W. H. Channing": "Things are in the saddle, and ride mankind."

Nowhere is Chapman's prose style better than in *William Lloyd Garrison*. Take the following passage from the introduction, which, for understanding, requires quotation at length:

> The Civil War,—that war with its years of interminable length, its battles of such successive and monstrous carnage, its dragged-out reiterations of horror and agony, and its even worse tortures of hope deferred,—hope all but extinct,—that war of which it is impossible to read even a summary without becoming so worn out by distress that you forget everything that went before in the country's history and emerge, as it were, a new man at the close of your perusal;—that war was no accident. It was involved in every syllable which every inhabitant of America uttered or

neglected to utter in regard to the slavery question between 1830 and 1860. The gathering and coming on of that war, its vaporous distillation from the breath of every man, its slow, inevitable formation in the sky, its retreats and apparent dispersals, its renewed visibilities—all of them governed by some inscrutable logic—and its final descent in lightning and deluge;—these matters make the history of the interval between 1830 and 1865. That history is all one galvanic throb, one course of human passion, one Nemesis, one deliverance. And with the assassination of Lincoln in 1865 there falls from on high the great, unifying stroke that leaves the tragedy sublime. No poet ever invented such a scheme of curse, so all-involving, so remotely rising in an obscure past and holding an entire nation in its mysterious bondage—a scheme based on natural law, led forward and unfolded from mood to mood, from climax to climax, and plunging at the close into the depths of a fathomless pity. The action of the drama is upon such a scale that a quarter of the earth has to be devoted to it. Yet the argument is so trite that it will hardly bear statement. Perhaps the true way to view the whole matter is to regard it as the throwing off by healthy morality of a little piece of left-over wickedness—that bad heritage of antiquity, domestic slavery. The logical and awful steps by which the process went forward merely exhibit familiar, moral, and poetic truth. What else could they exhibit?

The sentences arise—it seems hardly appropriate to say that they are built, so inevitable does the unfolding progress feel—out of an intricate series of parallel clauses and phrases, many of them so recursively embedded in the clauses that precede them as to make the extrication of any single one of them an act of vandalism. The reader must take the passage whole or not at all. Two metaphors integrate and control the writing here: the metaphor of a storm and the metaphor of a dramatic "tragedy." The storm begins imperceptibly in the "vaporous distillation" of the breath of every American; no man, no woman, lives without giving vent to it. And out of this vapor, over the course of thirty-five years, condense clouds that inevitably darken

the skies until a "deluge" falls upon a nation cursed by its own wickedness. The war had, for Chapman, a moral necessity—even what might be called an Old Testament sort of necessity—just as it had for Abraham Lincoln in the Second Inaugural Address. And Lincoln becomes, in Chapman's vision, the sacrifice finally demanded of a guilty nation from "on high," as by a final purifying bolt of lightning. The Civil War can be interpreted—can be said to have been "no accident" and to contain "poetic truth"—precisely because it has the unity and the terrible pity-inducing perfection of a dramatic "tragedy."

Sophocles could not have done it better. Notice how Chapman's tone varies from hyperbole (the war "was involved in every syllable which every inhabitant of America uttered or neglected to utter in regard to the slavery question between 1830 and 1860") to an almost winking understatement ("a little piece of left-over wickedness—that bad heritage of antiquity, domestic slavery"). He is most comfortable as a prose writer with exhortation and invective, but within that sphere he has range and nuance, as seen in passages like this one, which work at the height of intensity. In this he resembles no one so much as Garrison himself. Later, in but one of many unforgettable paragraphs in the book, Chapman sketches a portrait of the abolitionist that could well have been drawn from his own dressing-table mirror:

> We must imagine Garrison behind and underneath the machinery and in touch with all the forces at work, writing away at his terrible *Liberator*—fomenting, rebuking, retorting, supporting, expounding, thundering, scolding. The continuousness of Garrison is appalling, and fatigues even the retrospective imagination of posterity: he is like an all-night hotel: he is possessed: he is like something let loose. I dread the din of him.

Never in the history of American biography has an author been better matched with his subject than Chapman is in *William Lloyd Garrison.*

Still, one reads the book today for more than its exhilarating, if somewhat exhausting, style. The contribution to American historiography is real and enduring. Consider, for example, what might be called the "Slave Power" theory of antebellum history. The Garrisonians spoke of an America in thrall to a conspiracy they called the Slave Power or, alternatively, the Slaveocracy. Henry Wilson—an early member of the Republican Party and later vice president of the United States under Ulysses S. Grant—argues the thesis at great length in his three-volume *History of the Rise and Fall of the Slavepower in America* (1877). Any reader acquainted with it is apt to recall it when reading Chapman's far more succinct and stimulating *Garrison*. By 1850 thinking people saw, Wilson says, "that there must be some malignant and potent agency at work, that could accomplish such results and give such a character to the nation's history." He goes on:

> They called it the Slave Power. Though it had no "local habitation," it had a "name" that was a growing terror and alarm. They saw that there existed a commanding power in the land, which made its influence everywhere felt, by which all other influences were greatly modified, and before which all other interests were compelled in greater or less degree to bend. It was as if *somewhere* some imperious autocrat or secret conclave held court or council, in which slavery's every interest, necessity, and demand were considered and cared for, and from which were issued its stern and inexorable decrees.

Imagined here is a kind of shadow government, rapaciously antirepublican and, though feudal in disposition, as efficiently bureaucratic in its methods as the British Foreign Office. It is an incipiently totalitarian state, rising up in the midst of America's Shining City upon a Hill (as the Puritans once called it) and contained within that City always as a kind of potential nightmare state. The Slave Power is our national doppelganger, our double, our Mr. Hyde. Everywhere men like Wilson looked they saw

traces of it. Like God for Saint Augustine—but this God is infernal—the center of the Slave Power was everywhere and its circumference nowhere. Early post-Reconstruction historians treated the Slave Power thesis with scorn; it hardly accorded with the cherished claim that the South had fought not for slavery nor out of economic interest, but for states' rights and out of principle. Chapman's *Garrison* may be read as a full-bore attack on this conservative school of American historiography, which was regnant in the early decades of the twentieth century and was centered at Columbia University, where the influential historian William Dunning taught. Only lately has the Slave Power thesis again begun to be taken seriously, as in Leonard Richards's book *The Slave Power: The Free North and Southern Domination, 1780–1860* (2000).

In any case, Chapman, a most able expositor of the Slave Power argument, without quite knowing it laid the foundations for a powerful theory of antebellum American literature. As has often been noted, that literature is everywhere shadowed by anxiety, anger, and gloom—shadowed by what Herman Melville, in his essay "Hawthorne and His Mosses," called simply "the power of blackness." Nathaniel Hawthorne's story "Young Goodman Brown," first published in 1835, draws deeply on these anxieties. Its New England is a dubious place—a place of two aspects, radically opposed: there is a prosperous piety on the one hand (here is what meets the eye), but there is also the intimation of a seething corruption on the other (here is what haunts the conscience).

This is an eminently American portrait of an eminently American world, and the outlines of it are apparent in such popular films as Oliver Stone's *JFK* (1991) and *Nixon* (1995), in which a "secret conclave," as Henry Wilson might say, works behind the daylight show of our government. Writers in the post–World War II period (Norman Mailer, Gore Vidal, Allen Ginsberg, Gary Snyder, and Thomas Pynchon all come to mind) would find the American serpent not in the Slave Power, for which evil no longer had any use, but in the new National Security State. This was the entity that built up and maintained, during decades of cold war, an arsenal of thermonuclear weapons and that evolved what seemed to some a potentially totalitarian internal security bureaucracy.

In Pynchon's *Gravity's Rainbow* (1973) the secret conclave takes the form of what Pynchon simply calls "The Firm"; it is now transnational in reach and so intimate in its invasions as to have appropriated, for its own dark purposes, the body of the novel's hero, Tyrone Slothrop (who is descended, as it happens, from an old New England family of Puritans). Mailer, in *Armies of the Night* (1968), speaks of America as "Corporation Land"—he, too, draws on the language of commerce—and locates the black heart of it all in the Pentagon. Chapman, inveighing against a Slave Power that had hijacked the machinery of republican government—or fulminating, in *Causes and Consequences,* against the "commercial interests" that in the 1890s were doing the same thing— belongs to this countercultural tradition. His *Garrison* is best read along a line that extends backward to *History of the Rise and Fall of the Slavepower in America* and Melville's *Confidence-Man* (1857) and forward to *Armies of the Night.*

In the theory of American history implied by Chapman's, Mailer's, and Pynchon's writings, the nation has always harbored within it a totalitarian tendency, which here emerges and there is kept in check, but which is never entirely vanquished. According to Chapman, what Garrison saw so clearly in 1830 was simply that "the Slave Power was a Moloch which controlled the politics of the North and which, in the nature of things, could stick at nothing while engaged in perpetuating that control." (Readers of Ginsberg's *Howl* will recall—though the connection is coincidental—

that Moloch is also the name there given to America's wicked alter ego.) This Moloch did not work merely through the instruments of the Congress, the White House, and the federal judiciary (that is, through "gag rules" prohibiting the reading of antislavery petitions on the floor of the House of Representatives, through executive enforcement of the Fugitive Slave Bill of 1850, and through the Dred Scott decision in the U.S. Supreme Court); its power was also felt in what Chapman calls "a policy of silence": no one could speak honestly about the nation's affairs. It was, Chapman claims, as if a great "paving-stone" had been "placed upon the mouth of a natural spring." Americans could say nothing without resort to euphemism, circumlocution, and evasive gentility. "It is hard," Chapman explains, "to imagine the falsetto condition of life in the Northern States in 1829;—the lack of spontaneity and naturalness about everybody, so far as externals went."

In Chapman's view the great pattern for this habit of obfuscation was the Constitution itself, in the very framing of which one can trace a certain "suppression of truth, the trampling upon instinct." "All the parties to that instrument," writes Chapman, and with good reason, "thoroughly understood the iniquity of slavery and deplored it. All the parties were ashamed of slavery and yet felt obliged to perpetuate it. They wrapped up a twenty-years' protection of the African slave trade in a colorless phrase." Whereupon Chapman quotes the document itself: "The migration or importation of such persons as any of the states now existing shall think proper to admit, shall not be prohibited by the Congress prior to the year one thousand eight hundred and eight." The point Chapman would make is plain: "The African slave trade is probably the most brutal organized crime in history. Our fathers did not dare to name it." And their timidity, their reflexive self-censorship—a censorship so efficient as to deceive even the canniest American into thinking that he knew his own heart and mind—came to characterize the American personality. The "leaden touch of hypocrisy" radiated outward from the Constitution, which Chapman calls the "Ark of our Covenant," until it embraced us all. "Our whole civilization, our social life, our religious feelings, our political ideas, had all become accommodated to cruelty, representative of tyranny." No wonder Huckleberry Finn lights out for the territory; no wonder that even there he will not escape the debilitating oppression of his American conscience. Tyranny had been made internal to each of us, and to be American was to be unaware precisely of that fact.

Of course, the tyranny was never perfect. Through fissures in the crust that lay so uneasily over the volcano there occasionally emerged infernal flashes of light—as when in "Young Goodman Brown" readers were invited to suppose, if only through allegory, that our New England, our original "America," may well have been pervaded by a wickedness no one had the courage to name in open meeting. And Chapman's *Garrison* certainly helps us understand the latent Gothicism, the sense of ever-present evil, that darkens the great writings of the American renaissance. "Everyone ought to have been perfectly happy" in that period, he points out, and continues:

> Had not the country emerged from the War of the Revolution in the shape of a new and glorious Birth of Time—a sample to all mankind? Had it not survived the dangers of the second war with Great Britain? And what then remained for us except to go forward victoriously and become a splendid, successful, vigorous, and benevolent people?

And yet it was a fact, Chapman contends, that "during the decade that followed the Missouri Compromise," which seemed to have settled the slavery question, "everyone in America fell sick": all went forward "under the gradually descending fringe of a mist, an unwholesome-

feeling cloud of oppression." All Americans were Young Goodman Brown—cursed by guilt, by doubt, and by suspicion and certain that *somewhere,* even at the very hearthside of our faith, we harbored evil. Lincoln himself could not escape the disease. As Chapman puts it:

> One of Lincoln's chief interests in life, from early manhood onward, lay in emancipation. This he could not say and remain in politics; nay, he could not think it and remain in politics. He could not quite know himself and yet remain in politics. The awful weight of a creed that was never quite true—the creed of the Constitution—pressed down upon the intellects of our public men. That was the dower and curse of slavery.

In short, every American may see himself in Huck Finn—that naive boy who, though he might *do* the right thing for a fugitive slave, never is able to *think* his way beyond the horizon of what the Slave Power saw fit to allow. After all, in its name he willingly condemns himself to Hell.

And yet for Chapman the outcome is never really in doubt. Slavery, like all wickedness, is doomed, because it is contrary to what Chapman calls "the great creative force of the universe." Here Chapman stands alongside Emerson in the conviction that the universe is, at bottom, good—in the belief that physical law is reducible to moral law and that the tendency of moral law is inevitably to realize itself in practical action of the sort that Garrison's life exemplified. The angels always find their instrument. This faith that the order of things is a moral order and that anything out of harmony with it must in due course perish most marks Chapman as a belated antebellum thinker, for his contemporaries had certainly abandoned it. The cool, cynical temper of the 1890s was unfriendly to the development of what William James sympathetically called, in "The Will to Believe," the "hot young moralist." Chapman and Stephen Crane both came into their own in the 1890s and in New York City. It is nonetheless impossible to imagine two souls, two temperaments, more unlike. Here is Crane's word, from "The Open Boat" (1898), a story in which one can recognize the new way of thinking:

> When it occurs to a man that nature does not regard him as important, and that she feels she would not maim the universe by disposing of him, he at first wishes to throw bricks at the temple, and he hates deeply the fact that there are no bricks and no temples. Any visible expression of nature would surely be pelted with his jeers.
>
> Then, if there be no tangible thing to hoot, he feels, perhaps, the desire to confront a personification and indulge in pleas, bowed to one knee, and with hands supplicant, saying: "Yes, but I love myself."

A high cold star on a winter's night is the word he feels that she says to him. Thereafter he knows the pathos of his situation.

And here is Chapman's word in *Garrison,* in which the old way of thinking has its Indian summer:

> During all this time the stars were fighting against slavery. They fought behind clouds and darkly for two hundred years; and at last their influence began to develop visible symptoms of cure. A very small part of life or history is ever visible, and it is only by inference that we know what powers have been at work; but in 1829 it is plain that some terrible drug is in operation in America. Whether this hot liquid was born in the vitals of the slave we do not know. It seems to me that the origin of it must have been in the slave himself; and that it was mystically transmitted to the Abolitionist, in whom it appeared as pity. We know that the drops of this pity had a peculiar, stimulating power on the earth—a dynamic, critical power, a sort of prison-piercing faculty, which sent voltages of electrical shock through humanity.

In this assertion that the stars were all along fighting against slavery (which for Chapman as

for Emerson is no mere figure of speech), that the stars are not high or cold or indifferent to human purposes, lies Chapman's great difference with the America of the post-Reconstruction years. This is an epoch that, by the light he casts, must strike us now as a time of unthinking infidelity. In *The Red Badge of Courage,* Crane could see in the Civil War little more than a theater for the staging, with knowing condescension, of a crisis in his protagonist's adolescence; "courage" is for him an empty word. Chapman saw in the war nothing less than "a mirror of the soul," and a "thesaurus of moral illustration." "Courage," he tells us, "came back with the war" and was "but a sample thread of a new kind of life which trusts generous feelings, relies upon the unseen, is in union with the unconscious operations of the spirit."

"THE ONLY OBJECT REALLY WORTHY OF ENTHUSIASM"

In the preface to his 1898 volume of social and political criticism, *Causes and Consequences,* Chapman makes a startling claim: "A normal and rounded development can only come from a use of faculties very different from that practised by the average American since the discovery of the cotton gin." The remark comes by way of introduction to the chapter, in *Causes and Consequences,* on early childhood education—indeed, on the kindergarten—and the relevance to that subject of the cotton gin is, in Chapman's view, a matter to be taken seriously.

The cotton gin made cultivation of the crop on a large scale, and for export into a world market, immensely profitable. This development, in due course, led to the rise of the Slave Power, which battened the succubus of a wicked commerce, with its single appetite for cotton and its system of lifetime bond slavery, onto the whole body of the nation. The result was that by 1860 more than half of all export revenues derived from the crop. This astonishing expansion of economic power called up as its instrument a fully elaborated doctrine of white supremacy, which led, as Chapman shows in *William Lloyd Garrison,* to the suppression of free speech and free press, and ultimately—such is the long reach of tyranny—to the extinction of free thought itself. Not even people's minds were really private any longer (again, as *Huckleberry Finn* makes plain). People's minds were gears in the great machinery of what Chapman in his poem "Bismarck" called, in a related context, "organized hatred." The Union Army and Lincoln's policies crushed the Slave Power, but the forces of "commerce" were merely redirected by the catastrophe into new channels, there again, as Chapman believed, to "distort" human character. "The growth and concentration of capital which the railroad and the telegraph made possible," writes Chapman in 1898, "is the salient fact in the history of the last quarter-century." And a civilization "based upon commerce which is in all its parts corruptly managed," as, in his view, ours was during the age of the robber barons, "will present a social life which is unintelligent and mediocre, made up of people afraid of each other, whose ideas are shopworn, whose manners are self-conscious."

Immigration, which greatly accelerated during this period, did nothing to improve matters. Chapman explains:

> By a process of natural selection, the self-seekers of Europe have for sixty years been poured into the hopper of our great mill. The Suabian and the Pole each drops his costume, his language, and his traditions as he goes in. They come out American business men; and in the second generation they resemble each other more closely in ideals, in aims, and in modes of thought than two brothers who had been bred to different trades in Europe.

In short, "America turns out only one kind of man. Listen to the conversation of any two men in a street car. They are talking about the price of something—building material, advertising, bonds, cigars." In such a society, Chapman contends, "private opinion is a thing to be stamped out, like private law." The whole tendency of American civilization, whether during the epoch of the Slave Power or that of the oil and railroad barons, ran counter to what Chapman calls "the aim of life": namely, the "full development of individual character." "In so far as individuals are developed," he explains, "they differ from one another." Or, to put the matter in other words, as he does in the essay on Emerson, "The only object which is really worthy of enthusiasm or which can permanently excite it [is] the character of a man." "Personal liberty" is all, and "those who fought for it and those who enjoyed it are our heroes."

According to Chapman, this private liberty is not merely *compatible* with a social existence; it *requires* a social existence. "The complete development of every individual is necessary to our complete happiness," Chapman explains in the essay on education. "And there is no reason why any one who has ever been to a dull dinner party should doubt this. Nay, history gives proof that solitude is dangerous. Man cannot sing, nor write, nor paint, nor reform, nor build, nor do anything except die, alone." With the destruction of liberty of thought, social life is also destroyed; which explains why, in Chapman's view, American letters and politics—even American dinner parties—have, since "the discovery of the cotton gin," been soul-killing exercises in "affable reticence." Commerce—whether in cotton, in the bodies of the men and women who produce cotton, or in railroads and oil—alienates us. We neither know nor speak our own minds; indeed, we do not possess them.

For all these reasons, the ideas of the German educator Friedrich Froebel, as set out by Chapman in *Causes and Consequences,* are a revelation: "Unselfishness and intellectual development are one and the same thing," and "there is no failure of intellect which cannot be expressed in terms of selfishness." The theory on which commerce operated during the Gilded Age, Chapman reminds us, proceeded from the assumption—to which social Darwinism gave a specious scientific authority—that the human being is a selfish animal; the going metaphor was of a Hobbesian war of all against all. "The scientists look into a drop of water and see animals eating each other up. What they have not seen is that all this ferocity goes forward, subject to customs as rigid as a military code, and that it is this code which preserves the species," not callous self-interest on the part of individual animals. "The 'struggle for existence' as it is commonly conceived would exterminate in short order any species that indulged in it." Real Darwinians have lately returned—and with infinitely more sophistication than the "social Darwinians" ever possessed—to this problem of the evolution of altruism. But for Chapman it suffices simply to say, in concluding his essay on education, that "we need not attempt to adjust our ideas of man to the dogmas developed by the study of the lower animals." He implies, too, that in American life, at least since the invention of the cotton gin, commerce had adhered to exactly those dogmas. It had, at its worst, reduced men to mere bodies—to a kind of animal existence—and insofar as it had done this, it had extinguished the light of the mind.

It will not have escaped the reader's notice that Chapman provides in all this a theory of tyranny—of its origins, its operations, and its results. In his *Garrison* and elsewhere Chapman sketches out a disturbing portrait of what would, in the twentieth century, become the scourge of Europe. It is also what, he felt, had been realized in the United States between 1830 and 1860, when the Slave Power stalked the halls of the Senate and held the president on a leash: totalitarianism. He does this with greatest force in what is perhaps his best poem, "Bismarck," a poem that is an anatomy of all those tendencies of modernity that threaten the "only object re-

ally worthy of enthusiasm—the character of a man." The occasion for the poem was the chancellor's death in 1898, and it was published first as a supplement to Chapman's periodical, the *Political Nursery,* in the summer of that year. It begins:

> At midnight, Death dismissed the chancellor
> But left the soul of Bismarck on his face.
> Titanic, in the peace and power of bronze,
> With three red roses loosely in his grasp,
> Lies the Constructor. His machinery
> Revolving in the wheels of destiny
> Rolls onward over him. Alive, inspired,
> Vast, intricate, complete, unthinkable,
> Nice as a watch and strong as dynamite,
> An empire and a whirlwind, on it moves,
> While he that set it rolling lies so still.

Bismarck, of course, was the man who made Germany a nation, bringing "unity," as Chapman goes on to say, "out of chaos, petty courts, / Princelings and potentates." In fact, he made what was more—an "empire." To be sure, his methods were as severe as they were effective; he exercised nearly total control over domestic and foreign policy after 1871, prohibiting the distribution of political literature unfriendly to his interests or to the interests of his class. The result was a state whose vitality was the spiritual "death" of the men who comprised it. The state, Chapman writes, was "alive, inspired, / vast, intricate, complete." It was a kind of superorganism, with motives of its own, and the materials out of which it was built—the "fibres" out of which its fretwork was "twisted"—were "human strands." (Here again we find anticipated Pynchon's portrait of "The Firm," Mailer's rendition of "Corporation Land," and Ginsberg's representation of "Moloch.")

This new state attracted the loyalties of men "by vanity," and it compelled their actions "by fear." Everything at its disposal, writes Chapman—even the "souls" of men—this empire "used ... like electricity," whether to make roads, to build monuments, or to write verse (for literature and art, too, were a part of the machinery). The state made war against Austria and France and "kill[ed] what intellect it [could not] use." "The age is just beginning," Chapman concedes,

> yet we see
> The fruits of hatred ripen hourly
> And Germany's in bondage—muzzled press—
> The private mind suppressed, while shade on
>   shade
> Is darkening o'er the intellectual sky.
> And world-forgotten, outworn crimes and cries
> With dungeon tongue accost the citizen
> And send him trembling to his family.

So it was in Germany under Bismarck; so it had been in the Confederacy, and indeed in America as a whole, when John C. Calhoun dominated the Senate and when Daniel Webster gave his name to the Fugitive Slave Bill of 1850; and so would it be in the Germany of the Third Reich, which Chapman did not live to see. In Chapman we have one of the great voices against those forms of tyranny so peculiar to the modern era—the era that saw the rise of the slave trade, of colonialism, and of industrialism and which also saw the advent of fascism, into which vortex every one of these earlier currents ultimately converged. And yet in Chapman there works also the conviction that the stars themselves are on the side of right. Bleak and furious as his writings may sometimes be, they are never untouched by something of the splendor that attaches to the prophetic books of the Old Testament, which always say the covenant can be redeemed.

THE SHAPE OF THE CAREER

Chapman is too seldom read, but the reason for this is not far to seek. He is an impossible man to place, except perhaps as he has been placed here, in a line of compassionately apocalyptic American exponents of liberty—liberty even to the point of anarchic idiosyncrasy. These writers include, at one end, Emerson, Thoreau, and Garrison, and at the other end, writers as diverse as W. E. B. Du Bois, Mailer, Ginsberg, James Baldwin, and Pynchon. As a literary critic he is simply one of the two or three best this country has ever produced.

Chapman confined himself to no single genre, writing poetry, plays (many of them for children), criticism, political theory, and journalism and producing translations of the Greek dramatists and of Dante (among others). For some years after his death there was no good selection of his writings available. Jacques Barzun's *The Selected Writings of John Jay Chapman* remedied the problem in 1957, though it has since gone out of print. The much more recent *Unbought Spirit: A John Jay Chapman Reader* (1998), edited by Richard Stone, is a fine supplement to Barzun's volume. (Barzun, in fact, supplies the foreword to the book.) As of this writing, however, no comprehensive edition of Chapman has yet been undertaken. The most remarkable documents he left us are probably his letters, where the prose often approaches an intense, difficult beauty and often burns with a searing wit; they have no parallel in American literature. Mark Anthony DeWolfe Howe's *John Jay Chapman and His Letters* (1937), with its tactful biographical commentary, will doubtless remain, for many years to come, the volume with which any reader should begin.

Chapman's peculiar vehemence—which, it must be said, unbalanced him at times—found what strikes most Americans now as an unhappy outlet in his later years. He had always been suspicious of the Catholic Church—a suspicion perhaps attributable at least in part to his Huguenot ancestry. But beginning in the 1910s and continuing until the end of his life, Chapman undertook a bitter campaign against the church's influence, which he regarded as dangerously undemocratic. The animosity of his remarks against the church, together with a certain crankish aspect they sometimes display, remind the reader now of nothing so much as Ezra Pound in his fulminations against usury in the *Cantos* and elsewhere. That Chapman was off his balance in making these remarks is perhaps evident from the tentativeness that occasionally qualifies them—a tentativeness perfectly absent from his more confident pronouncements against what he took for wickedness.

Consider the following from a letter of 1925:

> I suppose that my Protestant inheritance makes me think that the Roman Church is the most serious and everlasting professional destroyer of private opinion and open talk, and so I rush to open the subject on that side—as being the side I best understand. But truly—it is the decay in the American brain that is the real danger.

"I suppose," "the side I best understand," "but truly": these qualifying phrases do not sort well with the extravagance of the main charge—that "the Roman Church is the most serious and everlasting professional destroyer of private opinion and open talk." Chapman was not a man accustomed to the art of compromise. His worrying contempt ultimately led him to write a sonnet titled "Cape Cod, Rome, and Jerusalem"—a poem not merely anti-Catholic but anti-Semitic as well. This poem, it seems, only the *Kourier,* the official journal of the Ku Klux Klan, saw fit to print, for there, indeed, it was published. The fever-pitch nerve that led Chapman to thrust his left hand into the fire in his Harvard days and that sent him into a years-long fit of agitated (and incapacitating) depression in middle life had deranged the better angels of his nature at last.

The reader does well to remember Chapman's own admonition in *William Lloyd Garrison,* that steadfast book written against every current in American life that found its bastard issue in the Klan:

> I confess that I had rather stand out for posterity in a hideous silhouette, as having been wrong on every question of my time, than be erased into a cipher by my biographer. But biographers do not feel in this way toward their heroes. Each one feels that he has undertaken to do his best by his patron. Therefore they stand the man under a north light in a photographer's attic, suggest his attitude, and thus take the picture;—whereas, in real life, the man was standing on the balcony of a burning building which the next moment collapsed, and in it he was crushed beyond the semblance of humanity.

No proper survey of Chapman's work should "suggest his attitude" in this flattering way. He must be taken, like Garrison himself, "all on fire"; if he was wrong on two or three of the questions of his time (what writer is not?), he was right on nearly every other.

Selected Bibliography

WORKS OF JOHN JAY CHAPMAN

ESSAYS
Emerson, and Other Essays. New York: Scribners, 1898; 2nd ed., with a new preface, 1909.
Causes and Consequences. New York: Scribners, 1898.
Practical Agitation. New York: Scribners, 1900.
Learning and Other Essays. New York: Moffat, Yard, 1910.
William Lloyd Garrison. New York: Moffat, Yard, 1913; 2nd ed., with a new preface, 1921.
Greek Genius, and Other Essays. New York: Moffat, Yard, 1915.
A Glance toward Shakespeare. Boston: Atlantic Monthly Press, 1922.

OTHER WORKS

Four Plays for Children. New York: Moffat, Yard, 1908.

Songs and Poems. New York: Scribners, 1919.

John Jay Chapman and His Letters. Edited by Mark Anthony DeWolfe Howe. Boston: Houghton Mifflin, 1937. (Includes letters quoted in the text and passages from his unpublished memoir.)

COLLECTED WORKS

The Selected Writings of John Jay Chapman. Edited and with an introduction by Jacques Barzun. New York: Farrar, Straus & Cudahy, 1957. (Includes all writings quoted in the text, except *Causes and Consequences,* the letters, and the poem "Bismarck.")

Unbought Spirit: A John Jay Chapman Reader. Edited and with an introduction by Richard Stone. Urbana: University of Illinois Press, 1998.

CRITICAL AND BIOGRAPHICAL STUDIES

Bernstein, Melvin H. *John Jay Chapman.* New York: Twayne, 1964.

Hovey, Richard B. *John Jay Chapman: An American Mind.* New York: Columbia University Press, 1959.

Kazin, Alfred. "A Left-Over Transcendentalist." In his *Contemporaries, from the Nineteenth Century to the Present.* Boston: Little, Brown, 1962. Pp. 64–69. Reprinted by the Horizon Press in 1982.

Wilson, Edmund. "John Jay Chapman." In his *The Triple Thinkers: Ten Essays on Literature.* New York: Harcourt, Brace and Company, 1938.

Wister, Owen. "John Jay Chapman." *Atlantic Monthly,* May 1934, pp. 524–539.

—MARK RICHARDSON

Charles W. Chesnutt

1858–1932

ON MARCH 14, 1862, Federal forces captured the inlet port city of New Bern, North Carolina, which they would hold through the rest of the Civil War. Slaves soon gathered behind the new Union lines; local white landholders fled; and a chaplain in one of the Massachusetts regiments occupying the city, the Rev. Horace James, undertook to organize the "contraband," as the dislocated slaves were then called. He arranged for them to settle along the Trent River on plots of land that had been abandoned. To honor their protector, the now freed slaves named their settlement James City. The freedmen prospered, and, according to James, by 1865 most of them had laid up considerable property in the form of livestock, carts, and the like, and a number had succeeded as merchants. And there they lived for twenty-eight years until, in 1893, Governor Elias Carr dispatched a regiment of the First North Carolina Militia to evict the men and women of James City. Title to the land had long been in dispute in the courts—that is, until a decision was made in 1891 to transfer the land to its antebellum owners. In 1893, when the eviction orders were put into effect, the black men of James City had no choice but to sign three-year leases to work the land they had owned, or so they believed, for thirty years.

The James City farmers' predicament, however sensational its details, was not unusual in the North Carolina that Charles Waddell Chesnutt knew. Although Chesnutt was born to free black parents in Cleveland, Ohio—on June 20, 1858—they had emigrated there from Fayetteville, North Carolina, two years earlier, and they moved back there right after the Civil War when the boy was eight years old. Chesnutt's father, Andrew Jackson Chesnutt, was a grocery store owner and a farmer. Something about the tenuous hold that black farmers always had on the land is subtly communicated in "The Goophered Grapevine," the first story in Chesnutt's first book, *The Conjure Woman* (1899), published when he was forty years old. In that story we are told of how Uncle Julius, who had since 1865 been making a "respectable revenue" on the land he once worked as a slave, is displaced in 1877 by a new white owner—an Ohioan who had been seduced southward into North Carolina by the promise of cheap land. In short order he secures a legally binding deed to Uncle Julius's old estate, the title to which had been in dispute amongst the old master's heirs since the war. Uncle Julius might as well have been living in James City.

What, then, was life like in North Carolina for black men and women such as Uncle Julius, of whom there were some 330,000 in 1865? They were, of course, subject to the same political and economic uncertainties that affected whites when the Confederacy collapsed, but their situation was unique, and new laws were passed (and old ones retained) that specifically limited their freedom of movement and their ability to seek employment on fair terms. The new "black codes," as they were called, allowed for five-hundred-dollar fines to be levied "from time to time" against blacks who entered North Carolina from other states; a native North Carolinian freedman, on leaving the state for six months, was liable to the same sanctions. Black girls were to be bound out as apprentices until the age of twenty-one, whereas white girls achieved their majority at eighteen. County courts could hire out the children of any black parents who were, in the eyes of the court, not profitably engaged in "some honest, industrious occupation"; no such provision existed in the case of white parents. And in all cases former masters were to be granted first right to apprentice men and women whom they had previously owned. Vagrancy laws, while artfully written to avoid mention of race, were clearly intended to apply disproportionately to blacks. White employers were allowed, under the law, to pay black laborers in kind (that is, in clothing, food, and so forth) rather than in cash. And marriage between whites and blacks was a criminal offense. In short, when Chesnutt's fictional Ohio couple strolls onto the old plantation in 1877 with an eye toward turning it again to profit, Uncle Julius has little choice but to charm them, by whatever wiles he has, into a relationship of patronage: on his own and without white protectors he would indeed be insecure. His sole asset—and his friends and family depend on him to use it well—is his wit. He must wear the mask and sing for his supper. *The Conjure Woman* tells the story of how he set about to do exactly that.

"THE GOOPHERED GRAPEVINE" AND *THE CONJURE WOMAN*

"The Goophered Grapevine" appeared first in 1887 in the *Atlantic Monthly,* and in that text Chesnutt makes clear at once when the action of the story takes place—"ten years ago," or 1877. That year saw the collapse of the last of the Reconstruction-era Republican state governments. Freedmen and their children were once again at the tender mercies of the Southern Democratic Party. And John and Annie, the white couple who have come south from Ohio to buy some land "for a mere song," typify certain post-Reconstruction developments—to wit, the influx of Northern capital into cheap Southern labor markets and the like. Chesnutt

has so arranged things as to represent, in this engagement between John and Uncle Julius, the new regime whereby Southern blacks answered not to white owners, as they had before the war, but to white capitalists. In this connection, consider John's account of his first impression of the plantation he ultimately buys:

I went several times to look at a place that I thought might suit me. It was a plantation of considerable extent, that had formerly belonged to a wealthy man by the name of McAdoo. The estate had been for years involved in litigation between disputing heirs, during which period shiftless cultivation had well-nigh exhausted the soil. There had been a vineyard of some extent on the place, but it had not been attended to since the war, and had lapsed into utter neglect. The vines—here partly supported by decayed and broken-down trellises, there twining themselves among the branches of the slender saplings which had sprung up among them—grew in wild and unpruned luxuriance, and the few scattered grapes they bore were the undisputed prey of the first comer.

John's eye is naturally proprietary. As we soon learn, and as John himself admits, the vineyard has not at all been neglected. Uncle Julius has been farming it, if on a modest scale, for twelve years—from 1865 to 1877—precisely the years of the Reconstruction. But John looks out on the land with what must be called a "white" gaze: a thing not used by a white man is, for him, a thing not genuinely "used." His sense of entitlement is manifest—as manifest as had been the entitlement of white settlers in the nineteenth century to the western lands that had so long been "neglected" by Native Americans. So there is inevitably a note of finger-wagging, if indulgent, disapproval in John's voice—as if he had caught a child nicking a bit of candy—when he first lays eyes on Uncle Julius: "Upon Annie's complaining of weariness I led the way back to the yard, where a pine log, lying under a spreading elm, afforded a shady though somewhat hard seat. One end of the log was already occupied by a venerable-looking colored man. He held on his knees a hat full of grapes, over which he was smacking his lips with great gusto, and a pile of grape skins near him indicated that the performance was no new thing."

John wastes no time in sizing Julius up, in an ethnological sort of way: "He was not entirely black, and this fact, together with the quality of his hair, which was about six inches long and very bushy, except on the top of his head, where he was quite bald, suggested a slight strain of other than negro blood. There was a shrewdness in his eyes, too, which was not altogether African, and which, as we afterwards learned from experience, was indicative of a corresponding shrewdness in his character." For John race is a question of blood, and in this he is a typical late-nineteenth-century American. In those days there was much interest, of a pseudoscientific nature, in character traits associated with Anglo-Saxon blood, or Gallic blood, or Teutonic blood, or Negro blood, and so on. Any cunning, or "shrewdness," Julius might display must of course derive from white blood of some sort. (As for Julius's authentic Negro blood: some indication of what its legacy means to John may perhaps be gleaned from his later report that Julius "was a marvelous hand in the management of horses and dogs, with whose mental processes he manifested a greater familiarity than mere use would seem to account for.") But all the while, in this story, Chesnutt lets us see that race is much more likely a role we learn to perform than simply an identity we are born into. And Julius is a consummate performer, shrewd in ways that John's facile theories make him utterly unable to understand. Julius always wears a mask; he puts John and Annie at ease by playing the deferential, self-deprecating "darky": "But ef you en young miss dere doan' min' lis'nin' ter a ole nigger run on a minute er two w'ile you er restin', I kin 'splain

to you how it all happen'," he says in introducing his tale of the "goophered," or bewitched, grapevine.

Julius evokes, when it suits his purposes, nothing so much as the minstrel stage: "Now, ef dey's an'thing a nigger lub, nex' ter 'possum, en chick'n, en watermillyums, it's scuppernon's. Dey ain' nuffin dat kin stan' up side'n de scuppernon' for sweetness; sugar ain't a suckumstance ter scuppernon'. W'en de season is nigh 'bout ober, en de grapes begin ter swivel up des a little wid de wrinkles er ole age,—w'en de skin git sof' en brown,—den de scuppernon' make you smack yo' lip en roll yo' eye en wush fer mo'; so I reckon it ain' very 'stonishin' dat niggers lub scuppernon'." He doesn't so much affect naiveté as affect an *affected* naiveté, a thing sure to delight the more paternalistic instincts of a man like John: "Nex' spring, w'en de sap commence' ter rise in de scuppernon' vime, Henry tuk a ham one night. Whar'd he git de ham? *I* doan know; dey wa'n't no hams on de plantation 'cep'n' w'at 'uz in de smokehouse, but *I* never see Henry 'bout de smokehouse. But ez I wuz a-sayin', he tuk de ham ober ter Aun' Peggy's ...." Surely this is calculated. Otherwise why all this coyness over a theft that supposedly happened decades earlier?

Notice also that Julius exercises great tact when criticizing—mocking, really—his old white master: "So atter a w'ile Mars Dugal' begin ter miss his scuppernon's. Co'se he 'cuse' de niggers er it, but dey all 'nied it ter de las'. Mars Dugal' sot spring guns en steel traps, en he en de oberseah sot up nights once't er twice't, tel one night Mars Dugal'—he 'uz a monst'us keerless man—got his leg shot full er cow-peas. But somehow er nudder dey could n' nebber ketch none er de niggers. I dunner how it happen, but it happen des like I tell you, en de grapes kep' on a-goin' des de same." Julius knows perfectly well how it happened: Old Massa was a fool. To call him a "monst'us keerless man" understates things in a highly artful fashion—all the more artful, given that the story allows us to suppose, without ever quite specifying the matter, that Julius is making most of this up on the spot. His portrait of Mars Dugal' is ingeniously satirical.

What does Julius intend to accomplish with the conjure tales that so delight his white auditors? First, of course, it appears that Julius hopes to dissuade John from buying the old plantation, which Julius can claim by right of long labor if not by legal title. And this is precisely what John thinks he is up to: "I found, when I bought the vineyard, that Uncle Julius had occupied a cabin on the place for many years, and derived a respectable revenue from the product of the neglected grapevines. This, doubtless, accounted for his advice to me not to buy the vineyard, though whether it inspired the goopher story I am unable to state." But the reader has to ask: Is Julius really naive enough to suppose that a conjure story might frighten a calculating, up-to-date white man like John out of buying a promising spread of land—a white man who amuses himself, as we later learn, by reading hyper-rationalist (and pretentious) treatises on epistemology? Hardly. Julius's motives must be much more complicated. Telling the stories gives him a sort of "mastery." At times he can affect John's behavior in ways beneficial to him; he gets a stipend out of John, and more.

Julius also exercises a certain moral and intellectual authority over John. The stories Julius tells are sophisticated parables about slavery and also about post-Reconstruction race relations. For example, in "The Goophered Grapevine" the slave Henry is bewitched in a special way: when the sap rises in the vines each spring, old Henry grows spry and energetic, even to the point of "cuttin' up his didos" with the women; his hair grows back and curls up "in little balls, des like dis yer reg'lar grapy ha'r, en by de time de grapes got ripe his head look des like a bunch er grapes." When the sap falls in autumn the transformation runs in reverse: Henry's hair falls out, and he begins to get "ole en stiff in de j'ints ag'in." Master McAdoo soon enough cashes in—it has to be "a monst'us cloudy night when a dollar git by him in de dahkness," Uncle Julius tells us—by selling Henry dear in the spring and buying him back cheap in the fall. In this way he makes five thousand dollars in five years. The parable couldn't be plainer: the body of the slave is identified with the land and with the crop; essentially the slave's body, like the land, is harrowed, plowed, inseminated, harvested. And Master McAdoo's exploitation of the slave's body perfectly complements his exploitation of the land, which he greedily exhausts and impoverishes to the point that, by the time the war breaks out, it yields nothing. In spinning his tale of the goophered grapevine, Julius subtly contrasts two sorts of ownership of the land, two kinds of relationships to it. The way of old Master McAdoo and of John alike is essentially capitalistic and exploitive; they subordinate the land. Julius's way—for he has been working the vineyard a considerable length of time—is altogether different. It is, as we say now, sustainable, and one inescapable moral of the "The Goophered Grapevine" is that slave agriculture is unsustainable: McAdoo was doomed to failure.

But does Julius really believe in all this conjure business? Likely he does not, at least not in any naively superstitious way. His interest in the tales he spins is moral, political, and by all appearances literary. Such tales as "Po' Sandy," "The Gray Wolf's H'ant" and "Hot-Foot Hannibal" seem made to order, as even John comes to believe. These and other tales so perfectly suit Julius's ulterior motives that it is hard to believe he hasn't designed them expressly for the purpose of realizing those motives. So Julius probably does not believe in the conjure stories in quite the way that he pretends to, though this is not to say that his relation to the folk culture of the slaves is purely instrumental and artful. What Julius seems to see in the old stories is how conjuring was itself a politically interested enterprise: almost always in these tales, conjuring is a way for slaves to exercise some kind of power over their masters.

So Chesnutt, through his mouthpiece Julius, offers what is really a penetrating analysis of the folklore of the slaves: he shows us how that folk culture arose from specific material conditions and how it was in fact a way of managing those conditions, both literarily (that is, symbolically) and practically. The old folktales Julius draws on, then, are complex in their motivation and social function—every bit as complex as the goopher stories Julius himself makes up (for we have to conclude that a good deal of what he relates is improvised). For this reason the issue of whether or not Julius "believes in" the "truth" of these tales is doubly complicated: the tales surely do, as he feels, have a kind of mythic truth, quite apart from any merely factual truths about the fates of Henry and of Tenie and Sandy that they may set forth.

CHESNUTT AND THE POST-RECONSTRUCTION PLANTATION TALE

The Conjure Woman, as many scholars have pointed out, belongs alike to the postwar genres of local-color fiction and the plantation tale. The development of both these genres is intimately linked to the social, economic, and cultural transformation of America in the post-Reconstruction years. These years saw the widespread expansion of markets for industrial and consumer goods, as intercontinental transportation and communication became a fait accompli; the general adoption—at least in the *letter* of the law—of nationwide patterns of social relations and civil rights as regional political differences were diminished, in part by passage of the thirteenth, fourteenth, and

fifteenth amendments to the Constitution; and, in a sense, the nationalization of a common American culture, as disseminated through such magazines as the *Atlantic Monthly,* which began to enjoy a truly national readership and in which a number of Chesnutt's stories first appeared. The inevitable effect of these developments was a gradual attrition of radical regional differences, though this took many years to work itself out. So local-color fiction, evolving out of this cultural matrix and existing against its background, performed what the critic Richard H. Brodhead calls "the work of mourning ways of life being eradicated at this time": precisely at the moment when authentic regional differences were vanishing, these same differences became a kind of literary fetish. Much local-color writing is therefore marked by nostalgia, and at times it tends, when it turns its attention to the past, to clothe the antebellum years in almost idyllic dress.

The "plantation tale" was a specific subgenre in the local-color tradition, and, as historians and literary critics have shown, its cultural function seems to have been complex: it arose as Reconstruction ended—that is to say, as the last Federal troops withdrew from the last of the Southern capitals that harbored them, and as political and economic reconciliation became a fact of American life. Against this backdrop it becomes clear that plantation tales, such as those published by Joel Chandler Harris (author of the Uncle Remus stories) and Thomas Nelson Page (who romanticized the antebellum South as a virtual prelapsarian Eden), had, as Brodhead explains, "the more or less overt function of excusing the North's withdrawal from the plight of the freed southern slave." Freed slaves in these stories seem to have little but nostalgia for the old days and remain with their former owners as what used to be called "faithful retainers."

A typical statement of the plantation ideal is given by Colonel Owen in Chesnutt's story

"The Passing of Grandison," collected in his second book, *The Wife of His Youth and Other Stories of the Color Line* (1899), and discussed at some length below. The colonel has just elicited from one of his slaves an expression of devotion, which, unbeknownst to him (so caught up in the myth is he), will prove to be terrifically disingenuous: "The colonel was beaming. This was true gratitude, and his feudal heart thrilled at such appreciative homage. What cold-blooded, heartless monsters they were who would break up this blissful relationship of kindly protection on the one hand, of wise subordination and loyal dependence on the other! The colonel always became indignant at the mere thought of such wickedness." In the plantation tales, black men and women seem perfectly content with a condition of political inequality, and the stories in which they appear often seem devoted to assuring Northern readers (and Southern ones) that things in the South really aren't so bad and that relations between former slaves and former owners are essentially cordial and healthy. Chesnutt was well aware that plantation tales, together with cognate media—from minstrelsy to popular novels—fulfilled precisely this function.

In any event, it was into these combined literary and economic circumstances that Chesnutt introduced his much more complex and subtle (even countercultural) version of the local-color plantation tale. There is an analogy to be drawn between the conjures described in Uncle Julius's stories and the stories themselves: both are exercised—partly effectively, partly not—against white authority. And we can regard *The Conjure Woman* itself in this light: as a partly effective, though not completely satisfactory, effort to subvert white literary authority. The antagonism here is played out even in the history of the book's composition and publication. Its contents were arrived at through a kind of compromise on Chesnutt's part with his (white) establishment publisher, Houghton Mifflin and

Company, of Boston. Chesnutt felt that the plantation-tale genre was too constricting. It did not allow a broad range of representation of African-American life, and he had determined to abandon it. Houghton, Mifflin, however, declined at first to publish the nonplantation fiction he had begun to write and asked him instead to submit a number of new "conjure" stories, together with those he had already published. Out of these, Houghton selected the tales that comprise *The Conjure Woman*. So Julius's position as a storyteller addressing, and being constricted by, an exclusively white audience is analogous in certain respects to Chesnutt's position as an African-American author writing within an almost exclusively white literary establishment: he is able to do remarkable things, many of them subtly and ironically subversive, but there is something unsatisfactory about the fact that he, like Julius, never receives complete liberty.

It is worth asking now what Chesnutt intends to accomplish in *The Conjure Woman*. We have already seen that he essentially dramatizes his relation to his white audience in the relationship between Julius and the white Northerner, John. The stories perform, for Chesnutt, a certain ironic educative role. Like Julius he at once charms his readers while criticizing and admonishing them, and he does this in ways that no doubt remain unknown to some of his white readers (for that matter many of his early readers assumed that he *was* white). Chesnutt also engages in an indirect sort of literary criticism: he revises and critiques the plantation-tale genre and the plantation myth itself (as he does in "The Passing of Grandison")—and he does so, moreover, in astonishingly ingratiating ways. Citing Chesnutt's aspiration, as expressed in an 1890 entry in his journal, to "elevate" his white readers, Joseph McElrath and Robert Leitz speak tellingly, in their introduction to a volume of Chesnutt's letters, of the writer's effort to "mask his condescension toward unregenerate white readers," the better to win their confidence. McElrath and Leitz continue, again quoting from Chesnutt's journal:

> The "trumpet tones" used by the abolitionists would not work: "the subtle almost undefinable feeling of repulsion toward the negro, which is common to most Americans—and easily enough accounted for—, cannot be stormed and taken by assault; the garrison will not capitulate: so their position must be mined, and we will find ourselves in their midst before they think it." [Chesnutt] would win "social recognition and equality" for the African American by accustoming "the public mind to the idea; and while amusing them ... lead them on imperceptibly, unconsciously step by step to the desired state of feeling."

This Chesnutt accomplishes, insofar as anyone can, in *The Conjure Woman*. In the years to come he would rely increasingly on the trumpet tones of the abolitionists in novels of bitter protest such as *The Marrow of Tradition* (1901) and *The Colonel's Dream* (1905). But first there would come *The Wife of His Youth and Other Stories of the Color Line*.

"THE WIFE OF HIS YOUTH"

Brilliant as the conjure stories are, Chesnutt could not long remain satisfied mining a vein adulterated by what literary historians now call the plantation myth and by the largely white-defined conventions of the dialect tale. In fact in 1889, ten years before *The Conjure Woman* appeared, we already find him writing the novelist Albion W. Tourgée to the following effect: "I think I have about used up the old Negro who serves as mouthpiece, and I shall drop him in future stories, as well as much of the dialect." The problem was that plantation tales particularly, and dialect tales more generally, narrowed a writer's range. "All of the good negroes," Chesnutt observes in a letter to George Washington Cable, "whose virtues have been given to the world through the columns of the *Century*

[a popular literary magazine], have been blacks, full-blooded, and their chief virtues have been their dog-like fidelity and devotion to their old masters. Such characters exist," he adds, "but I don't care to write about these people." He goes on to explain that he admires European novelists whose "colored characters" are lawyers, judges, doctors, botanists, and musicians: "These writers seem to find nothing extraordinary in a talented, well-bred colored man, nothing amorphous in a pretty, gentle-spirited colored girl." "The Wife of His Youth," the title story of his second volume, achieves precisely this, while at the same time obliquely registering the difficult relations that almost always exist between "vernacular" and "mainstream" cultures in African-American writing.

"Mr. Ryder was going to give a ball." So begins this penetrating story of the "color line." Mr. Ryder, Chesnutt's narrator tells us, is the "dean" of the Blue Vein Society of Groveland, a fictional city based on Chesnutt's native Cleveland, to which he had moved with his wife (née Susan W. Perry), two daughters, and son in November of 1883 when he was twenty-five years old. The Blue Veins of Groveland comprise a "little society of colored persons" established to "maintain correct social standards" and to foster the general appreciation of finer things (such as the poetry of Alfred, Lord Tennyson). "By accident, combined perhaps with some natural affinity," we are told with dry understatement that at times approaches sarcasm, "the society consisted of individuals who were, generally speaking, more white than black. Some envious outsider made the suggestion that no one was eligible for membership who was not white enough to show blue veins. The suggestion was readily adopted by those who were not of the favored few, and since that time the society, though possessing a longer and more pretentious name, had been known far and wide as the 'Blue Vein Society,' and its members as the 'Blue Veins.'" There is a nice equivocation here: the affiliation in question is grounded partly on what might be called biological, and partly on cultural, criteria. Clearly the Blue Vein Society is compromised by the late-nineteenth-century American tendency to make social distinctions a matter of "color." It might even be said that we find practiced among the Blue Veins a kind of intraracial racism and that for this reason the Blue Vein Society is a kind of ideological adjunct of white supremacy whereby men and women of color are taught to despise those aspects of themselves that the culture as a whole deems "colored."

The problem is well illustrated in the following passage in which Mr. Ryder is allowed to speak for himself: "'I have no race prejudice,' he would say, 'but we people of mixed blood are ground between the upper and the nether millstone. Our fate lies between absorption by the white race and extinction in the black. The one does n't want us yet, but may take us in time. The other would welcome us, but it would be for us a backward step. "With malice towards none, with charity for all," we must do the best we can for ourselves and those who are to follow us. Self-preservation is the first law of nature.'" The white-supremacist devil is in the details—in, for example, the unhappy asymmetry of terms that ought to be parallel: "*absorption* by the white race and *extinction* in the black." And in appealing to "the first law of nature," "self-preservation," Mr. Ryder inadvertently engages one of the most powerful of late-nineteenth-century racist metaphors—a metaphor, borrowed inappropriately from Darwin, of a struggle for existence. It was often said in those days that the races themselves were involved in a struggle that the white, or "Anglo-Saxon," race was destined to win.

In *Our Country* (1885) the Rev. Josiah Strong generously confessed his belief that "God, with infinite wisdom and skill, is training the Anglo-Saxon race for an hour sure to come in the world's future." "The time is coming," he predicted, "when the pressure of population on the means of subsistence will be felt here as it is now felt in Europe and Asia. Then will the world enter upon a new stage of its history—*the final competition of the races, for which the Anglo-Saxon is being schooled.* Mr. Ryder's thinking is not unaffected by these ideas, which include the corollary notion in Eurocentric anthropology that "black" is to "white" as "primitive" is to "advanced" (hence the "backward step" of which Mr. Ryder speaks). The sad confusion of it all is manifest: this social Darwinian talk of "law of nature" and "extinction" sorts uncomfortably, and not a little ironically, with the profoundly democratic sentiment of Lincoln's Second Inaugural Address (1865), which Mr. Ryder echoes: "With malice toward none; with charity for all; with firmness in the right, as God gives us to see the right, let us strive on to finish the work we are in; to bind up the nation's wounds; to care for him who shall have borne the battle, and for his widow, and his orphan—to do all which may achieve and cherish a just and lasting peace among ourselves, and with all nations."

Mr. Ryder's invocation of Lincoln in 1890, when the story takes place, reminds the reader how far the nation in general, and the Republican Party in particular, has moved from the proposition that all men are created equal: disenfranchisement is well under way. "The Wife of His Youth" is a story about the legacy of the war that had, by the time Lincoln spoke in 1865, become a war *for* enfranchisement. In fact, making her unsettling way into the Blue Vein Society is a woman whom the narrator calls "a bit of the old plantation life," a relic of the antebellum years. This woman is an illiterate former slave to whom Mr. Ryder was married before the war and from whom he has been separated since 1861.

Mr. Ryder, it happens, is in love with Molly Dixon, a young widow who was born into the highest circles of Washington's Reconstruction-era colored society and who now, having relocated to Groveland after her husband's death, is the most accomplished, sought-after (and light-skinned) of the Blue Veins. And on the afternoon of the evening of the ball that was to have afforded Mr. Ryder the perfect opportunity to propose to her, he receives a visit from Liza Jane, the wife of his youth: "She was very black,—so black that her toothless gums, revealed when she opened her mouth to speak, were not red, but blue." From underneath her bonnet protrude tufts of "short gray wool." And her speech, by contrast to the other black voices in the story, is thick with the plantation dialect spoken by Uncle Julius in *The Conjure Woman.* Mr. Ryder had long ago abandoned his antebellum name, Sam Taylor, and the changes of twenty-five years, together with a marked elevation in social class, have made him unrecognizable. Liza Jane chances upon him simply because he is a man of consequence in Groveland's black community. Can he, she wonders, help her find her long lost husband? She relates the story of her quarter-century quest, which has taken her through every major city in the South, and in due course she produces an old daguerreotype.

Mr. Ryder gazes "intently at the portrait," we are told. "It was faded with time, but the features were still distinct, and it was easy to see what manner of man it had represented." Into that last, quietly bitter clause are folded the regrets, the guilt, and the ambivalence of a lifetime of self-invention—all the shameful fears of suffering "extinction" in a blackness so complete as to show "blue gums" instead of "blue veins." When Liza Jane takes her leave—unwittingly making herself the occasion for the "kindly amusement" of passersby on the street outside—Mr. Ryder retires to his bedroom and stands "for a long time before the mirror of his dressing-case, gazing thoughtfully at the reflection of his own face." What manner of man has he become? Can he somehow bring this reflec-

tion into the same frame with the old daguerreotype? Must he always, when gazing in the mirror, see double? Must he always see there something dubious, even duplicitous? Must he forever see either a black body or a man, either "wool" or hair, either "black skin" or just plain skin, and never both at once?

As it happens, of course, he acknowledges this thing of darkness his. After hypothetically putting the case of such a man as himself to the Blue Veins, who have gathered in his house for the ball, he asks them all: what should a man in this situation do—acknowledge his first wife and bind himself to her or marry the woman of his later aspirations? Mrs. Dixon herself makes the answer: "She had listened, with parted lips and streaming eyes. She was the first to speak: 'He should have acknowledged her.'" When all in the company agree, as Mr. Ryder expected they would, he turns toward "the closed door of an adjoining room, while every eye followed him in wondering curiosity. He came back in a moment, leading by the hand his visitor of the afternoon, who stood startled and trembling at the sudden plunge into this scene of brilliant gayety …. 'Ladies and gentlemen,' he said, 'this is the woman, and I am the man, whose story I have told you. Permit me to introduce to you the wife of my youth.'"

To an extent, the story concerns the relation of vernacular black culture to the white standards against which it was always invidiously judged. Chesnutt hopes to achieve here a triple solidarity: solidarity of the black working class and the black middle class, upon which basis only, he felt, real progress in civil and political rights could be made; solidarity of vernacular and literary cultures, upon which basis only genuine literary art could be produced; and, of course, solidarity, or fusion, of blackness and whiteness, upon which basis only could the color line be transcended. And it may well be that in this restrained and affecting story Chesnutt confronts some measure of self-hatred that the culture of white supremacy had left even him with, for Chesnutt himself was so fair skinned as to appear entirely white, and he understood that such an appearance was essential to his social and artistic success—becoming for instance the first "black" author to be published in a prestigious, nationally circulated magazine like the *Atlantic*. Even though, much to his regret, he was never able to support himself and his family entirely by his writing, the considerable success he did have depended in good measure on his complexion. The fact that he was among America's finest writers was, at that time, a secondary matter.

"THE PASSING OF GRANDISON"

Eric Sundquist, in a fine reading of "The Wife of His Youth," expresses its complexities well: "Ryder's choice operates on [several] levels.... Included within his recognition of Liza Jane are several implicit indications of Chesnutt's own cultural obligations: to join with the lower classes in the struggle for rights; to put the good of the community before the advances of the few who are able to enter directly into the white social and cultural mainstream; and to take control of the popular conceptions of 'the old plantation life' that are being generated by racist commentary and unscrupulous artistry." Nowhere does Chesnutt better achieve this latter end than in "The Passing of Grandison," a brilliant satire of "popular conceptions of the old plantation life," which was collected first in *The Wife of His Youth.*

Set in the early 1850s when the passage of the Fugitive Slave Act had much aggravated the slavery question, the story concerns the spoiled and undistinguished first son of a Kentucky slaveholding family with marked aristocratic pretensions—the Owenses. Charity Lomax, the girl of Dick Owens's dreams, refuses to entertain his advances until such time as he proves himself a man. As an example of what she has

in mind—and in the meantime congratulating herself on her own Quaker ancestry—she points to the actions of a man who went to prison for attempting to help a fugitive slave escape. Not that Charity is a serious abolitionist; she admires the Yankee for his courage rather than for his convictions. In response to the challenge, young Dick conspires to free a slave himself: "I 'll run off one of the old man's," he says to Charity, "we 've got too many anyway." The problem is how to do it. Dick decides on a trip North with a slave, Grandison, as a servant. Colonel Owens, needless to say, has no idea what his frivolous son intends to do. In New York and Boston, Dick so arranges things that Grandison has every opportunity to escape; he even anonymously notifies the abolitionists in Boston, who sure enough seek Grandison out. But to Dick's utter vexation the slave never takes the bait. "Mars Dick," he says, "dese yer abolitioners is jes' pesterin' de life out er me tryin' ter git me ter run away. I don' pay no 'tention ter 'em, but dey riles me so sometimes dat I 'm feared I 'll hit some of 'em some er dese days, an' dat mought git me inter trouble. I ain' said nuffin' ter you 'bout it, Mars Dick, fer I did n' wanter 'sturb yo' min'; but I don' like it, suh; no, suh, I don'! Is we gwine back home 'fo' long, Mars Dick?" Dick has a good mind to scold Grandison, and yet, on reflection, he has to concede the point: "How could he, indeed, find fault with one who so sensibly recognized his true place in the economy of civilization, and kept it with such touching fidelity?"

No doubt Grandison acts and speaks and even gestures so as to flatter every instinct toward mastery that can animate a white man's heart. When, in an interview designed to determine his trustworthiness for the trip North, Grandison is asked whether he envies the "poor free negroes down by the plank road, with no kind master to look after them and no mistress to give them medicine when they're sick," he heartily replies: "'Well, I sh'd jes' reckon I is better off, suh, dan dem low-down free niggers, suh! Ef anybody ax 'em who dey b'long ter, dey has ter say nobody, er e'se lie erbout it. Anybody ax me who I b'longs ter, I ain' got no 'casion ter be shame' ter tell 'em, no, suh, 'deed I ain', suh!'" At this, the colonel beams: "This was true gratitude, and his feudal heart thrilled at such appreciative homage." Colonel Owens, of course, has persuaded himself that Grandison really is contented; he doesn't own a plantation so much as a "plantation myth," and the circumstance has placed him dangerously out of touch with reality. Grandison, like Uncle Julius, wears a mask; and to men like the colonel and Dick he is utterly opaque, completely invisible. They simply fail to see him—which is of course precisely what Grandison wants, for he is indeed up to something subversive of all good slave-holding order. Never once does it occur to Dick that Grandison may not wish to flee without first securing the freedom of his family and of his fiancée, who of course remain at his old Kentucky home.

In the end Dick resorts to a remarkable stratagem. He takes Grandison across the border into Canada, on the other side of Niagara Falls. "You are now in Canada, Grandison," Dick says on their arrival, "where your people go when they run away from their masters. If you wished, Grandison, you might walk away from me this very minute, and I could not lay my hand upon you to take you back." But the mask remains in place: "Let 's go back ober de ribber, Mars Dick," Grandison replies. "I 's feared I 'll lose you ovuh heah, an' den I won' hab no marster, an' won't nebber be able to git back home no mo'.'"

At this point Chesnutt does something very peculiar with the narrative; he briefly changes its point of view. Dick leaves Grandison alone, drops into a nearby inn for lunch, and returns, irritated, to find his faithful servant sound asleep, waiting for young Mars Dick. Whereupon we read:

Dick retraced his footsteps towards the inn. The young woman chanced to look out of the window and saw the handsome young gentleman she had waited on a few minutes before, standing in the road a short distance away, apparently engaged in earnest conversation with a colored man employed as hostler for the inn. She thought she saw something pass from the white man to the other, but at that moment her duties called her away from the window, and when she looked out again the young gentleman had disappeared, and the hostler, with two other young men of the neighborhood, one white and one colored, were walking rapidly towards the Falls.

This is a curious maneuver. Throughout the rest of the story the narrator is closely attached, so to speak, to the mind of Dick Owens. What Dick knows, we know; all his silly motives and machinations are laid bare. But here we witness the scene from the point of view of the waitress at the inn. Chesnutt hides from us, just as he does from her, the details of what passes between Dick and the colored hostler, and this is by no means without consequence.

Some weeks later, after Dick has gone home and after he has married Charity Lomax, Grandison reappears on the old plantation, telling a story of abduction and torture, the truth of which the reader has no means accurately to assess. Here is the story, as refracted through the "feudal heart" of Colonel Owens:

It's astounding, the depths of depravity the human heart is capable of! I was coming along the road three miles away, when I heard some one call me from the roadside. I pulled up the mare, and who should come out of the woods but Grandison. The poor nigger could hardly crawl along, with the help of a broken limb. I was never more astonished in my life. You could have knocked me down with a feather. He seemed pretty far gone,—he could hardly talk above a whisper,—and I had to give him a mouthful of whiskey to brace him up so he could tell his story. It's just as I thought from the beginning, Dick; Grandison had no notion of running away; he knew when he was well off, and where his friends were. All the persuasions of abolition liars and runaway niggers did not move him. But the desperation of those fanatics knew no bounds; their guilty consciences gave them no rest. They got the notion somehow that Grandison belonged to a nigger-catcher, and had been brought North as a spy to help capture ungrateful runaway servants. They actually kidnaped him—just think of it!—and gagged him and bound him and threw him rudely into a wagon, and carried him into the gloomy depths of a Canadian forest, and locked him in a lonely hut, and fed him on bread and water for three weeks. One of the scoundrels wanted to kill him, and persuaded the others that it ought to be done; but they got to quarreling about how they should do it, and before they had their minds made up Grandison escaped, and, keeping his back steadily to the North Star, made his way, after suffering incredible hardships, back to the old plantation, back to his master, his friends, and his home. Why, it 's as good as one of Scott's novels! Mr. Simms or some other one of our Southern authors ought to write it up.

It is indeed a story as good as one of Scott's novels and one altogether worthy of the pen of that proslavery apologist from South Carolina, William Gilmore Simms. But is it the truth, the whole truth, and nothing but the truth? Dick is in no position to contradict Grandison in front of the colonel, to whom he has lied about his misadventures in the North. He does, it is true, wonder aloud whether the "kidnaping yarn sounds a little improbable," if only as a hint to Charity that he hadn't acted *completely* ignobly. But Chesnutt leaves the reader in doubt. Has Grandison fabricated this tale the better to gladden the feudal heart of the colonel, who predictably is reduced nearly to tears at its recital and who in gratitude "kill[s] the fatted calf" for Grandison and relaxes his customary vigilance? Is Grandison—having somehow smoked Dick out—making things hot for his young master by allowing his bride to conclude that he is both callous and a fool? Has Grandison simply embellished a tale that essentially conveys the truth? What exactly did pass between Dick

Owens and that hostler? The reader cannot say; the narrative does not allow Grandison to emerge from behind his mask—that is, not until the last paragraph.

Grandison, it turns out, has returned to Kentucky for one purpose only: to free his family. "About three weeks after Grandison's return," we learn, "the colonel's faith in sable humanity was rudely shaken, and its foundations almost broken up."

> One Monday morning Grandison was missing. And not only Grandison, but his wife, Betty the maid; his mother, aunt Eunice; his father, uncle Ike; his brothers, Tom and John, and his little sister Elsie, were likewise absent from the plantation; and a hurried search and inquiry in the neighborhood resulted in no information as to their whereabouts. So much valuable property could not be lost without an effort to recover it, and the wholesale nature of the transaction carried consternation to the hearts of those whose ledgers were chiefly bound in black. Extremely energetic measures were taken by the colonel and his friends. The fugitives were traced, and followed from point to point, on their northward run through Ohio. Several times the hunters were close upon their heels, but the magnitude of the escaping party begot unusual vigilance on the part of those who sympathized with the fugitives, and strangely enough, the underground railroad seemed to have had its tracks cleared and signals set for this particular train. Once, twice, the colonel thought he had them, but they slipped through his fingers.

> One last glimpse he caught of his vanishing property, as he stood, accompanied by a United States marshal, on a wharf at a port on the south shore of Lake Erie. On the stern of a small steamboat which was receding rapidly from the wharf, with her nose pointing toward Canada, there stood a group of familiar dark faces, and the look they cast backward was not one of longing for the fleshpots of Egypt. The colonel saw Grandison point him out to one of the crew of the vessel, who waved his hand derisively toward the colonel. The latter shook his fist impotently—and the incident was closed.

All the colonel's power comes to nothing. He's been outfoxed by a man who understands much better than he ever will the illusions under which labors the nation he now leaves in his wake, and who understands as well how to exploit those illusions. The point is plain: Grandison is everywhere inaccessible to the colonel. The colonel owns him, supposes himself on intimate terms with him, but in fact Grandison is something less to him even than a total stranger. And perhaps a certain suspicion that his readers stand on the other side of the color line from him led Charles Chesnutt to shield Grandison from their scrutiny as well. The reader sees him always as from a distance, and his backward look, with its derisive jocularity, is as unsettling as *Brown v. Board of Education* to the pretensions of white supremacy.

"The Passing of Grandison" suggests many things, among them that the plantation myth didn't merely allow whites to misunderstand their real relations to people of color in such a way as happily and in good conscience to oppress them; it also dialectically allowed for a certain impenetrability, a certain privacy, a certain space within a veil, as W. E. B. DuBois might say—of which black Americans could at times avail themselves. It is quite as if the plantation myth were a one-way mirror. On one side of it stand white men who see in it (though of this they remain unaware) only their own reflections; on the other side stand black men for whom that mirror is in fact a window into the darkest recesses of the white man's heart. For a man such as Grandison, Colonel Owen and his ilk are perfectly transparent. Men like Grandison know all the codes. And when Chesnutt's art achieves its ends—and it often does much more than merely achieve them—it inverts the mirror, lays bare the codes, and begins the work of unencumbering white American readers of their chief embarrassment: the color-consciousness that blinds them to their own hearts of darkness. "The object of my writ-

ings," Chesnutt once wrote in his journal, "would be not so much the elevation of the colored people as the elevation of the whites."

THE HOUSE BEHIND THE CEDARS

Chesnutt's first novel, *The House Behind the Cedars,* appeared in 1900. The plot is relatively simple and follows the contours of what literary critics sometimes call the novel of "the tragic mulatto." Rena Walden and her brother John are born out of wedlock to a light-skinned "colored" mother and a white father. Though known in their native town of Patesville, North Carolina, as black, they are light enough in complexion to pass for white. And this they do in neighboring South Carolina in the fading plantation town of Clarence, to which John removed just before the Civil War broke out, and in which he has been living for ten years as a white man. As the action of the novel opens, he is a distinguished lawyer and moves at the highest level of white society, to which he gained admittance, in part, by marriage into a prominent white family, though he is now a widower. Rena, a young woman of remarkable beauty, attracts the attention of George Tryon, a highborn white man from eastern North Carolina who has retained the services of John to settle various legal affairs in South Carolina. Tryon proposes marriage, and, after an anguished week during which she wonders whether or not she should reveal that she is really "black," Rena decides to accept, and a date is set for the wedding. A series of accidents worthy of Thomas Hardy shortly brings out the novel's tragic dimension: Tryon, a proud white supremacist in the post-Reconstruction mode, discovers the truth about Rena; repudiates her; is beset by doubts about his convictions; resolves to marry her anyway, but is too late: the lingering shock of his rejection and the predatory attentions of an unscrupulous man named Wain drive Rena to despair and break her health. She dies of exposure after trying to make her way home on foot to her aging mother, who waits back in Patesville in the house behind the cedars where Rena was born.

What distinguishes this novel is its psychological complexity. *The House Behind the Cedars* is best read as a penetrating investigation of the psychosexual problem of the color line. It concerns "white" America's felt relationship to "blackness," which in turn concerns nothing less than white America's felt relationship to the body and to sexuality. At one point in the novel, before he discovers the truth about Rena's parentage, Tryon visits Patesville to see his mother's cousin, Dr. Green. The doctor is out, and while awaiting his return Tryon idly peruses a medical journal which contains an article on ethnology. "The writer maintained," Chesnutt's narrator tells us,

> that owing to a special tendency of the negro blood, however diluted, to revert to the African type, any future amalgamation of the white and black races, which foolish and wicked Northern negrophiles predicted as the ultimate result of the new conditions confronting the South, would therefore be an ethnological impossibility; for the smallest trace of negro blood would inevitably drag down the superior race to the level of the inferior, and reduce the fair Southland, already devastated by the hand of the invader, to the frightful level of Hayti, the awful example of negro incapacity.

Here Chesnutt directs the reader's attention to a kind of white panic. Nothing less than fear of a supposed animality motivates this article, whose argument is quite conventional to the 1890s. The white imagination—the imagination of what the article in question calls the "all-pervading, all-conquering" Anglo-Saxon race—felt itself everywhere in confrontation with a "savagery" that had to be disciplined, repressed, and, when possible, subjugated into useful enterprise, such as for agricultural and industrial labor.

It is savagery of this sort that Tryon imagines he can detect beneath the thin "veneer" of civilization with which Rena has bedecked herself. Having (temporarily) resolved to go through with the marriage, he approaches the house behind the cedars, only to find that a party is there in progress. In fact, it is simply a reception for the cousin of a friend of Rena's mother. He peers through the window and spies Rena dancing:

> To-night his eyes had been opened—he had seen her with the mask thrown off, a true daughter of a race in which the sensuous enjoyment of the moment took precedence of taste or sentiment or any of the higher emotions. Her few months of boarding-school, her brief association with white people, had evidently been a mere veneer over the underlying negro, and their effects had slipped away as soon as the intercourse had ceased. With the monkey-like imitativeness of the negro she had copied the manners of white people while she lived among them, and had dropped them with equal facility when they ceased to serve a purpose. Who but a negro could have recovered so soon from what had seemed a terrible bereavement?—she herself must have felt it at the time, for otherwise she would not have swooned. A woman of sensibility, as this one had seemed to be, should naturally feel more keenly, and for a longer time than a man, an injury to the affections; but he, a son of the ruling race, had been miserable for six weeks about a girl who had so far forgotten him as already to plunge headlong into the childish amusements of her own ignorant and degraded people. What more, indeed, he asked himself savagely,—what more could be expected of the base-born child of the plaything of a gentleman's idle hour, who to this ignoble origin added the blood of a servile race? And he, George Tryon, had honored her with his love; he had very nearly linked his fate and joined his blood to hers by the solemn sanctions of church and state.

A number of things bear mentioning here. First, there is the association, inevitable in the discourse of white supremacy, of "color" with the flesh, with the senses. To be "colored" is to have a uniquely intense relation to the body—

here, to "sensuous enjoyment." It is as if white is to black as mind is to body or as soul is to body; and, given that in the patriarchal Christian culture of which Tryon is a fine representative the pleasures of the flesh are always to be disciplined, always to be subordinated to "higher" purposes and emotions, any people thought to be peculiarly sensual were regarded with wariness, and were, in the post-Reconstruction South, subject to severe repression (the castrations that often accompanied lynchings and the white hysteria about black rape are the worst symptoms of this disease). A pathological anxiety about the body and about sexuality, which afflicts men like Tryon, has here been projected outward onto the racial Other: what Tryon would repress in himself he oppresses in the culture as a whole.

The second thing to notice about the above passage is the metaphor of a "mask" or of a "veneer": "civilization," Tryon believes, attaches to people of color only in the most contingent and superficial way. So went the argument with which reactionaries in the post-Reconstruction South defended segregation, disenfranchisement, lynching, and with which they also sought to divert funds that might have supported liberal education for blacks into industrial training programs (merely physical creatures, it was said, were best suited for purely physical labor). And at the bottom of it all there moves a kind of panic: to wit, Tryon's panicked refusal to think of himself as a body, as a thing that must some day fall, in the way of all flesh, to ashes and dust.

White racism, as Chesnutt reveals it, is in fact a hatred of the human condition—a hatred of the brute fact of mortality and an unwillingness to acknowledge this thing of clay that we simply are. It is a hatred of the fact that our roots are in the earth, not in the heavens. Or as James Baldwin was later to put it: "What Americans do not face when they regard a Negro" (from *The Fire Next Time*) is nothing less than "real-ity—the fact that life is tragic. Life is tragic," he explains, "simply because the earth turns and the sun inexorably rises and sets, and one day, for each of us, the sun will go down for the last, last time. Perhaps the whole root of our trouble, the human trouble, is that we will sacrifice all the beauty of our lives, will imprison ourselves in totems, taboos, crosses, blood sacrifices, steeples, mosques, races, armies, flags, nations, in order to deny the fact of death, which is the only fact we have." George Tryon has most certainly imprisoned himself in totems and taboos: he has thwarted the only love, his love for Rena Walden, that he ever sincerely felt. He is an alien in the country of his own heart and mind. And insofar as he represents white America in the post-Reconstruction years, the meaning of his alienation is plain: America had yet to discover itself, had yet to yield to what Lincoln called in his First Inaugural Address "the better angels of our nature."

THE MARROW OF TRADITION

The Marrow of Tradition (1901) certainly merits Eric Sundquist's placement of it among the most significant historical novels ever produced by an American. The novel, Chesnutt's second, presents in fictionalized form the terrible Wilmington, North Carolina, riot of November 1898. The riot had its origins in a conspiracy on the part of disaffected white Democrats to wrest control of the city away from a coalition of Republicans and Populists who had won the elections of 1894 and 1896. Blacks were in the majority in Wilmington and the surrounding area, and for that reason the Democratic conspirators—who included Alfred Moore Waddell, the model for Chesnutt's General Belmont; Mike Dowling, the model for his Captain McBane; and Thomas Clawson, the model for his Major Carteret—found it necessary to resort to intimidation and violence to secure victory for white supremacy, as they forthrightly put it, in the 1898 elections. In the days before the voting, white men armed themselves (in part with weapons and ammunition shipped in from other states); and what can be best described as the terrorist wing of the Democratic party, known popularly as the Red Shirts, poisoned the air with racist propaganda and threats. The conspiracy succeeded; the elections went to the Democrats. Nonetheless, as if a blood-sacrifice must attend this "redemption" of the city, whites rioted a few days after the election. They burned down the building that housed the local black newspaper, ordered prominent black citizens to leave town, murdered at least a dozen blacks (the number has never been determined), assaulted scores of men and women, and destroyed thousands of dollars worth of black people's property. The victory was complete—on the ballot also was a provision to disenfranchise blacks—and North Carolina did not fully recover for more than fifty years.

Chesnutt artfully weaves the riot, and the events leading up to it, into a story about two families related by ties of blood but separated by the color line: the Carterets and the Millers. Major Carteret has married Olivia Merkell, the daughter of a white man who, in the antebellum years, stood at the peak of Wellington society (Wellington is Chesnutt's fictional North Carolina city). As the novel opens, Olivia, a frail and delicate woman, is giving birth to the son who will redeem, as the major sees it, the legacy of his illustrious family, which had been ruined by the Civil War. The reader soon learns that after Olivia's mother died her father had taken as his mistress the family's black maid, Julia. By her he fathered another daughter, named Janet, who is fair-skinned and who looks like Olivia's twin. Janet, though cast out of the house at Mr. Merkell's death, secures a liberal education, travels widely, and ultimately marries Adam Miller, a physician. The son of a

black entrepreneur—who, after buying himself out of slavery, had built a profitable business on the wharfs of Wellington—Dr. Miller establishes a hospital to serve the black community, and wins the respect of the more liberal elements of white Wellington. He settles in the house formerly occupied by the Carterets, and the dignity and consequence of his family—indeed their very existence—is a constant humiliation to Olivia and the major.

Major Carteret, an ardent Democrat, uses the editorial page of the paper he owns to foment a popular movement to reinstate white supremacy and to purge from Wellington, and from the state as a whole, any vestige of the Radical Reconstruction. In this endeavor he recruits General Belmont, a calculating politician with designs on statewide office, and Captain McBane, a lowborn white man who heads the local Red Shirt faction and who was an activist in the Ku Klux Klan during its vicious heyday in the late 1860s. The plot of the novel moves inexorably toward the riot, which Chesnutt fixes, in a slight departure from the historical record, on the eve of the 1898 election. What emerges is a devastating and politically shrewd portrait of North Carolina, which may certainly stand, as Chesnutt no doubt intends, for the whole "New South" of the post-Reconstruction period. The success of the novel lies in its precision and economy: Chesnutt manages to personify in a small cast of characters virtually every development in late-nineteenth-century Southern politics.

All the figures are here: the fading but worthy aristocrat—a man who never liked slavery and now strives in good faith to overcome its bitter legacy and in whose eyes the agitation for white supremacy is as vulgar as it is dishonest (old Mr. Delamere); the men W. E. B. DuBois once called "the cracker third estate," who filled the ranks of the Klan and the Red Shirts, and who, having sprung from poor white origins, resented equally the freedmen and the planter class that dominated antebellum Southern politics (Captain McBane); the "New South" breed of Democrat, who sought to lure Northern capital into the states of the former Confederacy to rebuild its infrastructure on a "modern" and industrial basis (General Belmont and Major Carteret); the rising black middle class, who wished to cooperate with respectable white people and who favored compromise and patience instead of violence (Dr. Miller); the "New Negro," who, having come of age during Reconstruction, saw no reason whatsoever why they shouldn't be entitled to what the Constitution now guaranteed them—full citizenship, voting rights, and equal protection under the law—and who were prepared to meet white violence with their own violence (Josh Green, a character who anticipates such later figures as Bigger Thomas, the violent hero of Richard Wright's 1940 novel *Native Son*); and finally the tragic mulatto, caught between the worlds of black and white and never at ease in either (Janet).

On finishing the novel readers are left with the bleak intimation that, though there is perhaps time enough to recover American democracy at the turn of the twentieth century, there is certainly none to spare: the hope of the white South in the person of the infant son of the Carterets—a white family which, in the wake of the riot, stands in unbelieving horror at what it has wrought—lies on his deathbed racked with fever. And the sole doctor who can come to his aid is the very black man, Dr. Miller, whose cherished son lies dead from the bullet of a white rioter and whose presence in the Carteret house would, only a day before, have been thought a pollution.

In *The Marrow of Tradition* Chesnutt wants very much to find some way out of the great American impasse. In a note on the novel published in the *Cleveland World* he confessed his faith "that the forces of progress will in the end prevail, and that in time a remedy may be found for every social ill." But the terrible logic of white supremacy, as *The Marrow of Tradition* reveals it, operates with the grim force of a Fate, from which the nation may never be able fully to emancipate itself—at least not, as Lincoln intimated in his Second Inaugural Address, "until all the wealth piled by the bondsman's two hundred and fifty years of unrequited toil shall be sunk, and until every drop of blood drawn with the lash shall be paid by another drawn with the sword." An atmosphere of anxiety, even of doom, everywhere colors the novel, a fact which should not be surprising given that it stands perhaps at the lowest point of what historian Rayford Logan once called the "nadir" of African-American history.

No doubt its realpolitik bleakness accounts for the fact that *The Marrow of Tradition* sold as poorly as it did on its publication in 1901—a development that eventually put an end to Chesnutt's hopes that he might support himself solely by writing. In that era of the plantation tale, with its mammies, faithful retainers, cakewalks, and darkeys; in that period during which the Republican Party, imitating Pontius Pilate, washed its hands of the matter and consigned the freedmen to a resurgent Democratic Party; in that season when U.S. soldiers were fighting to quell a war for independence in America's newly acquired colony in the Philippines; Americans did not much want to hear the story Chesnutt had to tell. His work sits awkwardly "post-bellum" and "pre-Harlem," as he himself once put it in an essay—that is to say, in a kind of literary-historical wilderness, caught between the Egypt of slavery and the Canaan of what is aptly called the Harlem (or "New Negro") Renaissance, during which, at last, black writers began to secure a reliable market for serious literary writing. On the other side of the Harlem Renaissance, of course, lie such writers as Richard Wright, James Baldwin, and Gwendolyn Brooks, whose work, in so many respects, Chesnutt helped make possible.

A brilliant scene occurs in the chapter called "The Cakewalk." "A party of Northern visitors," the chapter begins, "had been staying for several days at the St. James Hotel. The gentlemen of the party were concerned in a projected cotton mill, while the ladies were much interested in the study of social conditions, and especially in the negro problem." Here is the conventional Victorian division of gender roles whereby practical affairs were given to men, sentiment and uplift to women. The vaguely humanitarian interests of the women cloak the business enterprise in a certain gentility, as if to suggest Northern capital really does care about the Negro. But as Chesnutt intimates, this is largely a pretense in which North and South alike conspire. Every encounter these philanthropic Northern visitors have with black folk is mediated by Southern whites, who, at "elaborate luncheons," expound upon the "disappearance of the good old negro of before the war" and who congratulate themselves on the money the South has poured into black education. Chesnutt's narrator explains the result:

> The visitors were naturally much impressed by what they learned from their courteous hosts, and felt inclined to sympathize with the Southern people, for the negro is not counted as a Southerner, except to fix the basis of congressional representation. There might of course be things to criticise here and there, certain customs for which they did not exactly see the necessity, and which seemed in conflict with the highest ideals of liberty; but surely these courteous, soft-spoken ladies and gentlemen, entirely familiar with local conditions, who descanted so earnestly and at times pathetically upon the grave problems confronting them, must know more about it than people in the distant North, without their means of information. The negroes who waited on them at the hotel seemed happy enough, and the teachers whom they had met at the mission school had been well-dressed, well-mannered, and apparently content with their position in life. Surely a people who made no complaints could not be very much oppressed.

The satire is rich. Exposed here is the unacknowledged tendency, even at the late date in which the novel is set, to think of the black population as foreign to the culture of the South: "the negro is not counted as a Southerner," we are told, "except to fix the basis of congressional representation." The South relies on the freedmen's sons and daughters to augment its power in Congress, but only so that the South may, with the indulgence of the North, more efficiently oppress them. Most important, though, is the way this passage typifies the post-Reconstruction rapprochement between North and South: as has been suggested, this reconciliation, for the purposes of profitable investment, was accompanied by a romantic idealization of the old plantation life that in effect excused the North of its responsibilities to the freedmen. If things weren't all that terrible (so went the argument), then why continue the reconstruction program of the Radicals? Wouldn't it be better simply to let the Southerners handle the Negro problem on their own?

The better to enforce the point these "courteous" North Carolina hosts stage a "genuine negro cakewalk" for their Northern guests. Here, they assure the visitors, shall be exemplified "the joyous, happy-go-lucky disposition of the Southern darky and his entire contentment with existing conditions." But the winner of the cakewalk, as it happens, is not a black man at all, but a white man—Tom Delamere, the dissolute grandson of old Mr. Delamere—dressed up in blackface and impersonating his grandfather's faithful retainer, Sandy. The "genuine negro cakewalk" is in fact a fraud; the "Southern darky" on exhibit is in a very real sense a white man's Negro. He is an imposter, a fiction; he is the artificial "darky" of plantation tales and minstrel shows.

The astonishing thing is that no one notices the fraud—least of all the Southerners who claim so intimate a knowledge of black folk and who ought to be able to detect the ruse:

they dwell so entirely within the horizons of white supremacy as to mistake their own fantasy of black lives for the real thing. Tom Delamere, on being awarded the cake, returns his thanks in a speech which sends the white onlookers into "spasms of delight at the quaintness of the darky dialect and the darky wit." Only one man—Ellis, Major Carteret's protégé at the newspaper office—at all senses that things might be amiss, and even he can't put his finger on it. "There was a vague suggestion of unreality about this performance ... which Ellis did not attempt to analyze." He finds it passing strange that Sandy would abandon his usual courtly demeanor to take part in so undignified a spectacle. No white man, he reflects, "could possess two so widely varying phases of character" as Sandy apparently did; "but as to negroes, they were as yet a crude and undeveloped race, and it was not safe to make predictions concerning them. No one could tell at what moment the thin veneer of civilization might peel off and reveal the underlying savage."

To the white mind, black was to white as savage was to civil. The rule applied as well in North Carolina as in the Belgian Congo. And Chesnutt's novel—together with the facts of the case in the South—shows that this formula turns things upside down. Blackness is simply the name whites give to their own savagery, as this is projected onto a racial Other. Whites are themselves "double"—like Tom Delamere in blackface or like Robert Louis Stevenson's Dr. Jekyll/Mr. Hyde, to whom the rampaging white mob in *The Marrow of Tradition* is compared. To put on the mask of color for Tom is to cross a boundary into lawlessness and anarchy, not merely into a cakewalk; for later in the novel he blacks up his face again, and again borrows Sandy's distinctive clothes, in order to burglarize Mrs. Carteret's aunt, Mrs. Ochiltree (he needs the money to pay a gambling debt). Suspicion falls on Sandy, as Tom intends, and the poor fellow barely escapes a lynching, in

giddy anticipation of which the local railroads schedule special "excursion" trains, so that all in the outlying countryside can enjoy the grim spectacle. (For this latter detail Chesnutt likely relies on the real-life case of Sam Hose, who was lynched near Atlanta in 1897.) The charge of rape had fantastically been added to that of burglary: the white imagination always sensualizes "black" motives. The whole episode aggravates the racial tensions that Major Carteret has already deliberately inflamed, in the columns of his newspaper, in anticipation of the coming elections. And in due course the rioting breaks out in a terrifying display of white savagery. Old Mr. Delamere, devastated that a descendant of his—Tom—could have behaved so despicably, and shocked at the epidemic of lynchings that had been sweeping the South, bitterly observes: "I have lived to hear of white men, the most favored of races, the heirs of civilization, the conservators of liberty, howling like red Indians around a human being slowly roasting at the stake." The whole of the white population, he adds, had been turned into a "mob of primitive savages," very well capable, as we know, of mutilating the bodies of their victims and carrying away an ear, or worse, as a souvenir. The delusion of color, as Chesnutt sees it in this devastating novel, hopelessly confuses our efforts to understand, and therefore overcome, what must be called our own innate depravity.

THE LATER YEARS

In his lifetime Charles Chesnutt published only one more novel, *The Colonel's Dream* in 1905. The character who gives the book its title, Colonel Henry French, is a quixotic Southerner, who, after making his fortune in the North, returns to his native North Carolina in the years following the collapse of Reconstruction, with a view toward helping the state recover from the damage slavery did. He invests in a cotton mill, which he intends to operate under enlightened and "color-blind" labor policies, and for this he draws the ire of white reactionaries, chief among whom is a man aptly named William Fetters—a contractor of convict labor and thereby the beneficiary of one of the most infamous systems of labor relations ever to degrade the postbellum South. In the end the colonel's dream of a reconstructed South meets with bitter disappointment; he has no option but to retreat to his adopted city of New York, effectively abandoning his native Clarendon to the radical segregationists who would dominate the South until long after Chesnutt's own death of arteriosclerosis on November 15, 1932. *The Colonel's Dream* is the least hopeful of Chesnutt's novels of the South at the turn of the century, and it sold even more poorly than had *The Marrow of Tradition*. Chesnutt found himself compelled to abandon his own dream—the aspiration to support himself as an author in the American literary marketplace. For the remainder of his seventy-four years of life he supported himself and his family with his successful legal stenography business (in 1887 he had passed the Ohio bar exam with the highest grade in the group of lawyers with whom he took the test). He also worked vigorously for black rights in Cleveland, in Ohio, and in the South. True, he scattered short stories and essays in various periodicals from time to time, and he wrote at least two more novels, neither of which were published in his lifetime—*Paul Marchand, F.M.C.* (that is, "Free Man of Color"), first published in 1998 by the University Press of Mississippi, and *The Quarry*, which appeared for the first time in 1999 in an edition prepared for Princeton University Press by Dean McWilliams.

And so it happens that the best coda to Chesnutt's literary career is a curious story titled "Baxter's Procrustes," which appeared in the *Atlantic Monthly* in 1904. Baxter, a poet of sorts, belongs to a society of bibliophiles somewhat pretentiously styled the Bodelian Club. Now and then the club publishes literary works in fine bindings as collector's items. And when the club's publications committee learns of Baxter's poem-in-progress, titled "Procrustes," they offer to print it in a plush limited edition. Baxter accepts the offer with a sardonic gleam that fails to arouse suspicion—until too late. Baxter, it turns out, has submitted a ream of blank paper to the printer, and the resulting book, complete with its hand-tooled binding and rich linen paper, is entirely empty. No one on the editorial committee bothered to examine the manuscript before dispatching it to the printer; no one on the review committee—tasked with introducing the volume at a dinner celebrating its appearance—bothers to read the finished book (they were, to a man, loath to cut the pages for fear that this might reduce the value of the volume as a specimen of fine bookmaking). "Baxter's Procrustes" is a wicked satire of the American literary marketplace, with its procrustean demands for a standardized product and its readership of fools and unoriginal minds. And it makes a fitting farewell for a literary pioneer like Charles Chesnutt, whose brilliance the literary establishment failed to recognize until some fifty years after his death.

Selected Bibliography

WORKS OF CHARLES W. CHESNUTT

SHORT FICTION
The Conjure Woman. Boston: Houghton Mifflin, 1899. (Published in March.)
The Wife of His Youth and Other Stories of the Color Line. Boston: Houghton Mifflin, 1899. (Published on November 29.)

NOVELS
The House Behind the Cedars. Boston: Houghton Mifflin, 1900.

The Marrow of Tradition. Boston: Houghton Mifflin, 1901.

The Colonel's Dream. New York: Doubleday, 1905.

Mandy Oxendine. Edited by Charles Hackenberry. Urbana: University of Illinois Press, 1997. (The first publication of what is likely Chesnutt's earliest novel.)

Paul Marchand, F.M.C. Jackson: University Press of Mississippi, 1998. Reprint: Edited by Dean McWilliams. Princeton: Princeton University Press, 1999. (First publication of a novel written in the 1920s.)

The Quarry. Edited by Dean McWilliams. Princeton: Princeton University Press, 1999. (First publication of a novel written in the 1920s.)

BIOGRAPHY

Frederick Douglass. Small, Maynard, 1899.

MODERN COLLECTIONS

The Short Fiction of Charles W. Chesnutt. Edited by Sylvia L. Render. Washington, D.C.: Howard University Press, 1974.

The Conjure Woman and Other Conjure Tales. Edited by Richard Brodhead. Durham: Duke University Press, 1993. (Includes an excellent introductory essay by Brodhead.)

Essays and Speeches. Edited by Joseph R. McElrath, Jr., Robert C. Leitz III, and Jesse S. Crisler. Stanford: Stanford University Press, 1999. (Collects all of Chesnutt's known nonfiction works.)

Stories, Novels, & Essays. Edited by Werner Sollors. New York: Library of America, 2002. (The best single-volume edition of Chesnutt's writings; includes *The Conjure Woman, The Wife of His Youth and Other Stories of the Color Line, The House Behind the Cedars, The Marrow of Tradition,* nine uncollected short stories, and seven essays, with a detailed chronology of Chesnutt's life.)

LETTERS AND JOURNALS

The Journals of Charles W. Chesnutt. Edited by Richard Brodhead. Durham: Duke University Press, 1993.

"To Be an Author": Letters of Charles W. Chesnutt, 1889–1905. Edited by Joseph R. McElrath, Jr.,

and Robert C. Leitz III. Princeton: Princeton University Press, 1997.

An Exemplary Citizen: Letters of Charles W. Chesnutt, 1906–1932. Edited by Jesse S. Crisler, Robert C. Leitz III, and Joseph R. McElrath, Jr. Stanford: Stanford University Press, 2002.

CRITICAL AND BIOGRAPHICAL STUDIES

Andrews, William L. *The Literary Career of Charles W. Chesnutt.* Baton Rouge: Louisiana State University Press, 1980. A comprehensive overview of Chesnutt's writings, by one of his best editors and interpreters.

Bone, Robert A. *The Negro Novel in America.* Revised Edition. New Haven: Yale University Press, 1965. This classic study sets Chesnutt in the broad panorama of African-American literature.

Chesnutt, Helen M. *Charles Waddell Chesnutt: Pioneer of the Color Line.* Chapel Hill: University of North Carolina Press, 1952. A biography written by Chesnutt's daughter.

Duncan, Charles. *The Absent Man: The Narrative Craft of Charles W. Chesnutt.* Athens: Ohio University Press, 1998. A perceptive study of Chesnutt's artistry.

Ellison, Curtis W., and E. W. Metcalf, Jr. *Charles W. Chesnutt: A Reference Guide.* Boston: G. K. Hall, 1977.

Heermance, J. Noel. *Charles W. Chesnutt: America's First Great Black Novelist.* Hamden, Conn.: Archon Books, 1974

Holt, Sharon Ann. *Making Freedom Pay: North Carolina Freedpeople Working for Themselves, 1865–1900.* Athens: University of Georgia Press, 2000. Details the real-life situation of men like Chesnutt's fictional Uncle Julius.

Keller, Frances Richardson, *An American Crusade: The Life of Charles Waddell Chesnutt.* Provo, Utah: Brigham Young University Press, 1978.

Lefler, Hugh Talmage, editor. *North Carolina History Told by Contemporaries.* Chapel Hill: University of North Carolina Press, 1934. Revised and enlarged editions published 1948, 1956, and 1965. A documentary history; very helpful for setting Chesnutt's fiction in context.

McWilliams, Dean. *Charles W. Chesnutt and the Fictions of Race.* Athens: University of Georgia Press, 2002. A pathbreaking study, alert to recent developments in literary theory.

Pickens, Ernestine Williams. *Charles W. Chesnutt and the Progressive Movement.* New York: Pace University Press, 1994.

Render, Sylvia Lyons. *Charles W. Chesnutt.* Boston: Twayne, 1980.

Sundquist, Eric. *To Wake the Nations: Race in the Making of American Literature.* Cambridge, Mass.: Harvard University Press, 1993. A book of great breadth; includes an extensive, nuanced study of Chesnutt.

Wonham, Henry B. *Charles W. Chesnutt: A Study of the Short Fiction.* New York: Twayne Publishers, 1998.

—MARK RICHARDSON

Evan S. Connell

1924–

*T*HERE IS A scene early in *Mrs. Bridge: A Novel* (1959), Evan S. Connell's first and best-known novel, in which young Douglas Bridge constructs in the vacant lot beside his family's house a monolith out of cement and junk—"jugs and stones, tin cans, tree limbs, broken bottles, and all the other trash he could find." "My!" says Mrs. Bridge upon learning of the project. "I can see you're going to be an architect or an engineer when you grow up." But her son, Connell's semiautobiographical proxy, intends something at once less useful and more sublime: a towering monument that Mrs. Bridge finds far too "eccentric and mystifying." One day while Douglas is at school she asks the fire department to demolish it. "It was just getting too big," she explains to him that night. "People were beginning to wonder."

Connell has spent his career making people wonder. Every one of his twenty-one books is a protest against that smallness of mind, that timorous parochialism of the spirit, in which the Mrs. Bridges of the world seek solace and shelter. One morning while dusting the bookcase, Mrs. Bridge happens upon a novel by Joseph Conrad inherited from her husband's uncle; upon reading it she fleetingly understands that she has been "skimming over the years of existence … ignorant of life to the last, without ever having been made to see all it may contain." Connell's ambition has been to escape precisely that ignorance: to reckon human existence, to see for himself, and to make us see, what life may contain. This sensual yearning for knowledge, this insatiable wanderlust—what Anatole France called *un long désir* (a long desire)—is Connell's constant subject and his greatest theme.

In "Various Tourists," one of the essays originally collected under the title *A Long Desire* (1979), Connell writes, "Certain people do not travel the way most of us travel; not only do they sometimes choose odd vehicles, they take dangerous and unusual trips for incomprehensible reasons." The description could serve as a motto for his own career. Since publishing his first short story in the late 1940s, Connell in both his life and work has not traveled the way most writers travel. He has taken his readers on unusual trips, at times for incomprehensible reasons.

Two of his books, *Mrs. Bridge* and *Points for a Compass Rose* (1973), were nominated for National Book Awards. Two were best-sellers. Three have been adapted for film. In 1987 Connell was honored by the American Academy and Institute of Arts and Letters. In 2000 he received the prestigious Lannan Lifetime Achievement Award. Critics have decorated his dust jackets with superlatives, and eminent writers have honored him with the compliment of imitation. Yet despite these manifold successes several of his books, including some later ones, struggled to find a publisher, and many are out of print. A search for Connell's name in the database of the Modern Language Association turns up fewer than a dozen citations. In comparison, searches for John Updike and Philip Roth, who, like Connell, began publishing books in the late 1950s, turn up more than five hundred and three hundred citations, respectively.

As undeserved as it is, Connell's obscurity can be at least partly attributed to his distaste for publicity and to his defiant inclination to experiment. He abhors book tours and refuses to write under contract for fear that he will be tempted to bend his intentions to those of his publishers. "I do care about readers and sales," Connell told the *Los Angeles Times* in 1991; "after a book's out, I hope it sells like gangbusters. I'm just not going to manufacture something, though. Once in a while I do something that corresponds with popular interest, but I don't want to mechanically repeat myself." Thus, seven years after writing the immensely successful *Mrs. Bridge,* he offered readers *The Diary of a Rapist: A Novel,* (1966) a first-person psychological study of violent misogyny that remains among the most disturbing American novels ever published. *The Alchymist's Journal* (1991), the fugue of archaic monologues with which Connell chose to follow his best-selling *Son of the Morning Star: Custer and the Little Bighorn* (1984), is among the most impenetrable.

In addition to novels and collections of stories and essays, he has penned two notebooks of poetically enjambed prose fragments (*Notes from a Bottle Found on the Beach at Carmel,* published in 1962, and *Points for a Compass Rose*), referred to by most critics as "poems," though both grew (like two trees from a single acorn) out of what Connell considered to be an experimental short story; two books of other people's photographs for which Connell furnished captions; an epic narrative history of the Plains Wars (*Son of the Morning Star*); and another, in 2000, of the Crusades (*Deus Lo Volt!*), marketed by his publishers as a novel, though its subtitle labels it a "chronicle." These are indeed odd vehicles.

In 1979 when Connell published *A Long Desire,* his first volume of essays, Edward Hoagland, writing in the *New York Times Book Review,* politely dismissed it as "one of those pleasure books of nonfiction that a good novelist will pause to write once in a while as a relief from the rigors of invention." That assessment has proved in hindsight to be significantly off the mark. Not since *Double Honeymoon* in 1976 has he published anything resembling a novel as it is conventionally defined. Instead he has devoted himself to writing some of the most innovative and artful nonfiction in all of American literature.

Novelist, poet, essayist, historian—what Connell is above all else, regardless of genre, is a kind of literary archaeologist. In *Mrs. Bridge* and its companion, *Mr. Bridge* (1969), he salvages remarkable moments from the unremarkable life of an American family. In his 2001 volume of collected essays, *The Aztec Treasure House: New and Selected Essays*—the bibliography of which comprises nearly three hundred titles, including such esoteric works as *Travel and Discovery in the Renaissance, 1420–1620; Through Alchemy to Chemistry: A Procession of Ideas and Personalities;* and the memoirs of Cabeza de Vaca—he excavates and sifts several cubic tons of anthropological, scientific, and historical scholarship, rescuing and recombining the brightest shards he finds. What makes his essays so much more than the sum of the sources from which they are drawn is the very thing that makes the Bridges so much more interesting than other suburban families and *Son of the Morning Star* not just one more account of Custer's Last Stand but a genuine literary masterpiece: Connell is a virtuoso of noticing. He scrutinizes human behavior and human history with such forensic intensity that he attains a kind of curatorial omniscience, and he condenses his material with such draconian economy that his sentences read like paragraphs distilled, his paragraphs like distillations of chapters.

BEGINNING TO WONDER

There is discernible in Connell's life and work a common, exorbitant trajectory—the arc described by his "long desire." His first novel, *Mrs. Bridge,* is set in the affluent Kansas City suburbs of his childhood. *Deus Lo Volt!,* published forty-one years later, recounts events that occurred on battlefields in Europe, Byzantium, and the Holy Land more than seven hundred years earlier. Between these two antipodes, depression-era Kansas and medieval Palestine, Connell's work roams across continents and centuries. His life has been similarly peripatetic.

Evan Shelby Connell Jr. was born to Dr. Evan Shelby Connell, a surgeon, and Elton Williamson Connell, a judge's daughter, on August 17, 1924. In his 1985 essay for the *Contemporary Authors Autobiography Series (CAAS),* Connell describes Mission Hills, the Kansas City neighborhood where he grew up, as a suffocatingly proprietary world whose citizens were nearly as indistinguishable as their white houses—uniformly decorated with gauze curtains, needlepoint antimacassars, and overstuffed chairs. "It was like a European feudal society," Connell once said (quoted by Cathleen Schine).

Outwardly his boyhood appears to have been uneventful. He attended public schools, joined the Boy Scouts, built model airplanes, affixed decals of which his father disapproved to the fender of his bicycle, tormented his little sister, and pleaded for a family dog, which he eventually received. Inwardly, however, Connell seems to have detected early on a quiet desperation lurking behind the gauze curtains. In his *CAAS* essay he remembers his mother as a woman who cooked without enthusiasm, gardened without passion, who "felt threatened by allusions to sex" and "was concerned mostly that nothing outrageous should happen," but in whom he nonetheless detected a "mild artistic current." Dr. Connell was, according to his son's portrait, a somewhat domineering patriarch slavishly devoted to convention and breadwinning, a man who for fifty years went to work early and came home late. "Whether his grim routine

made him happy, I do not know," Connell says. "I think it satisfied him because he felt it was correct. Children went to school, wives kept house, husbands went to work. Accordingly there remained little space for poetry, ballet, storytelling, or grand opera"—little space, in other words, for the artistic life into which his son would seek to escape.

In his youth his heroes were explorers and adventurers, romantic figures who traveled bravely into the unknown and provided the doctor's son with an imaginary alternative to the feudalistic inevitability of marriage and medicine. When in 1939 Richard Halliburton attempted to cross the Pacific Ocean in a Chinese junk, Connell paid "something like $1.50" to have his hero carry a commemorative envelope on his voyage. When the junk vanished at sea, it was the envelope, not the explorer, whose loss Connell mourned—early evidence, perhaps, of his future obsession with artifacts. Influenced by *The Dawn Patrol,* a 1938 movie about aerial battles of World War I, Connell, like Douglas, his fictional counterpart in the *Bridge* novels, dreamed of becoming an aviator. In 1943, after two years at Dartmouth College, where he declared a major in premed and developed a fledgling interest in writing fiction, Connell enlisted in the navy as an aviation cadet, perhaps the single most fateful decision he would make.

Connell received his aviator's wings on May 8, 1945—the day the allies declared victory in Europe—and served as a flight instructor for the remainder of the war. Although he never saw action, he did witness several pilots die in accidents, and images of their deaths figure prominently in his work. Upon being discharged in 1945, he returned to college on the GI Bill, this time attending the University of Kansas, where he devoted himself to writing and art.

In 1947, after receiving his bachelor's degree, Connell embarked upon a decade of wandering, abandoning Kansas first for California, where he studied fiction with Wallace Stegner at Stanford, and then, in 1948, for New York City, where he studied both writing and sculpture at Columbia. While there, he acquired an agent and had his first success publishing short stories, one of which, "I'll Take You to Tennessee," was selected for inclusion in the O. Henry Award anthology of 1949. And yet Connell felt as out of place among Manhattan's literati as he had among Kansas City's bourgeoisie. When the GI Bill expired, he moved for no particular reason back to California, where he spent a few itinerant years in Los Angeles and Santa Cruz.

After World War II a second wave of expatriate American writers and artists, following the previous generation's example, flocked to Paris in pursuit of a more permissive and less expensive way of life than could then be had in the States. In 1952, increasingly sickened by rampant McCarthyite intolerance at home, Connell joined his compatriots abroad. He was soon bankrolled by a Eugene F. Saxton fellowship. During the several months he spent living and working in an eight-dollar-a-month hotel in Saint-Germain, he encountered some of the brightest literary talents of his generation, writers like Terry Southern, Max Steele, William Styron, Donald Hall, Peter Matthiessen, and the British poet Christopher Logue—who, Connell says in his *CAAS* essay, taught him more about the English sentence than anyone else "before or since." Matthiessen, along with Hall, Styron, Harold Humes, George Plimpton, and several others, had recently founded the *Paris Review.* Shortly after his arrival Connell began contributing illustrations and stories to the new literary journal, early issues of which also contained work by Simone de Beauvoir, Samuel Beckett, Saul Bellow, Adrienne Rich, and Philip Roth.

From France, Connell traveled to Barcelona, where he spent a cold, lonely spring in a boardinghouse, warming his hands over a hot plate, counting the days, writing short stories, and endeavoring to complete a novel about an art instructor named Andrev Andraukov that he would eventually abandon. "It was the worst emotional state I've ever been in," he told Barry Siegel in 1991. "If I hadn't fallen into a gibbering mess then,… I knew I never would." In 1954 he returned to the United States, settling in San Francisco. Apart from a few "untidy hegiras of various duration," including not one but two trips around the globe, he made that city his home for the next thirty-five years. "I had meant to stay perhaps a year," he writes in his *CAAS* essay, "but the panoramic view from the hillsides and a quality of light on San Francisco bay combined with a singularly un-American attitude on the part of most citizens to create an agreeable atmosphere."

Preferring to subsist on writing, he has purposefully abstained from the usual careers, such as teaching, with which many writers and artists of his generation have supported themselves. The impermanent work Connell has taken includes such odd jobs as reading gas meters, hauling ice, writing book reviews for newspapers, and clerking in a shipyard. In the early 1960s he toiled in the California unemployment office, an experience which he described to Schine as "Kafkaesque" and which he satirizes viciously in *The Diary of a Rapist.*

For Connell, San Francisco became less attractive with time (the attitude less un-American, the streets more crowded), and his writing became more lucrative. After selling the film rights to *Son of the Morning Star* and the two *Bridge* novels in the 1980s, Connell packed his scant belongings into his Honda Civic and moved to Santa Fe, New Mexico, where, alone in a sparsely furnished condominium, he has lived ascetically ever since.

WIDOWED IMAGES, NOISELESS SCREAMS, FORENSIC NARRATIVES

In his earliest memory, Connell is "seated on a rug near the bottom of some steps," which his mother suddenly descends, waving her arms. "And as she rushed down upon me," Connell recollects in his *CAAS* essay, "she was crying out in alarm, although I cannot remember any noise. This moment, like a dream, is forever noiseless." Readers of Connell's fiction and nonfiction will recognize the silent scream, variations on which echo throughout his work along with other, equally dreamlike images: they are irresolvable moments that contain within them inherent mysteries and ironic contradictions. Why is his mother screaming? Why is her scream noiseless? Why, after several decades, does her son remember it?

Connell says that his mother later shared with him her own recollection of this event. It seems that, while seated at the bottom of those steps, young Evan had been endeavoring to hoist his baby sister by the head with a pair of brass fire tongs. But this information, this backstory, fails to resolve satisfactorily the riddle of his mother's scream. The image possesses a talismanic power apart from or in excess of the immediate circumstances—the narrative—out of which it arose. It transcends the plot Connell's mother supplies. It glimmers with the incandescence of significance distilled.

The moment hints at something both uncanny and epiphanic, and yet neither of these terms seems altogether adequate to describe it. According to Sigmund Freud, uncanny moments are those in which the veneer of the familiar cracks and a repressed, estranging secret is revealed. As defined by James Joyce, an epiphany is an "evanescent" moment in which the spiritual suddenly becomes manifest. Connell's first memory, however, is powerful and enduring largely because it fails to disclose whatever truth, psychological or spiritual, it contains. It may very well be exactly the sort of moment Ezra Pound had in mind when he defined an "image" as "that which presents an intellectual and emotional complex in an instant of time." Or better yet it may be one of those images that Gerard Manley Hopkins referred to as "widowed"—fetishistic, misfit memories from which "some crucial part of their meaning had been stripped" (quoted by Charles Baxter).

The poet Robert Hass, who has perhaps thought as much and as well about the topic as anyone, explains the power of images this way:

> In the nineteenth century one would have said that what compelled us about them was a sense of the eternal. And it is something like that, some feeling in the arrest of the image that what perishes and what lasts forever have been brought into conjunction, and accompanying that sensation is a feeling of release from the self.

Yet we are perpetually awash with sensation, inundated with fleeting moments, and the great majority of our sensations evanesce instantaneously. Transforming sensation into image requires something more—trauma, perhaps, or art.

It is strange that we associate images primarily with poetry, when they are, according to Hass, a kind of "pure story." "In stories, in incidents that might be stories," Hass writes, "I suppose there is always a moment, different for different memories, when the image, the set of relationships that seem actually to reveal something about life, forms." All great works of fiction contain such moments, either revelatory of significance or pregnant with it, though, as in poetry, the moments become suddenly more prominent in fiction of the twentieth century. Presumably it is not coincidental that Joyce introduced his notion of the epiphany at approximately the same time Pound defined the image, nor that both of these events occurred soon after the impressionists began attempting to render the most ephemeral and delicate qualities of color and light. It is as if time itself were becoming more momentary, consciousness more fragmentary. In Joyce's work, as in that of Marcel Proust, Isaak Babel, or Ernest Hemingway (especially in such stories as "Indian Camp"), images begin to assume the importance of actions.

For instance, in Babel's "Crossing into Poland," the opening story of the *Red Cavalry* cycle, the ostensible protagonist, the narrator—who is, we later learn, a myopic war correspondent for a state-run propaganda organ—does almost nothing but describe what he sees, undergoing over the course of a mere two and a half pages a series of revelations that culminate in a kind of epiphany, a literal unveiling not of spiritual truth but of a previously hidden reality. Babel attains the kind of density and economy, almost entirely free of exposition, that we have come to associate with poetry. In the place of a dramatic climax, he gives us an imagistic one: a blanket is pulled back to reveal an old man murdered in a pogrom. "His throat had been torn out and his face cleft in two," Babel writes; "in his beard blue blood was clotted like a lump of lead." There is an inward as well as a forward movement to the story, a collapse in psychic distance, from the journalistic detachment of the opening paragraph to the traumatized silence that the story's climactic image leaves in its reverberating wake.

At least among American writers, Connell must certainly be one of the greatest living practitioners of narrative imagism. Although he never achieved the success as a graphic artist to which he initially aspired, Connell's intensely visual writing abounds with portraits of artists and references to art. The title story of his first book, *The Anatomy Lesson, and Other Stories,* published in 1957, is both a fictionalized exegesis on the art of life drawing and a virtuoso performance of that art. It is both a portrait of one particular artist—Andrev Andraukov, "Instructor of Drawing and Painting," about whom Connell had attempted but failed to write a novel—and a veiled declaration of Connell's own aesthetic credo: "The artist must not look at what he sees so much as what he

cannot see... ," Andraukov exhorts his class. "The artist must see around corners and through walls, even as he must see behind smiles, behind looks of pain." Few critics have so well described what is miraculous about Connell's portraits of Mr. and Mrs. Bridge, or of the rapist Earl Summerfield, or of George Armstrong Custer, or of the many adventurers, alchemists, astronomers, and explorers profiled in his historical essays. Everything Connell has written can be understood as a radical kind of life drawing, the product of his ongoing struggle to see not only behind smiles and through walls but across continents and centuries.

Much of his work consists almost exclusively of those moments, identified by Hass as when "the image, the set of relationships that seem actually to reveal something about life, forms." At the end of the same autobiographical essay in which he describes the memory of his mother's noiseless scream, Connell interrupts his otherwise chronological account to tell a story about storytelling—an *ars poetica* in the form of a parable. During the Second World War, a friend of his with the unlikely nickname of Blossom served as the copilot of a patrol bomber on search missions over the South Pacific. On most runs nothing turned up, but on one occasion Blossom and his crewmates spotted an empty yellow raft adrift on the ocean. After searching the water for a pilot and finding nothing, they destroyed the raft with machine-gun fire to keep the Japanese from discovering it. After the war, attending the University of Kansas and thinking he might like to become a writer, Blossom sketched a love story around this event—"a tedious, disorganized, sentimental story," says Connell, "in which the destruction of the raft was briefly mentioned." Years later, after Blossom had given up his writerly ambitions, Connell stole his friend's raft. "The image he had brought from the South Pacific was too significant to abandon," Connell says. Stripped of the narrative that would resolve it, yet hauntingly suggestive of that narrative, the image had become widowed. Connell continues, "I took what I needed and boiled it until almost nothing remained, not much more than a yellow dot." This process of salvaging and boiling down is typical of Connell's imagistic method.

"The Yellow Raft," the story with which *The Anatomy Lesson* concludes, consists of two long paragraphs that contain no dialogue or back-story and little characterization or conflict. Instead, beginning with the appearance of a "Navy fighter, high in the air, but gliding steadily down upon the ocean," Connell's aloof, omniscient narrator presents a series of images observed meticulously but from an enormous psychic distance. We hear the "dull whirring noise" of a broken propeller turned only by the wind, and we watch the shadow of the descending fighter leap "like some distraught creature … hastily through the whitecaps" until, with an eerie tranquility, the plane's engine dives into a wave: "The fuselage stood briefly erect, a strange blue buoy riddled by gunfire, and then, bubbling, inclining, it sank beneath the greasy water." Part of what makes this image, the first of several such images in the story, so powerful is its internal asymmetry. The drama of the event seems at odds with the affectlessness of the narrator's tone. It is, in effect, a kind of noiseless scream.

Moments after the plane sinks, a yellow raft bursts to the surface, immediately followed by the downed pilot's bloody, extended hand. Ah yes, we tell ourselves as the hero claws his way into the raft, a survival story: man against the sea, like something out of Jack London or Stephen Crane. And for a page or two, as the pilot takes stock of his few supplies and a storm begins to brew, our suspicions seem confirmed. However, Connell refuses to turn the man in the yellow raft into a protagonist. He remains name-less and faceless. We enter his consciousness rarely, and then only briefly and indirectly. Beginning with the appearance of the plane on the horizon in the opening sentence, the narra-tive proceeds in a single, unbroken paragraph of moving action that lasts three pages, until a wave sweeps the pilot into oblivion. This event, however, is not reported. It happens—and here's the quintessential Connell touch—between sentences. The understatement could not be more extreme. One moment the pilot is watch-ing colossal waves dive one after another "under the bounding yellow raft." In the next the storm has passed, it is nighttime again, and the constellations are shining overhead. We do not even realize the pilot is gone until, early in the story's second long paragraph, a search plane appears and finds the raft empty "except for the flashlight rolling idly back and forth and glitter-ing in the sunshine." Once again, we have the noiseless scream.

Everything up to and including the pilot's death, it turns out, is merely prelude, the introduction not to a survival story but to a forensic drama of seeing. The single paragraph break in the story functions like a hinge joining two mirrored halves. After spotting the yellow raft empty in the water, the second aircraft, a flying boat called a Catalina, begins searching for the pilot of the first. There is a kind of ironic parallel in the way the search plane seems to mimic the roving eye of the narrator, seeing nothing where the narrator sees all. Every detail Connell reports, in fact, ironizes the pilot's death, making it seem less tragic than absurd: after the Catalina has circled relentlessly for hours, a "blister" near its tail slides open, and "a moment later a cluster of empty beer cans" falls "in a smooth glittering trajectory toward the sea." The story ends with the similarly ironic image, at once awful and beautiful, of the yel-low raft after the search plane has riddled it with gunfire:

The strange dance ended. The yellow raft fell back, torn into fragments of cork and loose, deflated rubber. From these remains came floating an iridescent dye, as green as a rainbow. The Catalina, its work complete, began to rise. Higher and higher in the air, never changing course, it flew majestically toward the infinite horizon, leaving the darkness and the silence.

Everything is pitched to intensify the almost uncanny ironies and tonal contradictions of this final image, the one from which Connell's autobiographical essay says the entire story arose. Even having witnessed the pilot's death, we sense some irresolvable significance in that dreamlike iridescent dye, the stain of a horrible beauty leaking from the little life raft of narrative. The irony of the word "majestically" verges on the sardonic, a tone that modulates in the story's final note into existential despair. The darkness and silence with which this story ends punctuate all of Connell's narratives. More than the conflict between his characters, what gives his work intensity is the conflict between his images—his life drawings—and the silent darkness that engulfs them.

ART AND THE MEANING OF TIME

The stories Connell tells are dramas less of action than of perception. He practices what Andrev Andraukov preaches: his typically third-person narrators remain godlike and aloof, endeavoring to see what cannot be seen; looking around corners, through walls, behind smiles. *The Anatomy Lesson*'s title story opens with the narrator's extended investigation of the scene, an investigation during which nothing happens and no characters appear. Instead, Connell collects evidence, noticing the shabbiness of the art building where Andraukov spends his days, its windowsills "pocked by cigarette burns," its "creaking floors streaked and spattered with drops of paint." He peeks behind the locked door of Andraukov's studio and inventories the details he finds inside. Similarly, in "The Condor and the Guests," included in the same volume, nothing, so far as the characters can tell, happens. What the narrator ultimately

perceives, however—and what he makes us perceive—is beautiful and devastating.

The plot of "The Condor and the Guests" is almost too slight to summarize: at its beginning, J. D. Botkin (the character's name was changed to L. R. Botkin in Connell's *Collected Stories*) of the aptly named Parallel, Kansas, has just received illegal delivery of a Peruvian condor, an exotic pet which he intends to keep chained to the magnolia tree in his backyard. Botkin and the dinner guests for whom he shows off his new ornithological prize are not characters so much as types—small-minded provincials all. The condor, meanwhile, is essentially a metaphor with wings, an otherworldly, vaguely seraphic creature that, like that other exotic specimen, Andrev Andraukov in "The Anatomy Lesson," or the mysterious singing fisherman of "The Fisherman from Chihuahua," is the very embodiment of freedom and "long desire" and thus the consummate foil for the citizens of Parallel. What conflict there is in the story exists in the ironic discrepancy between the way Botkin and his guests see the condor ("What a simple bird"; "Now's the time to cook that turkey for Thanksgiving"; "Fowl … are not overly intelligent") and the way the story's painterly narrator sees it:

> The condor sat in the magnolia tree and looked across the fields of wheat, but just before sundown it lifted its wings and spread them to the fullest extent as if testing the wind; then with a slow sweep of utter majesty it rose into the air. It took a second leisurely sweep with its wings, and a third. However, on the third stroke, it came to the end of the chain. Then it made a sort of gasping noise and fell to the earth while the magnolia swayed from the shock. After its fall the gigantic bird did not move until long after dark when it got to its feet and climbed into the tree. Next morning as the sun rose it was on the same branch, looking south like a gargoyle taken from the ramparts of some cathedral.

This description of the condor's abbreviated vespertine flight, at once naturalistic and symbolic, is typical of Connell's method. Combining the verisimilitude of a realist with the moral intelligence of a parable teller, he imbues the condor with significance. He turns it into an artifact, freighting every detail—the "majestic" sweep of the condor's wings, the shocked magnolia, the gargoylelike gaze—with metaphor. It is not mere mimesis Connell is after, but illustration and, ultimately, instruction. In the collection's title story, Andrev Andraukov, midway through his anatomy lesson, conjectures rhetorically: "In this room perhaps now there sits young man who in this world discovers injustice. He would be conscience of the world. Mr. Dillon will now stand up. Mr. Dillon, you would draw picture which is to say, 'Behold! Injustice!'? You would do that?" Young Mr. Dillon declines. Young Mr. Connell did not.

As both the parable of Douglas' tower and "The Anatomy Lesson" suggest, Connell is a highly self-conscious, even self-referential (though never confessional) writer. His work is full of representations of and meditations upon the method and meaning of art. Like Andraukov, Connell, devoted to the figural tradition, distrusts abstract expressionism.

In painting, Andraukov's masters are the great practitioners of the art of seeing, the virtuosos of anatomy—Michelangelo, Leonardo da Vinci, Albrecht Dürer. In literature, Connell favors the great European realists—Leo Tolstoy, Gustave Flaubert, Anton Chekhov, Thomas Mann. Even at his most experimental, Connell is realism's heir. He represents, in a sense, surrealism's antithesis. Instead of abandoning himself to the irrationality of absurdists, in his best work he practices a brand of realism so rational, so omniscient, so "intensely verisimilitudinous" (to paraphrase Gus Blaisdell) that it reveals a hidden reality of absurdity and injustice. He observes so forensically that the evidence before him—whether it is firsthand experience or an archive of documents—begins to unravel, giving rise to a sense of emptiness, of uncanniness,

or of ontological vertigo. His realism approaches the mystical. Andraukov tells his students

> of how Rembrandt painted a young woman looking out an open window and said to them that ... she was more than one young woman, she was all. ... He told them that some afternoon they would glance up by chance and see her; then they would know the meaning of Time—what it could destroy, what it could not.

The meaning of time is the ultimate object of Connell's "long desire." "The condition of life," he writes in *Notes from a Bottle Found on the Beach at Carmel,* "is defeat." And yet, as Blaisdell points out, Connell is nonetheless "on the side of life alone, fragile in its beauties and terrible in its agonies." For him the act of seeing through walls and behind smiles is, ultimately, a moral endeavor as well as an aesthetic one. He is enraged by human savagery, and yet his rage, like Saint Augustine's, is "ameliorated by love," a love that stems from "untempered humanism." It is this love of the human that motivates his salvage operation, his rescue mission, his art.

The Anatomy Lesson also introduces two characters who reappear more prominently in later books, a lonely housewife named Mrs. Bridge and a lonely insurance executive named Muhlbach who would, in two novels, *The Connoisseur* (1974) and *Double Honeymoon* (1976), and in several short stories, become something of an authorial alter ego. Connell's enduring interest in these two characters makes sense in retrospect, for they are the most fully realized in the collection. What distinguishes them from the rest is complexity and, more important, sympathy—not theirs for others but Connell's for them. They are neither emblematically heroic figures, like Andraukov, the fisherman from Chihuahua, or the condor, nor caricatured provincials. Outwardly both appear to differ little from J. D. Botkin and his dinner guests, but in portraying them Connell does not limit himself to outward appearances. He succeeds at imagining their inner lives. He reveals that privately, even in the company of their spouses and children, both Muhlbach and Mrs. Bridge are profoundly isolated, as imprisoned as Botkin's condor by bourgeois existence, and as hungry for freedom. They, too, make small and pointless flights and discover the limits of their chains.

Whatever Mrs. Bridge and Muhlbach may have in common, formally the stories that introduce them, "The Beau Monde of Mrs. Bridge" and "Arcturus," respectively, could hardly represent time more differently. In "Arcturus," Connell dilates a single evening. Told in the present tense and in miniaturistic detail, the story seems to transpire moment by moment. The drama unfolds not in action but in the patterning of imagery, the counterpointing of characters (Otto with Donna, the cook with the nurse, Muhlbach with Sandy Kirk, the invalid Joyce with Dee Borowski), the modulations in tone, and the dueling of points of view. Although the story's setting (the Muhlbach residence in the suburbs of New York City) and its situation (a dinner party reuniting Muhlbach's dying wife with her former lover) remain fixed, the point of view does not. The narrator roves omnisciently and seamlessly from one character to the next, dramatizing the disparities among them and registering the subtle shifts in the sands of consciousness that occur over the course of the evening, an evening during which nearly all of Connell's creations are forced to contend with mortality, as intimations of it recur throughout the story. The narrative begins with a ghostlike moaning of the wind, and the story's central image—that of stars plummeting apocalyptically toward Earth—can be seen refracted everywhere: in the white snow leaping before the black windows; in the interior warmth and the exterior cold; and in the pattern of footprints a pair of hunters leaves in the snowy lawn, which looks to Muhlbach like an eight of spades. Imagistically, the Muhlbach residence becomes a sanctuary of light engulfed by a universe of silent darkness.

There is a moment in "Arcturus" when Muhlbach, the central character in the story's cast, "thinks over the shards remaining from his own childhood, but is conscious mostly of how much has perished." Connell takes up this theme fully in "The Beau Monde of Mrs. Bridge." In this story Connell represents the ravages wrought by time formally as well as imagistically; that is, instead of dilating time, he distills it into a mosaic composed of only the remaining shards of years—those shards that time could not destroy. His paratactic method is vaguely reminiscent of biblical and apocryphal stories about the life of Christ, and of folklore, such as the Brer Rabbit tales, wherein the purpose is not to provide a linear plot but to reveal a pattern of character and thought. The shortest of the vignettes included in "The Beau Monde of Mrs. Bridge," titled "Never Speak to Strange Men," is typical of his method:

> On a downtown street just outside a department store a man said something to her. She ignored him. But at that moment the crowd closed them in together.
>
> "How do you do?" he said, smiling and touching his hat.
>
> She saw that he was a man of about fifty with silvery hair and rather satanic ears.
>
> His face became red and he laughed awkwardly. "I'm Gladys Schmidt's husband."
>
> "Oh, for heaven's sake!" Mrs. Bridge exclaimed. "I didn't recognize you."

Connell is making fun of Mrs. Bridge here, but he is not merely making fun. This seemingly trivial anecdote is inflected with despair. By capturing this moment and fixing it, as if on a microscopic slide, Connell makes the latent manifest. Juxtaposing Mrs. Bridge's inner terror with her outer propriety, he reveals the dimensions of the gulf between them.

MRS. BRIDGE AS FEMINIST NOVEL

An imagistic short story is one thing, but an imagistic novel would in theory seem to require an impossibly chimerical union of the momentary and the grand. However, in writing *Mrs. Bridge,* Connell managed to concoct precisely this sort of fantastic literary creature. Asked by Patricia Holt about the novel's unconventional, mosaic structure, Connell explained his intentions as follows: "I had tried a traditional narrative ... but found that this story, as is true with most of our lives, had no dramatic climax. Mrs. Bridge's life was one incident after another. There was not one great, explosive event, so I had to break it down into the smaller moments." In her classic study of gender and literature, *Seduction and Betrayal: Women and Literature* (1974), Elizabeth Hardwick identifies in the plays of Henrik Ibsen a failure of form that this imagistic method of Connell's seems to redress. Ibsen's "people are not quite fixed," Hardwick complains.

> They are growing, moving, uncertain of their direction in life. With this sort of personality, dialogue and selected dramatic conflicts cannot tell us all we want to know. ...
>
> It is not a defect in dramaturgy; no, all of that is mastered perfectly. The trouble has to do with the sort of character Ibsen wanted to write about, particularly the women characters. Their motivation is true, but incomplete. Perhaps the fluid, drifting, poetic tone of Chekhov would have suited these women better. We would not have expected quite the same sort of resolution Ibsen's playmaking techniques demand. You look deeper into the plays and there are hints, little fragments here and there, stray bits of biography, detached, fascinating and mysterious suggestions.

It is entirely out of such "little fragments" that *Mrs. Bridge* is composed. In transforming "The Beau Monde of Mrs. Bridge" into a novel, Connell revised, reordered, and supplemented the original ten vignettes published in *The Anatomy Lesson.* Nearly every one of the book's 117 miniature chapters contains at its center one or more widowed images whose meaning Connell's heroine fails to grasp.

More than "uncertain of [her] direction in life," India Bridge is a kind of widowed image to herself, a character for whom her own name seems mysterious and from whom both biography and motive have been stripped, leaving behind a paralyzed nebula of distracted consciousness. As is suggested by the novel's epigraph from Walt Whitman—"But where is what I started for so long ago? / And why is it yet unfound?"—not only does Connell's novel lack a dramatic climax, but its protagonist's most defining characteristic is her lack of agency. Hers is an almost objectless quest that never actually begins, a quest motivated by ambient, misplaced, and perpetually interrupted desire.

For two centuries, from *Moll Flanders,* to *Pamela,* to *Emma,* to *Jane Eyre,* to *David Copperfield,* to *The Adventures of Huckleberry Finn,* to *Daisy Miller,* on down to *Sister Carrie* and *Babbitt,* British and American novels were predominantly biographical in form, narrating the fictional lives of the protagonists for which they were conventionally named. Such novels of character prototypically start at the logical beginning, with the protagonist's origins and childhood, and march relentlessly forward toward a defining crisis of selfhood, followed by a resolution commonly involving marriage or death. In one sense *Mrs. Bridge* belongs to this tradition—it narrates the life of its title character—but in another sense, as the novelist Charles Baxter observes (in private correspondence), it represents the tradition's terminus: "If [Mrs. Bridge] has an identity," Baxter comments, "she has achieved it passively, and though she certainly has a character, it is remarkably difficult to say what that character is. ... [It] can be defined only with the greatest difficulty, because it is nearly invisible."

In the brutally condensed childhood history with which the novel begins, we learn almost nothing of India Bridge's past, not her maiden name, not the profession of her parents, not her place of origin. Connell says only that as a child India had always wondered about her parents' reasons for giving her such an incongruous first name. "She was," Connell writes, "often on the point of inquiring, but time passed, and she never did." This statement, with which the novel's opening paragraph concludes, presages the entirety of the life that follows. In one small moment after another we see her there, on the verge of inquiry, on the verge of self-consciousness, on the verge of transforming widowed images into epiphanies, trembling at the threshold of her existential dollhouse—a threshold she never does, finally, cross.

Although Connell would likely resist characterizing his intentions as overtly feminist, *Mrs. Bridge* in both its form and subject matter can be meaningfully described as such. Set mainly in the 1920s and 1930s, in a world largely, though not entirely, immune to the infiltration of suffragists, the novel explicitly portrays its heroine as needing liberation. In her unmarried youth India Bridge imagines "that she could get along very nicely without a husband," a notion she does not relinquish until, as in a fairy tale, "there came a summer evening and a young lawyer named Walter Bridge," who enchants her with a promised tour of Europe and with verses of *The Rubáiyát*. It is not Walter Bridge she falls for, but the spell he casts: the dream of the alluring unknown. Her naïveté, her existential myopia, her submissiveness to her suitor's will are symptoms, Connell makes clear, not only of her character but of her circumstance. Keeping with patriarchal custom, she is passed from her father to her husband, marrying him, the text says, upon her father's death—an event Connell records almost parenthetically, and with no appeal whatsoever to our emotions nor with any mention of hers. Newly married, Mrs.

Bridge is still not certain what she wants from life, Connell writes, "or what to expect from it, for she had seen so little of it." She possesses, in other words, an incipient "long desire" that bourgeois domesticity repeatedly, permanently, and tragically interrupts.

Her repression, as Connell portrays it, is sexual as well as spiritual. She is the antithesis of what Andrev Andraukov means when he describes the nude model standing before his students as a woman "proud of body." Over the course of the novel Mrs. Bridge becomes increasingly disembodied, as if she were vanishing. During the brief interlude between marriage and motherhood—an interlude that in Connell's telling lasts only a few merciless paragraphs—Mrs. Bridge experiences an aborted sexual awakening:

> For a while after their marriage she was in such demand that it was not unpleasant when he fell asleep. Presently, however, he began sleeping all night, and it was then she awoke more frequently, and looked into the darkness, wondering about the nature of men, doubtful of the future, until at last there came a night when she shook her husband awake and spoke of her own desire. Affably he placed one of his long white arms around her waist; she turned to him then, contentedly, expectantly, and secure. However nothing else occurred, and in a few minutes he had gone back to sleep.

How devastating that word "expectantly" is. Connell has already said that Mrs. Bridge's "wants and expectations were the same." No longer. This interruption of her desire occurs on the novel's second page, and metaphorically speaking, it is as if the heroine has already died, smothered by Mr. Bridge's long, silencing arm. When, many chapters later, decades after marrying her, Mr. Bridge does finally take her to Europe, the bedside mirrors she encounters in their hotel rooms—mirrors posed to reveal "her intimacy with her husband"—fill her with "listless despair."

In the interior world Mrs. Bridge inhabits, the implements of repression are psychological and, therefore, largely invisible. She is not literally imprisoned after all. There are no sentries posted at the door of her house, no moat surrounding it. She is, rather, incarcerated by her own limitations in point of view, limitations that Connell's formal strategy is engineered to reveal to his readers, though never quite to his protagonist. The titles of the chapters, nearly all ironic, position the reader at a great distance. Thus the chapter in which Mrs. Bridge's best friend, Grace Barron (the most unambiguously sympathetic character in the book), commits suicide is titled, devastatingly, "Tuna Salad." In the text of the chapters, however, Connell plunges us into a vantage of extreme sympathy, making us aware of the awful disparity between Mrs. Bridge's inner life and outer life, between the claustrophobic world she is capable of imagining and the reality that the chapter titles imply. Immersed briefly into Mrs. Bridge's consciousness, we are snapped almost violently out again by the interrupting white space; our heroine recedes, diminishing, as if viewed through the wrong end of a telescope. On very few occasions it is not Mrs. Bridge's interior life we experience but that of one of the members of her family, yet even this outside perspective creates a sense of solitary confinement. It is as if Connell were slowly asphyxiating his heroine with psychic distance.

Mrs. Bridge is not an altogether passive victim, however. Within the domestic sphere, she is an agent of sorts, which may help explain why some early critics saw Connell's treatment of her as relentlessly satirical. Time after time, in gesture, word, and action, she records "her wish for the world to remain" as it is. When young Caroline Bridge befriends Alice Jones, the daughter of a black gardener, Mrs. Bridge intervenes, and Alice vanishes. When Douglas builds his tower, Mrs. Bridge has it destroyed. It is this doomed war against time that provides

Mrs. Bridge's life with the vestiges of a story line, a dramatic arc that ascends through a kind of rising action toward the crisis of Grace Barron's suicide. "The days passed, and the weeks, and the months," Connell writes in the novel's first chapter, "... and she felt no trepidation, except for certain moments in the depth of the night."

As the novel progresses, such moments grow more numerous, more frequent, and more ominous. Each vote that Mrs. Bridge casts in favor of immutability represents another lost battle against time, the passage of which Connell almost never explicitly signals. We experience it only obliquely through embedded cues— the aging of the children, for instance, or war beginning somewhere far away. Repressed, time seems only to grow more powerful. "[Mrs. Bridge] spent a great deal of time staring into space, oppressed by the sense that she was waiting," begins chapter 45, titled "The Clock,"

> but waiting for what? ... Each day proceeded like the one before. Nothing intense, nothing desperate, ever happened. Time did not move. The home, the city, the nation, and life itself were eternal; still she had a foreboding that one day, without warning and without pity, all the dear, important things would be destroyed.

Slowly, this "foreboding" metastasizes into "an evil, a malignancy" to which the androgynous, opinionated, free-spirited Grace Barron—a feminist canary in a mineshaft of despair— finally, depressively, succumbs. "Her friend was ill and suffering," Connell writes, "and Mrs. Bridge, too, was afflicted. Thinking back she was able to remember moments when this anonymous evil had erupted and left as its only cicatrice a sour taste in the mouth and a wild, wild desire." This is, perhaps, as close as Mrs. Bridge ever comes to an awakening.

The discrete incidents that make up the novel are related to one another, but not, as the events in a narrative usually are, by cause and effect. Rather, they play a series of imagistic variations on a theme. The dense patterning of image imbues seemingly irrelevant details with meaning and gives evanescent moments the heft of dramatic events. Again and again, for instance, Mrs. Bridge encounters uncanny representations of her own inanimate existence—a dressmaker's dummy at which she finds her son gazing with disturbing interest; a nightmarish electronic doll that rolls its eyes, broadcasts a nursery rhyme, and excretes "a thin, colorless liquid" on the statue of Winged Victory at the Louvre. "Have you ever felt like those people in the Grimm fairy tale—," Mrs. Bridge remembers Grace Barron asking her one afternoon, "the ones who were all hollowed out in the back?" Again and again, too, we see Mrs. Bridge holding still, more catatonic than calm, while the chaos of the outside world spins violently around her. Again and again, we come upon her son, Douglas, Connell's proxy, taking flight into the rafters of the garage or the branches of a tree, or finally to war. Again and again, clocks tick and chime.

And there are the silent screams. These chapters may blaze and gutter out like matches being struck one after another, but the ravages of time are here represented not by darkness but by obliterating whiteness and its aural counterpart, silence. Ruth Bridge's most vivid childhood memory, for instance, is of the sweltering day on which she removed her bathing suit and ran naked around the neighborhood swimming pool: she "squirmed out of the arms that reached for her from every direction," thinking mistakenly that this was a new game. "Then," Connell writes, "she noticed the expression on her mother's face." Little Ruth became "bewildered and then alarmed," and by the time she "was finally caught she was screaming hysterically." Connell ends the scene so that Ruth's scream reverberates into the white space. Only a few pages into the book, the narrative already echoes

subliminally the earlier, quieter, but no less desperate moment, in the novel's first chapter, when Mr. Bridge "affably" smothers his momentarily libidinous wife with "one of his long white arms." Many years and chapters later, seated before a mirror (another motif), Mrs. Bridge spreads cold cream on her face.

> The touch of the cream, the unexpectedness of it—for she had been thinking deeply about how to occupy tomorrow—the swift cool touch demoralized her so completely that she almost screamed.
>
> She continued spreading the cream over her features. … Rapidly, soundlessly, she was disappearing into white, sweetly scented anonymity.

In a sense, the abundant white space turns all of the novel's miniature chapters into noiseless screams, smothering the story of Mrs. Bridge's life with "long white arms," erasing it with "white, sweetly scented anonymity," interrupting it so abruptly that the silence becomes deafening. Charles Baxter describes the types of caesuras between Connell's vignettes as "expressive air-pockets of dead silence," a phrase he attributes to James Agee. Over the course of *Mrs. Bridge,* these air pockets grow ever more expressive, crescendoing during the book's final pages into a high C of inaudible distress.

What lends this profoundly undramatic drama—this mosaic of widowed images—its powerful sense of development, change, and heightening suspense are finely calibrated modulations of dynamics and tone. Many of the chapters early in the novel end with a punch line at Mrs. Bridge's expense. As time passes, however, the jokes become less comic and increasingly tragic; satire gives way to hysteria, which exhausts itself into elegy. In the penultimate chapter, ironically titled "Remembrance of Things Past," Mr. Bridge is dead and the children are gone. There is nothing left to interrupt Mrs. Bridge's life, which stalls even as the passage of time continues. She obsessively surveys the photographs in the family album, which presents a kind of counternarrative to the collection of images offered by the novel itself. In these snapshots of family vacations and birthday parties, she seeks refuge. The album contains a dreamlike vision of her vanished past, but this vision, we know, is profoundly incomplete, more illusion than reality, and the novel's final chapter obliterates it for good. Halfway out of the garage, Mrs. Bridge's Lincoln—like her life—stalls, its doors blocked on either side by walls. She taps her key against the glass. She calls out, inaudibly, "Hello?" And it is to this widowed image that Connell abandons his widowed heroine, trapped inside her car, buried alive, as it were, by the accumulating silence and snow.

Although *Mrs. Bridge* was both a popular and a critical success when it appeared in 1959, few reviewers appreciated what Connell had intended or accomplished in devising the novel's mosaic form. ("I have no idea why Mr. Connell chose to tell his lovely story in such a choppy manner," the reviewer for *Commonweal,* complained.) Deceived perhaps by the naïveté of the book's heroine, the hyperrealism of its uneventful plot, the aloofness of its narrator, and the understatement of its irony, an even greater number of reviewers failed to recognize just how subversive a portrait Connell had drawn. In praising the novel faintly as "easy reading," the *New York Times* called it "a wistful little book about a suburban wife and mother who goes through all the familiar motions." In a favorable review of *Mr. Bridge,* the companion novel Connell published ten years after *Mrs. Bridge,* the *New Republic* compared the earlier novel to "TV situation comedy." As would become more apparent in retrospect, this "wistful little book" (which is inarguably superior to *Mr. Bridge,* wherein the mosaic form feels inorganic, ill-suited to that novel's protagonist) quietly but witheringly indicts and exposes "the familiar motions" it describes, making visible the moral and spiritual bankruptcy lurking

beneath that most cherished of postwar icons, the nuclear family.

Set before and during World War II, the book nonetheless seems very much the product of the decade during which it was composed, the decade that witnessed the ascendance of the sitcom as well as that other form of televised entertainment, the Joseph McCarthy hearings. Superficially, of course, *Mrs. Bridge* and the 1950s sitcom do share a common subject matter (the American family) as well as certain formal elements (such as the use of semirelated but discrete episodes). These resemblances may help explain why the book sold well despite the novelty of its form. Yet its appeal must also lie in the vast differences between the Bridges and the typical TV family. They are, in a sense, mirror images of each other: *Mrs. Bridge* is a sitcom turned inside out. It is iconoclastic, designed to shatter the hagiographic imagery with which the nuclear family had come to be portrayed not only on television but also in magazine advertisements and political campaigns.

Sexual repression and middle-class malaise afflict many characters in mainstream literary fiction of the time—in the work of J. D. Salinger, for instance, or John Cheever, or Updike, or Roth. Connell's analysis, however, is considerably more political than that of most of his contemporaries. It has been remarked that aside from a few usually Southern exceptions (Flannery O'Connor, say, or William Faulkner), race is largely invisible in fiction by white Americans of the early and mid—twentieth century. Sympathetic portraits of female protagonists by male authors are also comparatively rare. After all, what was there to write about in the life of a housewife that could possibly sustain a prolonged, dramatic narrative? The same reviewer who compared *Mrs. Bridge* to a sitcom praised *Mr. Bridge* as the superior of the two novels. "Most simply," he wrote, "it is better because it is about a man." Not only does *Mrs. Bridge* dramatize the life both inner and outer of an unremarkable woman, it exposes the American housewife, that patron saint of postwar consumerism, as a suicidal prisoner of domesticity rather than its happy beneficiary. Moreover, it brings into relief the apartheid-like racism and quasi-feudalistic class system that most contemporary representations of suburbia—including literary ones—tend to romanticize or erase.

Although it fails to imagine the private lives of its black characters, the book succeeds in drawing attention to this failure, exposing the ways, unconscious and otherwise, that the Bridges misperceive and mistreat people of other races, ethnicities, and classes. It is, in a sense, a novel about whiteness, specifically of the affluent, Anglo-Saxon, Protestant variety (Italians are among the most recurrent objects of Mrs. Bridge's scorn). Connell's central palette of images—the white space between the chapters, Mr. Bridge's long white arm, the white cold cream, the snow falling at the novel's end—metonymically deconstructs the positive connotations that the residents of Mission Hills assume whiteness to carry.

Connell writes in his *CAAS* essay that he has "never forgiven anybody who lied to [him]," and reading his work one does not readily doubt the sincerity of this remark. His forensic brand of realism often seems inspired by a righteous anger against deceptions, delusions, and hypocrisies large and small, personal and collective, especially when they conceal or justify injustices. In *Mrs. Bridge,* when Grace Barron delivers a drunken jeremiad at a cocktail party, denouncing American "ethnocentricism," she is speaking as Connell's mouthpiece. Her indictment contains many of the American policies and atrocities that Connell's nonfiction would later document, including "Custer's deliberate violation of the treaty of eighteen-sixty-eight." "And what about the Seminoles?" she asks.

"They never harmed us but we invaded their swamps and cut them to ribbons." And Mrs. Bridge replies, "It does sound as though we've done some dreadful things, Grace, but isn't it possible that when you investigate fully you'll discover the Seminoles attacked us?" This is precisely the sort of lie, born of willful ignorance, that Connell cannot abide, the sort of lie that Earl Summerfield, the unreliable narrator of *The Diary of a Rapist* (in a sense the true companion novel to *Mrs. Bridge,* its dark antithesis) would rage sardonically against. Grace Barron's audience responds by silencing her, as it were, to death. Over the course of his career, Connell would come to her aid persistently, breaking her fatal silence, submitting for the jury's consideration a voluminous abecedarium of incriminating exhibits.

When, early in his second novel, *The Patriot,* (1960) Connell describes in minute detail the scene of a fatal plane crash, registering how the dead aviation cadet and flight instructor "hang head down from their safety belts" inside the plane's cabin, their hands resting on the cabin's roof, and how, when the cadet's corpse is removed from the cabin, a stream of coins won in a poker game the night before spills from his pockets onto the snow, the cumulative effect is not morbid or sensational but traumatic. Connell's goal is to transform a casualty statistic into a eulogy, to build out of scavenged moments a different sort of war memorial, to disturb his readers and make them—along with his protagonist, Melvin Isaacs, who over the course of the novel evolves from a flag-waving volunteer into a war-resisting artist—begin to wonder. Indeed, "wonder" is the single word that perhaps best characterizes Connell's response to the world. He is a collector of those unlikely artifacts of history and experience—coins spilled from the pockets of a dead cadet—that inspire a mixture of irony, awe, bewilderment, and, frequently, rage. He is a numismatist of ludicrous and luminous details.

TOWARD THE DOCUMENTARY NOVEL

There is another scene in *The Patriot* that contains within it the germ of everything Connell would write for the next forty-two years. Home in Kansas City on furlough, aviation cadet Melvin Isaacs, accompanied by his roommate and his father, visits the site of the Battle of Lexington, a battle in which his great grandfather fought on the side of the Confederates. A mansion on the property has been converted into a museum. For twenty-five cents apiece, the three visitors receive a guided tour from the curator, a woman wearing "an old quilted housecoat" who smells of "vinegar and beer." She points out one by one the traces of the past: a hole in the roof made by a cannonball; the burn marks left on a banister by a hangman's rope; the bloodstains on the varnished boards where those captured Union soldiers who preferred leaping over the upstairs banister to being hanged had landed atop a thicket of upright bayonets. After leaving the museum, Melvin and company visit the ruins of the house where Great-grandfather Isaacs once lived. "There was everywhere the silence of night and decay," Connell writes, yet Melvin

> had the impression that at any moment the crystal chandelier and the great marble mantel might reappear and a fire blaze on the hearth and the rooms fill with ghostly women and Confederate officers, and the vanished spinet would play a minuet while they danced and spoke of General Beauregard.

The Patriot, published in 1960, is Connell's *Portrait of the Artist as a Young Man,* a novel about how its protagonist came to resemble its author. Like Melvin, Connell is oppressed by the "senseless purpose, coursing perfectly as a torpedo and as indifferent to the consequence" that usually motivates human violence. Connell, too, is haunted by the past and has spent his life trying to rescue it from "the silence of night and decay," a phrase one can still hear echoing four decades later in the epigraph to Connell's

chronicle of the Crusades, *Deus Lo Volt!:* "The stream of Time, inexorable, constant," wrote the Byzantine princess Anna Comnena, "removes from our sight all things that are born and carries into the night deeds of little account, deeds worthy of notice."

"Worthy of notice" does not mean worthy of admiration. Connell aspires to see all, the most disturbing expressions of human nature as well as the beautiful and marvelous. The "nebulous goal" of his compulsive noticing, his relentless peregrinations, is similar to Proust's (for good reason the penultimate vignette of *Mrs. Bridge* is titled "Remembrance of Things Past"). The difference between the two authors' respective projects is primarily a matter of dimension: Proust's excavations are deeper; the site of Connell's excavations, far broader. It is humanity's past, and not merely his own, that Connell wishes to recover. His project, like Proust's, has required a new kind of storytelling. Just as he invented the mosaic form of *Mrs. Bridge* as a way to portray more accurately an undramatic life, so has he sought to represent the past with radical fidelity. "I think of this as a book about the Crusades," he remarks on the dust jacket of *Deus Lo Volt!,* "not an 'historical novel'—a term that suggests imaginary experiences and unlikely conversations. ... Every meeting, every conversation, every triumph or defeat, no matter how small, was recorded centuries ago."

Reviewing Susan Sontag's *In America* for the *New Republic* in 2000, the critic James Wood expressed similar misgivings about the historical novel. Such was the pace of historical change in the twentieth century, Wood argued, that historical fiction has increasingly come to resemble "science-fiction facing backwards, with the same crudities of detail." The only hope the historical novelist has of transcending the inherent "awkwardness of the genre," he wrote, is to become "self-conscious about his self-consciousness." Thus Sontag, in the opening chapter of *In America,* convenes her characters in a hotel dining room and wanders among them in the first person, "scattering seeds of prediction." Kevin Baker begins *Dreamland* with a self-conscious casting of the fictional spell: "'I know a story,' said Trick the Dwarf, and the rest of them leaned in close." Thomas Pynchon and his many offspring stage fantastic reenactments that unapologetically resemble "science-fiction facing backwards." William T. Vollmann intentionally archaizes. Robert Coover satirically anachronizes.

Connell's disavowal of "imaginary experiences and unlikely conversations" represents an altogether different solution to Wood's perceived dilemma. Whereas most postmodern historical novelists merrily confabulate the historical record in the service of fiction, Connell—along with, among others, Paul Metcalf, Guy Davenport, and the German writer W. G. Sebald—has in the service of historical detail resisted projecting what Davenport calls "an illusory, fictional world." "The old masks and artifices of conventional fiction ... were worn out ... ," Metcalf has said. "The simple facts of our situation, of our history, were the richest possible lode, begging to be mined." Davenport, Metcalf, and Sebald, like Connell, have created works not easily classified as fiction or nonfiction; they are collages constructed out of found materials— out of, in Davenport's phrase, "a mere handful of doubtful certainties." In a sense they have done for prose what Pound's *Cantos* and William Carlos Williams's *Paterson* did for poetry. Their work fulfills the prophecy made by the poet Charles Olson in 1951 that one direction the novel would take would be toward documentary. Rather than making things up, Olson wrote, the documentary novelist "juxtaposes, correlates, and causes to interact."

Shortly after finishing *Mrs. Bridge* and *The Patriot,* Connell embarked upon his first attempt at turning history into art. The result, an imaginary travelogue titled *Notes from a Bottle Found on the Beach at Carmel,* is his most ambitious experiment in collage. A composite of the great tourists of history (part Marco Polo, part Paracelsus, part Christopher Columbus), Connell's mythic notetaker sails across the oceans of time, accumulating a jumble of textual fragments as chaotic and as intricately patterned as the shards of a kaleidoscope (the analogy is Connell's). "I employ the procedure of Saint Gregory," the speaker says,

> which allows
> for the sake of the moral a juxtaposition of all
>   things,
> no matter how incompatible or contrary.

He quotes from documents (the diary of an ill-fated Viking, the Lord's Prayer in Latin, the cost-benefit analysis of an atomic bomb). He makes apothegmatic pronouncements and poses gnostic questions.

References to apocalyptic events (the bombing of Japan, the bubonic plague, the Inquisition) recur as a leitmotiv, and a basso continuo of postnuclear foreboding runs throughout the poem, as if the bottle containing these notes had been jettisoned from Western civilization's sinking wreck. A decade after *Notes,* incensed by, among other things, the war in Vietnam, Connell published a second prose poem, *Points for a Compass Rose,* a darker, angrier variation on its predecessor. Here the notetaker's anachronistic juxtapositions are more frequently and far more pointedly allegorical; the references to current events, far more numerous; his disappointment in humanity, far more bitter:

> I suggest that nothing exists more pitiable
> or presumptuous than Man. I cite as evidence
> a shipload of pilgrims returning from Mecca
> which was seized and set afire by Christians.

The book, largely a litany of such evidence, earned Connell a National Book Award nomination for poetry but is no longer in print.

The historical and biographical essays that Connell began publishing in the mid-1970s, collected in *A Long Desire* and *The White Lantern* (1980) and in 2001 in a single volume called *The Aztec Treasure House: New and Selected Essays,* are in many respects a continuation of the journey he began in *Notes from a Bottle Found on the Beach at Carmel*. With his two "poems," not only does Connell unearth an encyclopedic quantity of historical treasures, enough to fill many books; he discovers a way of representing history in far greater detail and with far greater fidelity to documents and artifacts than the historical novel allows. If *Notes* is a kaleidoscope, the essays are like stained-glass windows: they recycle many of the details and deeds of which the poems are composed, but with them Connell organizes his material topically into narratives that, though still miscellaneous, are comparatively coherent. And whereas the key signature of the poems is relentlessly dark, the essays show Connell at his most lighthearted. Humor is perhaps the least remarked aspect of his gift:

The title Connell gave his collected essays, *The Aztec Treasure House,* refers to an adventure novel of the same name that, in his boyhood, had been his favorite book. In the title essay Connell says that, after happening upon a copy of it in a San Francisco flea market as an adult, he began to suspect that this absurd romance, about a young American archaeologist known as Don Tomas who luckily inherits a hieroglyphic treasure map from a "mortally wounded cacique," may very well be the source of his obsessive and somewhat mysterious fascination with the ancient Mexican artifacts he passionately collects.

Again and again in his essays, Connell revisits some fable or adventure story, some "magic carpet" (as he quotes from Henry Hart's *Sea Road to the Indies*) that once upon a time had "annihilated time and space, and gilded all with the aura of the golden age of childhood," only to find that the carpet has lost much of its magic: the events are too imaginary, the dia- logue too unlikely, the rendering of historical detail too crude. The artifacts Connell excavates from beneath the many strata of sedimentary legend are invariably more wondrous than the legends themselves. One may interpret that Don Tomas' hieroglyphic map pointed the way to hidden treasure after all: not to imaginary Aztec gold, but to a museum's worth of singular individuals.

Connell's purpose, in his fiction and his nonfiction alike, is as simple and as ambitious as that. "I teach of the human body," Andrev Andraukov says, "and of the human soul."

The great advantage the historical novelist has always had over the historian is omniscience. Edward Gibbon's emperors cannot soliloquize; William Shakespeare's can. While biographers of Christ struggle in vain to resurrect their subject from a historical record riddled with lacunae and occluded by hearsay, the Russian novelist Mikhail Bulgakov shows what the weather was like on the morning of the Crucifixion. Even when the record is comparatively intact, the novelist's advantage pertains: no scholar of the Napoleonic Wars can compete with *War and Peace*.

And yet, for all his fidelity to fact, Connell's ambitions are artistic, not scholarly. By intertwining primary and secondary sources with meticulous description, he creates the illusion of novelistic omniscience. He can read the mind of a Neanderthal. He can tell us how the Antarctic explorer Sir Douglas Mawson felt after eating the head of a husky named Ginger for breakfast one morning in 1912. In *Son of the Morning Star,* an epic work of nonfiction that perhaps more than any other piece of American literature can compete with *War and Peace* (doing for the Plains Wars what Tolstoy's novel did for the Napoleonic ones), Connell assembles a *Guernica*-like mural of the Battle of the Little Bighorn composed from thousands of documents and refracted through hundreds of different, often conflicting points of view. He moves freely through time as well as space, flashing backward and forward but always circling and circling—like the war-hollering Sioux on their ponies—around the mystery of what happened on that Montana hillside where Custer made his stand. He pauses to draw portraits of dozens of figures centrally or tangentially involved in the battle, from General Custer and Sitting Bull all the way down to Captain Myles Keogh's intrepid steed, Comanche, one of the only horses to survive the slaughter of Custer's cavalry. After the death of his attendant, Comanche "grew increasingly morose. No longer did he root through garbage pails, which had been a special privilege and pleasure, and the beer he was issued at the enlisted men's canteen seemed to weaken him, so that he did nothing except lie gloomily in the barn or in a mud wallow." What the nineteenth-century Russian historian Constantine Leontiev said of Tolstoy thus applies equally well to Connell: "In [his] analysis ... there are no limits either in man's temperament, his age, or his sex, nor even in a zoological species, for at times he shows us what the bull felt, what the dog thought, what the horse was imagining."

Selected Bibliography

WORKS OF EVAN S. CONNELL

NOVELS AND SHORT STORIES

The Anatomy Lesson, and Other Stories. New York: Viking, 1957.

Mrs. Bridge: A Novel. New York: Viking, 1959.

The Patriot. New York: Viking, 1960.

At the Crossroads. New York: Simon & Schuster, 1965. (Stories.)

The Diary of a Rapist: A Novel. New York: Simon & Schuster, 1966; Hopewell, N.J.: Ecco, 1995.

Mr. Bridge. New York: Knopf, 1969.

The Connoisseur. New York: Knopf, 1974.

Double Honeymoon. New York: Putnam, 1976.

ESSAYS

A Long Desire. New York: Holt, Rinehart and Winston, 1979.

The White Lantern. New York: Holt, Rinehart and Winston, 1980.

"Evan S. Connell." In *Contemporary Authors Autobiography Series.* Edited by Adele Sarkissian. Vol. 2. Detroit: Gale, 1985. Pp. 97–112.

Mesa Verde. New York: Library Fellows of the Whitney Museum of American Art, 1992. (A limited edition of Connell's essay on the discovery and exploration of Mesa Verde, illustrated with a watercolor and etching by Robert Therrien.)

DOCUMENTARY NARRATIVES

Notes from a Bottle Found on the Beach at Carmel. New York: Viking, 1962. (Poem; novel; nonfiction. This title and others in this section may belong to more than one genre; they are identified in parentheses following each entry, with the customary classification listed first.)

Points for a Compass Rose. New York: Knopf, 1973. (Poem; novel; nonfiction.)

Son of the Morning Star: Custer and the Little Bighorn. San Francisco: North Point, 1984. (Nonfiction; novel.)

The Alchymist's Journal. San Francisco: North Point, 1991. (Novel; nonfiction.)

Deus Lo Volt! Chronicle of the Crusades. Washington, D.C.: Counterpoint, 2000. (Novel; nonfiction.)

Francisco Goya: A Life. New York: Counterpoint, 2004.

COLLECTED WORKS

Saint Augustine's Pigeon: The Selected Stories of Evan S. Connell. Edited by Gus Blaisdell. San Francisco: North Point, 1980.

The Collected Stories of Evan S. Connell. Washington, D.C.: Counterpoint, 1995.

The Aztec Treasure House: New and Selected Essays. Washington, D.C.: Counterpoint, 2001.

OTHER WORKS

Stoll, Jerry. *I Am a Lover.* With comment from various sources selected by Evan S. Connell Jr. Sausalito, Calif.: Angel Island, 1961. (Photographs with captions.)

Leonard, Joanne. *Woman by Three.* Photographs by Joanne Leonard, Michael E. Bry, and Barbara Cannon Myers. Prose and poetry selected by Evan S. Connell Jr. Menlo Park, Calif.: Pacific Coast, 1969.

FILMS BASED ON THE WORKS OF EVAN S. CONNELL

Mr. and Mrs. Bridge. Screenplay by Ruth Prawler Jhabvala. Directed by James Ivory. Cineplex Odeon/Merchant-Ivory/Miramax, 1990.

Son of the Morning Star. Teleplay by Melissa Mathison. Directed by Mike Robe. Republic Television, 1991.

INTERVIEWS

Holt, Patricia. "Evan S. Connell." *Publishers Weekly,* November 20, 1981, pp. 12–13.

Myers, Edward. "Notes from a Bottle Found on the Beach at Sausalito: An Interview with Evan S. Connell." *Literary Review* 35, no. 1:60–69 (fall 1991).

Tooker, Dan, and Roger Hofheins. "Evan S. Connell, Jr." In *Fiction!: Interviews with Northern California Novelists.* New York: Harcourt Brace Jovanovich/W. Kaufmann, 1976. Pp. 54–69.

MANUSCRIPTS AND PAPERS

The Evan Connell papers held at the Howard Gotlieb Archival Research Center at Boston University contain a hand-corrected, typewritten manuscript of *Notes from a Bottle Found on the Beach at Carmel* and correspondence related to *Contact* magazine, on the editorial staff of which Connell served in the early 1960s.

CRITICAL AND BIOGRAPHICAL STUDIES

Baker, Kevin. *Dreamland.* New York: HarperCollins, 1999.

Baxter, Charles. *Burning Down the House: Essays on Fiction.* Saint Paul, Minn.: Graywolf, 1997.

Bawer, Bruce. "The Luther of Science?" *New Criterion* 9, no. 10:30–35 (June 1991). (A helpful, though negative critique of *The Alchymist's Journal.*)

Blaisdell, Gus. "After Ground Zero: The Writings of Evan S. Connell, Jr." *New Mexico Quarterly* 36, no. 2:181–207 (summer 1966). (The best critical study of the early works, with an emphasis on Connell's postatomic mysticism and his relation to Saint Augustine.)

Bottoms, Greg. "Evan S. Connell." *Salon* (http://dir.salon.com/people/bc/2000/07/18/connell/index.html), July 18, 2000.

Crowther, Florence. "Stranded Matriarch." *New York Times Book Review,* February 1, 1959, pp. 30–31. (Review of *Mrs. Bridge;* cited in *Contemporary Literary Criticism.* Volume 45. Detroit: Gale, 1987. Pp. 106–118.)

Davenport, Guy. "Ernst Machs Max Ernst." In his *The Geography of the Imagination: Forty Essays.* San Francisco: North Point, 1981; New York: Pantheon, 1992. Pp. 373–384.

Dillard, Annie. "Winter Melons." *Harper's Magazine,* January 1974, pp. 87–90. (An eloquent and ecstatic review of *Notes from a Bottle Found on the Beach at Carmel* and *Points for a Compass Rose.*)

Gutwillig, Robert. "Ruthless Selection." *Commonweal* 69, no. 20:525–526 (February 13, 1959). (Review of *Mrs. Bridge;* cited in *Contemporary Literary Criticism.* Volume 45. Detroit: Gale, 1987. Pp. 106–118.)

Hardwick, Elizabeth. *Seduction and Betrayal: Women and Literature.* New York: Random House, 1974.

Hass, Robert. "Images." In his *Twentieth Century Pleasures: Prose on Poetry.* New York: Ecco, 1984. Pp. 269–308.

Hoagland, Edward. "Far Away from Home." *New York Times Book Review,* June 24, 1979, pp. 12, 37. (Review of *A Long Desire;* cited in *Contemporary Literary Criticism.* Volume 45. Detroit: Gale, 1987. Pp. 106–118.)

Hohn, Donovan. "Anatomy Lessons: Evan S. Connell and the Documentary School." *Harper's Magazine,* December 2001, pp. 79–83. (Review of *The Aztec Treasure House.*)

Joyce, James. "Epiphanies." In *Literature: An Introduction to Fiction, Poetry, and Drama.* Edited by X. J. Kennedy and Dana Gioia. 6th ed. New York: HarperCollins, 1995. P. 574.

Leontiev, Constantine. "The Greatness and Universality of *War and Peace.*" In *War and Peace: The*

Maude Translation, Backgrounds and Sources, Criticism, by Leo Tolstoy. Edited by George Gibian. New York: Norton, 1996. Pp. 1,109–1,110.

O'Brien, John. "Interview with Paul Metcalf." Center for Book Culture.(http://www.centerfor bookculture.org/interviews/interview_metcalf .html).

Pound, Ezra. "Vortex." In *Poems for the Millennium: The University of California Book of Modern and Postmodern Poetry.* Edited by Jerome Rothenberg and Pierre Joris. Vol. 1. Berkeley: University of California Press, 1995. Pp. 527–528.

Samuels, Charles Thomas. "Dead Center." *New Republic,* June 7, 1969, pp. 21–23. (Review of *Mr. Bridge;* cited in *Contemporary Literary Criticism.* Volume 45. Detroit: Gale, 1987. Pp. 106–118.)

Sawyer-Lauçanno, Christopher. "The Paris Review." In his *The Continual Pilgrimage: American Writers in Paris, 1944–1960.* New York: Grove, 1992. Pp. 145–161. (Provides context for Connell's time in Paris.)

Schine, Cathleen. "Going His Own Way in Santa Fe." *Newsday,* April 21, 1991, entertainment section, part 2, pp. 22–23.

Shapiro, Gerald. "Evan S. Connell: A Profile." *Ploughshares* 13, nos. 2–3:11–25 (fall 1987).

Siegel, Barry. "The Iconoclastic Mr. Connell." *Los Angeles Times Magazine,* June 9, 1991, pp. 24–27, 38.

Wood, James. "The Palpable Past-Intimate." *New Republic,* March 27, 2000, pp. 29–33. (Review of *In America* by Susan Sontag.)

—DONOVAN HOHN

Joseph Epstein

1937–

BEST KNOWN AS the editor of the *American Scholar* from 1975 until 1997 and as an accomplished writer of literary criticism, short stories, and perhaps most of all, personal or "familiar" essays, Joseph Epstein is a self-described "language snob," someone who believes that people should use words with clarity and precision but often do not. Epstein is not shy about taking the sloppy, vague, or just plain jargon-riddled to task. Add a wide conservative streak (which includes everything from his taste in music and literature to clothing and politics), and the result is often a curmudgeon of the first water.

Epstein's attacks on feminism have not endeared him to those who regard patriarchal hegemony as a force to be continually reckoned with. Moreover, many contemporary authors would prefer that Epstein not point out how tedious and inconsequential their books in fact are. He worries about political correctness and what he regards as an unsavory focus on postmodernist "theory," but the truth is that Epstein's crankiness casts a wide net. He is an equal opportunity scold, taking on nearly every aspect of the culture that strikes him as having gone sour since (at least) the mid-1960s. As a deliciously self-deprecating paragraph from *With My Trousers Rolled* (1995) puts it:

> I believe I began to feel out of it roughly in 1966. Around that time the curtain fell, dividing the country between the young and the not-so-young, and I found myself, even though only twenty-nine, on the not-young side of that curtain. The student revolution had begun, and I—in taste, temperament, in point of view—had *ancien régime* so clearly written all over me I might as well have worn a powdered wig.

Epstein protests a bit too much about his late membership in the ancien régime, but his playful, half-ironic tone makes an important point. He in fact wears $60 bow ties rather than a powdered wig, but the effect is nearly the same given a culture where every day seems to be "dress-down day."

Taken together, Epstein's essays make it clear he enjoys traveling against the cultural grain, not only because playing the naysayer gives his essays an in-your-face, edgy flavor but also because being a persuasive tastemaker is what literary-cultural critics at their best do. Some would argue that Epstein preaches to the already converted and that his iconoclastic posture, however much drenched in wit and learning, produces more exasperation than agreement. He would not be surprised to learn that some readers give up midway through one of his harangues on what he regards as bad taste and throw the magazine across the room; neither would he particularly care. He writes, as he once put it in an interview, for himself "and for strangers who might happen to share my interests." Over some forty years at the writing desk, a significant number of these "strangers" have discovered that Epstein is singing their tune and that he has put into carefully chiseled words precisely what they had in fact been thinking for some time.

EARLY LIFE

Joseph Epstein was born in Chicago on January 9, 1937, the son of Maurice and Barbara

(Abrams) Epstein. Chicago, along with its suburb Evanston, Illinois, is Epstein's familiar stamping ground, and while he may do stints of travel to give lectures, he has always returned to his roots, never sorry, he insists, that he did not land a teaching job in the Ivies. Evanston is, to use Epstein's word, "convenient": within a few blocks of his home are a first-rate library, good restaurants and bookstores, and his long-time barber. As the song lyric would have it, "Who could ask for anything more?" Certainly not Epstein, who first hit on the idea of becoming a serious intellectual when he was an undergraduate at the University of Chicago (A.B., 1959) and who devoted the years after graduation to teaching, lecturing, editing, and writing as precisely that—a serious intellectual.

Epstein was born in the cultural equivalent of a log cabin. In the opening pages of *Snobbery: The American Version* (2002), he describes his family history this way:

> Neither of my parents went to college. My father, growing up in Canada, in fact never finished high school; my mother took what was then known as "the commercial course" at John Marshall (public) High School in Chicago. They were both Jewish, but, against the positive stereotype of Jews loving culture and things of the mind, my parents had almost no cultural interests apart from occasionally going to musical comedies or, in later years, watching the Boston Pops on television. Magazines—*Life, Look,* later *Time*—and local newspapers came into our apartment, but no books. I don't recall our owning an English dictionary, though both my parents were well spoken, always grammatical and jargon-free.

Epstein's father was a salesman who, unlike the tragic figure of Arthur Miller's Willie Loman, managed to prosper. *Death of a Salesman* may be widely regarded as one of the triumphs of the American stage but not so far as Epstein is concerned. No doubt part of his animus can be chalked up to Miller's leftist stances over the years, but a larger part probably has to do with Epstein's fond memories of a father who

worked hard in America and who succeeded. True, Maurice Epstein did not care a whit for the niceties that so energized his son, and true, there was not a hint of snobbery in his bones, but what pleased him above all else was the fact that he supported his family and that, in his later years, they were well provided for. His unstinting financial support made it possible for the college-age Joseph to ruminate about the Good, the True, and the Beautiful.

As for Epstein's mother, she was no snob either, although she "had a greater awareness" of its power to hurt: "She was on the alert for snobberies used against her," Epstein remembers, "and could be vulnerable to them":

> In her friendships she sought out women who were goodhearted, for she was goodhearted and generous herself. She also had an unashamed taste for what, by her standard, passed for *luxe,* which meant driving big cars (Cadillacs), owning lavish furniture, dressing well (furs, expensive dresses, Italian shoes, jewelry). She was made a bit nervous by people who had more money than she, and tended to arrange her social life among people who were her financial equals or inferiors. But [and this is really the point] I never saw my mother—or father—commit a single socially mean act.

Given such a lineage, how did Epstein become such a self-admitted snob? *Snobbery: the American Version,* his book-length rumination on the subject, gives us clues. In Europe, status is largely determined by what one does or does not inherit at birth: an aristocratic title, a 400-year-old family mansion, the certainty of an Oxbridge education. In America, an individual's talent and ambition are what counts, and status is determined by what side of town you live on, what brand of automobile you drive, and where your children were accepted to college.

Epstein is, by contrast, a culture snob, a temperament he acquired as an undergraduate at the University of Chicago. There he acquired the habit of serious reading, and after graduation he was sufficiently equipped to make his way into the world of letters. After a short stint in the peacetime army, he worked at "a low-paying job on a political magazine in New York City" but soon returned to Chicago where, during the mid-1960s and early 1970s, he served as a senior editor for *Encyclopaedia Britannica* and then became an editor at Quadrangle Books. This editorial experience, combined with the attention that his occasional pieces in *Dissent* and *Commentary* brought him, helped him to land his first regular (and as it turned out, longtime) job as editor of the *American Scholar,* the quarterly journal of the Phi Beta Kappa Society.

Lest anyone unduly romanticize the knock-about years between college graduation and his mid-thirties, Epstein provides the following disclaimer in an autobiographical essay published in *Commentary* (February 2003) titled "Goodbye, Mr. Chipstein":

> After holding a number of mid-grade editorial and government jobs I had begun writing as a freelance, a phrase the reality behind which comes nowhere near matching the dash and romance it seems to suggest. … I had never held a position for more than four years, and did not so much plan my new jobs as flee my old ones.

As a thirty-six-year-old, Epstein could accurately have been described a rolling stone. This condition changed radically in the next few years, as he became the editor of a prestigious journal, a college professor, and an increasingly versatile writer. He made himself equally at home with the familiar essay—a form he so perfected that many critics came to regard him as its foremost practitioner—and with literary criticism, providing what many regarded as much-needed correctives (and sound sense) at a time when the reputations of many contemporary writers were overinflated. He also has written book-length studies on aspects of American sociology and even has tried his hand at the short story. Epstein is a prolific writer, and his four decades at the writing desk have made his

no-nonsense, sometimes crusty voice a part of our literary landscape.

BEGINNINGS AND THE BIRTH OF ARISTIDES

One of the places Epstein published his work during his early thirties was *Dissent,* the political magazine edited by Irving Howe. Epstein then numbered himself (loosely) as a man of the Left, and in that frame of mind he contributed an important essay titled "The New Conservatives: Intellectuals in Retreat" (reprinted in Lewis A. Coser and Irving Howe, eds., *The New Conservatives,* 1974). Within a few years Epstein would himself join the "retreat" he talked about, and while he remained more focused on literature than on partisan politics, he was rightly numbered among the neoconservative critics (also including Kenneth S. Lynn and Norman Podhoretz) that Mark Royden Winchell assembled in his 1991 study *Neoconservative Criticism.*

Winchell describes how Epstein, speaking before a well-heeled group at the swank San Diego City Club, quickly donned his characteristically self-deprecating mask: Here I am, Winchell records him as saying, "again speaking to the rich." The habit of hobnobbing with the wealthy would continue, often with Epstein pointing out which luminaries swelled the crowd and how grand (or ungrand) the dinner laid before them was. *Snobbery* provided Epstein with a chance to graze through manifestations of taste and how they insure, or nearly insure, superiority. Mostly, however, he slowly drifted toward the neoconservative Right because he was more comfortable there, and because he could no longer take America and its culture to task with the zeal required of those on the Left.

Irving Howe, while remaining a democratic socialist until his death in 1990, would have agreed with Epstein's general assessment of America, although he would no doubt quickly point out how socialized medicine, for example, would much improve the quality of life in America for its poorer citizens. Epstein generally has shied away from such discussions, preferring to cast his gaze at the culture's flotsam and jetsam, especially if he turns the ostensible subject at hand back to himself. In much the way that James Thurber, in *The Thurber Carnival* (1945), insists that humorists talk about large matters "smally" and about small matters "largely," Epstein's familiar essays are meant to be savored by the reader who has just curled up in an oversized armchair after enjoying a fine meal. If it is true that Epstein often writes from the perspective of a man nearly overwhelmed by the shallow culture swirling everywhere around him, it is not true that he is, finally, a version of Thurber's little man. Instead Epstein's harrumphy persona fights back using humor as much as a weapon as a shield. Even when he still thought of himself as a leftist in good standing, Epstein liked nothing better than to swap jokes with people who had good ones to share and who knew how to tell them.

No doubt part of the reason that Epstein was attracted to Howe had to do with Howe's familiarity with Yiddish culture and the way that humor is incorporated into the very fabric of its language. In the early 1970s, Howe, completing work on what would soon become *World of Our Fathers,* his encyclopedic study of Jewish immigrants on New York City's Lower East Side, came out to give a talk at Northwestern University in Evanston and stopped by to spend an afternoon with Epstein. Over drinks and literary chitchat, Howe suggested that a teaching career might not be a bad idea for Epstein. It would at the very least relieve him from writing under the gun of financial realities; moreover, Howe, once skeptical about academic life, had found it surprisingly pleasant. As Epstein remembers it, "He offered to do what he could," and in short order

Epstein was invited to the campus to deliver a lecture of his own. (He chose "The Man of Letters" as his topic.) The "audition" (Epstein's word) went well enough for him to be hired as a lecturer for the 1973–1974 academic year.

Epstein's run of good luck continued during the following year when he became editor of *American Scholar.* Each issue of *American Scholar* published during his editorship included a familiar essay written under the pseudonym of Aristides. Over his twenty-one years at the journal, Epstein wrote dozens of essays, hundreds of thousands of words (he puts the total at a whopping 600,000), and filled six book-length collections. If Aristides proved to be very good for Epstein's career, he was possibly even better for Epstein's readers, who looked forward to each new installment of what his lovable crank and mouthpiece had to say.

Historians of the ancient world tell us that Aristides (530–468 B.C.E.) was so esteemed as an example of probity in public life that he came to be known as "Aristides the Just." Given the huge volume of words that Epstein has written using the pseudonym, he makes the witty point that the man should now be known as "Aristides the Loquacious." But if Aristides turned out to be more talkative than just, at least he was never a "gasbag," which is how Epstein once described Ralph Waldo Emerson, whose essay "The American Scholar" is not only required reading in American high schools and colleges but also provided the title for the journal Epstein edited until the board of the Phi Beta Kappa Society fired him in 1996. In Aristides' last appearance in the journal's pages, he—and Epstein—took no small delight in saying just how dreary and repetitive Emerson's paragraphs had always struck "them."

Readers who had followed Aristides over the years were hardly surprised by his irreverence. In the essay "Life and Letters," his 1975 debut as Aristides, Epstein went immediately for the cultural jugular: "The most important influence of that assemblage of 1960s youth and its camp followers," Epstein/Aristides argues, "was not on politics, or philosophy, or art, or social organization, but on retailing." That said, the essay goes on to provide readers with a catalog that might have been the envy of Walt Whitman:

> Candle shops, leather-goods shops, organic food shops, macramé shops, needlepoint shops, handcrafted jewelry and dress shops have brought the commune into the home, or, more precisely, into the neighborhood. If one lives anywhere in any of the middle-to upper-middle-class neighborhoods in this country nowadays, one lives in Boutique America.

Having thus announced his counter-countercultural position, Epstein went on to write dozens of personal essays that invariably produced nods of agreement for their wisdom as well as smiles of recognition for their wit. Aristides had a long run, moving on, as Epstein himself did, in 1997.

What remains now that Aristides has been put out to pasture are the essays, most of which have been collected between hard covers. In the guise of Aristides, Epstein speaks to those who have the sinking feeling that things in general are sinking and to those increasingly exasperated by coinages ending in "ize." For those who harbor the deep suspicion that what "was" seems better, richer, and certainly more interesting than what "is," those who recognize the allusion to a poem by T. S. Eliot in an Epstein title such as *With My Trousers Rolled,* and most especially those who want to reach for a pistol when the words "popular culture" are uttered, Epstein's familiar essays tend to look very familiar indeed.

Epstein is a consummate stylist, but he is more than a writer's writer, however much the praise of people who care about the shape and ring of sentences must matter to him. There is a considerable market these days for the finely wrought familiar essay, that peculiar species of writing in which personal rumination grazes leisurely in the pastures of learning. As Epstein describes the phenomenon in his introduction to *The Norton Book of Personal Essays* (1997), the form allows for all manner of discovery and shaping. He goes on to argue that its subject is finally the self, the I, and that the burden of the good familiar essay is to convey the illusion that equal measures of candor and erudition can be hauled out as effortlessly as a pocket watch. Familiar essayists never let you see them sweat. The master of the genre, as well as its inventor, was Michel de Montaigne (1533–1592), and Epstein makes no secret about the French master's abiding influence.

At the same time, however, Epstein is clearly his own man. For example, he takes a measure of pride in being "out of it" at a time when being "in" is seen as everything, and given the joy he takes in pulling down pretentiousness he is hardly at a loss for fit targets, including academic radicals, solemn, tone-deaf theorists, and assorted cultural gurus. Epstein scours each and all with just the right mixture of condescension and playfulness, highbrow throw-offs and uncompromising common sense. If the world is divided among those men who pull their gray, thinning hair into tight pony tails, those who think about it but probably won't, and those who find the whole idea simultaneously ridiculous and appalling, Epstein clearly numbers himself in the last camp.

Yet, as personal as he seems to be in his pages, the truth is that Epstein jealously guards many aspects of his privacy. The illusion that he is a writer who confesses everything about himself is finally an illusion. He is decidedly not part of the boom in confessional writing that zeroes in on every detail, every peccadillo of one's sexual history. Epstein is in fact as far from the new school of confessional (*moi*) nonfiction as one could imagine. No doubt much of the reticence can be chalked up to taste, but one suspects the matter goes much deeper. Epstein worries about wallowing. We no longer live what Henry David Thoreau once described as "lives of quiet desperation"; rather, we shamelessly (and noisily) unpack our woes to anyone who will listen to them—not only to colleagues or fellow office workers but also to AM radio talk-show hosts and the ever-growing band of afternoon TV pseudo-therapists. Epstein, rightly, wants none of that.

FAMILIAR TERRITORY

Familiar Territory: Observations on American Life (1979) is composed of fourteen essays that originally appeared in *American Scholar.* As would be the case for subsequent Aristides essays, Epstein largely shied away from the polemical, preferring to write personal essays for his own magazine. This may or may not have been a conscious decision, but it is certainly true that when he wanted to address overtly political subjects he did so in the pages of magazines such as *Hudson Review* or, more typically, *Commentary.* In these venues Epstein could fly his neoconservative colors without compromising what he saw as the central mission of *American Scholar:* to print the most intelligent and most engagingly written essays on a wide variety of topics. As it turned out, Epstein's critics did not give a fig for niceties and felt that he had shut out certain radical opinion, be it postmodernist thought in general or feminist thinking in particular.

Nonetheless, the essays in *Familiar Territory* made good on the "familiar" part. Epstein has an eye and an ear for the quirks in American custom and language. Benjamin DeMott, writing in the *New York Times Book Review,* singled out Epstein for his flair in "apposite quotation and allusion" and went on to talk about how this confuses some readers. The rub, apparently, is that they do not get what lies just beneath the veneer: "the intention," DeMott argued, "is always humorous," even if "the reader hungers

for a stronger note, less affected and more self-respecting." What such readers miss, however, are the moments when Epstein drops the masks and makes it clear that he is, in DeMott's words, "a critic with real force of mind."

THE MIDDLE OF MY TETHER

One way to describe Epstein's familiar essays is to say that they are playfully serious or seriously playful. Among the topics he covers in this collection are book dedications, clichés, sending and receiving letters, and a wide range of childhood memories. As with *Familiar Territory,* all the pieces appeared originally in *American Scholar* and all of them fall squarely into the "personal essay" category. As Anatole Broyard pointed out in the *New York Times,* "Epstein looks closely at the very things most of us hardly notice," but after we share his vision of the small and often quirky, these unnoticed things become fully ours.

At the same time, however, there are signs in *The Middle of My Tether: Familiar Essays* (1983) that Aristides/Epstein is not always a jovial humorist. Mark Royden Winchell puts it this way:

> On occasion, even the genial Aristedes can, like the mild-mannered Clark Kent, jump into a phone booth and don his crimefighter's apparel. ... [In *The Middle of My Tether*] Epstein does precisely that in order to level the charge of vulgarity against American culture. In a neoconservative twist on those insipid "happiness is ... " cartoons, Epstein tells us that vulgarity is publicity, the Oscar awards, the Aspen Institute for Humanistic Studies, talk shows, Pulitzer Prizes, Barbara Walters, interviews with writers, Lauren Bacall, dialogue as an ideal, and (you guessed it) psychology.

At this point, Epstein's personal essays and his cultural criticism become nearly indistinguishable. One form nourishes the other as he continues to take a measure of the world around him. Much of what he sees strikes him as "vulgar," and increasingly, as worse than vulgar. This is particularly true when he realizes how out of touch he is with academic trendsetters and, conversely, how out of touch they are with the America outside classroom windows.

ONCE MORE AROUND THE BLOCK AND *A LINE OUT FOR A WALK*

More than any other Epstein collection, *Once More around the Block: Familiar Essays* (1987) pays full attention to just how deep his language snobbery runs. He will gently correct an amateur's gaffes, but the gloves come off with regard to anyone who "lives off language without caring about it." This includes writers, politicians, teachers, journalists, and others who supply him with a seemingly endless supply of fodder. Take, for example, President Jimmy Carter's famous prayer, "Let me live my life so that it will be meaningful." Epstein cannot resist asking, "Whatever can Carter have meant by meaningful? Hitler was meaningful, so was Gandhi, and Attila the Hun, and Jesus Christ, and Josef Stalin, and Saint Francis of Assisi. What Carter means only God knows, but since he is using the word in a prayer, perhaps that is sufficient." There is no end to Epstein's language peeves (e.g., people who say that things drive them "off the wall" drive Epstein, correctly, "*up* the wall"). Even famous writers come in for a scolding: "More recently … I discovered T. S. Eliot—T. S. Bloody Eliot, for God's sake, misusing *presently* to mean 'now' or 'currently.' … Believe me, I don't enjoy feeling superior to Shakespeare, Burke, and Eliot, yet what is a man of serious standards to do?" A man with Epstein's fixation on "serious standards" is likely to be a lonely fellow, which makes even more interesting the account of how, as an unsure adolescent, he craved popularity: "Since I was neither a first-rate athlete, nor a notably

successful Lothario, nor even a half-serious student," Epstein tells us, "all that was left on the buffet of roles for me to choose from was Good Guy—and I went for it in a big way." He collected friends as one might exotic stamps, and while he continues to value certain adult friendships, he has gained enough self-confidence not to care if he expresses an opinion that makes eyeballs roll.

A Line Out for a Walk: Familiar Essays (1991) focuses in large measure on his boyhood days in Chicago and compares a richer, more humane "then" with the lowered standards and general vulgarity of "now." Put so baldly, one might imagine that Epstein's essays would be doomed to repetition, but they are not, partly because they never sink into cliché and partly because his supply of fresh examples is so large. For a young man who seems on the whole to be nondescript—especially for those looking for a rebel with, or without, a cause—and an adult writer fully aware of what restrictions and responsibilities rightly come with the territory of adulthood, Epstein proves to be more interesting, and certainly more engaging, than one might think possible at first glance. His social conservatism arrives on the page with a wink and armed with a good, usually humorous story. Best of all, Epstein knows how to turn himself into the butt of a joke.

BEGINNING OF THE END FOR ARISTIDES

Epstein did not want his forced departure from the *American Scholar* to become a cause célèbre, much less an occasion for talk about his martyrdom. He went more or less "quietly," although he left certain clues about why his days at *American Scholar* were numbered after the publication of an incendiary article he wrote for the spring 1991 issue of the *Hudson Review* titled "The Academic Zoo: Theory—in Practice." In it, Epstein provided a stinging, no-holds-barred account of how many English departments, including the one he taught in at Northwestern, had abandoned their former mission of teaching literature in order to pursue what Epstein regarded as the highly dubious and often just plain daffy:

> Beginning in the 1970s a much more radical program [of literary criticism] emerged. It was more radical in two distinct senses: first, it tended to be much more openly political than other programmatic attempts to alter the teaching and professional study of literature; and, second, its methods were a direct challenge not alone to literary criticism but to literature itself. Whereas other, earlier disputes within literature departments [e.g., the New Criticism vs. literary historians] were about methodologies, about how literature could most profitably be studied, what was now being proposed was the quite original notion that literature was itself inherently false, corrupt, in need of destruction. I say "destruction," but the official word was of course "deconstruction," which as Alvin Kernan, in *The Death of Literature,* notes has been "the covering term increasingly used for the broad range of literary criticism that discredited the old literature ... and charged it with having been mystifying, illogical, and harmful rather than beneficial."

Feminist literary criticism earned his relentless bashing because Epstein saw it as an especially pernicious threat to everything he held dear:

> Perhaps the first significant bookish evidence of the new impulse to degrade literature came in 1970, with the publication of Kate Millet's *Sexual Politics,* which revealed that certain writers—Norman Mailer and Henry Miller prominent among them—did not treat women very kindly in their novels. What came to be known as "gender studies" were on their way, and would get goofier and goofier with the passage of time, though, doubtless my view of the matter is, as the academic feminists would put it, "phallocentric."

Epstein used his sharp wit to ridicule the ways in which literary discussion had become both reductive and dreary: "gender, class, and race / gender, class, and race / stop your blubbering and wash your face" went the mantra Epstein whispered to himself—and then consigned to print—as he watched political correctness bully any dissenter into silence. People in English departments, Epstein pointed out, "walk about in a state of high cussedness—ticked, as the kids say, to the max—ready at all times to be offended":

> The least miscue and they book you for sexism, racism, homophobia, sexual harassment. Heaven forfend you should refer to a department *chairman* rather than to the neutral and sillily elliptical *chair,* or say "Negro" (instead of black or African-American or whatever is the O.K. nomenclature of the week), or enunciate an unacceptable political opinion—and you are done for, morally cashiered, banished forever from the land of the enlightened and virtuous.

Not surprisingly, Epstein became a pariah in Northwestern's English department precisely because he expressed—in print—these opinions. As he remembers those days in his adieu to academe "Goodbye, Mr. Chipstein," the *Hudson Review* article, along with one he wrote for *Commentary* (September 1986) about what he regarded as an abuse of academic freedom, made him deep, lifelong enemies at Northwestern. His exasperated colleagues "averted their eyes when I walked past them in the hallway." No doubt a person less sure of himself would have cracked under the silent treatment doled out for years. But not Epstein. If he did not get invited to certain parties in Evanston, no matter. His real life, he insisted, "was elsewhere."

"Elsewhere" was in large measure defined by *American Scholar.* As its editor Epstein enjoyed the company of the best minds writing about science, politics, and culture. But his critiques of feminism in general and feminist literary criticism in particular were so unyielding that pressure began to mount for Epstein to be replaced at the helm of *American Scholar.* As those who lobbied against him pointed out, there was no shortage of evidence that he was a woman-basher: in the infamous *Hudson Review* article he had retold a joke in which a couple whose West Side apartment had been twice robbed quarrel about the best way to protect themselves. The husband wants to get a revolver; the wife wants to get a pit bull. So, Epstein wrote in "Academic Zoo," "they agree to compromise and instead get a feminist." Feminists did not find the joke either funny or appropriate, coming as it did from the editor of Phi Beta Kappa's journal—and things did not get markedly better as the paragraph rolled along and pilloried one of literary feminism's leading lights: "attacking conservatives, Catherine R. Stimpson, who is dean of the graduate school at Rutgers, says that 'under the guise of defending objectivity and intellectual rigor, which is a lot of mishmash, they [conservatives] are trying to preserve the cultural and political supremacy of white heterosexual males.' This not from a member of Dykes on Bikes but, you understand, from the woman who is the outgoing president of the Modern Language Association. So many loony tunes, so few merry melodies."

Even Joyce Carol Oates, better known as a fiction writer than as a political animal, called for Epstein's ouster—and she was hardly alone. As the composition of the Phi Beta Kappa Society board gradually changed over the next few years, it became harder and harder to argue, as many Epstein supporters did, that excellence alone ought to determine the journal's content. Those of a mind to have Epstein replaced insisted that he was not open-minded enough to be inclusive.

For years, many had regarded Epstein as courageous for taking strong, often unpopular positions, and when the editorial rug was yanked from beneath his feet, the word "martyr" began to be bandied about. Epstein, however, would have none of it—not when he first wrote the following words in "Knocking on Three, Winston," and not when he was *American Scholar*'s former editor:

> Whenever I have been cited for courage, it has been only for expressing forthright opinions on mildly controversial intellectual matters. The first thing to be said about this is that these matters never seemed all that controversial to me—they seemed, in fact, rather commonsensical—or I should not have been able to be so jollily forthright about them. The second thing to be said is that expressing any opinion in our country doesn't really require anything like courage; in the Soviet Union, in Nazi Germany, in China, saying what one thinks has been to court death. The only penalty one pays here is to be excluded from certain parties, which, to someone who prefers to stay home anyhow, is no penalty whatsoever. Speaking your mind in America is not my idea of courage and nowhere near my idea of heroism.

Epstein's voluntary retirement from Northwestern's English department in 2002 may have lacked the drama of his forced departure from *American Scholar*, but it still provided an occasion for him to reiterate his belief that words should be used precisely. As he told students during the last class meeting of his justly famous Fundamentals of Prose Style course, if they wanted their final essays returned, "they would have to leave an envelope with their address on it in my departmental mailbox. 'And I'm not talking about a self-addressed envelope either,' I said, 'for we all know, surely, that an envelop cannot address itself'" ("Goodbye Mr. Chipstein").

Thus Epstein ended his teaching career—not with a whimper and certainly not with a bang, but rather with something that to him "seemed entirely appropriate": a "small puff of pedantry." The word "pedantry" is quite consciously chosen here, for Epstein has always been well aware that he lacks a Ph.D. and therefore writes about literature as an amateur—albeit an enthusiastic and well-read one.

A SENSE OF ADVANCING AGE

As Epstein wistfully puts it in his author's note to *Narcissus Leaves the Pool: Familiar Essays* (1999) with this collection he began to see "an autobiography of sorts" and a "progression implicit" in his choice of earlier titles. He has no choice but to admit—and to admit as only his dry wit will have it—that he is growing old: "The time has come," Epstein writes, "for an end to preening, to thinking oneself still youthful, to regarding the future as endlessly expandable." Worse, he needs to get "serious"—as if he had not been, at bottom, a serious character for decades. Then and now, however, Epstein cannot resist the well-aimed quip or dry double entendre. If he, like all mortals, is destined to leave life's stage, he means to exit laughing. Here, for example, is how Epstein imagines his response to learning that his body has had it with the present occupant and that this is, as he puts it, the *ball game:*

> From my physician's office, I shall betake myself to an ice cream shop for a banana split, after which I shall stop off for a large packet of a candy I have always been partial to known as Spearmint Leaves. I may pick up a pack of cigarettes. A restaurant known as Chicago Joe's, a steak joint with a specialty in cheesecake and key lime pie, will, in the time remaining, get to see a lot of me. I shall cease flossing.

Epstein clearly enjoys playing the joker, although he is smart enough to know that the joke will in the final analysis be on him. At one point in the collection's title essay he takes a good deal of pleasure in quoting a passage from Henry James about the American businessman because he has never had to be one of those poor fellows:

> In an essay with the very Jamesian title "The Question of the Possibilities," [James] refers to the American businessman of his day as "seamed all over with the scars of the marketplace." I think

often about how lucky I am to have been spared such scars, both metaphorical and real, of the marketplace and of the medical office. I suppose the chief scar of our day is that left by heart surgery, the from simple to quintuple bypass. Lifesaving though this operation has proved to be, I am pleased to have avoided it and want ardently to depart the planet without its particular rococo medical tattoo. Hence my blasted careful diet.

A handful of essays later we learn that Epstein has joined the "zipper club"—those who sport a long scar down their sternums—despite his fastidious diet and overall sense that clogged arteries happen to people who richly deserve them. In "Taking the Bypass," Epstein reports on his own encounter with the surgeon's knife and how it confirmed what he had only vaguely suspected about the vagaries of the body that he reported on so graphically in "Narcissus Leaves the Pool":

> I note that my body seems slightly out of proportion to my head, which is a size 7 3/8. My shoulders are not wide—they are, more precisely, sloped—and my posture, a good deal less than perfect, has caused a slight humpiness where my neck runs into my back. Only the muscles in my calves and forearms could pass for youthful. My stomach is flat just now, but any weight I gain usually goes, like the blows of the late, punishing welterweight Carmen Basilio, straight to the midsection. The skin at my throat has begun to sag. I have old-guy elbows whose skin is dry, wrinkled, and reddish. ... My buttocks, I do believe, have begun to droop—not an inspiring sight, drooping buttocks.

"The trick with these essays," Epstein tells us, "is to take what seems a small or mildly amusing subject and open it up, allow it to exfoliate, so that by the end something arises that might be larger and more intricate than anyone—including the author—had expected" (foreword to *Narcissus Leaves the Pool*). In Epstein's case, this requires having a large supply of apt quotations and telling anecdotes at the ready to be pulled out when the essay takes an unexpected turn. Most of all, however, the familiar essay needs a voice, one that identifies the writer as uniquely as a thumbprint. Epstein can give us hints about the ways in which his essays resemble hothouse flowers (each "exfoliates" into something larger and more beautiful than the bulb in which it began), but of course to write like Epstein one must have lived the particulars of Epstein's life and sit at the writing desk (probably attired in sports coat, bow tie, and crisply pressed trousers) as none other than Epstein himself. No contemporary American writer has had more success and a longer run in turning the familiar essay into an art form.

LITERARY CULTURAL CRITICISM

It is hardly surprising that even one so confident as is Epstein might have reservations, not to mention doubts, about teaching in an English department without an advanced degree. Taking on professional literary criticism not only raised that ante but also added whole new dimensions: How, for example, would academic critics respond to the work of a self-declared amateur, and what would general readers think about the very opinionated Mr. Epstein? To answer the latter question, one need only say that many readers have found Epstein's literary criticism to their liking, but one must hasten to add that these are readers of magazines such as *The New Yorker* rather than of more specialized literary quarterlies such as *Modern Fiction Studies*. Epstein himself models his literary style on the pieces written by that Baltimore scold H. L. Mencken for the *American Mercury*. Epstein has made large claims for Mencken's lasting importance—"Along with Ernest Hemingway, H. L. Mencken devised one of the few original and unmistakable American prose styles of the current century"—and tries in his own fashion to continue Mencken's legacy of pulling down

inflated reputations through sarcasm, ridicule, and no-nonsense truth-telling. Epstein is no Mencken (at least not yet), but he too knows how to turn an opinion into a sustained argument and how to give the latter an air of plausibility.

Plausible Prejudices: Essays on American Writing (1985)—the title *phrase* comes from Mencken—consists of Epstein's views on the state of language and literature in the United States. The topic, admittedly a large one, has continued to dominate his literary criticism, for Epstein is one of the few writers who consciously links the way language is used by our best authors and the more general state of American culture. Writing in the *Chicago Tribune,* Stevenson Swanson argued that his "most interesting work has been his literary criticism," and that newspaper honored Epstein with its Heartland Prize for *Partial Payments: Essays on Writers and Their Lives* (1989), a collection in which Epstein praises an older generation of modern poets and takes a few well-aimed shots at the horde of, by his lights, lesser poets now teaching verse-writing workshops. As Winchell points out, most of these tribute essays "could easily double as obituaries. The exception that proves the rule is Epstein's laudatory discussion of V. S. Naipaul, the Anglo-Indian novelist who is described as 'far and away the most talented, the most truthful, the most honorable writer of his generation.'"

Epstein's collections of literary-cultural essays make no secret about the agenda neatly tucked into the pocket of his herringbone sports coat. He can, for example, mount a sustained case for the importance of Theodore Dreiser, a novelist no longer in fashion, even through Dreiser's valiant battle against the forces of censorship has led, in Epstein's view, to a situation in which the graphic but finally puerile sexuality found in the novels of John Updike, Norman Mailer, and Philip Roth "go directly to the best-seller tables." No doubt Epstein can take a measure of comfort, probably smaller than he might earlier have imagined, in the fact that none of these writers command the best-seller lists as they once did, superceded by writers considerably less able in terms of navigating their way through a paragraph.

Epstein's point, one he makes over and over again, is that contemporary fiction is going through a bad patch, a state of affairs all the more obvious if one is reminded of what excellence once was. Moreover, he brings up cases in which quite good writers are appropriated, hijacked, if you will, to serve ideological purposes. Willa Cather is a striking example of this tendency, partly because she is a writer Epstein much admires (when teaching at Northwestern, his course in Cather shared billing with courses in Joseph Conrad and Henry James) and partly because she is now regarded as a lesbian writer despite the fact that, for Epstein, there is no conclusive proof that this is the case.

Or there are writers like Philip Roth, whom Epstein once admired—with a few caveats. The stories in *Goodbye, Columbus* (1959) that got Roth so much attention as a twenty-six-year-old may have taken some cheap, mean-spirited shots, but they were part of a socio-realistic tradition that Epstein continues to admire; it is the later Roth, the one consumed with sex and full of postmodernist experimentation (see especially *Sabbath's Theater*) that so tick off the more decorous Mr. Epstein. (It is also worth noting here that it is the socio-realistic tradition that Epstein has drawn from for his own short stories, collected in *The Goldin Boys* and *Fabulous Small Jews*—stories that sing a wise, often sad song about family, love, and money as it affects middle-age Chicago Jews.)

In Life Sentences: Literary Essays (1997), Epstein discusses the lives and work of writers including Sydney Smith, Italo Svevo, George Orwell, Joseph Conrad, and a handful of others. Epstein takes the collection's title from his essay on Conrad. As he explains in the introduc-

tion, the phrase "life sentences" is packed with a double, perhaps even a triple, entendre. It means to suggest

> Conrad's travail with every sentence he wrote on his way to his triumph as an English prose stylist, his dark but dignified vision of men and women's destiny on earth, and his own long confinement to literary creation. A fourth possible meaning is that literature, for those who truly believe in its powers, is also a life sentence, but of a very different order. As such a believer, a true believer in literature, I feel that this particular sentence is one I myself can do, as they say out in the yard, standing on my head.

Much has, rightly, been made about Epstein's neoconservatism, but the deeper truth about his sensibility is that it has been far more formed by literature than by politics as those in political science departments understand the term. Epstein writes about literature because he is a self-described "autodidact," a term usually defined as "self-taught" but which Epstein insists applies to anybody who has "sat through endless lectures, and dutifully read all the prescribed books," and who, nonetheless, puts the responsibility for one's education where it should properly be—namely, in the person's own hands.

Whatever his subject, Epstein brings a distinctive prose style to his literary-cultural writing, just as he does to the other genres in which he works. As he wrote in an essay (in *Plausible Prejudices*) about *The New Yorker* sportswriter A. J. Leibling:

> Like Minnesota Fats with a cue ball, so Liebling with an English sentence—there was nothing he couldn't make it do, including the work of three normal paragraphs. He could make a single sentence ride the crest of a classical allusion, dip down to capture a passing irony, pick up a startling analogy along the way, curl over to the side for a comic touch, kiss off a serious observation, and, *plunk,* drop neatly into the pocket of a period to score a delicious original point.

Many of the same observations can be made about the characteristic Epstein sentence, especially with regard to the alternating rhythms of humor, irony, and serious observation. Epstein writes literary-cultural criticism in the same easygoing, never-let-them-see-you-sweat way that Perry Como, the mild-mannered crooner, once meandered his way through a love song.

SOCIOLOGICAL STUDIES

During his freelance phase, Epstein gained enough knowledge of marital discord for his first marriage to end in divorce and to prompt him to write his first book, *Divorced in America: Marriage in an Age of Possibility* (1974). Epstein's study was hardly the first, nor will it be the last, to analyze why it is that more than half of American marriages end in divorce, but his is an odds-on favorite to remain the most literate. *Newsweek* called it a "refreshingly thoughtful" and "personally insightful" book. Rather than an exercise in vindictiveness or in settling scores, Epstein well understood why it is that most one-sided accounts of divorce fail to arrive at any sort of "truth." This is a case where candor must be balanced by complexity and where the institution of marriage must be set against the assets and liabilities of "possibility."

Epstein divides his book into three sections: the first focuses on how and why marriage became such a beleaguered institution, the second looks at the legal proceedings of a divorce, and the final one talks about the effect of divorce on the individuals involved. The story of Epstein's own dissolving marriage is threaded through all three parts.

Epstein is wise enough not to view his divorce as a "creative" experience or to substitute psychobabble for the very real pain he felt; instead he regards divorce as a personal failure. Writing in the pages of the *New York Times Book Review,* Sara Sanborn thought that Ep-

stein's book was "generally perceptive and sometimes enlightening" but that it rehashed far too much of what had been known for far too long. The parts that ladled in material culled from other books on the subject seemed much less impressive than those parts in which Epstein talked about personal experience in his own voice.

Despite some minor reservations, Sonya Rudikoff, in the *Washington Post Book World,* praised Epstein's first book for its "poignancy" and for having "the nuance of domestic poetry about it, the poetry of making do and making the best of it with rueful dignity." What Epstein did not do was whine, and that, as the poet Robert Frost once said of two roads and a yellow wood, "has made all the difference" in Epstein's subsequent writing. For the personal essayist, wringing one's hands on the page is a sure way to lose one's reader, and Epstein understood this early in his career. Better to crack a joke, even a wisecrack, than to "fall upon the thorns of life" and "bleed" as Shelley, the English Romantic, once wrote. Granted divorce is no joking matter, but *Divorced in America* demonstrated that it can be talked about in something of the same neighborly key that distinguishes Epstein's unpretentious prose.

Ambition: The Secret Passion (1980) is an extended neoconservative prayer to the twin gods of Ambition and Success and a relentless attack on those who give the raspberry to the work ethic. The study also makes it clear that a staunch philistinism (namely, Epstein's) can coexist with elbow patches, an academic job, and the editorship of *American Scholar.*

Who is to blame, Epstein asks again and again, for the fish eye that many Americans—and particularly college undergraduates—give to success? And who, furthermore, is responsible for the contempt such students feel toward the unashamedly ambitious? The answer is simple: the backbiting currently being directed at portraits in ambition begins in, of all places, courses devoted to American literature classes:

> Certainly no major American literary figure has failed to get in his word on the subject of success, and most have not spoken kindly of it. James Fenimore Cooper, Nathaniel Hawthorne, Edgar Allan Poe, Herman Melville, William Dean Howells, Mark Twain, Robert Herrick, Frank Norris, Henry James—through the nineteenth century, from Cooper's distrust of the self-made man to James's deliciously sneering reference to his countrymen's "grope of wealth"—viewed success in America in terms ranging from equivocation to condemnation. In the twentieth century, the terms have been closer to those of unrelieved contempt. Antisuccess has been perhaps the strongest strain in American literature of the past half century. And to be against success is to put ambition in grave doubt.

Epstein so focuses on the naysaying strain in American literature that it is hardly surprising that he sums up his thumbnail account of our literary history this way: "It was not so much that [American] novelists preached failure but that they impugned success, and thus debunked ambition. They brought down the house but erected nothing in its place." What Epstein wants is nothing less than

> a novel … about a man who sets out to succeed in life and does so through work, decisive action, and discretion, without stepping on anyone's neck, without causing his family suffering, without himself becoming stupid or inhumane. … Yet it is a novel unlikely to be written so long as the other, more familiar novel—which has the ambitious man or woman confront society and either go under or win out only at the cost of his or her decency—provides, as it evidently does, so much comfort.

Writers are not the only ones who disappoint Epstein. Academics often take such delight in the negativity they pass off as required reading that their students have little choice but to mouth back the language of cynicism or to dummy up. "Excitement at the prospect of a career devoted to making money, even if it is felt, cannot be openly expressed," Epstein charges. Many English professors would take issue with this claim, not only because students are more independent-minded than Epstein imagines, but also because they very much want well-paying jobs after graduation. That is why business and accounting majors greatly outnumber those in the liberal arts.

Despite the palpable anxiety of graduating seniors who wonder if they will get a career-path job or undergraduates hoping to snag a plum summer internship, Epstein continues to insist that it is literature that killed the golden goose he calls Ambition. The reason, he argues, that students are so shamefaced about the prospect of "making money" is that

> it has been systematically downgraded for a number of decades now, and these students, often the best among them, have learned their lessons well. What are these lessons? Business, to begin with, is hypocritical and sterile (see *Babbitt*). Ambition is unseemly and everywhere suspect (see *What Makes Sammy Run, The Great Gatsby,* and for nonreaders, the movies *Citizen Kane* and *The Apprenticeship of Duddy Kravitz*). Middle-class life is essentially boring (see modern literature); upper-middle-class life, worse (see, these students say, their own families). Affluence is a sham, a greedy affair bringing no happiness (see Galbraith et al.).

Although *Ambition* was published in 1980, its arguments seem directed to the countercultural 1960s, a time when many undergraduates were in full rebellion against authority, whether manifested as their parents, the Establishment, or plain old-fashioned ambition. In this sense, Epstein's study has the feel of a rearguard action, one that does battle with enemies who have long ago departed the field.

Looking down one's nose at others has become an American pastime. In *Snobbery: The American Version*, Epstein turns his attention to the wide variety of complicated codes and cultural signals that flourish in a land where merit (supposedly) counts for more than aristocratic birth, and taste determines who has real class and who does not. In approaching this large and slippery subject, Epstein points out that snobbery "seems to have existed, in however attenuated a form, from the Tuesday of the week following that in which God created the universe." However, he has chosen to focus on snobbery in America since the decline of what he calls "Waspocracy." Not surprisingly, Epstein discovers that American snobbery is everywhere to be found—in the smug satisfaction many people take in driving an expensive, high-status automobile such as a Jaguar (interestingly enough, Epstein's car of choice) or in the reverse snobbery of those who buck the usual benchmarks of snobbery by driving a mid-size Chevrolet with cloth seats. As he lays out the various pieces in the snobbery puzzle, his narrative method blends personal anecdotes about his encounters—often in upscale restaurants—with the rich and famous, jokes (Epstein's Jewishness is perhaps most apparent in his sense of humor), well-chosen snippets from a wide variety of writers, and hard information culled from more "formal" scholarship.

Typically, *Snobbery: The American Version* is a deeply personal book. When Epstein talks about the special (read: snobbish) rush one feels when a son or daughter is accepted to an elitist college, he makes sure we know that he felt the same elation when his son got into Stanford—even though, Epstein being Epstein, he often daydreamed about telling people he meets at parties that he has a son at Tufts and a daughter at Taffeta.

Epstein's brand of snobbery can be traced to his undergraduate days at the University of Chicago. There he learned that

> only four kinds of work in life had any standing. These were: to be an artist; to be a scientist (and not some dopey physician, treating people for flu or urological problems—only a research physician

qualified); to be a statesman (of which there were none then extant); or—and here was the loophole—to be a teacher of potential artists, scientists, and statesmen. To be anything else, no matter how great one's financial or professional success, was to be rabble, just another commoner, a natural slave (in Aristotle's term), out there struggling under the blazing sun with the only shade available that provided by Plato's cave for the uninitiated ignorant.

Epstein once had kinder things to say about businessmen, but ambition, something he presumably still applauds, is a different matter from snobbery. It took him many years to shake off the self-righteousness bred into him at the University of Chicago, and some of the residue still sticks. Epstein just kept these snobbish notions buttoned in:

> I never came across as preposterous as I assuredly was in the inner drama I was then living. Still, deep down (deep down, that is, for a shallow young person) I tended to forgo the most innocent affectations by which people hope to establish superiority—through possessions, through memberships in clubs and groups, through socially favorable marriages—in favor of a heavy freight of artiness and intellectuality.

Snobbery: The American Version is filled with delightful observations of the social scene. When people turn the actor Humphrey Bogart into a cult figure, Epstein bristles, as he does when he watches people pretending to enjoy a piece of contemporary art he thinks of as crappy. At the same time, he freely admits that "good clothing" can elevate his spirits and that he is a

> sucker for the small fine things that a not really wealthy person can acquire: fine stationery, a splendid fountain pen, an elegant raincoat. I don't own an expensive watch, chiefly because I'm not much for jewelry, and spending a thousand dollars or more for a wristwatch is not my notion of a good time, but I am not opposed to buying a knockoff of a Cartier tank watch or of a Bvlgari

watch on the streets of New York or Washington, D.C., for fifteen or twenty-five dollars. ("An Andre Knokovsky," I say, if anyone asks what kind of watch I'm wearing.) Snobbery, I know, still courses through my bloodstream.

Indeed snobbery courses through *everybody's* bloodstream. For Epstein, it is—or at least seems to be—an unalterable fact of human nature. Like religion, snobbery works, Epstein claims, "through hope and fear": "The snob hopes to position himself securely among those whom he takes to be the best, most elegant, virtuous, fashionable, or exciting people. He also fears contamination from those he deems beneath him." Had Epstein done up snobbery as the topic of a magazine article, less might well have been more. As a book-length study, however, one begins to feel a sense of padding creeping in: there are too many side journeys and far too many historical recitations to sustain our interest.

About Epstein's writing one thing can be said with confidence: more collections of essays, short fiction, and criticism will most surely follow. He is a prolific writer, and even more than that, one able to take the temperature of our culture with insight, grace, and good humor.

Selected Bibliography

WORKS OF JOSEPH EPSTEIN

FAMILIAR ESSAYS

Familiar Territory: Observations on American Life. Oxford: Oxford University Press, 1979.

The Middle of My Tether: Familiar Essays. New York: Norton, 1983.

Once More around the Block: Familiar Essays. New York: Norton, 1987.

A Line Out for a Walk: Familiar Essays. New York: Norton, 1991.

With My Trousers Rolled. New York: Norton, 1995.

Narcissus Leaves the Pool: Familiar Essays. Boston: Houghton Mifflin, 1999.

LITERARY CRITICISM

Plausible Prejudices: Essays on American Writing. New York: Norton, 1985.

Partial Payments: Essays on Writers and Their Lives. New York: Norton, 1989.

Pertinent Players: Essays on the Literary Life. New York: Norton, 1993.

Life Sentences: Literary Essays. New York: Norton, 1997.

SOCIOLOGY

Divorced in America: Marriage in an Age of Possibility. New York: Dutton, 1974.

Ambition: The Secret Passion. New York: Dutton, 1980.

Snobbery: The American Version. Boston: Houghton Mifflin, 2002.

FICTION

The Goldin Boys. New York: Norton, 1991.

Fabulous Small Jews. New York: Houghton Mifflin, 2003.

UNCOLLECTED ESSAYS

"Knocking on Three, Winston." *American Scholar* 60, no. 3:327ff (1991).

CRITICAL AND BIOGRAPHICAL STUDIES

Bloom, James. Review of *Partial Payments. New York Times Book Review,* March 12, 1989, p. 23.

Bromwich, David. "A Regular Joe." *New Republic,* June 8, 1987, pp. 45–48. (Review of *Once More Around the Block.*)

Connarroe, Joel. "From Aristotle to Zelda." *New York Times Book Review,* June 7, 1987, p. 13. (Review of *Once More Around the Block.*)

Core, George. "Procrustes' Bed." *Sewanee Review* 96:xci–xcv (fall 1985).

DeMott, Benjamin. "Animadversions and Amusements." *New York Times Book Review,* November 4, 1979, pp. 12, 47. (Review of *Familiar Territory.*)

Iannone, Carol. "Payment in Full." *National Review,* April 21, 1989, pp. 46–47. (Review of *Partial Payments.*)

Jacoby, Russell. "Is 'Aristides' Just?" *Nation,* November 19, 1983, pp. 489–491. (Review of *The Middle of My Tether.*)

Larkin, Philip. "On Familiar Ground." *Times Literary Supplement,* January 13, 1984, p. 29. (Review of *The Middle of My Tether.*)

Lilla, Mark. Review of *The Middle of My Tether. American Spectator,* January 1984, pp. 39–40.

Miller, Stephen. "The Fuel of Achievement." *Commentary,* April 1981, pp. 79–82. (Review of *Ambition.*)

Pritchard, William H. "Kind to the Dead, Hard on the Living." *New York Times Book Review,* Febru

ary 24, 1985, p. 8. (Review of *Plausible Prejudices.*)

Rubin, Louis D., Jr. "Mr. Epstein Doesn't Like It." *Sewanee Review* 94:111–117 (winter 1986). (Review of *Plausible Prejudices.*)

Shechner, Mark. "The Ford in Our Past." *Nation,* January 17, 1981, pp. 53–56. (Review of *Ambition.*)

Winchell, Mark Royden. *Neoconservative Criticism: Norman Podhoretz, Kenneth S. Lynn, and Joseph Epstein.* Boston: Twayne, 1991.

Yardley, Jonathan. Review of *Plausible Prejudices. Washington Post,* February 20, 1985, p. C-2.

—*SANFORD PINSKER*

Sara Henderson Hay

1906–1987

*B*ECAUSE WOMEN AUTHORS have come to figure prominently in the literary landscape, it is difficult yet important to recall that for much of the twentieth century the odds were against a woman's building a career as a serious poet. Sara Henderson Hay was one of the relatively few who faced and bucked these odds, producing seven collections of poetry over a span of forty-nine years and enjoying frequent publication in midcentury literary and mainstream periodicals. At the peak of her career Hay was a regular contributor of poems to the *New Yorker,* the *New York Herald Tribune,* and the *Saturday Review.* Her work was anthologized among the most well-known poets of her time and was reviewed by such poet-critics as William Rose Benét, William Stafford, Robert Hayden, Louis Untermeyer, and John Holmes.

However, late-twentieth-century changes in literary tastes and cultural priorities regarding form and subject matter caused Hay's contributions to American letters to fade. Whereas Hay wrote traditionally formal—rhymed and metered—poetry that maintained a distanced decorum in relation to its subject matter, the 1960s and 1970s saw a radical shift to more open, raw, and explicit poetry. And whereas many women of Hay's generation avoided direct treatment of women's issues for fear of being treated differently by the mostly male literary establishment, later generations of American women writers, particularly following the second wave of the U.S. women's movement, strove for the removal of masks and deference in favor of direct and uncensored expression of women's emotions and experiences. By the mid-1960s Hay herself was aware that "alas, I am not in the current fashion," as she wrote to her editor at Doubleday, Maggie Cousins. At the same time, Hay had reservations about "the current outpourings of liberated expression." After 1970 much of Hay's work fell into obscurity.

A notable exception to this trend is her book *Story Hour: A Second Look at Cinderella, Bluebeard, and Company,* initially published by Doubleday in 1963 as a collection of thirty sonnets offering ironic revisions of traditional fairy tales. This collection was expanded to forty-one sonnets and published again in 1982 by the University of Arkansas Press. Many of its individual poems appear in anthologies devoted to fairy-tale scholarship and revision and in secondary and college-level curricula. That Hay's literary life continues primarily on the basis of her book-length revision of fairy tales is fitting because she was one of the first women authors to subject these traditional narratives to a more cynical, critical, and feminine—if not feminist—point of view.

Aside from these poems that provide "a second look at Cinderella, Bluebeard, and Company," one of Hay's earliest published poems, "For a Dead Kitten," which appeared in the *New York Times* in 1930, remains popular: it continues to be cherished by cat fanciers and language arts teachers:

> Put the rubber mouse away,
> Pick the spools up from the floor,
> What was velvet-shod, and gay,
> Will not want them, any more—
>
> What was warm, is strangely cold.
> Whence dissolved the little breath?

How could this small body hold
So immense a thing as Death?

In addition, Hay's more decidedly devotional poems have a following among Christian publishers and readers. Yet as a poet with secular literary appeal, Hay has been neglected, not unlike the poet she so greatly admired, Edna St. Vincent Millay, whose work saw renewed attention in the late twentieth and early twenty-first centuries, following decades of critical dismissal based on presuppositions about the derivativeness of her forms, the artificiality of her diction, and the amateurish sentimentality of her tone. As revived studies of and attention to Millay's oeuvre have amply demonstrated, such presuppositions are all too often the product of certain cultural biases, and looking past them makes it possible to see the writing strategies women used in the effort to be taken seriously by a male-dominated literary establishment. One finds, for instance, that writers like Hay had reason to take to heart Emily Dickinson's dictum—"Tell all the Truth but tell it slant"—in an era when women's suffrage, let alone their right to pursue roles other than housewife and mother, was still a very recent and fragile reality.

EARLY LIFE AND WORK

The daughter of Major Ralph Watson Hay and Daisy Henderson Baker Hay, Sara Henderson Hay was born in Pittsburgh, Pennsylvania, on November 13, 1906. Her father's family had a long and prestigious history in this northeastern industrial steel town, and her paternal great-grandfather, Alexander Hay, had been the city's mayor in the 1840s. Daisy Baker Hay's family lived in Anniston, Alabama, where Hay, at age ten, took up residence with her mother and her sister, Willa. Early on, Hay wrote poetry; the *Anniston Star* frequently published the young woman's work. In lectures Hay repeatedly spoke of her mother's role in encouraging her literary aspirations. Daisy Baker Hay, who had studied elocution, read aloud to Hay and her sister from Alfred, Lord Tennyson; Algernon Charles Swinburne; William Shakespeare; and Henry Wadsworth Longfellow. Hay once recalled being put to bed to "the soporific measures of 'The Song of Hiawatha.'"

She attended Brenau College in Georgia, where as a freshman she edited the college magazine. Then she transferred to Columbia University, where she studied with John Erskine, Joseph Auslander, Hoxie Fairchild, and John Hall Wheelock and received her bachelor's degree in 1929. At a time when few women did so, Hay sought out knowledgeable and influential mentors, envisioning for herself a literary life. Like the celebrated fiction writer Carson McCullers, who also attended Columbia, Hay was involved in the university literary magazine and in the Parnassus Club, a campus women's organization which put out a publication by the same name. Hay waited tables at the club to pay for her college residence.

Intent on a literary career following graduation from Columbia, Hay joined the Poetry Society of America, forged connections with other writers and editors, and published her poetry in magazines and anthologies, including *Younger Poets* and *Selected Magazine Verse*. She worked for the publisher Charles Scribner's Sons in New York from 1935 to 1942, mostly as a secretary and librarian, while taking on freelance writing and editing jobs, including the proofreading of Burton E. Stevenson's *Home Book of Shakespeare Quotations* (1937). Hay published her first book, *Field of Honor*, in 1933 through a contest sponsored by Kaleidograph Press of Dallas, Texas. The title poem is written in three sections and allegorizes the end of a love affair in heraldic terms, advocating the honorable though painful breakup as preferable to "a darker wound, a deadlier agony."

For it were surely treachery most base
To risk the sullying of so proud a shield—
To chance a single stain upon the face
Of what we bear in honor from the field,
Worthy to keep untarnished through the years,
Though polished daily with what meed of tears!

Perhaps the poem refers to a passion for someone who is already committed to another, or perhaps a platonic relationship is on the verge of "turning … / Into a way we may not walk together." Little material provides any autobiographical insight into Hay's relation to the poem's addressee. Like many women of her generation, she tended to underplay the connections between her personal life and her poetry, warned, it may be, by the example of Millay, who was more often a household word for her reputed bohemianism and "free love" experiments than for her finely crafted and startling poems. Still, Hay saw poetry as a mode, albeit indirect, of self-expression: "Not that all poems are autobiographical or even from the poet's personal experience, but … out of all the extraneous outlines a true likeness, to the discerning eye which reads between the lines, appears." By and large Hay's own work reflects her belief in indirect expression, for only by "read[ing] between the lines" is one able to find in her work a tie to autobiographical, social, and political contexts.

Hay's personal experience expanded when at age twenty-eight she took a job as an assistant to the journalist Gladys Baker on a European tour for the New York Times. Among the European potentates interviewed during this 1935 tour were Benito Mussolini, Pope Pius XI, and the Turkish president Kemal Atatürk. Traveling through Europe during the rise of fascism, Baker and Hay went to Berlin to interview top Nazi Party leaders, but the interviews failed to materialize. Very little in Hay's poetry would seem to evoke that time in her life when she was immersed in public-sphere political life and the world beyond the sonnet. In the early 1940s, with deepening U.S. involvement in the Second

World War, Hay did publish topical political poetry, including the poems "To the Nazi Leaders" and "Blood Donor," which appeared in the New York Herald Tribune, and "Blackout," which appeared in the New Yorker. Of these poems only "Blackout" was later included in one of Hay's book-length collections; it was published in The Delicate Balance (1951). This spare two-quatrain poem seeks out timeless essence rather than historical detail. It plays on an allusion to the Bible—"Let there be dark!"—to draw attention to the ironic destruction implied by wartime blackout exercises, in contrast to the fiat lux of the biblical creation account.

Hay so reveled in poetic license, the distancing and imaginative efficacy of poetry, that she wrote a series of poems to and about a son she did not have. They are collected in the fourth section of Hay's second book of poems, This, My Letter, which was published in 1939 and dedicated to the poet Raymond Holden, whom she had married in 1937. Of the fifteen poems addressed "To My Small Son" in various situations, all but the last are in sonnet form; the closing poem, "To My Small Son, Growing Up," is a mere ten lines, registering the speaker's reticence about the fact that her son, in putting away "childish things," must "at so great price become a man." Except for reprints of the "small son" poems in later volumes, Hay never published another poem to this imaginary boy, letting him go, as it were, once he had grown up.

Whether as a creative challenge or as an assertion of her femininity in a time when women writers were often branded unfeminine, Hay infuses such poems as "To My Small Son, on Certain Occasions" and "To My Small Son, at the Photographer's" with an intimacy and knowledge that led many reviewers, editors, and readers to assume that Hay was, in fact, a mother. This included Holden himself, who, prior to meeting Hay, had been an editor at the

Saturday Review and who was partial to the poems Hay submitted about her "son." When they finally met, according to the Hay biographer Agnes Dodds Kinard, Holden asked Hay how her son was; Hay responded that she was neither married nor a parent and added, "Mr. Holden, you, a poet, should know that having brain children now and then is our license." In any event, William Rose Benét, reviewing *This, My Letter* in 1939, seemed convinced enough that Hay was writing about "a most actual little boy." And John Ritchey, reviewing Hay's book for the *Christian Science Monitor,* wrote that it was "the most arresting book to appear in America so far this year" and saw Hay's work as exemplary of Robert Frost's "rule of symmetry," by which a poem should be so well constructed that not one word might be added or subtracted.

This, My Letter gets its title from a poem by John Donne in which the latter claims that a poem embodies all that is essential about the author. Using poetry to explore Christian themes was important to Hay throughout her life, and as in most of her collections, the last section of this book consists of religious and devotional poetry. The fact that she placed her most directly religious poetry at the end of her secular collections reflects her experience in New York publishing circles and her acumen in self-marketing; on a figurative level it could be seen as a gesture underscoring her religious faith as the "last word." Also found in this second book of Hay's is "In Memoriam," a poem that originally appeared in the *New Yorker* eulogizing the southern novelist Thomas Wolfe, who died young in 1938. This poem, with its echoes of the exuberant "Ohs!" that have made Wolfe's lyrical prose style famous, demonstrates the degree to which Hay's role in American letters was, even at this early point in her career, substantial.

Hay's marriage to Holden ended in a divorce at Reno, Nevada, in 1949. If Hay's poems from this period are any indication, the marriage's decline and breakup were the source of much anger and pain. A poem directly dealing with the experience of divorce, "Residence: Washoe County, Nevada… ," marvels with bittersweet candor at the ease with which a marriage can be legally dissolved:

> [The lawyer's] heard it all before.
> All that to you was terrible and unique
> Is an old story, lady; weep no more.

Characteristically, however, Hay chose not to include this poem in any of her collections.

Her third book, *The Delicate Balance,* was published in 1951 by Scribners and received the Poetry Society of America's Edna St. Vincent Millay Memorial Award. Like Millay's, Hay's poetry in this volume is interested in male-female relationships and the difficulties of making them work. Though never a declared feminist, Hay's life choices and many of her poems reflect a determination to maintain her own footing and balance in spite of social expectations. A common theme in this and later works is that of giving up romantic naïveté, suggesting that women would not suffer so much from betrayal if they believed less in "fairy tale" myths about what to expect from life and love. The especially sardonic poem that gives the collection its title refers to "Hope" as a drug that "Should Be Plainly Labeled 'Poison'" and teases out the paradox in four quatrains before coming to the conclusion that "There is a delicate balance set / Between Hope's virtue and its vice." Another poem in this volume, "Premonition," seems to address the betrayal of romantic hopes with an oblique evocation of the Genesis story of the Fall:

> What lustful root
> Wrought savagely the pained and innocent
>   ground
> To bear this bitter fruit?

Hope's opposite, despair or bitterness, rears its head frequently throughout this work, which seems to be devoted to finding a balance between the two extremes. In a review of the book Louis Untermeyer observes its "delicate balance" between "frail whimsicality and fine-spun strength," adding that the book's "prevailing bittersweetness saves even the most romantic lines from cloying." And the poet Robert Hayden, reviewing *The Delicate Balance* for the *New York Times,* emphasized the strength of Hay's irony.

THE POET IN PITTSBURGH

In 1950, while in residence at the MacDowell Colony, a Peterborough, New Hampshire, retreat for fine artists, Hay met the Russian American composer Nikolai Lopatnikoff. The two married in 1951, and Hay returned to Pittsburgh, Pennsylvania, where her second husband was on the music faculty at Carnegie Mellon University, then called the Carnegie Institute of Technology. The marriage appears to have been a nurturing and productive one, for they were together for twenty-five years until his death in 1976. In Pittsburgh, Hay continued to write poetry, give readings and lectures, and contribute essays to such journals and magazines as the *Lyric* and *Writer's Digest.* Always a closet fiction writer and avid mystery lover, Hay even published, in 1954, a short mystery titled "Mrs. Jellison" in *Ellery Queen's Mystery Magazine;* it appeared alongside works by such authors as Agatha Christie, L. Frank Baum, Jack London, and Roald Dahl. But Hay did not pursue prose writing with the vigor she gave to poetry.

Upon returning to her childhood home, Hay gave a good deal to the Pittsburgh area cultural community. Being married to a musician, she had occasion to collaborate with her husband's musical colleagues. More than two dozen of her poems were set to musical scores by Roland Leich. According to Kinard these collaborations were "sometimes serious, sometimes playful,

some were orchestral and some were for male chorus or Pittsburgh's Mendelssohn Choir." Hay's support for and involvement with the arts extended to the International Poetry Forum, a poetry and performance venue begun in the 1960s by the Pittsburgh poet Samuel Hazo. The Poetry Forum brought many of the world's most notable poets—Anne Sexton, Elizabeth Bishop, Chinua Achebe, and Jorge Luis Borges, to name but a few—to a city struggling to forge a cultural life from a legacy of smoke and steel. Recognized in her own right as a literary figure and married to a composer of international scope, Hay inevitably moved in "society." One striking moment in her role as a Pittsburgh society lady bears witness to her independence—her refusal of an offer by the *Pittsburgh Press* to name her as one of the city's "ten best-dressed women": in declining, Hay firmly asserted that the honor was not in keeping with her primary interests. Another understated yet firm plea to be taken seriously, found in Hay's bequest of her professional papers to Carnegie Mellon University's Hunt Library, allows for fair use quotation from her work and notebooks under the condition that she not be referred to by prospective researchers as a "poetess."

In 1959, Hay's fourth book, *The Stone and the Shell,* became the first book of poetry to be published by the University of Pittsburgh Press, whose Pitt Poetry Series has since become a showcase for numerous American poets of note, including the United States Poet Laureate Billy Collins. The poet and critic William Stafford wrote in *Poetry* magazine that *The Stone and the Shell* has "a remarkable unity of effect" partially because "many of the poems take off from references to Scripture and to universal, fundamental human predicaments" and maintain a "fluency of treatment and sharpness of turning." The book, which earned for Hay the 1960 Pegasus Award, centers around two dominant images—the shell as protective armor and the stone as an object both permanent and subject to erosion—which were emblematic for the poet throughout her career. As epigraphs to the book, she quotes three of her own previously published poems that evoke these images.

In *The Delicate Balance* Hay, like the poet Marianne Moore, looked to the "book of nature" for insights into selfhood and humanity, writing in the poem "Natural History Note" that she had been drawn to "hard things" such as stones because she was soft, and to "armored things" because she "unguarded was." In *The Stone and the Shell,* however, Hay seems to recognize that armor can also be a sign of weakness or even of greed and aggression, as is the case in the poem "Public Figure," which begins with a "natural history" epigraph about the hermit crab's habit of appropriating and occupying the abandoned shells of other creatures. The poem goes on to suggest connotatively that, like the crab, certain public figures lack "a rigid bone" of their own yet take ownership of and credit for the shell that "contain[s] no stuff of [them]." Still, the shell retains many positive attributes for the poet, particularly, as in "The Snail," by its evocation of self-sufficiency, a personal and poetic ideal for Hay.

The final portion of the book, "The Shape God Wears," consists of sixteen religious poems that reinterpret biblical stories in often unexpected and homely ways. One of these poems, "Witness for the Defense," received the Lyric Memorial Prize for 1959. This poem, written in smooth couplets and lines of varying lengths, takes a sympathetic view of characters cast as envious and self-righteous—such as the jealous workers in the vineyard (Matthew 20); Martha, who rebukes her sister Mary in Luke 10 for leaving housework undone to converse with Jesus; and the elder brother of the prodigal son (Luke 15). While these figures may be "posts whereon to pin the parable," the poem argues, their hard work and consistency is not without value. Samuel Hazo, in a newspaper review that went unpublished owing to a strike, remarked

on the strength of the biblically oriented poems in *The Stone and the Shell:* "These monologues are stylistic departures from Miss Hay's terse lyricism, but they work beautifully as poems and invite further experimentation and development." Hay's adoption of unorthodox viewpoints in the retelling of traditional stories adds tension and interest not only to her religious poetry, but also to her sustained revision of fairy tales.

In 1951 Hay published a sonnet, "Jack and the Beanstalk," in the *New York Herald Tribune.* In it she expresses, through the voice of an inquisitive child, amazement that Jack should be rewarded for trespass and homicide. The adult speaker in the sonnet's closing six lines, or sestet, reprimands the child for daring to question the story's logic and calls instead for a "gullible innocence" that "applauds the climber, and ignores the crime." This poem was reprinted in a 1959 issue of *McCall's* under the title "Story Hour." Finally, in 1963 the work became the title poem for Hay's best-selling, most heavily promoted, and most influential book of poems.

Story Hour, illustrated by Jim McMullan and published by Doubleday in time for the holiday shopping season, is a collection of sonnets parodying the logic of fairy tales and written, in Hay's words, as "ostensibly light verse" that at the same time, in the tradition of satire, seeks to make "a perfectly valid comment on social behavior and customs, in short, to say a true word in jest." Hay was known throughout her career for her ironic approach, but this is her first extensive deployment of full satire. It is a genre in which she was deeply interested, no doubt because it provides a time-tested means for leveling criticism without drawing undue controversy. In drafts toward an article on satire commissioned by *Writer's Digest* Hay wrote that irony and satire "can often be more compelling than downright positive frontal attack. A rapier is as lethal as a blunt instrument any day, and most of the time considerably less messy."

Publicity related to *Story Hour* included an appearance by Hay on the NBC *Today* show with Barbara Walters; an enactment of one of the poems on Burr Tillstrom's television program *That Was the Week That Was;* illustrated spreads in the *New York Herald Tribune, McCall's, Show* magazine, and the London edition of *Harper's Bazaar;* and the publication of individual poems in such widely read periodicals as the *Atlantic*. The composer Tom Rice undertook setting the poems of *Story Hour* to music, and seven poems were choreographed—without Hay's permission—and made part of the ballet repertoire of the Ethel Butler company of Washington, D.C.

Eight years following the appearance of *Story Hour,* the Pulitzer Prize–winning poet Anne Sexton published her own full-length verse revision of fairy tales, *Transformations* (1971), unaware of Hay's role as a precursor. Hay anticipated the revisionary spirit of the 1970s, when writers, many of them in the interest of feminism, satirized, questioned, and even rewrote fairy tales and other cultural narratives that were no longer accepted as reflective of timeless, universal values. In a letter to a reader who had written to Hay in praise of the 1982 expanded edition of *Story Hour,* Hay recalled that the book was "the first of such contemporary glimpses behind the scenes of fairy tales; there've been a good many since, including Anne Sexton's." Countless features and reviews of the original *Story Hour* emphasized that these worldly takes on Grimm and others were not intended for children. Ironically, many of the collection's poems, especially "The Builders," which retells the story of the three little pigs in the slangy "I-told-them-so" voice of the pig who built with bricks, have been used in elementary and high school reading curricula, perhaps because Hay's clarity of line makes it that much more likely that students will be able to devote attention to the subtle ironies of character and social interaction at play in the more didactic of the poems.

Hay's largest collection of poetry, *A Footing on This Earth,* a volume of new and selected poems, was issued by Doubleday in 1966. The book is the most comprehensive cross section of Hay's long writing career, which is brought full circle in this later volume by the use of the same poem, "Dedication for a Book," that Hay used thirty-three years earlier to open her first book, *Field of Honor.* The poem's claim that "More of my self will move in word and line / Than ever walked abroad in flesh and bone" taps into the poetic commonplace about immortality through the written word and does seem, by 1966, somewhat old-fashioned in a decade that saw the bursting-forth of beat and confessional modes in poetry.

The 220-page book divides Hay's work thematically rather than chronologically, with sections titled "Times and Seasons," "Inner Weather," "Seasons of the Heart," "Men and Women," "Another Story" (which contains selections from *Story Hour,* as well as poems written for a sequel on which she was working), and "Birds and Beasts," plus four sections consisting of spiritual and religious poetry. *A Footing on This Earth* provides the fullest sampling of Hay's styles and themes and marks Hay's "footing" in a type of poetry that was losing ground in the latter part of the twentieth century. She had long espoused the communicative function of poetry over what she termed its "obscurantist" or "avant-garde" tendencies; but clarity of communication did not, for her, amount to what she saw as the "raunchily explicit writing produced by women poets today" that "seems to verge on the exhibitionistic." Given the changing poetry climate of the 1960s, reviews for the book were not what Hay and her editor had hoped for: in a decade that fostered the "raw" work of Le Roi Jones, Allen Ginsberg, and Diane Di Prima, and the "cooked" expressivism of Adrienne Rich, Anne Sexton, and Robert Lowell, the widespread literary appeal and acceptance Hay had known before and at midcentury was fading.

What was unconventional or unorthodox about Hay's work seems mild when viewed in relation to the obscenity controversy sparked by Ginsberg's *Howl* or the confrontational styles of the black arts movement of the 1960s. In 1943, for instance, Hay's poem, "The Neighbors," unintentionally raised controversy among some readers. This seemingly benign poem, which was published in the equally benign *Good Housekeeping* magazine, opens with an epigraph from the Christian Bible (Mark 6), then playfully imagines what the gossip among Jesus' neighbors might sound like in a blue-collar American idiom; one neighbor offhandedly says,

He'd a been a better son
If he'd stayed home and raised a family
Like his brothers done.

The National Organization for Decent Literature, headed by Bishop John F. Noll, took issue with the reference to Jesus' brothers as "blasphemous"; religious organizations protested the poem and pressured *Good Housekeeping* editors for an apology; and the syndicated writer Drew Pearson devoted a column to the debate. Prudently, Hay decided against including "The Neighbors" in any of the collections produced in the 1940s and 1950s. By the time she selected poems for *A Footing on This Earth,* though, she let go of her prior caution and included the poem, emboldened, in her own conservative way, by the iconoclastic 1960s.

Hay's work papers suggest that she hoped to publish a book titled *Another Story,* consisting of new sonnet treatments of fairy tales, with a New York trade publisher. She was likely encouraged to pursue this project by the proliferation in the 1970s of interest in folklore, fairy tales, psychology, and cultural values. When the neo-Freudian psychologist Bruno Bettelheim

published his best-selling *The Uses of Enchantment: The Meaning and Importance of Fairy Tales* in 1976, Hay read the book avidly and briefly corresponded with the author. Her second set of fairy tales did not appear until 1982, when the University of Arkansas Press published an expanded edition of *Story Hour* with eleven new sonnets. This edition does not include illustrations, but a posthumous reissue of the title by the press in 1998 includes what appear to be public-domain illustrations.

The poet Miller Williams writes in his foreword to the reissue, "It's a joy to have available again Sara Henderson Hay's timeless gift to us all, so that a new generation of readers can go with her through the back doors of these old houses we thought we knew so well." These old, seemingly familiar houses to which Williams refers are not only the tales themselves, but also the sonnet form as Hay employs it, which "come[s] across as so natural, so relaxed, simply so very good that the poet seems almost to have thought in the form."

Late in Hay's life she saw the inclusion of her *Story Hour* poems in elementary and secondary language arts textbooks in the United States and abroad, as well as in Stephen Dunning's *Reflections on a Gift of Watermelon Pickle* (1966); Jack Zipes' *Don't Bet on the Prince: Contemporary Feminist Fairy Tales in North America and England* (1986); *The Oxford Book of Children's Verse in America* (1985), edited by the poet Donald Hall; and *Disenchantments: An Anthology of Modern Fairy Tale Poetry* (1985), edited by Wolfgang Mieder.

Hay had become an elder poetry stateswoman by the 1980s, her husband of twenty-five years having predeceased her. She volunteered her time and expertise to the Pittsburgh chapter of the National Society of Arts and Letters. In 1980 the *Kentucky Poetry Review* honored Hay by publishing an issue devoted to her life and work. Hay died in her sleep in her Pittsburgh home on July 7, 1987, at the age of eighty, having lived a life many women of her generation could not have secured for themselves. In her poem "Minor Poet"—one of the rare instances in which she refers to "the poet" as a "she"—she could be said to have assessed her career in advance and come to terms with the vagaries of taste and circumstance by which a poet's work lives or dies:

> She knows as well as anybody else
> How slight the pressure is
> Behind such trickling poetry as fills
> Only small pools and little crevices.

Even if the "minor" poet's work never floods forth with "resistless power," the poem continues, at least it will nourish the small amount of land through which it flows, and the poet "can kneel beside it on the sands / And touch her mouth to it, and cool her hands."

In 1989 Agnes Dodds Kinard compiled a collection of devotional poems by Hay titled *Seasons of the Heart: In Quest of Faith.* The book includes the once-troublesome "The Neighbors" as well as poems representing both Hay's fervent faith and her moments of doubt and questioning; her sense of humor and humanity; and her stylistic restraint and humility. The book, published by Pickwick Publications, a Pittsburgh imprint later based in San Jose, California, includes Kinard's "The Poet and the Person," the most complete biographical memoir available on Hay.

WRITING AS A WOMAN

Sara Henderson Hay, coming of age during the extension of the vote and the opening of new doors to women, fit into the "new woman" generation. "New woman" was a popular label—at times leveled critically, at times used approvingly—for the more independent, ambitious, and educated women (usually white and of upper-middle-class origins) whose increasing freedoms and participation in the public sphere were the result of urbanization, scientific advances, and the secularization of American culture. Traditional values and mores were reappraised in the "thoroughly modern" opening decades of the twentieth century. Hay's ability to pursue higher education and a writing career as a single woman in New York City owed something to this changing atmosphere.

Yet as a writer, Hay and other ambitious literary women had few precursors to whom they could look. Instead, women who received the mentorship and support of academic and literary men were often given male models and standards against which to measure their efforts and aspirations. It was inevitable that women like Hay would look askance at the women authors who did enjoy popularity and publication, influenced by the prevailing assumption that few of the "scribbling women" known in the mass literary market made significant contributions to serious belles lettres. Hay would, then, have patterned much of her work after the male authors to whom she was exposed at Columbia and in the prestigious literary publications of the day. She did greatly admire the work of her more flamboyant and controversial contemporary Edna St. Vincent Millay (1892–1950), writing a memorial poem upon her death and including it in her book *The Stone and the Shell.* The elegy "In Memoriam" asserts Hay's desire to mark the passing of

> one
> Whom only in her song I knew,
> But loved therefore, and more than most
> Whom daily I might look upon.

Hay also expressed admiration for the poet Sara Teasdale (1884–1933), and her work has been compared more than once with that of Elinor Wylie (1885–1928).

As for earlier female influences and affinities, Hay can be associated with Emily Dickinson (1830–1886) on the basis of their common use of poetry as a way to seek spiritual growth and solace, as well as their common adaptation of elements of Protestant hymns to their poetic prosody. But where Dickinson's work is idiosyncratic and enigmatic, Hay's seeks clarity and communication. A rare example of a Hay poem that, like the work of Dickinson, is convoluted, and in certain places hermetic, is "For Pot-Boiling":

Behold this scarlet shame,
This sin against the Name:
That with deliberate lime
I snared the brave bird, rhyme,
And did this monstrous wrong
To the light-pinioned song.
Know that the outrage wrought
Was well and subtly taught
By the deft mind, whose art
Betrayed the honest heart
With the entangling phrase
The syllable's smooth ways,
The honied verb, the sweet
Trap for guileless feet.
See how the innocent guest
Fouls his immaculate breast—
And that were shame enough
For one who spread the stuff,
Not from my self disguised,
And bitterly despised.

The poem's title helps the reader to tie the short-measure allegorical couplets to the writing practice of "pot-boiling," or hackwork in which appeal and profitability are based on superficial cleverness and devices that "snare" the reader's prurient attention. Without the title's reference one could read the poem itself as an example of that which the poet seems to be viewing critically, the subjection of the "brave bird, rhyme" to the disingenuous art of the mind rather than of the heart. The closing six lines so ensnare themselves inside the conceit Hay sets up that it is difficult to find a clear referent for "his immaculate breast" and "one who spread the stuff." This level of confusion is infrequent in the work of Hay, who swore by Sir Philip Sidney's mandate in *Astrophil and Stella*—"looke in thy heart and write"—and believed that feeling, rightly transferred to the page, was necessary to the making of meaningful poetry.

More than with Dickinson's poetry, Hay's work generally shares commonalities with that of an even earlier North American female precursor, Anne Bradstreet (1612–1672), particularly in the elevation of the "heart" over the "head" and the valuing of communication over complication. In her devotional lyrics, barring those more adventurous monologues that resee Scripture or attempt in the manner of Job to "reason with God," Hay keeps to an orthodox Protestantism, much as Anne Bradstreet, even in her moments of loss and doubt, does. Other possible female influences on Hay's work include the Pre-Raphaelite English poet Christina Rossetti (1830–1894) and, if Hay's respectful references are any indication, the American imagist poet Amy Lowell (1874–1925).

Hay recognized the cultural difficulties facing a woman who chose writing as a career. In a draft for a talk, she wrote:

If a woman has a tremendous talent, and the necessary ruthlessness, conscious or unconscious, to put its demands above any other obligation, then she has at least two alternatives; she can, like Emily Dickinson, withdraw from the world and write her poems from the imagined ecstasies of love and the sweet agonies of renunciation; or on the other hand she can, like Edna St. Vincent Millay, live a very full physical and emotional life and then marry a man who is willing to devote *his* life to be housekeeper, protector, guardian and shield against the world.

These alternatives—shut-away spinster or catered-to wife—gloss over other possibilities, which only serves to remind one of how restricted the cultural imagination was regarding women's work and living arrangements.

Attention to the work of Sara Henderson Hay reveals the effects of sociocultural restrictions on a woman's range of writing choices. While

Hay, an author of ingenuity and talent, was undoubtedly independent of many of the strictures on and expectations for women of her generation, the body of her work—in its form, style, approach, tone, and treatment of gender differences—is symptomatic of the ways in which the sociocultural position of a woman writer influences the kinds of texts she produces.

On the structural level Hay kept to traditional forms. She frequently employed the sonnet, at times faithful to its conventional diction, imagery, and tone, while at other times pushing against the limitations of the form to infuse it with humor and colloquial diction. A lifelong churchgoer, she was—as were many of her contemporaries—adept at the ballad form thanks to its adaptation to many American Protestant hymns. While in her earlier collections her line lengths and metrics tended to be textbook-pristine, in her later work Hay often varied line lengths to attain a more finely tuned fluctuation in rhythm and to register subtle shifts in tone, influenced no doubt by the opening up of forms during the modernist period and, later, in the 1950s and 1960s. However, one will not find a poem in free verse, or even blank verse, in any of Hay's published books.

William Rose Benét, reviewing Hay's 1939 book *This, My Letter* for the *Saturday Review,* observed, "This poet does not experiment with form. Her range in rhyme and meter is not great. She accepts certain conventions of statement." Indeed, as she told a Pittsburgh-area reporter in the 1980s, Hay owed her early popularity and critical success—and her post-1960s decline in audience—to her formal conservatism. The prominent American poet and critic Louise Bogan (1897–1970), who also wrote predominantly in rhyme and meter but who experimented more boldly with prosody and concept than did Hay, once observed that it is difficult for women to throw off "the more superficial fashions" of their societies; while Bogan did not provide extensive reasons for this observa-tion, it may well be that such conservatism in the fashion of traditional poetic forms was a means for women poets to assert their craftsmanship in decades when it was frequently seen as lacking in women's work, as well as a way of building aesthetic distance between the author and her subject matter. More recently the American feminist poet Adrienne Rich, writing of her coming of age as a poet in the 1940s and 1950s, has referred to formalism as "asbestos gloves" donned by women writers to protect themselves from their anger and frustration at a sociocultural situation that warranted that they suppress their feminine identity and emotions in order to be respected as artists.

Hay's style and approach to subject matter reflect the tastes and values of her generation; they also reflect her own ambition to be seen as a "poet" rather than as a mere "poetess." One approach that bears witness to this ambition is Hay's tendency to bypass specific, localizing, or topical detail in favor of broader outlines that evoke universal and timeless ideas and values. Seldom does one of Hay's poems exceed thirty lines, since Hay generally worked toward didactic or paradoxical essences in her work. Envisioning a more generalized scope in her work also made it possible for Hay to write as a gender-free speaker, an "I" who was not so much an individual as a member of a long tradition of faceless poetic voices. For instance, in "The Deeper Wisdom," which appears in *The Delicate Balance,* Hay treats the city and country as symbolic abstractions meant to heighten the discovery on the speaker's part that "the deeper wisdom" resides in "that word the meadow softly said, / The speaking silence of the land," as opposed to the worldly sophistry to which the speaker, "city born and bred," is accustomed. And in "Field of Honor," from Hay's first book, even as a love affair and breakup is allegorized, it is never clear that the speaker is a female party to a heterosexual relationship. Instead, the poem attempts to paint romantic love in the largely masculine colors of chivalric battle and decorum.

Even the landscape of personal feelings and inner struggles tends to be abstracted and generalized in Hay's work. Two examples are seen in "The Riddle" and "On Being Too Inhibited." In "The Riddle," which is found in *A Footing on This Earth,* Hay opens with a first-person speaker directly admitting to being full of anger:

> I am as one who has a starving anger,
> A metaphysical want in his soul's middle.
> And yet what food will satisfy that hunger
> Remains my stubborn riddle.

Although the subject matter is from the beginning personal and private, Hay enacts slight but effective means to generalize and abstract the emotional situation: for example, instead of stating "I am one," the poem transforms the "I" to a type by stating "I am *as* one." Further, through the use of words like "metaphysical" and "soul," the particular personal instance is subsumed into a perennial state endemic to the human condition. In "On Being Too Inhibited," which is in Hay's first book, the approach is similar to that of François, duc de La Rochefoucauld's *Reflexions; ou, Sentences et maximes morales* (1665) in that an introspective lesson learned too late becomes a cautionary lesson to all readers:

> Now may the pitying eye discern
> The pinched and wistful soul
> Of one who was so late to learn
> That often "self-control"
>
> Is neither more nor less, in truth,
> Than just the meager art
> Of planing the emotions smooth,
> And chiselling the heart!

The highly anonymous and hypothetical third-person pronoun "one" conveys the pithy lesson to readers, with an exclamation point serving to offset its clinical coldness.

Another brief meditation on inner emotional life, "On Suicide," which also appeared in *Field of Honor,* disposes with the particularities of despair and instead casts the specter of suicide as an epigrammatic "equation" which is, "save a certain conquerable fear, / Easily done" and solves "a sum or two of Fate." Such abstractions and generalizations of inner emotions would seem to work against Hay's own stated belief that feeling should take precedence over reason in poetry. A draft of Hay's essay for a 1956 issue of the *Lyric,* fittingly titled "Look to Thy Heart … ," may suggest some possible reasons for this disparity between Hay's poetic ideals and much of her practice:

> What is apt to come under fire today is not the technical pattern of a poem, but any tendency of its author to be warmly and directly and candidly emotional. Ingenuous and uncomplicated sentiment is, in these days, very likely to be mis-called sentimentality, something very different indeed.

Perhaps Hay, like many women writers of her generation, was wary of falling into this trap. Later generations of women poets, especially those fueled by the second wave of the U.S. women's movement, would take up the issue more directly and with fewer reservations.

Though formally very different from the modernist "exercises in composition" of Marianne Moore (1887–1972), Hay's work, like Moore's, frequently avoids the trap of "mis-called sentimentality" by looking to nature and natural history for inspiration. *The Stone and the Shell* is full of imagery from nature, most often used as object lessons for some insight about the human condition. The poem "Natural History Note" is one of the few that announces Hay's motives for drawing on nature to compensate for her own real or imagined lacks:

> I praise all armored things,
> With shells, and stings …
> That I unguarded was
> Must be the cause.

Other poems of Hay's that deal with nature move in the direction of fable. "Little Fable" tells in five quatrains the story of a snail convinced by a panther to abandon his shell and his "undaring, circumscribed and slow" life in order to lead the panther's more adventurous, free life. After the snail

> Strain[s] against his little roof,
> Uncoil[s] himself, and with a shout
> Step[s] out,

he finds he is at a loss to run, climb, leap, and kill as the panther does. The blunt moral comes in the stanza that follows:

> And while he wondered what to do
> And how to prove his mighty worth,
> Some passer-by's unheeding shoe
> Trampled him into earth.

Hay distances herself from the fable's central drama by employing the animals, the fabulistic conventions, and the masculine third-person pronoun to refer to the snail and the panther.

The fable has long functioned as a means for encoding specific social criticisms, and in the hands of a woman writer it may take on the additional function of indirectly voicing concerns of immediate significance to the author. It is possible to read "Little Fable" as a mediated expression of the dilemmas faced by a woman (or snail) trying to succeed in a man's (or panther's) world. To strengthen this approach one might read the fable in relation to a more socially explicit poem like "Career Woman," which appears in *This, My Letter* and is a well thought out, multilayered poem that addresses the complexity of women's issues more fully and less obliquely than the bulk of Hay's work.

In Hay's usual fashion, "Career Woman" is written more as a character case study than as an autobiographical reflection.

Also like the snail in "Little Fable," the woman, prodded by the thorn to succeed in the male public sphere, is puzzled by what makes her give up the safe shell of her sphere, the traditional role as homemaker and dependent. But unlike the snail, the woman is not faulted for foolishly trying to be other than herself: the poem's first line makes clear that it was God and the poem, in its final lines, reinforces this statement.

This poem's structure mirrors the complexity of the topic as it was debated in society and as Hay surely grappled with it in her own life. By extending a complex and embedded sentence over the last seven lines of the first stanza, the poem permits the reader to fall into productive misreadings. It is easy during initial readings to refer to the career woman's unnatural appetite, which would play into the stereotype of the ambitious woman as a monstrosity or travesty of her feminine nature. However, Hay's extreme economy of language may be the cause for such a misreading. This moment of ambiguity and productive misreading brings into play exactly the sorts of assumptions prevailing in the culture about the "career woman" type. A similar use of embedding and enjambment to heighten the ambiguity and so encourage active reading is found in the parenthetical "(who knows best?)" in the second stanza, whose punctuation makes it possible for the clause to be read as a complete question, but whose relation to the words "doom" and "blessing" in the following line suggests that these words may be read as the direct objects to the verb "knows" in the prior line. In other words, Hay's uncharacteristically dense structure and approach accommodate both the prevailing judgments against the "career woman" and their annulment.

In the end the poem explicitly acquits the "career woman," rendering moot judgment anyone might make of her choices by reasserting the fact that it was "her God ... Who shaped and thrust it." The complexity does not end here, however, for while in line 1 it was simply "God" who "thrust a thorn within her side," at the poem's conclusion a new possibility is entertained: that the woman has the right to conceive of "her God" in her own terms. But because "God" and "Who" are capitalized in this final line, it is unlikely that Hay is ironically suggesting that the woman compulsively serves some false god of her own creation.

So-called case studies such as "Career Woman" provided Hay with aesthetic distance while she explored issues that were of immediate relevance to her personal and professional life. Yet even in "Career Woman," which stands as one of Hay's more feminist poems, the speaker is at a remove, an omniscient voice with no clearly gendered identity. This was a dominating tendency in much of the poetry of the first half of the twentieth century by men and women alike. It was also a strategy used by women writers to keep attention on the work itself, not on the gender of the author. If Hay's poem "On Suicide," for instance, seems cold to an audience used to confessional poems like Anne Sexton's passionate and detailed "Wanting to Die," it nonetheless carried a heat that Hay, very much in step with the tastes of her mentors and contemporaries, had learned to temper with distance, abstraction, and formalism.

The use of personae, or poetic masks, is another distancing strategy Hay frequently employs. By writing in the voice of an imagined character, she was free to try on idioms and ideas with which she might have been less comfortable in a voice closer to her own. Hay's work with personae is extensively carried out in *Story Hour* and in the numerous monologues based on biblical characters published throughout her career. *Story Hour,* with its ostensibly parodic premise for seeing traditional fairy tales in a new light, is also a study of how crucial point of view is in shaping what people believe to be the truth. If history is always written by the winners, one might say that, for Hay, fairy tales are always written from the point of view

of the protagonist. To unsettle this dominant point of view and what it obscures, Hay often takes on the persona of a tale's villain or minor character. "Interview," written in the persona of Cinderella's stepmother, is an example. The poem imagines how the stepmother might speak to a local reporter interested in learning more about the childhood of the now celebrated princess, "Miss Glass Slipper of the Year." In the poem's sestet the stepmother refers disparagingly to Cinderella's lies, "those shameless tales about the way / We treated her," raising the possibility that the famed mistreatment of Cinderella may have been less than true. At the same time, the sestet allows for the possibility that the stepmother is simply saving face before the reporter, that—given the chance to tell her side of the story—she shapes it to her advantage:

> Oh, nobody denies
> That she was pretty, if you like those curls.
> But looks aren't everything, I always say.

The addition of "if you like those curls" betrays a certain cattiness and jealousy on the part of the stepmother just before she intones the old commonplace that "looks aren't everything." In "Interview" Hay serves up no ready-made conclusions about what *really* happened; rather she demonstrates that point of view makes the truth itself a slippery entity.

Personae and point of view also enabled Hay to explore gender relations in *Story Hour* and in other of her works. The most notable examples from *Story Hour* are her revisions of the Briar Rose tale, "The Sleeper 1" and "The Sleeper 2." In "The Sleeper 1" readers hear Briar Rose, or Sleeping Beauty, speak. Now married to the prince who awakened her after years of sleep behind impenetrable, thorny rosebushes, she bluntly announces in line 1, "I wish the Prince had left me where he found me." Immediately the poem recasts the "rescue" as a potentially negative act. What was she rescued from? According to the speaker in this sonnet, the prince saved her from "the cloistered world I've loved so long"—which is to say it was not so much a rescue as a disturbance. "The Sleeper 1" is a complaint on the part of a woman who, like the image frequently painted of Emily Dickinson, had come to love the safety of her "dearest privacy" because it allowed her to determine and live by "the pattern of [her] dream." As such, it also suggests that women may want other things from life besides rescue by and marriage to a "prince," despite the "happily ever after" insistence of the fairy-tale endings.

"The Sleeper 2," written in the persona of the prince, shows the ways in which the prince's expectations, too, have not been met by the marital aftermath of his dramatic rescue. Writing in this male persona gives Hay the opportunity to comment on the ways in which men, as well as women, are deprived of authentic experiences when they place too much faith in cultural myths:

> I used to think that slumbrous look she wore,
> The dreaming air, the drowsy-lidded eyes,
> Were artless affectation, nothing more.

Too late the prince discovers that the woman is as she seems, that what was charming to him as "affectation" is galling to him as a permanent personality trait. Recalling Hay's own reflections on the limited options for the woman who is committed to writing, "The Sleeper 2" dramatizes how, from the point of view of the male raised to expect complete devotion from his wife, the woman who is dedicated to her inner life and dreams appears to those around her to be asleep "behind a thorny wall / Of rooted selfishness."

As early as her first book, Hay wrote a poem in defense of her love of solitude and contemplation. The sonnet's title, "Retort," is the only suggestion that the poem is a response to the social expectation that women should be emotionally available to others at all times. Echoing Dickinson's assertions that "The Soul selects her own Society," "Retort" declares that it is "Inestimable privilege, to find / The quiet friend of one's congenial Mind!" But while this early poem eschews the gender-based conflicts around the choice of a contemplative life, Hay's work with personae in *Story Hour* sets the stage for seeing such conflicts in terms of sexual politics.

Hay's use of personae to deepen interpretations of religious texts also opened the way to problematizing gender relations. "Eden," a five-sonnet sequence that first appeared in *The Delicate Balance,* includes sonnets in Eve's and Adam's voices. The third sonnet of the sequence, in the persona of Eve, expresses her disappointment at Adam's cowardice in the face of God's censure:

> And here lies all the measure of my blame:
> That one for whom I dreamed so proud a span
> Fell short the very stature of a man,
> And would not even own our common shame;
> But mumbled, cringing at Jehovah's feet,
> "The woman tempted me, and I did eat."

There are several messages that this sestet conveys. For one, Eve is shown to be a sort of Lady Macbeth figure in her voicing of vicarious ambitions for Adam. At the same time, her respect for him and the idea of manhood is implicit in her disappointment at his falling short of "the very stature of a man." Finally, Eve does not disown her role in the Fall but simply expects that Adam would have recognized their "common shame."

For his part, Adam, in the fourth sonnet, claims that the only reason he blamed Eve was that he thought God's punishment would be less harsh, considering that it was God who created her to be weak and who made her "lovelier than all / Wisdom or caution or obedience." Adam's ploy, of course, failed, and so the poem in his voice exposes the irony of his assumption that Eve is the weaker of the two. It further exposes Adam's preoccupation with her physical beauty, a preoccupation that blinds him to her other potential virtues and vices. He describes her as "flower, and flint, and fragile air, / Gentle and wilful and withal most fair" but fails, in his disproportionate focus on her beauty, to recognize that "flint" and "fragile air" are two quite different qualities.

Irony and paradox are powerful literary devices that enable a text at once to say-and-not-say something. It is indeed probable that Hay excelled at irony not only because it is a time-tested strategy that adds multiple meanings to poetry, but also because, at a time when the serious female author figured as the "exception proving the rule," these devices promised a sanctioned means for telling the truth but "telling it slant." It may well be true that, as Hay herself wrote, she has attained the status of only a "minor poet." Nonetheless, she may have been able to come to terms with that truth because she understood how few women of her generation had a fair chance of becoming a poet at all.

Selected Bibliography

WORKS OF SARA HENDERSON HAY

POETRY

Field of Honor. Dallas: Kaleidograph Press, 1933.

This, My Letter. New York: Knopf, 1939.

The Delicate Balance. New York: Scribners, 1951.

The Stone and the Shell. Pittsburgh: University of Pittsburgh Press, 1959.

Story Hour: A Second Look at Cinderella, Bluebeard, and Company. Illustrated by Jim McMullan. New York: Doubleday, 1963.

A Footing on This Earth. New York: Doubleday, 1966. (New and selected poems.)

Story Hour. Fayetteville: University of Arkansas Press, 1982; 1998. (An expansion of the 1963 edition. The 1998 reissue is illustrated and has a foreword by Miller Williams.)

PROSE

"Mrs. Jellison." *Ellery Queen's Mystery Magazine,* November 1954, pp. 73–80. (Short fiction.)

"A Round-Eyed Listener Who Asks No Questions." *New York Sunday Herald Tribune Book Week Fall Children's Issue,* November 10, 1963, pp. 1–2.

COLLECTIONS

Kentucky Poetry Review 16, no. 1 (winter–spring 1980). (Issue devoted to Hay's life and work.)

Seasons of the Heart: In Quest of Faith: Poems. Edited and with a bibliographic memoir by Agnes Dodds Kinard. Allison Park, Pa.: Pickwick Publications, 1989. (Selection focuses on Hay's religious and devotional poetry).

MANUSCRIPT PAPERS

The personal archives of Sara Henderson Hay are kept in the Hunt Library special collections department at Carnegie Mellon University, Pittsburgh, Pennsylvania.

AUDIO RECORDINGS

Sara Henderson Hay Recording Her Poems at the City College of New York, June 7, 1938, and May 16, 1940. Library of Congress Archive of Recorded Poetry and Literature, 1938 and 1940.

CRITICAL AND BIOGRAPHICAL STUDIES

Baker, Gladys. "New York Lauds Sara Henderson Hay." *The Birmingham News-Age Herald,* April 15, 1935, p. 5.

Benét, William Rose. "Heart, Mind, and Wit." *Saturday Review,* October 21, 1939, p. 16. (Review of *This, My Letter.*)

French, Warren. "Redskin Verse Versus Paleface Verse." *Voices,* May–August 1964, pp. 39–41.

Hayden, Robert. "A Feel for Irony." *New York Times Book Review,* April 29, 1951, p. 22. (Review of *The Delicate Balance.*)

Ritchey, John. "A Major Lyricist." *Christian Science Monitor,* November 4, 1939. (Review of *This, My Letter.*)

Sheehy, Gail. "Who's Afraid of the Big Bad Fairy Tale?" *New York Herald Tribune,* September 20, 1963, p. 16. (Review of *Story Hour.*)

Spector, Robert D. "The Poet's Other Voices, Other Rooms." *Saturday Review,* February 1, 1964, pp. 36–38. (Review of *Story Hour.*)

Stafford, William. "Several Tongues." *Poetry* 95:248–257 (January 1960). (Review of *The Stone and the Shell.*)

—ELLEN MCGRATH SMITH

Herbert Huncke

1915–1996

Herbert Huncke was "beat" long before there was a Beat Movement. A high-school dropout, he made his way from Chicago to New York's Forty-second Street in 1939 by way of freight trains, hitched rides, and sexual liaisons with strangers. Huncke (rhymes with "junky") may have started his life as a beguiling young hustler, but a heavy drug habit and frequent prison sentences aged him prematurely. Slight of stature, with a heroin addict's knowing eyes and a memorably plaintive voice, Huncke mesmerized the future Beat writers William S. Burroughs, Allen Ginsberg, and Jack Kerouac with tales of his down-and-out youth and his volatile friendships with drug-using drifters. In a 1947 letter to Neal Cassady included in his *Selected Letters, 1940–1956,* Kerouac lauds Huncke as "the greatest storyteller I know, an actual genius at it, in my mind." All three of the primary Beats seemed to realize early on that Huncke was, as Burroughs expresses it in his foreword to *The Herbert Huncke Reader* (1997), "a character, a rarity, a real picaresque antihero in the classical tradition."

Herbert Edwin Huncke was born on January 9, 1915, in Greenfield, Massachusetts. His father was Herbert Spencer Huncke, a German American from Chicago who held an apprentice position with a machine parts company. His mother was Marguerite Bell Huncke, the teenaged daughter of a recently deceased Wyoming cattle rancher. A few years after Huncke's birth the family moved to Detroit, where a second son was born, and then they settled in Chicago. With financial help from his wife's inheritance, the elder Huncke founded H. S. Huncke & Company, a precision-tool business. Though their prospects appeared bright, the Hunckes' contentious marriage traumatized young Herbert. Decades later, he would break down in sobs when recalling his unhappy childhood.

Flanked by his quarreling parents, he grew up feeling alone and unprotected. Although he was close to his maternal grandmother, who often stayed in the Chicago household, her combative nature only exacerbated tensions. Complicating matters further, Marguerite treated Herbert more like a confessor than a son. She told the boy about her sexual difficulties and implied that the consummation of her marriage had been a virtual rape. Revelations such as these had a lifelong impact. As Huncke matured, he developed a profound empathy for others as well as a pained awareness of his own isolation. Although he was never a student of Buddhism in the way that Kerouac and Ginsberg were, he intuitively grasped the first Noble Truth, that all life is suffering.

Still, as Huncke recognized, that precept does not mean that life is all bad. In his stories and vignettes, his perceptions of beauty often give form and meaning to his deepest fears. This is evident in an autobiographical piece that provided the title for a 1980 collection of his writing, "The Evening Sun Turned Crimson," in which he recounts his stay as a young child at a country house. His host family had taken an overnight trip and left him on his own. Though he was just five or six, he had looked forward to a night by himself with only the resident dog for company. As we see in this excerpt from the story, which is reprinted in *The Herbert Huncke Reader,* the experience quickly devolves into one of existential terror:

On the evening of this story as I walked from the interior of the house out onto the porch, I became aware of the sky which had turned a wild furious crimson from the huge glowing red disk of the sun radiating shafts of gold light and at rushing speed plunged below the horizon. I stood—nearly riveted to the spot bathed in pinkish tint and surrounded by an almost red world—everything reflecting the sunset—and filled with awe and an inward fright I felt the intenseness of my being alone, and although I've suffered acute awareness of loneliness many many times throughout my life, I've never sensed it quite as thoroughly or traumatically as on that evening when all the world turned into burning flame and it was as though I was already in the process of being consumed. I was not brave at all any longer and was out-and-out afraid—plain scared—as I've ever been in my life.

The poet in Huncke could not ignore the duality of his experience. "The Evening Sun Turned Crimson" ends with this seeming contradiction: "There isn't much more except to say the sun setting on that warm summer evening was one of the most frightening experiences in my life. Today a sunset can fill me with an awareness of beauty that nothing else can." As is the case in much of his work, the story does not comment on the author's dramatic shift in perception. The delicacy of the omission implies that a lifetime of sunsets—a gradual rapprochement with beauty and fear—has intervened between the penultimate sentence and the last.

His parents' marriage ended when Herbert was just beginning to come into his own as a rebellious spirit with a taste for adventure. On a summer day in 1927, when he was twelve years old, he took the dime his mother had given him for trolley fare and rode to the outskirts of Chicago instead of going to his father's home. Then he hitchhiked east in hopes of reaching New York City by way of his birthplace in Greenfield, Massachusetts. Along the way he had a sexual encounter with a stranger, who quickly handed over a ten-dollar bill and sped off after learning his victim's age. Huncke later recalled how happy the windfall made him. It was the beginning of his career as a hustler.

His trip took him to Geneva, New York, where he paused to inhale the intoxicating scent of an onion field. Here was a natural tranquility unknown to him in his chaotic Chicago home. But soon thereafter a police officer took the young drifter into custody. In *Guilty of Everything: The Autobiography of Herbert Huncke,* published in its full form in 1990 and excerpted in *The Herbert Huncke Reader,* he describes this early encounter with the law:

> The next thing you know the big cop was saying, "You know, maybe you're not a boy at all." Oh man, I had never had anyone question my sex before. This was the ultimate, I thought. "Maybe you're a girl. Why don't you get up and walk across the room?" I got up, and my face must have turned red as a beet. Of course, I was so self-conscious, I don't know whether I walked like a man or the biggest faggot that ever came down the pike, but I did walk across that office. He said, "All right, now walk back." So I walked back. He said, "I don't know. Maybe there's someone looking for you someplace. Maybe you're a girl in boy's clothes." I was so mad I pulled my pants open and said, "Look, there's a cock. I'm a boy." That cracked those guys up. The motorcycle cop couldn't look at me he was laughing so much. "Oh yeah, well, you think you're pretty tough."

Huncke's experiences as a runaway foreshadowed the trips Kerouac describes in *On the Road.* Like Kerouac's Sal Paradise, the peripatetic young Huncke wanted to get out and experience America firsthand. Although his journey ended inauspiciously, when his embarrassed and angry father arrived from Chicago to take him home, Huncke had tasted freedom. In time he would elude his father's censorious gaze and lose contact with him altogether.

As a teenager Huncke yearned to be a writer, but the very powers of perception that stimulated that desire sometimes overwhelmed him with sadness. In "Song of Self," originally included in *Huncke's Journal* (1965) and reprinted in *The Herbert Huncke Reader*, he recalls an early attempt at writing poetry. Having stared at the predawn sky for hours, he ventured outside to see the sun "hurling and spiraling across a huge space of blue," an image that recalls the apocalyptic sunset in "The Evening Sun Turned Crimson." What he saw—blooming flowers and cheerful young women walking to work—left him feeling "more convinced each instant, I was doomed." He wrote a poem about the scene but lost it, "along with everything of myself at that time." The loss of the poem symbolizes a loss of connection with his own past; this brief sketch fully captures his feelings of psychological disenfranchisement. The title "Song of Self" refers to Walt Whitman's "Song of Myself," the omission of "my" hinting at the narrator's pathological self-doubt. It is as if Huncke is mourning a lost self even as he acknowledges that this loss is the very essence of his identity.

Disaffected but always deeply curious about the world, Huncke educated himself on the streets of Chicago rather than submit to the rigors of a classroom. "In the Park," which first appeared in *Huncke's Journal* and later in *The Herbert Huncke Reader*, offers a glimpse of his youth:

> I had adventures and strange experiences—frequently meeting and becoming involved with other night people. I learned much about sex and about the vast number of people who make up the so-called less desirable element in our American way of life. Haunted people—lonely people—misfits—outcasts—wanderers—those on the skids—drunkards—deviates of all kinds—hustlers of every description—male and female—old people and young people—and they come from every section of the country.

Huncke too was haunted and lonely. Primarily attracted to men yet not averse to an occasional tryst with a woman, he communed with the misfits, outcasts, and wanderers of Chicago because he recognized in them something of his own restive, despairing soul. The hustlers and addicts he met were not deviants in his eyes; they were his friends, fellow sufferers, Americans in pain.

BEAT GENERATION BEGINNINGS

By the time Huncke arrived in New York City in 1939, he had spent time in Miami, New Orleans, Memphis, Galveston, and Las Vegas, working odd jobs and developing a lifelong dependency on heroin and other illicit drugs. He had learned how to hop freight trains, and that was how he made it from Las Vegas back to his boyhood home of Chicago. But no one in his family wanted anything to do with him, so he headed for New York City just as he had as a young runaway. This time, at the ripe age of twenty-four, he reached his destination and made himself at home:

> I was always quick in picking up on the scenes, and I took to Forty-second Street. I was a natural for it. It was exciting. I didn't see all the tinsel and tawdriness about it then, and it took me quite a while to finally detect the horror of the surroundings. But the Pokerino with its neon flashing, the little passageways from one street to another that were off the record, guys sitting around talking about the clip they'd made—all of this was completely new to me, and I was captivated by it.
>
> I had led something of an open life in Chicago, but it was comparatively protected. I had never really been out scuffling on my own. No matter how bad things were in Chicago, if I couldn't get it from my father I could bum it from my mother. But in New York I didn't know anybody. I was strictly on my own for the first time.
>
> At this time there were a lot of drugstores in New York that were doing illegal business. They were selling hypodermic needles under the counter, Benzedrine pills. The first place I hit was on Eighth Avenue, between Forty-sixth and Forty-seventh, cold turkey. I didn't know anything about it except that it was near Forty-second Street. I had already cruised a couple of times, so I figured if push came to shove this would be a good

headquarters. As it turned out, it was.

Huncke made it his business to know every addict, prostitute, and thief who crossed his path. Between sex acts with johns and his constant quest for heroin or whatever drug was most readily available, there was still time to weave his new friends' stories into his own. As his autobiographical writings attest, Huncke's early partners in crime included Little Jack Melody, a hapless crook with a Mafia pedigree; Detroit Redhead, a Times Square prostitute; and Johnnie Terrell, a burglar from Detroit.

As much as he loved New York City, however, Huncke was not done with traveling. He and a friend joined the merchant marine during World War II, ostensibly so that they could kick their heroin addiction and see the world. In an interview with John Tytell published in *the unspeakable visions of the individual* many years later, Huncke said, "Going to sea had always been a dream of mine like joining the circus when I was a kid." There was something distinctly circuslike in Huncke's travels. In Colón he acquired a pet monkey that accompanied him for the rest of the voyage. Still hooked on drugs he discovered that the monkey shared his tastes, as he relates in a passage from *The Evening Sun Turned Crimson,* later included in *The Herbert Huncke Reader:*

Jocko—the monkey—took to pot like the proverbial duck to water, and as soon as I would light up would jump up on my shoulder and I would exhale the smoke into his little grinning face. He and I would get high and he would balance himself on the rail while I leaned up against it and looked at the sea. He would talk to me in little chittering sounds and I would tell him about how cute and how great I thought he was. One day we saw a huge fish leap out of the sea and plunge back in again. The sea was a molten gray mass with a veil of shimmering vapor hanging just above the surface—reflecting the burning sun— when suddenly it seemed almost to shatter. This huge fish—glistening in the light—exploded in the air for a moment amidst a spray of crystal drops of water—arched—and slid back into the sea. We were both surprised. Jocko actually screeched and I almost yelled to him, "Did you dig that?"

Huncke's delirious adventures on the high seas were rife with double meanings. Who else but a doped-up Huncke would literally have a monkey on his back?

For most of the 1940s, however, Huncke was a fixture in Manhattan's Times Square. Because he was so integral to the Forty-second Street scene, Huncke caught the eye of Dr. Alfred Kinsey, the famed sex researcher based at Indiana University. In the early 1940s Kinsey interviewed Huncke for his book on male sexuality and then, for two dollars a person, paid him to line up interviews with other interesting specimens. Of his relationship with Kinsey, Huncke writes in *Guilty of Everything:*

I sent a number of people I knew up to meet with Kinsey. I think I pretty much made his Times Square study. There were others, of course, whom he'd met through me that kind of took over for me. It got to be quite competitive for a while there, what with all the running about for interviewees.

In fact, I introduced Burroughs to Kinsey over at the Angler Bar. Bill, of course, is a very knowledgeable individual. He's been all over the world, and as a young man he had studied medicine in Vienna. The two of them talked the same language. When Kinsey came back to the city the second time, he spent more time out and we'd all meet at the Angler. Joan [Vollmer Adams] would come around, and Ginsberg, and though I'm not sure, each of them interviewed with Kinsey as well.

A voyeur with license to ask prurient questions, Kinsey must have felt like he had struck gold with Huncke, who knew sexual libertines from all walks of life.

Although Kinsey faded from the group, Burroughs and Huncke would be linked for the rest of their lives. Harvard-educated and bolstered by a family trust fund, Burroughs met Huncke in the mid-1940s, early in his own criminal career. Burroughs wanted to unload a stolen sawed-off shotgun and a stash of morphine syringes, and he approached Huncke's roommate in a Brooklyn tenement about the deal. Sizing up Burroughs, who resembled a well-dressed praying mantis, Huncke suspected that the surprise guest was an undercover cop. Although this story has entered Beat lore as a famous case of mistaken identity, Huncke was not entirely wrong: reserved and watchful, Burroughs stood apart from a crowd even as he sampled its dissipations.

Through Burroughs, Huncke soon met Ginsberg and Kerouac. Although he could not know that all three of his new friends would become celebrated authors, he recognized their potential in other ways: they were easy marks who could provide him with quick cash and a place to sleep. The fact that they listened to his stories with rapt attention was a decided bonus. In Huncke the others saw a conduit for their interest in New York's underworld. In *Literary Outlaw: The Life and Times of William S. Burroughs* (1980), biographer Ted Morgan memorably labels Huncke as the group's "Virgilian guide to the lower depths." Ginsberg concurred in his essay about Huncke, "Hipster's Hipster," noting that Huncke's "shrewd estimates based on his own experiences on the street cut through a lot of bourgeois stupidity and enlightened a lot of us." Taking Burroughs, Ginsberg, and Kerouac to the sordid Angler Bar and introducing them to a carnivalesque crowd of crooks, Huncke served essentially the same purpose for them as he had for Kinsey: their experiences with Huncke would show up later as material in their books.

Despite their later reputation as rebellious outsiders, Burroughs, Ginsberg, and Kerouac were decidedly mainstream compared to Huncke. Yet even as they waded into the intriguingly murky waters where Huncke flailed, not one of them intended to stay there for long. All three would be arrested not long after meeting Huncke—Kerouac for being an accessory in Lucien Carr's fatal knifing of David Kammerer, Ginsberg for possession of stolen goods, Burroughs for fatally shooting Joan Vollmer Adams Burroughs—but not one was sentenced to prison. Luck and good connections kept them afloat. Huncke, broke and alienated from his family, was not so fortunate. He was in prison on drug and theft charges off and on during the 1940s, for much of the 1950s, and during the 1960s as well.

In 1947 at Burroughs's invitation Huncke decamped for the rural Southwest. Living with Joan and her daughter on a farm outside New Waverly, Texas, Burroughs hoped to raise a cash crop of marijuana. He was well aware of the complications that ensued when Huncke was around but seemed to crave his companionship nonetheless. Perhaps this was because Huncke had a knack for sniffing out drugs. With little else to occupy him, Huncke spent a good deal of his time in Texas tracking down disreputable drugstores that would supply him with all of the pharmaceuticals that he and his hosts depended on. Still, the bucolic surroundings were not lost on the displaced hipster. Recalling one telling episode from his Texas sojourn in *Guilty of Everything,* Huncke observes

> In the summer there was a mass of all kinds of flowers, and everything was so lush and beautiful. And there were a lot of cedar trees draped in Spanish moss, hibiscus bushes, big coral-colored blossoms. Little chameleons all during the summer when they'd mate, with their little throats bubbled up rose-colored. Armadillos were all over the place. Once, Bill shot an armadillo on his property. I'm ashamed to say I suggested it. Afterward I buried it and said prayers over it.

It was not the last time Burroughs would shoot and kill recklessly. Four years later, in a Mexico City apartment, a drunken Burroughs shot and killed Joan Burroughs at close range. Intelligent and well read, helplessly addicted to Benzedrine, and thoroughly beat, Joan had housed most of the key Beat figures in her New York apartment during the mid-1940s. Her death in 1951, for which Burroughs spent a couple of weeks in a Mexican jail, effectively signaled the end of the Beat Movement's halcyon days, such as they were.

ANGELHEADED HIPSTER

Huncke's use of the slang term "beat" provided Kerouac with the label for a generation of young people both tormented and energized by their experiences in America during the cold war era. Huncke used the word in two ways: to signify exhaustion and to describe a drug deal gone awry. To say he *was* beat meant he was tired and worn out; to say he *got* beat meant that his connection had taken his money without delivering the goods. But Kerouac found musical and spiritual connotations in "beat" as well. The French-Canadian Catholic in him yearned for the beatific; the jazz aficionado sought the beat of a drum. The word "beat," which Huncke used frequently and casually, thus expanded in meaning in order to accommodate Kerouac's evolving notion of a Beat Generation.

In addition to providing Kerouac with an intriguing way to describe his peers, Huncke was himself a ready-made character. Many a writer friend discovered that merely describing this wraith of a man made for a lively passage of poetry or prose. Ginsberg, who was to take a lifelong interest in Huncke and his affairs, turned to him as a source of inspiration in "Howl," which was published in 1956. The poem famously begins, "I saw the best minds of my generation destroyed by madness, starving hysterical naked, / dragging themselves through the negro streets at dawn looking for an angry fix, / angelheaded hipsters burning for the ancient heavenly connection to the starry dynamo in the machinery of night." In *Howl:*

Original Draft Facsimile, Transcript and Variant Versions (1988), Ginsberg comments on the second verse: "Herbert Huncke cruised Harlem, Times Square areas at irregular hours, late forties, scoring junk." It seems as though Huncke was the original angelheaded hipster. The *Facsimile* reveals that several other passages about Huncke were edited out of the final draft of "Howl." One memorable verse about Huncke remains, however: "who walked all night with their shoes full of blood on the snowbank docks waiting for a door in the East River to open to a room full of steamheat and opium." The story behind this particular verse helps explain how "Howl" got written in the first place.

In February 1949 Huncke was released from Riker's Island prison after serving a brief sentence for marijuana possession. Initially he was afraid to seek shelter from Ginsberg because he had recently stolen a great many books and other possessions from the New York apartment Ginsberg was subletting. But desperation brought him to Ginsberg's doorstep. In Huncke's own recollection (as recorded in Barry Gifford's *Jack's Book: An Oral Biography of Jack Kerouac,* 1988), "One night when I was just too beat to continue doing anything—I was just about two steps this side of being dead—I knocked on his door, and he took me in, and I slept for two days and finally came out of the condition I was in." When Huncke finally roused himself, Ginsberg was delighted. He recalled in an interview with Barry Farrell that "one day [Huncke] went out and pulled off a burglary of an auto. Signs of springtime! I was really grateful, he was coming back to life, something! Regrettable though it was, it meant he was going to survive."

His pleasure was short-lived. Little Jack Melody and Detroit Redhead, Huncke's partners in crime, began to frequent the apartment, and Ginsberg had to step around the stolen goods that were filling every corner. In April 1949 the police arrested all four of them after a car chase in Queens that got written up in the *New York Times*. Trailing a lengthy rap sheet and lacking anyone to vouch for him, Huncke was dispatched to prison. Family members came to the rescue of the equally culpable Little Jack and Detroit Redhead. As for Ginsberg, his father, his lawyer brother, and a couple of Columbia University professors arranged for him to avoid a prison sentence by going to the Columbia Psychiatric Institute instead. It was there that Ginsberg met Carl Solomon, a brilliant fellow patient with radical leanings. Several years later Ginsberg dedicated "Howl" to Solomon and built the poem's third part around Solomon's (and his own) experience in psychiatric care. Although in hindsight Ginsberg appeared destined to write an important poem that would speak for his generation, clearly both Solomon and Huncke helped call that poem into being.

Even in the earliest years of their friendship Ginsberg saved Huncke's letters and hastily scrawled notes, as if he anticipated Huncke's later importance to literary and cultural history. But Ginsberg was not the first of the Beat writers to draw inspiration from him. In Kerouac's first novel, *The Town and the City,* published in 1950, the aptly named Junkey is easily recognizable as Huncke. Loitering in a streetside cafeteria, Junkey maintains

> his pale vigil of Forty-second Street—a vigil that went on a good eighteen hours a day, and sometimes, when he had no place to sleep, twenty-four hours around the clock. … Junkey always sat facing the street, and when he talked, sometimes with intense earnestness, his eyes kept nevertheless going back and forth as he combed the street sweepingly under drooping eyelids.

In the company of characters based on Ginsberg, Little Jack Melody, and Kerouac himself, Junkey is both malcontent and sage: "Junkey, with his eyes sarcastically lidded, his mouth turned down at the corners in a masklike expression of weary indifference and misery, listened to everything with earnest attentiveness and

knowledge. He was wise in his own right." Although he does not actually appear in *On the Road,* Huncke nevertheless functions as an intriguing off-stage character named Elmer Hassel. Just as narrator Sal Paradise and his buddy Dean sporadically look for Dean's missing father on their travels back and forth across the country, so do they keep an eye out for Elmer Hassel around Times Square. Looking for Hassel becomes another of the novel's exercises in futile longing as Sal and Dean career from coast to coast.

Burroughs also makes interesting use of Huncke in his prose. In his autobiographical novel *Junky,* originally published under a pseudonym in 1953, Burroughs's merciless description of "Herman" gives us a nearly photographic image of Huncke in the mid-1940s:

> Waves of hostility and suspicion flowed out from his large brown eyes like some sort of television broadcast. The effect was almost like a physical impact. The man was small and very thin, his neck loose in the collar of his shirt. His complexion faded from brown to a mottled yellow, and pancake make-up had been heavily applied in an attempt to conceal a skin eruption. His mouth was drawn down at the corners in a grimace of petulant annoyance.

A few pages later, narrator Bill Lee reveals that he has become friendly with Herman, though he still regards his new acquaintance with disapprobation. He reports that "soon I was buying his drinks and meals, and he was hitting me for 'smash' (change) at regular intervals. Herman did not have a habit at this time. In fact, he seldom got a habit unless someone else paid for it." This failure to repay debts seemed to bother Burroughs more than anything else about Huncke.

From the beginning, Burroughs, Ginsberg, and Kerouac viewed Huncke as their social inferior. Ginsberg and Burroughs, both of whom outlived Kerouac by three decades, never wavered from this stance. But all three (along with Neal Cassady, whose academic credentials were about the same as Huncke's) realized that Huncke was a kindred artistic spirit. Huncke could talk cogently about Kafka and Dostoyevsky, and he appeared to be Jean Genet's soul brother. He was a superb storyteller, and the stories he got down on paper demonstrated a natural flair for writing. His firsthand knowledge of marginalized subcultures gave his stories and sketches a street credibility to which Kerouac and Ginsberg could only aspire, and his descriptions of friends and lovers evince a tenderness the acerbic Burroughs could never muster. If not quite a diamond in the rough, he was at least a grit-covered pearl. In a 1952 letter that Kerouac wrote to Ginsberg, included in Kerouac's *Selected Letters, 1940–1956,* he declared that "our genuine literary movement" is "made up of you, me, Neal, Huncke (as yet unpublishable) and mebbe Lucien [Carr] someday." A decade later, convinced that Huncke was in fact publishable, Kerouac helped him place a story in a magazine called *Escapade.*

FIRST BOOK PUBLICATION

In 1965 Huncke's first book came about through the good offices of the poet Diane di Prima, who operated a grassroots enterprise called the Poets Press. Having already published a couple of Huncke's stories in *Floating Bear,* the journal she co-edited with Amiri Baraka, she asked whether she could publish a book of his writings. Huncke gladly handed over an armload of stories and sketches, leaving di Prima to sort through the random pile and assign a title to the finished volume. The Poets Press published one thousand copies of *Huncke's Journal,* a collection of twenty stories and sketches dating from approximately 1948 through 1964. By the time it was released, Arthur Knight writes in *Dictionary of Literary Biography,* "Huncke had given a number of readings in the Village, and he was

beginning to attract a following." When the first edition sold out, di Prima published a second edition with a brief introduction by Ginsberg. Interest in the book had run its course, however, and di Prima ended up taking most of the second edition with her when she moved to San Francisco in 1968. Rather than sell the book, she left boxes of *Huncke's Journal* on Haight Street where the disenfranchised "night people" (to use Huncke's own term) could help themselves to free copies.

Benjamin G. Schafer, the editor of *The Herbert Huncke Reader,* observes that *Huncke's Journal* "demonstrates Huncke's remarkable range within the memoir form. In it are prose poems, solitary musings, teenage memories, sketches of various New York City scenes, and magical flights of imagination describing the crush of activity, personalities, and energy surrounding the amphetamine scene of the early 1960s." The strength of *Huncke's Journal* lies in its portraits of people, including Huncke himself, in telling moments of vulnerability and paradox. Of all the Beat writers, Huncke seemed best equipped to convey the "sympathy" that Kerouac, in a 1957 appearance on *The Steve Allen Show,* said was the essence of Beat.

Huncke's Journal was a modest beginning, but it gave the author a professional status that he badly needed. Upon his release from prison in 1959, he had felt a bit like Rip Van Winkle. Ginsberg and the other recently christened Beat writers had become famous while Huncke alternately chafed and dozed behind iron bars. When he rejoined the group, he had taken on the aura of a museum piece, even though he was only in his midforties. Writing in a special issue of the little magazine *the unspeakable visions of the individual,* John Clellon Holmes—author of the 1952 novel *Go* (yet another book that fictionalizes Huncke)—gives his impressions of the former jailbird at a party in 1960:

He looked like a slightly miniaturized Ezra Pound—the same reddish beard, life-wise eyes, and arresting air of remoteness from the circumstances of the evening. We looked at one another, but in the perambulations of too many people in too small a space, we didn't speak. He may not have recognized me, after all. It had been years since we had seen each other.

Several of the pieces in *Huncke's Journal,* all of them reprinted in *The Herbert Huncke Reader,* show the author struggling to find a comfortable footing in a social circle, and society, that had changed in his absence. In "Hallowe'en," dated October 31, 1961, he recaps his blighted trajectory from hustler to thief, all in the name of addictive drugs:

> Always there had been the opiates—heroin—morphine—Dilaudid—Pantopon—and it was thru their mysterious chemical magic I became truly conscious of God—the world—and the great wonder of life, and—when all else failed to stir my inner being—the quick fix again revealed the splendor—giving me reason to live until death. Nor has there been a change. It is still from the exquisite beauty of the poppy I seek solace.

He then recollects his reentry into the world of the New York Beats:

> They—those of them—creative and basically honest—at least as they understood honesty—had moved forward and had started speaking aloud—and had written great poems and books—and the world had made a place for them—because of their beauty and fineness, and because they are beautiful and good they were kind in their knowledge of me and welcomed me back and—now part of Bohemia—asked me to join them attending several Hallowe'en parties and I accepted.

Delighted that his reputation as a raconteur had preceded him, Huncke welcomed the opportunity to renew old friendships and expand his circle of literary acquaintances. One might think that being among hip young writers would have buoyed his spirits, but Huncke, age forty-six at the time of the essay's composition, was too beat for that. He claims that, despite his new-found notoriety in New York Bohemia, he wants to die "not because I especially dislike life—but mostly because I have grown rather old and am tired."

His disaffection was not merely personal. Like everyone else in America, Huncke was anxious about the threat of nuclear war. Setting aside the topic of Halloween (which suggests both the ghoulishness of the times and the frivolity of his partying friends), he ends the essay on a somber note that echoes with meaning today:

> Yesterday's headlines—our great American president states, "We now have sufficient bomb power to blow Russia off the face of the earth."
>
> Enough of hate—breeding hate—resenting each other—we need more love.
>
> There is of course the possibility—in order for us to truly evolve into something worthwhile—beyond our meager little niche in the inconceivable vastness of the universe—we have—like the Phoenix—to end in fire—and be reborn of the ashes.

Taking the poet's path rather than the polemicist's, Huncke does not elaborate on the implied comparison between his own death wish and the nation's cold war mentality, but his closing remarks hint at provocative connections: perhaps annihilation is not the end of the story; perhaps there is a realm of hope and splendor beyond the immediate despair.

In pieces such as "Song of Self" and "Youth," we see the torment Huncke endured as an adolescent in Chicago. While "Song of Self" emphasizes his private feelings of doom, "Youth" portrays him as a teenager cruelly toying with the affections of his male suitors. Never one to hide his sexual nature, Huncke writes without a trace of self-consciousness about his relationship with a University of Chicago student:

> It was he who first introduced me to poetry—to great music—to the beauty of the world—and who was concerned with my wants and happiness. Who

spent hours making love to me, caressing and kissing me on every part of my body until I would collapse in a great explosion of beauty and sensation which I have never attained in exactly the same way with anyone since. He truly loved me and asked nothing in return but that I accept him—instead of which I delighted in hurting him and making him suffer in all manner of petty ways.

Although the story reveals that neither of Huncke's two suitors during this time was above reproach, Huncke shoulders all of the blame for the disastrous outcome of his simultaneous love affairs. Bemoaning his deceitful behavior, he writes, "And so it happened that I succeeded in twisting one of the few really wonderful things that occurred when I was young into a sordid, almost tragic experience which even now fills me with shame." The story is about aborted love and the high emotional price one pays for selfishness, not about a tormented man struggling with homosexuality. Perhaps because he had never tried to live up to his father's notions of proper manhood, Huncke's sexuality did not inspire self-loathing in him, as it did in Kerouac, nor did he allow it to become the overriding consideration in his connections with others, as it often seemed to be for Ginsberg and Burroughs.

In "Ponderosa Pine," the longest piece in *Huncke's Journal,* Huncke describes his brief but memorable time working at a ranger station near Potlatch, Idaho. The story has little plot to speak of—Huncke and a teenaged Norwegian boy are unable to start their car in a violent rainstorm and must be rescued by the boy's mother—but "Ponderosa Pine," like most of Huncke's works, derives its momentum from the author's powers of description. In a few phrases casually joined by dashes, Huncke conveys the heady rush of time, the heartbreak of mortal life in an impossibly beautiful universe. The description of a fight between two "red-faced heavy-bodied lumberjacks" yields effortlessly to a portrait of an equally violent and potent landscape:

I once saw two of them in a fight—and when one had fallen—the other stomped on his face in a fury until the face looked like a hunk of raw beef when he was finally rescued—and red and black—green and black—orange and black—blue and black checked shirts—and all of this in a flash in my mind as the road rounds the last of the houses—the evening darkening blue-black in the distance, bedizened with the lights of thousands upon thousands of cosmic worlds, the stars and planets. The road now heads into the forests—only the tops of the great trees still visible individually—seemingly brushing the sky—all below a great mass of blackness, the headlights penetrating the mass—revealing brown tree trunks on either side and green foliage—the limbs of the trees begin too high up for us to see them.

For a hipster so closely identified with city life, Huncke was well attuned to the shifts of mood within the natural world.

THE BEAUTY TRAP

During the 1960s Huncke's new friends included a younger generation of writers and intellectuals who enjoyed his companionship despite the demands he placed on them. Among those friends was Eila Kokkinen, who as a graduate student at the University of Chicago had helped edit the *Chicago Review.* Both Kokkinen and her friend and fellow editor Ira Rosenthal had resigned after the university censored the journal. She followed Rosenthal to New York in 1959 and eventually took a position at the Museum of Modern Art. Through Rosenthal, she met a number of Beat writers, including Huncke. Drawn to his friendly personality and impressed by his writing, she began typing up his manuscripts for him. In an unpublished letter from 2002, she recalled their relationship:

There was always an element of being conned in Huncke's relations with other people, but there was also understanding and affection and humor. I would get exasperated and I'm sorry to say cynical about his endless drug sagas, his manipulations of people, etc., but his charm would always win the day. ... I always said I'll give Huncke love but I won't give him money, and I didn't. But I got a lot of love back from Huncke, too, and whether it was genuine, I'll never know. There was a definite affinity there; you could have a real conversation with Huncke and enjoy his company.

Staying close to him involved a lot of work and forbearance, and not many people could sustain the emotional and financial commitment that Huncke demanded. Even his closest and most liberal-minded friends, like Kokkinen and Rosenthal, struggled to understand why they tolerated him.

Rosenthal tries to justify Huncke's hold on him in his 1967 novel *Sheeper*, in which Huncke is identified by his own name:

Huncke is no sooner out of jail, than he is hooked again and turns to theft. He is apprehended in a matter of months. Never was a criminal more petty and unsuccessful. And then he is always trying to draw his friends into witnessing his pathetic courtroom appearances, into raising bail for him, into writing him letters to keep up his morale. Why bother with him at all?

Because he is a Beauty Trap and the finest storyteller my spirit has ever lifted to. He always says he relates just what he remembers, but he picks and clips unconsciously, transposes and condenses on each retelling, till his stories conform wholly to the beautiful configuration of his mind. His tales light up with compassion the most blighted and bizarre personalities, and he can portray these unfortunates with such flash and splendor that they turn into creatures of gorgon beauty before your eyes, or their beauty, pathos, and horror may jar unresolved in your mind for several days afterwards, finally condensing into beauty pure and clear, but with that slight jangle or derangement to it, that fixes it forever.

Although not everyone fell under Huncke's spell quite the way Rosenthal did, those who met Huncke were unlikely to forget him or his strange tales. As friend in need, storyteller, and drug addict on the make, he knew above all else how to connect with people.

By the late 1960s Huncke's stature as a consummate con artist who "could talk the wings off an angel" was secure, as his friend Jerome Poynton expresses it in a biographical sketch in *The Herbert Huncke Reader*. Depending on an ever-expanding circle of friends to help him through his many rough patches, he would take a deep interest in a new acquaintance and then, when the moment seemed right, ask for a small loan. The money might well be repaid the first few times, but lenders soon became benefactors. The people who stuck by Huncke were willing victims. Like most truly inspired storytellers, he was also a good listener. He coaxed reticent souls into speech and comforted those who poured out their troubles to him. Although he exhausted many a relationship through repeated petitions for aid and occasional outright theft, he was never at a loss for finding new friends. His neediness was part of his singular appeal.

Huncke was not always wise in his choice of companions, however. Around 1970 he began a long, vexed relationship with Louis Cartwright, a failed hustler lately of San Francisco. Cartwright had come to New York with Rosebud Pettet, a friend of Ginsberg's. In an unpublished story titled "Louie," Pettet writes that Cartwright "fancied himself hard, and streetwise, and tried to get by on his tight body, dark curly hair, and long-lashed Italian eyes. But he was short, and had an unfortunate lisp. And when he smiled, the wide childish gap between his two front teeth belied the tough-boy stance." When Pettet grew weary of him, she was glad to foist him off on Ginsberg. Ginsberg in turn passed Cartwright on to Huncke. In her story Pettet writes that "Some spark of understanding passed between those two—Huncke and Louie. They were a pair, the wise old hustler and the lost young orphan, and they seemed to fall in love." While Cartwright generally preferred women as sexual partners, he and Huncke were intimate friends, if not lovers, until Cartwright's death in 1994. Unlike Huncke, he had little redeeming artistic talent. His sporadic efforts at photography and poetry would never be as important to him, or to anyone else, as his pursuit of drugs, a vocation he learned from Huncke.

In 1971 Huncke received the equivalent of manna from heaven. The publisher Harvey Brown of Frontier Press paid Huncke an advance of $12,000 for a collection of his stories. Although Brown later decided he did not like Huncke's work well enough to publish it, Huncke lived like a rich man for about five months on the generous advance. In pursuit of opium, he traveled to India, Nepal, and Afghanistan. He was going from one drug addict's paradise to another, or so at least it seemed for a while. On his way back home, having met up with Cartwright (who was benefiting from Huncke's largesse), Huncke stopped in Spain, at the vacation home of his friend R'lene Dahlberg, a New York City high-school English teacher. At an ebb point emotionally and physically, Huncke attempted suicide. The windfall from Frontier Press had enabled him to explore the world in a way that he had not done since his wartime travels in the merchant marine, but it had almost destroyed him in the process. Upon his return to New York, he became increasingly dependent on Ginsberg and other friends to help him pay his bills and manage his affairs.

Although he spent most of his time in Brooklyn and Manhattan, living in one small apartment or another, he was also a regular guest at Ginsberg's communal farm in Cherry Valley, New York. Gordon Ball, who managed the farm and later became one of Ginsberg's editors, maintained a cordial but guarded relationship with Huncke beginning in the 1970s. Ball resented the way Huncke flouted Ginsberg's rule against the use of "needle drugs" on the farm, even as he acknowledged Huncke's hold

on the people around him: "He was a really good storyteller, partly because of his voice itself. It was just rich, very pleasing," he said in an unpublished interview from 2002. When he was not slipping off to inject drugs into his arm or reeling from withdrawal symptoms, Huncke would putter around the kitchen, rearranging Ginsberg's pots and pans. Just as he had taken over Ginsberg's apartment in the 1940s, so would he leave his mark on the Cherry Valley farm.

Huncke's next book came out in 1979, when R'lene Dahlberg published the chapbook *Elsie John and Joey Martinez: Two Stories* through Pequod Press, her own letterpress. Once married to the writer Edward Dahlberg, R'lene Dahlberg had become one of Huncke's closest friends. Although they eventually parted ways—the friendship severely strained when Huncke "corrected" the tail on a valuable painting of a whale in Dahlberg's home—she was among the literary women, including di Prima, Kokkinen, and the poet Janine Pommy Vega, who believed in Huncke and went out of their way to help him.

The stories Dahlberg published (later included in *The Evening Sun Turned Crimson* and reprinted in *The Herbert Huncke Reader*) are profiles of two of Huncke's friends. Elsie John was a German-born transvestite whom Huncke had known during his teen years in Chicago. A towering figure with shining blue eyes, Elsie worked in circus sideshows and proudly proclaimed himself "the only true hermaphrodite in human life." He was in his midthirties when he and Huncke became friends. In Huncke's recollection, Elsie's hair

> was an exquisite shade of henna red which he wore quite long like a woman's. He gave it special care and I can see it reflecting the light from an overhead bulb which hung shadeless in the center of his room while he sat crosslegged in the center of a big brass bed fondling his three toy pekes who were his constant companions and received greatly of his love.

The story ends with the police bursting into Elsie's room after being tipped off to his drug pushing. They ransack the room, maligning Elsie's ambiguous sexuality all the while. Recalling "the shock and the terror of the moment the door was thrust open," Huncke writes, "It was when one of the cops stepped on a dog that Elsie began crying." We are left with a final, heartbreaking image of Elsie in jail, "cowering in the corner surrounded by a group of young Westside hoods who had been picked up the same night we were—who were exposing themselves to him and yelling all sorts of obscenities." In Huncke's hands Elsie John is a vulnerable human being rather than a criminal or a freak.

In "Joey Martinez" (titled "Joseph Martinez" in *The Evening Sun Turned Crimson* and *The Herbert Huncke Reader*), the title character is not as unusual as Elsie John, but he is memorable nonetheless. A twenty-four-year-old Puerto Rican whom Huncke meets in a hospital where both of them are undergoing treatment for drug addiction, Martinez comes to Huncke's room bearing candy bars. Characteristically, Huncke searches Martinez's eyes in order to sound the depths of his soul:

> His eyes were full of light and expression—communicating constantly—and I imagined I could detect a glimmer of love and I opened up to him a little, and soon we were beginning to know one another and he began telling me stories of his life—of his first love—and he told it to me with feeling and sensitivity.

Although closely supervised, Huncke and Martinez "became fairly steady companions and made a sort of comrade-like love scene—full of a sort of promise of becoming even more intense in the future." Huncke, however, is not ready to embark on that future just yet. He makes no effort to contact Martinez after they have been released from the hospital, nor does he mourn the lost friendship. Yet the final description of Martinez reveals that a fleeting

relationship can still leave an indelible impact:

> We were strolling down the corridor toward the nurses' station for the final medication of that day, and he suddenly began telling me of a dream and what message the dream had given him, and looking at me he said, "Nothing bad will ever happen to me because someone looks over me and takes care of me." I asked who he thought it was and he answered, "My guardian angel."

Although Huncke has attested to Martinez's sweetness and openness of heart, it is this innocent expression of faith that reveals the young man's spiritual nature. He will soon face the loss of Huncke's friendship, but perhaps that, too, will be an act of providence.

In 1980 Cherry Valley Editions published Huncke's second full-length collection of stories and sketches, *The Evening Sun Turned Crimson*. The publishers, Charles and Pam Plymell, had first come upon Huncke in San Francisco, where he had briefly lived in the 1960s. The first edition consisted of one thousand paperback copies with a cover showing a crazed addict sticking a needle in his arm. Because Huncke objected to this image, the second edition substituted a cover photo of the author taken by Louis Cartwright. The second edition consisted of 1,000 paperbacks and 200 hardcover copies. Containing stories and sketches that Huncke composed during the early to mid-1960s, the book appeared at a time when renewed interest in the Beat Generation was building momentum. Covering much of his life, from his Chicago youth through his cross-country travels as a young man through his experiences in New York in the 1950s and 1960s, *The Evening Sun Turned Crimson* raised Huncke's profile as a chronicler of the Beat Generation. Much more than a drug addict who occasionally scribbled down a story—which is how he would be regarded had he published only *Huncke's Journal*—Huncke was an engaging writer whose vignettes added up to a compelling whole. He recounted the people and places important to him with a unique blend of candor and kindness. His lack of artifice, something his friends had long admired in his oral narratives, spoke to the authenticity of his observations.

DUKE OF DECEPTION

Although Huncke never gave up illicit drugs permanently, he did achieve chemical stability through a city-sponsored methadone program. According to Raymond Foye in the introduction to *The Herbert Huncke Reader,* "Until Herbert entered his eighties, he was remarkably fit and healthy, maintaining a busy daily routine that began with a visit to his methadone clinic, usually followed by lunch with friends, visits to local booksellers, and various small errands around town. On occasion he would give readings or attend book signings." When Foye published a miniature (and abbreviated) edition of Huncke's autobiography, *Guilty of Everything,* in 1987, it was partly from recognizing the story's inherent interest and partly from fascination with the elderly author.

Upon meeting Huncke at a book party for Burroughs in 1978, Foye had been thoroughly charmed. In the introduction to *The Herbert Huncke Reader* he recalls their first meeting: "If ever someone's reputation preceded him, it was Herbert Huncke. Yet I was unprepared for the refined gracefulness of his speech and deportment. He was loquacious, but his choice of words was exacting. His manner was elevated and noble. He was aware of his charm, and wielded it deftly." Foye was not put off by Huncke's innate criminality: "To befriend Herbert was to enter into a consensual agreement in which nearly all rules of conduct were challenged, save those of acceptance and style. He was the Duke of Deception and bore the office with the haughty air of ruined nobility."

The Duke of Deception made an appearance in Boulder, Colorado, at the Naropa Institute's conference commemorating the twenty-fifth an-

niversary of the publication of *On the Road.* Amid great fanfare, the surviving Beats held a public reunion in July 1982 at the institution where in 1974 Ginsberg and the poet Anne Waldman had founded a creative writing program called the Jack Kerouac School of Disembodied Poetics. Participants included John Clellon Holmes, Diane di Prima, William Burroughs, Peter Orlovsky, David Amram, Robert Creeley, Timothy Leary, Carl Solomon, Robert Frank, Michael McClure, Abbie Hoffman, Ted Berrigan, Joyce Johnson, Gregory Corso, and Carolyn Cassady.

When Jerome Poynton arrived at Huncke's room to interview him, he discovered the renegade author in his underwear, sitting on his bed and mulling over his role in the Naropa proceedings. Skipping the preliminaries, Huncke immediately took Poynton into his confidence. He told his new acquaintance, who in time would become a close friend, that Ginsberg had paid for his flight from New York to Boulder with the understanding that Huncke would lead a writing workshop at the conference. Poynton remembered Huncke saying, "I don't know what a writing workshop is, but I don't like the sound of that word 'work'."

The expanded version of *Guilty of Everything: The Autobiography of Herbert Huncke* appeared in 1990 and was the last of Huncke's books published during his lifetime. A much-edited work that grew out of a series of interviews with Huncke, it lacks the fluidity of his earlier stories and sketches and sometimes rehashes episodes already covered in the story collections. But it makes for zesty reading nonetheless. Its title suggested by William Burroughs, *Guilty of Everything* traces Huncke's life from his runaway attempt at age twelve through the mid-1960s. As Jan Herman writes in the *New York Times Book Review,* Huncke's autobiography "reads like an oral history of urban survival and offers an uncommon tale of the streets from which the 75-year-old author is lucky to have emerged." By the time the book was published, Huncke was a cult figure who had caught the imagination of foreign journalists and independent filmmakers. Though his late-life celebrity never translated into a steady income, he enjoyed the attention.

In 1994 when his friend Louis Cartwright was murdered in a street fight Huncke was devastated. Friends feared that the shock would kill him, but the following year he summoned the energy to go abroad for a reading tour. Organized by Suzanne Hines, a promoter for a Belgian music production company, the tour took Huncke to several cities in England. Huncke's predilections did not make the trip easy, as an account in the *Daily Telegraph* reveals. According to the *Telegraph,* at one reading Huncke demanded a gram of cocaine as a condition of his appearance. To "mollify" him, the organizers said they had tried but failed to obtain any cocaine. As a substitute they "provided a couple of tumblers of vodka, which did the job. He performed well." The tour was a flop, but Huncke had become (at least in the eyes of the *Daily Telegraph* reporter) "King of the Beat Generation," a moniker usually assigned to Kerouac.

In October of 1995 Huncke appeared along with the singer Patti Smith at the Lowell Celebrates Kerouac! festival in the Massachusetts city where Kerouac was born. Alone on stage, a diminutive figure haloed by a spotlight, Huncke read a brief sketch of Kerouac that he had written in a notebook made of Tibetan rice paper. After comparing Kerouac to the notebook, which was "earthy in texture and handsome," Huncke said that he wished Kerouac "had been as loyal to himself and what I think of as his inner quality as I believe he tried being to his mother." For all of the ink spilled on Kerouac's unsettled and unsettling life, no one had ever taken the Beat Generation leader to task in quite this way. It was as if Elmer Hassel had emerged

from the margins of *On the Road* in order to chastise Sal Paradise. Huncke concluded, "Oddly enough, I didn't become aware of [Kerouac's] writing desire or ability until we became better acquainted, although even then, speaking honestly, I failed perceiving what a strong influence he would have on the literary history of the world." Was this a characteristic confession of Huncke's own shortcomings or a subtle indictment of a contemporary's undeserved success? Perhaps both. As usual, Huncke ended on an ambiguous note.

In his last months Huncke lived at the Chelsea Hotel, a fabled bohemian preserve on the Lower East Side of Manhattan. Friends and other supporters, including the Grateful Dead's Rex Foundation, paid some bills, but he still faced the grim specter of eviction for unpaid rent. He typically spent his monthly Social Security check on drugs; he freely shared with his latest coterie of friends, writers, and artists in their twenties who viewed Huncke as both icon and mascot. More mature friends cleaned up the mess after Huncke's parties and helped the host put himself back together in time for his daily trek to the methadone clinic.

Although Huncke's history of self-medication was remarkably long and varied, illegal drugs did not kill him. Huncke died on August 8, 1996, of system failure, sometimes euphemistically referred to as "old age." The *New York Times* marked his passing with a long obituary wherein is said, "Mr. Huncke had lived long enough to become a writer himself and a hero to a new generation of adoring artists and writers, not to mention a reproach to a right-thinking, clean-living establishment that had long predicted his imminent demise."

The Herbert Huncke Reader, which had been planned prior to his death, was published posthumously in 1997. The book contains all of his published works and a selection of twenty-two previously unpublished pieces. Along with his inclusion in the anthologies *The Portable Beat Reader* (1992) and *Beat Down to Your Soul: What Was the Beat Generation?* (2001), this volume helped solidify Huncke's reputation as a chronicler of the Beat Movement.

Huncke was a con man remembered for his honesty, a thief celebrated for his generous spirit. For those who did not know him, the riddle of his appeal is generously answered in his stories and sketches, which reveal a tender man with a loving, candid eye.

Selected Bibliography

WORKS OF HERBERT HUNCKE

Huncke's Journal. New York: The Poets Press, 1965. (Stories and sketches.)

Elsie John and Joey Martinez: Two Stories. New York: Pequod Press, 1979. (Stories.)

The Evening Sun Turned Crimson. Cherry Valley, N.Y.: Cherry Valley Editions, 1980. (Sketches and stories.)

Guilty of Everything. Madras, India, and New York: Hanuman Books, 1987. (Autobiography.)

Guilty of Everything: The Autobiography of Herbert Huncke. New York: Paragon House, 1990. (Expanded version of the autobiography issued in 1987.)

The Herbert Huncke Reader. Edited by Benjamin G. Schafer. New York: Morrow, 1997. (Includes a foreword by William S. Burroughs, an introduction by Raymond Foye, a biographical sketch by Jerome Poynton, and an editor's afterword by Benjamin G. Schafer. The selected bibliography includes works in which Huncke appears as a fictionalized character.)

ANTHOLOGIES CONTAINING WORKS OF HERBERT HUNCKE

The Portable Beat Reader. Edited by Ann Charters. New York: Penguin, 1992.

Beat Down to Your Soul: What Was the Beat Generation? Edited by Ann Charters. New York: Penguin, 2001.

JOURNALS AND MANUSCRIPTS

Herbert Huncke's papers, including journals and handwritten drafts of many of his stories and vignettes, are held at Columbia University's Butler Library.

FILM

Huncke and Louis. Directed and produced by Laki Vazakas. 1998. (Documentary film about Herbert Huncke and his friend Louis Cartwright.)

CRITICAL AND BIOGRAPHICAL STUDIES

Ball, Gordon. Unpublished interview with Hilary Holladay, March 23, 2002.

"Beat That." *Daily Telegraph,* May 26, 1995, p. 23.

Burroughs, William S. *Junky.* Ace Books, 1953. New York: Penguin, 1977.

Gifford, Barry, and Lawrence Lee. *Jack's Book: An Oral Biography of Jack Kerouac.* New York: St. Martin's, 1988.

Ginsberg, Allen. *Collected Poems, 1947–1980.* New York: Harper & Row, 1984.

Ginsberg, Allen. *Howl: Original Draft Facsimile, Transcript and Variant Versions.* New York: HarperCollins, 1988.

———. "The Hipster's Hipster." *New York Times Magazine,* December 29, 1996, p. 39.

Ginsberg, Allen, and Barry Farrell. "February 11, 1966, On the Road near Lawrence, Kansas." In *Spontaneous Mind: Selected Interviews, 1958–1996.* Edited by David Carter. New York: HarperCollins, 2001. Pp. 54–66.

Hackensberger, Alfred. *"I am beat": Das Leben des Hipsters Herbert Huncke—und seine Freunde Burroughs, Ginsberg, Kerouac.* Hamburg, Germany: Rotbuch, 1998.

Herman, Jan. "The Beatnik's Beatnik." *New York Times Book Review,* June 10, 1990, p. 23. (Review of *Guilty of Everything.*)

Holmes, John Clellon. Letter to Arthur and Glee Knight, reprinted in *the unspeakable visions of the individual* 3, nos. 1–2:18 (1973). (Special issue dedicated to Herbert Huncke.)

Kaufman, Michael T. "About New York: At 78, Someone Who Is Still Beat Yet Undefeated." *New York Times,* December 9, 1993, p. B3.

Kerouac, Jack. *The Town and the City.* New York: Harcourt, Brace, 1950; San Diego: Harcourt Brace Jovanovich, 1978.

———. *Selected Letters, 1940–1956.* Edited by Ann Charters. New York: Viking, 1995.

Knight, Arthur Winfield. "Herbert Huncke." In *Dictionary of Literary Biography.* Vol. 16, *The Beats: Literary Bohemians in Postwar America. Part I: A–L.* Edited by Ann Charters. Detroit: Gale, 1983. Pp. 262–267.

Knipfel, Jim. "Resurrecting Huncke." *New York Press,* June 14–20, 2000, pp. 15–16.

Kokkinen, Eila. Unpublished letter to Hilary Holladay, April 29, 2002.

Morgan, Ted. *Literary Outlaw: The Life and Times of William S. Burroughs.* New York: Holt, 1988.

Pettet, Rosebud. "Louie." Unpublished typescript of a story.

Poynton, Jerome. Conversation with Hilary Holladay, February 23, 2002.

Rosenthal, Irving. *Sheeper: "The Poet! The Crooked! The Extra-fingered!"* New York: Grove, 1967.

Schumacher, Michael. *Dharma Lion: A Critical Biography of Allen Ginsberg.* New York: St. Martin's, 1992.

Thomas, Robert McG., Jr. "Herbert Huncke, the Hipster Who Defined 'Beat,' Dies at 81." *New York Times,* August 9, 1996, p. B7.

Tytell, John. "An Interview with Herbert Huncke." *the unspeakable visions of the individual* 3, nos. 1–2:3–15 (1973).

—HILARY HOLLADAY

Christopher Isherwood

1904–1986

CHRISTOPHER ISHERWOOD IS often regarded as a wandering, ironic observer, but in 1939, when he emigrated to America, the wandering stopped. Some critics have maintained that this date marks a decline in Isherwood's career and a narrowing of his fictional range. Francis King, for example, writes in her 1976 study of Isherwood that "this narrowing is probably a reflection of a narrowing in his own life after his decision to settle in California." Critics such as David Garrett Izzo, by contrast, have argued on behalf of a steady improvement in Isherwood's writing that was made possible in part by his move to America where, in the Hindu philosophy of Vedanta, he "found something to believe in" that "gave him hope that there was meaning in a world that had seemed meaningless."

His first novels are set in Britain, where—a generation before John Osborne's play *Look Back in Anger* stunned London audiences in 1956—Isherwood expresses the angst of the "angry young man." In rebellion against the strictures of conventional English life, Isherwood moved to Germany in 1929, where his experiences over the next several years provided the background for the fiction collected as *The Berlin Stories* (1945), his most famous work—made more famous in American incarnations on the stage and in film versions, particularly as the 1972 musical film *Cabaret*. These stories celebrate the struggle for freedom but also the corruption of Germany between the wars.

With the rise of the Third Reich, Isherwood left for southern California, where he worked as a film writer, studied with a Hindu guru, and struggled with his desire to write about homosexual life within an insistently heterosexual

literary marketplace. In America, Isherwood produced his most underestimated works. Though there were lengthy gaps in Isherwood's production, the fiction and nonfiction from the second half of his life hardly represent a decline in his powers, and it can easily be argued that they live up to the promise of his early work. As an out-of-the-closet homosexual, as a practicing Hindu, as a pacifist during wartime, and as a literary artist working in Hollywood, Isherwood found himself at odds with his world in a number of important ways, but his American odyssey was a successful attempt to make a place for himself within a world that might have been too constrictive.

When, after a *wanderjahre* that continued into the second half of his life, Isherwood began to write as a settled southern Californian, he was still received as a British writer. In a sense this hybrid status has put him among the "lost and found" of literary history. He does not exactly fit in as an American writer because his literary personae often maintain recognizably British traits, and yet he has seemed too lax—too "California"—to British reviewers. Isherwood's prose shifted in ways that resemble main trends in postwar American writing, and his literary achievement is inseparable from this transformation. As Lisa M. Schwerdt points out in *Isherwood's Fiction* (1989), Isherwood stands apart from other autobiographers of his generation such as Louis MacNeice, George Orwell, and Edward Upward in his "exclusive concentration on self." For readers who see him primarily as a British writer who lived abroad, Isherwood is a literary modernist whose later work fails to live up to the way in which generic ambiguity and fragmentary presentation express social and moral degeneration in his early semiautobiographical fiction.

At worst Isherwood is considered a writer who was ruined by the movies, but this easy judgment does not survive a reading that is at once more sympathetic and more skeptical. Gore Vidal, in his introduction to the posthumous collection *Where Joy Resides* (1989), addresses the charge that Isherwood sold out to the so-called culture industry.

Vidal insightfully underscores the artistry of the real in-the-flesh Isherwood, which is also a mythological construction of sorts: everyday conversation is a campy performance, and the meanings expressed cannot be understood apart from the miniature theater in which the lines are performed. Isherwood's admonition, "Don't become a hack like me" expresses two contradictory meanings: that Isherwood paid a price for working in Hollywood but also that he was not nearly ruined by the processes of the Hollywood studio system, as many would claim. Isherwood's finest art can, in fact, be seen as a series of self-cancellations that, paradoxically, create the self they seem to undermine.

Personal identity, literary genre, and reputation are fluid matters in Isherwood's life and writing, and this protean, wandering quality is at times a matter of crisis and pain, but increasingly Isherwood's placelessness metamorphoses from the failure to find a specific role or form into the achievement of a fluid identity and artistry. Considering Isherwood as an American writer opens the way to understanding the ways in which his various life experiments were successful and bore significant literary fruit. Izzo's 2001 study divides Isherwood's writing life into two parts, the "frantic" and the "Vedantic": the "tearing down" before Isherwood came to America is marked by rebellion and frustration, whereas the "building up" after 1939 describes the artistic construction of alternative models and ideals.

Izzo's before-and-after division is appealing, but it tends to discount the long transitional phase during which Isherwood struggled with his relationship to the United States. In the first part of Isherwood's career, spanning from his 1928 novel *All the Conspirators* to the 1939 journalistic account of China that he coauthored with W. H. Auden, *Journey to a War,* Isherwood was writing as a British author, albeit one often in flight from British identity. The source materials and social relations treated in his work during this period are primarily expressions of what it meant to be an Englishman, whether in the United Kingdom, in Germany, or in China. *All the Conspirators* and *The Memorial: Portrait of a Family* (1932) are portraits of the artist as a young man, as one not yet able to fly over the nets of social convention. Isherwood satirizes these conventions in the plays he wrote with Auden during this period, and then his semiautobiographic fictional stand-in passively witnesses bohemian rebellion and moral corruption in the Weimar Germany of *The Berlin Stories.* From Germany, Isherwood returned to England, made a trip to China with Auden, and then the two writers left for America.

Isherwood's first two decades in the United States were a period of transition. He emigrated from England in 1939 and took American citizenship in 1946. (According to Francis King, Isherwood acquired not only citizenship, but also "an American accent, manner, and style of dress," but Paul Zall, a former colleague from California State University, claims Isherwood always had a clear British accent.) His transition to life in the United States was less comfortable than Auden's, and his first American book, one might say, was the 1944 English-language version of *The Song of God: Bhagavad-Gita.* Of course, Isherwood did not compose this work; he helped his guru, Swami Prabhāvānanda, create a successful translation. But his relationship with Prabhāvānanda and his exploration of Vedantism as a religion and as a spiritual practice initiated a period of transition in which Isherwood was, so to speak, *in* but not *of* America. Perhaps this period of transition never ended, but in that case the practice of Vedanta helped Isherwood become comfortable with being "in but not of" not just America but the world.

Between this translation and *An Approach to Vedanta* (1963), a work that consolidates Isherwood's thoughts on Vedantism in relation to pacifism, art, and his own life struggles, he wrote three fine novels concerning displaced and wandering people, including his first novel set in the United States, *The World in the Evening* (1954). While these works dramatize essentially secular issues (the film industry, the breakup of a marriage, and the interrelation of apparently isolated individuals), they are all flavored by Isherwood's growing interest in Hindu philosophy and spiritual discipline.

If the first part of Isherwood's writing life can be characterized as a mixture of fight-or-flight responses to conventional British life, and the second as an attempt to find a positive set of values to replace those he wished to reject, the third and final act of Isherwood's life drama is the development of a public persona that has outgrown the shame and pain of his previous existence. However self-deprecating the Isherwood of this period, the self is presented, warts and all, with a confident boldness. In 1964 Isherwood published *A Single Man,* a novel in which homosexuality is a central component rather than an important marginal one; and in this novel more than any other book, Isherwood can be considered an American writer.

The main themes of Isherwood's career continue across all of his works, but *A Single Man* and two memoirs he published in this period, *Christopher and His Kind: 1929–1939* (1976) and *My Guru and His Disciple* (1980), align him with several American writers who challenged taboos about lifestyle and representation head-on. Like the Allen Ginsberg of

"Howl" (1956) and the Norman Mailer of *Advertisements for Myself* (1959), Isherwood in this phase presents activist and confessional selves who fiercely resist social constraints. In *Christopher and His Kind,* Isherwood was able, as Paul Piazza demonstrates, to withdraw references to "Vedantist serenity" so as to produce an iconoclastic "anti-myth": "The role of shattering creeds and demolishing idols becomes a lifestyle, so that homosexuality is not merely his nature; much more, it is Isherwood's own particular form of rebellion." In this third phase of Isherwood's career, however, the representation of homosexuality grows beyond angry rebellion, as evidenced by his portrait of one month of life entitled *October* (1983).

The critics James Berg and Chris Freeman have made the most ambitious claims on Isherwood's behalf, titling a collection of essays about Isherwood's work, relationships, politics, and spirituality *The Isherwood Century* (2000). His connections with numerous important literary figures (Auden, Stephen Spender, E. M. Forster, Bertolt Brecht, Thomas Mann, Somerset Maugham, Aldous Huxley, Gore Vidal) and his literary reactions to important historical movements (the Third Reich, literary bohemianism across the century, Hollywood's effects on American culture, the explosion of postwar orientalist writing, and the assertion of gay pride in the wake of the civil rights struggle), make Isherwood a major figure in twentieth-century English writing even if he was not the central figure.

CHILDHOOD AND YOUTH

The three central facts of Isherwood's youth are that he was born into semiaristocratic circumstances, that he came to despise social convention and authority, and that literary imagination was the principle means of overcoming what was *for him* a disadvantageous upbringing.

Christopher William Bradshaw-Isherwood was born to his parents, Kathleen and Frank, on August 26, 1904, at Wyberslegh Hall in Cheshire, England. Frank Isherwood, whom John Lehmann describes as a man whose "real interest lay in the arts; music and painting," was forced, because he was the second son and did not inherit the family fortune, into becoming a professional soldier. When Isherwood was twelve years old, his father died in World War I. The boy resented the idealization of his father, "the war hero." His difficult relationship with his mother—who came from a merchant family but became, as Brian Finney puts it in *Christopher Isherwood: A Critical Biography* (1979), "more upper-class than the upper-class family into which she married"—is directly reflected in the mother figure of his first two novels, a fanatically controlling presence who defeats the ambitions of the young artist. Although he defined himself in opposition to familial roles in his youth, in later years Isherwood recognized how much he had in common with his parents, and he ultimately came to terms with his familial past in the memoir *Kathleen and Frank: The Autobiography of a Family* (1971), based on letters between his parents. (The pacifist convert to Vedantism was particularly surprised to learn that his soldier father had a sincere interest in Theosophy.)

Isherwood's days before preparatory school were mostly idyllic, although his relations with his parents were formal and distant. He was cared for by a nanny; his memoirs recall that he was not washed and dressed by his mother before he was five. His father, in the interest of educating the six-year-old boy, produced an illustrated daily newspaper titled "The Toy-Drawer Times." There were numerous homemade theatrical productions, and Kathleen wrote in her diary about young Christopher's penchant for storytelling: "he so easily gets overexcited and frightens himself over the stories he tells himself, and he is always telling himself stories." During this period Frank attempted to obtain release from the armed forces without success.

After his tenth birthday Isherwood was sent off to St. Edmund's Preparatory School in Surry, and less than two years later his father was killed in the second battle of Ypres. According to Finney, Isherwood's cousins, who were also students at St. Edmund's, "seized on his father's death to force their eleven-year-old upstart cousin to conform to their glamorised vision of war, patriotism and death." Frank Isherwood "became an heroic ideal with whom the son would be constantly compared to his disadvantage by his school teachers," and in this way did his teachers, his mother, and the "establishment at large" become the enemy. Isherwood, like Orwell and Cyril Connolly, scorned the residual Victorian ethos of his preparatory school years, and much of Isherwood's writing career can be construed as a reaction against the established form of society taught at St. Edmund's. In a memoir about his education, *Lions and Shadows: An Education in the Twenties* (1938), Isherwood complained that "the war years had given full licence to every sort of dishonest cant about loyalty, selfishness, patriotism, playing the game and dishonouring the dead. Now I wanted to be left alone."

But Isherwood did not remain alone. In his senior year he met the younger student W. H. Auden (called "Hugh Weston" in *Lions and Shadows*), and the two formed a rapport that was the best part of his experience at St. Edmund's. Isherwood and Auden later coauthored three plays and the journalistic narrative *Journey to a War.* Auden and Isherwood became reacquainted when they went to their respective universities, developing a private language they called "the *Waste Land* Game": "quotations and misquotations were allowed, together with bits of foreign languages, proper names and private jokes." Scholars scrimmage about whether to call the generation surrounding these two writers the "Auden generation" as Samuel Hynes has argued, or to give chief honors to Isherwood as Izzo does in his study and Berg and Freeman do in *The Isherwood Century.* All accounts agree, however, that the friendship was one of the most productive literary relationships of the twentieth century.

The best part of Isherwood's experience at Repton, near Derby, the public school he entered in 1919, was meeting Edward Upward. The two were literary allies even during school days. In *Lions and Shadows,* Isherwood writes admiringly of Upward's "natural hatred of all established authority" and confesses that he felt it would be "a weakness in myself not to share it." The friendship with Upward continued at Cambridge, and Upward appears as "Allen Chalmers" in *All the Conspirators, Lions and Shadows,* and *Down There on a Visit* (1962). With Upward, Isherwood also developed a fantasy world that they called "Mortmere." This private world took public form in 1994 with the publication of *The Mortmere Stories,* and before that Isherwood and Upward's satirical attacks on the social establishment (known variously as "the Others," "Them," and the "poshocracy") were known to readers through Isherwood's descriptions in *Lions and Shadows.* "Mortmere," writes Izzo, "signified an us-against-them mentality," and from the standpoint of their imagined community of resistors, Isherwood and Upward attacked those "who had caused the war in order to protect and preserve the British traditions and class divisions that had given them disproportionate advantages."

Within *The Mortmere Stories* and in *Lions and Shadows,* Isherwood shapes the rebellion he and Upward shared at Cambridge into a mythological dichotomy of the "truly strong" and the "truly weak" man. The former is confident and needs no outward display of heroism, but the latter is wracked by insecurity (and by the feeling that he does not measure up to the previous generation of war heroes). The

truly weak man seeks out the Test, an act of derring-do that, whether it is passed or failed, will never satisfy the would-be hero, because, as Izzo writes, "the underlying subconscious needs that are motivating the Tests are not really being assuaged." E. M. Forster is (in Izzo's account) an example of the truly strong man, whereas T. E. Lawrence exemplifies the truly weak man, though these archetypes may occur by turns in the same person.

One test for Isherwood was to reject the advantages of being born into the poshocracy. He entered Cambridge in 1923, but as John Lehmann writes, "In spite of having won an outstanding scholarship to Corpus Christi, Christopher gradually disengaged himself from Cambridge, making a joke of his exams, to the scandal of his tutor and his family." Isherwood made a half-hearted attempt to study medicine at King's College in 1928 (the same year that *All the Conspirators* was published), this being his last attempt to become a success in his mother's sense of the term. Isherwood did poorly on his first set of exams but was progressing well on his second novel, *The Memorial.* He stayed on for a second term to please his mother but left for Berlin on March 14, 1929.

REBEL WITHOUT A PAUSE

In the first decade of his writing career, Isherwood published *All the Conspirators, The Memorial: Portrait of a Family,* and the disjunctive array that was collected in 1939 as *Goodbye to Berlin* and has been read variously as a collection of short stories and as a fragmentary novel. The first two novels are stories of failed rebellions. The third, in which an Isherwood-like narrator has left England to teach English in Germany, recounts the experiences and interactions of a sometimes startled and sometimes bemused observer who witnesses the bohemian freedom of Weimar Germany and its loss as the Nazis rose to power.

Published when Isherwood was twenty-one years old, *All the Conspirators* is something of an anti-bildungsroman. Finney calls the novel "an anti-heroic *Portrait of the Artist as a Young Man* in which a pseudo-artist fails to elude the nets of family and class and is outmaneuvered by his mother's superior use of the modern artist's defences, silence and cunning." Isherwood's semibiographical would-be artist Philip Lindsay discusses aesthetics (often in somewhat snide tones) with his "fellow conspirator" Allen Chalmers. Philip and Allen especially dislike Victor Page and his uncle the Colonel, who represent the generational incarnations of Victorian manhood, but all resistance succumbs to compromise and surrender. Philip's sister Joan, also a conspirator, engages to marry Victor-the-poshocrat, and Allen—after his rebellious plan to leave England and take a post in Kenya collapses owing to his hypochondria—remains, childlike, in his mother's house. Isherwood called his own "compulsive hypochondria" a sign of his "tireless sense of guilt" after being sent down from Cambridge, and the novel captures the techniques by which these levers of guilt are used to produce conformity: "A neuralgic twinge had begun over Philip's left eye" after his mother lectures him on wasting his life. "Feeling giddy, he sat down beside his mother on the sofa."

Two technical aspects of this novel warrant special attention. First, it, like *The Memorial*, features a kind of dramatic understatement that Edward Upward referred to as "tea-tabling" and that owes much to the manner of E. M. Forster. In *Lions and Shadows*, Isherwood recounts Upward's theory that "we ought to aim at being essentially comic writers," as the writing of tragedy is not possible for contemporary society. Forster's solution, according to Upward, "is based on the tea-table: instead of trying to screw all the scenes up to the highest possible pitch, he tones them down until they sound like mother's-meeting gossip." Tea-tabling, then,

involves a strategic inversion of dramatic emphasis: "there's actually *less* emphasis laid on the big scenes than on the unimportant ones." The second technical characteristic—which Isherwood more or less rejected as being a form of passive-aggressive anger in his 1958 foreword to the New Directions edition of the novel—is occasional indulgence in modernist stream-of-consciousness writing and cryptic presentation of relationships.

The Memorial, which had the private title "War and Peace," concerns the aftereffects of World War I at a personal level and is generally considered the finer social portrait of the first two novels. As Izzo points out, the second novel continues many themes of the first: "hatred of the war, rejection of the traditions that led to the war, the widowed mother exerting the influence of guilt on a bound, Truly Weak son, and undertones of homosexual liaisons." But while *All the Conspirators* centers each of these themes tightly around Philip Lindsay's failed quest for freedom, *The Memorial* presents a more developed social architecture.

Homosexuality is certainly less important than class snobbery in Isherwood's early work, but it is always present in a muted way. (Piazza calls the homosexual references in the first novel "coy and sophomoric.") In Isherwood's first novel it was confined to tonal hints, such as Allen Chalmers' talk of sailors and "a certain boatman" when discussing aesthetic subject matter and artistic point of view with Philip Lindsay. Isherwood encountered more progressive psychoanalytic approaches to homosexuality in Germany via Auden's interest in the psychological work of Homer Lane and John Layard, who persuaded Auden that failure to obey one's impulses leads to serious illness. Consequently Auden chose to acknowledge his homosexuality, and in *The Memorial*, Isherwood begins the slow process of creating homosexual and bisexual characters who are not mere campy jokes or psychological failures. The war veteran Edward Blake, who struggles with his homosexuality and even attempts suicide (in the same way Layard did, by shooting himself in the mouth), is "a Test-driven homosexual," according to Izzo. He is a truly weak man who must prove himself by taking risks, but Blake is also a test drive of sorts for Isherwood in the sense that Isherwood was trying out this new model—the homosexual character.

Perhaps the key technical breakthrough of *The Memorial* is the way Isherwood creates a four-part disruption of chronology (starting in 1928 but shifting to 1920, 1925, and then closing in 1929) to show not the development of character through time but rather the static blockage of development. Claude J. Summers claims that the "shifting time scheme actually emphasizes the static quality of the internal lives of the characters, all of whom remain imprisoned in the past." At its best, Isherwood's artistry devises forms to show how people create hellish circumstances, and the idea that life is hell is hinted in Isherwood's later four-part work *Down There on a Visit,* in which the titular "there" indicates hell.

Isherwood's next work was to be titled "The Lost," but he reports that he was unable to pull this work together into a Balzacian epic: "What I actually produced was an absurd jumble of subplots and coincidences which defeated me whenever I tried to straighten it out on paper." Finney contests Isherwood's self-disparaging claim, saying that his method of taking up "all the broken bits" and putting them in *Goodbye to Berlin* "appears to be offering an essentially modernist justification for the form of a book which in most other respects constitutes a reaction against Modernism." The earlier title, "The Lost," indicates such ominous political events as the rise of the Nazi Party, but "the lost," Isherwood says in his foreword to the New Directions edition, can also refer satirically to "those

individuals whom respectable society shuns in horror: an Arthur Norris, a von Pregnitz, a Sally Bowles."

Their stories were told in several works published as novellas and stories before being gathered into the 1939 collection (or modernist novel?) *Goodbye to Berlin.* The parts, including "A Berlin Diary (autumn 1930)," "Sally Bowles," "The Nowaks," "The Landauers," and "Berlin Diary (winter 1932–1933)," are set and arranged chronologically in the volume to create an evolving portrait of Berlin from 1930 through 1933. They reflect the confusion and uncertainty of those times—while retrospectively the progress of the Third Reich has come to seem all too certain, this is not how Isherwood's Berliners experienced the events. *Mr. Norris Changes Trains* (*The Last of Mr. Norris* in the American version) was published by Hogarth Press in 1935, and in 1945 this novella was combined with *Goodbye to Berlin* to form the complete version of *The Berlin Stories.* As Carolyn Heilbrun has put it, the stories are "constructed around the disintegration and dehumanization of a modern city." Chronology and thematic unity are parlayed into an apparently fragmentary but actually well-organized collage: the story of the heterosexual outlaw Sally Bowles is set against the homotopia presented in "On Ruegen Island"; and the working-class Jews presented in "The Nowaks" are contrapuntally defined against the Jewish capitalists "The Landauers." "These formal polarities," writes Finney, "reflect the real polarisation of attitudes that characterised the final years of democracy in Germany."

Although Isherwood was said by the generously inclined Somerset Maugham to hold "the future of the English novel in his hands," his first two novels sold poorly and did little or nothing to alter the course of English fiction. His Berlin-inspired writings changed this fact with the introduction of challenging narrative strategies and the creation of memorable characters. Although some readers have attacked the passivity and apparent moral resignation epitomized in the famous line from "A Berlin Diary"—"I am a camera with its shutter open, quite passive, recording, not thinking"—G. S. Fraser and others have championed Isherwood's "documentary" fiction. Isherwood's experiments in *The Berlin Stories* with presenting himself (or a self called "Christopher Isherwood") as a fictional character were forerunners of postmodern American works that would challenge the border between fiction and nonfiction, including Truman Capote's *In Cold Blood* (1965), Norman Mailer's *Armies of the Night* (1968), and Maxine Hong Kingston's *The Woman Warrior* (1976).

The Berlin Stories are rich with seedy characters presented with an almost parental indulgence. Arthur Norris, for example, is in every sense a questionable character; he befriends "Christopher Isherwood" but he also behaves in various appalling ways, as when he blackmails the secretly homosexual Baron Kuno von Pregnitz. Sally Bowles, based on Isherwood's friend Jean Ross, has become an avatar of bohemian freedom, and she more than any other Isherwood character has entered American cultural memory, in part because of the ways in which *The Berlin Stories* have been retold: in 1951 John van Druten worked Isherwood's stories into a successful Broadway play, *I Am a Camera,* with Julie Harris in the Bowles role; the dramatic version of *Cabaret* was first performed in 1966; and the musical film directed by Bob Fosse, for which Liza Minelli won an Oscar for best actress, hit the theaters in 1972. Through Sally Bowles, Isherwood has also influenced American writers such as Truman Capote and even Norman Mailer—an early draft of Mailer's 1951 novel *Barbary Shore,* then called "Mrs. Guinevere," was intended as an Americanization of the Bowles material.

By the end of the 1930s, Isherwood had treated social paralysis in apprentice and journeyman works; he had created *Goodbye to Berlin,* which inaugurated the postwar boom in semiautobiographical fiction and altered readers' perceptions about cabaret and Berlin for decades to come; and he had developed in his autobiography *Lions and Shadows* a fully fledged theory of life. With Auden he had written three plays and the travel narrative *Journey to a War,* and he had cowritten with Desmond Vesey a translation of the verses to Bertolt Brecht's *Der Dreigroschenroman* (*A Penny for the Poor,* 1937). And yet 1939 marked a downward turn for Isherwood's critical reputation and career from which he did not really recover until the post-Stonewall gay rights movement began to gather force.

THE CORMORANT'S QUEER CRY: ISHERWOOD'S ATLANTIC CROSSING

Flight as a rebellion is the central theme of Isherwood's writings before World War II, and he first signals that such maneuvers are bound to fail in the final sentence of the first chapter of *All the Conspirators:* "A cormorant, startling them with its queer cry, broke flapping from unseen rocks below and vanished into the empty gulf of light westward, like an absurd impulse of desperation, towards America." In his 1958 foreword to the New Directions edition of the novel, Isherwood calls this sentence an "unconscious prophecy," noting that his first book, like its author, was just then migrating to America. What was "queer" or futile in 1923 had a different meaning in 1958. It was no longer futile to hope to escape, and the meaning of the word "queer" would, in the 1950s, 1960s, and 1970s, begin to undergo a sea change whereby the abusive term ultimately became—in a time when it is possible for a university professor to be hired as a "queer theorist"—a term of pride and solidarity.

Leaving Germany, where Isherwood and Auden had experienced sexual freedom unlike any they had known in England, was an experience of profound crisis for Isherwood, especially since he was forced to abandon his lover Heinz to an uncertain fate. This personal crisis was compounded by recent events, since the Spanish Civil War had been a death blow to progressive-leftist support of Russian communism. Isherwood and Auden's play *On the Frontier* (1938), which Izzo calls "a rote exercise of didactic leftist propaganda," reflects the "enervation of their peers."

The crisis was social as well. Heilbrun writes, "It was only in 1939, therefore, that Isherwood, crossing to America on a boat with Auden, realized, at sea, that he, like Forster, had always essentially been a pacifist," but the fact of becoming a pacifist at this particular moment led to abuse, which Heilbrun argues was entirely unfair:

> Isherwood and Auden, in coming to America as England stood on the brink of war, laid themselves open to enormous abuse from those left behind. In fact, both men had earlier planned to emigrate from England; both offered their services when war came. Isherwood, moreover, had scarcely lived in England for any length of time since his early twenties.

Although Isherwood portrays the movement to America at the conclusion of *Christopher and His Kind* in idyllic yet campy terms, the migration was more unsettling for him than for Auden. In *An Approach to Vedanta,* Isherwood recounts this difficult transition:

> The conquering confident mood in which I had approached America quickly disappeared. It had been based on the illusions of a tourist, and now I was a tourist no longer. I wanted to make my own niche in American life, and settle down and get to work. But I found that I couldn't write a line. I was paralyzed by apprehension.

While Auden settled into New York literary society with relative ease and began to write the most famous poetry of his career (such as "In Memory of W. B. Yeats" and "September 1, 1939"), Isherwood was feeling alienated and unproductive. He decided to move to California to be closer to his pacifist friend Gerald Heard, and he found work as a screenwriter. While writing for Hollywood, Isherwood became a devotee of Swami Prabhāvānanda, a Vedanta teacher in the Ramakrishna order. Brendan Bernhard describes the different paths of Auden and Isherwood in archetypally American terms:

> It was the old East Coast–West Coast dichotomy— New York versus L.A., crowds versus solitude, Judeo-Christianity versus "New Age" mysticism— turning up where you'd least expect it, between the two whiz kids of '30s British lit. Although Auden and Isherwood arrived as two apparently similar people, America, in a very short space of time, revealed that they were in fact far more different than either had realized. And those differences could be reduced, crudely but accurately, to a purely American paradigm.

Auden was a New Yorker. Isherwood was an Angeleno.

The British press was not enthusiastic about Isherwood's California lifestyle. In addition to veiled attacks on homosexuality, there were swipes at his religious leanings, as when Harold Nicholson complained in the *Spectator* in April 1940 that, while "Western civilization is bursting into flame," Isherwood had retreated "into the gentler solitudes of the Wisdom of the East." Even Isherwood's friend E. M. Forster once wrote to another friend, regarding Isherwood's conversion to Vedanta, "How he does go on about God!" adding "I suppose it wouldn't matter in conversation."

Although many readers considered Isherwood's spiritual concerns an intrusion within the world of writing, it is impossible to understand his life or works in America without considering his Vedantism. Stated briefly, the Hindu philosophical branch called Vedanta, meaning "the end of the Veda," draws from the

Upanishads and is a set of teachings in which the main purpose of human life is to realize one's inherent divinity. The inner divine component is called Atman. Beyond the illusory world of the senses, called maya, exists the true reality, called Brahman. Advaita Vedanta is one of three branches of Vedanta, the nondualist branch (*advaita* means "not two"). Shaped also by the writings of the seventh-century Hindu saint Adi Shankara, Advaita Vedanta declares that Atman and Brahman are really identical, but we fail to see this because our understanding is obscured by egoistic desire.

The practice of Vedantism in Western contexts usually involves renunciation of sensual desires; the performance of ritual prayers, called *pujas;* and devotion to one's spiritual teacher, the guru. Isherwood's particular community, the Vedanta Society of Southern California, was an offshoot of the Ramakrishna order, dedicated to the teachings of the Sri Ramakrishna (1836–1886), about whom Isherwood wrote *Ramakrishna and His Disciples* (1965); Ramakrishna's disciple Vivekananda introduced Vedantism to many Americans at the World Parliament of Religions in 1893. In the late 1890s Swami Vivekananda visited Pasadena, California, and laid the foundations for what would become the Vedanta Society of Southern California. Isherwood's own guru moved to America in 1914 and went to southern California to lead the Pasadena group in 1929. Isherwood's fellow expatriate friend Gerald Heard introduced him to Prabhavananda and Aldous Huxley when Isherwood arrived on the West Coast in 1939.

The literary fruit of Isherwood's Vedantism includes the novels and memoirs for which he is chiefly remembered, especially *My Guru and His Disciple,* but it also includes twenty-five years of writing that is less well-known, such as cotranslations and commentaries done with Prabhāvānanda such as *The Song of God: Bhagavad-Gita* (1944) and *How to Know God: The Yoga Aphorisms of Patanjali* (1953), edited collections such as *Vedanta for the Western World* (1945) and *Vedanta for Modern Man* (1951), and accounts of the religions and histories of its founders such as *An Approach to Vedanta* and *Ramakrishna and His Disciples.* Posthumously published, *The Wishing Tree: Christopher Isherwood on Mystical Religion* (1987) collects Isherwood's best writings on spirituality and mysticism.

"How I Came to Vedanta," drawn from *An Approach to Vedanta,* begins with the question "Why had I come to America?" Isherwood answers his own question: "I suppose because I couldn't stop traveling; I had become constitutionally restless." He had come to feel that the "hospitality of friends and strangers couldn't reassure me, for I felt that I was accepting it under false pretenses" since the "Christopher Isherwood they wanted to see was no longer myself." It became necessary to reinvent himself, a revision effected and reflected within the pages of his American writings.

FIRST NOVEL IN AMERICA: *PRATER VIOLET*

Isherwood's eight significant works between his exodus from Europe and his death in 1986 are the novels *Prater Violet* (1945), *The World in the Evening* (1954), *Down There on a Visit* (1962), *A Single Man* (1964), *A Meeting by the River* (1967), and the autobiographical works *Christopher and His Kind* (1976), *My Guru and His Disciple* (1980), and *October* (1980).

Isherwood did not yet feel comfortable with American settings, and so his portrait of the "culture industry" is set in London in the 1930s; but except for the fact of the setting *Prater Violet* can be read as an insightful Hollywood novel in disguise. The narrator "Christopher Isherwood" is not quite the passive figure of *The Berlin Stories,* as he actively hangs up the phone when Chatsworth, the arrogant figure from Imperial Bulldog Studios, first calls him to pressure him into working as an advisor and scriptwriter for a film titled *Prater Violet.* Isherwood, who is angry at distractions pulling him away from his novel, finally agrees to work on the film.

As a naturalistic description of artistic compromise in the marketplace, the novel shows the inherent conflict of interest between the capitalistic studio and the artist via the wrangling between Chatsworth and the film's director over the final shape of the film, but the film is also an allegory about the role of the artist in a time of political crisis. Like *The Berlin Stories* before and *The World in the Evening* after, *Prater Violet* presents craftsmen who use art as a way to turn away from the world, but all three books also complain about such patterns of flight. In Linda Hutcheon's phrase, these postmodern works offer a form of "complicitous critique" of the larger social and economic forces that determine or constrain the artist's attempts to forge a work that is at once interesting, personal, and truthful. There are also intimations of postmodern self-reflexivity in the novel: the character Christopher Isherwood is not always distinguishable from the author, and naming the novel after the film being made in the novel suggests that the novel itself does not transcend the crude economic and political compromises satirized in the fictional account of making the film *Prater Violet.*

The film's director, Friedrich Bergmann, is a fictional version of Isherwood's friend and mentor in the film world, Berthold Viertel. Bergmann, like Viertel, is a kind of father figure to Isherwood, and in their first meeting Bergmann praises Isherwood's novel *The Memorial,* focusing on the scene in which Edward Blake attempts suicide: "This I find clearly genial." Isherwood (the author) appears to be making fun of his earlier style, especially the "tea-tabling" in which extraordinary events were presented as if minor, and in *Prater Violet* a reversal of sorts is achieved, since the utterly trivial film and the idiocy of the studio process are allegorical analogues of the Nazi conquest of Europe.

Bergmann's emotionalism only *seems* inappropriate. Finney writes that "Bergmann's apparently paranoid reaction" to the studio "reveals a subtle criticism of the fascist assumptions underlying British society in general." Bergmann refers to Isherwood and himself as "fellow prisoners" and frequently makes parallels between those surrounding the film set and figures in Weimar Germany and Austria such as Engelbert Dollfuss. Because Bergmann is such a histrionic presence, Isherwood's passive protagonist works better in this novel than anywhere else. As Isherwood said to George Wickes (quoted in *Conversations,* 2001), the character "Christopher Isherwood"

> really worked best, in my opinion … in my little *Prater Violet* because there he was up against a real talker, a tremendous dynamic behaver and talker, and a person whom at the same time, although he regarded him with humor, he could regard with great affection and genuine admiration.

Bergmann is an emotionally intense character who wears out everyone in his presence, and there is much self-dramatization in his political analogies. In placing the justice of Bergmann's artistic and political passions alongside his excessive presentation, Isherwood adds nuance to his Vedantic theme by showing that the transcendence of self is not the abandonment of the world (although Random House downplayed the relationship between Isherwood and cultish mysticism by assuring readers, on the back cover, that the novel had "no trace of mysticism"). When a journalist tactlessly asks Bergmann about events in Germany, the director fulminates, hitting the table and saying, "I expect everyone to care!" He then expects Isherwood to comment, but Isherwood is utterly exhausted by Bergmann's constant demands.

He is annoyed by the journalist, Patterson, but he also resents Bergmann: "But the 'I' that thought this was both Patterson and Bergmann, Englishman and Austrian, islander and continental. It was divided, and hated its division."

Toward the end of the novel, the character Isherwood has a glimpse of the larger, undivided sense of self, but the vision leaves him suddenly:

"No," I think, "I could never do it. Rather the fear I know, the loneliness I know. … For to take that other way would mean that I should lose myself. I should no longer be a person. I should no longer be Christopher Isherwood. No, no. That's more terrible than the bombs."

The novel closes with a scathing review of the film (it is "an insult to the intelligence of a five-year-old child" and is "definitely counter-revolutionary"), but the film *Prater Violet* gets Bergmann a job in Hollywood, where Isherwood's next novel would begin.

THE WORLD IN THE EVENING

The decade after *Prater Violet* was difficult for Isherwood. Money was tight, his lover William Caskey was a tempestuous drinker, and Isherwood had serious doubts about his progress as a novelist. His next novel, *The World in the Evening,* caused him enormous difficulties for several reasons. It was his first novel in which his protagonist, instead of being a camera's eye focusing on other people's peccadilloes, would begin to emerge as a homosexual man. The fictional Isherwood who contemplates failure in the closing pages of *Prater Violet* considers the string of lovers who are part of his attachment to the world of self as opposed to the ego-transcending way of life that might otherwise be possible: "Love, at the moment, was J." and "after J., there would be K. and L. and M., right down the alphabet."

The "J." of Isherwood's life in the early 1940s had been the photographer William Caskey, who took the photographs for Isherwood's travel account of South America, *The Condor and the Cows: A South American Travel Diary* (1949). In 1953 while Isherwood was struggling with *The World in the Evening,* he met Don Bachardy, a young artist who was half his age and with whom he lived for the rest of his life. As King points out, the lettered lovers of *Prater Violet* are not given a name or a gender. Like Isherwood's earlier work, *Prater Violet* acknowledges the existence of homosexuality, but Isherwood had not yet found a way to present this aspect of his life in an uncensored way.

When *The World in the Evening* was published in 1954, it had many fierce critics, but none were harsher than Isherwood himself. When interviewer Stanley Poss asked him about the notion of religious progress in the book (in *Conversations*), Isherwood spoke of the book as a failure: "Well, perhaps that's the whole trouble. Maybe it should have been much more or much less than it was, you know. There's something there which is, to my mind, fundamentally wrong." When the same interviewer mentioned a strong review by John Wain, one that praised the characterization of Elizabeth Rydal, whom Isherwood based partly on the life of Katherine Mansfield, Isherwood again dismissed the work: "She somehow or another doesn't have any real roots for me in life. That is, she seems to me a sort of literary character, and I wish I had desanctified her more." Isherwood's judgment, which has swayed other critics such as Brian Finney into regarding *The World in the Evening* as a failure, is simply not to be trusted in this case. He had great difficulties finishing the book, but it came together much more successfully than the author himself was able to recognize.

The novel happens in three parts, beginning with "An End," then "Letters and Life," and concluding with "A Beginning." "An End" refers to the marriage of Stephen Monk and his wife Jane, whom he catches having sex with another man at a Hollywood party. Stephen's way of dealing with problems has always been to flee, so he runs away to his childhood home, Tawelfan (Welsh for "the quiet place"), in Pennsylvania. Just as he is about to flee Tawelfan, he has what Finney calls a "psychosomatic accident": he gets hit by a truck and so must endure ten weeks of convalescence in a body cast. This enforced stillness provides Isherwood with a secular way to dramatize meditation, which, externally regarded, is as undramatic a form of behavior as one can imagine.

In "Letters and Life," Stephen Monk rereads the letters of his first wife, the novelist Elizabeth Rydal, and learns a great deal about her and himself, mainly having to do with his selfishness and failure to love. Several strands come together as Stephen is forced to understand rather than flee his own story. He reviews his homosexual relationship with a young journalist, Michael Drummond—including two rather tame sex scenes that caused some readers discomfort—and the confrontation in which Drummond tries to force Stephen and Elizabeth apart by bluntly revealing his affair with Stephen. This line of memory is paralleled in Stephen's present-tense experience by his friendship with a gay couple, Charles Kennedy and Bob Wood.

Though Finney complains that these characters have nothing to do with Stephen's story, Kennedy and Wood represent alternative responses to the problem of being homosexual in a heterosexist society: Bob is militant and angry (as Uncle George will be in *A Single Man*), whereas Charles presents the "camp" theory of life and art in which one need never take oneself so seriously. Susan Sontag, who develops ideas from this famous passage in her 1964 essay "Notes on Camp," ungraciously refers to it as "a lazy two-page sketch" that has become a cornerstone of queer theory. Robert Caserio, by contrast, relates the Bob-Charles dyad to the basic choices facing American citizens in the postwar world: "In response to a dislike for what American victory makes of nationalism and citizenship, *The World in the Evening* sums a movement of thought in some immediately post–World War II fictions to recreate citizenship in the light of Quaker Camp." Paradoxically, Caserio demonstrates that Isherwood's novel affirms aesthetic and political passivism in a manner that can actually be construed as a form of political activism. Just as meditation is only apparently the antithesis of "action," so too is Isherwood's fictive defense of Quaker camp less quietist than it might at first seem.

As in T. S. Eliot's *Four Quartets* (1943), one's end is one's beginning and one's beginning is one's end. Stephen, having come to a better understanding of himself, arranges an amicable divorce from Jane and, presumably, moves on to a more honest life. Although many readers regard Aunt Sarah as the novel's saintly character, the final discussion between Stephen and his former wife Jane suggests that Elizabeth is the holy ghost of this novel, for her transmission of love to Stephen, and through Stephen to Jane, animates the love of Jane and her new husband. Isherwood has dismissed the ending of the novel as overly sentimental, but clearly he is working within the "high camp" aesthetic framework sketched for Stephen by Charles Kennedy. Sarah and Elizabeth are—Isherwood is quite serious—presented as saints of a sort, but Isherwood also pulls the rug out from the idea of saintliness in the novel's final paragraphs. Stephen and Jane forgive each other for all manner of transgressions, and when Stephen says, "It's these cocktails," Jane responds, "I know it! They're just loaded with faith, hope and charity. I think the bartender must be a saint in disguise. Another one of these and I'll even forgive Hitler." Stephen goes one better and says, as he empties his glass, "I'll even forgive myself."

DOWN THERE ON A VISIT

Isherwood's next novel is a semifictional, quasi-autobiographical reconnoitering in which "Isherwood" revisits four chronologically arranged episodes. The "down there" of *Down There on a Visit* refers to hell, and it is as if the self who remembers the life in four parts is looking back from an afterlife, perhaps at the way one's choices in one moment of life shape one's reincarnation in the next life. The parts of life that seem so separate, the narrator explains, are actually intimately interrelated; and Isherwood's achievement in this novel is to set explicit fragmentation and division against an implicit development across sections. The narrator announces that division is only apparent, an illusion, in the first paragraph of the first section, "Mr. Lancaster":

> I always used to think of him as an isolated character. Taken alone, he is less than himself. To present him entirely, I realize I must show how our meeting was the start of a new chapter in my life, indeed a whole series of chapters. And I must go on to describe some of the characters in those chapters. They are all, with one exception, strangers to Mr. Lancaster. (If he could have known what was to become of Waldemar, he would have cast him forth from the office in horror.) If he could ever have met Ambrose, or Geoffrey, or Maria, or Paul—but no, my imagination fails! And yet, through me, all these people are involved with each other, however much they might have hated to think so. And so they are all going to have to share the insult of each other's presence in this book.

Although the title, indicating that all worldly life is really hell, proposes a pessimistic outlook, the narrator who recounts the separations between lives, the failures of understanding, and the grasping quality of people in various situations offers knowledge of redemption:

> There has been no break in the sequence of daily statements that I am I. But *what* I am has refashioned itself throughout the days and years, until now almost all that remains constant is the mere awareness of being conscious. And that awareness belongs to everybody; it isn't a particular person.

Although they do not know it, all the characters in the novel—including the narrator himself at a younger age—need to know what the narrator himself knows. For lack of this knowledge, Mr. Lancaster, who is very much one of the "Others" against which Isherwood's work was a lifelong rebellion, kills himself. In the second episode, "Ambrose," a small group of friends develops a briefly utopian community, a kind of alternative world where homosexuality is the norm—but this world breaks apart. At the social level, characters begin to fight bitterly, and at the level of personal experience, the "Isherwood" whom the narrator recounts loses interest and even the ability to remember: "All this happened four, five, six days ago? I've lost track already. It might as well be six months." The narrative gives way to diary fragments, and the diary breaks down into shorter and shorter fragments, such as "Oh, Jesus, my head." The cycles of life on the island repeat themselves "like a play which had to be performed day after day in its original version but with a cast which was no longer big enough." The third section, "Waldemar," is set in England during the Munich Crisis, where Christopher fails to help Waldemar avoid returning to Germany, just as the actual Christopher Isherwood was unable to help his lover Heinz.

In the fourth section, "Paul," the fictional Isherwood has left Europe and the war behind for southern California. Isherwood in this novella-length section vacillates between the worlds of Augustus Parr (based on Gerald Heard) and Paul, the campy analogue of a saint or near-saint who, after some strenuous drug abuse, cleans himself up but then dies of a weak heart. Parr recognizes great potential in Paul's face, which he compares to a photo of a wild animal at bay: "one also saw something else—which no animal has or can have—despair. Not help-less, negative despair. Dynamic despair. The kind that makes dangerous criminals, and, very occasionally, saints." Paul becomes heavily involved in Vedantic meditation, even displac-ing Christopher as the primary disciple of the guru figure Augustus Parr. The largest part of Paul's earthy charm is that he has no tolerance for pious self-presentation: "He was prepared to take everything Augustus had told him quite literally, with no reservations. 'Are we going to be mystics or aren't we? Let's either shit or get off the pot.'"

Paul, however, is accused of having relations with an underage girl (it later turns out that the story was a complete fabrication), and the scandal that quickly engulfs the religious com-munity makes it clear that there are two kinds of people, hetero- and homosexual, and that there is great distrust between these two sides. The protagonist is relieved when he finds out that Paul did not behave in the extremely improper way of which he had been accused, but divisions arise between all the characters in this novel, and when Christopher sees a shock-ingly pale Paul on his final visit, Paul is moving fearlessly toward death and laughs at Christo-pher's desire to share a pipe of opium with him: "You know, you really *are* a tourist, to your bones. I bet you're always sending post cards with 'Down here on a visit' on them. That's the story of your life."

Francis King argues that "despite the fact that each of the sections is about people shut up in hells of their own making, with the author as spectator, the book remains scrappy and lacking in cohesion," but David Izzo and Brian Finney conclude that it is among Isherwood's best works. Finney writes that it warrants "the same critical attention that has been devoted to *Good-bye to Berlin*." One could say that the wander-ing self whom Isherwood tracks through the four parts of *Down There on a Visit* is a tourist both in a negative and a positive sense: the

character "Christopher Isherwood" may lack the actual commitment that a saint candidate like Paul has, evidenced by his "dynamic despair"; but the Isherwood who is incarnated four times in the episodes and then a fifth time as narrator is a tourist in a positive sense insofar as he moves from place to place without attachment. Such nonattachment can be negatively viewed as lack of concern, but it can also be the basis for genuine spiritual progress.

Claude J. Summers finds that Isherwood refuses "to depict the narrator's emergence into full maturity" but also suggests that Isherwood's emphasis on continuity between the protago-nist's consciousness and the narrator's voice is an optimistic sign. Of course, if there were no progress, then the mature narrative voice would not be able to look back upon his youthful self and say "He embarrasses me often, and so I'm tempted to sneer at him; but I will try not to. I'll try not to apologize for him, either. After all, I owe him some respect. In a sense he is my father, and in another sense my son." This at-titude might be called "auto-paternalism." It bespeaks a settled, authoritative perspective before which Isherwood's career-long espousal of generational rebellion—"As far as I was concerned, everyone over forty belonged … to an alien tribe"—could be construed as a mere phase of youth, were Isherwood not such a constant advocate of generational rebellion. *Down there*: by novel's end the phrase has come to refer to purgatory, not hell. The pain and suf-fering of rebellion, and hence of self-making, are presented in the later work as temporary rather than permanent. In memory one may visit "hell" as if a tourist.

A SINGLE MAN

A Single Man is strikingly different from *Down There on a Visit*—it is highly unified in plot, character, setting, and style—but it does share a technique Isherwood uses in *Prater Violet*, namely the ghostly narrator who hangs over the fictive world with equal measures of compassion and detachment. Whereas *Down There* fits the pattern of Isherwoodian "semiautobiographical fiction" described by the critic Katherine Bucknell, *A Single Man* features sharper differences between author and narrator. Like *The World in the Evening*'s Stephen Monk, George shares some of Isherwood's characteristics but is clearly not identical to him. Both author and protagonist are gay men, and George's San Tomas State College is recognizable as the Los Angeles branch of California State University at which Isherwood was teaching when he wrote the novel. Although Isherwood and Don Bachardy had become, within the homosexual community, "first couple" of Santa Monica, George is alone, as his lover Jim as recently died. George also differs from Isherwood in that he has no spiritual practices or particular beliefs; Isherwood describes him as "stoic."

More than anything else, George must be stoic about the death of Jim, which highlights his experience as a gay man in a heterosexual society—that is, as a member of a distinct minority group. This general situation allows the novel a claim to universality, since Isherwood resisted being ghettoized as a "gay writer" and since all people experience loss, but the dramatic situation becomes problematic as well. When Gore Vidal, to whom *A Single Man* is dedicated, sent Isherwood a copy of his first novel, *The City and the Pillar* (1948), Isherwood appreciated Vidal's frank treatment of homosexuality but complained about the novel's tragic ending: "This is what homosexuality brings you to, [the liberal reader] will say: tragedy, defeat, and death." *A Single Man* is not a tragic novel; it is comic in the sense that it affirms the world it describes—provided one takes a wide enough view of the conditions of this world.

But the plot of *A Single Man*—by involving a *single* man—sidesteps the difficulties of present-ing a homosexual couple and so can be said to accommodate the liberal heterosexist reader about whom Isherwood complains in his letter to Vidal. Still, the novel insightfully depicts the strains of being a gay man (which are not viewed as essentially different from the strains of being a member of any other minority group), and Isherwood is too hard on himself when he says he fails to portray adequately this minority position:

> You see, the element that goes very, very deep in the material, which is never satisfactorily expressed in any of these books and which now I am expressing, is the homosexuality, not so much from the point of view of the question of sexual preference as the whole thing of belonging to a rather small minority, a tribe, which is sometimes overtly persecuted but always sort of subtly slighted. And what this means, the boiling rage underneath the nicey-nice exterior.

In *A Single Man,* Isherwood expresses so brilliantly this rage and the ways in which people like George bottle it up that the novel, in retrospect, looks quite prophetic.

A MEETING BY THE RIVER

Isherwood's final novel, *A Meeting by the River,* attempts once again to resolve the conflicting claims of the spirit and flesh, incarnated in two brothers named Patrick and Oliver. At the novel's beginning, Oliver writes to his older brother Patrick to explain that he is about to take final monastic vows, and so Patrick decides to visit India (the river mentioned in the title is the Ganges) and make a final attempt to keep his brother from renouncing the world. There are no simple two-way struggles, however, as each apparent dichotomy reveals itself as a triangle. Oliver has had romantic feelings for Patrick's wife, Patrick has been cheating on his wife with a boy named Tommy, and both Patrick and Oliver conspire about how to communicate with their mother. These struggles are presented entirely in epistolary or diary form, and thus *A Meeting by the River* does not achieve a position of ironic semitranscendence, as do the narrative voices of *Prater Violet, Down There on a Visit,* and *A Single Man.* By the end of the novel, both Patrick and Oliver have had dream visions, and both dream visions confirm their lives as lived so far. One wonders: were all the letters necessary?

In his final novel, as in *A Single Man,* Isherwood attempts to present a minority position in a universalizing way, but as Lisa Schwerdt points out, "We are asked to complete the novel's intention without being shown how to do so." Oliver is obviously unusual because he is an Englishman becoming a Hindu monk, and Patrick, who is a successful publisher working in Los Angeles, nonetheless has a marginal role in relation to society because he is a closeted bisexual. Yet *A Meeting by the River* does less well than *A Single Man* at creating an actual meeting between the particular and the universal. By contrast, this meeting is made explicit in *A Single Man:* George, in speaking to students in his southern California classroom, describes the situation of the ethnic minority writer in relation to the mainstream audience; and George's various personality shifts, as he moves from context to context (for example, from the classroom to the neighbor's porch to the gay bar), demonstrate that *all* people are minorities.

In *A Meeting by the River,* Oliver's religious quest is not quite enlarged in the way George's secular quest is in *A Single Man,* and some readers find the novel dramatically lax. Isherwood himself admitted that "it ends with a deadlock." Schwerdt concludes that *"A Meeting by the River* is an anomaly in the Isherwood canon in that the narrator or his namesake is rendered redundant by the novel's form." Izzo finds the novel a successful allegorical representation of "dueling sides of Isherwood's psyche," but "Isherwood" is not, as Schwerdt points out, part of

this novel, as he is in *The Berlin Stories, Prater Violet,* and *Down There on a Visit.*

AUTOBIOGRAPHY

In the last fifteen years of his life, Isherwood wrote four autobiographical works that successfully manage the dilemmas he was able to stage but not to resolve in *A Meeting by the River.* In *Kathleen and Frank* he works through his mother and father's letters and diaries so to revise his personal mythology of generational strife, until he is able to thank his stubborn mother whose once-maddening behavior "saved him from being a mother's boy, a churchgoer, an academic, a conservative, a patriot and a respectable citizen." Izzo praises Isherwood's achievement of a "Vedantic reconciliation" of the opposition between himself and his mother, "an opposition without which the fission required to advance his evolving consciousness would never have been fueled."

The next autobiographical installment was *Christopher and His Kind.* Paul Piazza describes the book as "not an end, but an exuberant, sometimes playful, and altogether unexpected beginning"—unexpected because Isherwood chose to be as candid as possible in his self-presentation. On the first page of this memoir about Isherwood's Berlin years he tells the reader, "The book I am now going to write will be as frank and factual as I can make it." Telling this story required Isherwood to describe his failed efforts to get his lover Heinz out of Germany; his writing troubles, his psychosomatic illnesses, and his intense struggles with his mother; and his developing understanding of his sexuality.

In 1972 the Modern Language Association held its first panel on gay literature, which Isherwood attended. Isherwood insisted that this event did not bring him out of the closet—he had already brought himself out, incrementally, in a book-by-book fashion—but rather it was the Modern Language Association that came out of the closet. Isherwood's leadership in publicly affirming his homosexuality nevertheless involved a self-exposure that was not without risks to his literary reputation, and his autobiographical writings in the last twenty years of his writing life continued to offer an array of actual as opposed to idealized or stylized selves. "Actual" is perhaps misleading, since Isherwood the writer always refers to "Christopher" of a given year and not a single, unchanging self: *Christopher and His Kind* and the next installment, *My Guru and His Disciple*, form the history of these Christophers. One does not sense fear about such exposure at the end of *Christopher and His Kind*. The narrative closes with a slightly campy and utterly charming picture of Christopher leaning over the rail, looking at the ominous Statue of Liberty. The ghostly narrative voice, *in* the world it describes but not *of* it, pays homage to America as the land of freedom in which Auden and Isherwood would each find true love:

> Yes, my dears, each of you will find the person you came here to look for—the ideal companion to whom you can reveal yourself totally and yet be loved for what you are, not what you pretend to be. You, Wystan, will find him very soon, within three months. You, Christopher, will have to wait much longer for yours. He is already living in the city where you will settle. He will be near you for many years without your meeting. But it would be no good if you did meet him now. At present he is only four years old.

Christopher and His Kind and *My Guru and His Disciple* are both dedicated to Don Bachardy, who was four years old when Isherwood arrived in America.

If *A Meeting at the River* ended in a "deadlock," Isherwood found in *My Guru and His Disciple* a more congenial form through which to stage a dialogue between the parts of himself that were homosexual and the parts of himself that were Vedantic (if this word is understood

to mean a belief that the *maya* of this world is inherently unsatisfactory). In this spiritual autobiography, Isherwood reviews his early years in America and his relationship with Swami Prabhāvānanda through the swami's death in 1976. Whereas Isherwood's many fictional attempts to imagine saintly or near-saintly characters often left readers with the uncomfortable sense of a gap between the saintly ideal and its literary realization, in *Guru*, Isherwood more or less celebrates this gap.

The problem he discusses in "The Problem of the Religious Novel" (in *Vedanta for Modern Man*), that "perhaps the truly comprehensive religious novel could only be written by a saint," does not exist for this book, because Isherwood has, perhaps after the "deadlock" of *A Meeting by the River*, given up on the competitive struggle between these aspects of himself. Instead the memoir fleshes out a rather sweet and often wickedly funny friendship between the supposedly incommensurable worlds of sensual indulgence and Vedantic otherworldly discipline. Isherwood reports his great discomfort at the bad fit between these roles at certain moments, such as when he accompanied Prabhāvānanda to India and was asked to address a council of Vedantic monks: "*As long as I quite unashamedly get drunk, have promiscuous sex, and write books like* A Single Man, *I simply cannot appear before people as a sort of lay monk. Whenever I do, my life becomes divided and untruthful—or rather, the only truth left is in my drunkenness, my sex, and my art.*" Isherwood expresses his sense of an impossible division to Swami, who responds lovingly (he is often presented as a living saint, like Aunt Sarah in *The World in the Evening*) by saying, "*Chris, how can you say that? You're almost too good*" and "*I don't want to lose you, Chris.*" Isherwood confesses that some parts of his complaint are consciously overdramatic, that he is "playacting," but then he realizes the Swami is too: "*I knew that he, too, had begun to playact—to* call my bluff." Isherwood has said in a number of interviews that Hinduism, in his view, is not always as serious as it is made out to be— "What's great about the Hindu thing is that it's very lively and kind of campy and fun"—and in this book he is, most successfully, able to resolve the apparent contradiction between piety and campy fun, largely in favor of campy fun.

Isherwood's final work, *October,* is perhaps slight compared to works that have gotten more attention such as *The Berlin Stories, The World in the Evening, A Single Man,* and *My Guru and His Disciple,* but this final piece of autobiography, richly illustrated with drawings by Don Bachardy, is in its own way the perfect conclusion of Isherwood's writing career. If *A Single Man* suffered slightly for avoiding the representation of a happy homosexual union, then *October* makes good on the debt. And if Isherwood's long slow struggle was to try to imagine into existence a form of life in which one's spirituality, sexuality, and worldly commitments are all "friends" with one another, *October* is the work in which these themes come together. Vedantism is almost a silent partner in this work, but the work is a vision of gay happiness, and the definition of happiness comes from Swami Prabhavananda. As Isherwood meditates on Katherine Mansfield, whom he had once considered a "saint," he revises his admiration slightly in view of Prabhāvānanda's teaching: "years later, Prabhāvānanda taught me that a saint is a person who has attained enlightenment and whose chief characteristic is therefore happiness." *October* demonstrates that happiness, rather than suffering, had become the primary virtue for Isherwood.

Isherwood died of cancer on January 4, 1986, in Santa Monica at the age of eighty-one. The *Los Angeles Times* editorial page obituary functions as a preface to the posthumously published *Wishing Tree,* where it is titled "He Belonged": "His elegant, innovative, and unflinchingly honest prose made him one of this century's most important English-speaking writers. As such, he belonged not only to his native Britain and his adopted America, but also to the whole world of letters."

Selected Bibliography

WORKS OF CHRISTOPHER ISHERWOOD

FICTION

All the Conspirators. London: Jonathan Cape, 1928; New York: New Directions, 1958.

The Memorial: Portrait of a Family. London: Hogarth Press, 1932.

Mr. Norris Changes Trains. London: Hogarth Press, 1935. (Published in the United States as *The Last of Mr. Norris.* New York: Morrow, 1935.)

Sally Bowles. London: Hogarth Press, 1937.

Goodbye to Berlin. London: Hogarth Press, 1939.

The Berlin Stories. New York: New Directions, 1945. (This volume collects *The Last of Mr. Norris* with *Goodbye to Berlin,* which itself gathers "A Berlin Diary [autumn 1930]," "Sally Bowles," "The Nowaks," "The Landauers," and "Berlin Diary [winter 1932–1933].")

Prater Violet. New York: Random House, 1945.

The World in the Evening. New York: Random House, 1954.

Down There on a Visit. New York: Simon & Schuster, 1962.

A Single Man. New York: Simon & Schuster, 1964.

A Meeting by the River. New York: Simon & Schuster, 1967.

The Mortmere Stories. With Edward Upward. London: Enitharmon Press, 1994.

NONFICTION

Lions and Shadows: An Education in the Twenties. London: Hogarth, 1938.

Journey to a War. With W. H. Auden. London: Faber & Faber, 1939.

The Condor and the Cows: A South American Travel Diary. New York: Random House, 1949.

An Approach to Vedanta. Hollywood, Calif.: Vedanta Press, 1963.

Ramakrishna and His Disciples. New York: Simon & Schuster, 1965.

Kathleen and Frank: The Autobiography of a Family. New York: Simon & Schuster, 1971.

Christopher and His Kind: 1929–1939. New York: Farrar, Straus & Giroux, 1976.

My Guru and His Disciple. New York: Farrar, Straus & Giroux, 1980.

October. With drawings by Don Bachardy. London: Methuen, 1983.

The Wishing Tree: Christopher Isherwood on Mystical Religion. Edited by Robert Adjemian. San Francisco: Harper & Row, 1987.

Where Joy Resides: A Christopher Isherwood Reader. Edited by Don Bachardy and James P. White. New York: Farrar, Straus & Giroux, 1989.

Diaries: Volume 1, 1939–1960. Edited by Katherine Bucknell. New York: HarperCollins, 1997.

Lost Years: A Memoir, 1945–1951. Edited by Katherine Bucknell. New York: HarperCollins, 2000.

Conversations with Christopher Isherwood. Edited by James J. Berg and Chris Freeman. Jackson: University Press of Mississippi, 2001.

OTHER WORKS

The Dog beneath the Skin; or, Where Is Francis? With W. H. Auden. London: Faber, 1935. (Play.)

The Ascent of F6. With W. H. Auden. London: Faber, 1936. (Play.)

On the Frontier. With W. H. Auden. London: Faber, 1938. (Play.)

Exhumations: Stories, Articles, Verses. New York: Simon & Schuster, 1966.

Frankenstein: The True Story. With Don Bachardy. New York: Avon, 1973. (Screenplay, based on the novel by Mary Wollstonecraft Shelley.)

Jacob's Hands. With Aldous Huxley. New York: St. Martin's Press, 1998. (Screenplay.)

TRANSLATIONS

Anonymous. *The Song of God: Bhagavad-Gita.* With Swami Prabhavananda. Hollywood, Calif.: Vedanta Press, 1944. (Translation of *Bhagavad-Gita* from Sanskrit.)

Baudelaire, Charles. *Intimate Journals.* London: Blackamore Press, 1930. (Translation of *Journaux intimes* from French.)

Brecht, Bertolt. *A Penny for the Poor.* With Desmond Vesey. London: Hale, 1937. (Translation of *Der Dreigroschenroman* from German.)

Patanjali. *How to Know God: The Yoga Aphorisms of Patanjali.* With Swami Prabhavananda. New York: Harper, 1953. (Translation from Sanskrit.)

Shankara. *Shankara's Crest-Jewel of Discrimination.* With Swami Prabhavananda. Hollywood, Calif.: Vedanta Press, 1947. (Translation of *Vivekachudamani* from Sanskrit.)

EDITED VOLUMES

Vedanta for the Western World. Hollywood, Calif.: Marcel Rodd, 1945.

Vedanta for Modern Man. New York: Harper, 1951.

Great English Short Stories. New York: Dell, 1957.

MANUSCRIPTS AND PAPERS

The main collection of Isherwood's papers is at the Huntington Library in San Marino, California. The University of Texas, the University of California at Los Angeles, New York University, and Cambridge University also have collections of Isherwood's papers.

FILMS AND PLAYS BASED ON THE WORKS OF ISHERWOOD

I Am a Camera. Written by John Van Druten. First production: New York, Empire Theatre, November 1951. (Stage play.)

I Am a Camera. Directed by Henry Cornelius. Screenplay by John Collier. Remus Films, Ltd., 1955. (Motion picture.)

Cabaret. Book by Joe Masteroff, lyrics by Fred Ebb, music by John Kander. First production: New York, Broadhurst Theatre, November 1966. (Musical stage play.)

Cabaret. Directed by Bob Fosse. Screenplay by Jay Allen. Lorimar, 1972. (Musical motion picture.)

CRITICAL AND BIOGRAPHICAL STUDIES

Berg, James J., and Chris Freeman. *The Isherwood Century: Essays on the Life and Work of Christopher Isherwood.* Madison: University of Wisconsin Press, 1999.

Bernhard, Brendan. "Coming to America: Isherwood and Auden in the New World." *L.A. Weekly,* February 21–27, 1997. (Available at http://www.la weekly.com/ink/printme.php?eid=5947.)

Caserio, Robert L. "Queer Passions, Queer Citizenship: Some Novels about the State of the American Nation 1946–1954." *Modern Fiction Studies* 43: 170–205 (1997).

Finney, Brian. *Christopher Isherwood: A Critical Biography.* London: Faber & Faber, 1979.

Heilbrun, Carolyn. *Christopher Isherwood.* New York: Columbia University Press, 1970.

Hutcheon, Linda. *The Politics of Postmodernism.* London: Routledge, 1989.

Izzo, David Garrett. *Christopher Isherwood: His Era, His Gang, and the Legacy of the Truly Strong Man.* Columbia: University of South Carolina Press, 2001.

King, Francis. *Christopher Isherwood.* Harlow, Essex, U.K.: Longman, 1976.

Lehmann, John. *Christopher Isherwood: A Personal Memoir.* New York: Henry Holt, 1989.

Page, Norman. *Auden and Isherwood: The Berlin Years.* New York: St. Martin's, 1998.

Piazza, Paul. *Christopher Isherwood: Myth and Anti-Myth.* New York: Columbia University Press, 1978.

Schwerdt, Lisa M. *Isherwood's Fiction.* Houndsmills, U.K.: Macmillan, 1989.

Sontag, Susan. "Notes on Camp." *Partisan Review* 31:515–530 (fall 1964). Reprinted in her *Against Interpretation, and Other Essays.* New York: Farrar, Straus & Giroux, 1966.

Summers, Claude J. *Christopher Isherwood.* New York: Ungar, 1980.

Summers, Claude J. "Christopher Isherwood." In *Dictionary of Literary Biography.* Vol. 15, *British Novelists, 1930–1959.* Edited by Bernard Oldsey. Detroit: Gale/Bruccoli Clark, 1983.

Vidal, Gore. "Introduction." In Isherwood's *Where Joy Resides.* Edited by Don Bachardy and James P. White. New York: Farrar, Straus & Giroux, 1989.

——JOHN WALEN-BRIDGE

Aldo Leopold

1886–1948

THE AUTHOR OF natural histories, personal sketches, and scientific articles, Aldo Leopold defied disciplinary conventions to pursue a holistic vision of the natural world and humanity's place within it. His central work, the essay collection *A Sand County Almanac and Sketches Here and There* (1949), displays three main ambitions: to celebrate the beauty of a landscape whose wildness had been hitherto ignored; to bring about the resurrection of lands badly damaged by short-sighted farming and logging methods; and to inspire the development of a human role in the natural world as steward, not despoiler. The vision the book offers, of farmers and small landowners restoring a damaged landscape to ecological health, has influenced the environmental movement profoundly. Many in the field place Leopold's *Sand County Almanac* in the company of Henry David Thoreau's *Walden* (1854), John Muir's *My First Summer in the Sierra* (1911), Rachel Carson's *Silent Spring* (1962), Edward Abbey's *Desert Solitaire: A Season in the Wilderness* (1968), and Wendell Berry's *Unsettling of America: Culture and Agriculture* (1977) as a nonfiction work whose philosophical, ethical, and political implications transcend the genre of nature writing.

Thoreau's *Walden* clearly served as a model for Leopold's book in both its structure and its narrative voice. There are striking similarities in the retiring of Leopold's narrator to a rural "shack" and Thoreau's account of his year spent in a cabin near Walden Pond. Leopold's narrator possesses the same cantankerous sense of humor, the same jaundiced view of contempo-

rary social and economic attitudes, and the same inquisitive desire to look beyond the surface of the natural world in search of explanations and causes. Like Thoreau, Leopold's narrator arrives at belief in a community that includes all beings, wild and human.

Yet Leopold's philosophy, unlike Thoreau's, always was grounded in pragmatism. The critic William Barillas argues that Leopold derived his philosophical insights from such transcendentalists as Thoreau and Ralph Waldo Emerson but that his unique approach grounded their "romantic spirit of place" in "modern ecological science." Leopold's reverence for nature is clear in the *Almanac,* but he never approaches the dense spiritual rhapsodies of Thoreau or even the ecstatic proclamations of John Muir, aloft in a tree and howling the virtues of wildness. While Thoreau ignored or railed against any evidence of human intrusion on his Walden enclave, Leopold deliberately highlighted signs of human activity. He believed his neighbors were ignoring the wildlife potential of their own backyards and itching instead to visit national parks, an attitude that Thoreau's withdrawal from society encouraged. Thus Leopold's own retreat was not a renunciation of human company but a journey away from urban life toward an ecologically based vision of community.

As a writer Leopold often balanced the poetics of place with the practical sensibility of a land manager who knows his readers are intelligent and curious but not necessarily tolerant of either scientific jargon or spiritual rapture. He wanted the reader to be inspired enough by the beauty of the writing to put down the book and look around outside. The basis for the most literary of his essays was observation, the close monitoring of experience in the field that yielded both moral epiphany and scientific discovery. In fact, Leopold described natural history observation as the highest form of recreation, higher than hunting, which he loved from boyhood. Observation, he believed, brought pleasure to the observer without demanding that the land produce anything in return.

Elevated language, allegory, vivid sensory imagery—all were tools intended to spark the reader's interest, but Leopold often found them inadequate to the greater task of describing a new relationship with nature. *A Sand County Almanac* represents Leopold's struggle to come up with a new language that could convey an appreciation of the beauty of the natural world, an understanding of ecological principles, and an ethic of environmental stewardship. To create this ecological vocabulary, he believed that education should pursue the amalgamation of different disciplines, that philosophy, science, and literature were all features of the same whole. *A Sand County Almanac* demonstrates this interdisciplinary process at work.

Because of its experimental form, the book struggled to find a publisher. Those who read it felt that there was too little of what the public expected from nature writing: safe descriptions of charming wildlife and pastoral scenes or swashbuckling frontier adventures. Editors advised Leopold to expand the first portion of the book, which could be read as traditional nature writing, and to cut the political and ethical commentaries that were not in keeping with the fashion of the time. For Leopold, however, countering the general ignorance of the Midwest's natural heritage with scenes from the farm was not enough. The lack of regard for local wildlife was only a symptom of what he viewed as a greater societal detachment from the ecological community, and he therefore refused to soften the work's ethical imperative.

Leopold came of age in an era of unprecedented ecological controversy and excitement, with Theodore Roosevelt in the White House buying up acres of western land by the thousands, creating national parks, and establishing agencies to manage the acquisitions. The key question of the time was whether these resources existed to serve the purposes of humanity or had intrinsic worth of their own. The two protagonists in this debate, the forester and conservationist Gifford Pinchot and the naturalist John Muir, argued furiously over specific projects, such as the construction of the Hetch Hetchy Dam in the heart of Yosemite National Park, and over the greater philosophical questions of wilderness and development as well. Pinchot, who served as the first chief of the Division of Forestry of the U.S. Agriculture Department, thought the natural world should be managed according to human needs, with dams built in Yosemite if human civilization required the water, trees cut for lumber when it was needed, and mines developed where they promised to yield wealth. Muir, on the other hand, viewed wilderness areas as tantamount to religious shrines and their destruction as something akin to the desecration of a cathedral.

Wilderness was a central feature of Leopold's formative years as a writer and environmentalist; it offered experience of physical beauty, personal freedom, and an intense vitality that he associated with the frontier and thus with an era of American history that had run its course. The essays that feature wilderness, in contrast to the celebratory tone of those set on the Wisconsin farm, are nostalgic, even elegiac in tone. They convey a sense of loss that cannot be redeemed—the passing of the last grizzly, the extinguishing of wolves, the disappearance of the cowboy way of life. Leopold continued to advocate the preservation of wilderness areas until his death, but he was not content with what he termed a "rearguard action."

His return from the Southwest to the Midwest of his youth marked a transition in almost every sense: the departure from conventional notions of beauty, the loss of contact with traditional wilderness, and the removal from frontier culture. In their place Leopold discovered the intellectual terrain that would occupy him for the rest of his life and would lead him to search for an environmental ethic with an abiding sense of possibility and opportunity instead of nostalgia and loss.

Leopold's "Land Ethic," for which he is best known today, does not side with either party in the wilderness debate. While he certainly envisions humans utilizing natural resources, he breaks from Pinchot in his view of the natural world as valuable in its own right, an appreciation that at times borders on the spiritual. Unlike Muir, however, Leopold's natural system extends to include all landscapes, not just the stand of redwoods where humanity must leave no trace but also the agrarian fields where people live and work every day. Leopold was adamant in his belief that the future of wildlife depended on the actions of small landholders, who could begin the process of integrating themselves into the ecological community through the practice of what is now known as ecological restoration. He was the first to articulate the principles of ecological restoration, which calls for landowners to return degraded landscapes to their condition prior to human settlement, and he was the first to put these principles into practice.

In the years since *A Sand County Almanac*'s publication in 1949, numerous writers, activists, and scholars have taken up Leopold's challenge to live by an ethic of ecological responsibility. When Edward Abbey rails against the road building and profiteering of "industrial tourism," in *Desert Solitaire,* he echoes the complaints that Leopold lodges in the essay "Conser-vation Esthetic." When Wendell Berry, in *The Unsettling of America,* writes of a return to the family farm as the salvation of the country's ills, he indirectly recalls Leopold's move to his Sauk County farm. Berry's call for farming practices that are in harmony with the landscape and the ecological community could easily come from one of the environmentally conscious farmers Leopold envisioned in his work.

CHILDHOOD AND YOUTH

Rand Aldo Leopold was born on January 11, 1887, in Burlington, Iowa, the first child of Carl Leopold and Clara Starker Leopold. His sister, Marie, was born soon after, in 1888, and his brothers, Carl Jr. and Frederic, were born in 1892 and 1895, respectively. His early history reflects the insular nature of upper-middle-class life in a small but bustling town only recently carved from the great expanse of open prairie. His parents, for example, were first cousins who shared maternal grandparents—a fact that was considered unremarkable at the time.

Clara Starker, Leopold's mother, had attended a private school in Boston. She supplemented her children's public school education with selections of German literature. These readings probably introduced Leopold to the celebration of the natural world evident in the poetry and prose of German Romanticism and also to the strong sense of *heimat,* or the attachment to homeland, that pervaded German literature throughout this and earlier periods.

Leopold's father, Carl, was an avid hunter who nurtured his son's interest in the outdoors. The elder Leopold had established a successful furniture-making business, the Rand Leopold Desk Company, which kept the family in comfortable circumstances. In *Aldo Leopold: His Life and Work,* however, the biographer Curt Meine suggests that Carl's avocation troubled his conscience. He witnessed the agricultural transformation of the prairie, the epic slaughter of wildlife populations in the vicinity of Burlington, and the complete extinction of species like the passenger pigeon, and these changes left him uneasy about an income derived from cutting down northern forests. Carl Leopold's response was to set his own bag limits, restrict his use of firepower, and curtail the periods when he could fire. His actions clearly influenced his son's thinking. They set the tone for Aldo Leopold's political activism in favor of stricter game laws, and they also laid the ground for the emphasis on personal responsibility in his famous essay "The Land Ethic."

At the age of seventeen, Leopold went east for the first time, to attend Lawrenceville Preparatory School in New Jersey. His success there translated into a place at Yale, where he began studies in science and forestry in 1905. Forestry was a new field, full of unprecedented, dramatic action on a national scale, and Yale was one of the few places outside Europe with a professional school of forestry. In 1908 Leopold received a bachelor of science and in 1909 his master's degree from Yale and headed west to join the U.S. Forest Service. His first assignment took him to one of the wildest corners of the Arizona Territory, the newly established Apache National Forest. His first few jobs were mainly outdoors, cruising timber, making maps, and heading up teams of laborers. He adjusted quickly to the regional culture and landscape. The experience of this wilderness, with few roads, sparse settlements, and an enduring frontier spirit, left a lasting impression on Leopold that he recalls, nostalgically, in the "Sketches Here and There" section of the *Almanac.*

While working in the New Mexico Territory first as deputy supervisor and then as supervisor of the Carson National Forest, Leopold fell in love with Estella Luna Bergere, who had deep roots in the region and could trace her ancestors to the Spanish conquistadors. By marrying Estella (on October 9, 1912), Leopold entered a regional network of obligation and affiliation that bound him even more closely to the Southwest, but the extreme physical demands of the outdoor work nearly killed him. Suffering from kidney failure brought on by overexposure to harsh weather, Leopold required a long convalescence that left him unable to endure the physical hardships of fieldwork and changed the direction of his career. Leopold continued to work with the Forest Service as a consultant, but the nature of his work changed dramatically. He was put in charge of recreation policy for the entire region, a job that allowed him to shift his attention to issues of great personal significance: the management and protection of wildlife.

Many contemporary environmental organizations arose at this time out of sportsmen's clubs dedicated, like Leopold, to hunting. Leopold was instrumental in founding the New Mexico Game Protective Association, a private group pushing for the establishment of game refuges on public land. He became a political activist, lobbying state officials for better game protection laws and delivering speeches filled with the passionate convictions that eventually would make their way into the *Sand County Almanac.*

Leopold was well aware of such ecological problems as overgrazing, erosion, and the introduction of invasive non-native species, but he had not yet placed them within the context of the overall ecosystem or considered what he termed "land health" as a reflection of the health of all the members of the ecological community, as he would come to emphasize in his later work. In marked contrast to the *Almanac,* Leopold's writing from this era often displays antipathy toward wolves and other carnivores. Perhaps the most famous example comes from the first edition of the *Pine Cone,* a newsletter for which Leopold served as writer and editor. Published in 1915 and reprinted in the essay collection *The River of the Mother of God and Other Essays by Aldo Leopold* (1991), "The Varmint Question," states that "wolves, lions, coyotes, bob-cats, foxes, skunks and other varmints" are thriving, to the detriment of game populations. Not only does this statement contradict the facts on the ground (in which predators like the wolf and grizzly were on the verge of regional extermination), but it goes against the basic ecological tenet that predators and prey form a necessary system of checks and balances that benefits both species. Leopold later observed the damage wrought by the explosion of deer populations in the absence of natural predators, both in Wisconsin and the West, and refers directly to this predicament in the *Almanac* essay "Conservation Esthetic."

As with his appreciation of predators, Leopold's interest in wilderness preservation developed in his final years in the Southwest, as he witnessed rapid changes in the landscape. The wilds he had encountered upon arriving in Arizona ten years earlier were fading with the arrival of roads, cars, and people. Guided by the wilderness values of Thoreau and Muir, Leopold called for the preservation of large areas of national forest to be kept in their "natural state," and he proposed the headwaters of the Gila River in New Mexico as a prime candidate to begin the program. The Gila Wilderness Area eventually became the first in the country to receive this designation.

THE MIDWEST

As the debate over wilderness was just beginning to bear fruit, Leopold was asked to take a step that would transform his life and work: to leave New Mexico and the West for a position with the U.S. Forest Products Laboratory in Madison, Wisconsin. The drama of this uprooting cannot be overstated. Leopold had spent years working with the land, until he was intimately familiar with its features; he had married into the region's social system and produced five children with ties there too; and he was

engaged fully in the public debate over the future of the wild areas he had grown to love. He had rejected requests for his transfer to Washington in the past, on just these grounds. Leopold's reasons for accepting this time are not definitively known. *A Sand County Almanac* makes no mention of the momentous decision, exploring both eras of Leopold's life but not the journey that joined them.

To understand the context of Leopold's essays from this period, we must consider the tumult and devastation arising from the twofold calamity of the Great Depression. While the governing image of the era may be of the stock market collapse and its impact on urban life, a protracted drought was turning the prairie states into a cauldron of swirling dust at the time, with profound effects on the rural population of the country. The dust bowl exposed as nothing more than a delusion the prevailing view that great swaths of the region could be plowed up, planted in wheat, and expected to bear crops without access to irrigation. The failure could not be linked to the weather alone: farming practices had as much to do with the blowing soil as the lack of rain.

Many people left the Midwest for greener pastures to the west. The novelist John Steinbeck records one such family's travails on the way to California in *The Grapes of Wrath* (1939), and the photographer Dorothea Lange's images of dust bowl migrants reveal similar hardships. Leopold, however, made this journey in reverse. While others were abandoning played-out farms and heading west, Leopold was packing up his family and traveling east, to the landscape of his youth. It is important to view Leopold's writings in this context: as the return of a native, whose pleasures arise from rediscovering what he recalls from a boyhood spent roaming the region and whose pains are those of an adult recording what has disappeared in the time he has spent away.

Leopold quit the U.S. Forest Service after four years with the lab (1924–1928), when he was asked to conduct a game survey for the Sporting Arms and Ammunition Manufacturers' Institute. The position allowed him to enter the fray of yet another emerging field: game management. The group asked him to conduct an extensive survey of game populations in the region, something that had never been attempted. He published the results in 1931 as the *Report on a Game Survey of the North Central States,* making him the nation's leading expert on game populations just as the Great Depression was making its dire presence felt throughout the nation. Soon after, he published the textbook *Game Management* (1933), another landmark in the field that added to his growing national reputation. But funding from the institute dried up with the economic times, and like many at the time, Leopold found himself in precarious economic circumstances.

After several years of economic struggle and piecemeal stints with state and federal agencies, in 1933 Leopold was offered an endowed chair at the University of Wisconsin, as the nation's first Professor of Game Management. Soon after, the university dedicated its arboretum, with Leopold supervising the restoration of the five hundred acres. The project demonstrated the degree to which Leopold's thinking had changed as a result of the game survey work, which had revealed just how little of the original Midwestern landscape remained intact. He set about transforming the arboretum's crop fields into a tall-grass prairie as a demonstration of the potential for a harmonious relationship between humanity and nature.

In 1935 Leopold purchased the abandoned farm in Sauk County, Wisconsin, that was to become famous as the setting for the *Almanac.* The only structure still standing on the site was a chicken coop, which he converted into a cabin. The Leopold family began to spend every weekend working, hunting, and roaming the farm's 120 acres. The drought that brought on the dust bowl was already under way, but Leopold set about installing thousands of trees and shrubs on the site. Planting required a great deal of manual labor, and most of the trees died owing to the lack of moisture. Yet Leopold treated the setbacks as a series of experiments that he could observe, record, and write about.

Leopold maintained his involvement in national environmental politics, traveling to conventions and conferences to deliver speeches and confer with other leading figures. While he remained engaged in the drive to establish wilderness areas like the one he fought for on the Gila River, his focus had shifted to Wisconsin. He was one of the principal founders of the Wilderness Society, for example, but when he was offered its presidency in 1935, he declined, stating that the office would require him to pay too much attention to the politics of Washington. He already had begun the series of short essays that would provide the basis for the first section of *A Sand County Almanac,* and he was preoccupied with his plantings and observations at the farm.

A SAND COUNTY ALMANAC

Leopold's writings from his time in Wisconsin should be understood in a broad context of economic pain and agricultural disillusionment, but they also must be viewed in terms of the specific occasion for which they were written. *A Sand County Almanac and Sketches Here and There* consists of three sections—"A Sand County Almanac," "Sketches Here and There," and "The Upshot"—organized by Leopold to make up a whole, yet reflecting the different eras of his career and the distinct kinds of writing that he often was called upon to produce. Most of the book's essays had their genesis in earlier pieces of writing: Leopold reworked his speeches and articles to reflect the evolution of his thinking, but most of the pieces could, and did, stand alone in print. Landmark essays such as "The Land Ethic" had been in production and delivered on important occasions for more than a decade before they made their appearance in the *Almanac.*

The short, image-rich portraits that make up the "Almanac" section frequently derive from the series of sketches that Leopold contributed to the *Wisconsin Agriculturalist and Farmer,* a small monthly magazine. The progression of Leopold's thinking is clear from the tenor of these pieces, many of which are published in the collection *For the Health of the Land: Previously Unpublished Essays and Other Writings* (1999). The earliest pieces offer utilitarian advice that is safely within the expectations of a conservative audience. By the end of the period, however, as he began to envision the masterwork that would become *A Sand County Almanac,* the essays chart an increasingly radical course, challenging the utilitarian view to such an extent that several of the essays written for the magazine never gained publication in his lifetime.

The almanac is an ancient means of recording local wisdom, part prophesy, part history, part observation of the seasons, and part entertainment for people whose livelihood depends on the land. In conceiving of his work as a series of seasonal observations, Leopold aligns himself with an agrarian tradition of seasonal celebration whose Western roots lie in the work of the Roman poet Virgil and the ancient Greek poet Hesiod. Yet Leopold is not offering simply another entry in this traditional genre, for as his exhortations in favor of wildlife protection suggest, his didactic purpose extends well beyond marking the seasons for a farming audience.

Organized monthly, Leopold's "almanac" emphasizes the seasonal occasion for each of the essays as a means of connecting them to life beyond the page. Reading the essays becomes a form of participating in the seasonal flux, since the seasons of migration and dramatic change in the landscape, spring and fall, are mirrored in a flurry of essays each month, while the winter and summer months are each represented by only one essay. The almanac structure forces the reader to ponder the passage of seasons, the changes in weather, and the cyclical time of natural history to comprehend the essay's relevance fully.

The first essay, "January Thaw," is an introduction to the landscape of the farm, a superficially barren expanse of wet snow that Leopold's narrator transforms through a series of provocative questions into a vibrant microcosm filled with life-or-death struggles and romance. The essay can be viewed as an expansion of an earlier piece, "Stories in the Snow," which appeared in *The Wisconsin Agriculturalist and Farmer* (and was reprinted in *For the Health of the Land*). In contrast to this and the other earlier essays that were published for a narrow agricultural audience, this piece clearly abandons utility as a justification for its writing and for celebrating the natural world more generally. Leopold takes the reader under the snow, where, in a satiric reversal of the human obsession with economy and utility, a "mouse-engineer" is busy trying to salvage a tidy empire of stored grass from the collapsing snow. This witty anthropomorphizing of the mouse into a bureaucrat filled with the very human desire for "freedom from want and fear" is a frequent device in Leopold's natural history essays, because it helps the reader empathize with the smallest citizens of the farm while never straying far from the ecological truth. Before the reader can become too cozy with the mouse engineer, for example, a rough-legged hawk swoops down to make short work of the mouse and offer an ecological lesson: predators need freedom from want and fear too.

The essay closes with the narrator again testing the limits of the desire to impute human emotions to animals. In a seemingly prosaic but highly symbolic journey, the narrator follows the slushy tracks of a skunk across the farm. Like the narrator, the reader can only guess at the skunk's motivation for movement in a time of hibernation, because the skunk never appears. It leaves only the signs of its presence, the ghostly tracks in the snow. Just when the audience is about to give up on knowing anything more, however, the narrator notes the "tinkle of dripping water," a metaphor for the pleasurable stirring of curiosity in the landscape of the mind. "I fancy the skunk hears it too," the narrator reports, a suggestion that while Leopold is critical of anthropomorphism when it explains too much, he is unwilling to divorce himself from the kind of natural affinity that might come through close observation.

Paying close attention to wildlife behavior and changes in the landscape leads Leopold in two directions, one aesthetic and the other scientific. The aesthetic moment often evokes a sense of traditional beauty in untraditional places. A Romantic sensibility, for example, transforms the river in "The Green Pasture" into an artist whose canvas is a sandbar bedecked with flowers. The critic J. Baird Callicott, in his essay "The Land Aesthetic," identifies this comparison of landscape to painting as an aesthetic commonplace of the time: "The 'picturesque' aesthetic, as the name suggests, self-consciously canonized as beautiful those natural 'scenes' or 'landscapes' suitable as motifs for pictures." Leopold's accord with Romantic ideas extends even to the ability of the imagination to render transient beauty permanent. Just as the Romantic poet William Wordsworth reflects in tranquility on the beauty of daffodils in the poem "I Wandered Lonely as a Cloud," so Leopold's pleasurable vision in "The Green Pasture" "exists only in my mind's eye," long after the riverbank painting has disappeared.

Having invoked a quintessentially "picturesque" scene, however, Leopold proceeds to undermine his readers' pleasure with irony.

Whereas Wordsworth's delight occurs after a view of the well-recognized Lake District, Leopold's moment of beauty in "The Green Pasture" arrives on a silty stretch of the frequently disregarded Wisconsin River. This dissonance between traditional description and untraditional location forces the audience to reappraise the aesthetic appeal of the Midwestern landscape.

Leopold's search for a Midwestern aesthetic also leads him to experimental forms that read more like poetry than prose. Such is the case with "If I Were the Wind," a meditation on a stiff fall breeze that bears many of the hallmarks of a wistful poem. Leopold repeats words and phrases to achieve a rhythm that mimics the wind's chaotic force, as in the description of geese "dipping and rising, blown up and blown down, blown together and blown apart." The assonance and alliteration of such phrases as "the wind wrestling lovingly with each winnowing wing" also heighten the sense of a poetic sensibility at work. The piece ends with an invocation of the wind as imaginary force, another hallmark of Romantic verse.

The other direction Leopold pursues is scientific—musing over hypotheses, gathering data, and coming to conclusions about animal behavior and the interaction of land, weather, and life. The scientific method is implicit in his response to every question about the ecological nature of the farm. In "Home Range," Leopold unfolds the process step by step, observing curious grouse behavior, asking a question about how the birds could traverse the land without leaving tracks, and discovering clues from the other signs they have left behind. Finally, he arrives at a conclusion: uncharacteristically, the birds have flown from place to place to avoid deep snow. The essay "65290" shows the narrator engaged in formal data gathering—he and the family are banding chickadees to learn about their survival. Yet Leopold avoids the dry and formulaic structure of the scientific paper. His results are explained in the heroic tale of a single chickadee, surviving for five years against all odds. Scientific research becomes family entertainment.

Leopold fervently believed that the farm could be an educational resource. "Every farm is a textbook on animal ecology," he contends in "Home Range," which, as he argues in "A Mighty Fortress," "should provide its owner a liberal education." The blame for poor management of wildlife habitat lay with ignorance, not malevolence, Leopold believed, which the government fostered with misinformation. Many of his short essays from the 1930s, such as "Fifth Column of the Fencerow" (collected in *For the Health of the Land*), rail against the bad advice coming from standard sources like the Farm Bureau, and his lessons in the *Almanac* run counter to such standard management prescriptions. While conventional wisdom might demand the immediate removal of diseased trees, for example, Leopold leaves them standing. "A Mighty Fortress" is, in fact, a litany of reasons for letting dead and diseased trees stand, for "dead trees are transmuted into living animals."

"Good Oak" continues the educational process, this time through the revelations of an unconventional environmental history. The narrator can read the growth rings of an old oak like a historical text, a record of human interaction with the landscape. Yet the version of American history the lightning-felled oak reveals is decidedly revisionist, for it provides an annual catalogue of the human abuse of natural resources, not a celebration of frontier conquest. As the narrator saws through the rings, he enumerates the crimes of the previous owner, a bootlegger who "hated this farm" and "skinned it of residual fertility." The bootlegger is only a footnote, however, in the long march back through the extinction of the passenger pigeon in the area, the burning of forests, the droughts that blew away the topsoil, the blunders and mishaps of farmers and politicians—all the way back to 1865. Leopold's rhetorical strategy in this repetition of despairing facts is not to pull any punches but to offer a periodic respite in the present, in the wholesome action of the sawyer, harvesting wood for his own hearth. When he cries "Rest!" we "pause for breath" with the narrator just long enough to cope with the losses we have witnessed. The present, then, becomes a refuge of hope, in which better land management, symbolized by the appropriately harvested wood, can bring human activity into harmony with the landscape. But Leopold also finds solace in the moment of the tree's birth. The tree's birth year, he writes, coincided with John Muir's attempt to purchase land nearby to create a haven for wildflowers, and thus the year 1865 "still stands in Wisconsin history as the birth-year of mercy for things natural, wild, and free."

Leopold's own concern for wildflowers surfaces in essays like "Prairie Birthday," which makes the case for valuing botanical remnants of the native prairie as part of the region's history. This piece has served as the touchstone for the present-day ecological restoration movement, because in it Leopold provides the ethical basis for respecting native plants, demonstrates techniques for locating rare specimens, and attempts to restore these species to his farm. Leopold focuses on silphium, a rare and showy species he finds blooming in an obscure corner of an old cemetery, the area's "sole remnant" of what once were thousands of plants. To restore the plant to its former range, he tries to transplant a specimen and then successfully plants seeds on his own land. Yet he finds his efforts countered by the ignorance of "mechanized man," who is busy mowing down and digging up the very specimens Leopold is striving to save. Leopold's response is a declaration of rhetorical war against "Progress," in which he verges on the religious passion of Muir: "If I were to tell a preacher of the adjoining church

186 / AMERICAN WRITERS

that the road crew has been burning history books in his cemetery, under the guise of mowing weeds, he would be amazed and uncomprehending." Native plants are the last living links to the region's history, a history that can continue to be read only if certain "idle corners" of land are allowed to remain untouched by machines. In effect, Leopold demands recognition that the highest value of some areas is their natural value, even when the land in question is only a highway shoulder.

The short passage "Draba" suggests the extremes to which Leopold is willing to go in his rejection of utility as a measure of natural value. Having finished a long appreciation of the spectacle of Canada geese in migration, Leopold turns in counterpoint to a modest corner of the ground. Draba, a tiny plant that grows in mud, whose flower is ignored almost universally in favor of "bigger, better blooms," serves as a metaphor for the prairie landscape in its entirety. "No poets sing of it," Leopold writes, for the plant "plucks no heartstrings," yet the narrator forces us to acknowledge its value by devoting a section to it alone. Implicit in this attention to the seemingly insignificant is Leopold's recognition of what we now call biodiversity, the value of all members of the ecological community, not just the charismatic ones.

Like "Draba," the essays "Sky Dance" and "Back from the Argentine" focus on small, hidden wonders, but in these pieces Leopold challenges conventional notions of utility, not by rejecting it entirely, as he does with "Draba," but by offering an unconventional view of what is valuable. "Sky Dance" begins with an extended metaphor that disguises the identity of the actual creature in soaring language. The sky becomes a stage on which the dancers perform in "romantic light"; and only after several paragraphs of description do we learn that the dancer is a male woodcock. The plover's performance is similarly pleasing—the plover is the embodiment of "grace." Like most of Le-

opold's metaphors, the literary device leads to a statement about human behavior: "The drama of the sky dance is enacted nightly on hundreds of farms, the owners of which sigh for entertainment, but harbor the illusion that it is to be sought in theaters." Thus woodcock and plover can offer more than just the traditional bird on toast: they have entertainment value, if they are kept alive. Leopold is foreshadowing here the point he will make explicit in the essay "Conservation Esthetic," that the highest form of recreation involves appreciation, not killing.

We can see Leopold's narrator struggling with this dilemma in a series of hunting-related essays, in which the central figure cannot quite relinquish his love of sport but nevertheless is unsuccessful as a hunter. These stories of game that gets away and shots that go awry challenge the traditional structure of the hunting narrative that ends in the conquest of a successful shot. Leopold is much more interested in the "olfactory poems" his dog might translate for him than in shooting wildlife. The narrator confesses in "Smoky Gold" that "it's hard on such a day to keep one's mind on grouse, for there are many distractions," including hawks to identify and chickadees to contemplate. In "Too Early," the narrator revels in the sensory rewards for getting out on the marsh when it is too dark to shoot; he enjoys an "adventure in pure listening" that hunting would only spoil. The essay "The Alder Fork" features the narrator actually capturing his quarry, but the piece is a parody of the typical fishing yarn. After a climactic battle scene, when the audience might expect the author to display a trophy, Leopold offers his version: nothing more than a fingerling. The real prize, he writes, was being out on the stream.

The "Sketches" section of A Sand County Almanac differs significantly from the preceding section in both theme and tone. The critic Robert Finch, in his introduction to the 1987 edition, describes the "Sketches" as a chronicle "not only of loss but of doubt," whose tone reflects "genuine bitterness and pain." While the "Almanac" section describes the little-known joys to be found in a single Midwestern locale, the "Sketches" roam through time and place to deal more explicitly with questions of environmental ethics and land management. Many of the sketches offer Leopold the chance to reappraise and even atone for his earlier beliefs, particularly when it comes to the relationship of the land manager to the land. Leopold may be harshly critical of government policy at times, but the "Sketches" reveal that he does not hold himself above reproach. In his description of the Southwest in particular, he implicates himself in poor management decisions and describes his own process of ethical education.

A profound sense of nostalgia and loss pervades "Marshland Elegy," the first sketch, which sets the tone for the remainder of the "Sketches." The sandhill crane is the Midwestern equivalent of the grizzly bear, a charismatic symbol of wildness from a previous age. Leopold always is highly attuned to the sounds that signify the presence of wildlife, and his description of the cranes begins with an almost mystical series of aural images, in which the birds' "high horns" and "trumpets" rival a symphony. Yet the crane marsh is peculiar in its sense of time, which "lies thick and heavy on such a place." Time in the marsh appears to be cyclical, not chronological, since an "endless caravan" of cranes has returned "yearly since the ice age," to the "sodden pages of their own history."

Leopold's bitterness comes from the disappearance of cranes from most of their range, for marshes without cranes "stand humbled, adrift in history." For Leopold, the missing cranes represent the passing of a golden age of human and animal coexistence, in which "man and beast, plant and soil lived on and with each other in mutual toleration, to the mutual benefit of all." All life, including humans, once existed

in cyclical time, and the marsh could have continued benefiting wildlife and human beings "forever," were it not for the arrival of the "high priests of progress." The advent of chronological time disrupted the cyclical harmony of the marsh, and the series of destructive events chronicled in "Good Oak" began to govern human experience.

The value of the marsh, like native prairie, is not in marginal farmland, but in "wildness." The crane is not merely a useless denizen of untamed ground to be swept aside by engineers, but "wildness incarnate," the noble, timeless "symbol of our untamable past." Yet Leopold also makes clear his continuing frustration with the inadequacy of this symbolic language to express the true significance of the birds. The crane has immense value, he suggests, but its value is "as yet uncaptured by language." Most people, he suggests, speak only the language of progress, which they share with the engineers who drain marshes. While we might expect Leopold to demand marshland preservation, his frustration with language leads to a bitter assessment of humanity, who cannot value wildlife without killing it, and to a despairing vision of the crane's future. "The last crane," he writes, will one day ascend to the heavens, leaving a "never to be broken" silence behind.

The extinction of the passenger pigeon, on the other hand, leads Leopold to a more hopeful conclusion, that perhaps humanity can learn from its past mistakes. "On a Monument to a Pigeon" continues to identify the shortcomings of the American ethical vocabulary, but the new alphabet is beginning to develop through an appreciation of ecology and history. "To love what *was* is a new thing under the sun, unknown to most people and to all pigeons," he argues. "To see America as history, to conceive of destiny as a becoming, to smell a hickory tree through the still lapse of ages—all these things are possible for us." The possibility exists, then, to develop a sense of time that draws upon the past to survive in the present, which is a hopeful kind of nostalgia.

Leopold justifies this nascent ethical sense by drawing specifically upon Charles Darwin's discovery of evolution as evidence of the "kinship" of all forms of life. The famous essay "Thinking like a Mountain," a phrase that Leopold originally had hoped to use as the title of the entire book, describes the evolution of his personal sense of kinship. Leopold struggled to overcome a deep prejudice against predators, and for most of his time in the West he ascribed to the view that the only good predator was a dead one. By the time of his return to the Midwest, his writing had shifted to a kind of utilitarian cost/benefit analysis, in which the control of pests outweighed the occasional loss of livestock. A piece entitled "The Farmer and the Fox" for example, written for the *Wisconsin Agriculturalist and Farmer* in the late 1930s (reprinted in *For the Health of the Land*), argues that owls and foxes are valuable because the number of mice they eat is far greater than the occasional chicken they kill.

"Thinking like a Mountain" however, suggests that the seed for a change in Leopold's thinking was planted during the earliest days of his career in Arizona, when he participated in the slaughter of a mother wolf and her pups. The attack he describes is senseless, and it scandalizes Leopold's conscience, particularly when he approaches the wounded but still conscious mother and looks into her eyes. "I realized then, and have known ever since, that there was something new to me in those eyes— something known only to her and to the mountain," Leopold explains. To think like a mountain is to move beyond anthropocentrism, to appreciate the role of all life-forms in an ecological community. Without wolves as part of the community, deer overpopulate, destroy the range, and starve.

Yet the "green fire" Leopold sees in the dying wolf's eyes signifies more than her useful role in controlling deer—Leopold has identified the same mystical force that powers the crane and that dies with the last grizzly in "Escudilla." The big bear is the embodiment of the frontier, a tangible presence that gives the mountains their wildness. When a government trapper kills the bear, again without justification, the result is therefore far more than the loss of a single animal—the entire experience of the mountains has been diminished. The loss causes Leopold to reflect on the paradox of the frontier—that in subduing the land, he and the other settlers killed the thing they loved.

Leopold longs to revisit the frontier, but he can do so only through sentimental memoir pieces, such as "On Top" and "The Green Lagoons," because the places he loved have disappeared into history. Frontier time is different from the timeless cycle of the cranes; it is the initial intoxicating phase of progress. The "Sketches" reveal that Leopold was himself caught up in the delights of discovering "virgin" country, as he recalls with vivid sentimentality a lost world in which young, virile horsemen ruled a vast, uncharted, and sublime landscape. The "green lagoons," for instance, were an Edenic land of plenty, in which game was "too abundant to hunt." But the death of the grizzly suggests that the narrator cannot return to the landscapes that seemed "new" when he was there. "I have never returned to the White Mountain," Leopold laments in "On Top." "I prefer not to see what tourists, roads, sawmills and logging railroads have done for it, or to it." Without the bear, Escudilla is just a mountain, not a mystical force.

In "Guacamaja," Leopold attempts to provide the missing language that will describe the value of the grizzly, the crane, and the wolf. In doing so, he draws upon the work of the Russian philosopher Peter Ouspensky, who supplied both a terminology and a conceptual framework. Ouspensky believed that all matter was imbued with a life force, so that even a seemingly inanimate object like a mountain could have a mind of its own. He also thought that the life force of all animate and inanimate elements was connected in a greater living system, much like the brain might be connected to the rest of the body. His theory inspired Leopold's description of Escudilla's palpable power, and it led directly to the essay title "Thinking like a Mountain." Thus Leopold describes the "green fire" in the wolf's eyes with Ouspensky's term "numenon." Leopold describes the numenon as an "imponderable essence," which differs from the concrete and predictable "phenomenon" in that it cannot be quantified, only sensed. "Song of the Gavilan" meditates further on this mystical force, describing the feeling that arises in the presence of a river as something akin to a divine music, a "vast pulsing harmony" of ecological cycles. To hear it, the listener must know the speech of hills and rivers, a language that is not taught in university classrooms, where the professors are too busy studying the biological parts to perceive the ecological whole.

Leopold's understanding of ecology emphasized the stability of ecosystems. Landscapes and their inhabitants evolved through cycles over long periods of time, but the components stayed the same in the short term. "Cheat Takes Over" records Leopold's dismay at the interruption of this stability with the introduction of exotic species from other continents. Not only has the grizzly been lost, Leopold asserts, but its replacement are inferior "ecological stowaways" who take over the entire system and leave no room for other species. Cheat grass is Leopold's poster child for land sickness, carpeting the hills of the West Coast, increasing the fire risk, and decreasing the food value of the range. Yet to Leopold's dismay, the plant has invaded the landscape to such an extent that most people regard its eradication as hopeless. Cheat grass represents not just a massive biological invasion but also the lack of an ethic that cares for native communities. In "Illinois

Bus Ride," Leopold bitterly condemns the willful ignorance on the part of his fellow passengers, who see only weeds where they should see valuable native plants and who do not notice when the natives are missing from the roadside. Having lost its native plant community, Illinois has lost its identity—a sea of nothingness unfurls beside the bus.

The final sketch, "Clandeboye," echoes the fatalism and frustration of the first sketch "Marshland Elegy." Clandeboye is a marsh and thus a refuge from the onward march of time for ancient creatures like the grebe. In elegiac tones the narrator honors the grebe as a "timeless" symbol of the marshland's ecological cycles. The invasion of progress, however, looms over this last refuge. The narrator envisions a bleak future in which progress drains the marsh, and the sketch ends when the grebe joins the crane in the flight into extinction.

The third and final section of *A Sand County Almanac,* "The Upshot," makes explicit the philosophical and ethical arguments that appear by implication throughout the book. The first section of the *Almanac* illustrates the ethic at work, with little didactic commentary; the second portion travels outside the farm to record the tragedy taking place in the American countryside. "The Upshot," Leopold hopes, will guide his readers as they seek to change the prevailing view of land and wildlife as nothing more than resources for human consumption. Because the earlier sections have laid the emotional foundation, rhetorical argument, not narrative, takes precedence in these pieces. These essays are best viewed as the culmination of Leopold's thinking on ecology, community, wilderness, and aesthetics.

"Conservation Esthetic" finds Leopold confronting a conundrum: too many people are loving the outdoors, particularly in the most scenic areas. "Recreation," he writes, "has become a self-destructive process of seeking but never quite finding, a major frustration of mechanized society." Tourists swarm like ants across the continent, while the wildness and solitude they seek inevitably retreat behind the approach of their automobiles. Leopold responds by distinguishing between those pursuits that take a heavy toll on land and wildlife and those that tread lightly. The typical approach to recreation is economic, but tourist dollars do not describe its real value. What drives people outdoors is the pursuit of pleasure, whether their goal is the capture of a fish or recording a new species of bird on their species list. The "trophy," Leopold argues, must be redefined not as a physical object but as an emotional experience. If the trophy is a duck or a fish, mass use leads to extinction of species or to the degradation of the ecological community. There simply is not enough to go around. If the trophy is an experience, on the other hand, it has the potential to be enjoyed by many people. "Nature study" is an experience that requires no consumption—its trophies are enjoyed in the mind, and they can be found in the backyard as easily as the national park.

Ultimately Leopold arrives at a strongly worded repudiation of the blood sport he enjoyed in his youth. He loved to hunt; the "Sketches" are replete with references to the joy he found with a gun. Yet their mournful tone suggests that the time for these pleasures passed with the end of the frontier, and in this essay Leopold no longer bemoans its passing. The trophy hunter is "the caveman reborn," and hunting is a "rudimentary" form of recreation. The hunter's pleasures belong to youth, and neither Leopold nor the country is young any longer. The aesthetic appreciation of the wild is the mature form of recreation, and it represents the hope for the future.

"Wildlife in American Culture" continues the examination of the cultural value of outdoor recreation in an increasingly mechanized age. Leopold believes that the cultural value of outdoor experience can be divided into three components: the "split-rail" value, or knowing the connection between the native biota and local history, the "man-earth" value, which acknowledges human dependence on the ecological community for food, and "sportsmanship," which limits the harvest of game. An increasing number of gadgets, representing the intrusion of progress into the outdoors, are destroying these values, however. The factory is moving into the woods, and the contrast between urban and wild is disappearing. Once again, Leopold offers wildlife research as a new form of sport that does not destroy habitat or wildlife.

Leopold is best known for his advocacy of agricultural lands that would not qualify as wilderness, yet as the essay "Wilderness" suggests, he never ceased in his efforts to preserve wild areas from the influences of an expanding civilization. While this essay makes "a plea for the preservation of some tag-ends of wilderness, as museum pieces," Leopold's view of wilderness is actually far less modest—he sees wilderness as the fundamental source of all human culture, and his goal is to preserve as broad an expanse as he can.

Wilderness areas should be preserved as places for outdoor recreation, as experimental terrain for science, and as refuges for wildlife. The biology of Montana cannot be studied in the Amazon, and the national parks cannot provide enough habitat for animals that require large areas to roam and become trapped in geographical islands. He defends the wilderness concept against those critics who claim that wilderness is either irrelevant or the exclusive playground of the rich. Yet wilderness preservation is at best a "rearguard" action that minimizes losses, because wilderness can shrink, but it cannot grow. He surveys the American landscape to locate the last remnants of wilderness and finds only small, threatened expanses that will never rival the abundance of the frontier. While his tone remains strident, the clear limitations of the wilderness movement set the stage for a more hopeful and extensive ethic, which Leopold offers in his famous essay, "The Land Ethic."

The problem he confronts in the first three essays of "The Upshot" has an ethical basis: Americans expect too much from the land, and they do not feel a duty to give anything in return. The solution, Leopold believes, is the extension of the ethics that govern human society to the entire ecological community. To enlarge the community, of course, is to challenge the very notion of the hierarchy, with humans at the top, and replace it with a web of relations in which humans are only a small part in a system. Bacteria might play a more vital role in creating and supporting the community than do human beings. The land ethic, as Leopold puts it in "The Land Ethic," is therefore a radical counter to utilitarianism, for it changes the role of "*Homo sapiens* from conqueror of the land-community to plain member and citizen of it."

The essay begins with a reference to Homer's *Odyssey,* which is meant to disturb and even shock the reader. Leopold's allusion to Odysseus' return from Troy makes no mention of the Greek hero's familiar triumph over adversity. Instead the statement focuses on Odysseus' decision to hang a dozen slave girls who behaved badly in his absence. Leopold expects outrage from the audience, but his reply is ironically blasé: the girls were only property, and "the disposal of property was then, as now, a matter of expediency, not of right and wrong." The analogy between the mistreatment of women and the abuse of the land not only conveys Leopold's outrage at the current state of land management but also provides the rationale for his central argument—that human ethics have evolved in the past to cover those unjustly excluded from the system of rights and that they must continue to do so. The ecological community is the next logical beneficiary of an ethical advance.

While Leopold considers the extension of rights a cultural development, he also explains it as an advance in ecological terms. In "Wildlife in American Culture," Leopold suggests that human behavior could be clarified through research on animal behavior, because humans, after all, are animals governed by the same ecological rules. "The Land Ethic" follows a similar rhetorical path by applying ecological principles to human society. From an ecological perspective, the economic and political extension of rights is, in fact, a recognition of the value of symbiotic relationships, in which interdependence and cooperation triumph over competition and destruction. Leopold calls for an understanding of human history as a record of human interactions with the land, much as he illustrated in the "Almanac" section with "Good Oak."

While the land ethic ultimately demands an ecological reorganization of society, change cannot develop as a government project. Leopold argues forcefully that political change can come only from the bottom up, with a dramatic shift in the mind of the individual. The private landowner must develop a sense of obligation to the land through the social influence of the local community. Numerous critics have suggested that this view of government places Leopold in the company of Thomas Jefferson, who also saw the independent-minded yeoman farmer as the backbone of a participatory democracy. Jefferson's *Notes on the State of Virginia* (1781–1782) envisions a land of small farmers bound together by a constitutional guarantee of rights and responsibilities. Leopold's land ethic calls for the Jeffersonian farmer to extend these rights to the other members of the biotic community.

Many critics have noted Leopold's preference for the integrity of the ecological community as a whole over the rights of the individual. The historian Roderick Nash, in the essay "Aldo Leopold's Intellectual Heritage," asserts that Leopold's land ethic closely follows the evolutionary ideas found in Charles Darwin's *On the Origin of Species* (1859) and *The Descent of Man* (1871) and also draws upon the ecological framework developed by the famed University of Wisconsin ecologist Charles Elton, among others. Like Darwin, Leopold seeks to extend rights to the nonhuman world. Leopold breaks with Darwin, however, by envisioning a community whose interests might supersede the rights of the individual. Leopold never mourns the passing of an individual animal, except when that animal represents the extinction of an entire population. The scientific basis Leopold provides for the land ethic is actually an explanation of nutrient cycles, and he views the death of individual animals as an inevitable and justified part of the system. "The Land Ethic" explains what is now recognized in science education but was known less widely at the time—that all life exists in a series of hierarchical food chains Leopold calls the "biotic pyramid," with predators at the top and decomposers at the bottom; that nutrients cycle continuously through the system; and that changes in the flow of energy occur slowly enough that the system evolves over time.

Leopold concludes with the clearest statement of his ecologically inspired ethic: "A thing is right when it tends to preserve the integrity, stability, and beauty of the biotic community. It is wrong when it tends otherwise." With this statement in mind, the overall coherence of Leopold's book becomes clear. Each of the earlier pieces is a meditation on these three central themes. Leopold has visited landscapes in which these principles have been violated, and he has described places where they exist under threat. But he also has illustrated the way to live in harmony with the biotic community. "The Land Ethic" invites the reader to think back to the first series of essays, in which we can now recognize a figure who lives by the land ethic. His stewardship entails an entirely different attitude toward the land, one that respects every member of the community and therefore preserves its integrity. The narrator promotes stability in the landscape by planting trees to halt erosion, and he recognizes and preserves the beauty of his community by eschewing hunting in favor of observation.

AFTER *A SAND COUNTY ALMANAC*

Aldo Leopold never saw his great work in print. His health had declined in the year of editorial wrangling and rejection that preceded publication. On April 21, 1948, he saw smoke coming from his neighbor's farm and blowing toward the stand of trees his family had labored to plant. He rushed to the blaze and began trying to establish a containment line. Witnesses, including his family, said that he did not appear to be working very hard, but the stress and fatigue of the battle apparently overwhelmed him. He collapsed alone and was found later, dead of an apparent heart attack. He was buried in Burlington, Iowa.

A Sand County Almanac appeared a year after his death. The book sold slowly at first, but it benefited enormously from the explosion of environmental interest that lead to the first Earth Day in 1970 and has since sold millions of copies. Leopold's work has served as the touchstone for the ecological restoration movement, which seeks to remedy past abuses of the biotic community and improve land health. Local restoration projects, modeled after the seminal plantings conducted at the University of Wisconsin Arboretum, have sprung up across the United States, much as Leopold hoped. His work continues to be invoked by advocates of wilderness, who find in Leopold's essays a scientifically grounded counterweight to economically motivated threats to wilderness areas. Most view Leopold as a visionary, a writer whose ethical stance was far ahead of his time. As the western writer Wallace Stegner wrote for a 1987 edition of *Wilderness* magazine (reprinted as "The Legacy of Aldo Leopold" in the critical essay collection *Companion to "A Sand County Almanac"*): "When this forming civilization assembles its Bible ... *A Sand County Almanac* will belong in it, one of the prophetic books, the utterance of an American Isaiah."

Selected Bibliography

WORKS OF ALDO LEOPOLD

Report on a Game Survey of the North Central States. Madison, Wis.: Sporting Arms and Ammunition Manufacturers' Institute, 1931. (Nonfiction.)

Game Management. New York: Scribners, 1933. Revised edition, Madison: University of Wisconsin Press, 1986. (Nonfiction.)

A Sand County Almanac and Sketches Here and There. New York: Oxford University Press, 1949. Revised, with an introduction by Robert Finch, 1987. (Essays.)

Round River: From the Journals of Aldo Leopold. Edited by Luna B. Leopold. New York: Oxford University Press, 1953. Revised, 1993. (Journals.)

Aldo Leopold's Southwest. Edited by David E. Brown and Neil B. Carmony. Albuquerque: University of New Mexico Press, 1990. (Collection.)

Aldo Leopold's Wilderness: Selected Early Writings by the Author of "A Sand County Almanac." Edited by David E. Brown and Neil B. Carmony. Harrisburg, Pa.: Stackpole Books, 1990. (Collection.)

The River of the Mother of God and Other Essays by Aldo Leopold. Edited by Susan L. Flader and J. Baird Callicott. Madison: University of Wisconsin Press, 1991. (Collection.)

For the Health of the Land: Previously Unpublished Essays and Other Writings. Edited by J. Baird Callicott and Eric T. Freyfogle. Washington, D.C.: Island Press, 1999. (Collection.)

MANUSCRIPTS AND PAPERS
The primary archive of Leopold's papers is at the Memorial Library, University of Wisconsin, Madison. The collection includes papers, letters, diaries, and photographs.

CRITICAL AND BIOGRAPHICAL STUDIES

Barillas,William. "Aldo Leopold and Midwestern Pastoralism." *American Studies* 37:61–81 (fall 1996).

Berthold-Bond, Daniel. "The Ethics of 'Place': Reflections on Bioregionalism." *Environmental Ethics* 22:5–24 (spring 2000).

Cafaro, Philip. "Thoreau, Leopold, and Carson: Toward an Environmental Virtue Ethics." *Environmental Ethics* 23:3 (spring 2001).

Callicott, J. Baird, ed. *Companion to "A Sand County Almanac": Interpretive and Critical Essays.* Madison: University of Wisconsin Press, 1987. (Includes the essays: J. Baird Callicott, "The Land Aesthetic"; Roderick Nash, "Aldo Leopold's Intellectual Heritage"; Wallace Stegner, "The Legacy of Aldo Leopold"; and others.)

Flader, Susan L. *Thinking Like a Mountain: Aldo Leopold and the Evolution of an Ecological Attitude Toward Deer, Wolves, and Forests.* Columbia: University of Missouri Press, 1974.

Fromm, Harold. "Aldo Leopold: Aesthetic 'Anthropocentrist.'" *Isle: Interdisciplinary Studies in Literature and Environment* 1:43–49 (spring 1993).

Knight, Richard L., and Suzanne Riedel. *Aldo Leopold and the Ecological Conscience.* New York: Oxford University Press, 2002. (Includes the essays: Mary Anne Bishop, "Great Possessions: Leopold's Good Oak"; Reed Noss, "Aldo Leopold Was a Conservation Biologist"; Edwin P. Pister, "The A–B Dichotomy and the Future"; Jack Ward Thomas, "'What Would Aldo Have Done?': A Personal Story"; and others.)

———. "Aldo Leopold, the Land Ethic, and Ecosystem Management." *Journal of Wildlife Management* 60, no. 3:471–474 (1996).

Lea, Sydney. "'I Recognize Thy Glory': On the American Nature Essay." *Sewanee Review* 106:478–486 (summer 1998).

McCabe, Robert A. *Aldo Leopold, the Professor.* Madison, Wis.: Rusty Rock Press, 1987.

McClintock, James I. *Nature's Kindred Spirits: Aldo Leopold, Joseph Wood Krutch, Edward Abbey, Annie Dillard, and Gary Snyder.* Madison: University of Wisconsin Press, 1994.

Meine, Curt. *Aldo Leopold: His Life and Work.* Madison: University of Wisconsin Press, 1988.

————. "The Secret Leopold, or Who Really Wrote *A Sand County Almanac?*" *Transactions of the Wisconsin Academy of Sciences, Arts and Letters* 88:1–21 (2000).

Nash, Roderick. "Aldo Leopold and the Limits of American Liberalism." In *Aldo Leopold: The Man and His Legacy.* Edited by Thomas Tanner. Ankeny, Iowa: Soil Conservation Society of America, 1987. Pp. 53–86.

Nelson, Michael P. "Aldo Leopold: Environmental Ethics and the Land Ethic." *Wildlife Society Bulletin* 28, no. 4:741–746 (winter 1998).

Rolston, Holmes. "The Land Ethic at the Turn of the Millennium." *Biodiversity and Conservation* 9:1045–1058 (August 2000).

Scheese, Don. "'Something More Than Wood': Aldo Leopold and the Language of Landscape." *North Dakota Quarterly* 58, no. 1:72–89 (winter 1990).

Shaw, Bill. "A Virtue Ethics Approach to Aldo Leopold's Land Ethic." *Environmental Ethics* 19, no. 1:53–68 (spring 1997).

Tanner, Thomas, ed. *Aldo Leopold: The Man and His Legacy.* Ankeny, Iowa: Soil Conservation Society of America, 1987.

Westra, Laura. "From Aldo Leopold to the Wildlands Project: The Ethics of Integrity." *Environmental Ethics* 23, no. 3:261 (fall 2001).

Worster, Donald. *Nature's Economy: The Roots of Ecology.* San Francisco: Sierra Club Books, 1977.

—JAMES BARILLA

Alain Locke

1885–1954

ALAIN LEROY LOCKE—philosopher, race leader, art critic, adult educator, essayist, and anthologist—was the leading African American intellectual of his day after W. E. B. Du Bois (1868–1963). A social genius, Locke was the mastermind behind the Harlem Renaissance, that explosion in the 1920s and 1930s of "New Negro" literature, drama, music, and art that bolstered black pride and earned reciprocal white respect on a national scale never before achieved. The December 1925 publication of Locke's anthology, *The New Negro,* was a stellar event in American cultural history. A volume that spoke volumes, *The New Negro: An Interpretation* was art as manifesto—a secular liberation theology. For this and other reasons Columbus Salley, in *The Black 100* (1999), ranks Locke as the thirty-sixth most influential African American in history. Alain LeRoy Locke is the Martin Luther King Jr. of American culture.

"RACE MAN" AND "FATHER OF MULTICULTURALISM"

Locke was a "prophet of democracy," whose grand (though not systematic) theory of democracy sequenced local, moral, political, economic, and cultural stages of democracy as they arced through history, with racial, social, spiritual, and world democracy completing the trajectory. Adjunct notions of natural, practical, progressive, creative, intellectual, equalitarian democracy crystallized the paradigm. Seeing America as "a unique social experiment," Locke's larger goal was to "Americanize Americans," with the simple yet profound message that equality

benefits everyone and that democracy itself is at stake. The essence of Locke's philosophy of democracy is captured in the title "Cultural Pluralism: A New Americanism," a public lecture he gave at Howard University on November 8, 1950. In raising democracy to a new level of consciousness, Locke internationalized the race issue, making the crucial connection between American race relations and international relations. Racial justice, he predicted, would serve as a social catalyst of world peace. Thus there are two major streams of thought in Locke's work—the African American historical, cultural, and intellectual tradition, and a cosmopolitan, global outlook intensified by the Bahá'í principles he embraced. Locke is both a "race man" (cultural racialist) and a philosopher (cultural pluralist). How Locke should be read depends on which of these two roles predominates.

"Race men" were black leaders who came of age during the era of scientific racism. They embraced nineteenth-century middle-class values and held a deep faith in the meliorative powers of liberalism. Cultural pluralists compensated for the deficiencies of liberalism by promoting social justice and community; they accorded respect to culturally diverse groups and valued their diversity. A Harlem Renaissance immortal, Locke is no less historic in his role as a cultural pluralist. Locke has been called "the father of multiculturalism"—as cultural pluralism is now known—although his Harvard colleague Horace Kallen was the one who actually coined the term "cultural pluralism" in conversations with Locke that took place at Oxford University in 1907 and 1908.

How should Locke be thought of as a writer? Beyond his historic roles as critic, editor, and cultural ambassador, to what extent does he leap from history onto the printed page and demand to be read? The answers depend largely on how much of Locke *can* be read. While Locke did publish widely, a great deal of his work remains in manuscript form, including lectures, speeches, and unfinished essays that are often the clearest exposition of what he really thought. Two editions of his writings relied heavily on archival research and the subsequent editing of texts for publication: Leonard Harris' *The Philosophy of Alain Locke: Harlem Renaissance and Beyond* (1989) and Jeffrey C. Stewart's edition of Locke's *Race Contacts and Interracial Relations: Lectures on the Theory and Practice of Race* (1992). A third collection, *The Critical Temper of Alain Locke: A Selection of His Essays on Art and Culture* (1983), also edited by Jeffrey Stewart, reprints a number of reviews and essays. These posthumous publications and reprints have effectively brought Locke's work back to influential life. How Locke is *now* being read is becoming as important as how Locke *was* read.

LIFE AND CAREER

Harvard, Harlem, Haifa—place names that represent Locke's special involvement in philosophy, art, and religion—are keys to understanding his life and thought. Harvard prepared Locke for the distinction of becoming in 1907 the first black Rhodes Scholar, and in 1918 it awarded him a Ph.D. in philosophy (for his dissertation, *Problems of Classification in the Theory of Value,* submitted on September 1, 1917), which eventually secured his position as chair of the Department of Philosophy at Howard University from 1927 until his retirement in 1953. Harlem was the mecca of the Harlem Renaissance, whereby Locke, as a spokesman for his race, revitalized racial

solidarity and fostered the group consciousness among African Americans that proved a necessary precondition of the civil rights movement. Haifa is the world center of the Bahá'í Faith, the religion to which Locke converted in 1918, the same year he received his doctorate from Harvard. Until recently Locke's religion has been the least understood aspect of his life. During the Jim Crow era, at a time when black people saw little possibility of interracial harmony, this new religious movement offered hope through its "race amity" efforts, which Locke was instrumental in organizing. These three spheres of activity—the academy, the art world, and spiritual society—converge to create a composite picture of Locke as an integrationist whose model was not assimilation but rather "unity through diversity."

For reasons that have eluded historians, Locke always stated that he was born in 1886, but he was really born a year earlier—on September 13, 1885, in Philadelphia. Although his birth name was Arthur his parents may actually have named him Alan. At the age of sixteen Locke adopted the French spelling ("Alain," close to the American pronunciation of "Allen"), and added the middle name LeRoy (probably because he was called Roy as a child). He was the only son of Pliny Locke and Mary (Hawkins) Locke, who had been engaged for sixteen years before they married. A child of Northern Reconstruction (which focused on the post-Civil War economic revolution, while Southern Reconstruction dealt more with laws pertaining to blacks), the boy was given an enlightened upbringing and a private education. As a child of privilege Locke led a somewhat sheltered life. He was raised as an Episcopalian, and during his youth he became enamored with classical Greek philosophy.

Locke was predisposed to music and reading owing to his physical condition. In infancy he was stricken with rheumatic fever, which permanently damaged his heart. Locke dealt with his "rheumatic heart" by seeking, as Michael R. Winston says, "compensatory satisfactions" in books, piano, and violin. Only six years old when his father died, Locke was sent by his mother to one of the Ethical Culture schools—a pioneer experimental program of Froebelian pedagogy, a philosophy of childhood education named after Friedrich Froebel (1782–1852), who opened the first kindergarten. By the time he enrolled in Central High School in 1898, Locke was already an accomplished pianist and violinist. In 1902 he began studies at the Philadelphia School of Pedagogy, graduating second in his class in 1904. That year Locke entered Harvard College with honors, where he was among precious few African American undergraduates.

During the "golden age of philosophy at Harvard," Locke studied at a time when Josiah Royce, William James, George Herbert Palmer, Hugo Münsterberg, and Ralph Barton Perry were on the faculty. Elected to Phi Beta Kappa, in 1907 Locke won the Bowdoin Prize—Harvard's most prestigious academic award—for an essay he wrote, "The Literary Heritage of Tennyson." He also passed a qualifying examination in Latin, Greek, and mathematics for the Rhodes scholarship, which had just been established by the diamond magnate Cecil Rhodes in 1902. Remarkably Locke completed his four-year undergraduate program at Harvard in three years, graduating magna cum laude with his bachelor's degree in philosophy. Then Locke made history and headlines in May 1907 as America's first—and only, until the 1960s—African American Rhodes scholar. While his Rhodes scholarship provided for study abroad at Oxford, it was no guarantee of admission. Rejected by five Oxford colleges because of his race, Locke was finally admitted to Hertford College, where he studied from 1907 to 1910.

During his senior year at Harvard, Locke met Horace Kallen, a German-born Jew who was a graduate teaching assistant in a course on Greek philosophy—taught by George Santayana—in which Locke had enrolled. Thus began a lifetime friendship. Kallen recorded some valuable personal observations about Locke as a young man. First, Locke was "very sensitive, very easily hurt." As Kallen relates in "Alain Locke and Cultural Pluralism," Locke would strenuously insist that we are all human beings, that "the Negro is ... an American fact," and that color should make no difference in the "inalienable rights to life, liberty, and the pursuit of happiness." This sentiment is corroborated by a letter he wrote to his mother shortly after receiving his Rhodes scholarship; in it he insists: "I am not a race problem. I am Alain LeRoy Locke." Unfortunately color made all the difference in that era. The prevailing social reality was that Locke's self-image was really a wish-image.

In 1907, on a Sheldon traveling fellowship, Kallen ended up at Oxford at the same time as Locke. In "Alain Locke and Cultural Pluralism" Kallen describes a racial incident over a Thanksgiving Day dinner hosted at the American Club at Oxford. Locke was not invited because of "gentlemen from Dixie who could not possibly associate with Negroes." Elsewhere Kallen is more blunt: "We had a race problem because the Rhodes scholars from the South were bastards. So they had a Thanksgiving dinner which I refused to attend because they refused to have Locke." In fact, even before they left for Oxford these southern Rhodes Scholars had "formally appealed to the Rhodes trustees to overturn Locke's award"—but to no avail. "What got Kallen particularly upset, however," according to Louis Menand in *The Metaphysical Club* (2001), "was the insult to Harvard." In support of this, Menand cites a letter to Harvard English professor Barrett Wendell, in which Kallen speaks of overcoming his aversion to blacks through his loyalty to Harvard and by virtue of his personal respect for Locke. After having invited Locke to tea in lieu of the

Thanksgiving dinner, Kallen writes that, "tho' it is personally repugnant to me to eat with him … Locke is a Harvard man and as such he has a definite claim on me." The irony is that Kallen harbored some of the very same prejudices as the southern Rhodes Scholars who shunned Locke, but not to the same degree. "As you know, I have neither respect nor liking for his race," Kallen writes, "—but individually they have to be taken, each on his own merits and value, and if ever a Negro was worthy, this boy is." Locke was deeply wounded by the incident. And it wasn't just the prejudice of his American peers that disaffected him, for he was almost as critical of British condescension as he was of American racism. In 1909 Locke published a critique of Oxford, particularly of its aristocratic pretensions.

At Oxford, resuming their conversation begun at Harvard, Locke asked Kallen, "What difference does the difference [of race] make?" "In arguing out those questions," Kallen recounts, "the phrase 'cultural pluralism' was born." While the term itself was thus coined by Kallen in his historic conversation with Locke, it was Locke who developed the concept into a full-blown philosophical framework for the melioration of African Americans. Distancing himself from Kallen's purist and separatist conception of it, Locke was part of the cultural pluralist movement that flourished between the 1920s and the 1940s. Indeed it was at Oxford that a crucial transformation took place: Locke saw himself as a cultural cosmopolitan when he entered Oxford; by the time he left he had resolved to be a race leader, although he did not know then how he would fulfill that role. While at Oxford, Locke founded the African Union Society and served as its secretary, thereby greatly broadening his international contacts in Africa and the Caribbean, which proved valuable in later life.

So acutely did the Thanksgiving Day incident traumatize Locke that he left Oxford without taking a degree and spent the 1910–1911 academic year studying Immanuel Kant at the University of Berlin and touring Eastern Europe. During his stay in Berlin, Locke became conversant with the Austrian school of anthropology, known as philosophical anthropology, under the tutelage of Franz Brentano, Alexius Meinong, Christian Freiherr von Ehrenfels, Paul Natorp, and others. Locke much preferred Europe to America. Indeed there were moments when Locke resolved never to return to the United States. But reluctantly he did return in 1911.

In the spring of that year Locke would taste firsthand the bitterness and alacrity of the racialized Deep South. For the first eight days of March Locke traveled with Booker T. Washington through Florida, beginning in Pensacola. Beyond this the extent of Locke's travels is unclear, but his trip probably lasted through the summer. There were moments during that trip when he feared for his life. As a direct result of his experience with racism in the South, Locke resolved to promote the interests of African Americans—and thereby of all Americans—using culture as a strategy. This was another turning point in his life. At Oxford, Locke knew that he had been prepared and destined to become a race leader. But he did not know in what capacity he would lead. It was during this trip in the South that Locke had his vision of promoting racial pride and equality through the influence of culture. Unlike politics, culture is a means of expressing and effectively communicating the aspirations and genius of a people.

Later, in an unpublished autobiographical note, Locke reflected on the circumstances that led to this momentous decision in his life and career:

Returning home in 1911, I spent six months travelling in the South,—my first close-range view of the race problem, and there acquired my life-long avocational interest in encouraging and interpreting the artistic and cultural expression of Negro life, for I became deeply convinced of its efficacy as an internal instrument of group integration and morale and as an external weapon of recognition and prestige.

On September 3, 1912, with the help of Booker T. Washington, Locke joined the faculty of the Teachers College at Howard University. There Locke taught literature, English, education, and ethics—and later, ethics and logic—although he did not have an opportunity to teach a course on philosophy until 1915. In the spring of 1915 Locke proposed a course on the scientific study of race and race relations. His rationale was that "a study of race contacts is the only scientific basis for the comprehension of race relations." But the white ministers on Howard University's Board of Trustees rejected his petition. They opposed him because they felt that "controversial" subjects such as race had no place at a school whose mission was to educate young, black professionals. However, the Howard chapter of the National Association for the Advancement of Colored People (NAACP) and the Social Science Club sponsored a two-year extension course of public lectures (1915–1916), which Locke called "Race Contacts and Inter-Racial Relations: A Study in the Theory and Practice of Race." (See below for an account of these lectures.)

In the 1916–1917 academic year Locke took a sabbatical from Howard University to become Austin Teaching Fellow at Harvard. In that brief span of time, Locke wrote the two hundred sixty-three pages of his dissertation, *The Problem of Classification in the Theory of Value,* evidently an extension of an earlier essay he had written at Oxford. It was the Harvard professor of philosophy Josiah Royce who originally inspired Locke's interest in the philosophy of value. Of all the major American pragmatists to date, only Royce had published a book dealing with racism: *Race Questions, Provincialism, and Other American Problems* (1908). In formulating his own theory of value,

Locke synthesized the Austrian school of value theory (Franz Brentano and Alexius Meinong) with American pragmatism (George Santayana, William James, and Josiah Royce), along with the anthropology of Franz Boas and Kant's theories of aesthetic judgment.

The essence of Locke's philosophy of value is captured in the first sentence of his 1935 essay "Values and Imperatives," which recapitulates his dissertation: "All philosophies, it seems to me, are in ultimate derivation philosophies of life and not of abstract, disembodied 'objective' reality; products of time, place and situation, and thus systems of timed history rather than timeless eternity." In anchoring philosophy in social reality, Locke studied the determinative role of values in the human experience, and developed a typology of values. In his dissertation Locke expresses his "psychology of value-types" in one cognitive breath: "We have therefore taken values classed, rather roughly and tentatively, as Hedonic, Economic, Aesthetic, Ethical and Moral, Religious, and Logical, aiming to discover in terms of the generic distinctions of a value-psychology their type-unity, character, and specific differentiae with respect to other types." Later, in "Values and Imperatives," Locke reduces his taxonomy to four types of values: Religious; Ethical/Moral; Aesthetic/Artistic; and Logical Truth/Scientific Truth.

When awarded his Ph.D. in philosophy from Harvard in 1918, Locke emerged as perhaps the most exquisitely educated and erudite African American of his generation. The year 1918 marked another milestone in Locke's life when he found a "spiritual home" in the Bahá'í Faith, a new world religion whose gospel was the unity of the human race. The recent discovery of Locke's signed "Bahá'í Historical Record" card (1935), in which Locke fixes the date of his conversion in 1918, restores a "missing dimension" of Locke's life (as documented in Buck, "Alain Locke: Bahá'í Philosopher," and more fully in *Alain Locke: Faith and Philosophy*). In a letter dated June 28, 1922, written shortly after the death of his mother, Locke states: "Mother's feeling toward the [Bahá'í] cause, and the friends who exemplify it, was unusually receptive and cordial for one who had reached conservative years,—it was her wish that I identify myself more closely with it." Locke honored her wish.

The Bahá'í Faith (known then as the Bahá'í Cause) was attractive to some African Americans wherever it had made significant inroads, as was the case in Washington, D.C. Its message of world unity—particularly its gospel of interracial unity (then called "race amity")—was quite radical in its stark contrast to the "separate but equal" American apartheid of the Jim Crow era. One instance of this new religion's appeal is the fact that W. E. B. Du Bois's first wife, Nina, was a member of the Bahá'í community of New York City. The Bahá'í World Center is located on Mt. Carmel in Haifa, Israel, and is a place of pilgrimage for Bahá'ís. As a Bahá'í Locke undertook two pilgrimages to the Holy Land, in 1923 and again in 1934. His first pilgrimage was immortalized in a travel narrative published in 1924, reprinted three times in 1926, 1928, and 1930, and endorsed by Bahá'í leader, Shoghi Effendi (1897–1957).

It is significant that Locke's trips to Israel (then called Palestine) were for the primary purpose of visiting the Bahá'í shrines rather than Jerusalem, the spiritual magnet that attracts most pilgrims bound for the Holy Land. The fact that Haifa was his principal destination attests the primacy of Locke's religious identity as a Bahá'í rather than as an Episcopalian, as he was always designated in the brief biographical notices of him published during his lifetime. It was not until an article, "Bahá'í Faith: Only Church in World That Does Not Discriminate," appeared in the October 1952 issue of *Ebony* magazine that Locke's Bahá'í identity was ever publicized in the popular media. Although he

studiously avoided references to the Bahá'í Faith in his professional life, Locke's four *Bahá'í World* essays served as his public testimony of faith.

As previously mentioned, Locke was actively involved in the early "race amity" initiatives sponsored by the Bahá'ís. "Race amity" was the Bahá'í term for ideal race relations (interracial unity). The Bahá'í "race amity" era lasted from 1921–1936, followed by the "race unity" period of 1939–1947, with other socially significant experiments in interracial harmony (such as "Race Unity Day") down to the present. The Bahá'í statement, "The Vision of Race Unity," together with the video "The Power of Race Unity," which was broadcast on the Black Entertainment Network and across the country in 1997, has its roots in early Bahá'í race-relations endeavors, in which Alain Locke played an important role. The first four Race Amity conventions were held in Washington, D.C. (May 19–21, 1921); Springfield, Massachusetts (December 5–6, 1921); New York (March 28–30, 1924); and Philadelphia (October 22–23, 1924). Locke participated in all but the second, and was involved in the planning and execution of these events as well. Beginning with the task force that organized and successfully executed the first convention, Locke served on race-amity committees from 1924 to 1932. There are records of Locke's having spoken (albeit sporadically) at Bahá'í-sponsored events from 1921 to 1952. Locke's last-known public talk ("fireside") on the Bahá'í Faith was given on March 23, 1952, in Toronto, Ontario.

In 1924 Locke left for the Sudan and Egypt. He was granted sabbatical leave to collaborate with the French Archaeological Society of Cairo. The highlight of his research trip was the reopening of the tomb of Tutankhamen. On his return from Egypt, however, he found his campus in upheaval from a student strike. In June 1925 Locke was fired from Howard

University by its white president, J. Stanley Durkee, for Locke's support of an equitable faculty pay scale and for student demands to end mandatory chapel and ROTC. Following his dismissal, since he was no longer gainfully employed, Locke needed to find a patron for support of his intellectual work. He found his benefactor in Charlotte Mason, a wealthy white woman with whom Locke faithfully corresponded until her death in 1940. Mason financed Locke's annual trips to Europe for thirteen years and enabled Locke to begin building his invaluable collection of African art, which he later bequeathed to Howard University.

That very year (1925) the Harlem Renaissance was born. It was conceived a year earlier when Locke was asked by the editor of the *Survey Graphic* to produce an issue on Harlem, a community located in Manhattan in New York. That special issue, *Harlem, Mecca of the New Negro,* Locke subsequently recast as an anthology, *The New Negro: An Interpretation,* published in December 1925. A landmark in black literature, it was an instant success. Locke wrote the foreword plus four essays appearing in the anthology: "The New Negro," "Negro Youth Speaks," "The Negro Spirituals," and "The Legacy of the Ancestral Arts." *The New Negro* featured five white contributors as well, making this artistic tour de force a genuinely interracial collaboration, with much support from white patronage (not without some strings attached, however).

The Harlem Renaissance—known also as the New Negro Movement, of which Locke was both the prime organizer and spokesman—sought to advance freedom and equality for blacks through art. The term "New Negro" dates back to Booker T. Washington, Norman Barton Wood, and Fannie Barrier Williams's *A New Negro for a New Century* (1900). From 1925 onward Locke engendered what was called "race pride" among African Americans by fostering a new sense of the distinctiveness of

black culture and its enrichment of the American experience for all Americans. Not merely a great creative outburst during the Roaring Twenties, the Harlem Renaissance was actually a highly self-conscious modern artistic movement. In an unpublished report on race relations, Locke stated that the New Negro Movement "deliberately aims at capitalizing race consciousness for group inspiration and cultural development. But it has no political or separatist motives, and is, in this one respect, different from the nationalisms of other suppressed minorities." In its mythic and utopian sense, Harlem was the "race capital" and the largest "Negro American" community in the world. The Harlem Renaissance, consequently, presented itself to America and to the world as a microcosm or self-portraiture of black culture. With its epic scope and lyric depth, the movement was an effusion of art borne of the everyday African American experience. The Harlem Renaissance would establish Locke as the elder statesman of African American art in later life, when his towering prestige wielded enormous authority.

In principle Locke was an avowed supporter of W. E. B. Du Bois's idea of a cultural elite (the "Talented Tenth") but differed from Du Bois in the latter's insistence that art should serve as propaganda. Even so, as Locke reveals in *The New Negro,* he hoped the Harlem Renaissance would provide "an emancipating vision to America" and would advance "a new democracy in American culture." He spoke of a "race pride," "race genius," and the "race-gift." This "race pride" was to be cultivated through developing a distinctive culture, a hybrid of African and African American elements. In Locke's opinion, art ought to contribute to the improvement of life—a pragmatist aesthetic principle sometimes called "meliorism." But the Harlem Renaissance was more an aristocratic than a democratic approach to culture. Criticized by some African American contemporaries, Locke himself came to regret the Harlem

Renaissance's excesses of exhibitionism as well as its elitism. Its dazzling success was short-lived.

A little-known fact is that at the very time *The New Negro* was published Locke went on an extended teaching trip in the South, giving public lectures on the Bahá'í vision of race unity. Between October 1925 and sometime in the spring of 1926, Locke spoke in the Dunbar Forum of Oberlin, at Wilberforce University, in Indianapolis, Cleveland, and Cincinnati, and before what the Southern Regional Teaching Committee in 1926 called "the best Negro institutions in the Middle South and Northern Florida," including the Daytona Industrial Institute and the Hungerford School near Orlando.

Locke returned to Howard under its new black president, Mordecai Johnson, who reinstated him in June 1927, although Locke did not resume teaching there until June 1928. (During the 1927–1928 academic year, Locke was an exchange professor at Fisk University.) In a letter dated May 5, 1927, Du Bois had written to Howard administrator Jesse Moorland to lobby for Locke's reinstatement. Du Bois states: "Mr. Locke is by long odds the best trained man among the younger American Negroes." Locke was subsequently promoted to chair of the philosophy department. He is credited with having first introduced the study of anthropology, along with philosophy and aesthetics, into the curriculum at Howard. A pioneer in the Negro theater movement, Locke coedited the first African American drama anthology, *Plays of Negro Life: A Source-Book of Native American Drama* (1927), which consisted of twenty one-act plays and dramatic sketches—ten by white playwrights (including Eugene O'Neill) and ten by black dramatists.

Strange to say, Locke did not publish a formal philosophical essay until he was fifty, when "Values and Imperatives" (1935) appeared. Apart from his dissertation Locke published only four other major philosophical articles in a philosophy journal or anthology: "Three Corollaries of Cultural Relativism" (1941), "Pluralism and Intellectual Democracy" (1942), "Cultural Relativism and Ideological Peace" (1944), and "Pluralism and Ideological Peace" (1947).

In 1936, under the auspices of the Associates in Negro Folk Education (ANFE), Locke established the *Bronze Booklets on the History, Problems, and Cultural Contributions of the Negro* series, written by such leading African American scholars as Sterling A. Brown and Ralph Bunche. Locke himself wrote two Bronze Booklets: *The Negro and His Music* (1936, Bronze Booklet No. 2) and *Negro Art: Past and Present* (1936, Bronze Booklet No. 3). Published between 1936 and 1942, the nine Bronze Booklets became a standard reference for teaching African American history. In 1940 the ANFE issued Locke's *The Negro in Art: A Pictorial Record of the Negro Artist and of the Negro Theme in Art,* which was Locke's best-known work after *The New Negro* and the leading book in its field. In 1942 Locke coedited (with Bernhard J. Stern) *When Peoples Meet: A Study of Race and Culture.* This anthology was international in scope, promoting interracial and ethnic contacts through intercultural exchange. In November 1942 Locke served as guest editor for a special edition of the *Survey Graphic,* an issue entitled "Color: The Unfinished Business of Democracy."

In 1943 Locke was on leave as Inter-American Exchange Professor to Haiti under the joint auspices of the American Committee for Inter-American Artistic and Intellectual Relations and the Haitian Ministry of Education. Toward the end of his stay there, Haitian President Lescot personally decorated Locke with the National Order of Honor and Merit, grade of Commandeur. There Locke wrote *Le rôle du Nègre dans la culture des Amériques* (1943), the nucleus of a grand project that he believed would be his magnum opus. That project, *The Negro in*

American Culture, was completed in 1956 by Margaret Just Butcher, daughter of Locke's close friend and Howard colleague Ernest E. Just. It is not, however, considered to be an authentic work of Locke.

In 1944 Locke became a charter member of the Conference on Science, Philosophy, and Religion, which published its annual proceedings. When in 1945 Locke was elected president of the American Association for Adult Education, he became the first black president of a predominantly white institution. During the 1945–1946 academic year Locke was a visiting professor at the University of Wisconsin, and in 1947 he was a visiting professor at the New School for Social Research. One of Locke's former students at Wisconsin, Beth Singer, describes her professor as follows: "Locke was a quiet, extremely scholarly, and well organized lecturer; I do not recall his speaking from notes." After mentioning the fact that Locke was a member of the Bahá'í Faith, Singer recalls that "Dr. Locke seemed somehow aloof, and my friends and I were pretty much in awe of him."

Among his many other accomplishments, Locke served on the editorial board of the *American Scholar,* was the philosophy editor for the *Key Reporter* of Phi Beta Kappa, and a regular contributor to various national magazines and journals, most notably *Opportunity* (1929–1940) and *Phylon* (1947–1953). Locke also contributed articles on Negro culture and Harlem to the *Encyclopedia Britannica* from 1940 to 1954. From 1948–1952 Locke taught concurrently at the City College (now City University) of New York and Howard University. Howard granted Locke a leave of absence for the 1951–1952 academic year to produce *The Negro in American Culture,* conceived in Haiti but left unfinished. Locke retired in June 1953 as a professor emeritus with an honorary doctorate of human letters conferred by Howard University. On June 5, 1953, Locke said in his unpublished acceptance speech:

> In coming to Howard in 1912, I was fortunate, I think, in bringing a philosophy of the market place not of the cloister. For, however much a luxury philosophy may be in our general American culture, for a minority situation and a trained minority leadership, it is a crucial necessity. This, because free, independent and unimposed thinking is the root source of all other emancipations. ... A minority is only safe and sound in terms of its social intelligence.

He moved to New York in July. For practically his entire life, Locke had sought treatment for his rheumatic heart. On June 9, 1954, nearly a year after moving to New York, Locke died of heart failure in Mount Sinai Hospital. On June 11 at Benta's Chapel, Brooklyn, Locke's memorial was presided over by Dr. Channing Tobias with cremation following at Fresh Pond Crematory in Little Village, Long Island. The brief notice that appeared in the *Baha'i News* in 1954 states that "quotations from the Baha'i Writings and Baha'i Prayers were read at Dr. Locke's funeral."

LOCKE'S PHILOSOPHY OF DEMOCRACY

Before describing the three principle collections of Locke's writings, it is important to explain how democracy provided the real basis of Locke's body of work. To this end, manuscript sources must be drawn on as well as actual publications. Access to the full range of Locke's writings permits one to see the breadth of his vision of America and the world. A survey of Locke's writings, both published and unpublished, reveals his overarching interest in democracy, and all of his writings on race are referenced to it. For Locke, race relations are at the heart of what democracy is all about. Locke's grand theory of democracy provides a necessary framework of analysis for comprehending what his views on race relations actually were. His multidimensional approach to democracy has already been noted. The first five dimensions are historical; they appear in Locke's paradigm of social evolution. In his 1941 unpublished farewell address at Talladega College, Locke spoke of local, moral, political, economic, and cultural stages of democracy.

Locke traces the origins of democracy back to Athens, where "democracy was a concept of local citizenship." By analogy he compares this "local democracy" to "college fraternities and sororities" in which the bonds are of "like-mindedness," thereby excluding others:

> The rim of the Greek concept of democracy was the barbarian: it was then merely the principle of fraternity within a narrow, limited circle. There was a dignity accorded to each member on the basis of membership in the group. It excluded foreigners, slaves and women. This concept carried over into the Roman empire.

Christianity would provide spiritual and social resources for the next stage in the evolution of democracy. Christianity gave rise to what Locke calls "moral democracy":

> We owe to Christianity one of the great basic ideals of democracy—the ideal of the moral equality of human beings. The Christian ideal of democracy was in its initial stages more democratic than it subsequently became. ... But the Christian church was a political institution and in making compromises often failed in bringing about real human equality.

Democracy in America began with a quest for "freedom of worship and the moral liberty of conscience." Yet "it had not even matured to the adult principle of abstract freedom of conscience as the religious intolerances of colonial settlers proved; migrating non-conformists themselves, they still could not stand the presence of non-conformity in their midst." Thus Christianity, while representing a necessary advance in the notion of democracy, was not a sufficient advance.

"It is a sad irony," Alain Locke wrote, "that the social institution most committed and potentially most capable of implementing social democracy should actually be the weakest and most inconsistent, organized religion." Indeed Locke takes Christianity to task for what is now called "self-segregation": "Of all the segregated bodies, the racially separate church is the saddest and most obviously self-contradicting. The separate Negro church, organized in self-defensive protest, is nonetheless just as anaomolous [sic], though perhaps, more pardonably so."

This is where secularism comes in, that is, "political democracy." According to Locke:

> The third great step in democracy came from protestant [sic] lands and people who evolved the ideal of political equality: (1) equality before the law; (2) political citizenship. This political democracy pivoted on individualism, and the freedom of the individual in terms of what we know as the fundamental rights of man. It found its best expression in the historic formula of "Liberty, equality and fraternity."

Here Locke acknowledges the influence of the French Revolution. "In terms of this ideology our country's government was founded," Locke explains, and continues:

> But for generations after[,] many of the fundamentals of our democracy were pious objectives, not fully expressed in practice. In the perspective of democracy's long evolution, we must regard our country's history as a progressive process of democratization, not yet fully achieved, but certainly progressing importantly in terms of the thirteenth, fourteenth and fifteenth amendments [sic], and the amendment extending the right of franchise to women. It is still imperfect.

What, then, is beyond political democracy? In Locke's view, "If we are going to have effective democracy in America we must have the democratic spirit as well as the democratic tradition, we must have more social democracy and more economic democracy in order to have or keep political democracy." Economic reform, then, was considered a necessary development of democracy:

The fourth crucial stage in the enlargement of democracy began, I think, with the income tax amendment. ... The income tax amendment was an initial step in social [economic] democracy as distinguished from the purely political,—a step toward economic equality through the partial appropriation of surplus wealth for the benefit of the commonwealth.

History is the measure of how far America has come. "In this country for many generations we thought we had economic equality," Locke goes on to say.

What we really had was a frontier expansion which developed such surpluses and offered such practical equality of opportunity as to give us the illusion of economic equality. We later learned that we did not have economic democracy, and that in order to have this, we must have guaranteed to all citizens certain minimal standards of living and the right to earn a living.

Locke then shows how the New Deal and the creation of the social security system represented further advances in economic democracy, by which he means economic equality of rights and opportunities. In the conclusion of an unpublished essay, "Peace Between Black and White in the United States," Locke stresses the importance of economic development:

We used to say that Christianity and democracy were both at stake in the equitable solution of the race question. They were; but they were abstract ideals that did not bleed when injured. Now we think with more realistic logic, perhaps, that economic justice cannot stand on one foot; and economic reconstruction is the dominant demand of the present-day American scene.

This relatively timeless statement attests Locke's contemporary relevance.

Locke continues in his Talladega speech:

A fifth phase of democracy, even if the preceding four are realized, still remains to be achieved in order to have a fully balanced society. The present crisis forces us to realize that without this also democracy may go into total eclipse. This fifth phase is the struggle for cultural democracy, and rests on the concept of the right of difference,— that is, the guarantee of the rights of minorities.

In his small book *World View on Race and Democracy: A Study Guide in Human Group Relations* (1943), Locke sums up the problem he is addressing as follows: "Less acute than race prejudice, but by no means unrelated to it, is the social bias and discrimination underlying the problem of cultural minorities. ... Cultural bias, like that directed against the Mexican, Orientals, the Jew, the American Indian, often intensifies into racial prejudice." At this stage in the social evolution of democracy Locke begins to address the problem of racism:

These contemporary problems of democracy can be vividly sensed if we realize that the race question is at the very heart of this struggle for cultural democracy. Its solution lies beyond even the realization of political and economic democracy, although of course that solution can only be reached when we no longer have extreme political inequality and extreme economic inequality.

The first four stages of democracy, developmental in nature, are still in process. These dimensions are not merely historical. Rather, they are challenges that America continues to face.

Locke looked beyond political democracy, which is merely the structure and machinery of the American experiment: "Constitutional guarantees, legal and civil rights, political machinery of democratic action and control are, of course, the skeleton foundation of democracy," Locke concedes,

but you and I know that attitudes are the flesh and blood of democracy, and that without their vital reenforcement [*sic*] democracy is really moribund or dead. That is my reason for thinking that in any democracy, ours included, the crucial issue, the test touchstone of democracy is minority status, minority protection, minority rights.

Not only is the race question America's "most challenging issue," as Locke's fellow Bahá'ís would say, it is also the single greatest challenge facing the world.

"The race question," wrote Locke in 1949, "has become the number one problem of the world." The next statement follows from the first: "Race really is a dominant issue of our thinking about democracy." In *World View on Race and Democracy,* Locke states this another way: "Of all the barriers limiting democracy, color is the greatest, whether viewed from a standpoint of national or world democracy." And in an unpublished report on racism Locke writes:

So, as between the white and the black peoples, the American situation is the acid test of the whole problem; and will be crucial in its outcome for the rest of the world. This makes America, in the judgment of many, the world's laboratory for the progressive solution of this great problem of social adjustment.

Thus Locke defines America's world role.

Locke speaks of "religious liberals" who represent "renewed hope for some early progress toward racial and social and cultural democracy." In a letter dated November 7, 1943, to the editor of the *Washington Star* Locke cites, with approval, a story that appeared in the November 2nd *Salt Lake Tribune,* which quoted him as saying:

There must be complete consistency between what democracy professes and what democracy practices. ... Public opinion in America has got to be sold on racial democracy. Now is the time for the people to face this question. Race equality alone can secure world peace. ... To save the United

States from moral bankruptcy we must solve the color problem.

Locke's rhetoric here is a direct echo of his Bahá'í convictions.

The next dimension is social democracy. In "Reason and Race: A Review of the Literature of the Negro for 1946" (1947) Locke underscores "the fact that the contemporary world situation clearly indicates that social democracy is the only safe choice for the survival of Western and Christian civilization." In the Seventeenth Annual Convention and Bahá'í Congress (July 5, 1925), Locke is reported to have remarked on "the great part which America can play in the establishment of world peace, if alive to its opportunity." He went on to say that "the working out of social democracy can be accomplished here. To this end we should not think in little arcs of experience, but in the big, comprehensive way. ... In final analysis, peace cannot exist anywhere without existing everywhere." To get from national democracy to world democracy, the world will have to be spiritualized.

Locke's views on "spiritual democracy" have received scant attention. In "The Gospel for the Twentieth Century," an evidently unpublished Bahá'í essay, Locke expresses his conviction that spiritual democracy is our greatest resource for realizing the full range of democracy: "The gospel for the Twentieth Century rises out of the heart of its greatest problems. ... Much has been accomplished in the name of Democracy, but Spiritual Democracy, its largest and most inner meaning, is so below our common horizons." Locke follows with this telling criticism of American materialism: "The land that is nearest to material democracy is furthest away from spiritual democracy." Then, presumably for the benefit of his Bahá'í audience, Locke cites Bahá'í scripture:

The word of God is still insistent, ... and we have ... Bahá'u'lláh's "one great trumpet-call to humanity": "That all nations shall become one in faith, and all men as brothers; that the bonds of affection and unity between the sons of men should be strengthened; that diversity of religion should cease, and differences of race be annulled. ... These strifes and this bloodshed and discord must cease, and all men be as one kindred and family."

Locke's direct citation of Bahá'u'lláh (1817–1892), prophet-founder of the Bahá'í Faith, makes his point abundantly clear: spiritual democracy is democracy taken to heart, internalized and universalized. This alone can ensure world democracy.

"World democracy," writes Locke, "presupposes the recognition of the essential equality of all peoples and the potential parity of all cultures." On a radio program, "Woman's Page of the Air" with Adelaide Hawley, broadcast August 6, 1944, while World War II was in full furor, Locke said: "Just as the foundation of democracy as a national principle made necessary the declaration of the basic equality of persons, so the founding of *international* democracy must guarantee the basic equality of human *groups*." This is where Locke registers his support for the United Nations:

> Significantly enough, the Phalanx of the United Nations unites an unprecedented assemblage of the races, cultures and peoples of the world. Could this war-born assemblage be welded by a constructive peace into an effective world order—one based on the essential parity of peoples and a truly democratic reciprocity of cultures—world democracy would be within reach of attainment.

He then draws a moral analogy:

> Moreover, the United States, with its composite population sampling all the human races and peoples, is by way of being almost a United Nations by herself. We could so easily and naturally, with the right dynamic, become the focus of thoroughgoing internationalism—thereby realizing, one might say, our manifest destiny.

Note that Locke has not only redefined the idea of manifest destiny—he has revolutionized it.

In "Moral Imperatives for World Order" (1944), Locke incorporates nation, race, and religion as the three "basic corporate ideas" that are integral to America's world role. Locke explored the relationship between America and world democracy. In "Color: The Unfinished Business of Democracy" (1942) he states: "World leadership ... must be moral leadership in democratic concert with humanity at large." In so doing, America must perforce "abandon racial and cultural prejudice." "A world democracy," he adds, "cannot possibly tolerate what a national democracy has countenanced too long."

Beyond these nine dimensions of democracy—or collateral with them—is the contribution of youth. On May 28, 1946, in his commencement address at the University of Wisconsin High School, Locke spoke of "the gallant natural democracy of youth," stating as its cause the simple reason that "youth, generally speaking, are typically the most free of deeply engrained prejudice." Another variation on the theme of democracy is Locke's use of the term "practical democracy" in a variety of contexts. For instance, in reporting on a Bahá'í-sponsored race amity convention, Locke wrote: "Washington, which the penetrating vision of Abdul Baha [Bahá'í leader, 1844–1921] in 1912 saw as the crux of the race problem and therefore of practical democracy in America, was for that reason selected as the place for the first convention under Bahá'í auspices for amity in inter-racial relations."

Democracy has always been a creative human project, according to Locke. We should "keep constantly in mind how indisputably democracy has historically changed and enlarged its meaning, acquiring from generation to generation new scope, added objectives, fresh sanctions." Democracy, of course, has not always been democratic. Locke shows the dissonance between the ideal and the real in the inherent contradictions of democracy as practiced by the founding fathers:

> We can scarcely make a fetish of our own or even our generation's version of democracy if we recall that once in the minds of all but a few radical democrats like Jefferson, democracy was compatible with such obvious contradictions as slavery and has even much later seemed adequate in spite of such limitations equally obvious to us now as the disenfranchisement of women, complete disregard of public responsibility for education, no provision for social security and the like.

Democracy is ongoing in its development. In an unpublished essay, "Creative Democracy," Locke rhetorically asks:

> If democracy hasn't always meant the same thing, how can we be so sure that its present compass of meaning is so permanent or so fully adequate? It seems absolutely essential, then, to treat democracy as a dynamic, changing and developing concept, to consider it always in terms of an expanding context, and to realize that like any embodiment of human values, it must grow in order to keep alive. Except as progressive and creative, democracy both institutionally and ideologically stagnates.

In one of his formal philosophical essays, "Pluralism and Intellectual Democracy," Locke declares: "The intellectual core of the problems of the peace ... will be the discovery of the necessary common denominators and the basic equivalences involved in a democratic world order or democracy on a world scale." To this end Locke advocated a "democracy of values"—that is, value pluralism. In this essay Locke argues for the "re-vamping of democracy" and advocates the adoption of "'cultural pluralism' as a proposed liberal rationale for our national democracy." Conceived differently, Locke sees pluralism as an extension of eighteenth-century democratic values.

This inventory of the dimensions of democracy in the philosophy of Alain Locke does not exhaust his expansive use of the concept. Perhaps the summary lies in Locke's felicitous expression "equalitarian democracy." At the heart of this view of democracy is interracial unity, Locke's paramount Bahá'í ideal. In *The Negro in America* (1933), Locke explains:

> If they will but see it, because of their complementary qualities, the two racial groups [blacks and whites] have great spiritual need, one of the other. It would be truly significant in the history of human culture, if two races so diverse should so happily collaborate, and the one return for the gift of a great civilization the reciprocal gift of the spiritual cross-fertilization of a great and distinctive national culture.

In his speech "America's Part in World Peace" (1925) Locke reportedly said:

> America's democracy must begin at home with a spiritual fusion of all her constituent peoples in brotherhood, and in an actual mutuality of life. Until democracy is worked out in the vital small scale of practical human relations, it can never, except as an empty formula, prevail on the national or international basis. Until it establishes itself in human hearts, it can never institutionally flourish. Moreover, America's reputation and moral influence in the world depends on the successful achievement of this vital spiritual democracy within the lifetime of the present generation. (Material civilization alone does not safeguard the progress of a nation.) Bahá'í Principles and the leavening of our national life with their power, is to be regarded as the salvation of democracy. In this way only can the fine professions of American ideals be realized.

This rare religious sentiment by Locke should not be misconstrued. In his own lifetime the Bahá'ís were the only predominantly white group, with the possible exception of the Quakers, who collectively reached out to African Americans for the purpose of fostering interracial unity—a sacred Bahá'í value. Far from asserting any parochial ownership of this ideal, Locke wanted to promote the principle of interracial unity within the broader context of democracy. Evidence suggests that he first encountered Bahá'ís in 1915, which, if true, coincides with his remarkable series of five lectures, first delivered in 1915 and again in March and April of 1916, "Race Contacts and Inter-Racial Relations."

"RACE CONTACTS AND INTERRACIAL RELATIONS"

Jeffrey Stewart edited *Race Contacts and Interracial Relations: Lectures on the Theory and Practice of Race* (1992) from transcripts of Locke's 1916 lectures preserved in the Alain Locke Papers, held in the archives of the Manuscript Division of the Moorland-Spingarn Research Center at Howard University. Locke drew heavily on the work of Franz Boas (1858–1942), whose paper "The Instability of Race Types" Locke may have heard at the Universal Race Congress (July 26–29, 1911). In the fourth lecture Locke directly cites Boas' pioneer work, *The Mind of Primitive Man* (1911), which, as Stewart observes in the introduction to his book, "revolutionized theories of race and culture." Stewart goes on to acknowledged that Boas, the "father of American anthropology," exploded the myth that race had any real basis in scientific fact, and sought to establish "culture" as a "central social science paradigm." In so doing Boas was widely regarded by intellectual historians as one who did more to combat the ideological rationalization of race prejudice than any other person in history. Yet in 1916 only a handful of Americans knew of Boas' work. Stewart notes that Locke "was the intellectual who most fully comprehended the implications of Boas' theories for African Americans." Boas, who had significant contacts with Bahá'ís, was a touchstone of truth for Locke. His lectures thus represent a further development of ideas of Boas, whom Locke eulogized as a "major prophet of democracy."

In the first lecture, "The Theoretical and Scientific Conceptions of Race," Locke leads with the question, "What is race?" He then traces the origins of race theory to Joseph Arthur Comte de Gobineau (1816–1882), the founder of scientific racism. "We should expect naturally," said Locke, stating the obvious, "that race theory should be a philosophy of the dominant groups." Apart from the serious social issues involved, the integrity of the scientific method itself was at stake. Scientific racism could no longer maintain its scientific pretense. Addressing the connection between bias and theory, Locke stresses Boas' distinction between racial difference and racial inequality. Racial difference is biological; racial inequality is social. Race, therefore, is socially—not biologically—determined. There may indeed be a cause-and-effect relationship between the two. "Consequently, any true history of race," Locke goes on to say, "must be a sociological theory of race." The paradox is that race "amounts practically to social inheritance[,] and yet it parades itself as biological or anthropological inheritance." Races are socially constructed, and their cultures expressive of core values, even though those values themselves are in flux.

This is a theoretical reversal of the old-school anthropological approach to race. Locke debunks Social Darwinism, the belief that distinct races exist and are genetically determined to express certain traits. Science must be brought to bear on the race question, to dispel "false conceptions of race." And he predicts that "science will ultimately arrive" at the conclusion that "there are no static factors of race." Locke successfully removed race from its biological basis, arguing that race is culture. Accordingly Locke supported the move from "biological" anthropology to cultural anthropology.

In the second lecture, "The Political and Practical Conceptions of Race," Locke states that dominant groups are "imperialistic." He gives the Roman Empire as a perfect example.

Then there are "the exploitations of modern *imperialism.*" On a personal note, Locke says, "I lived for three years in close association with imperial folk at the 'Imperial Training School' at the University of Oxford. Oxford and Cambridge rule the English Empire." Imperialism generates its own race myths. Anglo-Saxon superiority is a rationalization and justification of its own imperialism. Another form of imperialism is "commercial imperialism," exercised "to further trade dominance." In the modern age, "empire is the political problem." As a corollary to this problem, Locke discusses race and class in the third lecture, "The Phenomena and Laws of Race Contacts."

In the fourth lecture, "Modern Race Creeds and Their Fallacies," Locke compares "racial antipathy" with Francis Bacon's concept of "social idols." Examples range from the Rhine District (French and German), the Alsace-Lorraine question, the Brown Provinces of Austria, to anti-Semitism in Prussia. Locke then enumerates a series of social fallacies: the "biological fallacy," the "fallacy of the masses," the "fallacy of the permanency of race types" (which Locke takes to be a "race creed"), the "fallacy of race ascendancy," and the fallacy of "automatic adjustment." In the end prejudice "is simply an abnormal social sense, a [perversion] of a normal social instinct."

In the fifth and final lecture, "Racial Progress and Race Adjustment," Locke concludes the series with a discourse on "social race," citing the Hindu caste system as the oldest instance of it. Then he baldly states: "Every civilization produces its type." He goes on to say that "conformity to civilization type is something which society exacts of all its members." What does Locke mean by this? America's social metaphor of the melting pot instantly comes to mind. The pressure to conform is the pressure to assimilate. Historically, because they were forcibly cut off from their African traditions, African Americans were exposed to, immersed in, and assimilated to American culture. Segregation is one of the barriers that prevents their full participation in American life.

Paradoxically, race pride is a loyalty that can coexist within a larger loyalty to the "common civilization type." The reader is left to presume that America is its own "civilization type." As his own theory of social conservation, Locke goes so far as to propose the reinvention of the "race type," advocating the development of a "secondary race consciousness." This eventually leads to "culture-citizenship," or group contribution to a joint civilization, where "race type blends into the 'civilization type.'" Racial pride is analogous to an individual's sense of self-respect. Here Locke differs from Boas in his theory of race in that Locke saw value in maintaining race consciousness. In "The Negro's Contribution to American Culture" (1939) Locke projected that race would matter less and less in the future, when the "ultimate biological destiny, perhaps, of the human stock" would be mulatto, or mixed, "like rum in the punch." Sadly Locke's lectures had no influence on his philosophical contemporaries.

THE CRITICAL TEMPER OF ALAIN LOCKE

Stewart has again made Locke far more available than ever before, with the publication of his anthology of Locke's essays on art and culture. The book is organized in sections: "Renaissance Apologetics"; "Poetry"; "Drama"; "African Art"; "Contemporary Negro Art"; "Retrospective Reviews"; "Race and Culture." The majority of these reprinted articles originally appeared in the journals *Phylon* and *Opportunity*. In these, as in other works by Locke, the reader must hunt for the occasional "gold nugget"—when Locke is at his timeless best. Otherwise the reviews can be somewhat tedious. Locke's prefatory remarks in each article often repay the effort, however.

In the opening paragraph of "Dawn Patrol: A Review of the Literature of the Negro for 1948" (1949), Locke states that "the race question has become [the] number one problem of the world." This is this crisis of Western civilization. Art, literature, and drama counteract racism through creating "new sensitivities of social conscience, of radically enlarged outlooks of human understanding." "Race and Culture," the last section in Stewart's collection, is the most interesting from the standpoint of understanding Locke's thought. "The American Temperament" (1911) is a critique of American popular culture, which failed to live up to Locke's belief that the function of art is to enlighten, to engender social change. "Race Contacts and Inter-Racial Relations" was a privately printed syllabus of Locke's 1915–1916 lectures. "The Ethics of Culture" (1923) is an address by Locke to freshmen at Howard University. This is one of Locke's most straightforward talks, in which he tells his students that "a brilliant Englishman once characterized America as a place where everything had a price, but nothing a value. ... There is a special need for a correction of this on your part." America is largely a cultural wasteland, with "Saharas of culture" across the country. Locke exhorts his students to strive for excellence, to be "well-bred." "In fact," Locke concludes, "one suspects that eventually the most civilized way of being superior will be to excel in culture."

In "The Negro's Contribution to American Culture" Locke reflects on the Harlem Renaissance. He refers to it as "cultural racialism" which was "the keynote of the Negro renaissance." Between 1925 and 1939 "three schools of Negro cultural expression" appeared in succession. The first was the "enthusiastic cult of idealistic racialism" that characterized the "Negro renaissance" (Locke's preferred term of reference to the Harlem Renaissance in his later writings). The movement was marred by a certain degree of "irresponsible individualism

and eccentric exhibitionism." This was followed by a period of folk realism (which the depression intensified), giving rise to a school of "iconoclast" social protest literature. (In his own iconoclastic vein, Locke refers to *Gone With the Wind* as a "contrary to fact romance.") Ideally "Negro art" should fulfill its primary purpose as "an instrument for social enlightenment and constructive social reform." This is what Locke means by "culture politics." But this is not a "racially exclusive" task, since it is "the ultimate goal of cultural democracy, the capstone of the historic process of American acculturation."

In "The Negro in the Three Americas" (1944), the English version of a May 1943 lecture given in French while in Haiti, Locke points to the shared historical legacy of slavery in North America, the Caribbean, and South America. The effects of slavery still need to be eradicated. Poverty, illiteracy, and all related social ills are the direct consequence of persisting "undemocratic social attitudes" and "anti-democratic social policies." Locke sees the effort to remedy this situation as a crusade to save democracy by expanding it. "For historical and inescapable reasons," Locke explains, "the Negro has thus become ... a conspicuous symbol ... of democracy." Locke is optimistic about the "radiant" prospects for "inter-American cultural democracy," but achieving a "larger social democracy" is a broader issue. Speaking "as a philosopher," Locke concedes that the emergence and influence of the elite remains "a necessary though painful condition for mass progress." The reader can see that Locke placed a great deal of faith in the power of the elite to amplify social democracy through the instrumentality of cultural democracy.

THE PHILOSOPHY OF ALAIN LOCKE

Leonard Harris has done an invaluable service in assembling *The Philosophy of Alain Locke:*

Harlem Renaissance and Beyond (1989), a truly representative selection of Locke's work. Harris even includes two of Locke's Bahá'í essays, "The Orientation of Hope" (1933) and "Unity through Diversity" (1936). This volume is divided into four parts: "Epistemological Foundations"; "Valuation: Commentaries and Reviews"; "Identity and Plurality"; "Identity and Education." Each section is ordered historically, with three of the essays in the first section published for the first time.

Locke did not publish a formal philosophical essay until he was fifty. Accordingly Harris has chosen "Values and Imperatives" as the first essay. In many ways the essay is a condensation of Locke's doctoral dissertation. His classification of "value types" and their associated "value predicates" and "value polarity" are reduced to a schematic chart. Locke's theory of values provides the epistemological foundation for his subsequent philosophical formulations. In "Pluralism and Intellectual Democracy," Locke posits a "vital connection between pluralism and democracy" that can give rise to "a flexible, more democratic nexus, a unity in diversity." Crediting William James with rejecting "intellectual absolutism," Locke outlines his vision of "intellectual democracy." Radical empiricism leads to "anarchic pluralism." Midway between these two extremes, Locke proposes a "systematic relativism." Through objective comparison of different value systems, one may discover "functional constants" that can "scientifically" supplant arbitrary universals, such as "sole ways of salvation" and "perfect forms of the state or society." In so doing, not only will traditional value systems "make peace with one another" but will also make "an honorable peace with science"—an echo of the Bahá'í ideal of the harmony of science and religion, which Locke professed.

The practical corollaries of value pluralism are tolerance and reciprocity. World democracy—a "democratic world order"—cannot be based "on an enlarged pattern of our own." Rather, "the intellectual core of the problems of the peace, should it lie in our control and leadership, will be the discovery of the necessary common denominators and the basic equivalences involved in a democratic world order or democracy on a world scale." Some of the dogmatisms to be overcome are "culture bias, nation worship, and racism." The duty of intellectuals is to reconstruct democracy to make it truly pluralistic.

In "Cultural Relativism and Ideological Peace," Locke is concerned with the implementation of cultural pluralism. It is a "new age," and a "new scholarship" is needed. Cultural relativity is, in effect, the new methodology. It is based on three basic corollaries: "the principle of *cultural equivalence*" (a search for "culture-correlates"), "the principle of *cultural reciprocity*," and "the principle of *limited cultural convertibility*." The scholarly "task of the hour" is to discover an underlying "unity in diversity." These unities, however, have a functional rather than content character, and are pragmatic rather than ideological.

In "Pluralism and Ideological Peace," Locke argues that cultural parity, tolerance, and reciprocity are "an extension of democracy beyond individuals and individual rights" to group rights. In this essay Locke repeats verbatim a statement he made in "Cultural Relativism" that the "Utopian dream of the idealist" is "that somehow a single faith, a common culture, an all-embracing institutional life and its confraternity should some day unite man by merging all his loyalties and culture values." But that day seems distant, which is why cultural pluralism is far more attainable.

The second section of this anthology opens with "The Orientation of Hope." As a professed Bahá'í, Locke gives an oblique testimony of faith in saying that "the true principles and hopes of a new and universal human order" may be realized through "an inspired extension of the potent realism of 'Abdu'l-Bahá by which he crowned and fulfilled the basic idealism of Bahá'u'lláh." In "Unity through Diversity: A Bahá'í Principle," Locke urges Bahá'ís to apply "the precious legacy of the inspired teachings of 'Abdu'l-Bahá and Bahá'u'lláh" by translating the Bahá'í principles into action and carrying them into "the social and cultural fields" where "the support and adherence of the most vigorous and intellectual elements in most societies can be enlisted." This will result in the "application and final vindication of the Bahá'í principles" and "a positive multiplication of spiritual power." In "Moral Imperatives for World Order," Locke abandons his role as an advocate of the rights of African Americans to address the current world crisis. He identifies nation, race, and religion as the three basic group loyalties. "The moral imperatives of a new world order," Locke concludes, "are an internationally limited idea of national sovereignty, a non-monopolistic and culturally tolerant concept of race and religious loyalties freed of sectarian bigotry."

Skipping over several essays, three of which also appear in *The Critical Temper of Alain Locke* ("The Ethics of Culture," "The Concept of Race as Applied to Social Culture," and "Who and What is 'Negro'?"), one can see how Locke for his entire professional life advocated a "pragmatically functional type of philosophy, to serve as a guide to life and living rather than what Dewey calls 'busy work for a few professionals' refining the techniques and polishing the tools of rational analysis." Locke wanted to "extend the scientific method and temper beyond the domain of science ... to all other intellectual domains." He attempted to provide a model for this in coediting *When Peoples Meet: A Study of Race and Culture* (1942), which was "an integrated analysis" of "basic problems of human group relations" and a "wide-scale comparative study of universal forces in group interaction."

In "Frontiers of Culture" (1950), Locke reflects on how "culture" was "once a favorite theme-song word with me. Now I wince at its mention." In retrospect Locke claims the New Negro Movement as his "brain child." "Having signed that 'New Negro's' birth certificate, I assume some right to participate in the post-mortem findings." The movement died because of "exhibitionism and racial chauvinism." Late in life Locke believed that "there is no room for any consciously maintained racialism in matters cultural." Locke then questions the utility of self-segregation: "Let us ask boldly and bravely, what then are the justifications of separate Negro churches, of separate Negro fraternities, schools, colleges?" Thus the new "frontier of culture" is integration. The enemies remain the same—class bias and group bias.

CONCLUSION

History has both immortalized and obscured Locke. Given his cynicism toward it in later life, it is ironic, although not surprising, that Locke should forever be associated with the Harlem Renaissance, much to the exclusion of his broader role as a cultural pluralist. With new information that has come to light regarding his Bahá'í identity, it is now possible to understand how Locke could function simultaneously as a cultural racialist and cultural pluralist. Together the two combine to produce "unity through diversity"—the Bahá'í principle that Locke held sacred. Locke's philosophy of democracy, which previous literature never holistically described, is the key to integrating the various facets of his thought. As a philosopher Locke had no appreciable impact in his own lifetime. In the end, however, he may enjoy a delayed influence. That will depend largely on whether the new information that recent scholarship has provided can bring Locke back to influential life as a prophet of democracy.

Selected Bibliography

WORKS OF ALAIN LOCKE

BOOKS AND PAMPHLETS

"Race Contacts and Inter-Racial Relations: A Study in the Theory and Practice of Race." Syllabus of an Extension Course of Lectures. Washington, D. C.: Howard University, 1916. (Pamphlet.)

The Problem of Classification in the Theory of Value. Ph.D. dissertation. Cambridge, Mass.: Harvard, 1918.

The Negro in America. Chicago: American Library Association, 1933.

The Negro and His Music. Washington, D.C.: Associates in Negro Folk Education, 1936 (Bronze Booklet No. 2). Reprints: Port Washington, N.Y.: Kennikat Press, 1968; New York: Arno Press, 1969.

Negro Art: Past and Present. Washington, D.C.: Associates in Negro Folk Education, 1936 (Bronze Booklet No. 3). Reprint: New York: Arno Press, 1969.

Le rôle du Nègre dans la culture des Amériques. Port-au-Prince, Haiti: Imprimerie de l'état, 1943.

World View on Race and Democracy: A Study Guide in Human Group Relations. Chicago: American Library Association, 1943.

Diversity within National Unity. Washington, D.C.: National Council for Social Studies, 1945. (Pamphlet.)

ESSAYS ON PHILOSOPHY

"Values and Imperatives." In *American Philosophy Today and Tomorrow.* Edited by Horace M. Kallen and Sidney Hook. New York: Lee Furman, 1935. Pp. 312–333. Reprints: Freeport, N. Y.: Books for Libraries Press, 1968; in *The Philosophy of Alain Locke.* Edited by Leonard Harris. Philadelphia: Temple University Press, 1989. Pp. 31–50.

"Three Corollaries of Cultural Relativism." In *Proceedings of the Second Conference on the Scientific Spirit and the Democratic Faith.* New York: Conference on Science, Philosophy and Religion, 1941.

"Pluralism and Intellectual Democracy." In *Conference on Science, Philosophy, and Religion, Second Symposium.* New York: Conference on Science, Philosophy and Religion, 1942. Pp. 196–212. Reprinted in *The Philosophy of Alain Locke.* Pp. 51–66.

"Cultural Relativism and Ideological Peace." In *Approaches to World Peace.* Edited by Lyman Bryson, Louis Finfelstein, and R. M. MacIver. New York: Harper & Brothers, 1944. Pp. 609–618. Reprinted in *The Philosophy of Alain Locke.* Pp. 67–78.

"Pluralism and Ideological Peace." In *Freedom and Experience: Essays Presented to Horace M. Kallen.* Edited by Milton R. Konvitz and Sidney Hook. Ithaca, N.Y.: New School for Research and Cornell University Press, 1947. Pp. 63–69.

ESSAYS ON THE HARLEM RENAISSANCE AND NEGRO ART

"Art of the Ancestors." *Survey Graphic* 53:673 (March 1925).

"Enter the New Negro." *Survey Graphic* 53:631–634 (March 1925).

"Harlem." *Survey Graphic* 53:629–630 (March 1925).

Foreword. In *The New Negro: An Interpretation.* New York: Albert and Charles Boni, 1925.

"The Legacy of the Ancestral Arts." In *The New Negro: An Interpretation.* New York: Albert and Charles Boni, 1925. Pp. 254–267.

"The New Negro." In *The New Negro: An Interpretation.* New York: Albert and Charles Boni, 1925. Pp. 3–16. Reprinted in *Within the Circle: An Anthology of African American Literary Criticism from the Harlem Renaissance to the Present.* Edited by Angelyn Mitchell. Durham, N.C.: Duke University Press, 1994. Pp. 21–31.

"The Negro Spirituals." In *The New Negro: An Interpretation.* New York: Albert and Charles Boni, 1925. Pp. 199–213.

"Negro Youth Speaks." In *The New Negro: An Interpretation.* New York: Albert and Charles Boni, 1925. Pp. 47–53.

"The Negro and the American Stage." *Theatre Arts Monthly* 10:112–120 (February 1926).

"American Literary Tradition and the Negro." *The Modern Quarterly* 3:215–222 (May–July 1926). Reprinted in *Interracialism: Black-White Intermarriage in American History, Literature, and Law.* Edited by Werner Sollors. Oxford: Oxford University Press, 2000. Pp. 269–274.

"Our Little Renaissance." In *Ebony and Topaz.* Edited by Charles S. Johnson. New York: National Urban League, 1927. Pp. 117–118.

"The High Cost of Prejudice." *The Forum* 78:500–510 (December 1927).

"Art or Propaganda?" *Harlem* 1:12–13 (November 1928).

"The Negro's Contribution to American Art and Literature." *Annals of the American Academy of Political and Social Science* 140:234–247 (1928).

"The Negro in American Culture." In *Anthology of American Negro Literature.* Edited by V. F. Calverton. New York: Modern Library Series, 1929. Pp. 248–266.

"The Negro's Contribution in Art to American Culture." *Proceedings of the National Conference of Social Work.* New York, 1933. Pp. 315–322.

"Propaganda—or Poetry?" *Race* 1:70–76, 87 (summer 1936).

"Harlem: Dark Weather-vane." *Survey Graphic* 24:457–462, 493–495 (August 1936).

"The Negro's Contribution to American Culture." *Journal of Negro Education* 8:521–529 (July 1939).

"On Literary Stereotypes." In *Fighting Words.* Edited by Donald Ogden Stewart. New York: Harcourt, Brace and Company, 1940. Pp. 75–78.

"Spirituals." In *75 Years of Freedom.* Washington, D. C.: Library of Congress, 1940. Pp. 7–15.

"The Negro Minority in American Literature." *English Journal* 35:315–320 (1946).

"The Negro in American Literature." *New World Writing* 1:18–33 (1952).

ESSAYS ON DEMOCRACY AND RACE

"Democracy Faces a World Order." *Harvard Educational Review* 12:121–128 (March 1942).

"Color: The Unfinished Business of Democracy." *Survey Graphic* 31:455–459 (November 1942).

"Race, Culture et Democratie." *Cahiers d'Haiti* 8:6–14 (March 1944).

"Moral Imperatives for World Order." *Summary of Proceedings.* Institute of International Relations. Oakland, Calif.: Mills College, June 18–28, 1944. Pp. 19–20.

"Whither Race Relations? A Critical Commentary." *Journal of Negro Education* 13:398–406 (summer 1944).

"Major Prophet of Democracy." Review of *Race and Democratic Society* by Franz Boas. *Journal of Negro Education* 15:191–192 (spring 1946).

"Are Negroes Winning Their Fight for Civil Rights?" *Harlem Quarterly* 1, no. 1:23 (1949–1950).

ESSAYS ON THE BAHÁ'Í

"Impressions of Haifa." *Star of the West* 15:13–14 (April 1924). Reprints: *Bahá'í Year Book.* Vol. I, April 1925–April 1926. Compiled by the National Spiritual Assembly of the Bahá'ís of the United States and Canada. New York: Bahá'í Publishing Committee, 1926. Pp. 81, 83; *The Bahá'í World: A Biennial International Record.* Vol. II, April 1926–April 1928. Compiled by the National Spiritual Assembly of the Bahá'ís of the United States and Canada. New York: Bahá'í Publishing Committee, 1928. Pp. 125, 127; *The Bahá'í World: A Biennial International Record.* Vol. III, April 1928–April 1930. Compiled by the National Spiritual Assembly of the Bahá'ís of the United States and Canada. New York: Bahá'í Publishing Committee, 1930. Pp. 280, 282.

"America's Part in World Peace." Quoted in Harlan Ober's "The Bahá'í Congress at Green Acre." *The Bahá'í Magazine (Star of the West)* 16:525 (August 1925).

"A Bahá'í Inter-Racial Conference." *The Bahá'í Magazine (Star of the West)* 18:315–316 (January 1928).

"The Orientation of Hope." In *The Bahá'í World: A Biennial International Record,* Vol. IV, 1930–1932. New York: Bahá'í Publishing Committee, 1933. Pp. 527–528. Reprinted in *The Philosophy of Alain Locke.* Pp. 130–132.

"Unity through Diversity: A Bahá'í Principle." In *The Bahá'í World: A Biennial International Record,* Vol. V, 1932–1934. New York: Bahá'í Publishing Committee, 1936. Pp. 372–374. Reprinted in *The Philosophy of Alain Locke.* Pp. 133–138.

"Lessons in World Crisis." In *The Bahá'í World: A Biennial International Record,* Vol. IX, 1940–1944. Wilmette, Ill.: Bahá'í Publishing Trust, 1945. Pp. 745–747. Reprint: Wilmette, Ill.: Bahá'í Publishing Trust, 1980.

"The Gospel for the Twentieth Century." Unpublished. Undated. Alain Locke Papers, Moorland-

Spingarn Research Center, Manuscript Division, Box 164–143, Folder 3 (Writings by Locke— Notes. Christianity spirituality, religion). Washington, D. C.: Howard University.

WORKS EDITED BY ALAIN LOCKE

"Harlem: Mecca of the New Negro." Special issue of the *Survey Graphic* 53 (March 1925). Reprint: Baltimore, Md.: Black Classic Press, 1981.

"Harlem: Mecca of the New Negro." A Hypermedia Edition of the *Survey Graphic* (March 1925). Prepared by Matthew G. Kirschenbaum and Catherine Tousignant. University of Virginia's Electronic Text Center. http://etext.lib.virginia.edu/harlem/index.html.

The New Negro: An Interpretation. New York: Albert and Charles Boni, 1925.

Four Negro Poets. New York: Simon & Schuster, 1927.

Plays of Negro Life: A Source-Book of Native American Drama. Coedited with Montgomery Gregory. New York: Harper and Brothers, 1927. Reprint: Westport, Conn.: Negro Universities Press, 1970.

A Decade of Negro Self-Expression: Occasional Paper No. 26. With foreword by Howard W. Odum. Charlottesville, Va.: Trustees of the John S. Slater Fund, 1928.

Americans All: Immigrants All. Washington, D.C.: Office of Education *Bulletin,* 1939.

The Negro in Art: A Pictorial Record of the Negro Artist and of the Negro Theme in Art. Washington, D.C.: Associates in Negro Folk Education, 1940. Reprint: New York: Hacker Art Books, 1971.

"Color: Unfinished Business of Democracy." Special issue of the *Survey Graphic* 31 (November 1942).

When Peoples Meet: A Study of Race and Culture. Coedited with Bernhard J. Stern. New York: Committee on Workshops, Progressive Education Association, 1942. Revised edition: New York: Hinds, Hayden & Eldredge, 1946.

The Negro Artist Comes of Age: A National Survey of Contemporary American Artists. With John Davis Hatch. Albany, N.Y.: Albany Institute of History and Art, 1945.

OTHER WORKS

"Oxford Contrasts." *Independent* 67:139–142 (July 15, 1909).

"The American Temperament." *North American Review* 194:262–270 (August 1911).

"The Role of the Talented Tenth." *Howard University Record* 12:15–18 (December 1918).

"The Ethics of Culture." *Howard University Record* 17:178–185 (January 1923).

"The Problem of Race Classification." *Opportunity* 1:261–264 (September 1923).

"The Concept of Race as Applied to Social Culture." *Howard Review* 1:290–299 (June 1924).

"Minorities and the Social Mind." *Progressive Education* 12:141–150 (March 1935).

"The Dilemma of Segregation." *Journal of Negro Education* 4:406–411 (July 1935).

"Lessons of Negro Adult Education." In *Adult Education in Action.* Edited by Mary L. Fly. New York: American Association for Adult Education, 1936. Pp. 126–131.

"Ballad for Democracy." *Opportunity* 18:228–229 (August 1940).

"Autobiographical Sketch." In *Twentieth Century Authors.* Edited by Stanley Kunitz and Howard Haycroft. New York: Wilson, 1942. P. 837.

"The Negro in the Three Americas." *Journal of Negro Education* 13:7–18 (winter 1944).

"Reason and Race: A Review of the Literature of the Negro for 1946." *Phylon* 8:17–27 (first quarter 1947). Reprinted in *The Critical Temper of Alain Locke.* Edited by Jeffrey C. Stewart. New York: Garland, 1983. Pp. 319–327.

"The Need for a New Organon in Education." In *Goals for American Education.* New York: Conference on Science, Philosophy and Religion, 1950. Pp. 201–212. Reprinted in *The Philosophy of Alain Locke.* Pp. 263–276.

"Self-Criticism: The Third Dimension in Culture." *Phylon* 11:391–394 (1950). Reprinted in *Remembering the Harlem Renaissance.* Edited by Cary D. Wintz. New York: Garland, 1996. Pp. 164–168.

"The Social Responsibility of the Scholar." *Proceedings of the Conference of the Division of Social Sciences.* Washington, D.C.: Howard University Press, 1953. Pp. 143–146.

"Minority Side of Intercultural Relations." In *Education for Cultural Unity: Seventeenth Yearbook.*

California Elementary School Principals Association, n.d. Pp. 60–64.

CORRESPONDENCE AND MANUSCRIPTS

Alain Locke Collection. Papers, 1841–1954 (bulk 1898–1954). 220 Boxes. Washington, D.C.: Moorland-Spingarn Research Center, Howard University.

Alain Locke Papers. Collection 164–1 to 164–233. Prepared by Helen Rutt. Assisted by Joellen El-Bashir. Washington, D.C.: Manuscript Division, Moorland-Spingarn Research Center, Howard University, December 1993.

COLLECTED WORKS

The Critical Temper of Alain Locke: A Selection of His Essays on Art and Culture. Edited by Jeffrey C. Stewart. New York: Garland, 1983.

The Philosophy of Alain Locke: Harlem Renaissance and Beyond. Edited by Leonard Harris. Philadelphia: Temple University Press, 1989.

Race Contacts and Interracial Relations: Lectures on the Theory and Practice of Race. Edited by Jeffery C. Stewart. Washington, D. C.: Howard University Press, 1992.

BIBLIOGRAPHIES

Harris, Leonard. "Chronological Bibliography." In *The Philosophy of Alain Locke: Harlem Renaissance and Beyond.* Edited by Leonard Harris. Philadelphia: Temple University Press, 1989. Pp. 301–319.

Martin, Robert. "A Bibliography of the Writings of Alain Leroy Locke." In *The New Negro Thirty Years Afterward: Papers Contributed to the Sixteenth Annual Spring Conference ... April 20, 21, and 22, 1955.* Edited by Rayford Whittingham Logan, Eugene C. Holmes, and G. Franklin Edwards. Washington, D.C.: Howard University Press, 1956. Pp. 89–96.

Midgette, Lillian Avon. *A Bio-bibliography of Alain LeRoy Locke.* M.S.L.S. thesis. Atlanta: Atlanta University, 1963.

Stewart, Jeffrey. *Alain Locke: A Research Guide.* New York: Garland, 1988.

Tidwell, John Edgar and John Wright. "Alain Locke: A Comprehensive Bibliography." *Bulletin of Bibliography* 42, no. 2:95–104 (1985).

Tidwell, John Edgar and John Wright. "Alain Locke: A Comprehensive Bibliography of Published Writings." *Callaloo* 4:175–192 (February–October 1981).

CRITICAL AND BIOGRAPHICAL STUDIES

Akam, Everett H. "Community and Cultural Crisis: The 'Transfiguring Imagination' of Alain Locke." *American Literary History* 3, no. 2:255–276 (1991).

Braithwaite, William. "Alain Locke's Relationship to the Negro in American Literature." *Phylon* 18, no. 2:166–173 (1957). Reprinted in *Remembering the Harlem Renaissance.* Edited by Cary D. Wintz. New York: Garland, 1996. Pp. 420–427.

Braithwaite, William Stanley, Ralph J. Bunche, C. Glenn Carrington, W. E. B. Du Bois, Benjamin Karpman, Yervant H. Krikorian, and William Stuart Nelson. *Alain LeRoy Locke Funeral Orations Brochure, 1954.* In Rare Books and Manuscripts, University Libraries, Pennsylvania State University, University Park, Penn. 1954.

Buck, Christopher. "Alain Locke: Bahá'í Philosopher." *Bahá'í Studies Review* 10:7–49 (2001–2002).

Bunche, Ralph J., et al. "The Passing of Alain Leroy Locke." *Phylon* 15, no. 3:243–252 (1954).

Burgett, Paul Joseph. "Vindication as a Thematic Principle in Alain Locke's Writings on the Music of Black Americans." *The Harlem Renaissance: Revaluations.* Edited by Amritjit Singh, William S. Shiver, and Stanley Brodwin. New York: Garland, 1989. Pp. 139–157.

Fitchue, M. Anthony. "Locke and Du Bois: Two Major Black Voices Muzzled by Philanthropic Organizations." *Journal of Blacks in Higher Education* 14:111–116 (winter 1996–1997).

Fraser, Nancy. "Another Pragmatism: Alain Locke, Critical 'Race' Theory, and the Politics of Culture." In *The Revival of Pragmatism: New Essays on Social Thought, Law, and Culture.* Edited by Morris Dickstein. Durham, N.C.: Duke University Press, 1998. Pp. 157–175. Reprint: *The Critical Pragmatism of Alain Locke: A Reader on Value Theory, Aesthetics, Community, Culture, Race, and Education.* Edited by Leonard Harris. Lanham, Md.: Rowman & Littlefield, 1999. Pp. 3–20.

Gyant, LaVerne. "Contributors to Adult Education:

Booker T. Washington, George Washington Carver, Alain L. Locke, and Ambrose Caliver." *Journal of Black Studies* 19:97–110 (September 1988).

Harris, Leonard, ed. *The Critical Pragmatism of Alain Locke: A Reader on Value Theory, Aesthetics, Community, Culture, Race, and Education.* Lanham, Md.: Rowman & Littlefield, 1999.

Harris, Leonard. "Locke, Alain Leroy." *American National Biography.* Edited by John A. Garraty and Mark Carnes. New York: Oxford University Press, 1999. Vol. 13, pp. 796–798.

———. "Alain Locke: Community and Citizenship." *Modern Schoolman* 74:337–346 (May 1997).

———. "Identity: Alain Locke's Atavism." *Transactions of the Charles S. Pierce Society* 24:65–83 (winter 1988).

———. "Rendering the Subtext: Subterranean Deconstructive Project." In *The Philosophy of Alain Locke: Harlem Renaissance and Beyond.* Edited by Leonard Harris. Philadelphia: Temple University Press, 1989. Pp. 279–289.

———. "Rendering the Text." In *The Philosophy of Alain Locke.* Edited by Leonard Harris. Philadelphia: Temple University Press, 1989. Pp. 3–27.

Helbling, Mark. "Alain Locke: Ambivalence and Hope." *Phylon* 40:291–300 (September 1979).

Holmes, Eugene. "Alain LeRoy Locke and the Adult Education Movement." *Journal of Negro Education* 34, no. 1:5–10 (1965).

———. "Alain Locke and the New Negro Movement." *Negro American Literature Forum* 2:60–68 (autumn 1968).

Hutchinson, George B. "The Whitman Legacy and the Harlem Renaissance." In *Walt Whitman: The Centennial Essays.* Edited by Ed Folsom. Iowa City: University of Iowa Press, 1994. Pp. 201–216.

Kallen, H. M. "Alain Locke and Cultural Pluralism." *Journal of Philosophy* 54:119–127 (February 28, 1957).

Logan, Rayford Wittingham, Eugene C. Holmes, and G. Franklin Edwards, eds. *The New Negro Thirty Years Afterward; Papers Contributed to the Sixteenth Annual Spring Conference ... April 20, 21, and 22, 1955.* Washington, D.C.: Howard University Press, 1956.

Long, Richard. "The Genesis of Locke's *The New Negro.*" *Black World* 25, no. 4:14–20 (1976).

Lott, Tommy Lee. "Alain LeRoy Locke." In *Encyclopedia of Aesthetics.* Vol. 3. Edited by Michael P. Kelly. New York: Oxford University Press, 1998. Pp. 160–165.

———. "Du Bois and Locke on the Scientific Study of the Negro." *Boundary 2: An International Journal of Literature and Culture* 27, no. 3:135–152 (2000).

———. "Nationalism and Pluralism in Alain Locke's Social Philosophy." In *Defending Diversity: Contemporary Philosophical Perspectives on Pluralism and Multiculturalism.* Edited by Lawrence Foster and Patricia Herzog. Amherst: University of Massachusetts Press, 1994. Pp. 103–119.

Mason, Ernest. "Alain Locke." In *Dictionary of Literary Biography.* Vol. 51: *Afro-American Writers from the Harlem Renaissance to 1940.* Edited by Trudier Harris. Detroit, Mich.: Gale Research, 1987. Pp. 313–321.

Mason, Ernest. "Alain Locke on Race and Race Relations." *Phylon* 40:342–350 (December 1979).

Mason, Ernest. "Alain Locke's Social Philosophy." *World Order* 13:25–34 (winter 1979).

Napier, Winston. "Affirming Critical Conceptualism: Harlem Renaissance Aesthetics and the Formation of Alain Locke's Social Philosophy." *Massachusetts Review* 39:93–112 (spring 1998).

Ochillo, Yvonne. "The Race-Consciousness of Alain Locke." *Phylon* 47:173–181 (September 1986).

Salley, Columbus. "Alain Locke." In his *The Black 100: A Ranking of the Most Influential African-Americans, Past and Present.* Revised and Updated. Secaucus, N.J.: Citadel Press, 1999. Pp. 137–139.

Scruggs, Charles. "Alain Locke and Walter White: Their Struggle for Control of the Harlem Renaissance." *Black American Literature Forum* 14:91–99 (autumn 1980).

Stafford, Douglas K. "Alain Locke: The Child, the Man, and the People." *Journal of Negro Education* 30:25–34 (winter 1961).

Stewart, Jeffrey C. *A Biography of Alain Locke: Philosopher of the Harlem Renaissance, 1886–1930.* Ph.D. Dissertation. Cambridge: Yale University, 1979.

————. "A Black Aesthete at Oxford." *Massachusetts Review* 34:411–428. (autumn 1993).

————. Introduction. In Alain Locke's *Race Contacts and Interracial Relations: Lectures on the Theory and Practice of Race.* Edited by Jeffrey C. Stewart. Washington, D.C.: Howard University Press, 1992. Pp. xix–lix.

Washington, Johnny. *Alain Locke and Philosophy: A Quest for Cultural Pluralism.* Westport, Conn.: Greenwood, 1986.

Washington, Johnny. *A Journey into the Philosophy of Alain Locke.* Westport, Conn.: Greenwood, 1994.

Watts, Eric King. "African American Ethos and Hermeneutical Rhetoric: An Exploration of Alain Locke's *The New Negro.*" *Quarterly Journal of Speech* 88, no.1:19–32 (2002).

Weithman, Paul J. "Deliberative Democracy and Community in Alain Locke." *Modern Schoolman* 74:347–353 (May 1997).

Wright, John S. "Alain Leroy Locke." *Encyclopedia of African-American Culture and History.* Vol. 3. Edited by Jack Salzman, David Lionel Smith, and Cornel West. New York: MacMillan Library Reference, 1996. Pp. 1641–1643.

— CHRISTOPHER BUCK

Norman Maclean

(1902–1990)

"A FEW THINGS WELL"

"*I* KNEW WHEN I started that it was too late for me to be a writer, that all I could hope to do was write a few things well," said Norman Fitzroy Maclean at age seventy-nine, speaking with Pete Dexter in an interview from the log cabin he had built with his father in 1922 in Seeley Lake, Montana. At the time of the interview, Maclean was trying to complete a manuscript about the fire that had killed thirteen Forest Service Smokejumpers in 1949 during a forest fire in Mann Gulch in western Montana. In 1981 when Dexter's profile appeared in *Esquire,* only five years had passed since the publication of *A River Runs Through It and Other Stories* (1976), a book that is now accepted as a classic in American literature. Before that Maclean had published only a smattering of critical essays derived from his years of teaching Shakespeare and Romantic poetry at the University of Chicago, where he taught for forty-three years. Yet based on this slim collection (two stories and a "novella," as it was then termed), his reputation was growing.

The Mann Gulch manuscript, *Young Men and Fire,* was published posthumously in 1992 after it had been revised by Maclean's son, John, and the editors at the University of Chicago Press. It won the 1992 National Book Critics Circle Award. By the time of his death at the age of eighty-seven on August 2, 1990, Maclean had not only written a few things well; he had clearly earned the right to be considered a writer.

While Maclean's interest in writing came from several sources, at its center were his father's early lessons. John Norman Maclean was a Presbyterian minister who had moved his family from Scotland to Nova Scotia and then to Missoula, Montana, in 1909, less than thirty years after the railroad opened Montana to homesteaders. John Maclean taught his son Norman to read and write. In his essay "The Woods, Books, and Truant Officers" (1977) Maclean describes his father's methods:

> Being a Scot, he tried to make me write economically. He tried to make me write primarily with nouns and verbs, and not to fool around with adjectives and adverbs, not even when I wanted to write soul stuff. At nine o'clock, when the first period began, he would assign me a 200-word theme; at the end of the ten o'clock period he would tell me, "Now rewrite it in 100 words"; and he concluded the morning by telling me, "Now, throw it away."

By noon the two would be walking in the woods, often with Norman's younger brother, Paul, learning the names of trees and flowers and especially learning to fish. Not just to fish—to fish with flies. Maclean's early years were spent learning the ways of nature as much as the ways of books. When he was fourteen he began working summers for the U.S. Forest Service, spending much of his time in logging camps and lookout towers, as well as fighting fires. In fact, he had decided to make his career in the Forest Service. "We were all young, but we all worked in the woods in the summer, and I don't think you can be a Montana story-teller unless you have worked in the woods or on ranches," says Maclean in a speech entitled "Montana Memory" (1977).

The Bible, his father's sermons, his early forays into nature, his later forays into the logging camps, then later hanging around pool halls and streetcorners with his friends—everything conspired to teach him the art of storytelling. And storytelling, as Maclean saw it, is a Western art; it derives from the oral tradition in a frontier world full of adventure, a place that generates the comic tall tale: "Comedy is a Western way of playing down the big thing." In the world of Maclean's youth history could be seen in the making. Montana had been a state for only thirteen years when he was born, and the Forest Service as an official entity was younger than he was. As an old man Maclean described his stories as attempting something more than mere storytelling: "They especially try to leave a record of how we did things in the world just before this one—the world of hand and horse and hand tools and horse tools. The history in these stories, then, is a kind of a history of hand craft, and the chief characters are experts with their hands—expert packers, expert sawyers, expert fishermen. ...."

In 1920, Norman enrolled in Dartmouth College in Hanover, New Hampshire—a far cry from the wilderness of Montana, yet rural enough that he could spend much time out of doors. There he studied under Robert Frost, among others, taking from him his fierce independence of spirit and his atypical teaching habits. After receiving his degree in 1924 and spending an additional two years at Dartmouth as a teaching assistant, Maclean returned in 1926 to Montana (while his brother attended Dartmouth) where he worked with the Forest Service for two years. During this time he met the woman who was to be his wife, Jessie Burns, the Scotch-Irish daughter of another frontier family. In 1928, Maclean went east again, this time to the University of Chicago where he began graduate studies in English and, at the same time, served as a graduate assistant—a job teaching three sections of compo-

sition, which, as he described it, entailed spending all weekend in bed grading a hundred papers each week. He returned to Montana in the summers and in 1931, when he was promoted to instructor, he and Jessie were married with John Maclean performing the ceremony.

Jessie and Norman had two children, a daughter, Jean, and a son, John Norman, born in 1942 and 1943 at the height of World War II when Norman was engaged in at least three positions at the university, serving not only in the classroom but as dean of students and director of the Institute for Military Studies which trained students for positions in the military. The marriage was stable, lasting until Jessie's death in 1968, and Maclean credits her with, among many other things, teaching him to appreciate the beauty of Chicago: "You can't be provincial about beauty."

In 1932 he received the Quantrell Award for Excellence in Undergraduate Teaching, and against all tradition the university bestowed this award on him twice more before his retirement in 1973. From 1963 to 1973, Maclean was the William Rainey Harper Professor of English Literature. Thus the world of the university provided him with two other important influences on his writing: literature and the teaching of literature. How one teaches literature is integrally linked to how one reads literature and, although Maclean was exposed to any number of critical approaches over his tenure at the University of Chicago, he was primarily interested in the art of storytelling, which translates into the craft by which a writer allows his story to unfold. In his essay "The Pure and the Good: On Baseball and Backpacking" (1979) Maclean says, "I believe that one must know something about craftsmanship to come to know and love an art in its purity. ... Even the ordinary baseball fan operates on these assumptions."

Maclean's best-known work, "A River Runs Through It," is the story of his brother, Paul—

"the tragedy of my brother who was one of the finest fishermen in the northwest, a reporter for the *Helena Independent,* a big gambler at Hot Springs, and who knows what else." This is a true story—of his brother's art and his mysteries—and Maclean felt custodial responsibilities for its authenticity. When offered a movie contract that would allow the studio to take creative license, he responded with ferocity: "Not with my family, my stories." Eventually a movie, produced posthumously by Robert Redford and carefully monitored by the co-producer Annick Smith, did justice to the story—and to Maclean's real, remembered family. It was almost as though he could foretell the imminent controversies surrounding the emerging genre of "creative nonfiction" when, at the end of the story, his father raises the salient question:

> "You like to tell true stories, don't you?" he asked, and I answered, "Yes, I like to tell stories that are true."

"A RIVER RUNS THROUGH IT": THE STORY

> A man has to have a lot of reasons for writing his first book after becoming 70, and at least a couple of them should be good in case at that age the book isn't. I have one I am sure is pretty good. Before I die and disintegrate altogether, I wanted to put some of the pieces of myself together, and I have some pretty big splits in my personality. We talk as if the problem of identity is a problem of youth—but we always have problems of trying to find out who we are, and life is very persistent in splitting us into pieces. Yet we all yearn—if I may use a theological phrase—to achieve some kind of unity of the soul somewhere along the way.
> —"Montana Memory"

So it was that Norman Maclean set out in his seventies to discover the meanings of his own experience and to lock the pieces of the puzzle into place. The story of the publication of the resulting book is the stuff of legend. Over a period of two years it was rejected by several major publishing houses. One editor, finding the content too "western," said in a dismissive letter, "This book has trees in it." Eventually the University of Chicago Press brought out the book, its first and only publication of "fiction." At first by word of mouth, then by virtue of stunning reviews, *A River Runs Through It and Other Stories* began to be noticed. It was nominated for the Pulitzer Prize in 1977, but the prize was not awarded in what was termed a "lean year" for fiction. Later, when the book had become famous, the editor who initially rejected it wrote to ask if Maclean would send him his next book. Not one to mince words Maclean wrote back, "If the time should ever come when you are the last publisher in the world and I am the last author, then that will be the end of books, as we know them."

Over the decades since its publication *A River Runs Through It and Other Stories* has never been out of print (and in fact has been reprinted in several deluxe editions, one with engravings by the celebrated artist Barry Moser), has been translated into a dozen languages, and has sold well over a million copies. Known today as a classic in twentieth-century American literature, it has a life in the classroom and with the common reader.

The title story, though centered in the summer of 1937, encompasses a lifetime. It begins with the famous opening line, "In our family, there was no clear line between religion and fly fishing," proceeds to question that statement, and ends by demonstrating its validity. Along the way the reader learns the basics of fly-fishing, including its underlying psychology, gleans a fair amount of knowledge about Montana's geology and topography and some of its history, ponders what it is to love and be loved, laughs out loud at moments of high comedy, and grieves at the story's inherent—and inevitable—tragedy. For all its religious terminology (in later years conventional religion meant nothing to Maclean), he did not intend it as religious allegory. He entered its terrain, as writers do, to discover the line between religion and fly-fishing, to brush up against the limits of faith, and if possible to reconcile what he knew with what he could never know.

The tale begins by teaching us (as young Norman and Paul were taught by their father) the elements of casting. So the story begins with youth and the knowledge that Paul is a "natural." The father and other son are good, but Paul becomes a master. And Paul is willing to bet on himself, determining all subsequent employment by the amount of time it will give him for fly-fishing. Norman becomes the responsible teacher, Paul the flamboyant journalist, the gambler, the womanizer, the good-natured rogue, the one with the mysterious darker side. Soon we are deep into the summers of their early adulthood. Their father is less able to keep up with them, and the brothers go out to fish the Big Blackfoot alone.

Thus we learn about the origins of the rough terrain that constitutes their favorite fishing spot—and about the Big Blackfoot River that runs through it. We learn what it takes to read the water, to see where the fish are biting, to determine what kind of fly works best in the given conditions. In each scene, we see Paul and his art at work. The descriptions of nature illuminate Paul's mastery of it; the descriptions of Paul make him a part of the natural beauty. One of the best examples—one that culminates in religious imagery—is the description of Paul swimming out to stand on a rock in the middle of the river in order to get a better perch:

> Below him was the multitudinous river, and, where the rock had parted it around him, big-grained vapor rose. The mini-molecules of water left in the wake of his line made momentary loops of gossamer, disappearing so rapidly in the rising big-grained vapor that they had to be retained in memory to be visualized as loops. The spray emanating from him was finer-grained still and enclosed him in a halo of himself.

Again and again we see Paul as the beautiful object neither his father nor his brother can quite understand. These scenes are rendered in great detail, while Paul's other sides are given only glimpses, as when, fairly early in the book, Norman is called to come pick him up at the county jail. The desk sergeant asks, "Can't you help him straighten out?" to which Norman replies, "I don't know what to do." Norman finds his brother in the drunk tank with an Indian woman, a Northern Cheyenne known to be trouble, but as "beautiful a dancer as [Paul] was a fly caster." They are both drunk and incoherent. Paul, standing near the jailhouse window, knows just enough of what is happening to cover his face with his "enlarged casting hand."

Often the dark side is tempered with the humorous one, as when Norman and Paul are inveigled to take Norman's brother-in-law, Neal, fishing with them. Neal is a lazy bait fisherman, a term of supreme contempt, and the brothers find him despicable. Yet Norman has no choice but to honor his wife's mother's wishes. One of the more hilarious scenes occurs when Neal has brought the whore Old Rawhide along. The brothers fish while Neal manages to steal the beer they have left cooling in the rapids. They return to see the two sleeping naked on a sandbar, sunburned to the point of injury. The whore's buttocks have LO tattooed on one cheek, VE on the other, and Paul kicks her where the letters meet. Neal simply spells disaster for the brothers, who take him back to the "three Scottish women" who will nurse him back to health.

Late in the book we learn about fishing different kinds of water, and at the end we learn how to hook and play a fish. We learn by watching Paul at his competitive best. Norman and his father stand above him on the bank. From this angle the scene appears at a distance, as though Paul were an abstraction, no longer an individual but a part of something larger:

Then the universe stepped on its third rail. The wand jumped convulsively as it made contact with the magic current of the world. The wand tried to jump out of the man's right hand. … Everything seemed electrically charged but electrically unconnected. Electrical sparks appeared here and there on the river. … Although the act involved a big man and a big fish, it looked more like children playing. … The man put the wand down, got on his hands and knees in the sand, and, like an animal, circled another animal and waited.

Before it is over, Maclean, as though with a zoom lens, closes in until the man again has a name, is once more familiar: "This was the last fish we were ever to see Paul catch. My father and I talked about this moment several times later, and whatever our other feelings, we always felt it fitting that, when we saw him catch his last fish, we never saw the fish but only the artistry of the fisherman."

Within a page Paul is dead. He has been beaten to death with the butt of a revolver—a sordid back-alley death that left all the bones in his casting hand broken and unanswered questions abounding. The death is made more tragic by its proximity to the moment of transcendence.

The story has two tenses, so to speak: the present tense of the telling—a time in which an old man speaks from knowledge and hindsight—and the past tense of the story he tells. Because the story is told retrospectively, the end is present from the beginning. Only six pages into the book Maclean states, "[Paul] did not want any big brother advice or money or help, and, in the end, I could not help him." Paul's death is foreshadowed in this way throughout the telling, suggesting that what is important is not the events themselves, but what to make of them.

Whether Maclean discovered who he was in the telling of his tale remains unclear. The story ends in the present tense: "Now nearly all those I loved and did not understand when I was young are dead, but I still reach out to them."

The lack of understanding is as compelling as the love. Both are remembered with equal intensity. But it is clear that Maclean did achieve a kind of unity. The "reaching" recapitulates the tale. He goes on to say: "Then in the Arctic half-light of the canyon, all existence fades to a being with my soul and memories and the sounds of the Big Blackfoot River and a four-count rhythm and the hope that a fish will rise." The final five sentences move beyond the story, into the mystery:

> Eventually, all things merge into one, and a river runs through it. The river was cut by the world's great flood and runs over rocks from the basement of time. On some of the rocks are timeless raindrops. Under the rocks are the words, and some of the words are theirs.
>
> I am haunted by waters.

"A RIVER RUNS THROUGH IT": THE CRAFT

No discussion of Maclean's classic would be complete without noting its craft. The style is deceptive; it tends to ramble, taking its time to get to the point, and yet every digression deepens the complexities. The voice is conversational, capturing the rhythms of speech and yet veering toward something more formal—the accentual rhythms of poetry.

Maclean was keenly aware of rhythm—much of his teaching career had been devoted to the metrical craft of poetry, especially in Shakespeare and the Psalms. Attentive readers soon notice the cadence of "A River Runs Through It." In sentences that alternate rhythmical patterns, much like the rhythmical patterns in fly-flishing, Maclean captures some of the sonorous beauty of the King James Bible and the dramatic flair of Shakespeare's finest plays. In "The Woods, Books, and Truant Officers," he states three tenets about rhythm and prose: (1) that "all prose should be rhythmical," and (2) that "one should practically never be consciously aware of the rhythms of prose," and

(3) that there are exceptions to the second rule. The fourth axiom is that there are places in prose writing that readers expect rhythm and would feel its absence. That no such void occurs in "A River Runs Through It" attests to Maclean's sure sense of how to fill readerly expectations.

Maclean the teacher often spoke of quantitative and grammatical rhythms. The quantitative is recurrent patterns of speech groups of similar length. The grammatical rhythm involves repetition of sentence structures—noun, verb, predicate, in that order. Often this is emphasized by repetitive vocabulary as well. The trick is to establish the rhythm and provide variants at the same time. A good example can be found in the following progression of sentences: "Either we don't know what part to give or maybe we don't like to give any part of ourselves. Then, more often than not, the part that is needed is not wanted. And even more often, we do not have the part that is needed."

Beyond Maclean's astute attention to rhythm is his attention to the overall structure of the piece. A key element in the structure is the dual nature of the narrator, combining youthful observation with retrospective reflection. Thus the outcome is never in question, since it is the given from which the story proceeds. Foreshadowing is instrumental. Maclean tells us over and over that Paul refuses to be helped. So we look for moments when he might be receptive or for moments his brother might have missed an opportunity. The reader thereby participates in the drama from which he has been excluded as surely as Norman was excluded some forty years prior to his telling of the tale. The reader enters the mind of the man who is thinking back, trying to fit the pieces of his life together. We are given what he knows and what he wants to understand.

Maclean uses humor to undercut and underscore the pathos. He orchestrates comic relief, peppering the story with levity. These scenes are rarely essential to the basic story, but they are developed with gusto, and they give readers some breathing room. Often the humor is turned back on the narrator, who makes a wry comment about himself, noting his own naïveté. In an often deadpan voice, he reveals his wit, as when he says, "A man is at a disadvantage talking to a woman as tall as he is, and I had tried long and hard to overcome this handicap." Thus Maclean humanizes the teller of the tale.

In numerous instances Maclean highlights the humor of a situation with brief slapstick. When the brothers encounter Norman's brother-in-law naked with the prostitute and chase them away from the riverbank, the scene concludes:

> Even Neal tried to pull himself together. He tried to put on some clothes before the women saw him. He piled his clothes outside the car, and, when he couldn't find his underwear, he started trying to get into his pants, but he stumbled and kept stumbling. He held his pants out in front of him and tried to catch up to them. He was stumbling so fast he was running after them.

At other times he reaches for the comedic by turning negatives into positives. He is especially deft in doing so within a sentence, giving it the effect of a one-liner. Again in reference to the hapless prostitute Maclean says, "After she got near home, she stopped several times to look back, and Paul and I didn't like what we couldn't hear she was saying."

A careful orchestration of contrasts further characterizes Maclean's craft: good and evil, wilderness and civilization, male and female, youth and age, nature and religion, salvation and damnation, idea and emotion. And contrasts lie within these contrasts, so that, for example, the women in the story fall into two groups, those who love and sustain family and the whores who, for all their energy and strength, represent an unhealthy alternative. Yet those who nurture can also smother and emasculate, and so the subdivisions multiply. Religion, too, is presented with differentiations: the father's is based on quiet faith, the Word coming from first principles; the son's is tested, more secular, finally aesthetic. And Paul, who is the book's figure of saving grace as well as its emblem of the Fall, remains mysteriously silent on all counts.

Coursing through the whole is a concentrated precision of instruction. "A River Runs Through It" might substitute for a manual on fly-fishing. Each aspect of fly-fishing is treated separately so that the reader learns by stages what is necessary in order to comprehend what comes next. Almost every scene depends on prior knowledge; the tale is so tightly built that nothing can be extracted to stand on its own. In part that derives from Maclean's intuitive understanding of psychology. One needs to have met Norman's mother-in-law and wife in order to know precisely why his brother-in-law's unhappy episodes inevitably backfire and the blame falls neatly on Norman and Paul. One needs to have seen Paul deflect offers of help in order to feel Norman's inability to say more. Maclean develops the story in a way that makes the reader aware of every component, while an element of surprise still awaits in the end. The surprise comes not from what happens (the reader already knows this), nor from the response to what happens (the reader can predict how the author will feel), but from the depth of the reader's response to what he already knows has happened.

The tragedy, then, is threefold, and each strand weaves throughout as an integral part of the story. The first is Paul's death—the stuff of tragedy, the young and beautiful and damned, brought down by his own intemperance and recklessness. The second is Norman's inability to prevent that death, his knowledge that his brother doesn't want his help. Time after time, we see Paul deflect and deny until his self-imposed isolation appears in opposition to his natural grace on the water. Filled with reticence, Norman comes face to face with the limits of love. If he is to love his brother well, he must grant him the right to his own life—and to his own death. This is the dark knowledge at the center of the book, a knowledge that Maclean, for all his eloquence, never quite articulates but allows his reader to confront. The third tragedy provides the overriding impulse behind the book—the expressed hope that writing might bridge the gaps and supply the answers. The fact that, no matter how many ways he looks at the past, the old man telling the story will remain locked in "Arctic light," haunted by the waters of memory and desire, establishes the book as a definitive statement on the human condition.

"A RIVER RUNS THROUGH IT": THE THEMES AND MEANINGS

For all its easygoing tone "A River Runs Through It" takes on the dimensions of a classic. Scholars have often compared the piece to Ernest Hemingway's "Big Two-Hearted River" (1925) and to Henry David Thoreau's *A Week on the Concord and Merrimack Rivers* (1849) and *Walden* (1854). Following the tradition of Herman Melville, James Fenimore Cooper, Stephen Crane, Jack London, even of Lewis and Clark, it evokes a clear strain in American literature: adventure, the wilderness, individualism, an untamed natural world that offers transcendence. "A River Runs Through It" also stands as an early exemplar of another type of literature—the nature writing prevalent in contemporary literature of the West—found in the work of Barry Lopez, Ivan Doig, Rick Bass, Gretel Ehrlich, Mary Clearman Blew, and a host of other writers who have established a distinctive set of concerns.

The story is, in Maclean's words, "a love poem to my family." It asks the age-old question: am I my brother's keeper? Long before the reader can understand its significance, Paul tells Norman a story about driving home drunk one dark night, "feeling in need of a friend to keep him awake, when suddenly a jackrabbit jumped on to the road and started running with the headlights." The rabbit, bathed in moonlight, keeps a steady pace with the car, taking on legendary dimensions. "I don't know how to explain what happened next," Paul says "but there was a right-angle turn in this section-line road, and the rabbit saw it, and I didn't." With the humorous twist of a tall tale, Paul diffuses the reality of his wrecked car and the threat to his own life. Only retrospectively does his "need of a friend" take on significance.

Later, when Norman tentatively offers assistance and Paul curtly turns him down, Paul softens the blow by talking about the unfortunate brother-in-law, Neal. "Maybe what he likes is somebody trying to help him," Paul says, probably talking as much about himself as about Neal. Norman is forced to conclude that love may not be a saving grace. He makes a clear decision not to interfere. Near the end he outlines for his father what he learned: "you can love completely without complete understanding."

The tone is elegiac, and the story is an elegy. The writer mourns for more than a lost brother. He looks back to an Edenic past, a pristine river filled with fish. There was beauty in that world and beauty in the men who could, however briefly, tame it. At stake is a state of grace, seen as Wordsworthian "spots of time" in which eternity is "compressed into a moment." Norman has brief intimations of such a state:

> I sat there and forgot and forgot, until what remained was the river that went by and I who watched. On the river the heat mirages danced with each other and then they danced through each other and then they joined hands and danced around each other. Eventually the watcher joined the river, and there was only one of us.

Then in a wry summation worthy of Twain he quips: "I believe it was the river."

Not surprisingly critics have discovered in this short piece the religious and philosophical underpinnings of Western literature. The theological argument—begun in the first sentence—has to do with the place of humanity in the universe, with fate versus free will. Maclean's father, a devout Calvinist, holds to the primacy of an all-knowing, all-powerful God, and to the fallen state of human beings. Maclean seems to contemplate a more benign deity and the concept of free will. The argument takes place as father and son wait on the riverbank for Paul to catch his limit:

> "What have you been reading?" I asked. "A book," he said. It was on the ground on the other side of him. So I would not have to bother to look over his knees to see it, he said, "A good book."
>
> Then he told me, "In the part I was reading it says the Word was in the beginning, and that's right. I used to think water was first, but if you listen carefully you will hear that the words are underneath the water."
>
> "That's because you are a preacher first, and then a fisherman," I told him. "If you ask Paul, he will tell you that the words are formed out of water."
>
> "No," my father said, "you are not listening carefully. The water runs over the words. Paul will tell you the same thing.

Maclean's tightly-woven narrative accommodates its many strands well. They flicker like glints of sun on water, revealing themselves incompletely. Norman describes the three aspects of any good fishing hole—the rapids or head, the big turn (the pool), and the quiet, shallow tail. "Of course, at the time I did not know that stories of life are often more like rivers than books." Thus literature, too, becomes a theme: the power of literature to create unity.

Rich in its confluence of themes and allusions "A River Runs Through It" positions itself at the center of American literature's traditional concerns. It raises the spectres of history, philosophy, religion, culture (the forces of civilization), and at the same time, it offers up the challenge of the frontier. Wilderness plays a dual role. At once physical and metaphysical, it provides the basis for the realism of the story even as it poses large questions about the nature of the universe. "All things merge into one, and a river runs through it." The river that runs through "it" is both real and metaphorical, recognizable in either guise; yet the "it" the river runs through is nebulous and undefined. The implied referent is missing, and never more tellingly than in the title, which establishes the philosophical nature of the piece before the book is even opened.

Maclean's enigmatic "it" has much in common with the most mysterious line in Robert Frost's "Desert Places": "The woods around it have it—it is theirs." Whatever "it" is, it does not invite people to partake of its essence. Frost goes on to provide a snow-ridden context in which the woods take on deeper meanings, smothering the animals "in their lairs," creating a wintry loneliness of the soul. Maclean's solitary "it" feels more inclusive, more open and available to humankind, assuming, as it does, that we understand instinctively that which cannot be pinned down by theory or theology. It encompasses everything: river, wilderness, time, confusion, desire, family, love, death. And fly-fishing.

The universe persists; if there is redemption, it resides in the image of perfection: "[Paul] would complete this grand circle four or five times, creating an immensity of motion which culminated in nothing if you did not know, even if you could not see, that now somewhere out there a small fly was washing itself on a wave. Shockingly, immensity would return as the Big Blackfoot and the air above it became iridescent with the arched sides of a great Rainbow."

AND OTHER STORIES

Two stories, one short and one long, follow "A River Runs Through It." Neither has the depth or breadth of the title story, but they provide background material and set the scene, so to speak. Written first, they served as trial runs. The shorter is set in the logging camps where Maclean worked summers while he was in graduate school. "Logging and Pimping and 'Your Pal, Jim'" establishes the physical world of the "working stiff"—lumberjacks, cowboys, gamblers—and the physicality that accompanies it. Norman is chosen by Jim to "gyppo" with him for a summer: that is, to elect to be paid by the number of trees cut down rather than to receive a monthly wage. Only the hardiest could profit from this arrangement, and Jim pushes Norman beyond his capacities. Jim becomes not only his "partner" but his nemesis. Norman begins to hate Jim with the slow, smoldering hate born of initial admiration.

Jim—an early, wilderness version of a Communist who sees through and hates the Company—stirs up the men by showing them ways that they are being exploited. But his physical and mental prowess keep him an outsider. Norman, too, is an outsider, doomed to observe the dynamics of the camp even as he tries to participate in them. So he spends his summer sabotaging his own best interests, altering the rhythms of the saw slightly, pausing a bit too long, reaching for Jim's wedge, anything to throw Jim off his stride without being detected. The summer becomes a battle of wits.

The story reaches no real denouement; it simply ends when the two part ways, except for occasional letters that Norman receives from Jim. Nothing is resolved, and the reader does not quite understand Norman's antipathy for Jim. The narrator himself seems a bit hazy about just what it was he didn't like, but he knew he didn't like Jim. As fiction the story fails: no real plot, no character development, no climax. But as storytelling it instructs in the art of logging, depicts the conditions in the camps, reveals the thoughts and motivation of the narrator, speculates, reminisces, lingers over the mysteries.

The narrator remembers his former self with good humor and not a little mystification.

Thinking back to his youth, the same narrator tackles an even earlier period in his life in the longer story, "USFS 1919: The Ranger, the Cook, and a Hole in the Sky" (USFS stands for United States Forest Service, and the summer of 1919 is when the events take place). Here, too, we see the interplay between an older man's consciousness and the boy's perception: "I don't suppose Bill would have sent me up to the lookout if he knew how much I needed a couple of days of rest, a thought that gave me a good deal of pleasure." Over the interval in time, the teller can see the whole picture while, for the purposes of the story, the boy remains naive.

Firefighters were often only drunks dragged from barstools, drifters enlisted for a few days of hard work on the line. The head ranger needed to be as tough as they were, and the cowboy, Bill Bell, fit the description. For a summer he stands in as a father figure. Bill is a demon with a lariat, can tie any knot and balance a pack on a mule by instinct, knows how to fight fires in a variety of circumstances, but cannot play cards. The cook, an ornery, hot-tempered cardsharp, becomes Norman's nemesis for the summer.

The stage is set for competition, even altercation, but before things can blow up in the camp, Norman is banished to the high lookout station where he watches over the mountain range for evidence of fire and savors his imposed solitude. When he returns to camp, a plan has been hatched. Everyone will stake some of his wages for the cook to clean out the gamblers in town. They have no doubt the cook can do this, though they worry a bit about their roles in the ensuing fight. Norman perceives that he will be the first one hit since his job is to rake in the money. Everything goes according to plan, including the rather grisly fight, leaving each of the men with a $7.20 profit from the encounter.

Underlying the story, though, is the narrator's growing awareness that he is in this life, but he is not of it. The early weeks spent fighting a large fire teach him something about his own resiliency, and the later weeks in isolation restore his confidence. The solitary twenty-eight-mile walk into town leaves him dehydrated but unconstrained. Bill looks out for him when he is wounded in the fight and asks for his help with the pack animals the next morning. Norman shows up after staking the destitute cook to the price of a train ticket to Butte and promises to work for Bill the next summer. But as he watches Bill retrace his steps back into the Bitterroots, he senses that he is watching an alternative life fade away. By the next summer, when he returns from college, he will be working with the engineering department on a mapping crew. Someone else will fight the fires, and someone else will do the gambling.

As fiction the story has too much the feel of something recollected rather than created. In a critical article on *A River Runs Through It and Other Stories*, Wallace Stegner says, "The stories are so frankly autobiographical that one suspects he hasn't even bothered to alter names." Maclean confirms this fact in subsequent talks in which he describes the ranger—a man named Bill Bell—along with others in the camp and on the fire line. Even the narrator suspects that the ending is anticlimactic. With a finality that foreshadows the ending of his next, great story, his last paragraphs speak directly to the reader:

Everything that was to happen had happened and everything that was to be seen had gone. It was now one of those moments when nothing remains but an opening in the sky and a story—and maybe something of a poem. Anyway, as you possibly remember, there are these lines in front of the story:

And then he thinks he knows
The hills where his life rose ...
These words are now part of the story.

The divide is complete. Maclean's life rose in the mountains of Montana, but he was unable to inhabit completely the ethos of that life. Maybe it was his "Presbyterian father" giving voice to his misgivings just before he landed his first punch. Maybe it was the rattlesnake he almost didn't see. Maybe it was the way Bill Bell could balance a pack. Whatever it was, Norman will resist the very elements to which Paul is fatally drawn. The boy of "USFS 1919" will go east and when he returns he will be the young man of "A River Runs Through It."

YOUNG MEN AND FIRE

After publication of *A River Runs Through It and Other Stories* when he was seventy-four, Maclean started work on his book about the famous Mann Gulch fire in which thirteen elite young Smokejumpers perished. He spent the last decade of his writing life perusing Forest Service reports and documents; he interviewed the two remaining survivors of the jump, walked the forbidding terrain where the fire overtook the men, studied contemporary techniques for putting out forest fires, spoke with rangers and scientists. Thirty years after its tragic outcome, the fire was still controversial; there were suggestions that evidence had been suppressed or altered. Because the deaths had sparked threats of lawsuits, Maclean wanted to do a thorough job of explaining what had happened on August 5, 1949, and why. Having worked on it for ten years—until he became too ill in 1987 to continue—Maclean produced a fine piece of investigative journalism.

Young Men and Fire has its roots in those first three stories Maclean wrote. The Mann Gulch fire is mentioned almost exactly half way through "A River Runs Through It," and the description of how a fire can "crown" found in "USFS 1919" is a practice run for the expanded explanation found in *Young Men and Fire*. In the intervening years Maclean had been asked

to give several talks and lectures, and some of them centered around Montana history, especially the history in which he had participated. He had been in on mopping up the Mann Gulch fire, and this particular piece of history had haunted Maclean for years. He felt he had the practical knowledge to put the pieces of the puzzle together—a task not unlike the one he had claimed for his first book.

> Although young men died like squirrels in Mann Gulch, the Mann Gulch fire should not end there, smoke drifting away and leaving terror without consolation of explanation, and controversy without lasting settlement. ... So this story is a test of its own belief—that in this cockeyed world there are shapes and designs, if only we have some curiosity, training, and compassion and take care not to lie or be sentimental.

Again Maclean teaches his reader what he will need to know: the nature of fire under different conditions and over different terrains, the effect of the weather, the function and application of tools, the training and preparation of the men. He imparts the necessary information with precision so that when the "blowup" occurs the reader can experience the full drama. For this purpose Maclean enlists the help of several experts, foremost among them the fire behavior scientist Harry T. Gisborne whose analysis in the 1950s of blowups made him legendary. Gisborne himself had become a victim of the tragedy, for it was on a final trip to Mann Gulch to test his theories that he suffered a heart attack near the top of the ridge. Another was a young ranger named Laird Robinson who became Maclean's friend and companion. Together they made four trips into the remote gulch in search of its mysteries.

But the mysteries are not only physical; they are also psychological. Maclean is meticulous about giving us a sense of the personalities of the men involved, especially the leader, R. Wagner ("Wag") Dodge. It had been his decision to jump, and then his decision to work their way down the gulch, his order to turn back when the fire proved too strong. And he was the one who had lit the "escape" fire, buried himself in its ashes, and survived. He lived five years after the tragedy, haunted by his inability to save the others who would not follow him into his fire. Maclean goes behind the scenes:

> To see how Dodge's life as a woodsman shaped his thoughts in an emergency and to follow his thoughts closely, one more tick must be added to the tock of his makeup. In an emergency he thought with his hands. He had an unusual mechanical skill that helped him think, that at least structured his thoughts. ... And in fact that spring he had been excused from training with the Smokejumpers so that he could be maintenance man for the whole Smokejumper base—no doubt part of the cause of the tragedy he was about to face with a crew only three of whom he knew.

Trusting in Dodge's expertise, Maclean began his research only to find conflicting versions. With Robinson, Maclean walked the terrain, stopping at the crosses that mark where the men had fallen. Still they could never fully reconstruct the scene. Finally they agreed that they needed to find the remaining two survivors, Robert Sallee and Walter Rumsey, for confirmation. And confirmation entailed one more trip into the gulch. Maclean found himself with three younger men who did not want him to suffer Gisborne's fate, but, like Gisborne before him, he insisted on making the climb. Even after both men identified the crevice through which they had crawled and pulled themselves to safety, the geometries did not fit the prior testimony. It was necessary to take one last trip in grueling heat for Maclean and Robinson to discover that the crevice had been misidentified.

Good teachers are willing to learn. In the thirty years since the Mann Gulch fire, scientists had invented the computer model. By coincidence Maclean met Arthur P. Brackebusch, a former student of Gisborne who worked at the Northern Forest Fire Laboratory, and there he

and Robinson were able to simulate the conditions of the late afternoon on which the Smokejumpers died. With what the scientists now knew about the behavior of fire, it was finally possible to explain most of the conflicting perspectives and to understand that Dodge's escape fire had burned quickly upslope, that it had not been the cause of the death of his men. The Forest Service may have been covering up something that had never happened.

The mystery of the fire was at last unlocked—or as much as it could ever be, given the vagaries of the universe—a universe Maclean described in an interview with Kay Bonetti as "brutal and beautiful," as having a design of some sort "but I can't make sense of it ultimately." The universe, according to Maclean's father, needs some explanation from good men. Maclean would seem to concur, although he adds, with tongue in cheek, "A mystery of the universe is how it has managed to survive with so much volunteer help."

In the end the fire was the easiest thing to understand; Maclean was more interested in the human lives that delineate the tragedy. To some extent *Young Men and Fire* is a study in the shape of tragedy. For Maclean there is a moment when time seems to stop and life offers up the stuff of literature: "It is in the world of slow-time that truth and art are found as one." His aim was art, and the art was story: "If a storyteller thinks enough of storytelling to regard it as a calling, unlike a historian he cannot turn from the sufferings of his characters. ... They were young and did not leave much behind them and need someone to remember them."

Maclean ends his book looking back, thinking about the nature of tragedy. It is different, he thinks, for the old. And the emphasis in his book has been on the word "young." One cannot help but remember the youthful version of Maclean in the logging camps and Forest Service. Nor can one forget that young man's younger brother, Paul, whose beauty seemed almost to foretell his death. Sallee, only seventeen at the time of the jump, had lied about his age in order to become a Smokejumper. All the men in the crew had youthful stamina, physical prowess, and relative inexperience—a bit like the students to whom Maclean had devoted a lifetime. In telling their story he was in a way retelling his own. This impulse is evident as he speaks of his young friend Laird Robinson:

> It is a great privilege to possess the friendship of a young man who is as good or better than you at what you intended to be when you were his age just before you changed directions—all the way from the woods to the classroom. It is as if old age fortuitously had enriched your life by letting you live two lives, the life you finally chose to live and a working copy of the one you started out to live.

"RETURN TO THE RIVER": AN ARGUMENT FOR GENRE

Young Men and Fire is clearly nonfiction, and Maclean speaks of it as such. Constantly aware that the story of the fire and its victims resides outside himself, he considered the book to be a quest for truth. And to find truth he included charts and graphs, mathematical computations, photographs, documents, interviews, all the trappings of nonfiction reportage.

When Maclean refers to "A River Runs Through It," however, his use of the word "story" is more self-conscious. He had difficulty seeing it as nonfiction when he was aware of all the subtle adjustments he had made: conflation of time and events, changes in location, the use of imagination, slight exaggerations, deliberate omissions, composite characters, the shaping hand of the author. His son, John, claims that he "fictionalized too much for autobiography." Maclean admitted, "if I had still another life to live I couldn't conceive of a novel—I would be sure ahead of time that a novel would be mostly wind, as most novels are." The "story" does not conform to the usual standards of fiction. As Wallace Stegner observes, the author's voice intrudes, speaking to the readers; he speculates, supplies motivation, sums up. The characters do not develop. "No wonder he couldn't find an orthodox publisher," says Stegner.

For all his scholarly discipline Maclean seemed to make little or no distinction between storytelling and the stories that are told. His aesthetic stance mirrors his father's religious tenet: the Word is underneath the water; the story is underneath the art. The impulse is toward truth. Only then can the storytelling urge—a desire to make order out of chaos— also find the order *in* the chaos: "True, though, it must be. Far back in the impulses to find this story is a storyteller's belief that at times life takes on the shape of art and that the remembered remnants of these moments are largely what we come to mean by life. ... They become almost all of what we remember of ourselves." This might appear to be almost an argument for the blurring of genre, as though the fiction and the nonfiction are indistinguishable in memory. And the continuation of this passage from *Young Men and Fire* does little to clarify Maclean's position:

> Although it would be too fancy to take these moments of our lives that seemingly have shape and design as proof we are inhabited by an impulse to art, yet deep within us is a counterimpulse to the id or whatever name is presently attached to the disorderly, the violent, the catastrophic both in and outside us. As a feeling, this counterimpulse to the id is a kind of craving for sanity, for things belonging to each other, and results in a comfortable feeling when the universe is seen to take a garment from the rack that seems to fit. Of course, both impulses need to be present to explain our lives and our art, and probably go a long way to explain why tragedy, inflamed with the disorderly, is generally regarded as the most composed art form.

Gordon G. Brittan, Jr., writes, "Maclean doesn't so much *tell* us there's a pattern as *show* us the pattern." But that statement assumes that the pattern is of Maclean's making. Instead Maclean *finds* the underlying pattern that he perceives to be there, shapes and sculpts to allow the preexisting pattern to emerge. In "USFS 1919," bringing to bear the wisdom of experience on his young protagonist (himself), Maclean actually gives voice to this objective:

> I had as yet no notion that life every now and then becomes literature—not for long, of course, but long enough to be what we best remember, and often enough so that what we eventually come to mean by life are those moments when life, instead of going sideways, backwards, forward, or nowhere at all, lines out straight, tense and inevitable, with a complication, climax, and, given some luck, a purgation, as if life had been made and not happened.

What we recognize as literary is the shape of the story within the life. In looking at the story of his brother, he is not *making* the story; he is making something *of* the story—something we might recognize as art.

In an interview Maclean noted that his memory was made up of "golden moments"—composed moments in which he seemed to be a character in his own story. Perhaps if the art of the literary memoir had been more developed at the time, Maclean would have resolved the essential conflict in his rhetoric. By the time of Maclean's death, and certainly thereafter, "A River Runs Through It" was referred to as memoir as often as it was called fiction. Memoir would be a more fitting term, and it is possible Maclean would have come to appreciate its precision. In "Teaching and Story Telling" (1978) he spoke of the world of his writing: "a world of moonlight and garbage cans and French-Canadians working on mill ponds, and my brother, and unhappy endings, and, of course a big river running through all of it. I call this the real world, and a lot happens in it."

The big test of genre is whether a textual analysis (using standard critical terminology) will yield further insight. So it is instructive that when "A River Runs Through It" is treated as a novella much of the critical commentary trivializes the story, gives it the feel of something heavily plotted or planned. Critics refer to the symbolic aspects, yet this story is rooted in actuality. If anything, Maclean is a natural symbolist; that is, he instinctively understands when his particulars intersect with a universal, where the individual story resonates with a cultural norm. If symbols are there, they rise from the material rather than shape it. They offer up their implications rather than impose their meanings.

"Plot," as a term, is suspect here, though in an interview with Kay Bonetti, Maclean confessed that the story is "highly designed, while looking as if it is just reality." Plot implies fabrication and the expected twists of plot. Yet the events of this story—and their sequence—had already occurred. There was room for shaping but not for invention. The piece moves of its own momentum, taking on a trajectory that will, eventually, provide insight. Maclean's retrospection is evaluative; in looking back over what happened and when it happened, he hopes to *discover* meaning: "it is not fly fishing if you are not looking for answers to questions."

The word "character" is also problematic, suggesting that Maclean could set an invented character in motion, could provide impulse and motivation and response. Yet the underlying tragedy of the piece is how he could not know his actual brother, how he could not guess the response; it is about the way in which real people resist becoming characters, even in their own stories. Thus, when Maclean looks at his brother fishing, he draws on what he knows; he observes—and records—but does not characterize. The word "character" also would suggest that Maclean provided his various women as instructive tools—those who represented the civilizing force of family, those who provided an alluring alternative. But the Cheyenne and Old Rawhide were not mere inventions to offer up a "dark" side, as though they fit neatly into themes in American literature. They were women Maclean knew, women he admired or despised, not an "idea" of women who could provide a contrived tension.

The word "theme," too, resists its fictional trappings. It would imply that, should Maclean choose to weight the story differently or should he decide on a different set of values, the story could be altered. But this is not so, and almost everything Maclean himself said about the story in later talks and essays points to his emphatic desire to get at the truth through telling a story that is true.

If we substitute the word "indication" for "symbol," the word "trajectory" for "plot," "concern" for "theme," "person" for "character," we come closer to the spirit of "A River Runs Through It." Even without corroborating photographs to prove the point (some editions of the book have them), the reader rests easier knowing that these events carry the weight of lived experience. When it is spoken of as memoir, it changes the register of the discussion, and the story is all the more powerful.

Finally there is the issue of "metaphor." If the river were metaphorical, as it is in Hemingway's "Big Two-Hearted River," it would carry that function throughout. But the river is the Big Blackfoot, a section that runs wild and straight from the Continental Divide through the Bitterroots to the Columbia. Of course, the word "river" brings with it metaphorical implications (river of time, waters of memory, etc.), and this confluence of cultural connotations and personal detail adds to the story's richly symbolic nature.

If the river becomes fully metaphorical, however, it does so only once, and it's not when Norman and his father have their conversation about the nature of the Word, because the water

then is simply idea: a way of looking at the world. No, the river becomes metaphorical at the moment the story discovers its title: "Eventually, all things merge into one, and a river runs through it." Briefly, from within the story, from within its source, the river represents the whole. Object and meaning are fused. And then the metaphor subsides: "The river was cut by the world's great flood and runs over rocks from the basement of time." The Big Blackfoot reemerges, fraught with all the realities of geology and history and, yes, of religion, thereby retaining some of its metaphorical implications: "On some of the rocks are timeless raindrops. Under the rocks are the words, and some of the words are theirs." Whose? Certainly not the rocks'. Probably not the river's. Nothing in the penultimate paragraph supplies the referent. Nor does the preceding paragraph which describes how and where Maclean fishes now as an old man.

But the one-sentence paragraph before that, removed by time and distance, says, "Now nearly all those I have loved and did not understand when I was young are dead, but I still reach out to them." Reaching across time, as one can do only in writing, he hears some of "their" words. The reader shivers into the coat of the first person: "I am haunted by waters." Plural. The metaphor has surfaced from within the material, revealing itself as a shaping force to anyone willing to be persuaded by its power and possibility, the reader who is haunted by waters of his own.

Selected Bibliography

WORKS OF NORMAN MACLEAN

FICTION

A River Runs Through It and Other Stories. Chicago: University of Chicago Press, 1976; 25th anniversary edition, 2001. (Both editions contain the title novella, the short story "Logging and Pimping and 'Your Pal, Jim,'" and a second novella, "USFS 1919: The Ranger, the Cook, and a Hole in the Sky.")

A River Runs Through It. Chicago: University of Chicago Press, 1983. (Reprint of the novella, with photographs by Joel Snyder.)

A River Runs Through It. Chicago: University of Chicago Press, 1989. (Reprint of the novella, with wood engravings by Barry Moser.)

OTHER WORKS

"Episode, Scene, Speech, and Word: The Madness of Lear." In *Critics and Criticism: Ancient and Modern.* Edited by R. S. Crane. Chicago: University of Chicago Press, 1952. Pp. 595–615.

"From Action to Image: Theories of the Lyric in the Eighteenth Century." In *Critics and Criticism: Ancient and Modern.* Edited by R. S. Crane. Chicago: University of Chicago Press, 1952. Pp. 408–460.

Norman Maclean: American Authors Series. Edited by Ron McFarland and Hugh Nichols. Lewiston, Idaho: Confluence Press, 1988. (Ten selected essays by Norman Maclean, most written after the publication of *A River Runs Through It,* several given as lectures, one from Studs Terkel's *American Dreams: Lost and Found,* others reprinted from these journals: *Association of Departments of English Bulletin, Chicago, Esquire,* and the *University of Chicago Magazine.*)

Young Men and Fire. Chicago: University of Chicago Press, 1992.

PRINT INTERVIEWS

Dexter, Pete. "The Old Man and the River." *Esquire* 95:86–91 (June 1981).

Kittredge, William, and Annick Smith. "The Two Worlds of Norman Maclean: Interviews in Montana and Chicago." *TriQuarterly* 60:412–432 (summer 1984).

SOUND RECORDINGS

Norman Maclean. Columbia, Mo.: American Audio Prose Library, 1985. Audiocassette. 38 minutes. (The tape contains an interview with Kay Bonetti in which Maclean discusses both "A River Runs Through It" and the Mann Gulch fire.)

Norman Maclean Collection. United States: HighBridge, 1993. 8 audiocassettes. Unabridged. 11 hours. (Includes *A River Runs Through It,* read by Ivan Doig; *Young Men and Fire,* read by John Maclean, Norman Maclean's son; *On the Big Blackfoot,* archival reading by and interviews with Norman Maclean, along with recollections by John Maclean.)

On the Big Blackfoot: Recollections of the River and Life that Inspired the Book "A River Runs Through It." Minocqua, Wis.: NorthWord Audio Press, 1995. Audiocassette. 1 hour. (The tape contains two interviews broadcast on National Public Radio's "All Things Considered," one on November 9, 1985, and the other on October 15, 1992. Also included is an archival recording with narration copyrighted by John N. Maclean, 1994.)

CRITICAL AND BIOGRAPHICAL STUDIES

Butler, Douglas R. "Norman Maclean's 'A River Runs Through It': Word, Water and Text." *Critique: Studies in Contemporary Fiction* 33:263–273 (summer 1992).

Ford, James E. "When 'Life … Becomes Literature': The Neo-Aristotelian Poetics of Norman Maclean's 'A River Runs Through It.'" *Studies in Short Fiction* 30:525–534 (fall 1993).

Lojeck, Helen. "Casting Flies and Recasting Myths with Norman Maclean." *Western American Literature* 25:145–156 (summer 1990).

McFarland, Ron. *Norman Maclean.* Western Writers Series Number 107. Boise, Idaho: Boise State University Press, 1993.

McFarland, Ron, and Hugh Nichols, eds. *Norman Maclean: American Authors Series.* Lewiston, Idaho: Confluence Press, 1988. (Seven critical essays by Wendell Berry, Mary Clearman Blew, Gordon Brittan, Jr., Walter Hesford, Glen A. Love, Harold P. Simonson, and Wallace Stegner.)

Sale, Roger. "Bradley and Maclean." In his *On Not Being Good Enough: Writings of a Working Critic.* New York: Oxford University Press, 1979. Pp. 84–93.

Weltzien, O. Alan. "Norman Maclean and Tragedy." *Western American Literature* 30:139–149 (summer 1995).

———. "The Two Lives of Norman Maclean and the Text of Fire in *Young Men and Fire*." *Western American Literature* 29:3–24 (spring 1994).

Womack, Kenneth. "'Haunted by Waters': Narrative Reconciliation in Norman Maclean's 'A River Runs Through It.'" *Critique: Studies in Contemporary Fiction* 42:192–204 (winter 2001).

FILM BASED ON THE WORK OF NORMAN MACLEAN

A River Runs Through It. Screenplay by Richard Friedenberg. Directed by Robert Redford. Columbia Pictures, 1992.

—*JUDITH KITCHEN*

David Mamet

1947–

Dᴀᴠɪᴅ Mᴀᴍᴇᴛ, ʜɪs reputation boosted by a successful career in Hollywood as both scriptwriter and director, has the highest profile of any living English-language dramatist: a handful of his stage plays—*Sexual Perversity in Chicago and the Duck Variations* (1978), *American Buffalo* (1977), and *Glengarry Glen Ross* (1984) prominent among them—have been so frequently and so successfully revived on both sides of the Atlantic that they are now staples of the modern theatrical repertoire. Unlike many popular dramatists, however, Mamet is also well regarded in academic circles, where he is proclaimed a true heir of Samuel Beckett, of Harold Pinter, and (though with significant reservations) of Arthur Miller. "You know, Arthur," Mamet once told Miller after seeing a revival of *Death of a Salesman,* "I felt I was watching my own story." Yet behind the heartfelt acknowledgment there is an element of reprimand; Miller fails to make clear, Mamet complains, that the Lomans (like the Millers and the Mamets) are a Jewish family.

Mamet's widespread acclaim is not altogether easy to understand, for in every phase of his career his plays have been littered with verbal profanities and indecencies that might easily have caused offense: the ceaseless torrent of "strong" language in *Sexual Perversity in Chicago* was truly unsettling a quarter of a century ago and has not entirely lost its power to shock even today. In some of his plays too Mamet embraces (or perhaps, since he is one American writer whose ironic powers are in full working order, he merely *seems* to embrace) controversial positions in racial and sexual matters that could ordinarily be guaranteed to provoke

hostility and opposition. But on the whole, although *Oleanna* (1992) might mark a turning point in this respect, critics who have praised Mamet have drawn approving attention to his dialogue, to its muscular strength and speed and power to rouse, but have been oddly reticent in their assessment of other aspects of his work. This selectiveness is surprising when we remember Mamet's own insistence—backed up, he suggests, by the example of Eugene O'Neill—that good dialogue is a peripheral dramatic virtue that is far less important than plot or action.

LIFE AND WORK

David Alan Mamet was born on November 30, 1947 in Flossmoor, an Illinois suburb of Chicago. His parents—Bernard Mamet, a lawyer specializing in employer-labor relations, and Lenore Mamet, a schoolteacher—were the children of Jewish immigrants from Poland and the Russian-Polish borderlands who had settled in the United States just before and just after World War I. Mamet's upbringing was what he would later characterize and criticize as "assimilationist," for his parents, while neither denying their Jewish ancestry nor renouncing their faith (thus assimilationist rather than assimilated), chose to stress their own and their children's need to succeed as Americans. This "nondenominational" attitude, Mamet has said, was the natural response of insecure people anxious to make their way in a new country, but he has also argued that assimilationist Jews weaken their own and their children's religious and ethnic identity.

"I came from a Broken Home. The most important institution in America," Carol reminds her father in *Reunion* (1982). So too does Mamet: his parents divorced when he was ten, and his mother married one of her husband's closest friends. Six years later, as soon as he was old enough to express a preference, Mamet moved back in with his father. Though reticent about his personal life, he paints a vivid picture in "The Rake," an essay in *The Cabin: Reminiscence and Diversions* (1992), of a deeply unpleasant childhood in which, in his eyes at least, his mother and stepfather behaved with complete disregard for all emotional needs save their own. Both *The Cryptogram* (1995), a play that has puzzled and divided audiences, and *Jolly,* the second of the three playlets that make up *The Old Neighborhood* (1998), are directly influenced by their author's experience of this troubled household.

From 1965 to 1969—because "only one school accepted me"—Mamet studied at Goddard College in Plainfield, Vermont. There he developed a love of the unspoiled countryside that surrounded him; he still maintains a house in Vermont and has written a *National Geographic* guidebook to the area. But the school itself failed to impress; there is a ferocious denunciation of Goddard College, of its dissembling ethos and its failure to invest in its own supposed principles, in "Sex Camp," an essay in *Make-Believe Town: Essays and Remembrances* (1996):

> Like had found like, and I'd landed not in a utopia of Stoic, self-directed scholars, but, rather, in the midst of a community that had no interest whatever in education. The unanimity of our support for Progressive Education knew no bounds. For neither the teachers nor the students were about to rat the other group out.

"The whole thing is a sort of orange blur," he has said of his Goddard experience. Yet out of this blur a considerable dramatist began to emerge. Mamet spent his junior year acting at

New York's Neighborhood Playhouse under the direction of Sanford Meisner (1905–1997), a disciple and interpreter of Konstantin Stanislavsky (1863–1938) and Richard Boleslavsky (1889–1937). Meisner, taking his lead from his distinguished mentors, taught the paramount importance of action in performance: every character in a well-constructed play works toward the attainment of an emotional goal that, once understood, reveals the intimate relationship between motivation and action. This view of the essential unity of plot and character deeply informs Mamet's own theory and practice of playmaking.

Back at Goddard, Mamet worked on initial drafts of *Duck Variations* (1978) and *Sexual Perversity in Chicago* (1978), two short plays often performed in tandem that are frequently revived. *Duck Variations,* an extended revue exercise of a kind held up for mild derision in *Squirrels* (1982), is the first full flowering of Mamet's talent for dialogue. *Sexual Perversity in Chicago,* an altogether more substantial piece, is a surreal and acerbic exploration of failed relationships that for many critics remains very near the heart of Mamet's achievement as a dramatist. At this time he also worked on *Reunion,* about an alcoholic father who reestablishes contact with his daughter after a twenty-year absence. In its emphasis on family issues and tensions, *Reunion* gives an early airing to subject-matter to which Mamet has returned explicitly in more recent plays, especially in *The Cryptogram* (1995) and *The Old Neighborhood.* After graduation and a brief period working in the real estate office that inspired *Glengarry Glen Ross,* Mamet spent 1970–1971 teaching at Marlboro College, Vermont, where *Lakeboat* was first performed. Revised and restaged in 1980, revived for its British premiere in 1998, and filmed in 2000, *Lakeboat*—discovered by many critics thirty years after its first appearance—is a reminder of aspects of his dramatic talent that its author has for the most part chosen not to develop. During 1971–1973, while working at Goddard College as artist in residence, Mamet helped to form the St. Nicholas Theatre Company, which moved to Chicago in 1974.

Mamet's account of his emergence as a playwright is charming and disarming. Faced with a theater company that needed scripts and with no money to pay royalties, he started to write out of economic necessity. Behind this benign joke, however, lies a story of conviction and determination and of a wholly uncompromised dedication to his chosen art form. Not surprisingly, this most actor-directed of dramatists frequently writes plays that reflect upon the art that the actor practices: *A Life in the Theatre* (1978), which traces the rising and falling fortunes of a younger and an older actor, is merely the most extended and explicit example. Other examples are briefer but equally forceful: "I love the theater," Glenna tells Edmond in the scene in *Edmond* (1983) in which he kills her, because in the act of acting "what you must ask respect for is yourself." The relationship between actor and audience is, Mamet has always insisted, the dynamic of theater and its most distinctive feature. In that crucial scene in *Edmond,* Glenna has been speaking of the integrity of the acting process but then reveals that she has performed only in class and in workshops. "Then you are not an actress. Face it," is Edmond's withering reply. This reply Mamet echoes in his own person in *True and False: Heresy and Common Sense for the Actor* (1997): "That is what acting is. Doing the play for the audience. The rest is just practice."

Mamet's own "life in the theatre" has not been uneventful; he has married twice, both wives being actresses, and has two daughters from his first marriage and a third daughter from his second. His renewed interest in Judaism and his absorption in the responsibilities of family life are reflected in his later work, sometimes in ways that began to generate critical disapproval.

Another important development—with, some have argued (though Mamet dissents vigorously), a malign impact upon his work as a playwright—is his move into filmmaking. In 1981 he wrote the screenplay for Bob Rafelson's *The Postman Always Rings Twice,* and this began a long and productive relationship with the movie industry as scriptwriter, director, and "script doctor." Inevitably, just as he has written plays about plays, so he has written plays and films about filmmaking. *Speed-the-Plow* (1988) is a theater piece that exposes the sexual power politics of the film industry. *State and Main* (released in 2000), more genial and more expansive but at least equally insightful, is a film that both satirizes and celebrates the chaos and compromise and downright bad faith that goes into the making of movies.

Mamet has also written three novels, three treatises on acting and playmaking, short stories and plays for children, and a large number of occasional essays. In the face of such a range of achievement and of such immense productivity, and however one ultimately judges the worth of his work, one can scarcely doubt that Mamet was born to write.

LANGUAGE, ACTION, AND PLOT

Mamet has said that *American Buffalo, The Woods* (performed in 1977), *Oleanna,* and *The Old Neighborhood* are "all written in free verse." Though most of his other plays could be added to the list, this claim about verse, like the parallel claim (voiced by the critic of the *New York Times*) that Mamet's dialogue "makes poetry out of common usage," is formally suspect, but undeniably Mamet crafts his dialogue with careful attention to how his words will fall upon the ear. His style is marked by colorful utterance ("Because you're a prince among men and you're Yertle the Turtle"); by the fractured but artfully manipulated syntax that has come to be known as Mametspeak; and perhaps most often of all, by an insistent use of repetition. When, in *Glengarry Glen Ross,* for instance, Dave Moss tries to persuade George Aaronow to rob the office and Aaronow protests that doing so would be a crime, Moss's reply is precisely structured:

(a) "That's right. It's a crime. It is a crime. It's also very safe."

One can see this precision most clearly if one tries to replace Mamet's line with any of the following near-equivalents, all of which must surely have been buzzing around in his head at the time of writing:

(b) "That's right. It's a crime. It's also very safe."

(c) "That's right. It is a crime. It's also very safe."

(d) "That's right. It's a crime. It's a crime. It's also very safe."

(e) "That's right. It is a crime. It is a crime. It's also very safe."

None of these is unspeakable, of course, but (b) is simply too speedy and (d) and (e) are merely repetitive; (d) is hectoring and (e) is ponderous. One can perhaps make (c) work if one speaks "It is a crime" with precisely the right weight of emphasis, but only (a) properly mixes the seemingly flippant and the pseudo-solemn by reaping the benefit of a repetition that is not exactly a repetition. ("It's a crime. It is a crime.") Such analyses are always clumsy when frozen in print, but very nearly every sentence that Mamet writes can be glossed in this way and will have to be in the rehearsal room.

Nevertheless, despite the consistently high quality of his dialogue, Mamet is certain that a dramatist's principal task is the production of great plots (see, for example, "A Playwright in Hollywood," in *Writing in Restaurants,* 1986). In this matter, however, praise of his work is less uniform: one critic, writing when *American*

Buffalo first came out, thought there was evidence even at that early stage in Mamet's career of a decline in his ability to construct plot coherently. (But against what at that date was he judging the decline?) Others have suggested that in *Glengarry Glen Ross,* his other unquestionably major play, there are elements of plot that are not fully integrated into the action as a whole. (Perhaps in confirmation of this point, when *Glengarry Glen Ross* was filmed Mamet wrote a new scene for a new character in order to make explicit the competitive pressure under which the salesmen are working. He also boosted Levene's motivation by stressing his daughter's illness and his need for money to pay her hospital bills.) Later, with hostile criticism a shade commoner than was once the case, John Heilpern vigorously attacked the plotlessness of *The Old Neighborhood* in a collection of essays (only two of which are about Mamet) provocatively titled *How Good Is David Mamet, Anyway?* (2000). By the middle of the 1990s, "the dramatist of earlier, superior plays," Heilpern argued, had "long since settled for dramatically less." The more usual response, however, has been to defend Mamet by conflating dialogue and plot as equal expressions of dramatic "action." "Action counts," Don tells Bobby at the beginning of *American Buffalo.* "Action talks and bullshit walks." What, however, is action? And can it properly substitute for plot?

Dramatic characters do some at least of the following things: they pass examinations, fall in love, get pregnant, rob a bank, cook meals badly, dance a gavotte, win the lottery, murder their father, die. These things comprise a play's plot. In many plays—those of Chekhov, a particular favorite of Mamet, are often cited as examples—plot is subordinate to character in the sense that it serves to reveal character. But in other plays (including, Aristotle says, the best tragedies) plot is paramount, character being at best the fuel that keeps the plot's engine ticking over. Playwrights, according to Aristotle's *Poetics,* do not create action in order to portray characters but include characters for the sake of the action. However, for many modern playwrights and critics, especially for those who work within naturalistic traditions of theater, there is a need to reconcile character and plot, to see in each the reflection of the other.

Mamet is proud of his Aristotelian allegiance and is firmly committed to plot or action. Indeed "characters are nothing but habitual action," he said in an interview in 1981: "You don't create a character; you describe what he does." When we remember that two of Konstantin Stanislavsky's most famous books are *Creating a Role* and *Building a Character,* we might think that Mamet is taking a potshot at the Russian director's famous System. And, indeed, in *True and False,* Mamet declares that many of Stanislavsky's rehearsal techniques are useless and dismisses the System as a cult. Things, however, are not quite as they seem, for some Stanislavskian precepts are central to Mamet's thinking about theater. In 1987, in another interview, he owned up to a quartet of major debts: "The most important thing I learned at the Neighborhood Playhouse [under Sanford Meisner] was the idea of a through-line, which was Aristotle filtered through Stanislavski and Boleslavsky."

Aristotle's view of plot, like Newtonian physics, operates on a large scale: "We have laid it down," he says, "that a tragedy is the imitation of an action that is complete in itself, as a whole of some magnitude ... a story or Plot must be of some length." He is principally concerned with identifying large expanses of action that configure a play as either tragic (where the protagonist, having recognized his error, moves downward toward ruin or death) or comic (where threatened confusion is dissolved and equilibrium restored). But Stanislavsky and Boleslavsky take the argument far beyond Aristotle. What emerges from their work—and this

is what Mamet seizes upon—is a belief that microscopically small actions may serve to reveal character; that indeed a character's "character" is no more than the product of an audience's interpretation of the totality of a character's small actions. The consistency of these actions—their pointing, when properly interpreted, in the same direction—is what constitutes a character's "through-line of action," and it is this through-line that reconciles character and plot.

Because action "talks," it always tells an audience something and is indeed what con men call a "tell." In *House of Games* (1987), the first film Mamet both wrote and directed, Mike, a master craftsman of deception, eases Margaret Ford, an inquisitive and thereby vulnerable psychotherapist, into his trap by means of seemingly confidential disclosures. He asks her:

MIKE: You know what a "tell" is?

FORD: A "tell"?

He then explains by guessing, time after time, in which hand she has hidden a coin:

MIKE: Okay, now I can do that all day. How? You got a "tell." You're "telling" me the hand that has the coin.

FORD: I *am*?

MIKE: Yes.

FORD: How?

MIKE: It's not important. Ah, okay—you're doing it with your nose. You're pointing your nose slightly at the hand that has the coin. Okay? That's a "tell."

That slight pointing of the nose, a gesture so small that it would ordinarily escape notice, becomes an "action" once we are alerted to it. And "actions" can be slighter still. In *The Shawl and Prairie du Chien: Two Plays* (1985), the bogus clairvoyant John believes that Miss A, the woman he intends to fleece, is unmarried because she is not wearing a wedding ring. But he seeks confirmation by testing her: "I mentioned the word 'husband' … and her eyes did nothing. So we *confirm* she isn't married. Always confirm."

Mamet requires his audiences to develop these habits of close inspection. Imagine a character called upon to act decisively when he would rather do nothing at all: by way of subterfuge, or to purchase thinking time or to hide his embarrassment, he does something that would be utterly trivial were it not serving the purpose that he wishes to conceal. But to the watchful and perpetually interpretative eye of the audience, the actor reveals this embarrassment that accompanies the disguise, and by revealing it exposes the attempted concealment, whether or not other characters notice it. There is an unusually clear instance of this kind of effect in *American Buffalo*. Don and Bobby are planning a burglary; Teach, who always imagines himself as the leader of the pack, is anxious to cut himself into (and cut Bobby out of) any lucrative deal; Don does not wish to take Teach on board; he needs to further his plan by making a telephone call; he wants to make the call in private but does not want to arouse Teach's suspicions by deliberately shutting him out of the room; Teach has driven up to Don's shop and has parked his car on a meter. Out of these simple facts Mamet builds a far-reaching action, which occurs between the first [1] and second [2] pauses in the following extract:

DON: What time is it?

TEACH: Noon.

DON: (Noon.) (Fuck.)

TEACH: What? (*Pause.*) [1]

DON: You parked outside?

TEACH: Yeah.

DON: Are you okay on the meter?

TEACH: Yeah. The broad came by already. (*Pause.*) [2]

DON: Good. (*Pause.*)

TEACH: Oh, yeah, she came by.

DON: Good.

TEACH: You want to tell me what this thing is?

DON (*pause*): The thing?

TEACH: Yeah. *Pause.* What is it?

Teach knows (and an alert audience knows that Teach knows) that Don's question about the meter is an intended diversion that fails miserably. The seeds of the entire play lie half-buried and half-displayed in this small incident. Teach is quick to learn (quick at any rate to take offense) but, despite his nickname, is, like every teacher in the Mamet canon, an unreliable mentor. Don's eminently reasonable distrust of him is suppressed by a politeness that proceeds from weakness. This distrust resurfaces later in much tougher form when, angry with himself for having been persuaded to exclude Bobby from the deal, Don insists that Fletch, another of his criminal acquaintances, be brought in as a safeguard. Teach, rightly understanding that Don lacks confidence in his reliability, interprets Fletch's nonappearance later that evening as evidence that Bobby and Fletch have joined forces to defraud them—an intelligent interpretation bred of suspicion, but quite false. Teach's violent physical assault on Bobby, with Don's momentary but momentous cooperation, is the result. Don, in Mamet's own unusually explicit commentary, is "tempted by the devil into betraying all his principles [and] betrays himself into allowing Teach to beat up this young fellow whom he loves." By dropping Bobby, and by then disbelieving him in order to justify having dropped him, Don fails the play's moral test of friendship but ends the play (so Mamet insists) having recognized his failure. By a still greater irony Don's true kinship with Teach is also revealed: "I'm trying to teach you something here," Don had told Bobby at the beginning of the play, but as the play proceeds he proves to be the teacher who learns that he has more to learn than he has to teach. This reversal of fortune can be identified as the play's larger action.

The value of this kind of analysis is that it enables us to see that two of Mamet's other plays have exactly the same "action" or "plot" or "theme," terms that tend to coalesce in the analysis of Mamet's work. In the reversal (a true Aristotelian *peripeteia*) that is the climax of *Glengarry Glen Ross,* Shelly "The Machine" Levene—anxious to teach a thing or two to Williamson, his hated office manager—forgets to follow his own best advice ("Be sure it will *help* or keep your mouth closed," he tells Williamson), exposes himself badly ("You've got a big mouth," Williamson tells him in return), and must bear the disastrous consequences, dismissal and imprisonment, as a bitter lesson (a true Aristotelian *anagnorisis*). And what is *Oleanna* deep down, below the level at which it has proved so controversial, but another play about a teacher who is taught a lesson?

MAMET AND CONTROVERSY

Despite Mamet's considerable popularity there are two aspects of his work that have made him an object of controversy: his treatment of women and of black characters. The issues and arguments involved in this discussion are complex and delicate; critics who pursue them with reductive simplicity risk endangering a dramatist's right to express his own vision of the world. However, to adopt for a moment the inappropriate language of a court of law, the outlines of the case against Mamet are clear and are as follows: there are too few women (and blacks) in his plays, they are dealt with unsympathetically, and they are marginalized.

Even the way in which Mamet presents a female character in speech headings can, to unsympathetic eyes, reveal her to be no more than an anonymous plot accessory. *The Shawl*—a brief and minor but by no means unrepresentative play—features two men, John ("a man in his fifties") and Charles ("a man in his thirties"), and Miss A ("a woman in her late thirties"), no longer young, unmarried and unlikely ever to marry, a "miss" in every sense of the term. When Mamet says, as he has done several times in interviews, that a good dramatist provides only the information that is essential, we might wonder what the absence of Miss A's name is telling us about her, and about the play in which she is present but from which her name is excluded. Of course, in his defense, Mamet may be using *The Shawl* to tell us—deliberately and openly—that confidence tricksters are more interested in assigning their victims to categories than in responding to them as autonomous individuals. Charles, Mamet has said, is John's lover (something that never clearly emerges from the play itself); Miss A, by contrast, is merely his intended dupe.

Too few women? Too few for whom? Here developments in social history are relevant. Though Shakespeare made no attempt to achieve gender balance in his plays, no blame attaches to him since the very assumptions that make imbalance an issue for us were scarcely visible to him or his contemporaries. In any case, since all of Shakespeare's actors were male, women's parts were a technical challenge to the young men who had to appear in skirts. Restricting, in both number and complexity, the female characters that a dramatist created was a sensible response to a practical problem. It is Mamet's misfortune, it might be argued, that, now that everybody is counting, his failure—or his refusal—to provide equal opportunities for male and female actors is glaringly obvious. In *American Buffalo* and *Glengarry Glen Ross,* his best plays, we see and hear no women at all. It is true that Grace and Ruthie (lesbian partners who thrive in a man's world) and Mrs. Lingk (the stronger half of the Lingk marriage) are powerful "offstage presences," but an offstage presence is, however one dresses up the matter, an onstage absence. When *Speed-the-Plow,* sometimes linked with *American Buffalo* and *Glengarry Glen Ross* as the third item in a very informal trinity of "business plays," is added to the account, the situation scarcely changes. Here indeed a woman does appear, and casting the pop star Madonna in the role ensured that her character achieved artificial prominence in the play's original production. But Karen, the temporary secretary drafted into a workplace awash with testosterone, is, like Miss A, little more than an instrument of the plot. By bedding her, Bobby Gould confirms his right to perch on a high branch of the management tree, but her classic bid for power through the bedroom door is deeply flawed and scarcely competent, since she uses it to back a film project of self-parodying awfulness. Her reduction to the ranks by Charlie Fox is a triumph of male bonding against female intrusion and a vindication of the essential rightness of masculine judgment. "You squat to pee," Fox tells Bobby as the highest expression of his contempt for him, and it is only when Gould learns to stand up and pass his water like a man that sanity and equilibrium return.

There is an odd sentence (odd because of its tone as much as its content) in an essay—"True Stories of Bitches" in *Writing in Restaurants*—in which Mamet deliberately tests the limits of good taste. He says that "in husband-and-wife arguments, or, as they are generally known, 'marriage,' the ultimate response the man feels is, of course, physical violence." Ten years earlier, in an interview conducted shortly after winning an off-Broadway award, he defended himself against the charge that *Sexual Perversity in Chicago* was misogynist by arguing that it is a picture of various kinds of emotional inadequacy: all of the characters in the play are losers and his dialogue simply records and reports their failings. At one level this defense is entirely satisfying: in the first scene, Bernie, egged on by the ever-gullible Danny, tells of a date so hot that at a vital moment in their lovemaking the young woman douses the bedroom in gasoline and sets fire to it. The absurdity of Bernie's description never entirely loses contact with an underlying reality. Mamet is telling us—what Bernie and Danny would never be honest enough to admit to themselves or to others—that these young men reassure themselves by disparaging a vigorous female sexual responsiveness of which they are secretly in awe: "It's these young broads. They don't know what the fuck they want." Similarly, in the final scene, where they are on the beach looking at attractive women, their misogyny is just the cowardly face they put upon sexual disappointment: "Coming out here on the beach. Lying all over the beach, flaunting their bodies … I mean who the fuck do they think they are all of a sudden, coming out here and just flaunting their bodies all over?" Again when, in a moment of fury in *American Buffalo,* Teach tells Don that he is "not your nigger … not your wife," the gender and racial offensiveness of the remark is so clearly embedded in what we know of Teach's relations with Don, and of his values in general, that we can easily separate him from his creator.

But *Sexual Perversity in Chicago* has some darker moments that are less easily put to one side. One involves Joan Webber, a nursery school teacher who may or may not be lesbian, who has a low view of men, and who (the inexcusable part of her personality) takes out her sexual frustrations on the children she teaches:

> Were you playing "Doctor"? (*Pause.*) Don't play dumb with me, just answer the question. (You know, that attitude is going to get you in a lot of trouble someday.) Were you playing with each other's genitals? Each others ... "pee-pees"?—whatever you call them at home, that's what I'm asking (and don't play dumb, because I saw what you were doing, so just own up to it). (*Pause.*) All right ... no. No, stop that, there's no reason for tears ... it's perfectly ... natural. But ... there's a time and a place for everything. Now ... no, it's alright. Come on. Come on, we're all going into the other room, and we're going to watch our hands. And then Miss Webber is going to call our parents.

This is masterly writing (the "our" of "our parents" especially) and a great gift for an actress. But it is undeniably sinister, for what it chronicles, unlike the play's opening and closing scenes, are not the consequences of repression but its origins—and of course the origin of repression is repression, just as the consequence of repression is repression. But at this point of origin, and acting as the agent of transmission is—significantly and not by happenstance—a woman.

In embryo the case against Mamet is not that some of the men in his plays behave badly toward women or that some of his women behave badly in return—"Of course they do" would be an adequate response to that complaint—but that his plays disproportionately portray women as uncaring and self-obsessed, perpetually demanding of men (and contemptuously dismissive of them) whether as husbands or lovers or sons. In *Reunion*, Carol's complaint that you cannot just reacquire a father after twenty years is couched in reasonable terms when she tells Bernie that she feels cheated by

him—"I never had a father. ... And I don't want to be pals and buddies; I want you to be my father." But it is unreasonable when it coincides with her brutal dismissal of the husband who, through an act of caring and kindness, has brought father and daughter together: "He's a lousy fuck." Or consider how cruelly and with what deliberateness Donny, the mother in *The Cryptogram,* damages her young son, John, by forcing him into an emotional relationship that he is too immature to sustain while she blames him for his failure to sustain it. "I'm going to speak to you as an adult," Donny rather laboriously tells John at one point, but one of the oddities of the play, and perhaps its principal defect, is that nothing in the way in which Mamet has them speak to each other suggests that one of them is a ten-year-old child. In Donny's skewed view of things, John—like her husband, who has deserted her, or her homosexual friend, who cannot substitute for him—is yet another man who brings in his wake all of the disappointments that are incidental to his maleness.

Boston Marriage (2001), a play for three female performers, is written as though in conscious rebuttal of these charges. Apparently inspired by Mamet's overhearing the theatrical banter of actresses (one of them his wife) in the Green Room, it is this origin, perhaps, that explains the extreme theatricality of the piece: so camp are the verbal antics of Anna and Claire (a "Boston marriage" is a lesbian liaison), so outrageous the flouncing and posturing that accompanies their speeches, that the play could easily be performed by men in drag without loss of force or credibility. *Boston Marriage* may signal, some critics have suggested, a new, more lighthearted and less intense development in Mamet's playmaking, but it does nothing to address the gender issue and nothing much to redress the gender imbalance.

According to this argument, women are marginalized and exploited in Mamet's masculine world; a similar argument, more telling in its impact, has also been applied to his black characters. On October 16, 1998 the *Columbus Dispatch* ran an item about an unsavory row that had enveloped Otterbein College and its student theater. At the center of this row was *Edmond,* one of Mamet's darkest, most puzzling, and least typical plays, which had first been staged in Chicago and New York sixteen years earlier. The play begins with a conversation between a fortune-teller and Edmond Burke, its principal character, a white American of presumably Irish descent (whose name, a minor spelling discrepancy apart, echoes that of the great Anglo-Irish conservative politician and political thinker). In this conversation there is raised the question of how far one is morally responsible for one's actions if one is genetically or otherwise predisposed to act in certain ways. But how the play answers this question, some students said, both employs and encourages the fixing of racial stereotypes that are a slur on the black community:

(*Edmond is at the bar. A Man is next to him. They sit for a while.*)

MAN: ... I'll tell you who's got it *easy* ...

EDMOND: Who?

MAN: The niggers. (*Pause.*) Sometimes I wish I was a nigger.

EDMOND: Sometimes I do, too.

MAN: I'd rob a store. I don't blame them. I swear to God. Because I want to tell you: we're *bred* to do the things that we do.

EDMOND: Mm.

MAN: Northern races *one* thing, and the southern races something else. And what *they* want to do is sit beneath the tree and watch the elephant.

Of course—a point that needs always to be borne in mind—no playwright is to be naively identified with one of his characters. Nevertheless this extract clearly shows why the play might cause offense. Otterbein's college authorities, caught in an administrator's nightmare, responded by describing the play as "a dark portrait of an unhappy white man whose frustrations are expressed through self-hatred, misogyny and bigotry." They added that they believed strongly that the play "also contains a journey of individual redemption and a spiritual awakening" that involves the "shedding of past narrow-minded belief systems." In short, despite its heavy disguise, this is fundamentally a liberal play from which at the end, once we learn to see it aright, liberal values emerge not merely intact but strengthened. Some students, however, were unconvinced by a play that seemed to offer its spiritual salvation selectively: Edmond, one student said, curses, spits on, and kicks the black pimp who tries to rob him and is later sodomized by a black prisoner with whom he shares a cell, but he emerges at the end of the play "smelling like a rose when he discovers his own spirituality." If indeed—it is a disputed point—Edmond can be said to undergo spiritual rejuvenation in this play, then the contrast with the play's black characters (who, being symbolically as well as physically black, do not simply happen to be the color they are) is one that any black viewer might find offensive. Of course this entire dispute might also be seen, as some at Otterbein clearly saw it, as an exercise in the kind of political correctness that, with reference to gender rather than race, Mamet had made central to *Oleanna,* a play whose recent notoriety doubtless fed into the Otterbein dispute.

Other explanations—other kinds of explanation—are possible, however. Perhaps Mamet is telling us that we desire what we fear, and loathe the unacknowledged desire as much as we loathe the fear itself. Edmond, on this interpretation, seems to be (and seems to be because he obviously is) a "nigger"-hating homophobe but is also (or is really) a "nigger"-loving homosexual. He hates women though he seems to love them and, symbolizing the concurrence of hatred and love, stabs Glenna, a white woman—after they have had sex, so that stabbing and penetration are equated—whereas what he really wants is to be penetrated by a big black man. ("*His cellmate,*" Mamet's stage direction explicitly states, "*is a large, black Prisoner.*") Self-acceptance, for Edmond, involves reversing the polarity of his prejudice and accepting his dark secret love. Beneath that reversed polarity, however, the structure of prejudice remains intact. Mamet is perfectly able to see that Edmond's rape by a black prisoner is an erotic stereotype. Indeed he puts exactly this same bit of plot into the dismal Douggie Brown buddy-movie that Charlie Fox sells to Bobby Gould in *Speed-the-Plow:*

Fox: Doug's in prison.

Gould: ... prison ...

Fox: Right. These guys, they want to get him.

Gould: *Black* guys ...

Fox: Black guys in the prison.

Gould (*into phone*): Coffee, quickly, can you get some coffee in here? (*Hangs up.*)

Fox: And the black guys going to rape his ass.

Gould: Mmm.

What lies behind the Otterbein student protest and gives it basic credibility is that *Edmond,* when we see the negative that lies behind the positive, is a play in which blacks feature not as fully formed characters in their own right but as stage properties in Edmond's white man's theater of self-regarding self-imagining.

ASSIMILATION

Right from the beginning of his career, Mamet's plays have been densely populated with Jewish characters: Emil Varec and George S. Aronovitz, the "two gentlemen in their sixties" whose talk on a park bench is recorded in *The Duck Variations,* are surely immigrants or the children of immigrants; a generation or so below them, at least three of the characters in *Sexual Perversity in Chicago,* and perhaps all four, are Jewish too. Neither play, however, develops specifically Jewish issues or themes: Emil and George whittle away their spare time as any old men might; the sexual competitiveness and emotional egotism of Dan, Bernard, Deborah, and Joan are those of their age and situation rather than of a precisely identified ethnic or religious group. However, during the mid-1980s—when *The Disappearance of the Jews* (first performed in 1983), the initial part of *The Old Neighborhood,* was written and first performed—Jewish self-identity and the external and internal threats to which it is subject began to emerge as dominant themes in Mamet's work.

This development has not been without critics, who blame it for what they perceive as doctrinaire rigidity and dramatic thinness in *The Old Neighborhood,* but this cryptic and elliptical triplet of plays has also been saluted as a major work, evidence that, at a time when he is increasingly preoccupied with filmmaking, Mamet's commitment to live theater is undiminished. Granted his subject matter and the way in which he constructed these plays (by, for example, omitting essential characters), this sharp division of opinion is scarcely surprising. On whichever side of the division one falls, however, one can scarcely discuss *The Old Neighborhood* without engaging with Mamet's high-profile and unashamedly visible Jewishness. This visibility directly contradicts his parents' (and his parents' generation's) assimilationism.

In modern American theater, Tennessee Williams told an interviewer as recently as 1981 that "you hardly dare use the word *Jew*." The objection to doing so, he added, came from the exaggerated sensitivity of Jews themselves, who, perhaps understandably in view of recent history, are "frightened of any criticism, whatsoever." But, with the reality of anti-Semitism undiminished, it is hard to present "a picture of the world as it truly is without on occasion allowing a voice to those sentiments." What does Mamet, a great admirer of Williams' "dramatic poetry," make of this argument? Clearly some version of its conclusion, directed toward blacks rather than Jews, is needed if *Edmond,* a play pledged to the recording of unpleasant truths, is to be defended against charges of racism and sexism.

Lesley Kane, in *Weasels and Wisemen: Ethics and Ethnicity in the Work of David Mamet* (1999), a detailed study of Mamet's pervasive interest in Jewish matters, has argued that whether a character is Jewish or not is something we need to know if we are to understand the hidden motivation of Mamet's plots. Two examples she gives are striking, though only intermittently convincing. When, at the end of *Glengarry Glen Ross,* Levene asks Williamson why he is taking pleasure in exposing him to the police, Williamson's reply—"Because I don't like you"—is interpreted as evidence of Williamson's anti-Semitism. (But Williamson has excellent reasons for disliking Levene.) Still more unsettling is Kane's reading of *Oleanna* as a conflict between Jewish scholarship (John) and anti-Semitic anti-intellectualism (Carol) that relives the battle for scriptural authority fought out between the Catholic Church and the Jewish community in the Middle Ages. John, Kane argues, is a thoroughly assimilated Jew who, in his quest for invisibility, has adopted the signs and signals of non-Jews. However, these very signals become evidence of assimilation once they are recognized as its product; absence of evidence is itself evidence; evidence, moreover, of John's Jewishness. The argument is plainly circular, yet the conclusion may still be correct. "What has led you to this place?" Carol asks the now thoroughly defeated John, before (an example of the play's power reversal) answering on his behalf: "Not your sex. Not your race. Not your class. YOUR OWN ACTIONS." But what is John's race? And, if it is truly insignificant, why does Carol mention it at all? Much here will depend upon a director and his or her decisions. A Jewish John and gentile Carol? A gentile John and Jewish Carol? A Jewish John and Jewish Carol? A black John and white Carol? A white John and black Carol? A black John and black Carol? Mamet's stage directions rule out none of these possibilities. (By contrast his dialogue probably does rule out some of them: John, an assimilated black, need not sound black; Carol, unassimilated in every respect, would surely do so.) Whether or not one sees a racial aspect to any of this, *Oleanna* makes a good deal of sense if it is interpreted as a battle between the assimilated and the unassimilated in which the assimilated is overthrown.

A third example, less contentious than the two that Kane gives, also reveals an otherwise hidden motivation. Are Bobby Gould and Charlie Fox, the film executives in *Speed-the-Plow,* Jewish? Not a great deal within the play (just one passing reference) helps one to decide, but the answer is clear when one goes back five years and turns to *The Disappearance of the Jews.* Its principal character, also named Bobby Gould, is a secular Jew anxious to rediscover his lost spiritual and ethnic inheritance. A conversation about the "five smart Jew boys from Russia" who founded the Hollywood film industry generates the following exchange:

BOBBY: Mayer. Warners. Fox.

JOEY: Fox? Fox is Jewish?

BOBBY: Sure.

JOEY: Fox is a Jewish name?

BOBBY: Sure.

JOEY: Who knew that?

BOBBY: Everyone.

Just before this passage Bobby and Joey have been talking of the pleasures of fooling around with gentile women (while arguing that, for the preservation of family integrity, wives should be Jewish), so we have perhaps another explanation—in addition to the obviously sexual one—of why Karen does not really fit into *Speed-the-Plow* and of why she is eventually evicted from the play.

Many of Mamet's characters are Jewish, some are not, others may be, but the evidence that allows one to decide is weak or missing. This state of affairs prompts a more basic question that runs throughout *The Old Neighborhood:* "What is a Jew?" This question, very hotly contested within the recent history of Judaism, is one that Mamet's triplet of plays raises at a popular or anecdotal level but does not develop at length. In *The Disappearance of the Jews,* Bobby and Joey (they are men in their thirties or forties, though they seem much older) treat assimilated Jewishness as something akin to closeted homosexuality. This image, calculated to irritate Jews and gays and Jewish gays, is one that Mamet explicitly draws in an essay ("The Jew for Export") in *Make-Believe Town* in which he contrasts the openness with which American popular culture (supposedly) accepts gays and their lifestyle, free from stereotype or parody, with the fact that "Jews remain in the closet." True to this image, Bobby and Joey

begin the play with their humorous but unfunny outing of Howie Greenberg:

BOBBY: Whatever happened to Howie?

JOEY: Howie.

BOBBY: Yeah.

JOEY: Are you ready for this … ? Howie turned out to be a fag.

BOBBY: You're kidding.

JOEY: No.

BOBBY: You're kidding.

JOEY: No.

BOBBY: He's a fag.

JOEY: That he is.

BOBBY: How about that.

JOEY: Isn't that something.

BOBBY: Yeah.

Then Bobby and Joey, assimilationist Jews not wholly at ease with themselves, start "outing"—as Jews, not as homosexuals—other Jews that they deem to be assimilated: Charlie Chaplin ("I know that, Joe") and even the seemingly goyish Jerry White of Miller-White Shoes ("He was the shamus. Temple Zion, thirty years"). This game has no rules and, once you start playing it, knows no limits: a man who has taken an active part in worship in his synagogue for thirty years scarcely needs to be outed, and Charlie Chaplin was not Jewish. It is a game, however, that both Mamet and his characters play with gusto: in "The Jew for Export," for example, he gives a long list of Jewish actors who have built their careers upon non-Jewish roles. But are these actors Jewish? "How would one know if one did not know?" What, once again, is a Jew?

Mamet's answer is that, first and foremost, a Jew is a member of a particular community or family. In "Poor but Happy," an essay in *Jafsie and John Henry: Essays on Hollywood, Bad Boys, and Six Hours of Perfect Poker* (1999), he states his point of view with maximum bluntness: "The only peace, if one is a Jew, is to be a member of the tribe and to resent deprecation of it (others *and* one's own), just as one would of one's family." Those Jews who openly criticize any aspect of being Jewish—even if they simply say, "I am a Jew, but I disagree with the conduct of Israel"—place themselves "outside the group." This strict, and many will think unacceptable, standard sets great store by notions of inclusion and exclusion. In pursuit of it Mamet puts his characters in *The Old Neighborhood* under immense pressure as he attempts to weave together his twinned themes: on the one hand, they want to bring a vanished Jewishness back into visibility; on the other, they struggle to rearticulate, out of the ruins of failed relationships, a traditional Jewish family and its values.

How fiercely intestinal the struggle to keep these themes together becomes is clearly shown when Bobby's defense of the integrity of his family turns against Judaism itself. His marriage in tatters, he blames his gentile wife for suggesting that their children are not Jewish: "I should never have married a shiksa," he tells Joey. But what he is blaming Laurie for is something over which she has—and has, moreover, in specifically Jewish terms—no control at all. Joey may not be very articulate (we need to supply the missing "ifs" in his sentence), but he is right: "Well, Bob, the law says he's a Jew, [if] his, you know what the law says, he's a Jew [if] his mother is a Jew." And Bobby's response ("Fuck the law") is, however forceful, wrong by the very standards that he seeks to invoke, for the law that Bobby treats with such disrespect is Jewish religious and ceremonial law—*halakah*—that states that a Jew is a person born of a Jewish mother, or is a convert, who has no other religious affiliation. In 1982, when Mamet was writing *The Disappearance of the Jews,* the issue was certainly topical, for that was the year when Reform Jews in Britain and the United States agreed to accept that Jewishness was also transmissible through the male line. But this concession, a very recent event in the long history of Judaism, is not universally accepted even among Reform Jews and is decisively rejected by Conservative Jews and by the Orthodox and ultra-Orthodox.

There is more at stake here than a dispute, however passionate, within Judaism, for Bobby toughens up his case against Laurie by telling Joey that she has said that Jews owe their permanent victimhood to a basic failing within themselves, an unacknowledged emotional participation in the lives and attitudes of those who persecute them. This is a slander that Mamet raises time and time again in his essays and which he always opposes. In "Brompton Cocktail" (in *Jafsie and John Henry*), he tells of a woman at dinner ("I had known [her] for thirty years, foreign-born, raised in Europe, multilingual, cultured") who, speaking of a thirteenth-century extermination, said "Well … I'm sure to a certain extent they brought it on themselves." In "True Stories of Bitches," he relates how his sister, when cracking a complex joke, told him (he interprets her as meaning) that his inability to rule his life according to his perceptions "is an unfortunate trait and, doubtless, it was in some wise responsible for the murder of the European Jewry." But as this second example shows (it is Mamet's interpretation of a "bitchy" joke that he admires rather than a direct expression of what his sister said or meant), a calumny, once it is widely enough disseminated, can end up deeply embedded in the thinking of those that it victimizes: "There is nothing unlovely about our people or practices," Mamet writes in "Poor but Happy." "There is only internalized self-hatred," he adds bleakly.

This process of internalization is investigated most thoroughly in *The Old Religion* (1997), Mamet's second novel, which tells the true story of Leo Frank, a New York Jew who owned and managed a factory in Georgia; who in 1913 was falsely accused of raping and murdering "a *working* girl, a *Southern* girl" (poor, white, but Christian); who is reviled in the public press as an outsider and an intruder ("The Kike. The 'Nigger to the nth degree'—as the paper had called him"); is convicted and sentenced to death (a sentence commuted to life imprisonment); and is then kidnapped by a mob and castrated and lynched. Mamet concentrates so much attention upon Frank's emotional and intellectual response to his arrest that the outline of the story is left frequently obscure. Nonetheless it is clear that Mamet blames a fundamentalist Christian society that supports the activities of the Ku Klux Klan. ("Jews and Catholics. You are not required. Leave now or be eliminated.") Less clear, but ultimately much more important, is that Frank himself is blamed for conspiring in his own destruction. He is a secular Jew and to that extent assimilated. He is not, however, in either disguise or denial, and he neither changes his name nor adopts the Christian faith. Instead, every Sunday he sits out on his porch breakfasting and drinking coffee as his neighbors make their way to church. Nevertheless Mamet equates this partial assimilation—Frank's belief that if he does not make an issue of his difference nobody else will—with his acceptance of the values of the country in which he lives. But one of that society's principal values, its belief that justice is achieved through a system of fair trials, is travestied unless Frank is guilty. Since Frank has not killed the girl, his treatment is unjust; it becomes just only if he learns to accept that he has killed her. Thus the logic of assimilation requires him to fabricate guilt in order to defend

the injustice under which he suffers: "Then the one event, if I had misremembered it, would make it right. If I had killed her, if I could avow the fact, then it would all come out right. I would be saved. And that is what the Rabbi meant when he talked of the Christian Outlook."

The rabbi means that Christians can forgive Christian murderers (even though they hang them) because such murderers, when they confess their sins and repent, fit into a pattern that conforms to a Christian expectation that excludes believing Jews. Murderers are more amenable than Jews because, though it is appropriate to hope that a murderer will repent, it is not appropriate to expect anyone to repent for sincerely held religious beliefs. Therefore religious difference is subversive of a well-ordered and uniform society in a way and to an extent that murder is not. Frank (so the novel implies) is killed to preserve the purity of a Protestant Christian ascendancy, and mentally at least, he has taught himself to accept and acknowledge that ascendancy. *The Old Religion* is, thus, powerfully and unapologetically an anti-assimilationist tract: on the one hand Mamet reasserts his belief that American Jews must not try to seek safety through invisibility; on the other hand, because he sympathetically identifies with his beleaguered hero, he is able to spell out a thought that runs through Frank's troubled mind: Jews, in the person of Jesus of Nazareth, have connived at their own persecution by raising from among themselves a force that will destroy them. These two views, however, are quite different: Mamet in his own person refuses victim-status and angrily rejects it, but shows through the way in which he characterizes Frank, how tempting and how insidious it can be.

"Because I want to tell you what she says to me one night," Bobby tells Joey: "If you've been persecuted so long, eh, you must have brought it on yourself." But this is what Bobby tells us that his wife has said: Laurie herself—

another offstage presence that is an onstage absence—is given no voice at all. Her embittered and frustrated retort (perhaps she does not like being called a "shiksa") is robbed of its immediate context in an acrimonious and failing marriage. Mamet's reduction of marital dialogue to (Bobby's) monologue is evidence of the dramatic impoverishment of *The Disappearance of the Jews.* Exactly the same point needs to be made against those interpretations of *Jolly,* the second play in the triplet, that entirely endorse Jolly's view of her stepfather. (Initially, in her rambling and scarcely coherent monologue, she seems to be complaining about her stepbrother's maladministration of the parental estate, but eventually her stepfather emerges as the principal object of her hatred.) The issue is artistic rather than biographical: however deeply the play may be rooted in Mamet's own childhood and that of his sister, it remains—like all plays—an invention and a fiction that cannot be checked off against a reality to which we have easy, or indeed any, access. Rather the problem is one of the constraints of monologue and of an essentially monocular vision, and that problem is simply stated. How do we decide between two interpretations? Does the play chronicle the appalling effects of parental and stepparental emotional abuse? Or is Jolly, for reasons of self-centeredness and self-esteem, reviling her innocent stepfather unfairly? All we hear, and all we shall ever hear, is what Jolly tells us happened, in a play in which—and this, again, is evidence of dramatic impoverishment—we have no evidence upon which to base a judgment of her honesty.

FAMILY DRAMA

The plays that make up *The Old Neighborhood* deal with dark material and with family matters. In an interview in 1986, faced with an interviewer who correctly identified "family drama" as an abiding interest and strength of American

theater, Mamet admitted that, with the partial and slight exception of *Reunion,* he had not attempted to write such a play but would like to do so. Then, with deliberate provocativeness, he added that *American Buffalo,* "sneakily enough, is really a tragedy about life in the family." Moreover it is, he insists, this play—rather than *Glengarry Glen Ross,* the one that critics always cite in this respect—that invites comparison with Arthur Miller's *Death of a Salesman.* Because Miller's principal concern is with Willy Loman's relationship with his wife and children, at heart his play is "a tragedy about a man who happens to be a salesman" rather than a play about salesmanship itself. But an immediate reaction to Mamet's claim is to say that if *American Buffalo* is—however sneakily—a family drama, the question "Who is mother?" needs urgently to be asked. As Teach tells Don, at a point when Don is cradling the injured Bobby much as a mother (or father?) might cradle an injured child: "You want kids, you go have them. *I* am not your *wife.* This doesn't mean a thing to me." Teach is being cruel but not trivial: a family (at least the standard family of Jewish and Christian and Western tradition) is a uniquely difficult aggregation of human beings that depends upon the expression of a strong sexual attraction between husband and wife and the suppression or sublimation of any sexual attraction between parents and children. Moreover, this expression and suppression and sublimation must be done under the banner of love on a battlefield where sexual jealousies and generational conflicts work themselves out.

Mamet has explained the very nearly universal unpopularity of *The Woods* (first performed in 1977)—and a Mamet play that is not widely admired needs explanation—by arguing that its subject matter is a heterosexual relationship, and that the depiction of such relationships is not a very marketable commodity in modern theater. The explanation is suspect on numerous grounds, including the untruth of its final assertion, but it is clear that this play about a man (Nick) and a woman (Ruth) who fail to get together cannot, precisely because they do fail to get together, be counted as even the beginnings of a family drama. It does, however, like many of Mamet's plays, depict a relationship that mirrors isolated aspects of the complex of relationships that composes a family, but it does so in typically ambiguous fashion. The physical violence that Ruth visits on Nick infantilizes him:

(*Ruth hits him.*)

RUTH: You *shit.* You stupid *shit.* You sit down and don't *move.* You are *alright.* You are alright. (*She hits him again.*)

Can't you *hear* me?

Are you *deaf*?

You are alright. There's nothing wrong with you.

This speech sounds like a less well-controlled (and for that reason slightly less disturbing) premonition of how Donny addresses her son in *The Cryptogram,* that strange play about inequality and exploitation. The only way of reducing the unpleasantness of this incident is to render Nick and Ruth more equal by rendering them equally childlike, and this is what Ruth does when, in the play's mawkish ending, she imagines that Nick and she are small children, curling up in the forest to sleep with their arms around each other. (*The Woods* and *The Cryptogram* are linked through their shared symbolism of the woods, in the latter play a place of escape and fulfillment to which no one escapes and in which no one is fulfilled.)

Husband and wife, parent and child: families have their vertical as well as their horizontal alignments. "I felt … that you had written the story of my father and me," Mamet once told Miller, recognizing (as perhaps everyone now

does) that *Death of a Salesman* is not so much a satire on the American business dream as a profound probing of the relationship between a father and his son, between past and present, between present and future. Mamet was right to point out that *American Buffalo,* in its depiction of the relationships between Teach and Don and between Don and Bobby gets closer to Miller's family drama than does the superficially more comparable *Glengarry Glen Ross.* Alerted to this point, we can see that *A Life in the Theatre* is a Mamet family play too: Robert ("an older actor") and John ("a younger actor") are a team and a partnership, in which John, a generation below Robert, will eventually supplant him, as sons supplant their fathers. Just like *American Buffalo,* however, *A Life in the Theatre* is not entirely and not exactly a family drama: Don and Bobby, Robert and John are like fathers and sons only to the very limited extent to which those who are *like* fathers and sons are like those who *are* fathers and sons. Remarkably, in Mamet's by now extensive canon, there is no play in which these scattered family fragments—reflected so widely throughout his work—are brought together into a satisfying whole; none in which the simple structure but emotional complexity of the modern nuclear family is displayed and explored. There are plenty of Boston marriages but no true ones.

Selected Bibliography

WORKS OF DAVID MAMET

PLAYS
American Buffalo. New York: Grove, 1977.
A Life in the Theatre. New York: Grove, 1978.
Sexual Perversity in Chicago and The Duck Variations. New York: Grove, 1978.
The Water Engine: An American Fable and Mr. Happiness. New York: Grove, 1978.

Reunion; Dark Pony; The Sanctity of Marriage. New York: French, 1982.

Squirrels. New York: French, 1982.

Edmond: A Play. New York: Grove Press, 1983.

Glengarry Glen Ross. New York: Grove, 1984.

Goldberg Street: Short Plays and Monologues. New York: Grove, 1985.

The Shawl and Prairie du Chien: Two Plays. New York: Grove, 1985.

Three Children's Plays. New York: Grove, 1985. (Includes *The Poet and the Rent, The Frog Prince,* and *The Revenge of the Space Pandas.*)

Three Jewish Plays. New York: French, 1987. (Includes *The Disappearance of the Jews, The Luftmensch,* and *Goldberg Street.*)

Speed-the-Plow. New York: Grove, 1988.

The Woods, Lakeboat, Edmond: Three Plays. New York: Grove, 1989.

Oh, Hell! New York: French, 1989. (Includes *Bobby Gould in Hell.*)

Oleanna. New York: Pantheon, 1992.

No One Will Be Immune and Other Plays and Pieces. New York: Dramatists Play Service, 1994.

An Interview. In *Death Defying Acts: Three One-Act Comedies.* New York: French, 1995.

The Cryptogram. New York: Vintage, 1995.

The Old Neighborhood: Three Plays. New York: Vintage Books, 1998.

Short Plays and Sketches. New York, 1999.

Boston Marriage. London: Methuen, 2001; New York: Vintage, 2002.

COLLECTED WORKS

Five Television Plays. New York: Grove Weidenfeld, 1990. (Includes *The Museum of Science and Industry Story, We Will Take You There, A Waitress in Yellowstone; or, Always Tell the Truth, A Wasted Weekend,* and *Bradford.*)

Plays One. London: Methuen, 1994. (Includes *Duck Variations, Sexual Perversity in Chicago, Squirrels, American Buffalo, The Water Engine,* and *Mr. Happiness.*)

Plays Two. London: Methuen, 1996. (Includes *Reunion, Dark Pony, A Life in the Theatre, The Woods, Lakeboat,* and *Edmond.*)

Plays Three. London: Methuen, 1996. (Includes *Glengarry Glen Ross, Prairie du Chien, The Shawl,* and *Speed-The-Plow.*)

Plays Four. London: Methuen, 2002. (Includes *Oleanna, The Cryptogram,* and *The Old Neighborhood.*)

ADAPTATIONS OF CHEKHOV

The Cherry Orchard. Translated by Peter Nelles and adapted by David Mamet. New York: French, 1986; Grove, 1987.

Uncle Vanya. Translated by Vlada Chernomordik and adapted by David Mamet. New York: French, 1988; Grove, 1989.

The Three Sisters. Translated by Vlada Chernomordik and adapted by David Mamet. New York: Grove Weidenfeld, 1991.

SCREENPLAYS

House of Games. New York: Grove, 1987.

Things Change. With Shel Silverstein. New York: Grove, 1988.

We're No Angels. New York: Grove Weidenfeld, 1990.

Homicide. New York: Grove Weidenfeld, 1992.

The Spanish Prisoner and The Winslow Boy: Two Screenplays. New York: Vintage, 1999.

State and Main. London: Methuen, 2001.

NOVELS

The Village: A Novel. Boston: Little, Brown, 1994.

The Old Religion. New York: Free Press, 1997.

Wilson: A Consideration of the Sources, Containing the Original Notes, Errata, and Commentary. London: Faber and Faber, 2000; Woodstock, N.Y.: Overlook Press, 2001.

OTHER PROSE WORKS

Writing in Restaurants. New York: Viking, 1986.

Some Freaks. New York: Viking, 1989.

On Directing Film. New York: Viking, 1991.

The Cabin: Reminiscence and Diversions. New York: Turtle Bay, 1992.

A Whore's Profession: Notes and Essays. London: Faber and Faber, 1994.

Passover. New York: St. Martin's Press, 1995. (Reprints the four preceding items.)

Make-Believe Town: Essays and Remembrances. Boston: Little, Brown, 1996.

True and False: Heresy and Common Sense for the Actor. New York: Pantheon, 1997.

Three Uses of the Knife: On the Nature and Purpose of Drama. New York: Columbia University Press, 1998.

Jafsie and John Henry: Essays on Hollywood, Bad Boys, and Six Hours of Perfect Poker. New York: Free Press, 1999.

On Acting. New York: Viking, 1999.

South of the Northeast Kingdom. Washington, D.C.: National Geographic Society, 2002.

CRITICAL AND BIOGRAPHICAL STUDIES

Berkowitz, Gerald M., *American Drama of the Twentieth Century* (London and New York: Longman, 1992)

Bigsby, C. W. E. *David Mamet.* London: Methuen, 1985.

Bloom, Harold, ed. *David Mamet.* Philadelphia: Chelsea House, 2004.

Brewer, Gay. *David Mamet and Film: Illusion and Disillusion in a Wounded Land.* Jefferson, N.C.: McFarland, 1993.

Carroll, Dennis. *David Mamet.* London: Macmillan, 1987.

Cohn, Ruby. *Anglo-American Interplay in Recent Drama.* Cambridge and New York: Cambridge University Press, 1995.

Dean, Anne. *David Mamet: Language as Dramatic Action.* Rutherford, N.J.: Fairleigh Dickinson University Press, 1990.

Grossberg, Michael. "Otterbein Shifts Gears after Uproar about Mamet Play." *Columbus Dispatch,* October 16, 1998.

Hayes, John. "On Stage: '*The Cryptogram.*' Mothers and Sons: Mamet's *Cryptogram* Is a Real-Life Drama for Theatrical Family." *Post-Gazette,* October 23, 1998.

Heilpern, John. *How Good Is David Mamet, Anyway? Writings on Theater and Why It Matters.* New York and London: Routledge, 2000.

Hudgins, Christopher C., and Leslie Kane, eds. *Gender and Genre: Essays on David Mamet.* New York: Palgrave, 2001.

Joki, Ilkka. *Mamet, Bakhtin, and the Dramatic: The Demotic as a Variable of Addressivity.* Åbo, Finland: Åbo Akademis Förlag, 1993.

Jones, Nesta, and Steven Dykes, comps. *File on Mamet.* London: Methuen Drama, 1991.

Kane, Leslie, ed. *David Mamet: A Casebook.* New York: Garland, 1992.

———, ed. *David Mamet's* Glengarry Glen Ross, *Text and Performance.* New York and London: Garland, 1996.

Kane, Leslie. *Weasels and Wisemen: Ethics and Ethnicity in the Work of David Mamet.* New York: St. Martin's Press, 1999.

Lahr, John. "Fortess Mamet." *The New Yorker,* November 17, 1997, p. 70.

Malkin, Jeanette R. *Verbal Violence in Contemporary Drama: From Handke to Shepard.* Cambridge and New York: Oxford University Press, 1992.

McDonough, Carla J. *Staging Masculinity: Male Identity in Contemporary American Drama.* Jefferson, N.C., and London: McFarland, 1997.

Simon, John. "Two David Mamet Plays: Two Early Plays Remind Us of a Time When David Mamet Still Mattered." *New York Magazine,* January 24, 2000.

Vorlicky, Robert. *Act Like a Man: Challenging Masculinities in American Drama.* Ann Arbor: University of Michigan Press, 1995.

INTERVIEWS

Harriott, Esther. "Interview with David Mamet." In her *American Voices: Five Contemporary Playwrights in Essays and Interviews.* Jefferson, N.C.: McFarland, 1988. Pp. 77–97.

Kane, Leslie, ed. *David Mamet in Conversation.* Ann Arbor: University of Michigan Press, 2001.

Plimpton, George, ed. "David Mamet (1997)." In *Playwrights at Work: "The Paris Review" Interviews.* New York: Modern Library, 2000. Pp. 369–388.

Savran, David. "David Mamet." In his *In Their Own Words: Contemporary American Playwrights.* New York: Theatre Communications Group, 1988. Pp. 132–144.

FILMS

The Postman Always Rings Twice, directed by Bob Rafelson, Lorimar, 1981.

About Last Night, directed by Edward Zwick, Tri-Star, 1986. (Loosely based on *Sexual Perversity in Chicago,* but disowned by Mamet)

House of Games, directed by David Mamet, Orion, 1987.

Things Change, directed by David Mamet, Columbia, 1988.

Homicide, directed by David Mamet, Triumph, 1991.

Glengarry Glen Ross, directed by James Foley, New Line, 1992.

The Water Engine, directed by Steven Schachter, Amblin Televisions, 1992.

Oleanna, directed by David Mamet, MGM, 1994.

American Buffalo, directed by Michael Corrente, Capitol, 1996.

The Spanish Prisoner, directed by David Mamet, Magnolia, 1997.

The Winslow Boy, directed by David Mamet, Tri-Star, 1999.

Heist, Warner, directed by David Mamet, 2000.

State and Main, directed by David Mamet, New Line, 2000.

Lakeboat, directed by Joe Mantegna, One Vibe, 2001.

Spartan, directed by David Mamet, Franchise, 2004.

—*PHILIP PARRY*

Linda McCarriston

1943–

LINDA MCCARRISTON IS a poet of enormous skill, one whose work encompasses both great sorrows and great hopes. Her poems and essays deal with the family in its most extreme moments, the class structure of society, relations between the sexes, and the healing force of nature.

EARLY LIFE AND INFLUENCES

McCarriston was born at Chelsea Naval Hospital in Chelsea, Massachusetts, on July 30, 1943, the daughter of William McCarriston and Leona Parent McCarriston. Her father was then serving in the U.S. Coast Guard during World War II. Linda McCarriston grew up in the industrial town of Lynn, Massachusetts, renowned for its long-standing role in the U.S. labor movement. In her autobiographical essay "Weed" (1998), McCarriston expresses pride in Lynn's union history, but she remains aware of the stigma attached to its working-class character. She refers to her hometown as the "Vatican of Tackiness."

McCarriston's paternal grandparents, Patrick and Margaret Reavey McCarriston, were immigrants from Northern Ireland. Soon after arriving in the United States in 1911 Margaret started organizing for the shoeworker's union. McCarriston's maternal grandfather was John Telesphore Parent, an Ojibwa Indian born on a reservation in Matane, Quebec. Her maternal grandmother, Marie Gosselin, crossed the Atlantic from Paris at the age of sixteen to work in the mills in Salem, Massachusetts. Eventually she bore sixteen children by John Parent, of whom the second to last was the poet's mother. McCarriston's immigrant and Native American heritage played a large role in molding her worldview.

"Childhood is the barrel they give you / to go over the falls in," writes McCarriston in *Eva-Mary* (1991), her second book of poems. The harshness of this statement reflects McCarriston's difficult youth. Her blue-collar upbringing made her sharply aware of the way opportunity is often denied those without wealth, and this awareness dramatically influenced her career and goals as a writer. In McCarriston's childhood home, clothes were all hand-me-downs or homemade, medical care almost unheard of, food never plentiful, books not present, music lessons impossible. In the social class in which she grew up, girls were expected to marry and mother and not much more. Even the smartest females—like McCarriston, who "had a troublesomely high IQ for a girl"—could aspire to careers only as nurses or teachers.

Her childhood influenced her work in other ways as well. Even before she was a teenager McCarriston's father began abusing her sexually, attacks that went on for years. He also beat her and her mother and brother. In her poetry and in her autobiographical prose, McCarriston is remarkably balanced in describing her father as a many-faceted person, an intelligent and politically aware man who enjoyed playing the ukulele and pennywhistle but who was uneducated and bigoted, embittered by lack of opportunity, his alcoholism finally washing away all that was good in his character.

Even though Linda McCarriston grew up in a small city, she always gravitated toward nature. In the backyard of her parents' home in Lynn, a trio of huge oak trees provided a haven where she could hide, think, and feel protected. The oaks formed for her "a circle endowed, or endowed by me, with almost sentient presence." McCarriston's sense of the healing power of nature, an important current in her poetry, flowed from this refuge and from her voracious reading as a child of animal stories borrowed from the local library.

She was educated in Catholic schools from fifth grade through her Bachelor of Arts degree. The parish scholarship for a graduate of St. Mary's Catholic High School in Lynn helped pay for her undergraduate degree at Emmanuel College in Boston. McCarriston accuses her parochial education of omitting vital lessons in politics and civics, and of stuffing her full of worn-out notions of gender roles. She credits her schooling, though, with giving her both the vision and the tools to see herself and to express herself as a complete human being.

MARRIAGES AND A WRITING CAREER

While in college McCarriston became involved with a Harvard medical student. They married one month after her college graduation in 1965. She took a job as a high-school English teacher in Salem, Massachusetts, and helped support her husband during his studies until they started a family. The couple had two sons: Michael, born in 1969; and David, in 1971. The family lived at an army base in Karlsruhe, Germany, from 1972 until 1974 while McCarriston's husband fulfilled his military duty in the Army Medical Corps.

Although McCarriston writes nostalgically about her first marriage in one poem, in a later autobiographical essay she describes the union as unsatisfying in every respect. In the early 1970s she became increasingly depressed and started drinking heavily. She was teetering and has written that her husband frequently suggested she be hospitalized. Instead the couple divorced in 1977. In the course of a bitter legal

fight that continued for many years, McCarriston at one point lost all custody of her two sons, forbidden even to speak to them on the phone.

Before the end of her first marriage McCarriston had begun to make a new life for herself as a writer. In 1976 she was admitted to the Master of Fine Arts in Writing Program at Goddard College, where she fell in love with a poet on the faculty; he later became her second husband. McCarriston finished her MFA in 1978 and started to publish poems. Her second marriage also ended in divorce.

On her own in the late 1980s, she found help for her depression and alcoholism. Struggling economically as an adjunct faculty member at Vermont College, at age forty-seven she returned to waiting tables, a job she had done in high school and college to pay for her education. Two grants from the National Endowment for the Arts (the first in 1984 and the second in 1988) also helped support her writing. Following the breakthrough publication in 1991 of her award-winning *Eva-Mary,* she was invited to be a visiting writer at Radcliffe College's Bunting Institute (1992–1993) and at George Washington University (1993–1994). In 1994 she was offered a tenure-track teaching position at the University of Alaska in Anchorage. She accepted and set off on her own, driving 4,700 miles from Vermont in a pickup truck with her horse in a trailer. In 1996 McCarriston married a university professor in Anchorage, but that brief union also ended in divorce the following year. McCarriston was promoted to full professor at the University of Alaska in 1997.

TALKING SOFT DUTCH

McCarriston's first book of poetry was honored with an Associated Writing Programs Award Series selection, chosen by Josephine Jacobsen. Published in 1984 by Texas Tech University Press, the book has remained continuously in print, exceptional for a volume of poetry. These poems do not have the roughness of many first collections. Unified in theme and imagery, the book represents the work of a poet who has mastered her craft and has formulated a strong point of view.

The book's intriguing title, *Talking Soft Dutch* (1984) comes from the poem, "The Tulip Man." In this poem the speaker suggests that merely observing pretty flowers is not the best way to appreciate them. Truly to take in the tulips in a square in Holland, for instance, the viewer has to know about the man who works at sunrise each day to cultivate the flowers, getting soil under his nails as he "talks / soft Dutch" to them. The imagined gardener returns in the afternoon, not only to admire the flowers but also to watch others who get pleasure from them, completing the circle of humanity interacting with nature.

"The Tulip Man" embodies some of McCarriston's most fundamental ideas. The gardener, someone we might never encounter or even think of, is essential to the tulips' beauty. Until we use our imaginations to see not just the flowers, but the human labor and warmth that radiates from their color, we have not experienced the Dutch square. In this poem and elsewhere in her writings McCarriston reminds the reader of the dignity of those who toil with their hands. Significantly the gardener works closely with nature, speaking to it with tenderness in the service of creating for others. This formula also fits McCarriston as a poet.

The poet's voice in the book is often quiet, inward, as if reflecting on the forest from a clearing. This voice and the regional landscape in the book recall the work of another New Englander, the meditative lyrics of Emily Dickinson. But *Talking Soft Dutch* also introduces many of the key themes that McCarriston makes her own in later volumes. The book is divided into four sections, the first of which, "On

Horseback," sketches moments of healing, only dimly suggesting the hurt that prompted the recovery.

The opening poem, "Birthday Girl: 1950," dedicated and addressed to the poet's mother, is a camera-sharp picture of a working-class home on a day imprinted in the speaker's memory. The mother is ironing and smoking, listening by radio as the Red Sox lose yet another chance at the World Series. In setting the scene, McCarriston shows early in her career the incredible gift for figurative language that distinguishes her poetry:

> the smells of workclothes—Tide
> and oil—rose up together
> in steam around you, like the roar
> of the crowd at Fenway.

But it is not only aromas that are rising—also the shouts of the downstairs neighbor whose husband is beating her.

In the midst of this drudgery and domestic violence, there is one "slab of light"—a wonderful phrase—in which the mother stands. The mother has ordered by mail a pair of harlequin sandals for her daughter, and the birthday girl is buoyed by this gift. The scene might have a Hallmark quality to it if McCarriston did not preface it with the gritty details that make clear how much is at stake here. She describes the small gestures between people who love one another, gestures that make it possible to survive a desperate situation. The fact that the poem is in the second person, directed to the speaker's mother, highlights the urgency.

Another poem in this section of the book, one that also deals with healing, is the first in which McCarriston treats a favorite subject—horses. Again, this could be corny, as in the girls' novels about ponies that the poet devoured as a child. But there is no sentimentality in "Aubade: November." The language is fresh, the details clear and realistic. The small act of feeding a horse allows for a large realization, the speaker's awakening to the fact that her life is "neither earned nor fair," yet contains the possibilities of joy and forgiveness.

Traditionally an aubade is a love poem in which a couple wakes together and laments having to part at dawn. McCarriston's aubade is radically different in that there are no lovers, only a woman giving feed to a mare (the gender of the horse links her to the speaker). The poem retains the essence of the aubade, though, because it turns around a bittersweet dawn. The extent of the bitterness is only hinted in the poem, when the poet compares birds circling a snow-covered garden to "a single mind in torment." But the birds do come to rest at the poem's conclusion, suggesting a peace earned over time.

The second section of *Talking Soft Dutch,* called "Mammals," concerns encounters with creatures of the natural world and the process of healing, both in the animals and in the narrator. One of the most dramatic of these poems is "With the Horse in the Winter Pasture," the poem that concludes this section. The landscape is at zero degrees with no wind, a still point frozen in the depth of winter. From this spot, motion starts—"barely / the January sun has begun to ripen"—suggesting the first inkling of better things to come.

The physical closeness of the horse provides a chance for the speaker to feel that "today, I am victim / of nothing, nor am I mistress." The poet cleverly uses the word "mistress" to mean both a kept woman and the lady of a fine house, linking those two roles. McCarriston's ear is always tuned to the way the sound of language can strengthen her meaning, and she is agile in sprinkling in rhyme and half-rhyme to match the speaker's giddiness: "as if it were after school, a fool, / a woman carrying on like a girl." In this poem as well we have a sense that dire events have preceded this heady relief—the speaker reveals that as a child she prayed to die. This is one of several doors McCarriston

leaves slightly ajar in *Talking Soft Dutch,* doors she enters boldly in her next book.

A similar opening occurs in "Eve," the next section of *Talking Soft Dutch.* Here McCarriston begins to take on another key topic: the contradiction between the stated biblical and democratic values of American society and the way that society actually treats certain individuals and groups. The Eve of McCarriston's retelling of the myth has not been through a romp in the garden with the serpent. McCarriston's Eve has experienced a shock, an attack, something she cannot even speak about: "What she learned / in the trees / was beyond him."

Landscape as a locus of hurt and healing recurs in the book's title section, which is also its last. In "Second Marriage," the woman in the poem almost misses the failed bond of her youth:

> How happy, even sadly, to have been
> young together, to have held off loneliness
> with the shiny locket of *we.*

McCarriston's knack for surprising but apt metaphor is at its finest here. Describing her daring step away from this comfortable failure, the narrator says,

> She sees the land take shape beneath her,
> as birds must, on the first migration,
> trusting their bodies as they veer away.

That dizzying jump of the imagination, entering into the eyes of a bird headed south for the first time, fuses many of the themes of *Talking Soft Dutch* into one—the search for human regeneration, supported by nature.

This same alliance of the human and the natural continues in the last poem in the book, "Riding Out at Evening." Here the speaker is actually on horseback, not just tending to a horse or getting thrown by one, as in earlier poems. That vantage point opens up an enormous horizon, made poignant by the light of dusk, which McCarriston describes beautifully: "The fields and hills pull up/the first slight sheets of evening." The landscape is humanized, while the speaker is in harmony with the horse she rides.

Traditionally in art, since the equestrian statues of caesars and generals of ancient times, a figure astride a horse has been the quintessential symbol of male power. McCarriston has feminized this image to create a figure who is powerful in her ability to wish for grace for all that she sees:

> And who is to say it is useless
> or foolish to ride out in the falling light
> alone, wishing, or praying,
> for particular good to particular beings
> on one small road in a huge world?

The authority of this equestrian figure comes not from political or military might but from humility, vision, and lyricism. It also derives from the autochthonous origin of the animal and its rider. The speaker attributes the power of this horse and woman not to a celestial source, but to the earth itself, inverting the divine right that kings on horseback once claimed.

The originality, imagery, and depth of feeling of "Riding Out at Evening" make it one of McCarriston's strongest poems to this point in her career. The presence here of the female rider prefigures images found in her later work, as does the theme of healing in partnership with nature.

EVA-MARY

In her second collection of poems, *Eva-Mary,* McCarriston not only opens the secret doors she left cracked in *Talking Soft Dutch,* she blows them off their hinges. When McCarriston wrote *Talking Soft Dutch* in the late 1970s and early 1980s, she found little support for poetry about topics that reflected her own experience. "Class and gender (and surely race) as conditions that may have savaged the life of the speaker were forbidden," she recounts in her autobiographical essay. "One wrote only from deep inside the world of the saved." By the time she composed *Eva-Mary* in the late 1980s and early 1990s, McCarriston was leading her own workshop of women writers who viewed her as a mentor, and she had read widely in women's studies, from Simone de Beauvoir to Adrienne Rich. The writers she knew personally together with the writers she read helped create a climate in which she felt she could finally address the difficult circumstances of her own experience.

Eva-Mary also emerged from a new political climate in North America. At the time McCarriston began to write poems, domestic violence and abuse were still taboo subjects. By the late 1980s, however, the resurgent feminist movement and high-profile court cases brought new attention to these issues. Abuse victims were coming forward to tell their stories in forums from the legal arena to television talk shows. Additionally, labor history was reemerging as a topic taught in universities, and McCarriston began to read about the epic events that had happened in her hometown, validating her heritage.

Even with all that foundation McCarriston's *Eva-Mary* is still startling and visceral. Published in 1991, it was the second book to win the Terrence Des Pres Prize for Poetry and was a finalist for the National Book Award. The book's first four poems set the tone for the entire collection.

As in *Talking Soft Dutch,* McCarriston begins this book with a poem dedicated to her mother. But from the first lines of this poem, "The Apple Tree," beginning with a long sentence that spans more than nine lines, it is clear that the author is now in full voice. The speaker addresses a tree in winter, past its bloom and years of bearing, like an older woman who is luminous in her white hair. Instead of the mother offering solace to the child, as in the poem that begins McCarriston's first book, here the daughter is consoling the maternal figure of the tree. In painterly images and resounding diction the speaker tells the mother/tree to drink deeply and long; those who used her are gone now. The mention of apples ties this poem both to the "Eve" section of *Talking Soft Dutch* and to an allusion to the Edenic myth found in the title *Eva-Mary*.

The next poem in *Eva-Mary* smashes the silence McCarriston's family maintained about the abuse they endured at the hands of her father. Interestingly McCarriston chooses to address the poem not to a family member but to the judge to whom her mother appealed, asking him to take action to prevent the violent attacks. "To Judge Faolain, Dead Long Enough: A Summons" is a devastating indictment, trial, and verdict; an exposé of a system that failed to help a desperate family. The poem refers to the fact that when McCarriston and her mother attempted to get assistance to halt the father's abuse, both judge and priest did nothing except advise them to obey. (The events McCarriston describes in the poem correspond with the term on the bench of a Judge John V. Phelan of Lynn, Massachusetts, and "Faolain" is the Gaelic spelling of "Phelan.") McCarriston's mother is portrayed not as passive in the face of her father's violence, but as ignored by a hypocritical social order.

McCarriston says in an interview with Maxine Scates that, though the poem is about her family history, she started to write it when she read a newspaper account of an abusive father in Vermont who was finally shot in his trailer by a relative who had had enough. The spark for the poem indicates that McCarriston is addressing more than her own family's experience.

"To Judge Faolain" begins with a sarcastic nod to "Your Honor." The speaker then presents her first exhibit, her mother with Pan-Cake makeup to cover the bruises her father inflicted, chin knocked askew by the force of his blows. Throughout the poem it is clear that the gap between the mother's social class and the judge's is part of what prevents her from getting a fair hearing—the mother has to style her own hair, while the judge speaks "in the tones / of parlors overlooking the harbor."

McCarriston is such a strong poet that she makes this scene not just the record of a memory but a work of art:

> you ferried us back down to *the law*,
> the black ice eye, the maw, the mako
> that circles the kitchen table nightly.

In these few lines, striking imagery, classical allusion, alliteration, rhyme, and assonance all work to recreate the nightmare that her family faced. The poem is whittled into a symmetrical arrangement of four stanzas of twelve lines each. It's as if the poet must express this scene as perfectly as possible in order to salvage and preserve the lesson in her mother's suffering.

The final stanza is the coup de grâce. The speaker calls the dead judge back to life, but not as himself. Using her imagination like a knife, she peels away the judge's official trappings, removing even his delicate hand and "half-lit Irish eye." She wills him to be reborn in a trailer (emblematic of the working class), the daughter of an abusive father. Employing a rare but majestic grammatical structure, the subjunctive mood, the poet then turns the tables and passes sentence on the judge:

> Let your name be
> Eva-Mary. Let your hour of birth
> be dawn. Let your life be long
> and common, and your flesh endure.

The judge is condemned to live out the fate of those to whom he was deaf in life. His new name, Eva-Mary, brings together both the figure of Eve as the object of the serpent's attack, and Mary as the type in Christianity of the suffering female.

The next poem in *Eva-Mary* details the father's brutal beating of McCarriston's brother. The poem's title is her brother's actual name, "Billy," giving us a clue that she is not using merely what Sharon Olds has called "the apparently personal." Olds is another poet who has written powerfully about domestic abuse, but in Olds's concept the speaker of a poem, even in a poem written in the first person, is *not* assumed to be the poet. McCarriston herself, however, is bearing witness to the events in her poems, events that it is crucial the reader believe actually occurred. "I wrote those poems in the first person not because I felt the experiences were only *mine* but to prevent their being read as fictions," McCarriston tells Maxine Scates.

In the unforgettable basement scene of "Billy," the underground setting and the coal furnace create a hellish light. The poem concludes with an ironic metaphor—the father's heavy breathing is likened to that of a parent "trying to lift a Buick off the body of / a loved child"—and this contrast heightens the reader's sense that something is violently and terribly wrong.

The next poem in *Eva-Mary,* "A Castle in Lynn," is in some ways the most devastating in the book. To this point in the collection she has documented only physical abuse. In this poem McCarriston lays bare her father's sexual assaults on her as a young girl. The poem's point of view is surprising. The poet never directly recounts an incident of abuse. Instead she fast-forwards to a moment many years later when the abusive father is too old to assault anyone. He is masturbating while calling to mind his own abusive behavior, savoring it in memory as pornography for his arousal. This account of the abuse—in the mind of the father as seen by an omniscient narrator—though indirect, produces perhaps a greater shock than would more direct narration; the reader must fathom the soul of a man so without heart that he can not only violate his daughter but also, years later, recall his actions not with regret but with satisfaction.

The poem's title refers to one of the father's rationales, the classic line that "*A man is king in his own / castle.*" The irony is that this house is not at all a castle. It is the last refuge of an alcoholic workingman. The advanced age and weakness of the old man disarm him and allow a safe setting for the poet to enter. The emotions of this poem are so outside the way people generally present themselves in public that the diction of the poem bends to portray this distorted, private world:

> Now hand
> —square hand, cruel as a spade—
>
> splits the green girlwood of her body.

Pronouns fall out of the language and nouns combine in strange ways. Although McCarriston is testifying, it is by means of the imagination, and the odd diction of the thoughts the reader overhears reflects the extremity of the old man's consciousness.

The poem's final quatrain is not easy to read, but it clinches the poem in the sense that it follows the abusive father's consciousness to its "logical" end:

> in a lifetime
> of used ones, second-hand, one girl
> he could spill like a shot of whiskey,
> the whore only he could call *daughter.*

The metaphor of whiskey recalls the alcoholism that sped McCarriston's father's decline, and the phrases "used" and "second-hand" suggest ragged surroundings. The end of the poem, where the father is thinking of his daughter as a prostitute, shakes the reader by the collar and shouts out for recognition of the humanity transgressed by the acts he is recalling.

After this depiction of her father, it's unexpected that McCarriston dedicates a poem in

Eva-Mary to him. "October 1913" recounts an incident that happened when her father was just five days old. Again the poet portrays her father at a time in life when he is harmless, and here he is also innocent. The poet's grandmother Margaret, named in the poem, has recently given birth to her fifth child. The reader gathers that there is little money to feed even the children who came before, and Margaret is tempted to drop her baby into the stove to solve the problem of the extra mouth to feed. Ironically McCarriston's father actually worked much of his life tending giant furnaces in factories, and the poem's second stanza admiringly portrays him at this difficult work. The description of this kind of workplace as a hell on earth is precise and dynamic.

While the mother is poised over the stove to dispose of her infant, the second youngest child comes in, and the mother retreats from the brink of murder. The poem's conclusion is heartbreaking:

> She crushed the flames
> back under the black lids. She would have
> nursed you then. She would have sat down
> to do it, unbuttoning the bodice on her
> scalding breasts. We do not know if,
> as she nursed you, she wept.
>
> She wept.

The mother's unfastening her blouse to feed her child recalls the description at the beginning of the poem of how Margaret used to bare her breasts, unashamed of her naked beauty. At the poem's end, though, the mood is not defiance but a blend of resignation and love. What emerges is a picture of a family caught in decade after decade of strife, from the sectarian violence of Northern Ireland, to the labor conflicts of New England, to the battles with alcoholism that carried on from generation to generation. McCarriston's ability to place her domestic story in the context of history and class deepens the reader's understanding of all the characters in this tragedy, including her father.

The possibility of peace of mind does emerge from the background of another poem in *Eva-Mary,* "Girl from Lynn Bathes Horse!!" The mock headline of the title indicates that the poem is taking a lighter tone than the book's earlier works. As in *Talking Soft Dutch,* the nearness of a horse opens new vistas.

In this poem a nine-year-old girl tries to bathe a mare with a garden hose as she holds the horse at the end of a short rope with the other hand. The arrangement is incredibly awkward, not to mention dangerous, but it works because the girl loves the horse, as she loved the mute animals she identified with in children's books and on television. The poet insists that no directions or blueprints for bathing the horse are necessary or even desirable, and, looking back to one of the book's key images, she insists that this cleansing involves a kind of knowledge like that of the Garden of Eden, beyond instruction. A child, according to the poem, must take from the trials of youth just one idea he or she can carry, clenched in the fist, "as earth expresses a diamond."

What this redemptive idea might be for McCarriston becomes clearer in the poem "A Thousand Genuflections," which in 1986 won the Poetry Society of America's Consuelo Ford Award. The speaker here is giving food and drink to her horse, and she unreels a gorgeous picture of this majestic animal running when called to eat, "her tail and mane / made flame by movement." This hymn to the beauty of a living thing has a Whitmanesque quality. The mare seems to possess almost supernatural powers, as McCarriston compares the animal's senses to scouts sent ahead and behind her. The speaker kneels to offer the bucket to the horse in this daily ritual, the action that in the title is linked to worship. It is almost as if the speaker is praying to the horse.

Suddenly a realization clicks and the speaker sees the horse in all its corporeal reality. The horse is not otherworldly; it possesses all the things an animal does—hunger for its food and drink, flesh, and attention. The horse's grandeur is its *body,* and this realization reflects back to the speaker, as she sees herself and humanity not as shadows of another reality but as beings charged with the vitality of life. The poem moves from the Catholic imagery of the title, to the almost pagan nature-worship of the horse, to a kind of Zen satori at the end. By unburdening her heart of the fury she felt in reaction to the abuse her family suffered, McCarriston has left room for a great wonder to fill her.

In *Eva-Mary,* McCarriston tries to make sense of her childhood, partly by setting the record straight. In it she also addresses with more honesty than in her first book the subject of her adult relationships, including the collapse of her first marriage and the ensuing custody battle.

Several poems deal with more recent issues in the poet's life. One of the most powerful is "Bad Lay." In this poem the speaker addresses a lover who was introduced to sex by buying prostitutes in Mexican border towns. His idea of women was formed by these illusory encounters with girls whom the poet characterizes with her usual verbal acumen as "hard nulliparous / bodies." His ideas of women and sex have been shaped by one-sided economic transactions, and he has no way of seeing a woman clearly enough to learn how actually to make love with her. The title refers to the man's dismissive attitude toward the women he has met later in life through more natural circumstances. The speaker of the poem would like to heal him with her love, but his ignorance is a vault that cannot be opened.

The image she uses of her anger as a cauldron has deep resonances by this point in the book, with echoes of the grandmother's stove, the boilers of her father's work experience, and the furnace in the childhood basement. It is remark-able that McCarriston is able so to unify the imagery in *Eva-Mary* despite the explosive emotions in the book. The cauldron image also suggests witches, but in a pagan sense, not a demonic one. At the poem's end she takes responsibility for her own ignorance in allowing her lover to assume the role of authority and teacher.

One of the most dramatic poems in *Eva-Mary* seems on the surface not to fit in the book. "Le Coursier de Jeanne d'Arc" (French for "Joan of Arc's Steed") is an unabashedly historical poem, set in Europe in the year 1431. The poem retells the moment when France's national heroine was burned at the stake, ostensibly for heresy but in reality for trying to rid her country of English domination. Though the time and place and characters do not match the rest of *Eva-Mary,* on closer look this poem vibrates with all of the themes and images of the book. McCarriston writes the poem in quatrains, but the sentences are long and breathless, conveying the rapid pace of events. McCarriston's poetry becomes most formal and musical when she is on fire with the strongest emotions.

The story of Joan of Arc has had a lifelong appeal for McCarriston. Joan is her saint's name. In addition McCarriston recalls that when as a girl she was granted early access to the adult section of her local library, "the first book I found there was a biography of Joan of Arc, pictured on the cover astride her charger." In McCarriston's family her trim and petite figure is often compared to that of her Parisian grandmother, making the French connection a natural one for her.

In McCarriston's own very individual narrative of the Joan of Arc story, the emphasis is on Joan's horse. McCarriston imagines that Joan's persecutors have decided to burn her horse in front of her eyes, before they burn her, in order to get her to recant her belief in her angelic voices. Joan refuses, despite the suffering of the horse. The poet depicts the charger in all its beauty and agony. Linking this poem to the others in the book, McCarriston portrays the martyrdom of Joan not in terms of the sovereignty of France or of that saint's connection to God, but in terms of Joan's insistence on the truth of her own perceptions and her love of her horse's natural grace. Her judges, on the other hand, are men with

> cruelty that can make
> of what a woman hears *a silence,*

> that can make of what a woman sees
> *a lie.*

In characterizing Joan's executioners in this light McCarriston is linking them to men who suppressed women's reports of abuse, including the judge who refused justice to her mother. McCarriston transforms Joan of Arc, a warrior in man's armor atop a steed, into a patron saint for women's soothsaying. As in much of McCarriston's poetry, telling the truth involves an act of the imagination—in this poem, seeing the immolation of the horse. Like many other poems in *Eva-Mary,* "Le Coursier de Jeanne d'Arc" explores the depths of human cruelty. By concentrating on the pain of an animal McCarriston escapes the maudlin snare and allows the reader to feel deeply the human misery that partakes of the fate of the horse. The pain in *Eva-Mary* is not just McCarriston's own, nor is it only Joan of Arc's in this poem.

This poem also gathers together all the images in *Eva-Mary.* The burning stakes reflect the fire imagery throughout the book, the horse resonates with the ones in earlier poems, and even the anthropomorphic fuel of the pyre "of greenwood stakes / head-high" recalls both the violated "green girlwood" of "A Castle in Lynn" and the maternal wood of "The Apple Tree."

McCarriston's last daring move in *Eva-Mary* is made with the final poem. The reader does a double take, realizing that it is word for word "The Apple Tree," the poem that begins the collection. Rereading the poem after the others in the book, the words sink in more deeply. At this point the reader knows who damaged that mother/tree, how deep the scars go, and how great is the solace now that those tormentors are gone.

RESPONSES TO *EVA-MARY*

Eva-Mary generated a response that few books of poetry achieve. The book has sold thousands of copies and has stayed in print since 1991. Even more remarkable is how audiences reacted when McCarriston read from the book. In public events from Burlington to Berkeley, larger than usual crowds turned out to hear her. After the readings women lined up to make personal contact with McCarriston. The women often spoke to her about their own experiences with abuse, or sought advice on how to escape dangerous situations at home. Precisely because of the power of the poetry in *Eva-Mary,* McCarriston was asked to be more than a poet— she was called upon to act as a healer. To one woman, who asked "for my friend" how to get out of an abusive situation, McCarriston responded, "She must become spiritually and economically self-sufficient. She must gain that inner and outer safety. ... So that, if she chooses, she may make a just and loving partnership, and if she chooses, she may not."

Critical reaction to the book has often been polarized, depending on the reader's opinion about the inclusion in poetry of autobiographical material related to incest and abuse. The reactions of two former teachers of McCarriston at Goddard College, both Pulitzer Prize–winning poets, are diametrically opposed. In a jacket blurb for *Eva-Mary,* Lisel Mueller hails the work as "an immensely moving book, fearless in its passion. Linda McCarriston accomplishes a near miracle, transforming memories of trauma into poems that are luminous and often sacramental."

Louise Glück states the other side in an essay called "The Forbidden," first printed in the summer 1993 issue of the *Threepenny Review* and collected in 1994 in Glück's *Proofs & Theories: Essays on Poetry*. In this essay on confessional poetry Glück specifically criticizes McCarriston and *Eva-Mary:* "The test for emotional authority is emotional impact, and the great flaw in Linda McCarriston's *Eva-Mary* is that, cumulatively, it isn't moving." Glück goes on to attack what she sees as the book's simplistic division of characters into either heroes or villains.

Judith Harris defends McCarriston in the December 1994 issue of the Associated Writing Programs' *Writer's Chronicle*. In her article "Breaking the Code of Silence: Ideology and Women's Confessional Poetry," which was reprinted in 2001 in *After Confession: Poetry as Autobiography*, Harris argues that, "in strong poets like McCarriston or [Sharon] Olds, confession is a personal outcry that seeks to address a community's consciousness."

CONFESSIONAL POET?

The extremely revealing and autobiographical nature of some of McCarriston's work in some ways links her with poets termed "confessional," including her fellow Massachusetts natives Robert Lowell, Anne Sexton, and Sylvia Plath. (It's not surprising that Massachusetts, with its Puritan heritage of emphasizing the individual's internal struggle for a pure soul, should be the birthplace of so many confessional poets.) McCarriston shares an intent with these poets to use a frank account of personal and family history as the material of her verse.

In fact McCarriston has personal connections to these poets. When she was still in college McCarriston gave a reading with Robert Lowell as part of an award she won, and he encouraged her writing. Also, as McCarriston points out in a forthcoming essay entitled "Coming Home to Vermont," she and Plath grew up in neighboring towns in Massachusetts. In that essay McCarriston identifies herself as "eleven years younger than she was, and from a town close enough to hers to know the ring of her economic peril." But important differences between these confessional poets and McCarriston exist.

Confessional poets try to unburden themselves of personal or familial weaknesses or errors. Think of Robert Lowell's famous admission in "Skunk Hour" that his "mind's not right," or Allen Ginsberg's revelation in *Kaddish* of his mother's madness. McCarriston builds on their urgency to make public what is usually kept quiet or in the family, but in her case the impulse is not so much to expose herself as to bear witness to an injustice. Her pulling the veil off her father's abuse is not confession, but testimony. Her model is not the Puritan battle for the individual's soul, but the insistence of the martyr against the opposition of the disbelieving status quo.

Despite these differences McCarriston has publicly defended confessional poetry as the forerunner of the personal-as-political writing of her generation. In remarks that she made as a panelist at the Associated Writing Programs Annual Conference in Albany, New York, on April 17, 1999, McCarriston praised these poets' willingness to break taboos, even though it meant that critics labeled them as "confessional," a term that still carries a stigma. Arguing against these critics McCarriston stated that their dismissal of confessional poets "was a social judgment of the kind one might incur breaking the dinner party trust by raising issues of politics or religion. What has stuck to the term is only that—but all of that: *bad taste, poor taste. You won't be asked back.*"

LITTLE RIVER

It took McCarriston nine years to assemble her next collection of poems after the tumultuous *Eva-Mary.* This third book, *Little River: New* and *Selected Poems* (2000), was first published in Ireland in 2000 by a press called, appropriately, Salmon Publishing. It was released in the United States in 2002.

For a writer who discovers as deep a source as McCarriston did in her *Eva-Mary* poems on domestic abuse, it is tempting to dip back into the same well. McCarriston refuses to do that with *Little River*. She continues to explore relations between the sexes, but deals with issues that primarily affect adult relationships. She develops her critique of the social system and widens her search for a spirituality that is liberating, not constraining. Her probe of her family history extends back to the root cultures of her ancestors.

Little River consists of four sections bookended by an introductory and a concluding poem. The selected section of the book assembles nine horse-related poems from her first two collections and includes a new poem in this vein. All the rest is new material, including much work from her adopted home in Alaska, a series of poems inspired by trips to Ireland, and poems dealing with Native American themes.

This book highlights an important aspect of McCarriston's poetic work: almost all of it has a setting. Many contemporary poets, moving as they do from teaching job to teaching job and from region to region, write from a nonspecific sense of place. McCarriston's poetry has a distinctive locale, whether it is working-class Lynn or the Alaskan wilderness. In fact one of the poems in *Little River* is titled "Local," which is also the Irish term for pub.

After "Kitchen Terrarium: 1983," the introductory poem, the next seven poems are set on the rural west coast of Ireland and are written in a voice close to the lyrical, pastoral style of *Talking Soft Dutch*, but with an ear to the harsh terrain and fates of that landscape. "*This is the wind they say makes people / mad here*" begins "In Off the Cliffs of Moher," the first of these poems. In Ireland McCarriston discovers many of the problems that beset her family, but she also finds a sense of peace and belonging. The lilt of the Irish brogue informs the diction of these poems, playing with the syntax and heightening the musicality of McCarriston's verse.

McCarriston first visited Ireland in 1991, traveling mostly in Counties Clare and Mayo. In 1991 she also became a dual citizen of Ireland and the United States. She returned to Ireland in 1997 and 1998 on her way back from teaching at the Spoleto Symposium in Italy. During her 1998 trip to Ireland she wrote most of the poems in this section of *Little River*.

In "Local," set in a pub, the speaker thinks back to an era when her Irish progenitors caroused in such a spot. McCarriston describes the warm communal glow of the bar, but there is a strong undertow of tragedy in the scene. Referring to an Irish euphemism for alcoholism, she describes Ireland as "the land / of *an honest man's failing*." The drinking in the bar reminds her of how that problem decimated her family. The man who is entertaining the patrons with a mock dance does not delight the poem's speaker, who recalls that this man's brother recently died as a result of drink, which she compares to the riptides of the coast.

Another standout in this section of the book is "In Clare," a whole story in only seven lines. Like an Irish ballad the poem recounts in flowing language how a girl's love was unrequited, "though she was lovely as a silken thing, blue-eyed and good." The reader sees her in a small boat in the rain on her way to an island as "the wind wrapped her face in her yellow hair." The poet emphasizes the openness of the girl's field of vision and her soul in ironic contrast to her inward brooding on her one-sided love, implying that a better way exists for women to engage in relationships. The poem is based on an actual encounter McCarriston had in Ireland with a nurse who was going to take up a position on the remote island of Clare. With few words Mc-

Carriston captures a scene that has emotion, color, and depth.

"Aubade," also in this section, is perhaps the most innocent and uncomplicated love poem McCarriston has written. Unlike the aubade in *Talking Soft Dutch,* this work fits the traditionally prescribed mold of such a poem. The lover is a farmer in a small Irish community. The poem is cozy with details, warm and close. Before the lovers can go off to their privacy the farmer must escort a drunk home from the pubs, where he knows every fiddler. Here the drunkenness is harmless, indicative of the lover's part in a caring circle.

The farmer is the county *Da,* or father, who looks after others. He lives surrounded by animals, so much so that his goats wait for his car to return so that they can fall asleep on the warm hood, and his hours for loving are governed by when he must wake up to milk the cows. The animals and the labor of caring for them seem to provide protection, as they do in McCarriston's horse poems, but the proliferation of animals adds a note of domestic safety beyond any of her earlier poems.

The scene is a northern summer's night, when the sun sets late, and that luminousness carries through the whole poem, lighting up the imagery. The only note that is less than delicious comes at the very end when the poet compares the two lovers to "worn meadows / along a historied wall." The word "worn" tells us that these lovers are not young and that they have not led easy lives. The long history of the wall bonds them in their Irish ancestry. The fact that McCarriston can write a love poem in such a warm light at this point in her career is indicative of how far she has come in healing the wounds of her childhood and marriages.

In this collection McCarriston affirms her Native American roots as well. Some of the poems present either an American Indian perspective or a perspective on American Indians. In two poems written about a trip to the Southwest,

McCarriston reflects on her distance from and connection to the Native Americans who work menial jobs. In "At the Indian Store" the speaker is in some ways like any tourist buying crafts and Indian music at this stand in Tulsa, tied to those who broke promises to the tribe of the Comanche salesman. What unites her with the Indian workers here is that she is a woman who has herself experienced lies and injuries at the hands of the powers that be. More than that, she knows what it feels like to exchange "handiwork, for pennies," being a poet who works with little recompense, and a former waitress and university adjunct. There is a similar dynamic in the poem "Indian Country," which appears later in the collection.

This perspective is also evident in the poem "The Greeks." Here the poet describes the other end of the American class structure, privileged white males living in a fraternity house near the seat of power in Washington, D.C. She describes these preppies as "sons of moneyed fathers, / monotheists." This introduction of religion into a poem that is largely about social class is intriguing. It seems as if McCarriston is now moving further from her Catholic upbringing toward a belief in the holiness of nature, a belief grounded more in the Native American worldview than in the European.

Her differences with her Catholic education are evident in "Reading *Ode to the West Wind* 25 Years Later." In this poem, one of McCarriston's funniest, she describes the nun who tried to teach literature to her parochial-school class as if it were like memorizing dates of battles:

I don't recall we ever read
a fiery word, but took
her dictation—*understanding*—
hunk by hunk down in the margins.

As a result of this dry approach to poetry even Percy Bysshe Shelley's masterpiece "Ode to the West Wind" about a whirl of passion and prophecy becomes "windless, tone-deaf, and unsexed."

McCarriston's writing on class, a crucial topic for her, takes on a different expression in "Song of the Scullery." This poem represents a new venture for the poet since it is a dramatic monologue in the persona of a maid, possibly in a nineteenth-century house of means. The lustful master of the house is, interestingly, a writer, who likes to romanticize the earthy world of his servants in his scribbling. But he is the type of person who could tell his own story. McCarriston uses her inventiveness to sing the song of a person who paradoxically says she has no song. The poem is a reflection by the maid who has no time to write; she is too busy peeling and preparing food to do anything but ruin her beautiful young hands. She feels she has more in common with the house's workhorse than with the writer upstairs.

Some of the poems about Alaska and McCarriston's trip there also have a diction that is new for the poet. The sentences are clipped, spare, as if the cold climate and the press of the years is starting to make her more frugal with her words. In "Last Frontier," about her cross-country road trip to Anchorage, her phrasing and tone sound almost like Ezra Pound's *Hugh Selwyn Mauberley*. The two poems share abbreviated clauses, use of the third person to write about personal experience, and the sense of being out of step with one's time. McCarriston now reflects on her life with a wry humor, describing the highlight of the year she moved as being the manicures she got every other week at a strip mall.

In another Alaska poem in *Little River*, McCarriston makes her most definitive statement about how relations between men and women could change, are changing. "Wrought Figure" is a poem told by a woman who is attracted to a man who, by his own admission, is "hard on women." He reveals this to the speaker at the end of a candlelight dinner in the short summer of the north, pieces of shellfish scattered over the table like the bodies of the smart and beauti-

ful partners in his past. McCarriston's use of color in this poem is particularly skillful. Everything is red, suggesting emotional carnage—the barn, the lobster, and the man's cayenne beard.

But the speaker does not shy away from this attractive and bright suitor, despite the procession of loves who've passed through his life, despite the speaker's jealousy of each woman's "second language, hair / and eyes, height, even the fights." Her use of alliteration and rhyme is effective in this passage and in this poem in general. Instead the speaker takes time to contemplate the paradigm this man puts forward in which the woman is used by the male user, comparing it in an intricate metaphor to the "figure / ground problem" in psychology, in which two images interact dynamically, taking turns being in the foreground. She realizes that she is equally hard on men, and goes back to explain this in a spirited comeback to the man.

At the end of the poem the speaker invites the man to dance with her on the summer lawn, both aware of their own attractions, both confident in their ability to pull for themselves in an adult relationship,

> a woman turned by
> a man who loves women, and a man turned
> by a woman who loves men.

Neither one is leading the other, neither dominates—McCarriston's vision of harmony between the sexes.

CONTROVERSY OVER "INDIAN GIRLS"

In early December of 2000 McCarriston published a poem entitled "Indian Girls" in a magazine called *Ice-Floe*. The poem refers to sexual abuse of Native American children and its leading to alcoholism in adulthood. A Tlingit

Indian student of McCarriston claimed that the poem is "racist" and "insulting." Responding to this student's call to action, about twenty Native American women protested outside McCarriston's class at the University of Alaska, drawing media attention. In the *Anchorage Daily News* on December 16, 2000, McCarriston publicly apologized, saying that her intent was "to comfort the afflicted and afflict the comfortable, not the reverse." The department chair responded to the protest by declaring that a dean was investigating the matter. First Amendment advocates and editorial writers nationally decried the investigation as a violation of McCarriston's right to free speech. The matter went to the university president, Mark R. Hamilton, who stated publicly that there were no grounds for investigation of constitutionally protected speech. In April 2002 federal investigators issued a report saying that neither the university nor McCarriston had violated her student's civil rights.

McCARRISTON'S PROSE

Since 1993 McCarriston has been writing and publishing essays that question the assumptions of U.S. intellectual life. Her prose seeks to keep class and gender as participants in the debate at a time when many artists in the country are preoccupied with formal experimentation and individual expression.

Her autobiographical essay "Weed" was published in 1998 in the *Contemporary Authors Autobiography Series*. McCarriston's narrative about her development as an artist is itself a work of art, full of the sorts of details that thrive in her poetry. When she writes about how her father took her as a child with him to bars in Lynn, for instance, she recalls how the red dye of the pistachio nuts came off on her fingers. When she discusses class and gender she does not treat them as abstractions but as real forces that made her hold an aspirin to a rotting tooth

to ease the ache when as a child she had no dental care, or undermined the trust between her and her second husband when, because of differences in their backgrounds and resources, he wrote her out of his will.

One of the chief points in her prose is that American artistic life is compromised by the insistence on keeping it clear of politics. According to McCarriston, a pervasive bias against art with a social message shows up in poetry in the form of fragmented verse that makes no attempt to find lessons in lived experience. In "God the Father and the Empty House" (2001), an essay published in a collection by Wolfhound Press in Ireland, she writes, "As nowhere else, the United States defines art as that which marks the furthest reach from political social consciousness. A radical, atomising individualism, requisite for our upwardly mobile consumerist identity, finds its perfection in our modern and postmodern 'high end' poetry." McCarriston is questioning no less than the American dream, with its emphasis on individual success. She contrasts it with a vision that would restructure society to remedy social ills.

As McCarriston indicates in an important but unpublished prose work written as a long letter to the poet Hayden Carruth, the individualism of the American dream also plays out in creative writing programs. The letter was occasioned by Carruth's refusal to accept a presidential invitation to attend a poetry evening at the White House on April 22, 1998. McCarriston notes in the letter that she observes many students splintering or ignoring material from their own lives in order to create poems that are fashionably obscure but empty of content. Alternatively she sees students from communities that are traditionally underrepresented in universities being encouraged to write laments about their exclusion from the American dream but discouraged from questioning the isolating effects of that myth. Either of these paths may lead to jobs in academia, but McCarriston questions their consequences for young writers: "When student poets strive for the balcony view of their own street experience, they strive for an aesthetic *victory* over their own knowledge," she contends.

In the letter to Carruth, McCarriston is equally critical of the primacy of the lyric mode in contemporary poetry, maintaining that it is a young person's form that privileges the individual voice over collective aspirations. For students in MFA programs that emphasize fragments over content and exclusively promote the lyric, the cumulative effect is a drastic limiting of the writing tools at their disposal. Such programs place "the broad range of human condition and earned response, off limits: lucid, powerful language, off limits: strict forms and musical variations, off limits; history, off limits. Narrative, syntax, discourse, off limits."

Just as McCarriston is one of the most heart-grabbing voices in contemporary poetry, her criticism is direct and forceful. She represents an important pole in the spectrum of views on contemporary American poetry; she is willing to say what many think but are too timid to express because of a climate in which academic advancement and secure employment are dependent on diplomacy.

McCarriston is also an astute critic of contemporary society and the global economy. In her unpublished essay "Of 'The Frill'" she unpacks the consumer impulses in herself and contrasts them with what she knows about the labor conditions of those who produce the goods she desires. The title of this essay comes from a Pearl S. Buck story called "The Frill," one of the few pieces of political writing McCarriston encountered as a young adult. In that story a rich woman constantly criticizes the needlework of her Chinese servant who is stitching her frill. McCarriston identifies with the servant, but she confesses that her appetites as a consumer are more like those of the master. She describes how she tries to tailor her tastes to her politics,

boycotting chain stores that use cheap labor in third world countries, companies "that reap grotesque profits in the abyss between the cost of production and the cost of purchase."

McCarriston finds herself identifying with the factory workers in those sweatshops, so like the factories where her grandmother worked in Lynn: "That *Lynn* is wherever the factories are now. My grandmother is making the shoes there. She is Costa Rican or Indonesian. I'm not born." She describes the irony of former factory workers supporting the labor practices that their grandparents struggled to eliminate, caught in the American rush to possess status symbols and comforts. But McCarriston does not accept the inevitability of this arrangement: "Why should my bedding have to be made at slave wages?" she asks. "Why should the fabric? Who is sewing my frill?"

McCarriston's view of literature and culture draws from a familiar source, John Keats's maxim that "Beauty is truth, truth beauty." She believes that a poem needs to contain an idea and that the idea should point toward justice. Despite a difficult life and a controversial career, despite her deep criticisms of the state of the world, McCarriston is positive about the possibilities for writing and for change in this era. As she says in an interview with Maxine Scates, "We live in a wonderful moment of course; I mean we live in a moment of really transforming consciousness. And the job is not done."

Selected Bibliography

WORKS OF LINDA McCARRISTON

POETRY

Talking Soft Dutch. Lubbock, Tex.: Texas Tech University Press, 1984.

Eva-Mary. Chicago and Evanston, Ill.: Another Chicago Press and TriQuarterly Books/ Northwestern University Press, 1991; Evanston,

Ill.: TriQuarterly Books/Northwestern University Press, 1994.

Little River: New and Selected Poems. Cliffs of Moher, County Clare, Ireland: Salmon Publishing, 2000; Evanston, Ill.: TriQuarterly Books/ Northwestern University Press, 2002.

CRITICAL ESSAYS AND AUTOBIOGRAPHICAL WRITINGS

"Class Unconsciousness and an American Writer." *New England Review* 15:65–75 (spring 1993).

"The Grace of Form." In *Liberating Memory: Our Work and Our Working-Class Consciousness.* Edited by Janet Zandy. New Brunswick, N.J.: Rutgers University Press, 1994. Pp. 97–110.

"Horse and Writer" *Sojourners* 25:22 (May–June 1996).

"Weed." In *Contemporary Authors Autobiography Series,* Vol. 28. Edited by Linda R. Andres. Detroit: Gale Group, 1998. Pp. 189–229.

"One Hand Clapping: Free Speech under Attack in America." *Anchorage Press,* April 5–11, 2001, p. 8.

"God the Father and the Empty House." In *Irish Spirit: Pagan, Celtic, Christian, Global.* Edited by Patricia Monaghan. Dublin, Ireland: Wolfhound Press, 2001. Pp. 235–244.

UNPUBLISHED ESSAYS AND PAPERS

"An Unreconstructed *Townie:* Thomas McGrath among the *Gownies.*" (A study of the poet McGrath and the relationship between feminism and socialism.)

"Coming Home to Vermont." (A lengthy essay on various topics including McCarriston's relationship to confessional poetry and the role of class in the literary community.)

"Of 'The Frill.'" (A personal essay on consumerism inspired by a rethinking of Pearl S. Buck's short story "The Frill.")

Letter to Hayden Carruth. (A meditation on the sociology of American poetry and creative writing departments.)

"Who If Not Us: Writers and Teachers Talk about Literary Silence." (Remarks made on April 17, 1999, as a panelist at the Associated Writing Programs Annual Conference in Albany, New York.)

INTERVIEWS

Grimes, Carol. *Kalliope* 18, no. 1:70–77 (1995).

Moyers, Bill. "Linda McCarriston." In his *The Languages of Life: A Festival of Poets.* New York: Doubleday, 1995. Pp. 270–286.

Scates, Maxine. "The Denial of Class." *Poetry Flash* 258:1, 6–11 (January 1995).

CRITICAL AND BIOGRAPHICAL STUDIES

Berger, Rose Marie. "Got Poetry?" *Sojourners* 29:62–64 (July–August 2000).

Corey, Stephen. Review of *Eva-Mary. Georgia Review* 46:184–185 (spring 1992).

Cotter, James Finn. "Prized Poetry." *Hudson Review* 45:518–524 (autumn 1992).

Cramer, Stephen. "Self-Defense." *Poetry* 161:159–181 (December 1992).

Glück, Louise. "The Forbidden." In her *Proofs & Theories: Essays on Poetry.* Hopewell, N.J.: Ecco/Harper Trade, 1994. Pp. 53–63.

Harris, Judith. "Breaking the Code of Silence: Ideology and Women's Confessional Poetry." In *After Confession: Poetry as Autobiography.* Edited by Kate Sontag and David Graham. Saint Paul, Minn.: Graywolf Press, 2001. Pp. 254–268.

McGuiness, Daniel. Review of *Eva-Mary. Antioch Review* 50:778 (fall 1992).

Oktenberg, Adrian. "Formal but Unconstrained." *Women's Review of Books* 20:36 (July 2003).

Ruskin, Liz. "Indian Women Protest Poem on Sexual Abuse: University Professor's Class Center of Debate." *San Francisco Chronicle,* December 23, 2000, p. A9.

Shetley, Vernon. Review of *Talking Soft Dutch. Poetry* 146:38–39 (April 1985).

Solari, Rose. "The Sound of What Matters." *Common Boundary* 14:24–32 (January–February 1996).

Townsend, Alison. "Poetry Out of Pain." *Women's Review of Books* 9:11–12 (March 1992).

—ZACK ROGOW

Charles Reznikoff

1894–1976

*I*T IS THE pure nobility of his character, as much as the disarming simplicity of his poems, that distinguishes Charles Reznikoff from the menagerie of twentieth-century poets. The son of Jewish Russian immigrants in turn-of-the-century New York, he set his compass to poetry at an early age and pursued it until, literally, his dying hour. He earned a degree in law, but declined to practice in order to concentrate fully on his writing. When he did not have a publisher, as was the case for the vast majority of his eighty-two years, he paid to have his poems printed privately so that he could preserve his work and freely move on to his next project. His unfaltering dedication to poetry compromised his marriage, denied him all sorts of material comforts, and essentially precluded him from having children. But it was as much a desire to honor the traditions of his ancestry as it was to honor an abstract notion of art that induced him to forego the pleasures and sustenance of a family. He applied his singular focus on endless walks of ten and twenty miles through Manhattan and Brooklyn, producing lyrics so uniquely forthright in their imagery that they continually dared their readers to declare them prose. "To me the use of language means communication," he told the interviewer L. S. Dembo late in his life. "If you write, you write to be understood, and if you're not understood, you've failed." By this standard, he never failed.

"THE WORK WAS THE THING"

Charles Reznikoff was born on August 30, 1894, in the Jewish ghetto of Brownsville, a small town in a then-rural section of Brooklyn. With the exception of a few brief interludes working as a film factotum for a movie producer friend in Hollywood in the 1930s, Reznikoff lived his entire life in New York City. His parents, Nathan and Sarah Yetta (Wolvovsky) Reznikoff, had emigrated like many Jews of their time and place from Russia in the 1880s to escape the pogroms of Tsar Alexander III. Their lives and struggles naturally dominated Reznikoff's self-understanding and became the subject matter for much of his own work. He recorded their oral autobiographies in "Early History of a Seamstress" and "Early History of a Sewing-Machine Operator," which, after publishing separately, he added to his own memoir "Needle Trade" in the three-part *Family Chronicle: An Odyssey from Russia to America* (1963). He lifted much of this material, particularly from his mother's story, for his first novel *By the Waters of Manhattan: An Annual,* self-published in 1930. His mother made it clear that the educational aspirations she and her husband privately harbored in the Old World, and traded for escape from social persecution and an immigrant's eighty-hour work week, would be left to Charles to try to fulfill. "We are a lost generation," she pronounced through her son's pen in "Early History of a Seamstress." "It is for our children to do what they can."

Reznikoff was not, however, the first poet in the family. When Sarah's father, who shared Charles' Hebrew name Ezekiel, died far from home in Russia while searching for work, a bundle of verses, heretofore unknown to his family, was discovered on his person and returned to his wife. The poems were written in

Hebrew, which none of his family could read or speak. As Jews were routinely being deported, tortured, and killed for the alleged dissemination of politically subversive writings, Sarah's mother immediately burned her husband's poems, fearing they might contain politically subversive sentiments and not wanting to even risk soliciting a translator to learn their content. The loss of his grandfather's poems, in addition to his mother's hopes, was taken up by Reznikoff as a filial burden that he wholeheartedly accepted:

> All his verse was lost—except for what
> still speaks through me
> as mine.

In 1910, with an inkling of an interest in literature and an adolescent's desire to get away from home, Reznikoff left New York for the University of Missouri School of Journalism. Deciding that journalism and literature were not of a piece but actually antithetical, he returned after just one year. His professors explained that what made a good story was "man bites dog;" Reznikoff realized that he was instead interested in the commonplace "dog bites man"—"the news that stays news," as he later put it.

Striking out on his own for an unlikely career in middle America had caused some trepidation within his immigrant family, as he later memorialized in his long autobiographical poem "Early History of a Writer:"

> my grandfather turned aside and burst into tears
> ...
> ... in spite of all the learning I had acquired in
> high school,
> I knew not a word of the sacred text of the Torah
> and was going out into the world
> with none of the accumulated wisdom of my
> people to guide me,
> with no prayers with which to talk to the God of
> my people. ...

Although he only ever learned a rudimentary Hebrew and could never have been considered a practicing Jew, the tradition of his family and ancestors comprised an enormous share of Reznikoff's self-identity and, as with poetry, he was keenly aware of receiving the family torch. Though he never became an expert in Talmudic law, as his paternal grandfather had, he built his own bridge to his faith tradition by applying himself to civil law, enrolling in New York University Law School in 1912 and passing the bar in 1916. To his surprise, he found his studies stimulating and liberating:

> I found it delightful
> to climb those green heights,
> to bathe in clean waters of reason,
> to use words for their daylight meaning
> and not as prisms
> playing with the rainbows of connotation

He pursued a law degree no doubt in part to ameliorate his parents' high hopes (his only brother, never close to Charles as an adult, became a doctor) and pay homage to his ancestor's traditional honor for reason and scripture, but the law's scrupulous attention to language also profoundly influenced Reznikoff's own writing, becoming a source of inspiration to which he returned throughout his career.

As Reznikoff was known for his fanatical devotion to his art and the prodigious body of work he ultimately produced, so he was also known for never letting the petty concerns of food, money, or shelter intrude upon his writing. He passed the bar but never practiced. With the exception of a few years working as a researcher for the law encyclopedia *Corpus Juris,* he never put his degree to any "practical" application, and indeed never successfully maintained a full-time job. Nor cared to. After years of grueling textile labor, his parents had a fantastically successful run with their own hat company, the Artistic Millinery Company, in the late 1910s, and Charles worked for them as a traveling salesman, living for years afterward on a monthly stipend they sent him for his contribution to the business. He passionately believed that a poet's first responsibility must be to his work, and he religiously observed this code of honor throughout his life. When the leading journals of the day were not quick to accept his poems, he hit upon the strategy that would keep his books in print through good times and bad:

> But since I did not hope for a publisher
> ...
> nor did I relish the pretence—
> why, I thought, I should print privately,
> that is, pay the printer and make no pretence of
> having a publisher at all.
> There was little notice to be had that way, I
> knew,
> among the crowd of new books;
> but, besides the stimulation to write and revise,
> I would clear my head and heart
> for new work. Yes, the work was the thing.

Until New Directions signed him to a contract in 1962, Reznikoff would print several hundred copies each of more than two dozen volumes of his work, most on a turn-of-the-century printing press he stored in his parents' basement.

He published his first book, *Rhythms,* in 1918 and brought out a revised and expanded edition each of the next three years. He assembled all of this work in his collection *Five Groups of Verse* in 1927. Mostly, however, what Reznikoff did in the 1920s was walk. He regularly covered twenty miles per day throughout his adult life, still managing as many as six miles when he was in his late seventies. Walking the streets of New York was his office, synagogue, and sanctuary. "Unless he walked a number of miles ... he suffered psychic deprivation," his wife, Marie Syrkin, remembered in a memoir. "'I did not walk today,' he would announce with an air of tragic loss that the simple fact did not seem to justify." Reznikoff married Syrkin in 1930 after a somewhat formal and protracted courtship, necessarily prolonged by the fact that at the time Syrkin was only legally separated from

her second husband. She was, however, by all accounts, the one and only great love of Reznikoff's life, and the two were married for more than forty years. The brief nadir of the Objectivist poetry movement in the early 1930s, created and very much improvised by the poet Louis Zukofsky, who presented Reznikoff's work as sort of Platonic ideal of poetry, brought Reznikoff some fleeting recognition, but little work and less money. He and Syrkin agreed that he would have to find some employment to support the pair, and it was at this time that he went to work for *Corpus Juris.* Essentially, Reznikoff was charged with reviewing court testimony and writing case histories for law encyclopedias. The long hours spent researching cases ultimately served as the genesis of one of Reznikoff's most innovative and important works, *Testimony,* which Reznikoff first published in 1934 and then published in more complete form beginning in 1965. But as a pure researcher, Reznikoff apparently left something to be desired. A premium was placed on efficiency and uniformity, but Reznikoff liked to ponder the evidence before him and write his histories in such a way that satisfied his literary standards. He at first was favored with forgiving bosses, then was not, and was fired after a couple of years.

A friend from his school days fortuitously interceded. As students, Reznikoff and Albert Lewin were both interested in literature, trading poems and reading assignments, and the two managed to keep up a healthy correspondence after they went their separate ways. Reznikoff stuck to poems, but Lewin moved to Hollywood and became a film producer. With Reznikoff out of work and the Great Depression at its bleakest, Lewin offered his old friend a position as a researcher and fact checker for his studio. The $75 per week salary was so modest that none of Lewin's superiors or associates bothered to question Reznikoff's role or qualifications, but to the poet, it was a small gold mine. Meanwhile

Syrkin worked as high school teacher in the New York City public schools, a job she greatly resented as beneath her, being a Cornell-educated woman used to moving in intellectual circles. Nevertheless it provided the lion's share of her family's income, as well as support for her son by her previous marriage.

"AT THE COMMON TABLE"

The poet of the New York City streets could encounter no greater juxtaposition than life in Hollywood, and, like the law, his time in the movies provided Reznikoff a valuable fresh perspective and a wealth of new material. Lewin's patronage, however, was ultimately compromised by Reznikoff's essential uselessness around the studio, and the poet was obliged to return to New York. As a writer, Reznikoff remained as productive as ever throughout the 1930s. After the novel *By the Waters of Manhattan* in 1930, he printed and published the poetry collections *Jerusalem the Golden* (1934), *In Memoriam: 1933* (1934), and *Separate Way* (1936), as well as the first installment of his landmark *Testimony*. Shortly after returning from California, he also received a commission to write a sociological history of the Jews of Charleston, South Carolina, a work that remains one of the finest immigrant community histories ever produced. But Reznikoff's reluctance and inability to work took its toll on his marriage. "He did not womanize, drink or even smoke; he was often prissily prudish," Syrkin remembered. "All in all quite the reverse of the stereotype of the manic poet. But on a more fundamental level he rejected the basic conventions as to how life should be led. He would assume no obligations, such as support of a family, that might hamper his true vocation."

When Syrkin was offered a teaching position at the new Brandeis University in Massachusetts, she accepted it, and for years she and Reznikoff essentially lived separate lives. He remained absolutely devoted to her through these lean years, but his refusal to contribute his share to the household income left his wife, also a mother, little choice. She respected her husband's artistic integrity—he was only living as he ever had—but would not allow both their souls to be sacrificed on the altar of his art. She made the trip to New York to visit him perhaps one weekend a month, sometimes less.

Private works that Reznikoff wrote in the 1940s and 1950s, only discovered after his death in 1976, revealed this time to be the saddest of his life. Still, he printed and published, bringing out the poetry collection *Going To and Fro and Walking Up and Down* in 1941 and a historical novel about Jews in Arthurian England, *The Lionhearted: A Story about the Jews of Medieval England,* in 1944. In the 1950s he completed several German translations of Jewish works. While at Brandeis, Syrkin assumed the editorship of the magazine *The Jewish Frontier,* and she procured some editorial work for Reznikoff at its New York office. Again, his work suffered from tardiness and idiosyncrasy, but he charmed his coworkers as he charmed most everyone and got along well. Each day he would walk from his apartment in Riverdale, on Manhattan's Upper West Side, to the *Frontier*'s offices in Brooklyn, covering the entire Manhattan Hudson River shoreline, traversing the downtown financial district and crossing the Brooklyn Bridge. In the evenings he would leave at six, walk two hours, stop for a modest dinner in an automat along the river, then cover the last 90 minutes or so to arrive home around ten, a round trip of more than twenty miles.

Reznikoff, in both his work and his vocational devotion to it, was very much the poet's poet. He attracted a notable list of admirers throughout his years of relative obscurity, from Lionel Trilling to William Carlos Williams to Allen Ginsberg, and their combined advocacy ultimately provided him his first significant book contract, with New Directions in 1962, who published a book of his selected poems for which Reznikoff resurrected the title *By the Waters of Manhattan: Selected Verse.* New Directions next backed publication of an expanded edition of Reznikoff's *Testimony: The United States (1885–1890): Recitative* in 1965, but, to the poet's bitter disappointment, meager sales and a cool critical reception led his publisher to drop him from its list. Now, however, the die had been cast, and Reznikoff's days of anonymity were finally over. The National Institute of Arts and Letters awarded him the $2,500 Morton Dauwen Zabel Prize in 1971 for his lifetime contribution to literature. More important, after self-publishing two more books of poetry (in one volume) in 1969—*By the Well of Living and Seeing and The Fifth Book of the Maccabees*—he found a publisher that committed to keeping all of his works in print in perpetuity. The Black Sparrow Press in Santa Rosa, California, brought out *By the Well of Living and Seeing: New and Selected Poems 1918–1973* in 1974 and then published a touchstone of Reznikoff's career, *Holocaust,* in 1975. Reznikoff was reviewing the proofs of the first volume of his *Complete Poems* when he died in 1976.

His final decade was infinitely happier at home as well. Syrkin accepted a directorial position with the executive of the World Zionist Organization and moved back to New York; the two moved into the modern Lincoln Towers on the Upper West Side in 1966, quite a step up from the tenement buildings in which Reznikoff spent most of his life. Aside from his tedious penchant for turning their weekly *New Yorker* over to the doorman before Syrkin had a chance to read it, and his stubborn insistence on elaborately and laboriously cleaning the apartment himself rather than hire a weekly maid service, the two got along well. After being mugged in Riverside Park, he finally curtailed his extensive wanderings, but he developed a new route around and across Central Park to the Upper East Side, befriending several leisure sidewalk and park bench regulars along the way. One such gentleman would regale Reznikoff with tales of his past business glory, leading him miles off his course to whatever appointment he was obliged to keep. After the man's death, Reznikoff and Syrkin were astonished to discover that this acquaintance had bequeathed them $10,000 in his will, by far the largest windfall of Reznikoff's life. Even Syrkin had to acknowledge the karmic justice.

On January 21, 1976, after an early dinner in their apartment, Reznikoff suffered a stroke, and he died in the hospital early the following morning. In an absurdly timely reflection earlier that day, he had remarked to Syrkin: "You know, I have never made money, but I have done everything that I most wanted to do." Of the many memories she recalled in her arrestingly frank and affectionate memoir, she remembered a certain awards ceremony they were obliged to attend in the latter half of her husband's life. Syrkin's organization was the host, and she was seated at the long banquet table in the front of the room, while Reznikoff was left to fend with a number of strangers at one of the circular tables in the center. Much as he had during his time in Hollywood, he surprised his closest acquaintances with an absolute knack for getting along with unfamiliar people and a love, even anticipation, for large parties. Later, Syrkin wondered if this evening in particular was the inspiration for a short, telling poem in his *Inscriptions, 1944–1956* (1959), "Te Deum:"

Not because of victories
I sing,
having none,

            ...

Not for victory
but for the day's work done
as well as I was able;
not for a seat upon the dais
but at the common table.

RHYTHMS, AND THE EARLY POEMS

This subway station
with its electric lights, pillars of steel, arches of
  cement, and trains—
quite an improvement on the caves of the cave-
  men;
but, look! on this wall
a primitive drawing.

Reznikoff's most admired poems remain the short, untitled lyrics of a wandering New Yorker from his earliest collections, such as this poem XVIII from *Going To and Fro*. His 1927 *Five Groups of Verse* included poems from *Rhythms* (1918), *Rhythms II* (1919), *Poems* (1920), and *Uriel Accosta: A Play and a Fourth Group of Verse* (1921). The poems, numbered and occasionally titled, typically comprise two or three stanzas of two or three lines each, as in poem 6 from *Rhythms II*:

Stubborn flies buzzing
in the morning when she wakes.

The flat roofs, higher, lower,
chimneys, water-tanks, cornices.

Those poems without contemporary objects among their images can easily be mistaken for haiku and other short lyrics of the ancient Chinese poets, and Reznikoff alluded to these poetics in explaining his strategies to L. S. Dembo: "'Poetry presents the thing in order to convey the feeling,'" he said, quoting an eleventh-century Chinese poet. "It should be precise about the thing and reticent about the feeling." Removing the feeling and indeed himself from his poetry remained of absolutely paramount importance to him throughout his career. It was in large part this asceticism that led Louis Zukofsky to champion Reznikoff as the model of his Objectivist movement. While the postmodern reader would likely and rightly question what exactly could be meant by "objectivism," the poet of the Zukofsky-Reznikoff program was to observe the world, above all, dispassionately and, not unlike a photographer, record exactly what is seen, leaving value judgments to the reader.

Rhythms and *Rhythms II* each contained around twenty numbered, short lyrics, the exact number fluctuating a bit as Reznikoff reprinted and revised the collections in *Poems* and *Five Groups of Verse*. *Rhythms'* first poem is its most uncharacteristic, a seven-stanza poem of couplets and quatrains with a regular rhyme scheme:

The stars are hidden
the lights are out;
the tall black houses
are ranked about.

With the exception of a few instances in this first collection, Reznikoff rarely employed rhyme, and it would not be too grandiose a reading to suggest that he begins his first collection with a nod to the canonical work of the premodernist era before embarking upon a career of his own trademark and contemporary free verse. Indeed, he concludes his first book with the short poem:

My work done, I lean on the window-sill,
watching the dripping trees.
The rain is over, the wet pavement shines.
From the bare twigs
rows of drops like shining buds are hanging.

The even meter or "rhythm" of the first poem has become uneven or even atonal; simple quatrains of two beats per line have morphed into poems with five beats per line, then three, five, two, and so forth, a familiar but no less bold launch into the murky modernist waters.

Readers have heard in the concluding couplet of *Rhythms'* second poem—"I raised on each a brown hill, / the dead are walking slow and still"—an echo of Edgar Lee Masters' *Spoon River Anthology* (1915): "All, all, are sleeping on the hill." Reznikoff qualified the comparison in an interview with Robert Franciosi, saying, cryptically, that he did not care for how Masters' tour de force was written but was "interested in the subject matter." The comparison, though, is indeed fruitful. As Masters' is a book of voices from the grave, so much of Reznikoff's career was devoted to reclaiming the notion of a poet as a tribal historian, animating biblical and Jewish historical figures as characters in his poems, as Reznikoff liked to think of his own grandfather speaking through him. His 1929 collection "Editing and Glosses" (in the anthology *By the Waters of Manhattan*) included the long poems "Israel" and "King David," dramatizing biblical stories in verse, and many of his verse plays of the 1920s, such as *Captive Israel* (1923), did the same. His early collections, then, can be seen as an exercise in developing a voice for these communal functions, becoming a tribal teller of tales—an artist—and critics have traced a Joycean, *Portrait of the Artist* arc through the early books. *Rhythms'* first poem ends:

    all I say
    blown by the wind
    away.

The poet's words are not yet truly his own and lack gravitas. By the end of the first book, the poet is resting weary but satisfied on his windowsill, the rain over and the pavement shining, and *Rhythms II* concludes with

    no wind.

    Far off,
    a white horse
    in the green gloom
    of the meadow

—a clear and confident "Imagist" image. The poet has weathered "the lonely marsh" and "the outer frozen blackness" of his early collections, earning the honor to speak what he sees into existence.

In *Poems* and the subsequent editions of the 1920s, Reznikoff began to attempt to address the immigrant experience he knew as a child. Rather than always employ the simple voice of the pedestrian observer, he would sometimes adopt the tone of a community storyteller, explaining the lives and tragedies of his neighbors, as well as write in character, animating both contemporary fictitious figures and figures from Jewish history, such as King David. In the eleventh poem of *Poems,* he describes a young immigrant woman in desperate need of a husband to sustain her life in America, waiting to meet a suitor proposed by her aunt:

    If he would have her, she would marry whatever
      he was.
    A knock. She lit the gas and opened her door.
    Her aunt and the man—skin loose under his eyes,
      the face slashed with wrinkles.
    "Come in," she said as gently as she could and
      smiled.

In recorded lessons to his poetry students on Reznikoff, Allen Ginsberg described poems such as this one as, in just a few short lines, encompassing "a complete moral lifetime." While there is a constant obsession among poets about showing emotions in their poetry, Ginsberg claimed, Reznikoff accomplishes this "by simply being totally accurate to what stimulated the emotion in him." Many critics have pointed out that images in Reznikoff's poetry are not used for symbolic or allusive effect, but simply to convey the facts of the scene. Though he found journalism so at odds with literature, it is a journalist's sense of duty and indeed objectivity that Reznikoff brings to his poems time and again.

Another recurring theme in these increasingly mature editions, particularly as Reznikoff began to dare to speak boldly as a Jewish poet in full possession of his people's histories and tragedies, is that of communicative failure, of "talk" being swallowed in "darkness." "The talk fell apart and bit by bit slid into a lake," he writes in the twenty-second poem of the 1920 volume *Poems,* describing something like a group of friends on a weekend retreat together. "In and about the house darkness lay, a black fog; / and each on his bed spoke to himself alone, making no sound." The idea of speaking to oneself in stillness, alone, and indeed in silence, would reappear throughout his career. Then, in the eleventh poem of *A Fourth Group of Verse,* subtitled "Visiting:"

> Almost midnight. "Good night." "Good night."
> I close the heavy door behind me.
> The black courtyard smells of water: it has been
> raining.
> What were we talking about?

Readers will hear the "Good night, ladies, good night" of T. S. Eliot's *The Waste Land,* though that modernist classic was not published until 1922. As these poems of disconnection are interspersed with autobiographical poems of his Brownsville childhood and versified dramas of other struggling and persecuted Jewish immigrants, Reznikoff seems to be playing the psalmist or Old Testament prophet, calling for God and receiving no answer, asking "why have you forsaken me?" There is talk but there is no understanding. Yet the tribal historian goes on telling the story of his people, defiantly, as is his solemn charge.

Reznikoff's lyrics also beg comparison to the preeminent short lyricist of the American canon, Emily Dickinson. Reznikoff seldom alluded to Dickinson in interviews (he wrote almost no critical prose about his own work or poetry), yet the two are strikingly similar in form and posture. "I'm nobody. Who are you?" Dickinson famously asks. In his poems Reznikoff is always the invisible observer, at the scene but not of the scene (as in the fourth verse of poem 2 from *Going To and Fro,* subtitled "Autobiography: New York"):

> I like the sound of the street—
> but I, apart and alone,

> beside an open window
> and behind a closed door.

Both Dickinson and Reznikoff employ short poems with short lines of two or three beats; more importantly, both share a conviction that the most singular individual or object is a microcosm of the entire human or natural drama and merely awaits the poet to exploit its story. Compare Dickinson—

> The Mountains—grow unnoticed—
> Their Purple figures rise
> Without attempt—Exhaustion—
> Assistance—or Applause—

—with Reznikoff—"Among the heaps of brick and plaster lies / a girder, still itself among the rubbish." There is certainly an immigrant's political sensibility to these poetics: every thing has its story, and the story gives it dignity.

Reznikoff began writing poems in the heyday of imagism, and its high priests William Carlos Williams and Ezra Pound both had a significant impact on the young poet's sensibility. Williams' one-line manifesto "no ideas but in things" (from the 1927 poem "Paterson") was essentially the starting point of the Objectivist movement. Zukofsky appreciated Williams' rigorous minimalism and depersonalization but wanted to lend his short Imagist poems a kind of structure so that they were not merely a verbal photograph but represented a "rested totality." Pound insisted that images were not merely "ornaments," that "the image itself is the speech." Reznikoff's ultraminimalist early poems—"Streamers of crepe idling before doors" is the entirety of poem 15 from *Rhythms II*—clearly heed this advice, and Pound expressed admiration for Reznikoff's early poems, which he read after Zukofsky sent them to the exile in Italy as part of a furious courtship of the elder poet's patronage. Pound's famous two-line poem "In a Station of the Metro" so closely resembles Reznikoff's characteristic poetry that one might think Reznikoff had written the lines himself: "The apparition of these faces in the crowd; / Petals on a wet, black bough." Still, for Zukofsky, the mere image was not the speech; the triumvirate of the image, the poet, and the sociopolitical context was the speech, and in spite of his exhortations, what he really advocated was not so much that it be expressed "objectively" as it be expressed, simply, clearly.

Zukofsky, Williams, Reznikoff, and George Oppen were partners in the short-lived Objectivist Press in the early 1930s, which in 1934 published Williams' *Collected Poems 1921–1931* and Reznikoff's *Jerusalem the Golden, In Memoriam: 1933,* and the first volume of *Testimony,* though each poet was expected to cover the costs of his book's publication. Williams remained a tireless fan of Reznikoff's throughout his life, praising each new book and writing him notes encouraging him to continue his work even when the commercial and critical reception was slim to none. In comparison to Williams' lyrics, Reznikoff offers a little more and a little less. Williams' pure imaginative powers took his poems from ordinary plums in the icebox to the "pure products of America" gone crazy. Imagine Williams' creative landscape as a circle emanating from a focus, encompassing everything it touches in every direction. Reznikoff's creative palette was linear, stretching from the ancient origins of his people, through the sagas of the centuries and concluding in the arena of twentieth-century Manhattan. The images to which he returns in all of his poems are those of streetlights, sidewalks, subways, and bridges. But Reznikoff also attempts something that Williams passes over. Williams states that

> so much depends
> upon
>
> a red wheel
> barrow

and that is that. Reznikoff (in poem VIII of *Going To and Fro*) tries something like:

> A dead gull in the road,
> the body flattened
> and the wings spread—
>
> ...
>
> and a robin dead beside a hedge,
> the little claws drawn up
> against the dusty bundle:
> has there been a purge of Jews
> among the birds?

Reznikoff too trades primarily in imagery, but adds to it a context, and with that context, an entire moral dimension to the image.

The Reznikoff-Williams comparison hits upon the central critical disagreement about Reznikoff's early, trademark poems: whether they distinguish him as indeed an Objectivist, dispassionate, a worthy inheritor of Imagist aesthetics, or quite the opposite, whether they reveal Reznikoff to be a rabid moralist, a didactic poet in a modernist era uniformly opposed to didacticism. Both camps find a wealth of evidence. A poet can be no more invisible than in *Poems'* "Moonlit Night," comprised entirely of: "The trees's shadows lie in black pools on the lawns." At the same time, Reznikoff's characters and subjects come almost exclusively from the proletarian working class, naturally the people he knew best, and the poet's keen sense of justice, or injustice, is present almost everywhere. In one early lyric he describes the plight of an elevator attendant, made to work long hours for little money, but who nevertheless

> must also greet each passenger
> pleasantly:
> to be so heroic
> he wears a uniform.

And the objectivist poet could also be deeply personal in his poems. In more than one instance, he addresses a nameless woman who once dismissed his inquiries or appeals because he was "not at all important." "That was true. But I wonder / whom you thought important," Reznikoff asks, before ultimately answering his own question after a series of speculations:

Yourself, no doubt:
looking like one
who has been a great beauty.

The poem is not only personal, but emotionally charged and plainly vindictive. And the moral dimension is the poem's essential battleground: the speaker begins by assuming an equal footing between the two; the woman then suggests that she is a worthier person than her interlocutor; and the poet concludes by implying that perhaps in fact the reverse is true.

Reznikoff does not simply present the facts in these early lyrics. He plainly writes as the child of Russian Jewish immigrants and of the Brooklyn ghetto, and that sensibility is everywhere. Furthermore, he is clearly capable and adept at writing a poem not about mere images or circumstances, but about emotions and human tragedy, as he does about the dismissive woman, and as he writes of the young immigrant girl in need of a husband, "If he would have her, she would marry whatever he was." There, he is completely inside his character's mind. Yet, to a degree that is no less than astonishing when compared to the poets of that time and the times that followed, Reznikoff lets the image do the talking. Poem 39 of *Jerusalem the Golden* consists of these lines:

What are you doing in our street among the
   automobiles
horse?
How are your cousins, the centaur and the
   unicorn?

If we strain our mind's ears and eyes, we can perhaps imagine Dickinson or Williams writing something like those lines. No one else.

THE OBJECTIVISTS

Reznikoff's privately printed editions did attract some positive attention, in particular from the young poets Louis Zukofsky and George Oppen. The two had become friends in 1928. Zukofsky had recently concluded his masters in English at Columbia University, while the younger Oppen had just arrived in New York with his wife Mary after a cross-country elopement, abandoning their parents' comfortable California life, marrying in Dallas, Texas, and itching to launch careers of literary and political revolution. Both Zukofsky and Oppen were admirers of Reznikoff's work and soon managed to befriend the older poet.

Zukofsky's cultivated friendship with Ezra Pound eventually induced Pound to ask his friend Harriet Monroe to let Zukofsky guest-edit one issue of her influential Chicago-based journal, *Poetry*. In what would have been Reznikoff's first big "break," Monroe had accepted two poems of his several years earlier, but when she made a handful of editorial suggestions, Reznikoff politely declined and withdrew his work. Now, under his friend Zukofsky's shepherding, he would have his *Poetry* debut after all. Monroe believed that the issue would sell more copies if the poets whom Zukofsky was collecting belonged to some kind of movement, and she implored him to brand them as such in his introduction to the issue. It is no overstatement to say that, by this motivation alone, the Objectivist school was born.

Zukofsky adopted his introduction from an essay he was writing on Reznikoff, titling it "Sincerity and Objectification: With Special Reference to the Work of Charles Reznikoff." Like many of his essays, it seemed to begin in midsentence, apropos of nothing, and veer wildly from subject to subject, tossing off obscure allusions at whim. The February 1931 "Objectivist" issue of *Poetry* included poems from, among others, Reznikoff, Zukofsky, Oppen, Williams, Carl Rakosi, and Basil Bunting. While Zukofsky had not plucked the term "objectivist" out of the blue—he, Oppen, and Reznikoff had talked plenty of poetry and were in some general agreement on aesthetics—many of the contributors spent the rest of their careers questioning, qualifying, or openly rejecting the label. "His [Zukofsky's] aloof tone, the distant hauteur, the reasoning and language icily severe and rebuffing, I found that disturbing," Rakosi later said of Zukofsky's manifesto. (quoted in *The Complete Prose of Carl Rakosi,* 1983) Yet in spite of the word's accidental genesis, Reznikoff for one would readily use the term in reference to his work throughout his career, and several of the group soon incorporated themselves, after the *Poetry* issue, as the Objectivist Press.

The press's first publication was *An Objectivist Anthology* (1932), an expanded edition of the Objectivist *Poetry,* and in this second chance at an introduction Zukofsky attempted to quell the critical furor he induced both within and outside the flock. "The interest of the issue was in the few recent lines of poetry which could be found, and in the craft of poetry, NOT in a movement," Zukofsky wrote. "The contributors did not get up one morning all over the land and say 'objectivists' between tooth-brushes." In the anthology, he added Pound, T. S. Eliot, and Kenneth Rexroth to the already impressive roster, yet even these beacons of high modernism were not enough to counter Zukofsky's knack for generating negative criticism. "Mr. Zukofsky's preface is so badly written that it is next to impossible to disentangle more than a few intelligible remarks," sneered Yvor Winters (quoted in *Yvor Winters: Uncollected Essays and Reviews,* 1973), whose New Criticism school would thoroughly outmaneuver the Objectivists on the literary battleground, driving the latter into obscurity. Each new attempt by Zukofsky to explain what he meant seemed only to confuse the matter more. "A poem. A poem as object—And yet certainly it arose in the veins and capillaries, if only in the intelligence—," he wrote in the introduction. "Experienced—parenthesis—(every word can't be overdefined)

experienced as an object. ..." The press disbanded after a couple of years.

The spare lyrics of Reznikoff's early work were clearly the model for Zukofsky's frenetic aesthetics, and the brief Objectivist hullabaloo afforded him a level of attention far above what he had previously experienced; yet by all accounts, the entire episode had no impact on his poetry whatsoever. He was not, by nature, a collaborator. "Rezy never talked poetry," Oppen remembered fondly. Objectivism had basically come to him, rather than the other way around as with some of his younger colleagues, and Reznikoff remained as commercially obscure when it passed as before it began. Strangely, all of the Objectivists independently arose to critical prominence twenty-five years or more after their brief appearance on the literary scene. As Reznikoff finally garnered a book contract with New Directions in the early 1960s, Zukofsky attracted his first established publisher, W. W. Norton, at the same time. After abandoning poetry for more than twenty years and living as a political exile in Mexico, Oppen returned to America and to writing and in the span of three new collections won the Pulitzer Prize. Rakosi also attracted a new and vibrant readership after leaving poetry for more than two decades, and a young poet from Wisconsin who had admired the Objectivist *Poetry* and embarked on a long, intimate correspondence with Zukofsky, Lorine Niedecker, began publishing in earnest in the 1960s, her work generating as much posthumous critical attention as any of her brethren. In Oppen's, Rakosi's, and Niedecker's poems, Reznikoff's influence is plain. On the other hand, none of their work seems to have influenced Reznikoff's whatsoever. The three-line lyrics of 1969's *By the Well of Living and Seeing* are practically interchangeable with those of *Rhythms.* This does not seem be the result of any obstinance or pride on Reznikoff's part; simply, as tribal historian and as artist, he naturally looked to his ancestors and predecessors for direction, rather than to his contemporaries. He regarded himself as a necessarily solitary craftsman. "The objectivist, then, is one *person,* not a group," Zukofsky explained in an interview with L. S. Dembo in the late 1960s. That description seemed to fit.

PLAYS AND PROSE

"I divide [my writing] into work horizontal and vertical," Reznikoff told his friend and chief critical champion, Milton Hindus:

> The "vertical" is the moment, the as/is; if possible from the top of the sky to the bottom of the earth. For that my instrument is the poem. … That brings me to the "horizontal"—the succession of events, the story, the years. As for that I work at the "novel"—in prose.

He is remembered, of course, for his vertical writing, but the horizontal provides a valuable perspective on the vertical work.

Throughout the 1920s, Reznikoff wrote a series of verse plays, among them the collections *Uriel Accosta; Chatterton, The Black Death, and Meriwether Lewis* (1922); and *Coral and Captive Israel* (1923), all of which were ultimately compiled with several others in his 1927 *Nine Plays.* Between Reznikoff and Syrkin, at least, there was some disagreement concerning the plays' merit, or at least genre. Syrkin thought them "dramatic verse" whereas Reznikoff insisted they were pure "drama." When he was assembling work for his *Selected Poems* late in his career, Syrkin suggested that he use "Rashi," one of his plays, because "it's only a few pages." "It's a play," Reznikoff said. "It's not a play," Syrkin responded. For his part, Reznikoff later confessed in interviews that he was heavily under the influence of the German Expressionist theater when he was writing his plays, and he did not actually intend for them ever to be performed. Syrkin's characterization of her husband's drama as worthy poems that would nevertheless make for stilted dialogue is fair. But as he was beginning to experiment with writing in character and writing about history in his poems at this time, the plays are indicative of his search for voice and growing confidence in expanding his literary repertoire.

Reznikoff's first serious prose effort was his novel *By the Waters of Manhattan* (1930), published by the modest independent printer Charles Boni. The story borrowed liberally from the autobiographical accounts he had transcribed from his parents and later collected in *Family Chronicle.* In the first of two parts, Ezekiel, the namesake and stand-in for Reznikoff's grandfather, is swindled out of his land in Russia, but he refuses to turn in the thief, a fellow Jew, for Ezekiel knows the culprit will be deported to Siberia. The family is destitute. His daughter, Sarah, cannot find a worthy suitor, and so she emigrates to New York where she ultimately marries Saul. Meanwhile, Ezekiel dies penniless in Russia, and when his wife discovers a secret trove of poems written by her husband in Hebrew (which she cannot read), she burns them in fear that they contain political heresy. Part 2 follows Sarah's son Ezekiel from the ages of nineteen to twenty-two. He establishes a bookstore in New York and conducts an ill-fated affair with a young woman. He manages in the end to achieve a peace of mind that eluded his mother and grandfather, as he finds some harmony between his artistic sensibilities and his practical responsibilities, rather than depend on the workaday world to support his literary endeavors.

By the Waters of Manhattan was "the first story of the Jewish immigrant that is not false," Lionel Trilling declared in the October 1930 *Menorah Journal* in a review that was astonishingly prescient in its description and appreciation of Reznikoff's peculiar talents. Reznikoff's novel was not, however, the Jewish immigrant's story that was to make a splash in the literary world that year; that was Michael Gold's *Jews without Money.* Gold's spirited novel had everything an immigrant's tale was supposed to have: a muckraker's description of substandard living conditions, hatred, bigotry, persecution, religious turmoil and hypocrisy, long hours, low wages, heroic success stories, and a healthy dose of political rabble-rousing. Reznikoff's novel soared critically and suffered commercially in its trademark understatement, its attention to the odd detail, and its simple rejection of such fiction conventions of plot, conflict, and resolution. For his part, Trilling found Gold's "admirable and moving" work a study of "filth and misery ... but it deals with it so ... melodramatically that its stench becomes racy and Chaucerian." *By the Waters of Manhattan,* on the other hand, had "a quality of privacy which is startling." The *Portrait of the Artist* arc that can be traced through Reznikoff's *Rhythms* is also present in his first novel. The novel's first section essentially explains who the young artist is at the time of his birth, and the second section traces the formation of his artistic posture in relation to the world. Of course the 1930 book market liked its Chaucer and liked its Gold, and Reznikoff's first novel remained little more than a personal footnote for many years.

He did continue writing prose. In 1944 the Jewish Publication Society of America published his historical novel *The Lionhearted: A Story about the Jews of Medieval England.* Reznikoff had included his mother's memoir "Early History of a Seamstress" in his 1929 self-published hodgepodge *By the Waters of Manhattan: An Annual* (he would employ the title throughout his career); he published his father's memoir *Early History of a Sewing-Machine Operator* in 1936; and he had submitted his own memoir, "Needle Trade," under a different title to a 1951 issue of *Commentary:* he finally collected the three memoirs in 1963's *Family Chronicle: An Odyssey from Russia to America,* also self-published. As with his debut novel, the sense in each memoir is of a reticent narrator with little

taste for romance or nostalgia but a deep sense of responsibility for getting things right. And the episode of his grandmother burning her late husband's poems plays a prominent role in each. As he recorded his mother's recollections: "There was too much to burn at one time, so Mother burnt a few sheets every morning until all were gone. As she put the first into the fire she said, 'Here's a man's life'" (quoted in Homberger).

Though he neither pursued nor received any critical or commercial reception for it, the publication of *Family Chronicle* proved deeply satisfying for Reznikoff. By the time it was completed he had finally begun to receive some attention for his poetry, and now, fulfilling the role of tribal historian, he had successfully preserved the story of his family for the ages. It is in some respects his high-water mark as a prose writer, though many reserve that honor for his innovative *Testimony.*

A WORLD OF VIOLENCE

The posthumously published *Poems 1918–1975: The Complete Poems of Charles Reznikoff* (1989), meticulously edited by Seamus Cooney, does not include any of the hundreds of poems from the various editions of Reznikoff's *Testimony.* In the list of Reznikoff's complete works on the first page of the *Complete Poems,* the first volume of *Testimony,* printed in 1934, is listed under his works of prose. Reznikoff always maintained, however, that this peculiar book was not only a collection of verse, but also the most perfect reflection of his poetics.

Testimony's genesis is easily accounted for: while working at the law encyclopedia *Corpus Juris* in the early 1930s Reznikoff had the occasion to read thousands upon tens of thousands of collections of court testimony, which he distilled into case summaries for the encyclopedia. Stories and personal accounts that particularly moved him he would save, and a very few

("few" by the standard of the extraordinary number he read) he would scrupulously edit into perhaps six dozen lines and call a poem. "Found poems"—poems in which the text is extracted from another source and then edited by the poet into verse—were in large part invented by the French surrealists of the 1920s and 1930s and later made popular in America by the writers of the Beat Generation, the Black Mountain poets, and the first and second generations of the New York School of poets. Reznikoff seems to have hit upon the idea entirely as a product of his own standards as to what makes good poetry, coupled with the rigorous attention to language he acquired via his legal training. In the poem "Early History of a Writer," Reznikoff disagreeably cites the symbolists' dictum that "to name is to destroy," juxtaposing it with a law curriculum's

> ... plain sunlight of the cases
> the sharp prose,
> the forthright speech of the judges.

In *Testimony* he would name not to destroy but to create, endeavoring to present a truly objective account of the facts and leave judgment to the reader.

He divided the book by geographical sections—"The North," "The South," and "The West"—and used subtitles such as "Social Life," "Domestic Scenes," "Machine Age," "Property," and "Railroads" to organize his familiarly numbered poems. A typical *Testimony* poem details an apparently harmless scene that immediately devolves into swift and gruesome violence, often with undertones of social injustice or the individual's hopeless struggle against technological innovation. There are many innocent travelers being run over by trains, spouses murdering each other, factory machinery chewing up women and children, and socially marginalized figures such as unwed mothers, "Negroes," or "Chinese" being brutally persecuted by the powers-that-be. In the third poem in the "Children" section of "The South" (from the second part of volume 1, "1891–1900"), we learn "Jimmie was about eight years old / when put to work in the factory ..." The child's toying with the cogwheels of a waste machine immediately results in his injury, even though

> the boy had been repeatedly "advised"
> by other employees—
> and even by the assistant superintendent of the
>   company—
> as to the danger
> of "a negligent attention to his business."

Critics attacked Reznikoff's *Testimony* on two fronts: that it was unreasonably, disproportionately violent and that it was not poetry. To the charge that he saw only a world of horror and violence, he responded, "I didn't invent the world, but I felt it." A reader may read *Testimony* and conclude that everyone who lived in turn-of-the-century America eventually became the victim of a violent crime. But to a child of immigrants whose parents fled brutal political persecution in their native land, whose own grandfather and uncle would come to his Brooklyn home—after a simple shopping errand—beaten bloody in an anti-Semitic attack, and who witnessed all manner of human cruelty while wandering the streets of New York, such violence would hardly seem unusual or even remarkable. To the second charge, that his found poems were not poems, Reznikoff appealed to T. S. Eliot's well-considered concept of the objective correlative. Eliot famously argued that the sum total of the images in a properly constructed poem produces a coherent feeling in the reader; the relationship between the images and the feeling may or may not be logical, or evident, but the connection is definite. The whole is more than the sum of its parts. This is what Reznikoff had in mind in *Testimony*. As he understood the objective correlative, he told L. S. Dembo, "Something happens and it expresses something that you feel, not necessarily because of *those* facts, but because of entirely different facts that give you the same kind of feeling." He described his style as "recitative," which to him implied an adherence to fact and a passivity of judgment. Much as a witness in court does not relate what he felt, but what he saw or heard, so the poet presents only the sensory images and buries the feeling in between the lines. The strategy is much the same as he pursued in his short lyrics. The poet selects imagesthat, to the poet, convey a certain feeling and lets the images summon the emotions.

"A little *Testimony* went a long way with me," Syrkin remembered. "Like any philistine I saw it in the main as chopped up prose." Among the book-buying public, there were apparently many philistines. Reznikoff self-published a first volume of *Testimony* in 1934. After publishing his *By the Waters of Manhattan: Selected Verse* in 1962, New Directions brought out a revised and expanded edition of *Testimony: The United States (1885–1890): Recitative* in 1965. Sales were dismal, reviews were cruel, and New Directions promptly dropped Reznikoff from its list. Characteristically undaunted, he again self-published a second volume, *Testimony: The United States (1891–1900): Recitative,* in 1968. To the non–poetry reader, *Testimony* is unusually readable, coming off as dozens of little short stories with sensational endings, broken into lines. To the poetry reader steeped in the language of irony, allusion, and double entendre, *Testimony* is baffling. "Andy, I am going to write a letter that may seem / hardhearted," begins the second stanza of the third poem of "Domestic Scenes" in "The West":

Don't you think it best
to give me a divorce?
If you do,
I will not have to sell the house in Denver
that you gave me,
and I will give you back the ranch in Delta.
After we are divorced,
if you care for me and I care for you,
we will marry again. Polly.

Time and again we are presented with the trivial affairs—real estate and marital arrangements, for instance,—of ordinary people in *Testimony.* Is this poetry? Of course it is the pure triviality of the particulars, the house in Denver, that make them remarkable and, when these affairs turn brutally violent, that make them personal and painful. Reznikoff believed he had dipped his poetry in an acid wash, removing all the blemishes and corrosions and leaving only the pure essentials. "With respect to the treatment of subject matter in verse and the use of the term 'objectivist' and 'objectivism,'" he wrote in a posthumously published broadside titled *First There Is the Need* (1977), the only article he ever composed on poetry and his own work, "let me again refer to the rules with respect to testimony in a court of law." He continues (as quoted in Milton Hindus, ed., *The Manner Music*):

> Evidence to be admissible in a trial cannot state conclusions of fact: it must state the facts themselves. For example, a witness in an action for negligence cannot say: the man injured was negligent in crossing the street. He must limit himself to a description of how the man crossed: did he stop before crossing? Did he look? Did he listen? The conclusions of fact are for the jury and let us add, in our case, for the reader.

HOLOCAUST

Late in his career, his friend Milton Hindus asked Reznikoff, a writer whose Judaism was plainly integral to his work, why he had not addressed the attempted annihilation of European Jewry in his poetry. Reznikoff responded that he believed *Testimony* spoke to the issue at stake in illustrating man's basic inhumanity to man. Then, in 1975, Black Sparrow published Reznikoff's *Holocaust.*

In *Holocaust,* Reznikoff employs the same technique he used to produce *Testimony,* only in this case his source material is the Nuremberg and Eichmann trials. He divided his slender volume into sections with titles including "Deportation," "Massacres," "Work Camps," "Entertainment," and "Mass Graves." The second poem of the section "Research" describes one of the sadistic experiments to which the Nazis subjected their prisoners:

A number of Jews had to drink sea water only
to find out how long they could stand it.
In their torment
they threw themselves on the mops and rags
used by the hospital attendants
and sucked the dirty water out of them
to quench the thirst
driving them mad.

Hindus and many other critics regarded *Holocaust* as Reznikoff's crowning achievement, no less than the triumph for which he had unwittingly been preparing his entire career. Comparisons are naturally made to *Testimony*. It can be convincingly argued that while the two books are the product of the same technique, the effect of that technique is exactly opposite. In *Testimony*, Reznikoff's recitative style heightens the interest of ordinary affairs, such as Polly and Andrew's marital discord, while in *Holocaust* the strategy subdues the extraordinary, otherworldly events of genocide, such as a Nazi officer making casual target practice of his Jewish prisoners from the vantage of his office tower, and allows the events to approach comprehension. For *Testimony*, Reznikoff selected an epigraph from the biblical book of Ephesians 4:31: "Let all bitterness, and wrath, and anger, and clamour, and railing, be put away from you, with all malice." For *Holocaust,* there is no epigraph, only a cryptic footnote on the first page of poems, stating that in 1933 the Nazis instigated their policies against the Jews, their initial official objective being only exportation. *Testimony* is populated by proper names throughout; *Holocaust* has none.

Others have found *Holocaust* to be the least satisfying of Reznikoff's work. In his superb, affectionate essay on Reznikoff, "The Decisive Moment," Paul Auster finds the recitative strategy ill-suited for the most inconceivable event of at least the twentieth century, if not all of modern history. The problem is threefold. One, Reznikoff's best subjects are the individual and the particular—the boy injured at the face of the factory waste machine—and the Holocaust, simply, is huge. Two, Andrew and Polly's marital troubles, while mundane, are new, a surprise to the reader, while the facts of the Holocaust are horrifyingly familiar, depriving Reznikoff's court-reporting style of its usual powers of disarmament. Three, Reznikoff's strategy is to dispassionately present the facts of a "case" and, ostensibly, leave moral judgment to the reader. On the matter of the Holocaust, judgment has long since been passed and reconsideration is well out of the question. The pretense of objectivity is exactly that. One cannot come to any of these atrocities anew.

It can and has likewise been argued that this greatest of human atrocities is actually composed of countless individual atrocities, and Reznikoff's style is perfectly suited to illuminate these particular instances of terror. The incident of a Nazi officer placing a bottle on a prisoner's head and performing his version of the William Tell exploit is not generally known in itself, and the poet surely endows it with the power to morally offend. Strangely, Reznikoff concludes his book with a section titled "Escapes," detailing several episodes where a small number of Jews managed to evade their torturers. The sixth poem of the section concerns an effective Danish rescue operation:

...the Jews were escorted to the coast by the
 Danes—
many of them students—
and ferried to safety in Sweden:
about six thousand Danish Jews were rescued
and only a few hundred captured by the
 Germans.

What is Reznikoff's intention by ending with these facts? Perhaps the question he is asking is not if these acts of salvation and altruism redeem humanity for its unspeakable sins, but whether they can provide any small measure of redemption whatsoever. The ambivalent ending goes to the heart of a central paradox within Reznikoff himself. He was an unfalteringly gentle man whose family bore considerable physical hardship, whose ancestors have known thousands of years of brutal persecution, and whose own writing was largely concerned with fatal injustice and even brute violence. Whatever the resolution to the conclusion of his last book and to these personal antitheses, all of it seems to speak to the central nobility of his character and integrity of his work. *Holocaust* does not pique, arrest, or even shock as *Testimony* does, and the morally dulling, numbing effect may be precisely the objective.

POSTSCRIPT: *THE MANNER MUSIC*

In the late 1940s, when Reznikoff was ostensibly separated from Syrkin and was at perhaps the one true low ebb of his poetry production, he received an encouraging note from William Carlos Williams. Williams related that he had been ill, and his illness afforded him the opportunity to, for the first time, with apologies, examine a present Reznikoff had made to him many years earlier: a signed copy of his first novel *By the Waters of Manhattan.* Williams said he thought it one of the finest books he had ever read and, knowing his friend and former collaborator had never achieved much in the way of critical or commercial success, heartily implored Reznikoff to keep writing, saying that if he was having trouble finding new material for poetry, perhaps he should try another novel.

It is not known for sure that Williams' exhortations led Reznikoff to write *The Manner Music* (1977). What is known is that when Milton Hindus was organizing his friend's papers

after Reznikoff's death in 1976, he discovered a perfectly typed and formatted manuscript of fiction that the poet had never spoken of to anyone and that he had apparently composed sometime in the 1950s. Reznikoff typically kept his wife, his friend Albert Lewin, and other acquaintances apprised of all his writing projects through letters or otherwise. Thus the discovery was particularly curious. A review of the contents suggested the reason for secrecy.

The Manner Music is a roman à clef, one that stars loose approximations of Reznikoff and the few central figures in his life, and one that was written in the most despairing period of his life. Everyone comes off badly. The hero of the novel is Jude Dalsimer, a struggling composer whose music has received no commercial or critical reception whatsoever. He lives in a constant state of acrimony with his wife, Lucy, in their tiny New York apartment during the Great Depression. The nameless narrator of the book is an old friend from adolescence, now a traveling salesman, who happens to run into Jude one day and finds their paths cross on several occasions over the next few years. As Reznikoff traveled selling hats for his parents for several years, it is reasonable to suppose there may be some of the author in the narrator; but the character of Jude is the central repository for Reznikoff's bitter self-reproach.

Lucy insists that Jude earn money for the household; Jude insists that he is an artist and must dedicate all his energies to composing. Lucy calls Jude a selfish no-talent to his face and in awkward quarrels in front of the narrator. The unhappy couple catches a break when another old friend of Jude's, Paul Pasha, offers Jude a job as a fact checker at his movie studio in Hollywood. Jude moves to California and continually proves himself to be utterly worthless. He advocates projects that would be commercial disasters and dismisses movies that become blockbusters. At parties attended by

Hollywood's rich and famous, Jude fails to acquit himself and is isolated as a pariah. Paul must continually apologize for his friend's professional futility and social gracelessness. Finally Jude is fired and returns to the East, where relations with Lucy further deteriorate. When the narrator happens upon him a final time, he hardly recognizes him as a homeless man foraging for food on the street. He forces him into a diner and buys him dinner; Jude struggles to uphold a semblance of dignity before tearing into his food ravenously. Lucy has left him. In the end we learn that Jude was ultimately committed to the Bellevue mental hospital, where he died.

As bleak as the plot is, Reznikoff reserves his most lethal barbs for his hero's art. The author makes clear that Jude is completely delusional about his musical abilities, that no listener could ever reasonably be expected to enjoy his compositions, and that no musician would ever purchase or perform them. Throughout the novel, Jude imposes upon the narrator with his latest masterpieces, which the narrator, whom we are given to understand is an otherwise polite and decent person, can't help but greet with "weariness and annoyance." In one instance, the narrator comes to see Jude to find out how a certain job prospect unfolded that day. He finds Jude playing the piano and, after waiting for him to finish, asks him what happened. "I told you what happened," Jude says. "When you came in. I played it for you on the piano." "I tried to remember what I had heard," the narrators says, "whether sad or gay. I could not decide." Jude sends his compositions to a famous singer, hears nothing, writes her, hears nothing, finally receives his compositions returned to him unopened, and so it goes. Lucy makes it clear that she cannot stand his music and, worse, cannot stand being poor, and the narrator is continually forced to conclude that the pieces Jude plays for him "do not move me." Reznikoff's doppelganger is a talentless hack who drives all of his relations into frustration and poverty.

Readers have searched for charms in Reznikoff's antihero, likening him to Bartleby the Scrivener in his artistic resilience, trying to weave *The Manner Music* into the fabric of Reznikoff's oeuvre. Others simply conclude that the book is a savage personal admonishment. While Reznikoff is always humble and self-deprecating in letters, interviews, and in his poetry, nowhere else in his body of work does he profess the fundamental artist's doubt that his work is worthless, a sham. And he pairs his antihero with a scornful, loveless wife, a portrait that naturally troubled Syrkin after her husband's death. A comparison with *By the Waters of Manhattan* proves illuminating. The earlier novel concerned a young man's successful assimilation of his artistic aspirations with the demands of the practical world. This challenge, on the other hand, is precisely where Jude Dalsimer fails. He cannot rectify the two, and he dies poor and alone. *The Manner Music* is not a great novel, but neither does it in anyway detract from Reznikoff's body of work. It is, at least, a unique, and (like everything of Reznikoff's) unfalteringly honest insight into the psyche of a poet.

Of course, Reznikoff wrote his terrible confessional when he was down and out, before things got better. And things got wonderfully better. A survey of Reznikoff's work reveals many Reznikoffs: the artist, the historian, the Jew, the New Yorker, the immigrant's child, the proletarian. But *The Manner Music,* like no other of his works, reveals the mortal human being, one paralyzed by insecurity, tortured by guilt, and plagued with resentment. Along with a photographer's sense of image and totality, the novel proves that Reznikoff could get man's basest passions down on the page as well. It not only provides a more complete picture of the man, it also makes the emotional reticence he practiced in the sum total of work all the more admirable.

It is not that he did not feel. It is that he chose the image in place of the emotion, in the hope that others might feel.

What a strange character was this Charles Reznikoff. At the age of seventy-five, without a publisher, he was privately printing poems such as poem 11 of *By the Well of Living and Seeing*:

> You must not suppose
> that all who live on Fifth Avenue
> are happy: I have heard the gulls screaming
> from the reservoir in Central Park.

as he had then been doing for fifty-one years. The word for this shy gentleman, seldom photographed without a coat and tie, is *radical*. He assumed what was to him a sacred errand and pursued it without reference to the standards of his society. Surcly someone else would come along and worry about the publishing, the publicity, the sales, the criticism: the ephemera. He was an artist, and his noble concerns were few.

Selected Bibliography

WORKS OF CHARLES REZNIKOFF

POETRY

Rhythms. New York: Charles Reznikoff, 1918.

Rhythms II. New York: Charles Reznikoff, 1919.

Poems. New York: S. Roth at New York Poetry Bookshop, 1920.

Five Groups of Verse. New York: Charles Reznikoff, 1927.

In Memoriam: 1933. New York: Objectivist Press, 1934.

Jerusalem the Golden. New York: Objectivist Press, 1934.

Testimony. New York: Objectivist Press, 1934.

Separate Way. New York: Objectivist Press, 1936.

Going To and Fro and Walking Up and Down. New York: Futuro Press, 1941.

Inscriptions: 1944–1956. New York: Charles Reznikoff, 1959.

By the Waters of Manhattan: Selected Verse. New York: New Directions, 1962.

Testimony: The United States (1885–1890): Recitative. New York: New Directions, 1965.

Testimony: The United States (1891–1900): Recitative. New York: Charles Reznikoff, 1968.

By the Well of Living and Seeing and The Fifth Book of the Maccabees. New York: Charles Reznikoff, 1969.

By the Well of Living and Seeing: New and Selected Poems 1918–1973. Los Angeles, Calif.: Black Sparrow Press, 1974.

Holocaust. Los Angeles, Calif.: Black Sparrow Press, 1975.

Poems 1918–1936: Volume 1 of the Complete Poems of Charles Reznikoff. Santa Barbara, Calif.: Black Sparrow Press, 1976.

Poems 1937–1975: Volume 2 of the Complete Poems of Charles Reznikoff. Santa Barbara: Black Sparrow Press, 1977.

Testimony: The United States (1885–1915): Recitative. 2 vols. Santa Barbara: Black Sparrow Press. 1978–1979.

Poems, 1918–1975: The Complete Poems of Charles Reznikoff. Edited by Seamus Cooney. Santa Rosa, Calif.: Black Sparrow Press, 1989.

CORRESPONDENCE, PLAYS, AND PROSE

Uriel Accosta: A Play and a Fourth Group of Verse. New York: Cooper Press, 1921.

Chatterton, The Black Death, and Meriwether Lewis. New York: Charles Reznikoff, 1922.

Coral and Captive Israel. New York: Charles Reznikoff, 1923.

Nine Plays. New York: Charles Reznikoff, 1927.

By the Waters of Manhattan: An Annual. New York: Charles Reznikoff, 1929. (Anthology.)

By the Waters of Manhattan. New York: Charles Boni, 1930. (Novel.)

Early History of a Sewing-Machine Operator. With Nathan Reznikoff. New York: Charles Reznikoff, 1936.

The Lionhearted: A Story about the Jews of Medieval England. Philadelphia, PA.: Jewish Publication Society of America, 1944.

The Jews of Charleston: A History of an American Jewish Community. With Uriah Engelmann. Philadelphia: Jewish Publication Society of America, 1950.

Family Chronicle: An Odyssey from Russia to America. With Nathan and Sarah Reznikoff. New York: Charles Reznikoff, 1963.

First There Is the Need. Santa Barbara, Calif.: Black Sparrow Press, 1977.

The Manner Music. Edited and introduced by Milton Hindus. Santa Barbara, Calif.: Black Sparrow Press, 1977.

By the Waters of Manhattan. New York: Markus Wiener, 1986.

Family Chronicle: An Odyssey from Russia to America. New York: Markus Wiener, 1988.

Selected Letters of Charles Reznikoff: 1917–1976. Edited by Milton Hindus. Santa Rosa, Calif.: Black Sparrow Press, 1997.

PAPERS

Archives of Reznikoff's papers are held at the libraries of the University of California, San Diego, and the University of Arizona.

CRITICAL AND BIOGRAPHICAL STUDIES

Auster, Paul. "The Decisive Moment." In his *The Art of Hunger and Other Essays.* London: Menard Press, 1982.

Dembo, L. S., ed. "The Objectivist Poet: Four Interviews." *Contemporary Literature* 10: 155–219 (spring 1969).

DuPlessis, Rachel, and Peter Quartermain. *The Objectivist Nexus: Essays in Cultural Poetics.* Tuscaloosa: University of Alabama Press, 2002.

Fredman, Stephen. *A Menorah for Athena: Charles Reznikoff and the Jewish Dilemmas of Objectivist Poetry.* Chicago: University of Chicago Press, 2001.

Heller, Michael. *Conviction's Net of Branches: Essays on the Objectivist Poets and Poetry.* Carbondale: Southern Illinois University Press, 1985.

Hindus, Milton. *Charles Reznikoff: A Critical Essay.* Santa Barbara, Calif.: Black Sparrow Press, 1977.

Hindus, Milton, ed. *Charles Reznikoff: Man and Poet.* Orono: National Poetry Foundation, University of Maine at Orono, 1984.

Omer-Sherman, Ranen. *Diaspora and Zionism in Jewish American Literature: Lazarus, Syrkin, Reznikoff, and Roth.* Hanover, N.H.: Brandeis University Press, University Press of New England, 2001.

—*DAVE GUNTON*

Richard Rodriguez

1944–

*I*N THE OPENING of his first book, *Hunger of Memory: The Education of Richard Rodriguez* (1982), Richard Rodriguez began his quest—not for identity, but for an adequate expression of his identity.

> The name on the door. The name on my passport. The name I carry from my parents—who are no longer my parents, in a cultural sense. This is how I pronounce it: Rich-heard Road-ree-guess. *This is how I hear it most often.*

Rodriguez is fairly well-known to the general public as a journalist and essayist. He is an editor with the Pacific News Service in San Francisco, a contributing editor for *Harper's* and the Sunday "Opinion" section of the *Los Angeles Times,* and is a commentator and photo-essayist on public television's *NewsHour with Jim Lehrer.* He has produced hundreds of short pieces on topics ranging from painters, musicians, movies, cities, religions, and the Twin Towers to cell phones, front porches, food, the Gold Rush, the homeless, and the absence of the Twin Towers. Sometimes humorous, always provocative, these "essays" convey the range and the raucous variety of contemporary American culture. In 1997, he received a George Foster Peabody Award for his *NewsHour* essays on American life. The Peabody Award is designed to recognize "outstanding achievement in broadcast and cable" and is one of television's highest honors. In many ways, Rodriguez' commentary on public issues has been an affirmation of his public identity. The three books that comprise a twenty-year examination of the nature of his private identity become, retrospectively, a "reading" of American literature as well as a chronicle of cultural assimilation.

With each successive book, Richard Rodriguez has emphasized one aspect of identity even as he reexamines his initial concerns. And with each additional book, he has become increasingly controversial. Critics have been inclined to include Rodriguez in discussions of ethnic literatures, where they often use such terms as "miseducation" or "guilty vision."

In 2002, Rodriguez completed his third collection of essays, *Brown: The Last Discovery of America.* In its preface, he refers to his three collections of essays as a "trilogy" in which he takes a cumulative look at American public and private life by examining class, ethnicity, and race. It is fairly evident that Rodriguez did not set out to write a trilogy, but the collections evolved in such a way that a retroactive assessment allows him to bring together twenty years of concentrated thought to form a larger, more comprehensive, statement. Indeed, read consecutively, the three books do add up to one prolonged examination of the culture. Although there are some redundancies when the books are read in this way, it is also possible to see how his thought (and his style) has evolved.

Born in 1944, in San Francisco, the third of four children of immigrant Mexican parents, Rodriguez spent his childhood and adolescence in Sacramento. His mother had arrived with her family as an adolescent. His father, who came alone to the United States as a young man from Colima in western Mexico, made false teeth for a group of local dentists. Rodriguez was educated in Catholic schools by Irish nuns. The young Richard entered school with a vocabulary of around fifty words in English, graduated from high school as a top student in the mid-sixties, and went on to study literature at Stanford University. He did graduate work at Columbia University and the Warburg Institute (London). In 1974, he began work on his Ph.D. at the University of California at Berkeley, where he earned his doctorate in English Renaissance literature. He spent a year in England on a Fulbright scholarship and in 1976 was offered a position at Yale. And then, abruptly, his academic career came to a halt. Rodriguez turned down the invitation from Yale in order to begin his life as a freelance writer and editor. His first book, *Hunger of Memory,* chronicles the experiences that led up to his decision. It also takes a critical, even judgmental, stance on bilingual education. It was for that reason that it first came to the attention of the educational community and the name Richard Rodriguez, almost from the beginning, became synonymous with controversy.

Twenty years later, Rodriguez is still concerned about education. In an interview with Virginia Postrel and Nick Gillespie for the online magazine *Reason,* he stated:

Education is not about self-esteem. Education is demeaning. It should be about teaching you what you don't know, what you yet need to know, how much there is yet to do. Part of the process of education is teaching you that you are related to people who are not you, not your parents—that you are related to black runaway slaves and that you are related to suffragettes in the 19th century and that you are related to Puritans. That you are related to some continuous flow of ideas, some linkage, of which you are the beneficiary, the most recent link.

The first book not only angered proponents of bilingual education; it disturbed academic theorists as well. If *Hunger of Memory* was about class, then its critics wanted it to be about ethnicity. Rodriguez was dodging the issues, they suggested. His second book, *Days of Obligation: An Argument with My Mexican Fa-*

ther (1992), answered the critics of the first book by addressing his Hispanic roots. Possibly because of its stylistic changes, it did not gain such a wide readership and therefore it did not engender quite so much controversy. Yet it, too, provoked discomfort. Its characterization of Mexican and American ethnicities did not take into account the old American nemesis—race. Nor did its somewhat reticent discussion of what it is to be gay in either culture satisfy the more militant critical cadre. *Brown* addresses both of those issues in depth, but it, too, invites opposition. Rodriguez simply does not toe the critical line; his perceptions are as individualistic as his voice. The trilogy, then, is the story of how he achieved that voice—and the reason he is willing to stand alone in order to preserve it.

HUNGER OF MEMORY: THE EDUCATION OF RICHARD RODRIGUEZ

I remained a child longer than most; I lingered too long, poised at the edge of language—often frightened by the sounds of los gringos, *delighted by the sounds of Spanish at home.*

Published by David R. Godine, a small press in Boston, the growing reputation of *Hunger of Memory* was earned mostly by word of mouth. Over time, it received several awards, including the Gold Medal for nonfiction from the Commonwealth Club of California, the Frankel Medal from the National Endowment for the Humanities, and the Ansfeld-Wolf Prize for Civil Rights from the Cleveland Foundation. The title suggests that Rodriguez has taken a passionate look backward in order to discover his educational roots. The subtitle positions his experience squarely in the mainstream of American literature. *Hunger of Memory* covers the years from grade school to graduate school—and just a bit beyond. Its focus is not only the manner (and tenor) of his particular education, but also the role of education itself in the life of American immigrants. As it was in the nineteenth-century memoir *The Education of Henry Adams,* education, and especially self-education, is still a way of defining the nation as much as the self. In this way, the book, although functioning much like a memoir, is also social commentary.

Hunger of Memory consists of six "chapters," each of which acts as a discrete essay. In the first, the reader sees the young Rodriguez as he learns to negotiate the classroom. Shy and fearful, he rarely spoke up in class, listening instead to "the high nasal notes of middle-class American speech." After his continued reticence, the nuns visited his home and requested that his parents speak to their children only in English. Suddenly Rodriguez found himself caught between the intimate sounds of the home and the public expectations of the schoolroom. For Rodriguez, these differences were cloaked in language. More sensitive than his older brother or his two sisters, Richard found himself making distinctions between public words and private sounds.

When he finally began to succeed in school, Rodriguez noticed that his parents "spoke a hesitant, accented, not always grammatical English." He became self-conscious about his Spanish. In fact, it all but disappeared, so much so that his uncles and aunts called him *Pocho*—traitor—to indicate that he had sold out his heritage. Constantly aware that he was trading intimacy for social and intellectual progress, Rodriguez realized early the nature of his true education: "What I needed to learn in school was that I had the right—and the obligation—to speak the public language of *los gringos.*"

The obligation to speak in English led Rodriguez to another concept—individuality. If Spanish was a collective language, if its construction was often in the first-person plural, English offered up its singular "I" and expected him to supply the verb to follow. English demanded that he form an opinion and that he state it openly. "Only when I was able to think

of myself as an American, no longer an alien in *gringo* society, could I seek the rights and opportunities necessary for full public individuality." The cost was alienation from his family. And, although Rodriguez speaks forcefully about the need for this process, the book betrays some of his ambivalence. He is self-conscious as he notes that, at family gatherings, his father sometimes glances away, or that he and his brother and sisters make small talk in place of an intimate connection with their parents. True to his own sense of privacy, however, he never names his parents or siblings in his pieces, letting them function not so much as individuals but as roles.

In school, Rodriguez embraced the English language as a means to enter the public arena. And yet he felt that education had changed and separated him from the culture of his family. He concludes that this was, perhaps, the only way in which to become fully a part of the society in which he was living. So he worries that bilingual education will, in effect, impede that process for others, leaving them in what he later refers to as a "linguistic limbo." And language, he suspects, is not the only problem. One chapter, "The Achievement of Desire," spends considerable time looking at the concept of "the scholarship boy." While reading in the British Museum, he had encountered Richard Hoggart's *The Uses of Literacy* (1957), a study of the underlying psychology of the impoverished student given an opportunity to study in a school well beyond his means. The book had a profound effect. Although he had entered high school having read hundreds of books, had been awarded scholarships to Stanford and, later, fellowships to graduate school, Rodriguez recognized himself in Hoggart's descriptions: "The scholarship boy is a very bad student. He is the great mimic; a collector of thoughts, not a thinker; the very last person in the class who ever feels obliged to have an opinion of his own." At this point, Rodriguez began to understand his own estrangement to be one of class as much as one of language.

If education is discovery, it is at this point that the education of Richard Rodriguez began. He was forced to rethink his early experience in order to have an opinion of his own. The first admission is that he had "intended to hurt my mother and father." In the face of their children's newly acquired skills, his parents had retreated into the background, his father silent, his mother self-conscious. In a recapitulation of a familiar immigrant pattern, Rodriguez had allowed that to happen in order to become American. This recognition seems to be a turning point in the book. The remainder of the book examines other factors that influenced his "education."

A first important factor was religion. In a chapter that foreshadows many of the concerns found in *Days of Obligation,* Rodriguez touches on the role religion played in his early education. The church's education was ancient and evocative. It was learned through the senses. The year revolved around a sequence of events, each with its rituals, its scents, and its associations. Long before the mind could form an opinion, the body learned the cycle of the liturgical year. Religion was a physical experience. And yet, as Rodriguez matured, he sensed differences between his parents' Spanish Catholicism and the English version he was learning from the nuns and priests in school. In Spanish, his parents were expected to think. In English, the church thought for them. Here, too, he encountered the unbridgeable schism between the private and the public.

Looking back at the way the church was a part of the seamless fabric of his childhood, in the wake of Vatican II, Rodriguez predicts a devaluation of the newly altered Catholic church—with its Mass in English and folksongs, its handshakes and jazzy combos. "I would protest this simplification of the liturgy if I could. I would protest as well the diminished sense of the sacred in churches today."

A second major element that shaped Rodriguez' experience was his complexion. In a chapter that foreshadows the primary concerns of *Brown,* Rodriguez recounts the way his dark skin (darker than that of his brother and sisters) and Indian features affected his self-image. His mother kept him out of the sun, worrying that if his skin got any darker he would look like *los pobres,* the workers in the fields. The young boy understood color as shame, a symbol of a life of poverty. When asked in school to draw a self-portrait, he refused. His self-consciousness persisted until one summer, while in college, he took a summer job that involved hard outdoor labor. His skin grew dark, but his body grew strong and capable.

Richard worked mostly with other college students, yet sometimes the foreman hired temporary workers—Mexicans who kept themselves apart, spoke only to each other. Once Rodriguez was asked to act as a translator. He did so uneasily, speaking in halting Spanish, realizing that he was, and was not, one of them. This moment left a lasting impression. At the end of the summer, Rodriguez felt at home with his body, even beginning to dress like a "dandy." He felt less at home with his divided identity.

A third factor that played a strong role in Rodriguez' education was the academic policy of affirmative action. This factor is addressed in the chapter titled "Profession," which became instantly controversial within the higher education community. While Richard Rodriguez was in college, an identity was handed to him—the word "Hispanic" was coined, and Mexican-Americans were granted rights under affirmative action. Almost overnight, he became a professional "minority student." The chapter reviews the history of the civil rights movement in order to probe the origins of affirmative action: "The aim was to integrate higher education in the North. So no one seemed troubled by the fact that those who were in the best position to benefit from such reforms were those blacks least victimized by racism or any other social oppression—those culturally, if not always economically, of the middle class."

Although he benefited from the new policies, Rodriguez did not recognize himself in the affirmative action profile. He felt uncomfortable in the role, and the memoir gives voice to his reservations: "The policy of affirmative action, however, was never able to distinguish someone like me (a graduate student of English, ambitious for a college teaching career) from a slightly educated Mexican-American who lived in a barrio and worked as a menial laborer, never expecting a future improved. Worse, affirmative action made me the beneficiary of his condition."

Affirmative action had entered the realm of the scholarship boy, and the collision gave educators a solution that was not, at least in his terms, resolution. "Here was the source of the mistaken strategy—the reason why activists could so easily ignore class and could consider race alone a sufficient measure of social oppression." But class, Rodriguez had concluded, had been a profound influence on his own psychology.

In addition, Rodriguez unwittingly found himself at the beginning of the "culture wars" in English departments. "I didn't think that there was such a thing as minority literature," he remembers. Literature had been his ticket into the mainstream of American culture; through reading, he had felt himself included. Now he was expected to represent an "excluded" minority, to become the border-crosser he had never felt himself to be.

The education of Richard Rodriguez was coming to an end. He was completing his degree and receiving offers of employment from prestigious schools. But something felt wrong. His friends and colleagues were not receiving such offers. Their resentment was palpable. Years later, in an interview with Scott London, he recalls this time: "I was being chosen because Yale University had some peculiar idea about what my skin color or ethnicity signified. … The people who offered me the job thought there was nothing wrong with that. I thought there was something very wrong with that. I still do. I think race-based affirmative action is crude and absolutely mistaken."

Under these circumstances, Rodriguez was forced to look at the gap between his realities and his ideals, and he concluded that the only honest course was to reject the offers and leave academics entirely. "My decision was final. No, I would say to them all. Finally, simply, no." Thus was born Richard Rodriguez, thinker. And, naturally, thus was born further controversy.

A final factor is the role of secrecy in the making of his adult identity. *Hunger of Memory* is told in a fairly straightforward manner, each chapter unfolding in a similar chronology: recollection, introspection, conclusion. Thus the chapters function more like essays—they aim at idea. In the final chapter, "Mr. Secrets," Rodriguez seems to have found what will come to be a distinctive style. The voice becomes gradually less formal, more personal, even experimental with its innovative use of parentheses. The book ends at its beginning, with a discussion of privacy. Richard's mother accuses him of being too secret and, at the same time, feels that he has violated the family's privacy in making his memoir public. Speaking sometimes to her, sometimes about her, sometimes in a parenthetical whisper to himself, Rodriguez confesses, "I am writing about those very things my mother has asked me not to reveal." Rodriguez is forced, yet again, to take a hard look at what he is doing—and why. When he was a child, he never revealed his personal feelings when he was writing school assignments. He pretended a self. As an adult, with a clearly defined sense of self, he explores what drives him to write. He names his reader; he is *un gringo*. He faces him in the mirror:

I write very slowly because I write under the obligation to make myself clear to someone who knows nothing about me. It is a lonely adventure. Each morning I make my way along a narrowing precipice of written words. I hear an echoing voice—my own resembling another's. Silent! The reader's voice silently trails every word I put down. I reread my words, and again it is the reader's voice I hear in my mind, sounding my prose.

DAYS OF OBLIGATION: AN ARGUMENT WITH MY MEXICAN FATHER

I have come at last to Mexico, to the place of my parents' birth. I have come under the protection of an American credit-card company. I have canceled this trip three times.

In the years between 1982 and 1992, the culture had undergone numerous changes—becoming simultaneously more divisive and more open. When Rodriguez revisited some of the issues that had haunted him in *Hunger of Memory,* he found some of them passé, some more pertinent than ever. In the ten intervening years, Rodriguez had also honed his writing style. Less a memoir and more a collection of loosely related essays, *Days of Obligation* is a study in contrasts: Mexico/the United States, tragedy/comedy, Catholicism/Protestantism, past/future, mother/father, and, naturally, private/public. In doing so, it also becomes a discussion of ethnicity, especially as it functions in the California of today.

The book opens with "India," an essay in which Rodriguez repeats some of the personal information found in *Hunger of Memory.* He stares at the Indian in the mirror, the man with the brown skin and long, narrow face. "I grew up in Sacramento thinking of Indians as people who had disappeared. I was a Mexican in California; I would no more have thought of myself as an Aztec in California than you might imagine yourself a Viking or a Bantu." Here,

this leads him not to the more intricate discussion of racial assimilation that figures in *Brown,* but to the specificity of the *mestizo*—and the disappearance (or the pervasiveness) of the Indian. In Mexico, he is identified. "Each face looks like mine. No one looks at me." In the mirror, the conquistador has been conquered: "I take it as an Indian achievement that I am alive, that I am Catholic, that I speak English, that I am an American. My life began, it did not end, in the sixteenth century."

Most of the essays take one issue or another and work through the contrasting attitudes seen in Mexico and the United States, thus creating the "argument" alluded to in the book's subtitle. For example, in "Mexico's Children," Rodriguez combines the language and customs of the countries to demonstrate the difference between private and public: "In Mexico, one is most oneself in private. The very existence of *tú* must undermine the realm of *usted.* In America, one is most oneself in public." Gone is the overt statement found in *Hunger of Memory.* In its place, Rodriguez gives free rein to the associative mind. He takes the reader into his thought process. His style is confident, even daring. The effect is the intimacy he once perceived in the sounds of Spanish. "If I were to show you Mexico, I would take you home; with the greatest reluctance I would take you home, where family snapshots crowd upon the mantel. For the Mexican, the past is firmly held from within."

Rodriguez is imaginative, even inventive, as though he has given himself permission to reveal the inner feelings he had so long denied. One can sense the pleasure in the writer as the United States is portrayed through a long, extended metaphor:

In order to show you America I would have to take you out. I would take you to the restaurant—OPEN 24 HOURS—alongside a freeway, any freeway in the U.S.A. The waitress is a blond or a redhead—not the same color as at her last job.

She is divorced. Her eyebrows are jet-black migraines painted on, or relaxed, clownish domes of cinnamon brown. Morning and the bloom of youth are painted on her cheeks. She is at once antimaternal—the kind of woman you're not supposed to know—and supramaternal, the nurturer of lost boys.

… Your table may yet be littered with bitten toast and spilled coffee and a dollar tip. Now you will see the greatness of America. As one complete gesture, the waitress pockets the tip, stacks dishes along one strong forearm, produces a damp rag soaked in lethe water, which she then passes over the Formica.

There! With that one swipe of the rag, the past has been obliterated. The Formica gleams like new. You can order anything you want.

Mexico is mother, is intimate, is Catholic, is pessimistic. America (the name is noted for its ironic implications) is father, is public, is optimistically Protestant. They tug equally at the immigrant, more so than other waves of immigrants because of Mexico's proximity, because of what Rodriguez calls "confluence of history." Mexican-Americans can look over their shoulders and remind themselves of where they came from, can return and briefly turn their backs on the freeways and Tex-Mex and T-shirts before they leave again. They can pay homage to memory.

Rodriguez conjures up the Mexico his mother left, with its dusty village streets and whispered prayers. But he does not fool himself. They are not his memories. In "In Athens Once," he spends the Holy Week in Tijuana, touring the city with a variety of guides, spending an evening on the border patrol, helping a priest who feeds the poor, visiting the mall. Each night he returns to San Diego to sleep in a hotel. Like any good tourist, he is afraid to drink the water.

The focus of the book begins to shift. What began as a study in ethnicity becomes a discussion of religion. "The Missions" is an account of Rodriguez' tour of the old Spanish missions along the California coast. It is also a reflection

on a unique brand of Catholicism. The difference between the mission as sanctuary and the mission as historical artifact becomes the difference between the living faith of Mexico and the sterile utilitarianism of Puritan America. "The Head of Joaquín Murrieta" recounts the legend of a Western-world Robin Hood, robbing the rich and (sometimes) giving to the poor. Rodriguez is caught up in the search for the head by a Father Huerta, who wants to bring closure to the tale by burying the head with the rest of the body. The essay is picaresque, yet Rodriguez' droll account becomes increasingly serious as it offers up yet more contrast, yet more food for thought. "Father Huerta believes in the power of memory. Californians are linked by memory—mainly unconscious—to a founding Hispanic culture." Rodriguez writes to find the conscious memory, and to lay it, too, to rest.

The essays of *Days of Obligation* are peppered with characters: Uncle Raj, the Indian dentist who married the author's Mexican aunt; Larry Faherty, the flippant high school buddy gone hippie before his time; Helen Hunt Jackson, who wrote the 1884 novel *Ramona* (which focuses on the plight of Native Americans in southern California); Junípero Serra, who preached to the Indians; Cesar Romero, probably most famous as a villain on television's *Batman* series; the painter David Hockney; Oliver North; St. Augustine; Elizabeth Taylor. The past and the present converge. Taken as a whole, these essays make the point that modern California is a mix of cultures—was, in fact, a mix of cultures on the day the first white settler arrived.

In an otherwise unified collection—one in which the essays goad each other into dialogue—one essay stands apart. "Late Victorians" is firmly located in present-day San Francisco, and it is even more firmly, and somewhat stoically, personal. Yet it may also be an argument with Rodriguez' Mexican father, or, at the very least, an argument with the *machismo* that has been translated from the mother country into something that parodies itself in the United States. Chronicling the renovation of Victorian San Francisco, Rodriguez also chronicles the gay movement in its bid for cultural and political recognition. Characteristically, Rodriguez forces intellectual connections, finds metaphor: "The nineteenth century was remarkable for escalating optimism even as it excavated the backstairs, the descending architecture of nightmare—Freud's labor and Engels's" and "I live on the second story, in rooms that have been rendered as empty as Yorick's skull—gutted, unrattled, in various ways unlocked—added skylights and new windows, new doors."

The added skylight here is Rodriguez' open declaration of his homosexuality. Uncomfortable in this public display of private life (and reminiscent of his mother's accusation that he was too secretive), he retreats to the more familiar realm of the analyst. But the personal intervenes; the story of AIDS becomes the story of acceptance:

> It was not as in some Victorian novel—the curtains drawn, the pillows plumped, the streets strewn with sawdust. It was not to be a matter of custards in covered dishes, steaming possets, *Try a little of this, my dear.* Or gathering up the issues of *Architectural Digest* strewn about the bed. Closing the biography of Diana Cooper and marking its place. Or the unfolding of discretionary screens, morphine, parrots, pavillions.

AIDS was the reality, and Rodriguez recognizes its public entry into his personal life. The essay is quietly elegiac as, in italicized sections, it reconstructs obituaries. At times, they merge into one: "*He was born in Puerto La Libertad, El Salvador. He attended Apple Valley High School, where he was their first male cheerleader. From El Paso. From Medford. From Germany. From Long Island.*"

With characteristic honesty, Rodriguez paints himself as a reluctant participant in a showy extravaganza. He watches himself work out at his club. He describes the "false shutters" in his bedroom. He attends the memorial services. But he also notes that he does not stand in the front of the church when they ask members of the AIDS support group to come forward:

> So this is it—this, what looks like a Christmas party in an insurance office, and not as in Renaissance paintings, and not as we had always thought, not some flower-strewn, some sequined curtain call of greasepainted heroes gesturing to the stalls. A lady with a plastic candy cane pinned to her lapel. A Castro clone with a red bandana exploding from his hip pocket. A perfume-counter lady with an Hermès scarf mantled upon her shoulder. A black man in a checkered sports coat. The pink-haired punkess with a jewel in her nose. Here, too, is the gay couple in middle age; interchangeable plaid shirts and corduroy pants. Blood and shit and Mr. Happy Face. These know the weight of bodies.

Rodriguez sits tight, facing his paralyzing ambivalence. "These learned to love what is corruptible, while I, barren skeptic, reader of St. Augustine, curator of the earthly paradise, inheritor of the empty mirror, I shift my tailbone upon the cold, hard, pew." The private man mourns in the only way he knows how—within the piercing eye of the public essay.

The essays of *Days of Obligation* are characterized by this unforgiving look at the self, and yet critics often overlook this, as though they must chide Rodriguez for what he has already confronted. Because he does not espouse a militant stance, because he often questions the very tenets of a movement or a cause, because he remains so steadfastly individualistic, he is often the target of anger. Critics will not take him on his own terms. "Late Victorians" was not celebrated for what it had accomplished–clear-eyed compassion, wry self-appraisal–so much as it was denigrated for its refusal to subscribe to any "approved" cultural perspective. An example of the language and focus on the part of critics can be found in William Nericcio's review of *Days of Obligation* in *World Literature Today:*

> Richard Rodriguez's new book rehearses a Chicano, fin-de-siècle Narcissus. Like some mutation born of Roy Cohn and Jack Webb, our self-loathing/loving narrator polices the precincts of the Americas. Readers marvel as we await Rodriguez's tragic fall (simulcast nationally), his declared attraction to Milton's Satan echoing throughout. A Mexican-American who seethes at Chicanos, a gay man who sets himself apart from gay men, an English scholar who leaves the academy. I envision Rodriguez's next book: on the cover, Rodriguez's face in a mirror (pensive); looking back, a horse—with Richard's eyes and soul (our Chicano Houyhnynm: Rodriguez as Gulliver, *estilo latino*).

The criticism is almost always aimed at the content of the essays, and Rodriguez is condemned for refusing to be a representative Hispanic spokesman. This is perhaps inevitable, for in the broadest sense the "argument" is ongoing. If there is a point in this book, it is that there is a struggle for the soul of the immigrant, and that the battle renews itself as Mexico and American redefine themselves. Rodriguez is held accountable for the very mutability that he calls to our attention.

But *Days of Obligation* is a literary achievement even more than it is social commentary, and it was one of three finalists for a Pulitzer prize in nonfiction in 1993. In the ten years between books, Rodriguez had developed a fluid style, at once associative and incisively intellectual. He relied on his extensive reading to connect the tissues of his argument, but the argument itself remained elusive, shape-shifting, full of nuance. The scholarship boy grew up, and Richard Rodriguez learned to trust his own instincts. In doing so, he forged a technique that could accommodate the complexities of his subjects. The offhandedness of parenthetical asides, the intimacy of direct address, the historical insistence of italicized passages, the shouted hilarity or commanding attention of

capital letters—all combine to create an audible interior space within the reader, a space where Rodriguez' liberated voice can be heard singing his own HAIIII-EEE. HAI. HAI. HAI.

BROWN: THE LAST DISCOVERY OF AMERICA

> I write about race in America in hopes of undermining the notion of race in America.

On the cover of *Brown,* Richard Rodriguez' face (pensive), eyes shifting to the side (like a horse?), the dark skin and hair shading into the brown of the background, the brown of his shirt, and then his hands—catching the light until they appear almost an abstraction. The face is creased, the mouth serious, not quite defiant, but set. Ten years later, he mocks his critics. Or else he takes them so seriously that he is once again compelled to respond. "Brown forms at the border of contradiction," he states, and then boldly the first page of the preface announces: "I write about race in America in hopes of undermining the notion of race in America."

In *Brown,* Rodriguez has renounced contrast in favor of contradiction. The memoir takes its gathering principle from William Gass's 1975 *On Being Blue*—and it, too, pays homage to the long trajectory of American literature. America, Rodriguez contends, has always thought of itself in terms of black and white. But, as he stated in a televised address at the Seventh Annual Texas Book Festival, "assimilation is way ahead of our language about it." We have become "a global culture within a single border." So *Brown* becomes past *and* future, history *and* challenge. In the course of nine essays Rodriguez examines such a range of ideas it is impossible to enumerate them. There is no one central "theme" in this book, no one overriding concept, no point Rodriguez is trying to make, except that thought itself is complex, is all-inclusive, is assimilatory. In the name of true diversity, *Brown* is radically political in its intent to undermine everything its readers have been taught about diversity.

The nine essays each explore the concept of "brown" from a different angle. Brown is the color that is created when the child has swirled all the finger paints into one happy coincidence. Neither a primary nor a secondary color, brown is the fortuitous happenstance of impurity. "Brown" is, finally, what and who we all become: alike in our differences, linked by our shared histories, implicated in each other's fate. *Brown* is about *being* American.

As the book expands, it becomes a study in mixtures, in black and white—and red. Rodriguez begins with a reexamination of a scene from Alexis de Tocqueville's mid–nineteenth–century classic *Democracy in America.* Traveling in Alabama, the European comes upon an Indian woman, a "Negress," and a small white girl. As he approaches, the Indian retreats into the woods, the Negress waits passively, and the young girl already shows signs of an assumed superiority. De Tocqueville reads into the scene the various ways that history has already marginalized the women. Rodriguez speaks directly to him: *"But cher Monsieur: You saw the Indian sitting beside the African on a drape of baize. They were easy together. The sight of them together does not lead you to wonder about a history in which you are not the narrator?"* Rodriguez establishes a device—the interior voice that will characterize this collection. The reader is treated to the mercurial observations and quicksilver interrogations that precede formal thought, the path the mind travels as it sifts through possibilities on its way to conclusions.

The path is circuitous, and Rodriguez returns to the image of the two women throughout the book. His contemplation of its significance sparks numerous strains, among them the powerful memory of reading Carl T. Rowan's 1957 memoir *Go South to Sorrow,* an adult book Rodriguez found on the shelves of his fifth grade classroom. He remembers the feeling of identification he felt with the young African American's story. On hearing of Rowan's death, he found himself mourning "the voice that spoke through my eyes." This, in turn, leads to a riff on reading itself:

> It is a kind of possession, reading. Willing the Other to abide in your present. His voice, mixed with sunlight, mixed with Saturday, mixed with my going to bed and then getting up, with the pattern and texture of the blanket, with the envelope from a telephone bill I used as a bookmark. With going to Mass. With going to the toilet. With my mother in the kitchen, with whatever happened that day and the next; with clouds forming over the Central Valley, with the flannel shirt I wore, with what I liked for dinner, with what was playing at the Alhambra Theater. I remember Carl T. Rowan, in other words, as myself, as I was. Perhaps that is what one mourns.

This is the first of many such moments of identification, as many of them with African American literature as with white writers. Rodriguez calls on T. S. Eliot and William Faulkner and Ralph Ellison and Malcolm X (as a boy, he had seen him speak), on Hollywood films (*Psycho* and *Blackboard Jungle* and *Invasion of the Body Snatchers*), and on Mexicans (especially Octavio Paz), among others, to make a case for the evolutionary mix of idea and language that forged—and continues to forge—the identity of the United States as a country. The dialogue was open to Rodriguez, perhaps even more because of his brown skin, his felt need to place himself in the ongoing dialectic. So *Brown* pays homage to the work of James Baldwin and Philip J. DeLoria, Thackeray, Shakespeare, Benjamin Franklin and even Richard Milhous Nixon. Little did Richard Nixon know when he coined the term "Hispanic" that Richard Rodriguez, his affirmative-action success, would come along to deconstruct it:

Hi.spa´.nick. 1. Spanish, *adjective.* 2. Latin American, *adjective.* 3. Hispano, *noun.* An American citizen or resident of Spanish descent. 4. Ducking under the cyclone fence, *noun.* 5. Seen running from the scene of the crime, *adjective.* Clinging to a raft off the Florida coast. Elected mayor in New Jersey. Elevated to bishop or traded to the San Diego Padres. Awarded the golden pomegranate by the U. S. Census Bureau: "most fertile." Soon, an oxymoron: America's largest minority. An utter absurdity: "destined to outnumber blacks." A synonym for the future (salsa having replaced catsup on most American kitchen tables). Madonna's daughter. Sammy Sosa's son. Little Elián and his Great Big Family. A jillarioso novel about ten sisters, their sorrows and joys and intrauterine devices. The new face of American Protestantism: Evangelical minister, tats on his arms; wouldn't buy a used car from. Highest high school dropout rate: magical realism.

This passage might easily have come from *Days of Obligation.* Rodriguez' pattern seems to be to develop ideas—and arguments—over a period of years, testing them as they are presented in a variety of ways. Slowly, they begin to form a coherent argument.

Many of the central ideas of *Brown* can be found in a speech Rodriguez made in 1997 to a group of librarians in California. The speech anticipated the coming book, telling the story of de Tocqueville's women ("nowhere does de Tocqueville wonder about what the Indian and the African were talking about"), then moves on to muse about the information age and the role of libraries. "You didn't give me information," he says. "You gave me the deepest intuitions of a life and that is that we are connected to each other at some deeply human level." In response to a question from Gregory Wolfe in an interview for *Image,* Rodriguez adds, "What bothers me about the rhetoric of victimization is that it implies that we can belong to only one side of history, whereas the moment you participate in history, you participate in impurities." You can feel his arguments feeding off each other, forming themselves through cross-fertilization. The

arguments for "the browning of America" were beginning to find a mode of expression.

Those arguments are complex, convoluted, controversial. Essentially, Rodriguez sets out to demonstrate that we are all implicated in each other's lives. To this end, he makes several cases: the historical, the cultural, and the intellectual. In other words, he plays the role of historian, sociologist, anthropologist, politician. But, as he stated in an interview with Stan Rubin in 2002, he wanted to "deconstruct" the barrage of public language from those fields by "running it against my heart and soul." So, in *Brown,* he also makes an emotional case—at once highly personal and intuitively communal. The essays become a mix of personal anecdote, philosophical introspection, analytical assessment, italicized intrusion, literary criticism, observed behavior, and abstract meditation. All of these collide on any given page, and all are brought to bear on the contemporary proclivity to define the self in terms of ethnic identities, something Rodriguez sees as the antithesis to his concept of brown: "The trouble with today's ethnic and racial and sexual identifications is that they become evasions of citizenship. Groups beget subgroups."

And to which subgroup would Richard Rodriguez belong? Hispanic, or gay, or intellectual? Refusing to be marginalized, he opts for American—claiming, along with his citizenship, the right to be an individual, the right not to belong to any defining group.

The "melting pot" as Rodriguez describes it is far more complex than the originator of the metaphor assumed. As he stated to Scott London, "I am no more in favor of assimilation than I am in favor of the Pacific Ocean. Assimilation is not something to oppose or favor—it just happens" (interview with Scott London, *Insight & Outlook*). The melting process is fraught with difficulty, and the end result is loss as well as gain—for both the country and the individual. But that discussion covers old territory, and *Brown* is trying for originality as it celebrates the ways in which America has taken in—and taken over—the images and foods and languages of its immigrants. The metaphor of "brown" encompasses Madonna and Elvis and the thumping boom box on the street. We are in transition, and Rodriguez senses that the end results will be positive: "Brown people know there is nothing in the world—no recipe, no water, no city, no motive, no lace, no locution, no candle, no corpse that does not—I was going to say descend—that does not ascend to brown. Brown might be making."

How does the writer striving for accuracy— the writer of nonfiction—deal with the knowledge that whatever words go on the page, they will only approximate a truth? Rodriguez has skirted this issue by choosing what he calls a "rhetorical counterpart" of the mixing of cultures—a form that allows for the inevitable lapses, the disparities between versions, the inescapable opinions that cloud the picture. Sequence be damned—he is proceeding by association. The essays unfold in snippets; they progress in an untimely manner, dependent on the mind's circularities; they allow for discontinuity, making use of white space as a natural tool, something to be leapt over, bridged, stopped *at* and then begun again *from*. They trust the mind and its seemingly random connections to shape a full story—in its own sweet timelessness.

This style, coupled with the metaphor of brown, allows for—even courts—contradiction. Each essay acts as a collage of ideas, a mixture that proceeds more from emotion and intuition than from logic. For example, in "Gone West" (the title fully past tense), Rodriguez looks not only at the history of westward expansion but at the concept of the West as it evolved over time. He begins from the west of Los Angeles, looking eastward. How different things look from this perspective. "The old east-west dialectic in America moved between city and country, the settled and the unsettled." Brown reaches the Pacific, and then turns around again, discerning that the new orientation is north-south. "From the perspective of California, Oregon is a northern state; Seattle is a northern city; Vancouver becomes a part of the continuum without regard to international borders." What is endangered is the familiar *notion* of the West.

Along the way, Rodriguez indulges whatever other thoughts occur. The environmental movement receives his scrutiny. "In fact, protection is human intrusion," he says. In the light of the reality of Latin America, U.S. environmental policies seem determinedly nostalgic: "Weeping Conscience has become the patron saint of an environmental movement largely made up of the descendants of pioneers. More curiously, the dead Indian has come to represent pristine Nature in an argument made by some environmentalists against 'overpopulation' (the fact that so many live Indians in Latin America are having so many babies and are advancing north)."

Nothing is sacred. Just as Americans invented the West in order to be able to settle it, they have invented the homeland of "Africa" as a "prelapsarian savanna." They coined the term "Hispanic" and thus individual roots disappeared in the conglomerate. Now "Asians" are being born in the new country. "Asians do not exist anywhere in Asia."

In the culminating essay, "Peter's Avocado," Rodriguez describes himself as an "observer." He notes the sense of singularity—the "American I"—as a distinctive product of American culture. In an earlier essay, he claimed that American individualism is a "communally derived value, not truly an expression of individuality." Now he explores the idea:

I may be unwise, I may be mistaken, I may be guilty. But the essence of the American I is that I am irreducible.

I can be punished for my crime, in other words. Isn't that odd? My body can bear the weight of punishment for a crime weighed in the apprehension of others who did not see, who do not know what I know.

Americans are so individualistic, they do not realize their individualism is a communally derived value. The American I is deconstructed for me by Paolo, an architect who was raised in Bologna: "You Americans are not truly individualistic, you merely are lonely. In order to be individualistic, one must have a strong sense of oneself within a group." (The "we" is a precondition for saying "I.") Americans spend all their lives looking for a community: a chatroom, a church, a support group, a fetish magazine, a book club, a class-action suit.

Rodriguez is not "merely lonely"—but he is lonely. Loneliness becomes a motif, at times "a chord or a descending scale," at times a solitude so deep it yearns for complement. *Brown* carries with it the urgency of the repressed secret, the unspoken contradiction that fuels all other contradictions. The "last discovery" of the book's subtitle is the one that breaks down all barriers: love. For Rodriguez, love has been fraught with the forbidden. The very nature of individuality must be honored before the argument for sexual preference can be mounted. At the end of "Peter's Avocado," Rodriguez recounts his courageous stand. He has entered the territory of legislated morality. Is he Catholic? Yes. Is he gay? Yes. Very well then, he contains contradictions. The child who felt so out of place at last finds his voice in a mixture of analysis and anecdote and admonition:

Homosexuality requires cubism to illustrate itself, perhaps. But homosexuality is not a lifestyle. Homosexuality is an emotion—a physiological departure from homeostasis. ...

Do not say "I love him" before a convention of Anglican educators at the Fairmont Hotel in San Francisco, though, as I did. ... [T]alk about separate races and distinct ethnicities and the divisions in American social life, talk about literature, talk about God. (But do not speak about love.)

In his talk to the librarians in 1997, Rodriguez explained, "There will always be ways in which I am one, single, I. And I deeply am grateful to this country, especially its Anglo-Saxon judicial system, for honoring my I-ness, for honoring all the ways in which I am separate from you." And then, as though the very mention of the tradition from which his rights were derived had reminded him of his original alienation, he went on: "Separate even from the people who love me. Separate even from my family. Those incredible subtle ways in which a child is always separated from its parents. That mystery when you look you're your child's eyes and realize that separation."

Perhaps Rodriguez felt the separation more keenly because of his secrets. If so, either as a measure of the changing climate of the country or a measure of his growing comfort with the intimacy of the written word, in *Brown* he was able to admit—and explore—the implications of his singularity. In the end, love accounts for the mix that has colored America. And love will persist.

Brown is an important book, even a necessary one. It is not reactionary, but visionary. The nine essays are each a spoke on a wheel. Follow the spoke to the hub and you will see this: the clay of creation, the fired clay of conclusion cracked open to reveal the alloy, the compound, compounded.

THE STYLE IS THE MAN

The three books that make up the trilogy of Rodriguez' work over the years 1982 to 2002 have overlapping concerns; often, they seem to cover the same territory, if from slightly altered perspectives. In the preface to *Brown*, Rodriguez addressed this issue: "I believe it is possible to describe a single life thrice, if from three isolations." Thus it is that one book concentrates on the Spanish-speaking child in the English-speaking classroom, one on the tug-of-war for the child's soul by Mexico and the United States, and one on the child's growing awareness that his dark skin sets him apart, culminating in his celebration of that very darkness. At the center of each book is the same child, the same adult, but Rodriguez has chosen to isolate the isolations, concentrating on the effects of one aspect of his life at a time. Together, they add up to a whole.

But it is possible that the division of "isolations" also simplifies the experience, makes it possible to imagine solutions that are not so readily available when the child is simultaneously Spanish-speaking, dark-skinned, and conscious that he does not belong to mainstream America. Class, ethnicity, and race (to say nothing of religion and sexual preference) cannot be isolated from each other—are, in fact, part of an integral experience of growing up. Rodriguez calls himself "a queer Catholic Indian Spaniard at home in a temperate Chinese city in a fading blond state in a post-Protestant nation" (*Brown,* 35). Yet he has found it necessary to separate one discussion from another in order to bring all his intellectual power to bear on the issue at hand. Still, the totality of the experience of twenty years of struggle with identity can be seen more in the evolution of his style than in the development of the argument.

Hunger of Memory had a story to tell, a life to recount, essential points to be made. It acts like a conventional memoir in more than structure—its style is expository, clean and analytical. "Education created this voice," Rodriguez told Stan Rubin. Recalling his admiration for the way D. H. Lawrence "remained true to his memory of his working class past," Rodriguez understands that "class is not our great drama." But he emulated Lawrence in his determination to capture the physical detail and the emotional nuance of his early experiences.

In *Days of Obligation,* Rodriguez opened up the story in new ways, and for these he needed a new style. He needed a vehicle by which to convey the sense of mystery he felt in the presence of the Mexican side of his heritage. The answer was the lyric. Almost every essay is constructed as a mosaic; short segments ranging from approximately one to four pages are connected—fused—through simple juxtaposition. Each segment acts somewhat like a poem—a moment of felt insight, caught in nuance, given metaphorical import. The words circle and circle, held in suspension, a part of the ultimate meaning to be unlocked. And the argument is interrupted with italicized commentary, creating an effect that Rodriguez himself has termed "baroque." It is, he feels, his most Mexican voice.

Reading *Brown* is turning toward the tangential. One touches down on idea, sets the surface rippling; the idea gives way to conjecture, conjecture to opinion, opinion to fact: blunt, official fact. Rodriguez's style is associational—association at its fluid best: nervous energy as the skipping stone touches down, again and again, on familiar waters, stirring them into motion. Ideas and impressions and attitudes overlap, collide, circle each other, tightening the noose of interconnection. Opposites attract. Opposites define a larger, inclusive whole.

It is not possible to demonstrate how such rhythmic urgency and elastic association create a complete essay without reproducing an entire essay. But sometimes Rodriguez gives an example in microcosm. A paragraph can take him from origin to example to convolution to irony. His is a new style, fit for a new century. Rodriguez gives himself over to language, but it is a language infused with idea, popping with principle and paradox:

> I can see him now, yes, I can see him, a proper Chinatown dragon with silver pompons nodding so gaily upon his spine, his beard of silver fringe, his four, six, eight, hundreds, thousands of athletic,

hairless legs, rosy at the calf—*crash-gong-crash-gong*—mincing up to where I stand. He tosses his leonine head. He regards me silently. I tie a garland of green leaves and red firecrackers onto a bamboo pole to feed the droll monster. I raise the pole sky-high. The silver dragon rolls his ping-pongy eyes and rocks from side to side and then begins to writhe upward into the sky, one segment standing upon the shoulders of the next; his mouth clacking open and shut with puppet relish.

East meets East upon this shore. The dragon will discover his tail at last. And within bright paradox another lies: The numerical rise of the Hispanic in America today is paralleled by the numerical rise of the Asian. The Asian moves east into the American West to meet the Hispanic immigrant who moves north to reach the American West. The Hispanic brings the idea of a continuous past into a country that preferred to think of time as forward thrust. The Asian brings the idea of moment, of the present, into an America that was preoccupied by the westward movement into the future. American is fated to recognize itself as intersection—no, nothing so plain as intersection—as coil, pretzel, Gordian knot with a wagging tail.

Precisely because he has given himself so completely to the instrument of association, one segment standing upon the shoulders of the next, Richard Rodriguez functions as the Picasso of American literature. Simultaneously aesthetic and political, his writing weds the public and the private dream.

Even though *Brown* was nominated for the National Book Critics Circle Award, the irony, as Rodriguez sees it, is that he is not regularly thought of as a writer. More often, he is considered a journalist. The questions he is asked are political, sociological, cultural. In some odd way, he has been forced to become the spokesman he never wanted to be. Part of this, he suspects, is because of the compartmentalization of literature, both in the academy and in the society at large. He is being isolated from the very literature that fueled his imagination.

His ambition is to be shelved under L for Literature, not L for Latino:

> Acknowledgment came at a price, then as now. (Three decades later, the price of being a published brown author is that one cannot be shelved near those one has loved. The price is segregation.)
>
> I remain at best ambivalent about those Hispanic anthologies where I end up; about those anthologies where I end up the Hispanic; about shelves at the bookstore where I look for myself and find myself. The fact that my books are published at all is the result of the slaphappy strategy of the northern black Civil Rights movement.

Sometimes Rodriguez is worried that he is invited to speak only in the name of "diversity." The term, for him, is a negative one, as he makes clear in his interview with Scott London. "For me, diversity is not a value. Diversity is what you find in Northern Ireland. Diversity is Beirut. Diversity is brother killing brother. Where diversity is *shared*—where I share with you my difference—that can be valuable. But the simple fact that we are unlike each other is a terrifying notion."

Asked for his response to angry student groups protesting his presentations on campuses, he told his interviewers Virginia Postrel and Nick Gillespie:

> Multiculturalism, as it is expressed in the platitudes of the American campus, is not multiculturalism. It is an idea about culture that has a specific genesis, a specific history, and a specific politics. What people mean by multiculturalism is different hues of themselves. ... It isn't diversity. It's a pretense to diversity. And this is an exposure of it—they can't even tolerate my paltry opinion.

Richard Rodriguez is angry. He says so openly. He leads with his anger in the preface to his third book: "It is that brown faculty I uphold by attempting to write brownly. And I defy anyone who tries to unblend me or to say what is appropriate to my voice." His voice in *Brown* is urgent in its insistence that these are "dangerous times": the forces that drive us apart defeat us.

> (I reopen this book in the terrible dusk of September 11, 2001. On that day, several medieval men in the guise of multicultural America and in the manner of American pop culture, rode dreadnoughts through the sky. These were men from a world of certainty, some hours distant—a world where men presume to divine, to enforce, to protectively wear the will of God: a world where men wage incessant war against the impurity that lies without [puritans!] and so they mistrust, they wither whatever they touch; ... These several inauthentic men, of fake I.D., of brutish sentimentality, went missing from U.S. immigration rolls, were presumed lost and assimilated into brown America, these men of certainty refused to be seduced by modernity, postmodernity; by what I have been at pains to describe as brown, as making.)

Rodriguez wonders if there is any substantial audience for the essay—for the "drama of idea." "We have too many narratives," Rodriguez says. "The trouble is that we don't know what they mean." In graduate school, students describe how to analyze the story, but they don't seem to understand the story. Sometimes he hears his own voice on television; his words sound too thin as they roll off his tongue. That, he has said, is when he knows he needs to pull back, needs to look inward in order to complicate the issue. In other words, he feels the need to write a book. After the book has been completed, it will have a life of its own. Rodriguez will put it aside, almost as having been written by someone else—someone he can hardly recognize, someone from whom he has been definitively freed.

In an interview with Timothy Sedore in 1999, Rodriguez articulated that sense that the person who wrote the book (in this case, *Hunger of Memory*) is not the person speaking in the present: "I must tell you that I am not sure that I would like Richard Rodriguez were I not he. At some very simple level I can tell you that I

don't like the voice. ... He whimpers too much. He's too soft. He's not what I want."

In the years since their publication these challenging books have been treated to different forms of criticism. The emphasis has shifted from the "Chicano" critics whose focus was ethnicity to those whose interest is in the various faces of "solitude." Most notably, Randy A. Rodriguez (no relation) has addressed the work of Richard Rodriguez from the perspective of "queer theory." He sees Rodriguez's identification with literature as a kind of coded coming-out story. Finally, what characterizes all of Rodriguez' work is the collision and encounter of the past and present, of identities and selves, the tradition offering new perspectives on the future. *Brown* begins with de Tocqueville and ends with Walt Whitman. Each essay reveals the way Rodriguez' thought is anchored in literature, how books inform his very way of looking at the world, the world made new as it assimilates the old. The old masters accompany him on his journey; they nudge him one way or another; they argue with his latest ideas—and he talks back.

Selected Bibliography

WORKS OF RICHARD RODRIGUEZ

AUTOBIOGRAPHY

Hunger of Memory: The Education of Richard Rodriguez. Boston: Godine, 1982.

Days of Obligation: An Argument with My Mexican Father. New York: Viking, 1992.

Brown: The Last Discovery of America. New York: Viking, 2002.

TALKS AND ORAL PRESENTATIONS

"Remarks of Richard Rodriguez." Convocation on Providing Public Library Service to California's

21st Century Population, May 23, 1997. Available at www.library.ca.gov. (These remarks cover many of the same points Rodriguez makes in *Brown*.)

"Seventh Annual Texas Book Festival," Nov. 16–17, 2002. Televised on C-Span 2.

The texts of a number of original short pieces for television or newspapers can be found at http://www.pbs.org/newshour/essays/richard_rodriguez.html and at http://www.pacificnews.org/contribu tors/rodriguez/.

INTERVIEWS

London, Scott. "A View from the Melting Pot: An Interview with Richard Rodriguez." On his radio series *Insight & Outlook*. Script available at http://www.scottlondon.com/insight/scripts/rodriguez.html.

Postrel, Virginia I., and Nick Gillespie. "The New, New World." *Reason Magazine,* February 19, 2000. Available at http://www.reason.com/Rodri.shtml.

Rubin, Stan Sanvel. "A Conversation with Richard Rodriguez." Brockport Writers Forum Videotape Library, 2002. (This interview, given upon the presentation of the Brockport Writers Forum/M&T Bank Art of Fact Award, April 25, 2002, discusses the evolution of the trilogy and looks at Rodriguez the writer, talking about style as well as his approach to his subject.)

Sedore, Timothy S. "Violating the Boundaries: An Interview with Richard Rodriguez." *Michigan Quarterly Review* 38, no. 3: 425–446 (summer 1999).

Wolfe, Gregory. "A Conversation with Richard Rodriguez." *Image: A Journal of the Arts and Religion,* no. 34: 53–68 (spring 2002).

CRITICAL AND BIOGRAPHICAL STUDIES

Alarcon, Norma. "Tropology of Hunger: The 'Miseducation' of Richard Rodriguez." In *The Ethnic Canon: Histories, Institutions, and Interventions.* Edited by Liu D. Palumbo. Minneapolis: University of Minnesota Press, 1995. Pp. 140–152.

Danahay, Martin A. "Richard Rodriguez's Poetics of Manhood." In *Fictions of Masculinity: Crossing Cultures, Crossing Sexualities.* Edited by Peter F. Murphy. New York: New York University Press, 1994. Pp. 290–307.

Limon, Jose E., ed. "Richard Rodriguez: Public Intellectual." *Texas Studies in Literature and Language* 40, no. 4: 389–459 (winter 1998).

Marquez, Antonio C. "Richard Rodriguez's *Hunger of Memory* and New Perspectives on Ethnic Autobiography." In *Teaching American Ethnic Literatures: Nineteen Essays.* Edited by John R. Maitino and David R. Peck. Albuquerque: University of New Mexico Press, 1996. Pp. 237–254.

Nericcio, William. Review of *Days of Obligation. World Literature Today* 68, no. 1: 141–143 (winter 1994).

Rodriguez, Randy A. "Richard Rodriguez Reconsidered: Queering the Sissy (Ethnic) Subject." *Texas Studies in Literature and Language* 40, no. 4: 396–423 (winter 1998).

Sanchez, Rosaura. "Calculated Musings: Richard Rodriguez's Metaphysics of Difference." In *The Ethnic Canon: Histories, Institutions, and Interventions.* Edited by Liu D. Palumbo. Minneapolis: University of Minnesota Press, 1995. Pp. 153–173.

Schilt, Paige. "Anti-Pastoral and Guilty Vision in Richard Rodriguez's *Days of Obligation.*" *Texas Studies in Literature and Language* 40, no. 4: 424–441 (winter 1998).

Tilden, Norma. "Word Made Flesh: Richard Rodriguez's 'Late Victorians' as Nativity Story." *Texas Studies in Literature and Language* 40, no. 4: 442–459 (winter 1998).

Waxman, Barbara F. "Feeding the 'Hunger of Memory' and an Appetite for the Future: The Ethnic 'Storied' Self and the American Authored Self in Ethnic Autobiography." In *Cross-Addressing: Resistance Literature and Cultural Borders.* Edited by John C. Hawley. Albany: State University of New York Press, 1996. Pp. 207–116.

——JUDITH KITCHEN

John Patrick Shanley

1950–

JOHN PATRICK SHANLEY writes impressively if incongruously about the brutality of love and human communication. Shanley's two most celebrated works—the play *Danny and the Deep Blue Sea: An Apache Dance* (1984) and the Oscar-winning screenplay for the comedy *Moonstruck* (1987)—are equally startling, but in radically different ways: the former for its brooding mood and looming threat of violence, the latter for its old-fashioned romance and robust sentimentality. Both works typify the best of Shanley's drama. Stranded somewhere between heart attack and heartbreak, the mostly blue-collar denizens of Shanley's plays and screenplays find themselves traversing a landscape of psychological extremes in which the largeness of their emotions is gradually closed down by a world of possibilities that is frustratingly small. By marrying a vernacular flair rivaling David Mamet's to a sense of local color akin to Tennessee Williams', Shanley's work for stage and screen is tragicomic, quirky, and endlessly inventive.

Shanley was born in the New York City borough of the Bronx on October 13, 1950. His father was a meat packer of Irish-American descent, and his mother worked as a telephone operator. A poet at the age of eleven, Shanley later won statewide essay competitions in his early teens. He was expelled by no fewer than three Bronx high schools before a Roman Catholic priest helped him enroll in a New Hampshire prep school. Shanley found his way to New York University, but he dropped out after his first year to enlist in the U.S. Marine Corps. Following this stint with the Marine

Corps—which Shanley has described as "a continuation of the Bronx—but more civilized"—he returned to New York City. Dissatisfied with a series of low-paying jobs, Shanley decided to reenroll at New York University. Although he had been away from academia for five years, he graduated as class valedictorian with a degree in educational theater and went on to pursue a master's degree. When Shanley characteristically dropped out of graduate school to tend bar, paint apartments, and devote himself more completely to his writing, the move paid off. Early works such as *Saturday Night at the War* (1978), *George and the Dragon* (1979), *Ketchup* (c. 1980), *Rockaway* (1982), and especially *Welcome to the Moon* (produced in 1982, published in 1985) showed him to be a promising young playwright. In 1984 the off-Broadway production of *Danny and the Deep Blue Sea* brought him to a new level of success. Shanley's reputation was cemented by critically acclaimed productions such as *Savage in Limbo: A Concert Play* (produced in 1985, published in 1986); *Women of Manhattan: An Upper West Side Story* (1986); *the dreamer examines his pillow* (produced in 1986, published in 1987); and *Italian American Reconciliation: A Folktale* (produced in 1988, published in 1989).

Though these plays were critical successes, they were not financially rewarding, and Shanley was forced to consider other means of earning money. Disheartened by the idea of having to return to the mundane duties of bartending and apartment-painting, he did what many of his contemporaries from Sam Shepard to David Mamet had already done: he turned to Hollywood. Sources as unlikely as Oliver Stone's script for the Brian De Palma remake of *Scarface* influenced his first original screenplay, *Five Corners,* which was produced in 1988 (after the release of his second screenplay, *Moonstruck*). With its beaten-down Bronx losers, urban desperation, displaced penguins and bow-and-arrow assassinations, *Five Corners* is the most uncompromising of all Shanley's screenplays, particularly in its comic mixture of pathos and violence. Though not commercially successful, the film was critically well received and went on to win a Special Jury Prize at the Barcelona Film Festival.

Moonstruck began as a script titled *The Bride and the Wolf,* which Shanley wrote for actress Sally Field. Field passed on the project, but veteran director Norman Jewison snapped it up, changing the title to *Moonglow* and ultimately *Moonstruck.* Garnering Oscars for Cher and Olympia Dukakis in lead and supporting roles, respectively, this whimsical story of an Italian American bachelorette and the two brothers who farcically woo her earned Shanley a Writers Guild of America Award as well as the Oscar for Best Original Screenplay.

Despite its promising start, Shanley's career as a Hollywood screenwriter peaked early. Six screenplays followed, none equaling either *Five Corners* or *Moonstruck* in critical reception. *The January Man,* released in 1989, is an unconventional crime story featuring Kevin Kline. *Joe versus the Volcano,* produced in 1990, is a big-budget, Frank Capra–style fable with Tom Hanks and Meg Ryan. It was directed by Shanley and produced by Shanley's early champion Steven Spielberg. *Alive* (1993) is Shanley's re-creation of a true-life Andes plane crash disaster. Also appearing in 1993 was *We're Back! A Dinosaur's Story,* an animated movie for children. Shanley also wrote the screenplays for *Congo* (1995), an adaptation of the Michael Crichton best-seller, and the HBO teleplay *Live*

from Baghdad (2002), a dissection of the role of the American media during the 1991 Persian Gulf War.

Shanley's profitable relationship with Hollywood did not mean the end of his artistically rewarding relationship with American theater. He has continued to write plays and see them produced. His works from the 1990s and 2000s include *The Big Funk: A Casual Play* (produced in 1990, published in 1991); *Beggars in the House of Plenty* (produced in 1991, published in 1992); *Four Dogs and a Bone and The Wild Goose* (1995); *Missing/Kissing: Missing Marisa, Kissing Christine* (1997); *Psychopathia Sexualis* (produced in 1997, published in 1998); *Cellini* (2001); *Where's My Money?* (produced in 2001, published 2002); and the Arab/Israeli allegory *Dirty Story* (2003). Like his screenplays, Shanley's earlier plays tended to earn stronger critical receptions than his later ones. But Shanley's theater remains a compelling arena of love, violence, desperation, and hope in which, as Shanley explains in the preface to *13 by Shanley* (1992), "All the really exciting things possible during the course of a lifetime require a little more courage than we currently have."

WELCOME TO THE MOON AND OTHER PLAYS

First presented by the Ensemble Studio in New York City in the fall of 1982, *Welcome to the Moon and Other Plays* is a suite of one-act plays showcasing Shanley's considerable linguistic and imaginative range. As an early work, *Welcome to the Moon and Other Plays* provides a comprehensive tour of an emerging dramatic consciousness. Themes that will come to preoccupy Shanley—the redemptive power of love, the curse of the imagination, the precariousness of friendship, the difficulties of communication, and the rocky terrain of a borough named the Bronx—are all on display in miniature here.

In the opening one-act, *The Red Coat,* an abstracted seventeen-year-old boy named John confesses his love to Mary, a sixteen-year-old girl who has just arrived at a party. But the facile declarations of teenage infatuation are instantly jolted by a lyric sensibility. John is ecstatic with love, and Shanley's dialogue— poetic and heightened without becoming self-conscious or precious—tags along. When Mary confides her attraction to John, the moonlit exchange becomes charged with a poetry beyond the verbal reach of the average teenage crush. This is *Romeo and Juliet* in contemporary rhetoric—with a street-corner, unpretentious, native-Bronx inflection. Revealing their feelings for one another beneath "a street light that's more beautiful than the sun," John speaks fondly of Mary's red coat, and his poetic appreciation of the item of clothing enables her to realize that he alone understands her. In this funny valentine of a sketch—a foreshadowing of *Moonstruck,* minus the Hollywood trappings—love heightens all, and the dramatic language follows suit.

In the hilarious allegory *Down and Out,* thinly-drawn characters named Love and the Poet sit down to a dinner of "water and beans" while a deathly "Figure" demands the return of the Poet's library card. After the heady lyricism of *The Red Coat, Down and Out* offers a welcome decompression. Shanley manages to parody the myth of the starving artist—one to which he could clearly relate—while paying homage to it. "I remember when the wolf was at the door," the Poet says, lamenting the loss of more important things than library cards, "and I was not afraid."

Fear is also central to *Let Us Go into the Starry Night,* the title of which evokes the tortured ecstasies of artist Vincent Van Gogh. The figure of a suffering artist is also suggested by the startling opening image of *"a tormented young man"* at a cafe table *"surrounded by ghosts and monsters"* that *"chew on his head, claw his stomach, whisper in his ear."* Approached by a skinny woman with more than philosophy on her mind, the young man banters with her sophomorically about God. "I think there's a sophomore in a lot of people, just waiting to get out," the woman quips, offering the young man a glass of champagne. "It tastes like I'm drinking little sparks," he observes. Monsters banished, the two fall in love. Like *The Red Coat, Let Us Go into the Starry Night* is another unabashed valentine, but with monsters in the wings the stakes are clearly much higher.

Out West, the fourth piece in the suite, combines Wild-West rhetoric with the inflated romantic diction of the opening sketches. Archetypes named the Cowboy and the Girl are attracted to one another, but their romance is interrupted by a bizarre cast of characters. Shanley sends up saddle-sore sentimentality while allowing the Girl to display the occasional flashy costume-jewel of dialogue: "I have fixed my heart with a star like a pin to the bosom of the night." Although the Girl is killed at the climax in a tragic gunfight, the tongue-in-cheek rhetoric of her dying words points the audience to a tragicomic message about the redemptive power of love:

> GIRL: I have been living in my room all my life waiting for the world ta notice me. I have been a slave to my parents. The only dreams I had were from lookin' out at the prairie. I never was alive until I saw you. At least now I'm dyin' after I was alive.

> MIKE: Poor little thing. She's dead.

Love also looms large in *A Lonely Impulse of Delight,* the penultimate one-act about Walter, a dreamy man who takes his skeptical best friend Jim to Central Park Lake to meet Sally, the elusive freshwater mermaid for whom he has improbably fallen:

> WALTER: ... Do you know what I'm talking about, Jimmy? You're my best friend in the world. If

you don't know what I'm talking about then there's nobody.

JIM: I don't know what the fuck you're talking about.

WALTER: Just wait a minute. Just one more minute. Sally? Sally? Please?

As much about the possibilities of love as it is about the impossibility of communicating the possibilities of love, *A Lonely Impulse of Delight* ends on a bittersweet note when the unconvinced friend exits just as the belated mermaid emerges. "Sally, why didn't you come?" Walter laments. "He was my best friend." Love has survived, but a friendship is over. Walter is less and more lonely than before.

Shanley rounds out this suite of early one acts with the title piece, *Welcome to the Moon.* The most grounded and realistic of the sketches, *Welcome to the Moon* also boasts the distinction of introducing the most important unbilled character in Shanley's canon: the Bronx. "*A lowdown Bronx bar,*" the stage directions read, and the verbal rhythms and scenic touches of Shanley's signature borough distinguish this economic and tragicomic one-act. Gone is the inflated diction of the previous five sketches. In its place is gritty verbal phrasing: "I threw myself in front of the A train, but the fuckin' thing broke down before it got to me." The Byzantine plot—which involves a double-suicide pact, unrequited love, homosexual longing, and Canadian bacon and cheese sandwiches—keeps twisting and turning until, in an irresistible *coup de théâtre,* the redeemed hero Stephen breaks into an Irish love song, and the girl of his dreams is perhaps finally attainable. Simultaneously surreal and real, *Welcome to the Moon* walks a profoundly thin line between dreams and reality—a line Shanley will navigate to even more remarkable effect in his breakout play, *Danny and the Deep Blue Sea.*

DANNY AND THE DEEP BLUE SEA

"This play is emotionally real," Shanley writes in the stage directions to the work that would locate him on the theatrical map, "but does not take place in a realistic world." Written and performed a year after *Welcome to the Moon and Other Plays,* the psychologically perilous universe of *Danny and the Deep Blue Sea* could not be any further from the heightened romantic dialogue of its predecessor. In *Danny and the Deep Blue Sea,* Shanley lowers the language in the most unsparing way imaginable in order to capture the emotional realism of two embattled, embittered lovers hurtling toward each other in a seedy urban bar. In fact, *Danny and the Deep Blue Sea* picks up where the closing one-act of *Welcome to the Moon* left off—with yet another set of lower-class casualties dry-docked in yet another "lowdown Bronx bar." Unlike the promising ending of *Welcome to the Moon and Other Plays,* here the promise of love comes across more like a threat. Were this bar any lower it would be subterranean.

Roberta, a thirty-one-year-old unwed mother in a "cheap dress-up blouse that's gotten ratty," is nursing a beer when Danny—a twenty-nine-year-old whose "*hands are badly bruised*"—enters with a pitcher and asks her for a pretzel. She gives him one, reluctantly. But after listening to Danny's street-brawling braggadocio, Roberta's response—"I don't get it"—elicits from him an explosion of profanity, all in the opening moments of the play: "Who the fuck asked you to get it! Ain't none a your fuckin business I lock horns with anybody! Nobody crosses my fuckin line, man! They can do what they want out there, but nobody crosses my fuckin line!"

But Roberta *does* cross Danny's line, and with increasing fearlessness. After confiding in Danny about the glue she used to sniff, the mentally ill child she does not particularly want to care for, the husband who did not bother to stick around, and the sexual encounter with her father that has wrecked her life, Roberta dares to join the hair-triggered loner at his table. Although Danny confesses to a possible murder ("I think I killed a guy last night"), Roberta invites him back to her apartment. His hesitancy causes her to bait him even further. In one of the play's most nerve-wracking scenes, Roberta slaps the already wired Danny repeatedly in the face while berating and emasculating him:

> ROBERTA: You don't scare me, asshole. I see worse than you crawlin around in my sink. You're about as bad as a faggot in his Sunday dress! Your mama probably still gives you her tit when you get shook up! (*She starts slapping him.*) What's the matter, badass? Somebody get your matches wet?

Danny's response is to attempt to choke Roberta to death. But when she fails to resist, Danny *"Lets her go in horror."* "Why'd you stop?" Roberta asks. "Don't talk to me," Danny answers. Only in a Shanley play would a moment so brutal be a prelude to a kiss.

Scene Two has Danny and Roberta naked in bed in Roberta's closet-sized apartment drinking red wine that "tastes like piss" and planning, of all things, their wedding day. The implausibility of this self-destructive duo plunging headlong into plans for the future is overcome by the emotional reality of their need, a desperation that causes them to spin out of control in the one direction perhaps least available to them: hope. The ugliness of the opening act is mitigated here by an almost impossible romantic optimism. In one of the play's more affectionate exchanges, the lovers awkwardly catalogue one another's bodies. "You got friendly ears," Roberta says. "You got a nice nose," says Danny. "It looks right at ya, your nose, and it says Hello!" Discovering one another, these two are essentially discovering themselves, and their hope, however pathetic, knows no bounds. "It's good. It's good," Danny says. "Maybe that's what we oughta do. Build a

boat and sail the fuck away. Get married on some island where everybody speaks Booga Booga. Are you asleep? I love you."

Although the lovers drift off to pipe dreams of the future, the morning after paints a starker picture altogether. Roberta rejects the promises of the night before and dismisses Danny for being "all fucked up." Danny protests: "Ya kissed my hands. Ya kissed my hands." In typical Shanley fashion, the emotional lives of these eviscerated characters are richer and deeper than the options life has made available to them. Realizing the futility of their future together, Roberta hysterically orders Danny to "Go beat up a wall! Go watch yar dishrag mother puke her dishrag guts!" The confrontation ends as Roberta *"collapses, sobbing."* When she recovers Danny is right there waiting for her, still intent on planning their wedding day. Danny's hope has miraculously outdistanced her despair. The closing exchange is doggedly upbeat:

> DANNY: … We can plan a weddin, an the weddin'll happen the way we plan. …
>
> ROBERTA: Yeah? You think so?
>
> DANNY: Yeah. I do. I definitely definitely think I do.

Subtitled "An Apache Dance"—which Shanley describes in the play's opening notes as "a violent dance for two people, originated by … gangsters or ruffians"—*Danny and the Deep Blue Sea* portrays love as an embroiled psychic battlefield, bruising to combatants already bruised and raw. But however damaged they may be, and however tentatively healed, Danny and Roberta, like all of Shanley's couples, see love as the only plausible option.

SAVAGE IN LIMBO

Receiving its first full staging at the Double Image Theatre in New York City in 1985, *Savage in Limbo* shares with *Danny and the Deep Blue Sea* the two common denominators of Shanley's early drama—the blistering exchanges of young men and women attempting to communicate as lovers and friends and the humble surroundings of the Bronx.

Set in the interior of yet another seedy New York watering hole—this one outfitted with two dead plants, a funereal bartender, and the symbolic name Scales—*Savage in Limbo* is even more relentless than *Danny and the Deep Blue Sea.* Undivided by acts, the play unfolds on an intensely lit minimalist set that exudes the existential dread of dramas such as Jean-Paul Sartre's *No Exit. Savage in Limbo* presents a turbulent world in which five dead-end characters rebound off one another on an "emotionally real" plane. Individuals seem incapable of any kind of small talk. Even the most seemingly trivial exchanges come across as undisguised cries from the heart. As the heroine Denise Savage announces to the bartender when she first enters Scales:

> I don't feel like watching television once more for the rest of my life and I can't sit in that apartment that smells like a catbox with my mother who looks like a dead walrus for one more second or I will die. I will. So I put on a dress and my black pumps and I got lotsa cash and here I am. What's happening?

The plot involves the attempts of the belligerent Savage and the "*overripe Italian*" Linda Rotunda to win the affections of "the streamlined Italian stud" Tony Aronica. Tired of his relationship with Linda—with whom he has a son—and gun-shy as a womanizer, Tony is determined from now on to sleep only with "ugly girls." Tony is also intrigued when Savage unceremoniously offers him her virginity, an offer that enrages the recently jilted Linda, with whom Savage has arranged to move in. Overseeing all of these developments are the stoic bartender Murk, who insists that his patrons drink almost constantly, and his favorite customer April, a former nun in an alcoholic stupor for whom he periodically dresses up as Santa Claus in order to help her avert a mental breakdown:

> April: Is that you, Santa?
>
> Murk: Ho ho ho. It's me, April. ... Now promise me you'll be a good girl.
>
> April: I promise.
>
> Murk: And you'll say your prayers?
>
> April: Yes.
>
> Murk: And you won't go crazy?
>
> April: No.
>
> Murk: All right then. ... Jingle bells jingle bells, jingle all the way.

Like Eugene O'Neill, Shanley prefers extreme emotional states. And it does not take much to put his characters there. When Savage tells a weepy Linda to do her best to cheer up, Linda replies:

> I hate that. ... People tryin to cheer me up. Who asked you? I feel bad. ... I got no friends. I got nobody who loves me. My future looks like shit. I'm gettin fat. ... My life sucks. Your life sucks. ... Don't you tell me to stop cryin. You should start cryin. ... Miserable buncha two-faced Doris Days.

Approximately the same age as Shanley when he composed the play, each of the characters in *Savage In Limbo* is thirty-two, in crisis, and determined to get out of it. April says, "I'm only thirty-two. I've got too much time to kill. I could live thirty, forty more years just staring at the meter runnin." In defense of his improbable marriage proposal to April, Murk says self-evidently, "I'm thirty two years old. Well?" Even the relatively unrefined Tony wraps up the play's longest monologue with the telling admission: "I wanna look at somethin else. I wanna know somethin else. I'm thirty-two years old. I wanna change." Savage, also thirty-two, is crippled by the most profoundly radical doubt of all, and she is looking to escape from it through the equally disastrous options of cohabitation with Linda or marriage to Tony. She sums up the crises facing each of the characters in an unforgettable speech near the close of the play:

> This is not life. This is not life. This is not life. … God, gimme somethin else cause this is definitely not it. New eyes new ears new hands. Gimme back my soul from where you took it, gimme back my friends, gimme back my priests an my father, and take this goddamn virginity from off my life. HUNGER HUNGER HUNGER. If somebody don't gimme somethin, I'm gonna die.

Shanley subtitles *Savage in Limbo* "*A Concert Play,*" and the notes his tortured quintet hits are consistently unharmonious and discordant. Every bit as dazed as the punch-drunk lovers in *Danny and the Deep Blue Sea,* their narrowing options are perhaps even narrower, as they themselves are the first to admit. "Opportunity knocks like almost fuckin never," Savage tells her betrayed friend Linda in the process of seducing Tony. In one of the play's most significant exchanges, the mentally ill April asserts an agency Murk realizes she will never truly have:

APRIL: I like havin my options open.

MURK: Uh-huh.

APRIL: I like it that if we got somethin goin it's cause we choose to have somethin goin, an it's not outta feelin we should or somethin weird like that. Do you understand what I mean?

MURK: Yeah. You're cut off. No more credit. No more drinks.

Where *Danny and the Deep Blue Sea* opens up its lovers to the impossible option of solace through love, *Savage in Limbo* shuts down this option altogether. "I. AM. ALONE," Savage says at the climax to the play as the dour Murk cries out: "Closing time. Last call. Last call. Last call." How Shanley achieves this transition from unrelenting existential despair to the unabashed romanticism of his screenplay for *Moonstruck* is simple enough to understand: his miserable lovers have nowhere to go but up.

MOONSTRUCK

"I came up with the premise of a woman who makes the choice of marrying a man she likes but does not love," Shanley explains in the introduction to the Grove Press edition of *Moonstruck.* "And once she agrees to marry him, *then* have Mr. Right show up and claim her."

The woman in question is Loretta Castorini, a dutiful accountant played by Cher. When we first see her, she is balancing the books at her client Zito's store. Only thirty-seven, her black hair is "*flecked with gray.*" Zito offers her coffee; Loretta refuses and leaves. Dressed in "*sensible but unfashionable clothes of a dark color,*" Loretta is next pictured balancing the books in the backroom of a funeral parlor. Loretta's heart—Shanley argues in these few deft strokes, with a screenwriter's gift for the quickly telling detail—is slowly undergoing a kind of full-embalming. Her prospects look progressively grimmer at the florist's shop where she is next pictured tabulating figures. Filling "*a long white box … with red roses,*" her cheerfully occupied client observes: "Very romantic. The man who sends these knows what he's doing." "The man who sends those," Loretta snaps back, "spends a lot of money on something that ends up in the garbage can." The opening credits have yet to finish, and Loretta has already earned the dubious distinction of being one of Hollywood's great romantic grumps. To revive Loretta, Shanley will bury her in roses.

At dinner that night with Johnny Cammareri, portrayed with bumbling charm by Danny Aiello, Johnny proposes marriage, and Loretta disapproves of the manner in which he does it. Haunted by the memory of her late husband—who was hit by a bus, one of many things Loretta obsessively attributes to *"bad luck"*—Loretta superstitiously insists that Johnny propose properly:

> LORETTA: Right from the start, we didn't do it right. Could you kneel down?
>
> MR. JOHNNY: On the floor?
>
> LORETTA: Yes, on the floor.
>
> MR. JOHNNY: This is a good suit.
>
> LORETTA: I helped you buy it. It came with two pairs of pants. It's for luck, Johnny. When you propose marriage to a woman, you should kneel down.
>
> MR. JOHNNY: All right.

Loretta feels jinxed by the death of her husband; Johnny is concerned about the state of his trousers; a diner confuses Johnny's proposal for praying; Johnny, not surprisingly, forgets to bring a ring: in short, the engagement is doomed from the start. But desperate for romance, Loretta accepts anyway. Johnny *"stands up, brushes off his knees. … They embrace. Loretta kisses him quickly."* In the quickness of that kiss the relationship is over. Johnny leaves that evening by plane for his Sicilian mother's deathbed but not before extracting a promise from Loretta to inform his estranged brother, Ronny, of their impending wedding.

That evening at home news of the engagement does not impress Loretta's jaded parents, Rose and Cosmo, played with deadpan gusto by Olympia Dukakis and Vincent Gardenia. Cosmo dislikes Johnny and refuses to pay for the wedding. Unruffled by Cosmo, Rose questions her daughter:

> ROSE: … Do you love him, Loretta?
>
> LORETTA: No.
>
> ROSE: Good. When you love them, they drive you crazy 'cause they know they can. But you like him?
>
> LORETTA: Oh yeah. He's a sweet man.

Rose's words have a deeper relevance because she knows that her husband, Cosmo, is having an affair. This places Rose and her daughter in heartbroken cahoots: Rose is deeply in love with a husband who is fooling around on her, while Loretta is clearly not in love with the fiancé she intends to marry. Both retreat behind a cynicism neither one believes in. To be in love, Shanley argues, is to be driven crazy: Rose is crazy in a sadly stoic way, while Loretta, as her mother suspects, is too sane.

Enter Ronny Cammareri, Johnny's untamed brother, who is indelibly portrayed by Nicolas Cage. Loretta meets him for the first time when she goes to inform him of the wedding. Ronny is the script's Mr. Right, and only a screenwriter as playfully perverse as Shanley could picture him as an opera-obsessed baker with only one hand—the other having been lost to an automatic bread slicer. In fact, as Ronny informs Loretta, the bread-slicer incident is the root of his long-standing grudge against Johnny. He blames Johnny for his injury because the two were talking when the accident took place. Ronny also believes that his brother robbed him of a wife because "when my fiancé saw that I was maimed, she left me for another man." Loretta has a hard time accepting this:

> LORETTA: That's the bad blood between you and Johnny?
>
> RONNY: That's it.
>
> LORETTA: But that wasn't Johnny's fault.

RONNY: I don't care! I ain't no freakin' monument
to justice!

If not for the expert comic delivery of Cher and
Cage, we might be back in the grotesquely
shaded territory of *Danny and the Deep Blue
Sea* and *Savage in Limbo:* two characters meet,
both hopelessly mismatched, and find themselves sucked into one another's loony orbits.
But *Moonstruck* uses its characters' hyperbolic
frustrations in the seriously ridiculous service of
comedy. The sacrificial hand, the outsized emotions, the fondness for Puccini—in short, all of
the romantic aspects of Ronny's character make
Loretta realize that she has chosen the wrong
brother. Because he is such a mess Ronny *is*
Mr. Right. "This is the most tormented man I
have ever known," Chrissy, Ronny's co-worker,
confesses to Loretta, adding as an afterthought:
"I am in love with this man." In Shanley's
algebra of romance, torment equals love, and
love equals torment.

Loretta follows the weeping Ronny up to his
apartment, where both drink whiskey and Loretta cooks a steak:

RONNY: Loretta. What's that smell?

LORETTA: I'm making you a steak.

RONNY: You don't have to help me.

LORETTA: I know that. I do what I want.

RONNY: I like it well done.

LORETTA: You'll eat this bloody to feed your
blood.

That last line, both poetic and prosaic, suggests
Loretta's reason for fortifying Ronny is so that
he may finally overcome the hatred for his
brother that is slowly consuming him mentally
and physically. But it also suggests an ulterior
motive: she wants to feed his blood so Ronny
will seduce her. Whichever its intention, the latter is achieved. Ronny accuses Loretta of being
a "bride without a head!" Loretta accuses Ronny
of being a "wolf without a foot!" In a scene
that is simultaneously comic and erotic, Ronny
*"stiff-arms everything off the dining table and
grabs* LORETTA. *They kiss passionately. He pulls
her up on the table and over the table to him.
They are in each other's arms. They are on fire."*
Loretta breaks away shouting: "Wait a minute!
Wait a minute!" Then she *"changes her mind
and lunges into another kiss."* Like a slapstick
version of *Last Tango in Paris,* Shanley has
Loretta erupt in histrionic dialogue that, despite
its hilarity, is psychologically telling:

LORETTA: You're mad at him, take it out on me,
take your revenge on me! Take everything,
leave nothing for him to marry! Hollow me
out so there's nothing left but the skin over my
bones. Suck me dry!

RONNY: All right. All right. There will be nothing
left.

On the evening that Loretta and Ronny find
one another, a fabulous moon hovers over the
nightscape, inspiring other couples—Rose's
brother Raymond and wife Rita among
them—to make love. Its effects are lost only on
Rose and Cosmo. Snoring after too much wine
and satisfied by another lover earlier, the obliv-
ous Cosmo is kissed by Rose who *"puts her
face in her hands and quietly cries."* Shanley
understands that the reward of eventually bringing Loretta and Ronny together—the inevitable
conclusion to this old-fashioned fairytale—must
be tempered by a harder look at marital reality:
new lovers sleep while old lovers cry.

As in *Danny and the Deep Blue Sea,* daybreak
for Ronny and Loretta does not prove to be
particularly happy. "*What* have we done?" Loretta shrieks the next morning. Failing to convince Ronny that the two of them should take
their indiscretion "to our coffins," Loretta and
Ronny engage in the film's most famous comic
exchange:

RONNY: I can't do that!

LORETTA: Why not?

RONNY: I'm in love with you!

(*Loretta stares at him in alarm, slaps his face, then studies his face to see the effect of the slap. She is dissatisfied and slaps him again.*)

LORETTA: Snap out of it!

Unlike Roberta's mistreatment of Danny in *Danny and the Deep Blue Sea,* Loretta's slap is intended to bring the two back to their senses. She is striking Ronny, but she is striking herself *through* him. Confronted by a world that is too impossibly joyful, Loretta is in a state of shock. Not Ronny: a romantic, he is totally in love and absolutely ready for it.

The two agree to meet one last time at the Metropolitan Opera for a performance of Puccini's *La Bohème,* then to never see each other again. There, Loretta discovers her father with his mistress: both father and daughter are revealed as unfaithful—Loretta to Johnny, Cosmo to Rose. Disturbed, but enchanted by the pathos of *La Bohème,* Loretta sleeps again with Ronny. The next morning in the kitchen at the Castorini household, Ronny appears to claim Loretta's hand. At that moment, Johnny returns, shockingly early, from Sicily to announce the miraculous recovery of his mother:

> The breath had almost totally left her body. She was as white as snow. And then she completely pulled back from death and stood up and put on her clothes and began to cook for everyone in the house. The mourners. And me. And herself! She ate a meal that would choke a pig!

The recovery of Johnny's mother parallels that of Loretta. Both have been pulled from the brink and, stronger than ever, are ravenously hungry.

Johnny announces he cannot marry Loretta, Loretta feigns outrage and accepts Ronny's proposal, Cosmo agrees to pay for the wedding, Rose secures a promise of fidelity from Cosmo, and the brothers ultimately resolve their differences. The happiness of the ending would be unequivocal if not for an incisive final exchange between Rose and Loretta:

ROSE: Do you love him, Loretta?

LORETTA: Yeah, Ma, I love him awful.

ROSE: Oh God, that's too bad.

Somewhere Oscar Wilde would be smiling: Shanley demonstrates, as Wilde does in *The Importance of Being Earnest,* that love is the happiest and most inexplicable calamity of all. The film closes with a shot of "*red roses on the white tabletop.*" The grump has been trumped: Loretta has her bouquet and gets to smell it, too.

ITALIAN AMERICAN RECONCILIATION

Following the success of *Moonstruck, Italian American Reconciliation* proves that the affectionate free-for-all of *Moonstruck* was no happy fluke. The play is warmly imbued with the movie's rosy glow. Not only do *Moonstruck* and *Italian American Reconciliation* complement one another, as a pair they offset the darker duo of *Danny and the Deep Blue Sea* and *Savage in Limbo.* It is almost as if Shanley had decided to write his upbeat works to rescue his audience from the disheartening spaces in which his early plays had thrust them. *Italian American Reconciliation* features yet another boisterous set of romantically challenged Mediterraneans who wear their hearts on their sleeves and who like their opera loud. The mood in both is similarly sunny, and the dialogue just as Wildean in its flair for the epigram.

As a benign cousin to *Savage in Limbo*'s Tony Aronica, Aldo Scalicki of *Italian American*

Reconciliation makes his grand entrance wearing a sweetheart rose, announcing to the audience his embarrassing tendency to sport erections, handing out quarters like a flush uncle at Christmas, and gleefully smashing the fourth wall to smithereens. "How you doin? How's it goin?" he says, working the crowd. Spotting a pretty girl, Aldo gives her his rose. "Watch her like a hawk," he whispers to her boyfriend. "A word to the wise, man to man." After informing the audience that his mom is in attendance, and telling off an ex-girlfriend who is apparently stalking him, Aldo gets down to the business of the play: "And what I'm gonna do is, I'm gonna tell you a story. About my friend Huey and me, and what happened to him. And from this story, I'm gonna teach you something." There's a good reason why Shanley subtitled the play "*A Folktale.*" Where *Moonstruck* was a fairy tale, an elaborate excuse for an old-fashioned happy ending, *Italian American Reconciliation* will *teach,* and Aldo Scalicki is our unlikely instructor. "You wanna think of it that way, you're my class," he matter-of-factly informs his audience.

Aldo introduces us to Huey, who is involved in a relationship with Teresa but still in love with his ex-wife Janice. Huey convinces Aldo—in classic Italian folktale fashion—to help him win back the love of the hot-tempered Janice, a prospect that does not sit particularly well with Aldo:

> ALDO: It's like you get the Hong Kong Flu, you get rid of it, now you want it back? ... The woman shot your dog with a zip gun. ... Why?

> HUEY: Love?

> ALDO: I'm listening.

Traumatized by an emotionally unavailable father—a trauma that has led him to fear commitment to women—Aldo underscores his desire to help Huey with a desperate admission that makes for one of the most unique and moving exchanges in all of contemporary American theater:

> ALDO: I got things in me I gotta fix between me an men, before I even get to the women. Huey, we gotta be friends for each other! ...

> HUEY: What are you sayin, Aldo?

> ALDO: That I love you. And I'm petrified to say that. ... I love you, man to man, and I'm here for you. Alright?

> HUEY: Alright.

Latter day versions of Antonio and Bassanio in Shakespeare's *Merchant of Venice,* Huey and Aldo feel an affection for one another as deep as that of the despair of Shanley's earlier duos. *Italian American Reconciliation* is a love story, but Shanley understands what Shakespeare understood: that friends, like lovers, must declare their feelings, too. So as a declaration of love to his heartsick friend, Aldo agrees to disarm the zip-gun-toting Janice while Huey will break up with Teresa. But before the plan goes forward, Aldo demands something from Huey:

> ALDO: You know what I think, Huey? I think you should definitely tell me that you love me. If I am doing this, you should say it, you should carve it into a freakin tree.

> HUEY: I love you.

> ALDO: Don't lie to me.

> HUEY: I do love you, Aldo.

Scene Two begins with Teresa telling her Aunt May that she plans to break up with Huey, but she does not seem sure of her decision. Teresa and May have one of the play's many

Wildean exchanges ("Teresa: I want your moral support. May: I don't have no morals"), before Huey arrives and tells Teresa he is going back to Janice. Thus, Teresa is jilted by Huey before she can jilt him, and by the end of the play Teresa has unexpectedly decamped to Canada.

Aldo, on the other hand, decides that Huey is making a mistake in leaving Teresa for Janice. To stop that from happening, he announces his plan to "go to Janice tonight, and I am gonna seduce her. … In this way, I'm going to save my friend." But Janice is not so easily seduced, nor is she easily disarmed:

ALDO: (*Comes out from under the table.*) You shot a gun at me.

JANICE: Don't be obvious.

ALDO: You tried to kill me!

JANICE: I burned my finger. That's what I get for usin zip guns. …

ALDO: I should come up there and give you a spankin!

JANICE: Oh yeah? Try it. I'll cut your heart out.

Not surprisingly, Aldo and Janice nearly end up in bed, but Huey arrives in the nick of time, woos Teresa, and surprisingly succeeds. Shanley's stage directions set the winning mood: "*He kisses her. The music swells. They break apart and look at each other. He picks her up. The music! The music! The music! Blackout.*"

For all its brio, *Italian American Reconciliation* ends on an abrupt, dark note. Teresa does not return, Aldo and May make melancholy small talk about the differences between the sexes, and Huey stumbles onstage after his romantic tryst with Janice apparently longing for the AWOL Teresa. Aldo tries to wrap everything up with the moral lesson he forecasted earlier: "The greatest, the only success, is to be able to love." *Italian American Recon-* *ciliation* extends Shanley's range while confirming the sweet romantic promise of *Moonstruck*. The pleasures here are manifold, and the playwright's fondness for his comic world and characters is contagious, even though the ending is not a classically happy one.

OTHER EARLY PLAYS

Staged in 1986 at the Manhattan Theatre Club—a company with which Shanley would have a long and mutually profitable relationship—*Women of Manhattan* marks a departure for Shanley. Focusing on the largely upper-class concerns of three sophisticated women in a borough of New York that is a far cry from the Bronx, this chatty, catty comedy is refreshing in its presentation of a feminine point-of-view and an erotic interracial relationship:

DUKE: I didn't expect you to look like you look.

JUDY: I didn't expect you to look like you. Look.

DUKE: You mean black?

JUDY: Yeah!

DUKE: Does it bother you?

JUDY: No! …

…

Do you go through a lot of women?

DUKE: Like a hot knife through butter.

Women of Manhattan captures the social and sexual shenanigans of a set of New York women higher up the social ladder than Shanley's usual assortment of blue-collar brawlers. Though the pace at first appears to be dramatically more casual than that of the majority of his early plays, the startling final scene—with its discussion of marital bedwetting and violence between a man and wife—ups the dramatic ante in true Shanley fashion.

Even more true-to-form is *the dreamer examines his pillow,* Shanley's fascinating follow-up to *Women of Manhattan,* staged at the Double Image Theatre later that same year. Recalling in some ways the work of Sam Shepard in its jarring dislocations of reality, this expressionistic play about Tommy, a predatorial artist-loner, and Mona, the woman who loves him, is dedicated to Shanley's family. Punctuated by primal drums and ominous refrigerators that communicate silently with its unhinged hero ("O my refrigerator. Is my self in you?"), *the dreamer examines his pillow* is the most experimental and opaque of Shanley's early works. Featuring a threatening father figure named Dad who claims, "I hate kids. Especially my own," the play unravels in a Daliesque dreamscape of skewed familial and sexual misalliances. By the end of the play, when Dad is sent by his daughter Donna to rough up Tommy for sleeping with both her and Donna's sister Mona, things become aggressively surreal: Donna materializes in a wedding dress, Dad puts the tux he is wearing on Tommy, the newlyweds scream, and the play ends. With the pretzel logic of a dream and the visual stab of a nightmare, *the dreamer examines his pillow* is an oddly unforgettable work.

The Big Funk, which was directed by Shanley, was originally staged at Joseph Papp's New York Shakespeare Festival in 1990. It anticipates the anxieties of Y2K by a decade and was perhaps too far ahead of its time: it was received with critical indifference on its release. The play is marked by some singular moments, including a scene in which an Englishman covers the character Jill's head with gobs of petroleum jelly and another in which Jill's lover, Austin, treats her to a rejuvenating onstage bubble-bath. *The Big Funk* traces the relationships of two

couples: the aforementioned Jill and Austin and the depressed knife-thrower Omar and his pregnant wife Fifi. Shanley begins the play by providing his characters with a series of extended monologues and ends it by having them speculate on the sad state of the world, which a nude Austin apocalyptically dismisses in a monologue that closes the play with a whimper: "This is the big funk. The big fear. The big before. ... All we're doing now is sweating. We can hear our breathing. Everything is halted. We're waiting for the Big Storm."

It is difficult to ignore the autobiographical elements at work in *Beggars in the House of Plenty.* The play includes an Irish-American father who works in a slaughterhouse and its protagonist, John, is expelled from several schools before eventually enlisting in the U.S. Marines Corps. In some ways this is Shanley's most traditional play, with three definable acts and a reasonably realistic setting. On the other hand, it is his most experimental work: A five-year-old character is portrayed by a full-grown man, and an infernal basement doubles as an oedipal war zone. The dialogue is filled with non sequiturs:

> JOEY: ... I fell in love with this girl. Nadine. Garvin. She was a Salvation Army lass.
>
> JOHNNY: A lass? She was a lass?
>
> JOEY: I'm gonna get a Jaguar XKE.
>
> JOHNNY: We switched, right? We're talking about a car now?

A dysfunctional family in the tradition of O'Neill's *Long Day's Journey into Night,* Shepard's *Buried Child,* and even George S. Kaufman and Moss Hart's *You Can't Take It with You,* the Fitzgeralds display a bewildering array of eccentricities that keep this troubling play forever on the edge. Pyromaniac Johnny begs his mother for "breast milk" before routinely setting fire to the house; Pop nibbles the teenage Johnny's ears and calls him outrageously "my little gossoon"; Johnny's adult brother Jerry offers to show the teenage hero his genitalia; and in a sacrilegious parody of Catholic piety the Fitzgeralds recite a blasphemous prayer: "Hail Mary, full of grace, the Lord sides with you. Blessed art thou amongst chicken houses fulla squallin women, and blessed is the lucky fine fat of yer womb, Jesus." The fearlessness with which Shanley exorcises his family's demons is reminiscent of O'Neill, with less of the control. But control has never been a dramatic priority of Shanley's. His characters are often loose cannons, and the family Fitzgerald is a loose nuke. When John rejects his father's love in the play's climactic exchange, the language is poetic, the emotions ferocious, and the pain as excruciating as anything in Shanley's entire canon:

> I've stopped stealin and I've stopped settin fires and I've stopped breakin windows. And now, now I'm gonna stop waitin for you. To reach down to me. To touch my face. To kiss my wounds. There's been a kinda silence fallen between us like a long drop onta sharp rocks. ... I will never think of you without being shocked by your lovelessness.

An enigmatic and challenging play whose reputation is only bound to increase over the years, *Beggars in the House of Plenty* suggests the power and shape of Shanley's subsequent plays.

HOLLYWOOD, THE RENAISSANCE, AND MORE

"Biting the hand that feeds you" is practically a rite of passage for once-obscure American playwrights who end up making a killing in Hollywood. In *Four Dogs and A Bone*—Shanley's trenchant satire of the movie industry, which had a healthy run at the Manhattan Theatre Club in 1995—the playwright does more than bite Hollywood's hand. Like a great white shark, he goes after the whole arm.

Reportedly based on Shanley's experience turning his first original screenplay into Tony Bill's 1987 independent feature, *Five Corners*. *Four Dogs and A Bone* chronicles the Machiavellian moves one producer, one writer, and two competitive actresses put on one another in their attempts to keep afloat a low-budget film and the careers that may be dragged under in its awful wake. Unlike *Where's My Money?*—Shanley's 2002 send-up of marital greed—or *Italian American Reconciliation*—which lampoons marital loyalty—the greed and disloyalty on display in *Four Dogs and A Bone* points to something darker and more sinister altogether. As in the grotesque world of *The Day of the Locust* (1939)—novelist Nathanael West's last word on the screenwriter's nightmare in the Hollywood dream factory—the masks these characters wear keep slipping, and what lies beneath is a frightening sight.

Brenda, the ingenue who is conniving to steal the lead role from her co-star Collette, trades on her celebrity brother's superstar status, pretends she was the victim of incest to win sympathy, and chants a mantra ("I am famous") that sounds to everybody else like "Uncle Remus." Collette summarily informs Brenda that she walks through her scenes "like Bambi with polio" and entertains the suggestion of performing oral sex on screenwriter Victor to garner more screen time. Meanwhile, Victor is trying to cling to what remains of his artistic integrity and is too busy editing his overwrought screenplay to attend the funeral of his recently deceased mother. Bradley, the predatorial producer willing to sacrifice anyone and everyone for the sake of the project, cannot seem to stop complaining about a "surface ulcer" on his rectum "the size of a jumbo shrimp." When these characters speak frankly, they do so from a blasted ground zero of obscenity:

BRENDA: Fuck you.

BRADLEY: Fuck you.

BRENDA: Fuck you.

BRADLEY: Fuck you. Good. Now that we've established a common language, what do you think?

In such a profane world even attraction is registered as the absence of repulsion. As the charmless Bradley says, making a pass at the uncharmable Brenda:

BRADLEY: Do you find me repulsive?

BRENDA: Are you coming on to me?

BRADLEY: No.

BRENDA: I didn't think so.

Uncoiling as it does inside the viscera of Hollywood, *Four Dogs and a Bone* demonstrates all the comic distance of a tapeworm. Thankfully, this world is as funny as it is appalling. When someone finally expresses sympathy to the barely grieving Victor about the death of his mother, the audience breathes a sigh of sympathetic relief. But sympathy, even in this world, has a price tag:

BRENDA: I'm sorry about your mother.

VICTOR: Thank you.

BRENDA: Please don't cut all my scenes.

Four Dogs and A Bone is a devastating and devastatingly funny insider's portrait of a ravenous community. And given the dark comedy of the works that would follow, Shanley was just beginning to hit his stride.

Psychopathia Sexualis, which debuted in 1998, set out to do what no Shanley play in over a decade had attempted: strictly entertain.

The title (with a nod to the German psychiatrist Richard von Krafft-Ebing) and the subject matter (fetishism) are admittedly heavy, but unlike the black humor of *Four Dogs and A Bone,* the comic delivery here is undeniably light. The shaggy plot involves Arthur, a husband-to-be who can only have sex with his Southern belle fiancée in the perplexing presence of his father's argyle socks. Arthur enlists the help of his best friend Howard to rescue these socks from the evil Dr. Block, a devout Freudian who has stolen the footwear to break Arthur of his embarrassing fetish. Howard fails to convince the diabolical Block to give them back, but when Howard's wife Ellie informs Lucille about Arthur's neurotic dilemma, Lucille swoops down on Block's office like a Texas-sized tornado. Block is thwarted, the socks are snatched, and all live happily ever after. The second scene—an uproarious parody of psychotherapy in which Block decodes Howard's strange dreams—provides Shanley the opportunity for a comic field day.

After the venom of *Four Dogs and A Bone* and the dysfunctional family vertigo of *Beggars in the House of Plenty,* the self-consciously silly *Psychopathia Sexualis* was a more than welcome crowd-pleaser. With gimcrack comic dialogue (Lucille on masculinity: "Don't try and hide behind your penis. It won't provide enough cover") and a terrifically zippy pace, *Psychopathia Sexualis* played to packed houses for over eight weeks at Shanley's familiar Manhattan Theatre Club.

Shanley set his sights on a more ambitious story for his next play, *Cellini,* which was produced in 2002. The author took five years to write this hugely ambitious stage adaptation of John Addington Symonds' translation of the autobiography of Renaissance sculptor Benvenuto Cellini. The play feels like a dramatic summing up for Shanley. Familiar themes reappear: the power of the imagination, the consequences of human pride, the hunger of the artist to communicate a message that an apathetic world refuses to hear. Cellini makes baubles for corrupt kings and popes while contemplating the masterpiece that would prove to be his legacy: the bronze sculpture of Perseus decapitating Medusa for the Loggia dei Lanzi in Florence, Italy. Instead of contemplating love, friendship, and family—the usual terrain of Shanley's plays—*Cellini* is primarily about the challenge of reconciling the artist's vision with an uncooperative world. Threatened with jail for his unflinching hubris, Cellini engages Pope Paolo in one of the play's testier exchanges:

PAOLO: Remember who I am.

CELLINI: … It is not for you to intimidate me … but to entice me with the possibility of achieving fame. Good Shepherd. I want a large commission. A sculpture of at least seventeen feet in height. I want to cast a giant man. A Zeus. A Hercules. Award me that which I crave or I go to serve another throne.

PAOLO: Are you insane? … You must go to prison. We will subtract your art from you and leave the dull remains to idle suffering.

Cutting a broadly historical swath, which constitutes a real departure for this very contemporary playwright, *Cellini* aspires to be Shanley's theatrical equivalent of Cellini's *Perseus*: a masterpiece. Many critics felt that it fell short of this task. The play seems too conscious of its own history: "I hope I am not talking too loud," the boy-narrator shouts at the audience at the outset. "I raise my voice because it is 1558 and you are 443 years away." Also, *Cellini* is too cursory in its psychology to attain the combination of historical piquancy and artistic awareness that distinguishes works like Peter Shaffer's *Amadeus.* In many ways, the play is well crafted, but the cast balloons to Brechtian proportions. The most provocative characters—a prostitute named Caterina and the affable boy-narrator, both of whom serve Cellini in similar

capacities as models, confessors, and objects of desire—are obscured by the comings-and-goings of too many blurry minor figures. Cellini himself is a marvelous creation—vain, murderous, and forever alive to the possibilities of art, whether they are found in his legendary sculpture of Perseus or in the construction of a fantastic salt shaker. But by the end of *Cellini* one longs for the artless losers of *Savage in Limbo,* who slew their own Medusas just as artfully as Perseus.

Where's My Money? produced in 2002, lampoons the materialism of contemporary American culture so mercilessly that lovers return from the grave to demand financial compensation, and the ultimate expression of affection for young couples is not sex or pillow talk but the consensual establishment of joint checking accounts. The plot, an ingenious Rubik's cube of fidelities and infidelities, involves two second-rate matrimonial lawyers, their wives and jealous girlfriends, and ghosts of lovers past who steal scenes. Shanley's dialogue has not been this whip-smart since *Italian American Reconciliation,* but the comic tone is decidedly more caustic than the previous play. He skewers the superficiality of young New York marrieds who confuse love for money and money for love:

NATALIE: Goddammit, I'm not some hustler trying to get over on you, Henry! I'm your fucking wife!

HENRY: Oh, you're flashing the credential! … Why do you want a joint checking account?

NATALIE: So I can write checks.

HENRY: You tell me the check, I'll write it.

NATALIE: I wanna write the check!

HENRY: What check?

NATALIE: No check in particular. If you died, I'd get the money!

HENRY: So you're fantasizing my death.

Death, love, friendship, fidelity—it all comes down to dollars in *Where's My Money?* Even the soul is reduced to a wallet that has been pickpocketed:

MARCIA MARIE: I'm damned. Why shouldn't I be? You stole my soul.

SIDNEY: Go ahead. Frisk me!

The New York hotshots of *Where's My Money?* are the antitheses of Shanley's early has-beens: financially alive, emotionally dead. But after the lofty historical drama of *Cellini,* Shanley seemed back at home in the contemporary world.

Indeed, Shanley's next play—2003's *Dirty Story,* a politically loaded allegory of the Arab/Israeli conflict staged at the LAByrinth Theatre—could not be any more contemporary if it tried. The play received mixed reviews for its attempt to offer a bracing perspective on the morass that is the contemporary Middle East, but it revealed yet another aspect of Shanley's multifaceted career. Certainly, Shanley's dramatic universe is much broader and richer than the "lowdown" Bronx bars of his earlier triumphs, but despite a broader canvas, it remains just as rich and big-spirited, and essential.

"My work has saved my life," Shanley told *American Film* with characteristic frankness in 1989. "It has revealed to me that everything that I knew when I was a child was true. And that we are in the grip of enormous powers and beauty beyond our comprehension." Though he has specialized in characters who struggle with limited options, Shanley himself seems unencumbered by boundaries. The dramatic possibilities of this ingenious, prolific and phenomenally original American writer remain decidedly open.

Selected Bibliography

WORKS OF JOHN PATRICK SHANLEY

PLAYS

Danny and the Deep Blue Sea: An Apache Dance. New York: Dramatists Play Service, 1984.

Welcome to the Moon and Other Plays. New York: Dramatists Play Service, 1985.

Savage In Limbo: A Concert Play. New York: Dramatists Play Service, 1986.

Women of Manhattan: An Upper West Side Story. New York: Dramatists Play Service, 1986.

the dreamer examines his pillow. New York: Dramatists Play Service, 1987.

Italian American Reconciliation: A Folktake. New York: Dramatists Play Service, 1989.

The Big Funk: A Casual Play. New York, Dramatists Play Service, 1991.

Beggars in the House of Plenty. New York: Dramatists Play Service, 1992.

Four Dogs and A Bone and The Wild Goose. New York: Dramatists Play Service, 1995.

Missing/Kissing: Missing Marisa, Kissing Christine. New York, Dramatists Play Service, 1997.

Psychopathia Sexualis. New York: Dramatists Play Service, 1998.

Cellini. New York: Dramatists Play Service, 2001.

Where's My Money? New York: Dramatists Play Service, 2002.

Dirty Story. New York: Dramatists Play Service, 2003.

UNPUBLISHED PLAYS

Saturday Night at the War. 1978.

George and the Dragon. 1979.

Ketchup. Staged reading: New York, New Dramatists, c. 1980.

Rockaway. Produced: New York, Vineyard Theater, 1982.

All For Charity. Produced: New York, Ensemble Studio Theater, 1987.

What Is This Everything? 1992.

SCREENPLAYS

Moonstruck. Directed by Norman Jewison. Metro-Goldwyn-Mayer, 1987.

Five Corners. Directed by Tony Bill. Handmade Films, 1988.

The January Man. Directed by Pat O'Connor. United International Pictures/Metro-Goldwyn-Mayer, 1989.

Joe versus the Volcano. Directed by John Patrick Shanley. Warner/Amblin Entertainment, 1990.

Alive. Directed by Frank Marshall. United International Pictures/Paramount, 1993.

We're Back! A Dinosaur's Story. Directed by Dick Zondag, Phil Nibbelink, Ralph Zondag, and Simon Wells. Disney, 1993.

Congo. Directed by Frank Marshall. United International Pictures/Paramount, 1995.

Live From Bagdhad. Directed by Mick Jackson. HBO Films, 2002.

COLLECTED WORKS

13 by Shanley. New York: Applause, 1992.

Moonstruck, Joe Versus The Volcano, and Five Corners. New York: Grove Press, 1996.

CRITICAL AND BIOGRAPHICAL STUDIES

"Dialogue on Film: John Patrick Shanley." *American Film* 14:20–24 (September 1989).

Ghoulson, Craig. "John Patrick Shanley." *BOMB,* summer 1988, pp. 21–25.

Hischak, Thomas S. *American Theatre: A Chronicle of Comedy and Drama, 1969–2000.* Oxford: Oxford University Press, 2001. Pp. 237, 264, 267, 294, 317, 328, 352, 401.

Johnson, Brian D. "Writing His Own Ticket." *Maclean's,* April 4, 1988, p. 40.

McMurray, Emily J., and Owen O'Donnell, eds. *Contemporary Theatre, Film and Television.* Vol. 9. Detroit: Gale Research, 1992. Pp. 347–348.

Riggs, Thomas, ed. *Contemporary American Dramatists.* 6th ed. Detroit: St. James Press, 1999. Pp. 619–621.

Roberts, Polly. "Bard of the Bronx." *Harper's Bazaar,* February 1988, pp. 110, 112, 206.

PLAY AND MOVIE REVIEWS

Ansen, David. "Fort Apache, the Bronx: A Murdered Algebra Teacher, A Damsel in Distress." *Newsweek,* January 25, 1988, p. 69. (Review of *Five Corners.*)

Brantley, Ben. "Well, You See, Doctor, Someone's Stolen Dad's Argyle Socks." *New York Times,* February 27, 1997, p. C13. (Review of *Psychopathia Sexualis.*)

Brustein, Robert. "Why Plays Fail." *New Republic* 228:25 (April 14, 2003). (Review of *Dirty Story.*)

Isherwood, Charles. "Off Broadway: *Cellini.*" *Variety,* February 19–25, 2001, pp. 49–50.

Kael, Pauline. "The Current Cinema: Loony Fugue." *The New Yorker,* January 25, 1988, pp. 99–100. (Review of *Moonstruck.*)

Kanfer, Stefan. "Two Quartets." *New Leader* 77:22–23 (January 17, 1994). (Review of *Four Dogs and a Bone.*)

Oliver, Edith. "The Theatre: Off Broadway." *The New Yorker,* June 18, 1984, p. 89. (Review of *Danny and the Deep Blue Sea.*)

———. "Off Broadway: Noise in the Bronx." *The New Yorker,* October 7, 1985, pp. 110–111. (Review of *Savage in Limbo.*)

Radin, Victoria. "Theater: A Louder Silence." *The New Statesman* 114:23 (October 16, 1987). (Review of *Savage in Limbo.*)

Review of *The Big Funk. Variety,* December 17, 1990, p. 63.

Rich, Frank. "The Stage: Welcome to the Moon." *New York Times,* November 24, 1982, p. C14. (Review of *Welcome to the Moon and Other Plays.*)

———. "Author and Actor Converge to Resolve Old Family Horror." *The New York Times,* October 24, 1991, pp. C17, C24. (Review of *Beggars in the House of Plenty.*)

Weber, Bruce. "Shaky Marriages Sunk by Emotional Baggage." *New York Times,* November 12, 2001, p. E5. (Review of *Where's My Money?*)

—*DANIEL VILMURE*

Logan Pearsall Smith

1865–1946

*L*OGAN PEARSALL SMITH was born in Millville, New Jersey, on October 18, 1865, to a prominent family of Quakers descended from the founding father William Penn's secretary James Logan. Smith's parents, Robert Pearsall Smith (1827–1898) and Hannah Whitall Smith (1832–1911), were Quaker preachers and writers in nineteenth-century Philadelphia.

As an infant, Smith was described by his mother as a "gorilla for screaming." In his memoir, *Unforgotten Years* (1938), Smith recalls that as a young boy he was taken to P. T. Barnum's circus in Philadelphia. While watching the show, he experienced the "first awakenings" of sexual feeling. His parents allowed their children to watch the animal acts but ordered them to cover their eyes when the scantily clad acrobats performed. Smith tells of the "guilty peep through his fingers" as he "gazed on a show of muscular limbs moving, slowly moving, in pink tights." Smith's father managed glass factories in New Jersey, and Smith also recalls admiring "half-naked glass blowers moving like devils among the flames" of fiery furnaces. The association of hellfire with sensual pleasures would continue throughout his life.

At age four, Smith was "converted" to belief in Jesus by his elder sister. His father published a pamphlet entitled *As Little Children*, describing the boy's acceptance of religion at that age. (Decades later, Smith rediscovered this pamphlet, and his friends Robert Gathorne-Hardy and Kyrle Leng reissued it in 1934 with the semi-ironic title *How Little Logan Was Brought to Jesus*.) In 1872 the family traveled to Europe so that Smith's parents could continue their evangelical preaching. There they stayed at English country houses, at one of which Smith had an early masturbatory experience, recounted in *Unforgotten Years* with his usual irony:

> Anyone seeking for the home of unspotted purity would probably not pause in his search at an English public school; but the behavior and conversation of these polite Etonians, though they would have interested Proust, could not have been expected to reveal to the holy little Samuel of Philadelphia anything that was not innocent and pure. I remember one of these boys taking me up into a walnut tree in his father's park, and treating me to a display which, though it had no interest for me at the time, yet I felt, as a mark of friendliness from an English to an American boy, was a demonstration of international good will.

While in Europe, Smith's mother wrote what would prove to be her most popular book, selling one million copies in America alone: *The Christian's Secret of a Happy Life*. Originating with a series of newspaper articles in 1873, it was published in book form in 1875. In her preface, she disarmingly claims no special expertise:

> This is not a theological book. I frankly confess I have not been trained in theological schools, and do not understand their methods nor their terms. But the Lord has taught me experimentally and practically certain lessons out of his Word, which have greatly helped me in my Christian life, and have made it a very happy one.

Hannah Whitall Smith's homespun approach to Christianity stretched domestic experiences into a larger theological context. She addressed in one chapter the subject of hidden evil by describing a barrel in the cellar of her home, which she had ignored, until it turned out to be full of thousands of moths. In other chapters she addressed the subject of religious fanaticism and often misguided religious sects in nineteenth-century America. This debunking or skeptical attitude would later be reflected in the prose of her son, who, like his mother, offered didactic texts while sometimes disingenuously claiming not to be an expert in the subjects involved.

In 1882, having returned to America and settled in Germantown, Pennsylvania, the Smith family struck up a friendship with the poet Walt Whitman, then living as a semi-invalid in nearby Camden, New Jersey. Whitman would go on almost daily buggy rides with Smith's father to follow, if possible, a pair of lovers and voyeuristically watch them embrace. Afterward Whitman and the elder Smith, "who had ever honored that joy-giving power of nature symbolized under the name of Venus, would return home with happy hearts." Whitman introduced the Smith family to his working-class male friends, and Smith recalls in *Unforgotten Years* that he described his poetic method as "receptivity to experience, and of a complete surrender to it, combined with a patient effort to grasp its deepest meaning and to embody that meaning in significant words." Quoting Ralph Waldo Emerson, Smith describes Whitman's poetry collection *Leaves of Grass* as a book which took its "rank in our lives with parents and lovers and passionate experiences." Smith says that he yielded to it "in absolute surrender":

Much that was suppressed in the young people of my generation found a frank avowal in the *Leaves of Grass;* feelings and affections for each other, which we had been ashamed of, thoughts which we had hidden as unutterable, we found printed in its pages ... his delight in his own body and the bodies of his friends.

Smith's own frequent personal meetings with Whitman were equally significant. In a letter to his sister Mary he related one visit in the 1880s:

When I see him I never think of him as a grand poet, but simply as a dear old man. I first got interested in his poetry coming up in the train from Atlantic City, in about an hour my ideas on many subjects were entirely changed, especially the way I looked at vulgar and stupid people. Now they seem like beautiful souls temporarily uninviting in attire, of manners, habits, etc.

In 1882 Smith caught his first glimpse of another key figure in gay history, the Irish poet and playwright Oscar Wilde. Wilde was on a lengthy lecture tour of America, a country he called "an extensive lunatic asylum." During his stay in the Pennsylvania area, Wilde also paid a visit to Walt Whitman. It is uncertain whether Smith and his family saw the twenty-seven-year-old Wilde socially, but they definitely heard him lecture, as Hannah Whitall Smith wrote to a friend in 1882:

Oscar Wilde is a "sell." He looks like two radishes set up on their thin ends. He does say now and then a fine thing about art, just about what I would say about religion. But his manner is so poor and his style so excessively "Rose Matilda" that I believe everybody is disgusted. Logan did not get *one* idea from him, but I got several. For instance, he said—"To the true artist there is no time but the artistic moment; and no land but the land of beauty." There is a meaning in this, but what could *Logan* make out of it? And such a Logan!

It is possible that Smith received impressions which he did not divulge to his mother from this early exposure to Wilde, the "Apostle of Aestheticism." Around 1895, when Wilde was convicted of "gross indecency," Smith's mother recommended castration as the "only effectual remedy I know" for Wilde's behavior. Smith himself displayed far more sympathy in an 1898 letter to his friend the poet Robert C. Trevelyan, after Wilde was released from prison. He said that his sister Mary had visited with Wilde in Italy and found him lonely and depressed. Smith urged Trevelyan to ask their mutual acquaintances to write to Wilde so that he would feel less abandoned.

Smith first studied at Haverford College, a Quaker institution in Pennsylvania, and in 1884, at age nineteen, he transferred to Harvard. There his fellow students included the art historian Bernard Berenson and the philosopher George Santayana, although he only got to know them in later years. He did become friendly with a professor, William James, whom he describes in his memoir as "the most charming man I ever met." A major literary influence for Smith at Harvard was the poet and critic Matthew Arnold, who like other writers of the day, such as Robert Browning and Henry James, "had formed the habit of wearing masks" in social life, according to Smith.

After finishing his studies, Smith worked for a year at his family's business in New York. He was then given $25,000 dollars by his father, with which he bought an annuity that supported him for almost thirty years. (About authors who marketed their works to make a living, Smith said, "Writers who write for money don't write for me.") In 1888 he left America for Oxford, England, where he could be closer to his sister Mary, then living in London with her husband, Frank Costelloe, a barrister. At Oxford, Smith was active in sports such as cycling and rowing on the Thames River. He studied with renowned professors, including the classicist Benjamin Jowett, whom he describes in *Unforgotten Years* as "looking like an old pink and white parrot." Jowett's bowdlerized translations of Plato were notorious for deleting passages that describe gay love, and these suppressions were later criticized by students, particularly the art historian and translator John Addington Symonds.

On an evening in 1888 Smith first encountered the American-born novelist Henry James, the brother of his former professor William James. Smith's first impression of James was mostly negative: in an 1888 letter to his sister Alys, he said James was "small and very French in his appearance and has a disagreeable, sneering way

of talking." Soon, however, James became an indispensable colleague, one of the contemporaries Smith admired most. Although both men were émigrés, Henry James, unlike Smith, did not loathe his native country. The two men got along because of a shared sexuality and love for gossip, apart from literary concerns.

In one early letter James urgently asked Smith about Marc-André Raffalovich, a Russian-born poet and advocate of homosexuality in such books as *Uranisme et Unisexualité* (1896). Raffalovich claimed that gay love can be noble and pure when practiced by what he termed a "sublime invert," or someone who sublimates his urges into friendships, religion, and the arts. Smith, and possibly James as well, conformed to this sublimated gay paradigm. On hearing the news of James's death in 1916, Smith wrote to a friend:

> It's a great loss to feel that he is no longer in the world. I feel as if a great cathedral had disappeared from the sky-line, a great country with all its civilization been wiped from the map, a planet lost to the solar system. Things will happen and he won't be there to tell them to, and the world will be a poorer and more meagre place. We shall all miss the charm and danger of our relation with the dear elusive man, the affectionate and wonderful talks, the charming letters, the icy and sad intervals, and the way he kept us all allured and aloof, and shone on us, and hid his light, like a great variable but constant moon.

In 1891 Smith's sister Mary began a love affair with Bernard Berenson, whom she later married. It has been suggested that Mary's extramarital affair was a major reason for the Smith family's estrangement from Walt Whitman, who, presumably, would have approved of her impetuous acts which scandalized the family.

After he graduated from Oxford in 1891, Smith moved to Paris, where he frequented the American painter James Abbott McNeill Whistler. To help Whistler fulfill a commission,

Smith posed as the body model for a portrait of Comte Robert de Montesquiou-Fezensac, the gay poet upon whom Proust based his character Baron de Charlus in his novel *A la recherche du temps perdu.* Smith adopted Montesquiou-Fezensac's aristocratic pose, standing with a fur coat flung over his arm. Whistler clearly saw useful resemblances between Smith and his subject. While in France, Smith also became friendly with the British art critic Roger Fry and the Cambridge University literature professor Goldsworthy Lowes Dickinson, who was a key figure in the Apostles society, a college group much influenced by gay Hellenic ideals.

Smith avidly read the newly published letters of Gustave Flaubert, which, he says in *Unforgotten Years,* stated that "the true writer is a kind of priest." Imitating the mature Flaubert's rejection of amorous relationships, Smith practiced the renunciation of human attachments to further his literary efforts. He also read Guy de Maupassant and in 1895 self-published a book of his own short stories about Oxford life, *The Youth of Parnassus, and Other Stories.* In his memoir Smith describes these tales as "impressionist in their coloring, and matching in form the neat, accomplished construction of Maupassant. This labored, imitative, rather lifeless book … fell completely flat." Nevertheless his stories were praised by the discerning critic and musicologist Théodore de Wyzewa. England's future poet laureate Robert Bridges also enjoyed them and asked to meet Smith, whereas Henry James, who lost the book on the London Underground, merely reacted with "kindly but tepid" praise. James advised Smith that he must inscribe the word "loneliness" on his personal banner, advice that Smith was all too ready to take.

During a lengthy stay near his family's country home in Sussex, England, Smith socialized with neighbors, including Katherine Bradley and her niece, Edith Cooper, lesbian lovers who published plays and poetry under the pen name Michael Field. He also visited with the lesbian American writer Gertrude Stein and her gay brother, Leo Stein, also an author. Smith became one of the few early boosters of Gertrude Stein's literary career. He wrote about a later visit in a letter to his sister Mary:

> [Stein] seemed to me as fat as ever, but better dressed and generally improved in appearance. She is amusing and jolly and tells good stories about people. Her post-Impressionistic prose is fantastically absurd, of course, but to invent anything so crazy shows a kind of originality— There has certainly never been anything else like it.

SMITH'S SISTERS AND BROTHERS-IN-LAW

In 1897 Smith visited Mary and Bernard Berenson at their Italian villa, I Tatti. During the visit, Smith and the Berensons printed the *Golden Urn,* which in his memoir Smith calls a "pretentious little review." It contained early versions of Smith's book *Trivia: Printed from the Papers of Anthony Woodhouse, Esq.* (1902) as well as famous lines from English poetry and information about great European paintings.

Over the years Smith would make frequent visits to I Tatti, which later became a renowned dwelling place and social center for the arts (it is now a research center, the Harvard University Center for Italian Renaissance Studies at Villa I Tatti). There he socialized with famed European cultural figures, including the actress Eleonora Duse and the poet Gabriele D'Annunzio. He also made closer contacts with English writers, such as the distinguished musicologist and composer Sir Donald Francis Tovey. Smith wrote to Alys from I Tatti in 1906:

> Tovey is a most marvelous natural phenomenon. One hardly thinks of him as a person, he is so like the Aurora Borealis darting up into the sky and corruscating in wonderful shapes—a perpetual fountain of shining, illuminating talk, clear as

crystal, profound beyond our fathoming and absolutely inexhaustible. One has only to turn the tap and off he goes. ... So, the house sings with music and talk and a Bacchic thrill runs through the corridors.

Smith also forged a friendship with the American novelist Edith Wharton, whom he met in 1903 when she stayed at a villa near I Tatti. Despite their personal closeness, Smith failed to appreciate Wharton's literary achievement, as he wrote to Gathorne-Hardy in 1935:

[Wharton] gets faintly good ideas, and treats them in a workmanlike fashion, but good God, her style, or rather her appalling lack of that quality! After reading Henry James' prefaces (which I have enjoyed to the limit of enjoyment) poor Edith's flatness really turned my stomach—and I am fond too of the lady, and she is a gracious and affectionate friend. But can one forgive such platitude of style? I really can't do it;—but still she had a marvellous cook.

Smith and Bernard Berenson got along well. Both men delighted in malicious gossip, although Berenson warned Smith that as a writer he tended to be "too facetious." In a letter to Mary, Smith offered what he called "a sentiment for B. B. 'Je voudrais noyer mes contemporains dans les latrines [I'd like to drown my contemporaries in the latrines].'" Smith had a more troubled relationship with his other brother-in-law, the philosopher Bertrand Russell, who married his sister Alys in 1894. Biographers assert that Russell was uncomfortable with homosexuals and believed Smith's personal limits would prevent him from achieving his high aims. In her 1992 book about Russell's life, Caroline Moorehead says that Russell blamed Hannah Whitall Smith for beating Logan when he was a boy, thereby making him "malicious and frivolous" for life. In 1898 Russell wrote to Alys that Smith "has the passion to be first rate, and says other people's good work makes him miserable. ... [This passion] is an unfortunate one for him, as he will obvi-

ously not get it satisfied." In 1903 Smith went to hear one of the philosopher's public lectures and reported to his sister Mary:

It was very clear and intellectual and even witty. ... It seems like using a razor to chop wood, but such people are necessary to the State. ... [H]e is conscientious, public-spirited and likes excitement, so I suppose he will always be popping out of his cloister into the world.

Alys and Russell separated in 1911 after Russell confessed his affair with Lady Ottoline Morrell, who, with her husband, the lawyer and politician Philip Morrell, ran an important salon frequented by such luminaries as D. H. Lawrence, Aldous Huxley, Virginia Woolf, and Russell himself. After the separation Alys went to live with her brother. Smith carried a lasting grudge against Russell for the rest of his life, and Alys would reestablish contact with Russell only after Smith's death in 1946.

TRIVIA

Around 1895 Smith began to write short prose pieces inspired, he claimed, by Charles Baudelaire's book of prose poems, *Le Spleen de Paris* (1869). Instead of imitating Baudelaire's passionate and sometimes heroic tone, Smith created little observations—he called them "prose Minims"—which remain valid as turn-of-the-century expressions of masked rebellion against normality. Smith took his title for these writings from a narrative poem by the British poet John Gay, *Trivia; Or, the Art of Walking the Streets of London* (1716). In his long poem, Gay relates the thrills and terrors of walking through the city, including sexual trysts "where winding Alleys lead the doubtful Way." Viewing himself as a similarly tempted pedestrian, Smith toiled over the next several years on his most famous work, *Trivia.*

In 1902 Smith privately published the first edition of *Trivia*. He presented the forty short prose pieces as "Printed from the Papers of Anthony Woodhouse, Esq.," using a pseudonym in the tradition of Oscar Wilde's Bunbury in *The Importance of Being Earnest*. The book, of which three hundred copies were printed, was generally overlooked by critics, although Hannah Whitall Smith stated, "It is certainly very quaint and interesting, but it is what I would suppose would be called very 'precious,' as it begins nowhere and ends nowhere and leads to nothing." *Trivia* was reprinted by Constable in 1918 with several dozen more prose sketches. This edition, reflecting a widespread feeling of disillusionment after the First World War, elicited considerable response. *Trivia*'s tone of the futility of all human efforts struck a responsive chord in readers. The book was even more celebrated in France than in England after a translation appeared in 1921 by Philippe Neel, done with Smith's cooperation. The distinguished French man of letters Valéry Larbaud wrote the introduction to the French edition. Larbaud used a translated phrase from the work, *Ce vice impuni, la lecture* ("that unpunished vice, reading," which was Neel's version of Smith's original phrase, "reading … this polite and unpunishable vice"), as the title of his own book of essays published in France in 1924.

Beyond initial reviews, *Trivia* has attracted little sustained critical attention. Some reviewers of earlier editions, such as Edmund Wilson, returned to the subject later: In his forward to the 1984 edition of *All Trivia*, Gore Vidal notes that almost a half-century after the book's initial publication, Wilson found *Trivia* "overrated … yet there *is* something in it, something dry, independent, even tough." *Trivia* remains a challenging subject for close reading, particularly with knowledge of the author's homosexuality and with subsequent generations' respect for what is fragmentary or anthological in literature. A highly coded, allusive, and elliptical text, it reflects not just Baudelaire but also Arthur Rimbaud's *Illuminations*, prose poems which defy—some critics say deliberately—literal understanding.

The "Author's Note" at the beginning of *Trivia* describes the author as "a large Carnivorous Mammal" who is related to "the Baboon with his bright blue and scarlet bottom." The book's first chapter, entitled "Happiness," presents an Arcadian scene populated by male athletes: "Cricketers on village greens, haymakers in the evening sunshine … a piece of the old Golden World." Like other gay Americans, such as Whitman and the painter Thomas Eakins, Smith hearkens back to an earlier age of pagan, or Pan-like, ritual. This reference to a previous time continues in the chapter called "Stonehenge," in which schoolmasters and other elders frown while "in the bright center and sunlight I leap, I caper, I dance my dance." Some other passages, such as "In the Street," are closely allied to Whitman's practice of "adhesiveness," calling out in the midst of the crowd for human contact. Smith's narrator's words have a poignant, unrealized tone: "These oglings and eye-encounters in the street, little touches of love-liking; faces that ask, as they pass, 'Are you my new lover?' Shall I one day—in Park Lane or Oxford Street perhaps—see the unknown face I dread and look for?"

But Smith's narrator's dread is greater than his longing, and passages about pagan rituals, such as when he "dance[s] under the new Moon, naked and tattooed and holy," are eventually smothered by his acknowledgment that his kind of love must not speak its name. "Daydream" evokes the death of Orpheus, ripped to shreds by the Maenads, according to one legend, for inventing homosexuality: "In the cold and malicious society in which I live, I must never mention the Soul, nor speak of my aspirations. If I ever once let these people get a glimpse of the higher side of my nature, they would tear me in pieces." The narrator is fated to solitude, as expressed in "Loneliness": "Is there, then, no friend? ... Must I live all my life as mute as a mackerel, companionless and uninvited, and never tell anyone what I think of my famous contemporaries? Must I plough always a solitary furrow, and tread the winepress alone?"

Wryly observing that a young man may take "to his bed with a new Sex Theory," the narrator refuses any possibility of a successful relationship. "The Quest" suggests that seeking a male beloved is an activity doomed to failure:

"We walk alone in the world," the Moralist, at the end of his essay on Ideal Friendship, writes somewhat sadly. "Friends such as we desire are dreams and fables." Yet we never quite give up the hope of finding them. But what awful things happen to us, what snubs, what set-downs we experience, what shames and disillusions. We can never really tell what these new unknown persons may do to us. ... And yet we brush our hats, pull on our gloves, and go out and ring door-bells.

In "My Map" Smith's narrator depicts gay love as belonging to wild, unexplored, mythical regions, the cartography of which includes "pictures of the supposed inhabitants of these unexplored regions, Dog-Apes, Satyrs, Paiderasts and Bearded Women, Cimmerians involved in darkness, Amazons, and Headless Men." Linking pederasts, amazons, bearded ladies, and satyrs with actual historical groups like Cimmerians, an ancient nomadic tribe from the Ukraine, the narrator compares living as a sexual minority to dwelling in remote history and mythology.

In "Misapprehension" the narrator disguises his real self in society, like the hero of Wilde's comedy *The Importance of Being Earnest:* "People often seem to take me for some one else; they talk to me as if I were a person of earnest Views and unalterable Convictions. ... By means of grave looks and evasive answers, I conceal—or at least I hope I conceal—my discreditable secret." This secret may in part be his triviality or his lack of earnestness as an at-

tribute of homosexuality. In "Guilt" this lack of seriousness turns into self-reproach over his neglect of some sober literary accomplishments, such as that of Polish poets:

But a sense of guilt oppressed me. What had I done, or left undone? And the shadowy figures that seemed to menace and pursue me? Yes, I had wronged them; it was again those Polish Poets, it was Mickiewicz, Slowacki, Szymonowicz, Krasicki, Kochanowski;—and I'd never read one word of all their works!

Ultimately, in "The Alien," the narrator is resigned to feeling like a stranger in society: "The older I grow, the more of an alien I find myself in the world; I cannot get used to it, cannot believe that it is real. I think I must have been made to live on some other Star."

Trivia was followed by *More Trivia* in 1922, *Afterthoughts* in 1931, and the compendium *All Trivia: Trivia, More Trivia, Afterthoughts, Last Words* in 1933. *Afterthoughts,* which continues the sense of permanent dislocation, is a series of succinct, aphoristic observations which aspire to the tradition of Georg Christoph Lichtenberg and Friedrich Wilhelm Nietzsche, with varying success:

If we shake hands with icy fingers, it is because we have burnt them so horribly before.

We live in a world of monkeys; but often monkeys, at a distance, look like men.

Eunuchs are no longer procurable to guard the chastity of females; but there are gentlemen who can be absolutely trusted.

What are the Queens of Sodom to do when their sons come from school?

I might give my life for my Friend, but he'd better not ask me to do up a parcel.

Unrequited affections are in youth unmitigated woes; only later on in life do we learn to appreciate the charm of these bogus heart-breaks.

In a state of ironclad physical suppression, literary love was the only unconstrained possibility for Smith. In *Trivia,* his narrator assigns special praise to the learned Pierre-Daniel Huet, "that gay old Bishop of Avranches ... who lived to be ninety-one and read Theocritus every year in his favorite month of May." Stressing the longevity of writers he admired most, he also lauds the "octogenarian" Persian poet Firdawsī; Baron Charles Athanase Walckenaer, a venerable authority on insects; "the octogenarian poet" Edmund Waller; and the centenarian Bernard de Fontenelle, even observing "I shouldn't mind, though, living to my hundredth year."

In 1924 a teenage Dwight Macdonald, who grew up to be one of America's most distinguished political journalists, wrote Smith a fan letter about *Trivia.* Macdonald even sent along some of his own *Trivia*-style prose efforts. Smith praised him, offering advice and encouragement along with suggestions for further reading, apart from the Greek and Latin classics:

> Among modern writers the ones I find most useful, and who have most helped me are Montaigne and Charles Lamb and Flaubert and Pater. Montaigne taught me to look into my own mind; Pater and Lamb gave me an ideal of what good English prose should be, and Flaubert's letters were a kind of Bible, which preached to me the religion of art, and the contempt of the rewards and joys and successes of ordinary existence.

Among the more mature readers of *Trivia,* George Santayana offered the most enthused reaction. He wrote to Smith in 1918:

> Where did you get your humility? I thought that was an extinct virtue. And I very much like your love of pleasure, and your humour and *malice:* it is so delightful to live in a world that is full of pictures, and incidental *divertissements,* and amiable absurdities. Why shouldn't things be largely absurd, futile, and transitory? They are so, and we are so, and they and we go very well together. ... Now, if what is our inevitable fate is *ignominious,* I understand what [Robert] Bridges says of Trivia,

that it is the most immoral book ever written, although every word of it can be read aloud. But I don't think so; it is not immoral at all unless you take it to be complete and ultimate, which of course is the last thing you would think of pretending. Your point is to be incomplete, fugitive, incidental.

BACK TO THE SEVENTEENTH CENTURY: SIR HENRY WOTTON

In 1907 Smith published the two-volume *Life and Letters of Sir Henry Wotton.* A British poet and diplomat, Wotton left a treasure trove of unpublished letters, which Smith incorporated into his narrative. Smith enjoyed rediscovering his correspondence so much that he would later dig up letters by the eighteenth-century French writer Madame du Deffand, Thomas Carlyle, and other masters of the epistolary art.

Wotton was known during his lifetime for his wit and panache. In a 1901 letter to a friend, Smith described him as:

> a courtier, scholar, poet, wit and at last a kindly old saint—it is a real pleasure to find among old dust-heaps some trace of him; and when I untie a great bundle of manuscripts and at last come upon his beautiful clear handwriting and some account of his feelings and adventures—so alive, so humorous and charming among dead intrigues and diplomacies, it is as delightful and exciting as the sight of a friend in the crowd of a foreign city.

Wotton's friendship with John Donne helped ensure his lasting fame, along with an elegy on his death by Abraham Cowley and a biography by Izaak Walton. His most popular lyric, anthologized in Francis Turner Palgrave's important *Golden Treasury of the Best Songs and Lyrical Poems in the English Language* (1861), begins:

> You meaner beauties of the night,
> Which poorly satisfy our eyes
> More by your number than your light,

You common people of the skies,
What are you, when the Moon shall rise?

Smith's own poems, collected in 1909 in *Songs and Sonnets,* were pallid attempts by comparison, as he himself admitted.

FOCUS ON LANGUAGE AND ANTHOLOGIES

In 1912 Smith and his sister Alys moved to a country house in Sussex, near Arundel. While continuing his ardent reading and writing, he also invested in an antiques shop with Philip Morrell. One of Smith's most durable books soon appeared, *The English Language* (1912). In a sometimes ironic tone, Smith described what he called "the Genius of the Language," asserting that every English speaker possesses "speech-feeling," or "a sense of what is worthy of adoption and what should be avoided and condemned." Smith believed that :

Grammarians can help this corporate will by registering its decrees and extending its analogies; but they fight against it in vain. ... If the Genius of the Language finds the split infinitive useful to express certain shades of thought, we can safely guess that all opposition to it will be futile.

Smith was naturalized as a British subject in 1913 and bought an Elizabethan manor house on the Hampshire coast. Also that year he was asked to become a founding member of the Society for Pure English, formed by the poet Robert Bridges. Aiming for a linguistic ideal, the society published pamphlets, in some of which Smith indulged his passion for finicky pedantry about "pure" use of language. Smith was one of the four authors of the society's initial prospectus (the others were Henry Bradley, Bridges, and Sir Walter Raleigh). The prospectus, announcing the ideals and goals of the group, was also signed by a bevy of top British literary figures, including Thomas Hardy, Sir Edmund Gosse, Austin Dobson, Maurice

Hewlett, Gilbert Murray, George Saintsbury, Sir Arthur Thomas Quiller-Couch, and W. P. Ker. The kind of subject that excited these writers and critics was the assimilation of foreign words in the English language. The prospectus attacked this "tendency of modern taste":

Literary taste at the present time, with regard to foreign words recently borrowed from abroad, is on wrong lines, the notions which govern it being scientifically incorrect, tending to impair the national character of our standard speech, and to adapt it to the habits of classical scholars. On account of these alien associations our borrowed terms are now spelt and pronounced, not as English, but as foreign words, instead of being assimilated, as they were in the past, and brought into conformity with the main structure of our speech. And as we more and more rarely assimilate our borrowings, so even words that were once naturalized are being now one by one made un-English, and driven out of the language back into their foreign forms; whence it comes that a paragraph of serious English prose may be sometimes seen as freely sprinkled with italicized French words as a passage of Cicero is often interlarded with Greek. The mere printing of such words in italics is an active force towards degeneration. The Society hopes to discredit this tendency, and it will endeavour to restore to English its old reactive energy.

In 1914 Smith moved to 11 St. Leonard's Terrace in the Chelsea neighborhood of London, an address he would occupy for the rest of his life. His life followed a quiet routine of reading and writing, receiving and answering letters. With enough means to live modestly, he had no need to seek paid employment, for which his periodic mood swings—he defined himself as a manic-depressive—would not have suited him.

He continued to offer examples of ideal English usage in his 1919 book *A Treasury of English Prose.* Virginia Woolf responded enthusiastically to his focus on English prose rhythms, which could match the intensity of poetry. In a 1920 review of Smith's *Treasury* in the *Saturday*

Review, Woolf expressed a "sigh of wonder that when there is prose before us with its capacities and possibilities, its power to say new things, make new shapes, express new passions, young people should still be dancing to a barrel organ and choosing words because they rhyme." Robert Bridges disapproved of the *Treasury of English Prose* because of its inclusion of writers such as Sir Thomas Browne. In an exchange of letters with Kenneth Clark in 1926, Smith admitted that he might well have added a portion of Lytton Strachey's acclaimed biography *Queen Victoria* (1921), except that he regarded that book as a "stunt piece [which] suffers from Lytton's great defect, a poverty and slight commonness of diction."

Another anthology from 1919, *Donne's Sermons: Selected Passages,* presented Smith's literary passions in a sympathetic light. In addition to his sermons and other religious writings, John Donne also wrote satires, elegies, and epigrams, as well as supreme love poems. Apart from his powerful achievement in poetry and prose, Donne's combination of sensuality—he fathered twelve children—and piety fascinated Smith. Smith was no doubt amused by Donne's epigrams, such as "The Jughler," which ridiculed gay love: "Thou call'st me effeminat, for I love womens joyes; / I call not thee manly, though thou follow boyes."

In 1920 Smith published *Little Essays Drawn from the Writings of George Santayana,* excerpts from the noted philosopher's writings. In the preface Smith wrote that he pursued the project despite his qualms about offering a selection of "elegant extracts" from Santayana:

> Mr. Santayana is by race and temperament a representative of the Latin tradition: his mind is a Catholic one; it has been his aim to reconstruct our modern, miscellaneous, shattered picture of the world, and to build, not of clouds, but of the materials of this common earth, an edifice of thought, a fortress or temple for the modern mind, in which every natural impulse could find, if pos-

sible, its opportunity for satisfaction, and every ideal aspiration its shrine and altar. It was from this edifice of Reason that I had been taking the ornaments, and I now saw the much greater beauty they would have if they could appear in their appropriate setting.

Santayana cooperated on the project by arranging the excerpts which Smith chose and rewriting some of them to better suit the brief format. He also gave the excerpts titles, such as "The Suppressed Madness of Sane Men" and "Knowledge of Nature is Symbolic," which added vivacity.

Smith next published a fifty-three-page pamphlet with Leonard and Virginia Woolf's Hogarth Press, *Stories from the Old Testament Retold* (1920). In the pamphlet he reexamined eleven biblical stories, including Jonah, Moses, and Jezebel, in a wry, more modern tone. Smith's retelling of the Old Testament was in the vein of the American gay novelist Glenway Wescott's *A Calendar of Saints for Unbelievers* (1932), an oblique look at religious tradition. In a 1932 letter to Virginia Woolf, Smith discussed the book of Old Testament stories ironically:

> I find they have helped many to find salvation, and I have thus been carrying on my family trade of saving souls, and hope to wear these diamonds in my heavenly crown. Of rubies I shall have an abundance, since a tract published by my father long ago, called *How Little Logan Was Brought to Jesus* ... had an enormous circulation at the time, and produced an especially powerful effect on the Red Indians of the West, who were quite unable to withstand it.

In 1921 increasing prostate trouble caused Smith to return to America for surgery at Johns Hopkins University hospital in Baltimore, Maryland. His prostate operation did not resolve the problem, which plagued him intermittently for the remainder of his life and seems to have slowed down his literary productivity in the early 1920s.

MORE LANGUAGE STUDIES

With *Word and Idioms: Studies in the English Language* (1925), Smith continued his gimlet-eyed observations of linguistic developments:

> Plainly, a language which was all idiom and unreason would be impossible as an instrument of thought; but all languages permit the existence of a certain number of illogical expressions: and the fact that, in spite of their vulgar origin and illiterate appearance, they have succeeded in elbowing their way from popular speech into our prose and poetry, our learned lexicons and grammars, is a proof that they perform a necessary function in the domestic economy of speech.

As he grew older, Smith was seen more and more in his adopted country as a literary authority. In 1926 the BBC formed the Spoken English Advisory Committee to determine a uniform pronunciation for many words on the radio. The committee was chaired by Robert Bridges and also included George Bernard Shaw and the noted phonetician A. Lloyd James. Smith was asked to represent the Society for Pure English. In 1929 the committee produced its first report, which was disputed by some readers but was nevertheless implemented by the BBC:

> Affectation and pedantry are to be found wherever language is spoken; they are not confined to any one local or class variety of speech. The indiscriminate use of *h,* for instance, among some uneducated speakers is a pretension to superiority that may merely amuse us. Such pronunciations as *nevaa, faa, waaliss,* for *never, fire, wireless,* will appear an offensive affectation to those who are unacquainted with the class variant of which these pronunciations are so characteristic a feature.

In 1933 Smith wrote to Virginia Woolf to ask her to join the committee, which at the time had no female participant. Who, asked Smith, "could 'voice' her sex better than" Woolf? At first Woolf accepted the honor, but a few months later she withdrew, stating that she had never served on a committee before and now it was too late to start.

Smith's growing prestige was accompanied by a certain starchy conservatism which led him to reject aspects of modernism. He dismissed the young French poet René Crevel, the only overtly gay participant in the surrealist movement. After attending a posh Bloomsbury party in 1926, Smith reported to his bisexual protégé Cyril Connolly:

> This audience was addressed by a pert, self-confident French boy with a big mouth and a brazen voice [Crevel] who dinned our ears with a galimatias of what I thought pretentious and incomprehensible nonsense, a new gospel of *surréalisme* composed of Freud, Rimbaud, Valéry, Keyserling and Mussolini—an anti-intellectual gospel and attack on reason, chanted and bellowed at us in a kind of figurative and bombastic prose which, though we pretended to follow it, I am sure none of us really understood. The whole thing—the brazen pretentious boy and the anxious pretentious audience, was extremely funny.

Smith's derisory reaction may have been meant in part as a warning to Connolly, who would later be swept away by this sort of trendy European intellectual and artistic fashion as editor of the British arts magazine *Horizon.*

In 1927 Smith contributed a booklet, *The Prospects of Literature,* to a series published by the Hogarth Press. Smith saw literature as a subversive art and believed that to offer no help at all to young writers was better than to stifle them with praise and honors:

> No; the old, hard conditions were surely better. It was much better to stone the prophets than to crown them, as we now crown them at once, with roses. They are stifled by the roses, but the stones in the old days of stoning only drove them out into the desert to meditate on their mission and perfect their gifts, so that they might return at last to take their revenge on the world which had scorned them.

Smith developed a habit of reading for eight hours every day early on in his career, and he continued the habit throughout his life. One of his most satisfying and useful books resulted from this activity: *A Treasury of English Aphorisms* (1928). This collection, with a long historical introduction, bears reexamination in a day when writers of fragments and compilers of literary anthologies, such as Walter Benjamin, have enjoyed renewed respect from critics. For Smith aphorisms expressed "disenchantment and the ever-accumulating stores of wise disillusion and worldly wisdom." He categorized the material in his anthology under subject headings, including "Fools and Folly," "Knaves," "Prudence," "Quarrels," "Envy," "Calumny," and "Lies." He pointed out that:

> The greatest aphorists, the most accomplished masters of this form, have been sardonic observers of their fellow human beings; and it was the most famous of them all, La Rochefoucauld, [who depicted] … all-devouring egotism and the littleness and meanness of [man's] moral character. Pascal added to this picture a truly appalling indictment of the imbecility and impotence of the mind of man, and the general disgrace of his mortal condition.

Smith quoted some aphorisms from John Selden's seventeenth-century book *Table Talk,* including the suggestion that a man should pay his wife's bills, for "He that will keep a Monkey, 'tis fit he should pay for the glasses she breaks." Smith countered this misogynistic statement with an aphorism attributed to Mrs. Poyser, a character in George Eliot's novel *Adam Bede* (Smith considered Eliot to be "our great female aphorist of fiction."): "I'm not denyin' the women are foolish; God almighty made 'em to match the men." Smith also praised the aphorisms of Lord Halifax and Ralph Waldo Emerson. Although Smith also approved of William Blake and Algernon Charles Swinburne as aphorists, in general he disliked nineteenth-century efforts in the genre: "From the writings of Disraeli and Oscar Wilde collections of sayings and maxims have been made; but Disraeli's pretentious aphorisms and Oscar Wilde's paradoxes (for all their shining wit) must for the most part be classed among the counterfeit currency of thought."

FRIENDSHIPS AND SEXUAL EXPRESSION

In 1928 Smith met a young man, Robert Gathorne-Hardy, whom he employed as a secretary and research assistant for almost two decades. Gathorne-Hardy was gay and lived with the male photographer Kyrle Leng in a country home, the Mill House, at Stanford Dingley, Berkshire, where they ran a small literary press. He was an authority on gardening and a skilled bibliographer, and after Smith's death he wrote a telling memoir of his relationship with Smith entitled *Recollections of Logan Pearsall Smith: The Story of a Friendship* (1949). In the book he stated that he would not be surprised to learn that Smith had died a virgin. Smith's friend and heir, the critic John Russell, also states in a personal communication with the present writer, that although Smith was certainly gay, he had no physical expression of his homosexuality. Instead, Smith dealt with gay love by making allusions to it in letters and books. He also let off steam in the presence of younger friends with outlandish "naughty stories" and tales of sexual woe: "The prenuptial suicide of male virgins was a favourite subject of discussion with Logan," wrote Gathorne-Hardy.

In his racy correspondence with young male friends, Smith sometimes indulged in sexual innuendos, such as when he informed Gathorne-Hardy in 1929 that Jeremy Taylor's book *Golden Grove* "slept beside me (not with me). … Perhaps your method of going to bed with them is the best. I hope you had a happy night with [Taylor's Latin] Grammar—you deserve it after your audacity in making it your own."

When Gathorne-Hardy offered to buy some books from Smith's collection, Smith responded, "You are corrupting me, but that is not unpleasant, especially when (which must be unique at my age) the process is lucrative as well." In a 1931 letter Smith playfully suggested to Gathorne-Hardy that they take a "pilgrimage" to the home of the gay nineteenth-century author Edward FitzGerald in order to "pay my tribute to the memory of Posh." (Posh was the nickname of a young fisherman, Joseph Fletcher, who was FitzGerald's male lover.)

These japes did not conceal the fact that dealing with people exasperated Smith sooner or later, as his oft-quoted assertion in *Afterthoughts* implies: "People say that Life is the thing, but I prefer Reading." As he grew older, Smith's manic-depressive temperament veered more dramatically. When he was in high spirits, he played wild practical jokes on friends: he liked to send them fake blackmail letters and once paid his maid to purchase a dead cat and throw it into his neighbor's yard. These moods alternated with despair, when all he could do was read.

A friend of Smith's once commented that Smith "must be mad, or else with his brains and his power of writing, he'd have been a really great writer." Indeed, fear of insanity may have motivated what Gathorne-Hardy calls Smith's "characteristic vertiginous avoidance of deep feeling, which alone kept him from actual greatness." Smith's deepest emotions were reserved for books, as when he devoured *The Conway Letters,* a collection of seventeenth-century documents published in 1930. Smith wrote to Gathorne-Hardy that the collection offered him "as much pleasure as I can bear. Only I have no one but you to whom I can describe my ravishment." Gathorne-Hardy believed that Smith was emotionally "crippled" by his fear of deep emotions: "Sorrows and perplexities of the heart were matters not allowable in his life."

JEREMY TAYLOR AND FURTHER LITERARY REFLECTIONS

In 1930 Smith published *The Golden Grove: Selected Passages from the Sermons and Writings of Jeremy Taylor.* The seventeenth-century Anglican bishop and theologian Jeremy Taylor, like Donne, was a liberating influence, particularly in such books as *A Discourse of the Liberty of Prophesying,* which argued for freedom of conscience and speech in religious matters. Some of Taylor's statements seem to jibe with Smith's resigned, superior analysis of human foibles, such as when Taylor declared in a sermon, for instance, "It is impossible to make people understand their ignorance; for it requires knowledge to perceive it and therefore he that can perceive it hath it not." A confirmed bachelor when he was working on the book, Smith must also have reflected that he would never achieve the wedded state praised by Taylor:

Celibate, like the flie in the heart of an apple, dwels in a perpetuall sweetnesse, but sits alone, and is confin'd and dies in singularity; but marriage, like the usefull Bee, builds a house and gathers sweetnesse from every flower, and labours and unites into societies and republicks, and sends out colonies, and feeds the world with delicacies, and obeys their king, and keeps order, and exercises many vertues, and promotes the interest of mankinde, and is that state of good things to which God hath designed the present constitution of the world.

Smith's book *On Reading Shakespeare,* published in 1933, presented his personal impressions over a lifetime of reading the great playwright. Smith offered generalized opinions about the plays: "It is only in the *Two Gentlemen of Verona* ... that [Shakespeare's] power over words becomes a magic power, and his golden mastery of speech begins to almost blind us with its beauty." In the first chapter, "On Not Reading Shakespeare," Smith warns that "the world's great writers are apt to become the world's great bores." He points out that scholars have uselessly tried to deny Shakespeare's apparent bisexuality, which is expressed in the sonnets:

What are we to do about those sonnets he was fond of writing, his brutal sonnets to the Dark Lady, and his sentimental sonnets to the Lovely Boy? The story Shakespeare recounts of his moral—or rather his immoral—predicament between these "two loves" of his—

Two loves I have of comfort and despair—

must certainly, in the interests of the British Empire, be smothered up; the business of proving and re-proving, and proving over again—and then proving still once more, just to be absolutely certain—that our Shakespeare cannot possibly mean what he so frankly tells us, has become almost a national industry. ...

In the Sonnets I find described a sex-quandary which psycho-analysis has taught us to regard as not at all unusual.

Smith's arguments about Shakespeare's sexuality suggest a conscious awareness of human sexuality that some of his friends may not have credited him with. For example, in a letter Virginia Woolf once stated that she believed there to be "a good deal of the priest, it may be of the eunuch, in [Smith]." Woolf was referring to Smith's precious habit of extracting what he saw as ideal sentences from works of literature and treasuring them out of context: "He has several of these sentences always on his person, and [during a visit] read them aloud in a high nasal chant." Smith's discomfort with sex may have been an obstacle in appreciating Shakespeare, whether his great tragedies or rudely punning comedies, as Smith noted:

Even worse than this ithyphallic fun in which Shakespeare so plainly delighted, is the evidence of a more distressing kind of sex-preoccupation, by which, during a certain period of his life, he seems to have been obsessed. Lear's obscene rail-

ings against the mere fact of sex, which are quite inappropriate to his circumstances and situation, and in which he seems to scream and spit from horror, and Timon's even more terrible outbursts of sex-nausea, sound like the incoherent ravings of an unbalanced mind, driven to madness by a loathing for men and women in their natural intercourse together.

For Smith, Shakespeare's plays—and not just *Lear*—brushed too close to madness to be read without discomfort. A number of his contemporaries dismissed Smith as a fatally inhibited observer who would never dare delve deeply enough into basic motivations to create a work of permanent literary value. *On Reading Shakespeare* contains chapters appreciating the Bard's poetry and dramatic characters, but there is no sign that Smith is willing to allow his own reading of Shakespeare to be a life-changing experience. Instead, trying to express his own excitement in reading Shakespeare, Smith falls into flowery evocations:

The reader feels a dark strain, a far off-sound ... from dreaded histories, of great men and women caught in an older web of Destiny, wrecked by some flaw in themselves, or rendered helpless amid a crushing environment of evil, and swept down by terrible non-human forces on the remorseless flood of fate. ... For what is the meaning of a poem after all, but a pretext for fine poetry? If that meaning be involved in haze, may not the poetry be all the finer for it ... to dream, to meditate, to lose ourselves in thoughts beyond the reaches of our souls, to love the gay appearances of the world and know them as illusions— this temper of an ironic mind, of a happy, enjoying, and yet melancholy nature, expresses itself in a secret rhythm, a cadence, a delicate and dreamlike music which is, for me, the loveliest poetry in the world.

In a retrospective mood, Smith next gathered essays he had written from 1898 to 1936 for his collection *Reperusals and Re-Collections* (1936). This volume included a pamphlet which was published the same year by Clarendon

Press, *Fine Writing.* Smith revised and enlarged almost all of the essays from their original format. He doubled the size of the essay which originally introduced his anthology of aphorisms, adding new material and mentioning aphorists whom he had previously not dealt with. As with much of Smith's work in this period, his faithful research assistant, Gathorne-Hardy, took on all of the considerable library work required to make the material of renewed interest to the reader.

UNFORGOTTEN YEARS AND LATE EVENTS

While on a cruise trip with his friend Edith Wharton, Smith began *Unforgotten Years,* a memoir of his early years which, according to Gathorne-Hardy, he said was written "as if to please the youthful brilliance of Sir Kenneth Clark." The book, published in 1938, recounts how Smith fled Quakerism, a business career, and America, although he never escaped his mother's powerful influence. Perhaps this lack of escape was the reason he claimed to friends that he had never been in love and why he looked at sex as "merely a source of delicious absurdities." He opposed marriage, telling his (married) friend John Russell that his "idea of a happy ending of a love story is to begin at the engagement, where the hack writer ends, and show how they escape from the storms and the wild beasts back into the safe harbor of celibacy!" *Unforgotten Years* became an unexpected bestseller, selling over 100,000 copies through the Book-of-the-Month Club in America. John Russell wrote:

> The account of his career which he gives, or feigns to give, in *Unforgotten Years* is as fragmentary and elusive as everything else in that wonderfully-manipulated volume. ... So far from gushing forth uncontrollably, his work was strained off drop by drop, through the muslin of a super-sensitive critical sense.

Gathorne-Hardy would say as much in his *Recollections* when he alluded to the material that was omitted from *Unforgotten Years,* and to Smith's "crippled" spirit:

> It wasn't that he could not deal with deeper themes, but, in effect, that he dared not. This I believe to be the clue to his artistic nature. The unspoken fear was an incentive which heightened immeasurably the apparently trivial matters which he wrote about most often. ...
>
> *Unforgotten Years* is a history of escapes, from religion, from business, from America, from sordid ambition. But there is no record of escape from the silken cord of maternal chains; nor, in fact, did Logan ever make such an escape.

In the same year his memoir was published, Smith traveled with Gathorne-Hardy to Iceland, where he fell ill and became temporarily insane. Smith recovered when he returned to England, but he harbored lasting vindictive feelings toward Gathorne-Hardy, his longtime friend and employee. In 1940 Smith produced his final book, *Milton and His Modern Critics,* a wry debunking of influential modernists such as T. S. Eliot and Ezra Pound, whom Smith accused of diminishing John Milton's reputation. Smith's polemic particularly provided an occasion for him to attack Pound, whom he considered "the most slipshod and illiterate of published writers."

Smith's book appeared before the full extent of Pound's fascist sympathies became known, and it is unlikely that Smith's quarrel with Pound had its root in Pound's anti-Semitic views. But Smith was not neutral on the issue. In 1938, as war approached in Europe, Smith wrote a letter expressing solidarity with the persecuted Jewish minority, perhaps reflecting his friendship with Berenson, who was of Jewish origin:

> What purpose is gained by beating and banning the most intelligent, most cultivated and cosmo-

politan race of Europe? The Jews are lovers of the countries in which they are born. ... They are not lovers of bloodshed or propagandists of any religion; without their patronage painting and music would collapse in almost every city of Europe and America; the Jews are the best doctors and scientists in the world, and three of them, Marx, Freud and Einstein, have made the most brilliant contributions to modern thought. Europe also derives its religion from them since the Virgin Mary, Christ and all the apostles were Jews. Like the rest of us they have their faults, and are supposed to be fonder of money than we are. But a twentieth part of what we are now spending on armaments would satisfy them, and leave enough over to transport, say to Central Australia, those who don't like them, with an ample supply of bombs with which to exterminate each other. ...

For the Jews do love civilization, and the liberty of which it is the flower; and I happen to love them too.

Smith could be less enlightened about other minorities: Gathorne-Hardy recalls that Smith snobbily described an American scholar's work as "like an enthusaistic negro writing about Horace." Smith also reported in a 1925 letter to Virginia Woolf that Henry James "used to say that the best story writer in America was a Negro, William Du Bois, but the fact was hushed up on account of color prejudice." It is not known whether Smith shared this high view of the writings of W. E. B. Du Bois.

Besides Gathorne-Hardy, Smith hired other gifted young writers to assist him over the years, including the literary critic Cyril Connolly, a tormented bisexual who first visited Smith in 1926 with Kenneth Clark's recommendation. Smith found him to be, as he wrote to his sister Mary in 1926, "a little creature and as ugly as an ape, but full of the things he wants to write." Smith decided to give Connolly a chance. Just after the start of the Second World War, he met another protégé, the historian Hugh Trevor-Roper, to whom he wrote teasing letters with suggestive jokes, such as one in 1942:

Speaking of saints, Her Sanctity of Hinde Street [the novelist Rose Macaulay] telephoned to me yesterday with the voice of the female sex, which she has now resumed. She has sent me a postcard also to say that Tiresias was wrong when he said the fair sex gets more fun out of fucking than the male.

More than just joshing with them, Smith actively promoted his protégés, taking Kenneth Clark's first book, *The Gothic Revival: An Essay on the History of Taste,* to his publisher Constable, who accepted it. He also wrote to the editor of the *Atlantic Monthly* in 1945 to recommend Hugh Trevor-Roper and John Russell for journalistic jobs. (Trevor-Roper would later become a prolific and wide-ranging historian, and Russell went on to have a long career at the *New York Times.*) Smith's letters reflect some attempts to maintain a social circle of gay writers, such as in 1943, when he described the gay British biographer James Pope-Hennessy as a "Triviolator" (admirer of *Trivia*) and mentioned that the French novelist André Gide took an interest in only two English writers, one of whom was Smith.

DEATH AND POSTHUMOUS REPUTATION

Smith's estrangement from Gathorne-Hardy continued until Smith's death, and he left his estate to John Russell, a relatively recent acquaintance. Still, Gathorne-Hardy visited the sometimes addled and sickly Smith, despite Smith's verbal abuse and wistful reflections such as "I want ... to be old and gay and obscene." Smith died on March 2, 1946, in his London house. His friend the novelist Rose Macaulay, who twelve years before had included excerpts from *Trivia* in an anthology, *The Minor Pleasures of Life* (1934), wrote perhaps the most heartfelt obituary in the March 9, 1946, issue of *Time and Tide.* It is quoted in the introduction to *A Chime of Words: The Letters of Logan Pearsall Smith* (1984):

His going leaves an unfillable gap. His was the kind of ripe and scholarly culture that links yesterday (not today) with past centuries; he was at home with the great littérateurs, French and English, of the Nineteenth century, the Eighteenth, and (pre-eminently) the Seventeenth. Whenever and wherever men and women have made beauty out of words, there was his quarry. ... It was partly the scholar too, that quested after curious and beautiful words, collecting them like coins; but it was the artist and stylist who delighted in fashioning out of them mosaics of lovely color and pattern. For he was, of course, first and last a stylist; his aim from youth was to "master the powers of magical evocation, the elfin music, the ironic echoes which are latent in English prose. The golden sceptre of style gilds everything it touches and can make immortal those who grasp it." So he wrote in one of his most characteristic essays, his tract on Fine Writing.

Friends and readers best retained Smith's indubitable love for writing and books. In his memoir Gathorne-Hardy described Smith's advice for beginning writers:

> He had three rules which he imposed as essential on all aspiring writers. Carry a notebook, and write down any striking words or phrases which you hear, or which come into your mind: mark the passages in your reading which take your fancy, and make an index of them (if he lent me a book of his own, he asked me to mark and note such passages in it): read the dictionary. To fall short in any of thses rules implied a lack of seriousness and a distatste for proper application.

But despite these methods, Gathorne-Hardy said, Smith "shrunk, shudderingly from the fullness of life, and didn't care to question overmuch convenient, carelessly accepted, and comfortable assertions." Among such assertions were numerous hasty judgments about literature: in his books and letters he dismissed a variety of writers, from Thomas Hardy to Anton Chekhov, whose accomplishments are far greater than his own.

The still-faithful Gathorne-Hardy arranged for the posthumous publication of two of Smith's books: *The Golden Shakespeare: An Anthology* (1949), which was a collection of best bits from the Bard, and *A Religious Rebel: The Letters of "H. W. S." (Mrs. Pearsall Smith)* (1949), a selection of his mother's correspondance. While reading over his mother's letters as preparation for writing *Unforgotten Years,* Smith had been struck by the admirable energy of her writing.

Gathorne-Hardy's memoir of Smith also appeared in 1949, followed by *A Portrait of Logan Pearsall Smith, Drawn from His Letters and Diaries,* edited by John Russell in 1950. The personality therein revealed is so decisively repugnant that it may have discouraged readers from revisiting Smith's oeuvre. Decades of obscurity have followed for Smith, as he has received hardly any critical attention. Smith's preference for briefer forms also may have worked against him, although in a 1926 letter to his sister Mary he claimed he was merely agreeing with an old lady to the effect that "an hour is enough of anything." Smith has also been overlooked by gay studies specialists, although his work is ripe for a gender studies approach. Henry James often referred to him as "poor dear Logan," perhaps with as much pity for his unrealized personal life as for his constrained literary work. A modest revival of interest in Smith that takes into account both his achievements and impediments seems overdue.

Selected Bibliography

WORKS OF LOGAN PEARSALL SMITH

PROSE POEMS AND APHORISMS
Trivia: Printed from the Papers of Anthony Woodhouse, Esq. London: Chiswick, 1902.
Trivia. London: Constable, 1918.
More Trivia. London: Constable, 1922.

Afterthoughts. London: Constable, 1931.

All Trivia: Trivia, More Trivia, Afterthoughts, Last Words. London: Constable, 1933; New York: Ticknor & Fields, 1984; Harmondsworth, England: Penguin, 1986.

BIOGRAPHICAL AND CRITICAL WORKS

The Life and Letters of Sir Henry Wotton. Oxford: Clarendon, 1907.

The English Language. London: Williams and Norgate, 1912; Oxford University Press, 1952.

A Few Practical Suggestions. Society for Pure English, no. 3. Oxford: Clarendon, 1920.

English Idioms. Society for Pure English, no. 12. Oxford: Clarendon, 1923.

Four Words: Romantic, Originality, Creative, Genius. Society for Pure English, no. 17. Oxford: Clarendon, 1924.

Words and Idioms: Studies in the English Language. London: Constable, 1925.

The Prospects of Literature. Hogarth Essays, second series, no. 8. London: Hogarth, 1927.

Needed Words. Society for Pure English, no. 31. Oxford: Clarendon, 1928. (The volume also includes *Words Wanted in Connexion with Arts* by Roger Fry and *Jeremy Bentham and Word-Creation* by Professor Graham Wallas.)

Robert Bridges: Recollections. Society for Pure English, no. 35. Oxford: Clarendon, 1931.

On Reading Shakespeare. London: Constable, 1933.

Fine Writing. Society for Pure English, no. 46. Oxford: Clarendon, 1936.

Reperusals and Re-Collections. London: Constable, 1936.

Milton and His Modern Critics. London: Oxford University Press, Humphrey Milford, 1940.

COLLECTIONS EDITED BY LOGAN PEARSALL SMITH

Donne's Sermons: Selected Passages. Oxford: Clarendon, 1919. (Includes an essay by Smith.)

A Treasury of English Prose. London: Constable, 1919.

Little Essays Drawn from the Writings of George Santayana. London: Constable, 1920.

A Treasury of English Aphorisms. London: Constable, 1928.

The Golden Grove: Selected Passages from the Sermons and Writings of Jeremy Taylor. Oxford: Clarendon, 1930.

The Golden Shakespeare: An Anthology. London: Constable, 1949. (Posthumous publication arranged by Robert Gathorne-Hardy.)

A Religious Rebel. The Letters of "H. W. S." (Mrs. Pearsall Smith), by Hannah Whitall Smith. London: Nisbet, 1949. (Posthumous publication arranged by Robert Gathorne-Hardy.)

OTHER WORKS

The Youth of Parnassus, and Other Stories. London; New York: Macmillan, 1895.

Golden Urn. nos. 1–3 (March 1897–July 1898). (A literary and art review compiled by Smith, along with Bernhard Berenson, and Mary Costelloe, afterward Bernard Berenson and Mary Berenson.)

Songs and Sonnets. London: Elkin Mathews, 1909.

Stories from the Old Testament Retold. Richmond, England: Hogarth, 1920.

The Lady Hilda Trevelyan Rescue Fund Balance Sheet. Stanford Dingley: Mill House, 1932.

Death in Iceland. Reading, England: s.n., 1938. (This volume also included *Iceland: A Poem* by Robert Gathorne-Hardy.)

Unforgotten Years. London: Constable, 1938.

Saved from the Salvage. With a memoir of the author by Cyril Connolly. Edinburgh: Tragara, 1982.

JOURNALS, CORRESPONDENCE, AND MANUSCRIPTS

A Chime of Words: The Letters of Logan Pearsall Smith. Edited with an introduction by Edwin Tribble. New York: Ticknor & Fields, 1984.

A collection of Logan Persall Smith papers is also located at the following libraries: Kent State University Library (http://speccoll.library.kent.edu/literature/prose/lsmith.html); The University of Tulsa McFarlin Library (http://www.lib.utulsa.edu/speccoll/smithlp0.htm); and Indiana University Library (http://www.indiana.edu/~liblilly/lilly/mss/html/smithlp.html)

CRITICAL AND BIOGRAPHICAL STUDIES

Bridges, Robert, ed. *The B.B.C.'s Recommendations for Pronouncing Doubtful Words, Reissued with*

Criticisms. Society for Pure English, no. 32. Oxford: Clarendon, 1929.

Burman, Edward, ed. *An Anthology of Logan Pearsall Smith.* London: Constable, 1989.

Chanler, Margaret Terry. *Autumn in the Valley.* Boston: Little, Brown, 1936.

Clark, Kenneth. *Another Part of the Wood: A Self Portrait.* New York: Harper & Row, 1974.

————. *The Other Half: A Self Portrait.* New York: Harper & Row, 1977.

Clark, Ronald William. *The Life of Bertrand Russell.* New York: Knopf, 1976.

Connolly, Cyril. *A Romantic Friendship: The Letters of Cyril Connolly to Noel Blakiston.* London: Constable, 1975.

Dunn, Richard M. *Geoffrey Scott and the Berenson Circle: Literary and Aesthetic Life in the Early 20th Century.* Lewiston, N.Y.: Edwin Mellen, 1998.

Gathorne-Hardy, Robert. *Recollections of Logan Pearsall Smith: The Story of a Friendship.* London: Constable, 1949.

Heaney, Howell J. "A Logan Pearsall Smith Collection." *The Princeton University Library Chronicle* 23:181–183.

Henry, Marie. *Secret Life of Hannah Whitall Smith.* Grand Rapids, Mich.: Chosen Books, 1984; Minneapolis, Minn.: Bethany House, 1993.

James, Henry, *Henry James: A Life in Letters.* Edited by Philip Horne. London: Allen Lane, 1999.

Krieg, Joann P. "'Don't Let Us Talk of That Anymore': Whitman's Estrangement from the Costelloe-Smith Family." *Walt Whitman Quarterly Review* 17, no. 3: 91–120 (winter 2000).

Larbaud, Valéry. Introduction to *Trivia.* Translated by Philippe Neel with the collaboration of the author. Paris: B. Grasset, 1921.

Lewis, Jeremy. *Cyril Connolly: A Life.* London: Jonathan Cape, 1997.

Moorehead, Caroline. *Bertrand Russell: A Life.* London: Sinclair-Stevenson, 1992.

Parker, Robert Allerton. *A Family of Friends: The Story of the Transatlantic Smiths.* London: Museum, 1959.

Russell, Bertrand. *The Selected Letters of Bertrand Russell.* Edited by Nicholas Griffin. Boston: Houghton Mifflin, 1992.

Russell, John. Introduction to *A Portrait of Logan Pearsall Smith, Drawn from His Letters and Diaries,* by Logan Pearsall Smith. London: Dropmore, 1950.

Santayana, George. *Persons and Places: Fragments of Autobiography.* Edited by William G. Holzberger and Herman J. Saatkamp Jr. Cambridge, Mass.: MIT Press, 1986.

————. *The Letters of George Santayana.* Edited by William G. Holzberger. Cambridge, Mass.: MIT Press, 2001.

Secrest, Meryle. *Kenneth Clark: A Biography.* New York: Holt, Rinehart & Winston, 1985.

Smith, Hannah Whitall. *The Christian's Secret of a Happy Life.* Boston: Willard Tract Repository, 1875; Chicago: Fleming H. Revell, 1883.

————. *My Spiritual Autobiography; or, How I Discovered the Unselfishness of God.* New York: Revell, 1903.

————. *Religious Fanaticism: Extracts from the Papers of Hannah Whitall Smith.* Edited by Ray Strachey. London: Faber & Gwyer, 1928; New York: AMS Press, 1976.

Smith, Robert Pearsall. *How Little Logan Was Brought to Jesus.* Edited with a preface by Logan Pearsall Smith. Stanford Dingley, Berkshire: Mill House, 1934.

Strachey, Barbara. *Remarkable Relations: The Story of the Pearsall Smith Women.* New York: Universe Books, 1982.

Strachey, Ray. *A Quaker Grandmother, Hannah Whitall Smith.* New York: Revell, 1914.

Vidal, Gore. Foreword to *All Trivia: Trivia, More Trivia, Afterthoughts, Last Words.* New York : Ticknor & Fields, 1984; Harmondsworth, England: Penguin, 1986.

Whitman, Walt. *The Correspondence.* Edited by Edwin Haviland Miller. 6 vols. New York: New York University Press, 1961–1977.

Woolf, Virginia. *The Diary of Virginia Woolf, Volume One: 1915–1919.* London: Harcourt, 1979.

————. *The Letters of Virginia Woolf.* Edited by Nigel Nicolson and Joanne Trautmann. London: Hogarth, 1975–1980.

—BENJAMIN IVRY

Index

Arabic numbers printed in bold-face type refer to extended treatment of a subject.

"A" (Zukofsky), **Supp. III Part 2:** 611, 612, 614, 617, 619, 620, 621, 622, 623, 624, 626, 627, 628, 629, 630, 631; **Supp. IV Part 1:** 154

Aal, Katharyn, **Supp. IV Part 1:** 332

Aaron, Daniel, **IV:** 429; **Supp. I Part 2:** 647, 650

Aaron's Rod (Lawrence), **Supp. I Part 1:** 255

Abacus (Karr), **Supp. XI: 240–242,** 248, 254

Abádi-Nagy, Zoltán, **Supp. IV Part 1:** 280, 289, 291

"Abandoned Newborn, The" (Olds), **Supp. X:** 207

Abbey, Edward, **Supp. VIII:** 42; **Supp. X:** 24, 29, 30, 31, 36; **Supp. XIII: 1–18; Supp. XIV:** 179

Abbey's Road (Abbey), **Supp. XIII:** 12

Abbott, Edith, **Supp. I Part 1:** 5

Abbott, George, **Supp. IV Part 2:** 585

Abbott, Grace, **Supp. I Part 1:** 5

Abbott, Jack Henry, **Retro. Supp. II:** 210

Abbott, Jacob, **Supp. I Part 1:** 38, 39

Abbott, Lyman, **III:** 293

Abbott, Sean, **Retro. Supp. II:** 213

ABC of Color, An: Selections from Over a Half Century of Writings (Du Bois), **Supp. II Part 1:** 186

ABC of Reading (Pound), **III:** 468, 474–475

"Abdication, An" (Merrill), **Supp. III Part 1:** 326

Abel, Lionel, **Supp. XIII:** 98

Abel, Sam, **Supp. XIII:** 199

Abelard, Peter, **I:** 14, 22

Abeles, Sigmund, **Supp. VIII:** 272

Abercrombie, Lascelles, **III:** 471; **Retro. Supp. I:** 127, 128

Abernathy, Milton, **Supp. III Part 2:** 616

Abhau, Anna. *See* Mencken, Mrs. August (Anna Abhau)

"Ability" (Emerson), **II:** 6

Abish, Walter, **Supp. V:** 44

"Abishag" (Glück), **Supp. V:** 82

"Abortion, The" (Sexton), **Supp. II Part 2:** 682

"Abortions" (Dixon), **Supp. XII:** 153

"About Hospitality" (Jewett), **Retro. Supp. II:** 131

"About Kathryn" (Dubus), **Supp. VII:** 91

About the House (Auden), **Supp. II Part 1:** 24

About Town: "The New Yorker" and the World It Made (Yagoda), **Supp. VIII:** 151

"Above Pate Valley" (Snyder), **Supp. VIII:** 293

Above the River (Wright), **Supp. III Part 2:** 589, 606

"Abraham" (Schwartz), **Supp. II Part 2:** 663

Abraham, Nelson Algren. *See* Algren, Nelson

"Abraham Davenport" (Whittier), **Supp. I Part 2:** 699

"Abraham Lincoln" (Emerson), **II:** 13

Abraham Lincoln: The Prairie Years (Sandburg), **III:** 580, 587–589, 590

Abraham Lincoln: The Prairie Years and the War Years (Sandburg), **III:** 588, 590

Abraham Lincoln: The War Years (Sandburg), **III:** 588, 589–590

"Abraham Lincoln Walks at Midnight" (Lindsay), **Supp. I Part 2:** 390–391

"Abram Morrison" (Whittier), **Supp. I Part 2:** 699

Abramovich, Alex, **Supp. X:** 302, 309

"Absalom" (Rukeyser), **Supp. VI:** 278–279

Absalom, Absalom! (Faulkner), **II:** 64, 65–67, 72, 223; **IV:** 207; **Retro. Supp. I:** 75, 81, 82, 84, 85, 86, 87, 88, 89, 90, 92, 382; **Supp. V:** 261; **Supp. X:** 51; **Supp. XIV:** 12–13

"Absence of Mercy" (Stone), **Supp. V:** 295

"Absentee, The" (Levertov), **Supp. III Part 1:** 284

Absentee Ownership (Veblen), **Supp. I Part 2:** 642

"Absent Thee from Felicity Awhile" (Wylie), **Supp. I Part 2:** 727, 729

"Absolution" (Fitzgerald), **Retro. Supp. I:** 108

"Abuelita's Ache" (Mora), **Supp. XIII:** 218

Abysmal Brute, The (London), **II:** 467

"Academic Story, An" (Simpson), **Supp. IX:** 279–280

"Academic Zoo, The: Theory—in Practice" (Epstein), **Supp. XIV:** 107–108, 109

"Accident" (Minot), **Supp. VI: 208–209**

"Accident, The" (Southern), **Supp. XI:** 295

"Accident, The" (Strand), **Supp. IV Part 2:** 624

Accident/A Day's News (Wolf), **Supp. IV Part 1:** 310

Accidental Tourist, The (Tyler), **Supp. IV Part 2:** 657, 668–669; **Supp. V:** 227

Accordion Crimes (Proulx), **Supp. VII:** 259–261

"Accountability" (Dunbar), **Supp. II Part 1:** 197, 204

"Accusation, The" (Wright), **Supp. III Part 2:** 595

"Accusation of the Inward Man, The" (Taylor), **IV:** 156

"Accusing Message from Dead Father" (Karr), **Supp. XI:** 244

Ace, Goodman, **Supp. IV Part 2:** 574

Achievement in American Poetry (Bogan), **Supp. III Part 1:** 63–64

Acker, Kathy, **Supp. XII:1–20**

Ackerman, Diane, **Supp. XIII:** 154

"Acknowledgment" (Lanier), **Supp. I Part 1:** 364

Ackroyd, Peter, **Supp. V:** 233

"Acquaintance in the Heavens, An" (Dillard), **Supp. VI:** 34

"Acquainted with the Night" (Frost), **II:** 155; **Retro. Supp. I:** 137

Across Spoon River (Masters), **Supp. I**

Part 2: 455, 457, 459, 460, 466, 474–475, 476

Across the Layers: Poems Old and New (Goldbarth), **Supp. XII:** 181, **187–189**

Across the River and into the Trees (Hemingway), **I:** 491; **II:** 255–256, 261; **Retro. Supp. I:** 172, **184–185**

"Actfive" (MacLeish), **III:** 18–19, 22

Actfive and Other Poems (MacLeish), **III:** 3, 17–19, 21

Action (Shepard), **Supp. III Part 2:** 446

Active Anthology (Pound), **Supp. III Part 2:** 617

Active Service (Crane), **I:** 409

Acton, Patricia Nassif, **Supp. X:** 233

Actual, The (Bellow), **Retro. Supp. II:** 33

"Actual Experience, Preferred Narratives" (Julier), **Supp. IV Part 1:** 211

Acuff, Roy, **Supp. V:** 335

Ada (Nabokov), **Retro. Supp. I:** 265, 266, 270, 276–277, 278, 279

"Ada" (Stein), **IV:** 43

Ada; or Ardor (Nabokov), **III:** 247

"Adagia" (Stevens), **IV:** 78, 80, 88, 92

"Adam" (Hecht), **Supp. X:** 62

"Adam" (W. C. Williams), **Retro. Supp. I:** 422, 423

"Adam and Eve" (Eugene), **Supp. X:** 204

"Adam and Eve" (Shapiro), **Supp. II Part 2:** 708, 712

Adam Bede (Eliot), **II:** 181

Adamé, Leonard, **Supp. XIII:** 316

Adam & Eve & the City (W. C. Williams), **Retro. Supp. I:** 423

"Adamic Purity as Double Agent" (Whalen-Bridge), **Retro. Supp. II:** 211–212

Adams, Althea. *See* Thurber, Mrs. James (Althea Adams)

Adams, Annie. *See* Fields, Annie Adams

Adams, Brooks, **Supp. I Part 2:** 484

Adams, Charles, **Supp. I Part 2:** 644

Adams, Charles Francis, **I:** 1, 4; **Supp. I Part 2:** 484

Adams, Franklin P., **Supp. I Part 2:** 653; **Supp. IX:** 190

Adams, Henry, **I:** **1–24**, 111, 243, 258; **II:** 278, 542; **III:** 396, 504; **IV:** 191, 349; **Retro. Supp. I:** 53, 59; **Retro. Supp. II:** 207; **Supp. I Part 1:** 299–300, 301, 314; **Supp. I Part 2:** 417, 492, 543, 644; **Supp. II Part 1:** 93–94, 105; **Supp. III Part 2:** 613; **Supp. IV Part 1:** 31, 208

Adams, Henry B., **Supp. I Part 1:** 369

Adams, J. Donald, **IV:** 438

Adams, James Truslow, **Supp. I Part 2:** 481, 484, 486

Adams, John, **I:** 1; **II:** 103, 301; **III:** 17, 473; **Supp. I Part 2:** 483, 506, 507, 509, 510, 511, 517, 518, 520, 524

Adams, John Luther, **Supp. XII:** 209

Adams, John Quincy, **I:** 1, 3, 16–17; **Supp. I Part 2:** 685, 686

Adams, Léonie, **Supp. I Part 2:** 707; **Supp. V:** 79; **Supp. IX:** 229

Adams, Luella, **Supp. I Part 2:** 652

Adams, Mrs. Henry (Marian Hooper), **I:** 1, 5, 10, 17–18

Adams, Phoebe, **Supp. IV Part 1:** 203; **Supp. VIII:** 124

Adams, Samuel, **Supp. I Part 2:** 516, 525

"Ad Castitatem" (Bogan), **Supp. III Part 1:** 50

Addams, Jane, **Supp. I Part 1: 1–26;** **Supp. XI:** 200, 202

Addams, John Huy, **Supp. I Part 1:** 2

"Addendum" (Wright), **Supp. V:** 339

Addiego, John, **Supp. XII:** 182

Adding Machine, The (Rice), **I:** 479

Adding Machine, The: Selected Essays (Burroughs), **Supp. III Part 1:** 93, 97

Addison, Joseph, **I:** 8, 105, 106–107, 108, 114, 131, 300, 304; **III:** 430

"Addressed to a Political Shrimp, or, Fly upon the Wheel" (Freneau), **Supp. II Part 1:** 267

"Address to My Soul" (Wylie), **Supp. I Part 2:** 729

Address to the Government of the United States on the Cession of Louisiana to the French, An (Brown), **Supp. I Part 1:** 146

"Address to the Scholars of New England" (Ransom), **III:** 491

"Address with Exclamation Points, A" (Simic), **Supp. VIII:** 283

"Adjutant Bird, The" (Banks), **Supp. V:** 5

Adkins, Nelson F., **II:** 20

Adler, Alfred, **I:** 248

Adler, Betty, **III:** 103

Adler, George J., **III:** 81

Adler, Renata, **Supp. X:** 171

Admiral of the Ocean Sea: A Life of Christopher Columbus (Morison), **Supp. I Part 2:** 486–488

"Admirals" (Chabon), **Supp. XI:** 72

"Admonition, An" (Brodsky), **Supp. VIII:** 33

"Adolescence" (Dove), **Supp. IV Part 1:** 245

"Adolescence" (Olds), **Supp. X:** 211

"Adolescence II" (Dove), **Supp. IV Part 1:** 242, 244–245

"Adonais" (Shelley), **II:** 516, 540

Adorno, Theodor, **Supp. I Part 2:** 645, 650; **Supp. IV Part 1:** 301

"Adrienne Rich: The Poetics of Change" (Gelpi), **Supp. I Part 2:** 554

"Adultery" (Banks), **Supp. V:** 15

"Adultery" (Dubus), **Supp. VII:** 85

Adultery and Other Choices (Dubus), **Supp. VII:** 83–85

Adulthood Rites (O. Butler), **Supp. XIII:** 63, **64–65**

Adult Life of Toulouse Lautrec by Henri Toulouse Lautrec, The (Acker), **Supp. XII:** 5, 6, **8–9**

Adventure (London), **II:** 466

Adventures in Ancient Egypt (Goldbarth), **Supp. XII:** 191

Adventures in Value (Cummings), **I:** 430

"Adventures of a Book Reviewer" (Cowley), **Supp. II Part 1:** 137, 142

Adventures of Augie March, The (Bellow), **I:** 144, 147, 149, 150, 151, 152–153, 154, 155, 157, 158–159, 164; **Retro. Supp. II:** 19, 20, **22–23,** 24, 30; **Supp. VIII:** 234, 236–237

Adventures of a Young Man (Dos Passos), **I:** 488, 489, 492

Adventures of Captain Bonneville (Irving), **II:** 312

Adventures of Huckleberry Finn, The (Twain), **I:** 307, 506; **II:** 26, 72, 262, 266–268, 290, 418, 430; **III:** 101, 112–113, 357, 554, 558, 577; **IV:** 198, 201–204, 207; **Retro. Supp. I:** 188; **Retro. Supp. II:** 121; **Supp. I Part 1:** 247; **Supp. IV Part 1:** 247, 257; **Supp. IV Part 2:** 502; **Supp. V:** 131; **Supp. VIII:** 198; **Supp. X:** 230; **Supp. XII:** 16

Adventures of Roderick Random, The (Smollett), **I:** 134

Adventures of the Letter I (Simpson), **Supp. IX:** 266, **273–274**

Adventures of Tom Sawyer, The (Twain), **II:** 26; **III:** 223, 572, 577; **IV:** 199–200, 203, 204; **Supp. I Part 2:** 456, 470

Adventures While Preaching the Gospel of Beauty (Lindsay), **Supp. I Part 2:** 374, 376, 381, 382–384, 389, 399

Adventures with Ed (Loeffler), **Supp. XIII:** 1

Advertisements for Myself (Mailer), **III:** 27, 35–38, 41–42, 45, 46;

Retro. Supp. II: 196, 199, 200, 202, 203, 212; Supp. IV Part 1: 90, 284; Supp. XIV: 157

"Advertisements for Myself on the Way Out" (Mailer), III: 37

"Advice to a Prophet" (Wilbur), Supp. III Part 2: 555–557

Advice to a Prophet and Other Poems (Wilbur), Supp. III Part 2: 554–558

"Advice to a Raven in Russia" (Barlow), Supp. II Part 1: 65, 74, 80, 83

Advice to the Lovelorn (film), Retro. Supp. II: 328

Advice to the Privileged Orders, Part I (Barlow), Supp. II Part 1: 80

"Aeneas and Dido" (Brodsky), Supp. VIII: 24–25

"Aeneas at Washington" (Tate), IV: 129

Aeneid (Virgil), I: 396; II: 542; III: 124

Aeneus Tacticus, I: 136

Aerial View (Barabtarlo), Retro. Supp. I: 278

Aeschylus, I: 274, 433; III: 398; IV: 358, 368, 370; Retro. Supp. I: 65; Supp. I Part 2: 458, 494

Aesop, I: 387; II: 154, 169, 302; III: 587

Aesthetic (Croce), III: 610

"Aesthetics" (Mumford), Supp. II Part 2: 476

"Aesthetics of Silence, The" (Sontag), Supp. III Part 2: 459

"Aesthetics of the Shah" (Olds), Supp. X: 205

"Affair at Coulter's Notch, The" (Bierce), I: 202

"Affair of Outposts, An" (Bierce), I: 202

Affliction (Banks), Supp. V: 15, 16

Affluent Society, The (Galbraith), Supp. I Part 2: 648

"Aficionados, The" (Carver), Supp. III Part 1: 137

"Afloat" (Beattie), Supp. V: 29

Afloat and Ashore (Cooper), I: 351, 355

Africa, Its Geography, People, and Products (Du Bois), Supp. II Part 1: 179

Africa, Its Place in Modern History (Du Bois), Supp. II Part 1: 179

"Africa, to My Mother" (D. Diop), Supp. IV Part 1: 16

African American Writers (Smith, ed.), Supp. XIII: 115, 127

"African Book" (Hemingway), II: 259

"African Chief, The" (Bryant), Supp. I Part 1: 168

"African Fragment" (Brooks), Supp. III Part 1: 85

African Queen, The (film), Supp. XI: 17

"African Roots of War, The" (Du Bois), Supp. II Part 1: 174

African Silences (Matthiessen), Supp. V: 203

African Treasury, An (Hughes, ed.), Supp. I Part 1: 344

"Afrika Revolution" (Baraka), Supp. II Part 1: 53

"AFRO-AMERICAN LYRIC" (Baraka), Supp. II Part 1: 59

After All: Last Poems (Matthews), Supp. IX: 155, 167–169

After and Before the Lightning (Ortiz), Supp. IV Part 2: 513

"After a Party" (Salinas), Supp. XIII: 327

"After Apple-Picking" (Frost), Retro. Supp. I: 126, 128

"After Arguing against the Contention That Art Must Come from Discontent" (Stafford), Supp. XI: 327

After Confession: Poetry as Autobiography (Harris), Supp. XIV: 269

After Experience (Snodgrass), Supp. VI: 314–316, 317

"After great pain, a formal feeling comes" (Dickinson), Retro. Supp. I: 37

"After Hearing a Waltz by Bartók" (Lowell), II: 522

After Henry (Didion), Supp. IV Part 1: 195, 196, 199, 207, 208, 211

"After Henry" (Didion), Supp. IV Part 1: 211

"After Holbein" (Wharton), IV: 325; Retro. Supp. I: 382

After Ikkyu and Other Poems (Harrison), Supp. VIII: 42

"After-Image" (Caldwell), I: 309

After-Images: Autobiographical Sketches (Snodgrass), Supp. VI: 314, 319–323, 324, 326–327

After I's (Zukofsky), Supp. III Part 2: 628, 629

Afterlife (Monette), Supp. X: 153

Afterlife (Updike), Retro. Supp. I: 322

Afterlife, The (Levis), Supp. XI: 259, 260–264

"After Magritte" (McClatchy), Supp. XII: 264

"After Making Love" (Dunn), Supp. XI: 153

Aftermath (Longfellow), II: 490

"Aftermath" (Longfellow), II: 498

"Afternoon" (Ellison), Supp. II Part 1: 238

"Afternoon at MacDowell" (Kenyon), Supp. VII: 159

"Afternoon Miracle, An" (O. Henry), Supp. II Part 1: 390

Afternoon of a Faun (Hearon), Supp. VIII: 63–64

Afternoon of an Author: A Selection of Uncollected Stories and Essays (Fitzgerald), II: 94

"Afternoon of a Playwright" (Thurber), Supp. I Part 2: 620

Afternoon of the Unreal (Salinas), Supp. XIII: 311, 316–318

"Afternoon with the Old Man, An" (Dubus), Supp. VII: 84

"After Punishment Was Done with Me" (Olds), Supp. X: 213

"After Reading Barely and Widely," (Zukofsky), Supp. III Part 2: 625, 631

"After Reading 'In the Clearing' for the Author, Robert Frost" (Corso), Supp. XII: 130

"After Reading Mickey in the Night Kitchen for the Third Time before Bed" (Dove), Supp. IV Part 1: 249

"After Reading Tu Fu, I Go Outside to the Dwarf Orchard" (Wright), Supp. V: 343

"After Reading Wang Wei, I Go Outside to the Full Moon" (Wright), Supp. V: 343

After Shocks, Near Escapes (Dobyns), Supp. XIII: 80–82

"After Song, An" (W. C. Williams), Retro. Supp. I: 413

After Strange Gods (Eliot), I: 588

"After the Alphabets" (Merwin), Supp. III Part 1: 356

"After the Argument" (Dunn), Supp. XI: 149

"After the Burial" (Lowell), Supp. I Part 2: 409

"After the Curfew" (Holmes), Supp. I Part 1: 308

"After the Death of John Brown" (Thoreau), IV: 185

"After the Denim" (Carver), Supp. III Part 1: 144

"After the Dentist" (Swenson), Supp. IV Part 2: 645

After the Fall (A. Miller), III: 148, 149, 156, 161, 162, 163–165, 166

"After the Fire" (Merrill), Supp. III Part 1: 328

After the Fox (film), Supp. IV Part 2: 575

After the Genteel Tradition (Cowley),

Supp. II Part 1: 143

"After the Heart's Interrogation" (Komunyakaa), **Supp. XIII:** 120

After the Lost Generation: A Critical Study of the Writers of Two Wars (Aldridge), **Supp. IV Part 2:** 680

"After the Night Office—Gethsemani Abbey" (Merton), **Supp. VIII:** 195–196

"After the Persian" (Bogan), **Supp. III Part 1:** 64

"After the Pleasure Party" (Melville), **III:** 93

"After the Resolution" (Dunn), **Supp. XI:** 151

After the Stroke (Sarton), **Supp. VIII:** 264

"After the Surprising Conversions" (Lowell), **I:** 544, 545; **II:** 550; **Retro. Supp. II:** 187

"After 37 Years My Mother Apologizes for My Childhood" (Olds), **Supp. X:** 208

Afterthoughts (L. P. Smith), **Supp. XIV:** 339, 345

"Afterthoughts on the Rosenbergs" (Fiedler), **Supp. XIII:** 99

"After Twenty Years" (Rich), **Supp. I Part 2:** 559–560

"Afterwake, The" (Rich), **Supp. I Part 2:** 553

"Afterward" (Wharton), **Retro. Supp. I:** 372

"After Working Long" (Kenyon), **Supp. VII:** 170

"After Yitzl" (Goldbarth), **Supp. XII:** 186

"After You, My Dear Alphonse" (Jackson), **Supp. IX:** 119

"Again" (Dixon), **Supp. XII:** 157

"Again, Kapowsin" (Hugo), **Supp. VI:** 141

"Against" (Goldbarth), **Supp. XII:** 193

"Against Decoration" (Karr), **Supp. XI:** 248

Against Interpretation (Sontag), **Supp. III Part 2:** 451, 455; **Supp. XIV:** 15

"Against Interpretation" (Sontag), **Supp. III Part 2:** 456–458, 463

"Against Modernity" (Ozick), **Supp. V:** 272

"Against Nature" (Karr), **Supp. XI:** 243

Against Nature (Updike), **Retro. Supp. I:** 323

"Against the Crusades" (Stern), **Supp. IX:** 300

Against the Current: As I Remember F.

Scott Fitzgerald (Kroll Ring), **Supp. IX:** 63

Agapida, Fray Antonio (pseudonym). *See* Irving, Washington

"Agassiz" (Lowell), **Supp. I Part 2:** 414, 416

Agassiz, Louis, **II:** 343; **Supp. I Part 1:** 312; **Supp. IX:** 180

Agee, Emma, **I:** 26

Agee, James, **I: 25–47,** 293; **IV:** 215; **Supp. IX:** 109; **Supp. XIV:** 92

"Agent, The" (Wilbur), **Supp. III Part 2:** 557–561

Age of Anxiety, The (Auden), **Supp. II Part 1:** 2, 19, 21

"Age of Conformity, The" (Howe), **Supp. VI:** 117

Age of Grief, The: A Novella and Stories (Smiley), **Supp. VI:** 292, **299–301**

Age of Innocence, The (Wharton), **IV:** 320–322, 327–328; **Retro. Supp. I:** 372, 374, **380–381; Supp. IV Part 1:** 23

Age of Longing, The (Koestler), **I:** 258

Age of Reason, The (Paine), **Supp. I Part 2:** 503, 515–517, 520

"Age of Strolling, The" (Stern), **Supp. IX:** 297

"Ages, The" (Bryant), **Supp. I Part 1:** 152, 155, 166, 167

"Aging" (Jarrell), **II:** 388

Aging and Gender in Literature (George), **Supp. IV Part 2:** 450

"Agio Neró" (Mora), **Supp. XIII:** 224

"Agitato ma non Troppo" (Ransom), **III:** 493

"Agnes of Iowa" (Moore), **Supp. X:** 165, 178

Agnes of Sorrento (Stowe), **Supp. I Part 2:** 592, 595–596

Agnon, S. Y., **Supp. V:** 266

"Agosta the Winged Man and Rasha the Black Dove" (Dove), **Supp. IV Part 1:** 246–247

Agrarian Justice (Paine), **Supp. I Part 2:** 517–518

"Agricultural Show, The" (McKay), **Supp. X:** 139

Agua Fresca: An Anthology of Raza Poetry (Rodríguez, ed.), **Supp. IV Part 2:** 540

Agua Santa/Holy Water (Mora), **Supp. XIII: 222–225**

Agüero Sisters, The (García), **Supp. XI: 185–190**

Aguiar, Sarah Appleton, **Supp. XIII:** 30

Ah, Wilderness! (O'Neill), **III:** 400–401; **Supp. IV Part 2:** 587

Ah, Wilderness!: The Frontier in American Literature (Humphrey), **Supp. IX:** 104

Ahearn, Barry, **Retro. Supp. I:** 415

Ahearn, Frederick L., Jr., **Supp. XI:** 184

Ahearn, Kerry, **Supp. IV Part 2:** 604

Ahmed Arabi Pasha, **I:** 453

Ahnebrink, Lars, **III:** 328

Ah Sin (Harte), **Supp. II Part 1:** 354–355

"Ah! Sun-flower" (Blake), **III:** 19

AIDS and Its Metaphors (Sontag), **Supp. III Part 2:** 452, 466–468

Aids to Reflection (Coleridge), **II:** 10

Aiieeeee! An Anthology of Asian-American Writers (The Combined Asian Resources Project), **Supp. X:** 292

Aiken, Conrad, **I: 48–70,** 190, 211, 243; **II:** 55, 530, 542; **III:** 458, 460; **Retro. Supp. I:** 55, 56, 57, 58, 60, 62; **Supp. X:** 50, 115

"Aim Was Song, The" (Frost), **Retro. Supp. I:** 133

Ainsworth, Linda, **Supp. IV Part 1:** 274

Ainsworth, William, **III:** 423

Air-Conditioned Nightmare, The (H. Miller), **III:** 186

Airing Dirty Laundry (Reed), **Supp. X:** 241

"Air Plant, The" (Crane), **I:** 401

Air Raid: A Verse Play for Radio (MacLeish), **III:** 21

"Airs above the Ground" (Sarton), **Supp. VIII:** 261

Air Tight: A Novel of Red Russia. See We the Living (Rand)

"Airwaves" (Mason), **Supp. VIII:** 146

Airways, Inc. (Dos Passos), **I:** 482

Aitken, Robert, **Supp. I Part 2:** 504

Akhmadulina, Bella, **Supp. III Part 1:** 268

Akhmatova, Anna, **Supp. III Part 1:** 268, 269; **Supp. VIII:** 20, 21, 25, 27, 30

Akhmatova Translations, The (Kenyon), **Supp. VII:** 160

"Akhnilo" (Salter), **Supp. IX:** 260

Aksenev, Vasily P., **Retro. Supp. I:** 278

"Al Aaraaf" (Poe), **III:** 426–427

Al Aaraaf, Tamerlane, and Minor Poems (Poe), **III:** 410

"Alain Locke: Bahá'í Philosopher" (Buck), **Supp. XIV:** 199

Alain Locke: Faith and Philosophy (Buck), **Supp. XIV:** 200

"Alain Locke and Cultural Pluralism"

(Kallen), **Supp. XIV:** 197

Alarcón, Justo, **Supp. IV Part 2:** 538, 539, 540

À la Recherche du Temps Perdu (Proust), **IV:** 428

"Alastor" (Shelley), **Supp. I Part 2:** 728

"Alatus" (Wilbur), **Supp. III Part 2:** 563

"Alba" (Creeley), **Supp. IV Part 1:** 150

Albee, Edward, **I:** 71–96, 113; **II:** 558, 591; **III:** 281, 387; **IV:** 4, 230; **Retro. Supp. II:** 104; **Supp. VIII:** 331; **Supp. XIII:** 196, 197

Albers, Joseph, **Supp. IV Part 2:** 621

Albright, Margery, **Supp. I Part 2:** 613

"Album, The" (Morris), **III:** 220

Alcestiad, The (Wilder), **IV:** 357, 374

"Alchemist, The" (Bogan), **Supp. III Part 1:** 50

"Alchemist in the City, The" (Hopkins), **Supp. IV Part 2:** 639

Alchymist's Journal, The (Connell), **Supp. XIV:** 80

"Alcmena" (Winters), **Supp. II Part 2:** 801

Alcott, Abba. *See* Alcott, Mrs. Amos Bronson (Abigail May)

Alcott, Amos Bronson, **II:** 7, 225; **IV:** 172, 173, 184; **Retro. Supp. I:** 217; **Supp. I Part 1:** 28, 29–32, 35, 39, 41, 45; **Supp. II Part 1:** 290

Alcott, Anna. *See* Pratt, Anna

Alcott, Louisa May, **IV:** 172; **Supp. I Part 1: 28–46; Supp. IX:** 128

Alcott, May, **Supp. I Part 1:** 41

Alcott, Mrs. Amos Bronson (Abigail May), **IV:** 184; **Supp. I Part 1:** 29, 30, 31, 32, 35

Alcuin: A Dialogue (Brown), **Supp. I Part 1:** 126–127, 133

Alden, Hortense. *See* Farrell, Mrs. James T. (Hortense Alden)

Alden, John, **I:** 471; **II:** 502–503

"Alder Fork, The" (Leopold), **Supp. XIV:** 186

Aldington, Mrs. Richard. *See* Doolittle, Hilda

Aldington, Perdita, **Supp. I Part 1:** 258

Aldington, Richard, **II:** 517; **III:** 458, 459, 465, 472; **Retro. Supp. I:** 63, 127; **Supp. I Part 1:** 257–262, 270

Aldo Leopold: His Life and Work (Meine), **Supp. XIV:** 179

"Aldo Leopold's Intellectual Heritage" (Nash), **Supp. XIV:** 191–192

Aldrich, Thomas Bailey, **II:** 400; **Supp. II Part 1:** 192; **Supp. XIV:** 45

Aldrich, Tom, **Supp. I Part 2:** 415

Aldridge, John W., **Supp. I Part 1:** 196; **Supp. IV Part 1:** 286; **Supp. IV Part 2:** 680, 681; **Supp. VIII:** 189; **Supp. XI:** 228

Aleck Maury Sportsman (Gordon), **II:** 197, 200, 203–204

Alegría, Claribel, **Supp. IV Part 1:** 208

Aleichem, Sholom, **IV:** 3, 10; **Supp. IV Part 2:** 585

"Alert Lovers, Hidden Sides, and Ice Travelers: Notes on Poetic Form and Energy" (Dunn), **Supp. XI:** 153

"Aleš Debeljak" (Simic), **Supp. VIII:** 279

"Alex" (Oliver), **Supp. VII:** 232

Alexander, George, **II:** 331

Alexander, Michael, **Retro. Supp. I:** 293

"Alexander Crummell Dead" (Dunbar), **Supp. II Part 1:** 207, 208–209

Alexander's Bridge (Cather), **I:** 313, 314, 316–317, 326; **Retro. Supp. I:** 1, 6, 7, 8

Alexander the Great, **IV:** 322

"Alexandra" (Cather), **Retro. Supp. I:** 7, 9, 17

Alexandrov, V. E., **Retro. Supp. I:** 270

Algonquin Round Table, **Supp. IX:** 190, 191, 197

Algren, Nelson, **I:** 211; **Supp. V:** 4; **Supp. IX: 1–18; Supp. XII:** 126; **Supp. XIII:** 173; **Supp. XIV:** 3

Alhambra, The (Irving), **II:** 310–311

Alias Grace (Atwood), **Supp. XIII:** 20, **31–32**

"Alice Doane's Appeal" (Hawthorne), **II:** 227

Alice in Wonderland (Carroll), **Supp. I Part 2:** 622

"Alicia and I Talking on Edna's Steps" (Cisneros), **Supp. VII:** 64

"Alicia Who Sees Mice" (Cisneros), **Supp. VII:** 60

Alison, Archibald, **Supp. I Part 1:** 151, 159

Alison's House (Glaspell), **Supp. III Part 1:** 182, 188, 189

Alive (screenplay, Shanley), **Supp. XIV:** 316

Alive and Writing: Interviews with American Authors of the 1980s (McCaffery and Gregory), **Supp. X:** 260

"Alki Beach" (Hugo), **Supp. VI:** 135

ALL: The Collected Poems, 1956–1964 (Zukofsky), **Supp. III Part 2:** 630

ALL: The Collected Short Poems, 1923–1958 (Zukofsky), **Supp. III Part 2:** 629

"All Around the Town" (Benét), **Supp. XI:** 48, 58

All at Sea (Lardner), **II:** 427

"All Boy" (Rawlings), **Supp. X:** 222

Allegiances (Stafford), **Supp. XI: 322– 323,** 329

"Allegory of the Cave" (Dunn), **Supp. XI:** 150

"Allegro, L' " (Milton), **Supp. XIV:** 8

Allen, Brooke, **Supp. VIII:** 153

Allen, Dick, **Supp. IX:** 279

Allen, Donald, **Supp. VIII:** 291; **Supp. XIII:** 112

Allen, Frank, **Supp. XI:** 126; **Supp. XII:** 186

Allen, Frederick Lewis, **Supp. I Part 2:** 655

Allen, Gay Wilson, **IV:** 352; **Supp. I Part 2:** 418

Allen, Paula Gunn. *See* Gunn Allen, Paula

Allen, Walter, **I:** 505; **III:** 352; **Supp. IV Part 2:** 685; **Supp. IX:** 231

Allen, Woody, **Supp. I Part 2:** 607, 623; **Supp. IV Part 1:** 205; **Supp. X:** 164; **Supp. XI:** 307

"Aller et Retour" (Barnes), **Supp. III Part 1:** 36

Aller Retour New York (H. Miller), **III:** 178

Aller Retour New York (Miller), **III:** 182, 183

Allessandrini, Goffredo, **Supp. IV Part 2:** 520

Alleys of Eden, The (R. O. Butler), **Supp. XII:** 62, **62–64,** 68

All God's Children Need Traveling Shoes (Angelou), **Supp. IV Part 1:** 2, 9–10, 12–13, 17

All God's Chillun Got Wings (O'Neill), **III:** 387, 391, 393–394

All Gone (Dixon), **Supp. XII:** 148, 149

"All Hallows" (Glück), **Supp. V:** 82

"All I Can Remember" (Jackson), **Supp. IX:** 115

"Alligators, The" (Updike), **IV:** 219

"ALL IN THE STREET" (Baraka), **Supp. II Part 1:** 53

"All I Want" (Tapahonso), **Supp. IV Part 2:** 508

"All Little Colored Children Should Play the Harmonica" (Patchett), **Supp. XII:** 309

"All Mountains" (Doolittle), **Supp. I Part 1:** 271

All My Friends Are Going to Be Strangers (McMurtry), **Supp. V:** 224, 228, 229

All My Pretty Ones (Sexton), **Supp. II**

Part 2: 678, 679–683

"All My Pretty Ones" (Sexton), **Supp. II Part 2:** 681–682

"All My Sad Captains" (Jewett), **Retro. Supp. II:** 134

All My Sons (A. Miller), **III:** 148, 149, 150, 151–153, 154, 155, 156, 158, 159, 160, 164, 166

"All Night, All Night" (Schwartz), **Supp. II Part 2:** 665

All Night Long (Caldwell), **I:** 297

"All Our Lost Children: Trauma and Testimony in the Performance of Childhood" (Pace), **Supp. XI:** 245

"All Out" (Hecht), **Supp. X:** 72

All Over (Albee), **I:** 91–94

"Allowance" (Minot), **Supp. VI:** 206, 207–208

"Alloy" (Rukeyser), **Supp. VI:** 279

"All Parrots Speak" (Bowles), **Supp. IV Part 1:** 89

Allport, Gordon, **II:** 363–364

All Quiet on the Western Front (Remarque), **Supp. IV Part 1:** 380, 381

"ALL REACTION IS DOOMED-!-!-!" (Baraka), **Supp. II Part 1:** 59

"All Revelation" (Frost), **II:** 160–162

"All Souls" (Wharton), **IV:** 315–316; **Retro. Supp. I:** 382

"All Souls' Night" (Yeats), **Supp. X:** 69

All Souls' Rising (Bell), **Supp. X:** 12, **13–16,** 17

"All-Star Literary Vaudeville" (Wilson), **IV:** 434–435

Allston, Washington, **II:** 298

All Stories Are True (Wideman), **Supp. X:** 320

"All That Is" (Wilbur), **Supp. III Part 2:** 563

"All the Bearded Irises of Life: Confessions of a Homospiritual" (Walker), **Supp. III Part 2:** 527

"All the Beautiful Are Blameless" (Wright), **Supp. III Part 2:** 597

All the Conspirators (Isherwood), **Supp. XIV:** 156, 159, 160

All the Dark and Beautiful Warriors (Hansberry), **Supp. IV Part 1:** 360, 374

All the Days and Nights: The Collected Stories (Maxwell), **Supp. VIII:** 151, 158, 169

"All the Dead Dears" (Plath), **Retro. Supp. II:** 246; **Supp. I Part 2:** 537

All the Good People I've Left Behind (Oates), **Supp. II Part 2:** 510, 522, 523

"All the Hippos Were Boiled in Their Tanks" (Burroughs and Kerouac), **Supp. III Part 1:** 94

All the King's Men (Warren), **I:** 489; **IV:** 243, 248–249, 252; **Supp. V:** 261; **Supp. VIII:** 126; **Supp. X:** 1

All the Little Live Things (Stegner), **Supp. IV Part 2:** 599, 604, 605, 606, 609–610, 611, 613

All the Pretty Horses (film), **Supp. VIII:** 175

All the Pretty Horses (McCarthy), **Supp. VIII:** 175, **182–183,** 188

All the Sad Young Men (Fitzgerald), **II:** 94; **Retro. Supp. I:** 108

"All the Time in the World" (Dubus), **Supp. VII:** 91

"All the Way to Flagstaff, Arizona" (Bausch), **Supp. VII:** 47, 49

"All This and More" (Karr), **Supp. XI:** 243

"All Too Real" (Vendler), **Supp. V:** 189

All Trivia: Triva, More Trivia, Afterthoughts, Last Words (L. P. Smith), **Supp. XIV:** 339

All-True Travels and Adventures of Lidie Newton (Smiley), **Supp. VI:** 292, **305–307**

All We Need of Hell (Crews), **Supp. XI: 114**

Almack, Edward, **Supp. IV Part 2:** 435

al-Maghut, Muhammad, **Supp. XIII:** 278

"Almanac" (Swenson), **Supp. IV Part 2:** 641

Almanac of the Dead (Silko), **Supp. IV Part 2:** 558–559, 560, 561, 570–571

Almon, Bert, **Supp. IX:** 93

Almost Revolution, The (Priaulx and Ungar), **Supp. XI:** 228

Alnilam (Dickey), **Supp. IV Part 1:** 176, 186, 188–189

"Alone" (Levine), **Supp. V:** 184, 185, 186

"Alone" (Poe), **Retro. Supp. II:** 266

"Alone" (Singer), **IV:** 15

"Alone" (Winters), **Supp. II Part 2:** 786, 811

Aloneness (Brooks), **Supp. III Part 1:** 85, 86

Alone with America (Corso), **Supp. XII:** 131

Alone with America (Howard), **Supp. IX:** 326

"Along the Color Line" (Du Bois), **Supp. II Part 1:** 173

Along the Illinois (Masters), **Supp. I Part 2:** 472

"Alphabet" (Nye), **Supp. XIII:** 283

Alphabet, An (Doty), **Supp. XI:** 120

Alphabet of Grace, The (Buechner), **Supp. XII:** 52

"Alphabet of My Dead, An" (Pinsky), **Supp. VI:** 235, 250

"Alphabet of Subjects, An" (Zukofsky), **Supp. III Part 2:** 624

"Alpine Christ, The" (Jeffers), **Supp. II Part 2:** 415, 419

Alpine Christ and Other Poems, The (Jeffers), **Supp. II Part 2:** 419

"Alpine Idyll, An" (Hemingway), **II:** 249; **Retro. Supp. I:** 176

Al Que Quiere! (W. C. Williams), **Retro. Supp. I:** 414, 416, **417,** 428

Alsop, Joseph, **II:** 579

"Altar, The" (Herbert), **Supp. IV Part 2:** 646

"Altar, The" (MacLeish), **III:** 4

"Altar Boy" (Fante), **Supp. XI:** 160, 164

"Altar of the Dead, The" (James), **Retro. Supp. I:** 229

"Altars in the Street, The" (Levertov), **Supp. III Part 1:** 280

Alter, Robert, **Supp. XII:** 167

Altgeld, John Peter, **Supp. I Part 2:** 382, 455

Althea (Masters), **Supp. I Part 2:** 455, 459

Altick, Richard, **Supp. I Part 2:** 423

Altieri, Charles, **Supp. VIII:** 297, 303

Altman, Robert, **Supp. IX:** 143

"Altra Ego" (Brodsky), **Supp. VIII:** 31–32

A Lume Spento (Pound), **Retro. Supp. I:** 283, 285

"Aluminum House" (F. Barthelme), **Supp. XI:** 26

Alvares, Mosseh, **Supp. V:** 11

Alvarez, A., **Supp. I Part 2:** 526, 527; **Supp. II Part 1:** 99; **Supp. IX:** 248

Alvarez, Julia, **Supp. VII: 1–21; Supp. XI:** 177

Always Outnumbered, Always Outgunned (Mosley), **Supp. XIII:** 242

"Always the Stories" (Ortiz), **Supp. IV Part 2:** 499, 500, 502, 504, 512

Always the Young Strangers (Sandburg), **III:** 577–578, 579

Amadeus (Shaffer), **Supp. XIV:** 330

"Amahl and the Night Visitors: A Guide to the Tenor of Love" (Moore), **Supp. X:** 167

"Am and Am Not" (Olds), **Supp. X:** 212

"Amanita, The" (Francis), **Supp. IX:** 81

Amaranth (Robinson), **III:** 509, 510,

512, 513, 522, 523

Amazing Adventures of Kavalier and Clay, The (Chabon), **Supp. XI:** 68, 76, **77–80**

Amazons: An Intimate Memoir by the First Woman to Play in the National Hockey League (DeLillo), **Supp. VI:** 2

Ambassadors, The (H. James), **II:** 320, 333–334, 600; **III:** 517; **IV:** 322; **Retro. Supp. I:** 215, 218, 219, 220, 221, **232–233**

Ambelain, Robert, **Supp. I Part 1:** 260, 273, 274

Ambition: The Secret Passion (Epstein), **Supp. XIV:** 113–114

"Ambition Bird, The" (Sexton), **Supp. II Part 2:** 693

Ambler, Eric, **III:** 57

Ambrose Holt and Family (Glaspell), **Supp. III Part 1:** 175, 181, 184, 187, 188

"Ambrose Seyffert" (Masters), **Supp. I Part 2:** 464

"Ambush" (Komunyakaa), **Supp. XIII:** 122

Amen Corner, The (Baldwin), **Retro. Supp. II:** 5, 7; **Supp. I Part 1:** 48, 51, 54, 55, 56

America (Benét), **Supp. XI:** 46, 47, 51

"America" (Ginsberg), **Supp. II Part 1:** 58–59, 317

"America" (song), **IV:** 410

"America, America!" (poem) (Schwartz), **Supp. II Part 2:** 665

"America, Seen Through Photographs, Darkly" (Sontag), **Supp. III Part 2:** 464

America: The Story of a Free People (Commager and Nevins), **I:** 253

"America! America!" (story) (Schwartz), **Supp. II Part 2:** 640, 658–659, 660

America and Americans (Steinbeck), **IV:** 52

"America and the Vidal Chronicles" (Pease), **Supp. IV Part 2:** 687

America as a Civilization (Lerner), **III:** 60

"America Independent" (Freneau), **Supp. II Part 1:** 261

America Is Worth Saving (Dreiser), **Retro. Supp. II:** 96

American, The (James), **I:** 226; **II:** 326–327, 328, 331, 334; **IV:** 318; **Retro. Supp. I:** 220, **221**, 228, 376, 381

Americana (DeLillo), **Supp. VI:** 2, **3**, 5, 6, 8, 13, 14

American Adam, The (R. W. B. Lewis),

II: 457–458; **Supp. XIII:** 93

American Almanac (Leeds), **II:** 110

American Anthem (Doctorow and Suares), **Supp. IV Part 1:** 234

"American Apocalypse" (Gunn Allen), **Supp. IV Part 1:** 325

American Blood, (Nichols), **Supp. XIII:** 268

American Blues (T. Williams), **IV:** 381, 383

American Buffalo (Mamet), **Supp. XIV:** 239, 241, 242, 244–245, 246, 254, 255

American Caravan: A Yearbook of American Literature (Mumford, ed.), **Supp. II Part 2:** 482

American Cause, The (MacLeish), **III:** 3

American Childhood, An (Dillard), **Supp. VI:** 19–21, 23, 24, 25, 26, 30, 31

"American Childhood in the Dominican Republic, An" (Alvarez), **Supp. VII:** 2, 5

American Child Supreme, An: The Education of a Liberation Ecologist (Nichols), **Supp. XIII:** 256, 257, 258, 264, 265, 266, 267, 268, 269

American Claimant, The (Twain), **IV:** 194, 198–199

American Crisis I (Paine), **Supp. I Part 2:** 508

American Crisis II (Paine), **Supp. I Part 2:** 508

American Crisis XIII (Paine), **Supp. I Part 2:** 509

"American Critic, The" (J. Spingarn), **I:** 266

American Democrat, The (Cooper), **I:** 343, 346, 347, 353

American Diary (Webb), **Supp. I Part 1:** 5

American Drama since World War II (Weales), **IV:** 385

American Dream, An (Mailer), **III:** 27, 33–34, 35, 39, 41, 43, 44; **Retro. Supp. II:** 203, **204–205**

American Dream, The (Albee), **I:** 74–76, 77, 89, 94

"American Dreams" (Simpson), **Supp. IX:** 274

American Earth (Caldwell), **I:** 290, 308

"American Emperors" (Poirier), **Supp. IV Part 2:** 690

American Exodus, An (Lange and Taylor), **I:** 293

American Experience, The (Parkes), **Supp. I Part 2:** 617–618

American Express (Corso), **Supp. XII:** 129

"American Express" (Salter), **Supp. IX:** 260–261

"American Fear of Literature, The" (Lewis), **II:** 451

American Fictions (Hardwick), **Supp. X:** 171

American Fictions, 1940–1980 (Karl), **Supp. IV Part 1:** 384

"American Financier, The" (Dreiser), **II:** 428

American Folkways (book series), **I:** 290

American Heroine: The Life and Legend of Jane Addams (Davis), **Supp. I Part 1:** 1

American Historical Novel, The (Leisy), **Supp. II Part 1:** 125

"American Horse" (Erdrich), **Supp. IV Part 1:** 333

American Humor (Rourke), **IV:** 339, 352

American Hunger (Wright), **Supp. IV Part 1:** 11

American Indian Anthology, An (Tvedten, ed.), **Supp. IV Part 2:** 505

"American Indian Women: At the Center of Indigenous Resistance in Contemporary North America" (Jaimes and Halsey), **Supp. IV Part 1:** 331

"American in England, An" (Wylie), **Supp. I Part 2:** 707

American Jitters, The: A Year of the Slump (Wilson), **IV:** 427, 428

American Journal (Hayden), **Supp. II Part 1:** 367

"American Land Ethic, An" (Momaday), **Supp. IV Part 2:** 488

American Landscape, The, **Supp. I Part 1:** 157

American Language, The (Mencken), **II:** 289, 430; **III:** 100, 104, 105, 108, 111, 119–120

American Language, The: Supplement One (Mencken), **III:** 111

American Language, The: Supplement Two (Mencken), **III:** 111

"American Letter" (MacLeish), **III:** 13

"American Liberty" (Freneau), **Supp. II Part 1:** 257

American Literary History (Harrison), **Supp. VIII:** 37

American Mercury, **Supp. XI:** 163, 164

American Mind, The (Commager), **Supp. I Part 2:** 650

American Moderns: From Rebellion to Conformity (Geismar), **Supp. IX:** 15; **Supp. XI:** 223

"American Names" (Benét), **Supp. XI:** 47

American Nature Writers (Elder, ed.), **Supp. IX:** 25

American Nature Writers (Winter), **Supp. X:** 104

American Negro, The (W. H. Thomas), **Supp. II Part 1:** 168

American Notebooks, The (Hawthorne), **II:** 226

American Novel Since World War II, The (Klein, ed.), **Supp. XI:** 233

"American Original, An: Learning from a Literary Master" (Wilkinson), **Supp. VIII:** 164, 165, 168

American Pastoral (P. Roth), **Retro. Supp. II:** 279, 289, **292–293; Supp. XI:** 68

American Places (Porter, Stegner and Stegner), **Supp. IV Part 2:** 599

"American Poet" (Shapiro), **Supp. II Part 2:** 701

"American Poetry" (Simpson), **Supp. IX:** 272

"American Poetry and American Life" (Pinsky), **Supp. VI:** 239–240

American Poetry since 1945: A Critical Survey (Stepanchev), **Supp. XI:** 312

American Poetry since 1960 (Mesic), **Supp. IV Part 1:** 175

American Primer, An (Boorstin), **I:** 253

American Primer, An (Whitman), **IV:** 348

"American Primitive" (W. J. Smith), **Supp. XIII:** 333

American Primitive: Poems (Oliver), **Supp. VII:** 234–237, 238

American Procession, An: The Major American Writers from 1830–1930—-the Crucial Century (Kazin), **Supp. VIII: 105–106,** 108

"American Realist Playwrights, The" (McCarthy), **II:** 562

American Register, or General Repository of History, Politics, and Science, The (Brown, ed.), **Supp. I Part 1:** 146

American Renaissance (Matthiessen), **I:** 259–260; **III:** 310; **Supp. XIII:** 93

"American Rendezvous, An" (Beauvoir), **Supp. IX:** 4

American Scene, The (James), **II:** 336; **III:** 460; **Retro. Supp. I:** 232, 235

American Scenes (Kozlenko, ed.), **IV:** 378

"American Scholar, The" (Emerson), **I:** 239; **II:** 8, 12–13; **Retro. Supp. I:** 62, 74–75, 149, 298; **Retro.**

Supp. II: 155; **Supp. I Part 2:** 420; **Supp. IX:** 227, 271; **Supp. XIV:** 104

"American Soldier, The" (Freneau), **Supp. II Part 1:** 269

American Songbag, The (Sandburg), **III:** 583

"American Student in Paris, An" (Farrell), **II:** 45

"American Sublime, The" (Stevens), **IV:** 74

"American Temperament, The" (Locke), **Supp. XIV:** 211

American Tragedy, An (Dreiser), **I:** 497, 498, 499, 501, 502, 503, 511–515, 517, 518, 519; **III:** 251; **IV:** 35, 484; **Retro. Supp. II:** 93, 95, **104–108**

"American Triptych" (Kenyon), **Supp. VII:** 165

"American Use for German Ideals" (Bourne), **I:** 228

American Village, The (Freneau), **Supp. II Part 1:** 256, 257

"American Village, The" (Freneau), **Supp. II Part 1:** 256

America's Coming-of-Age (Brooks), **I:** 228, 230, 240, 245, 258; **IV:** 427

America's Humor: From Poor Richard to Doonesbury (Blair and Hill), **Retro. Supp. II:** 286

"America's Part in World Peace" (Locke), **Supp. XIV:** 208

America's Rome (Vance), **Supp. IV Part 2:** 684

America Was Promises (MacLeish), **III:** 16, 17

"Amerika" (Snyder), **Supp. VIII:** 301

Ames, Fisher, **Supp. I Part 2:** 486

Ames, Lois, **Supp. I Part 2:** 541, 547

Ames, William, **IV:** 158

Ames Stewart, Beatrice, **Supp. IX:** 200

Amichai, Yehuda, **Supp. XI:** 267

Amidon, Stephen, **Supp. XI:** 333

Amiel, Henri F., **I:** 241, 243, 250

Amis, Kingsley, **IV:** 430; **Supp. IV Part 2:** 688; **Supp. VIII:** 167; **Supp. XIII:** 93

Amis, Martin, **Retro. Supp. I:** 278

Ammons, A. R., **Supp. III Part 2:** 541; **Supp. VII: 23–38; Supp. IX:** 41, 42, 46; **Supp. XII:** 121

Ammons, Elizabeth, **Retro. Supp. I:** 364, 369; **Retro. Supp. II:** 140

"Among Children" (Levine), **Supp. V:** 192

Among My Books (Lowell), **Supp. I Part 2:** 407

"Among School Children" (Yeats), **III:** 249; **Supp. IX:** 52; **Supp. XIV:** 8

"Among the Hills" (Whittier), **Supp. I Part 2:** 703

Among the Isles of Shoals (Thaxter), **Supp. XIII:** 152

"Among Those Present" (Benét), **Supp. XI:** 53

"Amoral Moralist" (White), **Supp. I Part 2:** 648

Amory, Cleveland, **Supp. I Part 1:** 316

Amory, Fred, **Supp. III Part 1:** 2

Amos (biblical book), **II:** 166

Amran, David, **Supp. XIV:** 150

"Am Strand von Tanger" (Salter), **Supp. IX:** 257

"AMTRAK" (Baraka), **Supp. II Part 1:** 60

Amy and Isabelle (Strout), **Supp. X:** 86

Amy Lowell: Portrait of the Poet in Her Time (Gregory), **II:** 512

"Amy Lowell of Brookline, Mass." (Scott), **II:** 512

"Amy Wentworth" (Whittier), **Supp. I Part 2:** 694, 696

Anabase (Perse), **III:** 12

"Anabasis (I)" (Merwin), **Supp. III Part 1:** 342, 346

"Anabasis (II)" (Merwin), **Supp. III Part 1:** 342, 346

Anagrams: A Novel (Moore), **Supp. X:** 163, 164, 167, **169–171,** 172

Analects (Confucius), **Supp. IV Part 1:** 14

Analects, The (Pound, trans.), **III:** 472

Analogy (J. Butler), **II:** 8

"Analysis of a Theme" (Stevens), **IV:** 81

Anarchiad, The, A Poem on the Restoration of Chaos and Substantial Night, in Twenty Four Books (Barlow), **Supp. II Part 1:** 70

Anatomy Lesson, and Other Stories, The (Connell), **Supp. XIV:** 84, 87, 89

"Anatomy Lesson, The" (Connell), **Supp. XIV:** 84, 86, 87

Anatomy Lesson, The (P. Roth), **Retro. Supp. II:** 286, 290; **Supp. III Part 2:** 422–423, 425

Anatomy of Criticism (Frye), **Supp. XIII:** 19; **Supp. XIV:** 15

Anatomy of Melancholy (Burton), **III:** 78

Anatomy of Nonsense, The (Winters), **Supp. II Part 2:** 811, 812

Anaya, Rudolfo A., **Supp. IV Part 2:** 502; **Supp. XIII:** 213, 220

Ancestors (Maxwell), **Supp. VIII:** 152, 168

"Ancestors, The" (Tate), **IV:** 128

Ancestral Voice: Conversations with N. Scott Momaday (Woodard), **Supp. IV Part 2:** 484, 485, 486, 489, 493

"Anchorage" (Harjo), **Supp. XII:** 220–221

Ancient Child, The: A Novel (Momaday), **Supp. IV Part 2:** 488, 489–491, 492, 493

"Ancient Egypt/Fannie Goldbarth" (Goldbarth), **Supp. XII:** 191–192

Ancient Evenings (Mailer), **Retro. Supp. II:** 206, 210, 213

Ancient Law, The (Glasgow), **II:** 179–180, 192

Ancient Musics (Goldbarth), **Supp. XII:** 191–192

"Ancient Semitic Rituals for the Dead" (Goldbarth), **Supp. XII:** 191–192

"Ancient World, The" (Doty), **Supp. XI:** 122

& (And) (Cummings), **I:** 429, 431, 432, 437, 445, 446, 448

Andersen, Hans Christian, **I:** 441; **Supp. I Part 2:** 622

Anderson, Charles R., **Supp. I Part 1:** 356, 360, 368, 371, 372

Anderson, Frances, **I:** 231

Anderson, Guy, **Supp. X:** 264, 265

Anderson, Henry J., **Supp. I Part 1:** 156

Anderson, Irwin M., **I:** 98–99

Anderson, Jon, **Supp. V:** 338

Anderson, Judith, **III:** 399

Anderson, Karl, **I:** 99, 103

Anderson, Margaret, **I:** 103; **III:** 471

Anderson, Margaret Bartlett, **III:** 171

Anderson, Mary Jane. *See* Lanier, Mrs. Robert Sampson (Mary Jane Anderson)

Anderson, Maxwell, **III:** 159

Anderson, Mrs. Irwin M., **I:** 98–99

Anderson, Mrs. Sherwood (Tennessee Mitchell), **I:** 100; **Supp. I Part 2:** 459, 460

Anderson, Quentin, **Retro. Supp. I:** 392

Anderson, Robert, **Supp. I Part 1:** 277; **Supp. V:** 108

Anderson, Sally, **Supp. XIII:** 95

Anderson, Sherwood, **I: 97–120,** 211, 374, 375, 384, 405, 423, 445, 480, 487, 495, 506, 518; **II:** 27, 38, 44, 55, 56, 68, 250–251, 263, 271, 289, 451, 456–457; **III:** 220, 224, 382–383, 453, 483, 545, 576, 579; **IV:** 27, 40, 46, 190, 207, 433, 451, 482; **Retro. Supp. I:** 79, 80, 177; **Supp. I Part 2:** 378, 430, 459, 472, 613; **Supp. IV Part 2:** 502; **Supp. V:** 12,

250; **Supp. VIII:** 39, 152; **Supp. IX:** 14, 309; **Supp. XI:** 159, 164; **Supp. XII:** 343

Anderson, T. J., **Supp. XIII:** 132

Anderssen, A., **III:** 252

"And Hickman Arrives" (Ellison), **Retro. Supp. II:** 118, 126; **Supp. II Part 1:** 248

And in the Hanging Gardens (Aiken), **I:** 63

And I Worked at the Writer's Trade (Cowley), **Supp. II Part 1:** 137, 139, 141, 143, 147, 148

Andorra (Cameron), **Supp. XII:** 79, 81, **88–91**

Andral, Gabriel, **Supp. I Part 1:** 302

Andre, Michael, **Supp. XII:** 117–118, 129, 132, 133–134

Andre's Mother (McNally), **Supp. XIII:** 206

Andress, Ursula, **Supp. XI:** 307

"Andrew Jackson" (Masters), **Supp. I Part 2:** 472

Andrews, Bruce, **Supp. IV Part 2:** 426

Andrews, Roy Chapman, **Supp. X:** 172

Andrews, Tom, **Supp. XI:** 317

Andrews, Wayne, **IV:** 310

Andrews, William L., **Supp. IV Part 1:** 13

Andreyev, Leonid Nikolaevich, **I:** 53; **II:** 425

Andria (Terence), **IV:** 363

"Andromache" (Dubus), **Supp. VII:** 84

"And Summer Will Not Come Again" (Plath), **Retro. Supp. II:** 242

"And That Night Clifford Died" (Levine), **Supp. V:** 195

And the Band Played On (Shilts), **Supp. X:** 145

"And the Moon Be Still as Bright" (Bradbury), **Supp. IV Part 1:** 106

"And the Sea Shall Give up Its Dead" (Wilder), **IV:** 358

And Things That Go Bump in the Night (McNally), **Supp. XIII: 196–197,** 205, 208

"And *Ut Pictura Poesis* Is Her Name" (Ashbery), **Supp. III Part 1:** 19

"Anecdote and Storyteller" (Howe), **Supp. VI:** 127

"Anecdote of the Jar" (Stevens), **IV:** 83–84

"Anemone" (Rukeyser), **Supp. VI:** 281, 285

"Angel, The" (Buck), **Supp. II Part 1:** 127

Angela's Ashes (McCourt), **Supp. XII: 271–279,** 283, 285

"Angel at the Grave, The" (Wharton),

IV: 310; **Retro. Supp. I:** 365

"Angel Butcher" (Levine), **Supp. V:** 181

Angel City (Shepard), **Supp. III Part 2:** 432, 445

"Angel Is My Watermark!, The" (H. Miller), **III:** 180

Angell, Carol, **Supp. I Part 2:** 655

Angell, Katharine Sergeant. *See* White, Katharine

Angell, Roger, **Supp. I Part 2:** 655; **Supp. V:** 22; **Supp. VIII:** 139

Angel Landing (Hoffman), **Supp. X: 82–83**

"Angel Levine" (Malamud), **Supp. I Part 2:** 431, 432, 433–434, 437

Angel of Bethesda, The (Mather), **Supp. II Part 2:** 464

"Angel of the Bridge, The" (Cheever), **Supp. I Part 1:** 186–187

"Angel of the Odd, The" (Poe), **III:** 425

Angelo Herndon Jones (Hughes), **Retro. Supp. I:** 203

"Angel on the Porch, An" (Wolfe), **IV:** 451

Angelou, Maya, **Supp. IV Part 1: 1–19; Supp. XI:** 20, 245; **Supp. XIII:** 185

"Angel Poem, The" (Stern), **Supp. IX:** 292

Angels and Earthly Creatures (Wylie), **Supp. I Part 2:** 709, 713, 724–730

Angels in America: A Gay Fantasia on National Themes (Kushner), **Supp. IX:** 131, 134, **141–146**

"Angels of the Love Affair" (Sexton), **Supp. II Part 2:** 692

"Angel Surrounded by Paysans" (Stevens), **IV:** 93

Angel That Troubled the Waters, The (Wilder), **IV:** 356, 357–358

"Anger" (Creeley), **Supp. IV Part 1:** 150–152

Anger (Sarton), **Supp. VIII: 256**

"Anger against Children" (Bly), **Supp. IV Part 1:** 73

Angle of Ascent (Hayden), **Supp. II Part 1:** 363, 367, 370

"Angle of Geese" (Momaday), **Supp. IV Part 2:** 485

Angle of Geese and Other Poems (Momaday), **Supp. IV Part 2:** 487, 491

Angle of Repose (Stegner), **Supp. IV Part 2:** 599, 605, 606, 610–611

"*Angle of Repose* and the Writings of Mary Hallock Foote: A Source Study" (Williams-Walsh), **Supp. IV Part 2:** 611

Anglo-Saxon Century, The (Dos Passos), **I:** 474–475, 483
Angoff, Charles, **III:** 107
"Angola Question Mark" (Hughes), **Supp. I Part 1:** 344
Angry Wife, The (Sedges), **Supp. II Part 1:** 125
"Angry Women Are Building: Issues and Struggles Facing American Indian Women Today" (Gunn Allen), **Supp. IV Part 1:** 324
"Animal, Vegetable, and Mineral" (Bogan), **Supp. III Part 1:** 66
"Animal Acts" (Simic), **Supp. VIII:** 278
Animal and Vegetable Physiology Considered with Reference to Natural Theology (Roget), **Supp. I Part 1:** 312
Animal Dreams (Kingsolver), **Supp. VII:** 199, 204–207
"Animals, The" (Merwin), **Supp. III Part 1:** 348
"Animals Are Passing from Our Lives" (Levine), **Supp. V:** 181, 182
Animals in That Country, The (Atwood), **Supp. XIII:** 20, 33
Animals of the Soul: Sacred Animals of the Oglala Sioux (Brown), **Supp. IV Part 2:** 487
"Animula" (Eliot), **Retro. Supp. I:** 64
Ankor Wat (Ginsberg), **Supp. II Part 1:** 323
"Annabelle" (Komunyakaa), **Supp. XIII:** 117
"Annabel Lee" (Poe), **Retro. Supp. I:** 273; **Retro. Supp. II:** 266
Anna Christie (O'Neill), **III:** 386, 389, 390
Anna Karenina (Tolstoy), **I:** 10; **II:** 290; **Retro. Supp. I:** 225; **Supp. V:** 323
"Anna Karenina" (Trilling), **Supp. III Part 2:** 508
"Anna Who Was Mad" (Sexton), **Supp. II Part 2:** 692
"Ann Burlak" (Rukeyser), **Supp. VI:** 280
"Anne" (Oliver), **Supp. VII:** 232
"Anne at the Symphony" (Shields), **Supp. VII:** 310
"Anne Bradstreet's Poetic Voices" (Requa), **Supp. I Part 1:** 107
Anne Sexton: The Artist and Her Critics (McClatchy), **Supp. XII:** 253
"Ann from the Street" (Dixon), **Supp. XII:** 146–147
"Ann Garner" (Agee), **I:** 27
"Anniad, The" (Brooks), **Supp. III Part 1:** 77, 78

Annie (musical), **Supp. IV Part 2:** 577
Annie Allen (Brooks), **Supp. III Part 1:** 76–79
Annie Dillard Reader, The (Dillard), **Supp. VI:** 23
Annie Hall (film), **Supp. IV Part 1:** 205
Annie John (Kincaid), **Supp. VII:** 184–186, 193
Annie Kilburn, a Novel (Howells), **II:** 275, 286, 287
Anniversary (Shields), **Supp. VII:** 320, 322, 323, 324
"Annunciation, The" (Le Sueur), **Supp. V:** 130
Ann Vickers (Lewis), **II:** 453
"A No-Account Creole, A" (Chopin), **Retro. Supp. II:** 64
"Anodyne" (Komunyakaa), **Supp. XIII:** 130
Another America/Otra America (Kingsolver), **Supp. VII:** 207–209
"Another Animal" (Swenson), **Supp. IV Part 2:** 639
Another Animal: Poems (Swenson), **Supp. IV Part 2:** 639–641, 649
Another Antigone (Gurney), **Supp. V:** 97, 98, 100, 101, 102, 105
"Another August" (Merrill), **Supp. III Part 1:** 326
"Another Beer" (Matthews), **Supp. IX:** 158
Another Country (Baldwin), **Retro. Supp. II:** 9–11, 14; **Supp. I Part 1:** 51, 52, 56–58, 63, 67, 337; **Supp. II Part 1:** 40; **Supp. VIII:** 349
"Another Language" (Jong), **Supp. V:** 131
Another Mother Tongue: Gay Words, Gay Worlds (Grahn), **Supp. IV Part 1:** 330
"Another Night in the Ruins" (Kinnell), **Supp. III Part 1:** 239, 251
"Another Old Woman" (W. C. Williams), **Retro. Supp. I:** 423
Another Part of the Forest (Hellman), **Supp. I Part 1:** 282–283, 297
Another Republic: 17 European and South American Writers (Strand, trans.), **Supp. IV Part 2:** 630
Another Roadside Attraction (Robbins), **Supp. X:** 259, 261, 262, 263, 264, 265–266, **267–269,** 274, 275, 277, 284
"Another Spring Uncovered" (Swenson), **Supp. IV Part 2:** 644
Another Thin Man (film), **Supp. IV Part 1:** 355
Another Time (Auden), **Supp. II Part 1:** 15

Another Turn of the Crank (Berry), **Supp. X:** 25, 35
"Another upon the Same" (Taylor), **IV:** 161
"Another Voice" (Wilbur), **Supp. III Part 2:** 557
"Another Wife" (Anderson), **I:** 114
Another You (Beattie), **Supp. V:** 29, 31, 33–34
Anouilh, Jean, **Supp. I Part 1:** 286–288, 297
Ansky, S., **IV:** 6
Ansky, Shloime, **Supp. IX:** 131, 138
"Answer, The" (Jeffers), **Supp. III Part 2:** 423
Answered Prayers: The Unfinished Novel (Capote), **Supp. III Part 1:** 113, 125, 131–132
"Answering the Deer: Genocide and Continuance in the Poetry of American Indian Women" (Gunn Allen), **Supp. IV Part 1:** 322, 325
"Answer of Minerva, The: Pacifism and Resistance in Simone Weil" (Merton), **Supp. VIII:** 204
Antaeus (Wolfe), **IV:** 461
"Ante-Bellum Sermon, An" (Dunbar), **Supp. II Part 1:** 203–204
Antheil, George, **III:** 471, 472; **IV:** 404
Anthem (Rand), **Supp. IV Part 2:** 523
Anthology of Holocaust Literature (Glatstein, Knox, and Margoshes, eds.), **Supp. X:** 70
Anthology of Twentieth-Century Brazilian Poetry, An (Bishop and Brasil, eds.), **Retro. Supp. II:** 50; **Supp. I Part 1:** 94
Anthon, Kate, **I:** 452
Anthony, Saint, **III:** 395
Anthony, Susan B., **Supp. XI:** 200
"Anthropologist as Hero, The" (Sontag), **Supp. III Part 2:** 451
"Anthropology of Water, The" (Carson), **Supp. XII: 102–103**
Anthropos: The Future of Art (Cummings), **I:** 430
Antichrist (Nietzsche), **III:** 176
"Anti-Father" (Dove), **Supp. IV Part 1:** 246
"Anti-Feminist Woman, The" (Rich), **Supp. I Part 2:** 550
Antigone (Sophocles), **Supp. I Part 1:** 284; **Supp. X:** 249
Antin, David, **Supp. VIII:** 292; **Supp. XII:** 2, 8
Antin, Mary, **Supp. IX:** 227
Anti-Oedipus: Capitalism and Schizophrenia (Deleuze and Guattari), **Supp. XII:** 4

Antiphon, The (Barnes), **Supp. III Part 1:** 43–44

"Antiquities" (Mather), **Supp. II Part 2:** 452

"Antiquity of Freedom, The" (Bryant), **Supp. I Part 1:** 168

"Antislavery Tocsin, An" (Douglass), **Supp. III Part 1:** 171

Antoine, Andre, **III:** 387

Antonioni, Michelangelo, **Supp. IV Part 1:** 46, 47, 48

Antony and Cleopatra (Shakespeare), **I:** 285

"Antony on Behalf of the Play" (Burke), **I:** 284

"An trentiesme de mon Eage, L'" (MacLeish), **III:** 9

"Ants" (Bly), **Supp. IV Part 1:** 71

Anxiety of Influence, The (Bloom), **Supp. XIII:** 46

"Any Object" (Swenson), **Supp. IV Part 2:** 640

"Any Porch" (Parker), **Supp. IX:** 194

"Anywhere Out of This World" (Baudelaire), **II:** 552

Any Woman's Blues (Jong), **Supp. V:** 115, 123, 126

Anzaldúa, Gloria, **Supp. IV Part 1:** 330; **Supp. XIII:** 223

"Aphorisms on Society" (Stevens), **Retro. Supp. I:** 303

Apollinaire, Guillaume, **I:** 432; **II:** 529; **III:** 196; **IV:** 80; **Retro. Supp. II:** 326

Apologies to the Iroquois (Wilson), **IV:** 429

"Apology, An" (Malamud), **Supp. I Part 2:** 435, 437

"Apology for Bad Dreams" (Jeffers), **Supp. II Part 2:** 427, 438

"Apology for Crudity, An" (Anderson), **I:** 109

Apology for Poetry (Sidney), **Supp. II Part 1:** 105

"Apostle of the Tules, An" (Harte), **Supp. II Part 1:** 356

"Apostrophe to a Dead Friend" (Kumin), **Supp. IV Part 2:** 442, 451, 452

"Apostrophe to a Pram Rider" (White), **Supp. I Part 2:** 678

"Apostrophe to Man (on reflecting that the world is ready to go to war again)" (Millay), **III:** 127

"Apostrophe to Vincentine, The" (Stevens), **IV:** 90

"Apotheosis" (Kingsolver), **Supp. VII:** 208

"Apotheosis of Martin Luther King, The" (Hardwick), **Supp. III Part 1:** 203–204

Appalachia (Wright), **Supp. V:** 333, 345

"Appalachian Book of the Dead III" (Wright), **Supp. V:** 345

"Appeal to Progressives, An" (Wilson), **IV:** 429

Appeal to Reason (Paine), **I:** 490

Appeal to the World, An (Du Bois), **Supp. II Part 1:** 184

Appearance and Reality (Bradley), **I:** 572

"Appendix to 'The Anniad'" (Brooks), **Supp. III Part 1:** 77

Apple, Max, **Supp. VIII:** 14

"Apple, The" (Kinnell), **Supp. III Part 1:** 250

Applegarth, Mabel, **II:** 465, 478

"Apple of Discord, The" (Humphrey), **Supp. IX:** 109

"Apple Peeler" (Francis), **Supp. IX:** 82

Appleseed, Johnny (pseudonym). *See* Chapman, John (Johnny Appleseed)

Appleton, Nathan, **II:** 488

Appleton, Thomas Gold, **Supp. I Part 1:** 306; **Supp. I Part 2:** 415

"Apple Tree, The" (McCarriston), **Supp. XIV:** 263, 268

"Applicant, The" (Plath), **Retro. Supp. II:** 252; **Supp. I Part 2:** 535, 544, 545

"Applications of the Doctrine" (Hass), **Supp. VI:** 100–101

Appointment, The (film), **Supp. IX:** 253

Appointment in Samarra (O'Hara), **III:** 361, 363–364, 365–367, 371, 374, 375, 383

Appreciation of Sarah Orne Jewett (Cary), **Retro. Supp. II:** 132

"Approaches, The" (Merwin), **Supp. III Part 1:** 350

"Approaching Artaud" (Sontag), **Supp. III Part 2:** 470–471

"Approaching Prayer" (Dickey), **Supp. IV Part 1:** 175

Approach to Literature, An: A Collection of Prose and Verse with Analyses and Discussions (Brooks, Warren, and Purser), **Supp. XIV:** 4

"Approach to Thebes, The" (Kunitz), **Supp. III Part 1:** 265–267

Approach to Vedanta, An (Isherwood), **Supp. XIV:** 157, 163, 164

"Après-midi d'un faune, L'" (Mallarmé), **III:** 8

"April" (Winters), **Supp. II Part 2:** 788

"April" (W. C. Williams), **Retro. Supp. I:** 422

April Galleons (Ashbery), **Supp. III Part 1:** 26

"April Galleons" (Ashbery), **Supp. III Part 1:** 26

April Hopes (Howells), **II:** 285, 289

"April Lovers" (Ransom), **III:** 489–490

"April Showers" (Wharton), **Retro. Supp. I:** 361

"April Today Main Street" (Olson), **Supp. II Part 2:** 581

April Twilights (Cather), **I:** 313; **Retro. Supp. I:** 5

"Apt Pupil" (King), **Supp. V:** 152

Arabian Nights, **I:** 204; **II:** 8; **Supp. I Part 2:** 584, 599; **Supp. IV Part 1:** 1

"Arabic Coffee" (Nye), **Supp. XIII:** 276

"Araby" (Joyce), **I:** 174; **Supp. VIII:** 15

Aragon, Louis, **I:** 429; **III:** 471; **Retro. Supp. II:** 85, 321

Arana-Ward, Marie, **Supp. VIII:** 84

Ararat (Glück), **Supp. V:** 79, 86–87

Arbre du voyageur, L' (W. J. Smith; Haussmann, trans.), **Supp. XIII:** 347

Arbus, Diane, **Supp. XII:** 188

Arbuthnott, John (pseudonym). *See* Henry, O.

Archaeologist of Morning (Olson), **Supp. II Part 2:** 557

"Archaic Maker, The" (Merwin), **Supp. III Part 1:** 357

Archer (television show), **Supp. IV Part 2:** 474

Archer, William, **IV:** 131; **Retro. Supp. I:** 228

Archer at Large (Macdonald), **Supp. IV Part 2:** 473

Archer in Hollywood (Macdonald), **Supp. IV Part 2:** 474

"Archetype and Signature: The Relationship of Poet and Poem" (Fiedler), **Supp. XIII:** 101

"Archibald Higbie" (Masters), **Supp. I Part 2:** 461

"Architect, The" (Bourne), **I:** 223

Arctic Dreams (Lopez), **Supp. V:** 211

Arctic Refuge: A Circle of Testimony (Haines), **Supp. XII:** 205

"Arcturus" (Connell), **Supp. XIV:** 88

Arendt, Hannah, **II:** 544; **Retro. Supp. I:** 87; **Retro. Supp. II:** 28, 117; **Supp. I Part 2:** 570; **Supp. IV Part 1:** 386; **Supp. VIII:** 98, 99, 100, 243; **Supp. XII:** 166–167

Arensberg, Walter, **IV:** 408; **Retro. Supp. I:** 416

Aren't You Happy for Me? (Bausch), **Supp. VII:** 42, 51, 54

Areopagitica (Milton), **Supp. I Part 2:** 422

"Are You a Doctor?" (Carver), **Supp. III Part 1:** 139–141

"Are You Mr. William Stafford?" (Stafford), **Supp. XI:** 317

"Argonauts of 49, California's Golden Age" (Harte), **Supp. II Part 1:** 353, 355

Aria da Capo (Millay), **III:** 137–138

Ariel (Plath), **Retro. Supp. II:** 250–255; **Supp. I Part 2:** 526, 539, 541; **Supp. V:** 79

"Ariel" (Plath), **Supp. I Part 2:** 542, 546

"Ariel Poems" (Eliot), **I:** 579

Arise, Arise (Zukofsky), **Supp. III Part 2:** 619, 629

Aristides. See Epstein, Joseph

"Aristocracy" (Emerson), **II:** 6

Aristocracy and Justice (More), **I:** 223

Aristophanes, **I:** 436; **II:** 577; **Supp. I Part 2:** 406

Aristotle, **I:** 58, 265, 280, 527; **II:** 9, 12, 198, 536; **III:** 20, 115, 145, 157, 362, 422, 423; **IV:** 10, 18, 74–75, 89; **Supp. I Part 1:** 104, 296; **Supp. I Part 2:** 423; **Supp. IV Part 1:** 391; **Supp. IV Part 2:** 526, 530; **Supp. X:** 78; **Supp. XI:** 249; **Supp. XII:** 106; **Supp. XIV:** 242–243

Aristotle Contemplating the Bust of Homer (Rembrandt), **Supp. IV Part 1:** 390, 391

"Arkansas Traveller" (Wright), **Supp. V:** 334

"Armadillo, The" (Bishop), **Supp. I Part 1:** 93

Armadillo in the Grass (Hearon), **Supp. VIII:** 58–59

"Armageddon" (Ransom), **III:** 489, 492

Armah, Aiy Kwei, **Supp. IV Part 1:** 373

Armies of the Night, The (Mailer), **III:** 39–40, 41, 42, 44, 45, 46; **Retro. Supp. II:** 205, 206–207, 208; **Supp. IV Part 1:** 207; **Supp. XIV:** 49, 162

"Arm in Arm" (Simpson), **Supp. IX:** 267–268

Arminius, Jacobus, **I:** 557

Armitage, Shelley, **Supp. IV Part 2:** 439

Arm of Flesh, The (Salter), **Supp. IX:** 251

"Armor" (Dickey), **Supp. IV Part 1:** 179

Armored Attack (film), **Supp. I Part 1:** 281

Arms, George W., **Supp. I Part 2:** 416–417

Armstrong, George, **Supp. I Part 2:** 386

Armstrong, Louis, **Retro. Supp. II:** 114

"Army" (Corso), **Supp. XII:** 117, 127

Army Brat (W. J. Smith), **Supp. XIII:** 331, 347

Arna Bontemps Langston Hughes: Letters 1925–1967 (Nichols), **Retro. Supp. I:** 194

Arner, Robert D., **Retro. Supp. II:** 62

Arnold, Edwin T., **Supp. VIII:** 189

Arnold, George W., **Supp. I Part 2:** 411

Arnold, Marilyn, **Supp. IV Part 1:** 220

Arnold, Matthew, **I:** 222, 228, 275; **II:** 20, 110, 338, 541; **III:** 604; **IV:** 349; **Retro. Supp. I:** 56, 325; **Supp. I Part 2:** 416, 417, 419, 529, 552, 602; **Supp. IX:** 298; **Supp. XIV:** 11, 335

Arnold, Thurman, **Supp. I Part 2:** 645

Aronson, Steven M. L., **Supp. V:** 4

Around about America (Caldwell), **I:** 290

"Arrangement in Black and White" (Parker), **Supp. IX:** 198

"Arrival at Santos" (Bishop), **Retro. Supp. II:** 46; **Supp. IX:** 45–46

"Arrival of the Bee Box, The" (Plath), **Retro. Supp. II:** 255

Arrivistes, The: Poem 1940–1949 (Simpson), **Supp. IX:** 265, **267–268**

"Arrow" (Dove), **Supp. IV Part 1:** 250

Arrowsmith (Lewis), **I:** 362; **II:** 445–446, 449

"Arsenal at Springfield, The" (Longfellow), **Retro. Supp. II:** 168

"Arson Plus" (Hammett), **Supp. IV Part 1:** 343

"Ars Poetica" (Dove), **Supp. IV Part 1:** 250

"Ars Poetica" (Dunn), **Supp. XI:** 154

"Ars Poetica" (MacLeish), **III:** 9–10

"*Ars Poetica:* A Found Poem" (Kumin), **Supp. IV Part 2:** 455

"Ars Poetica; or, Who Lives in the Ivory Tower" (McGrath), **Supp. X:** 117

"Ars Poetica: Some Recent Criticism" (Wright), **Supp. III Part 2:** 603

"Art" (Emerson), **II:** 13

"Art and Neurosis" (Trilling), **Supp. III Part 2:** 502

Art and Technics (Mumford), **Supp. II Part 2:** 483

Art & Ardor: Essays (Ozick), **Supp. V:** 258, 272

Art as Experience (Dewey), **I:** 266

Art by Subtraction (Reid), **IV:** 41

Art de toucher le clavecin, L' (Couperin), **III:** 464

Artemis to Actaeon and Other Verse (Wharton), **Retro. Supp. I:** 372

Arte of English Poesie (Puttenham), **Supp. I Part 1:** 113

Arthur, Anthony, **Supp. IV Part 2:** 606

Arthur Mervyn; or, Memoirs of the Year 1793 (Brown), **Supp. I Part 1:** 137–140, 144

Articulation of Sound Forms in Time (Howe), **Supp. IV Part 2:** 419, 431–433

"Artificial Nigger, The" (O'Connor), **III:** 343, 351, 356, 358; **Retro. Supp. II:** 229, 232

Artist, The: A Drama without Words (Mencken), **III:** 104

"Artist of the Beautiful, The" (Hawthorne), **Retro. Supp. I:** 149

Artistry of Grief (Torsney), **Retro. Supp. I:** 224

"Artists' and Models' Ball, The" (Brooks), **Supp. III Part 1:** 72

"Art of Disappearing, The" (Nye), **Supp. XIII:** 287

Art of Fiction, The (Gardner), **Supp. VI:** 73

"Art of Fiction, The" (H. James), **Retro. Supp. I:** 226; **Retro. Supp. II:** 223

Art of Hunger, The (Auster), **Supp. XII:** 22

"Art of Keeping Your Mouth Shut, The" (Heller), **Supp. IV Part 1:** 383

"Art of Literature and Commonsense, The" (Nabokov), **Retro. Supp. I:** 271

Art of Living and Other Stories, The (Gardner), **Supp. VI:** 72

"Art of Poetry, The" (McClatchy), **Supp. XII:** 262

"Art of Romare Bearden, The" (Ellison), **Retro. Supp. II:** 123

"Art of Storytelling, The" (Simpson), **Supp. IX:** 277

Art of Sylvia Plath, The (Newman), **Supp. I Part 2:** 527

Art of the Moving Picture, The (Lindsay), **Supp. I Part 2:** 376, 391–392, 394

Art of the Novel (H. James), **Retro. Supp. I:** 227

"Art of Theodore Dreiser, The"

(Bourne), **I:** 235

Art of the Personal Essay, The (Lopate), **Supp. XIII:** 280–281

Art of the Self, The: Essays a Propos "Steps" (Kosinski), **Supp. VII:** 222

Arts and Sciences (Goldbarth), **Supp. XII: 184–186**

"Art's Bread and Butter" (Benét), **Retro. Supp. I:** 108

Arvin, Newton, **I:** 259; **II:** 508; **Retro. Supp. I:** 19, 137

Asali, Muna, **Supp. XIII:** 121, 126

Asbury, Herbert, **Supp. IV Part 1:** 353

Ascent of F6, The (Auden), **Supp. II Part 1:** 11, 13

Ascent to Truth, The (Merton), **Supp. VIII:** 208

Asch, Sholem, **IV:** 1, 9, 11, 14; **Retro. Supp. II:** 299

Ascherson, Neal, **Supp. XII:** 167

As Does New Hampshire and Other Poems (Sarton), **Supp. VIII:** 259

"As Evening Lays Dying" (Salinas), **Supp. XIII:** 319

"As Flowers Are" (Kunitz), **Supp. III Part 1:** 265

Ashbery, John, **Retro. Supp. I:** 313; **Supp. I Part 1:** 96; **Supp. III Part 1: 1–29; Supp. III Part 2:** 541; **Supp. IV Part 2:** 620; **Supp. VIII:** 272; **Supp. IX:** 52; **Supp. XI:** 139; **Supp. XIII:** 85

"Ashes" (Levine), **Supp. V:** 188

Ashes: Poems Old and New (Levine), **Supp. V:** 178, 188–189

"Ashes of the Beacon" (Bierce), **I:** 209

Ashford, Margaret Mary (Daisy), **II:** 426

Ash Wednesday (Eliot), **I:** 570, 574–575, 578–579, 580, 582, 584, 585; **Retro. Supp. I:** 64

"Ash Wednesday" (Eliot), **Supp. IV Part 2:** 436

"Ash Wednesday" (Garrett), **Supp. VII:** 109–110

"Ash Wednesday" (Merton), **Supp. VIII:** 199

Asian American Authors (Hsu and Palubinskas, eds.), **Supp. X:** 292

Asian American Heritage: An Anthology of Prose and Poetry (Wand), **Supp. X:** 292

Asian Figures (Mervin), **Supp. III Part 1:** 341

Asian Journal of Thomas Merton, The (Merton), **Supp. VIII:** 196, 206, 208

"Asian Peace Offers Rejected without Publication" (Bly), **Supp. IV Part 1:** 61

"Asides on the Oboe" (Stevens), **Retro.**

Supp. I: 305

"As I Ebb'd with the Ocean of Life" (Whitman), **IV:** 342, 345–346; **Retro. Supp. I:** 404, 405

As I Lay Dying (Faulkner), **II:** 60–61, 69, 73, 74; **IV:** 100; **Retro. Supp. I:** 75, 82, 84, 85, 86, 88, 89, 91, 92; **Supp. IV Part 1:** 47; **Supp. VIII:** 37, 178; **Supp. IX:** 99, 103, 251; **Supp. XIV:** 24

"As I Lay with My Head in Your Lap, Camerado" (Whitman), **IV:** 347

Asimov, Isaac, **Supp. IV Part 1:** 116

Asinof, Eliot, **II:** 424

"As Is the Daughter, So Is Her Mother" (Patchett), **Supp. XII:** 310

"As It Was in the Beginning" (Benét), **Supp. XI:** 56

"As I Walked Out One Evening" (Auden), **Supp. II Part 1:** 13

"As I Went Down by Havre de Grace" (Wylie), **Supp. I Part 2:** 723

"Ask Me" (Stafford), **Supp. XI:** 326–327

Ask Me Tomorrow (Cozzens), **I:** 365–367, 379

Ask the Dust (Fante), **Supp. XI:** 159, 160, 166, **167–169,** 172, 173, 174

Ask Your Mama (Hughes), **Supp. I Part 1:** 339, 341–342

Ask Your Mama: 12 Moods for Jazz (Hughes), **Retro. Supp. I:** 210, 211

As Little Children (R. P. Smith), **Supp. XIV:** 333

"As One Put Drunk into the Packet Boat" (Ashbery), **Supp. III Part 1:** 18

Aspects of the Novel (Forster), **Retro. Supp. I:** 232; **Supp. VIII:** 155

"Aspen and the Stream, The" (Wilbur), **Supp. III Part 2:** 555, 556

Aspern Papers, The (James), **Supp. V:** 101, 102

"Aspern Papers, The" (James), **Retro. Supp. I:** 219, 227, 228

Asphalt Jungle (film, Huston), **Supp. XIII:** 174

"Asphodel" (Welty), **IV:** 265, 271

"Asphodel, That Greeny Flower" (W. C. Williams), **Retro. Supp. I:** 429

"Aspic and Buttermilk" (Olds), **Supp. X:** 213

Asquith, Herbert Henry, **Retro. Supp. I:** 59

"Ass" (Cisneros), **Supp. VII:** 67

Assante, Armand, **Supp. VIII:** 74

Assassins, The (Oates), **Supp. II Part 2:** 512, 517–519

"Assault" (Millay), **III:** 130–131

"Assemblage of Husbands and Wives,

An" (Lewis), **II:** 455–456

Assembly (O'Hara), **III:** 361

Assignment, Wildlife (LaBastille), **Supp. X: 99,** 104

Assistant, The (Malamud), **Supp. I Part 2:** 427, 428, 429, 431, 435, 441–445, 451

Assommoir, L' (Zola), **II:** 291; **III:** 318

Assorted Prose (Updike), **IV:** 215–216, 218; **Retro. Supp. I:** 317, 319, 327

Astor, Mary, **Supp. IV Part 1:** 356; **Supp. XII:** 173

Astoria, or, Anecdotes of an Enterprise beyond the Rocky Mountains (Irving), **II:** 312

"Astounding News by Electric Express via Norfolk! The Atlantic Crossed in Three Days Signal Triumph of Mr. Monck's Flying-Machine . . ." (Poe), **III:** 413, 420

Astraea (Holmes), **III:** 82

Astro, Richard, **Supp. I Part 2:** 429, 445

"Astrological Fricassee" (H. Miller), **III:** 187

Astrophil and Stella (Sidney), **Supp. XIV:** 128

"As Weary Pilgrim" (Bradstreet), **Supp. I Part 1:** 103, 109, 122

As We Know (Ashbery), **Supp. III Part 1:** 9, 21–25

"As We Know" (Ashbery), **Supp. III Part 1:** 21–22

Aswell, Edward C., **IV:** 458, 459, 461

"As You Like It" (Chopin), **Supp. I Part 1:** 217

As You Like It (Shakespeare), **Supp. I Part 1:** 308

"At a Bar in Charlotte Amalie" (Updike), **IV:** 214

"At a Lecture" (Brodsky), **Supp. VIII:** 33

"At a March against the Vietnam War" (Bly), **Supp. IV Part 1:** 61

"At a Reading" (McClatchy), **Supp. XII:** 256–257

"At avism of John Tom Little Bear, The" (O. Henry), **Supp. II Part 1:** 410

"At Chênière Caminada" (Chopin), **Supp. I Part 1:** 220

"At Chinese Checkers" (Berryman), **I:** 182

Atchity, Kenneth John, **Supp. XI:** 227

At Eighty-Two (Sarton), **Supp. VIII:** 264

"At Every Gas Station There Are Mechanics" (Dunn), **Supp. XI:** 144

At Fault (Chopin), **Retro. Supp. II:** 57, 60, **62–63; Supp. I Part 1:** 207,

209–211, 220

At Heaven's Gate (Warren), **IV:** 243, 247–248, 251

Atheism Refuted: in a Discourse to Prove the Existence of God (Paine), **Supp. I Part 2:** 517

"Athénaïse" (Chopin), **Retro. Supp. II:** 66, 67; **Supp. I Part 1:** 219–220

Atherton, Gertrude, **I:** 199, 207–208

Athey, Jean L., **Supp. XI:** 184

At Home: Essays, 1982–1988 (Vidal), **Supp. IV Part 2:** 682, 687, 688

"At Kino Viejo, Mexico" (Ríos), **Supp. IV Part 2:** 541

Atkinson, Brooks, **IV:** 288; **Supp. IV Part 2:** 683

Atlantis (Doty), **Supp. XI:** 121, **126–129**

"Atlantis" (Doty), **Supp. XI:** 127–128

Atlas, James, **Supp. V:** 233

Atlas Shrugged (Rand), **Supp. IV Part 2:** 517, 521, 523, 524–526, 528, 531

At Liberty (T. Williams), **IV:** 378

"At Melville's Tomb" (H. Crane), **I:** 393; **Retro. Supp. II:** 76, 78, 80, 82

"At Mother Teresa's" (Nye), **Supp. XIII:** 276

At Night the Salmon Move (Carver), **Supp. III Part 1:** 142

"At North Farm" (Ashbery), **Supp. III Part 1:** 1–2

At Paradise Gate (Smiley), **Supp. VI:** 292, **293–294**

"At Paso Rojo" (Bowles), **Supp. IV Part 1:** 87

At Play in the Fields of the Lord (Matthiessen), **Supp. V:** 199, 202, 204–206, 212

"At Pleasure By" (Pinsky), **Supp. VI:** 245

At Risk (Hoffman), **Supp. X:** 87

"At Sea" (Hemingway), **II:** 258

"At Shaft 11" (Dunbar), **Supp. II Part 1:** 212

"At Slim's River" (Haines), **Supp. XII:** 208–209

"At St. Croix" (Dubus), **Supp. VII:** 83, 87

At Sundown (Whittier), **Supp. I Part 2:** 704

"At Sunset" (Simic), **Supp. VIII:** 282

Attebery, Brian, **Supp. IV Part 1:** 101

"At That Time, or The History of a Joke" (Paley), **Supp. VI:** 229–230

At the Back of the North Wind (Macdonald), **Supp. XIII:** 75

"At the Birth of an Age" (Jeffers), **Supp. II Part 2:** 432

"At the Bomb Testing Site" (Stafford), **Supp. XI:** 317–318, 321, 323

At the Bottom of the River (Kincaid), **Supp. VII:** 182–184, 185

"At the 'Cadian Ball" (Chopin), **Retro. Supp. II:** 64, 65, 68

"At the Chelton-Pulver Game" (Auchincloss), **Supp. IV Part 1:** 27

"At the Drugstore" (Taylor), **Supp. V:** 323

At the Edge of the Body (Jong), **Supp. V:** 115, 130

At the End of the Open Road (Simpson), **Supp. IX:** 265, 269, **271–273,** 277

At the End of This Summer: Poems 1948–1954, **Supp. XII:** 211

"At the End of War" (Eberhart), **I:** 522–523

"At the Executed Murderer's Grave" (Wright), **Supp. III Part 2:** 595, 597

"At the Fishhouses" (Bishop), **Retro. Supp. II:** 45; **Supp. I Part 1:** 90, 92

"At the Grave of My Guardian Angel: St. Louis Cemetery, New Orleans" (Levis), **Supp. XI:** 268–269

"At the Gym" (Doty), **Supp. XI:** 135

"At the Indian Store" (McCarriston), **Supp. XIV:** 271

"At the Lake" (Oliver), **Supp. VII:** 244

"At the Landing" (Welty), **IV:** 265–266; **Retro. Supp. I:** 348

At the Root of Stars (Barnes), **Supp. III Part 1:** 34

"At the Slackening of the Tide" (Wright), **Supp. III Part 2:** 597

"At the Tomb of Walt Whitman" (Kunitz), **Supp. III Part 1:** 262

"At the Tourist Centre in Boston" (Atwood), **Supp. XIII:** 33

"At the Town Dump" (Kenyon), **Supp. VII:** 167

"At the Worcester Museum" (Pinsky), **Supp. VI:** 251

"Atticus Finch and the Mad Dog: Harper Lee's *To Kill a Mockingbird*" (Jones), **Supp. VIII:** 128

"Atticus Finch—Right and Wrong" (Freedman), **Supp. VIII:** 127–128

"Attic Which Is Desire, The" (W. C. Williams), **Retro. Supp. I:** 422

"At Times in Flight: A Parable" (H. Roth), **Supp. IX:** 234

Attitudes toward History (Burke), **I:** 274

"At White River" (Haines), **Supp. XII:** 208–209

Atwood, Margaret, **Supp. IV Part 1:** 252; **Supp. V:** 119; **Supp. XI:** 317; **Supp. XIII: 19–39,** 291, 306

"Atwood's Gorgon Touch" (Davey), **Supp. XIII:** 33

"Aubade" (McCarriston), **Supp. XIV:** 271

"Aubade: November" (McCarriston), **Supp. XIV:** 261–262

"Aubade: Opal and Silver" (Doty), **Supp. XI:** 129

"Au Bal Musette" (Van Vechten), **Supp. II Part 2:** 735

Auchincloss, Hugh D., **Supp. IV Part 2:** 679

Auchincloss, Louis, **I:** 375; **III:** 66; **Retro. Supp. I:** 370, 373; **Supp. IV Part 1: 21–38**

"Auction" (Simic), **Supp. VIII:** 278

"Auction, The" (Crane), **I:** 411

"Auction Model 1934" (Z. Fitzgerald), **Supp. IX:** 61

Auden, W. H., **I:** 71, 381, 539; **II:** 367, 368, 371, 376, 586; **III:** 17, 134, 269, 271, 292, 476–477, 504, 527, 530, 542, 615; **IV:** 136, 138, 240, 430; **Retro. Supp. I:** 430; **Retro. Supp. II:** 183, 242, 244, 323; **Supp. I Part 1:** 270; **Supp. I Part 2:** 552, 610; **Supp. II Part 1: 1–28; Supp. III Part 1:** 2, 3, 14, 26, 60, 61, 64, 341; **Supp. III Part 2:** 591, 595; **Supp. IV Part 1:** 79, 84, 136, 225, 302, 313; **Supp. IV Part 2:** 440, 465; **Supp. V:** 337; **Supp. VIII:** 19, 21, 22, 23, 30, 32, 155, 190; **Supp. IX:** 94, 287, 288; **Supp. X:** 35, 57, 59, 115–116, 117, 118–119; **Supp. XI:** 243, 244; **Supp. XII:** 253, 264–265, 266, 269–270; **Supp. XIV:** 156, 158, 160, 162, 163

"Auden's OED" (McClatchy), **Supp. XII:** 264–265

"Audition" (Alvarez), **Supp. VII:** 10

Audubon, John James, **III:** 210; **IV:** 265; **Supp. IX:** 171

Auer, Jane. *See* Bowles, Jane

Auerbach, Eric, **III:** 453

Auerbach, Nina, **Supp. I Part 1:** 40

"August" (Oliver), **Supp. VII:** 235

"August" (Rich), **Supp. I Part 2:** 564

"August 1968" (Auden), **Supp. II Part 1:** 25

"August Darks, The" (Clampitt), **Supp. IX:** 43, **50–51,** 52

Augustine, Saint, **I:** 279, 290; **II:** 537; **III:** 259, 270, 292, 300; **IV:** 69, 126; **Retro. Supp. I:** 247; **Supp. VIII:** 203; **Supp. XI:** 245; **Supp. XIII:** 89

August Snow (Price), **Supp. VI:** 264

"Au Jardin" (Pound), **III:** 465–466

Aunt Carmen's Book of Practical Saints

(Mora), **Supp. XIII:** 227–229

"Aunt Cynthy Dallett" (Jewett), **II:** 393

"Aunt Gladys" (Karr), **Supp. XI:** 241

"Aunt Imogen" (Robinson), **III:** 521

"Aunt Jemima of the Ocean Waves" (Hayden), **Supp. II Part 1:** 368, 379

Aunt Jo's Scrapbooks (Alcott), **Supp. I Part 1:** 43

"Aunt Mary" (Oliver), **Supp. VII:** 232

"Aunt Mary" (Stowe), **Supp. I Part 2:** 587

"Aunt Moon's Young Man" (Hogan), **Supp. IV Part 1:** 400

"Aunt Sarah" (Lowell), **II:** 554

"Aunt Sue's Stories" (Hughes), **Retro. Supp. I:** 197, 199

"Aunt Violet's Canadian Honeymoon/ 1932" (Shields), **Supp. VII:** 311

"Aunt Violet's Things" (Shields), **Supp. VII:** 311–312

"Aurelia: Moon Jellies" (Mora), **Supp. XIII:** 224

Aurora Leigh (E. Browning), **Retro. Supp. I:** 33; **Supp. XI:** 197

Auroras of Autumn, The (Stevens), **Retro. Supp. I:** 297, 300, **309–312**

"Auroras of Autumn, The" (Stevens), **Retro. Supp. I:** 311, 312; **Supp. III Part 1:** 12

Auslander, Joseph, **Supp. XIV:** 120

"Auspex" (Frost), **Retro. Supp. I:** 122

"Auspex" (Lowell), **Supp. I Part 2:** 424

Austen, Jane, **I:** 130, 339, 375, 378; **II:** 272, 278, 287, 568–569, 577; **IV:** 8; **Retro. Supp. I:** 354; **Supp. I Part 1:** 267; **Supp. I Part 2:** 656, 715; **Supp. IV Part 1:** 300; **Supp. VIII:** 125, 167; **Supp. IX:** 128; **Supp. XII:** 310

Auster, Paul, **Supp. XII: 21–39; Supp. XIV:** 292

Austerities (Simic), **Supp. VIII: 276–278,** 283

"Austerities" (Simic), **Supp. VIII:** 277

Austin, Mary Hunter, **Retro. Supp. I:** 7; **Supp. IV Part 2:** 503; **Supp. X:** 29; **Supp. XIII:** 154

"Authentic Unconscious, The" (Trilling), **Supp. III Part 2:** 512

Author and Agent: Eudora Welty and Diarmuid Russell (Kreyling), **Retro. Supp. I:** 342, 345, 347, 349–350

"Author at Sixty, The" (Wilson), **IV:** 426

"Author of 'Beltraffio,' The" (James), **Retro. Supp. I:** 227

"Author's House" (Fitzgerald), **Retro. Supp. I:** 98

"Author's Reflections, An: Willie Lo-

man, Walter Younger, and He Who Must Live" (Hansberry), **Supp. IV Part 1:** 370

"Author to Her Book, The" (Bradstreet), **Supp. I Part 1:** 119; **Supp. V:** 117–118

"Autobiographical Note" (H. Miller), **III:** 174–175

"Autobiographical Notes" (Baldwin), **Supp. I Part 1:** 54

"Autobiographical Notes" (Holmes), **Supp. I Part 1:** 301

"Autobiographic Chapter, An" (Bourne), **I:** 236

Autobiography (Franklin), **II:** 102, 103, 108, 121–122, 302

Autobiography (James), **I:** 462

"Autobiography" (MacLeish), **III:** 20

Autobiography (Van Buren), **III:** 473

Autobiography (W. C. Williams), **Supp. I Part 1:** 254

Autobiography (Zukofsky), **Supp. III Part 2:** 627

"Autobiography of a Confluence, The" (Gunn Allen), **Supp. IV Part 1:** 321

Autobiography of Alice B. Toklas, The (Stein), **IV:** 26, 30, 35, 43; **Supp. IV Part 1:** 11, 81

Autobiography of an Ex-Colored Man, The (Johnson), **Supp. II Part 1:** 33, 194

Autobiography of Benjamin Franklin (Franklin), **Supp. IV Part 1:** 5

Autobiography of LeRoi Jones, The (Baraka), **Retro. Supp. I:** 411

Autobiography of Malcolm X (Little), **Supp. I Part 1:** 66; **Supp. X:** 27; **Supp. XIII:** 264

Autobiography of Mark Twain, The (Twain), **IV:** 209

Autobiography of My Mother, The (Kincaid), **Supp. VII:** 182, 188–190, 191, 192, 193

Autobiography of Red: A Novel in Verse (Carson), **Supp. XII:** 97, **106–110**

Autobiography of Upton Sinclair, The (Sinclair), **Supp. V:** 276, 282

Autobiography of W. E. B. Du Bois, The (Du Bois), **Supp. II Part 1:** 159, 186

Autobiography of William Carlos Williams, The (W. C. Williams), **Retro. Supp. I:** 51, 428

Autocrat of the Breakfast-Table, The (Holmes), **Supp. I Part 1:** 306–307

"Automatic Gate, The" (Southern), **Supp. XI:** 294

"Automotive Passacaglia" (H. Miller), **III:** 186

"Autopsy Room, The" (Carver), **Supp. III Part 1:** 137

"Auto Wreck" (Shapiro), **Supp. II Part 2:** 706

"Autre Temps" (Wharton), **IV:** 320, 324

"Autumn Afternoon" (Farrell), **II:** 45

"Autumnal" (Eberhart), **I:** 540–541

"Autumn Begins in Martins Ferry, Ohio" (Wright), **Supp. III Part 2:** 599

"Autumn Courtship, An" (Caldwell), **I:** 309

Autumn Garden, The (Hellman), **Supp. I Part 1:** 285–286, 290

"Autumn Garden, The: Mechanics and Dialectics" (Felheim), **Supp. I Part 1:** 297

"Autumn Holiday, An" (Jewett), **II:** 391; **Retro. Supp. II:** 140–141

"Autumn Musings" (Harte), **Supp. II Part 1:** 336

"Autumn Within" (Longfellow), **II:** 499

"Autumn Woods" (Bryant), **Supp. I Part 1:** 164

"Au Vieux Jardin" (Aldington), **Supp. I Part 1:** 257

"Aux Imagistes" (W. C. Williams), **Supp. I Part 1:** 266

Avakian, Aram, **Supp. XI:** 294, 295, 309

Avedon, Richard, **Supp. I Part 1:** 58; **Supp. V:** 194; **Supp. X:** 15

"Avenue" (Pinsky), **Supp. VI:** 248

Avenue Bearing the Initial of Christ into the New World: Poems 1946– 1964 (Kinnell), **Supp. III Part 1:** 235, 239–241

"Avenue of the Americas" (Simic), **Supp. VIII:** 278

"Average Torture" (Karr), **Supp. XI:** 243

Avery, John, **Supp. I Part 1:** 153

"Avey" (Toomer), **Supp. IX:** 317

Avon's Harvest (Robinson), **III:** 510

Awake and Sing! (Odets), **Supp. II Part 2:** 530, 531, 536–538, 550; **Supp. IV Part 2:** 587

Awakening, The (Chopin), **Retro. Supp. I:** 10; **Retro. Supp. II:** 57, 59, 60, 67, **68–71,** 73; **Supp. I Part 1:** 200, 201, 202, 211, 220–225; **Supp. V:** 304; **Supp. VIII:** 198; **Supp. XII:** 170

Awful Rowing Toward God, The (Sexton), **Supp. II Part 2:** 694–696

Awiakta, Marilou, **Supp. IV Part 1:** 319, 335

Awkward Age, The (James), **II:** 332;

Retro. Supp. I: 229, **230–231**

Axe Handles (Snyder), **Supp. VIII: 303–305**

Axel's Castle: A Study in the Imaginative Literature of 1870 to 1930 (Wilson), **I:** 185; **II:** 577; **IV:** 428, 431, 438, 439, 443; **Supp. VIII:** 101

"Ax-Helve, The" (Frost), **Retro. Supp. I:** 133

Azikewe, Nnamdi, **Supp. IV Part 1:** 361

"Aztec Angel" (Salinas), **Supp. XIII:** 314

Aztec Treasure House, The: New and Selected Essays (Connell), **Supp. XIV:** 80, 97

B. F.'s Daughter (Marquand), **III:** 59, 65, 68, 69

Babbitt (Lewis), **II:** 442, 443–445, 446, 447, 449; **III:** 63–64, 394; **IV:** 326

Babbitt, Irving, **I:** 247; **II:** 456; **III:** 315, 461, 613; **IV:** 439; **Retro. Supp. I:** 55; **Supp. I Part 2:** 423

Babcock, Elisha, **Supp. II Part 1:** 69

Babel, Isaac, **IV:** 1; **Supp. IX:** 260; **Supp. XII:** 308–309

Babel, Isaak, **Supp. XIV:** 83, 84

Babel to Byzantium (Dickey), **Supp. IV Part 1:** 177, 185

Babeuf, François, **Supp. I Part 2:** 518

"Babies, The" (Strand), **Supp. IV Part 2:** 625

Baby, Come on Inside (Wagoner), **Supp. IX: 335**

"Baby, The" (Barthelme), **Supp. IV Part 1:** 49

Baby Doll (T. Williams), **IV:** 383, 386, 387, 389, 395

"Baby Face" (Sandburg), **III:** 584

"Babylon Revisited" (Fitzgerald), **II:** 95; **Retro. Supp. I:** 109

"Baby or the Botticelli, The" (Gass), **Supp. VI:** 92

"Baby Pictures of Famous Dictators" (Simic), **Supp. VIII:** 276

"Baby's Breath" (Bambara), **Supp. XI:** 15, 16

"Babysitter, The" (Coover), **Supp. V:** 43–44

"Baby Villon" (Levine), **Supp. V:** 182

Bacall, Lauren, **Supp. IV Part 1:** 130

"Baccalaureate" (MacLeish), **III:** 4

Bacchae, The (Euripides), **Supp. VIII:** 182

Bach, Johann Sebastian, **Supp. I Part 1:** 363; **Supp. III Part 2:** 611, 612, 619

Bachardy, Don, **Supp. XIV:** 166, 170, 172, 173

Bache, Richard, **Supp. I Part 2:** 504

Bachelard, Gaston, **Supp. XIII:** 225

Bachmann, Ingeborg, **Supp. IV Part 1:** 310; **Supp. VIII:** 272

Bachofen, J. J., **Supp. I Part 2:** 560, 567

Back Bog Beast Bait (Shepard), **Supp. III Part 2:** 437, 438

Back Country, The (Snyder), **Supp. VIII: 296–299**

"Back fom the Argentine" (Leopold), **Supp. XIV:** 186

"Background with Revolutionaries" (MacLeish), **III:** 14–15

Back in The World (Wolff), **Supp. VII:** 345

Back in the World (Wolff), **Supp. VII:** 344

"Backlash Blues, The" (Hughes), **Supp. I Part 1:** 343

"Backlash of Kindness, A" (Nye), **Supp. XIII:** 285, 286

Back to China (Fiedler), **Supp. XIII: 102–103**

Back to Methuselah (Shaw), **IV:** 64

"Backwacking: A Plea to the Senator" (Ellison), **Retro. Supp. II:** 126; **Supp. II Part 1:** 248

Backward Glance, A (Wharton), **Retro. Supp. I:** 360, 363, 366, 378, 380, 382

"Backward Glance o'er Travel'd Roads, A" (Whitman), **IV:** 348

Bacon, Francis, **II:** 1, 8, 11, 15–16, 111; **III:** 284; **Retro. Supp. I:** 247; **Supp. I Part 1:** 310; **Supp. I Part 2:** 388; **Supp. IX:** 104; **Supp. XIV:** 22, 210

Bacon, Helen, **Supp. X:** 57

Bacon, Leonard, **II:** 530

Bacon, Roger, **IV:** 69

"Bacterial War, The" (Nemerov), **III:** 272

Bad Boy Brawly Brown (Mosley), **Supp. XIII:** 237, 239, 240–241

Bad Boys (Cisneros), **Supp. VII:** 58

"Bad Dream" (Taylor), **Supp. V:** 320

Badè, William Frederic, **Supp. IX:** 178

"Bad Fisherman, The" (Wagoner), **Supp. IX:** 328

Bad for Each Other (film), **Supp. XIII:** 174

"Badger" (Clare), **II:** 387

Badger, A. G., **Supp. I Part 1:** 356

"Bad Lay" (McCarriston), **Supp. XIV:** 267

Badley, Linda, **Supp. V:** 148

Bad Man, A (Elkin), **Supp. VI: 47**

Bad Man Blues: A Portable George Garrett (Garrett), **Supp. VII:** 111

"Bad Music, The" (Jarrell), **II:** 369

"Bad Woman, A" (Fante), **Supp. XI:** 165

Baeck, Leo, **Supp. V:** 260

Baecker, Diann L., **Supp. VIII:** 128

Baer, William, **Supp. XIII:** 112, 118, 129

Baez, Joan, **Supp. IV Part 1:** 200; **Supp. VIII:** 200, 202

Bag of Bones (King), **Supp. V:** 139, 148, 151

"Bagpipe Music" (MacNeice), **Supp. X:** 117

"Bahá'í Faith: Only Church in World That Does Not Discriminate" (Locke), **Supp. XIV:** 200

"Bahá'u'lláh in the Garden of Ridwan" (Hayden), **Supp. II Part 1:** 370, 378

"Bailbondsman, The" (Elkin), **Supp. VI:** 49, **50,** 58

Bailey, Gamaliel, **Supp. I Part 2:** 587, 590

Bailey, William, **Supp. IV Part 2:** 631, 634

Bailey's Café (Naylor), **Supp. VIII: 226–228**

Bailyn, Bernard, **Supp. I Part 2:** 484, 506

Bair, Deirdre, **Supp. X:** 181, 186, 187, 188, 192, 194, 195, 196, 197

Baird, Linnett, **Supp. XII:** 299

Baird, Peggy, **I:** 385, 401

Bakan, David, **I:** 59

Baker, Carlos, **II:** 259

Baker, David, **Supp. IX:** 298; **Supp. XI:** 121, 142, 153; **Supp. XII:** 175, 191–192

Baker, George Pierce, **III:** 387; **IV:** 453, 455

Baker, Gladys, **Supp. XIV:** 121

Baker, Houston A., Jr., **Retro. Supp. II:** 121; **Supp. IV Part 1:** 365; **Supp. X:** 324

Baker, Kevin, **Supp. XIV:** 96

Baker, Nicholson, **Supp. XIII: 41–57**

Bakerman, Jane S., **Supp. IV Part 2:** 468

Bakhtin, Mikhail, **Retro. Supp. II:** 273; **Supp. IV Part 1:** 301; **Supp. X:** 120, 239

Bakst, Léon, **Supp. IX:** 66

Bakunin, Mikhail Aleksandrovich, **IV:** 429

Balbuena, Bernado de, **Supp. V:** 11

Balch, Emily Greene, **Supp. I Part 1:** 25

Balcony, The (Genet), **I:** 84

Bald Soprano, The (Ionesco), **I:** 74

Baldwin, David, **Supp. I Part 1:** 47, 48, 49, 50, 51, 54, 65, 66

Baldwin, James, **Retro. Supp. II:**

1–17; **Supp. I Part 1:** 47–71, 337, 341; **Supp. II Part 1:** 40; **Supp. III Part 1:** 125; **Supp. IV Part 1:** 1, 10, 11, 163, 369; **Supp. V:** 201; **Supp. VIII:** 88, 198, 235, 349; **Supp. X:** 136, 324; **Supp. XI:** 288, 294; **Supp. XIII:** 46, 111, 181, 186, 294; **Supp. XIV:** 54, 71, 73, 306

Baldwin, Samuel, **Supp. I Part 1:** 48

Balkian, Nona, **Supp. XI:** 230

Ball, Gordon, **Supp. XIV:** 148

"Ballad: Between the Box Cars" (Warren), **IV:** 245

"Ballade" (MacLeish), **III:** 4

"Ballade at Thirty-Five" (Parker), **Supp. IX:** 192

"Ballade for the Duke of Orléans" (Wilbur), **Supp. III Part 2:** 556

"Ballade of Broken Flutes, The" (Robinson), **III:** 505

"Ballade of Meaty Inversions" (White), **Supp. I Part 2:** 676

"Ballad of Billie Potts, The" (Warren), **IV:** 241–242, 243, 253

"Ballad of Carmilhan, The" (Longfellow), **II:** 505

"ballad of chocolate Mabbie, the" (Brooks), **Supp. IV Part 1:** 15

"Ballad of Dead Ladies, The" (Villon), **Retro. Supp. I:** 286

"Ballad of East and West" (Kipling), **Supp. IX:** 246

"Ballad of Jesse Neighbours, The" (Humphrey), **Supp. IX:** 100

"Ballad of Jesus of Nazareth, A" (Masters), **Supp. I Part 2:** 459

"Ballad of John Cable and Three Gentlemen" (Merwin), **Supp. III Part 1:** 342

"Ballad of Nat Turner, The" (Hayden), **Supp. II Part 1:** 378

"Ballad of Pearl May Lee, The" (Brooks), **Supp. III Part 1:** 74, 75

Ballad of Remembrance, A (Hayden), **Supp. II Part 1:** 367

"Ballad of Remembrance, A" (Hayden), **Supp. II Part 1:** 368, 372, 373

"Ballad of Ruby, The" (Sarton), **Supp. VIII:** 259–260

"Ballad of Sue Ellen Westerfield, The" (Hayden), **Supp. II Part 1:** 364

Ballad of the Brown Girl, The (Cullen), **Supp. IV Part 1:** 167, 168, 169–170, 173

"Ballad of the Brown Girl, The" (Cullen), **Supp. IV Part 1:** 168

"Ballad of the Children of the Czar, The" (Schwartz), **Supp. II Part 2:** 649

"Ballad of the Girl Whose Name Is Mud" (Hughes), **Retro. Supp. I:** 205

"Ballad of the Goodly Fere," **III:** 458

"Ballad of the Harp-Weaver" (Millay), **III:** 135

"Ballad of the Sad Cafe, The" (McCullers), **II:** 586, 587, 588, 592, 595, 596–600, 604, 605, 606

"Ballad of the Sixties" (Sarton), **Supp. VIII:** 259

"Ballad of Trees and the Master, A" (Lanier), **Supp. I Part 1:** 370

"Ballad of William Sycamore, The" (Benét), **Supp. XI:** 44, 47

Ballads and Other Poems (Longfellow), **II:** 489; **III:** 412, 422; **Retro. Supp. II:** 157, 168

Ballads for Sale (Lowell), **II:** 527

"Ballads of Lenin" (Hughes), **Supp. I Part 1:** 331

Ballantyne, Sheila, **Supp. V:** 70

Ballard, Josephine. *See* McMurtry, Josephine

"Ballena" (Mora), **Supp. XIII:** 224

"Ballet in Numbers for Mary Ellen, A" (Karr), **Supp. XI:** 241

"Ballet of a Buffoon, The" (Sexton), **Supp. II Part 2:** 693

"Ballet of the Fifth Year, The" (Schwartz), **Supp. II Part 2:** 650

"Ball Game, The" (Creeley), **Supp. IV Part 1:** 140

"Balloon Hoax, The" (Poe), **III:** 413, 420

Balo (Toomer), **Supp. III Part 2:** 484

Balsan, Consuelo, **IV:** 313–314

Balthus, **Supp. IV Part 2:** 623

Balthus Poems, The (Dobyns), **Supp. XIII:** 87

Baltimore, Lord, **I:** 132

Balzac, Honoré de, **I:** 103, 123, 339, 376, 474, 485, 499, 509, 518; **II:** 307, 322, 324, 328, 336, 337; **III:** 61, 174, 184, 320, 382; **IV:** 192; **Retro. Supp. I:** 91, 217, 218, 235; **Retro. Supp. II:** 93; **Supp. I Part 2:** 647

Bambara, Toni Cade, **Supp. XI:** 1–23

Banana Bottom (McKay), **Supp. X:** 132, 139–140

Bancal, Jean, **Supp. I Part 2:** 514

Bancroft, George, **I:** 544; **Supp. I Part 2:** 479

Band of Angels (Warren), **IV:** 245, 254–255

Bang the Drum Slowly (Harris), **II:** 424–425

Banjo: A Story without a Plot (McKay), **Supp. X:** 132, 138–139

"Banjo Song, A" (Dunbar), **Supp. II Part 1:** 197

Bankhead, Tallulah, **IV:** 357; **Supp. IV Part 2:** 574

"Banking Potatoes" (Komunyakaa), **Supp. XIII:** 126

"Bank of England Restriction, The" (Adams), **I:** 4

Banks, Joanne Trautmann, **Supp. XIII:** 297

Banks, Russell, **Supp. V:** 1–19, 227; **Supp. IX:** 153; **Supp. X:** 85; **Supp. XI:** 178; **Supp. XII:** 295, 309, 343

"Banned Poem" (Nye), **Supp. XIII:** 282

Bannon, Barbara, **Supp. XI:** 228

"Banyan" (Swenson), **Supp. IV Part 2:** 651, 652

"Baptism" (Olsen). See "O Yes" (Olsen)

Baptism, The (Baraka), **Supp. II Part 1:** 40, 41–42, 43

Baptism of Desire (Erdrich), **Supp. IV Part 1:** 259

"B.A.R. Man, The" (Yates), **Supp. XI:** 341

Barabtarlo, Gennady, **Retro. Supp. I:** 278

Baraka, Imamu Amiri (LeRoi Jones), **Retro. Supp. I:** 411; **Retro. Supp. II:** 280; **Supp. I Part 1:** 63; **Supp. II Part 1:** 29–63, 247, 250; **Supp. III Part 1:** 83; **Supp. IV Part 1:** 169, 244, 369; **Supp. VIII:** 295, 329, 330, 332; **Supp. X:** 324, 328; **Supp. XIII:** 94; **Supp. XIV:** 125, 144

"Bar at the Andover Inn, The" (Matthews), **Supp. IX:** 168

"Barbados" (Marshall), **Supp. XI:** 281

"Barbara Frietchie" (Whittier), **Supp. I Part 2:** 695–696

Barbarella (film), **Supp. XI:** 293, 307–308

"Barbarian Status of Women, The" (Veblen), **Supp. I Part 2:** 636–637

Barbarous Coast, The (Macdonald), **Supp. IV Part 2:** 472, 474

Barbary Shore (Mailer), **III:** 27, 28, 30–31, 33, 35, 36, 40, 44; **Retro. Supp. II:** 199–200, 207; **Supp. XIV:** 162

Barber, David, **Supp. IV Part 2:** 550; **Supp. XII:** 188–189

Barber, Rowland, **Supp. IV Part 2:** 581

Barber, Samuel, **Supp. IV Part 1:** 84

"Barclay of Ury" (Whittier), **Supp. I Part 2:** 693

Bard of Savagery, The: Thorstein Ve-

blen and Modern Social Theory (Diggins), **Supp. I Part 2:** 650

"Barefoot Boy, The" (Whittier), **Supp. I Part 2:** 691, 699–700

Barefoot in the Park (Simon), **Supp. IV Part 2:** 575, 578–579, 586, 590

Bare Hills, The (Winters), **Supp. II Part 2:** 786, 788

"Bare Hills, The" (Winters), **Supp. II Part 2:** 790

Barely and Widely (Zukofsky), **Supp. III Part 2:** 627, 628, 635

Barenblat, Rachel, **Supp. XIII:** 274

Barfield, Owen, **III:** 274, 279

"Bargain Lost, The" (Poe), **III:** 411

Barillas, William, **Supp. XIV:** 177

Barker, Arthur, **Supp. XIII:** 167

Barker, Clive, **Supp. V:** 142

"Barking Man" (Bell), **Supp. X:** 9

Barking Man and Other Stories (Bell), **Supp. X:** 9

Barksdale, Richard, **Retro. Supp. I:** 202, 205; **Supp. I Part 1:** 341, 346

Barlow, Joel, **Supp. I Part 1:** 124; **Supp. I Part 2:** 511, 515, 521; **Supp. II Part 1: 65–86,** 268

Barlow, Ruth Baldwin (Mrs. Joel Barlow), **Supp. II Part 1:** 69

Barnaby Rudge (Dickens), **III:** 421

Barnard, Frederick, **Supp. I Part 2:** 684

Barnard, Rita, **Retro. Supp. II:** 324

Barn Blind (Smiley), **Supp. VI: 292– 293**

"Barn Burning" (Faulkner), **II:** 72, 73; **Supp. IV Part 2:** 682

Barnes, Djuna, **Supp. III Part 1: 31– 46; Supp. IV Part 1:** 79, 80

Barnett, Samuel, **Supp. I Part 1:** 2

Barnstone, Tony, **Supp. XIII:** 115, 126

Barnstone, Willis, **Supp. I Part 2:** 458

Barnum, P. T., **Supp. I Part 2:** 703

Baroja, Pío, **I:** 478

"Baroque Comment" (Bogan), **Supp. III Part 1:** 56, 58

"Baroque Sunburst, A" (Clampitt), **Supp. IX:** 49

"Baroque Wall-Fountain in the Villa Sciarra, A" (Wilbur), **Supp. III Part 2:** 553

Barr, Robert, **I:** 409, 424

Barracks Thief, The (Wolff), **Supp. VII:** 344–345

Barren Ground (Glasgow), **II:** 174, 175, 178, 179, 184–185, 186, 187, 188, 189, 191, 192, 193, 194; **Supp. X:** 228

Barrés, Auguste M., **I:** 228

Barrett, Elizabeth, **Supp. IV Part 2:** 430

Barrett, George, **Supp. IX:** 250

Barrett, Ralph, **Supp. I Part 2:** 462

Barron, Jonathan, **Supp. IX:** 299

Barrow, John, **II:** 18

Barrus, Clara, **I:** 220

Barry, Iris, **Supp. XIII:** 170

Barry, Philip, **Retro. Supp. I:** 104; **Supp. IV Part 1:** 83; **Supp. V:** 95

Bartas, Seigneur du, **IV:** 157

Barth, John, **I: 121–143; Supp. I Part 1:** 100; **Supp. III Part 1:** 217; **Supp. IV Part 1:** 48, 379; **Supp. V:** 39, 40; **Supp. IX:** 208; **Supp. X:** 263, 301, 302, 307; **Supp. XI:** 309; **Supp. XII:** 29, 289, 316; **Supp. XIII:** 41, 101, 104

Barth, Karl, **III:** 40, 258, 291, 303, 309; **IV:** 225; **Retro. Supp. I:** 325, 326, 327

Barthé, Richmond, **Retro. Supp. II:** 115

Barthelme, Donald, **Supp. IV Part 1: 39–58,** 227; **Supp. V:** 2, 39, 44; **Supp. VIII:** 75, 138; **Supp. X:** 263; **Supp. XI:** 25; **Supp. XII:** 29; **Supp. XIII:** 41, 46

Barthelme, Frederick, **Supp. XI: 25–41**

Barthelme, Peter, **Supp. XI:** 25

Barthelme, Steven, **Supp. XI:** 25, 27, 37

Barthes, Roland, **Supp. IV Part 1:** 39, 119, 126; **Supp. XIII:** 83

"Bartleby, the Scrivener; A Story of Wall-Street" (Melville), **III:** 88–89; **Retro. Supp. I:** 255

Bartleby in Manhattan and Other Essays (Hardwick), **Supp. III Part 1:** 204, 210

Bartlet, Phebe, **I:** 562

Bartlett, Lee, **Supp. VIII:** 291

Bartlett, Mary Dougherty, **Supp. IV Part 1:** 335

Barton, Bruce, **III:** 14; **Retro. Supp. I:** 179

Barton, Priscilla. *See* Morison, Mrs. Samuel Eliot (Priscilla Barton)

Barton, Rev. William E., **Retro. Supp. I:** 179

Bartram, John, **Supp. I Part 1:** 244

Bartram, William, **II:** 313; **Supp. IX:** 171; **Supp. X:** 223

Barzun, Jacques, **Supp. XIV:** 54

"Basement" (Bambara), **Supp. XI:** 5

"Base of All Metaphysics, The" (Whitman), **IV:** 348

"Base Stealer, The" (Francis), **Supp. IX:** 82

Bashevis, Isaac. *See* Singer, Isaac Bashevis

Basil Stories, The (Fitzgerald), **Retro.**

Supp. I: 109

Basin and Range (McPhee), **Supp. III Part 1:** 309

"Basin of Eggs, A" (Swenson), **Supp. IV Part 2:** 645

"Basket, The" (Lowell), **II:** 522

"Basketball and Beefeaters" (McPhee), **Supp. III Part 1:** 296

"Basketball and Poetry: The Two Richies" (Dunn), **Supp. XI:** 140

Baskin, Leonard, **Supp. X:** 58, 71

Bass, Rick, **Supp. XIV:** 227

Basso, Hamilton, **Retro. Supp. I:** 80

Bastard, The (Caldwell), **I:** 291, 292, 308

"Bat, The" (Kenyon), **Supp. VII:** 168

Bataille, Georges, **Supp. VIII:** 4; **Supp. XII:** 1

"Batard" (London), **II:** 468–469

Bate, W. J., **II:** 531

Bates, Arlo, **Retro. Supp. I:** 35

Bates, Kathy, **Supp. XIII:** 207

Bates, Lee, **Retro. Supp. II:** 46

Bates, Milton J., **Supp. XII:** 62

Bates, Sylvia Chatfield, **II:** 586

"Bath, The" (Carver), **Supp. III Part 1:** 144, 145

"Bath, The" (Snyder), **Supp. VIII:** 302

Bathwater Wine (Coleman), **Supp. XI:** 83, 90, **91**

"Batter my heart, three person'd God" (Donne), **Supp. I Part 2:** 726

"Battle, The" (Simpson), **Supp. IX:** 268–269

Battle-Ground, The (Glasgow), **II:** 175, 176, 177, 178, 193

"Battle Hymn of the Republic" (Sandburg), **III:** 585

"Battle Hymn of the Republic, The" (Howe), **III:** 505

"Battle Hymn of the Republic, The" (Updike), **Retro. Supp. I:** 324

Battle of Angels (T. Williams), **IV:** 380, 381, 383, 385, 386, 387

"Battle of Lovell's Pond, The" (Longfellow), **II:** 493

Battle of the Atlantic, The (Morison), **Supp. I Part 2:** 490

"Battle of the Baltic, The" (Campbell), **Supp. I Part 1:** 309

"Battle of the Bunker, The" (Snodgrass), **Supp. VI:** 319–320

"***Battle of the Century!!!, The***" (Goldbarth), **Supp. XII:** 193

Battle-Pieces and Aspects of the War (Melville), **II:** 538–539; **III:** 92; **IV:** 350; **Retro. Supp. I:** 257

"Battler, The" (Hemingway), **II:** 248; **Retro. Supp. I:** 175

"Baudelaire" (Schwartz), **Supp. II**

Part 2: 663

Baudelaire, Charles, **I:** 58, 63, 384, 389, 420, 569; **II:** 543, 544–545, 552; **III:** 137, 141–142, 143, 409, 417, 418, 421, 428, 448, 466, 474; **IV:** 74, 79, 80, 87, 211, 286; **Retro. Supp. I:** 56, 90; **Retro. Supp. II:** 261, 262, 322, 326; **Supp. I Part 1:** 271; **Supp. III Part 1:** 4, 6, 105; **Supp. XIII:** 77, 284

Baudrillard, Jean, **Supp. IV Part 1:** 45

Bauer, Dale, **Retro. Supp. I:** 381

Bauer, Douglas, **Supp. XII:** 290

Baum, L. Frank, **Supp. I Part 2:** 621; **Supp. IV Part 1:** 101, 113; **Supp. XII:** 42

Baumann, Walter, **III:** 478

Bausch, Richard, **Supp. VII:** 39–56

Bawer, Bruce, **Supp. VIII:** 153; **Supp. IX:** 135; **Supp. X:** 187

Baxter, Charles, **Supp. XII:** 22; **Supp. XIV:** 89, 92

Baxter, John, **Supp. XI:** 302

Baxter, Richard, **III:** 199; **IV:** 151, 153; **Supp. I Part 2:** 683

"Baxter's Procrustes" (Chesnutt), **Supp. XIV:** 76

"Bay City Blues" (Chandler), **Supp. IV Part 1:** 129

Baylies, William, **Supp. I Part 1:** 153

Baym, Nina, **Supp. IV Part 2:** 463; **Supp. X:** 229

Bayou Folk (Chopin), **Retro. Supp. II:** 64–65, 73; **Supp. I Part 1:** 200, 216, 218

Beach, Joseph Warren, **I:** 309, 500; **II:** 27; **III:** 319

Beach, Sylvia, **IV:** 404; **Retro. Supp. I:** 109, 422

"Beach Women, The" (Pinsky), **Supp. VI:** 241

"Beaded Pear, The" (Simpson), **Supp. IX:** 276

Beagle, Peter, **Supp. X:** 24

Beam, Jeffrey, **Supp. XII:** 98

Beaman, E. O., **Supp. IV Part 2:** 604

Bean, Michael, **Supp. V:** 203

Bean, Robert Bennett, **Supp. II Part 1:** 170

Bean Eaters, The (Brooks), **Supp. III Part 1:** 79–81

Be Angry at the Sun (Jeffers), **Supp. II Part 2:** 434

"Beanstalk Country, The" (T. Williams), **IV:** 383

Bean Trees, The (Kingsolver), **Supp. VII:** 197, 199–201, 202, 207, 209

"Bear" (Hogan), **Supp. IV Part 1:** 412

Bear, The (Faulkner), **Supp. VIII:** 184

"Bear, The" (Faulkner), **II:** 71–72, 73, 228; **IV:** 203; **Supp. IV Part 2:** 434; **Supp. IX:** 95; **Supp. X:** 30; **Supp. XIV:** 32

"Bear, The" (Kinnell), **Supp. III Part 1:** 244

"Bear, The" (Momaday), **Supp. IV Part 2:** 480, 487

Bear and His Daughter: Stories (Stone), **Supp. V:** 295, 308

Beard, Charles, **I:** 214; **IV:** 429; **Supp. I Part 2:** 481, 490, 492, 632, 640, 643, 647

Beard, James, **I:** 341

Beard, Mary, **Supp. I Part 2:** 481

"Bearded Oaks" (Warren), **IV:** 240

Bearden, Romare, **Retro. Supp. I:** 209; **Supp. VIII:** 337, 342

Beardsley, Aubrey, **II:** 56; **IV:** 77

"Beast" (Swenson), **Supp. IV Part 2:** 639

"Beast & Burden, The: Seven Improvisations" (Komunyakaa), **Supp. XIII:** 120, 121

Beast God Forgot to Invent, The (Harrison), **Supp. VIII:** 37, 46, 51–52

Beast in Me, The (Thurber), **Supp. I Part 2:** 615

"Beast in the Jungle, The" (James), **I:** 570; **II:** 335; **Retro. Supp. I:** 235; **Supp. V:** 103–104

Beast in View (Rukeyser), **Supp. VI:** 272, 273, 279, 280

"Beat! Beat! Drums!" (Whitman), **III:** 585

Beat Down to Your Soul: What Was the Beat Generation? (Charters, ed.), **Supp. XIV:** 152

"Beatrice Palmato" (Wharton), **Retro. Supp. I:** 379

Beattie, Ann, **Supp. V:** 21–37; **Supp. XI:** 26; **Supp. XII:** 80, 139, 294

Beatty, General Sam, **I:** 193

Beaty, Jerome, **Supp. IV Part 1:** 331

"Beau Monde of Mrs. Bridge, The" (Connell), **Supp. XIV:** 88, 89

Beaumont, Francis, **Supp. I Part 2:** 422

"Beauties of Santa Cruz, The" (Freneau), **Supp. II Part 1:** 260

Beautiful and Damned, The (Fitzgerald), **II:** 88, 89–91, 93, 263; **Retro. Supp. I:** 103–105, 105, 106, 110; **Supp. IX:** 56, 57

Beautiful Changes, The (Wilbur), **Supp. III Part 2:** 544–550

"Beautiful Changes, The" (Wilbur), **Supp. III Part 2:** 549, 550

"Beautiful Child, A" (Capote), **Supp. III Part 1:** 113, 125

"Beautiful & Cruel" (Cisneros), **Supp. VII:** 63, 67

"Beautiful Woman Who Sings, The" (Gunn Allen), **Supp. IV Part 1:** 326

"Beauty" (Emerson), **II:** 2, 5

"Beauty" (Wylie), **Supp. I Part 2:** 710

"Beauty and the Beast" (Dove), **Supp. IV Part 1:** 245

"Beauty and the Beast" (fairy tale), **IV:** 266; **Supp. X:** 88

"Beauty and the Shoe Sluts" (Karr), **Supp. XI:** 250

Beauty of the Husband, The: A Fictional Essay in Twenty-Nine Tangos (Carson), **Supp. XII:** 113–114

Beauty's Punishment (Rice), **Supp. VII:** 301

Beauty's Release: The Continued Erotic Adventures of Sleeping Beauty (Rice), **Supp. VII:** 301

Beauvoir, Simone de, **IV:** 477; **Supp. I Part 1:** 51; **Supp. III Part 1:** 200–201, 208; **Supp. IV Part 1:** 360; **Supp. IX:** 4

"Because I could not stop for Death—" (Dickinson), **Retro. Supp. I:** 38–40, 41, 43, 44

"Because It Happened" (Goldbarth), **Supp. XII:** 192

"Because of Libraries We Can Say These Things" (Nye), **Supp. XIII:** 283

"Because You Mentioned the Spiritual Life" (Dunn), **Supp. XI:** 154

Bech: A Book (Updike), **IV:** 214; **Retro. Supp. I:** 329, 335

Beck, Dave, **I:** 493

Beck, Jack, **Supp. IV Part 2:** 560

Becker, Carl, **Supp. I Part 2:** 492, 493

Becker, Paula. *See* Modersohn, Mrs. Otto (Paula Becker)

Beckett, Samuel, **I:** 71, 91, 142, 298, 461; **III:** 387; **IV:** 95; **Retro. Supp. I:** 206; **Supp. IV Part 1:** 297, 368–369; **Supp. IV Part 2:** 424; **Supp. V:** 23, 53; **Supp. XI:** 104; **Supp. XII:** 21, 150–151; **Supp. XIII:** 74; **Supp. XIV:** 239

Beckett, Tom, **Supp. IV Part 2:** 419

Beckford, William, **I:** 204

Beckonings (Brooks), **Supp. III Part 1:** 85

"Becky" (Toomer), **Supp. III Part 2:** 481, 483; **Supp. IX:** 312

Becoming a Man: Half a Life Story (Monette), **Supp. X:** 146, 147, 149, 151, 152, 155–157

"Becoming a Meadow" (Doty), **Supp. XI:** 124–125

"Becoming and Breaking: Poet and

Poem" (Ríos), **Supp. IV Part 2:** 539

Becoming Canonical in American Poetry (Morris), **Retro. Supp. I:** 40

Becoming Light: New and Selected Poems (Jong), **Supp. V:** 115

Bécquer, Gustavo Adolfo, **Supp. XIII:** 312

"Bed, The" (Dixon), **Supp. XII:** 154

Beddoes, Thomas Lovell, **III:** 469; **Retro. Supp. I:** 285

Bedichek, Roy, **Supp. V:** 225

Bedient, Calvin, **Supp. IX:** 298; **Supp. XII:** 98

"Bed in the Sky, The" (Snyder), **Supp. VIII:** 300

Bednarik, Joseph, **Supp. VIII:** 39

"Bedrock" (Proulx), **Supp. VII:** 253

"Bee, The" (Lanier), **Supp. I Part 1:** 364

Beecher, Catharine, **Supp. I Part 2:** 581, 582–583, 584, 586, 588, 589, 591, 599; **Supp. X:** 103; **Supp. XI:** 193

Beecher, Charles, **Supp. I Part 2:** 588, 589

Beecher, Edward, **Supp. I Part 2:** 581, 582, 583, 584, 588, 591

Beecher, Harriet. *See* Stowe, Harriet Beecher

Beecher, Henry Ward, **II:** 275; **Supp. I Part 2:** 581; **Supp. XI:** 193

Beecher, Lyman, **Supp. I Part 2:** 580–581, 582, 583, 587, 588, 599; **Supp. XI:** 193

Beecher, Mrs. Lyman (Roxanna Foote), **Supp. I Part 2:** 580–581, 582, 588, 599

Beeching, Jack, **Supp. X:** 114, 117, 118, 123, 125, 126

"Beehive" (Toomer), **Supp. IX:** 317

"Bee Hunt, The" (Irving), **II:** 313

"Beekeeper's Daughter, The" (Plath), **Retro. Supp. II:** 246–247

"Bee Meeting, The" (Plath), **Retro. Supp. II:** 254–255

Bee Poems (Plath), **Retro. Supp. II:** 254–255

Beer, Thomas, **I:** 405

Beerbohm, Max, **III:** 472; **IV:** 436; **Supp. I Part 2:** 714

"Beer in the Sergeant Major's Hat, or The Sun Also Sneezes" (Chandler), **Supp. IV Part 1:** 121

Beethoven, Ludwig van, **II:** 536; **III:** 118; **IV:** 274, 358; **Supp. I Part 1:** 363; **Supp. VIII:** 103

Beet Queen, The (Erdrich), **Supp. IV Part 1:** 259, 260, 264–265, 266, 273, 274, 275

Befo' de War: Echoes in Negro Dialect

(Gordon), **Supp. II Part 1:** 201

"Before" (Goldbarth), **Supp. XII:** 175

"Before" (Snyder), **Supp. VIII:** 301

Before Adam (London), **II:** 466

Before Disaster (Winters), **Supp. II Part 2:** 786, 800

"Before Disaster" (Winters), **Supp. II Part 2:** 801, 815

"Before I Knocked" (D. Thomas), **III:** 534

"Before March" (MacLeish), **III:** 15

"Before the Altar" (Lowell), **II:** 516

"Before the Birth of one of her children" (Bradstreet), **Supp. I Part 1:** 118

"Before the Sky Darkens" (Dunn), **Supp. XI:** 155

"Begat" (Sexton), **Supp. II Part 2:** 693

Beggar on Horseback (Kaufman and Connelly), **III:** 394

"Beggar Said So, The" (Singer), **IV:** 12

Beggars in the House of Plenty (Shanley), **Supp. XIV:** 316, **327–328**

Beggar's Opera, The (Gay), **Supp. I Part 2:** 523

Begiebing, Robert, **Retro. Supp. II:** 210

Begin Again (Paley), **Supp. VI:** 221

"Beginning and the End, The" (Jeffers), **Supp. II Part 2:** 420–421, 424

"Beginning of Decadence, The" (Jeffers), **Supp. II Part 2:** 420

"Beginning of Enthusiasm, The" (Salinas), **Supp. XIII:** 327–328

Beginning of Wisdom, The (Benét), **I:** 358; **Supp. XI:** 44

Be Glad You're Neurotic (Bisch), **Supp. I Part 2:** 608

"Begotten of the Spleen" (Simic), **Supp. VIII:** 277

"Behaving Like a Jew" (Stern), **Supp. IX: 290–291**, 294

"Behavior" (Emerson), **II:** 2, 4

Behavior of Titans, The (Merton), **Supp. VIII:** 201

Behind a Mask (Alcott), **Supp. I Part 1:** 36–37, 43–44

"Behind a Wall" (Lowell), **II:** 516

"Behold the Key" (Malamud), **Supp. I Part 2:** 437

Behrendt, Stephen, **Supp. X:** 204

Behrman, S. N., **Supp. V:** 95

Beidler, Peter G., **Supp. IV Part 2:** 557

Beidler, Philip D., **Supp. XII:** 69

Beige Dolorosa (Harrison), **Supp. VIII:** 40, 51

Beiles, Sinclair, **Supp. XII:** 129

Beiliss, Mendel, **Supp. I Part 2:** 427, 446, 447, 448

"Being a Lutheran Boy-God in Minnesota" (Bly), **Supp. IV Part 1:** 59, 67

Being and Race (Johnson), **Supp. VI:** 193, 199

Being and Time (Heidegger), **Supp. VIII:** 9

Being Busted (Fiedler), **Supp. XIII:** 95, 102, 104

Being There (Kosinski), **Supp. VII:** 215, 216, 222–223

Beiswanger, George, **Retro. Supp. II:** 220

Bel Canto (Patchett), **Supp. XII:** 307, 310, **320–322**

"Beleaguered City, The" (Longfellow), **II:** 498

Belfry of Bruges, The, and Other Poems (Longfellow), **II:** 489; **Retro. Supp. II:** 157, 168

"Belief" (Levine), **Supp. V:** 186, 190

"Beliefs of Writers, The" (Doctorow), **Supp. IV Part 1:** 235–236

"Believers, The/Los Creyentes" (Kingsolver), **Supp. VII:** 208

Belinda (Rice), **Supp. VII:** 301–302

"Belinda's Petition" (Dove), **Supp. IV Part 1:** 245

"Belita" (Ríos), **Supp. IV Part 2:** 541

Belitt, Ben, **Supp. XII:** 260

Bell, Clive, **IV:** 87

Bell, Daniel, **Supp. I Part 2:** 648

Bell, George Kennedy Allen, **Retro. Supp. I:** 65

Bell, Madison Smartt, **Supp. X: 1–20**

Bell, Marvin, **Supp. V:** 337, 339; **Supp. IX:** 152; **Supp. XI:** 316

Bell, Michael, **Retro. Supp. II:** 139

Bell, Pearl, **Supp. XI:** 233

Bell, Quentin, **Supp. I Part 2:** 636

Bell, Whitfield J., Jr., **II:** 123

Bellafante, Gina, **Supp. VIII:** 85

Bellamy, Edward, **II:** 276; **Supp. I Part 2:** 641; **Supp. XI:** 200, 203

Bellarosa Connection, The (Bellow), **Retro. Supp. II:** 31, 32

"Belle Dollinger" (Masters), **Supp. I Part 2:** 463

Belleforest, François de, **IV:** 370

"Belle Zoraïde, La" (Chopin), **Supp. I Part 1:** 215–216

Bell Jar, The (Plath), **Retro. Supp. II:** 242, **249–250; Supp. I Part 2:** 526, 527, 529, 531–536, 539, 540, 541, 542, 544

Belloc, Hilary, **III:** 176; **IV:** 432

Bellow, Saul, **I:** 113, 138–139, **144–166**, 375, 517; **II:** 579; **III:** 40; **IV:**

3, 19, 217, 340; **Retro. Supp. II: 19–36,** 118, 279, 307, 324; **Supp. I Part 2:** 428, 451; **Supp. II Part 1:** 109; **Supp. IV Part 1:** 30; **Supp. V:** 258; **Supp. VIII:** 98, 176, 234, 236–237, 245; **Supp. IX:** 212, 227; **Supp. XI:** 64, 233; **Supp. XII:** 159, 165, 170, 310; **Supp. XIII:** 106

"Bells, The" (Poe), **III:** 593; **Retro. Supp. II:** 266; **Supp. I Part 2:** 388

"Bells, The" (Sexton), **Supp. II Part 2:** 673

"Bells for John Whiteside's Daughter" (Ransom), **III:** 490

"Bells of Lynn, The" (Longfellow), **II:** 498

"Bells of San Blas, The" (Longfellow), **II:** 490–491, 493, 498

"Bell Tower, The" (Melville), **III:** 91

"Belly, The" (Dobyns), **Supp. XIII:** 87

Beloved (Morrison), **Supp. III Part 1:** 364, 372–379; **Supp. IV Part 1:** 13–14; **Supp. V:** 259; **Supp. VIII:** 343; **Supp. XIII:** 60

Beloved Lady: A History of Jane Addams' Ideas on Reform and Peace (Farrell), **Supp. I Part 1:** 24

Benchley, Robert, **I:** 48, 482; **II:** 435; **III:** 53; **Supp. IX:** 190, 195, 204

Benda, W. T., **Retro. Supp. I:** 13

Bend Sinister (Nabokov), **III:** 253–254; **Retro. Supp. I:** 265, 266, 270

"Beneath the Sidewalk" (Dunn), **Supp. XI:** 145

Benedict, Ruth, **Supp. IX:** 229

Benefactor, The (Sontag), **Supp. III Part 2:** 451, 455, 468, 469

"Benefit Performance" (Malamud), **Supp. I Part 2:** 431

Benét, Laura, **Supp. XI:** 44

Benét, Rosemary, **Supp. XI:** 44, 51

Benét, Stephen Vincent, **I:** 358; **II:** 177; **III:** 22; **IV:** 129; **Supp. XI: 43–61**

Benét, William Rose, **II:** 530; **Retro. Supp. I:** 108; **Supp. I Part 2:** 709; **Supp. XI:** 43, 44; **Supp. XIV:** 119, 122, 129

Ben Franklin's Wit and Wisdom (Franklin), **II:** 111

Ben-Hur (film), **Supp. IV Part 2:** 683

Benigna Machiavelli (Gilman), **Supp. XI:** 201, 208

Benitez, R. Michael, **Retro. Supp. II:** 264

Benito Cereno (Lowell), **II:** 546; **Retro. Supp. II:** 181

"Benito Cereno" (Melville), **III:** 91; **Retro. Supp. I:** 255; **Retro. Supp. II:** 188

Benito's Dream Bottle (Nye), **Supp. XIII:** 278

"Bênitou's Slave, The" (Chopin), **Retro. Supp. II:** 64

Benjamin, Walter, **Supp. IX:** 133

Benjamin Franklin (Van Doren), **Supp. I Part 2:** 486

"Benjamin Pantier" (Masters), **Supp. I Part 2:** 461

Bennett, Anne Virginia, **II:** 184

Bennett, Arnold, **I:** 103; **II:** 337

Bennett, Elizabeth, **Supp. VIII:** 58

Bennett, Patrick, **Supp. V:** 225

Bennett, Paula, **Retro. Supp. I:** 29, 33, 42

Bennett, William, **Supp. VIII:** 245

Benson, Jackson J., **Supp. IV Part 2:** 613

Benstock, Shari, **Retro. Supp. I:** 361, 368, 371, 382

Bentham, Jeremy, **I:** 279; **Supp. I Part 2:** 635

Bentley, Eric R., **IV:** 396

Bentley, Nelson, **Supp. IX:** 324

Bentley, Richard, **III:** 79, 86

Benton, Robert, **Supp. IV Part 1:** 236

Beowulf, **Supp. II Part 1:** 6

Beran, Carol, **Supp. XIII:** 25

"Berck-Plage" (Plath), **Retro. Supp. II:** 253–254

Bercovitch, Sacvan, **Retro. Supp. I:** 408; **Retro. Supp. II:** 325, 330; **Supp. I Part 1:** 99; **Supp. I Part 2:** 659

Berdyaev, Nikolai, **I:** 494; **III:** 292

"Bereaved Apartments" (Kingsolver), **Supp. VII:** 203

"Bereavement in their death to feel" (Dickinson), **Retro. Supp. I:** 43, 44

"Berenice" (Poe), **III:** 415, 416, 425; **Retro. Supp. II:** 270

Bérénice (Racine), **II:** 573

Berenson, Bernard, **Retro. Supp. I:** 381; **Supp. IV Part 1:** 314; **Supp. XIV:** 335, 336, 337

Berg, James, **Supp. XIV:** 157, 159

Berg, Stephen, **Supp. IV Part 1:** 60

Berger, Charles, **Retro. Supp. I:** 311

Berger, Roger, **Supp. XIII:** 237

Berger, Thomas, **III:** 258; **Supp. XII:** 171

Bergman, Ingmar, **I:** 291

Bergson, Henri, **I:** 224; **II:** 163, 165, 166, 359; **III:** 8, 9, 488, 619; **IV:** 86, 122, 466, 467; **Retro. Supp. I:** 55, 57, 80; **Supp. IV Part 1:** 42

Berkeley, Anthony, **Supp. IV Part 1:** 341

Berkeley, George, **II:** 10, 349, 357, 480, 554

Berkowitz, Gerald, **Supp. IV Part 2:** 590

Berlin Stories (Isherwood), **Supp. IV Part 1:** 82; **Supp. XIV:** 155, 156, 161, 162, 164, 165

Berlyne, Daniel E., **Supp. I Part 2:** 672

Bernard Clare (Farrell), **II:** 38, 39

Bernard of Clairvaux, Saint, **I:** 22; **II:** 538

Bernays, Thekla, **Retro. Supp. II:** 65

Berne, Suzanne, **Supp. XII:** 320

Berneis, Peter, **IV:** 383

Bernhard, Brendan, **Supp. XIV:** 163

Bernhardt, Sarah, **I:** 484; **Retro. Supp. I:** 377

Bernice (Glaspell), **Supp. III Part 1:** 179

"Bernice Bobs Her Hair" (Fitzgerald), **II:** 88; **Retro. Supp. I:** 103

Bernstein, Aline, **IV:** 455, 456

Bernstein, Andrea, **Supp. IX:** 146

Bernstein, Charles, **Supp. IV Part 2:** 421, 426

Bernstein, Elizabeth, **Supp. XII:** 318

Bernstein, Leonard, **I:** 28; **Supp. I Part 1:** 288, 289; **Supp. IV Part 1:** 83, 84

Bernstein, Melvin, **Supp. XIV:** 41, 46

Bernstein, Michael André, **Retro. Supp. I:** 427

Bernstein, Richard, **Supp. IX:** 253, 262; **Supp. XII:** 113; **Supp. XIV:** 33

Berrett, Jesse, **Supp. XIII:** 241, 242

Berrigan, Ted, **Supp. XIV:** 150

"Berry" (Hughes), **Supp. I Part 1:** 329, 330

Berry, Faith, **Retro. Supp. I:** 194, 201

Berry, Walter, **IV:** 313–314, 326

Berry, Wendell, **Supp. VIII:** 304; **Supp. X: 21–39; Supp. XII:** 202; **Supp. XIII:** 1–2; **Supp. XIV:** 179

"Berry Feast, A" (Snyder), **Supp. VIII:** 289, 297

Berryman, John, **I: 167–189,** 405, 441–442, 521; **II:** 554; **III:** 273; **IV:** 138, 430; **Retro. Supp. I:** 430; **Retro. Supp. II:** 175, 178; **Supp. I Part 2:** 546; **Supp. II Part 1:** 109; **Supp. III Part 2:** 541, 561, 595, 596, 603; **Supp. IV Part 2:** 620, 639; **Supp. V:** 179–180, 337; **Supp. IX:** 152; **Supp. XI:** 240

Berryman, Mrs. John, **I:** 168–169

Berryman's Sonnets (Berryman), **I:** 168, 175–178

"Berry Territory" (Snyder), **Supp. VIII:** 304

Berthoff, Warner, **Supp. I Part 1:** 133

Bertolucci, Bernardo, **Supp. IV Part 1:** 94

"Bertrand Hume" (Masters), **Supp. I Part 2:** 463–464

Best American Essays 1988, The (Dillard, ed.), **Supp. VIII:** 272

Best American Essays 1997, The (Frazier, ed.), **Supp. VIII:** 272

Best American Poetry, The: 1988 (Ashbery, ed.), **Supp. III Part 1:** 26

Best American Short Stories, **I:**174; **II:** 587; **III:** 443; **Supp. IV Part 1:** 102, 315; **Supp. IX:** 114; **Supp. X:** 301

Best American Short Stories, 1915–1050, The, **Supp. IX:** 4

Best American Short Stories of 1942, The, **Supp. V:** 316

Best American Short Stories of 1944, The, **Supp. IX:** 119

Best American Short Stories of the Century (Updike, ed.), **Supp. X:** 163

Best American Short Stories of the Eighties, The (Ravenal, ed.), **Supp. IV Part 1:** 93

"Best China Saucer, The" (Jewett), **Retro. Supp. II:** 145–146

Best Hour of the Night, The (Simpson), **Supp. IX:** 277–279

Bestiaire, Le (Apollinaire), **IV:** 80

Bestiary, A (Wilbur), **Supp. III Part 2:** 552

"Bestiary for the Fingers of My Right Hand" (Simic), **Supp. VIII:** 274, 275

Best Man, The: A Play About Politics (Vidal), **Supp. IV Part 2:** 683

"Best of Everything, The" (Yates), **Supp. XI:** 341

Best Short Plays, The (Mayorga), **IV:** 381

Best Short Stories, The (O'Brien, ed.), **I:** 289

Best Short Stories by Negro Writers, The (Hughes, ed.), **Supp. I Part 1:** 345

Best Times, The: An Informal Memoir (Dos Passos), **I:** 475, 482

Best Words, Best Order: Essays on Poetry (Dobyns), **Supp. XIII:** 74, **76–78,** 87

"BETANCOURT" (Baraka), **Supp. II Part 1:** 33, 34

Bête humaine, La (Zola), **III:** 316, 318

"Bethe" (Hellman), **Supp. I Part 1:** 293

Bethea, David, **Supp. VIII:** 27

Bethel Merriday (Lewis), **II:** 455

Bethlehem in Broad Daylight (Doty), **Supp. XI:** 121, **122–123**

Bethune, Mary McLeod, **Retro. Supp. I:** 197; **Supp. I Part 1:** 333

Bethurum, Dorothy, **IV:** 121

"Betrayal" (Lanier), **Supp. I Part 1:** 364

"Betrothed" (Bogan), **Supp. III Part 1:** 49–51

Bettelheim, Bruno, **Supp. I Part 2:** 622; **Supp. X:** 77, 84; **Supp. XIV:** 126

Better Days (Price), **Supp. VI:** 264

Better Sort, The (James), **II:** 335

Betty Leicester (Jewett), **II:** 406

Betty Leicester's Christmas (Jewett), **II:** 406; **Retro. Supp. II:** 145

Between Angels (Dunn), **Supp. XI: 149–159**

"Between Angels" (Dunn), **Supp. XI:** 150

Between Fantoine and Agapa (Pinget), **Supp. V:** 39

"Between the Porch and the Altar" (Lowell), **II:** 540–541

"Between the World and Me" (Wright), **Supp. II Part 1:** 228

Between Time and Timbuktu (Vonnegut), **Supp. II Part 2:** 753, 759

Bevis, Howard L., **Supp. I Part 2:** 611

Bevis, John, **Supp. I Part 2:** 503

"Bewitched" (Wharton), **IV:** 316

Bewley, Marius, **I:** 336

Beyle, Marie Henri. *See* Stendhal

Beyond (Goldbarth), **Supp. XII:** 192

Beyond Black Bear Lake (LaBastille), **Supp. X:** 95, **99–102,** 108

"Beyond Charles River to the Acheron" (Lowell), **II:** 541

Beyond Criticism (Shapiro), **Supp. II Part 2:** 703, 711

Beyond Culture (Trilling), **Supp. III Part 2:** 508–512

Beyond Desire (Anderson), **I:** 111

Beyond Document: The Art of Nonfiction Film (Warren, ed.), **Supp. IV Part 2:** 434

Beyond Good and Evil (Nietzsche), **Supp. IV Part 2:** 519

"Beyond Harm" (Olds), **Supp. X:** 210

"Beyond the Alps" (Lowell), **II:** 547, 550

"Beyond the Bayou" (Chopin), **Supp. I Part 1:** 215

Beyond the Horizon (O'Neill), **III:** 389

Beyond the Hundredth Meridian: John Wesley Powell and the Second Opening of the West (Stegner), **Supp. IV Part 2:** 599, 603–604, 611

"Beyond the Kittery Bridge" (Hatlen), **Supp. V:** 138

Beyond the Law (film) (Mailer), **Retro. Supp. II:** 205

"Beyond the Sea (at the sanatorium)" (Salinas), **Supp. XIII:** 325

Beyond the Wall: Essays from the Outside (Abbey), **Supp. XIII:** 13

Beyond Tragedy (Niebuhr), **III:** 300–303

Bezner, Kevin, **Supp. XII:** 202

Bhagavad Gita, **III:** 566; **IV:** 183

"Biafra: A People Betrayed" (Vonnegut), **Supp. II Part 2:** 760

Bianchi, Martha Dickinson, **I:** 470; **Retro. Supp. I:** 35, 37, 38

Bible, **I:** 191, 280, 414, 421, 490, 506; **II:** 6, 12, 15, 17, 108, 231, 237, 238, 252, 267, 302; **III:** 28, 199, 308–309, 341, 343, 350, 356, 402, 492, 519, 565, 577; **IV:** 11, 13, 42, 57, 60, 67, 152, 153, 154, 155, 164, 165, 296, 337, 341, 367, 369, 370, 371, 438; **Retro. Supp. I:** 91; **Supp. I Part 1:** 4, 6, 63, 101, 104, 105, 113, 193, 369; **Supp. I Part 2:** 388, 433, 494, 515, 516, 517, 583, 584, 587, 589, 653, 689, 690, 691; **Supp. IV Part 1:** 284; **Supp. VIII:** 20; **Supp. IX:** 246; **Supp. XIV:** 225. *See also* names of biblical books; New Testament; Old Testament

Biblia Americana (Mather), **Supp. II Part 2:** 442

Bibliography of the King's Book, A; or, Eikon Basilike (Almack), **Supp. IV Part 2:** 435

"Bibliography of the King's Book, A, or, Eikon Basilike" (Howe), **Supp. IV Part 2:** 435

Bickel, Freddy. *See* March, Fredric

Bidart, Frank, **Retro. Supp. II:** 48, 50, 52, 182, 183, 184

Bid Me to Live (Doolittle), **Supp. I Part 1:** 258, 260, 268, 269, 270

"*Bien* Pretty" (Cisneros), **Supp. VII:** 70

"Bienvenidos" (Mora), **Supp. XIII:** 220

Bierce, Albert, **I:** 191, 209

Bierce, Ambrose, **I: 190–213,** 419; **II:** 74, 264, 271; **IV:** 350; **Retro. Supp. II:** 72

Bierce, Day, **I:** 195, 199

Bierce, General Lucius Verus, **I:** 191

Bierce, Helen, **I:** 210

Bierce, Leigh, **I:** 195, 198, 208

Bierce, Marcus, **I:** 190, 191

Bierce, Mrs. Ambrose, **I:** 194–195, 199

Bierce, Mrs. Marcus, **I:** 190, 191

Biffle, Kent, **Supp. V:** 225

"Bi-Focal" (Stafford), **Supp. XI:** 318, 321

Big as Life (Doctorow), **Supp. IV Part 1:** 231, 234

"Big Bite" (Mailer), **Retro. Supp. II:** 204

"Big Blonde" (Parker), **Supp. IX:** 189, 192, 193, 195, 196, 203

Big Bozo, The (Glaspell), **Supp. III Part 1:** 182

Bigelow, Gordon, **Supp. X:** 222, 227, 229

Bigelow, Jacob, **Supp. I Part 1:** 302

Bigelow Papers, Second Series, The (Lowell), **Supp. I Part 2:** 406, 415–416

Bigelow Papers, The (Lowell), **Supp. I Part 2:** 406, 407, 408, 410, 411–412, 415, 417, 424

Big Funk, The: A Casual Play (Shanley), **Supp. XIV:** 316, **327**

"Bight, The" (Bishop), **Retro. Supp. II:** 38, 45

Big Hunger: Stories 1932–1959 (Fante), **Supp. XI:** 160

Big Knife, The (Odets), **Supp. II Part 2:** 546, 547, 548

Big Knockover, The (Hammett), **Supp. I Part 1:** 292; **Supp. IV Part 1:** 344, 345, 356

Big Laugh, The (O'Hara), **III:** 362, 373–375

Big Money, The (Dos Passos), **I:** 482, 483, 486–487, 489; **Supp. I Part 2:** 646, 647

"Big Rock Candy Figgy Pudding Pitfall, The" (Didion), **Supp. IV Part 1:** 195

Big Rock Candy Mountain, The (Stegner), **Supp. IV Part 2:** 596, 597, 598, 599, 600, 603, 604, 605, 606–607, 608, 610–611

Bigsby, C. W. E. (Christopher), **Supp. IX:** 137, 140

Big Sea, The (Hughes), **Retro. Supp. I:** 195, 197, 199, 201, 204; **Supp. I Part 1:** 322, 332, 333; **Supp. II Part 1:** 233–234

Big Sky, The (Mora), **Supp. XIII:** 221

Big Sleep, The (Chandler), **Supp. IV Part 1:** 122–125, 127, 128, 134

Big Sleep, The (film), **Supp. IV Part 1:** 130

Big Sur (Kerouac), **Supp. III Part 1:** 230

Big Sur and the Oranges of Hieronymous Bosch (H. Miller), **III:** 189–190

Big Town, The (Lardner), **II:** 426, 429

"Big Two-Hearted River" (Hemingway), **II:** 249; **Retro. Supp. I:** 170–171; **Supp. IX:** 106; **Supp. XIV:** 227, 235

"Big Wind" (Roethke), **III:** 531

"Big Winner Rises Late, The" (Dunn), **Supp. XI:** 146

"Bilingual Christmas" (Mora), **Supp. XIII:** 216–217

"Bilingual Sestina" (Alvarez), **Supp. VII:** 10

"Bill" (Winters), **Supp. II Part 2:** 792

"Bill, The" (Malamud), **Supp. I Part 2:** 427, 430, 434

Billings, Gladys. *See* Brooks, Mrs. Van Wyck

Bill of Rites, a Bill of Wrongs, a Bill of Goods, A (Morris), **III:** 237

"Bill's Beans" (Nye), **Supp. XIII:** 283

"Billy" (Gordon), **Supp. IV Part 1:** 306

"Billy" (McCarriston), **Supp. XIV:** 265

Billy Bathgate (Doctorow), **Supp. IV Part 1:** 217, 219, 222, 224, 227, 229–231, 231, 232, 233, 238

Billy Bathgate (film), **Supp. IV Part 1:** 236

Billy Budd, Sailor (Melville), **III:** 40, 93–95; **IV:** 105; **Retro. Supp. I:** 249, **258–260**

Billy Phelan's Greatest Game (Kennedy), **Supp. VII:** 131, 132, 134, 135, 142–147, 149, 151, 153, 155

Billy the Kid, **Supp. IV Part 2:** 489, 490, 492

Biloxi Blues (Simon), **Supp. IV Part 2:** 576, 577, 584, 586–587, 590

"Bimini" (Hemingway), **II:** 258

Bingham, Millicent Todd, **I:** 470; **Retro. Supp. I:** 36

Bingo Palace, The (Erdrich), **Supp. IV Part 1:** 259, 260, 261, 263–264, 265, 266–267, 268–269, 270, 271–273, 274, 275

"Binsey Poplars" (Hopkins), **Supp. I Part 1:** 94; **Supp. IV Part 2:** 639

Biographia Literaria (Coleridge), **II:** 10; **Retro. Supp. I:** 308

"Biography" (Francis), **Supp. IX:** 77

"Biography" (Pinsky), **Supp. VI:** 235, 236, 239, 241, **243**, 249, 250

Biography and Poetical Remains of the Late Margaret Miller Davidson (Irving), **II:** 314

"Biography in the First Person" (Dunn), **Supp. XI:** 144

"Biography of an Armenian Schoolgirl" (Nye), **Supp. XIII:** 275, 280

"Biography of a Story" (Jackson), **Supp. IX:** 113

Biondi, Joann, **Supp. XI:** 103

"Biopoetics Sketch for *Greenfield Review*" (Harjo), **Supp. XII:** 216

"Birchbrook Mill" (Whittier), **Supp. I Part 2:** 699

"Birches" (Frost), **II:** 154; **Retro. Supp. I:** 132; **Supp. XIII:** 147

Bird, Alan, **Supp. I Part 1:** 260

Bird, Gloria, **Supp. XII:** 216

Bird, Isabella, **Supp. X:** 103

Bird, Robert M., **III:** 423

"Bird, The" (Simpson), **Supp. IX:** 269–270

"Bird, the Bird, the Bird, The" (Creeley), **Supp. IV Part 1:** 149

"Bird came down the Walk, A" (Dickinson), **Retro. Supp. I:** 37

"Bird Frau, The" (Dove), **Supp. IV Part 1:** 245

"Bird in Hand" (screen story) (West and Ingster), **Retro. Supp. II:** 330

Bird Kingdom of the Mayas (LaBastille), **Supp. X:** 96

Birds and Beasts (W. J. Smith), **Supp. XIII:** 346

Bird's Nest, The (Jackson), **Supp. IX:** **124–125**

Birds of America (McCarthy), **II:** 579–583; **Supp. X:** 177

Birds of America (Moore), **Supp. X:** 163, 165, 167, 168, 171, **177–179**

"Birds of Killingsworth, The" (Longfellow), **Retro. Supp. II:** 164

Birds of North America (Audubon Society), **Supp. X:** 177

"Bird-Witted" (Moore), **III:** 214

Birkerts, Sven, **Supp. IV Part 2:** 650; **Supp. V:** 212; **Supp. VIII:** 85; **Supp. X:** 311

Birkhead, L. M., **III:** 116

"Birmingham Sunday" (Hughes), **Supp. I Part 1:** 343

Birnbaum, Henry, **Supp. XII:** 128

Birnbaum, Robert, **Supp. X:** 13

Birney, James G., **Supp. I Part 2:** 587, 588

Birstein, Ann, **Supp. VIII:** 100

Birthday Basket for Tía, A (Mora), **Supp. XIII:** 221

"Birthday Cake for Lionel, A" (Wylie), **Supp. I Part 2:** 721

"Birthday Girl: 1950" (McCarriston), **Supp. XIV:** 261

"Birthday of Mrs. Pineda, The" (Ríos), **Supp. IV Part 2:** 542, 546

"Birthday Poem, A" (Hecht), **Supp. X:** 64

"Birthday Present, A" (Plath), **Supp. I Part 2:** 531

"Birthmark, The" (Ellison), **Retro.**

Supp. II: 116; **Supp. II Part 1:** 237–238

"Birth-mark, The" (Hawthorne), **Retro. Supp. I:** 152

Birth-mark, The: Unsettling the Wilderness in American Literary History (Howe), **Supp. IV Part 2:** 422, 431, 434

Birth of a Nation, The (film), **Supp. I Part 1:** 66

Birth of the Poet, The (Gordon), **Supp. XII:** 7

Birth of Tragedy, The (Nietzsche), **Supp. IV Part 1:** 105, 110; **Supp. IV Part 2:** 519; **Supp. VIII:** 182

"Birth of Venus, The" (Botticelli), **IV:** 410

"Birth of Venus, The" (Rukeyser), **Supp. VI:** 281

"Birthplace Revisited" (Corso), **Supp. XII:** 123

"Birthright" (McKay), **Supp. X:** 136

Bisch, Louis E., **Supp. I Part 2:** 608

Bishop, Elizabeth, **Retro. Supp. I:** 140, 296, 303; **Retro. Supp. II: 37–56,** 175, 178, 189, 233, 234, 235; **Supp. I Part 1: 72–97,** 239, 320, 326; **Supp. III Part 1:** 6, 7, 10, 18, 64, 239, 320, 326; **Supp. III Part 2:** 541, 561; **Supp. IV Part 1:** 249, 257; **Supp. IV Part 2:** 439, 626, 639, 641, 644, 647, 651, 653; **Supp. V:** 337; **Supp. IX:** 40, 41, 45, 47, 48; **Supp. X:** 58; **Supp. XI:** 123, 136; **Supp. XIII:** 115, 348

Bishop, James, Jr., **Supp. XIII:** 1, 5, 6, 7, 9, 11, 15

Bishop, John Peale, **I:** 432, 440; **II:** 81, 85, 86–87, 91, 209; **IV:** 35, 140, 427; **Retro. Supp. I:** 109; **Supp. I Part 2:** 709

Bishop, John W., **Supp. I Part 1:** 83

Bishop, Morris, **Supp. I Part 2:** 676

Bishop, William Thomas, **Supp. I Part 1:** 83

"Bishop's Beggar, The" (Benét), **Supp. XI:** 56

"Bismarck" (Chapman), **Supp. XIV:** 52, 53

Bismark, Otto von, **Supp. I Part 2:** 643

"Bistro Styx, The" (Dove), **Supp. IV Part 1:** 250–251

Bitov, Andrei, **Retro. Supp. I:** 278

"Bitter Drink, The" (Dos Passos), **Supp. I Part 2:** 647

"Bitter Farce, A" (Schwartz), **Supp. II Part 2:** 640, 657–658

"Bitter Pills for the Dark Ladies" (Jong), **Supp. V:** 118

Bitterroot (Burke), **Supp. XIV:** 34, 35

Bitter Victory (Hardy; Kinnell, trans.), **Supp. III Part 1:** 235

Bixby, Horace, **IV:** 194

Bjorkman, Frances Maule, **Supp. V:** 285

Björnson, Björnstjerne, **II:** 275

Black 100, The (Salley), **Supp. XIV:** 195

Blackamerican Literature, 1760-Present (R. Miller), **Supp. X:** 324

Black American Literature Forum, **Supp. XI:** 86, 92, 93

"Black and Tan" (Bell), **Supp. X:** 9

Black Armour (Wylie), **Supp. I Part 2:** 708, 709, 712–714, 729

"Black Art" (Baraka), **Supp. II Part 1:** 49, 50–51, 59, 60

"Black Art, The" (Sexton), **Supp. II Part 2:** 682

"Black Ball, The" (Ellison), **Retro. Supp. II:** 124

Black Bart and the Sacred Hills (Wilson), **Supp. VIII:** 330, 331

Black Beetles in Amber (Bierce), **I:** 204, 209

"Blackberries" (Komunyakaa), **Supp. XIII:** 126

"Blackberry Eating" (Kinnell), **Supp. III Part 1:** 250

Blackberry Winter (Warren), **IV:** 243, 251, 252

Black Betty (Mosley), **Supp. XIII:** 237, **Supp. XIII:** 240, 243

"Black Birch in Winter, A" (Wilbur), **Supp. III Part 2:** 561

Black Boy (Wright), **IV:** 477, 478, 479, 480–482, 488, 489, 494; **Retro. Supp. II:** 117; **Supp. II Part 1:** 235–236; **Supp. IV Part 1:** 11

"Black Boys and Native Sons" (Howe), **Retro. Supp. II:** 112

Blackburn, Alex, **Supp. XIII:** 112

Blackburn, William, **IV:** 100

"Black Buttercups" (Clampitt), **Supp. IX:** 42

Black Cargo, The (Marquand), **III:** 55, 60

Black Cargoes: A History of the Atlantic Slave Trade (Cowley), **Supp. II Part 1:** 140

"Black Cat, The" (Poe), **III:** 413, 414, 415; **Retro. Supp. II:** 264, 267, 269, 270

Black Cherry Blues (Burke), **Supp. XIV:** 30

"Black Christ, The" (Cullen), **Supp. IV Part 1:** 170, 171–172

Black Christ and Other Poems, The (Cullen), **Supp. IV Part 1:** 166, 170

"Black Cottage, The" (Frost), **Retro. Supp. I:** 128

"BLACK DADA NIHILISMUS" (Baraka), **Supp. II Part 1:** 39, 41

"Black Death" (Hurston), **Supp. VI:** 153

Black Dog, Red Dog (Dobyns), **Supp. XIII:** 87, **88–89**

"Black Dog, Red Dog" (Dobyns), **Supp. XIII:** 89

"Black Earth" (Moore), **III:** 197, 212

Black Fire (Jones and Neal, eds.), **Supp. X:** 324, 328

Black Fire: An Anthology of Afro American Writing (Baraka, ed.), **Supp. II Part 1:** 53

Black Flame, The (Du Bois), **Supp. II Part 1:** 159, 185–186

Black Folk, Then and Now: An Essay in the History and Sociology of the Negro Race (Du Bois), **Supp. II Part 1:** 159, 178, 183, 185

"Black Fox, The" (Whittier), **Supp. I Part 2:** 692

Black Freckles (Levis), **Supp. XI:** 257, 271

"Black Gang," **IV:** 406, 407

Black Genius (Mosley, ed.), **Supp. XIII:** 246

"Black Hood, The" (Francis), **Supp. IX:** 83, 91

Black House, The (Theroux), **Supp. VIII:** 319

Black Humor (Johnson), **Supp. VI:** 187, 199

Black Image in the White Mind, The (Fredrickson), **Supp. I Part 2:** 589

"Black Is My Favorite Color" (Malamud), **Supp. I Part 2:** 437

"Black Jewel, The" (Merwin), **Supp. III Part 1:** 355

Black Light (Kinnell), **Supp. III Part 1:** 235, 243

"Blacklist and the Cold War, The" (Kramer), **Supp. I Part 1:** 295

Black Literature in America (Baker), **Supp. X:** 324

Black Magic, A Pictorial History of the Negro in American Entertainment (Hughes), **Supp. I Part 1:** 345

Black Magic: Collected Poetry 1961–1967 (Baraka), **Supp. II Part 1:** 45, 49–50

"Blackmailers Don't Shoot" (Chandler), **Supp. IV Part 1:** 121–122

Black Manhattan (Johnson), **Supp. IV Part 1:** 169

Black Mass, A (Baraka), **Supp. II Part 1:** 46, 48–49, 56, 57

"Black Mesa, The" (Merrill), **Supp. III Part 1:** 328

Black Metropolis (Cayton and Drake), **IV:** 475, 486, 488

Black Misery (Hughes), **Supp. I Part 1:** 336

Blackmur, Helen Dickson (Mrs. R. P. Blackmur), **Supp. II Part 1:** 90

Blackmur, Richard P., **I:** 50, 63, 67, 280, 282, 386, 455, 472; **II:** 320, 537; **III:** 194, 208, 462, 478, 497; **Supp. II Part 1: 87–112,** 136; **Supp. II Part 2:** 543, 643; **Supp. XII:** 45

Black Music (Baraka), **Supp. II Part 1:** 47, 51

Black Nativity (Hughes), **Retro. Supp. I:** 196

"Blackout" (Hay), **Supp. XIV:** 121

"Black Panther" (Hughes), **Retro. Supp. I:** 211

Black Power (Wright), **IV:** 478, 488, 494

"Black Rainbow, A: Modern Afro-American Poetry" (Dove and Waniek), **Supp. IV Part 1:** 244

Black Reconstruction (Du Bois), **Supp. II Part 1:** 159, 162, 171, 182

Black Riders and Other Lines, The (Crane), **I:** 406, 419

"Black Rook in Rainy Weather" (Plath), **Supp. I Part 2:** 543, 544

Blacks (Brooks), **Supp. III Part 1:** 69, 72, 86, 87

Blacks, The (Genet), **Supp. IV Part 1:** 8

Black Skin, White Masks (Fanon), **Retro. Supp. II:** 118

Black Spear, The (Hayden), **Supp. II Part 1:** 375

Black Spring (H. Miller), **III:** 170, 175, 178, 180–182, 183, 184; **Supp. X:** 187

"Black Stone Lying on a White Stone" (Vallejo), **Supp. XIII:** 324

Black Sun (Abbey), **Supp. XIII:** 4, **8–9,** 17

"Black Swan, The" (Jarrell), **II:** 382

Black Swan, The (Merrill), **Supp. III Part 1:** 319, 320

"Black Tambourine" (Crane), **I:** 387–388; **II:** 371

"Black Tuesday" (Swenson), **Supp. IV Part 2:** 646

Black Voices (Chapman), **IV:** 485

"Blackwater Mountain" (Wright), **Supp. V:** 335, 340

"Black Wedding, The" (Singer), **IV:** 12–13

Blackwell, Alice Stone, **Supp. XI:** 195, 197

Blackwell, Elizabeth, **Retro. Supp. II:** 146

Black Woman, The (Bambara, ed.), **Supp. XI:** 1

"Black Workers" (Hughes), **Retro. Supp. I:** 202

"Black Writer and the Southern Experience, The" (Walker), **Supp. III Part 2:** 521

Black Zodiac (Wright), **Supp. V:** 333, 344, 345

Blade Runner (film), **Supp. XI:** 84

Blaine, Anita McCormick, **Supp. I Part 1:** 5

Blair, Hugh, **II:** 8, 17; **Supp. I Part 2:** 422

Blair, Robert, **Supp. I Part 1:** 150

Blair, Walter, **II:** 20; **Retro. Supp. II:** 286

Blaisdell, Gus, **Supp. XIV:** 87

Blake, William, **I:** 381, 383, 389, 390, 398, 447, 476, 525, 526, 533; **II:** 321; **III:** 5, 19, 22, 195, 196, 197, 205, 485, 528, 540, 544–545, 567, 572; **IV:** 129; **Retro. Supp. II:** 76, 300; **Supp. I Part 1:** 80; **Supp. I Part 2:** 385, 514, 517, 539, 552, 708; **Supp. V:** 208, 257, 258; **Supp. VIII:** 26, 99, 103; **Supp. X:** 120; **Supp. XII:** 45; **Supp. XIV:** 344

Blakely, Barbara, **Supp. XIII:** 32

Blanc, Marie Thérèse, **Retro. Supp. II:** 135

Blanc-Bentzon, Mme. Thérèse, **II:** 405

Blanchard, Paula, **Retro. Supp. II:** 131, 133–134, 135

Blancs, Les (Hansberry), **Supp. IV Part 1:** 359, 364, 365, 369, 372–374

Blancs, Les: The Collected Last Plays of Lorraine Hansberry (Nemiroff, ed.), **Supp. IV Part 1:** 365, 368, 374

"'Blandula, Tenulla, Vagula'" (Pound), **III:** 463; **Supp. V:** 336, 337, 345

Blankenship, Tom, **IV:** 193

Blanshard, Rufus A., **I:** 67

Blauvelt, William Satake, **Supp. V:** 171, 173

Blavatsky, Elena Petrovna, **III:** 176

"Blazing in Gold and Quenching in Purple" (Dickinson), **Retro. Supp. I:** 30

Bleak House (Dickens), **II:** 291; **Supp. IV Part 1:** 293

Blechman, Burt, **Supp. I Part 1:** 290

"Bleeder" (Dobyns), **Supp. XIII:** 88

"Bleeding" (Swenson), **Supp. IV Part 2:** 646–647

"Blessed Is the Man" (Moore), **III:** 215

"Blessed Man of Boston, My Grandmother's Thimble, and Fanning Island, The" (Updike), **IV:** 219

"Blessing, A" (Wright), **Supp. III Part 2:** 600, 606

"Blessing the Animals" (Komunyakaa), **Supp. XIII:** 129–130

"Blessing the Children" (Hogan), **Supp. IV Part 1:** 401

Bless Me, Ultima (Anya), **Supp. XIII:** 220

Blew, Mary Clearman, **Supp. XIV:** 227

Bligh, S. M., **I:** 226

Blind Assassin, The (Atwood), **Supp. XIII:** 20, **32**

Blind Bow-Boy, The (Van Vechten), **Supp. II Part 2:** 737, 740–742

Blind Date (Kosinski), **Supp. VII:** 215, 224–225

Blind Lion, The (Gunn Allen), **Supp. IV Part 1:** 324

"Blind Man's Holiday" (O. Henry), **Supp. II Part 1:** 401

Blindness and Insight (de Man), **Retro. Supp. I:** 67

"Blind Poet, The: Sidney Lanier" (Warren), **Supp. I Part 1:** 371, 373

Blithedale Romance, The (Hawthorne), **II:** 225, 231, 239, 241–242, 271, 282, 290; **IV:** 194; **Retro. Supp. I:** 63, 149, 152, 156–157, **162–163;** **Supp. I Part 2:** 579; **Supp. II Part 1:** 280; **Supp. VIII:** 153, 201

Blitzstein, Marc, **Supp. I Part 1:** 277

Blix (Norris), **III:** 314, 322, 327, 328, 333

Blixen, Karen Denisen Baroness. *See* Dinesen, Isak

"Blizzard in Cambridge" (Lowell), **II:** 554

Blok, Aleksandr Aleksandrovich, **IV:** 443

"Blood" (Singer), **IV:** 15, 19

Blood, Tin, Straw (Olds), **Supp. X: 212–215**

Blood and Guts in High School (Acker), **Supp. XII:** 5, 6, **11–12**

"Blood Bay, The" (Proulx), **Supp. VII:** 262–263

"Blood-Burning Moon" (Toomer), **Supp. III Part 2:** 483; **Supp. IX:** 314–315

"Bloodchild" (O. Butler), **Supp. XIII:** 61, **69–70**

Bloodchild and Other Stories (O. Butler), **Supp. XIII:** 69

"Blood Donor" (Hay), **Supp. XIV:** 121

Blood for a Stranger (Jarrell), **II:** 367,

368–369, 370–371, 375, 377
Blood Issue (Crews), **Supp. XI:** 103
Bloodlines (Wright), **Supp. V:** 332, 335, 340
Blood Meridian; or, The Evening Redness in the West (McCarthy), **Supp. VIII:** 175, 177, **180–182,** 188, 190
"Blood of the Conquistadores, The" (Alvarez), **Supp. VII:** 7
"Blood of the Lamb, The" (hymn), **Supp. I Part 2:** 385
Blood of the Martyr (Crane), **I:** 422
"Blood of the Martyrs, The" (Benét), **Supp. XI:** 56, 58
Blood of the Prophets, The (Masters), **Supp. I Part 2:** 458, 459, 461
Blood on the Forge (Attaway), **Supp. II Part 1:** 234–235
"Blood Returns, The" (Kingsolver), **Supp. VII:** 209
Bloodshed and Three Novellas (Ozick), **Supp. V:** 259–260, 261, 266–268
"Blood Stains" (Francis), **Supp. IX:** 86
Bloody Crossroads, The: Where Literature and Politics Meet (Podhoretz), **Supp. VIII: 241–242**
Bloom, Alice, **Supp. IV Part 1:** 308
Bloom, Allan, **Retro. Supp. II:** 19, 30, 31, 33–34
Bloom, Claire, **Retro. Supp. II:** 281; **Supp. IX:** 125
Bloom, Harold, **Retro. Supp. I:** 67, 193, 299; **Retro. Supp. II:** 81, 210, 262; **Supp. IV Part 2:** 620, 689; **Supp. V:** 178, 272; **Supp. VIII:** 180; **Supp. IX:** 146, 259; **Supp. XII:** 261; **Supp. XIII:** 46, 47; **Supp. XIV:** 14
Bloom, Larry, **Supp. XIII:** 133
Bloom, Leopold, **I:** 27, 150; **III:** 10
Bloom, Lynn Z., **Supp. IV Part 1:** 6
Bloomfield, Leonard, **I:** 64
"Blossom and Fruit" (Benét), **Supp. XI:** 52–53
Blotner, Joseph, **Retro. Supp. I:** 88
Blouin, Lenora, **Supp. VIII:** 266
"Blue Battalions, The" (Crane), **I:** 419–420
"Bluebeard" (Barthelme), **Supp. IV Part 1:** 47
"Bluebeard" (Millay), **III:** 130
"Blueberries" (Frost), **Retro. Supp. I:** 121, 128
Blue Calhoun (Price), **Supp. VI:** 265–266
Blue City (Macdonald, under Millar), **Supp. IV Part 2:** 466–467
Blue Dahlia, The (Chandler), **Supp. IV Part 1:** 130

Blue Estuaries, The: Poems, 1923–1968 (Bogan), **Supp. III Part 1:** 48, 57, 66
Blue Hammer, The (Macdonald), **Supp. IV Part 2:** 462
"Blue Hotel, The" (Crane), **I:** 34, 415–416, 423
"Blue Hour, The" (Komunyakaa), **Supp. XIII:** 130
Blue in the Face (Auster), **Supp. XII:** 21
Blue Jay's Dance, The: A Birth Year (Erdrich), **Supp. IV Part 1:** 259–260, 265, 270, 272
"Blue Juniata" (Cowley), **Supp. II Part 1:** 144
Blue Juniata: Collected Poems (Cowley), **Supp. II Part 1:** 140
Blue Light (Mosley), **Supp. XIII: 245–247,** 248, 249
"Blue Light Lounge Sutra for the Performance Poets at Harold Park Hotel" (Komunyakaa), **Supp. XIII:** 125
"Blue Meridian" (Toomer), **Supp. III Part 2:** 476, 487; **Supp. IX:** 320
"Blue Moles" (Plath), **Supp. I Part 2:** 539
Blue Mountain Ballads (music) (Bowles), **Supp. IV Part 1:** 84
Blue Movie (Southern), **Supp. XI:** 309
"Blue Notes" (Matthews), **Supp. IX:** 169
Blue Pastures (Oliver), **Supp. VII:** 229–230, 245
"Blueprints" (Kingsolver), **Supp. VII:** 203
"Blue Ribbon at Amesbury, A" (Frost), **Retro. Supp. I:** 138
"Blues Ain't No Mockin Bird" (Bambara), **Supp. XI:** 3
"Blues Chant Hoodoo Rival" (Komunyakaa), **Supp. XIII:** 117, 118
"Blues for Another Time" (Dunn), **Supp. XI:** 148
"Blues for Jimmy" (McGrath), **Supp. X:** 116
"Blues for John Coltraine, Dead at 41" (Matthews), **Supp. IX:** 157
Blues for Mister Charlie (Baldwin), **Retro. Supp. II:** 8; **Supp. I Part 1:** 48, 61–62, 63
"Blues for Warren" (McGrath), **Supp. X:** 116
Blues If You Want (Matthews), **Supp. IX:** 155, **163–165**
"Blues I'm Playing, The" (Hughes), **Retro. Supp. I:** 204

"Blue Sky, The" (Snyder), **Supp. VIII:** 306
"Blues on a Box" (Hughes), **Retro. Supp. I:** 208
"Blues People" (Ellison), **Retro. Supp. II:** 124
Blues People: Negro Music in White America (Baraka), **Retro. Supp. II:** 124; **Supp. II Part 1:** 30, 31, 33–35, 37, 41, 42, 53
Bluest Eye, The (Morrison), **Supp. III Part 1:** 362, 363–367, 379; **Supp. IV Part 1:** 2, 253; **Supp. VIII:** 213, 214, 227; **Supp. XI:** 4, 91
Bluestone, George, **Supp. IX:** 7, 15
Blue Swallows, The (Nemerov), **III:** 269, 270, 271, 274–275, 278, 284, 286–288
Blue Voyage (Aiken), **I:** 53, 56
Blum, Morgan, **I:** 169
Blum, W. C (pseudonym). *See* Watson, James Sibley, Jr.
Blumenthal, Nathaniel. *See* Branden, Nathaniel
Blumenthal, Sidney, **Supp. VIII:** 241
Blunt, Wilfrid Scawen, **III:** 459
Bly, Robert, **I:** 291; **Supp. III Part 2:** 599; **Supp. IV Part 1:** **59–77,** 177; **Supp. IV Part 2:** 623; **Supp. V:** 332; **Supp. VIII:** 279; **Supp. IX:** 152, 155, 265, 271, 290; **Supp. X:** 127; **Supp. XI:** 142; **Supp. XIII:** 284
"Boarder, The" (Simpson), **Supp. IX:** 269
Boarding House Blues (Farrell), **II:** 30, 43, 45
Boas, Franz, **I:** 214; **Supp. I Part 2:** 641; **Supp. VIII:** 295; **Supp. IX:** 329; **Supp. XIV:** 199, 209, 210
"Boat, The" (Oliver), **Supp. VII:** 247
"Boat, The" (Sexton), **Supp. II Part 2:** 692
Boating Party, The (Renoir), **Supp. XII:** 188
Boat of Quiet Hours, The (Kenyon), **Supp. VII:** 167–169, 171
"Boat of Quiet Hours, The" (Kenyon), **Supp. VII:** 168
"Bob and Spike" (Wolfe), **Supp. III Part 2:** 580
Bob the Gambler (F. Barthelme), **Supp. XI:** 30, 31, 32, 34–35, 36–37
Boccaccio, Giovanni, **III:** 283, 411; **IV:** 230
Bocock, Maclin, **Supp. X:** 79
Bodenheim, Maxwell, **II:** 42, 530; **Retro. Supp. I:** 417; **Supp. I Part 1:** 257
"Bodies" (Oates), **Supp. II Part 2:** 520

"Bodies and Souls: The Haitian Revolution and Madison Smartt Bell's *All Souls' Rising*" (Trouillot), **Supp. X:** 14

Bodies of Work: Essays (Acker), **Supp. XII:** 7

Bodily Harm (Atwood), **Supp. XIII: 25–27**

Bodley Head Jack London (London), **II:** 483

Body (Crews), **Supp. XI: 108–109**

"Body, The" (Heldreth), **Supp. V:** 151

"Body and Soul: A Meditation" (Kumin), **Supp. IV Part 2:** 442, 452

Body and the Song, The (Bishop), **Retro. Supp. II:** 40

Body of This Death: Poems (Bogan), **Supp. III Part 1:** 47, 49–52, 58

Body of Waking (Rukeyser), **Supp. VI:** 274, 281

"Body of Waking" (Rukeyser), **Supp. VI:** 279

Body Rags (Kinnell), **Supp. III Part 1:** 235, 236, 243–245, 250, 253, 254

"Body's Curse, The" (Dobyns), **Supp. XIII:** 87

"Body's Weight, The" (Dobyns), **Supp. XIII:** 89

Body Traffic (Dobyns), **Supp. XIII:** 87, 89

"'Body with the Lamp Lit Inside, The'" (Mills), **Supp. IV Part 1:** 64

Boehme, Jakob, **I:** 10

Bogan, Louise, **I:** 169, 185; **Retro. Supp. I:** 36; **Supp. I Part 2:** 707, 726; **Supp. III Part 1: 47–68**; **Supp. VIII:** 171, 265; **Supp. IX:** 229; **Supp. X:** 58, 102; **Supp. XIII:** 347; **Supp. XIV:** 129

Bogan, Major Benjamin Lewis, **IV:** 120

Bogart, Humphrey, **Supp. I Part 2:** 623; **Supp. IV Part 1:** 130, 356

Bogdanovich, Peter, **Supp. V:** 226

"Bohemian, The" (Harte), **Supp. II Part 1:** 339

"Bohemian Girl, The" (Cather), **Retro. Supp. I:** 7

"Bohemian Hymn, The" (Emerson), **II:** 19

Boissevain, Eugen, **III:** 124

Boit, Edward, **Retro. Supp. I:** 366

Bojorquez, Jennifer, **Supp. XII:** 318

"Bold Words at the Bridge" (Jewett), **II:** 394

Boleslavsky, Richard, **Supp. XIV:** 240, 243

Boleyn, Anne, **Supp. I Part 2:** 461

Bolivar, Simon, **Supp. I Part 1:** 283, 284, 285

Bolton, Guy, **Supp. I Part 1:** 281

Bolts of Melody: New Poems of Emily Dickinson (Todd and Bingham, eds.), **I:** 470; **Retro. Supp. I:** 36

"Bomb" (Corso), **Supp. XII:** 117, 124, 125–126, 127

Bombs Away (Steinbeck), **IV:** 51–52

"Bona and Paul" (Toomer), **Supp. IX:** 307, 318–319

Bonaparte, Marie, **III:** 418; **Retro. Supp. II:** 264, 266

"Bon-Bon" (Poe), **III:** 425

Bone, Robert, **Supp. IX:** 318–319; **Supp. XI:** 283

Bone by Bone (Matthiessen), **Supp. V:** 199, 212, 213, 214

"Bones" (Goldbarth), **Supp. XII: 173–174**

"Bones and Jewels" (Monette), **Supp. X:** 159

"Bones of a House" (Cowley). *See* "Blue Juniata"

Bonetti, Kay, **Supp. VIII:** 47, 152, 159, 160, 165, 168, 170, 223; **Supp. XII:** 61; **Supp. XIV:** 232, 234

Bonfire of the Vanities, The (Wolfe), **Supp. III Part 2:** 584–586

Bonhoeffer, Dietrich, **Supp. VIII:** 198

Boni, Charles, **Supp. XIV:** 288

Boni and Liveright, **Retro. Supp. I:** 59, 80, 178

Bonicelli, Vittorio, **Supp. XI:** 307

Bonifacius (Mather), **Supp. II Part 2:** 461, 464

Bonnefoy, Yves, **Supp. III Part 1:** 235, 243

Bonner, Robert, **Retro. Supp. I:** 246

Bonneville, Mme. Marguerite, **Supp. I Part 2:** 520, 521

Bonneville, Nicolas de, **Supp. I Part 2:** 511, 518, 519

Bonney, William. *See* Billy the Kid

Bontemps, Arna, **Retro. Supp. I:** 194, 196, 203; **Supp. I Part 1:** 325; **Supp. IV Part 1:** 170; **Supp. IX:** 306, 309

Book, A (Barnes), **Supp. III Part 1:** 36, 39, 44

Book about Myself, A (Dreiser), **I:** 515; **Retro. Supp. II:** 104

"Book as a Container of Consciousness, The" (Gass), **Supp. VI:** 92

"Bookies, Beware!" (Heller), **Supp. IV Part 1:** 383

Book of American Negro Poetry, The (Johnson), **Supp. IV Part 1:** 165, 166

Book of Americans, A (Benét), **Supp. XI:** 46, 47, 51

Book of Beb, The (Buechner), **Supp. XII:** 53

Book of Breeething, The (Burroughs), **Supp. III Part 1:** 97, 103

Book of Burlesques, A (Mencken), **III:** 104

Book of Common Prayer, A (Didion), **Supp. IV Part 1:** 196, 198, 203–205, 207, 208

Book of Daniel, The (Doctorow), **Supp. IV Part 1:** 218, 219, 220–222, 227, 231, 237–238, 238; **Supp. V:** 45

Book of Dreams (Kerouac), **Supp. III Part 1:** 225

"Book of Ephraim, The" (Merrill), **Supp. III Part 1:** 330–334

Book of Folly, The (Sexton), **Supp. II Part 2:** 691, 692–694

Book of Gods and Devils, The (Simic), **Supp. VIII: 281**

"Book of Hours of Sister Clotilde, The" (Lowell), **II:** 522

Book of Jamaica, The (Banks), **Supp. V:** 11, 12, 16

Book of Medicines, The (Hogan), **Supp. IV Part 1:** 397, 410, 411–414

"Book of Medicines, The" (Hogan), **Supp. IV Part 1:** 412, 413

"Book of Memory, The" (Auster), **Supp. XII:** 21–22

Book of Negro Folklore, The (Hughes, ed.), **Supp. I Part 1:** 345

Book of Nightmares, The (Kinnell), **Supp. III Part 1:** 235, 236, 243, 244, 246–254

Book of Prefaces, A (Mencken), **III:** 99–100, 105

Book of Repulsive Women, The (Barnes), **Supp. III Part 1:** 33

Book of Roses, The (Parkman), **Supp. II Part 2:** 597, 598

"Book of the Dead, The" (Rukeyser), **Supp. VI:** 272, 278, 279

"Book of the Grotesque, The" (Anderson), **I:** 106

Book of the Homeless, The (Wharton), **Retro. Supp. I:** 377

Book of the Hopi (Waters), **Supp. X:** 124

Book of Tobit (Bible), **Supp. XII:** 54

Book of Verses, A (Masters), **Supp. I Part 2:** 458

"Book of Yolek, The" (Hecht), **Supp. X:** 69, **70–71**

"Books Considered" (Bloom), **Supp. I Part 1:** 96

Books in My Life, The (H. Miller), **II:** 176, 189

"Books/P,L,E, The" (Goldbarth), **Supp. XII:** 190

Bookviews, **Supp. XI:** 216

"Boom" (Nemerov), **III:** 278

Boom! (T. Williams), **IV:** 383

Boom Town (Wolfe), **IV:** 456

"Boom Town" (Wolfe), **IV:** 469

Boone, Daniel, **II:** 207; **III:** 444; **IV:** 192, 193

Boorstin, Daniel, **I:** 253

Booth, Charles, **Supp. I Part 1:** 13

Booth, General William, **Supp. I Part 2:** 384, 386

Booth, John Wilkes, **III:** 588

Booth, Philip, **I:** 522; **Supp. IX:** 269; **Supp. XI:** 141; **Supp. XIII:** 277

Borah, William, **III:** 475

Borden, Lizzie, **II:** 5

Borderlands/La Frontera: The New Mestiza (Anzaldúa), **Supp. XIII:** 223

Borders (Mora), **Supp. XIII:** 213, **215–217**

Border Trilogy (McCarthy), **Supp. VIII:** 175, 182

Borel, Pétrus, **III:** 320

Borges, Jorge Luis, **I:** 123, 135, 138, 140, 142; **Supp. III Part 2:** 560; **Supp. IV Part 2:** 623, 626, 630; **Supp. V:** 238; **Supp. VIII:** 15, 348, 349; **Supp. XII:** 21, 147

"Borinken Blues" (Komunyakaa), **Supp. XIII:** 117

"Born a Square: The Westerner's Dilemma" (Stegner), **Supp. IV Part 2:** 595; **Supp. V:** 224

"Born Bad" (Cisneros), **Supp. VII:** 62

Borrowed Time: An AIDS Memoir (Monette), **Supp. X:** 145, 146, 147, 152, 154, 155

"Bosque del Apache Wildlife Refuge" (Mora), **Supp. XIII:** 218

"Boston" (Hardwick), **Supp. III Part 1:** 201

Boston (Sinclair), **Supp. V:** 282, 288–289

Boston, B. H., **Supp. XIII:** 312

Boston Adventure (Stafford), **Retro. Supp. II:** 177, 178

"Boston Common" (Berryman), **I:** 172

"Boston Hymn" (Emerson), **II:** 13, 19

Bostonians, The (James), **I:** 9; **II:** 282; **IV:** 202; **Retro. Supp. I:** 216, 225

Boston Marriage (Mamet), **Supp. XIV:** 247

"Boston Nativity, The" (Lowell), **II:** 538

Boswell: A Modern Comedy (Elkin), **Supp. VI:** 42, **44–45,** 57

Boswell, James, **IV:** 431; **Supp. I Part 2:** 656

Bosworth, Patricia, **Supp. IV Part 2:** 573, 591

Botticelli (McNally), **Supp. XIII:** 197

Botticelli, Sandro, **IV:** 410; **Retro. Supp. I:** 422

"Botticellian Trees, The" (W. C. Williams), **Retro. Supp. I:** 422

"Bottle of Milk for Mother, A" (Algren), **Supp. IX:** 3

"Bottle of Perrier, A" (Wharton), **IV:** 316

"Bottles" (Kenyon), **Supp. VII:** 171

Bottom: On Shakespeare (Zukofsky), **Supp. III Part 2:** 622, 624, 625, 626, 627, 629

"Bottom Line, The" (Elkin), **Supp. VI:** 52, **53**

Boucher, Anthony, **Supp. IV Part 2:** 473

Boulanger, Nadia, **Supp. IV Part 1:** 81

"Boulot and Boulette" (Chopin), **Supp. I Part 1:** 211

Boulton, Agnes, **III:** 403

Bound East for Cardiff (O'Neill), **III:** 388

"Bouquet, The" (Stevens), **IV:** 90

"Bouquet of Roses in Sunlight" (Stevens), **IV:** 93

Bourdin, Henri L., **Supp. I Part 1:** 251

Bourgeois Poet, The (Shapiro), **Supp. II Part 2:** 701, 703, 704, 713, 714–716

Bourget, James, **IV:** 319

Bourget, Paul, **II:** 325, 338; **IV:** 311, 315; **Retro. Supp. I:** 224, 359, 373

Bourjaily, Vance, **III:** 43; **Supp. IX:** 260

Bourke-White, Margaret, **I:** 290, 293, 295, 297

Bourne, Charles Rogers, **I:** 215

Bourne, Mrs. Charles Rogers, **I:** 215

Bourne, Randolph, **I:** **214–238,** 243, 245, 246–247, 251, 259; **Supp. I Part 2:** 524

Bowden, Charles, **Supp. XIII:** 17

Bowditch, Nathaniel, **Supp. I Part 2:** 482

Bowen, Barbara, **Supp. IX:** 311

Bowen, Elizabeth, **Retro. Supp. I:** 351; **Supp. IV Part 1:** 299; **Supp. VIII:** 65, 165, 251, 265; **Supp. IX:** 128

Bowen, Francis, **Supp. I Part 2:** 413

Bowen, Louise de Koven, **Supp. I Part 1:** 5

Bowen, Michael, **Supp. VIII:** 73

Bowers, John, **Supp. XI:** 217–218

"Bowlers Anonymous" (Dobyns), **Supp. XIII:** 86

Bowles, Jane (Jane Auer), **II:** 586; **Supp. IV Part 1:** 89, 92

Bowles, Paul, **I:** 211; **II:** 586; **Supp. II Part 1:** 17; **Supp. IV Part 1:** **79–99**

Bowles, Samuel, **I:** 454, 457; **Retro. Supp. I:** 30, 32, 33

"Bowl of Blood, The" (Jeffers), **Supp. II Part 2:** 434

"Bowls" (Moore), **III:** 196

Bowman, James, **I:** 193

"Bows to Drouth" (Snyder), **Supp. VIII:** 303

Box, Edgar (pseudonym). *See* Vidal, Gore

Box and Quotations from Chairman Mao Tse-tung (Albee), **I:** 89–91, 94

Box Garden, The (Shields), **Supp. VII:** 314–315, 320

"Box Seat" (Toomer), **Supp. III Part 2:** 484; **Supp. IX:** 316, 318

Boy, A (Ashbery), **Supp. III Part 1:** 5

Boyce, Horace, **II:** 136

Boyd, Brian, **Retro. Supp. I:** 270, 275

Boyd, Janet L., **Supp. X:** 229

Boyd, Nancy (pseudonym). *See* Millay, Edna St. Vincent

Boyd, Thomas, **I:** 99; **IV:** 427

Boyesen, H. H., **II:** 289

"Boyhood" (Farrell), **II:** 28

"Boy in France, A" (Salinger), **III:** 552–553

Boy in the Water (Dobyns), **Supp. XIII:** 75, **84**

Boyle, Kay, **IV:** 404

Boyle, T. C. (Thomas Coraghessan), **Supp. VIII:** 1–17

Boyle, Thomas John. *See* Boyle, T. C.

Boynton, H. W., **Supp. IX:** 7

Boynton, Percy Holmes, **Supp. I Part 2:** 415

"Boy on a Train" (Ellison), **Retro. Supp. II:** 124

"Boy Riding Forward Backward" (Francis), **Supp. IX:** 82

"Boys and Girls" (Cisneros), **Supp. VII:** 59–60

Boy's Froissart, The (Lanier), **Supp. I Part 1:** 361

Boy's King Arthur, The (Lanier), **Supp. I Part 1:** 361

Boy's Mabinogion, The (Lanier), **Supp. I Part 1:** 361

"Boys of '29, The" (Holmes), **Supp. I Part 1:** 308

Boys of '76, The (Coffin), **III:** 577

Boy's Percy, The (Lanier), **Supp. I Part 1:** 361

Boy's Town (Howells), **I:** 418

Boy's Will, A (Frost), **II:** 152, 153, 155–156, 159, 164, 166; **Retro.**

Supp. I: 124, 127, 128, 131; **Retro. Supp. II:** 168

"Boy Who Wrestled with Angels, The" (Hoffman), **Supp. X:** 90

"Boy with One Shoe, The" (Jewett), **Retro. Supp. II:** 132

"Brace, The" (Bausch), **Supp. VII:** 48

Bracebridge Hall, or, The Humorists (Irving), **I:** 339, 341; **II:** 308–309, 313

Bracher, Frederick, **I:** 378, 380; **Supp. I Part 1:** 185

Brackenridge, Hugh Henry, **Supp. I Part 1:** 124, 127, 145; **Supp. II Part 1:** 65

Brackett, Leigh, **Supp. IV Part 1:** 130

Bradbury, John M., **I:** 288–289; **IV:** 130, 135

Bradbury, Malcolm, **Supp. VIII:** 124

Bradbury, Ray, **Supp. I Part 2:** 621–622; **Supp. IV Part 1: 101–118**

Braddon, Mary E., **Supp. I Part 1:** 35, 36

Bradfield, Scott, **Supp. VIII:** 88

Bradford, Gamaliel, **I:** 248, 250

Bradford, Roark, **Retro. Supp. I:** 80

Bradford, William, **Retro. Supp. II:** 161, 162; **Supp. I Part 1:** 110, 112; **Supp. I Part 2:** 486, 494

Bradlee, Ben, **Supp. V:** 201

Bradley, Bill, **Supp. VIII:** 47

Bradley, F. H., **Retro. Supp. I:** 57, 58

Bradley, Francis Herbert, **I:** 59, 567–568, 572, 573

Bradshaw, Barbara, **Supp. XIII:** 313

Bradstreet, Anne, **I:** 178–179, 180, 181, 182, 184; **III:** 505; **Retro. Supp. I:** 40; **Supp. I Part 1: 98–123,** 300; **Supp. I Part 2:** 484, 485, 496, 546, 705; **Supp. V:** 113, 117–118; **Supp. XIII:** 152; **Supp. XIV:** 128

Bradstreet, Elizabeth, **Supp. I Part 1:** 108, 122

Bradstreet, Mrs. Simon. *See* Bradstreet, Anne

Bradstreet, Simon, **I:** 178; **Supp. I Part 1:** 103, 110, 116

Brady, Alice, **III:** 399

"Bragdowdy and the Busybody, The" (Thurber), **Supp. I Part 2:** 617

"Brahma" (Emerson), **II:** 19, 20

Brahms, Johannes, **III:** 118, 448

"Brain and the Mind, The" (James), **II:** 346

"Brain Damage" (Barthelme), **Supp. IV Part 1:** 44

"Brain to the Heart, The" (Komunyakaa), **Supp. XIII:** 120

Braithewaite, W. S., **Retro. Supp. I:** 131

Braithwaite, William Stanley, **Supp. IX:** 309

Brakhage, Stan, **Supp. XII:** 2

Bramer, Monte, **Supp. X:** 152

Branch Will Not Break, The (Wright), **Supp. III Part 2:** 596, 598–601; **Supp. IV Part 1:** 60; **Supp. IX:** 159

Brancusi, Constantin, **III:** 201; **Retro. Supp. I:** 292

Brande, Dorothea, **Supp. I Part 2:** 608

Branden, Nathaniel, **Supp. IV Part 2:** 526, 528

"Brand-Name Blues" (Kaufmann), **Supp. XI:** 39

Brand New Life, A (Farrell), **II:** 46, 48

Brando, Marlon, **II:** 588; **Supp. IV Part 2:** 560

Brandon, Henry, **Supp. I Part 2:** 604, 612, 618

Brandt, Alice, **Supp. I Part 1:** 92

Brandt, Carl, **Supp. XI:** 45

Brant, Sebastian, **III:** 447, 448

Braque, Georges, **III:** 197; **Supp. IX:** 66

Brashford, Jake, **Supp. X:** 252

Brasil, Emanuel, **Supp. I Part 1:** 94

"Brasília" (Plath), **Supp. I Part 2:** 544, 545

"Brass Buttons" (McCoy), **Supp. XIII:** 161

"Brass Candlestick, The" (Francis), **Supp. IX:** 89

Brass Check, The (Sinclair), **Supp. V:** 276, 281, 282, 284–285

"Brass Ring, The" (Carver), **Supp. III Part 1:** 137

"Brass Spittoons" (Hughes), **Supp. I Part 1:** 326–327

Brautigan, Richard, **III:** 174; **Supp. VIII:** 42, 43; **Supp. XII:** 139

Brave Cowboy, The (Abbey), **Supp. XIII:** 4–5

Brave New World (Huxley), **II:** 454; **Supp. XIII:** 29

"Brave New World" (MacLeish), **III:** 18

Bravery of Earth, A (Eberhart), **I:** 522, 524, 525, 526, 530

"Brave Words for a Startling Occasion" (Ellison), **Retro. Supp. II:** 118

Braving the Elements (Merrill), **Supp. III Part 1:** 320, 323, 325–327, 329

Bravo, The (Cooper), **I:** 345–346, 348

"Bravura" (Francis), **Supp. IX:** 90

Brawley, Benjamin, **Supp. I Part 1:** 327, 332

Brawne, Fanny, **I:** 284; **II:** 531

Braxton, Joanne, **Supp. IV Part 1:** 12, 15

Brazil (Bishop), **Retro. Supp. II:** 45; **Supp. I Part 1:** 92

"Brazil" (Marshall), **Supp. XI:** 281

Brazil (Updike), **Retro. Supp. I:** 329, 330, 334

"Brazil, January 1, 1502" (Bishop), **Retro. Supp. II:** 47

Braziller, George, **Supp. X:** 24

Brazzi, Rossano, **Supp. IV Part 2:** 520

"Bread" (Dickey), **Supp. IV Part 1:** 182

"Bread" (Olds), **Supp. X:** 206

"Bread Alone" (Wylie), **Supp. I Part 2:** 727

Bread in the Wilderness (Merton), **Supp. VIII:** 197, 208

Bread of Idleness, The (Masters), **Supp. I Part 2:** 460

"Bread of This World, The" (McGrath), **Supp. X:** 119, 127

Bread of Time, The (Levine), **Supp. V:** 180

Bread without Sugar (Stern), **Supp. IX: 297–298**

"Break, The" (Sexton), **Supp. II Part 2:** 689

Breakfast at Tiffany's (Capote), **Supp. III Part 1:** 113, 117, 119–121, 124, 126

Breakfast of Champions (Vonnegut), **Supp. II Part 2:** 755, 759, 769, 770, 777–778

Breaking Ice (McMillan, ed.), **Supp. XIII:** 182–183

Breaking Open (Rukeyser), **Supp. VI:** 274, 281

"Breaking Open" (Rukeyser), **Supp. VI:** 286

Breaking Ranks: A Political Memoir (Podhoretz), **Supp. VIII: 239–241,** 245

"Breaking the Code of Silence: Ideology and Women's Confessional Poetry" (Harris), **Supp. XIV:** 269

"Breaking Up of the Winships, The" (Thurber), **Supp. I Part 2:** 616

Breast, The (Roth), **Retro. Supp. II:** 287–288; **Supp. III Part 2:** 416, 418

"Breast, The" (Sexton), **Supp. II Part 2:** 687

"Breasts" (Simic), **Supp. VIII:** 275

"Breath" (Levine), **Supp. V:** 185

Breathing Lessons (Tyler), **Supp. IV Part 2:** 669–670

Breathing the Water (Levertov), **Supp. III Part 1:** 274, 283, 284

Breaux, Zelia, **Retro. Supp. II:** 114

382 / AMERICAN WRITERS

Brecht, Bertolt, **I:** 60, 301; **III:** 161, 162; **IV:** 394; **Supp. I Part 1:** 292; **Supp. II Part 1:** 10, 26, 56; **Supp. IV Part 1:** 359; **Supp. IX:** 131, 133, 140; **Supp. X:** 112; **Supp. XIII:** 206, 286; **Supp. XIV:** 162

Breen, Joseph I., **IV:** 390

Breit, Harvey, **I:** 433; **III:** 575; **Retro. Supp. II:** 230

Bremer, Fredrika, **Supp. I Part 1:** 407

Brendan: A Novel (Buechner), **Supp. XII:** 53

Brent, Linda, **Supp. IV Part 1:** 12, 13

Brentano, Franz, **II:** 350; **Supp. XIV:** 198, 199

Brer Rabbit (tales), **Supp. IV Part 1:** 11, 13; **Supp. XIV:** 88

Breslin, James E. B., **Retro. Supp. I:** 430

Breslin, John B., **Supp. IV Part 1:** 308

Breslin, Paul, **Supp. VIII:** 283

Bresson, Robert, **Supp. IV Part 1:** 156

"Bresson's Movies" (Creeley), **Supp. IV Part 1:** 156–157

Breton, André, **III:** 425; **Supp. XIII:** 114

Brett, George, **II:** 466; **Supp. V:** 286

Brevoort, Henry, **II:** 298

Brew, Kwesi, **Supp. IV Part 1:** 10, 16

"Brewing of Soma, The" (Whittier), **Supp. I Part 2:** 704

Brewsie and Willie (Stein), **IV:** 27

Brewster, Martha, **Supp. I Part 1:** 114

"Brian Age 7" (Doty), **Supp. XI:** 136

"Briar Patch, The" (Warren), **IV:** 237

Briar Rose (Coover), **Supp. V:** 52

"Briar Rose (Sleeping Beauty)" (Sexton), **Supp. II Part 2:** 690

Brice, Fanny, **II:** 427

"Brick, The" (Nye), **Supp. XIII:** 276

"Bricklayer in the Snow" (Fante), **Supp. XI:** 164–165

"Brick Layer's Lunch Hour, The" (Ginsberg), **Supp. II Part 1:** 318

"Bricks, The" (Hogan), **Supp. IV Part 1:** 413

"Bridal Ballad, The" (Poe), **III:** 428

Bridal Dinner, The (Gurney), **Supp. V:** 109, 110

"Bride Comes to Yellow Sky, The" (Crane), **I:** 34, 415, 416, 423

"Bride in the 30's, A" (Auden), **Supp. II Part 1:** 9

Bride of Lammermoor (Scott), **II:** 291

Bride of Samoa (film), **Supp. IV Part 1:** 82

Bride of the Innisfallen, The (Welty), **IV:** 261, 275–279

"Bride of the Innisfallen, The" (Welty), **IV:** 278–279; **Retro. Supp. I:** 353

Bride of the Innisfallen, The, and Other Stories (Welty), **Retro. Supp. I:** 352–353, 355

Brides of the South Wind: Poems 1917–1922 (Jeffers), **Supp. II Part 2:** 419

Bridge, Horatio, **II:** 226

"BRIDGE, THE" (Baraka), **Supp. II Part 1:** 32, 36

Bridge, The (H. Crane), **I:** 62, 109, 266, 385, 386, 387, 395–399, 400, 402; **IV:** 123, 341, 418, 419, 420; **Retro. Supp. I:** 427; **Retro. Supp. II:** 76, 77, 81, 83, **84–87**; **Supp. V:** 342; **Supp. IX:** 306

Bridge at Remagen, The (film), **Supp. XI:** 343

"Bridge Burners, The" (Van Vechten), **Supp. II Part 2:** 733

Bridge of San Luis Rey, The (Wilder), **I:** 360; **IV:** 356, 357, 360–363, 365, 366

Bridge of Years, The (Sarton), **Supp. VIII:** 253

"Bridges" (Kingsolver), **Supp. VII:** 208

Bridges, Harry, **I:** 493

Bridges, Robert, **II:** 537; **III:** 527; **Supp. I Part 2:** 721; **Supp. II Part 1:** 21; **Supp. XIV:** 336, 341, 342, 343

Bridgman, P. W., **I:** 278

"Bridle, The" (Carver), **Supp. III Part 1:** 138

"Brief Début of Tildy, The" (O. Henry), **Supp. II Part 1:** 408

"Brief Encounters on the Inland Waterway" (Vonnegut), **Supp. II Part 2:** 760

Briefings (Ammons), **Supp. VII:** 29

Brief Interviews with Hideous Men (Wallace), **Supp. X: 308–310**

"Brief Interviews with Hideous Men" (Wallace), **Supp. X:** 309

"Briefly It Enters, and Briefly Speaks" (Kenyon), **Supp. VII:** 174

Briffault, Robert, **Supp. I Part 2:** 560, 567

"Brigade de Cuisine" (McPhee), **Supp. III Part 1:** 307–308

Brigadier and the Golf Widow, The (Cheever), **Supp. I Part 1:** 184–185, 192

Briggs, Charles F., **Supp. I Part 2:** 411

"Bright and Morning Star" (Wright), **IV:** 488

Bright Book of Life: American Novelists and Storytellers from Hemingway to Mailer (Kazin), **Supp. VIII:** 102, 104

Bright Center of Heaven (Maxwell),

Supp. VIII: 153–155, 164

Brighton Beach Memoirs (Simon), **Supp. IV Part 2:** 576, 577, 584, 586–587, 590

Bright Procession (Sedges), **Supp. II Part 1:** 125

Bright Room Called Day, A (Kushner), **Supp. IX:** 133, **138–141,** 142

"Brilliance" (Doty), **Supp. XI:** 124, 128

"Brilliant Leaves" (Gordon), **II:** 199

"Brilliant Sad Sun" (W. C. Williams), **Retro. Supp. I:** 422

"Bringing Back the Trumpeter Swan" (Kumin), **Supp. IV Part 2:** 454

Bringing It All Back Home (McNally), **Supp. XIII:** 197–198

"Bringing the Strange Home" (Dunn), **Supp. XI:** 141

"Bring the Day!" (Roethke), **III:** 536

Brinkley, Douglas, **Supp. XIII:** 9

Brinkmeyer, Robert H., Jr., **Supp. XI:** 38

Brinnin, John Malcolm, **IV:** 26, 27, 28, 42, 46

Brissot, Jacques Pierre, **Supp. I Part 2:** 511

"Britain's Negro Problem in Sierra Leone" (Du Bois), **Supp. I Part 1:** 176

"British Guiana" (Marshall), **Supp. XI:** 281–282

"British Poets, The" (Holmes), **Supp. I Part 1:** 306

"British Prison Ship, The" (Freneau), **Supp. II Part 1:** 261

Brittan, Gordon G., Jr., **Supp. XIV:** 234

Britten, Benjamin, **II:** 586; **Supp. II Part 1:** 17; **Supp. IV Part 1:** 84

Broadwater, Bowden, **II:** 562

Broadway, Broadway (McNally). *See It's Only a Play* (McNally)

Broadway, J. William, **Supp. V:** 316

Broadway Bound (Simon), **Supp. IV Part 2:** 576, 577, 584, 586–587, 590

"Broadway Sights" (Whitman), **IV:** 350

Broccoli, Albert R. "Cubby," **Supp. XI:** 307

Bröck, Sabine, **Supp. XI:** 275, 277, 278

Brodhead, Richard, **Retro. Supp. II:** 139; **Supp. XIV:** 61

Brodkey, Harold, **Supp. VIII:** 151; **Supp. X:** 160

Brodskii, Iosif Alexsandrovich. *See* Brodsky, Joseph

Brodsky, Joseph, **Supp. VIII: 19–35; Supp. X:** 65, 73

Brodyar, Anatole, **Supp. XIV:** 106

"Brokeback Mountain" (Proulx), **Supp. VII:** 264–265

"Broken Balance, The" (Jeffers), **Supp. II Part 2:** 426

"Broken Field Running" (Bambara), **Supp. XI:** 10, 11

Broken Ground, The (Berry), **Supp. X:** 30

"Broken Home, The" (Merrill), **Supp. III Part 1:** 319, 325

"Broken Oar, The" (Longfellow), **Retro. Supp. II:** 169

"Broken Promise" (MacLeish), **III:** 15

Broken Span, The (W. C. Williams), **IV:** 419; **Retro. Supp. I:** 424

"Broken Tower, The" (H. Crane), **I:** 385, 386, 400, 401–402; **Retro. Supp. II:** 89, 90

Broken Vessels (Dubus), **Supp. VII:** 90–91; **Supp. XI:** 347

"Broken Vessels" (Dubus), **Supp. VII:** 90

"Broker" (H. Roth), **Supp. IX:** 234

Bromfield, Louis, **IV:** 380

"Brompton Cocktail" (Mamet), **Supp. XIV:** 252

Bromwich, David, **Retro. Supp. I:** 305; **Supp. XII:** 162

"Broncho That Would Not Be Broken, The" (Lindsay), **Supp. I Part 2:** 383

Brontë, Anne, **Supp. IV Part 2:** 430

Brontë, Branwell, **I:** 462

Brontë, Charlotte, **I:** 458; **II:** 175; **Supp. IV Part 2:** 430; **Supp. IX:** 128; **Supp. XII:** 104, 303

Brontë, Emily, **I:** 458; **Retro. Supp. I:** 43; **Supp. IV Part 2:** 430; **Supp. IX:** 128; **Supp. X:** 78, 89

"Bronze" (Francis), **Supp. IX:** 76

"Bronze" (Merrill), **Supp. III Part 1:** 336

Bronze Booklets on the History, Problems, and Cultural Contributions of the Negro series, **Supp. XIV:** 202

"Bronze Buckaroo, The" (Baraka), **Supp. II Part 1:** 49

"Bronze Horses, The" (Lowell), **II:** 524

"Bronze Tablets" (Lowell), **II:** 523

Bronzeville Boys and Girls (Brooks), **Supp. III Part 1:** 79

"Bronzeville Mother Loiters in Mississippi, A. Meanwhile, a Mississippi Mother Burns Bacon" (Brooks), **Supp. III Part 1:** 80

"Brooch, The" (Singer), **IV:** 20

Brook, Peter, **Retro. Supp. II:** 182

Brooke, Rupert, **II:** 82; **III:** 3

Brook Evans (Glaspell), **Supp. III Part 1:** 182–185

"Brooking Likeness" (Glück), **Supp. V:** 85

"Brooklyn" (Marshall), **Supp. XI:** 281, 282

Brooks, Cleanth, **I:** 280, 282; **III:** 517; **IV:** 236, 279; **Retro. Supp. I:** 40, 41, 90; **Retro. Supp. II:** 235; **Supp. I Part 2:** 423; **Supp. III Part 2:** 542; **Supp. V:** 316; **Supp. IX:** 153, 155; **Supp. X:** 115, 123; **Supp. XIV:1–20**

Brooks, David, **Supp. IV Part 2:** 623, 626, 630; **Supp. VIII:** 232

Brooks, Gwendolyn, **Retro. Supp. I:** 208; **Supp. III Part 1: 69–90;** **Supp. IV Part 1:** 2, 15, 244, 251, 257; **Supp. XI:** 1, 278; **Supp. XIII:** 111, 112, 296; **Supp. XIV:** 73

Brooks, Mel, **Supp. IV Part 1:** 390; **Supp. IV Part 2:** 591

Brooks, Mrs. Van Wyck (Eleanor Kenyon Stimson), **I:** 240, 245, 250, 252

Brooks, Mrs. Van Wyck (Gladys Billings), **I:** 258

Brooks, Paul, **Supp. IX:** 26, 31, 32

Brooks, Phillips, **II:** 542; **Retro. Supp. II:** 134; **Supp. XIII:** 142

Brooks, Van Wyck, **I:** 106, 117, 215, 222, 228, 230, 231, 233, 236, **239–263,** 266, 480; **II:** 30, 271, 285, 309, 337, 482; **III:** 394, 606; **IV:** 171, 312, 427, 433; **Retro. Supp. II:** 46, 137; **Supp. I Part 2:** 423, 424, 650; **Supp. II Part 1:** 137; **Supp. VIII:** 98, 101; **Supp. XIV:** 11

Broom of the System, The (Wallace), **Supp. X:** 301, **302–305,** 310

"Brooms" (Simic), **Supp. VIII:** 275

Brosnan, Jim, **II:** 424–425

Brother Carl (Sontag), **Supp. III Part 2:** 452

"Brother Death" (Anderson), **I:** 114

Brotherhood of the Grape, The (Fante), **Supp. XI:** 160, **171–172**

"Brothers" (Anderson), **I:** 114

Brothers, The (F. Barthelme), **Supp. XI:** 25, 28, 29, 30, 32–33

Brothers and Keepers (Wideman), **Supp. X:** 320, 321–322, 323, **325–327,** 328, 329–330, 331, 332

Brothers Ashkenazi, The (Singer), **IV:** 2

Brothers Karamazov, The (Dostoyevsky), **II:** 60; **III:** 146, 150, 283; **Supp. IX:** 102, 106; **Supp. XI:** 172; **Supp. XII:** 322

Brother to Dragons: A Tale in Verse and Voices (Warren), **IV:** 243–244, 245, 246, 251, 252, 254, 257

Broughton, Rhoda, **II:** 174; **IV:** 309, 310

Broun, Heywood, **I:** 478; **II:** 417; **IV:** 432; **Supp. IX:** 190

Broussais, François, **Supp. I Part 1:** 302

Browder, Earl, **I:** 515

Brower, David, **Supp. X:** 29

Brown, Alice, **II:** 523; **Retro. Supp. II:** 136

Brown, Ashley, **Retro. Supp. II:** 48; **Supp. I Part 1:** 79, 80, 82, 84, 92

Brown, Charles Brockden, **I:** 54, 211, 335; **II:** 74, 267, 298; **III:** 415; **Supp. I Part 1: 124–149; Supp. II Part 1:** 65, 292

Brown, Clifford, **Supp. V:** 195

Brown, Dee, **Supp. IV Part 2:** 504

Brown, Elijah, **Supp. I Part 1:** 125

Brown, George Douglas, **III:** 473

Brown, Harry, **Supp. IV Part 2:** 560

Brown, Harvey, **Supp. XIV:** 148

Brown, John, **II:** 13; **IV:** 125, 126, 172, 237, 249, 254; **Supp. I Part 1:** 345; **Supp. VIII:** 204

Brown, Joseph Epes, **Supp. IV Part 2:** 487

Brown, Leonard, **Supp. IX:** 117

Brown, Mary Armitt, **Supp. I Part 1:** 125

Brown, Mrs. Charles Brockden (Elizabeth Linn), **Supp. I Part 1:** 145, 146

Brown, Percy, **II:** 20

Brown, Robert E., **Supp. X:** 12

Brown, Scott, **Supp. XI:** 178

Brown, Slater, **IV:** 123; **Retro. Supp. II:** 79

Brown, Solyman, **Supp. I Part 1:** 156

Brown, Sterling, **Retro. Supp. I:** 198; **Supp. IV Part 1:** 169; **Supp. XIV:** 202

Brown: The Last Discovery of America (Rodriguez), **Supp. XIV:** 297, 298, 300, **305–309,** 310, 311–312

Brown, Wesley, **Supp. V:** 6

Brown Decades, The (Mumford), **Supp. II Part 2:** 475, 478, 491–492

Brown Dog (Harrison), **Supp. VIII:** 51

"Brown Dwarf of Rügen, The" (Whittier), **Supp. I Part 2:** 696

Browne, Charles Farrar, **II:** 289; **IV:** 193, 196

Browne, Roscoe Lee, **Supp. VIII:** 345

Browne, Thomas, **II:** 15–16, 304; **III:** 77, 78, 198, 487; **IV:** 147; **Supp. IX:** 136; **Supp. XII:** 45

Browne, William, **Supp. I Part 1:** 98

Brownell, W. C., **II:** 14

Brownell, William Crary, **Retro. Supp.**

I: 365, 366

Brown Girl, Brownstones (Marshall), **Supp. XI:** 275, 276, **278–280,** 282

Brownies' Book, The (Hughes), **Supp. I Part 1:** 321

Browning, Elizabeth Barrett, **I:** 458, 459; **Retro. Supp. I:** 33, 43

Browning, Robert, **I:** 50, 66, 103, 458, 460, 468; **II:** 338, 478, 522; **III:** 5, 8, 467, 469, 484, 511, 521, 524, 606, 609; **IV:** 135, 245, 366, 416; **Retro. Supp. I:** 43, 55, 217; **Retro. Supp. II:** 188, 190; **Supp. I Part 1:** 2, 6, 79, 311; **Supp. I Part 2:** 416, 468, 622; **Supp. III Part 1:** 5, 6; **Supp. IV Part 2:** 430; **Supp. X:** 65

Brownmiller, Susan, **Supp. X:** 252

"Brown River, Smile" (Toomer), **Supp. IV Part 1:** 16

Brownstone Eclogues and Other Poems (Aiken), **I:** 65, 67

Broyard, Anatole, **Supp. IV Part 1:** 39; **Supp. VIII:** 140; **Supp. X:** 186; **Supp. XI:** 348

Bruccoli, Matthew, **Retro. Supp. I:** 98, 102, 105, 114, 115, 359; **Supp. IV Part 2:** 468, 470

Bruce, Lenny, **Supp. VIII:** 198

Bruce, Virginia, **Supp. XII:** 173

Bruce-Novoa, Juan, **Supp. VIII:** 73, 74

Bruchac, Joseph, **Supp. IV Part 1:** 261, 319, 320, 321, 322, 323, 325, 328, 398, 399, 403, 408, 414; **Supp. IV Part 2:** 502, 506

Brueghel, Pieter, **I:** 174; **Supp. I Part 2:** 475

Brueghel, Pieter, the Elder, **Retro. Supp. I:** 430

Bruell, Edwin, **Supp. VIII:** 126

"Bruja: Witch" (Mora), **Supp. XIII:** 214, 220, 221, **Supp. XIII:** 222

Brulé, Claude, **Supp. XI:** 307

Brumer, Andy, **Supp. XIII:** 88

Brunner, Emil, **III:** 291, 303

Brustein, Robert, **Supp. VIII:** 331

Brutus, **IV:** 373, 374; **Supp. I Part 2:** 471

"Brutus and Antony" (Masters), **Supp. I Part 2:** 472

"Bryan, Bryan, Bryan, Bryan" (Lindsay), **Supp. I Part 2:** 394, 395, 398

Bryan, George, **Retro. Supp. II:** 76

Bryan, Sharon, **Supp. IX:** 154

Bryan, William Jennings, **I:** 483; **IV:** 124; **Supp. I Part 2:** 385, 395–396, 455, 456

Bryant, Austin, **Supp. I Part 1:** 152, 153

Bryant, Frances, **Supp. I Part 1:** 153

Bryant, Louise, **Supp. X:** 136

Bryant, Mrs. William Cullen (Frances Fairchild), **Supp. I Part 1:** 153, 169

Bryant, Peter, **Supp. I Part 1:** 150, 151, 152, 153. *See also* George, Peter

Bryant, William Cullen, **I:** 335, 458; **II:** 311; **III:** 81; **IV:** 309; **Retro. Supp. I:** 217; **Retro. Supp. II:** 155; **Supp. I Part 1: 150–173,** 312, 362; **Supp. I Part 2:** 413, 416, 420; **Supp. IV Part 1:** 165; **Supp. XIII:** 145

Bryer, Jackson R., **Supp. IV Part 2:** 575, 583, 585, 586, 589, 591; **Supp. XIII:** 200, **Supp. XIII:** 205

Bryher, Jackson R. (pseudonym). *See* Ellerman, Winifred

"Bubbs Creek Haircut" (Snyder), **Supp. VIII:** 306

Buber, Martin, **II:** 228; **III:** 45, 308, 528; **IV:** 11; **Supp. I Part 1:** 83, 88

Buccaneers, The (Wharton), **IV:** 327; **Retro. Supp. I:** 382

Buchanan Dying (Updike), **Retro. Supp. I:** 331, 335

Buchbinder, David, **Supp. XIII:** 32

Buchwald, Art, **Supp. XII:** 124–125

Buck, Dudley, **Supp. I Part 1:** 362

Buck, Gene, **II:** 427

Buck, Pearl S., **Supp. II Part 1: 113–134; Supp. XIV:** 274

"Buckdancer's Choice" (Dickey), **Supp. IV Part 1:** 191

Buckdancer's Choice (Dickey), **Supp. IV Part 1:** 176, 177, 178, 180

Bucke, Richard Maurice, **Retro. Supp. I:** 407

"Buck Fever" (Humphrey), **Supp. IX:** 109

"Buck in the Snow, The" (Millay), **III:** 135

Buckley, Christopher, **Supp. IX:** 169; **Supp. XI:** 257, 329

Buckminster, Joseph, **Supp. II Part 1:** 66–67, 69

Bucknell, Katherine, **Supp. XIV:** 170

Bucolics (Auden), **Supp. II Part 1:** 21, 24

Budd, Louis J., **IV:** 210

Buddha, **I:** 136; **II:** 1; **III:** 173, 179, 239, 567; **Supp. I Part 1:** 363; **Supp. I Part 2:** 397

"Buddha's Last Instruction, The" (Oliver), **Supp. VII:** 239

Budding Prospects: A Pastoral (Boyle), **Supp. VIII:** 8–9

Buechner, Frederick, **III:** 310; **Supp. XII: 41–59**

Buell, Lawrence, **Supp. V:** 209; **Supp. IX:** 29

"Buffalo, The" (Moore), **III:** 215

"Buffalo Bill." *See* Cody, William

Buffalo Girls (McMurtry), **Supp. V:** 229

Buffalo Girls (screenplay) (McMurtry), **Supp. V:** 232

Buffett, Jimmy, **Supp. VIII:** 42

Buffon, Comte de, **II:** 101

Buford, Fanny McConnell, **Retro. Supp. II:** 117

Bugeja, Michael, **Supp. X:** 201

"Buglesong" (Stegner), **Supp. IV Part 2:** 606

"Buick" (Shapiro), **Supp. II Part 2:** 705

"Builders" (Yates), **Supp. XI: 342–343**

Builders, The (Glasgow), **II:** 183–184, 193

"Builders, The" (Hay), **Supp. XIV:** 125

Builders of the Bay Colony (Morison), **Supp. I Part 2:** 484–485

"Builders of the Bridge, The" (Mumford), **Supp. II Part 2:** 475

"Building" (Snyder), **Supp. VIII:** 305

"Building, Dwelling, Thinking" (Heidegger), **Retro. Supp. II:** 87

Building a Character (Stanislavsky), **Supp. XIV:** 243

"Building of the Ship, The" (Longfellow), **II:** 498; **Retro. Supp. II:** 159, 167, 168

"Build Soil" (Frost), **Retro. Supp. I:** 138, 139

"Build Soil" (Snyder), **Supp. VIII:** 304

Build-Up, The (W. C. Williams), **Retro. Supp. I:** 423

Bukowski, Charles, **Supp. III Part 1:** 147; **Supp. XI:** 159, 161, 172, 173

Bulgakov, Mikhail, **Supp. XIV:** 97

"Bulgarian Poetess, The" (Updike), **IV:** 215, 227; **Retro. Supp. I:** 329

Bull, Ole, **II:** 504

"Bulldozer, The" (Francis), **Supp. IX:** 87

"Bullet in the Brain" (Wolff), **Supp. VII:** 342–343

Bullet Park (Cheever), **Supp. I Part 1:** 185, 187–193, 194, 195

Bullfight, The (Mailer), **Retro. Supp. II:** 205

Bullins, Ed, **Supp. II Part 1:** 34, 42

Bullock, Sandra, **Supp. X:** 80

"Bull-Roarer, The" (Stern), **Supp. IX:** 297

"Bully, The" (Dubus), **Supp. VII:** 84

Bultmann, Rudolf, **III:** 309

Bulwark, The (Dreiser), **I:** 497, 506,

516–517; **Retro. Supp. II:** 95, 96, 105, 108

Bulwer-Lytton, Edward George, **IV:** 350

"Bums in the Attic" (Cisneros), **Supp. VII:** 62

Bunche, Ralph, **Supp. I Part 1:** 343; **Supp. XIV:** 202

"Bunchgrass Edge of the World, The" (Proulx), **Supp. VII:** 263

"Bunner Sisters, The" (Wharton), **IV:** 317

Bunting, Basil, **Retro. Supp. I:** 422; **Supp. III Part 2:** 616, 620, 624; **Supp. XIV:** 286

Buñuel, Luis, **III:** 184; **Retro. Supp. II:** 337

Bunyan, John, **I:** 445; **II:** 15, 104, 228; **IV:** 80, 84, 156, 437; **Supp. I Part 1:** 32

Burana, Lily, **Supp. XI:** 253

Burbank, Luther, **I:** 483

Burbank, Rex, **IV:** 363

Burchfield, Alice, **Supp. I Part 2:** 652, 660

Burden of Southern History, The (Woodward), **Retro. Supp. I:** 75

Burdens of Formality, The (Lea, ed.), **Supp. X:** 58

Burger, Gottfried August, **II:** 306

Burgess, Anthony, **Supp. IV Part 1:** 227; **Supp. IV Part 2:** 685; **Supp. V:** 128

Burgh, James, **Supp. I Part 2:** 522

"Burglar of Babylon, The" (Bishop), **Retro. Supp. II:** 47; **Supp. I Part 1:** 93

Burgum, E. B., **IV:** 469, 470

Buried Child (Shepard), **Supp. III Part 2:** 433, 447, 448; **Supp. XIV:** 327

"Buried Lake, The" (Tate), **IV:** 136

Burke, Edmund, **I:** 9; **III:** 310; **Supp. I Part 2:** 496, 511, 512, 513, 523; **Supp. II Part 1:** 80

Burke, James Lee, **Supp. XIV:21–38**

Burke, Kenneth, **I: 264–287,** 291; **III:** 497, 499, 546; **IV:** 123, 408; **Retro. Supp. I:** 297; **Retro. Supp. II:** 117, 120; **Supp. I Part 2:** 630; **Supp. II Part 1:** 136; **Supp. VIII:** 105; **Supp. IX:** 229; **Supp. XIV:** 3

"Burly Fading One, The" (Hayden), **Supp. II Part 1:** 366

"Burned" (Levine), **Supp. V:** 186, 192

"Burned Diary, The" (Olds), **Supp. X:** 215

Burnett, David, **Supp. XI:** 299

Burnett, Frances Hodgson, **Supp. I Part 1:** 44

Burnett, Whit, **III:** 551; **Supp. XI:** 294

Burnham, James, **Supp. I Part 2:** 648

Burnham, John Chynoweth, **I:** 59

"Burning, The" (Welty), **IV:** 277–278; **Retro. Supp. I:** 353

Burning Angel (Burke), **Supp. XIV:** 30, 32

Burning Bright (Steinbeck), **IV:** 51, 61–62

Burning City (Benét), **Supp. XI:** 46, 58

Burning Daylight (London), **II:** 474, 481

Burning House, The (Beattie), **Supp. V:** 29

"Burning of Paper Instead of Children, The" (Rich), **Supp. I Part 2:** 558

Burning the Days: Recollections (Salter), **Supp. IX:** 245, 246, 248, 260, **261–262**

"Burning the Small Dead" (Snyder), **Supp. VIII:** 298

Burns, David, **III:** 165–166

Burns, Ken, **Supp. XIV:** 14

Burns, Robert, **II:** 150, 306; **III:** 592; **IV:** 453; **Supp. I Part 1:** 158; **Supp. I Part 2:** 410, 455, 683, 685, 691, 692; **Supp. IX:** 173; **Supp. XII:** 171; **Supp. XIII:** 3

Burnshaw, Stanley, **Retro. Supp. I:** 298, 303; **Supp. III Part 2:** 615

"Burn the Cities" (West), **Retro. Supp. II:** 338

Burnt Norton (Eliot), **I:** 575, 580–581, 582, 584, 585; **III:** 10

"Burnt Norton" (Eliot), **Retro. Supp. I:** 66

Burnt-Out Case, A (Greene), **Supp. VIII:** 4

"Burnt-out Spa, The" (Plath), **Retro. Supp. II:** 246

Burr, Aaron, **I:** 7, 549, 550; **II:** 300; **IV:** 264; **Supp. I Part 2:** 461, 483

Burr: A Novel (Vidal), **Supp. IV Part 2:** 677, 682, 684, 685, 687, 688, 689, 691

Burr Oaks (Eberhart), **I:** 533, 535

Burroughs, Edgar Rice, **Supp. IV Part 1:** 101

Burroughs, John, **I:** 220, 236, 506; **IV:** 346; **Supp. IX:** 171

Burroughs, William S., **III:** 45, 174, 258; **Supp. II Part 1:** 320, 328; **Supp. III Part 1: 91–110,** 217, 226; **Supp. IV Part 1:** 79, 87, 90; **Supp. XI:** 297, 308; **Supp. XII:** 1, 3, 118, 121, 124, 129, 131, 136; **Supp. XIV:** 137, 140–141, 143–144, 150

Burrow, Trigant, **Supp. II Part 1:** 6

Burrows, Ken, **Supp. V:** 115

Burt, Steve, **Supp. V:** 83

Burtis, Thomson, **Supp. XIII:** 163

Burton, Robert, **II:** 535; **III:** 77, 78; **Supp. I Part 1:** 349

Burton, William Evans, **III:** 412

"Burying Ground by the Ties" (MacLeish), **III:** 14

Bury My Heart at Wounded Knee (Brown), **Supp. IV Part 2:** 504

Bury the Dead (Shaw), **IV:** 381

"Bus Along St. Clair: December, A" (Atwood), **Supp. XIII:** 33

Busch, Frederick, **Supp. X:** 78; **Supp. XII:** 343

Bush, Barney, **Supp. XII:** 218, 222

Bush, Douglas, **Supp. I Part 1:** 268; **Supp. XIV:** 10

"Busher Comes Back, The" (Lardner), **II:** 422

"Busher's Letters Home, A" (Lardner), **II:** 418–419, 421

"Business Deal" (West), **IV:** 287

"Business Man, A" (Jewett), **Retro. Supp. II:** 132

Buss, Helen M., **Supp. IV Part 1:** 12

Butcher, Margaret Just, **Supp. XIV:** 203

"Butcher, The" (Southern), **Supp. XI:** 294

"Butcher Shop" (Simic), **Supp. VIII:** 273

Butler, Benjamin, **I:** 457

Butler, Dorothy. *See* Farrell, Mrs. James T. (Dorothy Butler)

Butler, Elizabeth, **Supp. I Part 1:** 260

Butler, Ethel, **Supp. XIV:** 125

Butler, James D., **Supp. IX:** 175

Butler, Joseph, **I:** 8, 9

Butler, Judith, **Supp. XII:** 6

Butler, Maud. *See* Falkner, Mrs. Murray C. (Maud Butler)

Butler, Nicholas Murray, **I:** 223; **Supp. I Part 1:** 23; **Supp. III Part 2:** 499

Butler, Octavia, **Supp. XIII: 59–72**

Butler, Robert Olen, **Supp. XII: 61–78,** 319

Butler, Samuel, **II:** 82, 86; **IV:** 121, 440; **Supp. VIII:** 171

Butler-Evans, Elliot, **Retro. Supp. II:** 121

"But Only Mine" (Wright), **Supp. III Part 2:** 595

Butscher, Edward, **Supp. I Part 2:** 526

"Buttercups" (Lowell), **Retro. Supp. II:** 187

Butterfield 8 (O'Hara), **III:** 361

Butterfield, R. W., **I:** 386

Butterfield, Stephen, **Supp. IV Part 1:** 3, 11

Butterfly (Harvey), **Supp. XIII:** 184

"Butterfly, The" (Brodksy), **Supp. VIII:** 26

"Butterfly and the Traffic Light, The" (Ozick), **Supp. V:** 263, 265

"Butterfly-toed Shoes" (Komunyakaa), **Supp. XIII:** 126

Butter Hill and Other Poems (Francis), **Supp. IX:** 88, 89

Buttons, Red, **Supp. IV Part 2:** 574

Buttrick, George, **III:** 301; **Supp. XII:** 47–48

"But What Is the Reader to Make of This?" (Ashbery), **Supp. III Part 1:** 25

Butz, Earl, **Supp. X:** 35

"Buz" (Alcott), **Supp. I Part 1:** 43

By Avon River (Doolittle), **Supp. I Part 1:** 272

"By Blue Ontario's Shore" (Whitman), **Retro. Supp. I:** 399, 400

"By Disposition of Angels" (Moore), **III:** 214

"By Earth" (Olds), **Supp. X:** 214

"By Fire" (Olds), **Supp. X:** 214

By Land and by Sea (Morison), **Supp. I Part 2:** 492

By-Line: Ernest Hemingway (Hemingway), **II:** 257–258

By Love Possessed (Cozens), **I:** 358, 365, 372–374, 375, 376, 377, 378, 379

"By Morning" (Swenson), **Supp. IV Part 2:** 642

"By Night" (Francis), **Supp. IX:** 76

Bynner, Witter, **II:** 513, 527; **Supp. XIII:** 347

Byrd, William, **Supp. IV Part 2:** 425

Byrne, Donn, **IV:** 67

Byron, George Gordon, Lord, **I:** 343, 568, 577; **II:** 135, 193, 296, 301, 303, 310, 315, 331, 566; **III:** 82, 137, 170, 409, 410, 412, 469; **IV:** 245, 435; **Supp. I Part 1:** 150, 312, 349; **Supp. I Part 2:** 580, 591, 683, 685, 719; **Supp. XIII:** 139

"Bystanders" (Matthews), **Supp. IX:** 160

By the North Gate (Oates), **Supp. II Part 2:** 504

"By the Waters of Babylon" (Benét), **Supp. XI:** 56, 58

By the Waters of Manhattan (Reznikoff), **Supp. XIV:** 288, 293, 294

By the Waters of Manhattan: An Annual (Reznikoff), **Supp. XIV:** 277, 280, 289

By the Waters of Manhattan: Selected Verse (Reznikoff), **Supp. XIV:** 281, 291

By the Well of Living and Seeing: New and Selected Poems 1918–1973 (Reznikoff), **Supp. XIV:** 281, 287–288, 295

By the Well of Living and Seeing and the Fifth Book of the Maccabees (Reznikoff), **Supp. XIV:** 281

By Way of Orbit (O'Neill), **III:** 405

"C 33" (H. Crane), **I:** 384; **Retro. Supp. II:** 76

Cabala, The (Wilder), **IV:** 356, 358–360, 369, 374

Cabaret (film), **Supp. XIV:** 155, 162

Cabaret (play), **Supp. XIV:** 162

Cabbages and Kings (O. Henry), **Supp. II Part 1:** 394, 409

Cabell, James Branch, **II:** 42; **III:** 394; **IV:** 67, 359, 360; **Retro. Supp. I:** 80; **Supp. I Part 2:** 613, 714, 718, 721; **Supp. X:** 223

"Cabin, The" (Carver), **Supp. III Part 1:** 137, 146

Cabin, The: Reminiscence and Diversions (Mamet), **Supp. XIV:** 240

Cabinet of Dr. Caligari, The (film), **Retro. Supp. I:** 268

Cable, George Washington, **II:** 289; **Retro. Supp. II:** 65; **Supp. I Part 1:** 200; **Supp. II Part 1:** 198; **Supp. XIV:** 63

Cables to the Ace; or, Familiar Liturgies of Misunderstanding (Merton), **Supp. VIII:** 208

Cabot, James, **II:** 14; **IV:** 173

Cabot, John, **Supp. I Part 2:** 496, 497

"Caddy's Diary, A" (Lardner), **II:** 421–422

"Cadence" (Dubus), **Supp. VII:** 84–85

Cadieux, Isabelle, **Supp. XIII:** 127

"Cadillac Flambé" (Ellison), **Retro. Supp. II:** 119, 126; **Supp. II Part 1:** 248

Cadillac Jack (McMurtry), **Supp. V:** 225

Cadillac Jukebox (Burke), **Supp. XIV:** 32

Cadle, Dean, **Supp. I Part 2:** 429

Cady, Edwin H., **II:** 272

"Caedmon" (Garrett), **Supp. VII:** 96–97

Caesar, Julius, **II:** 12, 502, 561–562; **IV:** 372, 373

Caesar, Sid, **Supp. IV Part 2:** 574, 591

"Cafeteria, The" (Singer), **Retro. Supp. II:** 316

Cage, John, **Supp. IV Part 1:** 84; **Supp. V:** 337, 341

"Cage and the Prairie: Two Notes on Symbolism, The" (Bewley), **Supp. I Part 1:** 251

Cage of Spines, A (Swenson), **Supp. IV Part 2:** 641–642, 647

Cagney, James, **Supp. IV Part 1:** 236; **Supp. XIII:** 174

Cagney, William, **Supp. XIII:** 174

Cahalan, James, **Supp. XIII:** 1, 2, 3, 4, 12

Cahan, Abraham, **Supp. IX:** 227; **Supp. XIII:** 106

Cahill, Tim, **Supp. XIII:** 13

Cain, James M., **III:** 99; **Supp. IV Part 1:** 130; **Supp. XI:** 160; **Supp. XIII:** 159, 165

Cairns, Huntington, **III:** 103, 108, 114, 119

Cairo! Shanghai! Bombay! (Williams and Shapiro), **IV:** 380

Cakes and Ale (Maugham), **III:** 64

Calabria, Frank, **Supp. XIII:** 164

Calamity Jane (Martha Jane Canary), **Supp. V:** 229–230; **Supp. X:** 103

"Calamus" (Whitman), **IV:** 342–343; **Retro. Supp. I:** 52, 403, 404, 407

Calasso, Roberto, **Supp. IV Part 1:** 301

Calderón, Hector, **Supp. IV Part 2:** 544

Caldwell, Christopher, **Supp. IV Part 1:** 211

Caldwell, Erskine, **I:** 97, 211, **288–311;** **IV:** 286; **Supp. IV Part 2:** 601

Caldwell, Mrs. Erskine (Helen Lannegan), **I:** 289

Caldwell, Mrs. Erskine (Margaret Bourke-White), **I:** 290, 293–295, 297

Caldwell, Mrs. Erskine (Virginia Fletcher), **I:** 290

Caldwell, Reverend Ira Sylvester, **I:** 289, 305

Caldwell, Zoe, **Supp. XIII:** 207

Caleb Williams (Godwin), **III:** 415

"Calendar" (Creeley), **Supp. IV Part 1:** 158

Calendar of Saints for Unbelievers, A (Wescott), **Supp. XIV:** 342

Calhoun, John C., **I:** 8; **III:** 309

"California" (Didion), **Supp. IV Part 1:** 195

"California, This Is Minnesota Speaking" (Dunn), **Supp. XI:** 146

California and Oregon Trail, The (Parkman), **Supp. I Part 2:** 486

Californians (Jeffers), **Supp. II Part 2:** 415, 418, 420

"California Oaks, The" (Winters), **Supp. II Part 2:** 798

"California Republic" (Didion), **Supp. IV Part 1:** 205

California Suite (film), **Supp. IV Part
2:** 589
California Suite (Simon), **Supp. IV
Part 2:** 581, 582
"Caligula" (Lowell), **II:** 554
Callahan, John F., **Retro. Supp. II:**
119, 126, 127
"Call at Corazón" (Bowles), **Supp. IV
Part 1:** 82, 87
Calle, Sophia, **Supp. XII:** 22
"Called Back" (Kazin), **Supp. VIII:**
104
Calley, Captain William, **II:** 579
Calley, John, **Supp. XI:** 305
Callicott, J. Baird, **Supp. XIV:** 184
Calligrammes (Apollinaire), **I:** 432
"Calling Jesus" (Toomer), **Supp. III
Part 2:** 484
Calling Myself Home (Hogan), **Supp.
IV Part 1:** 397, 399, 400, 401, 413
Call It Experience (Caldwell), **I:** 290–
291, 297
"Call It Fear" (Harjo), **Supp. XII:** 220
Call It Sleep (H. Roth), **Supp. VIII:**
233; **Supp. IX:** 227, 228, **229–231;**
Supp. XIII: 106
"Call Letters: Mrs. V. B." (Angelou),
Supp. IV Part 1: 15
Call Me Ishmael (Olson), **Supp. II
Part 2:** 556
Call of the Gospel, The (Mather),
Supp. II Part 2: 448
Call of the Wild, The (London), **II:**
466, 470–471, 472, 481
"Call of the Wild, The" (Snyder),
Supp. VIII: 301
"Calloway's Code" (O. Henry), **Supp.
II Part 1:** 404
"Call to Arms" (Mumford), **Supp. II
Part 2:** 479
Call to Arms, The (film), **Retro. Supp.
I:** 325
Calmer, Ned, **Supp. XI:** 219
Calvert, George H., **Supp. I Part 1:**
361
Calverton, V. F., **Supp. VIII:** 96
Calvin, John, **II:** 342; **IV:** 160, 490
Calvino, Italo, **Supp. IV Part 2:** 623,
678
*Cambridge Edition of the Works of F.
Scott Fitzgerald, The* (Bruccoli, ed.),
Retro. Supp. I: 115
"Cambridge Thirty Years Ago"
(Lowell), **Supp. I Part 2:** 419
Cambridge University Press, **Retro.
Supp. I:** 115
"Camellia Sabina" (Moore), **III:** 208,
215
"Cameo Appearance" (Simic), **Supp.
VIII:** 283

Camera Obscura (Nabokov), **III:** 255
Cameron, Elizabeth, **I:** 10, 17
Cameron, Kenneth W., **II:** 16
Cameron, Peter, **Supp. XII: 79–95**
Cameron, Sharon, **Retro. Supp. I:** 43;
Retro. Supp. II: 40
Camerson, Don, **I:** 10, 17
Camino, Léon Felipe, **Retro. Supp. II:**
89
Camino Real (T. Williams), **IV:** 382,
385, 386, 387, 388, 391, 392, 395,
398
Camões, Luiz Vaz de, **II:** 133; **Supp. I
Part 1:** 94
"Camouflaging the Chimera"
(Komunyakaa), **Supp. XIII: 122–
123**
Camp, Walter, **II:** 423
Campana, Dino, **Supp. V:** 337
Campbell, Alan, **Supp. IV Part 1:** 353;
Supp. IX: 196, 198, 201
Campbell, Alexander, **Supp. I Part 2:**
381, 395
Campbell, Donna, **Retro. Supp. II:**
139
Campbell, Helen, **Supp. XI:** 200, 206
Campbell, James, **Supp. XII:** 127
Campbell, James Edwin, **Supp. II Part
1:** 202
Campbell, Joseph, **I:** 135; **IV:** 369,
370; **Supp. IX:** 245
Campbell, Lewis, **III:** 476
Campbell, Thomas, **II:** 8, 303, 314; **III:**
410; **Supp. I Part 1:** 309, 310
Campbell, Virginia, **Supp. XIII:** 114
Campbell (Hale), Janet, **Supp. IV Part
2:** 503
"Campers Leaving: Summer 1981"
(Kenyon), **Supp. VII:** 169
"Camp Evergreen" (Kenyon), **Supp.
VII:** 168
"Camping in Madera Canyon"
(Swenson), **Supp. IV Part 2:** 649
Campion, Thomas, **I:** 439; **Supp. VIII:**
272
Camus, Albert, **I:** 53, 61, 292, 294,
494; **II:** 57, 244; **III:** 292, 306, 453;
IV: 6, 211, 236, 442, 487; **Retro.
Supp. I:** 73; **Retro. Supp. II:** 20;
Supp. I Part 2: 621; **Supp. VIII:**
11, 195, 241; **Supp. XI:** 96; **Supp.
XIII:** 74, 165, 233, 247
Camuto, Christopher, **Supp. V:** 212–
213
"Canadian Mosaic, The" (Beran),
Supp. XIII: 25
"Canadians and Pottawatomies"
(Sandburg), **III:** 592–593
"Can a Good Wife Be a Good Sport?"
(T. Williams), **IV:** 380

"Canal, The: A Poem on the Applica-
tion of Physical Science to Political
Economy" (Barlow), **Supp. II Part
1:** 73
Canary, Martha Jane. *See* Calamity
Jane (Martha Jane Canary)
"Canary for One, A" (Hemingway),
Retro. Supp. I: 170, 189
Canary in a Cat House (Vonnegut),
Supp. II Part 2: 758
"Canary in Bloom" (Dove), **Supp. IV
Part 1:** 248
Canby, Henry Seidel, **IV:** 65, 363
"Cancer" (McClatchy), **Supp. XII:** 266
"Cancer Match, The" (Dickey), **Supp.
IV Part 1:** 182
"Canción y Glosa" (Merwin), **Supp.
III Part 1:** 342
Candide (Hellman), **I:** 28; **Supp. I
Part 1:** 288–289, 292
Candide (Voltaire), **Supp. I Part 1:**
288–289; **Supp. XI:** 297
Candide (Voltaire; Wilbur, trans.),
Supp. III Part 2: 560
Candle in the Cabin, The (Lindsay),
Supp. I Part 2: 398, 400
"Candles" (Plath), **Retro. Supp. II:**
248, 257
Candles in Babylon (Levertov), **Supp.
III Part 1:** 283
Candles in the Sun (T. Williams), **IV:**
381
Candles of Your Eyes, The (Purdy),
Supp. VII: 278
Candy (Southern), **Supp. XI:** 297,
298–299, 305
"Candy-Man Beechum" (Caldwell), **I:**
309
Cane (Toomer), **Supp. III Part 2:** 475,
481–486, 488; **Supp. IV Part 1:**
164, 168; **Supp. IX:** 305, 306, 307,
308–320
"Cane in the Corridor, The" (Thurber),
Supp. I Part 2: 616
Canfield, Cass, **Supp. I Part 2:** 668
Canfield, Dorothy, **Retro. Supp. I:** 4,
11, 14, 18. *See also* Fisher, Dorothy
Canfield
Can Grande's Castle (Lowell), **II:** 518,
524
"Canicula di Anna" (Carson), **Supp.
XII: 101–102**
"Canis Major" (Frost), **Retro. Supp. I:**
137
Cannery Row (Steinbeck), **IV:** 50, 51,
64–65, 66, 68
Cannibal Galaxy, The (Ozick), **Supp.
V:** 270
Cannibals and Christians (Mailer), **III:**

38–39, 40, 42; **Retro. Supp. II:** 203, 204, 205

Canning, George, **I:** 7, 8

Canning, Richard, **Supp. X:** 147

Cannon, Jimmy, **II:** 424

Cannon, Steve, **Retro. Supp. II:** 111

Cannon between My Knees, A (Gunn Allen), **Supp. IV Part 1:** 324

"Canonization, The" (Donne), **Supp. XIV:** 8

"Canso" (Merwin), **Supp. III Part 1:** 344

Can Such Things Be? (Bierce), **I:** 203, 204, 205, 209

Canterbury Tales (Chaucer), **II:** 504; **III:** 411; **IV:** 65

"Canto Amor" (Berryman), **I:** 173

Canto I (Pound), **III:** 469, 470; **Retro. Supp. I:** 286

Canto II (Pound), **III:** 470

Canto III (Pound), **III:** 470

Canto IV (Pound), **III:** 470

Canto VIII (Pound), **III:** 472

Canto IX (Pound), **III:** 472

Canto X (Pound), **III:** 472

Canto XIII (Pound), **III:** 472

Canto XXXIX (Pound), **III:** 468

Canto LXV (Pound), **Retro. Supp. I:** 292

Canto LXXXI (Pound), **III:** 459; **Retro. Supp. I:** 293

Cantor, Lois, **Supp. IV Part 1:** 285

Cantos (Pound), **I:** 482; **III:** 13–14, 17, 457, 462, 463, 466, 467, 469–470, 472–473, 474, 475, 476, 492; **Retro. Supp. I:** 284, 292, 292–293, 293, 427; **Supp. I Part 1:** 272; **Supp. II Part 1:** 5; **Supp. II Part 2:** 420, 557, 564, 644; **Supp. IV Part 1:** 153; **Supp. V:** 343, 345; **Supp. VIII:** 305; **Supp. XIV:** 55, 96

"Cantus Planis" (Pound), **III:** 466

Cantwell, Robert, **Retro. Supp. I:** 85; **Supp. VIII:** 96; **Supp. XIII:** 292

"Can You Carry Me" (O'Hara), **III:** 369

Canzoneri, Robert, **IV:** 114, 116

Canzoni (Pound), **Retro. Supp. I:** 286, 288, 413

"Cap" (Shaw), **Supp. IV Part 1:** 345

"Cape Breton" (Bishop), **Supp. I Part 1:** 92; **Supp. IX:** 45

Cape Cod (Thoreau), **II:** 540

"Cape Cod, Rome, and Jerusalem" (Chapman), **Supp. XIV:** 55

Capitalism: The Unknown Ideal (Rand), **Supp. IV Part 2:** 518, 527, 531, 532

Caponi, Gena Dagel, **Supp. IV Part 1:** 95

Capote, Truman, **Supp. I Part 1:** 291, 292; **Supp. III Part 1:** 111–133; **Supp. III Part 2:** 574; **Supp. IV Part 1:** 198, 220; **Supp. VIII:** 105; **Supp. XII:** 43, 249

Capouya, Emile, **Supp. I Part 1:** 50

Cappetti, Carla, **Supp. IX:** 4, 8

Capra, Fritjof, **Supp. X:** 261

Capron, Marion, **Supp. IX:** 193

"Capsule History of Conservation, A" (Stegner), **Supp. IV Part 2:** 600

"Captain Carpenter" (Ransom), **III:** 491

Captain Craig (Robinson), **III:** 508, 523; **Supp. II Part 1:** 192

"Captain Jim's Friend" (Harte), **Supp. II Part 1:** 337

"Captain Jones's Invitation" (Freneau), **Supp. II Part 1:** 261

"Captain's Son, The" (Taylor), **Supp. V:** 314, 325, 327

"Captain's Wife, The" (Salter), **Supp. IX:** 261

"Capt Christopher Levett (of York)" (Olson), **Supp. II Part 2:** 576, 577

Captive Israel (Reznikoff), **Supp. XIV:** 283

"Captivity and Restoration of Mrs. Mary Rowlandson, The" (Howe), **Supp. IV Part 2:** 419, 431, 434

"Captivity of the Fly" (MacLeish), **III:** 19

"Captured Goddess, The" (Lowell), **II:** 520

Caputi, Jane, **Supp. IV Part 1:** 334, 335

Caputo, Philip, **Supp. XI:** 234

Capuzzo, Michael, **Supp. XIII:** 254

Car (Crews), **Supp. XI:** 110–111

Carabi, Angels, **Supp. VIII:** 223; **Supp. XII:** 215

"Caravaggio: Swirl & Vortex" (Levis), **Supp. XI:** 258, 269

Carby, Hazel B., **Supp. IV Part 1:** 13

"Carcassonne" (Faulkner), **Retro. Supp. I:** 81

Card, Antha E., **Supp. I Part 2:** 496

Cárdenas, Lupe, **Supp. IV Part 2:** 538, 539, 540

Cardinale, Ernesto, **Supp. XII:** 225

"Cardinal Ideograms" (Swenson), **Supp. IV Part 2:** 645

"Cards" (Beattie), **Supp. V:** 31

"Career Woman" (Hay), **Supp. XIV:** 131

"Careful" (Carver), **Supp. III Part 1:** 138

Careful and Strict Enquiry into the

Modern Prevailing Notions of That Freedom of Will, Which Is Supposed to be Essential to Moral Agency, Vertue and Vice, Reward and Punishment, Praise and Blame, A (Edwards), **I:** 549, 557, 558, 562

Carel: A Poem and Pilgrimage in the Holy Land (Melville), **III:** 92–93

"Carentan O Carentan" (Simpson), **Supp. IX:** 267

Carew, Thomas, **IV:** 453

Cargill, Oscar, **Supp. II Part 1:** 117

Caribbean as Columbus Saw It (Morison and Obregon), **Supp. I Part 2:** 488

Carl, K. A., **III:** 475

"Carlos Who Died, and Left Only This, The" (Ríos), **Supp. IV Part 2:** 547

Carlotta (empress of Mexico), **Supp. I Part 2:** 457

Carl Sandburg (Golden), **III:** 579

Carlyle, Thomas, **I:** 103, 279; **II:** 5, 7, 11, 15–16, 17, 20, 145, 315; **III:** 82, 84, 85, 87; **IV:** 169, 182, 338, 350; **Retro. Supp. I:** 360, 408; **Supp. I Part 1:** 2, 349; **Supp. I Part 2:** 410, 422, 482, 485, 552

"Carma" (Toomer), **Supp. III Part 2:** 481–483; **Supp. IX:** 312–313

"Carmen de Boheme" (Crane), **I:** 384

Carmen Jones (film), **Supp. I Part 1:** 66

Carmina Burana, **Supp. X:** 63

Carnegie, Andrew, **I:** 483; **IV:** 192; **Supp. I Part 2:** 639, 644; **Supp. V:** 285

Carnegie, Dale, **Supp. I Part 2:** 608

"Carnegie Hall: Rescued" (Moore), **III:** 215

Carne-Ross, D. S., **Supp. I Part 1:** 268, 269

Carnes, Mark C., **Supp. X:** 14

Carnovsky, Morris, **III:** 154

Caroling Dusk: An Anthology of Verse by Negro Poets (Cullen), **Supp. IV Part 1:** 166, 169

"Carol of Occupations" (Whitman), **I:** 486

"Carpe Diem" (Frost), **Supp. XII:** 303

"Carpe Noctem, if You Can" (Thurber), **Supp. I Part 2:** 620

Carpenter, Dan, **Supp. V:** 250

Carpenter, David, **Supp. VIII:** 297

Carpenter, Frederic I., **II:** 20

Carpentered Hen and Other Tame Creatures, The (Updike), **IV:** 214; **Retro. Supp. I:** 320

Carpenter's Gothic (Gaddis), **Supp. IV Part 1:** 288, 289–291, 293, 294

Carr, Dennis W., **Supp. IV Part 2:** 560

Carr, Elias, **Supp. XIV:** 57
Carr, Rosemary. *See* Benét, Rosemary
Carrall, Aaron, **Supp. IV Part 2:** 499
Carrel, Alexis, **IV:** 240
"Carrell/Klee/and Cosmos's Groom" (Goldbarth), **Supp. XII:** 183
"Carriage from Sweden, A" (Moore), **III:** 212
Carrie (King), **Supp. V:** 137
Carried Away (Harrison), **Supp. VIII:** 39
Carrier of Ladders (Merwin), **Supp. III Part 1:** 339, 346, 350–352, 356, 357
"Carriers of the Dream Wheel" (Momaday), **Supp. IV Part 2:** 481
Carriers of the Dream Wheel: Contemporary Native American Poetry (Niatum, ed.), **Supp. IV Part 2:** 484, 505
Carrington, Carroll, **I:** 199
"Carrion Spring" (Stegner), **Supp. IV Part 2:** 604
Carroll, Charles, **Supp. I Part 2:** 525
Carroll, Lewis, **I:** 432; **II:** 431; **III:** 181; **Supp. I Part 1:** 44; **Supp. I Part 2:** 622, 656
"Carrots, Noses, Snow, Rose, Roses" (Gass), **Supp. VI:** 87
Carrouges, Michel, **Supp. IV Part 1:** 104
"Carrousel, The" (Rilke), **III:** 558
Carruth, Hayden, **Supp. IV Part 1:** 66; **Supp. VIII:** 39; **Supp. IX:** 291; **Supp. XIII:** 112; **Supp. XIV:** 273–274
"Carry" (Hogan), **Supp. IV Part 1:** 412
"Carrying On" (Dunn), **Supp. XI:** 145
Cars of Cuba (García), **Supp. XI:** 190
Carson, Anne, **Supp. XII: 97–116**
Carson, Johnny, **Supp. IV Part 2:** 526
Carson, Rachel, **Supp. V:** 202; **Supp. IX: 19–36; Supp. X:** 99
Carson, Tom, **Supp. XI:** 227
Cart, Michael, **Supp. X:** 12
Carter, Elliott, **Supp. III Part 1:** 21
Carter, Hodding, **Supp. XIV:** 2
Carter, Jimmy, **Supp. I Part 2:** 638; **Supp. XIV:** 107
Carter, Marcia, **Supp. V:** 223
Carter, Mary, **Supp. IV Part 2:** 444
Carter, Stephen, **Supp. XI:** 220
Cartesian Sonata and Other Novellas (Gass), **Supp. VI: 92–93**
Cartier, Jacques, **Supp. I Part 2:** 496, 497
Cartier-Bresson, Henri, **Supp. VIII:** 98
"Cartographies of Silence" (Rich), **Supp. I Part 2:** 571–572

Cartwright, Louis, **Supp. XIV:** 147, 149, 151
Carver, Raymond, **Supp. III Part 1: 135–151; Supp. IV Part 1:** 342; **Supp. V:** 22, 23, 220, 326; **Supp. VIII:** 15; **Supp. X:** 85, 167; **Supp. XI:** 26, 65, 116, 153; **Supp. XII:** 79, 139, 289, 294
Cary, Alice, **Retro. Supp. II:** 145
Cary, Richard, **Retro. Supp. II:** 132, 137
"Casabianca" (Bishop), **Retro. Supp. II:** 42; **Supp. I Part 1:** 86
Casablanca (film), **Supp. VIII:** 61
Case of the Crushed Petunias, The (T. Williams), **IV:** 381
Case of the Officers of Excise (Paine), **Supp. I Part 2:** 503–504
Casey, John, **Supp. X:** 164
Cash, Arthur, **Supp. IV Part 1:** 299
Cashman, Nellie, **Supp. X:** 103
Casiero, Robert, **Supp. XIV:** 167
Casino Royale (film), **Supp. XI: 306–307**
Caskey, William, **Supp. XIV:** 166
"Cask of Amontillado, The" (Poe), **II:** 475; **III:** 413; **Retro. Supp. II:** 268, 269, 270, 273
Cassada (Salter), **Supp. IX: 251–252**
Cassady, Carolyn, **Supp. XIV:** 150
Cassady, Neal, **Supp. II Part 1:** 309, 311; **Supp. XIV:** 137, 144
"Cassandra Southwick" (Whittier), **Supp. I Part 2:** 693
Cassell, Verlin, **Supp. XI:** 315
Cassill, R. V., **Supp. V:** 323
Cassirer, Ernst, **I:** 265; **IV:** 87, 89
Cass Timberlane (Lewis), **II:** 455–456
Cast a Cold Eye (McCarthy), **II:** 566
Castaway (Cozzens), **I:** 363, 370, 374, 375, 379
"Caste in America" (Du Bois), **Supp. II Part 1:** 169
Castiglione, Baldassare, **I:** 279; **III:** 282
"Castilian" (Wylie), **Supp. I Part 2:** 714
Castillo, Ana, **Supp. XI:** 177
"Castle in Lynn, A" (McCarriston), **Supp. XIV:** 265, 268
"Castles and Distances" (Wilbur), **Supp. III Part 2:** 550
Castle Sinister (Marquand), **III:** 58
Castro, Fidel, **II:** 261, 434
"Casual Incident, A" (Hemingway), **II:** 44
"Cat, The" (Matthews), **Supp. IX: 157–158**
"Catbird Seat, The" (Thurber), **Supp. I Part 2:** 623

"Catch" (Francis), **Supp. IX:** 82
Catch-22 (Heller), **III:** 558; **Supp. IV Part 1:** 379, 380, 381–382, 383, 384–386, 387, 390, 391, 392, 393, 394; **Supp. V:** 244, 248; **Supp. XII:** 167–168
Catcher in the Rye, The (Salinger), **I:** 493; **III:** 551, 552, 553–558, 567, 571; **Retro. Supp. I:** 102; **Retro. Supp. II:** 222, 249; **Supp. I Part 2:** 535; **Supp. V:** 119; **Supp. VIII:** 242; **Supp. XI:** 65
"Catching Frogs" (Kenyon), **Supp. VII:** 170
catechism of d neoamerican hoodoo church (Reed), **Supp. X:** 240, 241
Catered Affair, The (film), **Supp. IV Part 2:** 683
"Cathay" (Goldbarth), **Supp. XII:** 185, 186
Cathay (Pound), **II:** 527; **Retro. Supp. I:** 289
Cathedral (Carver), **Supp. III Part 1:** 144–146; **Supp. XII:** 139
"Cathedral" (Carver), **Supp. III Part 1:** 144–145
Cathedral, The (Lowell), **Supp. I Part 2:** 407, 416–417
Cather, Willa, **I:** 312–334, 405; **II:** 51, 96, 177, 404, 412; **III:** 453; **IV:** 190; **Retro. Supp. I: 1–23,** 355, 382; **Retro. Supp. II:** 71, 136; **Supp. I Part 2:** 609, 719; **Supp. IV Part 1:** 31; **Supp. VIII:** 101, 102, 263; **Supp. X:** 103; **Supp. XIII:** 253; **Supp. XIV:** 112
Catherine, Saint, **II:** 211
Catherine II, **Supp. I Part 2:** 433
Catholic Art and Culture (Watkin), **Retro. Supp. II:** 187
"Catholic Novelist in the Protestant South, The" (O'Connor), **Retro. Supp. II:** 223, 224
"Cathy Queen of Cats" (Cisneros), **Supp. VII:** 59
Cat Inside, The (Burroughs), **Supp. III Part 1:** 105
"Cat in the Hat for President, The" (Coover), **Supp. V:** 44, 46–47
Cato, **II:** 114, 117
Cat on a Hot Tin Roof (T. Williams), **II:** 190; **IV:** 380, 382, 383, 386, 387, 389, 390, 391, 394, 395, 397–398
Cat's Cradle (Vonnegut), **Supp. II Part 2:** 758, 759, 767–768, 770, 771, 772; **Supp. V:** 1
Cat's Eye (Atwood), **Supp. XIII: 29–30**
"Cat's Meow, A" (Brodsky), **Supp. VIII:** 31

"Catterskill Falls" (Bryant), **Supp. I Part 1:** 160

Catullus, **Supp. XII:** 2, 13, **112**

Catullus (Gai Catulli Veronensis Liber) (Zukofsky), **Supp. III Part 2:** 625, 627, 628, 629

"Catullus: *Carmina*" (Carson), **Supp. XII: 112**

Catullus, Gaius Valerius, **I:** 381; **Supp. I Part 1:** 261; **Supp. I Part 2:** 728

Caudwell, Christopher, **Supp. X:** 112

"Caul, The" (Banks), **Supp. V:** 10–11

Cause for Wonder (Morris), **III:** 232–233

"Causerie" (Tate), **IV:** 129

Causes and Consequences (Chapman), **Supp. XIV:** 41, 49, 51

"Causes of American Discontents before 1768, The" (Franklin), **II:** 120

Cavafy, Constantine P., **Supp. IX:** 275; **Supp. XI:** 119, 123

Cavalcade of America, The (radio program), **III:** 146

Cavalcanti (Pound, opera), **Retro. Supp. I:** 287

Cavalcanti, Guido, **I:** 579; **III:** 467; **Supp. III Part 2:** 620, 621, 622, 623

Cavalieri, Grace, **Supp. IV Part 2:** 630, 631

"Cavalry Crossing the Ford" (Whitman), **IV:** 347

Cave, The (Warren), **IV:** 255–256

Cavell, Stanley, **Retro. Supp. I:** 306–307, 309

Cavender's House (Robinson), **III:** 510

Caviare at the Funeral (Simpson), **Supp. IX:** 266, **276–277**

"Cawdor" (Jeffers), **Supp. II Part 2:** 431

Caxton, William, **III:** 486

Cayton, Horace, **IV:** 475, 488

Cazamian, Louis, **II:** 529

Celan, Paul, **Supp. X:** 149; **Supp. XII:** 21, 110–111

"Celebrated Jumping Frog of Calaveras County, The" (Twain), **IV:** 196

Celebrated Jumping Frog of Calaveras County, The, and Other Sketches (Twain), **IV:** 197

Celebration (Crews), **Supp. XI:** 103, **108**

Celebration at Dark (W. J. Smith), **Supp. XIII:** 332

"Celebration for June 24th" (McGrath), **Supp. X:** 116

"Celery" (Stein), **IV:** 43

"Celestial Globe" (Nemerov), **III:** 288

Celestial Navigation (Tyler), **Supp. IV Part 2:** 662–663, 671

"Celestial Railroad, The" (Hawthorne), **Retro. Supp. I:** 152; **Supp. I Part 1:** 188

Celibate Season, A (Shields), **Supp. VII:** 323, 324

Cellini (Shanley), **Supp. XIV:** 316, **329–330**

"Cemetery at Academy, California" (Levine), **Supp. V:** 182

Cemetery Nights (Dobyns), **Supp. XIII:** 85, 87, 89

"Censors As Critics: *To Kill a Mockingbird* As a Case Study" (May), **Supp. VIII:** 126

"Census-Taker, The" (Frost), **Retro. Supp. I:** 129

"Centaur, The" (Swenson), **Supp. IV Part 2:** 641

Centaur, The (Updike), **IV:** 214, 216, 217, 218, 219–221, 222; **Retro. Supp. I:** 318, 322, 324, 331, 336

"Centennial Meditation of Columbia, The" (Lanier), **Supp. I Part 1:** 362

Centeno, Agusto, **IV:** 375

"Centipede" (Dove), **Supp. IV Part 1:** 246

"Central Man, The" (Bloom), **Supp. IV Part 2:** 689

"Central Park" (Lowell), **II:** 552

Century of Dishonor, A (Jackson), **Retro. Supp. I:** 31

"Cerebral Snapshot, The" (Theroux), **Supp. VIII:** 313

"Ceremonies" (Rukeyser), **Supp. VI:** 279

Ceremony (Silko), **Supp. IV Part 1:** 274, 333; **Supp. IV Part 2:** 557–558, 558–559, 559, 561–566, 570

Ceremony (Wilbur), **Supp. III Part 2:** 550–551

"Ceremony, The" (Harjo), **Supp. XII:** 230

Ceremony in Lone Tree (Morris), **III:** 229–230, 232, 238, 558

Ceremony of Brotherhood, A (Anaya and Ortiz, eds.), **Supp. IV Part 2:** 502

Cerf, Bennett, **III:** 405; **IV:** 288; **Retro. Supp. II:** 330; **Supp. XIII:** 172

"Certain Attention to the World, A" (Haines), **Supp. XII:** 201

Certain Distance, A (Francis), **Supp. IX:** 85

"Certain Music, A" (Rukeyser), **Supp. VI:** 273

Certain Noble Plays of Japan (Pound), **III:** 458

Certain People (Wharton), **Retro. Supp. I:** 382

"Certain Poets" (MacLeish), **III:** 4

"Certain Testimony" (Bausch), **Supp. VII:** 48

Certificate, The (Singer), **IV:** 1; **Retro. Supp. II: 314–315**

Cervantes, Lorna Dee, **Supp. IV Part 2:** 545

Cervantes, Miguel de, **I:** 130, 134; **II:** 8, 272, 273, 276, 289, 302, 310, 315; **III:** 113, 614; **IV:** 367; **Retro. Supp. I:** 91; **Supp. I Part 2:** 406; **Supp. V:** 277; **Supp. XIII:** 17

Césaire, Aimé, **Supp. X:** 132, 139; **Supp. XIII:** 114

"Cesarean" (Kenyon), **Supp. VII:** 173

Cézanne, Paul, **II:** 576; **III:** 210; **IV:** 26, 31, 407; **Supp. V:** 333, 341–342

Chabon, Michael, **Supp. XI: 63–81**

Chaboseau, Jean, **Supp. I Part 1:** 260

Chaikin, Joseph, **Supp. III Part 2:** 433, 436–437

"Chain, The" (Kumin), **Supp. IV Part 2:** 452

Chainbearer, The (Cooper), **I:** 351, 352–353

"Chain of Love, A" (Price), **Supp. VI: 258–259,** 260

Chains of Dew (Glaspell), **Supp. III Part 1:** 181

Challacombe, Robert Hamilton, **III:** 176

Chalmers, George, **Supp. I Part 2:** 514, 521

"Chambered Nautilus, The" (Holmes), **Supp. I Part 1:** 254, 307, 312–313, 314

Chamberlain, John, **Supp. I Part 2:** 647; **Supp. IV Part 2:** 525

Chamberlain, Neville, **II:** 589; **Supp. I Part 2:** 664

Chamber Music (Joyce), **III:** 16

Chambers, Richard, **Supp. III Part 2:** 610, 611, 612

Chambers, Whittaker, **Supp. III Part 2:** 610; **Supp. IV Part 2:** 526

"Champagne Regions" (Ríos), **Supp. IV Part 2:** 553

"Champion" (Lardner), **II:** 420–421, 428, 430

Champion, Laurie, **Supp. VIII:** 128

Champollion-Figeac, Jean Jacques, **IV:** 426

"Chance" (Doolittle), **Supp. I Part 1:** 271

Chance, Frank, **II:** 418

Chance Acquaintance, A (Howells), **II:** 278

"Chanclas" (Cisneros), **Supp. VII:** 61

Chandler, Raymond, **Supp. III Part 1:** 91; **Supp. IV Part 1: 119–138,** 341, 344, 345; **Supp. IV Part 2:** 461,

464, 469, 470, 471, 472, 473; **Supp. XI:** 160, 228; **Supp. XII:** 307; **Supp. XIII:** 159, 233; **Supp. XIV:** 21

Chaney, "Professor" W. H., **II:** 463–464

Chang, Leslie C., **Supp. IV Part 1:** 72

"Change, The: Kyoto-Tokyo Express" (Ginsberg), **Supp. II Part 1:** 313, 329

Changeling (Middleton), **Retro. Supp. I:** 62

"Changeling, The" (Lowell), **Supp. I Part 2:** 409

"Changeling, The" (Whittier), **Supp. I Part 2:** 697

Change of World, A (Rich), **Supp. I Part 2:** 551, 552

"Changes of Mind" (Baker), **Supp. XIII:** 52

"Change the Joke and Slip the Yoke" (Ellison), **Retro. Supp. II:** 118

Changing Light at Sandover, The (Merrill), **Supp. III Part 1:** 318, 319, 323, 327, 332, 335–336; **Supp. XII:** 269–270

"Changing Same, The" (Baraka), **Supp. II Part 1:** 47, 51, 53

Chanler, Mrs. Winthrop, **I:** 22; **IV:** 325

Channing, Carol, **IV:** 357

Channing, Edward, **Supp. I Part 2:** 479–480

Channing, Edward Tyrrel, **Supp. I Part 1:** 155; **Supp. I Part 2:** 422

Channing, William Ellery, **I:** 336; **II:** 224, 495; **IV:** 172, 173, 176, 177; **Retro. Supp. I:** 54; **Supp. I Part 1:** 103; **Supp. I Part 2:** 589

Channing, William Henry, **IV:** 178; **Supp. II Part 1:** 280, 285

Chanson de Roland, La, **I:** 13

"Chanson un Peu Naïve" (Bogan), **Supp. III Part 1:** 50–51

"Chanteuse" (Doty), **Supp. XI:** 119

"Chant for May Day" (Hughes), **Supp. I Part 1:** 331

Chants (Mora), **Supp. XIII: 214–215**

Chaos (Dove), **Supp. IV Part 1:** 243

"Chaperone, The" (Van Vechten), **Supp. II Part 2:** 728

Chaplin, Charles Spencer, **I:** 27, 32, 43, 386, 447; **III:** 403; **Supp. I Part 2:** 607; **Supp. IV Part 1:** 146; **Supp. IV Part 2:** 574

"Chaplinesque" (H. Crane), **Retro. Supp. II:** 79

"Chapman" (Rukeyser), **Supp. VI:** 273

Chapman, Abraham, **IV:** 485

Chapman, George, **Supp. I Part 2:** 422

Chapman, John (Johnny Appleseed), **Supp. I Part 2:** 397

Chapman, John Jay, **IV:** 436; **Supp. XIV:39–56**

Chapman, Stephen, **Supp. XIII:** 12

Chappell, Fred, **Supp. IV Part 1:** 69; **Supp. XI:** 317

Chapters in a Mythology: The Poetry of Sylvia Plath (Kroll), **Supp. I Part 2:** 541–543

Chapters on Erie (Adams and Adams), **Supp. I Part 2:** 644

Chapter Two (Simon), **Supp. IV Part 2:** 575, 586

"Chapter VI" (Hemingway), **II:** 252

"Character" (Emerson), **II:** 6

"Character of Presidents, The" (Doctorow), **Supp. IV Part 1:** 224

"Character of Socrates, The" (Emerson), **II:** 8–9

Character of the Poet, The (Simpson), **Supp. IX:** 273, 275, 278

"Characters in Fiction" (McCarthy), **II:** 562

"Charades" (Moore), **Supp. X:** 178

"Charge It" (Fante), **Supp. XI:** 164–165

Charlatan, The (Singer), **IV:** 1

"Charles" (Jackson), **Supp. IX:** 125

Charles Goodnight: Cowman and Plainsman (Haley), **Supp. V:** 226

Charles Simic: Essays on the Poetry (Weigl), **Supp. VIII:** 269

Charles the Bold, Duke of Burgundy, **III:** 487

Charleville, Victoria Verdon, **Supp. I Part 1:** 200–201, 205, 206, 210

Charley's Aunt (B. Thomas), **II:** 138

Charlie Chan Is Dead: An Anthology of Contemporary Asian American Fiction (Hagedorn), **Supp. X:** 292

"Charlie Christian Story, The" (Ellison), **Retro. Supp. II:** 121

"Charlie Howard's Descent" (Doty), **Supp. XI:** 122

Charlotte: A Tale of Truth (Rowson), **Supp. I Part 1:** 128

Charlotte's Web (White), **Supp. I Part 2:** 655, 656, 658, 667, 670

Charm, The (Creeley), **Supp. IV Part 1:** 139, 141, 144, 149–150

Charmed Life, A (McCarthy), **II:** 571–574

Charms for the Easy Life (Gibbons), **Supp. X:** 45, **47–48**

Charnel Rose, The (Aiken), **I:** 50, 57, 62

Charon's Cosmology (Simic), **Supp. VIII: 276–278**

Charterhouse, The (Percy), **Supp. III Part 1:** 388

Charvat, William, **II:** 244

Chase, Mary Ellen, **Retro. Supp. II:** 243, 245

Chase, Richard, **IV:** 202, 443; **Retro. Supp. I:** 40, 395

Chase, Salmon P., **Supp. I Part 2:** 584

Chase, Stuart, **Supp. I Part 2:** 609

Chase, The (Foote), **Supp. I Part 1:** 281

"Chaste Land, The" (Tate), **IV:** 122

Château, The (Maxwell), **Supp. VIII:** 152, 160, **165–167,** 168, 169

Chatham, Russell, **Supp. VIII:** 40

Chatterdon, The Black Death, and Meriwether Lewis (Reznikoff), **Supp. XIV:** 288

Chatterton, Thomas, **Supp. I Part 1:** 349; **Supp. I Part 2:** 410, 716

Chatterton, Wayne, **Supp. IX:** 2, 4, 11–12

Chatwin, Bruce, **Supp. VIII:** 322

Chaucer, Geoffrey, **I:** 131; **II:** 11, 504, 516, 542, 543; **III:** 283, 411, 473, 492, 521; **Retro. Supp. I:** 135, 426; **Supp. I Part 1:** 356, 363; **Supp. I Part 2:** 422, 617; **Supp. V:** 259; **Supp. XII:** 197

Chauncy, Charles, **I:** 546–547; **IV:** 147

Chavez, César, **Supp. V:** 199

Chávez, Denise, **Supp. IV Part 2:** 544; **Supp. XI:** 316

Chavez, Lydia, **Supp. VIII:** 75

Chavkin, Allan, **Supp. IV Part 1:** 259

Chavkin, Nancy Feyl, **Supp. IV Part 1:** 259

Chayefsky, Paddy, **Supp. XI:** 306

Cheang, Shu Lea, **Supp. XI:** 20

"Cheat Takes Over" (Leopold), **Supp. XIV:** 189

"Cheers" (Carver), **Supp. III Part 1:** 138

Cheetham, James, **Supp. I Part 2:** 521

Cheever, Benjamin Hale, **Supp. I Part 1:** 175

Cheever, David W., **Supp. I Part 1:** 304

Cheever, Ezekiel, **Supp. I Part 1:** 174, 193

Cheever, Federico, **Supp. I Part 1:** 175

Cheever, Fred, **Supp. I Part 1:** 174

Cheever, Frederick L., **Supp. I Part 1:** 174

Cheever, John, **Retro. Supp. I:** 116, 333, 335; **Supp. I Part 1: 174–199;** **Supp. V:** 23, 95; **Supp. VIII:** 151; **Supp. IX:** 114, 208; **Supp. XI:** 65, 66, 99; **Supp. XII:** 140; **Supp. XIV:** 93

Cheever, Mary Liley, **Supp. I Part 1:** 174

Cheever, Mrs. John (Mary Winternitz), **Supp. I Part 1:** 175

Cheever, Susan. *See* Cowley, Susan Cheever (Susan Cheever)

Cheever Evening, A (Gurney), **Supp. V:** 95

Chekhov, Anton, **I:** 52, 90; **II:** 27, 38, 44, 49, 198, 542; **III:** 362, 467; **IV:** 17, 53, 359, 446; **Retro. Supp. I:** 5, 355; **Retro. Supp. II:** 299; **Supp. I Part 1:** 196; **Supp. II Part 1:** 6; **Supp. IV Part 2:** 585; **Supp. V:** 265; **Supp. VIII:** 153, 332; **Supp. IX:** 260, 265, 274; **Supp. XI:** 66; **Supp. XII:** 94, 307; **Supp. XIII:** 79; **Supp. XIV:** 87, 242

"Chekhov's Sense of Writing as Seen Through His Letters" (Dobyns), **Supp. XIII:** 77–78

"Chemin de Fer" (Bishop), **Retro. Supp. II:** 41; **Supp. I Part 1:** 80, 85, 86

Cheney, Brainard, **Retro. Supp. II:** 229

Chenzira, Ayoka, **Supp. XI:** 19

Cherkovski, Neeli, **Supp. XII:** 118, 132, 134

Chernyshevski, Nikolai, **III:** 261, 262, 263; **Retro. Supp. I:** 269

Cherokee Lottery, The: A Sequence of Poems (W. J. Smith), **Supp. XIII:** 340–344

Cherry (Karr), **Supp. XI:** 239, **251– 254**

Cherry Orchard, The (Chekhov), **IV:** 359, 426; **Supp. VIII:** 153

Cheslock, Louis, **III:** 99, 118, 119

Chesnutt, Charles Waddell, **Supp. II Part 1:** 174, 193, 211; **Supp. IV Part 1:** 257; **Supp. XIV:57–78**

"Chess House, The" (Dixon), **Supp. XII:** 139

Chessman, Caryl, **Supp. I Part 2:** 446

Chester, Alfred, **Retro. Supp. II:** 111, 112; **Supp. X:** 192

Chesterfield, Lord, **II:** 36

Chesterton, Gilbert Keith, **I:** 226; **IV:** 432

Cheuse, Alan, **Supp. IV Part 2:** 570

Chevigny, Bell Gale, **Supp. XI:** 283

"Chicago" (Sandburg), **III:** 581, 592, 596; **Supp. III Part 1:** 71

Chicago (Shepard), **Supp. III Part 2:** 439

Chicago: City on the Make (Algren), **Supp. IX:** 1, 3

"*Chicago Defender* Sends a Man to Little Rock, The" (Brooks), **Supp. III Part 1:** 80–81

"Chicago Hamlet, A" (Anderson), **I:** 112

Chicago Loop (Theroux), **Supp. VIII:** 324

"Chicago Picasso, The" (Brooks), **Supp. III Part 1:** 70–71, 84

Chicago Poems (Sandburg), **III:** 579, 581–583, 586

"Chicano/Borderlands Literature and Poetry" (Ríos), **Supp. IV Part 2:** 537, 538, 542, 545

Chick, Nancy, **Supp. IV Part 1:** 1

"Chickamauga" (Bierce), **I:** 201

"Chickamauga" (Wolfe), **IV:** 460

Chickamauga (Wright), **Supp. V:** 333, 343–344

"Chickamauga" (Wright), **Supp. V:** 334

"Chiefly about War Matters" (Hawthorne), **II:** 227; **Retro. Supp. I:** 165

"Child" (Plath), **Supp. I Part 2:** 544

Child, Lydia Maria, **Supp. XIII:** 141

"Child, The" (Ríos), **Supp. IV Part 2:** 543

"Child by Tiger, The" (Wolfe), **IV:** 451

"Childhood" (Wright), **Supp. V:** 341

Childhood, A: The Biography of a Place (Crews), **Supp. XI:** 102–103, 245

"Childhood, When You Are in It . . ." (Kenyon), **Supp. VII:** 160, 170

"Childhood Sketch" (Wright), **Supp. III Part 2:** 589

"Child Is Born, A" (Benét), **Supp. XI:** 46

"Child Is the Meaning of This Life, The" (Schwartz), **Supp. II Part 2:** 659–660

"Childlessness" (Merrill), **Supp. III Part 1:** 323

"Childless Woman" (Plath), **Supp. I Part 2:** 544

Child-Life (Whittier and Larcom, eds.), **Supp. XIII:** 142

Child-Life in Prose (Whittier and Larcom, eds.), **Supp. XIII:** 142

Childlike Life of the Black Tarantula, The (Acker), **Supp. XII:** 4, 6, **7–8**

"Child Margaret" (Sandburg), **III:** 584

"Child of Courts, The" (Jarrell), **II:** 378, 379, 381

Child of God (McCarthy), **Supp. VIII:** **177–178**

"CHILD OF THE THIRTIES" (Baraka), **Supp. II Part 1:** 60

"Child on Top of a Greenhouse" (Roethke), **III:** 531

Children (Gurney), **Supp. V:** 95, 96

"Children" (Stowe), **Supp. I Part 2:** 587

Children, The (Wharton), **IV:** 321, 326; **Retro. Supp. I:** 381

"Children, the Sandbar, That Summer" (Rukeyser), **Supp. VI:** 274

Children and Others (Cozzens), **I:** 374

Children Is All (Purdy), **Supp. VII:** 277, 278, 282

"Children of Adam" (Whitman), **IV:** 342; **Retro. Supp. I:** 403, 405

Children of Light (Stone), **Supp. V:** 304–306

Children of Light and the Children of Darkness, The (Niebuhr), **III:** 292, 306, 310

Children of the Frost (London), **II:** 469, 483

"Children of the Lord's Supper, The" (Tegnér), **Retro. Supp. II:** 155, 157

Children of the Market Place (Masters), **Supp. I Part 2:** 471

"Children on Their Birthdays" (Capote), **Supp. III Part 1:** 114, 115

"Children Selecting Books in a Library" (Jarrell), **II:** 371

Children's Hour, The (Hellman), **Supp. I Part 1:** 276–277, 281, 286, 297

"Children's Rhymes" (Hughes), **Supp. I Part 1:** 340

Childress, Mark, **Supp. X:** 89

Child's Garden of Verses, A (Stevenson), **Supp. IV Part 1:** 298, 314; **Supp. XIII:** 75

"Child's Reminiscence, A" (Whitman), **IV:** 344

Childwold (Oates), **Supp. II Part 2:** 519–520

Chill, The (Macdonald), **Supp. IV Part 2:** 473

Chills and Fever (Ransom), **III:** 490, 491–492, 493

Chilly Scenes of Winter (Beattie), **Supp. V:** 21, 22, 23, 24, 26, 27

Chime of Words, A: The Letters of Logan Pearsall Smith (Tribble, ed.), **Supp. XIV:** 348–349

"Chimes for Yahya" (Merrill), **Supp. III Part 1:** 329

Chin, Frank, **Supp. V:** 164, 172

"China" (Johnson), **Supp. VI: 193–194**

"Chinaman's Hat" (Kingston), **Supp. V:** 169

China Men (Kingston), **Supp. V:** 157, 158, 159, 160, 161, 164–169; **Supp. X:** 292

China Trace (Wright), **Supp. V:** 332, 340, 341, 342

Chinese Classics (Legge), **III:** 472

Chinese Materia Medica (P. Smith), **III:** 572

"Chinese Nightingale, The" (Lindsay), **Supp. I Part 2:** 392–393, 394

Chinese Nightingale and Other Poems, The (Lindsay), **Supp. I Part 2:** 392

Chinese Siamese Cat, The (Tan), **Supp. X:** 289

"Chinoiseries" (Lowell), **II:** 524–525

Chirico, Giorgio de, **Supp. III Part 1:** 14

"Chiron" (Winters), **Supp. II Part 2:** 801

Chodorov, Jerome, **IV:** 274

"Choice, The" (Karr), **Supp. XI:** 251

"Choice of Profession, A" (Malamud), **Supp. I Part 2:** 437

Chomei, Kamo No, **IV:** 170, 171, 184

Chomsky, Noam, **Supp. IV Part 2:** 679

Choosing not Choosing (Cameron), **Retro. Supp. I:** 43

Chopin, Felix, **Supp. I Part 1:** 202

Chopin, Frédéric, **Supp. I Part 1:** 363

Chopin, Jean, **Supp. I Part 1:** 206

Chopin, Kate, **II:** 276; **Retro. Supp. I:** 10, 215; **Retro. Supp. II: 57–74; Supp. I Part 1: 200–226; Supp. V:** 304; **Supp. X:** 227

"Choral: The Pink Church" (W. C. Williams), **Retro. Supp. I:** 428

"Chord" (Merwin), **Supp. III Part 1:** 356

Choruses from Iphigenia in Aulis (Doolittle, trans.), **Supp. I Part 1:** 257, 268, 269

"Chosen Blindness" (Karr), **Supp. XI:** 251

Chosen Country (Dos Passos), **I:** 475, 490–491

Chosen Place, The Timeless People, The (Marshall), **Supp. XI:** 275, 276, **282–284**

Chosön (Lowell), **II:** 513

Choukri, Mohamed, **Supp. IV Part 1:** 92

Chovteau, Mane Thérèse, **Supp. I Part 1:** 205

Chrisman, Robert, **Supp. IV Part 1:** 1

Christabel (Coleridge), **Supp. IV Part 2:** 465

"Christ for Sale" (Lowell), **II:** 538

Christian, Graham, **Supp. XII:** 193

Christian Dictionary, A (Wilson), **IV:** 153

"Christian in World Crisis, The" (Merton), **Supp. VIII:** 203

Christianity and Power Politics (Niebuhr), **III:** 292, 303

"Christianity and the Survival of Cre-

ation" (Berry), **Supp. X:** 30

"Christian Minister, The" (Emerson), **II:** 10

Christian Philosopher, The (Mather), **Supp. II Part 2:** 463–464

Christian Realism and Practical Problems (Niebuhr), **III:** 292, 308

"Christian Roommates, The" (Updike), **IV:** 226–227; **Retro. Supp. I:** 319, 323

Christiansen, Carrie, **I:** 210

Christian's Secret of a Happy Life, The (H. W. Smith), **Supp. XIV:** 333–334

Christie, Agatha, **Supp. IV Part 1:** 341; **Supp. IV Part 2:** 469

Christine (King), **Supp. V:** 139, 148

"Christ Light, The" (Chopin), **Retro. Supp. II:** 61

"Christmas 1944" (Levertov), **Supp. III Part 1:** 274

"Christmas, or the Good Fairy" (Stowe), **Supp. I Part 2:** 586

"Christmas Banquet, The" (Hawthorne), **II:** 227

Christmas Card, A (Theroux), **Supp. VIII:** 322

Christmas Carol, A (Dickens), **Retro. Supp. I:** 196; **Supp. I Part 2:** 409–410; **Supp. X:** 252, 253

"Christmas Eve at Johnson's Drugs N Goods" (Bambara), **Supp. XI:** 11–12

"Christmas Eve in the Time of War: A Capitalist Meditates by a Civil War Monument" (Lowell), **II:** 538

"Christmas Eve under Hooker's Statue" (Lowell), **II:** 539–540

"Christmas Gift" (Warren), **IV:** 252–253

"Christmas Greeting, A" (Wright), **Supp. III Part 2:** 601

"Christmas Hymn, A" (Wilbur), **Supp. III Part 2:** 557

Christmas Memory, A (Capote), **Supp. III Part 1:** 118, 119, 129

"Christmass Poem" (West), **Retro. Supp. II:** 338

Christmas Story (Mencken), **III:** 111

"Christmas to Me" (Lee), **Supp. VIII:** 113

Christographia (Taylor), **IV:** 164–165

"*Christ on the Cross*/Nuestro Señor Crucificado" (Mora), **Supp. XIII:** 229

Christopher and His Kind: 1929–1939 (Isherwood), **Supp. XIV:** 157, 163, 164, 171

"Christopher Cat" (Cullen), **Supp. IV Part 1:** 173

Christopher Columbus, Mariner

(Morison), **Supp. I Part 2:** 488

Christopher Isherwood: A Critical Biography (Finney), **Supp. XIV:** 158

Christophersen, Bill, **Supp. IX:** 159, 167; **Supp. XI:** 155; **Supp. XIII:** 87

"Christ's Passion" (Karr), **Supp. XI:** 251

Christus: A Mystery (Longfellow), **II:** 490, 493, 495, 505–507; **Retro. Supp. II:** 161, 165, 166

Chroma (F. Barthelme), **Supp. XI:** 30, 33, 34

"Chroma" (F. Barthelme), **Supp. XI:** 31

"Chronicle of Race Relations, A" (Du Bois), **Supp. II Part 1:** 182

Chronicle of the Conquest of Granada (Irving), **II:** 310

"Chronologues" (Goldbarth), **Supp. XII:** 183, 184

"Chrysanthemums, The" (Steinbeck), **IV:** 53

"Chrysaor" (Longfellow), **II:** 498

Chu, Louis, **Supp. X:** 291

Chuang, Hua, **Supp. X:** 291

Chuang-Tzu, **Supp. VIII:** 206

"Chunk of Amethyst, A" (Bly), **Supp. IV Part 1:** 72

Church, Margaret, **IV:** 466

"Church and the Fiction Writer, The" (O'Connor), **Retro. Supp. II:** 223, 233

Churchill, Winston, **I:** 9, 490; **Supp. I Part 2:** 491

Church of Dead Girls, The (Dobyns), **Supp. XIII:** 75, **83–84**

"Church Porch, The" (Herbert), **IV:** 153

Church Psalmody, Selected from Dr. Watts and Other Authors (Mason and Greene, ed.), **I:** 458

Ciannic, Saint, **II:** 215

Ciano, Edda, **IV:** 249

Ciardi, John, **I:** 169, 179, 535; **III:** 268; **Supp. IV Part 1:** 243; **Supp. IV Part 2:** 639; **Supp. IX:** 269, 324; **Supp. XII:** 119

Cicada (Haines), **Supp. XII: 206–207**

"Cicadas" (Wilbur), **Supp. III Part 2:** 549

Cicero, **I:** 279; **II:** 8, 14–15; **III:** 23; **Supp. I Part 2:** 405

Cider House Rules, The (Irving), **Supp. VI:** 164, **173–175**

"Cigales" (Wilbur), **Supp. III Part 2:** 549

Cimarron, Rose (Burke), **Supp. XIV:** 22, 35

"Cimetière Marin, Le" (Valéry), **IV:** 91–92

Cimino, Michael, **Supp. X:** 126

Cincinnati Kid, The (film), **Supp. XI: 306**

"Cinderella" (Jarrell), **II:** 386

"Cinderella" (Perrault), **IV:** 266, 267

"Cinderella" (Sexton), **Supp. II Part 2:** 691

"Cinema, The" (Salter), **Supp. IX:** 257

Cinema of Tony Richardson, The: Essays and Interviews (Phillips), **Supp. XI:** 306

Cinthio, **IV:** 370

CIOPW (Cummings), **I:** 429

"Circe" (Welty), **Retro. Supp. I:** 353

Circle Game, The (Atwood), **Supp. XIII:** 20, 33

"Circle in the Fire, A" (O'Connor), **III:** 344–345, 349–350, 351, 353, 354; **Retro. Supp. II:** 229, 232

"Circle of Breath" (Stafford), **Supp. XI:** 318, 322

"Circles" (Emerson), **I:** 455, 460

"Circles" (Lowell), **II:** 554

"Circus, The" (Porter), **III:** 443, 445

"Circus Animals' Desertion" (Yeats), **I:** 389

"Circus in the Attic" (Warren), **IV:** 253

Circus in the Attic, The (Warren), **IV:** 243, 251–253

"Circus in Three Rings" (Plath), **Retro. Supp. II:** 243; **Supp. I Part 2:** 536

Circus of Needs, A (Dunn), **Supp. XI: 147–148**

"Cirque d'Hiver" (Bishop), **Supp. I Part 1:** 85

Cisneros, Sandra, **Supp. IV Part 2:** 544; **Supp. VII: 57–73; Supp. XI:** 177

Cities of the Interior (Nin), **Supp. X:** 182

Cities of the Plain (McCarthy), **Supp. VIII:** 175, **186–187**

Cities of the Red Night (Burroughs), **Supp. III Part 1:** 106

"Citizen Cain" (Baraka), **Supp. II Part 1:** 49

Citizen Kane (film), **Retro. Supp. I:** 115; **Supp. V:** 251; **Supp. XI:** 169

"Citizen of the World" (Goldsmith), **II:** 299

"City" (Francis), **Supp. IX:** 87

City and the Pillar, The (Vidal), **Supp. IV Part 2:** 677, 680–681; **Supp. XIV:** 170

"City and the Pillar, The, as Gay Fiction" (Summers), **Supp. IV Part 2:** 680–681

City in History, The (Mumford), **Supp.**

II Part 2: 495

"City in the Sea, The" (Poe), **III:** 411; **Retro. Supp. II:** 274

City Life (Barthelme), **Supp. IV Part 1:** 44, 47

City of Glass (Auster), **Supp. XII:** 22, **24–26**

City of God, The (St. Augustine), **IV:** 126

City of the Living and Other Stories, The (Stegner), **Supp. IV Part 2:** 599, 609, 613

City of Your Final Destination, The (Cameron), **Supp. XII:** 79, 82, **91–94**

"City on a Hill" (Lowell), **II: 552**

"City Person Encountering Nature, A" (Kingston), **Supp. V:** 170

"City Planners, The" (Atwood), **Supp. XIII:** 33

City Without Walls (Auden), **Supp. II Part 1:** 24

Civil Disobedience (Thoreau), **IV:** 185; **Supp. I Part 2:** 507

Civilization in the United States (Stearns), **I:** 245

"Civil Rights" (Lanier), **Supp. I Part 1:** 357

Cixous, Hélène, **Supp. X:** 102; **Supp. XIII:** 297

Claiborne, William, **I:** 132

Claiming of Sleeping Beauty, The (Rice), **Supp. VII:** 301

Clampitt, Amy, **Supp. IX: 37–54; Supp. X:** 120; **Supp. XI:** 249

Clancy's Wake, At (Crane), **I:** 422

"Clandeboye" (Leopold), **Supp. XIV:** 189

Clara Howard; or, The Enthusiasm of Love (Brown), **Supp. I Part 1:** 145

Clara's Ole Man (Bullins), **Supp. II Part 1:** 42

Clare, John, **II:** 387; **III:** 528

Clarel: A Poem and Pilgrimage in the Holy Land (Melville), **Retro. Supp. I:** 257

Clarissa (Richardson), **II:** 111; **Supp. I Part 2:** 714; **Supp. V:** 127

Clark, Alex, **Supp. XII:** 307

Clark, Charles, **I:** 470

Clark, Eleanor. *See* Warren, Mrs. Robert Penn (Eleanor Clark)

Clark, Francis Edward, **II:** 9

Clark, Geoffrey, **Supp. XI:** 342

Clark, Harry Hayden, **Supp. I Part 2:** 423

Clark, John Bates, **Supp. I Part 2:** 633

Clark, Kenneth, **Supp. XIV:** 342, 348

Clark, Thomas, **Supp. III Part 2:** 629; **Supp. IV Part 1:** 140, 145, 147

Clark, Walter, **Supp. XI:** 315

Clark, William, **III:** 14; **IV:** 179, 283

Clark, Willis Gaylord, **Supp. I Part 2:** 684

Clarke, James Freeman, **Supp. II Part 1:** 280

Clarke, John, **Supp. IV Part 1:** 8

Clarke, John J., **III:** 356

Clarke, Samuel, **II:** 108

Clark Lectures, **Retro. Supp. I:** 65

Clash by Night (Odets), **Supp. II Part 2:** 531, 538, 544–546, 550, 551

Classical Tradition, The (Highet), **Supp. I Part 1:** 268

Classic Ballroom Dances (Simic), **Supp. VIII:** 271, **276–278,** 283

Classics and Commercials: A Literary Chronicle of the Forties (Wilson), **IV:** 433

"CLASS STRUGGLE" (Baraka), **Supp. III Part 1:** 55

Claudel, Paul, **I:** 60

Claudelle Inglish (Caldwell), **I:** 304

Clavel, Marcel, **I:** 343

"CLAY" (Baraka), **Supp. II Part 1:** 54

Clay, Henry, **I:** 8; **Supp. I Part 2:** 684, 686

Clay's Ark (O. Butler), **Supp. XIII:** 63

Clayton, John J., **Supp. IV Part 1:** 238

"Clean, Well Lighted Place, A" (Hemingway), **Retro. Supp. I:** 181

"Clear, with Light Variable Winds" (Lowell), **II:** 522

"Clear Days" (White), **Supp. I Part 2:** 664, 665

Clearing (Berry), **Supp. X:** 22

"Clearing, A" (Simpson), **Supp. IX:** 280

"Clearing, The" (Kenyon), **Supp. VII:** 174

"Clearing the Title" (Merrill), **Supp. III Part 1:** 336

"Clearing Up the Question of Stesichoros' Blinding by Helen" (Carson), **Supp. XII:** 107–108

"Clear Morning" (Glück), **Supp. V:** 88

"Clearness" (Wilbur), **Supp. III Part 2:** 544, 550

"Clear Night" (Wright), **Supp. V:** 341

Clear Pictures: First Loves, First Guides (Price), **Supp. VI:** 253, 254, 255, 256, 265

Clear Springs (Mason), **Supp. VIII:** 134–136, 137–138, 139, 147

Cleaver, Eldridge, **Retro. Supp. II:** 12; **Supp. IV Part 1:** 206; **Supp. X:** 249

Cleland, John, **Supp. V:** 48, 127

Clemenceau, Georges, **I:** 490

Clemens, Jane, **I:** 247
Clemens, Mrs. Samuel Langhorne (Olivia Langdon), **I:** 197, 208, 247; **Supp. I Part 2:** 457
Clemens, Orion, **IV:** 193, 195
Clemens, Samuel Langhorne. *See* Twain, Mark
Clemens, Susie, **IV:** 208
Clementine Recognitions (novel), **Supp. IV Part 1:** 280
Clemons, Walter, **Supp. IV Part 1:** 305, 307
Cleopatra, **III:** 44; **IV:** 373; **Supp. I Part 1:** 114
"Clepsydra" (Ashbery), **Supp. III Part 1:** 10–15
"Clerks, The" (Robinson), **III:** 517–518
Cleveland, Carol, **Supp. IX:** 120, 125
Cleveland, Ceil, **Supp. V:** 222
Cleveland, Grover, **II:** 126, 128, 129, 130, 137, 138; **Supp. I Part 2:** 486
"Clever Magician Carrying My Heart, A" (Salinas), **Supp. XIII:** 323
Clifford, Craig, **Supp. IX:** 99
Clift, Montgomery, **III:** 161
Climate of Monastic Prayer, The (Merton), **Supp. VIII:** 205, 207
"Climber, The" (Mason), **Supp. VIII:** 140–141
"Climbing the Tower" (Crews), **Supp. XI:** 102
Clinton, De Witt, **I:** 338
"Clipped Wings" (H. Miller), **III:** 176–177
Clive, Robert, **Supp. I Part 2:** 505
Clock Winder, The (Tyler), **Supp. IV Part 2:** 661–662, 670
Clock Without Hands (McCullers), **II:** 587–588, 604–606
Clockwork Orange, A (Burgess), **Supp. XIII:** 29
Clorindy (Cook), **Supp. II Part 1:** 199
"Close Calls" (Wolff), **Supp. VII:** 332–333
"Closed Book, A" (Mosley), **Supp. XIII:** 237
Close Range: Wyoming Stories (Proulx), **Supp. VII:** 261–265
Close the Book (Glaspell), **Supp. III Part 1:** 179
"Close the Book" (Lowell), **II:** 554
Close to Shore: A True Story of Terror in an Age of Innocence (Capuzzo), **Supp. XIII:** 254
Closet Writing & Gay Reading: The Case of Melville's Pierre (Creech), **Retro. Supp. I:** 254
Closing Circle, The (Commoner), **Supp. XIII:** 264

Closing of the American Mind, The (Bloom), **Retro. Supp. II:** 19, 30, 31
"Closing of the Rodeo, The" (W. J. Smith), **Supp. XIII:** 332
Closing Time (Heller), **Supp. IV Part 1:** 382, 386, 391–394
Closset, Marie, **Supp. VIII:** 251, 265
"Cloud, The" (Shelley), **Supp. I Part 2:** 720
"Cloud and Fame" (Berryman), **I:** 173
Cloud Forest, The: A Chronicle of the South American Wilderness (Matthiessen), **Supp. V:** 202, 204
"Cloud on the Way, The" (Bryant), **Supp. I Part 1:** 171
"Cloud River" (Wright), **Supp. V:** 341
"Clouds" (Levine), **Supp. V:** 184
Cloudsplitter (Banks), **Supp. V:** 16
"Clover" (Lanier), **Supp. I Part 1:** 362–364
Clover and Other Poems (Lanier), **Supp. I Part 1:** 362
"Clown" (Corso), **Supp. XII:** 127
Clown in the Belfry, The: Writings on Faith and Fiction (Buechner), **Supp. XII:** 53
Cluck, Julia, **Supp. I Part 2:** 728
Clum, John M., **Supp. XIII:** 200, 201, 209
Cluny, Hugo, **IV:** 290
Clurman, Harold, **I:** 93; **IV:** 381, 385
Clytus, Radiclani, **Supp. XIII:** 128, **Supp. XIII:** 129, 132
"Coal: Beginning and End" (Winters), **Supp. II Part 2:** 791
Coale, Howard, **Supp. XIII:** 15
"Coast, The" (column), **Supp. IV Part 1:** 198
"Coast Guard's Cottage, The" (Wylie), **Supp. I Part 2:** 723
Coast of Trees, A (Ammons), **Supp. VII:** 24, 34
"Coast-Range Christ, The" (Jeffers), **Supp. II Part 2:** 414, 419
"Coast-Road, The" (Jeffers), **Supp. II Part 2:** 425
Coates, Joseph, **Supp. VIII:** 80
Coates, Robert, **I:** 54; **IV:** 298
"Coatlicue's Rules: Advice from an Aztec Goddess" (Mora), **Supp. XIII:** 223
"Coats" (Kenyon), **Supp. VII:** 172
Cobb, Lee J., **III:** 153
Cobb, Ty, **III:** 227, 229
Cobbett, William, **Supp. I Part 2:** 517
"Cobbler Keezar's Vision" (Whittier), **Supp. I Part 2:** 699
"Cobweb, The" (Carver), **Supp. III Part 1:** 148

Cobwebs From an Empty Skull (Bierce), **I:** 195
Coccimiglio, Vic, **Supp. XIII:** 114
"Cock-a-Doodle-Doo!" (Melville), **III:** 89
"Cockayne" (Emerson), **II:** 6
"Cock-Crow" (Gordon), **II:** 219
Cock Pit (Cozzens), **I:** 359, 378, 379
Cockpit (Kosinski), **Supp. XII:** 21
Cockpit: A Novel (Kosinski), **Supp. VII:** 215, 223–224, 225
"Cock Robin Takes Refuge in the Storm House" (Snodgrass), **Supp. VI:** 319
Cocktail Hour, The (Gurney), **Supp. V:** 95, 96, 100, 101, 103, 105, 108
Cocktail Hour and Two Other Plays: Another Antigone and *The Perfect Party* (Gurney), **Supp. V:** 100
Cocktail Party, The (Eliot), **I:** 571, 582–583; **III:** 21; **Retro. Supp. I:** 65; **Supp. V:** 101, 103
Cocteau, Jean, **III:** 471; **Retro. Supp. I:** 82, 378; **Supp. IV Part 1:** 82
"Coda: Wilderness Letter" (Stegner), **Supp. IV Part 2:** 595
"Code, The" (Frost), **Retro. Supp. I:** 121, 128
Codman, Florence, **Supp. II Part 1:** 92, 93
Codman, Ogden, Jr., **Retro. Supp. I:** 362, 363
Cody, William ("Buffalo Bill"), **I:** 440; **III:** 584; **Supp. V:** 230
Coffey, Michael, **Supp. V:** 243
Coffey, Warren, **III:** 358
Coffin, Charles, **III:** 577
Cogan, David J., **Supp. IV Part 1:** 362
Coghill, Nevill, **Supp. II Part 1:** 4; **Supp. XIV:** 13
Cohan, George M., **II:** 427; **III:** 401
Cohen, Hettie, **Supp. II Part 1:** 30
Cohen, Marty, **Supp. X:** 112
Cohen, Norman J., **Supp. IX:** 132, 143
Cohen, Sarah Blacher, **Supp. V:** 273
"Coin" (Goldbarth), **Supp. XII:** 187
Coindreau, Maurice, **III:** 339
Coiner, Constance, **Supp. XIII:** 297, 302
Coit, Lille Hitchcock, **Supp. X:** 103
"Coitus" (Pound), **III:** 466
"Cold, The" (Kenyon), **Supp. VII:** 164
"Cold, The" (Winters), **Supp. II Part 2:** 790–791, 809, 811
"Cold-blooded Creatures" (Wylie), **Supp. I Part 2:** 729
Colden, Cadwallader, **Supp. I Part 1:** 250
"Colder the Air, The" (Bishop), **Supp. I Part 1:** 86

Cold Feet (Harrison), **Supp. VIII:** 39

Cold Ground Was My Bed Last Night (Garrett), **Supp. VII:** 98

"Cold Ground Was My Bed Last Night" (Garrett), **Supp. VII:** 100

"Cold Night, The" (W. C. Williams), **Retro. Supp. I:** 418

"Cold Plunge into Skin Diving, A" (Knowles), **Supp. XII:** 241

Cold Spring, A (Bishop), **Retro. Supp. II:** 45

Cold Springs Harbor (Yates), **Supp. XI:** 348

Cold War American Poetry, **Supp. V:** 182

Cold War and the Income Tax, The (Wilson), **IV:** 430

Cole, Goody, **Supp. I Part 2:** 696–697

Cole, Lester, **Retro. Supp. II:** 329

Cole, Nat King, **Retro. Supp. I:** 334; **Supp. X:** 255

Cole, Thomas, **Supp. I Part 1:** 156, 158, 171

"Coleman" (Karr), **Supp. XI:** 244

Coleman, Wanda, **Supp. XI: 83–98**

Coleridge, Samuel Taylor, **I:** 283, 284, 447, 522; **II:** 7, 10, 11, 19, 71, 169, 273, 301, 502, 516, 549; **III:** 77, 83–84, 424, 461, 488, 523; **IV:** 74, 173, 250, 349, 453; **Retro. Supp. I:** 65, 308; **Supp. I Part 1:** 31, 311, 349; **Supp. I Part 2:** 376, 393, 422; **Supp. IV Part 2:** 422, 465; **Supp. V:** 258; **Supp. IX:** 38, 50; **Supp. XIII:** 139; **Supp. XIV:** 21–22

Coles, Katharine, **Supp. IV Part 2:** 630

Colette, **Supp. VIII:** 40, 171

"Coliseum, The" (Poe), **III:** 411

Collage of Dreams (Spencer), **Supp. X:** 196

"Collapse of Tomorrow, The" (Mumford), **Supp. II Part 2:** 482

Collected Earlier Poems (Hecht), **Supp. X:** 58, 59

Collected Earlier Poems (W. C. Williams), **Retro. Supp. I:** 414, 428

Collected Earlier Poems 1940–1960 (Levertov), **Supp. III Part 1:** 273, 275

Collected Essays (Tate), **IV:** 133–134

Collected Essays of Ralph Ellison, The (Ellison), **Retro. Supp. II:** 119

Collected Essays of Robert Creeley, The (Creeley), **Supp. IV Part 1:** 153, 154

Collected Later Poems (W. C. Williams), **Retro. Supp. I:** 428

Collected Plays (A. Miller), **III:** 158

Collected Plays, 1974–1983 (Gurney),

Supp. V: 99

Collected Poems (Aiken), **I:** 50

Collected Poems (Burke), **I:** 269

Collected Poems (Cummings), **I:** 430, 439, 441

Collected Poems (Doolittle), **Supp. I Part 1:** 264–267, 269

Collected Poems (Frost), **Retro. Supp. I:** 136

Collected Poems (Lindsay), **Supp. I Part 2:** 380, 387, 392, 396–397, 400

Collected Poems (Moore), **III:** 194, 215

Collected Poems (Price), **Supp. VI:** 267

Collected Poems (Simpson), **Supp. IX:** 279

Collected Poems (Winters), **Supp. II Part 2:** 791, 810

Collected Poems (Wright), **Supp. III Part 2:** 602

Collected Poems (W. C. Williams), **IV:** 415; **Retro. Supp. I:** 430

Collected Poems 1909–1935 (Eliot), **I:** 580; **Retro. Supp. I:** 66

Collected Poems 1909–1962 (Eliot), **I:** 583

Collected Poems 1917–1952 (MacLeish), **III:** 3, 4, 19

Collected Poems 1921–1931 (W. C. Williams), **Retro. Supp. I:** 422; **Supp. XIV:** 285

Collected Poems 1930–1960 (Eberhart), **I:** 522, 525–526, 540, 541

Collected Poems, 1923–1953 (Bogan), **Supp. III Part 1:** 64

Collected Poems, 1936–1976 (Francis), **Supp. IX:** 77, 80, **87**

Collected Poems: 1939–1989 (W. J. Smith), **Supp. XIII:** 332, 340, 343, 345

Collected Poems: 1940–1978 (Shapiro), **Supp. II Part 2:** 703, 717

Collected Poems: 1951–1971 (Ammons), **Supp. VII:** 24, 26–29, 32, 33

Collected Poems: 1956–1976 (Wagoner), **Supp. IX:** 323, **328–329**

Collected Poems, The (Stevens), **III:** 273; **IV:** 75, 76, 87, 93; **Retro. Supp. I:** 296, 309

Collected Poems of Amy Clampitt, The (Clampitt), **Supp. IX:** 37, 44, 53

Collected Poems of George Garrett (Garrett), **Supp. VII:** 109

Collected Poems of Hart Crane, The (Crane), **I:** 399–402

Collected Poems of James Agee, The (Fitzgerald, ed.), **I:** 27–28

Collected Poems of James T. Farrell, The (Farrell), **II:** 45

Collected Poems of Langston Hughes, The (Rampersad and Roessel, ed.), **Retro. Supp. I:** 194, 196, 212

Collected Poems of Muriel Rukeyser, The (Rukeyser), **Supp. VI:** 274

Collected Poems of Thomas Merton, The, **Supp. VIII:** 207, 208

Collected Poetry (Auden), **Supp. II Part 1:** 18

Collected Prose (Wright), **Supp. III Part 2:** 596

Collected Prose, The (Bishop), **Retro. Supp. II:** 51

Collected Recordings (W. C. Williams), **Retro. Supp. I:** 431

Collected Short Stories, The (Wharton), **Retro. Supp. I:** 362, 363, 366

Collected Sonnets (Millay), **III:** 136–137

Collected Stories, 1939–1976 (Bowles), **Supp. IV Part 1:** 92

Collected Stories, The (Paley), **Supp. VI:** 218

Collected Stories, The (Price), **Supp. VI:** 266

Collected Stories, The (Theroux), **Supp. VIII:** 318

Collected Stories, The (Wharton), **Retro. Supp. I:** 361

Collected Stories of Eudora Welty, The (Welty), **Retro. Supp. I:** 355

Collected Stories of Isaac Bashevis Singer (Singer), **Retro. Supp. II: 307–308**

Collected Stories of Katherine Anne Porter (Porter), **III:** 454

Collected Stories of Peter Taylor (Taylor), **Supp. V:** 314, 320, 323–324, 325, 326

Collected Stories of Richard Yates, The, **Supp. XI:** 349

Collected Stories of Wallace Stegner (Stegner), **Supp. IV Part 2:** 599, 605

Collected Stories of William Faulkner (Faulkner), **II:** 72; **Retro. Supp. I:** 75

Collected Stories of William Humphrey, The (Humphrey), **Supp. IX:** 106

Collected Works (Bierce), **I:** 204, 208–210

Collected Works of Buck Rogers in the 25th Century, The (Bradbury), **Supp. IV Part 1:** 101

Collected Writings, The (Z. Fitzgerald; Bruccoli, ed.), **Supp. IX:** 65, 68

Collection of Epigrams, **II:** 111

Collection of Poems, on American Af-

fairs, and a Variety of Other Subjects . . . (Freneau), **Supp. II Part 1:** 274

Collection of Select Aphorisms and Maxims (Palmer), **II:** 111

"Collectors" (Carver), **Supp. III Part 1:** 141–142

Collingwood, R. G., **I:** 278

Collins, Billy, **Supp. XI:** 143; **Supp. XIV:** 123

Collins, Doug, **Supp. V:** 5

Collins, Eddie, **II:** 416

Collins, Richard, **Supp. XI:** 171

Collins, Wilkie, **Supp. I Part 1:** 35, 36; **Supp. IV Part 1:** 341

Collins, William, **Supp. I Part 2:** 714

Collinson, Peter, **II:** 114

Collinson, Peter (pseudonym). *See* Hammett, Dashiell

Colloff, Pamela, **Supp. XIII:** 281

Colloque Sentimental (ballet), **Supp. IV Part 1:** 83

"Colloquy in Black Rock" (Lowell), **II:** 535; **Retro. Supp. II:** 178

"Colloquy of Monos and Una, The" (Poe), **III:** 412

Colonel's Dream, The (Chesnutt), **Supp. XIV:** 63, 75–76

Colônia, Regina, **Retro. Supp. II:** 53

Color (Cullen), **Supp. IV Part 1:** 164, 166, 167, 168

"Color: The Unfinished Business of Democracy" (Locke), **Supp. XIV:** 202, 207

"Colorado" (Beattie), **Supp. V:** 27

Color and Democracy: Colonies and Peace (Du Bois), **Supp. II Part 1:** 184, 185

Color Curtain, The (Wright), **IV:** 478, 488

"Colored Americans" (Dunbar), **Supp. II Part 1:** 197

"Color Line, The" (Douglass), **Supp. III Part 1:** 163–165

Color Line, The (W. B. Smith), **Supp. II Part 1:** 168

Color of a Great City, The (Dreiser), **Retro. Supp. II:** 104

Color of Darkness (Purdy), **Supp. VII:** 271

Color Purple, The (Walker), **Supp. III Part 2:** 517, 518, 520, 525–529, 532–537; **Supp. VIII:** 141; **Supp. X:** 252, 330

Color Schemes (Cheang; film), **Supp. XI:** 20

"Colors of Night, The" (Momaday), **Supp. IV Part 2:** 490

"Colors without Objects" (Swenson), **Supp. IV Part 2:** 645

Colossus, The (Plath), **Retro. Supp.**

II: 245–247; **Supp. I Part 2:** 529, 531, 536, 538, 540; **Supp. V:** 79; **Supp. XI:** 317

"Colossus, The" (Plath), **Retro. Supp. II:** 250

Colossus of Maroussi, The (H. Miller), **III:** 178, 185–186

"Colt, The" (Stegner), **Supp. IV Part 2:** 600

Coltelli, Laura, **Supp. IV Part 1:** 323, 330, 335, 409; **Supp. IV Part 2:** 493, 497, 559

Coltrane, John, **Supp. VIII:** 197

Colum, Mary, **I:** 246, 252, 256; **Supp. I Part 2:** 708, 709

Columbiad, The (Barlow), **Supp. II Part 1:** 67, 72, 73, 74, 75–77, 79

"Columbian Ode" (Dunbar), **Supp. II Part 1:** 199

"Columbia U Poesy Reading—1975" (Corso), **Supp. XII:** 134

Columbus, Christopher, **I:** 253; **II:** 6, 310; **III:** 8; **Supp. I Part 2:** 397, 479, 480, 483, 486–488, 491, 495, 497, 498

"Columbus to Ferdinand" (Freneau), **Supp. II Part 1:** 255

Comanche Moon (McMurtry), **Supp. V:** 232

"Come, Break With Time" (Bogan), **Supp. III Part 1:** 52

Come Along with Me (Jackson), **Supp. IX:** 117, 118, 122

Comeback, The (Gurney), **Supp. V:** 97

"Come Back to the Raft Ag'in, Huck Honey!" (Fiedler), **Supp. XIII:** 93, 96–97, 101

Come Blow Your Horn (Simon), **Supp. IV Part 2:** 574, 575, 577, 578, 586, 587, 591

"Come Dance with Me in Ireland" (Jackson), **Supp. IX:** 119

"Comedian as the Letter C, The" (Stevens), **IV:** 84–85, 88; **Retro. Supp. I:** 297, 301, 302

"Comedy Cop" (Farrell), **II:** 45

"Comedy's Greatest Era" (Agee), **I:** 31

"Come In" (Frost), **Retro. Supp. I:** 139

"Come on Back" (Gardner), **Supp. VI:** 73

"Come Out into the Sun" (Francis), **Supp. IX:** 82

Come Out into the Sun: Poems New and Selected (Francis), **Supp. IX:** 82–83

"Come out the Wilderness" (Baldwin), **Supp. I Part 1:** 63

Comer, Anjanette, **Supp. XI:** 305

Comer, Cornelia, **I:** 214

Come with Me: Poems for a Journey (Nye), **Supp. XIII:** 279

"Comforts of Home, The" (O'Connor), **III:** 349, 351, 355; **Retro. Supp. II:** 237

Comic Artist, The (Glaspell and Matson), **Supp. III Part 1:** 182

"Comic Imagination of the Young Dickens, The" (Wright), **Supp. III Part 2:** 591

Comic Tragedies (Alcott), **Supp. I Part 1:** 33

"Coming Close" (Levine), **Supp. V:** 192

Coming Forth by Day of Osiris Jones, The (Aiken), **I:** 59

"Coming Home" (Gordon), **Supp. IV Part 1:** 309

"Coming Home to Vermont" (McCarriston), **Supp. XIV:** 269

"Coming in From the Cold" (Walker), **Supp. III Part 2:** 526

Coming into Eighty (Sarton), **Supp. VIII:** 262

"Coming into Eighty" (Sarton), **Supp. VIII:** 262

Coming into the Country (McPhee), **Supp. III Part 1:** 298, 301–306, 309, 310

Coming Into Writing (Cixous), **Supp. X:** 102

Coming of Age in Mississippi (Moody), **Supp. IV Part 1:** 11

Comings Back (Goldbarth), **Supp. XII:** 180

Coming to Canada: Poems (Shields), **Supp. VII:** 311–312

"Coming to Canada—Age Twenty Two" (Shields), **Supp. VII:** 311

"Coming to the Morning" (Merwin), **Supp. III Part 1:** 356

"Coming to This" (Strand), **Supp. IV Part 2:** 627

Comiskey, Charles, **II:** 422

Commager, Henry Steele, **I:** 253; **Supp. I Part 1:** 372; **Supp. I Part 2:** 484, 647, 650

Command the Morning (Buck), **Supp. II Part 1:** 125

"Commencement Address, A" (Brodsky), **Supp. VIII:** 31

"Commencement Day Address, The" (Schwartz), **Supp. II Part 2:** 660

Commentaries (Caesar), **II:** 502, 561

"Commentary" (Auden), **Supp. II Part 1:** 13

"Comment on Curb" (Hughes), **Supp. I Part 1:** 340

"Commerce" (Nye), **Supp. XIII:** 281

Commins, Saxe, **Retro. Supp. I:** 73;

Retro. **Supp. II:** 337

Commodity of Dreams & Other Stories, A (Nemerov), **III:** 268–269, 285

Common Carnage (Dobyns), **Supp. XIII:** 87

"Common Ground, A" (Levertov), **Supp. III Part 1:** 277

"Common Life, The" (Auden), **Supp. IV Part 1:** 302, 313

Common Room, A: Essays 1954–1987 (Price), **Supp. VI:** 264–265, 267

Commons, John, **Supp. I Part 2:** 645

Common Sense (Paine), **II:** 117; **Supp. I Part 1:** 231; **Supp. I Part 2:** 505, 506–508, 509, 513, 516, 517, 521

"Communication" (Dobyns), **Supp. XIII:** 91

"Communion" (Dubus), **Supp. VII:** 91

Communion (Mora), **Supp. XIII:** 217–219

Communist Manifesto, The (Marx), **II:** 463

"Community Life" (Moore), **Supp. X:** 178

Comnes, Gregory, **Supp. IV Part 1:** 283, 284, 291

"Companions, The" (Nemerov), **III:** 269, 278, 287

Company of Poets, A (Simpson), **Supp. IX:** 265, 275

Company of Women, The (Gordon), **Supp. IV Part 1:** 302–304, 304, 306, 313

Company She Keeps, The (McCarthy), **II:** 562, 563–566

Compass Flower, The (Merwin), **Supp. III Part 1:** 353, 357

"Compassionate Friendship" (Doolittle), **Supp. I Part 1:** 257, 258, 259, 260, 271

"Compendium" (Dove), **Supp. IV Part 1:** 248

"Complaint" (W. C. Williams), **Retro. Supp. I:** 418

Complete Collected Poems of William Carlos Williams, 1906–1938, The (W. C. Williams), **Retro. Supp. I:** 424

"Complete Destruction" (W. C. Williams), **IV:** 413

"Complete Life of John Hopkins, The" (O. Henry), **Supp. II Part 1:** 405

Complete Poems (Frost), **II:** 155, 164

Complete Poems (Reznikoff), **Supp. XIV:** 281

Complete Poems (Sandburg), **III:** 590–592, 594, 596

Complete Poems, The (Bishop), **Retro. Supp. II:** 49; **Supp. I Part 1:** 72, 82, 94

Complete Poems, The (Bradbury), **Supp. IV Part 1:** 105

Complete Poems, The: 1927–1979 (Bishop), **Retro. Supp. II:** 51

Complete Poems of Emily Dickinson, The (Bianchi and Hampson, eds.), **Retro. Supp. I:** 35

Complete Poems of Emily Dickinson, The (Johnson, ed.), **I:** 470

Complete Poems of Frederick Goddard Tuckerman, The (Momaday), **Supp. IV Part 2:** 480

Complete Poems of Hart Crane, **Retro. Supp. II:** 81

Complete Poems to Solve, The (Swenson), **Supp. IV Part 2:** 652

Complete Poetical Works (Hulme), **III:** 464

Complete Poetical Works (Longfellow), **Retro. Supp. II:** 154

Complete Poetical Works (Lowell), **II:** 512, 516–517

Complete Stories (O'Connor), **Supp. X:** 1

"Complete with Starry Night and Bourbon Shots" (Goldbarth), **Supp. XII:** 192–193

Complete Works of Kate Chopin, The (Seyersted, ed.), **Supp. I Part 1:** 212, 225

Complete Works of the Gawain-Poet (Gardner), **Supp. VI:** 64, 65

"Complicated Thoughts About a Small Son" (White), **Supp. I Part 2:** 678

"Compliments of the Season" (O. Henry), **Supp. II Part 1:** 392, 399

"Compline" (Auden), **Supp. II Part 1:** 23

Composition as Explanation (Stein), **IV:** 32, 33, 38

"Composition as Explanation" (Stein), **IV:** 27, 28

"Compounding of Consciousness" (James), **II:** 358–359

Comprehensive Bibliography (Hanneman), **II:** 259

Compton-Burnett, Ivy, **I:** 93; **II:** 580

"Comrade Laski, C.P.U.S.A. [M.L.]" (Didion), **Supp. IV Part 1:** 200

Comstock, Anthony, **Retro. Supp. II:** 95

Comus (Milton), **II:** 12; **Supp. I Part 2:** 622

Conan Doyle, Arthur. *See* Doyle, Arthur Conan

Conceptions of Reality in Modern American Poetry (Dembo), **Supp. I Part 1:** 272

"Concept of Character in Fiction, The" (Gass), **Supp. VI:** 85, 86

Concept of Dread, The (Kierkegaard), **III:** 305

Concerning Children (Gilman), **Supp. XI:** 206

"Concerning Some Recent Criticism of His Work" (Doty), **Supp. XI:** 131

Concerning the End for Which God Created the World (Edwards), **I:** 549, 557, 559

Concerto for Two Pianos, Winds, and Percussion (Bowles), **Supp. IV Part 1:** 83

Conchologist's First Book, The (Poe), **III:** 412

Conclusive Evidence (Nabokov), **III:** 247–250, 252

"Concord Hymn" (Emerson), **II:** 19

"Concrete Universal, The: Observations on the Understanding of Poetry" (Ransom), **III:** 480

Concurring Beasts (Dobyns), **Supp. XIII:** 76

Condensed Novels and Other Papers (Harte), **Supp. II Part 1:** 342

Condition of Man, The (Mumford), **Supp. II Part 2:** 483, 484, 486, 495–496, 498

"Condolence" (Parker), **Supp. IX:** 191

"Condominium, The" (Elkin), **Supp. VI:** 49, **50–51**, 55, 56

Condon, Charles R., **Supp. XIII:** 163

Condor and the Cows, The: A South American Travel Diary (Isherwood and Caskey), **Supp. XIV:** 166

"Condor and the Guests, The" (Connell), **Supp. XIV:** 86

Condorcet, Marquis de, **Supp. I Part 2:** 511

Conduct of Life, The (Emerson), **II:** 1–5, 8

Conduct of Life, The (Mumford), **Supp. II Part 2:** 485, 496–497

"Conductor of Nothing, The" (Levine), **Supp. V:** 189

"Conference Male, The" (Mora), **Supp. XIII:** 218

Confession de Claude, La (Zola), **I:** 411

"Confession of a House-Breaker, The" (Jewett), **Retro. Supp. II:** 146–147

Confession of Jereboam O. Beauchamp, The (pamphlet), **IV:** 253

Confessions (Augustine), **I:** 279

Confessions (Rousseau), **I:** 226

Confessions of a Barbarian: Selections from the Journals of Edward Abbey, 1951–1989 (Abbey; Petersen, ed.), **Supp. XIII:** 2, 4

"Confessions of a Latina Author" (Mora), **Supp. XIII:** 221

Confessions of Nat Turner, The (Styron), **IV:** 98, 99, 105, 113–117; **Supp. X:** 16, 250

Confetti (Mora), **Supp. XIII:** 221

Confidence (James), **II:** 327, 328

Confidence-Man, The (Melville), **III:** 91; **Retro. Supp. I:** 255–256, 257; **Retro. Supp. II:** 121; **Supp. XIV:** 49

Confidence Man, The (Van Vechten), **Supp. II Part 2:** 737

Confidential Clerk, The (Eliot), **I:** 570, 571–572, 583, 584; **Retro. Supp. I:** 65

Confident Years, 1885–1915, The (Brooks), **I:** 257, 259; **Supp. I Part 2:** 650

"Configurations" (Ammons), **Supp. VII:** 28

Confronting the Horror: The Novels of Nelson Algren (Giles), **Supp. IX:** 11, 15

Confucius, **II:** 1; **III:** 456, 475; **Supp. IV Part 1:** 14

Confusion (Cozzens), **I:** 358, 359, 377, 378

Congo (film), **Supp. IV Part 1:** 83

Congo (screenplay, Shanley), **Supp. XIV:** 316

"Congo, The" (Lindsay), **Supp. I Part 2:** 388–389, 392, 395

Congo and Other Poems, The (Lindsay), **Supp. I Part 2:** 379, 382, 389, 390, 391

"Congress of the Insomniacs, The" (Simic), **Supp. VIII:** 281–282

Congreve, William, **III:** 195; **Supp. V:** 101

Coningsby (Disraeli), **II:** 127

Conjectures of a Guilty Bystander (Merton), **Supp. VIII:** 197, 206, 207

Conjugal Bliss: A Comedy of Marital Arts (Nichols), **Supp. XIII:** 269

"Conjugation of the Paramecium, The" (Rukeyser), **Supp. VI:** 271

"Conjuration" (Wilbur), **Supp. III Part 2:** 551

Conjure (Reed), **Supp. X:** 240, 242

Conjure (recording), **Supp. X:** 241

Conjure Woman, The (Chesnutt), **Supp. II Part 1:** 193; **Supp. XIV:** 57, **58–61,** 62, 63

Conklin, Grof, **Supp. I Part 2:** 672

Conkling, Hilda, **II:** 530

Conkling, Roscoe, **III:** 506

Conley, Robert J., **Supp. V:** 232

Conley, Susan, **Supp. XIII:** 111, 112

Connaroe, Joel, **Supp. IV Part 2:** 690

"Connecticut Lad, A" (White), **Supp. I Part 2:** 677

"Connecticut Valley" (Cowley), **Supp. II Part 1:** 141–142

Connecticut Yankee in King Arthur's Court, A (Twain), **I:** 209; **II:** 276; **IV:** 205

Connell, Evan S., **Supp. XIV:79–100**

Connell, Norreys (pseudonym). *See* O'Riordan, Conal Holmes O'Connell

Connelly, Marc, **III:** 394; **Supp. I Part 2:** 679; **Supp. IX:** 190

Connoisseur, The (Connell), **Supp. XIV:** 87

"Connoisseur of Chaos" (Stevens), **IV:** 89; **Retro. Supp. I:** 306

Connolly, Cyril, **Supp. XIV:** 158, 343, 348

Connors, Elizabeth. *See* Lindsay, Mrs. Vachel (Elizabeth Connors)

Conover, Roger, **Supp. I Part 1:** 95

Conquering Horse (Manfred), **Supp. X:** 126

"Conqueror Worm, The" (Poe), **Retro. Supp. II:** 261

Conquest of Canaan (Dwight), **Supp. I Part 1:** 124

Conquistador (MacLeish), **III:** 2, 3, 13–14, 15

Conrad, Alfred, **Retro. Supp. II:** 245

Conrad, Alfred H., **Supp. I Part 2:** 552

Conrad, David, **Supp. I Part 2:** 552

Conrad, Jacob, **Supp. I Part 2:** 552

Conrad, Joseph, **I:** 123, 343, 394, 405, 409, 415, 421, 485, 506, 575–576, 578; **II:** 58, 73, 74, 91, 92, 144, 263, 320, 338, 595; **III:** 28, 102, 106, 328, 464, 467, 491, 512; **IV:** 476; **Retro. Supp. I:** 80, 91, 106, 108, 231, 274, 377; **Retro. Supp. II:** 222; **Supp. I Part 1:** 292; **Supp. I Part 2:** 621, 622; **Supp. IV Part 1:** 197, 341; **Supp. IV Part 2:** 680; **Supp. V:** 249, 251, 262, 298, 307, 311; **Supp. VIII:** 4, 310; **Supp. XIV:** 112

Conrad, Paul, **Supp. I Part 2:** 552

Conrad, Peter, **Supp. IV Part 2:** 688

"Conrad Aiken: From Savannah to Emerson" (Cowley), **Supp. II Part 1:** 43

Conroy, Frank, **Supp. VIII:** 145; **Supp. XI:** 245

Conscience with the Power and Cases thereof (Ames), **IV:** 158

"Conscientious Objector, The" (Shapiro), **Supp. II Part 2:** 710

"Consciousness and Dining" (Harrison), **Supp. VIII:** 46

"Conscription Camp" (Shapiro), **Supp. II Part 2:** 705

"Consejos de Nuestra Señora de Guadalupe: Counsel from the Brown Virgin" (Mora), **Supp. XIII:** 224

"Conservation Esthetic" (Leopold), **Supp. XIV:** 179, 181, 186, 189–190

"Conserving Natural and Cultural Diversity: The Prose and Poetry of Pat Mora" (Murphy), **Supp. XIII:** 214

"Considerations by the Way" (Emerson), **II:** 2, 5

Considine, Bob, **II:** 424

"Consolation" (Bausch), **Supp. VII:** 48

"Consolations" (Stafford), **Supp. XI:** 329

"Conspiracy of History, The: E. L. Doctorow's *The Book of Daniel*" (Levine), **Supp. IV Part 1:** 221

Conspiracy of Kings, The (Barlow), **Supp. II Part 1:** 80

Conspiracy of Pontiac, The (Parkman), **Supp. II Part 2:** 590, 595, 596, 599–600

Constab Ballads (McKay), **Supp. X:** 131, 133

Constance (Kenyon), **Supp. VII:** 170–172

"Constructive Work" (Du Bois), **Supp. II Part 1:** 172

"Consumption" (Bryant), **Supp. I Part 1:** 169–170

"Contagiousness of Puerperal Fever, The" (Holmes), **Supp. I Part 1:** 303–304

"Contemplation in a World of Action" (Merton), **Supp. VIII:** 204

"Contemplation of Poussin" (Sarton), **Supp. VIII:** 261

"Contemplations" (Bradstreet), **Supp. I Part 1:** 112, 113, 119–122

Contemporaries (Kazin), **Supp. VIII:** 102, **103–104**

Contemporary American Poetry (Poulin, ed.), **Supp. IX:** 272; **Supp. XI:** 259

"Contentment" (Holmes), **Supp. I Part 1:** 307

"Contest, The" (Paley), **Supp. VI:** 223, 230, 231

"Contest for Aaron Gold, The" (Roth), **Supp. III Part 2:** 403

Continental Drift (Banks), **Supp. V:** 13–14, 16, 227

Continental Op, The (Hammett), **Supp. IV Part 1:** 344

Continuity of American Poetry, The (Pearce), **Supp. I Part 1:** 111; **Supp. I Part 2:** 475

Continuous Harmony, A: Essays Cul-

tural and Agricultural (Berry), **Supp. X:** 33

Continuous Life, The (Strand), **Supp. IV Part 2:** 630, 631–633

Contoski, Victor, **Supp. XII:** 181

"Contract" (Lardner), **II:** 432

"Contraption, The" (Swenson), **Supp. IV Part 2:** 643

"Contrariness of the Mad Farmer, The" (Berry), **Supp. X:** 35

"Contrition" (Dubus), **Supp. VII:** 84

"Control Burn" (Snyder), **Supp. VIII:** 301

"Control Is the Mainspring" (Komunyakaa), **Supp. XIII:** 122, 124

Control of Nature, The (McPhee), **Supp. III Part 1:** 310–313

"Conventional Wisdom, The" (Elkin), **Supp. VI:** 52–53

"Convergence" (Ammons), **Supp. VII:** 28

"Convergence of the Twain, The" (Hardy), **Supp. VIII:** 31, 32

Conversation (Aiken), **I:** 54

Conversation at Midnight (Millay), **III:** 138

"Conversation of Eiros and Charmion, The" (Poe), **III:** 412

"Conversation on Conversation" (Stowe), **Supp. I Part 2:** 587

"Conversations in Moscow" (Levertov), **Supp. III Part 1:** 282

Conversations on Some of the Old Poets (Lowell), **Supp. I Part 2:** 405

Conversations with Byron (Blessington), **Retro. Supp. II:** 58

Conversations with Eudora Welty (Prenshaw, ed.), **Retro. Supp. I:** 339, 340, 341, 342, 343, 352, 354

Conversations with Ishmael Reed (Dick and Singh, eds.), **Supp. X:** 244

Conversations with James Baldwin (Standley and Pratt, eds.), **Retro. Supp. II:** 6

Conversations with Richard Wilbur (Wilbur), **Supp. III Part 2:** 542–543

"Conversation with My Father, A" (Paley), **Supp. VI:** 220

"Conversion of the Jews, The" (Roth), **Retro. Supp. II:** 281; **Supp. III Part 2:** 404, 406

Convict, The: Stories (Burke), **Supp. XIV:** 25

Conway, Jill, **Supp. I Part 1:** 19

Coode, John, **I:** 132

Cook, Bruce, **Supp. XII:** 130, 131, 133–134

Cook, Captain James, **I:** 2

Cook, Eleanor, **Retro. Supp. I:** 311

Cook, Elisha, **Supp. IV Part 1:** 356

Cook, Elizabeth Christine, **II:** 106

Cook, Mercer, **Supp. IV Part 1:** 368

Cooke, Alistair, **III:** 113, 119, 120

Cooke, Delmar G., **II:** 271

Cooke, Grace MacGowan, **Supp. V:** 285

Cooke, Philip Pendleton, **III:** 420

Cooke, Rose Terry, **II:** 401; **Retro. Supp. II:** 51, 136, 138; **Supp. XIII:** 152

"Cookie" (Taylor), **Supp. V:** 320

"Cookies, The" (Nye), **Supp. XIII:** 281

Cook-Lynn, Elizabeth, **Supp. IV Part 1:** 325

Coolbrith, Ina, **I:** 193, 196

"Coole Park" (Yeats), **Supp. VIII:** 155, 159

"Coole Park and Ballylee" (Yeats), **Supp. VIII:** 156

Cooley, John, **Supp. V:** 214

Cooley, Peter, **Supp. XIII:** 76

Coolidge, Calvin, **I:** 498; **II:** 95; **Supp. I Part 2:** 647

"Cool Million, A" (screen story) (West and Ingster), **Retro. Supp. II:** 330

Cool Million, A (West), **III:** 425; **IV:** 287, 288, 297–299, 300; **Retro. Supp. II:** 321, 322–323, 328, **335–337**

"Cool Tombs" (Sandburg), **III:** 554

Coon, Ross, **IV:** 196

Cooney, Seamus, **Supp. XIV:** 289

"Coon Hunt" (White), **Supp. I Part 2:** 669

Co-op (Sinclair), **Supp. V:** 290

Cooper, Bernard, **Supp. XI:** 129

Cooper, Gary, **Supp. IV Part 2:** 524

Cooper, James Fenimore, **I:** 211, 257, **335–357; II:** 74, 277, 295–296, 302, 306, 309, 313, 314; **III:** 51; **IV:** 205, 333; **Retro. Supp. I:** 246; **Retro. Supp. II:** 160; **Supp. I Part 1:** 141, 155, 156, 158, 171, 372; **Supp. I Part 2:** 413, 495, 579, 585, 652, 660; **Supp. IV Part 1:** 80; **Supp. IV Part 2:** 463, 469; **Supp. V:** 209–210; **Supp. VIII:** 189; **Supp. XIV:** 227

Cooper, Mrs. James Fenimore (Susan A. De Lancey), **I:** 338, 351, 354

Cooper, Mrs. William, **I:** 337

Cooper, Susan Fenimore, **I:** 337, 354

Cooper, William, **I:** 337–338, 351

Coover, Robert, **Supp. IV Part 1:** 388; **Supp. V:** 39–55; **Supp. XII:** 152; **Supp. XIV:** 96

Copacetic (Komunyakaa), **Supp. XIII:** 116–118, 126

Copland, Aaron, **II:** 586; **Supp. I Part 1:** 281; **Supp. III Part 2:** 619; **Supp. IV Part 1:** 79, 80–81, 84

Coplas de Don Jorge Manrique (Longfellow, trans.), **II:** 488, 492

Coppée, François Edouard Joachim, **II:** 325

Copperhead, The (Frederic), **II:** 134–135

Copper Sun (Cullen), **Supp. IV Part 1:** 167, 168

Coppola, Francis Ford, **Supp. XI:** 171, 172; **Supp. XII:** 75

Coprolites (Goldbarth), **Supp. XII:** **177–178,** 180, 183

Coral and Captive Israel (Reznikoff), **Supp. XIV:** 288

"Coral Ring, The" (Stowe), **Supp. I Part 2:** 586

"Cora Unashamed" (Hughes), **Supp. I Part 1:** 329, 330

"Corazón del Corrido" (Mora), **Supp. XIII:** 225

Corbett, Gentlemen Jim, **II:** 416

Corbett, William, **Supp. XI:** 248

Corbière, Jean Antoine, **II:** 354–355, 528

Cording, Robert, **Supp. IX:** 328; **Supp. XII:** 184

Corelli, Marie, **III:** 579

Corey, Lewis, **Supp. I Part 2:** 645

"Corinna's Going a-Maying" (Herrick), **Supp. XIV:** 8, 9

"Coriolan" (Eliot), **I:** 580

"Coriolanus and His Mother" (Schwartz), **Supp. II Part 2:** 643, 644–645

"Corkscrew" (Hammett), **Supp. IV Part 1:** 345, 347

Corkum, Gerald, **I:** 37

Corliss, Richard, **Supp. VIII:** 73

Corman, Cid, **Supp. III Part 2:** 624, 625, 626, 627, 628; **Supp. IV Part 1:** 144; **Supp. VIII:** 292

"Corn" (Lanier), **Supp. I Part 1:** 352, 353, 354, 356–361, 364, 366

Corn, Alfred, **Supp. IX:** 156

Corneille, Pierre, **Supp. I Part 2:** 716; **Supp. IX:** 131

Cornell, Esther, **I:** 231

Cornell, Katherine, **IV:** 356

"Corners" (Dunn), **Supp. XI:** 148

Cornhuskers (Sandburg), **III:** 583–585

"Corn-Planting, The" (Anderson), **I:** 114

"Corporal of Artillery" (Dubus), **Supp. VII:** 84, 85

"Corpse Plant, The" (Rich), **Supp. I Part 2:** 555

Corpus Christi (McNally), **Supp. XIII:** **205–206,** 209

Corradi, Juan, **Supp. IV Part 1:** 208

"Correspondences" (Baudelaire), **I:** 63

"Corrido de Gregorio Cortez" (Mora), **Supp. XIII:** 225

"Corrigenda" (Komunyakaa), **Supp. XIII:** 115, 116

Corruption City (McCoy), **Supp. XIII:** 175

Corso, Gregory, **Supp. II Part 1:** 30; **Supp. IV Part 1:** 90; **Supp. XII:** **117–138; Supp. XIV:** 150

Corsons Inlet (Ammons), **Supp. VII:** 25–26, 28–29, 36

"Corsons Inlet" (Ammons), **Supp. VII:** 25–26

Cortázar, Julio, **Retro. Supp. I:** 278

"Cortège for Rosenbloom" (Stevens), **IV:** 81

Cortez, Hernando, **III:** 2

Coser, Lewis, **Supp. I Part 2:** 650

Cosgrave, Patrick, **Retro. Supp. II:** 185

Cosmic Optimism: A Study of the Interpretation of Evolution by American Poets from Emerson to Robinson (Conner), **Supp. I Part 1:** 73

Cosmological Eye, The (H. Miller), **III:** 174, 184

"Cosmological Eye, The" (H. Miller), **III:** 183

"Cosmos" (Beattie), **Supp. V:** 35

"Cost, The" (Hecht), **Supp. X:** 62–63

Costello, Bonnie, **Retro. Supp. II:** 40

Costner, Kevin, **Supp. VIII:** 45

"Cost of Living, The" (Malamud), **Supp. I Part 2:** 429, 437

"Cottage Street, 1953" (Wilbur), **Supp. III Part 2:** 543, 561

"Cottagette, The" (Gilman), **Supp. XI:** 207

Cotten, Joseph, **Supp. IV Part 2:** 524

Cotter, James Finn, **Supp. X:** 202

Cotton, John, **Supp. I Part 1:** 98, 101, 110, 111, 116

Cotton, Joseph, **Supp. XII:** 160

Cotton, Seaborn, **Supp. I Part 1:** 101

"Cotton Song" (Toomer), **Supp. IX:** 312

Couch, W. T., **Supp. X:** 46

Coughlin, Ruth Pollack, **Supp. VIII:** 45

Coulette, Henri, **Supp. V:** 180; **Supp. XIII:** 312

"Council of State, A" (Dunbar), **Supp. II Part 1:** 211, 213

"Countee Cullen at 'The Heights'" (Tuttleton), **Supp. IV Part 1:** 166

Counterfeiters, The (Gide), **Supp. IV Part 1:** 80; **Supp. IV Part 2:** 681

"Countering" (Ammons), **Supp. VII:** 28

Counterlife, The (Roth), **Retro. Supp. II:** 279, 280, 291; **Supp. III Part 2:** 424–426

Counter-Statement (Burke), **I:** 270–272; **IV:** 431

"Countess, The" (Whittier), **Supp. I Part 2:** 691, 694

Count Frontenac and New France Under Louis XIV (Parkman), **Supp. II Part 2:** 607, 609–610

"Counting Small-Boned Bodies" (Bly), **Supp. IV Part 1:** 62

"Counting the Mad" (Justice), **Supp. VII:** 117

Count of Monte Cristo, The (Dumas), **III:** 386, 396

"Country Boy in Boston, The" (Howells), **II:** 255

Country By-Ways (Jewett), **II:** 402

Country Doctor, A (Jewett), **II:** 391, 392, 396, 404–405; **Retro. Supp. II:** 131, 141, 146

"Country Full of Swedes" (Caldwell), **I:** 297, 309

Country Girl, The (Odets), **Supp. II Part 2:** 546, 547, 548–549

"Country House" (Kumin), **Supp. IV Part 2:** 446

"Country Husband, The" (Cheever), **Supp. I Part 1:** 184, 189

Countrymen of Bones (R. O. Butler), **Supp. XII:** 62, **65–66**

"Country Mouse, The" (Bishop), **Retro. Supp. II:** 37, 38, 51

Country Music: Selected Early Poems (Wright), **Supp. V:** 332, 335, 338, 342

Country of a Thousand Years of Peace, The (Merrill), **Supp. III Part 1:** 321, 322, 331

"Country of Elusion, The" (O. Henry), **Supp. II Part 1:** 407

Country of Marriage, The (Berry), **Supp. X:** 33

Country of the Pointed Firs, The (Jewett), **II:** 392, 399, 405, 409–411; **Retro. Supp. I:** 6; **Retro. Supp. II:** 134, 136, 139, 140, 141, 145, 146, 147; **Supp. VIII:** 126; **Supp. XIII:** 152

"Country Printer, The" (Freneau), **Supp. II Part 1:** 269

Coup, The (Updike), **Retro. Supp. I:** 331, 334, 335

"Coup de Grâce, The" (Bierce), **I:** 202

Couperin, François, **III:** 464

"Couple, The" (Olds), **Supp. X:** 206

"Couple of Hamburgers, A" (Thurber), **Supp. I Part 2:** 616

"Couple of Nuts, A" (Z. Fitzgerald), **Supp. IX:** 58, 71, 72

Couples (Updike), **IV:** 214, 215, 216, 217, 227, 229–230; **Retro. Supp. I:** 320, 327, 330; **Supp. XII:** 296

Cournos, John, **III:** 465; **Supp. I Part 1:** 258

"Course in Creative Writing, A" (Stafford), **Supp. XI:** 327

"Course of a Particular, The" (Stevens), **Retro. Supp. I:** 312

"Coursier de Jeanne d'Arc, Le" (McCarriston), **Supp. XIV:** 267–268

Courtier, The (Castiglione), **III:** 282

"'Courtin,' The" (Lowell), **Supp. I Part 2:** 415

"Courting of Sister Wisby, The" (Jewett), **Retro. Supp. II:** 134, 135, 146

"Courtship" (Dove), **Supp. IV Part 1:** 248

"Courtship, Diligence" (Dove), **Supp. IV Part 1:** 248

Courtship of Miles Standish, The (Longfellow), **II:** 489, 502–503; **Retro. Supp. II:** 155, **161–162,** 163, 166, 168

"Cousin Aubrey" (Taylor), **Supp. V:** 328

Cousine Bette (Balzac), **Retro. Supp. II:** 98

Couturier, Maurice, **Supp. IV Part 1:** 44

"Covered Bridges" (Kingsolver), **Supp. VII:** 203

Cowan, Lester, **III:** 148

Cowan, Louise, **IV:** 120, 125

Coward, Noel, **Retro. Supp. I:** 65; **Supp. I Part 1:** 332; **Supp. V:** 101

"Cowardice" (Theroux), **Supp. VIII:** 313

Cowboy Mouth (Shepard), **Supp. III Part 2:** 441–442

"Cowboys" (Salter). *See* "Dirt" (Salter)

Cowboys (Shepard), **Supp. III Part 2:** 432

Cowboys #2 (Shepard), **Supp. III Part 2:** 437, 438

Cowell, Henry, **Supp. IV Part 1:** 80, 82

Cowen, Wilson Walker, **Supp. IV Part 2:** 435

Cowie, Alexander, **IV:** 70

"Cow in Apple Time, The" (Frost), **II:** 154; **Retro. Supp. I:** 131

Cowl, Jane, **IV:** 357

Cowley, Abraham, **III:** 508; **IV:** 158;

Supp. I Part 1: 357

Cowley, Malcolm, I: 246, 253, 254, 255, 256, 257, 283, 385; II: 26, 57, 94, 456; III: 606; IV: 123; Retro. Supp. I: 73, 91, 97; Retro. Supp. II: 77, 83, 89, 221, 330; Supp. I Part 1: 174; Supp. I Part 2: 609, 610, 620, 647, 654, 678; Supp. II Part 1: 103, 135–156; Supp. VIII: 96

Cowley, Marguerite Frances Baird (Mrs. Malcolm Cowley), Supp. I Part 2: 615; Supp. II Part 1: 138, 139

Cowley, Muriel Maurer (Mrs. Malcolm Cowley), Supp. II Part 1: 139

Cowley, Susan Cheever (Susan Cheever), Supp. I Part 1: 175; Supp. IX: 133

Cowper, William, II: 17, 304; III: 508, 511; Supp. I Part 1: 150, 151, 152; Supp. I Part 2: 539

"Cow Wandering in the Bare Field, The" (Jarrell), II: 371, 388

Cox, Martha Heasley, Supp. IX: 2, 4, 11–12

Cox, Sidney, Retro. Supp. I: 131

Cox, Stephen, Supp. IV Part 2: 523, 524

Coxey, Jacob, II: 464

"Coxon Fund, The" (James), Retro. Supp. I: 228

Coyne, Patricia, Supp. V: 123

"Coyote Ortiz: *Canis latrans latrans* in the Poetry of Simon Ortiz" (P. C. Smith), Supp. IV Part 2: 509

Coyote's Daylight Trip (Gunn Allen), Supp. IV Part 1: 320, 324

Coyote Was Here (Ortiz), Supp. IV Part 2: 499

Cozzens, James Gould, I: 358–380; II: 459

Crabbe, George, II: 304; III: 469, 508, 511, 521

"Crab-Boil" (Dove), Supp. IV Part 1: 249

"Cracked Looking-Glass, The" (Porter), III: 434, 435, 446

"Cracker Chidlings" (Rawlings), Supp. X: 224, 228

Cracks (Purdy), Supp. VII: 277–278

"Crack-Up, The" (Fitzgerald), I: 509; Retro. Supp. I: 113, 114

Crack-Up, The (Fitzgerald), II: 80; III: 35, 45; Retro. Supp. I: 113, 115; Supp. V: 276; Supp. IX: 61

"Crack-up of American Optimism, The: Vachel Lindsay, the Dante of the Fundamentalists" (Viereck), Supp. I Part 2: 403

Cradle Will Rock, The (Blitzstein), Supp. I Part 1: 277, 278

Craft of Fiction, The (Lubbock), I: 504; Supp. VIII: 165

Craft of Peter Taylor, The (McAlexander, ed.), Supp. V: 314

Craig, Gordon, III: 394

Crain, Jane Larkin, Supp. V: 123; Supp. XII: 167, 168

Cram, Ralph Adams, I: 19

Cramer, Stephen, Supp. XI: 139

Crandall, Reuben, Supp. I Part 2: 686

Crane, Agnes, I: 406

Crane, Edmund, I: 407

Crane, Hart, I: 61, 62, 97, 109, 116, 266, 381–404; II: 133, 215, 306, 368, 371, 536, 542; III: 260, 276, 453, 485, 521; IV: 122, 123–124, 127, 128, 129, 135, 139, 140, 141, 341, 380, 418, 419; Retro. Supp. I: 427; Retro. Supp. II: 75–91; Supp. I Part 1: 86; Supp. II Part 1: 89, 152; Supp. III Part 1: 20, 63, 350; Supp. V: 342; Supp. VIII: 39; Supp. IX: 38, 229, 320; Supp. X: 115, 116, 120; Supp. XI: 123, 131; Supp. XII: 198

Crane, Jonathan, Jr., I: 407

Crane, Jonathan Townley, I: 406

Crane, Luther, I: 406

Crane, Mrs. Jonathan Townley, I: 406

Crane, Nellie, I: 407

Crane, R. S., Supp. I Part 2: 423

Crane, Stephen, I: 34, 169–170, 201, 207, 211, 405–427, 477, 506, 519; II: 58, 144, 198, 262, 263, 264, 276, 289, 290, 291; III: 314, 317, 334, 335, 454, 505, 585; IV: 207, 208, 256, 350, 475; Retro. Supp. I: 231, 325; Retro. Supp. II: 97, 123; Supp. I Part 1: 314; Supp. III Part 2: 412; Supp. IV Part 1: 350, 380; Supp. IV Part 2: 680, 689, 692; Supp. VIII: 98, 105; Supp. IX: 1, 14; Supp. X: 223; Supp. XI: 95; Supp. XII: 50; Supp. XIV: 21, 50, 51, 227

Crane, William, I: 407

Cranford (Gaskell), Supp. IX: 79

Crashaw, William, IV: 145, 150, 151, 165

"Crash Report" (McGrath), Supp. X: 116

Crater, The (Cooper), I: 354, 355

Cratylus (Plato), II: 10

"Craven Street Gazette" (Franklin), II: 119

Crawford, Brad, Supp. XI: 133

Crawford, Eva, I: 199

Crawford, F. Marion, III: 320

Crawford, Joan, Supp. I Part 1: 67

Crawford, Kathleen, I: 289

"Crayon House" (Rukeyser), Supp. VI: 273

Crayon Miscellany, The (Irving), II: 312–313

"Crazy about her Shrimp" (Simic), Supp. VIII: 282

"Crazy Cock" (H. Miller), III: 177

Crazy Gypsy (Salinas), Supp. XIII: 311, 313–315, 316

"Crazy Gypsy" (Salinas), Supp. XIII: 313–314

Crazy Horse, Supp. IV Part 2: 488, 489

Crazy Horse (McMurtry), Supp. V: 233

Crazy Horse in Stillness (Heyen), Supp. XIII: 344

Creating a Role (Stanislavsky), Supp. XIV: 243

"Creation, According to Coyote, The" (Ortiz), Supp. IV Part 2: 505

Creation: A Novel (Vidal), Supp. IV Part 2: 677, 685, 688

"Creation of Anguish" (Nemerov), III: 269

"Creation Story" (Gunn Allen), Supp. IV Part 1: 325

"Creative and Cultural Lag" (Ellison), Retro. Supp. II: 116; Supp. II Part 1: 229

Creative Criticism (Spingarn), I: 266

"Creative Democracy" (Locke), Supp. XIV: 208

Creative Present, The (Balkian and Simmons, eds.), Supp. XI: 230

Creatures in an Alphabet (illus. Barnes), Supp. III Part 1: 43

"Credences of Summer" (Stevens), IV: 93–94

"Credo" (Du Bois), Supp. II Part 1: 169

"Credo" (Jeffers), Supp. II Part 2: 424

"Credos and Curios" (Thurber), Supp. I Part 2: 606, 613

Creech, James, Retro. Supp. I: 254

"Creed for Americans, A" (Benét), Supp. XI: 52

"Creed of a Beggar, The" (Lindsay), Supp. I Part 2: 379

Creekmore, Hubert, II: 586

Creeley, Robert, Retro. Supp. I: 411; Supp. II Part 1: 30; Supp. III Part 1: 2; Supp. III Part 2: 622, 626, 629; Supp. IV Part 1: 139–161, 322, 325; Supp. XI: 317; Supp. XIII: 104, 112; Supp. XIV: 150

"Cremona Violin, The" (Lowell), II: 523

"Crêpe de Chine" (Doty), **Supp. XI:** 128

"Cressy" (Harte), **Supp. II Part 1:** 354, 356

"Cretan Woman, The" (Jeffers), **Supp. II Part 2:** 435

Crèvecoeur, Michel-Guillaume Jean de, **I:** 229; **Supp. I Part 1: 227–252**

Crèvecoeur's Eighteenth-Century Travels in Pennsylvania and New York (Adams), **Supp. I Part 1:** 251

Crevel, René, **Supp. XIV:** 343

Crewe Train (Macaulay), **Supp. XII:** 88

Crews, Harry, **Supp. X:** 11, 12; **Supp. XI: 99–117,** 245

Crichton, Michael, **Supp. XIV:** 316

"Crickets" (R. O. Butler), **Supp. XII:** 71

Criers and Kibitzers, Kibitzers and Criers (Elkin), **Supp. VI: 45–46,** 57

Crime and Punishment (Dostoyevsky), **II:** 60, 130; **IV:** 484; **Supp. IV Part 2:** 525; **Supp. VIII:** 282; **Supp. XII:** 281

Crisis papers (Paine), **Supp. I Part 2:** 508–509, 510

"Criteria of Negro Arts" (Du Bois), **Supp. II Part 1:** 181

"Critiad, The" (Winters), **Supp. II Part 2:** 794, 799

Critical Essays on Charlotte Perkins Gilman (Karpinski, ed.), **Supp. XI:** 201

Critical Essays on Peter Taylor (McAlexander), **Supp. V:** 319, 320, 323–324

Critical Essays on Robert Bly (Davis), **Supp. IV Part 1:** 64, 69

Critical Essays on Wallace Stegner (Arthur), **Supp. IV Part 2:** 606

Critical Fable, A (Lowell), **II:** 511–512, 527, 529–530

Critical Guide to Leaves of Grass, A (J. Miller), **IV:** 352

Critical Response to Joan Didion, The (Felton), **Supp. IV Part 1:** 210

Critical Temper of Alain Locke, The: A Selection of His Essays on Art and Culture (Stewart, ed.), **Supp. XIV:** 196, **210–211,** 213

"Critic as Artist, The" (Wilde), **Supp. X:** 189

Criticism and Fiction (Howells), **II:** 288

Criticism and Ideology (Eagleton), **Retro. Supp. I:** 67

Criticism in the Borderlands (Calderón and Saldívar, eds.), **Supp. IV Part 2:** 544

"Critics, The" (Jong), **Supp. V:** 119

"Critics and Connoisseurs" (Moore), **III:** 209

Critic's Notebook, A (Howe), **Supp. VI:** 126–128

"Critic's Task, The" (Kazin), **Supp. VIII:** 103

"Critic Who Does Not Exist, The" (Wilson), **IV:** 431

"Critique de la Vie Quotidienne" (Barthelme), **Supp. IV Part 1:** 50

Croce, Benedetto, **I:** 58, 255, 265, 273, 281; **III:** 610

Crockett, Davy, **II:** 307; **III:** 227; **IV:** 266; **Supp. I Part 2:** 411

Crofter and the Laird, The (McPhee), **Supp. III Part 1:** 301–302, 307

Croly, Herbert, **I:** 229, 231, 235; **IV:** 436

Cromwell, Oliver, **IV:** 145, 146, 156; **Supp. I Part 1:** 111

Cronin, Dr. Archibald, **III:** 578

Cronin, Justin, **Supp. X:** 10

Crooke, Dr. Helkiah, **Supp. I Part 1:** 98, 104

Crooks, Alan, **Supp. V:** 226

Crooks, Robert, **Supp. XIII:** 237

"Crop, The" (O'Connor), **Retro. Supp. II:** 223–225

Crosby, Caresse, **I:** 385; **III:** 473; **Retro. Supp. II:** 85; **Supp. XII:** 198

Crosby, Harry, **I:** 385; **Retro. Supp. II:** 85

"Cross" (Hughes), **Supp. I Part 1:** 325

Crossan, John Dominic, **Supp. V:** 251

"Cross Country Snow" (Hemingway), **II:** 249

Cross Creek (Rawlings), **Supp. X:** 223, 226, 228, **231–232,** 233, 234, 235

Cross Creek Cookery (Rawlings), **Supp. X:** 233

Crossing, The (McCarthy), **Supp. VIII:** 175, **184–186**

"Crossing, The" (Swenson), **Supp. IV Part 2:** 644

"Crossing Brooklyn Ferry" (Whitman), **IV:** 333, 340, 341; **Retro. Supp. I:** 389, 396, 397, 400–401

"Crossing into Poland" (Babel), **Supp. XIV:** 84

Crossings (Chuang), **Supp. X:** 291

"Crossings" (Hogan), **Supp. IV Part 1:** 412

Crossing the Water (Plath), **Retro. Supp. II:** 248; **Supp. I Part 2:** 526, 538

Crossing to Safety (Stegner), **Supp. IV Part 2:** 599, 606, 612, 613–614

"Cross of Snow, The" (Longfellow), **II:** 490; **Retro. Supp. II:** 169–170

"Crossover" (O. Butler), **Supp. XIII:** 61

"Cross-Roads, The" (Lowell), **II:** 523

"Crossroads of the World Etc." (Merwin), **Supp. III Part 1:** 347, 348

Cross-Section (Seaver), **IV:** 485

Cross the Border, Close the Gap (Fiedler), **Supp. XIII:** 104

"Croup" (Karr), **Supp. XI:** 243

Crouse, Russel, **III:** 284

"Crow" (Hogan), **Supp. IV Part 1:** 405

"Crow, The" (Creeley), **Supp. IV Part 1:** 148–149

"Crowded Street, The" (Bryant), **Supp. I Part 1:** 168

Crowder, A. B., **Supp. XI:** 107

"Crow Jane" (Baraka), **Supp. II Part 1:** 38

Crowninshield, Frank, **III:** 123; **Supp. IX:** 201

Crown of Columbus (Erdrich and Dorris), **Supp. IV Part 1:** 260

"Crows, The" (Bogan), **Supp. III Part 1:** 50, 51

Crucial Instances (Wharton), **Retro. Supp. I:** 365, 367

Crucible, The (A. Miller), **III:** 147, 148, 155, 156–158, 159, 166; **Supp. XIII:** 206

"Crucifix in the Filing Cabinet" (Shapiro), **Supp. II Part 2:** 712

"Crude Foyer" (Stevens), **Retro. Supp. I:** 310

"Cruel and Barbarous Treatment" (McCarthy), **II:** 562, 563

Cruise of the Dazzler, The (London), **II:** 465

Cruise of the Snark, The (London), **II:** 476–477

"'Crumbling Idols' by Hamlin Garland" (Chopin), **Supp. I Part 1:** 217

"Crusade of the Excelsior, The" (Harte), **Supp. II Part 1:** 336, 354

"Crusoe in England" (Bishop), **Retro. Supp. II:** 50; **Supp. I Part 1:** 93, 95, 96; **Supp. III Part 1:** 10, 18

Cry, the Beloved Country (Paton), **Supp. VIII:** 126

Cryer, Dan, **Supp. VIII:** 86, 88; **Supp. XII:** 164

Crying of Lot 49, The (Pynchon), **Supp. II Part 2:** 618, 619, 621, 630–633

"Crying Sisters, The" (Rand), **Supp. IV Part 2:** 524

Cryptogram, The (Mamet), **Supp. XIV:** 240, 247, 255

"Crystal, The" (Aiken), **I:** 60
"Crystal, The" (Lanier), **Supp. I Part 1:** 364, 370
"Crystal Cage, The" (Kunitz), **Supp. III Part 1:** 258
Cry to Heaven (Rice), **Supp. VII:** 300–301
"Cuba" (Hemingway), **II:** 258
"Cuba Libre" (Baraka), **Supp. II Part 1:** 33
Cudjoe, Selwyn, **Supp. IV Part 1:** 6
"Cudjo's Own Story of the Last American Slaver" (Hurston), **Supp. VI:** 153
Cudlipp, Thelma, **I:** 501
Cudworth, Ralph, **II:** 9, 10
"Cuentista" (Mora), **Supp. XIII:** 224
"Cuento de agua santa, Un" (Mora), **Supp. XIII:** 224
Cujo (King), **Supp. V:** 138–139, 143, 149, 152
Cullen, Countee, **Retro. Supp. I:** 207; **Retro. Supp. II:** 114; **Supp. I Part 1:** 49, 325; **Supp. III Part 1:** 73, 75, 76; **Supp. IV Part 1: 163–174;** **Supp. IX:** 306, 309; **Supp. X:** 136, 140; **Supp. XIII:** 186
"Cultivation of Christmas Trees, The" (Eliot), **I:** 579
"Cult of the Best, The" (Arnold), **I:** 223
"Cultural Exchange" (Hughes), **Supp. I Part 1:** 341
"Cultural Pluralism: A New Americanism" (Locke), **Supp. XIV:** 195
"Cultural Relativism and Ideological Peace" (Locke), **Supp. XIV:** 202, 212
"Culture" (Emerson), **III:** 2, 4
"Culture, Self, and Style" (Gass), **Supp. VI:** 88
"Culture and Religion" (Olds), **Supp. X:** 214
Culture of Cities, The (Mumford), **Supp. II Part 2:** 492, 494–495
Cummings, E. E., **I:** 44, 48, 64, 105, 176, **428–450,** 475, 477, 482, 526; **III:** 20, 196, 476; **IV:** 384, 402, 415, 427, 433; **Retro. Supp. II:** 178, 328; **Supp. I Part 2:** 622, 678; **Supp. III Part 1:** 73; **Supp. IV Part 2:** 637, 641; **Supp. IX:** 20
Cummings, Robert, **Supp. IV Part 2:** 524
Cunard, Lady, **III:** 459
Cunningham, Merce, **Supp. IV Part 1:** 83
Cunningham, Michael, **Supp. XII:** 80
Cup of Gold (Steinbeck), **IV:** 51, 53, 61–64, 67

"Cupola, The" (Bogan), **Supp. III Part 1:** 53
"Curandera" (Mora), **Supp. XIII:** 214, 222
Curé de Tours, Le (Balzac), **I:** 509
Cure for Dreams, A: A Novel (Gibbons), **Supp. X:** 45–47, 48, 50
Curie, Marie, **IV:** 420, 421; **Supp. I Part 2:** 569
Curie, Pierre, **IV:** 420
Curiosa Americana (Mather), **Supp. II Part 2:** 463
Curiosities (Matthews), **Supp. IX:** 151, 152
"Curious Shifts of the Poor" (Dreiser), **Retro. Supp. II:** 97
"Currents and Counter-Currents in Medical Science" (Holmes), **Supp. I Part 1:** 305
"Curried Cow" (Bierce), **I:** 200
Curry, Professor W. C., **IV:** 122
Curse of the Starving Class (Shepard), **Supp. III Part 2:** 433, 447–448
"Curtain, The" (Chandler), **Supp. IV Part 1:** 122
Curtain of Green, A (Welty), **IV:** 261–264, 268, 283
"Curtain of Green, A" (Welty), **IV:** 263–264
Curtain of Green and Other Stories, A (Welty), **Retro. Supp. I:** 343, 344, 345, 346, 347, 355
Curtain of Trees (opera), **Supp. IV Part 2:** 552
"Curtain Raiser, A" (Stein), **IV:** 43, 44
"Curtains" (Cisneros), **Supp. VII:** 66
Curtin, John, **Supp. IX:** 184
Curtis, George William, **Supp. I Part 1:** 307
Curve (Goldbarth), **Supp. XII:** 181
Curve of Binding Energy, The (McPhee), **Supp. III Part 1:** 301
Curzon, Mary, **III:** 52
Cushing, Caleb, **Supp. I Part 2:** 684, 686
Cushman, Howard, **Supp. I Part 2:** 652
Cushman, Stephen, **Retro. Supp. I:** 430
"Custard Heart, The" (Parker), **Supp. IX:** 201
Custer, General George, **I:** 489, 491
Custer Died for Your Sins (Deloria), **Supp. IV Part 1:** 323; **Supp. IV Part 2:** 504
"Custom House, The" (Hawthorne), **II:** 223; **Retro. Supp. I:** 147–148, 157
Custom of the Country, The (Wharton), **IV:** 318; **Retro. Supp. I:** 374, **375–376**

"Cut" (Plath), **Retro. Supp. II:** 253
"Cut-Glass Bowl, The" (Fitzgerald), **II:** 88
Cutting, Bronson, **III:** 600
"Cuttings, *later*" (Roethke), **III:** 532
"Cycles, The" (Pinsky), **Supp. VI:** 250–252
Cynic's Word Book, The (Bierce), **I:** 197, 205, 208, 209, 210
Cynthia Ozick (Lowin), **Supp. V:** 273
Cynthia Ozick's Comic Art (Cohen), **Supp. V:** 273
Cynthia Ozick's Fiction (Kauvar), **Supp. V:** 273
D. H. Lawrence: An Unprofessional Study (Nin), **Supp. X:** 182–183
Dacey, Philip, **Supp. IV Part 1:** 70
Dacier, André, **II:** 10
"Dad" (Cullen), **Supp. IV Part 1:** 167
"Daddy" (Plath), **Retro. Supp. II:** 250–251; **Supp. I Part 2:** 529, 542, 545, 546; **Supp. II Part 2:** 688
"Daemon, The" (Bogan), **Supp. III Part 1:** 58, 61
"Daemon Lover, The" (Jackson), **Supp. IX:** 116–117
"Daffodils" (Wordsworth), **Supp. XIII:** 284
"Daffy Duck in Hollywood" (Ashbery), **Supp. III Part 1:** 18
D'Agata, John, **Supp. XII:** 97, 98
Dago Red (Fante), **Supp. XI:** 160, 169
Dahl, Roald, **Supp. IX:** 114
Dahlberg, Edward, **I:** 231; **Retro. Supp. I:** 426; **Supp. III Part 2:** 624; **Supp. XIV:** 148
Dahlberg, R'lene, **Supp. XIV:** 148
Daiches, David, **Retro. Supp. II:** 243; **Supp. I Part 2:** 536
Daily Modernism (Podnieks), **Supp. X:** 189
Dain Curse, The (Hammett), **Supp. IV Part 1:** 348
"Daisies" (Glück), **Supp. V:** 88
"Daisy" (Oates), **Supp. II Part 2:** 523
Daisy Miller (James), **Retro. Supp. I:** 216, 220, 222, 223, 228, 231
"Daisy Miller" (James), **II:** 325, 326, 327, 329; **IV:** 316
Dale, Charlie, **Supp. IV Part 2:** 584
Dali, Salvador, **II:** 586; **Supp. IV Part 1:** 83; **Supp. XIII:** 317
Dalibard, Thomas-François, **II:** 117
"Dallas-Fort Worth: Redband and Mistletoe" (Clampitt), **Supp. IX:** 45
"Dalliance of Eagles, The" (Whitman), **IV:** 348
Dalva (Harrison), **Supp. VIII:** 37, 45, 46, **48–49**

Daly, Carroll John, **Supp. IV Part 1:** 343, 345

Daly, John, **II:** 25, 26

Daly, Julia Brown, **II:** 25, 26

"Dalyrimple Goes Wrong" (Fitzgerald), **II:** 88

"Dam, The" (Rukeyser), **Supp. VI:** 283

Damas, Leon, **Supp. X:** 139

Damascus Gate (Stone), **Supp. V:** 308–311

Damballah (Wideman), **Supp. X:** 319, 320, 321, 322, 323, 326, 327, 331, 333–334

Damnation of Theron Ware, The (Frederic), **II:** 140–143, 144, 146, 147; **Retro. Supp. I:** 325

"Damned Thing, The" (Bierce), **I:** 206

Damon, Matt, **Supp. VIII:** 175

Damon, S. Foster, **I:** 26; **II:** 512, 514, 515

"Damon and Vandalia" (Dove), **Supp. IV Part 1:** 252

Dana, H. W. L., **I:** 225

Dana, Richard Henry, **I:** 339, 351; **Supp. I Part 1:** 103, 154, 155; **Supp. I Part 2:** 414, 420

Dana, Richard Henry, Jr., **III:** 81

Dana, Robert, **Supp. V:** 178, 180

"Dance, The" (Crane), **I:** 109

"Dance, The" (Roethke), **III:** 541

Dance of Death, The (Auden), **Supp. II Part 1:** 10

Dance of Death, The (Bierce and Harcourt), **I:** 196

Dance of the Sleepwalkers (Calabria), **Supp. XIII:** 164

"Dance of the Solids, The" (Updike), **Retro. Supp. I:** 323

Dances with Wolves (film), **Supp. X:** 124

Dancing After Hours (Dubus), **Supp. VII:** 91

Dancing Bears, The (Merwin), **Supp. III Part 1:** 343–344

Dancing on the Stones (Nichols), **Supp. XIII:** 256, 257, 259, 267, 269

"Dancing the Jig" (Sexton), **Supp. II Part 2:** 692

Dandelion Wine (Bradbury), **Supp. IV Part 1:** 101, 109–110

Dandurand, Karen, **Retro. Supp. I:** 30

"Dandy Frightening the Squatters, The" (Twain), **IV:** 193–194

Dangerous Crossroads (film), **Supp. XIII:** 163

Dangerous Moonlight (Purdy), **Supp. VII:** 278

"Dangerous Road Before Martin Luther King" (Baldwin), **Supp. I Part 1:** 52

"Dangerous Summer, The" (Hemingway), **II:** 261

"Dangers of Authorship, The" (Blackmur), **Supp. II Part 1:** 147

Dangling Man (Bellow), **I:** 144, 145, 147, 148, 150–151, 153–154, 158, 160, 161, 162, 163; **Retro. Supp. II:** 19, 20–21, 22, 23; **Supp. VIII:** 234

Daniel (biblical book), **Supp. I Part 1:** 105

Daniel (film), **Supp. IV Part 1:** 236

Daniel, Arnaut, **III:** 467

Daniel, Robert W., **III:** 76

Daniel, Samuel, **Supp. I Part 1:** 369

Daniel Deronda (Eliot), **I:** 458

Danielson, Linda, **Supp. IV Part 2:** 569

D'Annunzio, Gabriele, **II:** 515

Danny and the Deep Blue Sea: An Apache Dance (Shanley), **Supp. XIV:** 315, **318–319,** 320, 321, 323, 324

Danny O'Neill pentalogy (Farrell), **II:** 35–41

Danse Macabre (King), **Supp. IV Part 1:** 102; **Supp. V:** 144

"Danse Russe" (W. C. Williams), **IV:** 412–413

"Dans le Restaurant" (Eliot), **I:** 554, 578

Dans l'ombre des cathédrales (Ambelain), **Supp. I Part 1:** 273

Dante Alighieri, **I:** 103, 136, 138, 250, 384, 433, 445; **II:** 8, 274, 278, 289, 490, 492, 493, 494, 495, 504, 508, 524, 552; **III:** 13, 77, 124, 182, 259, 278, 448, 453, 467, 533, 607, 609, 610–612, 613; **IV:** 50, 134, 137, 138, 139, 247, 437, 438; **Retro. Supp. I:** 62, 63, 64, 66, 360; **Retro. Supp. II:** 330; **Supp. I Part 1:** 256, 363; **Supp. I Part 2:** 422, 454; **Supp. III Part 2:** 611, 618, 621; **Supp. IV Part 2:** 634; **Supp. V:** 277, 283, 331, 338, 345; **Supp. VIII:** 27, 219–221; **Supp. X:** 120, 121, 125; **Supp. XII:** 98

Danziger, Adolphe, **I:** 199–200

Dar (Nabokov), **III:** 246, 255

"Dare's Gift" (Glasgow), **II:** 190

Dark Angel, The (Bolton), **Supp. I Part 1:** 281

"Dark Angel Travels With Us to Canada and Blesses Our Vacation, The" (Dunn), **Supp. XI:** 146

Dark Carnival (Bradbury), **Supp. IV Part 1:** 102

Darker (Strand), **Supp. IV Part 2:** 619, 626–628

Darker Face of the Earth, The (Dove), **Supp. IV Part 1:** 255–257

Dark Green, Bright Red (Vidal), **Supp. IV Part 2:** 677

Dark Half, The (King), **Supp. V:** 141

Dark Harbor: A Poem (Strand), **Supp. IV Part 2:** 633–634

"Dark Hills, The" (Robinson), **III:** 523

Dark Laughter (Anderson), **I:** 111, 116; **II:** 250–251

"Darkling Alphabet, A" (Snodgrass), **Supp. VI:** 323

Darkling Child (Merwin and Milroy), **Supp. III Part 1:** 346

"Darkling Summer, Ominous Dusk, Rumorous Rain" (Schwartz), **Supp. II Part 2:** 661

"Darkling Thrush" (Hardy), **Supp. IX:** 40

"Dark Men, The" (Dubus), **Supp. VII:** 86

Darkness and the Light, The (Hecht), **Supp. X:** 58

"Darkness on the Edge of Town" (O'Brien), **Supp. V:** 246

Darkness under the Trees/Walking behind the Spanish (Salinas), **Supp. XIII:** 311, **319–324**

Dark Night of the Soul, The (St. John of the Cross), **I:** 1, 585

"Dark Ones" (Dickey), **Supp. IV Part 1:** 182

Dark Princess: A Romance (Du Bois), **Supp. II Part 1:** 179, 181–182

Dark Room, The (T. Williams), **IV:** 381

"Dark Summer" (Bogan), **Supp. III Part 1:** 51, 53

Dark Summer: Poems (Bogan), **Supp. III Part 1:** 52–53, 57

"Dark Tower, The" (column), **Supp. IV Part 1:** 168, 170

Dark Tower, The: The Gunslinger (King), **Supp. V:** 152

Dark Tower IV, The: Wizard and Glass (King), **Supp. V:** 139

Dark Tunnel, The (Macdonald, under Millar), **Supp. IV Part 2:** 465, 466

"Dark TV Screen" (Simic), **Supp. VIII:** 282

"Dark Voyage, The" (McLay), **Supp. XIII:** 21

"Dark Walk, The" (Taylor), **Supp. V:** 320–321, 322, 326

Darkwater: Voices from Within the Veil (Du Bois), **Supp. II Part 1:** 178, 180, 183

Dark Waves and Light Matter (Goldbarth), **Supp. XII:** 176, 193

"Darling" (Nye), **Supp. XIII:** 283–284

"Darling, The" (Chekhov), **Supp. IX:** 202

Darnell, Linda, **Supp. XII:** 173

Darragh, Tina, **Supp. IV Part 2:** 427

Darreu, Robert Donaldson, **Supp. II Part 1:** 89, 98, 102

Darrow, Clarence, **Supp. I Part 1:** 5; **Supp. I Part 2:** 455

Darwin, Charles, **I:** 457; **II:** 323, 462, 481; **III:** 226, 231; **IV:** 69, 304; **Retro. Supp. I:** 254; **Retro. Supp. II:** 60, 65; **Supp. I Part 1:** 368; **Supp. IX:** 180; **Supp. XI:** 203

Daryush, Elizabeth, **Supp. V:** 180

Dash, Julie, **Supp. XI:** 17, 18, 20

Dashell, Alfred, **Supp. X:** 224

"DAS KAPITAL" (Baraka), **Supp. II Part 1:** 55

"Datum Centurio" (Wallace), **Supp. X:** 309

Daudet, Alphonse, **II:** 325, 338

"Daughter" (Caldwell), **I:** 309

Daughter of Earth (Smedly), **Supp. XIII:** 295

Daughter of the Snows, A (London), **II:** 465, 469–470

"Daughters" (Anderson), **I:** 114

Daughters (Marshall), **Supp. XI:** 275, 276, 277, **286–288,** 289, 290

Daughters, I Love You (Hogan), **Supp. IV Part 1:** 397, 399, 401

"Daughters of Invention" (Alvarez), **Supp. VII:** 9

Daughters of the Dust (Dash; film), **Supp. XI:** 17, 18

Daumier, Honoré, **IV:** 412

Dave, R. A., **Supp. VIII:** 126

Davenport, Abraham, **Supp. I Part 2:** 699

Davenport, Gary, **Supp. IX:** 98

Davenport, Guy, **Supp. XIV:** 96

Davenport, Herbert J., **Supp. I Part 2:** 642

Davenport, James, **I:** 546

Daves, E. G., **Supp. I Part 1:** 369

Davey, Frank, **Supp. XIII:** 33

"David" (Garrett), **Supp. VII:** 109–110

"David" (Gordon), **Supp. IV Part 1:** 298–299

David Copperfield (Dickens), **I:** 458; **II:** 290; **Retro. Supp. I:** 33

"David Crockett's Other Life" (Nye), **Supp. XIII:** 282

Davideis (Cowley), **IV:** 158

David Harum (Westcott), **I:** 216

"David Lynch Keeps His Head" (Wallace), **Supp. X:** 314

David Show, The (Gurney), **Supp. V:** 97

Davidson, Donald, **I:** 294; **III:** 495, 496; **IV:** 121, 122, 124, 125, 236; **Supp. II Part 1:** 139; **Supp. XIV:** 2

Davidson, John, **Retro. Supp. I:** 55

Davidson, Michael, **Supp. VIII:** 290, 293, 294, 302–303

Davidson, Sara, **Supp. IV Part 1:** 196, 198, 203

Davidsz de Heem, Jan, **Supp. XI:** 133

Davie, Donald, **III:** 478; **Supp. IV Part 2:** 474; **Supp. V:** 331; **Supp. X:** 55, 59

Davies, Arthur, **III:** 273

Davies, Sir John, **III:** 541

Da Vinci, Leonardo, **I:** 274; **II:** 536; **III:** 210

Davis, Allen F., **Supp. I Part 1:** 1, 7

Davis, Allison, **Supp. I Part 1:** 327

Davis, Angela, **Supp. I Part 1:** 66; **Supp. X:** 249

Davis, Bette, **I:** 78; **Supp. I Part 1:** 67

Davis, Bill, **Supp. XIII:** 267

Davis, Donald, **Supp. XIII:** 93

Davis, Elizabeth Gould, **Supp. I Part 2:** 567

Davis, George, **II:** 586

Davis, Glover, **Supp. V:** 180, 182, 186

Davis, Jefferson, **II:** 206; **IV:** 122, 125, 126

Davis, Katie, **Supp. VIII:** 83

Davis, L. J., **Supp. XI:** 234

Davis, Lydia, **Supp. XII:** 24

Davis, Ossie, Jr., **Supp. IV Part 1:** 362

Davis, Rebecca Harding, **Supp. I Part 1:** 45; **Supp. XIII:** 292, 295, 305

Davis, Richard Harding, **III:** 328; **Supp. II Part 1:** 393

Davis, Robert Gorham, **II:** 51; **IV:** 108

Davis, Stuart, **IV:** 409

Davis, Thulani, **Supp. XI:** 179; **Supp. XIII:** 233, 234, 239

Davis, William V., **Supp. IV Part 1:** 63, 64, 68, 69, 70

Dawn (Dreiser), **I:** 498, 499, 503, 509, 515, 519

Dawn (O. Butler), **Supp. XIII:** 63, **64**

"Dawnbreaker" (Hayden), **Supp. II Part 1:** 370

"Dawn Patrol: A Review of the Literature of the Negro for 1948" (Locke), **Supp. XIV:** 211

Dawn Patrol, The (film), **Supp. XIV:** 81

Dawson, Edward, **IV:** 151

Dawson, Emma, **I:** 199

Dawson, Ruth, **Supp. XI:** 120

Day, Dorothy, **II:** 215; **Supp. I Part 2:** 524; **Supp. X:** 142

Day, Georgiana, **Supp. I Part 2:** 585

Dayan, Joan, **Retro. Supp. II:** 270

Day Book, A (Creeley), **Supp. IV Part 1:** 155

"Daybreak" (Kinnell), **Supp. III Part 1:** 250

"Daybreak in Alabama" (Hughes), **Retro. Supp. I:** 211; **Supp. I Part 1:** 344

Day by Day (Lowell), **Retro. Supp. II:** 184, 186, 191

"Day-Care Field Trip: Aquarium" (Karr), **Supp. XI:** 243

"Day-Dream, A" (Bryant), **Supp. I Part 1:** 160

"Day for Poetry and Song, A" (Douglass), **Supp. III Part 1:** 172

Day Late and a Dollar Short, A (McMillan), **Supp. XIII:** 184, **Supp. XIII:** 185, **191–192**

"Day longs for the evening, The" (Levertov), **Supp. III Part 1:** 274

Day of a Stranger (Merton), **Supp. VIII:** 203

"Day of Days, A" (James), **II:** 322

Day of Doom (Wigglesworth), **IV:** 147, 155, 156

Day of the Locust, The (West), **I:** 298; **IV:** 288, 299–306; **Retro. Supp. II:** 321, 323, 324, 329, **337–338; Supp. II Part 2:** 626; **Supp. XI:** 296; **Supp. XII:** 173; **Supp. XIII:** 170; **Supp. XIV:** 328

"Day on the Big Branch, A" (Nemerov), **III:** 275–276

"Day on the Connecticut River, A" (Merrill), **Supp. III Part 1:** 336

Day Room, The (DeLillo), **Supp. VI:** 4

"Days" (Emerson), **II:** 19, 20

Days: Tangier Journal, 1987–1989 (Bowles), **Supp. IV Part 1:** 94

"Days and Nights: A Journal" (Price), **Supp. VI:** 265

Days Before, The (Porter), **III:** 433, 453

"Days of 1935" (Merrill), **Supp. III Part 1:** 325, 328

"Days of 1964" (Merrill), **Supp. III Part 1:** 328, 352

"Days of 1971" (Merrill), **Supp. III Part 1:** 328

"Days of 1981" (Doty), **Supp. XI:** 123

"Days of 1941 and '44" (Merrill), **Supp. III Part 1:** 336

"Days of Edward Hopper" (Haines), **Supp. XII:** 210

Days of Obligation: An Argument with My Mexican Father (Rodriguez), **Supp. XIV:** 298, 300, **302–305,** 307, 310

Days of Our Lives (soap opera), **Supp. XI:** 83

Days of Our Lives Lie in Fragments: New and Old Poems (Garrett), **Supp. VII:** 109–110, 111

Days of the Phoenix (Brooks), **I:** 266

Days of Wine and Roses (J. P. Miller), **Supp. XIII:** 262

Days to Come (Hellman), **Supp. I Part 1:** 276, 277–278

Days without End (O'Neill), **III:** 385, 391, 397

"Day's Work, A" (Capote), **Supp. III Part 1:** 120

"Day's Work, A" (Porter), **III:** 443, 446

"Day the Presidential Candidate Came to Ciudad Tamaulipas, The" (Caldwell), **I:** 309

Day the World ended, The (Coover), **Supp. V:** 1

"Day with Conrad Green, A" (Lardner), **II:** 428–429, 430

"Deacon's Masterpiece, The" (Holmes), **Supp. I Part 1:** 302, 307

"Dead, The" (Joyce), **I:** 285; **III:** 343

Dead and the Living, The (Olds), **Supp. X:** 201, **204–206,** 207

"Dead Body, The" (Olds), **Supp. X:** 210

"Dead by the Side of the Road, The" (Snyder), **Supp. VIII:** 301

Dead End (Kingsley), **Supp. I Part 1:** 277, 281

Dead Father, The (Barthelme), **Supp. IV Part 1:** 43, 47, 50–51

"Dead Fiddler, The" (Singer), **IV:** 20

Dead Fingers Talk (Burroughs), **Supp. III Part 1:** 103

"Dead Hand" series (Sinclair), **Supp. V:** 276, 277, 281

"Dead Languages, The" (Humphrey), **Supp. IX:** 109

Dead Lecturer, The (Baraka), **Supp. II Part 1:** 31, 33, 35–37, 49

Deadline at Dawn (Odets), **Supp. II Part 2:** 546

Dead Man's Walk (McMurtry), **Supp. V:** 231, 232

Dead Man's Walk (screenplay) (McMurtry and Ossana), **Supp. V:** 231

Dead Man Walking (opera libretto, McNally), **Supp. XIII:** 207

Dead Souls (Gogol), **I:** 296

"Dead Souls on Campus" (Kosinski), **Supp. VII:** 222

"Dead Wingman, The" (Jarrell), **II:** 374

"Dead Yellow Women" (Hammett),

Supp. IV Part 1: 345

Dead Zone, The (King), **Supp. V:** 139, 143, 144, 148, 152

Dean, James, **I:** 493

Dean, Man Mountain, **II:** 589

Deane, Silas, **Supp. I Part 2:** 509, 524

"Dean of Men" (Taylor), **Supp. V:** 314, 323

Dean's December, The (Bellow), **Retro. Supp. II:** 30–31

"Dear Adolph" (Benét), **Supp. XI:** 46

"Dear America" (Ortiz), **Supp. IV Part 2:** 503

"Dear Judas" (Jeffers), **Supp. II Part 2:** 431–432, 433

Dear Juliette (Sarton), **Supp. VIII:** 265

Dear Lovely Death (Hughes), **Retro. Supp. I:** 203; **Supp. I Part 1:** 328

"Dear Villon" (Corso), **Supp. XII:** 135

"Dear World" (Gunn Allen), **Supp. IV Part 1:** 321

"Death" (Corso), **Supp. XII:** 127

"Death" (Lowell), **II:** 536

"Death" (Mailer), **III:** 38

"Death" (West), **IV:** 286

"Death" (W. C. Williams), **Retro. Supp. I:** 422

"Death and Absence" (Glück), **Supp. V:** 82

Death and Taxes (Parker), **Supp. IX:** 192

"Death and the Child" (Crane), **I:** 414

"Death as a Society Lady" (Hecht), **Supp. X:** 71–72

Death before Bedtime (Vidal, under pseudonym Box), **Supp. IV Part 2:** 682

"Death by Water" (Eliot), **I:** 395, 578

Death Comes for the Archbishop (Cather), **I:** 314, 327, 328–330; **Retro. Supp. I:** 16–18, 21; **Supp. XIII:** 253

Death in the Afternoon (Hemingway), **II:** 253; **IV:** 35; **Retro. Supp. I:** 182; **Supp. VIII:** 182

"Death in the Country, A" (Benét), **Supp. XI:** 53–54

Death in the Family, A (Agee), **I:** 25, 29, 42, 45

Death in the Fifth Position (Vidal, under pseudonym Box), **Supp. IV Part 2:** 682

"Death in the Woods" (Anderson), **I:** 114, 115

Death in the Woods and Other Stories (Anderson), **I:** 112, 114, 115

Death in Venice (Mann), **III:** 231; **Supp. IV Part 1:** 392; **Supp. V:** 51

"Death in Viet Nam" (Salinas), **Supp.**

XIII: 315

Death Is a Lonely Business (Bradbury), **Supp. IV Part 1:** 102, 103, 111–112, 115

"Death Is Not the End" (Wallace), **Supp. X:** 309

Death Kit (Sontag), **Supp. III Part 2:** 451, 468–469

Death Likes It Hot (Vidal, under pseudonym Box), **Supp. IV Part 2:** 682

"*Death*/Muerta" (Mora), **Supp. XIII:** 228

Death Notebooks, The (Sexton), **Supp. II Part 2:** 691, 694, 695

"Death of a Jazz Musician" (W. J. Smith), **Supp. XIII:** 334

Death of a Kinsman, The (Taylor), **Supp. V:** 324, 326

"Death of an Old Seaman" (Hughes), **Retro. Supp. I:** 199

"Death of a Pig" (White), **Supp. I Part 2:** 665–668

Death of a Salesman (A. Miller), **I:** 81; **III:** 148, 149, 150, 153–154, 156, 157, 158, 159, 160, 163, 164, 166; **IV:** 389; **Supp. IV Part 1:** 359; **Supp. XIV:** 102, 239, 254, 255

"Death of a Soldier, The" (Stevens), **Retro. Supp. I:** 299, 312. *see also* "Lettres d'un Soldat" (Stevens)

"Death of a Soldier, The" (Wilson), **IV:** 427, 445

"Death of a Toad" (Wilbur), **Supp. III Part 2:** 550

"Death of a Traveling Salesman" (Welty), **IV:** 261; **Retro. Supp. I:** 344

"Death of a Young Son by Drowning" (Atwood), **Supp. XIII:** 33

Death of Bessie Smith, The (Albee), **I:** 76–77, 92

Death of Billy the Kid, The (Vidal), **Supp. IV Part 2:** 683

Death of Cock Robin, The (Snodgrass), **Supp. VI:** 315, **317–319,** 324

"Death of General Wolfe, The" (Paine), **Supp. I Part 2:** 504

"Death of Halpin Frayser, The" (Bierce), **I:** 205

"Death of Justina, The" (Cheever), **Supp. I Part 1:** 184–185

Death of Life, The (Barnes), **Supp. III Part 1:** 34

Death of Malcolm X, The (Baraka), **Supp. II Part 1:** 47

"Death of Marilyn Monroe, The" (Olds), **Supp. X:** 205

"Death of Me, The" (Malamud), **Supp. I Part 2:** 437

"Death of Slavery, The" (Bryant),

Supp. I Part 1: 168–169

"Death of St. Narcissus, The" (Eliot), **Retro. Supp. I:** 291

"Death of the Ball Turret Gunner, The" (Jarrell), **II:** 369–370, 372, 374, 375, 376, 378

"Death of the Fathers, The" (Sexton), **Supp. II Part 2:** 692

"Death of the Flowers, The" (Bryant), **Supp. I Part 1:** 170

Death of the Fox (Garrett), **Supp. VII:** 99, 101–104, 108

"Death of the Hired Man, The" (Frost), **III:** 523; **Retro. Supp. I:** 121, 128; **Supp. IX:** 261

Death of the Kapowsin Tavern (Hugo), **Supp. VI:** 133–135

"Death of the Kapowsin Tavern" (Hugo), **Supp. VI:** 137, 141

"Death of the Lyric, The: The Achievement of Louis Simpson" (Jarman and McDowell), **Supp. IX:** 266, 270, 276

"Death of Venus, The" (Creeley), **Supp. IV Part 1:** 143, 144–145

"Death on All Fronts" (Ginsberg), **Supp. II Part 1:** 326

"Deaths" (Dunn), **Supp. XI:** 147

"Death Sauntering About" (Hecht), **Supp. X:** 72

Deaths for the Ladies (and Other Disasters) (Mailer), **Retro. Supp. II:** 203

Death's Jest-Book (Beddoes), **Retro. Supp. I:** 285

Death Song (McGrath), **Supp. X:** 127

"Death the Carnival Barker" (Hecht), **Supp. X:** 72

"Death the Film Director" (Hecht), **Supp. X:** 72

"Death the Judge" (Hecht), **Supp. X:** 72

"Death the Mexican Revolutionary" (Hecht), **Supp. X:** 72

"Death the Oxford Don" (Hecht), **Supp. X:** 72

"Death the Painter" (Hecht), **Supp. X:** 72

Death the Proud Brother (Wolfe), **IV:** 456

"Death to Van Gogh's Ear!" (Ginsberg), **Supp. II Part 1:** 320, 322, 323

"Death Warmed Over!" (Bradbury), **Supp. IV Part 1:** 104–105, 112

Débâcle, La (Zola), **III:** 316

"Debate with the Rabbi" (Nemerov), **III:** 272

Debeljak, Aleš, **Supp. VIII:** 272

De Bellis, Jack, **Supp. I Part 1:** 366, 368, 372

De Bosis, Lauro, **IV:** 372

"Debriefing" (Sontag), **Supp. III Part 2:** 468–470

Debs, Eugene, **I:** 483, 493; **III:** 580, 581; **Supp. I Part 2:** 524; **Supp. IX:** 1, 15

Debt to Pleasure, The (Lanchester), **Retro. Supp. I:** 278

Debussy, Claude, **Retro. Supp. II:** 266; **Supp. XIII:** 44

Decameron (Boccaccio), **III:** 283, 411; **Supp. IX:** 215

"Deceased" (Hughes), **Retro. Supp. I:** 208

"December" (Oliver), **Supp. VII:** 245

"December 1, 1994" (Stern), **Supp. IX:** 299

"December Eclogue" (Winters), **Supp. II Part 2:** 794

Deception (Roth), **Retro. Supp. II:** 291; **Supp. III Part 2:** 426–427

"Deceptions" (Dobyns), **Supp. XIII:** 77

De Chiara, Ann. *See* Malamud, Mrs. Bernard (Ann de Chiara)

De Chirico, Giorgio, **Supp. XIII:** 317

"Decided Loss, A" (Poe), **II:** 411

"Decisions to Disappear" (Dunn), **Supp. XI:** 144

"Decisive Moment, The" (Auster), **Supp. XIV:** 292

Decker, James A., **Supp. III Part 2:** 621

Declaration of Gentlemen and Merchants and Inhabitants of Boston, and the Country Adjacent, A (Mather), **Supp. II Part 2:** 450

"Declaration of Paris, The" (Adams), **I:** 4

Declaration of the Rights of Man and the Citizen, **Supp. I Part 2:** 513, 519

Declaration of Universal Peace and Liberty (Paine), **Supp. I Part 2:** 512

Decline and Fall (Waugh), **Supp. I Part 2:** 607

Decline and Fall of the English System of Finance, The (Paine), **Supp. I Part 2:** 518

Decline and Fall of the Roman Empire, The (Gibbons), **Supp. III Part 2:** 629

"Decline of Book Reviewing, The" (Hardwick), **Supp. III Part 1:** 201–202

Decline of the West, The (Spengler), **I:** 270; **IV:** 125

"Decoration Day" (Jewett), **II:** 412;

Retro. Supp. II: 138

Decoration of Houses, The (Wharton and Codman), **IV:** 308; **Retro. Supp. I:** 362, 363–364, 366

"Decoy" (Ashbery), **Supp. III Part 1:** 13–14

"De Daumier-Smith's Blue Period" (Salinger), **III:** 560–561

"Dedication and Household Map" (Erdrich), **Supp. IV Part 1:** 272

"Dedication Day" (Agee), **I:** 34

"Dedication for a Book" (Hay), **Supp. XIV:** 125

"Dedication for a Book of Criticism" (Winters), **Supp. II Part 2:** 801

"Dedication in Postscript, A" (Winters), **Supp. II Part 2:** 801

Dedications and Other Darkhorses (Komunyakaa), **Supp. XIII:** 112, **113–114**

"Dedication to Hunger" (Glück), **Supp. V:** 83

"Dedication to My Wife, A" (Eliot), **I:** 583

Dee, Ruby, **Supp. IV Part 1:** 362

"Deep Breath at Dawn, A" (Hecht), **Supp. X:** 58

Deeper into Movies: The Essential Kael Collection from '69 to '72 (Kael), **Supp. IX:** 253

"Deeper Wisdom, The" (Hay), **Supp. XIV:** 129

Deep Green Sea (R. O. Butler), **Supp. XII:** 62, **74**

Deephaven (Jewett), **II:** 398–399, 400, 401, 410, 411; **Retro. Supp. II:** 133, 134, 135, 136, 137, 138, 140, 141, 143, 144

"Deep Sight and Rescue Missions" (Bambara), **Supp. XI:** 18–19

Deep Sightings and Rescue Missions: Fiction, Essays, and Conversations (Bambara), **Supp. XI:** 1, 3, **14–20**

Deep Sleep, The (Morris), **III:** 224–225

Deep South (Caldwell), **I:** 305, 309, 310

"Deep Water" (Marquand), **III:** 56

"Deep Woods" (Nemerov), **III:** 272–273, 275

"Deer at Providencia, The" (Dillard), **Supp. VI:** 28, 32

"Deer Dancer" (Harjo), **Supp. XII:** 224–225

"Deer Ghost" (Harjo), **Supp. XII:** 225

Deer Park, The (Mailer), **I:** 292; **III:** 27, 31–33, 35–36, 37, 39, 40, 42, 43, 44; **Retro. Supp. II:** **200–202**, 205, 207, 211

Deer Park, The: A Play (Mailer),

Retro. Supp. II: 205
Deerslayer, The (Cooper), I: 341, 349, 350, 355; Supp. I Part 1: 251
"Defence of Poesy, The" (Sidney), Supp. V: 250
"Defence of Poetry" (Longfellow), II: 493–494
"Defender of the Faith" (Roth), Retro. Supp. II: 281; Supp. III Part 2: 404, 407, 420
"Defenestration in Prague" (Matthews), Supp. IX: 168
Defenestration of Prague (Howe), Supp. IV Part 2: 419, 426, 429–430
Defense, The (Nabokov), III: 251–252; Retro. Supp. I: 266, 268, 270–272
"Defense of Poetry" (Francis), Supp. IX: 83–84
Defiant Ones, The (film), Supp. I Part 1: 67
"Defining the Age" (Davis), Supp. IV Part 1: 64
"Definition" (Ammons), Supp. VII: 28
Defoe, Daniel, I: 204; II: 104, 105, 159, 304–305; III: 113, 423; IV: 180; Supp. I Part 2: 523; Supp. V: 127
De Forest, John William, II: 275, 280, 288, 289; IV: 350
Degas, Brian, Supp. XI: 307
Degler, Carl, Supp. I Part 2: 496
"Degrees of Fidelity" (Dunn), Supp. XI: 148, 156
De Haven, Tom, Supp. XI: 39; Supp. XII: 338–339
Deitch, Joseph, Supp. VIII: 125
"Dejection" (Coleridge), II: 97
DeJong, Constance, Supp. XII: 4
DeJong, David Cornel, I: 35
de Kooning, Willem, Supp. XII: 198
Delacroix, Henri, I: 227
De La Mare, Walter, III: 429; Supp. II Part 1: 4
Delamotte, Eugenia C., Supp. XI: 279
De Lancey, James, I: 338
De Lancey, Mrs. James (Anne Heathcote), I: 338
De Lancey, Susan A. *See* Cooper, Mrs. James Fenimore
De Lancey, William Heathcote, I: 338, 353
Delano, Amasa, III: 90
Delattre, Roland A., I: 558
De Laurentiis, Dino, Supp. XI: 170, 307
De la Valdéne, Guy, Supp. VIII: 40, 42
De l'éducation d'un homme sauvage (Itard), Supp. I Part 2: 564

"Delft" (Goldbarth), Supp. XII: 189
Delft: An Essay-Poem (Goldbarth), Supp. XII: 187
Delicate Balance, A (Albee), I: 86–89, 91, 93, 94
Delicate Balance, The (Hay), Supp. XIV: 121, 122, 124, 129, 133–134
"Delicate Balance, The" (Hay), Supp. XIV: 122
"Delicate Prey, The" (Bowles), Supp. IV Part 1: 86
Delicate Prey and Other Stories, The (Bowles), Supp. IV Part 1: 86–87
Délie (Scève), Supp. III Part 1: 11
DeLillo, Don, Retro. Supp. I: 278; Retro. Supp. II: 279; Supp. VI: 1–18; Supp. IX: 212; Supp. XI: 68; Supp. XII: 21, 152
DeLisle, Anne, Supp. VIII: 175
Deliverance (Dickey), Supp. IV Part 1: 176, 186–188, 190; Supp. X: 30
Deliverance, The (Glasgow), II: 175, 176, 177–178, 181
"Delivering" (Dubus), Supp. VII: 87
Dell, Floyd, I: 103, 105; Supp. I Part 2: 379
"Della Primavera Trasportata al Morale" (W. C. Williams), Retro. Supp. I: 419, 422
DeLoria, Philip J., Supp. XIV: 306
Deloria, Vine, Jr., Supp. IV Part 1: 323; Supp. IV Part 2: 504
"Delta Autumn" (Faulkner), II: 71
"Delta Factor, The" (Percy), Supp. III Part 1: 386
Delta of Venus: Erotica (Nin), Supp. X: 192, 195
Delta Wedding (Welty), IV: 261, 268–271, 273, 281; Retro. Supp. I: 349–350, 351
Delusions (Berryman), I: 170
de Man, Paul, Retro. Supp. I: 67
DeMarinis, Rick, Supp. XIV: 22
DeMars, James, Supp. IV Part 2: 552
Dembo, L. S., I: 386, 391, 396, 397, 398, 402; III: 478; Supp. I Part 1: 272; Supp. XIV: 277, 282, 288, 290
Demetrakopoulous, Stephanie A., Supp. IV Part 1: 12
DeMille, Cecil B., Supp. IV Part 2: 520
Demme, Jonathan, Supp. V: 14
Democracy (Adams), I: 9–10, 20; Supp. IV Part 1: 208
Democracy (Didion), Supp. IV Part 1: 198, 208–210
"Democracy" (Lowell), Supp. I Part 2: 419
Democracy and Education (Dewey), I: 232

Democracy and Other Addresses (Lowell), Supp. I Part 2: 407
Democracy and Social Ethics (Addams), Supp. I Part 1: 8–11
Democracy in America (Tocqueville), Retro. Supp. I: 235; Supp. XIV: 306
Democratic Vistas (Whitman), IV: 333, 336, 348–349, 351, 469; Retro. Supp. I: 408; Supp. I Part 2: 456
Democritus, I: 480–481; II: 157; III: 606; Retro. Supp. I: 247
"Demon Lover, The" (Rich), Supp. I Part 2: 556
"Demonstrators, The" (Welty), IV: 280; Retro. Supp. I: 355
DeMott, Benjamin, Supp. IV Part 1: 35; Supp. V: 123; Supp. XIII: 95; Supp. XIV:106
DeMott, Robert, Supp. VIII: 40, 41
Demuth, Charles, IV: 404; Retro. Supp. I: 412, 430
"Demystified Zone" (Paley), Supp. VI: 227
Denmark Vesey (opera) (Bowles), Supp. IV Part 1: 83
Denney, Joseph Villiers, Supp. I Part 2: 605
Denney, Reuel, Supp. XII: 121
Dennie, Joseph, II: 298; Supp. I Part 1: 125
Denniston, Dorothy Hamer, Supp. XI: 276, 277
"Den of Lions" (Plath), Retro. Supp. II: 242
"Dental Assistant, The" (Simpson), Supp. IX: 280
Den Uyl, Douglas, Supp. IV Part 2: 528, 530
"Deodand, The" (Hecht), Supp. X: 65
"Departing" (Cameron), Supp. XII: 81
"Departure" (Glück), Supp. V: 89
"Departure" (Plath), Supp. I Part 2: 537
"Departure, The" (Freneau), Supp. II Part 1: 264
Departures (Justice), Supp. VII: 124–127
Departures and Arrivals (Shields), Supp. VII: 320, 322
"Depressed by a Book of Bad Poetry, I Walk Toward an Unused Pasture and Invite the Insects to Join Me" (Wright), Supp. III Part 2: 600
"Depressed Person, The" (Wallace), Supp. X: 309
"Depression Days" (Mora), Supp. XIII: 224–225
De Puy, John, Supp. XIII: 12
D'Erasmo, Stacey, Supp. IX: 121

De Reilhe, Catherine, **Supp. I Part 1:** 202

De Rerum Natura (Lucretius), **II:** 162

"De Rerum Virtute" (Jeffers), **Supp. II Part 2:** 424

De Rioja, Francisco, **Supp. I Part 1:** 166

"Derivative Sport in Tornado Alley" (Wallace), **Supp. X:** 314

Derleth, August, **Supp. I Part 2:** 465, 472

Deronda, Daniel, **II:** 179

Derrida, Jacques, **Supp. IV Part 1:** 45

Deruddere, Dominique, **Supp. XI:** 173

Der Wilde Jäger (Bürger), **II:** 306

Derzhavin, Gavrila Romanovich, **Supp. VIII:** 27

De Santis, Christopher, **Retro. Supp. I:** 194

Descartes, René, **I:** 255; **III:** 618–619; **IV:** 133

Descendents, The (Glasgow), **II:** 173, 174–175, 176

Descending Figure (Glück), **Supp. V:** 83–84

"Descending Theology: Christ Human" (Karr), **Supp. XI:** 251

"Descending Theology: The Garden" (Karr), **Supp. XI:** 251

"Descent, The" (W. C. Williams), **Retro. Supp. I:** 428, 429

"Descent from the Cross" (Eliot), **Retro. Supp. I:** 57, 58

"Descent in the Maelström, A" (Poe), **Retro. Supp. II:** 274

"Descent into Proselito" (Knowles), **Supp. XII:** 237

"Descent into the Maelström, A" (Poe), **III:** 411, 414, 416, 424

Descent of Man (Boyle), **Supp. VIII:** 1, 12–13

"Descent of Man" (Boyle), **Supp. VIII:** 14

Descent of Man, The (Darwin), **Supp. XIV:** 192

Descent of Man, The (Wharton), **IV:** 311; **Retro. Supp. I:** 367

Descent of Man and Other Stories, The (Wharton), **Retro. Supp. I:** 367

Descent of Winter, The (W. C. Williams), **Retro. Supp. I:** 419, 428

De Schloezer, Doris, **III:** 474

"Description" (Doty), **Supp. XI:** 126

"Description of the great Bones dug up at Clavarack on the Banks of Hudsons River A.D. 1705, The" (Taylor), **IV:** 163, 164

"Description without Place" (Stevens), **Retro. Supp. I:** 422

"Desert" (Hughes), **Retro. Supp. I:** 207

"Deserted Cabin" (Haines), **Supp. XII:** 203

Deserted Village, The (Goldsmith), **II:** 304

Desert Is My Mother, The/El desierto es mi madre (Mora), **Supp. XIII:** 214, 221

Desert Music, The (W. C. Williams), **IV:** 422; **Retro. Supp. I:** 428, 429

"Desert Music, The" (W. C. Williams), **Retro. Supp. I:** 428, 429

"Desert Places" (Frost), **II:** 159; **Retro. Supp. I:** 121, 123, 129, 138, 299; **Supp. XIV:** 229

Desert Rose, The (McMurtry), **Supp. V:** 225, 231

Desert Solitaire (Abbey), **Supp. X:** 30; **Supp. XIII: 7–8,** 12; **Supp. XIV:** 177, 179

"Design" (Frost), **II:** 158, 163; **Retro. Supp. I:** 121, 126, 138, 139; **Supp. IX:** 81

"Designated National Park, A" (Ortiz), **Supp. IV Part 2:** 509

Des Imagistes (Pound), **II:** 513; **Supp. I Part 1:** 257, 261, 262

"Desire" (Beattie), **Supp. V:** 29

"Désirée's Baby" (Chopin), **Retro. Supp. II:** 64, 65; **Supp. I Part 1:** 213–215

Desire under the Elms (O'Neill), **III:** 387, 390

"Desolate Field, The" (W. C. Williams), **Retro. Supp. I:** 418

"Desolation, A" (Ginsberg), **Supp. II Part 1:** 313

Desolation Angels (Kerouac), **Supp. III Part 1:** 218, 225, 230

"Desolation Is a Delicate Thing" (Wylie), **Supp. I Part 2:** 729

Despair (Nabokov), **Retro. Supp. I:** 270, 274

"Despisals" (Rukeyser), **Supp. VI:** 282

Des Pres, Terrence, **Supp. X:** 113, 120, 124

"Destiny and the Lieutenant" (McCoy), **Supp. XIII:** 171

"Destruction of Kreshev, The" (Singer), **IV:** 13; **Retro. Supp. II:** 307

Destruction of the European Jews, The (Hilberg), **Supp. V:** 267

"Destruction of the Goetheanum, The" (Salter), **Supp. IX:** 257

"Destruction of the Long Branch, The" (Pinsky), **Supp. VI:** 239, 240, 243–244, 245, 247, 250

Destructive Element, The (Spender), **Retro. Supp. I:** 216

"Detail & Parody for the poem 'Paterson'" (W. C. Williams), **Retro. Supp. I:** 424

Detmold, John, **Supp. I Part 2:** 670

Deuce, The (R. O. Butler), **Supp. XII:** 62, **69–70,** 72

Deus Lo Volt! (Connell), **Supp. XIV:** 80, 81, 95

Deuteronomy (biblical book), **II:** 166

Deutsch, Andre, **Supp. XI:** 297, 301

Deutsch, Babette, **Supp. I Part 1:** 328, 341

Deutsch, Michel, **Supp. IV Part 1:** 104

"Devaluation Blues: Ruminations on Black Families in Crisis" (Coleman), **Supp. XI:** 87

Devane, William, **Supp. XI:** 234

"Development of the Literary West" (Chopin), **Retro. Supp. II:** 72

"Development of the Modern English Novel, The" (Lanier), **Supp. I Part 1:** 370–371

DeVeriante (Herbert of Cherbury), **II:** 108

"Devil and Daniel Webster, The" (Benét), **III:** 22; **Supp. XI:** 45–46, 47, 50–51, 52

Devil and Daniel Webster and Other Writings, The (Benét), **Supp. XI:** 48

"Devil and Tom Walker, The" (Irving), **II:** 309–310

Devil At Large, The: Erica Jong on Henry Miller (Jong), **Supp. V:** 115, 131

Devil Finds Work, The (Baldwin), **Retro. Supp. II:** 14; **Supp. I Part 1:** 48, 52, 66–67

Devil in a Blue Dress (Mosley), **Supp. XIII:** 237, 239

"Devil in Manuscript, The" (Hawthorne), **II:** 226; **Retro. Supp. I:** 150–151

Devil in Paradise, A (H. Miller), **III:** 190

"Devil in the Belfry, The" (Poe), **III:** 425; **Retro. Supp. II:** 273

"Devil Is a Busy Man, The" (Wallace), **Supp. X:** 309

Devil's Dictionary, The (Bierce), **I:** 196, 197, 205, 208, 209, 210

Devil's Stocking, The (Algren), **Supp. IX:** 5, 16

Devil's Tour, The (Karr), **Supp. XI:** 240, **242–244**

Devil Tree, The (Kosinski), **Supp. VII:** 215, 222, 223

"Devising" (Ammons), **Supp. VII:** 28

De Voto, Bernard, **I:** 247, 248; **II:** 446; **Supp. IV Part 2:** 599, 601

"Devout Meditation in Memory of

Adolph Eichmann, A" (Merton), **Supp. VIII:** 198, 203

De Vries, Peter, **Supp. I Part 2:** 604

Dewberry, Elizabeth, **Supp. XII:** 62, 72

Dewey, John, **I:** 214, 224, 228, 232, 233, 266, 267; **II:** 20, 27, 34, 229, 361; **III:** 112, 294–295, 296, 303, 309–310, 599, 605; **IV:** 27, 429; **Supp. I Part 1:** 3, 5, 7, 10, 11, 12, 24; **Supp. I Part 2:** 493, 641, 647, 677; **Supp. V:** 290; **Supp. IX:** 179; **Supp. XIV:** 3

Dewey, Joseph, **Supp. IX:** 210

Dewey, Thomas, **IV:** 161

Dexter, Peter, **Supp. XIV:** 221

De Young, Charles, **I:** 194

Dhairyam, Sagari, **Supp. IV Part 1:** 329, 330

Dharma Bums, The (Kerouac), **Supp. III Part 1:** 230, 231; **Supp. VIII:** 289, 305

D'Houdetot, Madame, **Supp. I Part 1:** 250

"Diabetes" (Dickey), **Supp. IV Part 1:** 182

Diaghilev, Sergei, **Supp. I Part 1:** 257

Dial (publication), **I:** 58, 109, 115, 116, 215, 231, 233, 245, 261, 384, 429; **II:** 8, 430; **III:** 194, 470, 471, 485; **IV:** 122, 171, 427; **Retro. Supp. I:** 58; **Retro. Supp. II:** 78; **Supp. I Part 2:** 642, 643, 647; **Supp. II Part 1:** 168, 279, 291; **Supp. II Part 2:** 474; **Supp. III Part 2:** 611

"Dialectics of Love, The" (McGrath), **Supp. X:** 116

"Dialogue" (Rich), **Supp. I Part 2:** 560

Dialogue, A (Baldwin and Giovanni), **Supp. I Part 1:** 66

"Dialogue: William Harvey; Joan of Arc" (Goldbarth), **Supp. XII:** 178

"Dialogue Between Franklin and the Gout" (Franklin), **II:** 121

"Dialogue Between General Wolfe and General Gage in a Wood near Boston, A" (Paine), **Supp. I Part 2:** 504

"Dialogue between Old England and New" (Bradstreet), **Supp. I Part 1:** 105–106, 110–111, 116

"Dialogue between the Writer and a Maypole Dresser, A" (Taylor), **IV:** 155

Dialogues (Bush, ed.), **III:** 4

Dialogues in Limbo (Santayana), **III:** 606

"Diamond as Big as the Ritz, The" (Fitzgerald), **II:** 88–89

Diamond Cutters and Other Poems, The (Rich), **Supp. I Part 2:** 551, 552, 553

"Diamond Guitar, A" (Capote), **Supp. III Part 1:** 124

"Diana and Persis" (Alcott), **Supp. I Part 1:** 32, 41

Diaries of Charlotte Perkins Gilman (Knight, ed.), **Supp. XI:** 201

Diary of Anaïs Nin, The (1931–1974), **Supp. X:** 181, 185–189, 191, 192, 193, 195

Diary of a Rapist, The: A Novel (Connell), **Supp. XIV:** 80, 82, 94

Diary of a Yuppie (Auchincloss), **Supp. IV Part 1:** 31, 32–33

Diary of "Helena Morley," The (Bishop, trans.), **Retro. Supp. II:** 45, 51; **Supp. I Part 1:** 92

Díaz del Castillo, Bernál, **III:** 13, 14

Dickens, Charles, **I:** 152, 198, 505; **II:** 98, 179, 186, 192, 271, 273–274, 288, 290, 297, 301, 307, 316, 322, 559, 561, 563, 577, 582; **III:** 146, 247, 325, 368, 411, 421, 426, 572, 577, 613–614, 616; **IV:** 21, 192, 194, 211, 429; **Retro. Supp. I:** 33, 91, 218; **Retro. Supp. II:** 204; **Supp. I Part 1:** 13, 34, 35, 36, 41, 49; **Supp. I Part 2:** 409, 523, 579, 590, 622, 675; **Supp. IV Part 1:** 293, 300, 341; **Supp. IV Part 2:** 464; **Supp. VIII:** 180; **Supp. IX:** 246; **Supp. XI:** 277; **Supp. XII:** 335, 337; **Supp. XIII:** 233

Dickey, James, **I:** 29, 535; **III:** 268; **Retro. Supp. II:** 233; **Supp. III Part 1:** 354; **Supp. III Part 2:** 541, 597; **Supp. IV Part 1: 175–194;** **Supp. V:** 333; **Supp. X:** 30; **Supp. XI:** 312, 317

Dick Gibson Show, The (Elkin), **Supp. VI:** 42, **48–49**

Dickie, Margaret, **Retro. Supp. II:** 53, 84

Dickinson, Donald, **Retro. Supp. I:** 206, 212

Dickinson, Edward, **I:** 451–452, 453

Dickinson, Emily, **I:** 384, 419, 433, **451–473; II:** 272, 276, 277, 530; **III:** 19, 194, 196, 214, 493, 505, 508, 556, 572, 576; **IV:** 134, 135, 331, 444; **Retro. Supp. I: 25–50; Retro. Supp. II:** 39, 40, 43, 45, 50, 76, 134, 155, 170; **Supp. I Part 1:** 29, 79, 188, 372; **Supp. I Part 2:** 375, 546, 609, 682, 691; **Supp. II Part 1:** 4; **Supp. III Part 1:** 63; **Supp. III Part 2:** 600, 622; **Supp. IV Part 1:** 31, 257; **Supp. IV Part 2:** 434, 637, 641, 643; **Supp. V:** 79, 140, 332, 335; **Supp. VIII:** 95, 104, 106, 108, 198, 205, 272; **Supp. IX:** 37, 38, 53, 87, 90; **Supp. XII:** 226; **Supp. XIII:** 153, 339; **Supp. XIV:** 45, 127–128, 133, 261, 284

Dickinson, Gilbert, **I:** 469

Dickinson, Goldsworthy Lowes, **Supp. XIV:** 336

Dickinson, Lavinia Norcross, **I:** 451, 453, 462, 470

Dickinson, Mrs. Edward, **I:** 451, 453

Dickinson, Mrs. William A. (Susan Gilbert), **I:** 452, 453, 456, 469, 470

Dickinson, William Austin, **I:** 451, 453, 469

Dickinson and the Strategies of Reticence (Dobson), **Retro. Supp. I:** 29, 42

Dickson, Helen. *See* Blackmur, Helen Dickson

Dickstein, Morris, **Supp. XIII:** 106

"Dick Whittington and His Cat," **Supp. I Part 2:** 656

"DICTATORSHIP OF THE PROLE-TARIAT, THE" (Baraka), **Supp. II Part 1:** 54

Dictionary of Literary Biography (Kibler, ed.), **Supp. IX:** 94, 109; **Supp. XI:** 297

Dictionary of Literary Biography (Knight), **Supp. XIV:** 144

Dictionary of Modern English Usage, A (Fowler), **Supp. I Part 2:** 660

"Dictum: For a Masque of Deluge" (Merwin), **Supp. III Part 1:** 342–343

"Didactic Poem" (Levertov), **Supp. III Part 1:** 280

Diderot, Denis, **II:** 535; **IV:** 440

Didion, Joan, **Retro. Supp. I:** 116; **Retro. Supp. II:** 209; **Supp. I Part 1:** 196, 197; **Supp. III Part 1:** 302; **Supp. IV Part 1: 195–216; Supp. XI:** 221; **Supp. XII:** 307

Dido, **I:** 81

"Did You Ever Dream Lucky?" (Ellison), **Supp. II Part 1:** 246

"Die-Hard, The" (Benét), **Supp. XI:** 54–55, 56

Diehl, Digby, **Supp. IV Part 1:** 204

Dien Cai Dau (Komunyakaa), **Supp. XIII:** 121, **122–124,** 125, 131, 132

"Dies Irae" (Lowell), **II:** 553

Die Zeit Ohne Beispiel, (Goebbels), **III:** 560

Different Drummer, A (Larkin; film), **Supp. XI:** 20

Different Fleshes (Goldbarth), **Supp. XII:** 181–182, 188

Different Hours (Dunn), **Supp. XI:**

139, 142, 143, 155

Different Seasons (King), **Supp. V:** 148, 152

Different Ways to Pray (Nye), **Supp. XIII:** 274, 275, 277, 285, 287

"Different Ways to Pray" (Nye), **Supp. XIII:** 275

"Difficulties of a Statesman" (Eliot), **I:** 580

"Difficulties of Modernism and the Modernism of Difficulty" (Poirier), **Supp. II Part 1:** 136

Diff'rent (O'Neill), **III:** 389

DiGaetani, John L., **Supp. XIII:** 200

"Digging in the Garden of Age I Uncover a Live Root" (Swenson), **Supp. IV Part 2:** 649

Diggins, John P., **Supp. I Part 2:** 650

Digregorio, Charles, **Supp. XI:** 326

"Dilemma of Determinism, The" (James), **II:** 347–348, 352

"Dilettante, The" (Wharton), **IV:** 311, 313

"Dilettante, The: A Modern Type" (Dunbar), **Supp. II Part 1:** 199

Dillard, Annie, **Supp. VI:** 19–39; **Supp. VIII:** 272; **Supp. X:** 31; **Supp. XIII:** 154

Dillard, R. H. W., **Supp. XII:** 16

Dillman, Bradford, **III:** 403; **Supp. XII:** 241

Dillon, Brian, **Supp. X:** 209

Dillon, George, **III:** 141; **Supp. III Part 2:** 621

Dillon, Millicent, **Supp. IV Part 1:** 95

Dilsaver, Paul, **Supp. XIII:** 112

Dilthey, Wilhelm, **I:** 58

Dime-Store Alchemy: The Art of Joseph Cornell, **Supp. VIII:** 272

"Diminuendo" (Dunn), **Supp. XI:** 152–153

"Dimout in Harlem" (Hughes), **Supp. I Part 1:** 333

Dinesen, Isak, **IV:** 279; **Supp. VIII:** 171

Dining Room, The (Gurney), **Supp. V:** 105–106

"Dinner at ———, A" (O. Henry), **Supp. II Part 1:** 402

"Dinner at Sir Nigel's" (Bowles), **Supp. IV Part 1:** 94

Dinner at the Homesick Restaurant (Tyler), **Supp. IV Part 2:** 657, 667–668

"Dinner at Uncle Borris's" (Simic), **Supp. VIII:** 272

Dinner Bridge (Lardner), **II:** 435

Dinosaur Tales (Bradbury), **Supp. IV Part 1:** 103

"Diogenes Invents a Game" (Karr),

Supp. XI: 240–241

"Diogenes Tries to Forget" (Karr), **Supp. XI:** 241

Dionysis in Doubt (Robinson), **III:** 510

Diop, Birago, **Supp. IV Part 1:** 16

Diop, David, **Supp. IV Part 1:** 16

Di Prima, Diane, **Supp. III Part 1:** 30; **Supp. XIV:** 125, 144, 148, 150

Direction of Poetry, The: Rhymed and Metered Verse Written in the English Language since 1975 (Richman), **Supp. XI:** 249

"Directive" (Bishop), **Retro. Supp. II:** 42

"Directive" (Frost), **III:** 287; **Retro. Supp. I:** 140; **Supp. VIII:** 32, 33

"Dire Cure" (Matthews), **Supp. IX:** 168

"Dirge" (Dunbar), **Supp. II Part 1:** 199

"Dirge without Music" (Millay), **III:** 126

"Dirt" (Salter), **Supp. IX:** 257, 260, 261

"Dirt and Desire: Essay on the Phenomenology of Female Pollution in Antiquity" (Carson), **Supp. XII: 111**

"Dirty Memories" (Olds), **Supp. X:** 211

Dirty Story (Shanley), **Supp. XIV:** 316, 331

"Dirty Word, The" (Shapiro), **Supp. II Part 2:** 710

Disappearance of the Jews, The (Mamet), **Supp. XIV:** 249–250, 250–251, 252, 254

Disappearances (Auster), **Supp. XII:** 23

"Disappearances" (Hogan), **Supp. IV Part 1:** 401

Disappearing Acts (McMillan), **Supp. XIII:** 182, 183, **188–189,** 192

"Disappointment, The" (Creeley), **Supp. IV Part 1:** 143

"Disappointment and Desire" (Bly), **Supp. IV Part 1:** 71

"Discards" (Baker), **Supp. XIII:** 53, 55–56

Discerning the Signs of the Times (Niebuhr), **III:** 300–301, 307–308

"Disciple of Bacon, The" (Epstein), **Supp. XII:** 163–164

"Discordants" (Aiken), **I:** 65

Discourse on Method (Descartes), **I:** 255

"Discovering Theme and Structure in the Novel" (Schuster), **Supp. VIII:** 126

"Discovery" (Freneau), **Supp. II Part 1:** 258

"Discovery of the Madeiras, The" (Frost), **Retro. Supp. I:** 139

"Discovery of What It Means to Be an American, The" (Baldwin), **Supp. I Part 1:** 54–55

Discovery! The Search for Arabian Oil (Stegner), **Supp. IV Part 2:** 599

"Discrete Series" (Zukofsky), **Supp. III Part 2:** 616

"Discretions of Alcibiades" (Pinsky), **Supp. VI:** 241

"Disease, The" (Rukeyser), **Supp. VI:** 279

Disenchanted, The (Schulberg), **II:** 98; **Retro. Supp. I:** 113

Disenchantments: An Anthology of Modern Fairy Tale Poetry (Mieder), **Supp. XIV:** 126

"Dish of Green Pears, A" (Ríos), **Supp. IV Part 2:** 552

Dismantling the Silence (Simic), **Supp. VIII: 273–274,** 275, 276

Disney, Walt, **III:** 275, 426

"Disney of My Mind" (Chabon), **Supp. XI:** 63

Dispatches (Herr), **Supp. XI:** 245

"Displaced Person, The" (O'Connor), **III:** 343–344, 350, 352, 356; **Retro. Supp. II:** 229, 232, 236

"Disposal" (Snodgrass), **Supp. VI:** 314

Dispossessed, The (Berryman), **I:** 170, 172, 173, 174, 175, 176, 178

"Disquieting Muses, The" (Plath), **Supp. I Part 2:** 538

Disraeli, Benjamin, **II:** 127

Dissent (Didion), **Supp. IV Part 1:** 208

"Dissenting Opinion on Kafka, A" (Wilson), **IV:** 437–438

Dissent in Three American Wars (Morison, Merk, and Freidel), **Supp. I Part 2:** 495

Dissertation on Liberty and Necessity, Pleasure and Pain, A (Franklin), **II:** 108

Dissertations on Government; the Affairs of the Bank: and Paper Money (Paine), **Supp. I Part 2:** 510

"Distance" (Carver), **Supp. III Part 1:** 146

"Distance" (Paley), **Supp. VI:** 222

"Distance, The" (Karr), **Supp. XI:** 241

"Distance Nowhere" (Hughes), **Retro. Supp. I:** 207

"Distant Episode, A" (Bowles), **Supp. IV Part 1:** 84–85, 86, 90

Distant Episode, A: The Selected Stories (Bowles), **Supp. IV Part 1:** 79

Distinguished Guest, The (Miller), **Supp. XII: 299–301**

Distortions (Beattie), **Supp. V:** 21, 23, 24, 25, 27

"Distrest Shepherdess, The" (Freneau), **Supp. II Part 1:** 258

District of Columbia (Dos Passos), **I:** 478, 489–490, 492

Disturber of the Peace (Manchester), **III:** 103

Disturbing the Peace (Yates), **Supp. XI:** 345, 346

"Diver, The" (Hayden), **Supp. II Part 1:** 368, 372, 373

"Divided Life of Jean Toomer, The" (Toomer), **Supp. III Part 2:** 488

Divina Commedia (Longfellow, trans.), **II:** 490, 492, 493

"Divine Collaborator" (Simic), **Supp. VIII:** 282

Divine Comedies (Merrill), **Supp. III Part 1:** 324, 329–332

Divine Comedy (Dante), **I:** 137, 265, 400, 446; **II:** 215, 335, 490, 492, 493; **III:** 13, 448, 453; **Supp. V:** 283, 331, 338, 345; **Supp. X:** 253; **Supp. XIV:** 6

"Divine Image, The" (Blake), **Supp. V:** 257

Divine Pilgrim, The (Aiken), **I:** 50, 55

Divine Tragedy, The (Longfellow), **II:** 490, 500, 505, 506, 507; **Retro. Supp. II:** 165, 166

Divine Weekes and Workes (Sylvester, trans.), **Supp. I Part 1:** 104

Divine Weeks (Du Bartas), **IV:** 157–158

"Diving into the Wreck: Poems 1971–1972" (Rich), **Supp. I Part 2:** 550, 559–565, 569

Diving Rock on the Hudson, A (H. Roth), **Supp. IX:** 236, **237–238**

"Divinity in Its Fraying Fact, A" (Levis), **Supp. XI:** 271

"Divinity School Address" (Emerson), **II:** 12–13

"Divisions upon a Ground" (Hecht), **Supp. X:** 58

"Divorce" (Karr), **Supp. XI:** 244

Divorced in America: Marriage in an Age of Possibility (Epstein), **Supp. XIV:** 113

Dix, Douglas Shields, **Supp. XII:** 14

Dixie City Jam (Burke), **Supp. XIV:** 32

Dixon, Ivan, **Supp. IV Part 1:** 362

Dixon, Stephen, **Supp. XII: 139–158**

Dixon, Thomas, Jr., **Supp. II Part 1:** 169, 171, 177

Djinn (Robbe-Grillet), **Supp. V:** 48

D'Lugoff, Burt, **Supp. IV Part 1:** 362, 370

Do, Lord, Remember Me (Garrett), **Supp. VII:** 98–100, 110

"Doaksology, The" (Wolfe), **IV:** 459

Dobie, J. Frank, **Supp. V:** 225; **Supp. XIII:** 227

Dobriansky, Lev, **Supp. I Part 2:** 648, 650

Dobson, Joanne, **Retro. Supp. I:** 29, 31, 42

Dobyns, Stephen, **Supp. XIII: 73–92**

"Docking at Palermo" (Hugo), **Supp. VI:** 137–138

"Dock Rats" (Moore), **III:** 213

"Dock-Witch, The" (Ozick), **Supp. V:** 262, 264

"Doc Mellhorn and the Pearly Gates" (Benét), **Supp. XI:** 55

"Doctor, The" (Dubus), **Supp. VII:** 80–81

"Doctor and the Doctor's Wife, The" (Hemingway), **II:** 248; **Retro. Supp. I:** 174, 175

Doctor Breen's Practice, a Novel (Howells), **I:** 282

Doctor Faustus (Mann), **III:** 283

"Doctor Jekyll" (Sontag), **Supp. III Part 2:** 469

"Doctor Leavis and the Moral Tradition" (Trilling), **Supp. III Part 2:** 512–513

Doctor Martino and Other Stories (Faulkner), **II:** 72; **Retro. Supp. I:** 84

"Doctor of the Heart, The" (Sexton), **Supp. II Part 2:** 692

Doctorow, E. L., **Retro. Supp. I:** 97; **Supp. III Part 2:** 590, 591; **Supp. IV Part 1: 217–240; Supp. V:** 45

Doctor Sax (Kerouac), **Supp. III Part 1:** 220–222, 224–227

Doctor Sleep (Bell), **Supp. X: 9–11**

"Doctors' Row" (Aiken), **I:** 67

Doctor's Son and Other Stories, The (O'Hara), **III:** 361

Doctor Stories, The (W. C. Williams), **Retro. Supp. I:** 424

"Doctor's Wife, The" (Ozick), **Supp. V:** 262, 265

Doctor Zhivago (Pasternak), **IV:** 434, 438, 443

"Documentary" (Simic), **Supp. VIII:** 282

Dodd, Elizabeth, **Supp. V:** 77

Dodd, Wayne, **Supp. IV Part 2:** 625

Dodson, Owen, **Supp. I Part 1:** 54

Dodsworth (Lewis), **II:** 442, 449–450, 453, 456

Doenitz, Karl, **Supp. I Part 2:** 491

Does Civilization Need Religion? (Niebuhr), **III:** 293–294

"Does 'Consciousness' Exist?" (James), **II:** 356

"Does Education Pay?" (Du Bois), **Supp. II Part 1:** 159

Dog (Shepard), **Supp. III Part 2:** 434

"Dog Act, The" (Komunyakaa), **Supp. XIII:** 114–115

"Dog and the Playlet, The" (O. Henry), **Supp. II Part 1:** 399

Dog Beneath the Skin, The (Auden), **Supp. II Part 1:** 10

"Dog Creek Mainline" (Wright), **Supp. V:** 340

Dog in the Manger, The (Vega; Merwin, trans.), **Supp. III Part 1:** 341, 347

Dogs Bark, The: Public People and Private Places (Capote), **Supp. III Part 1:** 120, 132

Dog Soldiers (Stone), **Supp. V:** 298, 299–301

Dog & the Fever, The (Quevedo), **Retro. Supp. I:** 423

"Dogwood, The" (Levertov), **Supp. III Part 1:** 276

"Dogwood Tree, The: A Boyhood" (Updike), **IV:** 218; **Retro. Supp. I:** 318, 319

Doig, Ivan, **Supp. XIV:** 227

"Doing Battle with the Wolf" (Coleman), **Supp. XI:** 87–88

Doings and Undoings (Podhoretz), **Supp. VIII: 236–237**

"Dolce Far' Niente" (Humphrey), **Supp. IX:** 106

Dolci, Carlo, **III:** 474–475

"Dollhouse, The" (Haines), **Supp. XII:** 204

Dollmaker's Ghost, The (Levis), **Supp. XI:** 259, 260, **264–268**

Doll's House, A (Ibsen), **III:** 523; **IV:** 357

Dolmetsch, Arnold, **III:** 464

Dolores Claiborne (King), **Supp. V:** 138, 141, 147, 148, 149–150, 152

"Dolph Heyliger" (Irving), **II:** 309

Dolphin, The (Lowell), **Retro. Supp. II:** 183, 186, 188, **190–191; Supp. XII:** 253–254

"Dolphins" (Francis), **Supp. IX:** 83

Dome of Many-Coloured Glass, A (Lowell), **II:** 515, 516–517

Domesday Book (Masters), **Supp. I Part 2:** 465, 466–469, 471, 473, 476

"Domestic Economy" (Gilman), **Supp. XI:** 206

"Domestic Manners" (Hardwick), **Supp. III Part 1:** 211

"Dominant White, The" (McKay), **Supp. X:** 134

Dominguez, Robert, **Supp. VIII:** 83
Dominique, Jean. *See* Closset, Marie
Donahue, Phil, **Supp. IV Part 2:** 526; **Supp. X:** 311
Doña Perfecta (Galdós), **II:** 290
"DON JUAN IN HELL" (Baraka), **Supp. II Part 1:** 33
"Donna mi Prega" (Cavalcanti), **Supp. III Part 2:** 620, 621, 622
Donn-Byrne, Brian Oswald. *See* Byrne, Donn
Donne, John, **I:** 358–359, 384, 389, 522, 586; **II:** 254; **III:** 493; **IV:** 83, 88, 135, 141, 144, 145, 151, 156, 165, 331, 333; **Retro. Supp. II:** 76; **Supp. I Part 1:** 80, 364, 367; **Supp. I Part 2:** 421, 424, 467, 725, 726; **Supp. III Part 2:** 614, 619; **Supp. VIII:** 26, 33, 164; **Supp. IX:** 44; **Supp. XII:** 45, 159; **Supp. XIII:** 94, 130; **Supp. XIV:** 122
Donne's Sermons: Selected Passages (L. P. Smith, ed.), **Supp. XIV:** 342
Donoghue, Denis, **I:** 537; **Supp. IV Part 1:** 39; **Supp. VIII:** 105, 189
Donohue, H. E. F., **Supp. IX:** 2, 3, 15, 16
Donovan, Josephine, **Retro. Supp. II:** 138, 139, 147
Don Quixote (Cervantes), **I:** 134; **II:** 291, 434; **III:** 113, 614; **Supp. I Part 2:** 422; **Supp. IX:** 94
Don Quixote: Which Was a Dream (Acker), **Supp. XII:** 5, **12–14**
Don't Ask (Levine), **Supp. V:** 178
Don't Ask Questions (Marquand), **III:** 58
Don't Bet on the Prince: Contemporary Feminist Fairy Tales in North America and England (Zipes), **Supp. XIV:** 126
"Don't Shoot the Warthog" (Corso), **Supp. XII:** 123
Don't You Want to Be Free? (Hughes), **Retro. Supp. I:** 203; **Supp. I Part 1:** 339
"Doodler, The" (Merrill), **Supp. III Part 1:** 321
Doolan, Moira, **Retro. Supp. II:** 247
Doolittle, Hilda (H. D.), **II:** 517, 520–521; **III:** 194, 195–196, 457, 465; **IV:** 404, 406; **Retro. Supp. I:** 288, 412, 413, 414, 415, 417; **Supp. I Part 1:** 253–275; **Supp. I Part 2:** 707; **Supp. III Part 1:** 48; **Supp. III Part 2:** 610; **Supp. IV Part 1:** 257; **Supp. V:** 79
Doolittle, Thomas, **IV:** 150
"Doomed by Our Blood to Care" (Orfalea), **Supp. XIII:** 278

"Doomsday" (Plath), **Retro. Supp. II:** 242
Doomsters, The (Macdonald), **Supp. IV Part 2:** 462, 463, 472, 473
"Door, The" (Creeley), **Supp. IV Part 1:** 145, 146, 156–157
"Door, The" (White), **Supp. I Part 2:** 651, 675–676
"Door in the Dark, The" (Frost), **II:** 156
Door in the Hive, A (Levertov), **Supp. III Part 1:** 283, 284
"Door of the Trap, The" (Anderson), **I:** 112
"Doors, Doors, Doors" (Sexton), **Supp. II Part 2:** 681
Doors, The, **Supp. X:** 186
Doreski, William, **Retro. Supp. II:** 185
Dorfman, Ariel, **Supp. IX:** 131, 138
Dorfman, Joseph, **Supp. I Part 2:** 631, 647, 650
Dorman, Jen, **Supp. XI:** 240
Dorn, Edward, **Supp. IV Part 1:** 154
Dorris, Michael, **Supp. IV Part 1:** 260, 272
Dos Passos, John, **I:** 99, 288, 374, 379, **474–496,** 517, 519; **II:** 74, 77, 89, 98; **III:** 2, 28, 29, 70, 172, 382–383; **IV:** 340, 427, 433; **Retro. Supp. I:** 105, 113, 187; **Retro. Supp. II:** 95, 196; **Supp. I Part 2:** 646; **Supp. III Part 1:** 104, 105; **Supp. V:** 277; **Supp. VIII:** 101, 105; **Supp. XIV:** 24
"Dos Passos: Poet Against the World" (Cowley), **Supp. II Part 1:** 143, 145
Dostoyevsky, Fyodor, **I:** 53, 103, 211, 468; **II:** 60, 130, 275, 320, 587; **III:** 37, 61, 155, 174, 176, 188, 189, 267, 272, 283, 286, 354, 357, 358, 359, 467, 571, 572; **IV:** 1, 7, 8, 17, 21, 50, 59, 106, 110, 128, 134, 285, 289, 476, 485, 491; **Retro. Supp. II:** 20, 204, 299; **Supp. I Part 1:** 49; **Supp. I Part 2:** 445, 466; **Supp. IV Part 2:** 519, 525; **Supp. VIII:** 175; **Supp. X:** 4–5; **Supp. XI:** 161; **Supp. XII:** 322
Doty, M. R. *See* Dawson, Ruth; Doty, Mark
Doty, Mark, **Supp. IX:** 42, 300; **Supp. XI:** **119–138**
Double, The (Dostoyevsky), **Supp. IX:** 105
"Double, The" (Levis), **Supp. XI:** 260, **261–263**
Double, The (Rank), **Supp. IX:** 105
Double Agent, The (Blackmur), **Supp. II Part 1:** 90, 108, 146
Double Axe, The (Jeffers), **Supp. II**

Part 2: 416, 434
Doubleday, Frank, **I:** 500, 502, 515, 517; **III:** 327
Doubleday, Mrs. Frank, **I:** 500
Double Down (F. and S. Barthelme), **Supp. XI:** 27, 34, 35, 36–38
Double Dream of Spring, The (Ashbery), **Supp. III Part 1:** 11–13
Double Fold: Libraries and the Assault on Paper (Baker), **Supp. XIII:** 52, 56
Double Game (Calle), **Supp. XII:** 22
"Double Gap, The" (Auchincloss), **Supp. IV Part 1:** 33
"Double-Headed Snake of Newbury, The" (Whittier), **Supp. I Part 2:** 698
Double Honeymoon (Connell), **Supp. XIV:** 80, 87
Double Image, The (Levertov), **Supp. III Part 1:** 274, 276
"Double Image, The" (Sexton), **Supp. II Part 2:** 671, 677–678
Double Indemnity (film), **Supp. IV Part 1:** 130
"Double Limbo" (Komunyakaa), **Supp. XIII:** 132
Double Man, The (Auden), **Supp. III Part 1:** 16; **Supp. X:** 118
"Double Ode" (Rukeyser), **Supp. VI:** 282–283, 286
Double Persephone (Atwood), **Supp. XIII:** 19
Doubles in Literary Psychology (Tymms), **Supp. IX:** 105
Double Vision: American Thoughts Abroad (Knowles), **Supp. XII:** 249
"Doubt on the Great Divide" (Stafford), **Supp. XI:** 322
Dougherty, Steve, **Supp. X:** 262
Douglas, Aaron, **Supp. I Part 1:** 326
Douglas, Alfred, **Supp. X:** 151
Douglas, Ann, **Supp. XII:** 136
Douglas, Claire, **III:** 552
Douglas, George (pseudonym). *See* Brown, George Douglas
Douglas, Kirk, **Supp. XIII:** 5–6
Douglas, Lloyd, **IV:** 434
Douglas, Melvyn, **Supp. V:** 223
Douglas, Michael, **Supp. XI:** 67
Douglas, Paul, **III:** 294
Douglas, Stephen A., **III:** 577, 588–589; **Supp. I Part 2:** 456, 471
Douglas, William O., **III:** 581
Douglass, Frederick, **Supp. I Part 1:** 51, 345; **Supp. I Part 2:** 591; **Supp. II Part 1:** 157, 195, 196, 292, 378; **Supp. III Part 1: 153–174; Supp. IV Part 1:** 1, 2, 13, 15, 256; **Supp. VIII:** 202

Douglass Pilot, The (Baldwin, ed.), **Supp. I Part 1:** 49
Dove, Belle, **I:** 451
Dove, Rita, **Supp. IV Part 1: 241–258**
"Dover Beach" (Arnold), **Retro. Supp. I:** 325
Dow, Lorenzo, **IV:** 265
Dowd, Douglas, **Supp. I Part 2:** 645, 650
"Do We Understand Each Other?" (Ginsberg), **Supp. II Part 1:** 311
Dowie, William, **Supp. V:** 199
Do with Me What You Will (Oates), **Supp. II Part 2:** 506, 515–517
Dowling, Eddie, **IV:** 394
Down and Out (Shanley), **Supp. XIV:** 317
"Down at City Hall" (Didion), **Supp. IV Part 1:** 211
"Down at the Cross" (Baldwin), **Retro. Supp. II:** 1, 2, 7, 12, 13, 15; **Supp. I Part 1:** 60, 61
"Down at the Dinghy" (Salinger), **III:** 559, 563
"Down by the Station, Early in the Morning" (Ashbery), **Supp. III Part 1:** 25
Downhill Racer (film), **Supp. IX:** 253
"Down in Alabam" (Bierce), **I:** 193
Downing, Ben, **Supp. XII:** 175, 189, 190–191
Downing, Major Jack (pseudonym). *See* Smith, Seba
Down in My Heart (Stafford), **Supp. XI:** 313, 315
Down Mailer's Way (Solotaroff), **Retro. Supp. II:** 203
Down There on a Visit (Isherwood), **Supp. XIV:** 159, 161, 164, **168–169,** 170, 171
Down the River (Abbey), **Supp. XIII:** 12–13
"Down the River with Henry Thoreau" (Abbey), **Supp. XIII:** 12–13
Down These Mean Streets (P. Thomas), **Supp. XIII:** 264
Down the Starry River (Purdy), **Supp. VII:** 278
"Downward Path to Wisdom, The" (Porter), **III:** 442, 443, 446
"Down Where I Am" (Hughes), **Supp. I Part 1:** 344
Dowson, Ernest C., **I:** 384
Doyle, Arthur Conan, **Retro. Supp. I:** 270; **Supp. IV Part 1:** 128, 341; **Supp. IV Part 2:** 464, 469; **Supp. XI:** 63
Doyle, C. W., **I:** 199
"Dr. Bergen's Belief" (Schwartz), **Supp. II Part 2:** 650

"Dr. Jack-o'-Lantern" (Yates), **Supp. XI:** 340–341
Dr. Strangelove; or, How I Learned to Stop Worrying and Love the Bomb (film), **Supp. XI:** 293, **301–305**
"Draba" (Leopold), **Supp. XIV:** 186
Drabble, Margaret, **Supp. IV Part 1:** 297, 299, 305
Drabelle, Dennis, **Supp. XIII:** 13
Drach, Ivan, **Supp. III Part 1:** 268
Dracula (film), **Supp. IV Part 1:** 104
"Draft Horse, The" (Frost), **Retro. Supp. I:** 141
"Draft Lyrics for *Candide*" (Agee), **I:** 28
Draft of XVI Cantos, A (Pound), **III:** 472; **Retro. Supp. I:** 292
Draft of XXX Cantos, A (Pound), **III:** 196; **Retro. Supp. I:** 292
Drafts &Fragments (Pound), **Retro. Supp. I:** 293
Dragon Country (T. Williams), **IV:** 383
Dragon Seed (Buck), **Supp. II Part 1:** 124
Dragon's Teeth (Sinclair), **Supp. V:** 290
Drake, Benjamin, **Supp. I Part 2:** 584
Drake, Daniel, **Supp. I Part 2:** 584
Drake, Sir Francis, **Supp. I Part 2:** 497
Drake, St. Clair, **IV:** 475
Dramatic Duologues (Masters), **Supp. I Part 2:** 461
"Draught" (Cowley), **Supp. II Part 1:** 141, 142
Drayton, Michael, **IV:** 135; **Retro. Supp. II:** 76
"Dreadful Has Already Happened, The" (Strand), **Supp. IV Part 2:** 627
"Dream, A" (Ginsberg), **Supp. II Part 1:** 312
"Dream, A" (Tate), **IV:** 129
"Dream, The" (Hayden), **Supp. II Part 1:** 368, 377
Dream at the End of the World, The: Paul Bowles and the Literary Renegades in Tangier (Green), **Supp. IV Part 1:** 95
"Dream Avenue" (Simic), **Supp. VIII:** 282
"Dream Boogie" (Hughes), **Retro. Supp. I:** 208; **Supp. I Part 1:** 339–340
"Dreambook Bestiary" (Komunyakaa), **Supp. XIII:** 120
Dreamer (Johnson), **Supp. VI:** 186, **196–199**
dreamer examines his pillow, the (Shanley), **Supp. XIV:** 315, **327**
"Dreamer in a Dead Language"

(Paley), **Supp. VI:** 217
Dreaming in Cuban (García), **Supp. XI:** 178, **179–185,** 190
"Dreaming the Breasts" (Sexton), **Supp. II Part 2:** 692
"Dream Interpreted, The" (Paine), **Supp. I Part 2:** 505
Dream Keeper, The (Hughes), **Supp. I Part 1:** 328, 332, 333, 334
Dream Keeper and Other Poems, The (Hughes), **Retro. Supp. I:** 201, 202
Dreamland (Baker), **Supp. XIV:** 96
"Dream-Land" (Poe), **Retro. Supp. II:** 274
Dream Life of Balso Snell, The (West), **IV:** 286, 287, 288–290, 291, 297; **Retro. Supp. II:** 321, 322, 327, 328, **330–332**
Dream of a Common Language, The: Poems, 1974–1977 (Rich), **Supp. I Part 2:** 551, 554, 569–576
Dream of Arcadia: American Writers and Artists in Italy (Brooks), **I:** 254
Dream of Governors, A (Simpson), **Supp. IX:** 265, **269–270**
"Dream of Italy, A" (Masters), **Supp. I Part 2:** 458
"Dream of Mourning, The" (Glück), **Supp. V:** 84
"Dream of the Blacksmith's Room, A" (Bly), **Supp. IV Part 1:** 73
"Dream of the Cardboard Lover" (Haines), **Supp. XII:** 204
Dream of the Golden Mountains, The (Cowley), **Supp. II Part 1:** 139, 141, 142, 144
"Dream Pang, A" (Frost), **II:** 153
"Dreams About Clothes" (Merrill), **Supp. III Part 1:** 328–329
Dreams from Bunker Hill (Fante), **Supp. XI:** 160, 166, **172–173**
"Dreams of Adulthood" (Ashbery), **Supp. III Part 1:** 26
"Dreams of Math" (Kenyon), **Supp. VII:** 160–161
"Dreams of the Animals" (Atwood), **Supp. XIII:** 33
"Dream Variations" (Hughes), **Retro. Supp. I:** 198; **Supp. I Part 1:** 323
"Dream Vision" (Olsen), **Supp. XIII:** 295–296
Dream Work (Oliver), **Supp. VII:** 234–235, 236–238, 240
Dred: A Tale of the Great Dismal Swamp (Stowe), **Supp. I Part 2:** 592
Dreiser, Theodore, **I:** 59, 97, 109, 116, 355, 374, 375, 475, 482, **497–520;** **II:** 26, 27, 29, 34, 38, 44, 74, 89, 93, 180, 276, 283, 428, 444, 451,

456–457, 467–468; **III:** 40, 103, 106, 251, 314, 319, 327, 335, 453, 576, 582; **IV:** 29, 35, 40, 135, 208, 237, 475, 482, 484; **Retro. Supp. I:** 325, 376; **Retro. Supp. II: 93–110,** 114, 322; **Supp. I Part 1:** 320; **Supp. I Part 2:** 461, 468; **Supp. III Part 2:** 412; **Supp. IV Part 1:** 31, 236, 350; **Supp. IV Part 2:** 689; **Supp. V:** 113, 120; **Supp. VIII:** 98, 101, 102; **Supp. IX:** 1, 14, 15, 308; **Supp. XI:** 207; **Supp. XIV:** 111

"Drenched in Light" (Hurston), **Supp. VI:** 150–151

Dresser, Paul, **Retro. Supp. II:** 94, 103

Dress Gray (Truscott), **Supp. IV Part 2:** 683

Dress Gray (teleplay), **Supp. IV Part 2:** 683

"Dressing for Dinner" (Ríos), **Supp. IV Part 2:** 548

Dressing Up for the Carnival (Shields), **Supp. VII:** 328

Drew, Bettina, **Supp. IX:** 2, 4

Drew, Elizabeth, **Retro. Supp. II:** 242, 243

Dreyfus, Alfred, **Supp. I Part 2:** 446

Drift and Mastery (Lippmann), **I:** 222–223

"Drinker, The" (Lowell), **II:** 535, 550

"Drinking from a Helmet" (Dickey), **Supp. IV Part 1:** 180

Drinking Gourd, The (Hansberry), **Supp. IV Part 1:** 359, 365–367, 374

Drinks before Dinner (Doctorow), **Supp. IV Part 1:** 231, 234–235

"Drive Home, The" (Banks), **Supp. V:** 7

"Driver" (Merrill), **Supp. III Part 1:** 331

"Driving through Minnesota during the Hanoi Bombings" (Bly), **Supp. IV Part 1:** 61

"Driving through Oregon" (Haines), **Supp. XII:** 207

"Driving toward the Lac Qui Parle River" (Bly), **Supp. IV Part 1:** 61

"Drone" (Coleman), **Supp. XI:** 85–86

"Drowned Man, The: Death between Two Rivers" (McGrath), **Supp. X:** 116

Drowning Pool, The (film), **Supp. IV Part 2:** 474

Drowning Pool, The (Macdonald), **Supp. IV Part 2:** 470, 471

Drowning Season, The (Hoffman), **Supp. X: 82**

Drowning with Others (Dickey), **Supp. IV Part 1:** 176, 178, 179

"Drowsy Day, A" (Dunbar), **Supp. II Part 1:** 198

Drugiye Berega (Nabokov), **III:** 247–250, 252

"Drug Shop, The, or Endymion in Edmonstoun" (Benét), **Supp. XI:** 43

"Drug Store" (Shapiro), **Supp. II Part 2:** 705

"Drugstore in Winter, A" (Ozick), **Supp. V:** 272

Drukman, Steven, **Supp. XIII:** 195, 197, 202

"Drum" (Hogan), **Supp. IV Part 1:** 413

"Drum, The" (Alvarez), **Supp. VII:** 7

"Drumlin Woodchuck, A" (Frost), **II:** 159–160; **Retro. Supp. I:** 138

Drummond, William, **Supp. I Part 1:** 369

Drummond de Andrade, Carlos, **Supp. IV Part 2:** 626, 629, 630

Drum-Taps (Whitman), **IV:** 346, 347, 444; **Retro. Supp. I:** 406

"Drunken Fisherman, The" (Lowell), **II:** 534, 550

"Drunken Sisters, The" (Wilder), **IV:** 374

Drunk in the Furnace, The (Merwin), **Supp. III Part 1:** 345–346

"Drunk in the Furnace, The" (Merwin), **Supp. III Part 1:** 346

Druten, John van, **Supp. XIV:** 162

Dryden, John, **II:** 111, 542, 556; **III:** 15; **IV:** 145; **Retro. Supp. I:** 56; **Supp. I Part 1:** 150; **Supp. I Part 2:** 422; **Supp. IX:** 68; **Supp. XIV:** 5

Drye, Captain Frank, **Retro. Supp. II:** 115

Dry Salvages, The (Eliot), **I:** 581

"Dry Salvages, The" (Eliot), **Retro. Supp. I:** 66

"Dry September" (Faulkner), **II:** 72, 73

Dry Sun, Dry Wind (Wagoner), **Supp. IX:** 323, 324

D'Souza, Dinesh, **Supp. X:** 255

"Dual" (Goldbarth), **Supp. XII:** 188

"Dual Curriculum" (Ozick), **Supp. V:** 270

"Dualism" (Reed), **Supp. X:** 242

Duane's Depressed (McMurtry), **Supp. V:** 233

Du Bartas, Guillaume, **Supp. I Part 1:** 98, 104, 111, 118, 119

Duberman, Martin, **Supp. I Part 2:** 408, 409

"Dubin's Lives" (Malamud), **Supp. I Part 2:** 451

Dubliners (Joyce), **I:** 130, 480; **III:** 471; **Supp. VIII:** 146

Du Bois, Nina Gomer (Mrs. W. E. B. Du Bois), **Supp. II Part 1:** 158; **Supp. XIV:** 200

Du Bois, Shirley Graham (Mrs. W. E. B. Du Bois), **Supp. II Part 1:** 186

Du Bois, W. E. B., **I:** 260; **Supp. I Part 1:** 5, 345; **Supp. II Part 1:** 33, 56, 61, **157–189,** 195; **Supp. IV Part 1:** 9, 164, 170, 362; **Supp. X:** 133, 134, 137, 139, 242; **Supp. XIII:** 185, **Supp. XIII:** 186, 233, 238, 243, 244, 247; **Supp. XIV:** 54, 69, 72, 201, 202

Dubreuil, Jean, **Supp. IV Part 2:** 425

Dubus, Andre, **Supp. VII: 75–93; Supp. XI:** 347,**Supp. XI:** 349; **Supp. XIV:** 21

Duchamp, Marcel, **IV:** 408; **Retro. Supp. I:** 416, 417, 418, 430; **Supp. IV Part 2:** 423, 424; **Supp. XII:** 124

"Duchess at Prayer, The" (Wharton), **Retro. Supp. I:** 365

Duchess of Malfi, The (Webster), **IV:** 131

Duck Soup (film), **Supp. IV Part 1:** 384

Duck Variations, The (Mamet), **Supp. XIV:** 239, 240, 249

Dudley, Anne. *See* Bradstreet, Anne

Dudley, Joseph, **III:** 52

Dudley, Thomas, **III:** 52; **Supp. I Part 1:** 98, 99, 110, 116

"Duet, With Muffled Brake Drums" (Updike), **Retro. Supp. I:** 319

Duet for Cannibals (Sontag), **Supp. III Part 2:** 452, 456

Duffey, Bernard, **Supp. I Part 2:** 458, 471

Duffus, R. L., **Supp. I Part 2:** 650

Duffy, Martha, **Supp. IV Part 1:** 207

Dufy, Raoul, **I:** 115; **IV:** 80

Dugan, Alan, **Supp. XIII:** 76

Dujardin, Edouard, **I:** 53

"Duke de l'Omelette, The" (Poe), **III:** 411, 425

"Duke in His Domain, The" (Capote), **Supp. III Part 1:** 113, 126

Duke of Deception, The (G. Wolff), **Supp. II Part 1:** 97; **Supp. XI:** 246

"Duke's Child, The" (Maxwell), **Supp. VIII:** 172

"Dulham Ladies, The" (Jewett), **II:** 407, 408; **Retro. Supp. II:** 143

Duluth (Vidal), **Supp. IV Part 2:** 677, 685, 689, 691–692

Dumas, Alexandre, **III:** 386

"Dumb Oax, The" (Lewis), **Retro. Supp. I:** 170

"Dummy, The" (Sontag), **Supp. III**

Part 2: 469

"Dump Ground, The" (Stegner), **Supp. IV Part 2:** 601

Dunbar, Alice Moore (Mrs. Paul Laurence Dunbar), **Supp. II Part 1:** 195, 200, 217

Dunbar, Paul Laurence, **Supp. I Part 1:** 320; **Supp. II Part 1:** 174, **191–219**; **Supp. III Part 1:** 73; **Supp. IV Part 1:** 15, 165, 170; **Supp. X:** 136; **Supp. XI:** 277; **Supp. XIII:** 111

Duncan, Isadora, **I:** 483

Duncan, Robert, **Retro. Supp. II:** 49; **Supp. III Part 2:** 625, 626, 630, 631; **Supp. VIII:** 304

Dunciad, The (Pope), **I:** 204

Dunford, Judith, **Supp. VIII:** 107

Dunlap, William, **Supp. I Part 1:** 126, 130, 137, 141, 145

Dunn, Stephen, **Supp. XI: 139–158**

Dunne, Finley Peter, **II:** 432

Dunne, John Gregory, **Supp. IV Part 1:** 197, 198, 201, 203, 207

"Dunnet Shepherdess, A" (Jewett), **II:** 392–393; **Retro. Supp. II:** 139

Dunning, Stephen, **Supp. XIV:** 126

Dunning, William Archibald, **Supp. II Part 1:** 170; **Supp. XIV:** 48

Dunnock, Mildred, **III:** 153

Dunster, Henry, **Supp. I Part 2:** 485

"Duo Tried Killing Man with Bacon" (Goldbarth), **Supp. XII:** 176

Dupee, F. W., **I:** 254; **II:** 548; **Supp. VIII:** 231; **Supp. IX:** 93, 96

DuPlessis, Rachel Blau, **Supp. IV Part 2:** 421, 426, 432

Duplicate Keys (Smiley), **Supp. VI:** 292, **294–296**

Durable Fire, A (Sarton), **Supp. VIII:** 260

Durand, Asher, B., **Supp. I Part 1:** 156, 157

Durand, Régis, **Supp. IV Part 1:** 44

"Durango Suite" (Gunn Allen), **Supp. IV Part 1:** 326

"Durations" (Matthews), **Supp. IX:** 152–153, 154

Dürer, Albrecht, **III:** 212; **Supp. XII:** 44

"During Fever" (Lowell), **II:** 547

Durkheim, Émile, **I:** 227; **Retro. Supp. I:** 55, 57; **Supp. I Part 2:** 637, 638

Durrell, Lawrence, **III:** 184, 190; **IV:** 430; **Supp. X:** 108, 187

Dürrenmatt, Friedrich, **Supp. IV Part 2:** 683

Duse, Eleonora, **II:** 515, 528

Dusk and Other Stories (Salter), **Supp. IX: 260–261**

Dusk of Dawn: An Essay Toward an Autobiography of a Race Concept (Du Bois), **Supp. II Part 1:** 159, 183, 186

"Dusting" (Alvarez), **Supp. VII:** 4

"Dusting" (Dove), **Supp. IV Part 1:** 247, 248

"Dust of Snow" (Frost), **II:** 154

Dust Tracks on a Road (Hurston), **Supp. IV Part 1:** 5, 11; **Supp. VI:** 149, 151, 158–159

"Dusty Braces" (Snyder), **Supp. VIII:** 302

Dutchman (Baraka), **Supp. II Part 1:** 38, 40, 42–44, 54, 55

"Dutch Nick Massacre, The" (Twain), **IV:** 195

"Dutch Picture, A" (Longfellow), **Retro. Supp. II:** 171

Dutton, Charles S., **Supp. VIII:** 332, 342

Dutton, Clarence Earl, **Supp. IV Part 2:** 598

Duvall, Robert, **Supp. V:** 227

"Duwamish" (Hugo), **Supp. VI:** 136

"Duwamish, Skagit, Hoh" (Hugo), **Supp. VI:** 136–137

"Duwamish No. 2" (Hugo), **Supp. VI:** 137

Duyckinck, Evert, **III:** 77, 81, 83, 85; **Retro. Supp. I:** 155, 247, 248; **Supp. I Part 1:** 122, 317

Duyckinck, George, **Supp. I Part 1:** 122

"Dvonya" (Simpson), **Supp. IX:** 274

Dwellings: A Spiritual History of the Living World (Hogan), **Supp. IV Part 1:** 397, 410, 415–416, 417

Dwight, Sereno E., **I:** 547

Dwight, Timothy, **Supp. I Part 1:** 124; **Supp. I Part 2:** 516, 580; **Supp. II Part 1:** 65, 69

Dworkin, Andrea, **Supp. XII:** 6

Dybbuk, A, or Between Two Worlds: Dramatic Legend in Four Acts (Kushner), **Supp. IX:** 138

Dybbuk, The (Ansky), **IV:** 6

Dyer, Geoff, **Supp. X:** 169

Dyer, R. C., **Supp. XIII:** 162

Dying Animal, The (Roth), **Retro. Supp. II:** 288

"Dying Elm, The" (Freneau), **Supp. II Part 1:** 258

"Dying Indian, The" (Freneau), **Supp. II Part 1:** 262

"Dying Man, The" (Roethke), **III:** 540, 542, 543–545

Dylan, Bob, **Supp. VIII:** 202; **Supp. XIII:** 114, 119

Dynamo (O'Neill), **III:** 396

"Dysfunctional Nation" (Karr), **Supp. XI:** 245

Dyson, A. E., **Retro. Supp. II:** 247

E. E. Cummings (Marks), **I:** 438

E. E. Cummings: A Miscellany (Cummings), **I:** 429, 441

E. E. Cummings: A Miscellany, Revised (Cummings), **I:** 429

E. L. Doctorow (Harter and Thompson), **Supp. IV Part 1:** 217

E. M. Forster (Trilling), **Supp. III Part 2:** 496, 501, 504

"Each and All" (Emerson), **II:** 19

Each in His Season (Snodgrass), **Supp. VI:** 324, 327

"Each Like a Leaf" (Swenson), **Supp. IV Part 2:** 644

Eager, Allen, **Supp. XI:** 294

"Eagle, The" (Tate), **IV:** 128

"Eagle and the Mole, The" (Wylie), **Supp. I Part 2:** 710, 711, 713, 714, 729

"Eagle Poem" (Harjo), **Supp. XII:** 224, 226

"Eagles" (Dickey), **Supp. IV Part 1:** 186

Eagle's Mile, The (Dickey), **Supp. IV Part 1:** 178, 185–186

"Eagle That Is Forgotten, The" (Lindsay), **Supp. I Part 2:** 382, 387

Eagleton, Terry, **Retro. Supp. I:** 67

Eakin, Paul John, **Supp. VIII:** 167, 168; **Supp. XIII:** 225

Eakins, Thomas, **Supp. XIV:** 338

Eames, Roscoe, **II:** 476

"Earl Painter" (Banks), **Supp. V:** 14–15

"Early Adventures of Ralph Ringwood, The" (Irving), **II:** 314

Early Ayn Rand, The: A Selection of Her Unpublished Fiction (Rand), **Supp. IV Part 2:** 520

Early Dark (Price), **Supp. VI:** 262

Early Diary of Anaïs Nin, The, **Supp. X:** 184, 192

Early Elkin (Elkin), **Supp. VI: 42–43**, 45

"Early Evenin' Blues" (Hughes), **Retro. Supp. I:** 205

"Early History of a Seamstress" (Reznikoff), **Supp. XIV:** 277, 289

"Early History of a Sewing-Machine Operator" (Reznikoff), **Supp. XIV:** 277

Early History of a Sewing-Machine Operator (Reznikoff), **Supp. XIV:** 289

"Early History of a Writer" (Reznikoff), **Supp. XIV:** 278, 290

Early Lectures of Ralph Waldo Emerson, The (Emerson), **II:** 11

Early Lives of Melville, The (Sealts), **Retro. Supp. I:** 257

Early Martyr and Other Poems, An (W. C. Williams), **Retro. Supp. I:** 423

"Early Morning: Cape Cod" (Swenson), **Supp. IV Part 2:** 641

"Early Spring between Madison and Bellingham" (Bly), **Supp. IV Part 1:** 71

Earnhardt, Dale, **Supp. XII:** 310

Earnshaw, Doris, **Supp. IV Part 1:** 310

"Earth" (Bryant), **Supp. I Part 1:** 157, 164, 167

"Earth, The" (Sexton), **Supp. II Part 2:** 696

"Earth and Fire" (Berry), **Supp. X:** 27

"Earth Being" (Toomer), **Supp. IX:** 320

"Earthly Care a Heavenly Discipline" (Stowe), **Supp. I Part 2:** 586

"Earthly City of the Jews, The" (Kazin), **Retro. Supp. II:** 286

Earthly Possessions (Tyler), **Supp. IV Part 2:** 665–666, 671

Earth Power Coming (Ortiz, ed.), **Supp. IV Part 2:** 502

"Earth's Holocaust" (Hawthorne), **II:** 226, 231, 232, 242; **III:** 82; **Retro. Supp. I:** 152

East Coker (Eliot), **I:** 580, 581, 582, 585, 587

"East Coker" (Eliot), **Retro. Supp. I:** 66; **Supp. VIII:** 195, 196

"Easter" (Toomer), **Supp. III Part 2:** 486

"Easter, an Ode" (Lowell), **II:** 536

"Easter Morning" (Ammons), **Supp. VII:** 34

"Easter Morning" (Clampitt), **Supp. IX:** 45

"Easter Ode, An" (Dunbar), **Supp. II Part 1:** 196

Easter Parade, The (Yates), **Supp. XI:** 346, 349

"Easter Sunday: Recollection" (Gunn Allen), **Supp. IV Part 1:** 322

"Easter Wings" (Herbert), **Supp. IV Part 2:** 646

"East European Cooking" (Simic), **Supp. VIII:** 277

East Is East (Boyle), **Supp. VIII:** 1–3

Eastlake, William, **Supp. XIII:** 12

East Lynne (Wood), **Supp. I Part 1:** 35, 36; **Supp. I Part 2:** 459, 462

Eastman, Elaine Goodale, **Supp. X:** 103

Eastman, Max, **Supp. III Part 2:** 620; **Supp. X:** 131, 134, 135, 137

East of Eden (Steinbeck), **IV:** 51, 56–57, 59

"East of the Sun and West of the Moon" (Merwin), **Supp. III Part 1:** 344

Easton, Alison, **Retro. Supp. II:** 143, 144, 145

Easton, Bret Ellis, **Supp. XI:** 65

Easton, Robert, **Supp. IV Part 2:** 461, 474

East Wind (Lowell), **II:** 527

East Wind: West Wind (Buck), **Supp. II Part 1:** 114–115

Easy Rawlins mysteries, **Supp. XIII:** 236, **237–241,** 242

Easy Rider (film), **Supp. XI:** 293, **308,** 309

Eat a Bowl of Tea (Chu), **Supp. X:** 291

Eating Naked (Dobyns), **Supp. XIII: 78–79**

"Eating Poetry" (Strand), **Supp. IV Part 2:** 626

Eaton, Edith, **Supp. X:** 291

Eaton, Peggy, **Supp. I Part 2:** 461

Eaton, Winnifred, **Supp. X:** 291

"Eatonville Anthology, The" (Hurston), **Supp. VI:** 152

"Ebb and Flow, The" (Taylor), **IV:** 161

Eben Holden (Bacheller), **I:** 216

Eberhardt, Isabelle, **Supp. IV Part 1:** 92

Eberhart, Mrs., **I:** 521–522, 530

Eberhart, Richard, **I: 521–543; II:** 535–536; **III:** 527; **IV:** 416; **Retro. Supp. II:** 176, 178; **Supp. I Part 1:** 83; **Supp. XII:** 119

Eble, Kenneth E., **Supp. I Part 1:** 201

Eccentricities of a Nightingale (T. Williams), **IV:** 382, 385, 397, 398

Ecclesiastica Historia Integram Ecclesiae (Taylor), **IV:** 163

"Echo, The" (Bowles), **Supp. IV Part 1:** 84, 86, 87

Echoes inside the Labyrinth (McGrath), **Supp. X:** 127

Eckhart, Maria, **Supp. V:** 212

Eclipse (Hogan), **Supp. IV Part 1:** 397, 400, 402

Eclogues (Virgil), **Supp. VIII:** 31

"Ecologue" (Ginsberg), **Supp. II Part 1:** 326

"Ecologues of These States 1969–1971" (Ginsberg), **Supp. II Part 1:** 325

"Economics of Negro Emancipation in the United States, The" (Du Bois), **Supp. II Part 1:** 174

"Economic Theory of Women's Dress, The" (Veblen), **Supp. I Part 2:** 636

Economy of the Unlost: Reading Simonides of Keos with Paul Celan (Carson), **Supp. XII:** 110–111

Ecotactics: The Sierra Club Handbook for Environmental Activists (Mitchell and Stallings, eds.), **Supp. IV Part 2:** 488

"Ecstasy" (Olds), **Supp. X:** 206

"Ecstatic" (Komunyakaa), **Supp. XIII:** 131

Edda, **Supp. X:** 114

Eddy, Mary Baker, **I:** 583; **III:** 506

Edel, Leon, **I:** 20; **II:** 338–339; **Retro. Supp. I:** 218, 224, 231

Edelberg, Cynthia, **Supp. IV Part 1:** 155

"Eden and My Generation" (Levis), **Supp. XI:** 270

Edenbaum, Robert, **Supp. IV Part 1:** 352

Eder, Richard, **Supp. XII:** 189

Edgar Huntly; or, Memoirs of a Sleep-Walker (Brown), **Supp. I Part 1:** 140–144, 145

"Edge" (Plath), **Retro. Supp. II:** 256; **Supp. I Part 2:** 527, 547

Edge, Mary E., **II:** 316

"Edge of the Great Rift, The" (Theroux), **Supp. VIII:** 325

Edge of the Sea, The (Carson), **Supp. IX:** 19, **25–31,** 32

Edgeworth, Maria, **II:** 8

Edible Woman, The (Atwood), **Supp. XIII:** 19, 20, **20–21**

"Edict by the King of Prussia, An" (Franklin), **II:** 120

Edison, Thomas A., **I:** 483; **Supp. I Part 2:** 392

Edith Wharton (Joslin), **Retro. Supp. I:** 376

Edith Wharton: A Biography (Lewis), **Retro. Supp. I:** 362

Edith Wharton: A Woman in Her Time (Auchincloss), **Retro. Supp. I:** 370

Edith Wharton: Matters of Mind and Spirit (Singley), **Retro. Supp. I:** 373

Edith Wharton: Traveller in the Land of Letters (Goodwyn), **Retro. Supp. I:** 370

Edith Wharton's Argument with America (Ammons), **Retro. Supp. I:** 364

Edith Wharton's Brave New Politics (Bauer), **Retro. Supp. I:** 381

Edith Wharton's Letters from the Underworld (Waid), **Retro. Supp. I:** 360

"Editing and Glosses" (Reznikoff), **Supp. XIV:** 283

Editing of Emily Dickinson, The (Franklin), **Retro. Supp. I:** 41

"Editor and the Schoolma'am, The"

(Frederic), **II:** 130

"Editor's Easy Chair" (Howells), **II:** 276

"Editor's Study, The" (Howells), **II:** 275, 276, 285

"Editor Whedon" (Masters), **Supp. I Part 2:** 463

Edlin, Mari, **Supp. X:** 266

Edman, Irwin, **III:** 605

Edmond (Mamet), **Supp. XIV:** 241, 248, 249, 250

Edmundson, Mark, **Retro. Supp. II:** 262

Edsel (Shapiro), **Supp. II Part 2:** 703, 704, 717–719

Edson, Russell, **Supp. VIII:** 279

"Educated American Woman, An" (Cheever), **Supp. I Part 1:** 194

"Education, An" (Ozick), **Supp. V:** 267

Education and Living (Bourne), **I:** 252

"Education of a Storyteller, The" (Bambara), **Supp. XI:** 20

Education of Black People, The (Du Bois), **Supp. II Part 1:** 186

Education of Harriet Hatfield, The (Sarton), **Supp. VIII: 257–258**

Education of Henry Adams, The (Adams), **I:** 1, 5, 6, 11, 14, 15–18, 19, 20–21, 111; **II:** 276; **III:** 504; **Retro. Supp. I:** 53, 59; **Supp. IX:** 19; **Supp. XIV:** 299

"Education of Mingo, The" (Johnson), **Supp. VI:** 193, 194

"Education of Norman Podhoretz, The" (Goldberg), **Supp. VIII:** 238

Education of Oscar Fairfax, The (Auchincloss), **Supp. IV Part 1:** 25, 36

"Education of the Poet" (Glück), **Supp. V:** 78, 80

Education sentimentale (Flaubert), **III:** 315

Edwards, Eli. *See* McKay, Claude

Edwards, Esther, **I:** 545

Edwards, John, **I:** 478

Edwards, Jonathan, **I: 544–566; II:** 432; **Retro. Supp. II:** 187; **Supp. I Part 1:** 301, 302; **Supp. I Part 2:** 552, 594, 700; **Supp. IV Part 2:** 430; **Supp. VIII:** 205

Edwards, Sarah, **I:** 545

Edwards, Timothy, **I:** 545

Edwards-Yearwood, Grace, **Supp. VIII:** 81

"Edwin Arlington Robinson" (Cowley), **Supp. II Part 1:** 144

Edwin Arlington Robinson (Winters), **Supp. II Part 2:** 812

Edwin Booth (play), **Supp. IV Part 1:** 89

"Effects of Analogy" (Stevens), **Retro. Supp. I:** 297

"Effort at Speech between Two People" (Rukeyser), **Supp. VI:** 276, 284

"Efforts of Affection" (Moore), **III:** 214

"Efforts of Affection: A Memoir of Marianne Moore" (Bishop), **Retro. Supp. II:** 52

"Egg, The" (Anderson), **I:** 113, 114

"Egg, The" (Snyder), **Supp. VIII:** 302

"Eggplant Epithalamion, The" (Jong), **Supp. V:** 119

"Eggs" (Olds), **Supp. X:** 206

"Eggshell" (Stern), **Supp. IX:** 299

Egoist, The (Meredith), **II:** 186

Egorova, Lubov, **Supp. IX:** 58

"Egotism, or the Bosom Sergent" (Hawthorne), **II:** 227, 239

"Egyptian Pulled Glass Bottle in the Shape of a Fish, An" (Moore), **III:** 195, 213

Ehrenfels, Christian von, **Supp. XIV:** 198

Ehrenpreis, Irvin, **Supp. XII:** 128

Ehrlich, Gretel, **Supp. XIV:** 227

Eichmann, Adolf, **Supp. XII:** 166

Eichmann in Jerusalem (Arendt), **Retro. Supp. II:** 28; **Supp. VIII:** 243; **Supp. XII:** 166

"Eichmann in New York: The New York Intellectuals and the Hannah Arendt Controversy" (Rabinbach), **Supp. XII:** 166

"Eidolon" (Warren), **IV:** 239

Eight Cousins (Alcott), **Supp. I Part 1:** 29, 38, 42, 43

18 Poems from the Quechua (Strand, trans.), **Supp. IV Part 2:** 630

1876: A Novel (Vidal), **Supp. IV Part 2:** 677, 684, 688, 689, 691, 692

"18 West 11th Street" (Merrill), **Supp. III Part 1:** 323, 328

"Eighth Air Force" (Jarrell), **II:** 373–374, 377

Eight Harvard Poets, **I:** 429, 475

"Eighth Ditch, The" (Baraka), **Supp. II Part 1:** 40

"'80s Pastoral: Frederick Barthelme's *Moon Deluxe* Ten Years On" (Peters), **Supp. XI:** 39

Eight Men (Wright), **IV:** 478, 488, 494

80 Flowers (Zukofsky), **Supp. III Part 2:** 631

Eikon Basilike, The, **Supp. IV Part 2:** 435

Eileen (Masters), **Supp. I Part 2:** 460

Eimi (Cummings), **I:** 429, 433, 434, 439–440

"Einstein" (MacLeish), **III:** 5, 8, 10–11, 18–19

Einstein, Albert, **I:** 493; **III:** 8, 10, 21, 161; **IV:** 69, 375, 410, 411, 421; **Retro. Supp. I:** 63; **Supp. I Part 2:** 609, 643; **Supp. III Part 2:** 621; **Supp. V:** 290; **Supp. XII:** 45

Eiseley, Loren, **III:** 227–228

Eisenhower, Dwight D., **I:** 136, 376; **II:** 548; **III:** 215; **IV:** 75; **Supp. I Part 1:** 291; **Supp. III Part 2:** 624; **Supp. V:** 45

Eisenstein, Sergei, **I:** 481

Eisinger, Chester E., **I:** 302; **II:** 604; **Supp. IX:** 15

Eisner, Douglas, **Supp. X:** 155

Elam, Angela, **Supp. XI:** 290

El Bernardo (Balbuena), **Supp. V:** 11

Elbert, Sarah, **Supp. I Part 1:** 34, 41

Elder, Donald, **II:** 417, 426, 435, 437

Elder, John, **Supp. IX:** 25

Elder, Lonne, III, **Supp. IV Part 1:** 362

Elder, Richard, **Supp. XII:** 172

"Elder Sister, The" (Olds), **Supp. X:** 205–206

Elder Statesman, The (Eliot), **I:** 572, 573, 583; **Retro. Supp. I:** 53, 65

Eldredge, Kay, **Supp. IX:** 254, 259

Eldridge, Florence, **III:** 154, 403; **IV:** 357

Eleanor of Aquitaine, **III:** 470

Eleanor of Guienne, **I:** 14

"Elect, The" (Taylor), **Supp. V:** 323

"Elections, Nicaragua, 1984" (Kingsolver), **Supp. VII:** 208

Elective Affinities (Goethe; Bogan and Mayer, trans.), **Supp. III Part 1:** 63

Electra (Euripides), **III:** 398

Electra (Sophocles), **III:** 398; **IV:** 370; **Supp. IX:** 102

"Electra on Azalea Path" (Plath), **Supp. I Part 2:** 538

"Electrical Storm" (Bishop), **Supp. I Part 1:** 93

"Electrical Storm" (Hayden), **Supp. II Part 1:** 370

"Electric Arrows" (Proulx), **Supp. VII:** 256

"Electricity Saviour" (Olds), **Supp. X:** 215

Electric Kool-Aid Acid Test, The (Wolfe), **Supp. III Part 2:** 575–577, 582–584; **Supp. XI:** 239

Electric Lady, The (film), **Supp. XI:** 309

Elegant Extracts (Knox), **II:** 8

Elegiac Feelings American (Corso), **Supp. XII: 131–134**

Elegies (Rukeyser), **Supp. VI:** 273

"Elegies" (Rukeyser), **Supp. VI:** 272

"Elegies for Paradise Valley" (Hayden), **Supp. II Part 1:** 363

Elegy (Levis), **Supp. XI:** 257, 259, 261, **271–272**

"Elegy" (Merwin), **Supp. III Part 1:** 351

"Elegy" (Stafford), **Supp. XI:** 322

"Elegy" (Tate), **IV:** 128

"Elegy, for the U.S.N. Dirigible, Macon, An" (Winters), **Supp. II Part 2:** 810

"Elegy Ending in the Sound of a Skipping Rope" (Levis), **Supp. XI:** 271–272

"Elegy for D. H. Lawrence, An" (W. C. Williams), **Retro. Supp. I:** 421

"Elegy for My Father" (Strand), **Supp. IV Part 2:** 628

"Elegy for My Mother" (Wagoner), **Supp. IX:** 330

Elegy for September, An (Nichols), **Supp. XIII:** 268

"Elegy for Thelonious" (Komunyakaa), **Supp. XIII:** 118

"Elegy for the U.S.N. Dirigible, Macon, A" (Winters), **Supp. II Part 2:** 810

"Elegy of Last Resort" (Nemerov), **III:** 271

"Elegy with a Thimbleful of Water in the Cage" (Levis), **Supp. XI:** 272

Elegy Written in a Country Churchyard (Gray), **I:** 68

"Elegy Written in a Country Churchyard" (Gray), **Supp. XIV:** 8

"Elementary Scene, The" (Jarrell), **II:** 387, 388, 389

"Elements" (Frank), **Supp. X:** 213

Elements of Style, The (Strunk), **Supp. I Part 2:** 670

"Elenita, Cards, Palm, Water" (Cisneros), **Supp. VII:** 64

"Eleonora" (Poe), **III:** 412

Eleothriambos (Lee), **IV:** 158

"Elephants" (Moore), **III:** 203

"Elevator, The" (Dixon), **Supp. XII:** 154

"Elevator Boy" (Hughes), **Retro. Supp. I:** 200; **Supp. I Part 1:** 326

"Eleven" (Cisneros), **Supp. VII:** 69

Eleven Essays in the European Novel (Blackmur), **Supp. II Part 1:** 91, 111

Eleven Kinds of Loneliness (Yates), **Supp. XI:** **340–343,** 349

Eleven Poems on the Same Theme (Warren), **IV:** 239–241

"Eleven Times a Poem" (Corso), **Supp. XII:** 132, 133

El Greco (Doménikos Theotokópoulos), **I:** 387; **III:** 212

"El-Hajj Malik El-Shabazz" (Hayden), **Supp. II Part 1:** 379

"Eli, the Fanatic" (Roth), **Supp. III Part 2:** 407–408

Eliot, Charles W., **I:** 5; **II:** 345; **Supp. I Part 2:** 479; **Supp. IX:** 94

Eliot, Charles William, **Retro. Supp. I:** 55

Eliot, George, **I:** 375, 458, 459, 461, 467; **II:** 179, 181, 191–192, 275, 319, 324, 338, 577; **IV:** 311, 322; **Retro. Supp. I:** 218, 220, 225; **Supp. I Part 1:** 370; **Supp. I Part 2:** 559, 579; **Supp. IV Part 1:** 31, 297; **Supp. IV Part 2:** 677; **Supp. V:** 258; **Supp. IX:** 38, 43, 51; **Supp. XI:** 68; **Supp. XII:** 335; **Supp. XIV:** 344

Eliot, T. S., **I:** 48, 49, 52, 59, 60, 64, 66, 68, 105, 107, 215–216, 236, 243, 256, 259, 261, 266, 384, 386, 395, 396, 399, 403, 430, 433, 441, 446, 475, 478, 479, 482, 521, 522, 527, **567–591;** **II:** 65, 96, 158, 168, 316, 371, 376, 386, 529, 530, 532, 537, 542, 545; **III:** 1, 4, 5, 6, 7–8, 9, 10, 11, 14, 17, 20, 21, 23, 26, 34, 174, 194, 195–196, 205–206, 220, 236, 239, 269, 270–271, 277–278, 301, 409, 428, 435, 436, 453, 456–457, 459–460, 461–462, 464, 466, 471, 476, 478, 485, 488, 492, 493, 498, 504, 509, 511, 517, 524, 527, 539, 572, 575, 586, 591, 594, 600, 613; **IV:** 27, 74, 82, 83, 95, 122, 123, 127, 129, 134, 138, 140, 141, 191, 201, 237, 331, 379, 402, 403, 418, 419, 420, 430, 431, 439, 442, 491; **Retro. Supp. I:** **51–71,** 74, 80, 89, 91, 171, 198, 210, 283, 289, 290, 292, 296, 298, 299, 311, 324, 359, 411, 413, 414, 416, 417, 420, 428; **Retro. Supp. II:** 79, 178, 189, 262, 326; **Supp. I Part 1:** 257, 264, 268, 270, 274, 299; **Supp. I Part 2:** 387, 423, 455, 536, 554, 624, 659, 721; **Supp. II Part 1:** 1, 4, 8, 20, 30, 91, 98, 103, 136, 314; **Supp. III Part 1:** 9, 10, 26, 31, 37, 41, 43, 44, 48, 62–64, 73, 91, 99–100, 105–106, 273; **Supp. III Part 2:** 541, 611, 612, 617, 624; **Supp. IV Part 1:** 40, 47, 284, 380, 404; **Supp. IV Part 2:** 436; **Supp. V:** 79, 97, 101, 338, 343, 344; **Supp. VIII:** 19, 21, 93, 102, 105, 182, 195, 205, 290, 292; **Supp. IX:** 158–159, 229; **Supp. X:** 59, 115, 119, 124, 187, 324; **Supp. XI:** 242; **Supp. XII:** 45, 159, 198, 308; **Supp. XIII:** 77, 104, 115, 332, 341–342, 344, 346; **Supp. XIV:** 5, 13, 107, 287, 290, 306, 347

Eliot's Early Years (Gordon), **Retro. Supp. I:** 55

"Elizabeth" (Longfellow), **I:** 502

Elizabeth Appleton (O'Hara), **III:** 362, 364, 375–377

"Elizabeth Bishop (1911–1979)" (Merrill), **Retro. Supp. II:** 53

"Elizabeth Bishop in Brazil" (Brown), **Supp. I Part 1:** 96

"Elizabeth Bishop's *North & South*" (Lowell), **Retro. Supp. II:** 40–41

"Elizabeth Gone" (Sexton), **Supp. II Part 2:** 674, 681

Elk Heads on the Wall (Ríos), **Supp. IV Part 2:** 540

Elkin, Stanley, **Supp. VI:** **41–59**

"Elk Song" (Hogan), **Supp. IV Part 1:** 406

Ella in Bloom (Hearon), **Supp. VIII:** **70–71**

Elledge, Jim, **Supp. XIII:** 88

Ellen Foster: A Novel (Gibbons), **Supp. X:** 41, **42–44,** 46, 47, 49, 50

Ellen Rogers (Farrell), **II:** 42–43

Eller, Ernest, **Supp. I Part 2:** 497

Ellerman, Winifred, **Supp. I Part 1:** 258–259. *See also* McAlmon, Mrs. Robert (Winifred Ellerman)

"El libro de la sexualidad" (Simic), **Supp. VIII:** 283

Ellington, Duke, **Retro. Supp. II:** 115; **Supp. IV Part 1:** 360; **Supp. IX:** 164

Elliot, Charles, **Supp. V:** 161

Elliott, George B., **III:** 478

Ellis, Albert, **Supp. IV Part 2:** 527

Ellis, Bret Easton, **Supp. XII:** 81

Ellis, Brett Easton, **Supp. X:** 7

Ellis, Charles, **Supp. I Part 1:** 99

Ellis, Havelock, **II:** 276

Ellis, John Harvard, **Supp. I Part 1:** 103

Ellis, Katherine, **IV:** 114

Ellison, Harlan, **Supp. XIII:** 61

Ellison, Ralph, **IV:** 250, 493; **Retro. Supp. II:** 3, **111–130;** **Supp. II Part 1:** 33, **221–252;** **Supp. IV, Part 1:** 374; **Supp. VIII:** 105, 245; **Supp. IX:** 114, 316; **Supp. X:** 324; **Supp. XI:** 18, 92, 275; **Supp. XIII:** 186, 233, 305; **Supp. XIV:** 306

Ellmann, Maud, **Supp. IV Part 1:** 302

Ellmann, Richard, **Supp. VIII:** 105

Ellroy, James, **Supp. XIV:** 26

Elman, Richard, **Supp. V:** 40

"Elmer" (Faulkner), **Retro. Supp. I:** 79, 80

Elmer Gantry (Lewis), **I:** 26, 364; **II:** 447–449, 450, 455

Elmer the Great (Lardner), **II:** 427

"Elms" (Glück), **Supp. V:** 85

Eloges (Perse), **Supp. XIII:** 344

"Eloquence of Grief, An" (Crane), **I:** 411

"El Río Grande" (Mora), **Supp. XIII:** 224

"*El* Round up" (Alvarez), **Supp. VII:** 11

"El Salvador: Requiem and Invocation" (Levertov), **Supp. III Part 1:** 284

Elsasser, Henry, **I:** 226

"Elsa Wertman" (Masters), **Supp. I Part 2:** 462–463

Elsie John and Joey Martinez: Two Stories (Huncke), **Supp. XIV:** 148

Elsie Venner (Holmes), **Supp. I Part 1:** 243, 315–316

Elton, Charles, **Supp. XIV:** 192

Éluard, Paul, **III:** 528; **Supp. IV Part 1:** 80

Elvins, Kells, **Supp. III Part 1:** 93, 101

Ely, Richard T., **Supp. I Part 1:** 5; **Supp. I Part 2:** 640, 645

"Emancipation. A Life Fable" (Chopin), **Retro. Supp. II:** 59; **Supp. I Part 1:** 207–208

"Emancipation in the British West Indies" (Emerson), **II:** 13

"Emancipation Proclamation, The" (Emerson), **II:** 13

Emanuel, James, **Supp. I Part 1:** 346

Embargo, The (Bryant), **Supp. I Part 1:** 152–153

Embarrassments (James), **Retro. Supp. I:** 229

Embezzler, The (Auchincloss), **Supp. IV Part 1:** 24, 30–31

"Emerald" (Doty), **Supp. XI:** 131

"Emerald, The" (Merrill), **Supp. III Part 1:** 328

"Emergence of Flight from Aristotle's Mud, The" (Goldbarth), **Supp. XII:** 190

"Emergency Room" (Mora), **Supp. XIII:** 218

"Emerging Voices: The Teaching of Writing" (Mora), **Supp. XIII:** 220

Emerson, and Other Essays (Chapman), **Supp. XIV:** 41–44

Emerson, Ellen, **Supp. I Part 1:** 33

Emerson, Ralph Waldo, **I:** 98, 217, 220, 222, 224, 228, 239, 246, 251, 252, 253, 257, 260, 261, 283, 386, 397, 402, 424, 433, 444, 447, 455, 458, 460–461, 463, 464, 485, 561;

II: 1–24, 49, 92, 127–128, 169, 170, 226, 233, 237, 273–274, 275, 278, 289, 295, 301, 313, 315, 336, 338, 344, 402, 491, 503; **III:** 53, 82, 171, 174, 260, 277, 409, 424, 428, 453, 454, 507, 576–577, 606, 614; **IV:** 60, 167, 169, 170, 171, 172, 173–174, 176, 178, 183, 186, 187, 192, 201, 202, 211, 335, 338, 340, 342, 350; **Retro. Supp. I:** 34, 53, 54, 57, 62, 74–75, 76, 125, 148–149, 152–153, 159, 217, 250, 298, 392, 400, 403; **Retro. Supp. II:** 96, 113, 135, 142, 155, 207, 262; **Supp. I Part 1:** 2, 28–29, 31, 33, 188, 299, 308–309, 317, 358, 365, 366, 368; **Supp. I Part 2:** 374, 383, 393, 407, 413, 416, 420, 422, 474, 482, 580, 582, 602, 659, 679; **Supp. II Part 1:** 280, 288; **Supp. III Part 1:** 387; **Supp. IV Part 2:** 439, 597, 619; **Supp. V:** 118; **Supp. VIII:** 42, 105, 106, 108, 198, 201, 204, 205, 292; **Supp. IX:** 38, 90, 175, 176, 181; **Supp. X:** 42, 45, 121, 223; **Supp. XI:** 203; **Supp. XIII:** 141, 145, 233, 246, **Supp. XIII:** 247; **Supp. XIV:** 41–44, 46, 54, 104, 177

"Emerson and the Essay" (Gass), **Supp. VI:** 88

"Emerson the Lecturer" (Lowell), **Supp. I Part 2:** 420, 422

Emerson-Thoreau Award, **Retro. Supp. I:** 67

Emery, Clark, **III:** 478

Emily Dickinson: Woman Poet (Bennett), **Retro. Supp. I:** 42

"Emily Dickinson and Class" (Erkkila), **Retro. Supp. I:** 42–43

Emily Dickinson Editorial Collective, **Retro. Supp. I:** 47

Eminent Victorians (Strachey), **Supp. I Part 2:** 485

"Emma and Eginhard" (Longfellow), **III:** 505

"Emma Enters a Sentence of Elizabeth Bishop's" (Gass), **Supp. VI:** 93

Emperor Jones, The (O'Neill), **II:** 278; **III:** 391, 392

Emperor of Haiti (Hughes), **Supp. I Part 1:** 339

"Emperor of Ice Cream, The" (Stevens), **IV:** 76, 80–81

"Emperors" (Dunn), **Supp. XI:** 155

"Emperor's New Clothes, The" (Anderson), **I:** 441

"Empire" (Ford), **Supp. V:** 69

Empire: A Novel (Vidal), **Supp. IV Part 2:** 677, 684, 686, 690

"Empire Builders" (MacLeish), **III:** 14

Empire Falls (Russo), **Supp. XII:** 339–343

Empire of Summer, The (Doty), **Supp. XI:** 120

Empire of the Senseless (Acker), **Supp. XII:** 5, **6, 14–16**

"Empires" (Simic), **Supp. VIII:** 282

"Emporium" (Shapiro), **Supp. II Part 2:** 705

Empress of the Splendid Season (Hijuelos), **Supp. VIII: 86–89**

Empson, William, **I:** 522, 533; **II:** 536; **III:** 286, 497, 498, 499; **IV:** 136, 431; **Retro. Supp. I:** 263; **Retro. Supp. II:** 253

"Empty Hills, The" (Winters), **Supp. II Part 2:** 792, 793, 796

Empty Mirror, Early Poems (Ginsberg), **Supp. II Part 1:** 308, 311, 313–314, 319, 329

"Empty Room" (Hughes), **Supp. I Part 1:** 337

"Empty Threat, An" (Frost), **II:** 159

"Encantadas, The" (Melville), **III:** 89

Enchanter, The (Nabokov), **Retro. Supp. I:** 266

"Encomium Twenty Years Later" (Tate), **I:** 381

"Encounter, The" (Pound), **III:** 466

Encounter in April (Sarton), **Supp. VIII:** 259

"Encounter in April" (Sarton), **Supp. VIII:** 259

"Encountering the Sublime" (McClatchy), **Supp. XII:** 261

"Encounter on the Seine: Black Meets Brown" (Baldwin), **Retro. Supp. II:** 2

Encounters with Chinese Writers (Dillard), **Supp. VI:** 19, 23, 31

Encounters with the Archdruid (McPhee), **Supp. III Part 1:** 292–294, 301; **Supp. X:** 30

"End, The" (Olds), **Supp. X:** 205

"Endangered Species" (Mora), **Supp. XIII:** 219–220

Endecott and the Red Cross (Lowell), **II:** 545

Endgame (Beckett), **Supp. XIII:** 196

"Endgame" (Tan), **Supp. X:** 290

"Endicott and the Red Cross" (Hawthorne), **Retro. Supp. II:** 181, 187–188

"End of Books, The" (Coover), **Supp. V:** 53

End of Education, The (Postman), **Supp. XI:** 275

"End of Season" (Warren), **IV:** 239–240

"End of Something, The"

(Hemingway), **II:** 248

End of the Affair, The (Greene), **Supp. XI:** 99

End of the Age of Innocence, The (Price), **Retro. Supp. I:** 377

"End of the Line, The" (Jarrell), **III:** 527

"End of the Rainbow, The" (Jarrell), **II:** 386

End of the Road (film), **Supp. XI:** 309

End of the Road, The (Barth), **I:** 121, 122, 126–131; **Supp. XI:** 309

"End of the World, The" (MacLeish), **III:** 8

Endor (Nemerov), **III:** 269, 270, 279

"Ends" (Dixon), **Supp. XII:** 153

End to Innocence, An: Essays on Culture and Politics (Fiedler), **Supp. XIII:** 98–99

Endure: The Diaries of Charles Walter Stetson (Stetson), **Supp. XI:** 196

"Enduring Chill, The" (O'Connor), **III:** 349, 351, 357; **Retro. Supp. II:** 236

Enduring Vision of Norman Mailer, The (Leeds), **Retro. Supp. II:** 204

Endymion (Keats), **IV:** 405; **Retro. Supp. I:** 412

End Zone (DeLillo), **Supp. VI:** 2, 3, 4, 10, 11, 12

Enemies: A Love Story (Singer), **IV:** 1; **Retro. Supp. II:** 310–311

Enemy, The: Time (T. Williams), **IV:** 391

Enemy of the People, An (adapt. Miller), **III:** 154–156

"Energy Vampire" (Ginsberg), **Supp. II Part 1:** 326

"Enforcement of the Slave Trade Laws, The" (Du Bois), **Supp. II Part 1:** 161

"Engaging the Past" (Bell), **Supp. X:** 17

Engel, Bernard F., **I:** 532

Engels, Friedrich, **IV:** 429, 443–444; **Supp. I Part 1:** 13

Engineer of Moonlight (DeLillo), **Supp. VI:** 4

Engineers and the Price System, The (Veblen), **I:** 475–476; **Supp. I Part 2:** 638, 642, 648

"England" (Moore), **III:** 203, 207, 214

Engle, Paul, **III:** 542; **Retro. Supp. II:** 220, 221; **Supp. V:** 337; **Supp. XI:** 315; **Supp. XIII:** 76

English Elegy, The: Studies in the Genre from Spenser to Yeats (Sacks), **Supp. IV Part 2:** 450

English Hours (James), **II:** 337; **Retro. Supp. I:** 235

English Language, The (L. P. Smith),

Supp. XIV: 341

Englishmen of Letters (James), **II:** 327

English Notebooks, The (Hawthorne), **II:** 226, 227–228

English Novel, The (Lanier), **Supp. I Part 1:** 371

English Poets, The: Lessing, Rousseau (Lowell), **Supp. I Part 2:** 407

English Prosody and Modern Poetry (Shapiro), **Supp. II Part 2:** 710

English Traits (Emerson), **II:** 1, 5, 6–7, 8

"English Writers on America" (Irving), **II:** 308

Engstrand, Stuart, **Supp. I Part 1:** 51

"Enoch and the Gorilla" (O'Connor), **Retro. Supp. II:** 225

Enormous Changes at the Last Minute (Paley), **Supp. VI:** 218

"Enormous Changes at the Last Minute" (Paley), **Supp. VI:** 226, 232

"Enormous Radio, The" (Cheever), **Supp. I Part 1:** 175–177, 195

Enormous Radio and Other Stories, The (Cheever), **Supp. I Part 1:** 175–177

Enormous Room, The (Cummings), **I:** 429, 434, 440, 445, 477

"Enough for a Lifetime" (Buck), **Supp. II Part 1:** 127

Enough Rope (Parker), **Supp. IX:** 189, 192

Enquiry Concerning Political Justice (Godwin), **Supp. I Part 1:** 126, 146

Entered From the Sun (Garrett), **Supp. VII:** 105–106, 107–109

"Entering the Kingdom" (Oliver), **Supp. VII:** 234

Entertaining Strangers (Gurney), **Supp. V:** 98, 99

Entrance: Four Chicano Poets, **Supp. XIII:** 316

Entrance to Porlock, The (Buechner), **Supp. XII:** 52

Entries (Berry), **Supp. X:** 23

"Entropy" (Pynchon), **Supp. II Part 2:** 619, 621

Environmental Imagination, The (Buell), **Supp. V:** 209; **Supp. IX:** 29

"Envoys, The" (Merrill), **Supp. III Part 1:** 326

"Envy; or, Yiddish in America" (Ozick), **Supp. V:** 263, 265–266

"Eolian Harp, The" (Coleridge), **I:** 284

"Ephemera, The" (Franklin), **II:** 121

Ephesians (biblical book), **Supp. I Part 1:** 117

Epictetus, **III:** 566

"Epicurean, The" (Auchincloss), **Supp. IV Part 1:** 25

Epicurus, **I:** 59

"Epigram" (Lowell), **II:** 550

"Epilogue" (Lowell), **Retro. Supp. II:** 191

"Epimanes" (Poe), **III:** 411

"Epimetheus" (Longfellow), **II:** 494

"Epipsychidion" (Shelley), **Supp. I Part 2:** 718

Episode in Palmetto (Caldwell), **I:** 297, 307

Epistle to a Godson (Auden), **Supp. II Part 1:** 24

"Epistle to Be Left in the Earth" (MacLeish), **III:** 13

"Epistle to George William Curtis" (Lowell), **Supp. I Part 2:** 416

"Epistle to Léon-Paul Fargue" (MacLeish), **III:** 15

"Epitaph Ending in And, The" (Stafford), **Supp. XI:** 321–322

Epitaph for a Desert Anarchist (Bishop), **Supp. XIII:** 1

"Epitaph for Fire and Flower" (Plath), **Supp. I Part 2:** 537

"Epitaph for the Race of Man" (Millay), **III:** 127–128

"Epithalamium" (Auden), **Supp. II Part 1:** 15

"Epstein" (Roth), **Retro. Supp. II:** 281; **Supp. III Part 2:** 404, 406–407, 412, 422

Epstein, Jason, **Supp. VIII:** 233

Epstein, Joseph, **Supp. IV Part 2:** 692; **Supp. VIII:** 236, 238; **Supp. XIV:101–117**

Epstein, Leslie, **Supp. XII: 159–174**

Epstein, Philip, **Supp. XII:** 159

"Equal in Paris" (Baldwin), **Retro. Supp. II:** 3; **Supp. I Part 1:** 52

"Equilibrists, The" (Ransom), **III:** 490, 494

"Equipment for Pennies" (H. Roth), **Supp. IX:** 233

"Erat Hora" (Pound), **III:** 463; **Retro. Supp. I:** 413

Erdrich, Louise, **Supp. IV Part 1: 259–278,** 333, 404; **Supp. X:** 290

"Erectus" (Karr), **Supp. XI:** 243

"Ere Sleep Comes Down to Soothe the Weary Eyes" (Dunbar), **Supp. II Part 1:** 199, 207–208

Erikson, Erik, **I:** 58, 214, 218

Erisman, Fred, **Supp. VIII:** 126

Erkkila, Betsy, **Retro. Supp. I:** 42

"Ernest: or Parent for a Day" (Bourne), **I:** 232

Ernst, Max, **Retro. Supp. II:** 321

"Eros" (Komunyakaa), **Supp. XIII:** 130

Eros and Civilization (Marcuse), **Supp. XII:** 2

"Eros at Temple Stream" (Levertov), **Supp. III Part 1:** 278–279

Eros the Bittersweet (Carson), **Supp. XII:** 97, **98–99**

"Eros Turannos" (Robinson), **III:** 510, 512, 513–516, 517, 518

"Eroticism in Women" (Nin), **Supp. X:** 195

"Errand" (Carver), **Supp. III Part 1:** 149

Erskine, Albert, **IV:** 261; **Retro. Supp. II:** 117

Erskine, John, **I:** 223; **Supp. X:** 183; **Supp. XIV:** 120

Erstein, Hap, **Supp. IV Part 2:** 589, 590

"Escape" (MacLeish), **III:** 4

Escape Artist, The (Wagoner), **Supp. IX:** 324, **334–335**

Escher, M. C., **Supp. XII:** 26

"Escudilla" (Leopold), **Supp. XIV:** 188

Espen, Hal, **Supp. X:** 15

Espey, John, **III:** 463, 468, 478

Essais (Renouvier), **II:** 344–345

"Essay: The Love of Old Houses" (Doty), **Supp. XI:** 136

Essay Concerning Human Understanding, An (Locke), **I:** 554; **II:** 8, 348–349

Essay on American Poetry (Brown), **Supp. I Part 1:** 156

"Essay on Aristocracy" (Paine), **Supp. I Part 2:** 515

"Essay on Friendship, An" (McClatchy), **Supp. XII:** 258–259

Essay on Man (Pope), **II:** 111; **Supp. I Part 2:** 516

Essay on Our Changing Order (Veblen), **Supp. I Part 2:** 629, 642

"Essay on Poetics" (Ammons), **Supp. VII:** 29–31

Essay on Projects (Defoe), **II:** 104

"Essay on Psychiatrists" (Pinsky), **Supp. VI:** 237, 238, 241, 242, 249, 250

Essay on Rime (Shapiro), **I:** 430; **Supp. II Part 2:** 702, 703, 708–711

"Essay on Sanity" (Dunn), **Supp. XI:** 147

"Essay on the Character of Robespierre" (Paine), **Supp. I Part 2:** 515

Essay on the Chinese Written Character (Fenollosa), **III:** 474

"Essay on What I Think About Most" (Carson), **Supp. XII: 111–112**

Essays (Emerson), **II:** 1, 7, 8, 12–13, 15, 21

Essays, Speeches, and Public Letters by William Faulkner (Meriweather, ed.), **Retro. Supp. I:** 77

Essays in Anglo-Saxon Law (Adams), **I:** 5

Essays in London (James), **II:** 336

Essays in Radical Empiricism (James), **II:** 355, 356–357

Essays on Norman Mailer (Lucid), **Retro. Supp. II:** 195

Essays on the Nature and Principles of Taste (Alison), **Supp. I Part 1:** 151

Essays to Do Good (Mather), **II:** 104; **Supp. II Part 2:** 461, 467

"Essay Toward a Point of View, An" (Brooks), **I:** 244

Essential Haiku, The (Hass), **Supp. VI:** 102

Essential Keats (Levine, ed.), **Supp. V:** 179

"Essential Oils—are wrung" (Dickinson), **I:** 471; **Retro. Supp. I:** 43, 46

"Essentials" (Toomer), **Supp. III Part 2:** 486

Essentials: A Philosophy of Life in Three Hundred Definitions and Aphorisms (Toomer), **Supp. III Part 2:** 486

Essentials: Definitions and Aphorisms (Toomer), **Supp. IX:** 320

"Essentials of Spontaneous Prose" (Kerouac), **Supp. III Part 1:** 227–228

"Estate Sale" (Nye), **Supp. XIII:** 283

Estess, Sybil, **Supp. IV Part 2:** 449, 452

Esther (Adams), **I:** 9–10, 20

"Esther" (Toomer), **Supp. IX:** 313–314

"Esthétique du Mal" (Stevens), **IV:** 79; **Retro. Supp. I:** 300, 311, 312

"Estoy-eh-muut and the Kunideeyahs (Arrowboy and the Destroyers)" (film), **Supp. IV Part 2:** 560

Estrada, Genaro, **Retro. Supp. II:** 89

Estray, The (Longfellow, ed.), **Retro. Supp. II:** 155

Esty, William, **III:** 358

"Etching, An" (Masters), **Supp. I Part 2:** 458

"Eternal Goodness, The" (Whittier), **Supp. I Part 2:** 704

"Eternity, An" (W. C. Williams), **Retro. Supp. I:** 423

"Eternity Is Now" (Roethke), **III:** 544–545

"Ethan Brand" (Hawthorne), **II:** 227

Ethan Frome (Wharton), **IV:** 316–317, 327; **Retro. Supp. I:** 372–373; **Supp. IX:** 108

Ethics (Spinoza), **IV:** 12; **Retro. Supp. II:** 300

"Ethics of Culture, The" (Locke), **Supp. XIV:** 211

Etulain, Richard, **Supp. IV Part 2:** 597, 601, 604, 606, 607, 608, 610, 611

Euclid, **III:** 6, 620

"Euclid Alone Has Looked on Beauty Bare" (Millay), **III:** 133

Eugene, Frank, **Supp. X:** 204

Eugene Onegin (Pushkin), **III:** 246, 263

Eugene Onegin (Pushkin; Nabokov, trans.), **Retro. Supp. I:** 266, 267, 272

Eugénie, Empress, **IV:** 309

Eugénie Grandet (Balzac), **II:** 328

"Eugénie Grandet" (Barthelme), **Supp. IV Part 1:** 47

"Eulogy for Richard Hugo (1923–1982)" (Wagoner), **Supp. IX:** 330–331

"Eulogy on the Flapper" (Z. Fitzgerald), **Supp. IX:** 71

Eumenides (Aeschylus), **Retro. Supp. I:** 65

"E Unibus Pluram: Television and U.S. Fiction" (Wallace), **Supp. X:** 315–316

"Euphemisms" (Matthews), **Supp. IX: 167–168**

Eureka (Poe), **III:** 409, 424, 428–429

Eurekas (Goldbarth), **Supp. XII:** 181

Euripides, **I:** 325; **II:** 8, 282, 543; **III:** 22, 145, 398; **IV:** 370; **Supp. I Part 1:** 268, 269, 270; **Supp. I Part 2:** 482; **Supp. V:** 277

"Euripides and Professor Murray" (Eliot), **Supp. I Part 1:** 268

"Euripides—A Playwright" (West), **IV:** 286; **Retro. Supp. II:** 326

"Europe" (Ashbery), **Supp. III Part 1:** 7–10, 13, 18

European Discovery of America, The: The Northern Voyages (Morison), **Supp. I Part 2:** 496–497

European Discovery of America, The: The Southern Voyages (Morison), **Supp. I Part 2:** 497

Europeans, The (James), **I:** 452; **II:** 327, 328; **Retro. Supp. I:** 216, 220

"Europe! Europe!" (Ginsberg), **Supp. II Part 1:** 320, 322

Europe of Trusts, The: Selected Poems (Howe), **Supp. IV Part 2:** 420, 422, 426

Europe without Baedeker (Wilson), **IV:** 429

Eurydice in the Underworld (Acker), **Supp. XII:** 7

Eustace, Saint, **II:** 215

Eustace Chisholm and the Works (Purdy), **Supp. VII:** 273–274, 279–280

"Euthanasia" (Tate), **IV:** 122

Eva-Mary (McCarriston), **Supp. XIV:** 259, 260, **263–268**

"Evangeline" (Dixon), **Supp. XII:** 153

Evangeline (Longfellow), **II:** 489, 501–502; **Retro. Supp. II:** 155, **156–159,** 162, 164; **Supp. I Part 2:** 586

Evans, Mary Ann. *See* Eliot, George

Evans, Oliver, **Supp. IV Part 1:** 85, 91

Evans, Sandy, **Supp. XIII:** 129

Evans, Walker, **I:** 36, 38, 293; **Retro. Supp. II:** 85

"Eve" (W. C. Williams), **Retro. Supp. I:** 423

Even Cowgirls Get the Blues (Robbins), **Supp. X:** 259, 260, 261, 262–263, 264, 266, **269–271,** 272, 274, 277, 284; **Supp. XIII:** 11

"Evening" (Carver), **Supp. III Part 1:** 148

Evening (Minot), **Supp. VI:** 204–205, 208, **213–215**

"Evening at a Country Inn" (Kenyon), **Supp. VII:** 167

"Evening in a Sugar Orchard" (Frost), **Retro. Supp. I:** 133

"Evening in Nuevo Leon, An" (Caldwell), **I:** 309

"Evening in the Sanitarium" (Bogan), **Supp. III Part 1:** 61

"Evening on the Cote d'Azur" (Yates), **Supp. XI:** 349

Evening Performance, An: New and Selected Short Stories (Garrett), **Supp. VII:** 109

"Evenings at Home" (Hardwick), **Supp. III Part 1:** 195–196

"Evening's at Seven, The" (Thurber), **Supp. I Part 2:** 616

"Evening Star" (Bogan), **Supp. III Part 1:** 56

Evening Star, The (McMurtry), **Supp. V:** 230

Evening Star, The (screenplay) (McMurtry), **Supp. V:** 232

"Evening Sun" (Kenyon), **Supp. VII:** 168

Evening Sun Turned Crimson, The (Huncke), **Supp. XIV:** 140, 149–150

"Evening Sun Turned Crimson, The" (Huncke), **Supp. XIV:** 137–138, 139

"Evening Wind, The" (Bryant), **Supp. I Part 1:** 164

"Evening without Angels" (Stevens), **Retro. Supp. I:** 302

Evening with Richard Nixon, An (Vidal), **Supp. IV Part 2:** 683

"Even Sea, The" (Swenson), **Supp. IV Part 2:** 641

Even Stephen (Perelman and West), **Retro. Supp. II:** 328

"Event, An" (Wilbur), **Supp. III Part 2:** 547, 554

"Event, The" (Dove), **Supp. IV Part 1:** 242, 247–248

"Eventide" (Brooks), **Supp. III Part 1:** 73

"Eventide" (Purdy), **Supp. VII:** 270

Eve of Saint Agnes, The (Keats), **II:** 82, 531

"Eve of St. Agnes, The" (Clampitt), **Supp. IX:** 40

"Ever a Bridegroom: Reflections on the Failure of Texas Literature" (McMurtry), **Supp. V:** 225

Everett, Alexander Hill, **Supp. I Part 1:** 152

Everlasting Story of Nory, The (Baker), **Supp. XIII:** 52, **Supp. XIII: 53–55**

Evers, Medgar, **IV:** 280; **Retro. Supp. II:** 13; **Supp. I Part 1:** 52, 65

Everwine, Peter, **Supp. V:** 180; **Supp. XIII:** 312

"Everybody's Protest Novel" (Baldwin), **Retro. Supp. II:** 4; **Supp. I Part 1:** 50, 51

"Everybody's Reading Li Po' Silk-screened on a Purple T-Shirt" (Komunyakaa), **Supp. XIII:** 120

"Everybody Was Very Nice" (Benét), **Supp. XI:** 53

"Every-Day Girl, A" (Jewett), **Retro. Supp. II:** 132

"Everyday Use" (Walker), **Supp. III Part 2:** 534

"Every-Day Work" (Jewett), **Retro. Supp. II:** 132

Every Pleasure (Goldbarth), **Supp. XII:** 181

Every Soul Is a Circus (Lindsay), **Supp. I Part 2:** 384, 394, 399

"Everything Is a Human Being" (Walker), **Supp. III Part 2:** 527

Everything Is Illuminated (Foer), **Supp. XII:** 169

"Everything Stuck to Him" (Carver), **Supp. III Part 1:** 143

Everything That Rises Must Converge (O'Connor), **III:** 339, 348–349, 350–351; **Retro. Supp. II:** 235, **236–237**

"Everything That Rises Must Converge" (O'Connor), **III:** 349, 352, 357; **Retro. Supp. II:** 236

Eve's Diary (Twain), **IV:** 208–209

"Eve the Fox" (Gunn Allen), **Supp. IV Part 1:** 331

"Evidence" (Harjo), **Supp. XII:** 219

Evidence of the Senses, The (Kelley), **Supp. IV Part 2:** 529

Evidence of Things Not Seen, The (Baldwin), **Retro. Supp. II:** 15

"Evil Seekers, The" (Sexton), **Supp. II Part 2:** 696

"Evolution" (Swenson), **Supp. IV Part 2:** 639

Ewing, Jon, **Supp. X:** 253

Ewings, The (O'Hara), **III:** 383

"Examination of the Hero in a Time of War" (Stevens), **Retro. Supp. I:** 305–306, 308

"Excavation of Troy" (MacLeish), **III:** 18

Excellent Becomes the Permanent, The (Addams), **Supp. I Part 1:** 25

"Excelsior" (Longfellow), **Retro. Supp. II:** 169

"Excerpts from Swan Lake" (Cameron), **Supp. XII:** 80, **84**

"Excerpts from the Epistemology Workshops" (Rand), **Supp. IV Part 2:** 529

"Excess of Charity" (Wylie), **Supp. I Part 2:** 720

"Exchange, The" (Swenson), **Supp. IV Part 2:** 644

"Exclusive" (Olds), **Supp. X:** 206

"Excrement Poem, The" (Kumin), **Supp. IV Part 2:** 448

"Excursion" (Garrett), **Supp. VII:** 100

Excursions (Thoreau), **IV:** 188

Executioner's Song, The (Mailer), **Retro. Supp. II:** 108, 209

Ex-Friends: Falling Out with Allen Ginsberg, Lionel and Diana Trilling, Lillian Hellman, Hannah Arendt, and Norman Mailer (Podhoretz), **Supp. VIII:** 239, **242–244**

"Exhausted Bug, The" (Bly), **Supp. IV Part 1:** 73

"Exhortation" (Bogan), **Supp. III Part 1:** 58

"Exhortation" (McKay), **Supp. X:** 135

"Exile" (Gass), **Supp. VI:** 92

"Exile" (Oates), **Supp. II Part 2:** 523

Exile, The (Buck), **Supp. II Part 1:** 119, 131

"Exiles, The" (Bradbury), **Supp. IV**

Part 1: 113

"Exiles, The" (Whittier), **Supp. I Part 2:** 692–693

Exiles and Fabrications (Scott), **II:** 512

Exile's Daughter, The (Spencer), **Supp. II Part 1:** 121

"Exile's Departure, The" (Whittier), **Supp. I Part 2:** 683

Exiles from Paradise: Zelda and Scott Fitzgerald (Mayfield), **Supp. IX:** 65

"Exile's Letter" (Karr), **Supp. XI:** 241

Exile's Return (Cowley), **Supp. III Part 1:** 136, 138, 140, 141, 144, 147, 148

"Exile's Return, The" (Lowell), **II:** 539; **Retro. Supp. II:** 187

"Existences" (Stafford), **Supp. XI:** 324

Exit to Eden (Rampling), **Supp. VII:** 301–302

Exodus (biblical book), **IV:** 300

Exodus (Uris), **Supp. IV Part 1:** 379

"Exorcism" (Snodgrass), **Supp. VI:** 314

"Exorcism, An" (Malamud), **Supp. I Part 2:** 435

Exorcist, The (film), **Supp. I Part 1:** 66

"Expanses" (Dickey), **Supp. IV Part 1:** 186

"Ex Parte" (Lardner), **II:** 432

"Expectant Father Compares His Wife to a Rabbit, An" (White), **Supp. I Part 2:** 678

"Expedition to the Pole, An" (Dillard), **Supp. VI:** 32, 34

"Expelled" (Cheever), **Supp. I Part 1:** 174, 186

Expense of Greatness, The (Blackmur), **Supp. II Part 1:** 90, 107

Expense of Vision, The (Holland), **Retro. Supp. I:** 216

"Expensive Gifts" (Miller), **Supp. XII:** 294

"Expensive Moment, The" (Paley), **Supp. VI:** 222, **227–228,** 230

Expensive People (Oates), **Supp. II Part 2:** 509, 510–511

"Experience" (Emerson), **Supp. XIV:** 42

"Experience and Fiction" (Jackson), **Supp. IX:** 121

"Experience and the Objects of Knowledge in the Philosophy of F. H. Bradley" (Eliot), **I:** 572; **Retro. Supp. I:** 59

Experience of Literature, The (Trilling), **Supp. III Part 2:** 493

"Experiences and Principles of an

Historian" (Morison), **Supp. I Part 2:** 492

Experimental Death Unit # 1 (Baraka), **Supp. II Part 1:** 46

"Experimental Life, The" (Bourne), **I:** 217, 220

"Experiment in Misery, An" (S. Crane), **I:** 411; **Retro. Supp. II:** 97

Experiments and Observations on Electricity (Franklin), **II:** 102, 114–115

"Expiation" (Wharton), **Retro. Supp. I:** 367

"Explaining Evil" (Gordon), **Supp. IV Part 1:** 310

"Explanation" (Stevens), **IV:** 79

Explanation of America, An (Pinsky), **Supp. VI:** 237, **241–243**

"Exploit" (Wharton), **IV:** 324

"Exploration in the Great Tuolumne Cañon" (Muir), **Supp. IX:** 181

"Explorer, The" (Brooks), **Supp. III Part 1:** 79–80

"Exploring the Magalloway" (Parkman), **Supp. II Part 2:** 591

Expositor's Bible, The (G. A. Smith), **III:** 199

Expressions of Sea Level (Ammons), **Supp. VII:** 24, 28, 36

Extract from Captain Stormfeld's Visit to Heaven (Twain), **IV:** 209–210

Extracts from Adam's Diary (Twain), **IV:** 208–209

"Exulting, The" (Roethke), **III:** 544

"Eye, The" (Bowles), **Supp. IV Part 1:** 93

Eye, The (Nabokov), **III:** 251

Eye-Beaters, Blood, Victory, Madness, Buckhead and Mercy, The (Dickey), **Supp. IV Part 1:** 178, 182–183

"Eye for an Eye, An" (Humphrey), **Supp. IX:** 108

"Eye in the Rock, The" (Haines), **Supp. XII:** 208, 209

"Eye-Mote, The" (Plath), **Retro. Supp. II:** 246, 247

"Eye of Paris, The" (H. Miller), **III:** 183–184

Eye of the Poet, The: Six Views of the Art and Craft of Poetry (Citino, ed.), **Supp. XIII:** 115

"Eye of the Rock, The" (Haines), **Supp. XII:** 208

"Eye of the Story, The" (Porter), **IV:** 279

Eye of the Story, The: Selected Essays and Reviews (Welty), **Retro. Supp. I:** 339, 342, 344, 345, 346, 351, 354, 355, 356

"Eyes, The" (Wharton), **IV:** 315

"Eyes like They Say the Devil Has"

(Ríos), **Supp. IV Part 2:** 543, 544

Eyes of the Dragon, The (King), **Supp. V:** 139, 152

Eyes of the Heart: A Memoir of the Lost and Found (Buechner), **Supp. XII:** 53

"Eyes of Zapata" (Cisneros), **Supp. VII:** 70

"Eyes to See" (Cozzens), **I:** 374

Eye-to-Eye (Nye), **Supp. XIII:** 274

Eysturoy, Annie O., **Supp. IV Part 1:** 321, 322, 323, 328

Ezekiel (biblical book), **II:** 541

Ezekiel, Mordecai, **Supp. I Part 2:** 645

"Ezra Pound: His Cantos" (Zukofsky), **Supp. III Part 2:** 612, 619, 622

Ezra Pound's Mauberley (Espey), **III:** 463

"Ezra Pound's Very Useful Labors" (Schwartz), **Supp. II Part 2:** 644

"F. S. F., 1896–1996, R.I.P." (Doctorow), **Retro. Supp. I:** 97

F. Scott Fitzgerald: A Critical Portrait (Piper), **Supp. IX:** 65

Faas, Ekbert, **Supp. VIII:** 292

"Fabbri Tape, The" (Auchincloss), **Supp. IV Part 1:** 21–22

Faber, Geoffrey, **Retro. Supp. I:** 63

"Fable" (Merwin), **Supp. III Part 1:** 343

"Fable" (Wylie), **Supp. I Part 2:** 714

Fable, A (Faulkner), **II:** 55, 73; **Retro. Supp. I:** 74

"Fable, A" (Glück), **Supp. V:** 86

"Fable, The" (Winters), **Supp. II Part 2:** 792, 793, 796

Fable for Critics, A (Lowell), **Supp. I Part 2:** 406, 407–408, 409, 412–413, 416, 420, 422

"Fable of the War, A" (Nemerov), **III:** 272

Fables (Gay), **II:** 111

Fables and Distances: New and Selected Essays (Haines), **Supp. XII:** 197, 199, 207–208, 211

Fables for Our Time (Thurber), **Supp. I Part 2:** 610

Fables of Identity: Studies in Poetic Mythology (Frye), **Supp. X:** 80

Fables of La Fontaine, The (Moore), **III:** 194, 215

"Fables of the Fallen Guy" (Rosaldo), **Supp. IV Part 2:** 544

"Fables of the Moscow Subway" (Nemerov), **III:** 271

Fabulators, The (Scholes), **Supp. V:** 40

Fabulous Small Jews (Epstein), **Supp. XIV:** 112

Face against the Glass, The (Francis), **Supp. IX: 80–81**
Face of Time, The (Farrell), **II:** 28, 34, 35, 39
Faces of Jesus, The (Buechner), **Supp. XII:** 53
"Facing It" (Komunyakaa), **Supp. XIII:** 117, 124, 125
"Facing West from California's Shores" (Jeffers), **Supp. II Part 2:** 437–438
"Fact in Fiction, The" (McCarthy), **II:** 562
"Facts" (Levine), **Supp. V:** 193
"Facts" (Oliver), **Supp. VII:** 231–232
"Facts" (Snyder), **Supp. VIII:** 301
"Facts, The" (Lardner), **II:** 431
Facts, The: A Novelist's Autobiography (Roth), **Retro. Supp. II:** 280, 291; **Supp. III Part 2:** 401, 405, 417, 426
"Facts and Traditions Respecting the Existence of Indigenous Intermittent Fever in New England" (Holmes), **Supp. I Part 1:** 303
"Facts in the Case of M. Valdemar, The" (Poe), **III:** 416
Faderman, Lillian, **Retro. Supp. II:** 135; **Supp. XIII:** 313
Fadiman, Clifton, **II:** 430, 431, 443, 591–592; **Supp. IX:** 8
"Fado" (McClatchy), **Supp. XII:** 265–266
Faerie Queene, The (Spenser), **III:** 487; **IV:** 253; **Supp. XIV:** 6
Faery, Rebecca Blevins, **Retro. Supp. I:** 374
Fagan, Kathy, **Supp. V:** 180
Fahrenheit 451 (Bradbury), **Supp. IV Part 1:** 101, 102, 104, 107–109, 110, 113; **Supp. XIII:** 29
"Failure of David Barry, The" (Jewett), **Retro. Supp. II:** 132
Faint Perfume (Gale), **Supp. I Part 2:** 613
Fair, Bryan K., **Supp. VIII:** 128
Fairchild, Frances. *See* Bryant, Mrs. William Cullen (Frances Fairchild)
Fairchild, Hoxie, **Supp. XIV:** 120
Fairfield, Flora (pseudonym). *See* Alcott, Louisa May
Fairly Conventional Woman, A (Shields), **Supp. VII:** 312, 316, 318
"Fairly Sad Tale, A" (Parker), **Supp. IX:** 192
Fair Warning (R. O. Butler), **Supp. XII:** 62, **75–76**
Faith (Goldbarth), **Supp. XII:** 181, **182–183**
Faith and History (Niebuhr), **III:** 308
Faith and the Good Thing (Johnson),

Supp. VI: 187, **188–190,** 191, 193, 194, 196
Faith for Living (Mumford), **Supp. II Part 2:** 479–480
Faithful Narrative of the Surprising Works of God in the Conversion of Many Hundred Souls in Northampton, and the Neighboring Towns and Villages of New-Hampshire in New-England, A (Edwards), **I:** 545, 562
"Faith Healer" (Komunyakaa), **Supp. XIII:** 117
"Faith in a Tree" (Paley), **Supp. VI:** 217–218, 224, 230
"Faith in Search of Understanding" (Updike), **Retro. Supp. I:** 327
"Faith of an Historian" (Morison), **Supp. I Part 2:** 492
Falcoff, Mark, **Supp. VIII:** 88
Falcon (Hammett), **Supp. IV Part 1:** 351
Falconer (Cheever), **Supp. I Part 1:** 176, 193–195, 196
Falconer, A. F., **Supp. XIV:** 2
"Falcon of Ser Federigo, The" (Longfellow), **II:** 505
Falk, Peter, **Supp. XI:** 174
Falkner, Dean, **II:** 55
Falkner, John, **II:** 55
Falkner, Mrs. Murray C. (Maud Butler), **II:** 55
Falkner, Murray, **II:** 55
Falkner, Murray C., **II:** 55
Falkner, William C., **II:** 55
"Fall" (Francis), **Supp. IX:** 76
"Fall 1961" (Lowell), **II:** 550
"Fall in Corrales" (Wilbur), **Supp. III Part 2:** 556
Falling (Dickey), **Supp. IV Part 1:** 178, 181–182
"Falling" (Dickey), **Supp. IV Part 1:** 182
"Falling Asleep over the Aeneid" (Lowell), **II:** 542; **Retro. Supp. II:** 188
Falling in Place (Beattie), **Supp. V:** 28–29
"Falling into Holes in Our Sentences" (Bly), **Supp. IV Part 1:** 71
"Fall Journey" (Stafford), **Supp. XI:** 322
Fall of America, The: 1965–1971 (Ginsberg), **Supp. II Part 1:** 323, 325, 327
Fall of the City, The: A Verse Play for Radio (MacLeish), **III:** 20
"Fall of the House of Usher, The" (Poe), **III:** 412, 414, 415, 419; **Retro. Supp. II:** 270
Fallows, James, **Supp. VIII:** 241

Fall & Rise (Dixon), **Supp. XII:** 147–148, 148, 153, 157
"Falls, The" (Olds), **Supp. X:** 215
"Falls Fight, The" (Howe), **Supp. IV Part 2:** 431–432
Falon, Janet Ruth, **Supp. IV Part 2:** 422
"False Dawn" (Wharton), **Retro. Supp. I:** 381
"False Documents" (Doctorow), **Supp. IV Part 1:** 220, 236
"False Leads" (Komunyakaa), **Supp. XIII:** 116
Fame & Folly: Essays (Ozick), **Supp. V:** 272
"Familiar Epistle to a Friend, A" (Lowell), **Supp. I Part 2:** 416
Familiar Territory: Observations on American Life (Epstein), **Supp. XIV:106**
"Family" (Wilson), **IV:** 426
"Family Affair, A" (Chopin), **Retro. Supp. II:** 71
Family Arsenal, The (Theroux), **Supp. VIII:** 322
Family Chronicle: An Odyssey from Russia to America (Reznikoff), **Supp. XIV:** 277, 288, 289
"Family History" (Mora), **Supp. XIII:** 217
Family Life (Banks), **Supp. V:** 7
"Family Matters" (Alvarez), **Supp. VII:** 10
Family Moskat, The (Singer), **IV:** 1, 17, 20, 46; **Retro. Supp. II:** 304
"Family of Little Feet, The" (Cisneros), **Supp. VII:** 61
Family Party, A (O'Hara), **III:** 362
Family Pictures (Brooks), **Supp. III Part 1:** 69, 85, 86
Family Pictures (Miller), **Supp. XII:** 291, **295–297,** 299
Family Reunion, The (Eliot), **I:** 570–571, 572, 581, 584, 588; **Retro. Supp. I:** 62, 65
"Family Secrets" (Kingsolver), **Supp. VII:** 208
"Family Sideshow, The" (Karr), **Supp. XI:** 245
"Family Ties" (Mora), **Supp. XIII:** 215
"Family Tree" (Komunyakaa), **Supp. XIII:** 117–118, 126
Famous American Negroes (Hughes), **Supp. I Part 1:** 345
"Famous Gilson Bequest, The" (Bierce), **I:** 204
Famous Negro Music Makers (Hughes), **Supp. I Part 1:** 345
"Famous New York Trials" (Ellison), **Supp. II Part 1:** 230

Fanatics, The (Dunbar), **Supp. II Part 1**: 213–214
Fancher, Edwin, **Retro. Supp. II**: 202
"Fancy and Imagination" (Poe), **III**: 421
"Fancy Flights" (Beattie), **Supp. V**: 25
"Fancy's Show Box" (Hawthorne), **II**: 238
"Fancy Woman, The" (Taylor), **Supp. V**: 316–317, 319, 323
"Fang" (Goldbarth), **Supp. XII**: 190
Fanny: Being the True History of the Adventures of Fanny Hackabout-Jones (Jong), **Supp. V**: 115, 127
Fanny Hill (Cleland), **Supp. V**: 48, 127
Fan of Swords, The (al-Maghut), **Supp. XIII**: 278
Fanon, Frantz, **Retro. Supp. II**: 118; **Supp. X**: 131, 141
Fanshawe (Hawthorne), **II**: 223–224; **Retro. Supp. I**: 149, 151
"Fantasia on 'The Nut-Brown Maid'" (Ashbery), **Supp. III Part 1**: 19
"Fantasia on the Relations between Poetry and Photography" (Strand), **Supp. IV Part 2**: 631
"Fantastic Fables" (Bierce), **I**: 209
Fante, John, **Supp. XI**: **159–176**
Faraday, Michael, **I**: 480–481
"Farewell" (Emerson), **II**: 13
Farewell, My Lovely (Chandler), **Supp. IV Part 1**: 122, 125–126, 127, 128, 130
"Farewell, My Lovely!" (White), **Supp. I Part 2**: 661–663, 665
"Farewell Performance" (Merrill), **Supp. III Part 1**: 336–337
Farewell-Sermon Preached at the First Precinct in Northampton, after the People's Publick Rejection of their Minister, A (Edwards), **I**: 548, 562
"Farewell Sweet Dust" (Wylie), **Supp. I Part 2**: 727–728
Farewell to Arms, A (Hemingway), **I**: 212, 421, 476, 477; **II**: 68–69, 248–249, 252–253, 254, 255, 262, 265; **Retro. Supp. I**: 171, 178, **180–182**, 187, 189; **Retro. Supp. II**: 108; **Supp. IV Part 1**: 380–381, 381; **Supp. VIII**: 179; **Supp. XII**: 241–242
"Farewell to Miles" (Berryman), **I**: 173
Farewell to Reform (Chamberlain), **Supp. I Part 2**: 647
"Farewell to the Middle Class" (Updike), **Retro. Supp. I**: 321
Far Field, The (Roethke), **III**: 528, 529, 539, 545, 547–548
"Far Field, The" (Roethke), **III**: 537, 540

Far-Flung (Cameron), **Supp. XII**: 81
Far from the Madding Crowd (Hardy), **II**: 291
Faris, Athénaíse Charleville, **Supp. I Part 1**: 204
Farley, Abbie, **I**: 458
Farley, Harriet, **Supp. XIII**: 140
"Farm, The" (Creeley), **Supp. IV Part 1**: 155
Farmer (Harrison), **Supp. VIII**: 39, **44–45**
Farmer, Richard, **Supp. XIV**: 2
"Farmer and the Fox, The" (Leopold), **Supp. XIV**: 188
"Farmers' Daughters, The" (W. C. Williams), **Retro. Supp. I**: 423
Farmers Hotel, The (O'Hara), **III**: 361
"Farmer's Sorrow, A" (Jewett), **Retro. Supp. II**: 132
"Farmer's Wife, The" (Sexton), **Supp. II Part 2**: 676
"Farm Implements and Rutabagas in a Landscape" (Ashbery), **Supp. III Part 1**: 13
Farming: A Hand Book (Berry), **Supp. X**: 31, 35
"Farm on the Great Plains, The" (Stafford), **Supp. XI**: 322
Farnol, Jeffrey, **Supp. I Part 2**: 653
Far North (Shepard), **Supp. III Part 2**: 433, 435
"Far Northern Birch, The" (Francis), **Supp. IX**: 90
Farnsworth, Elizabeth, **Supp. XI**: 139
Farrand, Max, **II**: 122
Farrar, Geraldine, **Retro. Supp. I**: 10
Farrar, John, **II**: 191; **Supp. XI**: 47
Farrell, Barry, **Supp. XIV**: 142
Farrell, James Francis, **II**: 25, 26
Farrell, James T., **I**: 97, 288, 475, 508, 517, 519; **II**: **25–53**, 416, 424; **III**: 28, 114, 116, 118, 119, 317, 382; **IV**: 211, 286; **Retro. Supp. II**: 196, 327; **Supp. I Part 2**: 679; **Supp. VIII**: 96, 97; **Supp. XIV**: 3
Farrell, John, **II**: 26
Farrell, John C., **Supp. I Part 1**: 24
Farrell, Kevin, **II**: 26
Farrell, Mary, **II**: 25
Farrell, Mrs. James T. (Dorothy Butler), **II**: 26
Farrell, Mrs. James T. (Hortense Alden), **II**: 26, 27, 45, 48
"Far Rockaway" (Schwartz), **Supp. II Part 2**: 649
Far Side of the Dollar, The (Macdonald), **Supp. IV Part 2**: 473
Farther Off from Heaven (Humphrey), **Supp. IX**: 93, 96, 101, **103–104**, 105, 109

Far Tortuga (Matthiessen), **Supp. V**: 201, 206–207
"Fascinating Fascism" (Sontag), **Supp. III Part 2**: 465
"Fascination of Cities, The" (Hughes), **Supp. I Part 1**: 325
Fashion, Power, Guilt and the Charity of Families (Shields), **Supp. VII**: 323
Fasman, Jonathan, **Supp. V**: 253
Fast, Howard, **Supp. I Part 1**: 295
Fast, Jonathan, **Supp. V**: 115
Fast and Loose (Wharton), **Retro. Supp. I**: 361
"Fastest Runner on Sixty-first Street, The" (Farrell), **II**: 45
"Fat" (Carver), **Supp. III Part 1**: 141
Fatal Interview (Millay), **III**: 128–129, 130
"Fatality" (Bausch), **Supp. VII**: 54
Fatal Lady (film), **Supp. XIII**: 166
"Fate" (Emerson), **II**: 2–3, 4, 16; **Supp. XIV**: 42
"Fate" (Mailer), **Retro. Supp. II**: 207
"Fate of Pleasure, The" (Trilling), **Supp. III Part 2**: 510
Fate of the Jury, The (Masters), **Supp. I Part 2**: 466, 468, 469
"Fat Girl, The" (Dubus), **Supp. VII**: 84, 85
"Father" (Levine), **Supp. V**: 188
"Father" (Walker), **Supp. III Part 2**: 522
"Father, The" (Carver), **Supp. III Part 1**: 137, 140
Father, The (Olds), **Supp. X**: **209–211**
"Father Abraham" (Faulkner), **Retro. Supp. I**: 81, 82
Fatheralong: A Meditation on Fathers and Sons, Race and Society (Wideman), **Supp. X**: 320, 332–333, 334, 335
"Father and Daughter" (Eberhart), **I**: 539
Father and Glorious Descendant (Lowe), **Supp. X**: 291
"Father and Son" (Eberhart), **I**: 539
Father and Son (Farrell), **II**: 34, 35, 290, 291
Father and Son (Gosse), **Supp. VIII**: 157
"Father and Son" (Hughes), **Retro. Supp. I**: 204; **Supp. I Part 1**: 329, 339
"Father and Son" (Kunitz), **Supp. III Part 1**: 262
"Father and Son" (Schwartz), **Supp. II Part 2**: 650
Father Bombo's Pilgrimage to Mecca (Freneau), **Supp. II Part 1**: 254

"Father Guzman" (Stern), **Supp. IX: 293,** 296

"Father out Walking on the Lawn, A" (Dove), **Supp. IV Part 1:** 246

"Fathers" (Creeley), **Supp. IV Part 1:** 157–158

Fathers, The (Tate), **IV:** 120, 127, 130, 131–133, 134, 141; **Supp. X:** 52

"Fathers and Sons" (Hemingway), **II:** 249, 265–266; **Retro. Supp. I:** 175

"Father's Body, The" (Dickey), **Supp. IV Part 1:** 176

"Father's Story, A" (Dubus), **Supp. VII:** 88

"Father's Voice" (Stafford), **Supp. XI:** 322

"Fat Man, Floating" (Dunn), **Supp. XI:** 144

Faulkner: A Collection of Critical Essays (Warren), **Retro. Supp. I:** 73

Faulkner, William, **I:** 54, 97, 99, 105, 106, 115, 117, 118, 123, 190, 204–205, 211, 288, 289, 291, 292, 297, 305, 324, 374, 378, 423, 480, 517; **II:** 28, 51, **54–76,** 131, 174, 194, 217, 223, 228, 230, 259, 301, 306, 431, 458–459, 542, 594, 606; **III:** 45, 70, 108, 164, 218, 220, 222, 236–237, 244, 292, 334, 350, 382, 418, 453, 454, 482, 483; **IV:** 2, 4, 33, 49, 97, 98, 100, 101, 120, 131, 203, 207, 211, 217, 237, 257, 260, 261, 279, 280, 352, 461, 463; **Retro. Supp. I: 73–95,** 215, 339, 347, 356, 379, 382; **Retro. Supp. II:** 19, 221, 326; **Supp. I Part 1:** 196, 197, 242, 372; **Supp. I Part 2:** 450, 621; **Supp. III Part 1:** 384–385, 396; **Supp. IV Part 1:** 47, 130, 257, 342; **Supp. IV Part 2:** 434, 463, 468, 502, 677, 682; **Supp. V:** 58, 59, 138, 210, 226, 237, 261, 262, 334–336; **Supp. VIII:** 37, 39, 40, 104, 105, 108, 175, 176, 180, 181, 183, 184, 188, 189, 215; **Supp. IX:** 20, 95; **Supp. X:** 44, 228; **Supp. XI:** 92, 247; **Supp. XII:** 16, 289, 310, 313; **Supp. XIII:** 100, 169; **Supp. XIV:** 1, 12–13, 21, 24, 93, 306

Faulkner at Nagano (Jelliffe, ed.), **I:** 289; **II:** 63, 65

Faulkner-Cowley File, The: Letters and Memories 1944–1962 (Cowley, ed.), **Retro. Supp. I:** 73, 92; **Supp. II Part 1:** 140, 141

"Faun" (Plath), **Supp. I Part 2:** 537

"Fauna" (Jeffers), **Supp. II Part 2:** 415

Fauset, Jessie, **Supp. I Part 1:** 321, 325; **Supp. IV Part 1:** 164

Faust (Goethe), **I:** 396; **II:** 489; **III:** 395; **Supp. II Part 1:** 16; **Supp. IX:** 141

Faust, Clarence H., **II:** 20

Faute de l'Abbé Mouret, La (Zola), **III:** 322

Favor Island (Merwin), **Supp. III Part 1:** 346, 347

"Favrile" (Doty), **Supp. XI:** 131

Fay, Bernard, **IV:** 41

"Fear, The" (Frost), **Retro. Supp. I:** 128

"Fear & Fame" (Levine), **Supp. V:** 192

"Fearless" (Mosley), **Supp. XIII:** 241

Fearless Jones (Mosley), **Supp. XIII: 241–242**

Fear of Fifty: A Midlife Memoir (Jong), **Supp. V:** 114, 115, 116, 131

Fear of Flying (Jong), **Supp. V:** 113, 115, 116, 119–123, 124, 129

"Feast, The" (Kinnell), **Supp. III Part 1:** 239, 250

Feast of All Saints, The (Rice), **Supp. VII:** 299–301

Feast of Snakes, A (Crews), **Supp. XI:** 102, **107–108**

"Feast of Stephen, The" (Hecht), **Supp. X:** 63–64

"Featherbed for Critics, A" (Blackmur), **Supp. II Part 1:** 93, 151

Feather Crowns (Mason), **Supp. VIII: 146–147**

"Feathers" (Carver), **Supp. III Part 1:** 145

Feathers (Van Vechten), **Supp. II Part 2:** 736, 749

"Feathers, The" (Hogan), **Supp. IV Part 1:** 416

"February" (Ellison), **Supp. II Part 1:** 229

"February: Thinking of Flowers" (Kenyon), **Supp. VII:** 171

February in Sydney (Komunyakaa), **Supp. XIII: 124–125,** 129

"February in Sydney" (Komunyakaa), **Supp. XIII:** 125

"February 14th" (Levine), **Supp. V:** 194

"Feces" (McClatchy), **Supp. XII:** 266, 267–268

Fechner, Gustav, **II:** 344, 355, 358, 359, 363

Feder, Lillian, **IV:** 136

Federal Arts Project, **Supp. III Part 2:** 618

Federigo, or, The Power of Love (Nemerov), **III:** 268, 276, 282, 283–284, 285

"Fedora" (Chopin), **Supp. I Part 1:** 220

Fedorko, Kathy A., **Retro. Supp. I:** 361, 374

"Feeling and Precision" (Moore), **III:** 206

"Feeling of Effort, The" (James), **II:** 349

"Feel Like a Bird" (Swenson), **Supp. IV Part 2:** 639

"Feel Me" (Swenson), **Supp. IV Part 2:** 647

Feeney, Mary, **Supp. IX:** 152, 154

Feinstein, Sascha, **Supp. XIII:** 125

Feldman, Charles K., **Supp. XI:** 307

Fellini, Federico, **Supp. XII:** 172

"Fellow Citizens" (Sandburg), **III:** 553

Fellows, John, **Supp. I Part 2:** 520

"Felo de Se" (Wylie), **Supp. I Part 2:** 727, 729

Felton, Sharon, **Supp. IV Part 1:** 210

"Female Author" (Plath), **Retro. Supp. II:** 243

"Female Frailty" (Freneau), **Supp. II Part 1:** 258

"Female Voice in *To Kill a Mockingbird*, The: Narrative Strategies in Film and Novel" (Shakelford), **Supp. VIII:** 129

"Feminine Landscape of Leslie Marmon Silko's *Ceremony,* The" (Gunn Allen), **Supp. IV Part 1:** 324

Feminism and the Politics of Literary Reputation: The Example of Erica Jong (Templin), **Supp. V:** 116

"Feminismo" (Robbins), **Supp. X:** 272

"Feminist Criticism in the Wilderness" (Showalter), **Supp. X:** 97

"Fence, The" (Oliver), **Supp. VII:** 232

"Fence Posts" (Snyder), **Supp. VIII:** 304

Fences (Wilson), **Supp. VIII:** 329, 330, 331, **334–337,** 350

Fenick, Elizabeth, **Retro. Supp. II:** 221

"Fenimore Cooper's Literary Offenses" (Twain), **IV:** 204–205

Fenollosa, Ernest, **III:** 458, 465, 466, 474, 475, 477; **Retro. Supp. I:** 289; **Supp. IV Part 1:** 154

Fenollosa, Mrs. Ernest, **III:** 458

Fenton, Charles, **Supp. XI:** 43

Ferdinand: Including "It Was" (Zukofsky), **Supp. III Part 2:** 630

"Fergus" (Bourne), **I:** 229

Ferguson, James, **Supp. I Part 2:** 503

Ferguson, Otis, **Supp. IX:** 7

Ferguson, William, **Supp. XII:** 189

Ferguson Affair, The (Macdonald), **Supp. IV Part 2:** 473

Fergusson, Francis, **I:** 265, 440

Ferlinghetti, Lawrence, **Supp. IV Part**

1: 90; **Supp. VIII:** 290, 292; **Supp. XII:** 121, 125; **Supp. XIII:** 275

Fermata, The (Baker), **Supp. XIII: 49–52,** 54

"Fern" (Toomer), **Supp. III Part 2:** 481; **Supp. IX:** 313

Fern, Fanny, **Retro. Supp. I:** 246; **Supp. V:** 122

Fernández, Enrique, **Supp. VIII:** 73

Fernandez, Ramon, **Retro. Supp. I:** 302, 303

"Fern-Beds in Hampshire Country" (Wilbur), **Supp. III Part 2:** 558

"Fern Hill" (D. Thomas), **IV:** 93

"Fern-Life" (Larcom), **Supp. XIII:** 143

Ferreo, Guglielmo, **Supp. I Part 2:** 481

Fessenden, Thomas Green, **II:** 300

Fessier, Michael, **Supp. XIII:** 164

"Festival Aspect, The" (Olson), **Supp. II Part 2:** 585

Fêtes galantes (Verlaine), **IV:** 79

"Fetish" (McClatchy), **Supp. XII:** 256

Fetterley, Judith, **Retro. Supp. II:** 139

"Fever" (Carver), **Supp. III Part 1:** 145

"Fever 103°" (Plath), **Supp. I Part 2:** 541

Fever: Twelve Stories (Wideman), **Supp. X:** 320

Fever Pitch (Hornby), **Supp. XII:** 286

"Few Don'ts by an Imagiste, A" (Pound), **III:** 465; **Retro. Supp. I:** 288; **Supp. I Part 1:** 261–262

"Few Words of Introduction, A" (McNally), **Supp. XIII:** 198–199

Fiamengo, Janice, **Supp. XIII:** 35

Ficke, Arthur Davison, **Supp. XIII:** 347

"Fiction" (Stafford), **Supp. XI:** 327

"Fiction: A Lens on Life" (Stegner), **Supp. IV Part 2:** 595, 596, 600

Fiction and the Figures of Life (Gass), **Supp. VI:** 85

Fiction of Joseph Heller, The (Seed), **Supp. IV Part 1:** 391

Fiction of Paule Marshall, The (Denniston), **Supp. XI:** 276

Fiction of the Forties (Eisinger), **I:** 302; **II:** 604

"Fiction Writer and His Country, The" (O'Connor), **III:** 342; **Retro. Supp. II:** 223, 225; **Supp. II Part 1:** 148

Fidelity (Glaspell), **Supp. III Part 1:** 177

Fiedler, Leslie A., **II:** 27; **III:** 218; **Retro. Supp. II:** 280, 324; **Supp. II Part 1:** 87; **Supp. IV Part 1:** 42, 86; **Supp. IX:** 3, 227; **Supp. X:** 80;

Supp. XIII: 93–110; **Supp. XIV:** 11

Fiedler on the Roof: Essays on Literature and Jewish Identity (Fiedler), **Supp. XIII:** 106–107

"Fie! Fie! Fi-Fi!" (Fitzgerald), **Retro. Supp. I:** 100

Field, Eugene, **Supp. II Part 1:** 197

Field, John, **IV:** 179

Field Guide, (Hass), **Supp. VI:** 97–98, **99–101,** 102, 103, 106

Field Guide to Contemporary Poetry and Poetics (Friebert and Young, eds.), **Supp. XI:** 270

"Field Guide to the Western Birds" (Stegner), **Supp. IV Part 2:** 609

Fielding, Henry, **I:** 134; **II:** 302, 304–305; **III:** 61; **Supp. I Part 2:** 421, 422, 656; **Supp. IV Part 2:** 688; **Supp. V:** 127; **Supp. IX:** 128; **Supp. XI:** 277

"Field-larks and Blackbirds" (Lanier), **Supp. I Part 1:** 355

Field of Honor (Hay), **Supp. XIV:** 120–121, 125, 130

"Field of Honor" (Hay), **Supp. XIV:** 120–121, 129–130

Field of Vision, The (Morris), **III:** 226–228, 229, 232, 233, 238

"Field Report" (Corso), **Supp. XII:** 124, **136**

Fields, Annie Adams, **II:** 401, 402, 403–404, 406, 412; **IV:** 177; **Retro. Supp. II:** 134, 135, 142; **Supp. I Part 1:** 317

Fields, James T., **II:** 274, 279, 402–403; **Retro. Supp. II:** 135; **Supp. I Part 1:** 317; **Supp. XIII:** 150

Fields, Joseph, **IV:** 274

Fields, Mrs. James T., **Supp. XIV:** 44, 46. *See* Fields, Annie Adams

Fields, W. C., **II:** 427; **IV:** 335

"Fields at Dusk, The" (Salter), **Supp. IX:** 260

Fields of Wonder (Hughes), **Retro. Supp. I:** 206, 207; **Supp. I Part 1:** 333–334

Fierce Invalids Home from Hot Climates (Robbins), **Supp. X:** 267, 276–277, **282–285**

Fiery Chariot, The (Hurston), **Supp. VI:** 155–156

15 Poems (Banks), **Supp. V:** 5

"Fifteenth Farewell" (Bogan), **Supp. III Part 1:** 51, 58

"Fifth Avenue, Uptown" (Baldwin), **Supp. I Part 1:** 52

Fifth Book of Peace, The (Kingston), **Supp. V:** 173

Fifth Chinese Daughter (Wong), **Supp. X:** 291

Fifth Column, The (Hemingway), **II:** 254, 258; **Retro. Supp. I:** 184

"Fifth Column of the Fencerow" (Leopold), **Supp. XIV:** 185

Fifth Decad of Cantos, The (Pound), **Retro. Supp. I:** 292

"Fifth Movement: *Autobiography*" (Zukofsky), **Supp. III Part 2:** 611

Fifth Sunday (Dove), **Supp. IV Part 1:** 251, 252–253

"Fifth Sunday" (Dove), **Supp. IV Part 1:** 252

Fifty Best American Short Stories (O'Brien), **III:** 56

"Fifty Dollars" (Elkin), **Supp. VI: 43–44**

"55 Miles to the Gas Pump" (Proulx), **Supp. VII:** 264

55 Poems (Zukofsky), **Supp. III Part 2:** 611, 621

"Fifty Grand" (Hemingway), **II:** 250, 424; **Retro. Supp. I:** 177

50 Poems (Cummings), **I:** 430, 440, 442–443, 444–445, 446

"Fifty Suggestions" (Poe), **Retro. Supp. II:** 266

"52 Oswald Street" (Kinnell), **Supp. III Part 1:** 251

"Fifty Years Among the Black Folk" (Du Bois), **Supp. II Part 1:** 169

"Fifty Years of American Poetry" (Jarrell), **Retro. Supp. I:** 52

Fight, The (Mailer), **Retro. Supp. II:** 207, 208

Fight Back: For the Sake of the People, For the Sake of the Land (Ortiz), **Supp. IV Part 2:** 497, 498, 499, 503, 510–512, 514

Fight for Freedom (Hughes), **Supp. I Part 1:** 345

Fightin': New and Collected Stories (Ortiz), **Supp. IV Part 2:** 513

Fighting Angel (Buck), **Supp. II Part 1:** 119, 131

Fighting France; From Dunkerque to Belfort (Wharton), **Retro. Supp. I:** 377, 378

"Figlia che Piange, La" (Eliot), **I:** 570, 584; **III:** 9

Figliola, Samantha, **Supp. V:** 143

"Figure a Poem Makes, The" (Frost), **Retro. Supp. I:** 139

"Figured Wheel, The" (Pinsky), **Supp. VI:** 243, 244, 245, 246

Figured Wheel, The: New and Collected Poems (Pinsky), **Supp. VI:** 247–248

"Figure in the Carpet, The" (James),

Retro. Supp. I: 228, 229
"Figure in the Doorway, The" (Frost), **Retro. Supp. I:** 138
Figures from the Double World (McGrath), **Supp. X:** 118–119
"Figures in the Clock, The" (McCarthy), **II:** 561–562
Figures of Time (Hayden), **Supp. II Part 1:** 367
"Filling Out a Blank" (Wagoner), **Supp. IX:** 324
Fillmore, Millard, **III:** 101
Film Flam: Essays on Hollywood (McMurtry), **Supp. V:** 228
Films of Ayn Rand, The (Cox), **Supp. IV Part 2:** 524
Filo, John, **Supp. XII:** 211
Filson, John, **Retro. Supp. I:** 421
Final Beast, The (Buechner), **Supp. XII:** 49–51
"Finale" (Longfellow), **II:** 505, 506–507
"Final Fear" (Hughes), **Supp. I Part 1:** 338
Final Harvest: Emily Dickinson's Poems (Johnson, ed.), **I:** 470, 471
Final Payments (Gordon), **Supp. IV Part 1:** 297, 299, 300–302, 304, 306, 314
"Final Report, A" (Maxwell), **Supp. VIII:** 169
"Final Soliloquy of the Interior Paramour" (Stevens), **Retro. Supp. I:** 312
Final Solution, The (Reitlinger), **Supp. XII:** 161
Financier, The (Dreiser), **I:** 497, 501, 507, 509; **Retro. Supp. II:** 94, 101–102, 105
Finch, Robert, **Supp. XIV:** 186–187
Find a Victim (Macdonald), **Supp. IV Part 2:** 467, 472, 473
"Fin de Saison Palm Beach" (White), **Supp. I Part 2:** 673
Finding a Form (Gass), **Supp. VI:** 91–92, 93
Finding a Girl in America (Dubus), **Supp. VII:** 85–88
"Finding a Girl in America" (Dubus), **Supp. VII:** 87
"Finding Beads" (Hogan), **Supp. IV Part 1:** 400
"Finding of Zach, The" (Dunbar), **Supp. II Part 1:** 212
Findings and Keepings: Analects for an Autobiography (Mumford), **Supp. II Part 2:** 483
Finding the Center: Narrative Poetry of the Zuni Indians (Tedlock), **Supp. IV Part 2:** 509

Finding the Islands (Merwin), **Supp. III Part 1:** 353, 357
"Finding the Place: A Migrant Childhood" (Stegner), **Supp. IV Part 2:** 597
"Find the Woman" (Macdonald, under Millar), **Supp. IV Part 2:** 466
Fine, David, **Supp. XI:** 160
Fine Clothes to the Jew (Hughes), **Retro. Supp. I:** 200, 201, 203, 205; **Supp. I Part 1:** 326–328
"Fine Old Firm, A" (Jackson), **Supp. IX:** 120
Finer Grain, The (James), **II:** 335
Fine Writing (L. P. Smith), **Supp. XIV:** 347
Finished Man, The (Garrett), **Supp. VII:** 96, 97–98
Fink, Mike, **IV:** 266
Finley, John H., **II:** 418
Finn, David, **Supp. VIII:** 106–107
Finnegans Wake (Joyce), **III:** 7, 12, 14, 261; **IV:** 182, 369–370, 418, 421; **Supp. I Part 2:** 620; **Supp. II Part 1:** 2; **Supp. XIII:** 191
Finney, Brian, **Supp. XIV:** 158, 160, 161, 165, 166, 167, 169
"Finnish Rhapsody" (Ashbery), **Supp. III Part 1:** 26
Firbank, Ronald, **IV:** 77, 436
"Fire" (Hughes), **Supp. I Part 1:** 327
Fire: From "A Journal of Love," the Unexpurgated Diary of Anaïs Nin, 1934–1937, **Supp. X:** 184, 185, 189, 194, 195
"Fire and Cloud" (Wright), **IV:** 488
"Fire and Ice" (Frost), **II:** 154; **Retro. Supp. I:** 133
Fire and Ice (Stegner), **Supp. IV Part 2:** 598, 607–608
"Fire and the Cloud, The" (Hurston), **Supp. VI:** 158
"Fire and the Hearth, The" (Faulkner), **II:** 71
Firebird (Doty), **Supp. XI:** 119–120, 121, **132–133**, 134
"Firebombing, The" (Dickey), **Supp. IV Part 1:** 180–181, 187, 189–190
"Fireborn Are at Home in Fire, The" (Sandburg), **III:** 591
"Fire Chaconne" (Francis), **Supp. IX:** 87
Firecrackers (Van Vechten), **Supp. II Part 2:** 740, 742–744, 749
Fireman's Wife and Other Stories, The (Bausch), **Supp. VII:** 48, 54
Fire Next Time, The (Baldwin), **Retro. Supp. II:** 5, 8, 9; **Supp. I Part 1:** 48, 49, 52, 60–61
"Fire Next Time, The" (Baldwin). *See*

"Down at the Cross" (Baldwin)
"Fire of Driftwood, The" (Longfellow), **II:** 499; **Retro. Supp. II:** 159, 168
"Fire of Life" (McCullers), **II:** 585
Fire on the Mountain (Abbey), **Supp. XIII:** 6
"Fire Poem" (Merrill), **Supp. III Part 1:** 321
"Fires" (Carver), **Supp. III Part 1:** 136–139, 147
Fires: Essays, Poems, Stories (Carver), **Supp. III Part 1:** 136, 140, 142, 146–147
Fire Screen, The (Merrill), **Supp. III Part 1:** 319, 325–329
"Fire Season" (Didion), **Supp. IV Part 1:** 199
"Fire Sequence" (Winters), **Supp. II Part 2:** 791, 796, 800
Fire Sermon (Morris), **III:** 238–239
"Fire Sermon, The" (Eliot), **Retro. Supp. I:** 60–61
Fireside Travels (Lowell), **Supp. I Part 2:** 407, 419–420
Firestarter (King), **Supp. V:** 140, 141, 144; **Supp. IX:** 114
"fire the bastards" (Green), **Supp. IV Part 1:** 285
"Fire-Truck, A" (Wilbur), **Supp. III Part 2:** 556
"Fireweed" (Clampitt), **Supp. IX: 44–45**
"Firewood" (Banks), **Supp. V:** 15
"Fireworks" (Ford), **Supp. V:** 69
"Fireworks" (Shapiro), **Supp. II Part 2:** 707
Fir-Flower Tablets (Lowell), **II:** 512, 526–527
Firkins, Oscar W., **II:** 271
"Firmament, The" (Bryant), **Supp. I Part 1:** 162
Firmat, Gustavo Pérez, **Supp. VIII:** 76, 77, 79; **Supp. XI:** 184
"First American, The" (Toomer), **Supp. III Part 2:** 480, 487
"First Birth" (Olds), **Supp. X:** 212
First Book of Africa, The (Hughes), **Supp. I Part 1:** 344–345
First Book of Jazz, The (Hughes), **Supp. I Part 1:** 345
First Book of Negroes, The (Hughes), **Supp. I Part 1:** 345
First Book of Rhythms, The (Hughes), **Supp. I Part 1:** 345
First Book of the West Indies, The (Hughes), **Supp. I Part 1:** 345
Firstborn (Glück), **Supp. V:** 80, 81, 82, 84
"Firstborn" (Wright), **Supp. V:** 340
"First Chaldaic Oracle" (Carson),

Supp. XII: 111

"First Communion" (Fante), **Supp. XI:** 160

"First Day of School, The" (Gibbons), **Supp. X:** 41, 42

"First Death in Nova Scotia" (Bishop), **Supp. I Part 1:** 73

"First Formal" (Olds), **Supp. X:** 212

First Four Books of Poems, The (Glück), **Supp. V:** 81, 83

"First Grade" (Stafford), **Supp. XI:** 328

"First Hawaiian Bank" (Nye), **Supp. XIII:** 278

"First Heat" (Taylor), **Supp. V:** 323

"First Job, The" (Cisneros), **Supp. VII:** 62

"1st Letter on Georges" (Olson), **Supp. II Part 2:** 578

First Light (Wagoner), **Supp. IX:** 330

"First Love" (Welty), **IV:** 264; **Retro. Supp. I:** 347

First Man, The (O'Neill), **III:** 390

First Manifesto (McGrath), **Supp. X:** 115

"First Meditation" (Roethke), **III:** 545–546

"First Noni Daylight, The" (Harjo), **Supp. XII:** 219

"First Passover" (Longfellow), **II:** 500–501

"First Person Female" (Harrison), **Supp. VIII:** 40, 41, 48

"First Place, The" (Wagoner), **Supp. IX:** 328

First Poems (Buechner), **Supp. XII:** 45

First Poems (Merrill), **Supp. III Part 1:** 318–321, 323

First Poems 1946–1954 (Kinnell), **Supp. III Part 1:** 235, 238–239

"First Praise" (W. C. Williams), **Retro. Supp. I:** 413

First Principles (Spencer), **Supp. I Part 1:** 368

"First Ride and First Walk" (Goldbarth), **Supp. XII:** 182–183

"First Seven Years, The" (Malamud), **Supp. I Part 2:** 431

"First Sex" (Olds), **Supp. X:** 208

"First Snow in Alsace" (Wilbur), **Supp. III Part 2:** 545, 546, 559

"First Song" (Kinnell), **Supp. III Part 1:** 239

"First Spade in the West, The" (Fiedler), **Supp. XIII:** 103

"First Steps" (McClatchy), **Supp. XII:** 256

First There Is the Need (Reznikoff), **Supp. XIV:** 291

"First Things First" (Auden), **Supp. II Part 1:** 13

"First Thought, Best Thought" (Ginsberg), **Supp. II Part 1:** 327

"First Time I Saw Paris, The" (Fante), **Supp. XI:** 174

"First Travels of Max" (Ransom), **III:** 490–491

"First Tycoon of Teen, The" (Wolfe), **Supp. III Part 2:** 572

"First Views of the Enemy" (Oates), **Supp. II Part 2:** 508

"First Wife, The" (Buck), **Supp. II Part 1:** 127

"First World War" (White), **Supp. I Part 2:** 665

"Fish" (F. Barthelme), **Supp. XI:** 26

"Fish" (Levis), **Supp. XI:** 259–260

Fish, Stanley, **Supp. IV Part 1:** 48; **Supp. XIV:** 14, 15

"Fish, The" (Moore), **III:** 195, 197, 209, 211, 213–214

"Fish, The" (Oliver), **Supp. VII:** 236

"Fish and Shadow" (Pound), **III:** 466

Fishburne, Laurence, **Supp. VIII:** 345

"Fish Cannery" (Fante), **Supp. XI:** 167

Fisher, Alexander Metcalf, **Supp. I Part 2:** 582

Fisher, Alfred, **Retro. Supp. II:** 243

Fisher, Craig, **Supp. V:** 125

Fisher, Dorothy Canfield, **Retro. Supp. I:** 21, 133; **Supp. II Part 1:** 117. *See also* Canfield, Dorothy

Fisher, Mary, **Supp. I Part 2:** 455

Fisher, Phillip, **Retro. Supp. I:** 39

Fisher, Rudolph, **Retro. Supp. I:** 200; **Supp. I Part 1:** 325; **Supp. X:** 139

Fisher, Vardis, **Supp. IV Part 2:** 598

Fisher King, The (Marshall), **Supp. XI:** 275–276, **288–290**

"Fisherman, The" (Merwin), **Supp. II Part 1:** 346

"Fisherman and His Wife, The" (Welty), **IV:** 266

"Fisherman from Chihuahua, The" (Connell), **Supp. XIV:** 86

"Fishing" (Harjo), **Supp. XII:** 227–228

"Fish in the Stone, The" (Dove), **Supp. IV Part 1:** 245, 257

"Fish in the unruffled lakes" (Auden), **Supp. II Part 1:** 8–9

"Fish R Us" (Doty), **Supp. XI:** 135

Fisk, James, **I:** 4, 474

Fiske, John, **Supp. I Part 1:** 314; **Supp. I Part 2:** 493

"Fit Against the Country, A" (Wright), **Supp. III Part 2:** 591–592, 601

Fitch, Clyde, **Supp. IV Part 2:** 573

Fitch, Elizabeth. *See* Taylor, Mrs. Edward (Elizabeth Fitch)

Fitch, James, **IV:** 147

Fitch, Noël Riley, **Supp. X:** 186, 187

Fitts, Dudley, **I:** 169, 173; **Supp. I Part 1:** 342, 345; **Supp. XIII:** 346

FitzGerald, Edward, **Supp. I Part 2:** 416; **Supp. III Part 2:** 610

Fitzgerald, Ella, **Supp. XIII:** 132

Fitzgerald, F. Scott, **I:** 107, 117, 118, 123, 188, 221, 288, 289, 358, 367, 374–375, 382, 423, 476, 482, 487, 495, 509, 511; **II:** **77–100,** 257, 263, 272, 283, 415, 416, 417–418, 420, 425, 427, 430, 431, 432, 433, 434, 436, 437, 450, 458–459, 482, 560; **III:** 2, 26, 35, 36, 37, 40, 44, 45, 69, 106, 244, 284, 334, 350–351, 453, 454, 471, 551, 552, 572; **IV:** 27, 49, 97, 101, 126, 140, 191, 222, 223, 287, 297, 427, 471; **Retro. Supp. I:** 1, 74, **97–120,** 178, 180, 186, 215, 359, 381; **Retro. Supp. II:** 257, 321, 326, 328; **Supp. I Part 1:** 196, 197; **Supp. I Part 2:** 622; **Supp. III Part 2:** 409, 411, 585; **Supp. IV Part 1:** 123, 197, 200, 203, 341; **Supp. IV Part 2:** 463, 468, 607, 689; **Supp. V:** 23, 95, 226, 251, 262, 276, 313; **Supp. VIII:** 101, 103, 106, 137; **Supp. IX:** 15, 20, 55, 57–63, 199; **Supp. X:** 225; **Supp. XI:** 65, 221, 334; **Supp. XII:** 42, 173, 295; **Supp. XIII:** 170, 263

Fitzgerald, Robert, **I:** 27–28; **III:** 338, 348; **Retro. Supp. II:** 179, 221, 222, 223, 228, 229; **Supp. IV Part 2:** 631

"Fitzgerald: The Romance of Money" (Cowley), **Supp. II Part 1:** 143

Fitzgerald, Zelda (Zelda Sayre), **I:** 482; **II:** 77, 79, 82–85, 88, 90–91, 93, 95; **Supp. IV Part 1:** 310; **Supp. IX:** 55–73; **Supp. X:** 172. *See also* Sayre, Zelda

"Fitzgerald's Tragic Sense" (Schorer), **Retro. Supp. I:** 115

Five Came Back (West), **IV:** 287

Five Corners (screenplay, Shanley), **Supp. XIV:** 316

5 Detroits (Levine), **Supp. V:** 178

"Five Dollar Guy, The" (W. C. Williams), **Retro. Supp. I:** 423

Five Easy Pieces (film), **Supp. V:** 26

"Five Elephants" (Dove), **Supp. IV Part 1:** 244–245

Five Groups of Verse (Reznikoff), **Supp. XIV:** 279, 282

Five Hundred Scorpions (Hearon), **Supp. VIII:** 57, 65, **66**

Five Indiscretions (Ríos), **Supp. IV Part 2:** 545–547

Five Men and Pompey (Benét), **Supp. XI:** 43, 44

Five Plays (Hughes), **Retro. Supp. I:** 197, 209

Five Temperaments (Kalstone), **Retro. Supp. II:** 40

Five Young American Poets, **I:** 170; **II:** 367

Fixer, The (Malamud), **Supp. I Part 2:** 428, 435, 445, 446–448, 450, 451

Flaccus, Kimball, **Retro. Supp. I:** 136

Flacius, Matthias, **IV:** 163

Flag for Sunrise, A (Stone), **Supp. V:** 301–304

Flag of Childhood, The: Poems from the Middle East (Nye, ed.), **Supp. XIII:** 280

"Flag of Summer" (Swenson), **Supp. IV Part 2:** 645

Flagons and Apples (Jeffers), **Supp. II Part 2:** 413, 414, 417–418

Flags in the Dust (Faulkner), **Retro. Supp. I:** 81, 82, 83, 86, 88

Flamel, Nicolas, **Supp. XII:** 178

Flaming Corsage, The (Kennedy), **Supp. VII:** 133, 153–156

Flammarion, Camille, **Supp. I Part 1:** 260

Flanagan, John T., **Supp. I Part 2:** 464, 465, 468

"Flannery O'Connor: Poet to the Outcast" (Sister Rose Alice), **III:** 348

Flappers and Philosophers (Fitzgerald), **II:** 88; **Retro. Supp. I:** 103; **Supp. IX:** 56

Flash and Filigree (Southern), **Supp. XI:** 295, **296–297**

"Flashcards" (Dove), **Supp. IV Part 1:** 250

Flatt, Lester, **Supp. V:** 335

Flaubert, Gustave, **I:** 66, 123, 130, 272, 312, 314, 315, 477, 504, 506, 513, 514; **II:** 182, 185, 194, 198–199, 205, 209, 230, 289, 311, 316, 319, 325, 337, 392, 401, 577, 594; **III:** 196, 207, 251, 315, 461, 467, 511, 564; **IV:** 4, 29, 31, 37, 40, 134, 285, 428; **Retro. Supp. I:** 5, 215, 218, 222, 225, 235, 287; **Supp. III Part 2:** 411, 412; **Supp. XI:** 334; **Supp. XIV:** 87, 336

"Flavia and Her Artists" (Cather), **Retro. Supp. I:** 5

Flavoring of New England, The (Brooks), **I:** 253, 256

Flavor of Man, The (Toomer), **Supp. III Part 2:** 487

Flaxman, Josiah, **Supp. I Part 2:** 716

"Flèche d'Or" (Merrill), **Supp. III Part 1:** 328

Flecker, James Elroy, **Supp. I Part 1:** 257

"Flee on Your Donkey" (Sexton), **Supp. II Part 2:** 683, 685

Fleming, Ian, **Supp. XI:** 307

Fleming, Rene, **Supp. XII:** 321

"Fleshbody" (Ammons), **Supp. VII:** 27

Fletcher, H. D., **II:** 517, 529

Fletcher, John, **Supp. IV Part 2:** 621

Fletcher, John Gould, **I:** 243; **II:** 517, 529; **III:** 458; **Supp. I Part 1:** 263; **Supp. I Part 2:** 422

Fletcher, Phineas, **Supp. I Part 1:** 369

Fletcher, Virginia. *See* Caldwell, Mrs. Erskine (Virginia Fletcher)

Fleurs du mal, Les (Beaudelaire; Millay and Dillon, trans.), **III:** 141–142

"Flight" (Updike), **IV:** 218, 222, 224; **Retro. Supp. I:** 318

"Flight, The" (Haines), **Supp. XII:** 204–205

"Flight, The" (Roethke), **III:** 537–538

Flight among the Tombs (Hecht), **Supp. X:** 58, **71–74**

"Flight for Freedom" (McCoy), **Supp. XIII:** 170

"Flight from Byzantium" (Brodsky), **Supp. VIII:** 30–31

"Flight of Besey Lane, The" (Jewett), **Retro. Supp. II:** 139

Flight of the Rocket, The (Fitzgerald), **II:** 89

Flight to Canada (Reed), **Supp. X:** 240, **249–252**

Flint, F. S., **II:** 517; **III:** 459, 464, 465; **Retro. Supp. I:** 127; **Supp. I Part 1:** 261, 262

Flivver King, The (Sinclair), **Supp. V:** 290

Floating Opera, The (Barth), **I:** 121, 122–126, 127, 129, 130, 131

"Floating Poem, Unnumbered, The" (Rich), **Supp. I Part 2:** 572–573

Flood (Matthews), **Supp. IX:** 154, **160–161**

Flood (Warren), **IV:** 252, 256–257

"Flood of Years, The" (Bryant), **Supp. I Part 1:** 159, 170, 171; **Supp. I Part 2:** 416

"Floor and the Ceiling, The" (W. J. Smith), **Supp. XIII:** 345, 346

"Floor Plans" (Komunyakaa), **Supp. XIII:** 114

"Floral Decorations for Bananas" (Stevens), **IV:** 8

Florida (Acker), **Supp. XII:** 5

"Florida" (Bishop), **Retro. Supp. II:** 43

"Florida Road Workers" (Hughes), **Retro. Supp. I:** 203

"Florida Sunday, A" (Lanier), **Supp. I Part 1:** 364, 366

"Flossie Cabanis" (Masters), **Supp. I Part 2:** 461–462

Flow Chart (Ashbery), **Supp. VIII:** 275

"Flowchart" (Ashbery), **Supp. III Part 1:** 26

Flower-de-Luce (Longfellow), **II:** 490

Flower Fables (Alcott), **Supp. I Part 1:** 33

"Flower-Fed Buffaloes, The" (Lindsay), **Supp. I Part 2:** 398

"Flower Garden" (Jackson), **Supp. IX:** 119

"Flower-gathering" (Frost), **II:** 153

Flower Herding on Mount Monadnock (Kinnell), **Supp. III Part 1:** 235, 239, 241–244

"Flower Herding on Mount Monadnock" (Kinnell), **Supp. III Part 1:** 242

"Flowering Death" (Ashbery), **Supp. III Part 1:** 22

"Flowering Dream, The" (McCullers), **II:** 591

"Flowering Judas" (Porter), **III:** 434, 435–436, 438, 441, 445, 446, 450–451

Flowering Judas and Other Stories (Porter), **III:** 433, 434

Flowering of New England, The (Brooks), **IV:** 171–172; **Supp. VIII:** 101

Flowering of the Rod (Doolittle), **Supp. I Part 1:** 272

Flowering Peach, The (Odets), **Supp. II Part 2:** 533, 547, 549–550

"Flowering Plum" (Glück), **Supp. V:** 82

"Flowers for Marjorie" (Welty), **IV:** 262

"Flowers of the Fallow" (Larcom), **Supp. XIII:** 143, 145–146

"Flowers Well if anybody" (Dickinson), **Retro. Supp. I:** 30

"Fly, The" (Kinnell), **Supp. III Part 1:** 249

"Fly, The" (Shapiro), **Supp. II Part 2:** 705

"Fly, The" (Simic), **Supp. VIII:** 278

Flye, Father James Harold, **I:** 25, 26, 35–36, 37, 42, 46; **IV:** 215

"Fly in Buttermilk, A" (Baldwin), **Retro. Supp. II:** 8

"Flying High" (Levertov), **Supp. III Part 1:** 284

"Flying Home" (Ellison), **Retro. Supp.**

II: 117, **125–126; Supp. II Part 1:** 235, 238–239

"Flying Home" (Kinnell), **Supp. III Part 1:** 250

"Flying Home" and Other Stories (Ellison), **Retro. Supp. II:** 119, 124

"Flying Home from Utah" (Swenson), **Supp. IV Part 2:** 645

"Flying to Hanoi" (Rukeyser), **Supp. VI:** 279

Foata, Anne, **Supp. XI:** 104

Focillon, Henri, **IV:** 90

Focus (A. Miller), **III:** 150–151, 156

Foer, Jonathan Safran, **Supp. XII:** 169

Foerster, Norman, **I:** 222; **Supp. I Part 2:** 423, 424; **Supp. IV Part 2:** 598

"Fog" (Sandburg), **III:** 586

"Fog Galleon" (Komunyakaa), **Supp. XIII:** 127

"Foggy Lane, The" (Simpson), **Supp. IX:** 274

Folded Leaf, The (Maxwell), **Supp. III Part 1:** 62; **Supp. VIII: 159–162**

Folding Star, The (Hollinghurst), **Supp. XIII:** 52

Foley, Jack, **Supp. X:** 125

Foley, Martha, **II:** 587

Folks from Dixie (Dunbar), **Supp. II Part 1:** 211–212

Folkways (Sumner), **III:** 102

Follain, Jean, **Supp. IX:** 152, 154

Follett, Wilson, **I:** 405; **Supp. XIII:** 173

Follower of Dusk (Salinas), **Supp. XIII:** 326

Following the Equator (Twain), **II:** 434; **IV:** 208

Folly (Minot), **Supp. VI:** 205, 208, **210–213**

Folsom, Charles, **Supp. I Part 1:** 156

Folsom, Ed, **Retro. Supp. I:** 392

Folson, Marcia McClintock, **Retro. Supp. II:** 139

Fonda, Henry, **Supp. I Part 1:** 67; **Supp. IV Part 1:** 236

Fonda, Jane, **III:** 284; **Supp. XI:** 307

Fonda, Peter, **Supp. VIII:** 42; **Supp. XI:** 293, 308

Foner, Eric, **Supp. I Part 2:** 523

Fong and the Indians (Theroux), **Supp. VIII:** 314, 315, **316–317**

Fontanne, Lynn, **III:** 397

Fool for Love (Shepard), **Supp. III Part 2:** 433, 447, 448

Fools (Simon), **Supp. IV Part 2:** 584–585

Fool's Progress, The: An Honest Novel (Abbey), **Supp. XIII:** 4, **13–15**

Foote, Horton, **Supp. I Part 1:** 281; **Supp. VIII:** 128, 129

Foote, Mary Hallock, **Retro. Supp. II:** 72; **Supp. IV Part 2:** 611

Foote, Roxanna. *See* Beecher, Mrs. Lyman (Roxanna Foote)

Foote, Samuel, **Supp. I Part 2:** 584

Foote, Stephanie, **Retro. Supp. II:** 139

"Foot Fault" (pseudonym). *See* Thurber, James

Footing on This Earth, A (Hay), **Supp. XIV:** 125, 126, 130

"Footing up a Total" (Lowell), **II:** 528

"Footnote to Howl" (Ginsberg), **Supp. II Part 1:** 316–317

"Footnote to Weather Forecasts, A" (Brodsky), **Supp. VIII:** 32

Footprints (Hearon), **Supp. VIII: 69–70**

Footprints (Levertov), **Supp. III Part 1:** 272, 281

"Footsteps of Angels" (Longfellow), **II:** 496

For a Bitter Season: New and Selected Poems (Garrett), **Supp. VII:** 99–100

"For a Dead Kitten" (Hay), **Supp. XIV:** 119–120

"For a Dead Lady" (Robinson), **III:** 508, 513, 517

"For a Ghost Who Once Placed Bets in the Park" (Levis), **Supp. XI:** 265

"For a Lamb" (Eberhart), **I:** 523, 530, 531

"For All" (Snyder), **Supp. VIII:** 304

"For All Tuesday Travelers" (Cisneros), **Supp. VII:** 67–68

"For a Lost Child" (Stafford), **Supp. XI:** 329

"For a Marriage" (Bogan), **Supp. III Part 1:** 52

"For an Emigrant" (Jarrell), **II:** 371

"For Anna Akmatova" (Lowell), **II:** 544

"For Anna Mae Pictou Aquash, Whose Spirit Is Present Here and in the Dappled Stars" (Harjo), **Supp. XII:** 225

"For Anne, at a Little Distance" (Haines), **Supp. XII:** 207

"For Annie" (Poe), **III:** 427; **Retro. Supp. II:** 263

"For a Southern Man" (Cisneros), **Supp. VII:** 67

"For Bailey" (Angelou), **Supp. IV Part 1:** 15

Forbes, Malcolm, **Supp. IV Part 1:** 94

"Forbidden, The" (Glück), **Supp. XIV:** 269

For Bread Alone (Choukri), **Supp. IV Part 1:** 92

Forché, Carolyn, **Supp. IV Part 1:** 208

Ford, Arthur, **Supp. IV Part 1:** 140

Ford, Ford Madox, **I:** 288, 405, 409, 417, 421, 423; **II:** 58, 144, 198, 257, 263, 265, 517, 536; **III:** 458, 464–465, 470–471, 472, 476; **IV:** 27, 126, 261; **Retro. Supp. I:** 127, 177, 178, 186, 231, 286–287, 418; **Supp. II Part 1:** 107; **Supp. III Part 2:** 617; **Supp. VIII:** 107; **Supp. XIV:** 3

Ford, Harrison, **Supp. VIII:** 323

Ford, Harry, **Supp. V:** 179; **Supp. XIII:** 76

Ford, Henry, **I:** 295, 480–481; **III:** 292, 293; **Supp. I Part 1:** 21; **Supp. I Part 2:** 644; **Supp. III Part 2:** 612, 613; **Supp. IV Part 1:** 223; **Supp. V:** 290

Ford, John, **Supp. I Part 2:** 422; **Supp. III Part 2:** 619

Ford, Richard, **Supp. IV Part 1:** 342; **Supp. V:** 22, **57–75**

Ford, Webster (pseudonym). *See* Masters, Edgar Lee

"Fording and Dread" (Harrison), **Supp. VIII:** 41

"Ford Madox Ford" (Lowell), **II:** 547; **Retro. Supp. II:** 188

"For Dudley" (Wilbur), **Supp. III Part 2:** 558

Fordyce, David, **II:** 113

Foregone Conclusion, A (Howells), **II:** 278–279, 282

"Foreign Affairs" (Kunitz), **Supp. III Part 1:** 265

"Foreigner, The" (Jewett), **II:** 409–410; **Retro. Supp. II:** 133, 142

"Foreign Shores" (Salter), **Supp. IX:** 260

Forensic and the Navigators (Shepard), **Supp. III Part 2:** 439

Foreseeable Future, The (Price), **Supp. VI:** 265

Foreseeable Futures (Matthews), **Supp. IX:** 155, **163,** 169

"For Esmé with Love and Squalor" (Salinger), **III:** 560

"Forest" (Simic), **Supp. VIII:** 273

Forest, Jean-Claude, **Supp. XI:** 307

Forester's Letters (Paine), **Supp. I Part 2:** 508

"Forest Hymn, A" (Bryant), **Supp. I Part 1:** 156, 162, 163, 164, 165, 170

"Forest in the Seeds, The" (Kingsolver), **Supp. VII:** 203

Forest of the South, The (Gordon), **II:** 197

"Forest of the South, The" (Gordon), **II:** 199, 201

Forest without Leaves (Adams and Haines), **Supp. XII:** 209

"Forever and the Earth" (Bradbury), **Supp. IV Part 1:** 102

"For Fathers of Girls" (Dunn), **Supp. XI:** 146

"For/From Lew" (Snyder), **Supp. VIII:** 303

"For George Santayana" (Lowell), **II:** 547

Forgotten Helper, The: A Story for Children (Moore), **Supp. X:** 175

Forgotten Village, The (Steinbeck), **IV:** 51

Forgue, Guy J., **III:** 118, 119

"FOR HETTIE" (Baraka), **Supp. II Part 1:** 32

"FOR HETTIE IN HER FIFTH MONTH" (Baraka), **Supp. II Part 1:** 32, 38

"For Homer" (Corso), **Supp. XII:** 135

"For I'm the Boy" (Barthelme), **Supp. IV Part 1:** 47

"For Jessica, My Daughter" (Strand), **Supp. IV Part 2:** 629

"For John, Who Begs Me not to Enquire Further" (Sexton), **Supp. II Part 2:** 676

"For Johnny Pole on the Forgotten Beach" (Sexton), **Supp. II Part 2:** 675

"For Joy to Leave Upon" (Ortiz), **Supp. IV Part 2:** 508

"Fork" (Simic), **Supp. VIII:** 275

For Lancelot Andrewes (Eliot), **Retro. Supp. I:** 64

For Lizzie and Harriet (Lowell), **Retro. Supp. II:** 183, 186, 190

"Forlorn Hope of Sidney Lanier, The" (Leary), **Supp. I Part 1:** 373

For Love (Creeley), **Supp. IV Part 1:** 139, 140, 142–145, 147–149, 150, 154

"For Love" (Creeley), **Supp. IV Part 1:** 145

For Love (Miller), **Supp. XII: 297– 299,** 299

"Formal Elegy" (Berryman), **I:** 170

"Formalist Criticism: Its Principles and Limits" (Burke), **I:** 282

Forman, Milos, **Supp. IV Part 1:** 236

"Form and Function of the Novel, The" (Goldbarth), **Supp. XII:** 183

"For Marse Chouchoute" (Chopin), **Retro. Supp. II:** 60

"Formation of a Separatist, I" (Howe), **Supp. IV Part 2:** 427

"Form Is Emptiness" (Baraka), **Supp. II Part 1:** 51

"For Mr. Death Who Stands with His Door Open" (Sexton), **Supp. II Part 2:** 695

Forms of Discovery (Winters), **Supp. II Part 2:** 812, 813

Forms of Fiction, The (Gardner and Dunlap), **Supp. VI:** 64

"For My Children" (Karr), **Supp. XI:** 254

"For My Daughter" (Olds), **Supp. X:** 206

"For My Lover, Returning to His Wife" (Sexton), **Supp. II Part 2:** 688

"For Night to Come" (Stern), **Supp. IX:** 292

"For Once, Then, Something" (Frost), **II:** 156–157; **Retro. Supp. I:** 126, 133, 134

"For Pot-Boiling" (Hay), **Supp. XIV:** 128

"For Radicals" (Bourne), **I:** 221

"For Rainer Gerhardt" (Creeley), **Supp. IV Part 1:** 142–143, 147

Forrestal, James, **I:** 491; **Supp. I Part 2:** 489

"For Richard After All" (Kingsolver), **Supp. VII:** 208

"For Sacco and Vanzetti" (Kingsolver), **Supp. VII:** 208

"Forsaken Merman" (Arnold), **Supp. I Part 2:** 529

For Spacious Skies (Buck), **Supp. II Part 1:** 131

Forster, E. M., **I:** 292; **IV:** 201; **Retro. Supp. I:** 59, 232; **Supp. III Part 2:** 503; **Supp. V:** 258; **Supp. VIII:** 155, 171; **Supp. IX:** 128; **Supp. XII:** 79, 81; **Supp. XIV:** 159, 160, 163

Forster, John, **II:** 315

Fort, Paul, **II:** 518, 528, 529; **Retro. Supp. I:** 55

"For the Ahkoond" (Bierce), **I:** 209

For the Century's End: Poems 1990– 1999 (Haines), **Supp. XII: 211–213**

"For the Dedication of the New City Library, Boston" (Holmes), **Supp. I Part 1:** 308

"For the Fallen" (Levine), **Supp. V:** 188

For the Health of the Land: Previously Unpublished Essays and Other Writings (Leopold), **Supp. XIV:** 183

"For the Last Wolverine" (Dickey), **Supp. IV Part 1:** 182

"For the Lovers of the Absolute" (Simic), **Supp. VIII:** 278–279

"For the Man Cutting the Grass" (Oliver), **Supp. VII:** 235

"For the Marriage of Faustus and Helen" (H. Crane), **I:** 395–396, 399, 402; **Retro. Supp. II:** 78–79, 82

"For the Meeting of the National

Sanitary Association, 1860" (Holmes), **Supp. I Part 1:** 307

For the New Intellectual (Rand), **Supp. IV Part 2:** 521, 526–527, 527, 532

"For the New Railway Station in Rome" (Wilbur), **Supp. III Part 2:** 554

"For the Night" (Kenyon), **Supp. VII:** 163

"For Theodore Roethke: 1908–1963" (Lowell), **II:** 554

"For the Poem *Patterson*" (W. C. Williams), **Retro. Supp. I:** 424

"For the Poets of Chile" (Levine), **Supp. V:** 188

"FOR THE REVOLUTIONARY OUT-BURST BY BLACK PEOPLE" (Baraka), **Supp. II Part 1:** 55

"For the Sleepless" (Dunn), **Supp. XI:** 145

For the Time Being (Auden), **Supp. II Part 1:** 2, 17, 18

For the Time Being (Dillard), **Supp. VI:** 23, 27, 29, 32, **34–35**

For the Union Dead (Lowell), **II:** 543, 550–551, 554, 555; **Retro. Supp. II:** 181, 182, 186, 189; **Supp. X:** 53

"For the Union Dead" (Lowell), **II:** 551; **Retro. Supp. II:** 189

"For the Walking Dead" (Komunyakaa), **Supp. XIII:** 121

"For the West" (Snyder), **Supp. VIII:** 299

"For the Word Is Flesh" (Kunitz), **Supp. III Part 1:** 262–264

"Fortress, The" (Glück), **Supp. V:** 82

"Fortress, The" (Sexton), **Supp. II Part 2:** 682

Fortune, T. Thomas, **Supp. II Part 1:** 159

Fortune's Daughter (Hoffman), **Supp. X:** 77, 85

45 Mercy Street (Sexton), **Supp. II Part 2:** 694, 695, 697

Forty Poems Touching on Recent American History (Bly, ed.), **Supp. IV Part 1:** 61

42nd Parallel, The (Dos Passos), **I:** 482, 484–485

Forty Stories (Barthelme), **Supp. IV Part 1:** 47, 49, 53, 54

For Whom the Bell Tolls (Hemingway), **II:** 249, 254–255, 261; **III:** 18, 363; **Retro. Supp. I:** 115, 176–177, 178, **184,** 187

Foscolo, Ugo, **II:** 543

Foss, Sam Walter, **Supp. II Part 1:** 197

"Fossils, The" (Kinnell), **Supp. III Part 1:** 244

Foster, Edward, **Supp. IV Part 2:** 431, 434

Foster, Edward Halsey, **Supp. XII:** 120, 129, 130, 135

Foster, Emily, **II:** 309

Foster, John Wilson, **Supp. XIII:** 32–33

Foster, Phil, **Supp. IV Part 2:** 574

Foster, Stephen, **Supp. I Part 1:** 100–101; **Supp. I Part 2:** 699

Foucault, Michel, **Supp. VIII:** 5; **Supp. XII:** 98

"Founder, The" (Stern), **Supp. IX:** 297

Founding of Harvard College, The (Morison), **Supp. I Part 2:** 485

"Fountain, The" (Bryant), **Supp. I Part 1:** 157, 165, 166, 168

Fountain, The (O'Neill), **III:** 391

Fountain and Other Poems, The (Bryant), **Supp. I Part 1:** 157

Fountainhead, The (film), **Supp. IV Part 2:** 524

Fountainhead, The (Rand), **Supp. IV Part 2:** 517, 521–523, 525, 531

Fountainhead, The: A Fiftieth Anniversary Celebration (Cox), **Supp. IV Part 2:** 523

"Fountain Piece" (Swenson), **Supp. IV Part 2:** 641

"Four Ages of Man, The" (Bradstreet), **Supp. I Part 1:** 111, 115

Four American Indian Literary Masters (Velie), **Supp. IV Part 2:** 486

"Four Beasts in One; the Homo Cameleopard" (Poe), **III:** 425

Four Black Revolutionary Plays (Baraka), **Supp. II Part 1:** 45; **Supp. VIII:** 330

"Four Brothers, The" (Sandburg), **III:** 585

Four Dogs and a Bone and the Wild Goose (Shanley), **Supp. XIV:** 316, **328–329**

"Four Evangelists, The" (Komunyakaa), **Supp. XIII:** 131

"Four for Sir John Davies" (Roethke), **III:** 540, 541

"Four Girls, The" (Alvarez), **Supp. VII:** 7

4-H Club (Shepard), **Supp. III Part 2:** 439

"Four Horse Songs" (Harjo), **Supp. XII:** 220

"400-Meter Free Style" (Kumin), **Supp. IV Part 2:** 442

Fourier, Charles, **II:** 342

"Four in a Family" (Rukeyser), **Supp. VI:** 272

Four in Hand: A Quartet of Novels (Warner), **Supp. VIII:** 164

"Four Lakes' Days" (Eberhart), **I:** 525

"Four Meetings" (James), **II:** 327

Four Million, The (O. Henry), **Supp. II Part 1:** 394, 408

"Four Monarchyes" (Bradstreet), **Supp. I Part 1:** 105, 106, 116

"Four Mountain Wolves" (Silko), **Supp. IV Part 2:** 561

Four of a Kind (Marquand), **III:** 54, 55

"Four of the Horsemen (Hypertense and Stroke, Coronary Occlusion and Cerebral Insult)" (Karr), **Supp. XI:** 250

"Four Poems" (Bishop), **Supp. I Part 1:** 92

"Four Preludes on Playthings of the Wind" (Sandburg), **III:** 586

Four Quartets (Eliot), **I:** 570, 576, 580–582, 585, 587; **II:** 537; **III:** 539; **Retro. Supp. I:** 66, 67; **Supp. II Part 1:** 1; **Supp. IV Part 1:** 284; **Supp. V:** 343, 344; **Supp. VIII:** 182, 195; **Supp. XIII:** 344; **Supp. XIV:** 167

Four Saints in Three Acts (Stein), **IV:** 30, 31, 33, 43, 44–45

"Four Seasons" (Bradstreet), **Supp. I Part 1:** 112–113

"Four Sides of One Story" (Updike), **Retro. Supp. I:** 328

"Four Skinny Trees" (Cisneros), **Supp. VII:** 64

"14: In A Dark Wood: Wood Thrushes" (Oliver), **Supp. VII:** 244

Fourteen Hundred Thousand (Shepard), **Supp. III Part 2:** 439

"14 Men Stage Head Winter 1624/ 25" (Olson), **Supp. II Part 2:** 574

Fourteen Sisters of Emilio Montez O'Brien, The (Hijuelos), **Supp. VIII: 82–85**

Fourteen Stories (Buck), **Supp. II Part 1:** 126

14 Stories (Dixon), **Supp. XII:** 141, **145–147**

"Fourteenth Ward, The" (H. Miller), **III:** 175

Fourth Book of Peace, The (Kingston), **Supp. V:** 173

"Fourth Down" (Marquand), **III:** 56

Fourth Group of Verse, A (Reznikoff), **Supp. XIV:** 282, 284

"Fourth of July in Maine" (Lowell), **II:** 535, 552–553

Fourth Wall, The (Gurney), **Supp. V:** 109–110

Fowler, Douglas, **Supp. IV Part 1:** 226, 227

Fowler, Gene, **Supp. VIII:** 290

Fowler, Henry Watson, **Supp. I Part 2:** 660

Fowler, Singrid, **Supp. VIII:** 249, 258

Fowler, Virginia C., **Supp. VIII:** 224

Fox, Alan, **Supp. XIII:** 120

Fox, Dixon Ryan, **I:** 337

Fox, Joe, **Supp. IX:** 259, 261

Fox, John, **Supp. XIII:** 166

Fox, Linda C., **Supp. XIII:** 217–218

Fox, Ruth, **Supp. I Part 2:** 619

"Fox, The" (Levine), **Supp. V:** 181, 189

Fox-Genovese, Elizabeth, **Supp. IV Part 1:** 286

Fox of Peapack, The (White), **Supp. I Part 2:** 676, 677–678

"Fox of Peapack, The" (White), **Supp. I Part 2:** 677

Foye, Raymond, **Supp. XIV:** 150

Fraenkel, Michael, **III:** 178, 183

"Fragging" (Komunyakaa), **Supp. XIII:** 123

Fragile Beauty, A: John Nichols' Milagro Country: Text and Photographs from His Life and Work (Nichols), **Supp. XIII:** 268

"Fragility" (Shields), **Supp. VII:** 318

"Fragment" (Ashbery), **Supp. III Part 1:** 11, 13, 14, 19, 20

"Fragment" (Lowell), **II:** 516

"Fragment" (Ortiz), **Supp. IV Part 2:** 507

"Fragment of a Meditation" (Tate), **IV:** 129

"Fragment of an Agon" (Eliot), **I:** 579–580

"Fragment of a Prologue" (Eliot), **I:** 579–580

"Fragment of New York, 1929" (Eberhart), **I:** 536–537

"Fragments" (Emerson), **II:** 19

"Fragments for Fall" (Salinas), **Supp. XIII:** 320–321

"Fragments of a Liquidation" (Howe), **Supp. IV Part 2:** 426

Fragonard, Jean Honoré, **III:** 275; **IV:** 79

Fraiman, Susan, **Supp. IV Part 1:** 324

"Frame for Poetry, A" (W. J. Smith), **Supp. XIII:** 333

France, Anatole, **IV:** 444; **Supp. I Part 2:** 631; **Supp. XIV:** 79

France and England in North America (Parkman), **Supp. II Part 2:** 596, 600–605, 607, 613–614

Franchere, Hoyt C., **II:** 131

Franchiser, The (Elkin), **Supp. VI: 51–52,** 58

Franciosi, Robert, **Supp. XIV:** 283

Francis, Lee, **Supp. IV Part 2:** 499

Francis, Robert, **Supp. IX: 75–92**
Francis of Assisi, Saint, **III:** 543; **IV:** 69, 375, 410; **Supp. I Part 2:** 394, 397, 441, 442, 443
Franco, Francisco, **II:** 261
Franconia (Fraser), **Retro. Supp. I:** 136
"Franconia" tales (Abbott), **Supp. I Part 1:** 38
Frank, Anne, **Supp. X:** 149
Frank, Frederick S., **Retro. Supp. II:** 273
Frank, James M., **Supp. XIV:** 1
Frank, Jerome, **Supp. I Part 2:** 645
Frank, Joseph, **II:** 587
Frank, Mary, **Supp. X:** 213
Frank, Robert, **Supp. XI:** 295; **Supp. XII:** 127; **Supp. XIV:** 150
Frank, Waldo, **I:** 106, 109, 117, 229, 236, 245, 259, 400; **Retro. Supp. II:** 77, 79, 83; **Supp. IX:** 308, 309, 311, 320
Frankel, Charles, **III:** 291
Frankel, Haskel, **Supp. I Part 2:** 448
Frankenberg, Lloyd, **I:** 436, 437, 445, 446; **III:** 194
Frankenheimer, John, **Supp. XI:** 343
Frankenstein (film), **Supp. IV Part 1:** 104
Frankenstein (Gardner), **Supp. VI:** 72
Frankenstein (Shelley), **Supp. XII:** 79
Frankfurter, Felix, **I:** 489
Frankie and Johnny (film), **Supp. XIII:** 206
Frankie and Johnny in the Clair de Lune (McNally), **Supp. XIII: 200,** 201
Franklin, Benjamin, **II:** 6, 8, 92, **101–125,** 127, 295, 296, 302, 306; **III:** 74, 90; **IV:** 73, 193; **Supp. I Part 1:** 306; **Supp. I Part 2:** 411, 503, 504, 506, 507, 510, 516, 518, 522, 524, 579, 639; **Supp. VIII:** 202, 205; **Supp. XIII:** 150; **Supp. XIV:** 306
Franklin, Cynthia, **Supp. IV Part 1:** 332
Franklin, R. W., **Retro. Supp. I:** 29, 41, 43, 47
Franklin, Sarah, **II:** 122
Franklin, Temple, **II:** 122
Franklin, William, **II:** 122; **Supp. I Part 2:** 504
Franklin Evans (Whitman), **Retro. Supp. I:** 393
"Frank O'Connor and *The New Yorker*" (Maxwell), **Supp. VIII:** 172
Franks, Lucinda, **Supp. XIII:** 12
"Franny" (Salinger), **III:** 564, 565–566
Franny and Zooey (Salinger), **III:** 552, 564–567; **IV:** 216; **Supp. XIII:** 263

Franzen, Jonathan, **Retro. Supp. II:** 279
Fraser, G. S., **Supp. XII:** 128; **Supp. XIV:** 162
Fraser, Joe, **III:** 46
Fraser, Marjorie Frost, **Retro. Supp. I:** 136
Frayn, Michael, **Supp. IV Part 2:** 582
Frazee, E. S., **Supp. I Part 2:** 381
Frazee, Esther Catherine. *See* Lindsay, Mrs. Vachel Thomas (Esther Catherine Frazee)
Frazer, Sir James G., **I:** 135; **II:** 204; **III:** 6–7; **IV:** 70; **Retro. Supp. I:** 80; **Supp. I Part 1:** 18; **Supp. I Part 2:** 541
Frazier, Ian, **Supp. VIII:** 272
Freaks: Myths and Images of the Secret Self (Fiedler), **Supp. XIII:** 106, 107
"Freak Show, The" (Sexton), **Supp. II Part 2:** 695
Freddy's Book (Gardner), **Supp. VI: 72**
Frederic, Harold, **I:** 409; **II: 126–149,** 175, 276, 289; **Retro. Supp. I:** 325
"Frederick Douglass" (Dunbar), **Supp. II Part 1:** 197, 199
"Frederick Douglass" (Hayden), **Supp. II Part 1:** 363
Frederick the Great, **II:** 103; **Supp. I Part 2:** 433
Fredrickson, George M., **Supp. I Part 2:** 589
"Free" (O'Hara), **III:** 369
Free, and Other Stories (Dreiser), **Retro. Supp. II:** 104
Free Air (Lewis), **II:** 441
Freedman, Monroe H., **Supp. VIII:** 127
Freedman, Richard, **Supp. V:** 244
"Freedom" (White), **Supp. I Part 2:** 659
"Freedom, New Hampshire" (Kinnell), **Supp. III Part 1:** 238, 239, 251
Freedom Is the Right to Choose: An Inquiry into the Battle for the American Future (MacLeish), **III:** 3
"Freedom's a Hard-Bought Thing" (Benét), **Supp. XI:** 47, 48
"Freedom's Plow" (Hughes), **Supp. I Part 1:** 346
"Free Fantasia: Tiger Flowers" (Hayden), **Supp. II Part 1:** 363, 366
Freeing of the Dust, The (Levertov), **Supp. III Part 1:** 281–282
"Free Lance, The" (Mencken), **III:** 104, 105
Free-Lance Pallbearers, The (Reed), **Supp. X:** 240, **242–243,** 244

"Free Man" (Hughes), **Supp. I Part 1:** 333
Freeman, Chris, **Supp. XIV:** 157, 159
Freeman, Douglas Southall, **Supp. I Part 2:** 486, 493
Freeman, Joseph, **II:** 26; **Supp. I Part 2:** 610
Freeman, Mary E. Wilkins, **II:** 401; **Supp. IX:** 79
Freeman, Mary Wilkins, **Retro. Supp. II:** 51, 136, 138
Freeman, Morgan, **Supp. XII:** 317
Freeman, Suzanne, **Supp. X:** 83
"Free Man's Worship, A" (Russell), **Supp. I Part 2:** 522
Freinman, Dorothy, **Supp. IX:** 94
Frémont, John Charles, **Supp. I Part 2:** 486
Fremont-Smith, Eliot, **Supp. XIII:** 263
Fremstad, Olive, **I:** 319; **Retro. Supp. I:** 10
French, Warren, **Supp. XII:** 118–119
French Connection, The (film), **Supp. V:** 226
French Poets and Novelists (James), **II:** 336; **Retro. Supp. I:** 220
"French Scarecrow, The" (Maxwell), **Supp. VIII:** 169, 170
French Ways and Their Meaning (Wharton), **IV:** 319; **Retro. Supp. I:** 378
Freneau, Eleanor Forman (Mrs. Philip Freneau), **Supp. II Part 1:** 266
Freneau, Philip M., **I:** 335; **II:** 295; **Supp. I Part 1:** 124, 125, 127, 145; **Supp. II Part 1:** 65, **253–277**
Frescoes for Mr. Rockefeller's City (MacLeish), **III:** 14–15
Fresh Air Fiend: Travel Writings, 1985–2000 (Theroux), **Supp. VIII:** 325
Freud, Sigmund, **I:** 55, 58, 59, 66, 67, 135, 241, 242, 244, 247, 248, 283; **II:** 27, 370, 546–547; **III:** 134, 390, 400, 418, 488; **IV:** 7, 70, 138, 295; **Retro. Supp. I:** 80, 176, 253; **Retro. Supp. II:** 104; **Supp. I Part 1:** 13, 43, 253, 254, 259, 260, 265, 270, 315; **Supp. I Part 2:** 493, 527, 616, 643, 647, 649; **Supp. IV Part 2:** 450; **Supp. VIII:** 103, 196; **Supp. IX:** 102, 155, 161, 308; **Supp. X:** 193, 194; **Supp. XII:** 14–15; **Supp. XIII:** 75; **Supp. XIV:** 83
Freud: The Mind of the Moralist (Sontag and Rieff), **Supp. III Part 2:** 455
"Freud: Within and Beyond Culture" (Trilling), **Supp. III Part 2:** 508
"Freud and Literature" (Trilling),

Supp. III Part 2: 502–503

Freudian Psychology and Veblen's Social Theory, The (Schneider), Supp. I Part 2: 650

Freudian Wish and Its Place in Ethics, The (Holt), I: 59

"Freud's Room" (Ozick), Supp. V: 268

"Friday Morning Trial of Mrs. Solano, The" (Ríos), Supp. IV Part 2: 538, 548

Frieburger, William, Supp. XIII: 239

Friedenberg, Edgar Z., Supp. VIII: 240

Friedman, Bruce Jay, I: 161; Supp. IV Part 1: 379

Friedman, Lawrence S., Supp. V: 273

Friedman, Milton, Supp. I Part 2: 648

Friedman, Norman, I: 431–432, 435, 439

Friedman, Stan, Supp. XII: 186

Friedmann, Georges, Supp. I Part 2: 645

"Fried Sausage" (Simic), Supp. VIII: 270

Friend, Julius, Retro. Supp. I: 80

Friend, The (Coleridge), II: 10

"Friend Husband's Latest" (Sayre), Retro. Supp. I: 104

"Friendly Debate between a Conformist and a Non-Conformist, A" (Wild), IV: 155

Friend of the Earth (Boyle), Supp. VIII: 12, 16

"Friend of the Fourth Decade, The" (Merrill), Supp. III Part 1: 327

"Friends" (Beattie), Supp. V: 23, 27

"Friends" (Paley), Supp. VI: 219, 226

"Friends" (Sexton), Supp. II Part 2: 693

Friends: More Will and Magna Stories (Dixon), Supp. XII: 148, 149

Friend's Delight, The (Bierce), I: 195

"Friends from Philadelphia" (Updike), Retro. Supp. I: 319

"Friendship" (Emerson), Supp. II Part 1: 290

"Friends of Heraclitus, The" (Simic), Supp. VIII: 284

"Friends of Kafka, The" (Singer), Retro. Supp. II: 308

"Friends of the Family, The" (McCarthy), II: 566

"Friend to Alexander, A" (Thurber), Supp. I Part 2: 616

"Frigate Pelican, The" (Moore), III: 208, 210–211, 215

"Frill, The" (Buck), Supp. XIV: 274

Frobenius, Leo, III: 475; Supp. III Part 2: 620

Froebel, Friedrich, Supp. XIV: 52–53

Frog (Dixon), Supp. XII: 151

"Frog Dances" (Dixon), Supp. XII: 151

"Frog Pond, The" (Kinnell), Supp. III Part 1: 254

"Frog Takes a Swim" (Dixon), Supp. XII: 152

Frohock, W. M., I: 34, 42

Frolic of His Own, A (Gaddis), Supp. IV Part 1: 279, 291, 292–294

"From a Mournful Village" (Jewett), Retro. Supp. II: 146

"From an Old House in America" (Rich), Supp. I Part 2: 551, 565–567

"From a Survivor" (Rich), Supp. I Part 2: 563

From a Writer's Notebook (Brooks), I: 254

From Bauhaus to Our House (Wolfe), Supp. III Part 2: 580, 581, 584

From Bondage (H. Roth), Supp. IX: 236, 238–240

"From *Chants* to *Borders* to *Communion*" (Fox), Supp. XIII: 217–218

"From Chicago" (Anderson), I: 108–109

From Death to Morning (Wolfe), IV: 450, 456, 458

"From Feathers to Iron" (Kunitz), Supp. III Part 1: 261

"From Fifth Avenue Up" (Barnes), Supp. III Part 1: 33, 44

"From Gorbunov and Gorchakov" (Brodsky), Supp. VIII: 26

"From Grand Canyon to Burbank" (H. Miller), III: 186

"From Hell to Breakfast," Supp. IX: 326–327

From Here to Eternity (film), Supp. XI: 221

From Here to Eternity (Jones), I: 477; Supp. XI: 215, 216, 217, 218, 219–221, 223, 224, 226, 229, 230, 231, 232, 234

From Here to Eternity (miniseries), Supp. XI: 234

From Jordan's Delight (Blackmur), Supp. II Part 1: 91

Fromm, Erich, I: 58; Supp. VIII: 196

From Morn to Midnight (Kaiser), I: 479

"From Native Son to Invisible Man" (Locke), Supp. IX: 306

"From Pico, the Women: A Life" (Creeley), Supp. IV Part 1: 149

From Ritual to Romance (Weston), II: 540; III: 12; Supp. I Part 2: 439

From Room to Room (Kenyon), Supp.

VII: 163–165, 166, 167

"From Room to Room" (Kenyon), Supp. VII: 159, 163–165

From Sand Creek: Rising in this Heart Which Is Our America (Ortiz), Supp. IV Part 2: 512–513

"From Sea Cliff, March" (Swenson), Supp. IV Part 2: 649

"From the Antigone" (Yeats), III: 459

From the Barrio: A Chicano Anthology (Salinas and Faderman, eds.), Supp. XIII: 313

"From the Childhood of Jesus" (Pinsky), Supp. VI: 244–245, 247

"From the Corpse Woodpiles, From the Ashes" (Hayden), Supp. II Part 1: 370

"From the Country to the City" (Bishop), Supp. I Part 1: 85, 86

"From the Cupola" (Merrill), Supp. III Part 1: 324–325, 331

"From the Dark Side of the Earth" (Oates), Supp. II Part 2: 510

"From the Diary of a New York Lady" (Parker), Supp. IX: 201

"From the Diary of One Not Born" (Singer), IV: 9

"From the East, Light" (Carver), Supp. III Part 1: 138

From the First Nine: Poems 1946–1976 (Merrill), Supp. III Part 1: 336

"From the Flats" (Lanier), Supp. I Part 1: 364

From the Heart of Europe (Matthiessen), III: 310

"From the Memoirs of a Private Detective" (Hammett), Supp. IV Part 1: 343

"From the Nursery" (Kenyon), Supp. VII: 171

"From the Poets in the Kitchen" (Marshall), Supp. XI: 277

From the Terrace (O'Hara), III: 362

"From the Thirties: Tillie Olsen and the Radical Tradition" (Rosenfelt), Supp. XIII: 296, 304

"From Trollope's Journal" (Bishop), Retro. Supp. II: 47

"Front, A" (Jarrell), II: 374

Front, The (film), Supp. I Part 1: 295

"Front and the Back Parts of the House, The" (Maxwell), Supp. VIII: 169

Frontier Eden (Bigelow), Supp. X: 227

"Frontiers of Culture" (Locke), Supp. XIV: 213

"Front Lines" (Snyder), Supp. VIII: 301

Frost, A. B., Retro. Supp. II: 72

"Frost: A Dissenting Opinion" (Cowley), **Supp. II Part 1:** 143

Frost: A Time to Talk (Francis), **Supp. IX:** 76, **85–86**

"Frost: He Is Sometimes a Poet and Sometimes a Stump-Speaker" (News-Week), **Retro. Supp. I:** 137

Frost, Isabelle Moodie, **II:** 150, 151

Frost, Jeanie, **II:** 151

Frost, Robert, **I:** 26, 27, 60, 63, 64, 171, 229, 303, 326, 418; **II:** 55, 58, **150–172,** 276, 289, 388, 391, 471, 523, 527, 529, 535; **III:** 5, 23, 67, 269, 271, 272, 275, 287, 453, 510, 523, 536, 575, 581, 591; **IV:** 140, 190, 415; **Retro. Supp. I:** 67, **121–144,** 276, 287, 292, 298, 299, 311, 413; **Retro. Supp. II:** 40, 47, 50, 146, 178, 181; **Supp. I Part 1:** 80, 242, 263, 264; **Supp. I Part 2:** 387, 461, 699; **Supp. II Part 1:** 4, 19, 26, 103; **Supp. III Part 1:** 63, 74–75, 239, 253; **Supp. III Part 2:** 546, 592, 593; **Supp. IV Part 1:** 15; **Supp. IV Part 2:** 439, 445, 447, 448, 599, 601; **Supp. VIII:** 20, 30, 32, 98, 100, 104, 259, 292; **Supp. IX:** 41, 42, 75, 76, 80, 87, 90, 266, 308; **Supp. X:** 64, 65, 66, 74, 120, 172; **Supp. XI:** 43, 123, 150, 153, 312; **Supp. XII:** 130, 241, 303, 307; **Supp. XIII:** 143, 147, 334–335; **Supp. XIV:** 42, 122, 222, 229

Frost, William Prescott, **II:** 150–151

"Frost at Midnight" (Coleridge), **Supp. X:** 71

"Frost Flowers" (Kenyon), **Supp. VII:** 168

Frothingham, Nathaniel, **I:** 3

Frothingham, Octavius B., **IV:** 173

"Frozen City, The" (Nemerov), **III:** 270

"Frozen Fields, The" (Bowles), **Supp. IV Part 1:** 80

"Fruit Garden Path, The" (Lowell), **II:** 516

"Fruit of the Flower" (Cullen), **Supp. IV Part 1:** 167

Fruit of the Tree, The (Wharton), **IV:** 314–315; **Retro. Supp. I:** 367, **370–371,** 373

"Fruit of Travel Long Ago" (Melville), **III:** 93

Fruits and Vegetables (Jong), **Supp. V:** 113, 115, 117, 118, 119

Frumkes, Lewis Burke, **Supp. XII:** 335–336

Fry, Christopher, **Supp. I Part 1:** 270

Fry, Roger, **Supp. XIV:** 336

Frye, Joanne, **Supp. XIII:** 292, 296, 298, 302

Frye, Northrop, **Supp. I Part 2:** 530; **Supp. II Part 1:** 101; **Supp. X:** 80; **Supp. XIII:** 19; **Supp. XIV:** 11, 15

Fryer, Judith, **Retro. Supp. I:** 379

Fuchs, Daniel, **Supp. XIII:** 106

Fuchs, Miriam, **Supp. IV Part 1:** 284

Fuehrer Bunker, The (Snodgrass), **Supp. VI:** 314, 315–317, 319–321

Fuel (Nye), **Supp. XIII:** 277, **282–284**

"Fuel" (Nye), **Supp. XIII:** 283

Fuertes, Gloria, **Supp. V:** 178

Fugard, Athol, **Supp. VIII:** 330; **Supp. XIII:** 205

Fugitive Group, The (Cowan), **IV:** 120

Fugitive Kind, The (T. Williams), **IV:** 381, 383

Fugitives, The (group), **IV:** 122, 124, 125, 131, 237, 238

Fugitives, The: A Critical Account (Bradbury), **IV:** 130

"Fugitive Slave Law, The" (Emerson), **II:** 13

Fugitive's Return (Glaspell), **Supp. III Part 1:** 182–184

Fuller, B. A. G., **III:** 605

Fuller, Margaret, **I:** 261; **II:** 7, 276; **IV:** 172; **Retro. Supp. I:** 155–156, 163; **Retro. Supp. II:** 46; **Supp. I Part 2:** 524; **Supp. II Part 1:** 279–306; **Supp. IX:** 37

Fuller, Thomas, **II:** 111, 112

Fullerton Street (Wilson), **Supp. VIII:** 331

"Full Fathom Five" (Plath), **Supp. I Part 2:** 538

Full Monty, The (musical, McNally), **Supp. XIII:** 207

"Full Moon" (Hayden), **Supp. II Part 1:** 370

"Full Moon: New Guinea" (Shapiro), **Supp. II Part 2:** 707

Full Moon and Other Plays (Price), **Supp. VI:** 266

"Full Moon and You're Not Here" (Cisneros), **Supp. VII:** 71–72

"Fullness of Life, The" (Wharton), **Retro. Supp. I:** 363

Full of Life (Fante), **Supp. XI:** 160

Full of Life (film), **Supp. XI:** 170

Full of Lust and Good Usage (Dunn), **Supp. XI:** 145–147

"Full Summer" (Olds), **Supp. X:** 212

Fulton, Robert, **Supp. I Part 2:** 519; **Supp. II Part 1:** 73

Function of Criticism, The (Winters), **Supp. II Part 2:** 812, 813

"Fundamentalism" (Tate), **IV:** 125

"Fundamental Project of Technology, The" (Kinnell), **Supp. III Part 1:** 253

"Funeral of Bobò, The" (Brodsky), **Supp. VIII:** 27, 28

"Funnel" (Sexton), **Supp. II Part 2:** 675

"Furious Seasons, The" (Carver), **Supp. III Part 1:** 137

Furious Seasons and Other Stories (Carver), **Supp. III Part 1:** 142, 143, 146

"Furnished Room, The" (Hayden), **Supp. II Part 1:** 386–387, 394, 397, 399, 406, 408

"Furor Scribendi" (O. Butler), **Supp. XIII:** 70

Fur Person, The (Sarton), **Supp. VIII:** **264–265**

Further Fables for Our Time (Thurber), **Supp. I Part 2:** 612

"Further in Summer than the Birds" (Dickinson), **I:** 471

Further Poems of Emily Dickinson (Bianchi and Hampson, ed.), **Retro. Supp. I:** 35

Further Range, A (Frost), **II:** 155; **Retro. Supp. I:** 132, 136, 137, 138, 139

"Fury of Aerial Bombardment, The" (Eberhart), **I:** 535–536

"Fury of Flowers and Worms, The" (Sexton), **Supp. II Part 2:** 694

"Fury of Rain Storms, The" (Sexton), **Supp. II Part 2:** 695

Fury of the Jungle (film), **Supp. XIII:** 163

Fussell, Paul, **Supp. V:** 241

"Future, if Any, of Comedy, The" (Thurber), **Supp. I Part 2:** 620

Future is Ours, Comrade, The: Conversations with the Russians (Kosinski), **Supp. VII:** 215

Futureland: Nine Stories of an Imminent World (Mosley), **Supp. XIII:** **247–249**

"Future Life, The" (Bryant), **Supp. I Part 1:** 170

Future Punishment of the Wicked, The (Edwards), **I:** 546

"Gabriel" (Rich), **Supp. I Part 2:** 557

Gabriel, Ralph H., **Supp. I Part 1:** 251

Gabriel, Trip, **Supp. V:** 212

Gabriel Conroy (Harte), **Supp. II Part 1:** 354

"Gabriel's Truth" (Kenyon), **Supp. VII:** 166

Gaddis, William, **Supp. IV Part 1:** **279–296; Supp. IV Part 2:** 484; **Supp. V:** 52; **Supp. IX:** 208; **Supp. X:** 301, 302

Gadiot, Pud, **Supp. XI:** 295
Gain (Powers), **Supp. IX:** 212, **220–221**
Gaines, Ernest, **Supp. X:** 250
Gaines, Ernest J., **Supp. X:** 24
Gaines, James R., **Supp. IX:** 190
Galamain, Ivan, **Supp. III Part 2:** 624
Galatea 2.2 (Powers), **Supp. IX:** 212, **219–220**
"Galatea Encore" (Brodsky), **Supp. VIII:** 31
Galbraith, John Kenneth, **Supp. I Part 2:** 645, 650
Galdós, Benito Pérez. *See* Pérez Galdós, Benito
Gale, Zona, **Supp. I Part 2:** 613; **Supp. VIII:** 155
"Gale in April" (Jeffers), **Supp. II Part 2:** 423
Galignani, Giovanni Antonio, **II:** 315
Galileo Galilei, **I:** 480–481; **Supp. XII:** 180; **Supp. XIII:** 75
Gallant, Mavis, **Supp. VIII:** 151
Gallatin, Albert, **I:** 5
"Gallery" (Goldbarth), **Supp. XII:** 188
"Gallery of Real Creatures, A" (Thurber), **Supp. I Part 2:** 619
Gallows Songs (Snodgrass), **Supp. VI:** 317
Gallup, Donald, **III:** 404, 478
Galsworthy, John, **III:** 70, 153, 382
Galton Case, The (Macdonald), **Supp. IV Part 2:** 463, 473, 474
"Gal Young 'Un" (Rawlings), **Supp. X:** 228
"Gambler, the Nun, and the Radio, The" (Hemingway), **II:** 250
"Gambler's Wife, The" (Dunbar), **Supp. II Part 1:** 196
Gambone, Philip, **Supp. XII:** 81
"Gambrel Roof, A" (Larcom), **Supp. XIII:** 144
"Game at Salzburg, A" (Jarrell), **II:** 384, 389
Game Management (Leopold), **Supp. XIV:** 182
"Game of Catch, A" (Wilbur), **Supp. III Part 2:** 552
"Games Two" (Wilbur), **Supp. III Part 2:** 550
"Gamut, The" (Angelou), **Supp. IV Part 1:** 15
Gandhi, Indira, **Supp. X:** 108
Gandhi, Mahatma, **III:** 179, 296–297; **IV:** 170, 185, 367; **Supp. VIII:** 203, 204; **Supp. X:** 27
Gandhi on Non-Violence (Merton, ed.), **Supp. VIII:** 204–205
"Gang of Mirrors, The" (Simic), **Supp. VIII:** 283

Gansevoort, Guert, **III:** 94
Gansevoort, Peter, **III:** 92
Garabedian, Michael, **Supp. XIII:** 115
Garbage (Ammons), **Supp. VII:** 24, 35–36
Garbage (Dixon), **Supp. XII:** 147, 148
Garbage Man, The (Dos Passos), **I:** 478, 479, 481, 493
Garber, Frederick, **Supp. IX:** 294–295
Garbo, Greta, **Supp. I Part 2:** 616
García, Cristina, **Supp. VIII:** 74; **Supp. XI: 177–192**
"García Lorca: A Photograph of the Granada Cemetery, 1966" (Levis), **Supp. XI:** 264
García Lorca, Federico. *See* Lorca, Federico García
García Márquez, Gabriel, **Supp. V:** 244; **Supp. VIII:** 81, 82, 84, 85; **Supp. XII:** 147, 310, 316, 322; **Supp. XIII:** 226
"Garden" (Marvell), **IV:** 161
"Garden, The" (Glück), **Supp. V:** 83
"Garden, The" (Strand), **Supp. IV Part 2:** 629
"Garden by Moonlight, The" (Lowell), **II:** 524
Gardener's Son, The (McCarthy), **Supp. VIII:** 187
"Gardenias" (Doty), **Supp. XI:** 122
"Gardenias" (Monette), **Supp. X:** 159
"Garden Lodge, The" (Cather), **I:** 316, 317
Garden of Adonis, The (Gordon), **II:** 196, 204–205, 209
Garden of Earthly Delights, A (Oates), **Supp. II Part 2:** 504, 507–509
"Garden of Eden" (Hemingway), **II:** 259
Garden of Eden, The (Hemingway), **Retro. Supp. I:** 186, **187–188**
"Garden of the Moon, The" (Doty), **Supp. XI:** 122
"Gardens, The" (Oliver), **Supp. VII:** 236
"Gardens of Mont-Saint-Michel, The" (Maxwell), **Supp. VIII:** 169
"Gardens of the Villa D'Este, The" (Hecht), **Supp. X:** 59
"Gardens of Zuñi, The" (Merwin), **Supp. III Part 1:** 351
Gardiner, Judith Kegan, **Supp. IV Part 1:** 205
Gardner, Erle Stanley, **Supp. IV Part 1:** 121, 345
Gardner, Isabella, **IV:** 127
Gardner, John, **Supp. I Part 1:** 193, 195, 196; **Supp. III Part 1:** 136, 142, 146; **Supp. VI: 61–76**
Gardons, S. S. *See* Snodgrass, W. D.

Garfield, John, **Supp. XII:** 160
Garibaldi, Giuseppe, **I:** 4; **II:** 284
Garland, Hamlin, **I:** 407; **II:** 276, 289; **III:** 576; **Retro. Supp. I:** 133; **Retro. Supp. II:** 72; **Supp. I Part 1:** 217; **Supp. IV Part 2:** 502
Garland Companion, The (Zverev), **Retro. Supp. I:** 278
Garments the Living Wear (Purdy), **Supp. VII:** 278–279, 280–281
Garner, Dwight, **Supp. X:** 202
Garnett, Edward, **I:** 405, 409, 417; **III:** 27
Garrett, George P., **Supp. I Part 1:** 196; **Supp. VII: 95–113; Supp. X:** 3, 7; **Supp. XI:** 218
Garrigue, Jean, **Supp. XII:** 260
Garrison, Deborah, **Supp. IX:** 299
Garrison, Fielding, **III:** 105
Garrison, William Lloyd, **Supp. I Part 2:** 524, 588, 683, 685, 686, 687; **Supp. XIV:** 54
"Garrison of Cape Ann, The" (Whittier), **Supp. I Part 2:** 691, 694
Garry Moore Show (television show), **Supp. IV Part 2:** 575
"Garter Motif" (White), **Supp. I Part 2:** 673
Gartner, Zsuzsi, **Supp. X:** 276
Garvey, Marcus, **Supp. III Part 1:** 175, 180; **Supp. IV Part 1:** 168; **Supp. X:** 135, 136
Gas (Kaiser), **I:** 479
Gas-House McGinty (Farrell), **II:** 41–42
Gaskell, Elizabeth, A., **Supp. I Part 2:** 580
Gasoline (Corso), **Supp. XII:** 118, **121–123,** 134
Gass, William H., **Supp. V:** 44, 52, 238; **Supp. VI: 77–96; Supp. IX:** 208; **Supp. XII:** 152; **Supp. XIV:** 305
Gassner, John, **IV:** 381; **Supp. I Part 1:** 284, 292
Gates, David, **Supp. V:** 24; **Supp. XIII:** 93
Gates, Elmer, **I:** 515–516
Gates, Henry Louis, **Retro. Supp. I:** 194, 195, 203; **Supp. X:** 242, 243, 245, 247
Gates, Lewis E., **III:** 315, 330
Gates, The (Rukeyser), **Supp. VI:** 271, 274, 281
"Gates, The" (Rukeyser), **Supp. VI:** 286
Gates, Tudor, **Supp. XI:** 307
Gates of Ivory, the Gates of Horn, The (McGrath), **Supp. X:** 118
Gates of Wrath, The; Rhymed Poems

(Ginsberg), **Supp. II Part 1:** 311, 319

Gathering of Fugitives, A (Trilling), **Supp. III Part 2:** 506, 512

Gathering of Zion, The: The Story of the Mormon Trail (Stegner), **Supp. IV Part 2:** 599, 602–603

Gather Together in My Name (Angelou), **Supp. IV Part 1:** 2, 3, 4–6, 11

Gathorne-Hardy, Robert, **Supp. XIV:** 344, 347, 348, 349

Gaudier-Brzeska, Henri, **III:** 459, 464, 465, 477

Gauguin, Paul, **I:** 34; **IV:** 290; **Supp. IV Part 1:** 81; **Supp. XII:** 128

"Gauley Bridge" (Rukeyser), **Supp. VI:** 278

Gauss, Christian, **II:** 82; **IV:** 427, 439–440, 444

Gautier, Théophile, **II:** 543; **III:** 466, 467; **Supp. I Part 1:** 277

Gay, John, **II:** 111; **Supp. I Part 2:** 523; **Supp. XIV:** 337

Gay, Peter, **I:** 560

Gay, Sydney Howard, **Supp. I Part 1:** 158

Gay, Walter, **IV:** 317

Gayatri Prayer, The, **III:** 572

"Gay Chaps at the Bar" (Brooks), **Supp. III Part 1:** 74, 75

Gaylord, Winfield R., **III:** 579–580

"Gazebo" (Carver), **Supp. III Part 1:** 138, 144, 145

Gazer Within, The, and Other Essays by Larry Levis, **Supp. XI:** 270

Gazzara, Ben, **Supp. VIII:** 319

Gazzo, Michael V., **III:** 155

"Geese Gone Beyond" (Snyder), **Supp. VIII:** 304

"Gegenwart" (Goethe), **Supp. II Part 1:** 26

Geisel, Theodor Seuss (Dr. Seuss), **Supp. X:** 56

Geismar, Maxwell, **II:** 178, 431; **III:** 71; **Supp. IX:** 15; **Supp. XI:** 223

Gelb, Arthur, **IV:** 380

Gelbart, Larry, **Supp. IV Part 2:** 591

Gelder, Robert Van, **Supp. XIII:** 166

Gelfant, Blanche H., **II:** 27, 41

Gelfman, Jean, **Supp. X:** 3

Gellhorn, Martha. *See* Hemingway, Mrs. Ernest (Martha Gellhorn)

Gelpi, Albert, **Supp. I Part 2:** 552, 554, 560

Gelpi, Barbara, **Supp. I Part 2:** 560

Gemini: an extended autobiographical statement on my first twenty-five years of being a black poet (Giovanni), **Supp. IV Part 1:** 11

"Gen" (Snyder), **Supp. VIII:** 302

"Gender of Sound, The" (Carson), **Supp. XII:** **106**

"Genealogy" (Komunyakaa), **Supp. XIII:** 129

"General Aims and Theories" (Crane), **I:** 389

General Died at Dawn, The (Odets), **Supp. II Part 2:** 546

"General Gage's Confession" (Freneau), **Supp. II Part 1:** 257

"General Gage's Soliloquy" (Freneau), **Supp. II Part 1:** 257

General History of the Robberies and Murders of the Most Notorious Pyrates from Their First Rise and Settlement in the Island of New Providence to the Present Year, A (Johnson), **Supp. V:** 128

"General William Booth Enters into Heaven" (Lindsay), **Supp. I Part 2:** 374, 382, 384, 385–388, 389, 392, 399

General William Booth Enters into Heaven and Other Poems (Lindsay), **Supp. I Part 2:** 379, 381, 382, 387–388, 391

"Generations of Men, The" (Frost), **Retro. Supp. I:** 128; **Supp. XIII:** 147

Generous Man, A (Price), **Supp. VI:** 259, 260, 261

Genesis (biblical book), **I:** 279; **II:** 540; **Retro. Supp. I:** 250, 256; **Supp. XII:** 54

"Genesis" (Stegner), **Supp. IV Part 2:** 604

Genesis: Book One (Schwartz), **Supp. II Part 2:** 640, 651–655

Genet, Jean, **I:** 71, 82, 83, 84; **Supp. IV Part 1:** 8; **Supp. XI:** 308; **Supp. XII:** 1; **Supp. XIII:** 74

"Genetic Expedition" (Dove), **Supp. IV Part 1:** 249, 257

"Genetics of Justice" (Alvarez), **Supp. VII:** 19

"Genial Host, The" (McCarthy), **II:** 564

"Genie in the Bottle, The" (Wilbur), **Supp. III Part 2:** 542

"Genius, The" (MacLeish), **III:** 19

Genius and Lust: A Journey through the Major Writings of Henry Miller (Mailer), **Retro. Supp. II:** 208

"Genius Child" (Hughes), **Retro. Supp. I:** 203

"Genius," The (Dreiser), **I:** 497, 501, 509–511, 519; **Retro. Supp. II:** 94–95, **102–103,** 104, 105

"Genteel Tradition in American Phi-

losophy, The" (Santayana), **I:** 222

"Gentle Communion" (Mora), **Supp. XIII:** 218–219

Gentle Crafter, The (O. Henry), **Supp. II Part 1:** 410

"Gentle Lena, The" (Stein), **IV:** 37, 40

Gentleman Caller, The (T. Williams), **IV:** 383

"Gentleman from Cracow, The" (Singer), **IV:** 9

"Gentleman of Bayou Têche, A" (Chopin), **Supp. I Part 1:** 211–212

"Gentleman of Shalott, The" (Bishop), **Supp. I Part 1:** 85, 86

Gentleman's Agreement (Hobson), **III:** 151

Gentry, Marshall Bruce, **Supp. IV Part 1:** 236

"Genuine Man, The" (Emerson), **II:** 10

Geo-Bestiary (Harrison), **Supp. VIII:** 53

"Geode" (Frost), **II:** 161

Geographical History of America, The (Stein), **IV:** 31, 45

Geography and Plays (Stein), **IV:** 29–30, 32, 43, 44

Geography III (Bishop), **Retro. Supp. II:** 50; **Supp. I Part 1:** 72, 73, 76, 82, 93, 94, 95

Geography of a Horse Dreamer (Shepard), **Supp. III Part 2:** 432

Geography of Home, The: California's Poetry of Place (Bluckey and Young, eds.), **Supp. XIII:** 313

Geography of Lograire, The (Merton), **Supp. VIII:** 208

Geography of the Heart (Johnson), **Supp. XI:** 129

"Geometric Poem, The" (Corso), **Supp. XII:** 132, 133–134

George, Diana Hume, **Supp. IV Part 2:** 447, 449, 450

George, Henry, **II:** 276; **Supp. I Part 2:** 518

George, Jan, **Supp. IV Part 1:** 268

George, Lynell, **Supp. XIII:** 234–235, 237, 249

George, Peter, **Supp. XI:** 302, 303, 304

George and the Dragon (Shanley), **Supp. XIV:** 315

George Bernard Shaw: His Plays (Mencken), **III:** 102

George Mills (Elkin), **Supp. VI:** **53–54**

"George Robinson: Blues" (Rukeyser), **Supp. VI:** 279

George's Mother (Crane), **I:** 408

"George Thurston" (Bierce), **I:** 202

"Georgia: Invisible Empire State" (Du Bois), **Supp. II Part 1:** 179

Georgia Boy (Caldwell), **I:** 288, 305–

306, 308, 309, 310

"Georgia Dusk" (Toomer), **Supp. IX:** 309

"Georgia Night" (Toomer), **Supp. III Part 2:** 481

Georgia Scenes (Longstreet), **II:** 70, 313; **Supp. I Part 1:** 352

Georgics (Virgil), **Retro. Supp. I:** 135

Georgoudaki, Ekaterini, **Supp. IV Part 1:** 12

"Geraldo No Last Name" (Cisneros), **Supp. VII:** 60–61

Gerald's Game (King), **Supp. V:** 141, 148–150, 151, 152

Gerald's Party (Coover), **Supp. V:** 49–50, 51, 52

Gérando, Joseph Marie de, **II:** 10

"Geranium" (O'Connor), **Retro. Supp. II:** 221, 236

Gerber, Dan, **Supp. VIII:** 39

Gerhardt, Rainer, **Supp. IV Part 1:** 142

"German Girls! The German Girls!, The" (MacLeish), **III:** 16

"German Refugee, The" (Malamud), **Supp. I Part 2:** 436, 437

"Germany's Reichswehr" (Agee), **I:** 35

Germinal (Zola), **III:** 318, 322

Gernsback, Hugo, **Supp. IV Part 1:** 101

"Gerontion" (Eliot), **I:** 569, 574, 577, 578, 585, 588; **III:** 9, 435, 436; **Retro. Supp. I:** 290

Gerry, Elbridge, **Supp. I Part 2:** 486

"Gerry's Jazz" (Komunyakaa), **Supp. XIII:** 125

Gershwin, Ira, **Supp. I Part 1:** 281

"Gert" (Monette), **Supp. X:** 158

Gertrude of Stony Island Avenue (Purdy), **Supp. VII:** 281–282

Gertrude Stein (Sprigge), **IV:** 31

Gertrude Stein: A Biography of Her Work (Sutherland), **IV:** 38

"Gertrude Stein and the Geography of the Sentence" (Gass), **Supp. VI:** 87

Gesell, Silvio, **III:** 473

"Gestalt at Sixty" (Sarton), **Supp. VIII:** 260

"Gesture toward an Unfound Renaissance, A" (Stafford), **Supp. XI:** 323

Getlin, Josh, **Supp. V:** 22; **Supp. VIII:** 75, 76, 78, 79

"Getting Along" (Larcom), **Supp. XIII:** 144

"Getting Along with Nature" (Berry), **Supp. X:** 31–32

"Getting Away from Already Pretty Much Being Away from It All" (Wallace), **Supp. X:** 314–315

"Getting Born" (Shields), **Supp. VII:** 311

"Getting Out of Jail on Monday" (Wagoner), **Supp. IX:** 327

"Getting There" (Plath), **Supp. I Part 2:** 539, 542

"Getting to the Poem" (Corso), **Supp. XII:** 135

Getty, J. Paul, **Supp. X:** 108

"Gettysburg: July 1, 1863" (Kenyon), **Supp. VII:** 172

Gettysburg, Manila, Acoma (Masters), **Supp. I Part 2:** 471

Ghachem, Malick, **Supp. X:** 17

"Ghazals: Homage to Ghalib" (Rich), **Supp. I Part 2:** 557

Ghost, The (Crane), **I:** 409, 421

"Ghost Chant, et alii" (Komunyakaa), **Supp. XIII:** 114

Ghost in the Music, A (Nichols), **Supp. XIII:** 267

"Ghostlier Demarcations, Keener Sounds" (Vendler), **Supp. I Part 2:** 565

"Ghostly Father, I Confess" (McCarthy), **II:** 565–566

Ghostly Lover, The (Hardwick), **Supp. III Part 1:** 194–196, 208, 209

"Ghost of the Buffaloes, The" (Lindsay), **Supp. I Part 2:** 393

Ghosts (Auster), **Supp. XII:** 22, **24, 26–27**

Ghosts (Ibsen), **III:** 152

Ghosts (Wharton), **IV:** 316, 327

Ghost Town (Coover), **Supp. V:** 52–53

Ghost Writer, The (Roth), **Retro. Supp. II:** 22, 290, 291; **Supp. III Part 2:** 420–421

"G.I. Graves in Tuscany" (Hugo), **Supp. VI:** 138

Giachetti, Fosco, **Supp. IV Part 2:** 520

"Giacometti" (Wilbur), **Supp. III Part 2:** 551

Giacometti, Alberto, **Supp. VIII:** 168, 169

Giacomo, Padre, **II:** 278–279

Giant's House, The: A Romance (McCracken), **Supp. X:** 86

"Giant Snail" (Bishop), **Retro. Supp. II:** 49

Giant Weapon, The (Winters), **Supp. II Part 2:** 810

"Giant Woman, The" (Oates), **Supp. II Part 2:** 523

Gibbon, Edward, **I:** 4, 378; **IV:** 126; **Supp. I Part 2:** 503; **Supp. III Part 2:** 629; **Supp. XIII:** 75; **Supp. XIV:** 97

Gibbons, Kaye, **Supp. X:** **41–54;** **Supp. XII:** 311

Gibbons, Reginald, **Supp. X:** 113, 124, 127

Gibbons, Richard, **Supp. I Part 1:** 107

"Gibbs" (Rukeyser), **Supp. VI:** 273

Gibbs, Barbara, **Supp. IV Part 2:** 644

Gibbs, Wolcott, **Supp. I Part 2:** 604, 618; **Supp. VIII:** 151

"GIBSON" (Baraka), **Supp. II Part 1:** 54

Gibson, Charles Dana, **Supp. X:** 184

Gibson, Graeme, **Supp. XIII:** 20

Gibson, Wilfrid W., **Retro. Supp. I:** 128

Giddins, Gary, **Supp. XIII:** 245

Gide, André, **I:** 271, 290; **II:** 581; **III:** 210; **IV:** 53, 289; **Supp. I Part 1:** 51; **Supp. IV Part 1:** 80, 284, 347; **Supp. IV Part 2:** 681, 682; **Supp. VIII:** 40; **Supp. X:** 187; **Supp. XIV:** 24, 348

Gideon Planish (Lewis), **II:** 455

Gielgud, John, **I:** 82; **Supp. XI:** 305

Gierow, Dr. Karl Ragnar, **III:** 404

Gifford, Bill, **Supp. XI:** 38

"Gift, The" (Creeley), **Supp. IV Part 1:** 153

"Gift, The" (Doolittle), **Supp. I Part 1:** 267

Gift, The (Nabokov), **III:** 246, 255, 261–263; **Retro. Supp. I:** 264, 266, **268–270,** 273, 274–275, 278

"Gift from the City, A" (Updike), **Retro. Supp. I:** 320

"Gift of God, The" (Robinson), **III:** 512, 517, 518–521, 524

Gift of the Black Folk, The: The Negroes in the Making of America (Du Bois), **Supp. II Part 1:** 179

"Gift of the Magi, The" (O. Henry), **Supp. II Part 1:** 394, 406, 408

"Gift of the *Osuo,* The" (Johnson), **Supp. VI:** 194

"Gift of the Prodigal, The" (Taylor), **Supp. V:** 314, 326

"Gift Outright, The" (Frost), **II:** 152; **Supp. IV Part 1:** 15

"Gigolo" (Plath), **Retro. Supp. II:** 257

"Gila Bend" (Dickey), **Supp. IV Part 1:** 185–186

Gilbert, Jack, **Supp. IX:** 287

Gilbert, Peter, **Supp. IX:** 291, 300

Gilbert, Roger, **Supp. XI:** 124

Gilbert, Sandra M., **Retro. Supp. I:** 42; **Retro. Supp. II:** 324; **Supp. IX:** 66

Gilbert, Susan. *See* Dickinson, Mrs. William A.

Gilbert and Sullivan, **Supp. IV Part 1:** 389

Gil Blas (Le Sage), **II:** 290

Gilded Age, The (Twain), **III:** 504; **IV:** 198

"Gilded Six-Bits, The" (Hurston), **Supp. VI:** 154–155

Gilder, R. W., **Retro. Supp. II:** 66; **Supp. I Part 2:** 418

Gildersleeve, Basil, **Supp. I Part 1:** 369

Giles, H. A., **Retro. Supp. I:** 289

Giles, James R., **Supp. IX:** 11, 15; **Supp. XI:** 219, 223–224, 228, 234

"Giles Corey of the Salem Farms" (Longfellow), **II:** 505, 506; **Retro. Supp. II:** 166, 167

Giles Goat-Boy (Barth), **I:** 121, 122–123, 129, 130, 134, 135–138; **Supp. V:** 39

Gill, Brendan, **Supp. I Part 2:** 659, 660

Gillespie, Nick, **Supp. XIV:** 298, 311

Gillette, Chester, **I:** 512

Gilligan, Carol, **Supp. XIII:** 216

Gillis, Jim, **IV:** 196

Gillis, Steve, **IV:** 195

Gilman, Charlotte Perkins, **Supp. I Part 2:** 637; **Supp. V:** 121, 284, 285; **Supp. XI: 193–211; Supp. XIII:** 295, 306

Gilman, Daniel Coit, **Supp. I Part 1:** 361, 368, 370

Gilman, Richard, **IV:** 115; **Supp. IV Part 2:** 577; **Supp. XIII:** 100

Gilmore, Eddy, **Supp. I Part 2:** 618

Gilpin, Charles, **III:** 392

Gilpin, Laura, **Retro. Supp. I:** 7

Gilpin, Sam, **Supp. V:** 213

Gilpin, William, **Supp. IV Part 2:** 603

"Gil's Furniture Bought & Sold" (Cisneros), **Supp. VII:** 61–62, 64

"Gimpel the Fool" (Singer), **IV:** 14; **Retro. Supp. II:** 22, 307

Gimpel the Fool and Other Stories (Singer), **IV:** 1, 7–9, 10, 12

"Gin" (Levine), **Supp. V:** 193

"Gingerbread House, The" (Coover), **Supp. V:** 42–43

Gingerbread Lady, The (Simon), **Supp. IV Part 2:** 580, 583–584, 588

Gingerich, Willard, **Supp. IV Part 2:** 510

Gingertown (McKay), **Supp. X:** 132, 139

Gingrich, Arnold, **Retro. Supp. I:** 113

Ginna, Robert, **Supp. IX:** 259

Ginsberg, Allen, **I:** 183; **Retro. Supp. I:** 411, 426, 427; **Retro. Supp. II:** 280; **Supp. II Part 1:** 30, 32, 58, **307–333; Supp. III Part 1:** 2, 91, 96, 98, 100, 222, 226; **Supp. III Part 2:** 541, 627; **Supp. IV Part 1:** 79, 90, 322; **Supp. IV Part 2:** 502; **Supp. V:** 168, 336; **Supp. VIII:** 239, 242–243, 289; **Supp. IX:** 299; **Supp. X:** 120, 204; **Supp. XI:** 135, 297; **Supp. XII:** 118–119, 121–122, 124, 126, 130–131, 136, 182; **Supp. XIV:** 15, 53, 54, 125, 137, 141, 142, 143–144, 148, 150, 269, 280, 283

Gioia, Dana, **Supp. IX:** 279; **Supp. XII:** 209; **Supp. XIII:** 337

Giotto di Bondone, **Supp. I Part 2:** 438; **Supp. XI:** 126

Giovanni, Nikki, **Supp. I Part 1:** 66; **Supp. II Part 1:** 54; **Supp. IV Part 1:** 11; **Supp. VIII:** 214

Giovanni's Room (Baldwin), **Retro. Supp. II:** 5, 6, **6–7**, 8, 10; **Supp. I Part 1:** 51, 52, 55–56, 57, 60, 63, 67; **Supp. III Part 1:** 125

Giovannitti, Arturo, **I:** 476

"Giraffe" (Swenson), **Supp. IV Part 2:** 651

Giraldi, Giovanni Battista. *See* Cinthio

"Girl" (Kincaid), **Supp. VII:** 182–183

"Girl, The" (Olds), **Supp. X:** 207

"Girl from Lynn Bathes Horse!!" (McCarriston), **Supp. XIV:** 266

"Girl from Red Lion, P.A., A" (Mencken), **III:** 111

Girl in Glass, The: Love Poems (W. J. Smith), **Supp. XIII:** 335

"Girl in the Grave, The" (McCoy), **Supp. XIII:** 170

"Girl of the Golden West" (Didion), **Supp. IV Part 1:** 195, 208, 211

Girl of the Golden West, The (Puccini), **III:** 139

"Girl on the Baggage Truck, The" (O'Hara), **III:** 371–372

Girls at Play (Theroux), **Supp. VIII:** 314, 315, 316, **317**

"Girls at the Sphinx, The" (Farrell), **II:** 45

Girl Sleuth, The: A Feminist Guide (Mason), **Supp. VIII:** 133, 135, **139**, 142

"Girl's Story, A" (Bambara), **Supp. XI:** 10–11

"Girl the Prince Liked, The" (Z. Fitzgerald), **Supp. IX:** 71

Girl Who Loved Tom Gordon, The (King), **Supp. V:** 138, 152

Girl with Curious Hair (Wallace), **Supp. X:** 301, **305–308**

"Girl with Curious Hair" (Wallace), **Supp. X:** 306

"Girl with Silver Eyes, The" (Hammett), **Supp. IV Part 1:** 344, 345

"Girl with Talent, The" (Z. Fitzgerald), **Supp. IX:** 71

Girodias, Maurice, **III:** 171; **Supp. XI:** 297

Giroux, Robert, **Retro. Supp. II:** 177, 229, 235; **Supp. IV Part 1:** 280; **Supp. VIII:** 195

Gish, Dorothy, **Retro. Supp. I:** 103

Gissing, George, **II:** 138, 144

Gittings, Robert, **II:** 531

"Give Us Back Our Country" (Masters), **Supp. I Part 2:** 472

"Give Way, Ye Gates" (Roethke), **III:** 536

"Give Your Heart to the Hawks" (Jeffers), **Supp. II Part 2:** 433

"Giving Blood" (Updike), **IV:** 226; **Retro. Supp. I:** 332

Giving Good Weight (McPhee), **Supp. III Part 1:** 307

"Giving Myself Up" (Strand), **Supp. IV Part 2:** 627

Glackens, William, **Retro. Supp. II:** 103

Gladden, Washington, **III:** 293; **Supp. I Part 1:** 5

Gladstone, William Ewart, **Supp. I Part 2:** 419

"Gladys Poem, The" (Alvarez), **Supp. VII:** 10

"Glance at German 'Kultur,' A" (Bourne), **I:** 228

Glance Away, A (Wideman), **Supp. X:** 320

"Glance from the Bridge, A" (Wilbur), **Supp. III Part 2:** 551

Glance toward Shakespeare, A (Chapman), **Supp. XIV:** 44

Glanville-Hicks, Peggy, **Supp. IV Part 1:** 84

Glare (Ammons), **Supp. VII:** 35–36

Glasgow, Cary, **II:** 173, 182

Glasgow, Ellen, **II: 173–195; IV:** 328; **Supp. X:** 228, 234

Glasmon, Kubec, **Supp. XIII:** 166

Glaspell, Susan, **Supp. III Part 1: 175–191; Supp. X:** 46

"Glass" (Francis), **Supp. IX:** 80

Glass, Irony, and God (Carson), **Supp. XII:** 97, **104–106**

"Glass Ark, The" (Komunyakaa), **Supp. XIII:** 129

Glass Bees, The (Jünger; Bogan and Mayer, trans.), **Supp. III Part 1:** 63

"Glass Blower of Venice" (Malamud), **Supp. I Part 2:** 450

"Glass Essay, The" (Carson), **Supp. XII: 104–105**

"Glass Face in the Rain, A: New Poems" (Stafford), **Supp. XI: 327–328**

Glass Key, The (Hammett), **Supp. IV**

Part 1: 351–353

"Glass Meadows" (Bausch), **Supp. VII:** 53–54

Glass Menagerie, The (T. Williams), **I:** 81; **IV:** 378, 379, 380, 382, 383, 385, 386, 387, 388, 389, 390, 391, 392, 393–394, 395, 398; **Supp. IV Part 1:** 84

"Glass Mountain, The" (Barthelme), **Supp. IV Part 1:** 47

Glatstein, Jacob, **Supp. X:** 70

Glazer, Nathan, **Supp. VIII:** 93, 243

"Gleaners, The" (Merwin), **Supp. III Part 1:** 346

Gleanings in Europe (Cooper), **I:** 346

Gleason, Ralph J., **Supp. IX:** 16

Glenday, Michael, **Retro. Supp. II:** 210

Glengarry Glen Ross (film), **Supp. XIV:** 242

Glengarry Glen Ross (Mamet), **Supp. XIV:** 239, 240, 242, 245, 246, 250, 254, 255

Glimcher, Arne, **Supp. VIII:** 73

"Glimpses" (Jones), **Supp. XI:** 218

Glimpses of the Moon, The (Wharton), **II:** 189–190; **IV:** 322–323; **Retro. Supp. I:** 381

"Glimpses of Vietnamese Life" (Levertov), **Supp. III Part 1:** 282

Glisson, J. T., **Supp. X:** 234

Gloria Mundi (Frederic), **II:** 144–145

Gloria Naylor (Fowler), **Supp. VIII:** 224

Glory of Hera, The (Gordon), **II:** 196–197, 198, 199, 217–220

Glory of the Conquered, The (Glaspell), **Supp. III Part 1:** 176

Glotfelty, Cheryll, **Supp. IX:** 25

Gluck, Christoph Willibald, **II:** 210, 211

Glück, Louise, **Supp. V: 77–94; Supp. VIII:** 272; **Supp. X:** 209; **Supp. XIV:** 269

"Glutton, The" (Shapiro), **Supp. II Part 2:** 705

"Glutton for Punishment, A" (Yates), **Supp. XI:** 341

Gnädiges Fräulein, The (T. Williams), **IV:** 382, 395, 398

Gnomes and Occasions (Nemerov), **III:** 269

Gnomologia (Fuller), **II:** 111

"Gnothis Seauton" (Emerson), **II:** 11, 18–19

Go (Holmes), **Supp. XIV:** 144

"Goal of Intellectual Men, The" (Eberhart), **I:** 529–530

Go-Between, The (Hartley), **Supp. I Part 1:** 293

Gobineau, Joseph Arthur de, **Supp. XIV:** 209

God and the American Writer (Kazin), **Supp. VIII: 108–109**

Godard, Jean-Luc, **Supp. I Part 2:** 558

Godbey (Masters), **Supp. I Part 2:** 472

God Bless You, Mr. Rosewater (Vonnegut), **Supp. II Part 2:** 758, 767, 768–769, 771, 772

Goddess Abides, The (Buck), **Supp. II Part 1:** 129, 131–132

Gödel, Kurt, **Supp. IV Part 1:** 43

Godfather (Puzo), **Supp. IV Part 1:** 390

"God in the Doorway" (Dillard), **Supp. VI:** 28

"God is a distant-stately Lover" (Dickinson), **I:** 471

Godkin, E. L., **II:** 274

God Knows (Heller), **Supp. IV Part 1:** 386, 388–389

God Made Alaska for the Indians (Reed), **Supp. X:** 241

God of His Fathers, The (London), **II:** 469

God of Vengeance (Asch), **IV:** 11

Go Down, Moses (Faulkner), **Retro. Supp. I:** 75, 82, 85, 86, 88, 89, 90, 92

"Go Down, Moses" (Faulkner), **II:** 71–72

Go Down, Moses (Hayden), **Supp. II Part 1:** 365

Go Down, Moses and Other Stories (Faulkner), **II:** 71; **Supp. X:** 52

"Go Down Death A Funeral Sermon" (Johnson), **Supp. IV Part 1:** 7

"God Rest Ye Merry, Gentlemen" (Hemingway), **IV:** 122

Godric (Buechner), **Supp. XII:** 53

Gods, The (Goldbarth), **Supp. XII:** 189, 190

Gods Arrive, The (Wharton), **IV:** 326–327; **Retro. Supp. I:** 382

"God Save the Rights of Man" (Freneau), **Supp. II Part 1:** 268

"Godsildren" (Swenson), **Supp. IV Part 2:** 645

"God's Christ Theory" (Carson), **Supp. XII:** 106

God's Country and My People (Morris), **III:** 238

Gods Determinations touching his Elect: and the Elects Combat in their Conversion, and Coming up to God in Christ together with the Comfortable Effects thereof (Taylor), **IV:** 155–160, 165

God-Seeker, The (Lewis), **II:** 456

God's Favorite (Simon), **Supp. IV Part 2:** 575, 586, 588, 590

God's Little Acre (Caldwell), **I:** 288, 289, 290, 297, 298–302, 305–306, 309, 310

God's Man: A Novel in Wood Cuts (Ward), **I:** 31

"God's Peace in November" (Jeffers), **Supp. II Part 2:** 420

"God Stiff" (Carson), **Supp. XII:** 106

God's Trombones (Johnson), **Supp. II Part 1:** 201

"God the Father and the Empty House" (McCarriston), **Supp. XIV:** 273

Godwin, William, **II:** 304; **III:** 415; **Supp. I Part 1:** 126, 146; **Supp. I Part 2:** 512, 513–514, 522, 709, 719

God without Thunder (Ransom), **III:** 495–496, 499

Goebbels, Josef, **III:** 560

Goebel, Irma, **Supp. X:** 95

Goen, C. C., **I:** 560

Goethe, Johann Wolfgang von, **I:** 181, 396, 587–588; **II:** 5, 6, 320, 344, 488, 489, 492, 502, 556; **III:** 395, 453, 607, 612, 616; **IV:** 50, 64, 173, 326; **Retro. Supp. I:** 360; **Retro. Supp. II:** 94; **Supp. I Part 2:** 423, 457; **Supp. II Part 1:** 26; **Supp. III Part 1:** 63; **Supp. IX:** 131, 308; **Supp. X:** 60; **Supp. XI:** 169

Gogol, Nikolai, **I:** 296; **IV:** 1, 4; **Retro. Supp. I:** 266, 269; **Supp. VIII:** 14

Going, William T., **Supp. VIII:** 126

Going After Cacciato (O'Brien), **Supp. V:** 237, 238, 239, 244–246, 248, 249

Going All the Way (Wakefield), **Supp. VIII:** 43

"Going Critical" (Bambara), **Supp. XI:** 14

Going for the Rain (Ortiz), **Supp. IV Part 2:** 499, 505–508, 509, 514

"Going Home by Last Night" (Kinnell), **Supp. III Part 1:** 244

"Going Home in America" (Hardwick), **Supp. III Part 1:** 205

"Going North" (Salinas), **Supp. XIII:** 316

Going South (Lardner and Buck), **II:** 427

Going To and Fro and Walking Up and Down (Reznikoff), **Supp. XIV:** 280, 282, 284, 285

Going to Meet the Man (Baldwin), **Supp. I Part 1:** 60, 62–63

"Going to Meet the Man" (Baldwin), **Retro. Supp. II:** 8, 9; **Supp. I Part 1:** 62–63

"Going to Naples" (Welty), **IV:** 278; **Retro. Supp. I:** 352, 353

"Going to Shrewsbury" (Jewett), **II:** 393

"Going to the Bakery" (Bishop), **Supp. I Part 1:** 93

Going-to-the-Stars (Lindsay), **Supp. I Part 2:** 398

Going-to-the-Sun (Lindsay), **Supp. I Part 2:** 397–398

Going to the Territory (Ellison), **Retro. Supp. II:** 119, 123–124

"Going towards Pojoaque, A December Full Moon/72" (Harjo), **Supp. XII:** 218

"Going Under" (Dubus), **Supp. VII:** 83

"Gold" (Francis), **Supp. IX:** 82

Gold (O'Neill), **III:** 391

Gold, Michael, **II:** 26; **IV:** 363, 364, 365; **Retro. Supp. II:** 323; **Supp. I Part 1:** 331; **Supp. I Part 2:** 609; **Supp. XIV:** 288

Goldbarth, Albert, **Supp. XII: 175–195**

Goldbarth's Book of Occult Phenomena (Goldbarth), **Supp. XII:** 181

Goldberg, S. L., **Supp. VIII:** 238

"Gold Bug, The" (Poe), **III:** 410, 413, 419, 420

Gold Bug Variations, The (Powers), **Supp. IX:** 210, 212, **216–217**, 219

Gold Cell, The (Olds), **Supp. X: 206–209**

Gold Diggers, The (Monette), **Supp. X:** 153

Golde, Miss (Mencken's Secretary), **III:** 104, 107

Golden, Harry, **III:** 579, 581; **Supp. VIII:** 244

Golden, Mike, **Supp. XI:** 294, 295, 297, 299, 303

Golden Age, The (Gurney), **Supp. V:** 101–103

Golden Apples (Rawlings), **Supp. X: 228–229**, 230, 234

Golden Apples, The (Welty), **IV:** 261, 271–274, 281, 293; **Retro. Supp. I:** 341, 342, 343, **350–351**, 352, 355

Golden Apples of the Sun, The (Bradbury), **Supp. IV Part 1:** 102, 103

Golden Book of Springfield, The (Lindsay), **Supp. I Part 2:** 376, 379, 395, 396

Golden Bough, The (Frazer), **II:** 204, 549; **III:** 6–7; **Supp. I Part 1:** 18; **Supp. IX:** 123; **Supp. X:** 124

Golden Bowl, The (James), **II:** 320, 333, 335; **Retro. Supp. I:** 215, 216, 218–219, 232, **234–235**, 374

Golden Boy (Odets), **Supp. II Part 2:** 538, 539, 540–541, 546, 551

Golden Calves, The (Auchincloss), **Supp. IV Part 1:** 35

Golden Day, The (Mumford), **Supp. II Part 2:** 471, 475, 477, 483, 484, 488–489, 493

Golden Fleece, The (Gurney), **Supp. V:** 97

Golden Grove, The: Selected Passages from the Sermons and Writings of Jeremy Taylor (L. P. Smith), **Supp. XIV:** 345

"Golden Heifer, The" (Wylie), **Supp. I Part 2:** 707

"Golden Honeymoon, The" (Lardner), **II:** 429–430, 431

Golden Journey, The (W. J. Smith and Bogan, comps.), **Supp. XIII:** 347

"Golden Lads" (Marquand), **III:** 56

Golden Legend, The (Longfellow), **II:** 489, 490, 495, 505, 506, 507; **Retro. Supp. II:** 159, 165, 166

Golden Mean and Other Poems, The (Tate and Wills), **IV:** 122

"Golden Retrievals" (Doty), **Supp. XI:** 132

Golden Shakespeare, The: An Anthology (L. P. Smith), **Supp. XIV:** 349

Goldensohn, Lorrie, **Retro. Supp. II:** 51

Golden Treasury of Best Songs and Lyrical Poems in the English Language (Palgrave), **Retro. Supp. I:** 124

Golden Treasury of the Best Songs and Lyrical Poems in the English Language (Palgrave), **Supp. XIV:** 340

Golden Whales of California and Other Rhymes in the American Language, The (Lindsay), **Supp. I Part 2:** 394–395, 396

"Goldfish Bowl, The" (Francis), **Supp. IX:** 78

Goldin Boys, The (Epstein), **Supp. XIV:** 112

Golding, Arthur, **III:** 467, 468

Golding, William, **Supp. IV Part 1:** 297

Goldini, Carlo, **II:** 274

Goldkorn Tales (Epstein), **Supp. XII: 163–164**

Goldman, Albert, **Supp. XI:** 299

Goldman, Emma, **III:** 176, 177; **Supp. I Part 2:** 524

Goldman, William, **Supp. IV Part 2:** 474

"Gold Mountain Stories" project (Kingston), **Supp. V:** 164

Goldring, Douglas, **III:** 458

Goldsmith, Oliver, **II:** 273, 282, 299, 304, 308, 314, 315, 514; **Retro.**

Supp. I: 335; **Supp. I Part 1:** 310; **Supp. I Part 2:** 503, 714, 716

Gold Standard and the Logic of Naturalism, The (Michaels), **Retro. Supp. I:** 369

Goldwater, Barry, **I:** 376; **III:** 38

Goldwyn, Samuel, **Retro. Supp. II:** 199; **Supp. I Part 1:** 281

Golem, The (Leivick), **IV:** 6

"Goliardic Song" (Hecht), **Supp. X:** 63

"Go Like This" (Moore), **Supp. X:** 165

Goll, Ivan, **Supp. III Part 1:** 235, 243–244; **Supp. III Part 2:** 621

Goncharova, Natalya, **Supp. IX:** 66

Goncourt, Edmond de, **II:** 325, 328; **III:** 315, 317–318, 321; **Retro. Supp. I:** 226

Goncourt, Jules de, **II:** 328; **III:** 315, 317–318, 321

Gone Fishin' (Mosley), **Supp. XIII: 235–236**, 240

"Gone West" (Rodriguez), **Supp. XIV:** 308

Gone with the Wind (film), **Retro. Supp. I:** 113

Gone with the Wind (Mitchell), **II:** 177; **Retro. Supp. I:** 340

Gongora y Argote, Luis de, **II:** 552

Gonzalez, David, **Supp. VIII:** 85

Gooch, Brad, **Supp. XII:** 121

Good, George, **Supp. XI:** 306

"Good and Not So Good, The" (Dunn), **Supp. XI:** 141

"Good Anna, The" (Stein), **IV:** 37, 40, 43

Good As Gold (Heller), **Supp. IV Part 1:** 386, 388, 394

Good Boys and Dead Girls and Other Essays (Gordon), **Supp. IV Part 1:** 309–310

"Good-by and Keep Cold" (Frost), **Retro. Supp. I:** 135

"Good-bye" (Emerson), **II:** 19

"Goodbye, Christ" (Hughes), **Retro. Supp. I:** 202, 203

Goodbye, Columbus (Roth), **Retro. Supp. II:** 280, 281, 290; **Supp. III Part 2:** 403–406; **Supp. XIV:** 112

"Goodbye, Columbus" (Roth), **Supp. III Part 2:** 401, 404, 408–409, 411

Goodbye, Columbus and Five Short Stories (Roth), **Retro. Supp. II:** 279

"Goodbye, Goldeneye" (Swenson), **Supp. IV Part 2:** 651

"Goodbye, Mr. Chipstein" (Epstein), **Supp. XIV:** 103, 108

"Goodbye, My Brother" (Cheever), **Supp. I Part 1:** 175, 177, 193

"Goodbye and Good Luck" (Paley),

Supp. VI: 219, 223

Goodbye Girl, The (film), **Supp. IV Part 2:** 589

Goodbye Girl, The (musical), **Supp. IV Part 2:** 576, 588

Goodbye Girl, The (Simon), **Supp. IV Part 2:** 575

Goodbye Look, The (Macdonald), **Supp. IV Part 2:** 473, 474

"Good-Bye My Fancy" (Whitman), **IV:** 348

"Goodbye to All That" (Didion), **Supp. IV Part 1:** 197

Goodbye to All That (Graves), **I:** 477

Goodbye to Berlin (Isherwood), **Supp. XIV:** 159, 161, 162, 169

"Good-Bye to the Mezzogiorno" (Auden), **Supp. II Part 1:** 19

"Goodbye to the Poetry of Calcium" (Wright), **Supp. III Part 2:** 599

"Good Company" (Matthews), **Supp. IX:** 160

"Good Country People" (O'Connor), **III:** 343, 350, 351, 352, 358; **Retro. Supp. II:** 229, 232

Good Day to Die, A (Harrison), **Supp. VIII:** 42–44, 45, 47

Good Doctor, The (Simon), **Supp. IV Part 2:** 575, 585

Good Earth, The (Buck), **Supp. I Part 1:** 49; **Supp. II Part 1:** 115–175, 118, 125, 132

Good European, The (Blackmur), **Supp. II Part 1:** 91

Good Evening Mr. & Mrs. America, and All the Ships at Sea (Bausch), **Supp. VII:** 41, 47, 52

Good Gray Poet, The (O'Connor), **Retro. Supp. I:** 407

Good Health and How We Won It (Sinclair), **Supp. V:** 285–286

Good Hearts (Price), **Supp. VI:** 259, 265

"Good Job Gone, A" (Hughes), **Retro. Supp. I:** 204

Good Journey, A (Ortiz), **Supp. IV Part 2:** 497, 499, 503, 505, 509–510, 514

Good Luck in Cracked Italian (Hugo), **Supp. VI:** 133, 137–138

Goodman, Allegra, **Supp. XII:** 159

Goodman, Paul, **I:** 218, 261; **III:** 39; **Supp. I Part 2:** 524; **Supp. VIII:** 239–240

Goodman, Philip, **III:** 105, 108

Goodman, Walter, **Supp. IV Part 2:** 532

Good Man Is Hard to Find, A (O'Connor), **III:** 339, 343–345

"Good Man Is Hard to Find, A"
(O'Connor), **III:** 339, 344, 353; **Retro. Supp. II:** 230–231

Good Man Is Hard to Find and Other Stories, A (O'Connor), **Retro. Supp. II:** 229, **230–232**

Good Morning, America (Sandburg), **III:** 592–593

"Good Morning, Major" (Marquand), **III:** 56

Good Morning, Midnight (Rhys), **Supp. III Part 1:** 43

"Good Morning, Revolution" (Hughes), **Retro. Supp. I:** 201, 203

Good Morning Revolution: Uncollected Writings of Social Protest (Hughes), **Retro. Supp. I:** 194, 201, 202, 209

Good Mother, The (Miller), **Supp. XII:** 289, **290–294,** 299, 301

Good News (Abbey), **Supp. XIII:** 11–12

"Good News from New-England" (Johnson), **Supp. I Part 1:** 115

Good News of Death and Other Poems (Simpson), **Supp. IX:** 265, **268–269**

Good Night, Willie Lee, I'll See You in the Morning (Walker), **Supp. III Part 2:** 520, 531

"Good Oak" (Leopold), **Supp. XIV:** 185, 187, 191

Goodrich, Samuel G., **Supp. I Part 1:** 38

Good Scent from a Strange Mountain, A (R. O. Butler), **Supp. XII:** 62, **70–72**

Good School, A (Yates), **Supp. XI:** 334, **346–347,** 348, 349

"*Good Shepherdess, The*/La Buena Pastora" (Mora), **Supp. XIII:** 228–229

Good Will (Smiley), **Supp. VI:** 292, **299–300**

Goodwin, K. L., **III:** 478

Goodwin, Stephen, **Supp. V:** 314, 316, 322, 323, 325

"Good Word for Winter, A" (Lowell), **Supp. I Part 2:** 420

Goodwyn, Janet, **Retro. Supp. I:** 370

"Goophered Grapevine, The" (Chesnutt), **Supp. XIV:** 57, **58–61**

"Goose Fish, The" (Nemerov), **III:** 272, 284

"Goose Pond" (Kunitz), **Supp. III Part 1:** 262

Goose-Step, The (Sinclair), **Supp. V:** 276

Gordon, A. R., **III:** 199

Gordon, Caroline, **II: 196–222,** 536, 537; **III:** 454, 482; **IV:** 123, 126–127, 139, 282; **Retro. Supp. II:** 177,
222, 229, 233, 235; **Supp. II Part 1:** 139

Gordon, Charles G., **I:** 454

Gordon, Don, **Supp. X:** 119

Gordon, Eugene, **Supp. II Part 1:** 170

Gordon, Fran, **Supp. XIII:** 111

Gordon, James Morris, **II:** 197

Gordon, Lois, **Supp. IV Part 1:** 48; **Supp. V:** 46

Gordon, Lyndall, **Retro. Supp. I:** 55

Gordon, Mary, **Supp. IV Part 1: 297–317**

Gordon, Peter, **Supp. XII:** 3–4, 4–5, 8

Gordon, Ruth, **IV:** 357

Gore, Thomas Pryor, **Supp. IV Part 2:** 679

Gorey, Edward, **IV:** 430, 436

Gorilla, My Love (Bambara), **Supp. XI:** 1, **2–7**

"Gorilla, My Love" (Bambara), **Supp. XI:** 2, 3–4

Gorki, Maxim, **I:** 478; **II:** 49; **III:** 402; **IV:** 299; **Supp. I Part 1:** 5, 51

Gorra, Michael, **Supp. V:** 71

Goslings, The (Sinclair), **Supp. V:** 276, 281

Go South to Sorrow (Rowan), **Supp. XIV:** 306

Gospel According to Joe, The (Gurney), **Supp. V:** 99

"Gospel According to Saint Mark, The" (Gordon), **Supp. IV Part 1:** 310

Gospel according to the Son (Mailer), **Retro. Supp. II:** 213

"Gospel for the Twentieth Century, The" (Locke), **Supp. XIV:** 206

"Gospel of Beauty, The" (Lindsay), **Supp. I Part 2:** 380, 382, 384, 385, 391, 396

Gospel Singer, The (Crews), **Supp. XI:** 102, **109**

Gosse, Edmund, **II:** 538; **IV:** 350; **Supp. VIII:** 157

Gossips, Gorgons, and Crones: The Fates of the Earth (Caputi), **Supp. IV Part 1:** 335

Go Tell It on the Mountain (Baldwin), **Retro. Supp. II:** 1, 2, 3, **4–5,** 7, 14; **Supp. I Part 1:** 48, 49, 50, 51, 52, 53–54, 55, 56, 57, 59, 61, 63, 64, 67; **Supp. II Part 1:** 170

Gotera, Vince, **Supp. XIII:** 115, 116, 119, 121, 127

Gothic Revival, The: An Essay on the History of Taste (Clark), **Supp. XIV:** 348

Gothic Writers (Thomson, Voller, and Frank, eds.), **Retro. Supp. II:** 273

"Go to the Devil and Shake Yourself"

(song), **Supp. I Part 2:** 580

"Go to the Shine That's on a Tree" (Eberhart), **I:** 523

Go to the Widow-Maker (Jones), **Supp. XI:** 214, **225–226,** 227, 229, 233

Gottfried, Martin, **Supp. IV Part 2:** 584

Gotthelf, Allan, **Supp. IV Part 2:** 528

Gottlieb, Robert, **Supp. IV Part 2:** 474

Gottschalk and the Grande Tarantelle (Brooks), **Supp. III Part 1:** 86

"Gottschalk and the Grande Tarantelle" (Brooks), **Supp. III Part 1:** 86–87

Gould (Dixon), **Supp. XII:** 152, **153**

Gould, Edward Sherman, **I:** 346

Gould, Janice, **Supp. IV Part 1:** 322, 327; **Supp. XII:** 229

Gould, Jay, **I:** 4

Gourd Dancer, The (Momaday), **Supp. IV Part 2:** 481, 487, 491, 493

Gourmont, Remy de, **I:** 270, 272; **II:** 528, 529; **III:** 457, 467–468, 477; **Retro. Supp. I:** 55

Gouverneurs de la Rosée (Roumain), **Supp. IV Part 1:** 360, 367

"Governors of Wyoming, The" (Proulx), **Supp. VII:** 264

Goyen, William, **Supp. V:** 220

"Grace" (Dubus), **Supp. VII:** 91

"Grace" (Harjo), **Supp. XII:** 224

Grace Notes (Dove), **Supp. IV Part 1:** 248–250, 252

"Graduation" (Dubus), **Supp. VII:** 84

Grady, Henry W., **Supp. I Part 1:** 370

Graeber, Laurel, **Supp. V:** 15

Graham, Billy, **I:** 308

Graham, Don, **Supp. XI:** 252, 254

Graham, Jorie, **Supp. IX:** 38, 52; **Supp. X:** 73; **Supp. XII:** 209; **Supp. XIII:** 85

Graham, Martha, **Supp. XI:** 152

Graham, Maryemma, **Retro. Supp. I:** 201, 204

Graham, Nan, **Supp. XII:** 272

Graham, Sheilah, **II:** 94; **Retro. Supp. I:** 97, 113–114, 115; **Supp. IX:** 63

Graham, Shirley, **Supp. I Part 1:** 51

Graham, Stephen, **Supp. I Part 2:** 397

Graham, Tom (pseudonym). *See* Lewis, Sinclair

Grahn, Judy, **Supp. IV Part 1:** 325, 330

Grainger, Percy, **Supp. I Part 2:** 386

Grain of Mustard Seed, A (Sarton), **Supp. VIII:** **259–260,** 263

Gramar (Lowth), **II:** 8

Grammar of Motives, A (Burke), **I:** 272, 275, 276–278, 283, 284

Granberry, Edwin, **I:** 288

Grand Design, The (Dos Passos), **I:** 489–490

"Grande Malade, The" (Barnes), **Supp. III Part 1:** 36

"Grandfather" (Dunn), **Supp. XI:** 147

"Grandfather and Grandson" (Singer), **Retro. Supp. II:** 307

"Grandfather's Blessing" (Alvarez), **Supp. VII:** 2

"Grand Forks" (Simpson), **Supp. IX:** 280–281

"Grand Inquisitor" (Dostoyevsky), **IV:** 106

Grandissimes (Cable), **II:** 291

"Grand-Master Nabokov" (Updike), **Retro. Supp. I:** 317

"Grand Miracle, The" (Karr), **Supp. XI:** 251

"Grandmother" (Gunn Allen), **Supp. IV Part 1:** 320, 325

"Grandmother in Heaven" (Levine), **Supp. V:** 186

"Grandmother of the Sun: Ritual Gynocracy in Native America" (Gunn Allen), **Supp. IV Part 1:** 328

Grandmothers of the Light: A Medicine Woman's Sourcebook (Gunn Allen, ed.), **Supp. IV Part 1:** 332, 333–334

"Grandmother Songs, The" (Hogan), **Supp. IV Part 1:** 413

"Grandpa and the Statue" (A. Miller), **III:** 147

"Grandparents" (Lowell), **II:** 550

"Grandstand Complex, The" (McCoy), **Supp. XIII:** 166

Grange, Red, **II:** 416

Granger's Index to Poetry (anthology), **Retro. Supp. I:** 37, 39

Grant, Lee, **Supp. XIII:** 295

Grant, Madison, **Supp. II Part 1:** 170

Grant, Richard, **Supp. X:** 282

Grant, Ulysses S., **I:** 4, 15; **II:** 542; **III:** 506, 584; **IV:** 348, 446; **Supp. I Part 2:** 418

Grantwood, **Retro. Supp. I:** 416, 417

"Grapes, The" (Hecht), **Supp. X:** 65–66

"Grape Sherbet" (Dove), **Supp. IV Part 1:** 246

Grapes of Wrath, The (Steinbeck), **I:** 301; **III:** 589; **IV:** 51, 53–55, 59, 63, 65, 67, 68, 69; **Supp. V:** 290; **Supp. XI:** 169; **Supp. XIV:** 181

"Grapevine, The" (Ashbery), **Supp. III Part 1:** 4

"Grass" (Sandburg), **III:** 584

Grass, Günter, **Supp. VIII:** 40

"Grasse: The Olive Trees" (Wilbur), **Supp. III Part 2:** 550

Grass Harp, The (Capote), **Supp. III Part 1:** 114–117, 123

Grass Still Grows, The (A. Miller), **III:** 146

Gratitude to Old Teachers (Bly), **Supp. IV Part 1:** 73

"Grave, A" (Moore), **III:** 195, 202, 208, 213

Grave, The (Blair), **Supp. I Part 1:** 150

"Grave, The" (Porter), **III:** 433, 443, 445–446

"Grave, The" (Winters), **Supp. II Part 2:** 795, 796

"Graven Image" (O'Hara), **III:** 320

Grave of the Right Hand, The (Wright), **Supp. V:** 332, 338, 339

"Grave Piece" (Eberhart), **I:** 533

Graves, Billy, **Supp. I Part 2:** 607

Graves, John, **Supp. V:** 220

Graves, Morris, **Supp. X:** 264

Graves, Peter, **Supp. IV Part 2:** 474

Graves, Rean, **Supp. I Part 1:** 326

Graves, Robert, **I:** 437, 477, 523; **Supp. I Part 2:** 541; **Supp. IV Part 1:** 280, 348; **Supp. IV Part 2:** 685

Graveyard for Lunatics, A (Bradbury), **Supp. IV Part 1:** 102, 114–116

Gravity's Rainbow (Pynchon), **Supp. II Part 2:** 617, 618–619, 621–625, 627, 630, 633–636; **Supp. IV Part 1:** 279; **Supp. V:** 44; **Supp. XIV:** 49

Gray, Cecil, **Supp. I Part 1:** 258

Gray, Francine Du Plessix, **Supp. V:** 169

Gray, James, **III:** 207; **Supp. I Part 2:** 410

Gray, Paul, **Supp. IV Part 1:** 305; **Supp. IV Part 2:** 639

Gray, Thomas, **I:** 68; **Supp. I Part 1:** 150; **Supp. I Part 2:** 422, 716

Gray, Thomas A., **Supp. I Part 2:** 710

"Gray Heron, The" (Kinnell), **Supp. III Part 1:** 250

"Gray Mills of Farley, The" (Jewett), **Retro. Supp. II:** 132, 144

Grayson, Charles, **Supp. XIII:** 171

"Gray Squirrel" (Francis), **Supp. IX:** 90

"Gray Wolf's H 'ant, The" (Chesnutt), **Supp. XIV:** 60

Grealy, Lucy, **Supp. XII:** 310

Greasy Lake (Boyle), **Supp. VIII:** **14–15**

"Greasy Lake" (Boyle), **Supp. VIII:** 15

"Great Adventure of Max Breuck, The" (Lowell), **II:** 522

Great American Novel, The (Roth),

Retro. **Supp. II:** 283, 288–289;
Supp. III Part 2: 414–416
Great American Short Novels (Phillips,
ed.), **Supp. VIII:** 156
Great Battles of the World (Crane), **I:**
415
*Great Christian Doctrine of Original
Sin Defended, The . . .* (Edwards), **I:**
549, 557, 559
Great Circle (Aiken), **I:** 53, 55, 57
"Great Class-Reunion Bazaar, The"
(Theroux), **Supp. VIII:** 312
Great Day, The (Hurston), **Supp. VI:**
154
Great Days (Barthelme), **Supp. IV
Part 1:** 39
Great Days, The (Dos Passos), **I:** 491
Great Digest (Pound, trans.), **III:** 472
"Great Elegy for John Donne"
(Brodsky), **Supp. VIII:** 21, 23
Greater Inclination, The (Wharton),
Retro. Supp. I: 363, **364–365,** 366
"Greater Torment, The" (Blackmur),
Supp. II Part 1: 92
Greatest Hits 1969–1996 (Salinas),
Supp. XIII: 311
"Greatest Thing in the World, The"
(Mailer), **Retro. Supp. II:** 196
Great Expectations (Acker), **Supp.
XII:** 5, **9–11**
Great Expectations (Dickens), **III:** 247;
Supp. I Part 1: 35
"Great Figure, The" (W. C. Williams),
IV: 414
"Great Fillmore Street Buffalo Drive,
The" (Momaday), **Supp. IV Part 2:**
493
Great Gatsby, The (Fitzgerald), **I:** 107,
375, 514; **II:** 77, 79, 83, 84, 85, 87,
91–93, 94, 96, 98; **III:** 244, 260,
372, 572; **IV:** 124, 297; **Retro.
Supp. I:** 98, 105, **105–108,** 110,
114, 115, 335, 359; **Retro. Supp.
II:** 107, 201; **Supp. II Part 2:** 626;
Supp. III Part 2: 585; **Supp. IV
Part 2:** 468, 475; **Supp. IX:** 57, 58;
Supp. X: 175; **Supp. XI:** 65, 69,
334
Great Gatsby, The (Fitzgerald)
(Modern Library), **Retro. Supp. I:**
113
Great God Brown, The (O'Neill), **III:**
165, 391, 394–395
Great Goodness of Life: A Coon Show
(Baraka), **Supp. II Part 1:** 47
Great Inclination, The (Wharton), **IV:**
310
"Great Infirmities" (Simic), **Supp.
VIII:** 277
Great Jones Street (DeLillo), **Supp.**

VI: 2, 3, 8–9, 11, 12
"Great Lawsuit, The: Man *versus* Men:
Woman *versus* Women" (Fuller),
Retro. Supp. I: 156; **Supp. II Part
1:** 292
"Great Men and Their Environment"
(James), **II:** 347
"Great Mississippi Bubble, The"
(Irving), **II:** 314
*Great Railway Bazaar, The: By Train
through Asia* (Theroux), **Supp. VIII:**
318, 319, **320–321,** 322
Great Stories of Suspense (Millar, ed.),
Supp. IV Part 2: 474
Great Topics of the World (Goldbarth),
Supp. XII: 187, 189, 191
Great Valley, The (Masters), **Supp. I
Part 2:** 465
Great World and Timothy Colt, The
(Auchincloss), **Supp. IV Part 1:** 25,
31, 32
"Greek Boy, The" (Bryant), **Supp. I
Part 1:** 168
*Greek Mind/Jewish Soul: The Con-
flicted Art of Cynthia Ozick*
(Strandberg), **Supp. V:** 273
"Greek Partisan, The" (Bryant), **Supp.
I Part 1:** 168
"Greeks, The" (McCarriston), **Supp.
XIV:** 271
Greeley, Horace, **II:** 7; **IV:** 197, 286–
287
Green, Ashbel, **Supp. IV Part 2:** 474
Green, Henry, **IV:** 279; **Retro. Supp.
I:** 354; **Supp. III Part 1:** 3; **Supp.
XI:** 294–295, 296, 297; **Supp. XII:**
315
Green, Jack, **Supp. IV Part 1:** 284–
285
Green, Martin, **Supp. I Part 1:** 299
Green, Michelle, **Supp. IV Part 1:** 95
"Green Automobile, The" (Ginsberg),
Supp. II Part 1: 322
Greenberg, Eliezer, **Supp. I Part 2:**
432
Greenberg, Jonathan, **Supp. XII:** 285
Greenberg, Samuel, **I:** 393
Green Bough, A (Faulkner), **Retro.
Supp. I:** 84
Green Centuries (Gordon), **II:** 196,
197–207, 209
"Green Crab's Shell, A" (Doty), **Supp.
XI:** 126
"Green Door, The" (O. Henry), **Supp.
II Part 1:** 395
Greene, A. C., **Supp. V:** 223, 225
Greene, Graham, **I:** 480; **II:** 62, 320;
III: 57, 556; **Retro. Supp. I:** 215;
Supp. I Part 1: 280; **Supp. IV Part
1:** 341; **Supp. V:** 298; **Supp. IX:**

261; **Supp. XI:** 99,**Supp. XI:** 104;
Supp. XIII: 233
Greene, Helga, **Supp. IV Part 1:** 134,
135
Greene, J. Lee, **Retro. Supp. II:** 121
Greene, Nathanael, **Supp. I Part 2:**
508
Greene, Richard Tobias, **III:** 76
"Greene-ing of the Portables, The"
(Cowley), **Supp. II Part 1:** 140
"Greenest Continent, The" (Stevens),
Retro. Supp. I: 304
Greenfeld, Josh, **III:** 364
Green Hills of Africa (Hemingway),
II: 253; **Retro. Supp. I:** 182, 186
"Green Lagoons, The" (Leopold),
Supp. XIV: 188
"Green Lampshade" (Simic), **Supp.
VIII:** 283
Greenlanders, The (Smiley), **Supp. VI:**
292, **296–298,** 299, 305, 307
Greenlaw, Edwin A., **IV:** 453
"Greenleaf" (O'Connor), **III:** 350, 351;
Retro. Supp. II: 233, 237
Greenman, Walter F., **I:** 217, 222
Green Memories (Mumford), **Supp. II
Part 2:** 474, 475, 479, 480–481
"Green Pasture, The" (Leopold), **Supp.
XIV:** 184
Green Pastures, The (Connelly), **Supp.
II Part 1:** 223
"Green Red Brown and White"
(Swenson), **Supp. IV Part 2:** 639
"Green River" (Bryant), **Supp. I Part
1:** 155, 164
Green Shadows, White Whale
(Bradbury), **Supp. IV Part 1:** 102,
103, 116
"Green Shirt, The" (Olds), **Supp. X:**
209
Greenslet, Ferris, **I:** 19; **Retro. Supp.
I:** 9, 10, 11, 13; **Retro. Supp. II:** 41
Greenspan, Alan, **Supp. IV Part 2:**
526
Greenstreet, Sydney, **Supp. IV Part 1:**
356
Greenwald, Ted, **Supp. IV Part 2:** 423
Green Wall, The (Wright), **Supp. III
Part 2:** 591, 593, 595
Green Wave, The (Rukeyser), **Supp.
VI:** 273, 280
"Green Ways" (Kunitz), **Supp. III
Part 1:** 265
Green with Beasts (Merwin), **Supp. III
Part 1:** 340, 344–346
Greenwood, Grace, **Supp. XIII:** 141
Gregerson, Linda, **Supp. IV Part 2:**
651; **Supp. X:** 204–205; **Supp. XI:**
142
"Gregorio Valdes" (Bishop), **Retro.**

Supp. II: 51

Gregory, Alyse, I: 221, 226, 227, 231

Gregory, Horace, II: 512; **Supp. III Part 2:** 614, 615; **Supp. IX:** 229

Gregory, Lady Isabella Augusta, III: 458

Gregory, Sinda, **Supp. X:** 260, 268

Grendel (Gardner), **Supp. VI:** 63, **67,** 68, 74

"Gretel in Darkness" (Glück), **Supp. V:** 82

Gretta (Caldwell), I: 301, 302

Greuze, Jean Baptiste, **Supp. I Part 2:** 714

Grey, Zane, **Supp. XIII:** 5

Griffin, Bartholomew, **Supp. I Part 1:** 369

Griffin, John Howard, **Supp. VIII:** 208

Griffin, Merv, **Supp. IV Part 2:** 526

Griffith, Albert J., **Supp. V:** 325

Griffith, D. W., I: 31, 481–482; **Retro. Supp. I:** 103, 325; **Supp. XI:** 45

Griffiths, Clyde, I: 511

Grile, Dod (pseudonym). *See* Bierce, Ambrose

Grimm, Herman, II: 17

Grimm brothers, II: 378; III: 101, 491, 492; IV: 266; **Supp. I Part 2:** 596, 622; **Supp. X:** 78, 84, 86

Gris, Juan, I: 442; **Retro. Supp. I:** 430

Griswold, Rufus Wilmot, III: 409, 429; **Retro. Supp. II:** 261, 262

Grogg, Sam, Jr., **Supp. IV Part 2:** 468, 471

Gromer, Crystal, **Supp. XII:** 297

Gronlund, Laurence, II: 276

"Groping for Trouts" (Gass), **Supp. VI:** 87

Grosholz, Emily, **Supp. XII:** 185

"Grosse Fuge" (Doty), **Supp. XI:** 126–127

Grossman, Allen, **Retro. Supp. II:** 83

Grosz, George, III: 172; IV: 438; **Retro. Supp. II:** 321; **Supp. X:** 137

"Groundhog, The" (Eberhart), I: 523, 530–532, 533

"Ground on Which I Stand, The" (Wilson), **Supp. VIII:** 331

Group, The (McCarthy), II: 570, 574–578

"Group of Two, A" (Jarrell), II: 368

Group Therapy (Hearon), **Supp. VIII: 64–65**

"Grove" (Goldbarth), **Supp. XII:** 176

Groves of Academe, The (McCarthy), II: 568–571

"Growing Season, The" (Caldwell), I: 309

Growing Up Gay: A Literary Anthol-ogy (Singer, ed.), **Supp. IV Part 1:** 330

"Growing Up Good in Maycomb" (Shaffer), **Supp. VIII:** 128

"Grown-Up" (Jewett), **Retro. Supp. II:** 134

"Growth" (Lowell), II: 554

Growth of the American Republic, The (Morison and Commager), **Supp. I Part 2:** 484

"Growtown Buggle, The" (Jewett), **Retro. Supp. II:** 132

Gruenberg, Louis, III: 392

Grumbach, Doris, II: 560

"Guacamaja" (Leopold), **Supp. XIV:** 188–189

Guardian Angel, The (Holmes), **Supp. I Part 1:** 315–316

Guard of Honor (Cozzens), I: 370–372, 375, 376–377, 378, 379

Guare, John, **Supp. XIII:** 196, 207

Gubar, Susan, **Retro. Supp. I:** 42; **Retro. Supp. II:** 324; **Supp. IX:** 66

Guerard, Albert, Jr., **Supp. X:** 79; **Supp. XIII:** 172

Guérin, Maurice de, I: 241

"Guerrilla Handbook, A" (Baraka), **Supp. II Part 1:** 36

Guess and Spell Coloring Book, The (Swenson), **Supp. IV Part 2:** 648

Guess Who's Coming to Dinner (film), **Supp. I Part 1:** 67

Guest, Val, **Supp. XI:** 307

"Guests of Mrs. Timms, The" (Jewett), II: 408; **Retro. Supp. II:** 135

"Guevara . . .Guevara" (Salinas), **Supp. XIII:** 312–313, 315

Guevara, Martha, **Supp. VIII:** 74

Guide in the Wilderness, A (Cooper), I: 337

"Guide to Dungeness Spit, A" (Wagoner), **Supp. IX:** 325–326, 329

Guide to Ezra Pound's Selected Cantos' (Kearns), **Retro. Supp. I:** 292

Guide to Kulchur (Pound), III: 475

Guide to the Ruins (Nemerov), III: 269, 270–271, 272

Guillén, Nicolás, **Retro. Supp. I:** 202; **Supp. I Part 1:** 345

Guillevic, Eugene, **Supp. III Part 1:** 283

"Guilty Man, The" (Kunitz), **Supp. II Part 1:** 263

Guilty of Everything: The Autobiography of Herbert Huncke (Huncke), **Supp. XIV:** 138, 140, 141, 150

Guilty Pleasures (Barthelme), **Supp. IV Part 1:** 44, 45, 53

Guinness, Alec, **Retro. Supp. I:** 65

"Gulf, The" (Dunn), **Supp. XI:** 149

Gulistan (Saadi), II: 19

Gullible's Travels (Lardner), II: 426, 427

Gulliver's Travels (Swift), I: 209, 348, 366; II: 301; **Supp. I Part 2:** 656; **Supp. XI:** 209

"Gulls" (Hayden), **Supp. II Part 1:** 367

"Gulls, The" (Nemerov), III: 272

"Gun, The" (Dobyns), **Supp. XIII:** 88

Günderode: A Translation from the German (Fuller), **Supp. II Part 1:** 293

Gundy, Jeff, **Supp. XI:** 315

Gunn, Thom, **Supp. IX:** 269

Gunn, Thomas, **Supp. V:** 178

Gunn Allen, Paula, **Supp. IV Part 1: 319–340,** 404; **Supp. IV Part 2:** 499, 502, 557, 568; **Supp. XII:** 218

"Guns as Keys; and the Great Gate Swings" (Lowell), II: 524

Gurdjieff, Georges, **Supp. V:** 199; **Supp. IX:** 320

Gurganus, Allan, **Supp. XII:** 308–309, 310

Gurko, Leo, III: 62

Gurney, A. R., **Supp. V: 95–112; Supp. IX:** 261

Gurney, Mary (Molly) Goodyear, **Supp. V:** 95

Gussow, Mel, **Supp. IX:** 93; **Supp. XII:** 325, 328, 341

Gustavus Vassa, the African (Vassa), **Supp. IV Part 1:** 11

Gusto, Thy Name Was Mrs. Hopkins: A Prose Rhapsody (Francis), **Supp. IX:** 89

Gute Mensch von Sezuan, Der (Brecht), **Supp. IX:** 138

Gutenberg, Johann, **Supp. I Part 2:** 392

Guthrie, A. B., **Supp. X:** 103

Gutman, Herbert, **Supp. I Part 1:** 47

Guttenplan, D. D., **Supp. XI:** 38

"Gutting of Couffignal, The" (Hammett), **Supp. IV Part 1:** 345

Guy Domville (James), II: 331; **Retro. Supp. I:** 228

"Gwendolyn" (Bishop), **Retro. Supp. II:** 51

Gypsy Ballads (Hughes, trans.), **Supp. I Part 1:** 345

Gypsy's Curse, The (Crews), **Supp. XI: 110**

"Gyroscope, The" (Rukeyser), **Supp. VI:** 271

Gysin, Brion, **Supp. XII:** 129

H. L. Mencken, a Portrait from Memory (Angoff), III: 107

H. L. Mencken: The American Scene (Cairns), **III:** 119

"H. L. Mencken Meets a Poet in the West Side Y.M.C.A." (White), **Supp. I Part 2:** 677

H. M. Pulham, Esquire (Marquand), **II:** 482–483; **III:** 58, 59, 65, 68–69

Haardt, Sara. *See* Mencken, Mrs. H. L. (Sara Haardt)

Habakkuk (biblical book), **III:** 200, 347

Habibi (Nye), **Supp. XIII:** 273, **279**

"Habit" (James), **II:** 351

Habitations of the Word (Gass), **Supp. VI:** 88

Hackett, David, **Supp. XII:** 236

Hadda, Janet, **Retro. Supp. II:** 317

Haeckel, Ernst Heinrich, **II:** 480

Hafif, Marcia, **Supp. IV Part 2:** 423

Hagedorn, Jessica, **Supp. X:** 292

Hagen, Beulah, **Supp. I Part 2:** 679

Haggard, Rider, **III:** 189

Hagoromo (play), **III:** 466

"Hail Mary" (Fante), **Supp. XI:** 160, 164

Haines, George, IV, **I:** 444

Haines, John, **Supp. XII: 197–214**

"Hair" (Corso), **Supp. XII:** 117, 126, 127

"Hair, The" (Carver), **Supp. III Part 1:** 137

"Haircut" (Lardner), **II:** 430, 436

Hairpiece: A Film for Nappy-Headed People (Chenzira; film), **Supp. XI:** 19–20

"Hairs" (Cisneros), **Supp. VII:** 59

Hairs/Pelitos (Cisneros), **Supp. VII:** 58

Hairy Ape, The (O'Neill), **III:** 391, 392, 393

"Haïta the Shepherd" (Bierce), **I:** 203

Haldeman, Anna, **Supp. I Part 1:** 2

Hale, Edward Everett, **Supp. I Part 2:** 584; **Supp. XI:** 193, 200

Hale, John Parker, **Supp. I Part 2:** 685

Hale, Nancy, **Supp. VIII:** 151, 171

Haley, Alex, **Supp. I Part 1:** 47, 66

Haley, J. Evetts, **Supp. V:** 226

"Half a Century Gone" (Lowell), **II:** 554

Half-a-Hundred: Tales by Great American Writers (Grayson, ed.), **Supp. XIII:** 171

Half Asleep in Frog Pajamas (Robbins), **Supp. X:** 259, **279–282**

Half-Century of Conflict, A (Parkman), **Supp. II Part 2:** 600, 607, 610

"Half Deity" (Moore), **III:** 210, 214, 215

"Half Hour of August" (Ríos), **Supp.**

*IV Part 2:** 552

Half-Lives (Jong), **Supp. V:** 115, 119

Half Moon Street: Two Short Novels (Theroux), **Supp. VIII:** 322, 323

Half of Paradise (Burke), **Supp. XIV:** 22, 24

Half-Past Nation Time (Johnson), **Supp. VI:** 187

"Half-Skinned Steer, The" (Proulx), **Supp. VII:** 261–262

Half Sun Half Sleep (Swenson), **Supp. IV Part 2:** 645–646

Halfway (Kumin), **Supp. IV Part 2:** 441–442

"Halfway" (Rich), **Supp. I Part 2:** 553

Halfway Home (Monette), **Supp. X:** 154

Halfway to Silence (Sarton), **Supp. VIII:** 261

Half You Don't Know, The: Selected Stories (Cameron), **Supp. XII:** 79, 80, 81

Haliburton, Thomas Chandler, **II:** 301; **IV:** 193; **Supp. I Part 2:** 411

Halifax, Lord, **II:** 111

Hall, Daniel, **Supp. XII:** 258

Hall, Donald, **I:** 567; **III:** 194; **Supp. IV Part 1:** 63, 72; **Supp. IV Part 2:** 621; **Supp. IX:** 269; **Supp. XIV:** 82, 126

Hall, James, **II:** 313; **Supp. I Part 2:** 584, 585

Hall, James Baker, **Supp. X:** 24

Hall, Timothy L., **Supp. VIII:** 127, 128

Halleck, Fitz-Greene, **Supp. I Part 1:** 156, 158

"Hallelujah: A Sestina" (Francis), **Supp. IX:** 82

"Hallelujah on the Bum" (Abbey), **Supp. XIII:** 2

"Haller's Second Home" (Maxwell), **Supp. VIII:** 169

Hallock, Rev. Moses, **Supp. I Part 1:** 153

Hall of Mirrors, A (Stone), **Supp. V:** 295, 296–299, 300, 301

"Hallowe'en" (Huncke), **Supp. XIV:** 145

"Halloween Party, The" (Chabon), **Supp. XI:** 72

Halloween Tree, The (Bradbury), **Supp. IV Part 1:** 102, 112–113

Hallwas, John E., **Supp. I Part 2:** 454

Halpern, Daniel, **Supp. IV Part 1:** 94–95, 95

Halsey, Theresa, **Supp. IV Part 1:** 330, 331

"Halt in the Desert, A" (Brodsky), **Supp. VIII:** 24

"Halves" (Dunn), **Supp. XI:** 149

Hamerik, Asger, **Supp. I Part 1:** 356

Hamill, Sam, **Supp. X:** 112, 125, 126, 127

Hamilton, Alexander, **I:** 485; **Supp. I Part 2:** 456, 483, 509

Hamilton, Alice, **Supp. I Part 1:** 5

Hamilton, David, **Supp. IX:** 296

Hamilton, Lady Emma, **II:** 524

Hamilton, Hamish, **Supp. I Part 2:** 617

Hamilton, Walton, **Supp. I Part 2:** 632

Hamilton Stark (Banks), **Supp. V:** 8, 9–10, 11

"Hamlen Brook" (Wilbur), **Supp. III Part 2:** 564

"Hamlet" (Laforgue), **I:** 573; **III:** 11

Hamlet (Miller and Fraenkel), **III:** 178, 183

Hamlet (Shakespeare), **I:** 53, 183, 205, 377, 586–587; **II:** 158, 531; **III:** 7, 11, 12, 183; **IV:** 116, 131, 227; **Supp. I Part 1:** 369; **Supp. I Part 2:** 422, 457, 471; **Supp. IV Part 2:** 612; **Supp. IX:** 14

Hamlet, The (Faulkner), **II:** 69–71, 73, 74; **IV:** 131; **Retro. Supp. I:** 82, 91, 92; **Supp. VIII:** 178; **Supp. IX:** 103; **Supp. XI:** 247

"Hamlet and His Problems" (Eliot), **I:** 586–587

Hamlet of A. MacLeish, The (MacLeish), **III:** 11–12, 14, 15, 18

Hamlin, Eva, **Retro. Supp. II:** 115

Hammer, Adam, **Supp. XIII:** 112

Hammer, Langdon, **Retro. Supp. II:** 45, 53; **Supp. X:** 65

"Hammer Man, The" (Bambara), **Supp. XI:** 4–5

Hammett, Dashiell, **IV:** 286; **Retro. Supp. II:** 327; **Supp. I Part 1:** 286, 289, 291, 292, 293, 294, 295; **Supp. III Part 1:** 91; **Supp. IV Part 1:** 120, 121, **341–357**; **Supp. IV Part 2:** 461, 464, 468, 469, 472, 473; **Supp. IX:** 200; **Supp. XI:** 228; **Supp. XIII:** 159; **Supp. XIV:** 21

Hammond, Karla, **Supp. IV Part 2:** 439, 442, 448, 637, 640, 644, 648

Hampl, Patricia, **Supp. IX:** 291; **Supp. XI:** 126

Hampson, Alfred Leete, **Retro. Supp. I:** 35–36, 38

"Hamrick's Polar Bear" (Caldwell), **I:** 309–310

Hamsun, Knut, **Supp. VIII:** 40; **Supp. XI:** 161, 167; **Supp. XII:** 21, 128

Hancock, John, **Supp. I Part 2:** 524

Handbook of North American Indians (Sando), **Supp. IV Part 2:** 510

Handcarved Coffins: A Nonfiction Ac-

count of an American Crime (Capote), **Supp. III Part 1:** 131

Handel, Georg Friedrich, **III:** 210; **IV:** 369

"Handfuls" (Sandburg), **III:** 584

"Handle with Care" (Fitzgerald), **Retro. Supp. I:** 114

Handmaid's Tale, The (Atwood), **Supp. XIII:** 19, 20, **27–29**

"Hand of Emmagene, The" (Taylor), **Supp. V:** 314, 325–326

Hand of the Potter, The: A Tragedy in Four Acts (Dreiser), **Retro. Supp. II:** 104

"Hands" (Anderson), **I:** 106, 107

"Hands" (Mora), **Supp. XIII:** 215

Hand to Mouth (Auster), **Supp. XII:** 21

"Hand to Mouth" (Auster), **Supp. XII:** 31

Handy, Lowney, **Supp. XI:** 217, 220, 221, 225

Handy, W. C., **Supp. VIII:** 337

Handy Guide for Beggars, A (Lindsay), **Supp. I Part 2:** 376–378, 380, 382, 399

Hanging Garden, The (Wagoner), **Supp. IX: 338–339**

"Hanging Gardens of Tyburn, The" (Hecht), **Supp. X:** 58

"Hanging of the Crane, The" (Longfellow), **Retro. Supp. II:** 169, 171

"Hanging Pictures in Nanny's Room" (Kenyon), **Supp. VII:** 164

"Hanging the Wash" (Alvarez), **Supp. VII:** 4

"Hangman, The" (Sexton), **Supp. II Part 2:** 680, 691

Hangsaman (Jackson), **Supp. IX:** 116, 123, **124**

Hanh, Thich Nhat, **Supp. V:** 199

Hanks, Lucy, **III:** 587

Hanks, Nancy. *See* Lincoln, Mrs. Thomas (Nancy Hanks)

Hanley, Lynne T., **Supp. IV Part 1:** 208

Hanna, Mark, **Supp. I Part 2:** 395

Hannah, Barry, **Supp. X:** 285

"Hannah Armstrong" (Masters), **Supp. I Part 2:** 461

"Hannah Binding Shoes" (Larcom), **Supp. XIII:** 141, 143

Hannah's House (Hearon), **Supp. VIII:** 58, **60–61**

Hanneman, Audre, **II:** 259

Hannibal Lecter, My Father (Acker), **Supp. XII:** 6

Hanoi (McCarthy), **II:** 579

Hansberry, Lorraine, **Supp. IV Part 1:**

359–377; **Supp. VIII:** 329

Hanscom, Leslie, **Supp. XI:** 229

Hansen, Erik, **Supp. V:** 241

Hansen, Harry, **IV:** 366

Han-shan, **Supp. VIII:** 292

Hanson, Curtis, **Supp. XI:** 67

Han Suyin, **Supp. X:** 291

"Happenings: An Art of Radical Juxtaposition" (Sontag), **Supp. III Part 2:** 456

"Happenstance" (Komunyakaa), **Supp. XIII:** 130

Happenstance (Shields), **Supp. VII:** 315–318, 320, 323, 324, 326

Happersberger, Lucien, **Supp. I Part 1:** 51

"Happiest I've Been, The" (Updike), **IV:** 219

"Happiness" (Oliver), **Supp. VII:** 236

"Happiness" (Sandburg), **III:** 582–583

Happiness of Getting It Down Right, The (Steinman, ed.), **Supp. VIII:** 172

"Happy Birthday" (Bambara), **Supp. XI:** 4

Happy Birthday, Wanda June (Vonnegut), **Supp. II Part 2:** 759, 776–777

Happy Birthday of Death, The (Corso), **Supp. XII: 127–129**

Happy Childhood, A (Matthews), **Supp. IX:** 155, 160, **161–163**

Happy Days (Beckett), **Retro. Supp. I:** 206

Happy Days, 1880–1892 (Mencken), **III:** 100, 111, 120

"Happy End" (Simic), **Supp. VIII:** 276–277

"Happy Failure, The" (Melville), **III:** 90

Happy Families Are All Alike (Taylor), **Supp. V:** 322–323, 325

Happy Isles of Oceania, The: Paddling the Pacific (Theroux), **Supp. VIII:** 324

"Happy Journey to Trenton and Camden, The" (Wilder), **IV:** 366

"Happy Marriage, The" (MacLeish), **III:** 15–16

Happy Marriage and Other Poems, The (MacLeish), **III:** 4

"Hapworth 16, 1924" (Salinger), **III:** 552, 571–572

"Harbor Lights" (Doty), **Supp. XI:** 122

Harcourt, Alfred, **II:** 191, 451–452; **III:** 587; **Retro. Supp. I:** 131

Harcourt, Brace, **Retro. Supp. I:** 83

Harcourt, T. A., **I:** 196

Hard Candy, a Book of Stories (T. Williams), **IV:** 383

"Hardcastle Crags" (Plath), **Supp. I Part 2:** 537

"Hard Daddy" (Hughes), **Retro. Supp. I:** 200

Hard Facts (Baraka), **Supp. II Part 1:** 54, 55, 58

Hard Freight (Wright), **Supp. V:** 332, 339–340

Hard Hours, The (Hecht), **Supp. X:** 57, **59–62,** 63, 64

Hardie, Kier, **Supp. I Part 1:** 5

Harding, Walter, **IV:** 177, 178

Harding, Warren G., **I:** 486; **II:** 253, 433; **Supp. I Part 1:** 24

"Hard Kind of Courage, The" (Baldwin), **Supp. I Part 1:** 52

"Hard Time Keeping Up, A" (Ellison), **Retro. Supp. II:** 124

Hard Times (Dickens), **Supp. I Part 2:** 675

"Hard Times in Elfland, The" (Lanier), **Supp. I Part 1:** 365

Hardwick, Elizabeth, **II:** 543, 554, 566; **Retro. Supp. II:** 179, 180, 183, 184, 190, 221, 228–229, 245; **Supp. I Part 1:** 196; **Supp. III Part 1: 193–215; Supp. IV Part 1:** 299; **Supp. V,** 319; **Supp. X,** 171; **Supp. XII:** 209; **Supp. XIV:** 89

"Hard Work 1956" (Dunn), **Supp. XI:** 147

Hardy, Barbara, **Supp. I Part 2:** 527

Hardy, Oliver, **Supp. I Part 2:** 607; **Supp. IV Part 2:** 574

Hardy, René, **Supp. III Part 1:** 235

Hardy, Thomas, **I:** 59, 103, 292, 317, 377; **II:** 181, 184–185, 186, 191–192, 271, 275, 372, 523, 542; **III:** 32, 453, 485, 508, 524; **IV:** 83, 135, 136; **Retro. Supp. I:** 141, 377–378; **Supp. I Part 1:** 217; **Supp. I Part 2:** 429, 512; **Supp. II Part 1:** 4, 26; **Supp. VIII:** 32; **Supp. IX:** 40, 78, 85, 108, 211; **Supp. X:** 228; **Supp. XI:** 311; **Supp. XIII:** 294, **Supp. XIII:** 130; **Supp. XIV:** 24

Harjo, Joy, **Supp. IV Part 1:** 325, 404; **Supp. IV Part 2:** 499, 507; **Supp. XII: 215–234**

"Harlem" (Hughes), **Retro. Supp. I:** 194, 204; **Supp. I Part 1:** 340; **Supp. VIII:** 213

Harlem, Mecca of the New Negro (Locke), **Supp. XIV:** 201

Harlem: Negro Metropolis (McKay), **Supp. X:** 132, 141, 142

"Harlem Dancer, The" (McKay), **Supp. X:** 134

Harlem Gallery (Tolson), **Retro. Supp. I:** 208, 209, 210

Harlem Glory: A Fragment of Aframerican Life (McKay), **Supp. X:** 132, **141–142**

"Harlem Runs Wild" (McKay), **Supp. X:** 140

Harlem Shadows (McKay), **Supp. X:** 131–132, 136

"Harlequin of Dreams, The" (Lanier), **Supp. I Part 1:** 365

Harlot's Ghost (Mailer), **Retro. Supp. II:** 211–212

Harlow, Jean, **IV:** 256; **Retro. Supp. I:** 110

Harmon, William, **Retro. Supp. I:** 37; **Supp. XI:** 248

"Harmonic" (F. Barthelme), **Supp. XI:** 26

Harmonium (Stevens), **III:** 196; **IV:** 76, 77, 78, 82, 87, 89, 92; **Retro. Supp. I:** 296, 297, 299, **300–302,** 301, 302

"Harmony of the Gospels" (Taylor), **IV:** 149

Harper (film), **Supp. IV Part 2:** 473

Harper, Donna, **Retro. Supp. I:** 194, 195, 209

Harper, Frances E. Watkins, **Supp. II Part 1:** 201–202

Harper, Gordon Lloyd, **Retro. Supp. II:** 23

Harper, Michael S., **Retro. Supp. II:** 116, 123

Harper, William Rainey, **Supp. I Part 2:** 631

Harper's Anthology of 20th Century Native American Poetry (Niatum, ed.), **Supp. IV Part 1:** 331

"Harriet" (Lowell), **II:** 554

Harrigan, Edward, **II:** 276; **III:** 14

Harrington, Michael, **I:** 306

Harris, Celia, **Retro. Supp. I:** 9

Harris, George, **II:** 70

Harris, Joel Chandler, **III:** 338; **Supp. I Part 1:** 352; **Supp. II Part 1:** 192, 201; **Supp. XIV:** 61

Harris, Judith, **Supp. XIV:** 269

Harris, Julie, **II:** 587, 601; **Supp. IX:** 125

Harris, Leonard, **Supp. XIV:** 196, 211–212

Harris, MacDonald, **Supp. XI:** 65

Harris, Marie, **Supp. IX:** 153

Harris, Peter, **Supp. X:** 206, 207

Harris, Thomas, **Supp. XIV:** 26

Harris, Victoria Frenkel, **Supp. IV Part 1:** 68, 69

Harrison, Colin, **Supp. XIV:** 26

Harrison, Hazel, **Retro. Supp. II:** 115

Harrison, Jim, **Supp. VIII: 37–56**

Harrison, Kathryn, **Supp. X:** 191

Harrison, Ken, **Supp. IX:** 101

Harrison, Oliver (pseudonym). *See* Smith, Harrison

Harryhausen, Ray, **Supp. IV Part 1:** 115

"Harry of Nothingham" (Hugo), **Supp. VI:** 146–147

"Harry's Death" (Carver), **Supp. III Part 1:** 146

"Harsh Judgment, The" (Kunitz), **Supp. III Part 1:** 264

Hart, Albert Bushnell, **Supp. I Part 2:** 479, 480, 481

Hart, Bernard, **I:** 241, 242, 248–250, 256

Hart, Henry, **Retro. Supp. II:** 187; **Supp. XIV:** 97

Hart, Lorenz, **III:** 361

Hart, Moss, **Supp. IV Part 2:** 574

Hart, Pearl, **Supp. X:** 103

"Hart Crane" (Tate), **I:** 381

"Hart Crane and Poetry: A Consideration of Crane's Intense Poetics with Reference to 'The Return'" (Grossman), **Retro. Supp. II:** 83

Harte, Anna Griswold, **Supp. II Part 1:** 341

Harte, Bret, **I:** 193, 195, 203; **II:** 289; **IV:** 196; **Retro. Supp. II:** 72; **Supp. II Part 1: 335–359,** 399

Harte, Walter Blackburn, **I:** 199

Harter, Carol C., **Supp. IV Part 1:** 217

Hartley, David, **III:** 77

Hartley, L. P., **Supp. I Part 1:** 293

Hartley, Lois, **Supp. I Part 2:** 459, 464–465

Hartley, Marsden, **IV:** 409, 413; **Retro. Supp. I:** 430; **Supp. X:** 137

Hartman, Geoffrey, **Supp. IV Part 1:** 119; **Supp. XII:** 130, 253

Harum, David, **II:** 102

"Harvard" (Lowell), **II:** 554

Harvard College in the Seventeenth Century (Morison), **Supp. I Part 2:** 485

"Harvesters of Night and Water" (Hogan), **Supp. IV Part 1:** 412

"Harvest Song" (Toomer), **Supp. III Part 2:** 483

Harvill Book of 20th Century Poetry in English, **Supp. X:** 55

"Harv Is Plowing Now" (Updike), **Retro. Supp. I:** 318

Haselden, Elizabeth Lee, **Supp. VIII:** 125

Hass, Robert, **Supp. VI: 97–111;** **Supp. VIII:** 24, 28; **Supp. XI:** 142, 270; **Supp. XIV:** 83, 84

Hassam, Childe, **Retro. Supp. II:** 136

Hassan, Ihab, **IV:** 99–100, 115; **Supp. XI:** 221

Hasse, Henry, **Supp. IV Part 1:** 102

Hasty-Pudding, The (Barlow), **Supp. II Part 1:** 74, 77–80

Hatful of Rain, A (Gazzo), **III:** 155

Hatlen, Burton, **Supp. V:** 138, 139–140

"Hattie Bloom" (Oliver), **Supp. VII:** 232

Haunch, Paunch, and Jowl (Ornitz), **Supp. IX:** 227

"Haunted Landscape" (Ashbery), **Supp. III Part 1:** 22

"Haunted Mind" (Simic), **Supp. VIII:** 282

"Haunted Mind, The" (Hawthorne), **II:** 230–231

"Haunted Oak, The" (Dunbar), **Supp. II Part 1:** 207, 208

"Haunted Palace, The" (Poe), **III:** 421

"Haunted Valley, The" (Bierce), **I:** 200

Haunting, The (film), **Supp. IX:** 125

Haunting of Hill House, The (Jackson), **Supp. IX:** 117, 121, 126

Hauptmann, Gerhart, **III:** 472

Haussmann, Sonja, **Supp. XIII:** 331, **Supp. XIII:** 347

"Havanna vanities come to dust in Miami" (Didion), **Supp. IV Part 1:** 210

Haven's End (Marquand), **III:** 55, 56, 63, 68

"Have You Ever Tried to Enter the Long Black Branches" (Oliver), **Supp. VII:** 247

"Having Been Interstellar" (Ammons), **Supp. VII:** 25

"Having It Out With Melancholy" (Kenyon), **Supp. VII:** 171

"Having Lost My Sons, I Confront the Wreckage of the Moon: Christmas, 1960" (Wright), **Supp. III Part 2:** 600

"Having Snow" (Schwartz), **Supp. II Part 2:** 652

Hawai'i One Summer (Kingston), **Supp. V:** 157, 160, 166, 169–170

"Hawk, The" (Francis), **Supp. IX:** 81

Hawke, David Freeman, **Supp. I Part 2:** 511, 516

Hawkes, John, **I:** 113; **Retro. Supp. II:** 234; **Supp. III Part 1:** 2; **Supp. V:** 40; **Supp. IX:** 212

Hawkins, William, **II:** 587

Hawk in the Rain, The (Hughes), **Retro. Supp. II:** 244; **Supp. I Part 2:** 537, 540

Hawk Is Dying, The (Crews), **Supp. XI:** 111

Hawk Moon (Shepard), **Supp. III Part 2:** 445

Hawks, Howard, **Supp. IV Part 1:** 130

"Hawk's Cry in Autumn, The" (Brodsky), **Supp. VIII:** 29

"Hawk's Shadow" (Glück), **Supp. V:** 85

Hawk's Well, The (Yeats), **III:** 459–460

Hawley, Adelaide, **Supp. XIV:** 207

Hawley, Joseph, **I:** 546

Hawthorne (James), **II:** 372–378; **Retro. Supp. I:** 220, **223–224**

"Hawthorne" (Longfellow), **Retro. Supp. II:** 169

"Hawthorne" (Lowell), **II:** 550

Hawthorne, Julian, **II:** 225; **Supp. I Part 1:** 38

Hawthorne, Mrs. Nathaniel (Sophia Peabody), **II:** 224, 244; **III:** 75, 86

Hawthorne, Nathaniel, **I:** 106, 204, 211, 340, 355, 363, 384, 413, 458, 561–562; **II:** 7, 8, 40, 60, 63, 74, 89, 127–128, 138, 142, 198, **223–246,** 255, 259, 264, 267, 272, 274, 277, 281, 282, 295, 307, 309, 311, 313, 322, 324, 326, 402, 408, 446, 501, 545; **III:** 51, 81–82, 83, 84, 85, 87, 88, 91, 92, 113, 316, 359, 412, 415, 421, 438, 453, 454, 507, 565, 572; **IV:** 2, 4, 167, 172, 179, 194, 333, 345, 453; **Retro. Supp. I:** 1, 53, 59, 62, 63, 91, **145–167,** 215, 218, 220, 223, 248–249, 252, 257, 258, 330, 331, 365; **Retro. Supp. II:** 136, 142, 153, 156–157, 158, 159, 187, 221; **Supp. I Part 1:** 38, 188, 197, 317, 372; **Supp. I Part 2:** 420, 421, 545, 579, 580, 582, 587, 595, 596; **Supp. III Part 2:** 501; **Supp. IV Part 1:** 80, 127, 297; **Supp. IV Part 2:** 463, 596; **Supp. V:** 152; **Supp. VIII:** 103, 105, 108, 153, 201; **Supp. IX:** 114; **Supp. X:** 78; **Supp. XI:** 51, 78; **Supp. XII:** 26; **Supp. XIII:** 102; **Supp. XIV:** 48

Hawthorne, Rose, **II:** 225

Hawthorne, Una, **II:** 225

"Hawthorne and His Mosses" (Melville), **Retro. Supp. I:** 254; **Supp. XIV:** 48

"Hawthorne Aspect [of Henry James], The" (Eliot), **Retro. Supp. I:** 63

"Hawthorne in Solitude" (Cowley), **Supp. II Part 1:** 143

Hay, John, **I:** 1, 10, 12, 14–15; **Supp. I Part 1:** 352

Hay, Mrs. John, **I:** 14

Hay, Sara Henderson, **Supp. XIV:119–135**

Hayakawa, S. I., **I:** 448; **Supp. I Part 1:** 315

Hayden, Robert, **Supp. II Part 1: 361–383; Supp. IV Part 1:** 169; **Supp. XIII:** 115, 127; **Supp. XIV:** 119, 123

Hayden, Sterling, **Supp. XI:** 304

Haydn, Hiram, **IV:** 100, 358

Hayduke Lives! (Abbey), **Supp. XIII: 16**

Hayek, Friedrich A. von, **Supp. IV Part 2:** 524

Hayes, Ira, **Supp. IV Part 1:** 326

Hayes, Richard, **Supp. V:** 320

Hayes, Rutherford B., **Supp. I Part 2:** 419

Haygood, Wil, **Supp. VIII:** 79

Hayne, Paul Hamilton, **Supp. I Part 1:** 352, 354, 355, 360, 372

Hayward, Florence, **Retro. Supp. II:** 65

Hayward, John, **Retro. Supp. I:** 67

Haywood, "Big" Bill, **I:** 483; **Supp. V:** 286

Hazard, Grace, **II:** 530

Hazard of Fortunes, A (Howells), **Retro. Supp. II:** 288

Hazard of New Fortunes, A (Howells), **II:** 275, 276, 286–297, 290

Hazel, Robert, **Supp. VIII:** 137, 138

Hazen, General W. B., **I:** 192, 193

Hazlitt, Henry, **Supp. IV Part 2:** 524

Hazlitt, William, **I:** 58, 378; **II:** 315

Hazmat (McClatchy), **Supp. XII: 265–270**

Hazo, Samuel, **I:** 386; **Supp. XIV:** 123, 124

Hazzard, Shirley, **Supp. VIII:** 151

H.D. *See* Doolittle, Hilda

"He" (Porter), **III:** 434, 435

"Head and Shoulders" (Fitzgerald), **Retro. Supp. I:** 101

"Head-Hunter, The" (O. Henry), **Supp. II Part 1:** 403

"Headless Hawk, The" (Capote), **Supp. III Part 1:** 124

Headlines (T. Williams), **IV:** 381

Headlong Hall (Peacock), **Supp. I Part 1:** 307

Headmaster, The (McPhee), **Supp. III Part 1:** 291, 294, 298

"Head of Joaquín Murrieta, The" (Rodriguez), **Supp. XIV:** 303

Headsman, The (Cooper), **I:** 345–346

"Headwaters" (Momaday), **Supp. IV Part 2:** 486

Healy, Eloise Klein, **Supp. XI:** 121, 124, 126, 127, 129, 137

Healy, Tim, **II:** 129, 137

Heaney, Seamus, **Retro. Supp. II:** 245;

Supp. IX: 41, 42; **Supp. X:** 67, 122; **Supp. XI:** 249

Hearn, Lafcadio, **I:** 211; **II:** 311

Hearon, Shelby, **Supp. VIII: 57–72**

Hearst, Patty, **Supp. IV Part 1:** 195

Hearst, William Randolph, **I:** 198, 207, 208; **IV:** 298

"Heart and the Lyre, The" (Bogan), **Supp. III Part 1:** 65

"Heartbeat" (Harjo), **Supp. XII:** 221–222

Heartbreak Kid, The (film), **Supp. IV Part 2:** 575, 589

Heart for the Gods of Mexico, A (Aiken), **I:** 54

"Hear the Nightingale Sing" (Gordon), **II:** 200

Heart is a Lonely Hunter, The (McCullers), **II:** 586, 588–593, 604, 605

Heart of a Woman, The (Angelou), **Supp. IV Part 1:** 2, 5, 7–9, 9, 14, 17

Heart of Darkness (Conrad), **Retro. Supp. II:** 292; **Supp. V:** 249, 311; **Supp. VIII:** 4, 316

"Heart of Darkness" (Conrad), **I:** 575, 578; **II:** 595

Heart of Darkness (Didion), **Supp. IV Part 1:** 207

Heart of Happy Hollow, The (Dunbar), **Supp. II Part 1:** 214

Heart of Knowledge, The: American Indians on the Bomb (Gunn Allen and Caputi, eds.), **Supp. IV Part 1:** 334–335

"Heart of Knowledge, The: Nuclear Themes in Native American Thought and Literature" (Caputi), **Supp. IV Part 1:** 335

"Heart of the Park, The " (O'Connor), **Retro. Supp. II:** 225

Heart of the West (O. Henry), **Supp. II Part 1:** 410

"Hearts, The" (Pinsky), **Supp. VI:** 245–247, 248

"'Hearts and Flowers'" (MacLeish), **III:** 8

"Hearts and Heads" (Ransom), **Supp. I Part 1:** 373

"Heart's Graveyard Shift, The" (Komunyakaa), **Supp. XIII:** 120

Heart-Shape in the Dust (Hayden), **Supp. II Part 1:** 365, 366

"Heart's Needle" (Snodgrass), **Supp. VI: 311–313,** 320

Heart's Needle (Snodgrass), **I:** 400

"Heart Songs" (Proulx), **Supp. VII:** 254

Heart Songs and Other Stories

(Proulx), **Supp. VII:** 252–256, 261

Heart to Artemis, The (Bryher), **Supp. I Part 1:** 259

Heartwood (Burke), **Supp. XIV:** 35

Heath Anthology of American Literature, The, **Supp. IX:** 4

Heathcote, Anne. *See* De Lancey, Mrs. James

"Heathen Chinee, The" (Harte), **Supp. II Part 1:** 350–351, 352

Heathen Days, 1890–1936 (Mencken), **III:** 100, 111

"Heaven" (Dunn), **Supp. XI:** 154

"Heaven" (Levine), **Supp. V:** 182

"Heaven" (Patchett), **Supp. XII:** 309

Heaven and Earth: A Cosmology (Goldbarth), **Supp. XII: 187**

"Heaven and Earth in Jest" (Dillard), **Supp. VI:** 24, 28

"Heaven as Anus" (Kumin), **Supp. IV Part 2:** 448

Heavenly Conversation, The (Mather), **Supp. II Part 2:** 460

Heavens and Earth (Benét), **Supp. XI:** 44

Heaven's Coast (Doty), **Supp. XI:** 119, 121, **129–130,** 134

Heaven's Prisoners (Burke), **Supp. XIV:** 23, 29

"Heavy Bear Who Goes with Me, The" (Schwartz), **Supp. II Part 2:** 646

"He Came Also Still" (Zukofsky), **Supp. III Part 2:** 612

Hecht, Anthony, **IV:** 138; **Supp. III Part 2:** 541, 561; **Supp. X: 55–75; Supp. XII:** 269–270

Hecht, Ben, **I:** 103; **II:** 42; **Supp. I Part 2:** 646; **Supp. XI:** 307; **Supp. XIII:** 106

Hecht, S. Theodore, **Supp. III Part 2:** 614

Heckewelder, John, **II:** 503

"Hedge Island" (Lowell), **II:** 524

Hedges, William I., **II:** 311–312

"He 'Digesteth Harde Yron'" (Moore), **Supp. IV Part 2:** 454

Hedin, Robert, **Supp. XII:** 200, 202

Hedylus (Doolittle), **Supp. I Part 1:** 259, 270

"Heel & Toe To the End" (W. C. Williams), **Retro. Supp. I:** 430

Heffernan, Michael, **Supp. XII:** 177

"HEGEL" (Baraka), **Supp. II Part 1:** 53

Hegel, Georg Wilhelm Friedrich, **I:** 265; **II:** 358; **III:** 262, 308–309, 480, 481, 487, 607; **IV:** 86, 333, 453; **Supp. I Part 2:** 633, 635, 640, 645

"Hegemony of Race, The" (Du Bois),

Supp. II Part 1: 181

Hegger, Grace Livingston. *See* Lewis, Mrs. Sinclair (Grace Livingston Hegger)

"He Had Spent His Youth Dreaming" (Dobyns), **Supp. XIII:** 90

Heidegger, Martin, **II:** 362, 363; **III:** 292; **IV:** 491; **Retro. Supp. II:** 87; **Supp. V:** 267; **Supp. VIII:** 9

Heidenmauer, The (Cooper), **I:** 345–346

Heidi Chronicles, The (Wasserstein), **Supp. IV Part 1:** 309

"Height of the Ridiculous, The" (Holmes), **Supp. I Part 1:** 302

Heilbroner, Robert, **Supp. I Part 2:** 644, 648, 650

Heilbrun, Carolyn G., **Supp. IX:** 66; **Supp. XI:** 208; **Supp. XIV:** 161, 163

Heilman, Robert Bechtold, **Supp. XIV:** 11, 12

Heilpern, John, **Supp. XIV:** 242

Heim, Michael, **Supp. V:** 209

Heine, Heinrich, **II:** 272, 273, 277, 281, 282, 387, 544; **IV:** 5

Heineman, Frank, **Supp. III Part 2:** 619

Heinlein, Robert, **Supp. IV Part 1:** 102

Heinz, Helen. *See* Tate, Mrs. Allen (Helen Heinz)

Heiress, The (film), **Retro. Supp. I:** 222

"Heirs" (Nye), **Supp. XIII:** 284

"Helas" (Creeley), **Supp. IV Part 1:** 150, 158

Helburn, Theresa, **IV:** 381

"Helen" (Lowell), **II:** 544

"Helen: A Courtship" (Faulkner), **Retro. Supp. I:** 81

"Helen, Thy Beauty Is to Me" (Fante), **Supp. XI:** 169

"Helen I Love You" (Farrell), **II:** 28, 45

Helen in Egypt (Doolittle), **Supp. I Part 1:** 260, 272, 273, 274

Helen Keller: Sketch for a Portrait (Brooks), **I:** 254

"Helen of Tyre" (Longfellow), **II:** 496

Heliodora (Doolittle), **Supp. I Part 1:** 266

Hellbox (O'Hara), **III:** 361

Heller, Joseph, **III:** 2, 258; **IV:** 98; **Retro. Supp. II:** 324; **Supp. I Part 1:** 196; **Supp. IV Part 1: 379–396; Supp. V:** 244; **Supp. VIII:** 245; **Supp. XI:** 307; **Supp. XII:** 167–168

Hellman, Lillian, **I:** 28; **III:** 28; **Supp.**

I Part 1: 276–298; Supp. IV Part 1: 1, 12, 83, 353, 355, 356; **Supp. VIII:** 243; **Supp. IX:** 196, 198, 200–201, 204

Hellmann, Lillian, **Retro. Supp. II:** 327

Hello (Creeley), **Supp. IV Part 1:** 155, 157

"Hello, Hello Henry" (Kumin), **Supp. IV Part 2:** 446

"Hello, Stranger" (Capote), **Supp. III Part 1:** 120

Hello Dolly! (musical play), **IV:** 357

Hellyer, John, **Supp. I Part 2:** 468

Helmets (Dickey), **Supp. IV Part 1:** 175, 178, 180

"Helmsman, The" (Doolittle), **Supp. I Part 1:** 266

"Help" (Barth), **I:** 139

"Help Her to Believe" (Olsen). See "I Stand There Ironing" (Olsen)

"Helsinki Window" (Creeley), **Supp. IV Part 1:** 158

Hemenway, Robert E., **Supp. IV Part 1:** 6

Hemingway, Dr. Clarence Edwards, **II:** 248, 259

Hemingway, Ernest, **I:** 28, 64, 97, 99, 105, 107, 117, 150, 162, 190, 211, 221, 288, 289, 295, 367, 374, 378, 421, 423, 445, 476, 477, 478, 482, 484–485, 487, 488, 489, 491, 495, 504, 517; **II:** 27, 44, 51, 58, 68–69, 78, 90, 97, 127, 206, **247–270,** 289, 424, 431, 456, 457, 458–459, 482, 560, 600; **III:** 2, 18, 20, 35, 36, 37, 40, 61, 108, 220, 334, 363, 364, 382, 453, 454, 471–472, 476, 551, 575, 576, 584; **IV:** 27, 28, 33, 34, 35, 42, 49, 97, 108, 122, 126, 138, 190, 191, 201, 216, 217, 257, 297, 363, 404, 427, 433, 451; **Retro. Supp. I:** 74, 98, 108, 111, 112, 113, 115, **169–191,** 215, 292, 359, 418; **Retro. Supp. II:** 19, 24, 30, 68, 115, 123; **Supp. I Part 2:** 621, 658, 678; **Supp. II Part 1:** 221; **Supp. III Part 1:** 146; **Supp. III Part 2:** 617; **Supp. IV Part 1:** 48, 102, 123, 197, 236, 342, 343, 344, 348, 350, 352, 380–381, 383; **Supp. IV Part 2:** 463, 468, 502, 607, 679, 680, 681, 689, 692; **Supp. V:** 237, 240, 244, 250, 336; **Supp. VIII:** 40, 101, 105, 179, 182, 183, 188, 189, 196; **Supp. IX:** 16, 57, 58, 94, 106, 260, 262; **Supp. X:** 137, 167, 223, 225; **Supp. XI:** 214, 221; **Supp. XIII:** 96, 255, 270; **Supp. XIV:** 24, 83

Hemingway, Mrs. Ernest (Hadley

Richardson), **II:** 257, 260, 263

Hemingway, Mrs. Ernest (Martha Gellhorn), **II:** 260

Hemingway, Mrs. Ernest (Mary Welsh), **II:** 257, 260

Hemingway, Mrs. Ernest (Pauline Pfeiffer), **II:** 260

"Hemingway: The Old Lion" (Cowley), **Supp. II Part 1:** 143

"Hemingway in Paris" (Cowley), **Supp. II Part 1:** 144

"Hemingway Story, A" (Dubus), **Supp. VII:** 91

"Hemp, The" (Benét), **Supp. XI:** 44

"Henchman, The" (Whittier), **Supp. I Part 2:** 696

Henderson, Alice Corbin, **Supp. I Part 2:** 387

Henderson, Darwin L., **Supp. XIII:** 213, 221–222

Henderson, Jane, **Supp. VIII:** 87

Henderson, Katherine, **Supp. IV Part 1:** 203, 207

Henderson, Linda. *See* Hogan, Linda

Henderson, Robert W., **Supp. VIII:** 124

Henderson, Stephen, **Supp. IV Part 1:** 365

Henderson, the Rain King (Bellow), **I:** 144, 147, 148, 152, 153, 154, 155, 158, 160, 161, 162–163; **Retro. Supp. II:** 19, **24–25,** 30

"Hen Flower, The" (Kinnell), **Supp. III Part 1:** 247–248

Henie, Sonja, **Supp. XII:** 165

Henle, James, **II:** 26, 30, 38, 41; **Supp. IX:** 2

Henri, Robert, **IV:** 411; **Supp. I Part 2:** 376

Henry, Arthur, **I:** 515; **Retro. Supp. II:** 97

Henry, DeWitt, **Supp. XI:** 342

Henry, O., **I:** 201; **III:** 5; **Supp. I Part 2:** 390, 462; **Supp. II Part 1: 385–412**

Henry, Robert, **Retro. Supp. II:** 103

Henry, William A., III, **Supp. IV Part 2:** 574

Henry and June (film), **Supp. X:** 186

Henry and June: From the Unexpurgated Diary of Anaïs Nin, **Supp. X:** 184, 185, 187, 194

Henry Holt and Company, **Retro. Supp. I:** 121, 131, 133, 136

Henry IV (Shakespeare), **III:** 166; **Supp. VIII:** 164

"Henry James, Jr." (Howells), **II:** 289; **Retro. Supp. I:** 220

"Henry James and the Art of Teaching" (Rowe), **Retro. Supp. I:** 216

"Henry Manley, Living Alone, Keeps Time" (Kumin), **Supp. IV Part 2:** 451

"Henry Manley Looks Back" (Kumin), **Supp. IV Part 2:** 451

"Henry Manley" poems (Kumin), **Supp. IV Part 2:** 446

Henry Miller Reader, The (Durrell, ed.), **III:** 175, 190

"Henry's Confession" (Berryman), **I:** 186

Henry VIII (Shakespeare), **Supp. IX:** 235

Henslee, **Supp. IV Part 1:** 217

Henson, Josiah, **Supp. I Part 2:** 589

Hentoff, Margot, **Supp. IV Part 1:** 205

Hentz, Caroline Lee, **Supp. I Part 2:** 584

Henze, Hans Werner, **Supp. II Part 1:** 24

"He of the Assembly" (Bowles), **Supp. IV Part 1:** 90

Hepburn, Katharine, **Supp. IX:** 189; **Supp. XI:** 17

Heraclitus, **II:** 1, 163; **IV:** 86

Herakles: A Play in Verse (MacLeish), **III:** 21, 22

Herald of the Autochthonic Spirit (Corso), **Supp. XII:** 134–136

Herberg, Will, **III:** 291

Herbert, Edward, **II:** 11

Herbert, Francis (pseudonym). *See* Bryant, William Cullen

Herbert, George, **II:** 12; **IV:** 141, 145, 146, 151, 153, 156, 165; **Retro. Supp. II:** 40; **Supp. I Part 1:** 80, 107, 108, 122; **Supp. IV Part 2:** 646

Herbert, Zbigniew, **Supp. VIII:** 20

Herbert Huncke Reader, The (Schafer, ed.), **Supp. XIV:** 137, 138, 139, 140, 145, 147, 150, 151–152

Herbert of Cherbury, Lord, **II:** 108

Herbst, Josephine, **Retro. Supp. II:** 325, 328; **Supp. XIII:** 295

"Her Choice" (Larcom), **Supp. XIII:** 144

"Her Dead Brother" (Lowell), **Retro. Supp. II:** 188

"Her Dream Is of the Sea" (Ríos), **Supp. IV Part 2:** 546

"Here" (Kenyon), **Supp. VII:** 164

Here and Beyond (Wharton), **Retro. Supp. I:** 382

Here and Now (Levertov), **Supp. III Part 1:** 275, 276

"Here and There" (Wallace), **Supp. X:** 305–306

Heredia, Juanita, **Supp. XI:** 185, 190

Heredity and Variation (Lock), **Retro.**

Supp. I: 375

Here Lies (Parker), **Supp. IX:** 192

Here on Earth (Hoffman), **Supp. X:** 77, 89

Heresy and the Ideal: On Contemporary Poetry (Baker), **Supp. XI:** 142

"Here to Learn" (Bowles), **Supp. IV Part 1:** 93

"Here to Yonder" (Hughes), **Retro. Supp. I:** 205

"Her Father's Letters" (Milburn), **Supp. XI:** 242

Herford, Reverend Brooke, **I:** 471

Hergesheimer, Joseph, **Supp. I Part 2:** 620

"Heritage" (Cullen), **Supp. IV Part 1:** 164–165, 168, 170, 171

"Heritage" (Hogan), **Supp. IV Part 1:** 413

"Her Kind" (Sexton), **Supp. II Part 2:** 687

Herland (Gilman), **Supp. XI:** 208–209

Herman, Florence. *See* Williams, Mrs. William Carlos (Florence Herman)

Herman, Jan, **Supp. XIV:** 150–151

Herman, William (pseudonym). *See* Bierce, Ambrose

"Her Management" (Swenson), **Supp. IV Part 2:** 642

"Herman Melville" (Auden), **Supp. II Part 1:** 14

Herman Melville (Mumford), **Supp. II Part 2:** 471, 476, 489–491

"Hermes of the Ways" (Doolittle), **Supp. I Part 1:** 266

Hermetic Definition (Doolittle), **Supp. I Part 1:** 271, 272, 273, 274

"Hermitage, The" (Haines), **Supp. XII:** 205–206

Hermit and the Wild Woman, The (Wharton), **IV:** 315; **Retro. Supp. I:** 371

"Hermit and the Wild Woman, The" (Wharton), **Retro. Supp. I:** 372

"Hermit Meets the Skunk, The" (Kumin), **Supp. IV Part 2:** 447

"Hermit of Saba, The" (Freneau), **Supp. II Part 1:** 259

Hermit of 69th Street, The: The Working Papers or Norbert Kosky (Kosinski), **Supp. VII:** 215, 216, 223, 226–227

"Hermit Picks Berries, The" (Kumin), **Supp. IV Part 2:** 447

"Hermit Thrush, A" (Clampitt), **Supp. IX:** 40

Hernández, Miguel, **Supp. V:** 194; **Supp. XIII:** 315, 323

Herne, James A., **II:** 276; **Supp. II Part 1:** 198

Hernton, Calvin, **Supp. X:** 240

"Hero, The" (Moore), **III:** 200, 211, 212

Hero, The (Raglan), **I:** 135

Hérodiade (Mallarmé), **I:** 66

Herodotus, **Supp. I Part 2:** 405

Heroes, The (Ashbery), **Supp. III Part 1:** 3

Hero in America, The (Van Doren), **II:** 103

"Heroines of Nature: Four Women Respond to the American Landscape" (Norwood), **Supp. IX:** 24

"Heron, The" (Roethke), **III:** 540–541

"Her One Bad Eye" (Karr), **Supp. XI:** 244

"Her Own People" (Warren), **IV:** 253

"Her Quaint Honour" (Gordon), **II:** 196, 199, 200

Herr, Michael, **Supp. XI:** 245

Herrick, Robert, **II:** 11, 18, 444; **III:** 463, 592; **IV:** 453; **Retro. Supp. I:** 319; **Retro. Supp. II:** 101; **Supp. I Part 2:** 646; **Supp. XIII:** 334; **Supp. XIV:** 8, 9

Herrmann, John, **Retro. Supp. II:** 328

Herron, George, **Supp. I Part 1:** 7

Herschel, Sir John, **Supp. I Part 1:** 314

"Her Sense of Timing" (Elkin), **Supp. VI:** 56, 58

Hersey, John, **IV:** 4; **Supp. I Part 1:** 196

"Her Sweet turn to leave the Homestead" (Dickinson), **Retro. Supp. I:** 44

Herzog (Bellow), **I:** 144, 147, 149, 150, 152, 153, 154, 155, 156, 157, 158, 159–160; **Retro. Supp. II:** 19, **26–27; Supp. IV Part 1:** 30

"He/She" (Dunn), **Supp. XI:** 149

"Hesitation Blues" (Hughes), **Retro. Supp. I:** 211

Hesse, Hermann, **Supp. V:** 208

"Hetch Hetchy Valley" (Muir), **Supp. IX:** 185

He Who Gets Slapped (Andreyev), **II:** 425

"He Who Spits at the Sky" (Stegner), **Supp. IV Part 2:** 605

"He Will Not Leave a Note" (Ríos), **Supp. IV Part 2:** 548

Hewlett, Maurice, **I:** 359

Heyen, William, **Supp. XIII:** 285, 344

"Hey! Hey!" (Hughes), **Supp. I Part 1:** 327–328

Hey Rub-a-Dub-Dub (Dreiser), **I:** 515; **II:** 26; **Retro. Supp. II:** 104, 105, 108

"Hey Sailor, What Ship?" (Olsen),

Supp. XIII: 293, 294, 298, **299**

Hiawatha (Longfellow), **Supp. I Part 1:** 79; **Supp. III Part 2:** 609, 610

"Hibernaculum" (Ammons), **Supp. VII:** 26–27

Hichborn, Mrs. Philip. *See* Wylie, Elinor

Hichborn, Philip, **Supp. I Part 2:** 707, 708

"Hic Jacet" (W. C. Williams), **Retro. Supp. I:** 414

Hickok, James Butler ("Wild Bill"), **Supp. V:** 229, 230

Hicks, Granville, **I:** 254, 259, 374; **II:** 26; **III:** 342, 355, 452; **Supp. I Part 1:** 361; **Supp. I Part 2:** 609; **Supp. IV Part 1:** 22; **Supp. IV Part 2:** 526; **Supp. VIII:** 96, 124; **Supp. XII:** 250; **Supp. XIII:** 263

Hicok, Bethany, **Retro. Supp. II:** 39

"Hidden" (Nye), **Supp. XIII:** 283

"Hidden Gardens" (Capote), **Supp. III Part 1:** 125

Hidden Law, The (Hecht), **Supp. X:** 58

"Hidden Name and Complex Fate" (Ellison), **Supp. II Part 1:** 245

Hidden Wound, The (Berry), **Supp. X:** 23, 25, 26–27, 29, 34, 35

"Hide-and-Seek" (Francis), **Supp. IX:** 81

"Hiding" (Minot), **Supp. VI:** 203, 206

Hiding Place (Wideman), **Supp. X:** 320, 321, 327, 329, 331–332, 333

Hienger, Jorg, **Supp. IV Part 1:** 106

Higgins, George, **Supp. IV Part 1:** 356

Higginson, Thomas Wentworth, **I:** 451–452, 453, 454, 456, 458, 459, 463, 464, 465, 470; **Retro. Supp. I:** 26, 31, 33, 35, 39, 40; **Supp. I Part 1:** 307, 371; **Supp. IV Part 2:** 430

"High Bridge above the Tagus River at Toledo, The" (W. C. Williams), **Retro. Supp. I:** 429

"High Dive: A Variant" (Kumin), **Supp. IV Part 2:** 442

"High Diver" (Francis), **Supp. IX:** 82

"Higher Keys, The" (Merrill), **Supp. III Part 1:** 335–336

Higher Learning in America, The (Veblen), **Supp. I Part 2:** 630, 631, 641, 642

Highet, Gilbert, **Supp. I Part 1:** 268

High Noon (film), **Supp. V:** 46

"High on Sadness" (Komunyakaa), **Supp. XIII:** 114

"High School Senior" (Olds), **Supp. X:** 212

Highsmith, Patricia, **Supp. IV Part 1:** 79, 94, 132

"High Tide" (Marquand), **III:** 56

High Tide in Tucson: Essays from Now or Never (Kingsolver), **Supp. VII:** 198, 201, 209

"High-Toned Old Christian Woman, A" (Stevens), **Retro. Supp. I:** 301

"Highway, The" (Merwin), **Supp. III Part 1:** 346

"Highway 99E from Chico" (Carver), **Supp. III Part 1:** 136

High Window, The (Chandler), **Supp. IV Part 1:** 127–129, 130, 131

Hijuelos, Oscar, **Supp. IV Part 1:** 54; **Supp. VIII: 73–91**

Hike and the Aeroplane (Lewis), **II:** 440–441

Hilberg, Raul, **Supp. V:** 267

Hildebrand, Al, **III:** 118

Hiler, Hilaire, **Retro. Supp. II:** 327; **Supp. III Part 2:** 617

"Hill, A" (Hecht), **Supp. X:** 59–60, 63

Hill, Hamlin, **Retro. Supp. II:** 286

Hill, James J., **Supp. I Part 2:** 644

Hill, Joe, **I:** 493

Hill, Lee, **Supp. XI:** 293, 294, 297, 299, 301, 305, 307

Hill, Patti, **I:** 289

Hill, Peggy, **Supp. XIII:** 163

"Hill, The" (Strand), **Supp. IV Part 2:** 627

"Hill, The" (Toomer), **Supp. III Part 2:** 486

Hill, Vernon, **Supp. I Part 2:** 397

"Hillcrest" (Robinson), **III:** 504

Hill-Lubin, Mildred A., **Supp. IV Part 1:** 13

Hillman, Sidney, **Supp. I Part 1:** 5

Hillringhouse, Mark, **Supp. IX:** 286, 288, 299

Hills Beyond, The (Wolfe), **IV:** 450, 451, 460, 461

"Hills Beyond, The" (Wolfe), **IV:** 460

Hillside and Seaside in Poetry (Larcom, ed.), **Supp. XIII:** 142

"Hillside Thaw, A" (Frost), **Retro. Supp. I:** 133

"Hills Like White Elephants" (Hemingway), **Retro. Supp. I:** 170

"Hill-Top View, A" (Jeffers), **Supp. II Part 2:** 417

"Hill Wife, The" (Frost), **II:** 154; **Retro. Supp. I:** 131

Hillyer, Robert, **I:** 475; **Supp. IX:** 75; **Supp. XIV:** 11

Hilton, James, **Supp. XIII:** 166

"Hiltons' Holiday, The" (Jewett), **II:** 391; **Retro. Supp. II:** 134

Him (Cummings), **I:** 429, 434–435

Himes, Chester, **Retro. Supp. II:** 117; **Supp. I Part 1:** 51, 325; **Supp. XIII:** 233

Himes, Norman, **Supp. V:** 128

"Him with His Foot in His Mouth" (Bellow), **Retro. Supp. II:** 34

Him with His Foot in His Mouth and Other Stories (Bellow), **Retro. Supp. II:** 31

Hinchman, Sandra K., **Supp. IV Part 1:** 210

Hindemith, Paul, **IV:** 357; **Supp. IV Part 1:** 81

Hindsell, Oliver, **Supp. XIII:** 162

Hindus, Milton, **Supp. XIV:** 288, 291, 292, 293

Hines, Suzanne, **Supp. XIV:** 151

Hinge Picture (Howe), **Supp. IV Part 2:** 423–424

"Hippies: Slouching towards Bethlehem" (Didion), **Supp. IV Part 1:** 200

Hippolytus (Euripides), **II:** 543; **Supp. I Part 1:** 270

Hippolytus Temporizes (Doolittle), **Supp. I Part 1:** 270

"Hips" (Cisneros), **Supp. VII:** 61, 62

"Hipster's Hipster" (Ginsberg), **Supp. XIV:** 141

Hirsch, Edward D., **Supp. V:** 177; **Supp. IX:** 262; **Supp. XIV:** 15

Hirsch, Sidney, **Supp. XIV:** 1. *See* Mttron-Hirsch, Sidney

Hirschorn, Clive, **Supp. IV Part 2:** 577, 579

Hirson, Roger, **Supp. XI:** 343

"His Bride of the Tomb" (Dunbar), **Supp. II Part 1:** 196

"His Chest of Drawers" (Anderson), **I:** 113, 114

"His Lover" (Dubus), **Supp. VII:** 86

"His Music" (Dunn), **Supp. XI:** 149

"His Own Key" (Ríos), **Supp. IV Part 2:** 543

His Religion and Hers (Gilman), **Supp. XI:** 209

"Hiss, Chambers, and the Age of Innocence" (Fiedler), **Supp. XIII:** 99

"His Shield" (Moore), **III:** 211

"His Story" (Cisneros), **Supp. VII:** 67

His Thought Made Pockets & the Plane Buckt (Berryman), **I:** 170

Histoire comparée des systèmes de philosophie (Gérando), **II:** 10

Historical and Moral View of the Origin and Progress of the French Revolution (Wollstonecraft), **Supp. I Part 1:** 126

"Historical Conceptualization" (Huizinga), **I:** 255

Historical Evidence and the Reading of Seventeenth-Century Poetry (Brooks), **Supp. XIV:** 11

"Historical Interpretation of Literature, The" (Wilson), **IV:** 431, 433, 445

Historical Jesus, The: The Life of a Mediterranean Jewish Peasant (Crossan), **Supp. V:** 251

"Historical Value of Crèvecoeur's *Voyage . . .,*" (Adams), **Supp. I Part 1:** 251

"History" (Emerson), **II:** 13, 15

"History" (Hughes), **Supp. I Part 1:** 344

History (Lowell), **Retro. Supp. II:** 183, 190

"History" (Simic), **Supp. VIII:** 279

"History, Myth, and the Western Writer" (Stegner), **Supp. IV Part 2:** 596, 601

"History among the Rocks" (Warren), **IV:** 252

History as a Literary Art (Morison), **Supp. I Part 2:** 493

"History as Fate in E. L. Doctorow's Tale of a Western Town" (Arnold), **Supp. IV Part 1:** 220

"History Is the Memory of Time" (Olson), **Supp. II Part 2:** 574

"History Lessons" (Komunyakaa), **Supp. XIII:** 126

"History of a Literary Movement" (Nemerov), **III:** 270

"History of a Literary Radical, The" (Bourne), **I:** 215, 235, 236

History of a Radical: Essays by Randolph Bourne (Brooks), **I:** 245

"History of Buttons, The" (Goldbarth), **Supp. XII:** 187

History of English Literature (Taine), **III:** 323

History of Fortus, The (Emerson), **II:** 8

History of Henry Esmond, The (Thackeray), **II:** 91, 130

History of Modern Poetry, A (Perkins), **Supp. I Part 2:** 475

History of My Heart (Pinsky), **Supp. VI:** 243, 244, 245

History of New York, from the Beginning of the World to the End of the Dutch Dynasty, A (Irving), **II:** 300–303, 304, 310

History of Pendennis, The (Thackeray), **II:** 291

"History of Red, The" (Hogan), **Supp. IV Part 1:** 411

History of Roxbury Town (Ellis), **Supp. I Part 1:** 99

History of the Conquest of Mexico (Prescott), **Retro. Supp. I:** 123

History of the Conquest of Peru (Morison, ed.), **Supp. I Part 2:** 494

History of the Dividing Line betwixt Virginia and North Carolina (Byrd), **Supp. IV Part 2:** 425

History of the Life and Voyages of Christopher Columbus, A (Irving), **II:** 310, 314

History of the Navy of the United States of America (Cooper), **I:** 347

History of the Rise and Fall of the Slavepower in America (Wilson), **Supp. XIV:** 48, 49

History of the United States of America during the Administrations of Thomas Jefferson and James Madison (Adams), **I:** 6–9, 10, 20, 21

History of the Work of Redemption, A (Edwards), **I:** 560

History of United States Naval Operations in World War II (Morison), **Supp. I Part 2:** 490–492

History of Womankind in Western Europe, The, **Supp. XI:** 197

"History Through a Beard" (Morison), **Supp. I Part 2:** 490

His Toy, His Dream, His Rest (Berryman), **I:** 169, 170, 183, 184–186

"His Words" (Roethke), **III:** 544

Hitchcock, Ada. *See* MacLeish, Mrs. Archibald (Ada Hitchcock)

Hitchcock, Alfred, **IV:** 357; **Supp. IV Part 1:** 132; **Supp. VIII:** 177

Hitchcock, George, **Supp. X:** 127

"Hitch Haiku" (Snyder), **Supp. VIII:** 297

"Hitch-Hikers, The" (Welty), **IV:** 262

Hitchins, Christopher, **Supp. VIII:** 241

Hitler, Adolf, **I:** 261, 290, 492; **II:** 146, 454, 561, 565, 592; **III:** 2, 3, 110, 115, 140, 156, 246, 298, 446; **IV:** 5, 17, 18, 298, 372; **Supp. I Part 2:** 431, 436, 446, 664; **Supp. V:** 290

Hitler, Wendy, **III:** 404

Hnizdovsky, Jacques, **Supp. XIII:** 346

Hoagland, Edward, **Supp. XIV:** 80

"Hoarder, The" (Sexton), **Supp. II Part 2:** 692

Hobb, Gormley, **I:** 203

Hobbes, Thomas, **I:** 277; **II:** 9, 10, 540; **III:** 306; **IV:** 88; **Supp. XII:** 33; **Supp. XIV:** 5, 7

Hobson, Geary, **Supp. IV Part 1:** 321; **Supp. IV Part 2:** 502

Hobson, J. A., **I:** 232

Hobson, John A., **Supp. I Part 2:** 650

Hobson, Laura Z., **III:** 151

Hocking, Agnes, **Supp. VIII:** 251

Hocking, William Ernest, **III:** 303

Hodges, Campbell B., **Supp. XIV:** 8

Hodgson, Captain Joseph, **III:** 328

Hoffa, Jimmy, **I:** 493

Hoffenberg, Mason, **Supp. XI:** 294, 297, 299, 305

Hoffer, Eric, **Supp. VIII:** 188

Hoffman, Abbie, **Supp. XIV:** 150

Hoffman, Alice, **Supp. X: 77–94; Supp. XIII:** 13

Hoffman, Daniel, **Retro. Supp. II:** 265

Hoffman, Daniel G., **I:** 405; **II:** 307; **Supp. XI:** 152

Hoffman, Dustin, **Supp. IV Part 1:** 236

Hoffman, Frederick J., **I:** 60, 67; **II:** 443; **IV:** 113

Hoffman, Josiah Ogden, **II:** 297, 300

Hoffman, Matilda, **II:** 300, 314

Hoffman, William M., **Supp. X:** 153

Hoffmann, E. T. A., **III:** 415

Ho for a Hat (W. J. Smith), **Supp. XIII:** 346

Hofstadter, Richard, **Supp. VIII:** 98, 99, 108

Hogan, Linda, **Supp. IV Part 1:** 324, 325, **397–418**

Hogarth, William, **Supp. XII:** 44

Hogg, James, **I:** 53; **Supp. I Part 1:** 349; **Supp. IX:** 275

Hoggart, Richard, **Supp. XIV:** 299

Hohne, Karen, **Supp. V:** 147

Hojoki (Chomei), **IV:** 170

Holbrook, David, **Supp. I Part 2:** 526–527, 546

Holcroft, Thomas, **Supp. I Part 2:** 514

Holden, Jonathan, **Supp. XI:** 143

Holden, Raymond, **Supp. XIV:** 121–122

Holden, William, **Supp. XI:** 307

"Holding On" (Levine), **Supp. V:** 184

Holding the Line: Women in the Great Arizona Mine Strike of 1983 (Kingsolver), **Supp. VII:** 197, 201–202, 204

"Holding the Mirror Up to Nature" (Nemerov), **III:** 275, 276

"Hold Me" (Levine), **Supp. V:** 186

Hold the Press (film), **Supp. XIII:** 163

"Hole in the Floor, A" (Wilbur), **Supp. III Part 2:** 556–557

Holiday (Barry), **Retro. Supp. I:** 104

"Holiday" (Porter), **III:** 454

Holiday, Billie, **Supp. I Part 1:** 80; **Supp. IV Part 1:** 2, 7

Holinshed, Raphael, **IV:** 370

Holland, Josiah, **Supp. I Part 2:** 420

Holland, Laurence Bedwell, **Retro. Supp. I:** 216

Holland, Mrs. Theodore, **I:** 453, 455, 465

Holland, Theodore, **I:** 453

Holland, William, **IV:** 381

Hollander, John, **Supp. III Part 2:** 541; **Supp. IV Part 2:** 642; **Supp. IX:** 50, 153, 155; **Supp. XII:** 254, 255, 260

Holley, Marietta, **Supp. XIII:** 152

Hollinghurst, Alan, **Supp. XIII:** 52

Hollis, Thomas Brand, **Supp. I Part 2:** 514

Hollow Men, The (Eliot), **I:** 574, 575, 578–579, 580, 585; **III:** 586; **Retro. Supp. I:** 63, 64

"Hollow Tree, A" (Bly), **Supp. IV Part 1:** 64, 66

Hollyberrys at the Shore, The, **Supp. X:** 42

"Hollywood!" (Vidal), **Supp. IV Part 2:** 688

Hollywood: American Movie-City (Rand, unauthorized), **Supp. IV Part 2:** 519

Hollywood: A Novel of America in the 1920s (Vidal), **Supp. IV Part 2:** 677, 684, 686, 688, 690, 691

Hollywood on Trial (film), **Supp. I Part 1:** 295

Holmes, Abiel, **Supp. I Part 1:** 300, 301, 302, 310

Holmes, John, **I:** 169; **Supp. II Part 1:** 87; **Supp. IV Part 2:** 440–441; **Supp. XIV:** 119

Holmes, John Clellon, **Supp. XII:** 118; **Supp. XIV:** 144, 150

Holmes, Mrs. Abiel (Sarah Wendell), **Supp. I Part 1:** 300

Holmes, Mrs. Oliver Wendell (Amelia Jackson), **Supp. I Part 1:** 303

Holmes, Oliver Wendell, **I:** 487; **II:** 225, 273–274, 402, 403; **III:** 81–82, 590, 591–592; **IV:** 429, 436; **Retro. Supp. II:** 155; **Supp. I Part 1:** 103, 243, 254, **299–319; Supp. I Part 2:** 405, 414, 415, 420, 593, 704, 705; **Supp. XI:** 194

Holmes, Oliver Wendell, Jr., **I:** 3, 19; **Supp. IV Part 2:** 422

Holmes, Steven J., **Supp. IX:** 172, 177

Holmes, Ted, **Supp. V:** 180

Holmes, William Henry, **Supp. IV Part 2:** 603–604

Holocaust (Reznikoff), **Supp. XIV:** 281, **291–293**

Holt, Edwin E., **I:** 59

Holt, Felix, **II:** 179

Holt, Henry, **II:** 348; **III:** 587

Holt, Patricia, **Supp. XIV:** 89

Holtby, Winifred, **Supp. I Part 2:** 720

Holy Ghostly, The (Shepard), **Supp. III Part 2:** 437–438, 447

"Holy Innocents, The" (Lowell), **II:** 539

Holy Sonnets (Donne), **IV:** 145; **Supp. I Part 1:** 367; **Supp. III Part 2:** 619; **Supp. XIII:** 130–131

"Holy Terror, A" (Bierce), **I:** 203

"Holy Terror, The" (Maxwell), **Supp. VIII:** 169

Holy the Firm (Dillard), **Supp. VI:** 23, **29,** 30, 31, 32

Holy War, The (Bunyan), **IV:** 156

"Homage to Arthur Rimbaud" (Wright), **Supp. V:** 339

"Homage to Che Guevara" (Banks), **Supp. V:** 5

Homage to Clio (Auden), **Supp. II Part 1:** 24

"Homage to Elizabeth Bishop" (Ivask, ed.), **Supp. I Part 1:** 96

"Homage to Ezra Pound" (Wright), **Supp. V:** 339

Homage to Frank O'Hara (Ashbery), **Supp. III Part 1:** 2–3

"Homage to Franz Joseph Haydn" (Hecht), **Supp. X:** 69

"Homage to Hemingway" (Bishop), **IV:** 35

Homage to Mistress Bradstreet (Berryman), **I:** 168, 169, 170–171, 172, 174, 175, 178–183, 184, 186

"Homage to Paul Cézanne" (Wright), **Supp. V:** 341–342

Homage to Sextus Propertius (Pound), **Retro. Supp. I:** 290

"Homage to Sextus Propertius" (Pound), **III:** 462, 476; **Supp. III Part 2:** 622

"Homage to Shakespeare" (Cheever), **Supp. I Part 1:** 180

"Homage to the Empress of the Blues" (Hayden), **Supp. II Part 1:** 379

"Homage to the Memory of Wallace Stevens" (Justice), **Supp. VII:** 126

Homage to Theodore Dreiser (Warren), **I:** 517

Homans, Margaret, **Supp. X:** 229

"Home" (Hughes), **Supp. I Part 1:** 329, 330

"Home" (Mora), **Supp. XIII:** 217

Home (Updike), **Retro. Supp. I:** 320

Home: Social Essays (Baraka), **Supp. II Part 1:** 45, 61

"Home, Sweet Home" (Fante), **Supp. XI:** 164, 165

Home, The (Gilman), **Supp. XI:** 206–207

"Home after Three Months Away" (Lowell), **II:** 547

Home and Colonial Library (Murray), **Retro. Supp. I:** 246

Home as Found (Cooper), **I:** 348, 349, 350, 351

"Home Away from Home, A" (Humphrey), **Supp. IX:** 101

Home Book of Shakespeare Quotations (Stevenson), **Supp. XIV:** 120

"Home Burial" (Frost), **Retro. Supp. I:** 124, 125, 128, **129–130; Supp. VIII:** 31

Homecoming (Alvarez), **Supp. VII:** 1, 3–5, 9

"Homecoming" (McGrath), **Supp. X:** 116

Homecoming, The (Wilson), **Supp. VIII:** 330

Homecoming Game, The (Nemerov), **III:** 268, 282, 284–285

"Home during a Tropical Snowstorm I Feed My Father Lunch" (Karr), **Supp. XI:** 241–242, 248

Home Economics (Berry), **Supp. X:** 28, 31–32, 35, 36, 37

Home from the Hill (film), **Supp. IX:** 95

Home from the Hill (Humphrey), **Supp. IX:** 93, 95, **96–98,** 104, 106, 109

"Homeland" (Merwin), **Supp. III Part 1:** 351

Homeland and Other Stories (Kingsolver), **Supp. VII:** 199, 202–204, 207

Home on the Range (Baraka), **Supp. II Part 1:** 47

Home Place, The (Morris), **III:** 221, 222, 232

Homer, **I:** 312, 433; **II:** 6, 8, 133, 302, 543, 544, 552; **III:** 14, 21, 278, 453, 457, 473, 567; **IV:** 54, 371; **Retro. Supp. I:** 59; **Supp. I Part 1:** 158, 283; **Supp. I Part 2:** 494; **Supp. X:** 36, 120, 122; **Supp. XIV:** 21

Homer, Louise, **Retro. Supp. I:** 10

"Home Range" (Leopold), **Supp. XIV:** 184, 185

"Homesick Blues" (Hughes), **Supp. I Part 1:** 327

Home to Harlem (McKay), **Supp. X:** 132, 137–138, **138–139**

Homeward Bound (Cooper), **I:** 348

Homewood trilogy (Wideman), **Supp. X:** 319

"Homework" (Cameron), **Supp. XII:** 80, **83,** 84

"Homily" (Tate), **IV:** 121–122

"Homme Moyen Sensuel, L'" (Pound), **III:** 462

Homme révolté, L' (Camus), **III:** 306

"Homoeopathy and Its Kindred Delusions" (Holmes), **Supp. I Part 1:** 303–304, 305

Homo Ludens (Huizinga), **II:** 416–417, 425

"Homosexual Villain, The" (Mailer), **III:** 36

"Homo Will Not Inherit" (Doty), **Supp. XI:** 128

Hone and Strong Diaries of Old Manhattan, The (Auchincloss, ed.), **Supp. IV Part 1:** 23

"Honey" (Beattie), **Supp. V:** 33

"Honey" (Wright), **Supp. III Part 2:** 589

"Honey, We'll Be Brave" (Farrell), **II:** 45

Honey and Salt (Sandburg), **III:** 594–596

"Honey and Salt" (Sandburg), **III:** 594

"Honey Babe" (Hughes), **Supp. I Part 1:** 334

"Honey Tree, The" (Oliver), **Supp. VII:** 236

Hong, Maxine. *See* Kingston, Maxine Hong

Hongo, Garrett, **Supp. X:** 292; **Supp. XIII:** 114

"Honkytonk" (Shapiro), **Supp. II Part 2:** 705

"Honky Tonk in Cleveland, Ohio" (Sandburg), **III:** 585

Honorable Men (Auchincloss), **Supp. IV Part 1:** 23

Hood, Tom, **I:** 195

"Hoodoo in America" (Hurston), **Supp. VI:** 153–154

"Hook" (Wright), **Supp. III Part 2:** 604

Hook, Sidney, **I:** 265; **Supp. IV Part 2:** 527; **Supp. VIII:** 96, 100; **Supp. XIV:** 3

Hooker, Adelaide. *See* Marquand, Mrs. John P. (Adelaide Hooker)

Hooker, Isabella Beecher, **Supp. XI:** 193

Hooker, Samuel, **IV:** 162, 165

Hooker, Thomas, **II:** 15–16; **IV:** 162

Hooper, Marian. *See* Adams, Mrs. Henry (Marian Hooper)

Hoosier Holiday, A (Dreiser), **Retro. Supp. II:** 104

Hoover, Herbert, **Supp. I Part 2:** 638

Hoover, J. Edgar, **Supp. XIII:** 170

"Hope" (Jarrell), **II:** 389

"Hope" (Matthews), **Supp. IX:** 163

Hope, A. D., **Supp. XIII:** 347

Hope, Lynn, **Supp. II Part 1:** 38

"Hope Atherton's Wanderings" (Howe), **Supp. IV Part 2:** 432

Hope of Heaven (O'Hara), **III:** 361

"Hop-Frog" (Poe), **Retro. Supp. II:** 264, 268, 269

Hopkins, Anne Yale, **Supp. I Part 1:** 100, 102, 113

Hopkins, Gerard Manley, **I:** 171, 179, 397, 401, 522, 525, 533; **II:** 537; **III:** 197, 209, 523; **IV:** 129, 135, 141, 421; **Retro. Supp. II:** 40; **Supp. I Part 1:** 79, 81, 94; **Supp. III Part 2:** 551; **Supp. IV Part 1:** 178; **Supp. IV Part 2:** 637, 638, 639, 641, 643; **Supp. V:** 337; **Supp. IX:** 39, 42; **Supp. X:** 61, 115; **Supp. XIII:** 294; **Supp. XIV:** 83

Hopkins, L. A., **I:** 502

Hopkins, Lemuel, **Supp. II Part 1:** 70

Hopkins, Miriam, **IV:** 381; **Supp. I Part 1:** 281

Hopkins, Samuel, **I:** 547, 549

Hopkins, Vivian, **II:** 20

Hopkinson, Francis, **Supp. I Part 2:** 504

Hopper (Strand), **Supp. IV Part 2:** 632

Hopper, Dennis, **Supp. XI:** 293, 308

Hopper, Edward, **IV:** 411, 413; **Supp. IV Part 2:** 619, 623, 631, 634

Hopwood, Avery, **Supp. IV Part 2:** 573

Horace, **II:** 8, 154, 169, 543, 552, 568; **III:** 15; **IV:** 89; **Supp. I Part 2:** 423; **Supp. IX:** 152; **Supp. X:** 65; **Supp. XII:** 258, 260, 262

Horae Canonicae (Auden), **Supp. II Part 1:** 21

"Horatian Ode" (Marvell), **IV:** 135

"Horatian Ode upon Cromwell's Return from Ireland" (Marvell), **Supp. XIV:** 10

Horkheimer, Max, **Supp. I Part 2:** 645; **Supp. IV Part 1:** 301

Horn, Mother, **Supp. I Part 1:** 49, 54

Hornby, Nick, **Supp. XII:** 286

"Horn of Plenty" (Hughes), **Retro. Supp. I:** 210; **Supp. I Part 1:** 342

Horowitz, James. *See* Salter, James

Horowitz, Mark, **Supp. V:** 219, 231

"Horse, The" (Levine), **Supp. V:** 182

"Horse, The" (Wright), **Supp. III Part 2:** 592, 601

Horse Eats Hay (play), **Supp. IV Part 1:** 82

Horse Feathers (film), **Supp. IV Part 1:** 384

Horse Has Six Legs, The (Simic), **Supp. VIII:** 272

"Horselaugh on Dibber Lannon" (Fante), **Supp. XI:** 164

Horseman, Pass By (McMurtry), **Supp. V:** 220–221, 224

"Horses" (Doty), **Supp. XI:** 122

Horses and Men (Anderson), **I:** 112–113, 114

"Horses and Men in Rain" (Sandburg), **III:** 584

"Horse Show, The" (W. C. Williams), **Retro. Supp. I:** 423

Horses Make a Landscape More Beautiful (Walker), **Supp. III Part 2:** 521, 533

"Horse Thief" (Caldwell), **I:** 310

"Horsie" (Parker), **Supp. IX:** 193

Horton, Philip, **I:** 383, 386, 387, 393, 441

Hosea (biblical book), **II:** 166

Hospers, John, **Supp. IV Part 2:** 528

Hospital, Janette Turner, **Supp. IV Part 1:** 311–302

Hospital Sketches (Alcott), **Supp. I Part 1:** 34, 35

Hostages to Fortune (Humphrey), **Supp. IX:** 96, **104–106,** 109

"Hot Dog" (Stern), **Supp. IX: 298–299**

"Hotel Bar" (McClatchy), **Supp. XII:** 269

Hotel Insomnia (Simic), **Supp. VIII:** 280, **281–282**

Hotel New Hampshire, The (Irving), **Supp. VI:** 163, 164, **172–173,** 177, 179

"Hot-Foot Hannibal" (Chesnutt), **Supp. XIV:** 60

"Hot Night on Water Street" (Simpson), **Supp. IX:** 269, 270

"Hot Time, A" (Gunn Allen), **Supp. IV Part 1:** 333

Houdini, Harry, **IV:** 437

"Hound of Heaven" (Thompson), **Retro. Supp. I:** 55

"Hour in Chartres, An" (Bourne), **I:** 228

Hours, The (Cunningham), **Supp. XII:** 80

"Hours before Eternity" (Caldwell), **I:** 291

House, Bridge, Fountain, Gate (Kumin), **Supp. IV Part 2:** 448, 449, 451, 454

House, Edward, **Supp. I Part 2:** 643

"House, The" (Merrill), **Supp. III Part 1:** 323

House at Pooh Corner, The (Milne), **Supp. IX:** 189

House Behind the Cedars, The (Chesnutt), **Supp. XIV:69–71**

Houseboat Days (Ashbery), **Supp. III Part 1:** 18–20

Housebreaker of Shady Hill and Other Stories, The (Cheever), **Supp. I Part 1:** 184

House by the Sea, The (Sarton), **Supp. VIII:** 264

House Divided, A (Buck), **Supp. II Part 1:** 118

"House Divided, The/La Casa Divida"

(Kingsolver), **Supp. VII:** 207

"House Guest" (Bishop), **Retro. Supp. II:** 49; **Supp. I Part 1:** 93

"House in Athens, The" (Merrill), **Supp. III Part 1:** 323

House in the Uplands, A (Caldwell), **I:** 297, 301, 306

"House in Turk Street, The" (Hammett), **Supp. IV Part 1:** 344

"House in Winter, The" (Sarton), **Supp. VIII:** 259

"Housekeeping" (Alvarez), **Supp. VII:** 3–5, 10

"Housekeeping for Men" (Bourne), **I:** 231

House Made of Dawn (Momaday), **Supp. IV Part 1:** 274, 323, 326; **Supp. IV Part 2:** 479, 480, 481–484, 485, 486, 504, 562

Houseman, John, **Supp. IV Part 1:** 173

House of Dust, The: A Symphony (Aiken), **I:** 50

House of Earth trilogy (Buck), **Supp. II Part 1:** 118, 123

House of Five Talents, The (Auchincloss), **Supp. IV Part 1:** 21, 25–27

"House of Flowers" (Capote), **Supp. III Part 1:** 123

House of Games (Mamet), **Supp. XIV:** 243

House of Houses (Mora), **Supp. XIII:** 213, 215, 218, 219, 223–224, **225–227,** 228, 229

House of Incest (Nin), **Supp. III Part 1:** 43; **Supp. X:** 187, 190, 193

House of Life, The: Rachel Carson at Work (Brooks), **Supp. IX:** 26

House of Light (Oliver), **Supp. VII:** 238–240

House of Mirth, The (Wharton), **II:** 180, 193; **IV:** 311–313, 314, 316, 318, 323, 327; **Retro. Supp. I:** 360, 366, 367, **367–370,** 373, 380

"House of Mist, The" (Rand), **Supp. IV Part 2:** 524

"House of My Own, A" (Cisneros), **Supp. VII:** 64

"House of Night, The" (Freneau), **Supp. II Part 1:** 259, 260

House of the Far and Lost, The (Wolfe), **IV:** 456

"House of the Injured, The" (Haines), **Supp. XII:** 203

House of the Prophet, The (Auchincloss), **Supp. IV Part 1:** 31

House of the Seven Gables (Hawthorne), **I:** 106; **II:** 60, 224, 225, 231, 237, 239, 240–241, 243,

244; **Retro. Supp. I:** 63, 149, **160–162,** 163, 164; **Supp. I Part 2:** 579

House of the Solitary Maggot, The (Purdy), **Supp. VII:** 274–275

House on Mango Street, The (Cisneros), **Supp. VII:** 58, 59–64, 65, 66, 67, 68, 72

"House on Mango Street, The" (Cisneros), **Supp. VII:** 59

House on Marshland, The (Glück), **Supp. V:** 81–83, 84

"House on the Heights, A" (Capote), **Supp. III Part 1:** 120

"House on the Hill, The" (Robinson), **III:** 505, 524

"House on 15th S.W., The" (Hugo), **Supp. VI:** 140

"Houses" (Hogan), **Supp. IV Part 1:** 402

"Houses, The" (Merwin), **Supp. III Part 1:** 354

"Houses of the Spirit" (Karr), **Supp. XI:** 250

"House Sparrows" (Hecht), **Supp. X: 68**

House That Tai Maing Built, The (Lee), **Supp. X:** 291

"House Unroofed by the Gale" (Tu Fu), **II:** 526

"House Where Mark Twain Was Born, The" (Masters), **Supp. I Part 2:** 472

"Housewife" (Sexton), **Supp. II Part 2:** 682

Housman, A. E., **III:** 15, 136, 606; **Supp. II Part 1:** 4; **Supp. IV Part 1:** 165

Houston Trilogy (McMurtry), **Supp. V:** 223–225

How" (Ginsberg), **Supp. XIV:** 142, 143

"How" (Moore), **Supp. X:** 167

"How About This?" (Carver), **Supp. III Part 1:** 141

"How Annandale Went Out" (Robinson), **III:** 513

Howard, Gerald, **Supp. XII:** 21

Howard, Jane, **Retro. Supp. I:** 334

Howard, June, **Retro. Supp. II:** 139

Howard, Leon, **Supp. I Part 2:** 408, 422, 423

Howard, Maureen, **Supp. XII:** 285

Howard, Richard, **Retro. Supp. II:** 43; **Supp. IV Part 2:** 624, 626, 640; **Supp. VIII:** 273; **Supp. IX:** 324, 326; **Supp. X:** 152; **Supp. XI:** 317; **Supp. XII:** 254; **Supp. XIII:** 76

Howard, Vilma, **Retro. Supp. II:** 111, 112

Howards, J. Z., **Supp. VIII:** 178

Howards End (Forster), **Supp. XII:** 87

Howarth, Cora, **I:** 408, 409

Howbah Indians (Ortiz), **Supp. IV Part 2:** 513

"How Black Sees Green and Red" (McKay), **Supp. X:** 136

"How David Did Not Care" (Bly), **Supp. IV Part 1:** 73

Howe, E.W., **I:** 106

Howe, Florence, **Supp. XIII:** 295, 306

Howe, Harriet, **Supp. XI:** 200, 201

Howe, Irving, **IV:** 10; **Retro. Supp. I:** 369; **Retro. Supp. II:** 112, 286; **Supp. I Part 2:** 432; **Supp. II Part 1:** 99; **Supp. VI: 113–129; Supp. VIII:** 93, 232; **Supp. IX:** 227; **Supp. X:** 203, 245; **Supp. XII:** 160; **Supp. XIII:** 98

Howe, Irwing, **Supp. XIV:** 103–104, 104

Howe, James Wong, **Supp. I Part 1:** 281; **Supp. V:** 223

Howe, Julia Ward, **III:** 505; **Retro. Supp. II:** 135

Howe, M. A. DeWolfe, **I:** 258; **II:** 406; **Supp. XIV:** 54

Howe, Mary Manning, **Supp. IV Part 2:** 422

Howe, Samuel, **Supp. I Part 1:** 153

Howe, Susan, **Retro. Supp. I:** 33, 43; **Supp. IV Part 2: 419–438**

Howell, Chris, **Supp. XIII:** 112

Howell, James, **II:** 111

Howells: His Life and World (Brooks), **I:** 254

Howells, Margaret, **II:** 271

Howells, Mrs. William Dean (Elinor Mead), **II:** 273

Howells, William C., **II:** 273

Howells, William Dean, **I:** 109, 192, 204, 210, 211, 254, 355, 407, 411, 418, 459, 469; **II:** 127–128, 130, 131, 136, 137, 138, 140, **271–294,** 322, 331–332, 338, 397–398, 400, 415, 444, 451, 556; **III:** 51, 118, 314, 327–328, 461, 576, 607; **IV:** 192, 202, 342, 349; **Retro. Supp. I:** 220, 334, 362, 378; **Retro. Supp. II:** 93, 101, 135, 288; **Supp. I Part 1:** 306, 318, 357, 360, 368; **Supp. I Part 2:** 414, 420, 645–646; **Supp. II Part 1:** 198, 352; **Supp. IV Part 2:** 678; **Supp. VIII:** 98, 101, 102; **Supp. XI:** 198, 200; **Supp. XIV:** 45–46

Howells, Winifred, **II:** 271

"Howells as Anti-Novelist" (Updike), **Retro. Supp. I:** 334

Hower, Edward, **Supp. XII:** 330, 343

Howes, Barbara, **Supp. XIII:** 331

How Good Is David Mamet, Anyway? (Heilpern), **Supp. XIV:** 242

"How I Became a Shadow" (Purdy), **Supp. VII:** 269

"How I Came to Vedanta" (Isherwood), **Supp. XIV:** 164

"How I Learned to Sweep" (Alvarez), **Supp. VII:** 4

"How It Began" (Stafford), **Supp. XI:** 327

"How It Feels to Be Colored Me" (Hurston), **Supp. VI:** 152

"How I Told My Child About Race" (Brooks), **Supp. III Part 1:** 78

"How I Went to the Mines" (Harte), **Supp. II Part 1:** 336

"How I Write" (Welty), **IV:** 279, 280

"How Jonah Did Not Care" (Bly), **Supp. IV Part 1:** 73

Howl (Ginsberg), **Retro. Supp. I:** 426; **Supp. III Part 1:** 92; **Supp. IV Part 1:** 90; **Supp. V:** 336; **Supp. VIII:** 290; **Supp. XIV:** 15, 126, 157

Howl: Original Draft Facsimile, Transcript and Variant Versions (Gimsberg), **Supp. XIV:** 142

Howl and Other Poems (Ginsberg), **Supp. II Part 1:** 308, 317–318, 319; **Supp. X:** 123

Howlett, William, **Retro. Supp. I:** 17

"How Many Midnights" (Bowles), **Supp. IV Part 1:** 86–87

"How Many Nights" (Kinnell), **Supp. III Part 1:** 245–246

How Much? (Blechman), **Supp. I Part 1:** 290

"How Much Are You Worth" (Salinas), **Supp. XIII:** 325–326

"How Much Earth" (Levine), **Supp. V:** 184

How Much Earth: The Fresno Poets (Buckley, Oliveira, and Williams, eds.), **Supp. XIII:** 313

"How Poetry Comes to Me" (Corso), **Supp. X:** 122

"How Poetry Comes to Me" (Snyder), **Supp. VIII:** 305

"How She Came By Her Name: An Interview with Louis Massiah" (Bambara), **Supp. XI:** 20

"How Soon Hath Time" (Ransom), **IV:** 123

How Stella Got Her Groove Back (McMillan), **Supp. XIII:** 185, **190–191**

How the Alligator Missed Breakfast (Kinney), **Supp. III Part 1:** 235, 253

"How the Devil Came Down Division Street" (Algren), **Supp. IX:** 3

How the García Girls Lost Their Accents (Alvarez), **Supp. VII:** 3, 5–9, 11, 15, 17, 18

How the Other Half Lives (Riis), **I:** 293

"How the Saint Did Not Care" (Bly), **Supp. IV Part 1:** 73

"How the Women Went from Dover" (Whittier), **Supp. I Part 2:** 694, 696, 697

"How to Be an Other Woman" (Moore), **Supp. X:** 165, 167, 168

"How to Become a Writer" (Moore), **Supp. X:** 167, 168

"How to Be Happy: Another Memo to Myself" (Dunn), **Supp. XI:** 145

How to Develop Your Personality (Shellow), **Supp. I Part 2:** 608

How to Know God: The Yoga Aphorisms of Patanjali (Isherwood and Prabhavananda)), **Supp. XIV:** 164

"How To Like It" (Dobyns), **Supp. XIII: 85–86**

"How to Live. What to Do" (Stevens), **Retro. Supp. I:** 302

"How to Live on $36,000 a Year" (Fitzgerald), **Retro. Supp. I:** 105

How to Read (Pound), **Supp. VIII:** 291

How to Read a Novel (Gordon), **II:** 198

How to Save Your Own Life (Jong), **Supp. V:** 115, 123–125, 130

"How to Study Poetry" (Pound), **III:** 474

"How to Talk to Your Mother" (Moore), **Supp. X:** 167, 172

How to Win Friends and Influence People (Carnegie), **Supp. I Part 2:** 608

How to Worry Successfully (Seabury), **Supp. I Part 2:** 608

How to Write (Stein), **IV:** 32, 34, 35

"How to Write a Blackwood Article" (Poe), **III:** 425; **Retro. Supp. II:** 273

"How to Write a Memoir Like This" (Oates), **Supp. III Part 2:** 509

"How to Write Like Somebody Else" (Roethke), **III:** 540

How to Write Short Stories (Lardner), **II:** 430, 431

"How Vincentine Did Not Care" (Bly), **Supp. IV Part 1:** 73

How We Became Human: New and Selected Poems (Harjo), **Supp. XII: 230–232**

"How We Danced" (Sexton), **Supp. II Part 2:** 692

"How You Sound??" (Baraka), **Supp. II Part 1:** 30

Hoy, Philip, **Supp. X:** 56, 58

Hoyer, Linda Grace (pseudonym). *See* Updike, Mrs. Wesley

Hoyt, Constance, **Supp. I Part 2:** 707

Hoyt, Elinor Morton. *See* Wylie, Elinor

Hoyt, Henry (father), **Supp. I Part 2:** 707

Hoyt, Henry (son), **Supp. I Part 2:** 708

Hoyt, Henry Martyn, **Supp. I Part 2:** 707

Hsu, Kai-yu, **Supp. X:** 292

Hubba City (Reed), **Supp. X:** 241

Hubbard, Elbert, **I:** 98, 383

Hubbell, Jay B., **Supp. I Part 1:** 372

"Hubbub, The" (Ammons), **Supp. VII:** 35

Huber, François, **II:** 6

Huckins, Olga, **Supp. IX:** 32

Huckleberry Finn (Twain). *See Adventures of Huckleberry Finn, The* (Twain)

Hud (film), **Supp. V:** 223, 226

Hudgins, Andrew, **Supp. X:** 206

Hudson, Henry, **I:** 230

"Hudsonian Curlew, The" (Snyder), **Supp. VIII:** 302

Hudson River Bracketed (Wharton), **IV:** 326–327; **Retro. Supp. I:** 382

Huebsch, B. W., **III:** 110

Hueffer, Ford Madox, **Supp. I Part 1:** 257, 262. *See also* Ford, Ford Madox

Hug Dancing (Hearon), **Supp. VIII:** **67–68**

Huge Season, The (Morris), **III:** 225–226, 227, 230, 232, 233, 238

Hugging the Jukebox (Nye), **Supp. XIII: 275–276,** 277

"Hugging the Jukebox" (Nye), **Supp. XIII:** 276

Hughes, Carolyn, **Supp. XII:** 272, 285

Hughes, Frieda, **Supp. I Part 2:** 540, 541

Hughes, Glenn, **Supp. I Part 1:** 255

Hughes, H. Stuart, **Supp. VIII:** 240

Hughes, James Nathaniel, **Supp. I Part 1:** 321, 332

Hughes, Ken, **Supp. XI:** 307

Hughes, Langston, **Retro. Supp. I: 193–214; Retro. Supp. II:** 114, 115, 117, 120; **Supp. I Part 1: 320–348; Supp. II Part 1:** 31, 33, 61, 170, 173, 181, 227, 228, 233, 361; **Supp. III Part 1:** 72–77; **Supp. IV Part 1:** 15, 16, 164, 168, 169, 173, 243, 368; **Supp. VIII:** 213; **Supp. IX:** 306, 316; **Supp. X:** 131, 136, 139, 324; **Supp. XI:** 1; **Supp. XIII:** 75, 111, 132, 233

Hughes, Nicholas, **Supp. I Part 2:** 541

Hughes, Robert, **Supp. X:** 73

Hughes, Ted, **IV:** 3; **Retro. Supp. II:** 244, 245, 247, 257; **Supp. I Part 2:**
536, 537, 538, 539, 540, 541

Hughes, Thomas, **Supp. I Part 2:** 406

"Hugh Harper" (Bowles), **Supp. IV Part 1:** 94

Hughie (O'Neill), **III:** 385, 401, 405

Hugh Selwyn Mauberley (Pound), **I:** 66, 476; **III:** 9, 462–463, 465, 468; **Retro. Supp. I: 289–290,** 291, 299; **Supp. XIV:** 272

Hugo, Richard, **Supp. VI: 131–148; Supp. IX:** 296, 323, 324, 330; **Supp. XI:** 315, 317; **Supp. XII:** 178; **Supp. XIII:** 112, 113, 133

Hugo, Victor, **II:** 290, 490, 543; **Supp. IV Part 2:** 518; **Supp. IX:** 308

Hui-neng, **III:** 567

Huis Clos (Sartre), **Supp. IV Part 1:** 84

Huizinga, Johan, **I:** 225; **II:** 416–417, 418, 425

Hulbert, Ann, **Supp. XI:** 38–39

Hull, Lynda, **Supp. XI:** 131

Hulme, Thomas E., **I:** 68, 69, 475; **III:** 196, 209, 463–464, 465; **IV:** 122; **Supp. I Part 1:** 261, 262

Human, All Too Human (Nietzsche), **Supp. X:** 48

"Human Culture" (Emerson), **II:** 11–12

Human Factor, The (Greene), **Supp. V:** 298

"Human Figures" (Doty), **Supp. XI:** 123–124

"Human Immortality" (James), **II:** 353–354

"Human Life" (Emerson), **II:** 11–12

Human Stain, The (Roth), **Retro. Supp. II:** 279, 289, 294–295

"Human Things" (Nemerov), **III:** 279

Human Universe (Olson), **Supp. II Part 2:** 571

"Human Universe" (Olson), **Supp. II Part 2:** 565, 567

Human Wishes (Hass), **Supp. VI:** 105–106, 107

Human Work (Gilman), **Supp. XI:** 206

Humbert, Humbert, **Supp. X:** 283

Humble Inquiry into the Rules of the Word of God, An, Concerning the Qualifications Requisite to a Complete Standing and Full Communion in the Visible Christian Church (Edwards), **I:** 548

Humboldt, Alexander von, **III:** 428

Humboldt's Gift (Bellow), **Retro. Supp. II:** 19, 28–29, 34; **Supp. XIII:** 320

Hume, David, **I:** 125; **II:** 349, 357, 480; **III:** 618

Humes, H. L. "Doc," **Supp. XI:** 294

Humes, Harold, **Supp. V:** 201; **Supp. XIV:** 82

"Hummingbirds, The" (Welty), **IV:** 273

Humphrey, William, **Supp. IX: 93–112**

Humphreys, Christmas, **Supp. V:** 267

Humphreys, David, **Supp. II Part 1:** 65, 69, 70, 268

Humphreys, Josephine, **Supp. XII:** 311

Humphries, Rolfe, **III:** 124; **Retro. Supp. I:** 137

Hunchback of Notre Dame, The (film), **Supp. IV Part 1:** 101

Huncke, Herbert, **Supp. XII:** 118; **Supp. XIV:137–153**

Huncke's Journal (Huncke), **Supp. XIV:** 139, 144, 145, 146

Hundred Camels in the Courtyard, A (Bowles), **Supp. IV Part 1:** 90

"Hundred Collars, A" (Frost), **Retro. Supp. I:** 128; **Supp. XIII:** 147

Hundred Secret Senses, The (Tan), **Supp. X:** 289, 293, 295, 297, 298, 299

Hundred White Daffodils, A: Essays, Interviews, Newspaper Columns, and One Poem (Kenyon), **Supp. VII:** 160–162, 165, 166, 167, 174

Huneker, James, **III:** 102

Hunger (Hamsun), **Supp. XI:** 167

"Hunger" (Hogan), **Supp. IV Part 1:** 411

"Hunger . . ." (Rich), **Supp. I Part 2:** 571

"Hungerfield" (Jeffers), **Supp. II Part 2:** 416–417, 436

Hungerfield and Other Poems (Jeffers), **Supp. II Part 2:** 422

Hunger of Memory: The Education of Richard Rodriguez (Rodriguez), **Supp. XIV:** 297, 298, **298–302,** 310

Hungry Ghosts, The (Oates), **Supp. II Part 2:** 504, 510

Hunnewell, Susannah, **Supp. VIII:** 83

Hunt, Harriot K., **Retro. Supp. II:** 146

Hunt, Leigh, **II:** 515–516

Hunt, Richard Morris, **IV:** 312

Hunt, William, **II:** 343

Hunter, Dr. Joseph, **II:** 217

Hunter, J. Paul, **Supp. IV Part 1:** 332

Hunter, Kim, **Supp. I Part 1:** 286

"Hunter of Doves" (Herbst), **Retro. Supp. II:** 325

"Hunter of the West, The" (Bryant), **Supp. I Part 1:** 155

Hunters, The (film), **Supp. IX:** 250

Hunters, The (Salter), **Supp. IX:** 246, **249–250**

"Hunters in the Snow" (Brueghel), **I:** 174; **Retro. Supp. I:** 430

"Hunters in the Snow" (Wolff), **Supp.**

VII: 339–340

"Hunter's Moon—Eating the Bear" (Oliver), **Supp. VII:** 234

"Hunter's Vision, The" (Bryant), **Supp. I Part 1:** 160

"Hunting Is Not Those Heads on the Wall" (Baraka), **Supp. II Part 1:** 45

Huntington, Collis P., **I:** 198, 207

"Hunt in the Black Forest, The" (Jarrell), **II:** 379–380

Huntley, Jobe, **Supp. I Part 1:** 339

Hurray Home (Wideman), **Supp. X:** 320

"Hurricane, The" (Crane), **I:** 401

"Hurricane, The" (Freneau), **Supp. II Part 1:** 262

"Hurry Kane" (Lardner), **II:** 425, 426, 427

"Hurry up Please It's Time" (Sexton), **Supp. II Part 2:** 694, 695

Hurston, Zora Neale, **Retro. Supp. I:** 194, 198, 200, 201, 203; **Supp. I Part 1:** 325, 326, 332; **Supp. II Part 1:** 33; **Supp. IV Part 1:** 5, 11, 12, 164, 257; **Supp. VI:** 149–161; **Supp. VIII:** 214; **Supp. X:** 131, 139, 232, 242; **Supp. XI:** 85; **Supp. XIII:** 185, 233, 236, 295, 306

Hurt, John, **Supp. XIII:** 132

Husband's Story, The (Shields), **Supp. VII:** 316. *See also* "Happenstance" (Shields)

Husserl, Edmund, **II:** 362, 363; **IV:** 491; **Supp. IV Part 1:** 42, 43

Hussey, Jo Ella, **Supp. XII:** 201

Hustler, The (film), **Supp. XI:** 306

Huston, John, **I:** 30, 31, 33, 35; **II:** 588; **III:** 161; **Supp. IV Part 1:** 102, 116, 355; **Supp. XI:** 307; **Supp. XIII:** 174

"Huswifery" (Taylor), **IV:** 161; **Supp. I Part 2:** 386

Hutchens, John K., **Supp. IX:** 276

Hutcheson, Francis, **I:** 559

Hutchins, Patricia, **III:** 478

Hutchinson, Abigail, **I:** 562

Hutchinson, Anne, **Supp. I Part 1:** 100, 101, 113; **Supp. IV Part 2:** 434; **Supp. VIII:** 202, 205

Hutton, James, **Supp. IX:** 180

Huxley, Aldous, **II:** 454; **III:** 281, 428, 429–430; **IV:** 77, 435; **Supp. I Part 2:** 714; **Supp. XIV:** 3, 164

Huxley, Julian, **Supp. VIII:** 251; **Supp. X:** 108

Huxley, Juliette, **Supp. VIII:** 251, 265

Huxley, Thomas, **III:** 102, 108, 113, 281; **Retro. Supp. II:** 60, 65, 93

Huxley, Thomas Henry, **Supp. I Part 1:** 368

Huysmans, Joris Karl (Charles Marie Georges), **I:** 66; **III:** 315; **IV:** 286; **Retro. Supp. II:** 326

"*Hwame, Koshkalaka,* and the Rest: Lesbians in American Indian Cultures" (Gunn Allen), **Supp. IV Part 1:** 330

Hwang, David Henry, **Supp. X:** 292

"Hyacinth Drift" (Rawlings), **Supp. X: 226–227**

"Hydras, The" (Merwin), **Supp. III Part 1:** 349

"Hydriotaphia; or, Urne-Buriall" (Browne), **Supp. IX:** 136–137

Hydriotaphia, The; or, Death of Dr. Browne: An Epic Farce about Death and Primitive Capital Accumulation (Kushner), **Supp. IX:** 133, **136–138**

Hyman, Stanley Edgar, **I:** 129, 264, 363, 377, 379; **Retro. Supp. II:** 118; **Supp. IX:** 113, 114, 117, 118, 121, 122, 128

Hymen (Doolittle), **Supp. I Part 1:** 266

"Hymie's Bull" (Ellison), **Retro. Supp. II:** 124; **Supp. II Part 1:** 229

"Hymn Books" (Emerson), **II:** 10

"HYMN FOR LANIE POO" (Baraka), **Supp. II Part 1:** 31, 37

"Hymn from a Watermelon Pavilion" (Stevens), **IV:** 81

"Hymn of the Sea, A" (Bryant), **Supp. I Part 1:** 157, 163, 165

"Hymns of the Marshes" (Lanier), **Supp. I Part 1:** 364

"Hymn to Death" (Bryant), **Supp. I Part 1:** 169, 170

"Hymn to Earth" (Wylie), **Supp. I Part 2:** 727–729

"Hymn to the Night" (Longfellow), **Supp. I Part 2:** 409

Hynes, Samuel, **Supp. XIV:** 159

Hyperion (Longfellow), **II:** 488, 489, 491–492, 496; **Retro. Supp. II:** 58, 155–156

"Hypocrite Auteur" (MacLeish), **III:** 19

"Hypocrite Swift" (Bogan), **Supp. III Part 1:** 55

"Hysteria" (Eliot), **I:** 570

I (Dixon), **Supp. XII:** 141, 155, **156–157**

I, etcetera (Sontag), **Supp. III Part 2:** 451–452, 469

I, Governor of California and How I Ended Poverty (Sinclair), **Supp. V:** 289

I: Six Nonlectures (Cummings), **I:** 430, 433, 434

"I, Too" (Hughes), **Retro. Supp. I:** 193, 199; **Supp. I Part 1:** 320

I Accuse! (film), **Supp. IV Part 2:** 683

"I Almost Remember" (Angelou), **Supp. IV Part 1:** 15

"'I Always Wanted You to Admire My Fasting'; or, Looking at Kafka"(Roth), **Retro. Supp. II:** 282

I am a Camera (Druten), **Supp. XIV:** 162

"I am a cowboy in the boat of Ra" (Reed), **Supp. X:** 242

"I Am a Dangerous Woman" (Harjo), **Supp. XII:** 216, 219

"I Am Alive" (Momaday), **Supp. IV Part 2:** 489

I Am a Sonnet (Goldbarth), **Supp. XII:** 181

"I Am a Writer of Truth" (Fante), **Supp. XI:** 167

"'I Am Cherry Alive,' the Little Girl Sang" (Schwartz), **Supp. II Part 2:** 663

"I Am Dying, Meester?" (Burroughs), **Supp. III Part 1:** 98

I Am Elijah Thrush (Purdy), **Supp. VII:** 274

"I Am in Love" (Stern), **Supp. IX:** 295

"I Am Not Flattered" (Francis), **Supp. IX:** 78

I Am! Says the Lamb (Roethke), **III:** 545

"I and My Chimney" (Melville), **III:** 91

I and Thou (Buber), **III:** 308

"I Apologize" (Komunyakaa), **Supp. XIII:** 120, **Supp. XIII:** 121

I Apologize for the Eyes in My Head (Komunyakaa), **Supp. XIII: 119–121,** 126

Ibsen, Henrik, **II:** 27, 276, 280, 291–292; **III:** 118, 145, 148, 149, 150, 151, 152, 154–155, 156, 161, 162, 165, 511, 523; **IV:** 397; **Retro. Supp. I:** 228; **Retro. Supp. II:** 94; **Supp. IV Part 2:** 522; **Supp. XIV:** 89

"I Came Out of the Mother Naked" (Bly), **Supp. IV Part 1:** 62–63, 68

"I Cannot Forget with What Fervid Devotion" (Bryant), **Supp. I Part 1:** 154

"I Can't Stand Your Books: A Writer Goes Home" (Gordon), **Supp. IV Part 1:** 314

"Icarium Mare" (Wilbur), **Supp. III Part 2:** 563

Icarus's Mother (Shepard), **Supp. III Part 2:** 446

"Ice" (Bambara), **Supp. XI:** 16

"Iceberg, The" (Merwin), **Supp. III Part 1:** 345

Ice-Cream Headache, The, and Other Stories (Jones), **Supp. XI:** 215, 227

Ice Fire Water: A Leib Goldkorn Cocktail (Epstein), **Supp. XII: 164–166**

"Ice House, The" (Gordon), **II:** 201

Iceman Cometh, The (O'Neill), **I:** 81; **III:** 151, 385, 386, 401, 402–403; **Supp. VIII:** 345

"Ice Palace, The" (Fitzgerald), **II:** 83, 88; **Retro. Supp. I:** 103

"Ice Storm, The" (Ashbery), **Supp. III Part 1:** 26

"Ice-Storm, The" (Pinsky), **Supp. VI:** 247–248

"Ichabod" (Whittier), **Supp. I Part 2:** 687, 689–690; **Supp. XI:** 50

"Icicles" (Francis), **Supp. IX:** 83

"Icicles" (Gass), **Supp. VI:** 83

Ickes, Harold, **Supp. I Part 1:** 5

Iconographs (Swenson), **Supp. IV Part 2:** 638, 646–648, 651

"Icosaphere, The" (Moore), **III:** 213

"I Could Believe" (Levine), **Supp. V:** 189

"I Cry, Love! Love!" (Roethke), **III:** 539–540

Ida (Stein), **IV:** 43, 45

"Idea, The" (Carver), **Supp. III Part 1:** 143

"Idea, The" (Strand), **Supp. IV Part 2:** 631

Ideal Husband (Wilde), **II:** 515

Idea of Florida in the American Literary Imagination, The (Rowe), **Supp. X:** 223

"Idea of Order at Key West, The" (Stevens), **IV:** 89–90; **Retro. Supp. I:** 302, 303, 313

Ideas of Order (Stevens), **Retro. Supp. I:** 296, 298, **302–303,** 303, 305

"Ideographs" (Olds), **Supp. X:** 205

Ides of March, The (Wilder), **IV:** 357, 372

"I Did Not Learn Their Names" (Ellison), **Retro. Supp. II:** 124

"I Died with the First Blow & Was Reborn Wrong" (Coleman), **Supp. XI:** 91

"Idiom of a Self, The" (Pinsky), **Supp. VI:** 240

"Idiot, The" (Crane), **I:** 401

Idiot, The (Dostoyevsky), **I:** 468

"Idiots First" (Malamud), **Supp. I Part 2:** 434–435, 437, 440–441

I Don't Need You Any More (A. Miller), **III:** 165

"I Dream I'm the Death of Orpheus" (Rich), **Supp. I Part 2:** 557–558

I Dreamt I Became a Nymphomaniac!

Imagining (Acker), **Supp. XII:** 4, 6, 8, 11

Idylls of the King (Tennyson), **III:** 487; **Supp. I Part 2:** 410; **Supp. XIII:** 146

Idyl of Work, An (Larcom), **Supp. XIII:** 139, 142, 146–147, 150

"If" (Creeley), **Supp. IV Part 1:** 158

If Beale Street Could Talk (Baldwin), **Retro. Supp. II:** 13–14; **Supp. I Part 1:** 48, 59–60, 67

If Blessing Comes (Bambara), **Supp. XI:** 1

I Feel a Little Jumpy around You (Nye and Janeczko, eds.), **Supp. XIII:** 280

"I felt a Funeral, in my Brain" (Dickinson), **Retro. Supp. I:** 38

"If I Could Be Like Wallace Stevens" (Stafford), **Supp. XI:** 327

"If I Could Only Live at the Pitch That Is Near Madness" (Eberhart), **I:** 523, 526–527

If I Die in a Combat Zone (O'Brien), **Supp. V:** 238, 239, 240, 245

"If I Had My Way" (Creeley), **Supp. IV Part 1:** 157

"If I Might Be" (Chopin), **Retro. Supp. II:** 61

"I Find the Real American Tragedy" (Dreiser), **Retro. Supp. II:** 105

If It Die (Gide), **I:** 290

"If I Were a Man" (Gilman), **Supp. XI:** 207

"If I Were the Wind" (Leopold), **Supp. XIV:** 184

If Morning Ever Comes (Tyler), **Supp. IV Part 2:** 658–659

If Mountains Die: A New Mexico Memoir (Nichols), **Supp. XIII:** 255, 257, 267

I Forgot to Go to Spain (Harrison), **Supp. VIII:** 39, **52–53**

If the River Was Whiskey (Boyle), **Supp. VIII:** 15–16

"If They Knew Yvonne" (Dubus), **Supp. VII:** 81

"If We Had Bacon" (H. Roth), **Supp. IX:** 232, 234

"If We Had Known" (Francis), **Supp. IX:** 78

"If We Must Die" (McKay), **Supp. IV Part 1:** 3; **Supp. X:** 132, 134

"If We Take All Gold" (Bogan), **Supp. III Part 1:** 52

I Gaspiri (Lardner), **II:** 435

"I Gather the Limbs of Osiris" (Pound), **Retro. Supp. I:** 287

"I Give You Back" (Harjo), **Supp. XII:** 223

Ignatius of Loyola, **IV:** 151; **Supp. XI:** 162

Ignatow, David, **Supp. XIII:** 275

"Ignis Fatuus" (Tate), **IV:** 128

"I Go Back to May 1937" (Olds), **Supp. X:** 207

I Go Dreaming Serenades (Salinas), **Supp. XIII:** 316

I Got the Blues (Odets), **Supp. II Part 2:** 530

Iguana Killer, The (Ríos), **Supp. IV Part 2:** 542–544

"I Had Eight Birds Hatcht in One Nest" (Bradstreet), **Supp. I Part 1:** 102, 115, 117, 119

"I had no time to Hate" (Dickinson), **Retro. Supp. I:** 44–45, 46

"I Have a Rendezvous with Life" (Cullen), **Supp. IV Part 1:** 168

"I Have Increased Power" (Ginsberg), **Supp. II Part 1:** 313

"I Have Seen Black Hands" (Wright), **Supp. II Part 1:** 228

"I Hear an Army" (Joyce), **Supp. I Part 1:** 262

"I heard a Fly buzz when I died" (Dickinson), **Retro. Supp. I:** 38

"I Heard Immanuel Singing" (Lindsay), **Supp. I Part 2:** 379

"I Hear It Was Charged against Me" (Whitman), **IV:** 343

"I Held a Shelley Manuscript" (Corso), **Supp. XII:** 128

"I Held His Name" (Ríos), **Supp. IV Part 2:** 547

I Knew a Phoenix (Sarton), **Supp. VIII:** 249, 251–252

"I Know a Man" (Creeley), **Supp. IV Part 1:** 147–148, 149

I Know Some Things: Stories about Childhood by Contemporary Writers (Moore, ed.), **Supp. X:** 175

I Know Why the Caged Bird Sings (Angelou), **Supp. IV Part 1:** 2–4, 5, 7, 11, 12, 13, 14, 15, 17

"Ikon: The Harrowing of Hell" (Levertov), **Supp. III Part 1:** 284

Ile (O'Neill), **III:** 388

"I Let Him Take Me" (Cisneros), **Supp. VII:** 71

Iliad (Bryant, trans.), **Supp. I Part 1:** 158

Iliad (Homer), **II:** 470; **Supp. IV Part 2:** 631; **Supp. IX:** 211; **Supp. X:** 114

Iliad (Pope, trans.), **Supp. I Part 1:** 152

"I like to see it lap the Miles" (Dickinson), **Retro. Supp. I:** 37

"I Live Up Here" (Merwin), **Supp. III**

Part 1: 349

"Illegal Alien" (Mora), **Supp. XIII:** 215

"Illegal Days, The" (Paley), **Supp. VI:** 222

Illig, Joyce, **Retro. Supp. II:** 20

"Illinois" (Masters), **Supp. I Part 2:** 458

"Illinois Bus Ride" (Leopold), **Supp. XIV:** 189

Illinois Poems (Masters), **Supp. I Part 2:** 472

"Illinois Village, The" (Lindsay), **Supp. I Part 2:** 381

Illness as Metaphor (Sontag), **Supp. III Part 2:** 452, 461, 466

I'll Take My Stand ("Twelve Southerners"), **II:** 196; **III:** 496; **IV:** 125, 237; **Supp. X:** 25, 52–53; **Supp. XIV:** 3

"I'll Take You to Tennessee" (Connell), **Supp. XIV:** 82

Illumination (Frederic), **II:** 141

Illumination Night (Hoffman), **Supp. X:** 85, **86,** 88, 89

Illusion comique, L' (Corneille), **Supp. IX:** 138

"Illusion of Eternity, The" (Eberhart), **I:** 541

Illusions (Dash; film), **Supp. XI:** 20

"Illusions" (Emerson), **II:** 2, 5, 14, 16

Illustrated Man, The (Bradbury), **Supp. IV Part 1:** 102, 103, 113

Illustrations of Political Economy (Martineau), **Supp. II Part 1:** 288

"I Look at My Hand" (Swenson), **Supp. IV Part 2:** 638, 647

I Love Myself When I Am Laughing . . . : A Zora Neale Hurston Reader (Walker), **Supp. III Part 2:** 531, 532

"I'm a Fool" (Anderson), **I:** 113, 114, 116; **Supp. I Part 2:** 430

Image and Idea (Rahv), **Supp. II Part 1:** 146

Image and the Law, The (Nemerov), **III:** 268, 269–271, 272

"Images" (Hass), **Supp. VI:** 103

"Images and 'Images'" (Simic), **Supp. VIII:** 274

"Images for Godard" (Rich), **Supp. I Part 2:** 558

"Images of Walt Whitman" (Fiedler), **IV:** 352

"Imaginary Friendships of Tom McGrath, The" (Cohen), **Supp. X:** 112

"Imaginary Iceberg, The" (Bishop), **Retro. Supp. II:** 42; **Supp. I Part 1:** 86, 88

"Imaginary Jew, The" (Berryman), **I:** 174–175

Imaginary Letters (Pound), **III:** 473–474

Imagination and Fancy; or, Selections from the English Poets, illustrative of those first requisites of their art; with markings of the best passages, critical notices of the writers, and an essay in answer to the question 'What is Poetry?' (Hunt), **II:** 515–516

"Imagination as Value" (Stevens), **Retro. Supp. I:** 298

"Imagination of Disaster, The" (Gordon), **Supp. IV Part 1:** 306

"Imagine a Day at the End of Your Life" (Beattie), **Supp. V:** 33

"Imagine Kissing Pete" (O'Hara), **III:** 372; **Supp. VIII:** 156

"Imagining How It Would Be to Be Dead" (Eberhart), **I:** 533

Imagining Los Angeles: A City in Fiction (Fine), **Supp. XI:** 160

Imagining the Worst: Stephen King and the Representations of Women (Lant and Thompson), **Supp. V:** 141

"Imagisme" (Pound), **Retro. Supp. I:** 288

Imagistes, Des: An Anthology of the Imagists (Pound, ed.), **III:** 465, 471; **Retro. Supp. I:** 288

Imago (O. Butler), **Supp. XIII:** 63, **65–66**

"Imago" (Stevens), **IV:** 74, 89

Imagoes (Coleman), **Supp. XI:** 89–90

I Married a Communist (Roth), **Retro. Supp. II:** 289, 293–294

"I May, I Might, I Must" (Moore), **III:** 215

"I'm Crazy" (Salinger), **III:** 553

"I'm Here" (Roethke), **III:** 547

Imitations (Lowell), **II:** 543, 544–545, 550, 555; **Retro. Supp. II:** 181, 187

"Imitations of Drowning" (Sexton), **Supp. II Part 2:** 684, 686

"Immaculate Man" (Gordon), **Supp. IV Part 1:** 311

"Immanence of Dostoevsky, The" (Bourne), **I:** 235

"Immigrants" (Mora), **Supp. XIII:** 216

"Immigrant Story, The" (Paley), **Supp. VI:** 230

Immobile Wind, The (Winters), **Supp. II Part 2:** 786

"Immobile Wind, The" (Winters), **Supp. II Part 2:** 788, 811

"Immolatus" (Komunyakaa), **Supp. XIII:** 126

"Immoral Proposition, The" (Creeley),

Supp. IV Part 1: 144

"Immortal Autumn" (MacLeish), **III:** 13

"Immortality Ode" (Nemerov), **III:** 87

Immortality Ode (Wordsworth), **II:** 17; **Supp. I Part 2:** 673

"Immortal Woman, The" (Tate), **IV:** 130, 131, 137

"I'm Not Ready to Die Yet" (Harjo), **Supp. XII:** 231

"I'm on My Way" (Salinas), **Supp. XIII:** 320

"Impasse" (Hughes), **Supp. I Part 1:** 343

Imperative Duty, An, a Novel (Howells), **II:** 286

Imperial Eyes: Travel Writing and Transculturation (Pratt), **Retro. Supp. II:** 48

Imperial Germany and the Industrial Revolution (Veblen), **Supp. I Part 2:** 642, 643

Imperial Way, The: By Rail from Peshawar to Chittagong (Theroux), **Supp. VIII:** 323

"Implosions" (Rich), **Supp. I Part 2:** 556

"Imp of the Perverse, The" (Poe), **III:** 414–415; **Retro. Supp. II:** 267

Impolite Interviews, **Supp. XI:** 293

"Importance of Artists' Biographies, The" (Goldbarth), **Supp. XII:** 183, 184, 191

Importance of Being Earnest, The (Wilde), **Supp. XIV:** 324, 339

"Important Houses, The" (Gordon), **Supp. IV Part 1:** 315

"Impossible to Tell" (Pinsky), **Supp. VI:** 247, 248

"Imposter, The" (West), **Retro. Supp. II:** 322, 327

"Impressionism and Symbolism in *Heart of Darkness*" (Watt), **Supp. VIII:** 4

"Impressions of a European Tour" (Bourne), **I:** 225

"Impressions of a Plumber" (H. Roth), **Supp. IX:** 228, 234

"Impressions of Europe, 1913–1914" (Bourne), **I:** 225

"I'm Walking behind the Spanish" (Salinas), **Supp. XIII:** 323–324

"I/Myself" (Shields), **Supp. VII:** 311

"In Absence" (Lanier), **Supp. I Part 1:** 364

"In Absentia" (Bowles), **Supp. IV Part 1:** 94

Inada, Lawson Fusao, **Supp. V:** 180

"In a Dark Room, Furniture" (Nye), **Supp. XIII:** 274

"In a Dark Time" (Roethke), **III:** 539, 547, 548

"In a Disused Graveyard" (Frost), **Retro. Supp. I:** 126, 133

In a Dusty Light (Haines), **Supp. XII:** 207

"In a Garden" (Lowell), **II:** 513

"In a Hard Intellectual Light" (Eberhart), **I:** 523

"In a Hollow of the Hills" (Harte), **Supp. II Part 1:** 354

In America (Sontag), **Supp. XIV:** 95–96

"In Amicitia" (Ransom), **IV:** 141

In a Narrow Grave: Essays on Texas (McMurtry), **Supp. V:** 220, 223

"In Another Country" (Hemingway), **I:** 484–485; **II:** 249

In April Once (Percy), **Retro. Supp. I:** 341

In A Shallow Grave (Purdy), **Supp. VII:** 272

"In a Station of the Metro" (Pound), **Retro. Supp. I:** 288; **Supp. I Part 1:** 265; **Supp. XIV:** 284–285

"In a Strange Town" (Anderson), **I:** 114, 115

"In Athens Once" (Rodriguez), **Supp. XIV:** 303

In Battle for Peace: The Story of My 83rd Birthday (Du Bois), **Supp. II Part 1:** 185

In Bed One Night & Other Brief Encounters (Coover), **Supp. V:** 49, 50

"In Bertram's Garden" (Justice), **Supp. VII:** 117

"In Blackwater Woods" (Oliver), **Supp. VII:** 244, 246

In Broken Country (Wagoner), **Supp. IX:** 330

"In California" (Simpson), **Supp. IX:** 271

"In Camp" (Stafford), **Supp. XI:** 329

"Incant against Suicide" (Karr), **Supp. XI:** 249

"In Celebration of My Uterus" (Sexton), **Supp. II Part 2:** 689

"In Certain Places and Certain Times There Can Be More of You" (Dunn), **Supp. XI:** 144

Incest: From "A Journal of Love," the Unexpurgated Diary of Anaïs Nin, 1932–1934 (Nin), **Supp. X:** 182, 184, 185, 187, 191

Inchbald, Elizabeth, **II:** 8

Inchiquin, the Jesuit's Letters (Ingersoll), **I:** 344

"Incident" (Cullen), **Supp. IV Part 1:** 165, 166

Incidental Numbers (Wylie), **Supp. I Part 2:** 708

Incidentals (Sandburg), **III:** 579

Incident at Vichy (A. Miller), **III:** 165, 166

Incidents in the Life of a Slave Girl (Brent), **Supp. IV Part 1:** 13

"Incipience" (Rich), **Supp. I Part 2:** 559

"In Clare" (McCarriston), **Supp. XIV:** 270–271

In Cold Blood: A True Account of a Multiple Murder and Its Consequences (Capote), **Retro. Supp. II:** 107–108; **Supp. I Part 1:** 292; **Supp. III Part 1:** 111, 117, 119, 122, 123, 125–131; **Supp. III Part 2:** 574; **Supp. IV Part 1:** 220; **Supp. XIV:** 162

In Cold Hell, in Thicket (Olson), **Supp. II Part 2:** 571

"In Cold Hell, in Thicket" (Olson), **Supp. II Part 2:** 558, 563–564, 566, 572, 580

"Incomparable Light, The" (Eberhart), **I:** 541

Incorporative Consciousness of Robert Bly, The (Harris), **Supp. IV Part 1:** 68

In Country (Mason), **Supp. VIII:** 133, **142–143,** 146

"Incredible Survival of Coyote, The" (Snyder), **Supp. VIII:** 297

"Increment" (Ammons), **Supp. VII:** 28

In Defense of Ignorance (Shapiro), **Supp. II Part 2:** 703, 704, 713–714

In Defense of Reason (Winters), **Supp. I Part 1:** 268

In Defense of Women (Mencken), **III:** 109

Independence Day (Ford), **Supp. V:** 57, 62–63, 67–68

Independence Day (film), **Supp. X:** 80

"Independent Candidate, The, a Story of Today" (Howells), **II:** 277

"Indestructible Mr. Gore, The" (Vidal), **Supp. IV Part 2:** 679

Index of American Design, **Supp. III Part 2:** 618

"India" (Rodriguez), **Supp. XIV:** 302

"Indian at the Burial-Place of His Fathers, An" (Bryant), **Supp. I Part 1:** 155–156, 167–168

"Indian Burying Ground, The" (Freneau), **Supp. II Part 1:** 264, 266

"Indian Camp" (Hemingway), **II:** 247–248, 263; **Retro. Supp. I:** 174–175, 176, 177, 181

Indian Country (Matthiessen), **Supp. V:** 211

"Indian Country" (McCarriston), **Supp. XIV:** 271

"Indian Country" (Simpson), **Supp. IX:** 274

"Indian Girls" (McCarriston), **Supp. XIV:** 272–273

"Indian Manifesto" (Deloria), **Supp. IV Part 1:** 323

"Indian Names" (Sigourney), **Retro. Supp. II:** 47

"Indian Student, The" (Freneau), **Supp. II Part 1:** 264

"Indian Student, The" (Simpson), **Supp. IX:** 280

Indian Summer (Howells), **II:** 275, 279–281, 282

Indian Summer (Knowles), **Supp. XII:** 249, 250

"Indian Uprising, The" (Barthelme), **Supp. IV Part 1:** 44

Indifferent Children, The (Auchincloss), **Supp. IV Part 1:** 25

Indiscretions (Pound), **Retro. Supp. I:** 284

"Indispensability of the Eyes, The" (Olds), **Supp. X:** 202

"In Distrust of Merits" (Moore), **III:** 201, 214

"Individual and the State, The" (Emerson), **II:** 10

Individualism, Old and New (Dewey), **Supp. I Part 2:** 677

In Dreams Begin Responsibilities (Schwartz), **Supp. II Part 2:** 642, 645–650

"In Dreams Begin Responsibilities" (Schwartz), **Supp. II Part 2:** 641, 649, 654

In Dubious Battle (Steinbeck), **IV:** 51, 55–56, 59, 63

"In Durance" (Pound), **Retro. Supp. I:** 285

"Industry of Hard Kissing, The" (Ríos), **Supp. IV Part 2:** 547

"In Duty Bound" (Gilman), **Supp. XI:** 196–197

"I Need, I Need" (Roethke), **III:** 535–536

"I Need Help" (Stern), **Supp. IX:** 290

"Inés in the Kitchen" (García), **Supp. XI:** 190

"I never saw a Moor" (Dickinson), **Retro. Supp. I:** 37

Inevitable Exiles (Kielsky), **Supp. V:** 273

"Inevitable Trial, The" (Holmes), **Supp. I Part 1:** 318

"Inexhaustible Hat, The" (Wagoner), **Supp. IX:** 327

"In Extremis" (Berry), **Supp. X:** 23

"Infancy" (Wilder), **IV:** 375

"Infant Boy at Midcentury" (Warren), **IV:** 244–245, 252

Infante, Guillermo Cabrera, **Retro. Supp. I:** 278

Inferno (Dante), **IV:** 139; **Supp. V:** 338; **Supp. VIII:** 219–221

Inferno of Dante, The (Pinsky), **Supp. VI:** 235, 248

"Infidelity" (Komunyakaa), **Supp. XIII:** 130

"Infiltration of the Universe" (MacLeish), **III:** 19

Infinite Jest: A Novel (Wallace), **Supp. X:** 301, **310–314**

"Infinite Reason, The" (MacLeish), **III:** 19

"Infirmity" (Lowell), **II:** 554

"Infirmity" (Roethke), **III:** 548

In Five Years Time (Haines), **Supp. XII:** 206

"In Flower" (Snodgrass), **Supp. VI:** 325

"Influence of Landscape upon the Poet, The" (Eliot), **Retro. Supp. I:** 67

"In Football Season" (Updike), **IV:** 219

Informer, The (film), **Supp. III Part 2:** 619

Ingersoll, Charles J., **I:** 344

Ingersoll, Robert Green, **Supp. II Part 1:** 198

Ingster, Boris, **Retro. Supp. II:** 330

Inhabitants, The (Morris), **III:** 221–222

Inheritors (Glaspell), **Supp. III Part 1:** 175, 179–181, 186, 189

"In Honor of David Anderson Brooks, My Father" (Brooks), **Supp. III Part 1:** 79

"Inhumanist, The" (Jeffers), **Supp. II Part 2:** 423, 426

"In Illo Tempore" (Karr), **Supp. XI:** 242

"In Interims: Outlyer" (Harrison), **Supp. VIII:** 38

"Injudicious Gardening" (Moore), **III:** 198

"Injustice" (Paley), **Supp. VI:** 220

Injustice Collectors, The (Auchincloss), **Supp. IV Part 1:** 25

Ink, Blood, Semen (Goldbarth), **Supp. XII:** 181, 183

Ink Truck, The (Kennedy), **Supp. VII:** 132, 133–138, 140, 141, 149, 152

In Life Sentences: Literary Essays (Epstein), **Supp. XIV:** 112

"In Limbo" (Wilbur), **Supp. III Part 2:** 544, 561

In Love and Trouble: Stories of Black Women (Walker), **Supp. III Part 2:** 520, 521, 530, 531, 532

In Mad Love and War (Harjo), **Supp. XII:** 224–226

"In Memoriam" (Emerson), **II:** 13

"In Memoriam" (Hay), **Supp. XIV:** 122, 127

"In Memoriam" (Tennyson), **Retro. Supp. I:** 325; **Supp. I Part 2:** 416

In Memoriam: 1933 (Reznikoff), **Supp. XIV:** 280, 285

In Memoriam to Identity (Acker), **Supp. XII:** 5, **16–18**

"In Memory of Arthur Winslow" (Lowell), **II:** 541, 547, 550; **Retro. Supp. II:** 187

"In Memory of Congresswoman Barbara Jordan" (Pinsky), **Supp. VI:** 250

"In Memory of W. B. Yeats" (Auden), **Supp. VIII:** 19, 30; **Supp. XI:** 243, 244

"In Memory of W. H. Auden" (Stern), **Supp. IX:** 288

"In Mercy on Broadway" (Doty), **Supp. XI:** 132

In Morocco (Wharton), **Retro. Supp. I:** 380; **Supp. IV Part 1:** 81

Inmost Leaf, The: A Selection of Essays (Kazin), **Supp. VIII:** 102, 103

In Motley (Bierce), **I:** 209

In My Father's Court (Singer), **IV:** 16–17; **Retro. Supp. II: 301–302**

"In My Life" (Dubus), **Supp. VII:** 81

Inner Landscape (Sarton), **Supp. VIII:** 259

Inner Room, The (Merrill), **Supp. III Part 1:** 336

"In Nine Sleep Valley" (Merrill), **Supp. III Part 1:** 328

Innocents, The: A Story for Lovers (Lewis), **II:** 441

Innocents Abroad, The; or, The New Pilgrim's Progress (Twain), **II:** 275, 434; **IV:** 191, 196, 197–198

Innocents at Cedro, The: A Memoir of Thorstein Veblen and Some Others (Duffus), **Supp. I Part 2:** 650

"In Off the Cliffs of Moher" (McCarriston), **Supp. XIV:** 270

In Old Plantation Days (Dunbar), **Supp. II Part 1:** 214

In Ole Virginia (Page), **Supp. II Part 1:** 201

In Orbit (Morris), **III:** 236

In Other Words (Swenson), **Supp. IV Part 2:** 650–652

In Our Terribleness (Some elements and meaning in black style) (Baraka), **Supp. II Part 1:** 52, 53

In Our Time (Hemingway), **I:** 117; **II:** 68, 247, 252, 263; **IV:** 42; **Retro. Supp. I:** 170, 173, 174, 178, 180; **Supp. IX:** 106

"In Our Time" (Wolfe), **Supp. III Part 2:** 584

"Inpatient" (Kenyon), **Supp. VII:** 169

In Pharaoh's Army: Memories of the Lost War (Wolff), **Supp. VII:** 331–334, 335, 338

"In Plaster" (Plath), **Supp. I Part 2:** 540

"In Praise of Johnny Appleseed" (Lindsay), **Supp. I Part 2:** 397

"In Praise of Limestone" (Auden), **Supp. II Part 1:** 20–21; **Supp. VIII:** 23

In Quest of the Ordinary (Cavell), **Retro. Supp. I:** 307

Inquiry into the Nature of Peace, An (Veblen), **Supp. I Part 2:** 642

In Radical Pursuit (Snodgrass), **Supp. VI:** 312, 316, 318

In Reckless Ecstasy (Sandburg), **III:** 579

In Recognition of William Gaddis (Kuehl and Moore), **Supp. IV Part 1:** 279

"In Retirement" (Malamud), **Supp. I Part 2:** 437

"In Retrospect" (Angelou), **Supp. IV Part 1:** 15

In Russia (A. Miller), **III:** 165

"In Sabine" (Chopin), **Supp. I Part 1:** 213

"In School-Days" (Whittier), **Supp. I Part 2:** 699–700

"Inscription for the Entrance to a Wood" (Bryant), **Supp. I Part 1:** 154, 155, 161–162

Inscriptions, 1944–1956 (Reznikoff), **Supp. XIV:** 281

In Search of Bisco (Caldwell), **I:** 296

"In Search of Our Mothers' Gardens" (Walker), **Supp. III Part 2:** 520–532, 524, 525, 527, 529, 532–533, 535, 536; **Supp. IX:** 306

"In Search of Thomas Merton" (Griffin), **Supp. VIII:** 208

"In Search of Yage" (Burroughs), **Supp. III Part 1:** 98

"In Shadow" (Crane), **I:** 386

"In Sickness and in Health" (Auden), **Supp. II Part 1:** 15

"In Sickness and in Health" (Humphrey), **Supp. IX:** 94

Inside His Mind (A. Miller), **III:** 154

"Insider Baseball" (Didion), **Supp. IV Part 1:** 211

Inside Sports magazine, **Supp. V:** 58, 61

"In So Many Dark Rooms" (Hogan), **Supp. IV Part 1:** 400

"Insomnia" (Bishop), **Supp. I Part 1:** 92

"Insomniac" (Plath), **Supp. I Part 2:** 539

"Inspiration for Greatness" (Caldwell), **I:** 291

"Instability of Race Types, The" (Boas), **Supp. XIV:** 209

"Installation #6" (Beattie), **Supp. V:** 33

Instinct of Workmanship and the State of the Industrial Arts, The (Veblen), **Supp. I Part 2:** 642

Instincts of the Herd in Peace and War, The (Trotter), **I:** 249

Institute (Calvin), **IV:** 158, 160

"Instruction Manual, The" (Ashbery), **Supp. III Part 1:** 6–7, 10, 12

"Instruction to Myself" (Brooks), **Supp. III Part 1:** 87

Instrument, The (O'Hara), **III:** 362, 364

"In Such Times, Ties Must Bind" (Nye), **Supp. XIII:** 286

"Insurance and Social Change" (Stevens), **Retro. Supp. I:** 297

Insurgent Mexico (Reed), **I:** 476

In Suspect Terrain (McPhee), **Supp. III Part 1:** 309, 310

"In Tall Grass" (Sandburg), **III:** 585

Intellectual History, An (Senghor), **Supp. X:** 139

"Intellectual Pre-Eminence of Jews in Modern Europe, The" (Veblen), **Supp. I Part 2:** 643–644

Intellectual Things (Kunitz), **Supp. III Part 1:** 260, 262–264

Intellectual versus the City, The (White), **I:** 258

Intentions (Wilde), **Retro. Supp. I:** 56

"Interest in Life, An" (Paley), **Supp. VI:** 222, 224–225

Interest of Great Britain Considered, with Regard to Her Colonies and the Acquisition of Canada and Guadeloupe, The (Franklin), **II:** 119

Interior Landscapes (Vizenor), **Supp. IV Part 1:** 262

Interiors (film), **Supp. IV Part 1:** 205

"Interlude" (A. Lowell), **Retro. Supp. II:** 46

Interlunar (Atwood), **Supp. XIII:** 35

"In Terms of the Toenail: Fiction and the Figures of Life" (Gass), **Supp. VI:** 85

"International Episode, An" (James), **II:** 327

International Workers Order, **Retro. Supp. I:** 202

Interpretation of Christian Ethics, An (Niebuhr), **III:** 298–300, 301, 302

"Interpretation of Dreams, The" (Matthews), **Supp. IX:** 162–163

Interpretation of Music of the XVIIth and XVIIIth Centuries, The (Dolmetsch), **III:** 464

Interpretations and Forecasts: 1922–1972 (Mumford), **Supp. II Part 2:** 481

Interpretations of Poetry and Religion (Santayana), **III:** 611

Interpreters and Interpretations (Van Vechten), **Supp. II Part 2:** 729, 733–734

"Interrogate the Stones" (MacLeish), **III:** 9

"Interrupted Conversation, An" (Van Vechten), **Supp. II Part 2:** 735

Intersect: Poems (Shields), **Supp. VII:** 310–311

Interstate (Dixon), **Supp. XII:** 140, 152–153, 153, 156

"Interview" (Hay), **Supp. XIV:** 132

"Interview, The" (Thurber), **Supp. I Part 2:** 616

"Interview With a Lemming" (Thurber), **Supp. I Part 2:** 603

Interview with the Vampire (Rice), **Supp. VII:** 287, 288–291, 297–298, 303

"Interview with the Vampire" (Rice), **Supp. VII:** 288

Interzone (Burroughs), **Supp. IV Part 1:** 90

"In the Absence of Bliss" (Kumin), **Supp. IV Part 2:** 453

"In the Afternoon" (Dunn), **Supp. XI:** 146

"In the Alley" (Elkin), **Supp. VI:** 46–47

In the American Grain (W. C. Williams), **Retro. Supp. I:** 420–421

In the American Tree (Silliman), **Supp. IV Part 2:** 426

In the Bar of a Tokyo Hotel (T. Williams), **IV:** 382, 386, 387, 391, 393

In the Beauty of the Lilies (Updike), **Retro. Supp. I:** 322, 325, 326, 327, 333

"In the Beginning . . ." (Simic), **Supp. VIII:** 270, 271

In the Belly of the Beast: Letters from Prison (Abbott), **Retro. Supp. II:** 210

"In the Black Museum" (Nemerov), **III:** 275

"In the Bodies of Words" (Swenson), **Supp. IV Part 2:** 651

"In the Cage" (Gass), **Supp. VI:** 85

In the Cage (James), **Retro. Supp. I:** 229

"In the Cage" (James), **II:** 332; **Retro. Supp. I:** 231

"In the Cage" (Lowell), **Retro. Supp. II:** 187

"In the Cave at Lone Tree Meadow" (Haines), **Supp. XII:** 212

"In the City Ringed with Giants" (Kingsolver), **Supp. VII:** 209

"In the Clearing" (Brodsky), **Supp. VIII:** 32

In the Clearing (Frost), **II:** 153, 155, 164; **Retro. Supp. I:** 121, 122, 141

"In the Closet of the Soul" (Walker), **Supp. III Part 2:** 526

"In the Confidence of a Story-Writer" (Chopin), **Retro. Supp. II:** 66–67; **Supp. I Part 1:** 217

In the Country of Last Things (Auster), **Supp. XII:** 23, **29–30,** 31, 32

"In the Courtyard of the Isleta Missions" (Bly), **Supp. IV Part 1:** 71

"In the Dark" (Levine), **Supp. V:** 194

"In the Dark New England Days" (Jewett), **Retro. Supp. II:** 139

"In the Days of Prismatic Colour" (Moore), **III:** 205, 213

In the Electric Mist with Confederate Dead (Burke), **Supp. XIV:** 30, 31–32

"In the Field" (Wilbur), **Supp. III Part 2:** 558

"In the Fleeting Hand of Time" (Corso), **Supp. XII:** 122–123

"In the Footsteps of Gutenberg" (Mencken), **III:** 101

"In the Forest" (Simpson), **Supp. IX:** 270

"In the Forties" (Lowell), **II:** 554

In the Garden of the North American Martyrs (Wolff), **Supp. VII:** 341–342

In the Garret (Van Vechten), **Supp. II Part 2:** 735

"In the Grove: The Poet at Ten" (Kenyon), **Supp. VII:** 160

"In the Hall of Mirrors" (Merrill), **Supp. III Part 1:** 322

In the Harbor (Longfellow), **II:** 491

In the Heart of the Heart of the Country (Gass), **Supp. VI: 82–83,** 84, 85, 93

In the Heat of the Night (film), **Supp. I Part 1:** 67

In the Hollow of His Hand (Purdy), **Supp. VII:** 278–280

In the Lake of the Woods (O'Brien), **Supp. V:** 240, 243, 250–252

In the Mecca (Brooks), **Supp. III Part 1:** 74

"In the Mecca" (Brooks), **Supp. III Part 1:** 70, 83–84

In the Midst of Life (Bierce), **I:** 200–203, 204, 206, 208, 212

"In the Miro District" (Taylor), **Supp. V:** 323

In the Miro District and Other Stories (Taylor), **Supp. V:** 325–326

In the Money (W. C. Williams), **Retro. Supp. I:** 423

"In the Naked Bed, in Plato's Cave" (Schwartz), **Supp. II Part 2:** 646–649

"In the Night" (Kincaid), **Supp. VII:** 183

In the Night Season: A Novel (Bausch), **Supp. VII:** 52–53

"In the Old Neighborhood" (Dove), **Supp. IV Part 1:** 241, 257

"In the Old World" (Oates), **Supp. II Part 2:** 503, 504

"In the Park" (Huncke), **Supp. XIV:** 139

"In the Pit" (Proulx), **Supp. VII:** 255, 261

In the Presence of the Sun (Momaday), **Supp. IV Part 2:** 489, 490, 491–493, 493

"In the Realm of the Fisher King" (Didion), **Supp. IV Part 1:** 211

"In the Red Room" (Bowles), **Supp. IV Part 1:** 93

"In the Region of Ice" (Oates), **Supp. II Part 2:** 520

In the Room We Share (Simpson), **Supp. IX:** 279

"In These Dissenting Times" (Walker), **Supp. III Part 2:** 522

"In the Shadow of Gabriel, A.D.1550" (Frederic), **II:** 139

In the Spirit of Crazy Horse (Matthiessen), **Supp. V:** 211

In the Summer House (Jane Bowles), **Supp. IV Part 1:** 83, 89

In the Tennessee Country (Taylor), **Supp. V:** 328

"In the Thick of Darkness" (Salinas), **Supp. XIII:** 325

"In the Time of the Blossoms" (Mervin), **Supp. III Part 1:** 352

In the Time of the Butterflies (Alvarez), **Supp. VII:** 1, 12–15, 18

"In the Tunnel Bone of Cambridge" (Corso), **Supp. XII:** 120–121

"In the Upper Pastures" (Kumin), **Supp. IV Part 2:** 453

In the Valley (Frederic), **II:** 133–134, 136, 137

"In the Village" (Bishop), **Retro. Supp. II:** 38; **Supp. I Part 1:** 73, 74–75, 76, 77, 78, 88

"In the Waiting Room" (Bishop), **Retro. Supp. II:** 50; **Supp. I Part 1:** 81, 94, 95; **Supp. IV Part 1:** 249

"In the Ward: The Sacred Wood" (Jarrell), **II:** 376, 377

"In the White Night" (Beattie), **Supp. V:** 30–31

"In the Wind My Rescue Is" (Ammons), **Supp. VII:** 25

In the Winter of Cities (T. Williams), **IV:** 383

"In the X-Ray of the Sarcophagus of Ta-pero" (Goldbarth), **Supp. XII:** 191

"In the Yard" (Swenson), **Supp. IV Part 2:** 647

In the Zone (O'Neill), **III:** 388

In This, Our Life (film), **Supp. I Part 1:** 67

"In This Country, but in Another Language, My Aunt Refuses to Marry the Men Everyone Wants Her To" (Paley), **Supp. VI:** 225

In This Hung-up Age (Corso), **Supp. XII: 119–120,** 129

In This Our Life (Glasgow), **II:** 175, 178, 189

In This Our World (Gilman), **Supp. XI:** 196, 200, 202

"In Those Days" (Jarrell), **II:** 387–388

"In Time of War" (Auden), **Supp. II Part 1:** 8, 13

"Into Egypt" (Benét), **Supp. XI:** 56, 57–58

"Into My Own" (Frost), **II:** 153; **Retro. Supp. I:** 127

"Into the Night Life . . ." (H. Miller), **III:** 180, 184

"Into the Nowhere" (Rawlings), **Supp. X:** 220

Into the Stone (Dickey), **Supp. IV Part 1:** 178

"Into the Stone" (Dickey), **Supp. IV Part 1:** 179

Into the Stone and Other Poems (Dickey), **Supp. IV Part 1:** 176

In Touch: The Letters of Paul Bowles (J. Miller, ed.), **Supp. IV Part 1:** 95

"Intoxicated, The" (Jackson), **Supp. IX:** 116

"Intrigue" (Crane), **I:** 419

"Introducing the Fathers" (Kumin), **Supp. IV Part 2:** 452

Introductio ad Prudentiam (Fuller), **II:** 111

"Introduction to a Haggadah" (Paley), **Supp. VI:** 219

Introduction to Objectivist Epistemology (Rand), **Supp. IV Part 2:** 527, 528–529

Introduction to Objectivist Epistemology 2nd ed. (Rand), **Supp. IV Part 2:** 529

"Introduction to Some Poems, An" (Stafford), **Supp. XI:** 311, 324

Introduction to the Geography of Iowa, The (Doty), **Supp. XI:** 120

"Introduction to the Hoh" (Hugo), **Supp. VI:** 136–137

"Introduction to *The New Writing in the USA*" (Creeley), **Supp. IV Part 1:** 153–154

"Introduction to William Blake, An" (Kazin), **Supp. VIII:** 103

Introitus (Longfellow), **II:** 505, 506–507

"Intruder, The" (Dubus), **Supp. VII:** 76–78, 91

Intruder, The (Maeterlinck), **I:** 91

Intruder in the Dust (Faulkner), **II:** 71, 72

"Invaders, The" (Haines), **Supp. XII:** 205

Invasion of Privacy: The Cross Creek Trial of Marjorie Kinnan Rawlings (Acton), **Supp. X:** 233

Inventing Memory: A Novel of Mothers and Daughters (Jong), **Supp. V:** 115, 129

Inventing the Abbotts (Miller), **Supp. XII: 294–295**

"Invention of God in a Mouthful of Milk, The" (Karr), **Supp. XI:** 250

Invention of Solitude, The (Auster), **Supp. XII:** 21–22

Inventions of the March Hare (Eliot), **Retro. Supp. I:** 55–56, 58

"Inventions of the March Hare" (Eliot), **Retro. Supp. I:** 55

"Inventory" (Parker), **Supp. IX:** 192

"Inverted Forest, The" (Salinger), **III:** 552, 572

"Investigations of a Dog" (Kafka), **IV:** 438

"Investiture, The" (Banks), **Supp. V:** 7

"Investiture at Cecconi's" (Merrill), **Supp. III Part 1:** 336

Invisible: Poems (Nye), **Supp. XIII:** 277

Invisible Man (Ellison), **IV:** 493; **Retro. Supp. II:** 3, 12, 111, 112, 113, 117, 119, **120–123,** 125; **Supp. II Part 1:** 40, 170, 221, 224, 226, 227, 230, 231–232, 235, 236, 241–245; **Supp. IX:** 306; **Supp. X:** 242; **Supp. XI:** 18, 92

Invisible Spectator, An (Sawyer-

Lauçanno), **Supp. IV Part 1:** 95

Invisible Swords (Farrell), **II:** 27, 46, 48–49

Invisible Worm, The (Millar), **Supp. IV Part 2:** 465

Invitation to a Beheading (Nabokov), **III:** 252–253, 254, 257–258; **Retro. Supp. I:** 265, 270, 273

"Invitation to the Country, An" (Bryant), **Supp. I Part 1:** 160

"Invocation" (McKay), **Supp. X:** 134

"Invocation to Kali" (Sarton), **Supp. VIII:** 260

"Invocation to the Social Muse" (MacLeish), **III:** 15

"In Weather" (Hass), **Supp. VI:** 102–103

"In Your Fugitive Dream" (Hugo), **Supp. VI:** 143

"In Your Good Dream" (Hugo), **Supp. VI:** 143–144

"Iola, Kansas" (Clampitt), **Supp. IX:** 45–46

Ion (Doolittle, trans.), **Supp. I Part 1:** 269, 274

Ion (Plato), **I:** 523

"Ione" (Dunbar), **Supp. II Part 1:** 199

Ionesco, Eugène, **I:** 71, 74, 75, 84, 295; **II:** 435; **Supp. VIII:** 201

"I Only Am Escaped Alone to Tell Thee" (Nemerov), **III:** 272, 273–274

"I Opened All the Portals Wide" (Chopin), **Retro. Supp. II:** 71

I Ought to Be in Pictures (Simon), **Supp. IV Part 2:** 584

I Promessi Sposi (Manzoni), **II:** 291

"I Remember" (Sexton), **Supp. II Part 2:** 680

"Irenicon" (Shapiro), **Supp. II Part 2:** 704

Irigaray, Luce, **Supp. XII:** 6

"Iris by Night" (Frost), **Retro. Supp. I:** 132

Irish Stories of Sarah Orne Jewett, The (Jewett), **Retro. Supp. II:** 142

Irish Triangle, An (Barnes), **Supp. III Part 1:** 34

"Iron Characters, The" (Nemerov), **III:** 279, 282

"Iron Hans" (Sexton), **Supp. II Part 2:** 691

Iron Heel, The (London), **II:** 466, 480

Iron John: A Book about Men (Bly), **Supp. IV Part 1:** 59, 67

"Iron Table, The" (Jane Bowles), **Supp. IV Part 1:** 82–83

"Iron Throat, The" (Olsen), **Supp. XIII:** 292, 297, 299

Ironweed (Kennedy), **Supp. VII:** 132, 133, 134, 135, 142, 144, 145–147, 148, 150, 153

"Irony as Art: The Short Fiction of William Humphrey" (Tebeaux), **Supp. IX:** 109

"Irony Is Not Enough: Essay on My Life as Catherine Deneuve" (Carson), **Supp. XII:** 112–113

Irony of American History, The (Niebuhr), **III:** 292, 306–307, 308

"Irrational Element in Poetry, The" (Stevens), **Retro. Supp. I:** 298, 301

"Irrevocable Diameter, An" (Paley), **Supp. VI:** 231–232

Irvine, Lorna, **Supp. XIII:** 26

Irving, Ebenezer, **II:** 296

Irving, John, **Supp. VI:** 163–183; **Supp. X:** 77, 85

Irving, John Treat, **II:** 296

Irving, Peter, **II:** 296, 297, 298, 299, 300, 303

Irving, Sir Henry, **IV:** 350

Irving, Washington, **I:** 211, 335, 336, 339, 343; **II:** 295–318, 488, 495; **III:** 113; **IV:** 309; **Retro. Supp. I:** 246; **Supp. I Part 1:** 155, 157, 158, 317; **Supp. I Part 2:** 377, 487, 585; **Supp. II Part 1:** 335; **Supp. IV Part 1:** 380

Irving, William, **II:** 296

Irving, William, Jr., **II:** 296, 297, 298, 299, 303

Irwin, Mark, **Supp. XII:** 21, 22, 24, 29

Irwin, William Henry, **Supp. II Part 1:** 192

Is 5 (Cummings), **I:** 429, 430, 434, 435, 440, 445, 446, 447

"Isaac and Abraham" (Brodsky), **Supp. VIII:** 21

"Isaac and Archibald" (Robinson), **III:** 511, 521, 523

"Isabel Sparrow" (Oliver), **Supp. VII:** 232

Isaiah (biblical book), **Supp. I Part 1:** 236; **Supp. I Part 2:** 516

"Isaiah Beethoven" (Masters), **Supp. I Part 2:** 461

"I Saw in Louisiana a Live-Oak Growing" (Whitman), **I:** 220

I Shall Spit on Your Graves (film), **Supp. I Part 1:** 67

Isherwood, Christopher, **II:** 586; **Supp. II Part 1:** 10, 11, 13; **Supp. IV Part 1:** 79, 82, 102; **Supp. XI:** 305; **Supp. XIV:155–175**

Isherwood Century, The (Berg and Freeman), **Supp. XIV:** 157, 159

Isherwood's Fiction (Schwerdt), **Supp. XIV:** 155

Ishiguro, Kazuo, **Supp. VIII:** 15

Ishi Means Man (Merton), **Supp. VIII:** 208

"Ishmael's Dream" (Stern), **Supp. IX:** 287

I Should Have Stayed Home (McCoy), **Supp. XIII:** 167, **168–170,** 171

"I Sigh in the Afternoon" (Salinas), **Supp. XIII:** 318

"I Sing the Body Electric" (Whitman), **Retro. Supp. I:** 394, 395

"Isis: Dorothy Eady, 1924" (Doty), **Supp. XI:** 122

"Is It True?" (Hughes), **Supp. I Part 1:** 342

"Island" (Hughes), **Supp. I Part 1:** 340

Island Garden, An (Thaxter), **Retro. Supp. II:** 136; **Supp. XIII:** 152

Island Holiday, An (Henry), **I:** 515

"Island of the Fay, The" (Poe), **III:** 412, 417

"Islands, The" (Hayden), **Supp. II Part 1:** 373

"Island Sheaf, An" (Doty), **Supp. XI:** 136

Islands in the Stream (Hemingway), **II:** 258; **Retro. Supp. I:** 186

Is Objectivism a Religion? (Ellis), **Supp. IV Part 2:** 527

"Isolation of Modern Poetry, The" (Schwartz), **Supp. II Part 2:** 644

"Israel" (Reznikoff), **Supp. XIV:** 283

Israel Potter, or Fifty Years of Exile (Melville), **III:** 90

"Israfel" (Poe), **III:** 411

Is Sex Necessary? (Thurber and White), **Supp. I Part 2:** 607, 612, 614, 653

"Issues, The" (Olds), **Supp. X:** 205

"I Stand Here Ironing" (Olsen), **Supp. XIII:** 292, 294, 296, 298, 300, 305

I Stole a Million (West), **IV:** 287

"Is Verse a Dying Technique?" (Wilson), **IV:** 431

It (Creeley), **Supp. IV Part 1:** 157, 158

IT (King), **Supp. V:** 139, 140, 141, 146–147, 151, 152

"It" (Olds), **Supp. X:** 208

Italian American Reconciliation: A Folktale (Shanley), **Supp. XIV:** 315, **324–326,** 328, 330

Italian Backgrounds (Wharton), **Retro. Supp. I:** 370

Italian Hours (James), **I:** 12; **II:** 337; **Retro. Supp. I:** 235

Italian Journeys (Howells), **II:** 274

"Italian Morning" (Bogan), **Supp. III Part 1:** 58

Italian Villas and Their Gardens (Wharton), **IV:** 308; **Retro. Supp. I:** 361, 367

It All Adds Up: From the Dim Past to the Uncertain Future (Bellow), **Retro. Supp. II:** 32

"It Always Breaks Out" (Ellison), **Retro. Supp. II:** 126; **Supp. II Part 1:** 248

Itard, Jean-Marc Gaspard, **Supp. I Part 2:** 564

"I taste a liquor never brewed" (Dickinson), **Retro. Supp. I:** 30, 37

It Came from Outer Space (film), **Supp. IV Part 1:** 102

It Can't Happen Here (Lewis), **II:** 454

"It Don't Mean a Thing If It Ain't Got That Swing" (Matthews), **Supp. IX: 164–165**

I Tell You Now (Ortiz), **Supp. IV Part 2:** 500

"Ithaca" (Glück), **Supp. V:** 89

It Has Come to Pass (Farrell), **II:** 26

"I think to live May be a Bliss" (Dickinson), **Retro. Supp. I:** 44

I Thought of Daisy (Wilson), **IV:** 428, 434, 435

"Itinerary of an Obsession" (Kumin), **Supp. IV Part 2:** 450

"It Is a Strange Country" (Ellison), **Supp. II Part 1:** 238

"It Is Dangerous to Read Newspapers" (Atwood), **Supp. XIII:** 33

"It Must Be Abstract" (Stevens), **IV:** 95; **Retro. Supp. I:** 307

"It Must Change" (Stevens), **Retro. Supp. I:** 300, 307, 308

"It Must Give Pleasure" (Stevens), **Retro. Supp. I:** 307, 308, 309

"'It Out-Herods Herod. Pray You, Avoid It'" (Hecht), **Supp. X:** 62, 64

It's Loaded, Mr. Bauer (Marquand), **III:** 59

"It's Nation Time" (Baraka), **Supp. II Part 1:** 53

It's Nation Time (Baraka), **Supp. II Part 1:** 52, 53

It's Only a Play (McNally), **Supp. XIII:** 198

It Was (Zukofsky), **Supp. III Part 2:** 630

It Was the Nightingale (Ford), **III:** 470–471

"It Was When" (Snyder), **Supp. VIII:** 300

Ivanhoe (Scott), **I:** 216; **Supp. I Part 2:** 410

Ivens, Joris, **I:** 488; **Retro. Supp. I:** 184

"Iverson Boy, The" (Simpson), **Supp. IX:** 280

"Ives" (Rukeyser), **Supp. VI:** 273, 283

Ives, George H., **Supp. I Part 1:** 153

Ivory Grin, The (Macdonald), **Supp. IV Part 2:** 471, 472

Ivory Tower, The (James), **II:** 337–338

"Ivy Winding" (Ammons), **Supp. VII:** 33

"I Wandered Lonely as a Cloud" (Wordsworth), **Retro. Supp. I:** 121–122; **Supp. X:** 73; **Supp. XIV:** 184

"I want, I want" (Plath), **Retro. Supp. II:** 246

"I Wanted to Be There When My Father Died" (Olds), **Supp. X:** 210

"I Want to Be a Father Like the Men" (Cisneros), **Supp. VII:** 71

"I Want to Be Miss America" (Alvarez), **Supp. VII:** 18

"I Want to Know Why" (Anderson), **I:** 114, 115, 116; **II:** 263

"I Want You Women Up North To Know" (Olsen), **Supp. XIII:** 292, 297

"I Was Born in Lucerne" (Levine), **Supp. V:** 181, 189

"I Went into the Maverick Bar" (Snyder), **Supp. VIII:** 301

"I Will Lie Down" (Swenson), **Supp. IV Part 2:** 640

I Wonder As I Wander (Hughes), **Retro. Supp. I:** 196, 203; **Supp. I Part 1:** 329, 332–333

"Iyani: It goes this Way" (Gunn Allen), **Supp. IV Part 1:** 321

"I years had been from home" (Dickinson), **I:** 471

Iyer, Pico, **Supp. V:** 215

Izzo, David Garrett, **Supp. XIV:** 155, 156, 159, 160, 161, 163, 169, 171

J. B.: A Play in Verse (MacLeish), **II:** 163, 228; **III:** 3, 21–22, 23; **Supp. IV Part 2:** 586

"Jachid and Jechidah" (Singer), **IV:** 15

Jack and Jill (Alcott), **Supp. I Part 1:** 42

"Jack and the Beanstalk" (Hay), **Supp. XIV:** 124

Jack Kelso (Masters), **Supp. I Part 2:** 456, 471–472

Jacklight (Erdrich), **Supp. IV Part 1:** 259, 270

Jack London, Hemingway, and the Constitution (Doctorow), **Supp. IV Part 1:** 220, 222, 224, 232, 235

Jackpot (Caldwell), **I:** 304

Jackson, Amelia. *See* Holmes, Mrs. Oliver Wendell (Amelia Jackson)

Jackson, Andrew, **I:** 7, 20; **III:** 473; **IV:** 192, 248, 298, 334, 348; **Supp. I Part 2:** 456, 461, 473, 474, 493, 695

Jackson, Blyden, **Supp. I Part 1:** 337

Jackson, Charles, **Supp. I Part 1:** 303

Jackson, George, **Supp. I Part 1:** 66

Jackson, Helen Hunt, **I:** 459, 470; **Retro. Supp. I:** 26, 27, 30–31, 32, 33

Jackson, J. O., **III:** 213

Jackson, James, **Supp. I Part 1:** 302, 303

Jackson, Joe, **Supp. I Part 2:** 441

Jackson, Katherine Gauss, **Supp. VIII:** 124

Jackson, Lawrence, **Retro. Supp. II:** 113, 115

Jackson, Melanie, **Supp. X:** 166

Jackson, Michael, **Supp. VIII:** 146

Jackson, Richard, **II:** 119; **Supp. IX:** 165

Jackson, Shirley, **Supp. IX: 113–130**

Jackson, Thomas J. ("Stonewall"), **IV:** 125, 126

"Jackson Square" (Levertov), **Supp. III Part 1:** 276

Jackstraws (Simic), **Supp. VIII:** 280, 282–283

"Jackstraws" (Simic), **Supp. VIII: 283**

Jack Tier (Cooper), **I:** 354, 355

"Jacob" (Garrett), **Supp. VII:** 109–110

"Jacob" (Schwartz), **Supp. II Part 2:** 663

"Jacob and the Indians" (Benét), **Supp. XI:** 47–48

Jacobs, Rita D., **Supp. XII:** 339

Jacobsen, Josephine, **Supp. XIII:** 346; **Supp. XIV:** 260

"Jacob's Ladder" (Rawlings), **Supp. X:** 224, 228

"Jacob's Ladder, The" (Levertov), **Supp. III Part 1:** 278

Jacob's Ladder, The (Levertov), **Supp. III Part 1:** 272, 276–278, 281

Jacobson, Dale, **Supp. X:** 112

Jacoby, Russell, **Supp. IV Part 2:** 692

"Jacquerie, The" (Lanier), **Supp. I Part 1:** 355, 356, 360, 364, 370

Jade Mountain, The (Bynner), **II:** 527

Jafsie and John Henry: Essays on Hollywood, Bad Boys, and Six Hours of Perfect Poker (Mamet), **Supp. XIV:** 252

Jaguar Totem (LaBastille), **Supp. X:** 99, 106, **107–109**

Jailbird (Vonnegut), **Supp. II Part 2:** 760, 779–780

Jaimes, M. Annette, **Supp. IV Part 1:** 330, 331

Jain, Manju, **Retro. Supp. I:** 53, 58

Jake's Women (Simon), **Supp. IV Part 2:** 576, 588

"Jakie's Mother" (Fante), **Supp. XI:** 164

Jakobson, Roman, **Supp. IV Part 1:** 155

"Jamaica Kincaid's New York" (Kincaid), **Supp. VII:** 181

James, A. Lloyd, **Supp. XIV:** 343

James, Alice, **I:** 454; **Retro. Supp. I:** 228, 235

James, Caryn, **Supp. X:** 302, 303

James, Etta, **Supp. X:** 242

James, Henry, **I:** 4, 5, 9, 10, 12, 15, 16, 20, 52, 93, 109, 211, 226, 228, 244, 246, 251, 255, 258, 259, 336, 363, 374, 375, 379, 384, 409, 429, 436, 439, 452, 454, 459, 461–462, 463, 464, 485, 500, 504, 513, 514, 517–518, 571; **II:** 38, 58, 60, 73, 74, 95, 138, 140, 144, 147, 196, 198, 199, 228, 230, 234, 243, 259, 267, 271, 272, 275, 276, 278, 281, 282, 283, 284, 285, 286, 287, 288, 290, 306, 309, 316, **319–341,** 398, 404, 410, 415, 427, 444, 542, 544, 547–548, 556, 600; **III:** 44, 51, 136, 194–195, 199, 206, 208, 218, 228–229, 237, 281, 319, 325, 326, 334, 409, 453, 454, 457, 460, 461, 464, 511, 522, 576, 607; **IV:** 8, 27, 34, 37, 40, 53, 58, 73, 74, 134, 168, 172, 182, 198, 202, 285, 308, 309, 310, 311, 314, 316, 317, 318, 319, 321, 322, 323, 324, 328, 347, 352, 359, 433, 439, 476; **Retro. Supp. I:** 1, 8, 53, 56, 59, 108, 112, **215–242,** 272, 283, 284, 362, 366, 367, 368, 371, 373, 374, 375, 376, 377, 378, 379; **Retro. Supp. II:** 93, 135, 136, 203, 223; **Supp. I Part 1:** 35, 38, 43; **Supp. I Part 2:** 414, 454, 608, 609, 612–613, 618, 620, 646; **Supp. II Part 1:** 94–95; **Supp. III Part 1:** 14, 200; **Supp. III Part 2:** 410, 412; **Supp. IV Part 1:** 31, 35, 80, 127, 197, 349, 353; **Supp. IV Part 2:** 613, 677, 678, 682, 689, 693; **Supp. V:** 97, 101, 103, 258, 261, 263, 313; **Supp. VIII:** 98, 102, 156, 166, 168; **Supp. IX:** 121; **Supp. XI:** 153; **Supp. XIII:** 102; **Supp. XIV:** 40, 110, 112, 335, 336, 348, 349

James, Henry (father), **II:** 7, 275, 321, 337, 342–344, 364; **IV:** 174; **Supp. I Part 1:** 300

James, Henry (nephew), **II:** 360

James, Horace, **Supp. XIV:** 57

James, William, **I:** 104, 220, 224, 227, 228, 255, 454; **II:** 20, 27, 165, 166, 276, 321, 337, **342–366,** 411; **III:** 303, 309, 509, 599, 600, 605, 606, 612; **IV:** 26, 27, 28–29, 31, 32, 34, 36, 37, 43, 46, 291, 486; **Retro.**
Supp. I: 57, 216, 227, 228, 235, 295, 300, 306; **Supp. I Part 1:** 3, 7, 11, 20; **Supp. XIV:** 40, 50, 197, 199, 212, 335

James, William (grandfather), **II:** 342

James Baldwin: The Legacy (Troupe, ed.), **Retro. Supp. II:** 15

James Baldwin—The Price of the Ticket (film), **Retro. Supp. II:** 2

James Dickey and the Politics of Canon (Suarez), **Supp. IV Part 1:** 175

"James Dickey on Yeats: An Interview" (Dickey), **Supp. IV Part 1:** 177

James Hogg: A Critical Study (Simpson), **Supp. IX:** 269, 276

James Jones: A Friendship (Morris), **Supp. XI:** 234

James Jones: An American Literary Orientalist Master (Carter), **Supp. XI:** 220

James Jones: Reveille to Taps (television documentary), **Supp. XI:** 234

"James Jones and Jack Kerouac: Novelists of Disjunction" (Stevenson), **Supp. XI:** 230

Jameson, F. R., **Supp. IV Part 1:** 119

Jameson, Sir Leander Starr, **III:** 327

James Shore's Daughter (Benét), **Supp. XI:** 48

"James Thurber" (Pollard), **Supp. I Part 2:** 468

"James Whitcomb Riley (From a Westerner's Point of View)" (Dunbar), **Supp. II Part 1:** 198

Jammes, Francis, **II:** 528; **Retro. Supp. I:** 55

Jan. 31 (Goldbarth), **Supp. XII:** 177, **178–179,** 180

"Jan, the Son of Thomas" (Sandburg), **III:** 593–594

Janeczko, Paul, **Supp. XIII:** 280

Janet, Pierre, **I:** 248, 249, 252; **Retro. Supp. I:** 55, 57

Jane Talbot: A Novel (Brown), **Supp. I Part 1:** 145–146

"Janet Waking" (Ransom), **III:** 490, 491

"Janice" (Jackson), **Supp. IX:** 117

Janowitz, Tama, **Supp. X:** 7

Jantz, Harold S., **Supp. I Part 1:** 112

"January" (Barthelme), **Supp. IV Part 1:** 54

January Man, The (screenplay, Shanley), **Supp. XIV:** 316

"January Thaw" (Leopold), **Supp. XIV:** 183–184

"Janus" (Beattie), **Supp. V:** 31

Janzen, Jean, **Supp. V:** 180

Japanese by Spring (Reed), **Supp. X:**
241, **253–255**

Jara, Victor, **Supp. IV Part 2:** 549

Jarman, Mark, **Supp. IV Part 1:** 68; **Supp. IX:** 266, 270, 276; **Supp. XII:** 209

Jarrell, Mrs. Randall (Mary von Schrader), **II:** 368, 385

Jarrell, Randall, **I:** 167, 169, 173, 180; **II:** **367–390,** 539–540; **III:** 134, 194, 213, 268, 527; **IV:** 352, 411, 422; **Retro. Supp. I:** 52, 121, 135, 140; **Retro. Supp. II:** 44, 177, 178, 182; **Supp. I Part 1:** 89; **Supp. I Part 2:** 552; **Supp. II Part 1:** 109, 135; **Supp. III Part 1:** 64; **Supp. III Part 2:** 541, 550; **Supp. IV Part 2:** 440; **Supp. V:** 315, 318, 323; **Supp. VIII:** 31, 100, 271; **Supp. IX:** 94, 268; **Supp. XI:** 311, 315; **Supp. XII:** 121, 260, 297

Jarry, Alfred, **Retro. Supp. II:** 326

Jarvis, John Wesley, **Supp. I Part 2:** 501, 520

Jaskoski, Helen, **Supp. IV Part 1:** 325

"Jasmine" (Komunyakaa), **Supp. XIII:** 132

"Jason" (Hecht), **Supp. X:** 62

"Jason" (MacLeish), **III:** 4

Jason and Medeia (Gardner), **Supp. VI:** 63, **68–69**

Jaspers, Karl, **III:** 292; **IV:** 491

Jay, William, **I:** 338

Jayber Crow (Berry), **Supp. X:** 28, 34

"Jaz Fantasia" (Sandburg), **III:** 585

"Jazz Age Clerk, A" (Farrell), **II:** 45

Jazz Country: Ralph Ellison in America (Porter), **Retro. Supp. II:** 127

"Jazzonia" (Hughes), **Supp. I Part 1:** 324

Jazz Poetry Anthology, The (Komunyakaa and Feinstein, eds.), **Supp. XIII:** 125

"Jazztet Muted" (Hughes), **Supp. I Part 1:** 342

"Jealous" (Ford), **Supp. V:** 71

Jealousies, The: A Faery Tale, by Lucy Vaughan Lloyd of China Walk, Lambeth (Keats), **Supp. XII:** 113

Jean Huguenot (Benét), **Supp. XI:** 44

"Jeff Briggs's Love Story" (Harte), **Supp. II Part 1:** 355

Jeffers, Robinson, **I:** 66; **III:** 134; **Retro. Supp. I:** 202; **Supp. II Part 2:** **413–440;** **Supp. VIII:** 33, 292; **Supp. IX:** 77; **Supp. X:** 112; **Supp. XI:** 312

Jeffers, Una Call Kuster (Mrs. Robinson Jeffers), **Supp. II Part 2:** 414

Jefferson, Blind Lemon, **Supp. VIII:** 349

Jefferson, Thomas, **I:** 1, 2, 5, 6–8, 14, 485; **II:** 5, 6, 34, 217, 300, 301, 437; **III:** 3, 17, 18, 294–295, 306, 310, 473, 608; **IV:** 133, 243, 249, 334, 348; **Supp. I Part 1:** 146, 152, 153, 229, 230, 234, 235; **Supp. I Part 2:** 389, 399, 456, 474, 475, 482, 507, 509, 510, 511, 516, 518–519, 520, 522; **Supp. X:** 26; **Supp. XIV:** 191

Jefferson and/or Mussolini (Pound), **Retro. Supp. I:** 292

"Jefferson Davis as a Representative American" (Du Bois), **Supp. II Part 1:** 161

J-E-L-L-O (Baraka), **Supp. II Part 1:** 47

"Jelly-Bean, The" (Fitzgerald), **II:** 88

"Jellyfish, A" (Moore), **III:** 215

Jemie, Onwuchekwa, **Supp. I Part 1:** 343

Jenkins, J. L., **I:** 456

Jenkins, Kathleen, **III:** 403

Jenkins, Susan, **IV:** 123

Jenks, Deneen, **Supp. IV Part 2:** 550, 554

Jennie Gerhardt (Dreiser), **I:** 497, 499, 500, 501, 504–505, 506, 507, 519; **Retro. Supp. II:** 94, **99–101**

"Jennie M'Grew" (Masters), **Supp. I Part 2:** 468

Jennifer Lorn (Wylie), **Supp. I Part 2:** 709, 714–717, 718, 721, 724

"Jenny Garrow's Lover" (Jewett), **II:** 397

"Jerboa, The" (Moore), **III:** 203, 207, 209, 211–212

Jeremiah, **Supp. X:** 35

Jeremy's Version (Purdy), **Supp. VII:** 274

"Jericho" (Lowell), **II:** 536

"Jersey City Gendarmerie, Je T'aime" (Lardner), **II:** 433

Jersey Rain (Pinsky), **Supp. VI:** 235, **247–250**

"Jerusalem" (Nye), **Supp. XIII:** 287

Jerusalem the Golden (Reznikoff), **Supp. XIV:** 280, 285, 286

Jessup, Richard, **Supp. XI:** 306

"Je Suis Perdu" (Taylor), **Supp. V:** 314, 321–322

Jesuits in North America in the Seventeenth Century, The (Parkman), **Supp. II Part 2:** 597, 603–605

Jesus, **I:** 27, 34, 68, 89, 136, 552, 560; **II:** 1, 16, 197, 198, 214, 215, 216, 218, 219, 239, 373, 377, 379, 537, 538, 539, 549, 569, 585, 591, 592; **III:** 39, 173, 179, 270, 291, 296–297, 300, 303, 305, 307, 311, 339, 340, 341, 342, 344, 345, 346, 347, 348, 352, 353, 354, 355, 436, 451, 489, 534, 564, 566, 567, 582; **IV:** 51, 69, 86, 107, 109, 117, 137, 138, 141, 144, 147, 149, 150, 151, 152, 155, 156, 157, 158, 159, 163, 164, 232, 241, 289, 293, 294, 296, 331, 364, 392, 396, 418, 430; **Supp. I Part 1:** 2, 54, 104, 107, 108, 109, 121, 267, 371; **Supp. I Part 2:** 379, 386, 458, 515, 580, 582, 583, 587, 588, 683; **Supp. V:** 280

"Jesus Asleep" (Sexton), **Supp. II Part 2:** 693

"Jesus of Nazareth, Then and Now" (Price), **Supp. VI:** 268

"Jesus Papers, The" (Sexton), **Supp. II Part 2:** 693

"Jesus Raises Up the Harlot" (Sexton), **Supp. II Part 2:** 693

Jetée, La (film), **Supp. IV Part 2:** 436

"Jeune Parque, La" (Valéry), **IV:** 92

"Jewbird, The" (Malamud), **Supp. I Part 2:** 435

"Jewboy, The" (Roth), **Supp. III Part 2:** 412

Jewett, Caroline, **II:** 396

Jewett, Dr. Theodore Herman, **II:** 396–397, 402

Jewett, Katharine, **Retro. Supp. II:** 46

Jewett, Mary, **II:** 396, 403

Jewett, Rutger, **Retro. Supp. I:** 381

Jewett, Sarah Orne, **I:** 313; **II:** 391–414; **Retro. Supp. I:** 6, 7, 19; **Retro. Supp. II:** 51, 52, 131–151, 156; **Supp. I Part 2:** 495; **Supp. VIII:** 126; **Supp. IX:** 79; **Supp. XIII:** 153

Jewett, Theodore Furber, **II:** 395

"Jew for Export, The" (Mamet), **Supp. XIV:** 251–252

Jew in the American Novel, The (Fiedler), **Supp. XIII:** 106

"Jewish Graveyards, Italy" (Levine), **Supp. V:** 190

"Jewish Hunter, The" (Moore), **Supp. X:** 163, 165, **174**

Jewison, Norman, **Supp. XI:** 306; **Supp. XIV:** 316

Jews of Shklov (Schneour), **IV:** 11

Jews without Money (Gold), **Supp. XIV:** 288–289

JFK (film), **Supp. XIV:** 48

Jig of Forslin, The: A Symphony (Aiken), **I:** 50, 51, 57, 62, 66

"Jig Tune: Not for Love" (McGrath), **Supp. X:** 116

"Jihad" (McClatchy), **Supp. XII:** 266

"Jilting of Granny Weatherall, The" (Porter), **III:** 434, 435, 438

Jim Crow's Last Stand (Hughes),

Retro. Supp. I: 205

Jiménez, Juan Ramón, **Supp. XIII:** 315, 323

Jimmie Higgins (Sinclair), **Supp. V:** 288

Jimmy's Blues (Baldwin), **Retro. Supp. II:** 8, 9, 15

Jim's Book: A Collection of Poems and Short Stories (Merrill), **Supp. III Part 1:** 319

Jitney (Wilson), **Supp. VIII:** 330, 331, 351

Jitterbug Perfume (Robbins), **Supp. X:** 273, **274–276**, 279

Joachim, Harold, **Retro. Supp. I:** 58

Joan, Pope, **IV:** 165

Joanna and Ulysses (Sarton), **Supp. VIII:** **254–255**

Joan of Arc, **IV:** 241; **Supp. I Part 1:** 286–288; **Supp. I Part 2:** 469

Joans, Ted, **Supp. IV Part 1:** 169

Job (biblical book), **II:** 165, 166–167, 168; **III:** 21, 199, 512; **IV:** 13, 158; **Supp. I Part 1:** 125

Job, The (Burroughs and Odier), **Supp. III Part 1:** 97, 103

Job, The: An American Novel (Lewis), **II:** 441

"Job History" (Proulx), **Supp. VII:** 262

Jobim, Antonio Carlos, **Supp. IV Part 2:** 549

"Job of the Plains, A" (Humphrey), **Supp. IX:** 101

"Jody Rolled the Bones" (Yates), **Supp. XI:** 335, 341

"Joe" (Alvarez), **Supp. VII:** 7–8

Joe Hill: A Biographical Novel (Stegner), **Supp. IV Part 2:** 599

Joe Turner's Come and Gone (Wilson), **Supp. VIII:** 334, **337–342**, 345

Joe versus the Volcano (screenplay, Shanley), **Supp. XIV:** 316

"Joey Martiney" (Huncke), **Supp. XIV:** 149

Johannes in Eremo (Mather), **Supp. II Part 2:** 453

John (biblical book), **I:** 68

"John" (Shields), **Supp. VII:** 310–311

"John, John Chinaman" (Buck), **Supp. II Part 1:** 128

John Addington Symonds: A Biographical Study (Brooks), **I:** 240, 241

John Barleycorn (London), **II:** 467, 481

John Brown (Du Bois), **Supp. II Part 1:** 171–172

"John Brown" (Emerson), **II:** 13

"John Brown" (Lindsay), **Supp. I Part 2:** 393

John Brown: The Making of a Martyr

(Warren), **IV:** 236

John Brown's Body (Benét), **II:** 177; **Supp. XI:** 45, 46, 47, **56–57**

John Bull in America; or, The New Munchausen (Paulding), **I:** 344

"John Burke" (Olson), **Supp. II Part 2:** 579, 580

"John Burns of Gettysburg" (Harte), **Supp. II Part 1:** 343

"John Carter" (Agee), **I:** 27

"John Coltrane: Where Does Art Come From?" (Baraka), **Supp. II Part 1:** 60

John Deth: A Metaphysical Legend and Other Poems (Aiken), **I:** 61

"John Endicott" (Longfellow), **II:** 505, 506; **Retro. Supp. II:** 165–166, 167

"John Evereldown" (Robinson), **III:** 524

John Fante: Selected Letters, 1932–1981 (Cooney, ed.), **Supp. XI:** 170

John Fante Reader, The (Cooper, ed.), **Supp. XI:** 174

"John Gardner: The Writer As Teacher" (Carver), **Supp. III Part 1:** 136, 146–147

John Jay Chapman and His Letters (Howe), **Supp. XIV:** 54

John Keats (Lowell), **II:** 530–531

"John L. Sullivan" (Lindsay), **Supp. I Part 2:** 394, 395

John Lane, **Retro. Supp. I:** 59

"John Marr" (Melville), **III:** 93

John Marr and Other Sailors (Melville), **III:** 93; **Retro. Supp. I:** 257

John Muir: A Reading Bibliography (Kimes and Kimes), **Supp. IX:** 178

Johnny Appleseed and Other Poems (Lindsay), **Supp. I Part 2:** 397

"Johnny Bear" (Steinbeck), **IV:** 67

"Johnny Panic and the Bible of Dreams" (Plath), **Retro. Supp. II:** 245

"Johnny Ray" (Ríos), **Supp. IV Part 2:** 543

John of the Cross (Saint), **I:** 585; **Supp. IV Part 1:** 284

John Paul Jones: A Sailor's Biography (Morison), **Supp. I Part 2:** 494–495

"John Redding Goes to Sea" (Hurston), **Supp. VI:** 150

Johns, George Sibley, **Retro. Supp. II:** 65

Johns, Orrick, **Retro. Supp. II:** 71

John Sloan: A Painter's Life (Brooks), **I:** 254

"John Smith Liberator" (Bierce), **I:** 209

Johnson, Alexandra, **Supp. X:** 86

Johnson, Alvin, **I:** 236

Johnson, Ben, **Retro. Supp. I:** 56

Johnson, Buffie, **Supp. IV Part 1:** 94

Johnson, Charles, **Supp. I Part 1:** 325; **Supp. V:** 128; **Supp. VI:** 185–201; **Supp. X:** 239; **Supp. XIII:** 182

Johnson, Charles S., **Supp. IX:** 309

Johnson, Claudia Durst, **Supp. VIII:** 126–127

Johnson, Diane, **Supp. XIII:** 127

Johnson, Dianne, **Retro. Supp. I:** 196

Johnson, Eastman, **IV:** 321

Johnson, Edward, **IV:** 157; **Supp. I Part 1:** 110, 115

Johnson, Fenton, **Supp. XI:** 129

Johnson, Georgia Douglas, **Supp. IV Part 1:** 164

Johnson, James Weldon, **Retro. Supp. II:** 114; **Supp. I Part 1:** 324, 325; **Supp. II Part 1:** 33, 194, 200, 202–203, 206–207; **Supp. III Part 1:** 73; **Supp. IV Part 1:** 7, 11, 15, 16, 164, 165, 166, 169; **Supp. X:** 42, 136, **246**

Johnson, Joyce, **Supp. XIV:** 150

Johnson, Lady Bird, **Supp. IV Part 1:** 22

Johnson, Lyndon B., **I:** 254; **II:** 553, 582; **Retro. Supp. II:** 27

Johnson, Marguerite. *See* Angelou, Maya

Johnson, Mordecai, **Supp. XIV:** 202

Johnson, Nunnally, **Supp. IV Part 1:** 355

Johnson, Pamela Hansford, **IV:** 469

Johnson, Rafer, **Supp. I Part 1:** 271

Johnson, Reed, **Supp. IV Part 2:** 589

Johnson, Richard, **Supp. XIII:** 132

Johnson, Robert, **Supp. IV Part 1:** 146; **Supp. VIII:** 15, 134

Johnson, Robert K., **Supp. IV Part 2:** 573, 584

Johnson, Robert Underwood, **Supp. IX:** 182, 184, 185

Johnson, Samuel, **II:** 295; **III:** 491, 503; **IV:** 452; **Retro. Supp. I:** 56, 65; **Supp. I Part 1:** 33; **Supp. I Part 2:** 422, 498, 503, 523, 656; **Supp. IV Part 1:** 34, 124; **Supp. XI:** 209; **Supp. XII:** 159; **Supp. XIII:** 55, 347

Johnson, Thomas H., **I:** 470–471; **IV:** 144, 158; **Retro. Supp. I:** 26, 28, 36, 39, 40, 41, 43

Johnson, Walter, **II:** 422

"Johnson Girls, The" (Bambara), **Supp. XI:** 7

Johnsrud, Harold, **II:** 562

Johnston, Basil, **Supp. IV Part 1:** 269

Johnston, Mary, **II:** 194

Johnston, Robert M., **Supp. I Part 1:** 369

"John Sutter" (Winters), **Supp. II Part 2:** 810

John's Wife (Coover), **Supp. V:** 51–52

John the Baptist, **I:** 389; **II:** 537, 591

John XXIII, Pope, **Supp. I Part 2:** 492

Jolas, Eugène, **Retro. Supp. II:** 85, 328; **Supp. IV Part 1:** 80

Jolie Blon's Bounce (Burke), **Supp. XIV:** 26, 33–34

Jolly (Mamet), **Supp. XIV:** 240, 254

"Jolly Corner, The" (James), **I:** 571; **Retro. Supp. I:** 235

"Jonah" (Lowell), **II:** 536

Jonah's Gourd Vine (Hurston), **Supp. VI:** 149, 155

"Jonathan Edwards" (Holmes), **Supp. I Part 1:** 302, 315

"Jonathan Edwards in Western Massachusetts" (Lowell), **II:** 550

Jonathan Troy (Abbey), **Supp. XIII:** 4, 13

Jones, Anne, **Supp. X:** 8

Jones, Carolyn, **Supp. VIII:** 128

Jones, E. Stanley, **III:** 297

Jones, Edith Newbold. *See* Wharton, Edith

Jones, Everett LeRoi. *See* Baraka, Imamu Amiri

Jones, George Frederic, **IV:** 309

Jones, Grover, **Supp. XIII:** 166

Jones, Harry, **Supp. I Part 1:** 337

Jones, Howard Mumford, **I:** 353; **Supp. IV Part 2:** 606; **Supp. XIV:** 11

Jones, James, **III:** 40; **IV:** 98; **Supp. XI:** 213–237

Jones, James Earl, **Supp. VIII:** 334; **Supp. XI:** 309

Jones, Jennifer, **Supp. IV Part 2:** 524

Jones, John Paul, **II:** 405–406; **Supp. I Part 2:** 479, 480, 494–495

Jones, LeRoi. *See* Baraka, Imamu Amiri

Jones, Lucretia Stevens Rhinelander, **IV:** 309

Jones, Madison, **Retro. Supp. II:** 235; **Supp. X:** 1

Jones, Major (pseudonym). *See* Thompson, William T.

Jones, Malcolm, **Supp. V:** 219

Jones, Robert Edmond, **III:** 387, 391, 394, 399

Jones, Tommy Lee, **Supp. V:** 227

"Jones's Private Argyment" (Lanier), **Supp. I Part 1:** 352

"Jones's *The Thin Red Line:* The End of Innocence" (Michel-Michot), **Supp. XI:** 224–225

Jong, Allan, **Supp. V:** 115

Jong, Erica, **Supp. V: 113–135**

Jong-Fast, Molly Miranda, **Supp. V:** 115

Jonson, Ben, **I:** 58, 358; **II:** 11, 16, 17, 18, 436, 556; **III:** 3, 463, 575–576; **IV:** 395, 453; **Retro. Supp. II:** 76; **Supp. I Part 2:** 423; **Supp. IV Part 2:** 585

Jonsson, Thorsten, **Retro. Supp. I:** 73

Joplin, Janis, **Supp. IV Part 1:** 206; **Supp. XI:** 239

Joplin, Scott, **Supp. IV Part 1:** 223

Jordan, Barbara, **Supp. VIII:** 63; **Supp. XI:** 249

Jordan, June, **Supp. XII:** 217

Jo's Boys (Alcott), **Supp. I Part 1:** 32, 35, 40–41, 42

Joseph Heller (Ruderman), **Supp. IV Part 1:** 380

"Josephine Has Her Day" (Thurber), **Supp. I Part 2:** 606

Josephine Stories, The (Fitzgerald), **Retro. Supp. I:** 109

"Joseph Martinez" (Huncke), **Supp. XIV:** 149

"Joseph Pockets" (Stern), **Supp. IX:** 292

Josephson, Matthew, **I:** 259

"José's Country" (Winters), **Supp. II Part 2:** 789, 790

Joshua (biblical book), **Supp. I Part 2:** 515

Joslin, Katherine, **Retro. Supp. I:** 376

Journal (Emerson), **Supp. I Part 1:** 309

Journal (Thoreau), **IV:** 175

Journal (Woolman), **Supp. VIII:** 202

"Journal for My Daughter" (Kunitz), **Supp. III Part 1:** 268

Journal of Arthur Stirling, The (Sinclair), **Supp. V:** 280

"Journal of a Solitary Man, The" (Hawthorne), **II:** 226

Journal of a Solitude (Sarton), **Supp. VIII:** 256, 262–263

Journal of My Other Self (Rilke), **Retro. Supp. II:** 20

Journal of the Fictive Life (Nemerov), **III:** 267, 268, 269, 272, 273, 274, 280–281, 284–285, 286, 287

Journal of the Plague Year, A (Defoe), **III:** 423

"Journal of the Year of the Ox, A" (Wright), **Supp. V:** 343

Journals (Thoreau), **Supp. I Part 1:** 299

Journals and Other Documents on the Life and Voyages of Christopher Columbus (Morison, ed.), **Supp. I Part 2:** 494

Journals of Ralph Waldo Emerson, The (Emerson), **II:** 8, 17, 21

Journals of Susanna Moodie, The: Poems (Atwood), **Supp. XIII:** 33

"Journey, A" (Wharton), **Retro. Supp. I:** 364

"Journey, The" (Winters), **Supp. II Part 2:** 795

"Journey, The" (Wright), **Supp. III Part 2:** 605–606

"Journey, The: For Jane at Thirteen" (Kumin), **Supp. IV Part 2:** 442

Journey and Other Poems, The (Winters), **Supp. II Part 2:** 786, 794, 795, 796, 799, 800, 801

Journey Around My Room: The Autobiography of Louise Bogan—A Mosaic (Bogan), **Supp. III Part 1:** 47, 48, 52, 53

Journey Down, The (Bernstein), **IV:** 455

Journey Home, The (Abbey), **Supp. XIII:** 2, 12

Journeyman (Caldwell), **I:** 297, 302–304, 307, 309

Journey of Tai-me, The (Momaday), **Supp. IV Part 2:** 485

"Journey of the Magi" (Eliot), **Retro. Supp. I:** 64

Journey to a War (Auden and Isherwood), **Supp. II Part 1:** 13; **Supp. XIV:** 156, 158, 162

Journey to Love (W. C. Williams), **IV:** 422; **Retro. Supp. I:** 429

Journey to My Father; Isaac Bashevis Singer (Zamir), **Retro. Supp. II:** 317

"Journey to Nine Miles" (Walker), **Supp. III Part 2:** 527

"Journey to the Interior" (W. J. Smith), **Supp. XIII:** 339, 340

Jowett, Benjamin, **Supp. XIV:** 335

"Joy" (Moore), **Supp. X:** 174

"Joy" (Singer), **IV:** 9; **Retro. Supp. II:** 307

Joyce, Cynthia, **Supp. X:** 194, 195, 196

Joyce, James, **I:** 53, 105, 108, 130, 174, 256, 285, 377, 395, 475–476, 478, 480, 483, 576; **II:** 27, 42, 58, 73, 74, 198, 209, 264, 320, 569; **III:** 7, 16, 26–27, 45, 174, 181, 184, 261, 273, 277, 343, 396, 398, 465, 471, 474; **IV:** 32, 73, 85, 95, 103, 171, 182, 211, 286, 370, 412, 418, 419, 428, 434, 456; **Retro. Supp. I:** 59, 63, 75, 80, 89, 91, 108, 109, 127, 287, 290, 292, 334, 335, 420; **Retro. Supp. II:** 221, 326; **Supp. I Part 1:** 257, 262, 270; **Supp. I Part 2:** 437, 546, 613, 620; **Supp. II Part 1:** 136; **Supp. III Part 1:** 35, 36, 65, 225, 229; **Supp. III Part 2:** 611, 617, 618; **Supp. IV Part 1:** 40, 47, 80, 227, 300, 310; **Supp. IV Part 2:** 424, 677; **Supp. V:** 261, 331; **Supp. VIII:** 14, 40, 103; **Supp. IX:** 211, 229, 235, 308; **Supp. X:** 115, 137, 194, 324; **Supp. XI:** 66; **Supp. XII:** 139, 151, 165, 191, 289; **Supp. XIV:** 83

Joy Luck Club, The (Tan), **Supp. X:** 289, 291, 293, 294, 296, 297, 298, 299

"Joy of Sales Resistance, The" (Berry), **Supp. X:** 36

J R (Gaddis), **Supp. IV Part 1:** 279, 280, 285–289, 291, 294; **Supp. IV Part 2:** 484

"Juan's Song" (Bogan), **Supp. III Part 1:** 50

Jubilate Agno (Smart), **Supp. IV Part 2:** 626

Judah, Hettie, **Supp. XIII:** 246

"Judas Maccabaeus" (Longfellow), **II:** 506; **Retro. Supp. II:** 165, 167

Judd, Sylvester, **II:** 290; **Supp. I Part 2:** 420

Judd Rankin's Daughter (Glaspell), **Supp. III Part 1:** 186–188

Jude the Obscure (Hardy), **Supp. I Part 1:** 217

"Judgement Day" (O'Connor), **III:** 349, 350; **Retro. Supp. II:** 236

Judgment Day (Farrell), **II:** 29, 31, 32, 34, 39

"Judgment of Paris, The" (Merwin), **Supp. III Part 1:** 350

Judgment of Paris, The (Vidal), **Supp. IV Part 2:** 680, 682

"Judgment of the Sage, The" (Crane), **I:** 420

Judith (Farrell), **II:** 46, 48

"Judith" (Garrett), **Supp. VII:** 109–110

"Jug of Sirup, A" (Bierce), **I:** 206

"Jugurtha" (Longfellow), **II:** 499

"Juice or Gravy" (Roth), **Retro. Supp. II:** 279

"Juke Box Love Song" (Hughes), **Retro. Supp. I:** 209

"Julia" (Hellman), **Supp. I Part 1:** 280, 293

"Julia Miller" (Masters), **Supp. I Part 2:** 461

Julian (Vidal), **Supp. IV Part 2:** 677, 684–685, 685, 689

Julian the Apostate, **Retro. Supp. I:** 247

"Julian Vreden" (Bowles), **Supp. IV Part 1:** 94

Julie and Romeo (Ray), **Supp. XII:** 308, 310

Julien, Isaac, **Supp. XI:** 19

Julier, Laura, **Supp. IV Part 1:** 211

Julip (Harrison), **Supp. VIII:** 51

Julius Caesar (Shakespeare), **I:** 284

"July Midnight" (Lowell), **II:** 521

Jumel, Madame, **Supp. I Part 2:** 461

Jumping Out of Bed (Bly), **Supp. IV Part 1:** 71

"Jump-Up Day" (Kingsolver), **Supp. VII:** 203

"June Light" (Wilbur), **Supp. III Part 2:** 545

June Moon (Lardner and Kaufman), **II:** 427

"June Recital" (Welty), **IV:** 272–273

Juneteenth (Ellison), **Retro. Supp. II:** 119, 124, **126–128**

"Juneteenth" (Ellison), **Retro. Supp. II:** 119, 126; **Supp. II Part 1:** 248

Jung, Carl, **I:** 58, 135, 241, 248, 252, 402; **III:** 400, 534, 543; **Supp. I Part 2:** 439; **Supp. IV Part 1:** 68, 69; **Supp. VIII:** 45; **Supp. X:** 193

Junger, Ernst, **Supp. III Part 1:** 63

Jungle, The (Sinclair), **III:** 580; **Supp. V:** 281–284, 285, 289

Jungle Lovers (Theroux), **Supp. VIII:** 314, 315, 316, **317**

"Junior Addict" (Hughes), **Supp. I Part 1:** 343

"Juniper" (Francis), **Supp. IX:** 79

"Junk" (Wilbur), **Supp. III Part 2:** 556

Junkie: Confessions of an Unredeemed Drug Addict (Burroughs), **Supp. III Part 1:** 92, 94–96, 101

Junky (Burroughs), **Supp. XIV:** 143

Juno and the Paycock (O'Casey), **Supp. IV Part 1:** 361

"Jupiter Doke, Brigadier General" (Bierce), **I:** 204

Jurgen (Cabell), **III:** 394; **IV:** 286; **Retro. Supp. I:** 80; **Supp. I Part 2:** 718

Jusserand, Jules, **II:** 338

Just above My Head (Baldwin), **Retro. Supp. II:** 14–15

"Just a Little One" (Parker), **Supp. IX:** 191

Just and the Unjust, The (Cozzens), **I:** 367–370, 372, 375, 377, 378, 379

Just an Ordinary Day (Jackson), **Supp. IX:** 120

Just Before Dark: Collected Nonfiction (Harrison), **Supp. VIII:** 41, 45, 46, 53

"Just Before the War with the Eskimos" (Salinger), **III:** 559

"Just Boys" (Farrell), **II:** 45

"Just for the Thrill: An Essay on the Difference Between Women and Men" (Carson), **Supp. XII: 103– 104**

"Justice" (Hughes), **Supp. I Part 1:** 331

"Justice, A" (Faulkner), **Retro. Supp. I:** 83

Justice, Donald, **Retro. Supp. I:** 313; **Supp. III Part 2:** 541; **Supp. V:** 180, 337, 338, 341; **Supp. VII: 115– 130; Supp. XI:** 141, 315; **Supp. XIII:** 76, 312

Justice and Expediency (Whittier), **Supp. I Part 2:** 686

"Justice Denied in Massachusetts" (Millay), **III:** 140

Justice of Gold in the Damnation of Sinners, The (Edwards), **I:** 559

"Justice to Feminism" (Ozick), **Supp. V:** 272

"Just Like Job" (Angelou), **Supp. IV Part 1:** 15

Just Wild About Harry (H. Miller), **III:** 190

Juvenal, **II:** 8, 169, 552

"K, The" (Olson), **Supp. II Part 2:** 558, 563, 569

Kabir, **Supp. IV Part 1:** 74

"Kabnis" (Toomer), **Supp. III Part 2:** 481, 484; **Supp. IX:** 309, 310, **319– 320**

Kachel, Elsie. *See* Stevens, Mrs. Wallace (Elsie Kachel)

"Kaddish" (Ginsberg), **Supp. II Part 1:** 319, 327

Kaddish and Other Poems, 1958–1960 (Ginsberg), **Supp. II Part 1:** 309, 319–320; **Supp. XIV:** 269

Kael, Pauline, **Supp. IX:** 253

Kafka, Franz, **II:** 244, 565, 569; **III:** 51, 253, 418, 566, 572; **IV:** 2, 113, 218, 437–439, 442; **Retro. Supp. II:** 20, 221, 282; **Supp. I Part 1:** 197; **Supp. III Part 1:** 105; **Supp. III Part 2:** 413; **Supp. IV Part 1:** 379; **Supp. IV Part 2:** 623; **Supp. VIII:** 14, 15, 103; **Supp. XII:** 21, 37, 98, 168; **Supp. XIII:** 305

Kaganoff, Penny, **Supp. XI:** 122

Kahane, Jack, **III:** 171, 178

Kahn, Otto, **I:** 385; **IV:** 123; **Retro. Supp. II:** 81, 84, 85

Kahn, R. T., **Supp. XI:** 216

"Kai, Today" (Snyder), **Supp. VIII:** 300

Kaiser, Georg, **I:** 479

Kaiser, Henry, **Supp. I Part 2:** 644

Kakutani, Michiko, **Supp. IV Part 1:** 196, 201, 205, 211, 212; **Supp. V:** 63; **Supp. VIII:** 81, 84, 86, 88, 141; **Supp. X:** 171, 301, 302, 310, 314; **Supp. XI:** 38, 179; **Supp. XII:** 165, 171, 172, 299

Kalem, T. E., **Supp. IV Part 2:** 585

Kalevala (Finnish epic), **II:** 503, 504; **Retro. Supp. II:** 155

Kalevala (Lönnrot), **Retro. Supp. II:** 159, 160

Kalki: A Novel (Vidal), **Supp. IV Part 2:** 677, 682, 685, 691, 692

Kallen, Horace, **I:** 229; **Supp. I Part 2:** 643; **Supp. XIV:** 195, 197, 198

Kallman, Chester, **II:** 586; **Supp. II Part 1:** 15, 17, 24, 26

"Kallundborg Church" (Whittier), **Supp. I Part 2:** 696

Kalstone, David, **Retro. Supp. II:** 40

Kamel, Rose, **Supp. XIII:** 306

Kamera Obskura (Nabokov), **III:** 255

Kamhi, Michelle Moarder, **Supp. IV Part 2:** 529, 530

Kandy-Kolored Tangerine-Flake Streamline Baby, The (Wolfe), **Supp. III Part 2:** 569, 573–576, 580, 581

Kane, Lesley, **Supp. XIV:** 250

Kanellos, Nicolás, **Supp. VIII:** 82; **Supp. XIII:** 213

Kanin, Garson, **Supp. IV Part 2:** 574

"Kansas City Coyote" (Harjo), **Supp. XII:** 219, 222

"Kansas Emigrants, The" (Whittier), **Supp. I Part 2:** 687

Kant, Immanuel, **I:** 61, 277, 278; **II:** 10–11, 362, 480, 580–581, 582, 583; **III:** 300, 480, 481, 488, 612; **IV:** 90; **Supp. I Part 2:** 640; **Supp. IV Part 2:** 527; **Supp. XIV:** 198, 199

Kanter, Hal, **IV:** 383

Kapital, Das (Marx), **III:** 580

Kaplan, Abraham, **I:** 277

Kaplan, Justin, **I:** 247–248; **Retro. Supp. I:** 392

Kaplan, Steven, **Supp. V:** 238, 241, 243, 248

Karate Is a Thing of the Spirit (Crews), **Supp. XI: 112–113**

Karbo, Karen, **Supp. X:** 259, 262

"Karintha" (Toomer), **Supp. IX:** 311

Karl, Frederick R., **Supp. IV Part 1:** 384

Karl Shapiro's America (film), **Supp. II Part 2:** 703

Karr, Mary, **Supp. XI: 239–256; Supp. XIII:** 285

Kasabian, Linda, **Supp. IV Part 1:** 206

Kate Chopin (Toth), **Retro. Supp. II:** 71

Kate Chopin: A Critical Biography (Seyersted), **Retro. Supp. II:** 65;

Supp. I Part 1: 225

Kate Chopin and Edith Wharton: An Annotated Bibliographical Guide to Secondary Sources (Springer), **Supp. I Part 1:** 225

Kate Chopin and Her Creole Stories (Rankin), **Retro. Supp. II:** 57; **Supp. I Part 1:** 200, 225

"Kate Chopin's *The Awakening* in the Perspective of Her Literary Career" (Arms), **Supp. I Part 1:** 225

Kate Vaiden (Price), **Supp. VI:** 264, 265

"Käthe Kollwitz" (Rukeyser), **Supp. VI:** 283, 284

Katherine and Jean (Rice), **Supp. VII:** 288

"Kathleen" (Whittier), **Supp. I Part 2:** 693

Kathleen and Frank: The Autobiography of a Family (Isherwood), **Supp. XIV:** 158, 171

Kathy Goes to Haiti (Acker), **Supp. XII:** 5

Katz, Jonathan, **Supp. XII:** 179

Katz, Steve, **Supp. V:** 44

Kauffman, Carol, **Supp. XI:** 295

Kauffmann, Stanley, **III:** 452; **Supp. I Part 2:** 391

Kaufman, George S., **II:** 427, 435, 437; **III:** 62, 71–72, 394; **Retro. Supp. II:** 327; **Supp. IV Part 2:** 574; **Supp. IX:** 190

Kaufmann, James, **Supp. XI:** 39

Kauvar, Elaine M., **Supp. V:** 273

Kavanaugh (Longfellow), **I:** 458; **II:** 489, 491; **Retro. Supp. II:** 156; **Supp. I Part 2:** 420

Kaveney, Roz, **Supp. XI:** 39

Kazan, Elia, **III:** 153, 163; **IV:** 383; **Supp. I Part 1:** 66, 295

Kazin, Alfred, **I:** 248, 417, 419, 517; **II:** 177, 459; **IV:** 236; **Retro. Supp. II:** 206, 243, 246, 286; **Supp. I Part 1:** 195, 196, 294, 295, 296; **Supp. I Part 2:** 536, 631, 647, 650, 678, 679, 719; **Supp. II Part 1:** 143; **Supp. IV Part 1:** 200, 382; **Supp. V:** 122; **Supp. VIII: 93–111; Supp. IX:** 3, 227; **Supp. XIII:** 98, 106; **Supp. XIV:** 11

Keach, Stacey, **Supp. XI:** 309

Keane, Sarah, **Supp. I Part 1:** 100

Kearns, Cleo McNelly, **Retro. Supp. I:** 57

Kearns, George, **Retro. Supp. I:** 292

Keating, AnnLouise, **Supp. IV Part 1:** 330

Keaton, Buster, **I:** 31; **Supp. I Part 2:** 607; **Supp. IV Part 2:** 574

Keats, John, **I:** 34, 103, 284, 314, 317–318, 385, 401, 448; **II:** 82, 88, 97, 214, 368, 512, 516, 530–531, 540, 593; **III:** 4, 10, 45, 122, 133–134, 179, 214, 237, 272, 275, 469, 485, 523; **IV:** 360, 405, 416; **Retro. Supp. I:** 91, 301, 313, 360, 395, 412; **Supp. I Part 1:** 82, 183, 266, 267, 312, 349, 362, 363, 365; **Supp. I Part 2:** 410, 422, 424, 539, 552, 675, 719, 720; **Supp. III Part 1:** 73; **Supp. IV Part 1:** 123, 168, 325; **Supp. IV Part 2:** 455; **Supp. VIII:** 41, 273; **Supp. IX:** 38, 39, 45; **Supp. XI:** 43, 320; **Supp. XII:** 9, 113, 255; **Supp. XIII:** 131, 281; **Supp. XIV:** 274

Keats, John (other), **Supp. IX:** 190, 195, 200

"Keela, the Outcast Indian Maiden" (Welty), **IV:** 263

"Keen Scalpel on Racial Ills" (Bruell), **Supp. VIII:** 126

"Keep A-Inchin' Along" (Van Vechten), **Supp. III Part 2:** 744

Keeping (Goldbarth), **Supp. XII:** 179–180, 180

"Keeping Informed in D.C." (Nemerov), **III:** 287

Keeping Slug Woman Alive: A Holistic Approach to American Indian Texts (Sarris), **Supp. IV Part 1:** 329

"'Keeping Their World Large'" (Moore), **III:** 201–202

"Keeping Things Whole" (Strand), **Supp. IV Part 2:** 624

Keep It Simple: A Defense of the Earth (Nichols), **Supp. XIII:** 268

Kees, Weldon, **Supp. X:** 118; **Supp. XII:** 198

Keillor, Garrison, **Supp. XII:** 343; **Supp. XIII:** 274

Keith, Brian, **Supp. IV Part 2:** 474

Keith, Minor C., **I:** 483

Keller, A. G., **III:** 108

Keller, Helen, **I:** 254, 258

Keller, Lynn, **Supp. IV Part 2:** 423; **Supp. V:** 78, 80

Kelley, David, **Supp. IV Part 2:** 528, 529

Kelley, Florence, **Supp. I Part 1:** 5, 7

Kellogg, Paul U., **Supp. I Part 1:** 5, 7, 12

Kellogg, Reverend Edwin H., **III:** 200

Kelly, **II:** 464

Kelly, Emmett, **Supp. XI:** 99, 106

Kelly, Walt, **Supp. XI:** 105

Kemble, Fanny, **Retro. Supp. I:** 228

Kemble, Gouverneur, **II:** 298

Kemble, Peter, **II:** 298

Kempton, Murray, **Supp. VIII:** 104

Kempton-Wace Letters, The (London and Strunsky), **II:** 465

Kennan, George F., **Supp. VIII:** 241

Kennedy, Albert J., **Supp. I Part 1:** 19

Kennedy, Arthur, **III:** 153

Kennedy, Burt, **Supp. IV Part 1:** 236

Kennedy, J. Gerald, **Retro. Supp. II:** 271

Kennedy, John F., **I:** 136, 170; **II:** 49, 152–153; **III:** 38, 41, 42, 234, 411, 415, 581; **IV:** 229; **Supp. I Part 1:** 291; **Supp. I Part 2:** 496; **Supp. VIII:** 98, 104, 203; **Supp. XII:** 132

Kennedy, John Pendleton, **II:** 313

Kennedy, Mrs. John F., **I:** 136

Kennedy, Robert, **Supp. V:** 291

Kennedy, Robert F., **I:** 294; **Supp. I Part 1:** 52; **Supp. XI:** 343

Kennedy, William, **Supp. VII: 131–157**

Kennedy, X. J., **Supp. V:** 178, 182

Kenner, Hugh, **III:** 475, 478; **IV:** 412; **Supp. I Part 1:** 255; **Supp. IV Part 2:** 474

Kenneth Millar/Ross Macdonald: A Checklist (Bruccoli), **Supp. IV Part 2:** 464, 469, 471

Kenny, Maurice, **Supp. IV Part 2:** 502

Kent, George, **Supp. IV Part 1:** 11

Kenton, Maxwell. *See* Burnett, David; Hoffenberg, Mason; Southern, Terry

"Kent State, May 1970" (Haines), **Supp. XII:** 211

Kenyatta, Jomo, **Supp. X:** 135

Kenyon, Jane, **Supp. VII: 159–177; Supp. VIII:** 272

Kepler, Johannes, **III:** 484; **IV:** 18

Keppel, Frederick P., **I:** 214

"Kéramos" (Longfellow), **II:** 494; **Retro. Supp. II:** 167, 169

Kéramos and Other Poems (Longfellow), **II:** 490

Kerim, Ussin, **Supp. IX:** 152

Kermode, Frank, **IV:** 133; **Retro. Supp. I:** 301

Kern, Jerome, **II:** 427

Kerouac, Jack, **III:** 174; **Retro. Supp. I:** 102; **Supp. II Part 1:** 31, 307, 309, 318, 328; **Supp. III Part 1:** 91–94, 96, 100, **217–234; Supp. IV Part 1:** 90, 146; **Supp. V:** 336; **Supp. VIII:** 42, 138, 289, 305; **Supp. IX:** 246; **Supp. XII:** 118, 121, 122, 123, 126, 131, 132; **Supp. XIII:** 275, 284; **Supp. XIV:** 137, 138, 141, 142, 143–144

Kerr, Deborah, **Supp. XI:** 307

Kerr, Orpheus C. (pseudonym). *See* Newell, Henry

Kerr, Walter, **Supp. IV Part 2:** 575, 579

Kesey, Ken, **III:** 558; **Supp. III Part 1:** 217; **Supp. V:** 220, 295; **Supp. X:** 24, 265; **Supp. XI:** 104

Kesten, Stephen, **Supp. XI:** 309

Ketchup (Shanley), **Supp. XIV:** 315

Kevane, Bridget, **Supp. XI:** 185, 190

"Key, The" (Welty), **IV:** 262

"Keys" (Nye), **Supp. XIII:** 281

Key to Uncle Tom's Cabin, A (Stowe), **Supp. I Part 2:** 580

Key West (H. Crane), **Retro. Supp. II:** 84

"Key West" (H. Crane), **I:** 400

Key West: An Island Sheaf (Crane), **I:** 385, 399–402

Khrushchev, Nikita, **I:** 136

Kid, The (Aiken), **I:** 61

Kid, The (Chaplin), **I:** 386

Kidder, Tracy, **Supp. III Part 1:** 302

Kidman, Nicole, **Supp. X:** 80

"Kidnapping in the Family, A" (Fante), **Supp. XI:** 164

"Kid's Guide to Divorce, The" (Moore), **Supp. X:** 167, 172

Kidwell, Clara Sue, **Supp. IV Part 1:** 333

Kielsky, Vera Emuma, **Supp. V:** 273

Kieran, John, **II:** 417

Kierkegaard, Søren Aabye, **II:** 229; **III:** 292, 305, 309, 572; **IV:** 438, 491; **Retro. Supp. I:** 326; **Retro. Supp. II:** 222; **Supp. V:** 9; **Supp. VIII:** 7–8

Kiernan, Robert F., **Supp. IV Part 2:** 684

Kieseritsky, L., **III:** 252

"Kilim" (McClatchy), **Supp. XII:** 258

"Killed at Resaca" (Bierce), **I:** 202

"Killed at the Ford" (Longfellow), **Retro. Supp. II:** 170–171

Killens, John Oliver, **Supp. IV Part 1:** 8, 369

"Killer in the Rain" (Chandler), **Supp. IV Part 1:** 122

"Killers, The" (Hemingway), **II:** 249; **Retro. Supp. I:** 188, 189

Killing Mister Watson (Matthiessen), **Supp. V:** 212, 214

"Killing of a State Cop, The" (Ortiz), **Supp. IV Part 2:** 499

Killing of Sister George, The (Marcus), **Supp. I Part 1:** 277

"Killings" (Dubus), **Supp. VII:** 85–86

"Killing the Plants" (Kenyon), **Supp. VII:** 167, 168

Kilmer, Joyce, **Supp. I Part 2:** 387

Kilpatrick, James K., **Supp. X:** 145

Kilvert, Francis, **Supp. VIII:** 172

Kim (Kipling), **Supp. X:** 230

Kim, Alfred, **Supp. XI:** 140

Kimball, J. Golden, **Supp. IV Part 2:** 602

Kimbrough, Mary Craig. *See* Sinclair, Mary Craig (Mary Craig Kimbrough)

Kimes, Maymie B., **Supp. IX:** 178

Kimes, William F., **Supp. IX:** 178

"Kin" (Welty), **IV:** 277; **Retro. Supp. I:** 353

Kinard, Agnes Dodds, **Supp. XIV:** 122, 123, 127

Kincaid, Jamaica, **Supp. VII: 179–196**

"Kindness" (Dunn), **Supp. XI:** 149, 150

"Kindness" (Nye), **Supp. XIII:** 285

"Kindness" (Plath), **Retro. Supp. II:** 256

Kind of Order, A Kind of Folly, A: Essays and Conversations (Kunitz), **Supp. III Part 1:** 262, 268

Kindred (O. Butler), **Supp. XIII: 59–60,** 69

"Kind Sir: These Woods" (Sexton), **Supp. II Part 2:** 673

Kinds of Love (Sarton), **Supp. VIII: 253–254,** 256

Kinfolk (Buck), **Supp. II Part 1:** 126

King, Alexander, **IV:** 287

King, Carole, **Supp. XII:** 308

King, Clarence, **I:** 1

King, Ernest, **Supp. I Part 2:** 491

King, Fisher, **II:** 425

King, Francis, **Supp. XIV:** 155, 156, 166, 169

King, Grace, **Retro. Supp. II:** 136

King, Martin Luther, Jr., **Retro. Supp. II:** 12, 13

King, Michael, **Supp. XII:** 182

King, Queen, Knave (Nabokov), **III:** 251; **Retro. Supp. I:** 270

King, Starr, **Supp. II Part 1:** 341, 342

King, Stephen, **Supp. IV Part 1:** 102, 104; **Supp. IV Part 2:** 467; **Supp. V: 137–155; Supp. IX:** 114; **Supp. XIII:** 53

King, Tabitha (Mrs. Stephen King), **Supp. V:** 137

King, The (Barthelme), **Supp. IV Part 1:** 47, 52

King Coffin (Aiken), **I:** 53–54, 57

"King David" (Benét), **Supp. XI:** 44

"King David" (Reznikoff), **Supp. XIV:** 283

Kingdom by the Sea, The: A Journey around Great Britain (Theroux), **Supp. VIII:** 323

Kingdom of Earth (T. Williams), **IV:** 382, 386, 387, 388, 391, 393, 398

"Kingdom of Earth, The" (T. Williams), **IV:** 384

Kingfisher, The (Clampitt), **Supp. IX:** 38

"Kingfishers, The" (Olson), **Supp. II Part 2:** 557, 558–563, 582

King Jasper (Robinson), **III:** 523

King Kong (film), **Supp. IV Part 1:** 104

King Lear (Shakespeare), **I:** 538; **II:** 540, 551; **Retro. Supp. I:** 248; **Supp. IV Part 1:** 31, 36; **Supp. IX:** 14; **Supp. XI:** 172

King Leopold's Soliloquy (Twain), **IV:** 208

King My Father's Wreck, The (Simpson), **Supp. IX:** 266, 267, 270, 275, 276

King of Babylon Shall Not Come Against You, The (Garrett), **Supp. VII:** 110–111; **Supp. X:** 3

"King of Folly Island, The" (Jewett), **II:** 394; **Retro. Supp. II:** 132, 133

King of Kings (film), **Supp. IV Part 2:** 520

"King of the Bingo Game" (Ellison), **Retro. Supp. II:** 117, 125; **Supp. II Part 1:** 235, 238, 240–241

"King of the Cats, The" (Benét), **Supp. XI:** 49–50

"King of the Clock Tower" (Yeats), **III:** 473

"King of the Desert, The" (O'Hara), **III:** 369

King of the Fields, The (Singer), **Retro. Supp. II:** 317

King of the Jews (Epstein), **Supp. XII:** 161, **166–170,** 172

King of the Mountain (Garrett), **Supp. VII:** 96, 97

"King of the River" (Kunitz), **Supp. III Part 1:** 263, 267–268

"King of the Sea" (Marquand), **III:** 60

"King over the Water" (Blackmur), **Supp. II Part 1:** 107

"King Pandar" (Blackmur), **Supp. II Part 1:** 92, 102

"King Pest" (Poe), **Retro. Supp. II:** 273

Kingsblood Royal (Lewis), **II:** 456

Kingsbury, John, **Supp. I Part 1:** 8

King's Henchman, The (Millay), **III:** 138–139

Kingsley, Sidney, **Supp. I Part 1:** 277, 281

"King's Missive, The" (Whittier), **Supp. I Part 2:** 694

Kingsolver, Barbara, **Supp. VII: 197–214; Supp. XIII:** 16

Kingston, Earll, **Supp. V:** 160

Kingston, Maxine Hong, **Supp. IV Part 1:** 1, 12; **Supp. V: 157–175,** 250; **Supp. X:** 291–292; **Supp. XI:** 18, 245

"King Volmer and Elsie" (Whittier), **Supp. I Part 2:** 696

Kinmont, Alexander, **Supp. I Part 2:** 588–589

Kinnaird, John, **Retro. Supp. I:** 399

Kinnell, Galway, **Supp. III Part 1: 235–256; Supp. III Part 2:** 541; **Supp. IV Part 2:** 623; **Supp. V:** 332; **Supp. VIII:** 39; **Supp. XI:** 139; **Supp. XII:** 241

Kinsey, Alfred, **IV:** 230; **Supp. XIV:** 140

Kinzie, Mary, **Supp. XII:** 181

"Kipling" (Trilling), **Supp. III Part 2:** 495

Kipling, Rudyard, **I:** 421, 587–588; **II:** 271, 338, 404, 439; **III:** 55, 328, 508, 511, 521, 524, 579; **IV:** 429; **Supp. IV Part 2:** 603; **Supp. X:** 255

Kirby, David, **Supp. XIII:** 89

Kirkland, Jack, **I:** 297

Kirkpatrick, Jeane, **Supp. VIII:** 241

Kirkwood, Cynthia A., **Supp. XI:** 177, 178, 179

Kirp, David L., **Supp. XI:** 129

Kirstein, Lincoln, **Supp. II Part 1:** 90, 97; **Supp. IV Part 1:** 82, 83

Kiss, The (Harrison), **Supp. X:** 191

"Kiss, The" (Sexton), **Supp. II Part 2:** 687

Kissel, Howard, **Supp. IV Part 2:** 580

Kissinger, Henry, **Supp. IV Part 1:** 388; **Supp. XII:** 9, 14

Kiss of the Spider Woman, the Musical (McNally), **Supp. XIII:** 207, **Supp. XIII:** 208

Kiss Tomorrow Good-bye (McCoy), **Supp. XIII:** 170, **172–173,** 174

"Kit and Caboodle" (Komunyakaa), **Supp. XIII:** 115

Kit Brandon: A Portrait (Anderson), **I:** 111

Kitchen, Judith, **Supp. IV Part 1:** 242, 245, 252; **Supp. IX:** 163; **Supp. XI:** 312, 313, 315, 317, 319, 320, 326, 329

"Kitchenette" (Brooks), **Retro. Supp. I:** 208

Kitchen God's Wife, The (Tan), **Supp. X:** 289, 292, 293, 294–295, 296–297, 298–299

"Kitchen Terrarium: 1983" (McCarriston), **Supp. XIV:** 270

Kit O'Brien (Masters), **Supp. I Part 2:** 471

Kittel, Frederick August. *See* Wilson, August

Kittredge, Charmian. *See* London, Mrs. Jack (Charmian Kittredge)

Kittredge, William, **Supp. VIII:** 39; **Supp. XI:** 316; **Supp. XII:** 209; **Supp. XIII:** 16

"Kitty Hawk" (Frost), **II:** 164; **Retro. Supp. I:** 124, 141

Klein, Joe, **Supp. XII:** 67–68

Klein, Marcus, **Supp. I Part 2:** 432; **Supp. XI:** 233

Kleist, Heinrich von, **Supp. IV Part 1:** 224

Kline, Franz, **Supp. XII:** 198

Kline, George, **Supp. VIII:** 22, 28

Klinkowitz, Jerome, **Supp. IV Part 1:** 40; **Supp. X:** 263; **Supp. XI:** 347

Knapp, Adeline, **Supp. XI:** 200

Knapp, Friedrich, **III:** 100

Knapp, Samuel, **I:** 336

Kneel to the Rising Sun (Caldwell), **I:** 304, 309

"Knees/Dura-Europos" (Goldbarth), **Supp. XII:** 185

"Knife" (Simic), **Supp. VIII:** 275

Knight, Arthur, **Supp. XIV:** 144

Knight, Etheridge, **Supp. XI:** 239

"Knight in Disguise, The" (Lindsay), **Supp. I Part 2:** 390

Knightly Quest, The (T. Williams), **IV:** 383

Knight's Gambit (Faulkner), **II:** 72

"Knock" (Dickey), **Supp. IV Part 1:** 182

"Knocking Around" (Ashbery), **Supp. III Part 1:** 22

"Knocking on Three, Winston" (Epstein), **Supp. XIV:** 109

Knockout Artist, The (Crews), **Supp. XI: 113–114**

Knopf, Alfred A., **III:** 99, 105, 106, 107; **Retro. Supp. I:** 13, 19, 317; **Supp. I Part 1:** 324, 325, 327; **Supp. IV Part 1:** 125, 354; **Supp. XIII:** 172

Knopf, Blanche, **Supp. I Part 1:** 324, 325, 327, 328, 332, 341; **Supp. IV Part 1:** 128, 346, 348; **Supp. XIII:** 169

"Knot, The" (Rich), **Supp. I Part 2:** 555

Knotts, Kristina, **Supp. XIII:** 238

"Knowing, The" (Olds), **Supp. X:** 215

"Knowledge Forwards and Backwards" (Stern), **Supp. IX:** 296

Knowles, John, **Supp. IV Part 2:** 679; **Supp. XII: 235–250**

Knox, Frank, **Supp. I Part 2:** 488, 489

Knox, Israel, **Supp. X:** 70

Knox, Vicesimus, **II:** 8

Knoxville: Summer of 1915 (Agee), **I:** 42–46

Knudson, R. Rozanne, **Supp. IV Part 2:** 648

Kober, Arthur, **Supp. I Part 1:** 292

Koch, Frederick, **IV:** 453

Koch, John, **Supp. VIII:** 88

Koch, Vivienne, **III:** 194; **IV:** 136, 140; **Retro. Supp. I:** 428, 430

"Kochinnenako in Academe: Three Approaches to Interpreting a Keres Indian Tale" (Gunn Allen), **Supp. IV Part 1:** 329

"Kodachromes of the Island" (Hayden), **Supp. II Part 1:** 367, 380

Koestler, Arthur, **I:** 258; **Supp. I Part 2:** 671

Kokkinen, Eila, **Supp. XIV:** 146, 148

Kolbenheyer, Dr. Frederick, **Supp. I Part 1:** 207

Kolodny, Annette, **Supp. X:** 97, 103, 229

Komunyakaa, Yusef, **Supp. XIII: 111–136**

Kon-Tiki (Heyerdahl), **II:** 477

Koopman, Harry Lyman, **Retro. Supp. I:** 40

Kora and Ka (Doolittle), **Supp. I Part 1:** 270

Kora in Hell (W. C. Williams), **Retro. Supp. I:** 416, **417–418,** 419, 430, 431

Korb, Rena, **Supp. XI:** 2

Korczak, Janosz, **Supp. X:** 70

Kort, Amy, **Supp. XIII:** 148

Kosinski, Jerzy, **Supp. VII: 215–228; Supp. XII:** 21

"Kostas Tympakianakis" (Merrill), **Supp. III Part 1:** 326

Koteliansky, S. S., **Supp. VIII:** 251, 265

Kowloon Tong (Theroux), **Supp. VIII:** 325

Kozlenko, William, **IV:** 378, 381

Kramer, Dale, **Supp. I Part 2:** 669

Kramer, Hilton, **III:** 537; **Supp. I Part 1:** 295, 296; **Supp. VIII:** 239

Kramer, Lawrence, **Supp. IV Part 1:** 61, 65, 66; **Supp. IX:** 291

Kramer, Stanley, **II:** 421, 587

Krapp's Last Tape (Beckett), **I:** 71; **III:** 387; **Retro. Supp. I:** 206

Krassner, Paul, **Supp. IV Part 1:** 385; **Supp. XI:** 293

Kreitman, Esther, **IV:** 2

Kreymborg, Alfred, **II:** 530; **III:** 465; **IV:** 76; **Retro. Supp. I:** 417

Kristeva, Julia, **Supp. XII:** 6

Kristofferson, Kris, **Supp. XIII:** 119

Kristol, Irving, **Supp. VIII:** 93, 244; **Supp. XIII:** 98

Kroll, Jack, **Supp. IV Part 2:** 590

Kroll, Judith, **Supp. I Part 2:** 541–543, 544, 546

Kroll Ring, Frances. *See* Ring, Frances Kroll

Krook, Dorothea, **Retro. Supp. II:** 243

Kropotkin, Peter, **I:** 493; **Supp. I Part 1:** 5; **Supp. IV Part 2:** 521

Kruif, Paul de, **II:** 446

Krupat, Arnold, **Supp. IV Part 2:** 500

Krutch, Joseph Wood, **II:** 459; **III:** 425; **IV:** 70, 175

Kublai Khan, **III:** 395

"Kubla Khan" (Coleridge), **Supp. XIII:** 131, 283

Kubrick, Stanley, **Supp. IV Part 1:** 392; **Supp. XI:** 293,**Supp. XI:** 301, 302–303

Kuehl, John, **Supp. IV Part 1:** 279, 284, 285, 287

Kuehl, Linda, **Supp. IV Part 1:** 199

Kukachin, Princess, **III:** 395

"Ku Klux" (Hughes), **Retro. Supp. I:** 205

Kulshrestha, Chirantan, **Retro. Supp. II:** 21

Kumin, Maxine, **Supp. IV Part 2:** 439–457; **Supp. XIII:** 294

Kundera, Milan, **Supp. VIII:** 241

Kunitz, Stanley, **I:** 179, 180, 181, 182, 521; **II:** 545; **Supp. III Part 1:** 257–270; **Supp. V:** 79; **Supp. XI:** 259; **Supp. XIII:** 341

Kuo, Helena, **Supp. X:** 291

Kuropatkin, General Aleksei Nikolaevich, **III:** 247–248

Kurzy of the Sea (Barnes), **Supp. III Part 1:** 34

Kushner, Tony, **Supp. IX:** 131–149

Kussy, Bella, **IV:** 468

Kuttner, Henry, **Supp. IV Part 1:** 102

LaBastille, Anne, **Supp. X:** 95–110

"Labours of Hercules, The" (Moore), **III:** 201

La Bruyère, Jean de, **I:** 58

La Bufera e Altro (Montale), **Supp. V:** 337

Labyrinth of Solitude, The (Paz), **Supp. XIII:** 223

Lacan, Jacques, **Supp. IV Part 1:** 45; **Supp. VIII:** 5; **Supp. XII:** 98

La Casa en Mango Street (Cisneros), **Supp. VII:** 58–59

Lachaise, Gaston, **I:** 434

"Lackawanna" (Merwin), **Supp. III Part 1:** 350

Lackawanna Elegy (Goll; Kinnell, trans.), **Supp. III Part 1:** 235, 243–244

Laclède, Pierre, **Supp. I Part 1:** 205

"Lacquer Prints" (Lowell), **II:** 524–525

Ladder of Years (Tyler), **Supp. IV Part 2:** 657, 671–672

Ladders to Fire (Nin), **Supp. X:** 185

"Ladies" (Coleman), **Supp. XI:** 93

Ladies Almanack (Barnes), **Supp. III Part 1:** 37–39, 42

"Ladies in Spring" (Welty), **IV:** 276–277; **Retro. Supp. I:** 353

Lady Audley's Secret (Braddon), **Supp. I Part 1:** 35, 36

"Lady Barberina" (James), **Retro. Supp. I:** 227

"Lady Bates" (Jarrell), **II:** 380–381

Lady Chatterley's Lover (Lawrence), **III:** 170; **IV:** 434

"Lady from Redhorse, A" (Bierce), **I:** 203

Lady in Kicking Horse Reservoir, The (Hugo), **Supp. VI:** 134, **138–139**

Lady in the Lake, The (Chandler), **Supp. IV Part 1:** 127, 129–130

"Lady in the Lake, The" (Chandler), **Supp. IV Part 1:** 129

Lady in the Lake, The (film), **Supp. IV Part 1:** 130

"Lady in the Pink Mustang, The" (Erdrich), **Supp. IV Part 1:** 270

"Lady Is Civilized, The" (Taylor), **Supp. V:** 315

Lady Is Cold, The (White), **Supp. I Part 2:** 653

"Lady Lazarus" (Plath), **Retro. Supp. II:** 250, 251, 255; **Supp. I Part 2:** 529, 535, 542, 545

Lady of Aroostook, The (Howells), **II:** 280

"Lady of Bayou St. John, A" (Chopin), **Retro. Supp. II:** 58

"Lady of the Lake, The" (Malamud), **Supp. I Part 2:** 437

Lady Oracle (Atwood), **Supp. XIII:** 21, **23–24**

Lady Sings the Blues (film), **Supp. I Part 1:** 67

"Lady's Maid's Tale, The" (Wharton), **IV:** 316

"Lady Wentworth" (Longfellow), **II:** 505

"Lady with a Lamp" (Parker), **Supp. IX:** 193

"Lady with the Heron, The" (Merwin), **Supp. III Part 1:** 343

La Farge, John, **I:** 1, 2, 20; **II:** 322, 338; **Retro. Supp. I:** 217

La Farge, Oliver, **Supp. IV Part 2:** 503

Lafayette, Marquis de, **I:** 344, 345; **II:** 405–406; **Supp. I Part 2:** 510, 511, 683

"La Figlia che Piange" (Eliot), **Retro. Supp. I:** 63

La Follette, Robert, **I:** 483, 485, 492; **III:** 580

La Fontaine, Jean de, **II:** 154; **III:** 194; **IV:** 80

Laforgue, Jules, **I:** 386, 569, 570, 572–573, 575, 576; **II:** 528; **III:** 8, 11, 466; **IV:** 37, 79, 80, 122; **Retro. Supp. I:** 55, 56; **Supp. XIII:** 332, 335, 346

La Gallienne, Eva, **Supp. VIII:** 251

"Lager Beer" (Dunbar), **Supp. II Part 1:** 193

"La Gringuita: On Losing a Native Language" (Alvarez), **Supp. VII:** 18

Laguna Woman (Silko), **Supp. IV Part 2:** 557, 560–561

Laing, R. D., **Supp. I Part 2:** 527

La kabbale pratique (Ambelain), **Supp. I Part 1:** 273

"Lake, The" (Bradbury), **Supp. IV Part 1:** 101

Lake, The (play), **Supp. IX:** 189

Lakeboat (Mamet), **Supp. XIV:** 240–241

"Lake Chelan" (Stafford), **Supp. XI:** 321

Lake Effect Country (Ammons), **Supp. VII:** 34, 35

"Lake Isle of Innisfree" (Yeats), **Retro. Supp. I:** 413

Lalic, Ivan V., **Supp. VIII:** 272

L'Alouette (Anouilh), **Supp. I Part 1:** 286–288

Lamantia, Philip, **Supp. VIII:** 289

Lamb, Charles, **III:** 111, 207; **Supp. VIII:** 125

Lamb, Wendy, **Supp. IV Part 2:** 658

Lambardi, Marilyn May, **Retro. Supp. II:** 45–46

"Lament" (Wilbur), **Supp. III Part 2:** 550

"Lamentations" (Glück), **Supp. V:** 83, 84

"Lament for Dark Peoples" (Hughes), **Retro. Supp. I:** 199

"Lament for Saul and Jonathan" (Bradstreet), **Supp. I Part 1:** 111

"Lament-Heaven" (Doty), **Supp. XI:** 125

"Lament of a New England Mother, The" (Eberhart), **I:** 539

Laments for the Living (Parker), **Supp. IX:** 192

"Lame Shall Enter First, The" (O'Connor), **III:** 348, 351, 352, 355, 356–357, 358; **Retro. Supp. II:** 237

Lamia (Keats), **II:** 512; **III:** 523

La Motte-Fouqué, Friedrich Heinrich Karl, **III:** 77, 78

L'Amour, Louis, **Supp. XIII:** 5

Lamp for Nightfall, A (Caldwell), **I:** 297

"Lance" (Nabokov), **Retro. Supp. I:** 266

Lancelot (Percy), **Supp. III Part 1:** 384, 395–396

Lancelot (Robinson), **III:** 513, 522

Lanchester, John, **Retro. Supp. I:** 278

"Land" (Emerson), **II:** 6

"Land Aesthetic, The" (Callicott), **Supp. XIV:** 184

Landau, Deborah, **Supp. XI:** 122, 123

"Land beyond the Blow, The" (Bierce), **I:** 209

"Land Ethic, The" (Leopold), **Supp. XIV:** 179, 180, 183, 191, 192

Landfall (Wagoner), **Supp. IX:** 330

"Landing in Luck" (Faulkner), **Retro. Supp. I:** 85

"Landing on the Moon" (Swenson), **Supp. IV Part 2:** 643

Landlord at Lion's Head, The (Howells), **II:** 276, 287–288

Landmarks of Healing: A Study of House Made of Dawn (Scarberry-García), **Supp. IV Part 2:** 486

Land of Little Rain, The (Dillard), **Supp. VI:** 27–28

Land of the Free U.S.A. (MacLeish), **I:** 293; **III:** 16–17

Land of Unlikeness (Lowell), **II:** 537–538, 539, 547; **Retro. Supp. II:** 177, 178, **184–185**

Landor, Walter Savage, **III:** 15, 469; **Supp. I Part 2:** 422

"Landscape" (Sarton), **Supp. VIII:** 259

"Landscape: The Eastern Shore" (Barth), **I:** 122

"Landscape as a Nude" (MacLeish), **III:** 14

Landscape at the End of the Century (Dunn), **Supp. XI:** 139, 143, **150–151**

"Landscape Chamber, The" (Jewett), **II:** 408–409

"Landscape for the Disappeared" (Komunyakaa), **Supp. XIII:** 120, 126

Landscape in American Poetry (Larcom), **Supp. XIII:** 142

"Landscape Painter, A" (James), **II:** 322; **Retro. Supp. I:** 219

"Landscape Symbolism in Kate Chopin's *At Fault*" (Arner), **Retro. Supp. II:** 62

"Landscape with Boat" (Stevens),

Retro. Supp. I: 306

"Landscape with the Fall of Icarus" (Brueghel), **Retro. Supp. I:** 430

"Land Where There Is No Death, The" (Benét), **Supp. XI:** 56

Lane, Ann, **Supp. XI:** 195, 208

Lane, Cornelia. *See* Anderson, Mrs. Sherwood

Lane, Homer, **Supp. II Part 1:** 6; **Supp. XIV:** 160

Lane, Nathan, **Supp. XIII:** 207

Lane, Rose Wilder, **Supp. IV Part 2:** 524

Lang, Andrew, **Retro. Supp. I:** 127

Lang, Violet, **Supp. XII:** 119

Langdon, Olivia. *See* Clemens, Mrs. Samuel Langhorne (Olivia Langdon)

Lange, Carl Georg, **II:** 350

Lange, Dorothea, **I:** 293; **Supp. XIV:** 181

Langland, Joseph, **III:** 542

Langston Hughes, American Poet (Walker), **Supp. III Part 2:** 530–531

Langston Hughes: Modern Critical Views (Bloom, ed.), **Retro. Supp. I:** 193

Langston Hughes: The Poet and His Critics (Barksdale), **Retro. Supp. I:** 202

Langston Hughes and the "Chicago Defender": Essays on Race, Politics, and Culture (De Santis, ed.), **Retro. Supp. I:** 194

Langston Hughes Reader, The (Hughes), **Retro. Supp. I:** 202; **Supp. I Part 1:** 345

"Language, Visualization and the Inner Library" (Shepard), **Supp. III Part 2:** 436, 438, 449

"Language and the Writer" (Bambara), **Supp. XI:** 18

Language As Gesture (Blackmur), **Supp. II Part 1:** 108

Language as Symbolic Action (Burke), **I:** 275, 282, 285

Language Book, The (Andrews and Bernstein), **Supp. IV Part 2:** 426

Language in Thought and Action (Hayakawa), **I:** 448

"Language of Being and Dying, The" (Gass), **Supp. VI:** 91

"Language of Home, The" (Wideman), **Supp. X:** 320, 323–324

Language of Life, The (Moyers, television series), **Supp. XIII:** 274, 276

Language of the American South, The (Brooks), **Supp. XIV:** 14

"Language of the Brag, The" (Olds), **Supp. X:** 204

"Language We Know, The" (Ortiz), **Supp. IV Part 2:** 500

Lanier, Clifford, **Supp. I Part 1:** 349, 350, 353, 355, 356, 371

Lanier, James F. D., **Supp. I Part 1:** 350

Lanier, Lyle H., **Supp. X:** 25

Lanier, Mrs. Robert Sampson (Mary Jane Anderson), **Supp. I Part 1:** 349

Lanier, Mrs. Sidney (Mary Day), **Supp. I Part 1:** 351, 355, 357, 361, 362, 364, 370, 371

Lanier, Robert Sampson, **Supp. I Part 1:** 349, 351, 355, 356, 361

Lanier, Sidney, **IV:** 444; **Supp. I Part 1:** 349–373; **Supp. I Part 2:** 416; **Supp. IV Part 1:** 165

"Lanier as Poet" (Parks), **Supp. I Part 1:** 373

"Lanier's Reading" (Graham), **Supp. I Part 1:** 373

"Lanier's Use of Science for Poetic Imagery" (Beaver), **Supp. I Part 1:** 373

Lannegan, Helen. *See* Caldwell, Mrs. Erskine

Lannin, Paul, **II:** 427

Lanny Budd novels (Sinclair), **Supp. V:** 290

Lant, Kathleen Margaret, **Supp. V:** 141

Lanthenas, François, **Supp. I Part 2:** 515

Lao-tse, **III:** 173, 189, 567

"Lapis Lazuli" (Yeats), **I:** 532; **III:** 40

Laplace, Pierre Simon de, **III:** 428

Lapouge, M. G., **Supp. I Part 2:** 633

Larbaud, Valery, **IV:** 404; **Supp. XIII:** 332; **Supp. XIV:** 338

Larcom, Lucy, **Retro. Supp. II:** 145; **Supp. XIII:** 137–157

Larcom's Poetical Works (Larcom), **Supp. XIII:** 142

Lardner, John, **II:** 437

Lardner, Ring, **I:** 487; **II:** 44, 91, 259, 263, **415–438;** **III:** 566, 572; **IV:** 433; **Retro. Supp. I:** 105; **Retro. Supp. II:** 222; **Supp. I Part 2:** 609; **Supp. IX:** 200

Lardner, Ring, Jr., **Supp. XI:** 306

"Lardner, Shakespeare and Chekhov" (Matthews), **II:** 430

"Large Bad Picture" (Bishop), **Retro. Supp. II:** 43; **Supp. I Part 1:** 73, 80–82, 85, 86, 89, 90

"Large Coffee" (Lardner), **II:** 437

Large Glass, or The Bride Stripped Bare by Her Bachelors, Even (Duchamp), **Supp. IV Part 2:** 423, 424

Largo (Handel), **IV:** 369

Lark, The (Hellman), **Supp. I Part 1:** 286–288, 297

Larkin, Philip, **Supp. I Part 2:** 536; **Supp. XI:** 243, 249; **Supp. XIII:** 76, 85

Larkin, Sharon Alile, **Supp. XI:** 20

Larmore, Phoebe, **Supp. X:** 266

La Rochefoucauld, François de, **I:** 279; **II:** 111; **Supp. XIV:** 130

"La Rose des Vents" (Wilbur), **Supp. III Part 2:** 550

Larry's Party (Shields), **Supp. VII:** 324, 326–327

Larsen, Nella, **Supp. I Part 1:** 325, 326; **Supp. IV Part 1:** 164

Larson, Charles, **Supp. IV Part 1:** 331

Larson, Clinton, **Supp. XI:** 328

"Larval Stage of a Bookworm" (Mencken), **III:** 101

La Salle and the Discovery of the Great West (Parkman), **Supp. II Part 2:** 595, 598, 605–607

Lasch, Christopher, **I:** 259

Lasher (Rice), **Supp. VII:** 299–300

Lask, Thomas, **III:** 576

Laski, Harold, **Supp. I Part 2:** 632, 643

Lassalle, Ferdinand, **IV:** 429

"Last Acts" (Olds), **Supp. X:** 210

Last Adam, The (Cozzens), **I:** 362–363, 364, 368, 375, 377, 378, 379

Last Analysis, The (Bellow), **I:** 152, 160, 161; **Retro. Supp. II:** 26

Last and Lost Poems of Delmore Schwartz (Phillips, ed.), **Supp. II Part 2:** 661, 665

Last Beautiful Days of Autumn, The (Nichols), **Supp. XIII:** 254, 255, 267, 269

Last Blue (Stern), **Supp. IX: 299–300**

Last Carousel, The (Algren), **Supp. IX:** 16

"Last Day in the Field, The" (Gordon), **II:** 200

"Last Day of the Last Furlough" (Salinger), **III:** 552–553

"Last Days of Alice" (Tate), **IV:** 129

"Last Days of August, The" (Nye), **Supp. XIII:** 284

"Last Days of John Brown, The" (Thoreau), **IV:** 185

Last Days of Louisiana Red, The (Reed), **Supp. X:** 240, **248–249**

Last Decade, The (Trilling), **Supp. III Part 2:** 493, 499

"Last Demon, The" (Singer), **IV:** 15, 21

Last Exit to Brooklyn (Selby), **Supp. III Part 1:** 125

Last Flower, The (Thurber), **Supp. I**

Part 2: 610

"Last Frontier" (McCarriston), **Supp. XIV:** 272

Last Gentleman, The (Percy), **Supp. III Part 1:** 383–388, 392–393

"Last Good Country, The" (Hemingway), **II:** 258–259

Last Good Time, The (Bausch), **Supp. VII:** 45–46

"Last Hiding Places of Snow, The" (Kinnell), **Supp. III Part 1:** 252

"Last Hours, The" (Dunn), **Supp. XI:** 141

Last Husband and Other Stories, The (Humphrey), **Supp. IX:** 94

Last Jew in America, The (Fiedler), **Supp. XIII:** 103

"Last Jew in America, The" (Fiedler), **Supp. XIII:** 103

Last Laugh, Mr. Moto (Marquand), **III:** 57

"Last Leaf, The" (Holmes), **Supp. I Part 1:** 302, 309

"Last Leaf, The" (Porter), **III:** 444

"Last Look at the Lilacs" (Stevens), **IV:** 74

"Last May" (Dixon), **Supp. XII: 143**

"Last Mohican, The" (Malamud), **Supp. I Part 2:** 437–438, 450, 451

"Lastness" (Kinnell), **Supp. III Part 1:** 248–249

"Last Night" (Olds), **Supp. X:** 212

"Last Night at Tía's" (Alvarez), **Supp. VII:** 5

Last Night of Summer, The (Caldwell), **I:** 292–293

Last of Mr. Norris, The (Isherwood), **Supp. XIV:** 161

"Last of the Brooding Miserables, The" (Karr), **Supp. XI:** 250

"Last of the Caddoes, The" (Humphrey), **Supp. IX:** 101

"Last of the Legions, The" (Benét), **Supp. XI:** 56, 57

Last of the Mohicans, The (Cooper), **I:** 341, 342, 349

Last of the Red Hot Lovers (Simon), **Supp. IV Part 2:** 575, 583, 589

"Last of the Valerii, The" (James), **II:** 327; **Retro. Supp. I:** 218

"Last One, The" (Merwin), **Supp. III Part 1:** 355

Last Picture Show, The (film), **Supp. V:** 223, 226

Last Picture Show, The (McMurtry), **Supp. V:** 220, 222–223, 233

Last Puritan, The (Santayana), **III:** 64, 600, 604, 607, 612, 615–617

"Last Ride Together, The" (Browning), **I:** 468

"Last River, The" (Kinnell), **Supp. III Part 1:** 236

Last Song, The (Harjo), **Supp. XII:** 218

"Last Song for the Mend-It Shop" (Nye), **Supp. XIII:** 283

"Last Tango in Fresno" (Salinas), **Supp. XIII:** 318

Last Tycoon, The: An Unfinished Novel (Fitzgerald), **II:** 84, 98; **Retro. Supp. I:** 109, 114, **114–115; Retro. Supp. II:** 337; **Supp. IV Part 1:** 203; **Supp. IX:** 63; **Supp. XII:** 173; **Supp. XIII:** 170

"Last WASP in the World, The" (Fiedler), **Supp. XIII:** 103

Last Watch of the Night: Essays Too Personal and Otherwise (Monette), **Supp. X:** 147, 148, 153, **157–159**

Last Word, The: Letters between Marcia Nardi and William Carlos Williams (O'Neil, ed.), **Retro. Supp. I:** 427

"Last Words" (Levine), **Supp. V:** 190

"Last Words" (Olds), **Supp. X:** 210

Last Worthless Evening, The (Dubus), **Supp. VII:** 87–88

"Las Vegas (What?) Las Vegas (Can't Hear You! Too Noisy) Las Vegas! ! ! !" (Wolfe), **Supp. III Part 2:** 572

"Late" (Bogan), **Supp. III Part 1:** 53

"Late Air" (Bishop), **Supp. I Part 1:** 89

"Late Autumn" (Sarton), **Supp. VIII:** 261

Late Child, The (McMurtry), **Supp. V:** 231

"Late Conversation" (Doty), **Supp. XI:** 122

"Late Encounter with the Enemy, A" (O'Connor), **III:** 345; **Retro. Supp. II:** 232

Late Fire, Late Snow (Francis), **Supp. IX: 89–90**

Late George Apley, The (Marquand), **II:** 482–483; **III:** 50, 51, 52, 56–57, 58, 62–64, 65, 66

Late George Apley, The (Marquand and Kaufman), **III:** 62

Late Hour, The (Strand), **Supp. IV Part 2:** 620, 629–630

"Lately, at Night" (Kumin), **Supp. IV Part 2:** 442

"Late Moon" (Levine), **Supp. V:** 186

"Late Night Ode" (McClatchy), **Supp. XII:** 262–263

Later (Creeley), **Supp. IV Part 1:** 153, 156, 157

Later Life (Gurney), **Supp. V:** 103, 105

La Terre (Zola), **III:** 316, 322

Later the Same Day (Paley), **Supp. VI:** 218

Late Settings (Merrill), **Supp. III Part 1:** 336

"Late Sidney Lanier, The" (Stedman), **Supp. I Part 1:** 373

"Late Snow & Lumber Strike of the Summer of Fifty-Four, The" (Snyder), **Supp. VIII:** 294

"Latest Freed Man, The" (Stevens), **Retro. Supp. I:** 306

"Latest Injury, The" (Olds), **Supp. X:** 209

Latest Literary Essays and Addresses (Lowell), **Supp. I Part 2:** 407

"Late Subterfuge" (Warren), **IV:** 257

"Late Supper, A" (Jewett), **Retro. Supp. II:** 137

"Late Victorians" (Rodriguez), **Supp. XIV:** 303–304

"Late Walk, A" (Frost), **II:** 153; **Retro. Supp. I:** 127

Latham, Edyth, **I:** 289

Lathrop, George Parsons, **Supp. I Part 1:** 365

Lathrop, H. B., **Supp. III Part 2:** 612

Lathrop, Julia, **Supp. I Part 1:** 5

Latière de Trianon, La (Wekerlin), **II:** 515

"La Tigresse" (Van Vechten), **Supp. II Part 2:** 735, 738

Latimer, Hugh, **II:** 15

Latimer, Margery, **Supp. IX:** 320

La Traviata (Verdi), **III:** 139

"Latter-Day Warnings" (Holmes), **Supp. I Part 1:** 307

La Turista (Shepard), **Supp. III Part 2:** 440

Lauber, John, **Supp. XIII:** 21

Laud, Archbishop, **II:** 158

"Lauds" (Auden), **Supp. II Part 1:** 23

"Laughing Man, The" (Salinger), **III:** 559

Laughing to Keep From Crying (Hughes), **Supp. I Part 1:** 329–330

Laughlin, J. Laurence, **Supp. I Part 2:** 641

Laughlin, James, **III:** 171; **Retro. Supp. I:** 423, 424, 428, 430, 431; **Supp. VIII:** 195

Laughlin, Jay, **Supp. II Part 1:** 94

Laughter in the Dark (Nabokov), **III:** 255–258; **Retro. Supp. I:** 270

Laughter on the 23rd Floor (Simon), **Supp. IV Part 2:** 575, 576, 588, 591–592

"Launcelot" (Lewis), **II:** 439–440

"Laura Dailey's Story" (Bogan), **Supp. III Part 1:** 52

Laurel, Stan, **Supp. I Part 2:** 607; **Supp. IV Part 2:** 574

Laurel and Hardy Go to Heaven (Auster), **Supp. XII:** 21

Laurence, Dan H., **II:** 338–339

Laurens, John, **Supp. I Part 2:** 509

Lautréamont, Comte de, **III:** 174

Law, John, **Supp. XI:** 307

Lawd Today (Wright), **IV:** 478, 492

Law for the Lion, A (Auchincloss), **Supp. I Part 1:** 25

"Law Lane" (Jewett), **II:** 407

"Law of Nature and the Dream of Man, The: Ruminations of the Art of Fiction" (Stegner), **Supp. IV Part 2:** 604

Lawrence, D. H., **I:** 291, 336, 377, 522, 523; **II:** 78, 84, 98, 102, 264, 517, 523, 532, 594, 595; **III:** 27, 33, 40, 44, 46, 172, 173, 174, 178, 184, 229, 261, 423, 429, 458, 546–547; **IV:** 138, 339, 342, 351, 380; **Retro. Supp. I:** 7, 18, 203, 204, 421; **Retro. Supp. II:** 68; **Supp. I Part 1:** 227, 230, 243, 255, 257, 258, 263, 329; **Supp. I Part 2:** 546, 613, 728; **Supp. II Part 1:** 1, 9, 20, 89; **Supp. IV Part 1:** 81; **Supp. VIII:** 237; **Supp. X:** 137, 193, 194; **Supp. XII:** 172; **Supp. XIV:** 310

Lawrence, Rhoda, **Supp. I Part 1:** 45

Lawrence, Seymour, **Supp. IX:** 107; **Supp. XI:** 335, 346, 348

Lawrence, T. E., **Supp. XIV:** 159

Lawrence of Arabia (Aldington), **Supp. I Part 1:** 259

Lawrence of Arabia (film), **Supp. I Part 1:** 67

Laws (Plato), **Supp. IV Part 1:** 391

Laws of Ice, The (Price), **Supp. VI:** 264

Lawson, John Howard, **I:** 479, 482

Lawton Girl, The (Frederic), **II:** 132–133, 144

Layachi, Larbi (Driss ben Hamed Charhadi), **Supp. IV Part 1:** 92, 93

Layard, John, **Supp. XIV:** 160

Lay Down My Sword and Shield (Burke), **Supp. XIV:** 22, 25, 34

"Layers, The" (Kunitz), **Supp. III Part 1:** 260, 266–267

"Layers, The: Some Notes on 'The Abduction'" (Kunitz), **Supp. III Part 1:** 266

"Lay-mans Lamentation, The" (Taylor), **IV:** 162–163

Lay of the Land, The: Metaphor as Experience and History in American Life and Letters (Kolodny), **Supp. X:** 97

"Layover" (Hass), **Supp. VI:** 109

"Lay Preacher" (Dennie), **Supp. I Part 1:** 125

Layton, Irving, **Supp. XII:** 121

Lazarillo de Tormes (Mendoza), **III:** 182

Lazarus Laughed (O'Neill), **III:** 391, 395–396

Lazer, Hank, **Supp. IX:** 265

Lea, Luke, **IV:** 248

Leacock, Stephen, **Supp. IV Part 2:** 464

"LEADBELLY GIVES AN AUTOGRAPH" (Baraka), **Supp. II Part 1:** 49

Leaflets: Poems, 1965–1968 (Rich), **Supp. I Part 2:** 551, 556–557

"League of American Writers, The: Communist Organizational Activity among American Writers 1929–1942" (Wolfe), **Supp. III Part 2:** 568

League of Brightened Philistines and Other Papers, The (Farrell), **II:** 49

Leaning Forward (Paley), **Supp. VI:** 221

"Leaning Tower, The" (Porter), **III:** 442, 443, 446–447

Leaning Tower and Other Stories, The (Porter), **III:** 433, 442, 443–447

"Leap, The" (Dickey), **Supp. IV Part 1:** 182

"Leaping Up into Political Poetry" (Bly), **Supp. IV Part 1:** 61, 63

Leap Year (Cameron), **Supp. XII:** 79–80, 81, **85–86**, 88

Lear, Edward, **III:** 428, 536

Lear, Linda, **Supp. IX:** 19, 22, 25, 26

Learned Ladies, The (Molière; Wilbur, trans.), **Supp. III Part 2:** 560

"Learning a Dead Language" (Merwin), **Supp. III Part 1:** 345

Learning a Trade: A Craftsman's Notebooks, 1955–1997 (Price), **Supp. VI:** 254, 255, 267

Learning to Love: Exploring Solitude and Freedom (Merton), **Supp. VIII:** 200

"Learning to Read" (Harper), **Supp. II Part 1:** 201–202

Leary, Lewis, **III:** 478

Leary, Paris, **Supp. IV Part 1:** 176

Leary, Timothy, **Supp. X:** 265; **Supp. XIV:** 150

Least Heat Moon, William, **Supp. V:** 169

Leather-Stocking Tales, The (Cooper), **I:** 335

Leatherwood God, The (Howells), **II:** 276, 277, 288

"Leaves" (Updike), **Retro. Supp. I:**

323, 329, 335

Leaves and Ashes (Haines), **Supp. XII:** 206

Leaves from the Notebook of a Tamed Cynic (Niebuhr), **III:** 293

Leaves of Grass (Whitman), **II:** 8; **IV:** 331, 332, 333, 334, 335, 336, 340, 341–342, 348, 350, 405, 464; **Retro. Supp. I:** 387, 388, 389, 390, **392–395,** 406, 407, 408; **Retro. Supp. II:** 93; **Supp. I Part 1:** 365; **Supp. I Part 2:** 416, 579; **Supp. III Part 1:** 156; **Supp. V:** 170; **Supp. VIII:** 275; **Supp. IX:** 265; **Supp. X:** 120; **Supp. XIV:** 334

"Leaves of Grass" (Whitman), **IV:** 463

Leaves of Grass (1856) (Whitman), **Retro. Supp. I:** 399–402

Leaves of Grass (1860) (Whitman), **Retro. Supp. I:** 402–405

Leaves of the Tree, The (Masters), **Supp. I Part 2:** 460

"Leaving" (Hogan), **Supp. IV Part 1:** 400

"Leaving" (Wilbur), **Supp. III Part 2:** 563

Leaving a Doll's House: A Memoir (C. Bloom), **Retro. Supp. II:** 281

Leaving Another Kingdom: Selected Poems (Stern), **Supp. IX:** 296

Leaving Cheyenne (McMurtry), **Supp. V:** 220, 221–222, 224, 229

"Leaving the Island" (Olds), **Supp. X:** 214

"Leaving the Yellow House" (Bellow), **Retro. Supp. II:** 27, 32

"Leaving Town" (Kenyon), **Supp. VII:** 163

Leavis, F. R., **I:** 522; **III:** 462–463, 475, 478; **Retro. Supp. I:** 67; **Retro. Supp. II:** 243; **Supp. I Part 2:** 536; **Supp. VIII:** 234, 236, 245

"Leavis-Snow Controversy, The" (Trilling), **Supp. III Part 2:** 512

Leavitt, David, **Supp. VIII:** 88

Le Braz, Anatole, **Supp. XIII:** 253

Lecker, Robert, **Supp. XIII:** 21

LeClair, Thomas, **Supp. IV Part 1:** 286

LeClair, Tom, **Supp. V:** 53; **Supp. XII:** 152

Le Conte, Joseph, **II:** 479; **III:** 227–228

"Lecture, The" (Singer), **IV:** 21

"LECTURE PAST DEAD CATS" (Baraka), **Supp. II Part 1:** 52

Lectures in America (Stein), **IV:** 27, 32, 33, 35, 36, 41, 42

"Lectures on Poetry" (Bryant), **Supp. I Part 1:** 159, 161

Lectures on Rhetoric (Blair), **II:** 8

"Leda and the Swan" (Yeats), **III:** 347; **Supp. IX:** 52

Ledger (Fitzgerald), **Retro. Supp. I:** 109, 110

Lee (Masters), **Supp. I Part 2:** 471

Lee, Don, **Supp. XII:** 295

Lee, Don L. *See* Madhubuti, Haki R.

Lee, Gypsy Rose, **II:** 586; **III:** 161; **Supp. IV Part 1:** 84

Lee, Harper, **Supp. VIII:** 113–131

Lee, James W., **Supp. IX:** 94, 97, 109

Lee, James Ward, **Supp. VIII:** 57

Lee, Robert E., **II:** 150, 206; **IV:** 126; **Supp. I Part 2:** 471, 486

Lee, Samuel, **IV:** 158

Lee, Spike, **Retro. Supp. II:** 12; **Supp. XI:** 19; **Supp. XIII:** 179, 186

Lee, Virginia Chin-lan, **Supp. X:** 291

Leeds, Barry, **Retro. Supp. II:** 204

Leeds, Daniel, **II:** 110

Leeds, Titan, **II:** 110, 111

Leeming, David, **Retro. Supp. II:** 4, 10

"Lees of Happiness, The" (Fitzgerald), **II:** 88

Left Out in the Rain: New Poems 1947–1985 (Snyder), **Supp. VIII:** 305

"Legacy" (Dunn), **Supp. XI:** 148

"Legacy" (Komunyakaa), **Supp. XIII:** 132

"Legacy of Aldo Leopold, The" (Stegner), **Supp. XIV:** 193

Legacy of Fear, A (Farrell), **II:** 39

"Legacy of the Ancestral Arts, The" (Locke), **Supp. XIV:** 201

Legacy of the Civil War, The: Meditations on the Centennial (Warren), **IV:** 236

"Legal Alien" (Mora), **Supp. XIII:** 215

"Legal Tender Act, The" (Adams), **I:** 5

Légende de la mort, La (Le Braz), **Supp. XIII:** 253

"Legend of Duluoz, The" (Kerouac), **Supp. III Part 1:** 218, 226, 227, 229

"Legend of Lillian Hellman, The" (Kazin), **Supp. I Part 1:** 297

"Legend of Monte del Diablo, The" (Harte), **Supp. II Part 1:** 339

"Legend of Paper Plates, The" (Haines), **Supp. XII:** 204

"Legend of Sammtstadt, A" (Harte), **Supp. II Part 1:** 355

"Legend of Sleepy Hollow, The" (Irving), **II:** 306–308

Legends (Lowell), **II:** 525–526

Legends of New England (Whittier), **Supp. I Part 2:** 684, 692

Legends of the Fall (Harrison), **Supp.**

VIII: 38, 39, **45–46,** 48

Legends of the West (Hall), **II:** 313

Léger, Fernand, **Retro. Supp. I:** 292

Legge, James, **III:** 472

Leggett, William, **Supp. I Part 1:** 157

"Legion, The" (Karr), **Supp. XI:** 243

Legs (Kennedy), **Supp. VII:** 133, 134, 138–142, 143, 151

Le Guin, Ursula K., **Supp. IV Part 1:** 333

Lehan, Richard, **Retro. Supp. II:** 104

Lehman, David, **Supp. IX:** 161; **Supp. XIII:** 130

Lehmann, John, **Retro. Supp. II:** 243; **Supp. XIV:** 158, 159

Lehmann, Paul, **III:** 311

Lehmann-Haupt, Christopher, **Retro. Supp. II:** 291; **Supp. IV Part 1:** 205, 209, 306; **Supp. IX:** 95, 103

Leibling, A. J., **Supp. XIV:** 112

Leibniz, Gottfried Wilhelm von, **II:** 103; **III:** 428

Leibowitz, Herbert A., **I:** 386

Leich, Roland, **Supp. XIV:** 123

Leithauser, Brad, **Retro. Supp. I:** 133

Leitz, Robert, **Supp. XIV:** 62

Leivick, H., **IV:** 6

Lekachman, Robert, **Supp. I Part 2:** 648

Leland, Charles, **Supp. II Part 1:** 193

Leland, Charles Godfrey, **I:** 257

Lem, Stanislaw, **Supp. IV Part 1:** 103

"Le marais du cygne" (Whittier), **Supp. I Part 2:** 687

Lemay, Harding, **Supp. VIII:** 125; **Supp. IX:** 98

Lemercier, Eugène, **Retro. Supp. I:** 299

Le Morte D'Arthur Notes (Gardner), **Supp. VI:** 65, 66

Lenin, V. I., **I:** 366, 439, 440; **III:** 14–15, 262, 475; **IV:** 429, 436, 443–444; **Supp. I Part 2:** 647

"Lenore" (Poe), **III:** 411

"Lenox Avenue: Midnight" (Hughes), **Retro. Supp. I:** 198

Leonard, Elmore, **Supp. IV Part 1:** 356; **Supp. X:** 5; **Supp. XIV:** 26

Leonard, John, **Supp. IV Part 1:** 24; **Supp. IV Part 2:** 474; **Supp. V:** 164, 223–224; **Supp. XI:** 13

Leonardo da Vinci, **Supp. XII:** 44

Leontiev, Constantine, **Supp. XIV:** 98

Leopard, The (Lampedusa), **Supp. XII:** 13–14

Leopardi, Giacomo, **II:** 543

"Leopard Man's Story, The" (London), **II:** 475

Leopard's Mouth Is Dry and Cold Inside, The (Levis), **Supp. XI:** 258

Leopold, Aldo, **Supp. V:** 202; **Supp. X:** 108; **Supp. XIV:177–194**

"Leper's Bell, the" (Komunyakaa), **Supp. XIII:** 118

Lerman, Leo, **Supp. X:** 188

Lerner, Max, **III:** 60; **Supp. I Part 2:** 629, 630, 631, 647, 650, 654

"Lesbos" (Plath), **Retro. Supp. II:** 254

Lesesne, Teri, **Supp. XIII:** 277

Leskov, Nikolai, **IV:** 299

Leslie, Alfred, **Supp. XII:** 127

Les Misérables (Hugo), **II:** 179; **Supp. I Part 1:** 280

Lesser, Wendy, **Supp. IV Part 2:** 453; **Supp. XII:** 297

Lessing, Gotthold, **Supp. I Part 2:** 422

"Lesson, The" (Bambara), **Supp. XI:** 5–6

"Lesson, The" (Dunbar), **Supp. II Part 1:** 199

"Lesson, The" (Olsen), **Supp. XIII:** 297

"Lesson of the Master, The" (James), **Retro. Supp. I:** 227

Lesson of the Masters: An Anthology of the Novel from Cervantes to Hemingway (Cowley-Hugo, ed.), **Supp. II Part 1:** 140

"Lesson on Concealment, A" (Brown), **Supp. I Part 1:** 133

"Lessons" (Epstein), **Supp. XII:** 163

"Lessons of the Body" (Simpson), **Supp. IX:** 267

Less than One (Brodsky), **Supp. VIII:** 22, 29–31

Lester, Jerry, **Supp. IV Part 2:** 574

Le Style Apollinaire (Zukofsky), **Supp. III Part 2:** 616

Le Sueur, Meridel, **Supp. V:** 113, 130; **Supp. XII:** 217

"Let America Be America Again" (Hughes), **Retro. Supp. I:** 202; **Supp. I Part 1:** 331

Let Evening Come (Kenyon), **Supp. VII:** 160, 169–171

Lethem, Jonathan, **Supp. IX:** 122

Let It Come Down (Bowles), **Supp. IV Part 1:** 87

"Let Me Be" (Levine), **Supp. V:** 181, 189

"Let Me Begin Again" (Levine), **Supp. V:** 181, 189

"Let No Charitable Hope" (Wylie), **Supp. I Part 2:** 713–714, 729

"Let one Eye his watches keep/While the Other Eye doth sleep" (Fletcher), **Supp. IV Part 2:** 621

"Letter . . ." (Whittier), **Supp. I Part 2:** 687

"Letter, A" (Bogan), **Supp. III Part 1:** 54

"Letter, May 2, 1959" (Olson), **Supp. II Part 2:** 579, 580

"Letter, Much Too Late" (Stegner), **Supp. IV Part 2:** 613

"Letter, The" (Malamud), **Supp. I Part 2:** 435–436

"Letter about Money, Love, or Other Comfort, If Any, The" (Warren), **IV:** 245

Letter Addressed to the People of Piedmont, on the Advantages of the French Revolution, and the Necessity of Adopting Its Principles in Italy, A (Barlow), **Supp. II Part 1:** 80, 81

"Letter for Marion, A" (McGrath), **Supp. X:** 116

"Letter from Aldermaston" (Merwin), **Supp. III Part 1:** 347

"Letter from a Region in My Mind" (Baldwin). *See* "Down at the Cross"

Letter from Li Po, A (Aiken), **I:** 68

"Letter from 'Manhattan'" (Didion), **Supp. IV Part 1:** 205

Letter from the End of the Twentieth Century (Harjo), **Supp. XII:** 223

"Letter from the End of the Twentieth Century" (Harjo), **Supp. XII:** 227

"Letter on Céline" (Kerouac), **Supp. III Part 1:** 232

Letters (Cato), **II:** 114

Letters (Landor), **Supp. I Part 2:** 422

Letters (White), **Supp. I Part 2:** 651, 653, 675, 680

Letters (Wolfe), **IV:** 462

Letters and Leadership (Brooks), **I:** 228, 240, 245, 246

"Letters for the Dead" (Levine), **Supp. V:** 186

Letters from an American Farmer (Crèvecoeur), **Supp. I Part 1:** 227–251

Letters from Maine (Sarton), **Supp. VIII: 261**

"Letters from Maine" (Sarton), **Supp. VIII:** 261

"Letters from My Father" (R. O. Butler), **Supp. XII:** 71

Letters from the Earth (Twain), **IV:** 209

Letters from the East (Bryant), **Supp. I Part 1:** 158

"Letters from the Ming Dynasty" (Brodsky), **Supp. VIII:** 28

Letters of a Traveller (Bryant), **Supp. I Part 1:** 158

Letters of a Traveller, Second Series (Bryant), **Supp. I Part 1:** 158

Letters of Emily Dickinson, The

(Johnson and Ward, eds.), **I:** 470; **Retro. Supp. I:** 28

Letters of William James (Henry James, ed.), **II:** 362

Letters on Various Interesting and Important Subjects . . . (Freneau), **Supp. II Part 1:** 272

Letters to a Niece (Adams), **I:** 22

Letters to a Young Poet (Rilke), **Supp. XIII:** 74

"Letters to Dead Imagists" (Sandburg), **I:** 421

"Letters Written on a Ferry While Crossing Long Island Sound" (Sexton), **Supp. II Part 2:** 683

"Letter to Abbé Raynal" (Paine), **Supp. I Part 2:** 510

Letter to a Man in the Fire: Does God Exist or Does He Care? (Price), **Supp. VI:** 267–268

"Letter to American Teachers of History, A" (Adams), **I:** 19

Letter to an Imaginary Friend (McGrath), **Supp. X:** 111, 112–113, 116, **119–125**

"Letter to a Young Contributor" (Higginson), **Retro. Supp. I:** 31

"Letter to a Young Writer" (Price), **Supp. VI:** 267

"Letter to Bell from Missoula" (Hugo), **Supp. VI:** 142–143

"Letter to E. Franklin Frazier" (Baraka), **Supp. II Part 1:** 49

"Letter to Elaine Feinstein" (Olson), **Supp. II Part 2:** 561

"Letter to Freddy" (music) (Bowles), **Supp. IV Part 1:** 82

"Letter to Garber from Skye" (Hugo), **Supp. VI:** 146

"Letter to George Washington" (Paine), **Supp. I Part 2:** 517

"Letter to His Brother" (Berryman), **I:** 172, 173

Letter to His Countrymen, A (Cooper), **I:** 346, 347, 349

"Letter to Kizer from Seattle" (Hugo), **Supp. VI:** 142

Letter to Lord Byron (Auden), **Supp. II Part 1:** 11

"Letter to Lord Byron" (Mumford), **Supp. II Part 2:** 494

"Letter to Matthews from Barton Street Flats" (Hugo), **Supp. VI:** 133

"Letter to Minnesota" (Dunn), **Supp. XI:** 146

"Letter to Mr." (Poe), **III:** 411

"Letter Too Late to Vallejo" (Salinas), **Supp. XIII:** 313, 324

"Letter to Sister Madeline from Iowa City" (Hugo), **Supp. VI:** 142–143

"Letter to Soto" (Salinas), **Supp. XIII:** 325

"Letter to the Lady of the House" (Bausch), **Supp. VII:** 48

"Letter to the Rising Generation, A" (Comer), **I:** 214

"Letter to Walt Whitman" (Doty), **Supp. XI:** 135–136

"Letter to Wendell Berry, A" (Stegner), **Supp. IV Part 2:** 600

"Letter Writer, The" (Singer), **IV:** 20–21

"Let the Air Circulate" (Clampitt), **Supp. IX:** 45

"Letting Down of the Hair, The" (Sexton), **Supp. II Part 2:** 692

Letting Go (Roth), **Retro. Supp. II:** 282, 283; **Supp. III Part 2:** 403, 404, 409–412

"Letting the Puma Go" (Dunn), **Supp. XI:** 149

"Lettres d'un Soldat" (Stevens), **Retro. Supp. I:** 299

Let Us Go into the Starry Night (Shanley), **Supp. XIV:** 317

Let Us Now Praise Famous Men (Agee and Evans), **I:** 25, 27, 35, 36–39, 42, 45, 293

Let Your Mind Alone! (Thurber), **Supp. I Part 2:** 608

Leutze, Emanuel, **Supp. X:** 307

Levels of the Game (McPhee), **Supp. III Part 1:** 292, 294, 301

Levertov, Denise, **Retro. Supp. I:** 411; **Supp. III Part 1: 271–287; Supp. III Part 2:** 541; **Supp. IV Part 1:** 325; **Supp. VIII:** 38, 39

Levi, Primo, **Supp. X:** 149

Leviathan (Auster), **Supp. XII:** 27, **33–34**

"Leviathan" (Lowell), **II:** 537, 538

"Leviathan" (Merwin), **Supp. III Part 1:** 345

Levin, Harry, **Supp. I Part 2:** 647

Levin, Jennifer, **Supp. X:** 305

Levine, Ellen, **Supp. V:** 4; **Supp. XI:** 178

Levine, Paul, **Supp. IV Part 1:** 221, 224

Levine, Philip, **Supp. III Part 2:** 541; **Supp. V: 177–197,** 337; **Supp. IX:** 293; **Supp. XI:** 123, 257, 259, 267, 271, 315; **Supp. XIII:** 312

Levine, Rosalind, **Supp. XII:** 123

Levine, Sherry, **Supp. XII:** 4

Le Violde Lucréce (Obey), **IV:** 356

Levis, Larry, **Supp. V:** 180; **Supp. IX:** 299; **Supp. XI: 257–274; Supp. XIII:** 312

Lévi-Strauss, Claude, **Supp. I Part 2:** 636; **Supp. IV Part 1:** 45; **Supp. IV Part 2:** 490

Levitation: Five Fictions (Ozick), **Supp. V:** 268–270

Levy, Alan, **Supp. IV Part 2:** 574, 589

Levy, G. Rachel, **Supp. I Part 2:** 567

Lévy-Bruhl, Lucien, **Retro. Supp. I:** 57

Levy Mayer and the New Industrial Era (Masters), **Supp. I Part 2:** 473

Lewes, George Henry, **II:** 569

Lewin, Albert, **Supp. XIV:** 279, 293

Lewis, C. Day, **III:** 527

Lewis, Dr. Claude, **II:** 442

Lewis, Edith, **I:** 313; **Retro. Supp. I:** 19, 21, 22

Lewis, Edwin, J., **II:** 439, 442

Lewis, Jerry, **Supp. IV Part 2:** 575; **Supp. X:** 172

Lewis, John L., **I:** 493

Lewis, Lilburn, **IV:** 243

Lewis, Lorene, **Supp. IV Part 2:** 596, 597

Lewis, Lucy, **IV:** 243

Lewis, Maggie, **Supp. V:** 23

Lewis, Meriwether, **II:** 217; **III:** 14; **IV:** 179, 243, 283

Lewis, Merrill, **Supp. IV Part 2:** 596, 597

Lewis, Michael, **II:** 451, 452

Lewis, Mrs. Sinclair (Dorothy Thompson), **II:** 449–450, 451, 453

Lewis, Mrs. Sinclair (Grace Livingston Hegger), **II:** 441

Lewis, R. W. B., **I:** 386, 561; **II:** 457–458; **Retro. Supp. I:** 362, 367; **Supp. I Part 1:** 233; **Supp. XIII:** 93

Lewis, Robert Q., **Supp. IV Part 2:** 574

Lewis, Sinclair, **I:** 116, 212, 348, 355, 362, 374, 378, 487, 495; **II:** 27, 34, 74, 79, 271, 277, 306, **439–461,** 474; **III:** 28, 40, 51, 60, 61, 63–64, 66, 70, 71, 106, 394, 462, 572, 606; **IV:** 53, 326, 366, 455, 468, 475, 482; **Retro. Supp. I:** 332; **Retro. Supp. II:** 95, 108, 197, 322; **Supp. I Part 2:** 378, 613, 709; **Supp. IV Part 2:** 678; **Supp. V:** 278; **Supp. IX:** 308; **Supp. X:** 137

Lewis, Wyndham, **III:** 458, 462, 465, 470; **Retro. Supp. I:** 59, 170, 292; **Supp. III Part 2:** 617

Lexicon Tetraglotton (Howell), **II:** 111

"Leyenda" (Mora), **Supp. XIII:** 214

Leyte (Morison), **Supp. I Part 2:** 491

"Liar, The" (Baraka), **Supp. II Part 1:** 36

"Liars, The" (Sandburg), **III:** 586

Liars' Club, The: A Memoir (Karr), **Supp. XI:** 239, 240, 241, 242, **244–248,** 252, 254

Liars in Love (Yates), **Supp. XI:** 348, 349

Libation Bearers, The (Aeschylus), **III:** 398; **Supp. IX:** 103

Libby, Anthony, **Supp. XIII:** 87

Libera, Padre, **II:** 278

Liberal Imagination, The (Trilling), **III:** 308; **Retro. Supp. I:** 97, 216; **Supp. II Part 1:** 146; **Supp. III Part 2:** 495, 498, 501–504

"Liberation" (Winters), **Supp. II Part 2:** 791

Liber Brunenesis (yearbook), **IV:** 286

Liberties, The (Howe), **Supp. IV Part 2:** 426–428, 430, 432

Liberty Jones (play), **Supp. IV Part 1:** 83

"Liberty Tree" (Paine), **Supp. I Part 2:** 505

Libra (DeLillo), **Supp. VI:** 2, **4, 5,** 6, **7,** 9, 10, 12, 13, 14, 16

Library for Juana, A (Mora), **Supp. XIII:** 218

Library of America, **Retro. Supp. I:** 2

"Library of Law, A" (MacLeish), **III:** 4

Lice, The (Merwin), **Supp. III Part 1:** 339, 341–342, 346, 348, 349, 355

Lichtenberg, Georg Christoph, **Supp. XIV:** 339

Lichtenstein, Roy, **Supp. I Part 2:** 665

"Liddy's Orange" (Olds), **Supp. X:** 209

Lieberman, Laurence, **Supp. XI:** 323–324

Liebestod (Wagner), **I:** 284, 395

Liebling, A. J., **IV:** 290; **Supp. VIII:** 151

Lie Down in Darkness (Styron), **IV:** 98, 99, 100–104, 105, 111; **Supp. XI:** 343

Lie of the Mind, A (Shepard), **Supp. III Part 2:** 433, 435, 441, 447–449

"Lies" (Haines), **Supp. XII:** 204

Lies Like Truth (Clurman), **IV:** 385

Lieutenant, The (Dubus), **Supp. VII:** 78

"Life" (Wharton), **Retro. Supp. I:** 372

Life along the Passaic River (W. C. Williams), **Retro. Supp. I:** 423

Life Among the Savages (Jackson), **Supp. IX:** 115, **125**

Life and Gabriella (Glasgow), **II:** 175, 176, 182–183, 184, 189

"Life and I" (Wharton), **Retro. Supp. I:** 360, 361, 362

"Life and Letters" (Epstein), **Supp.**

XIV: 104–105

Life and Letters of Harrison Gray Otis, Federalist, 1765–1848, The (Morison), **Supp. I Part 2:** 480–481

Life and Letters of Sir Henry Wotton (L. P. Smith), **Supp. XIV:** 340–341

Life and Times of Frederick Douglass, Written by Himself, The (Douglass), **Supp. III Part 1:** 155, 159–163

Life and Writings of Horace McCoy, The (Wolfson), **Supp. XIII:** 172, 174

"Life as a Visionary Spirit" (Eberhart), **I:** 540, 541

"Life at Angelo's, A" (Benét), **Supp. XI:** 53

Life at Happy Knoll (Marquand), **III:** 50, 61

Life Before Man (Atwood), **Supp. XIII:** 24–25

"Life Cycle of Common Man" (Nemerov), **III:** 278

"Lifecycle Stairmaster" (Karr), **Supp. XI:** 250

Life Estates (Hearon), **Supp. VIII:** 68–69

Life for Life's Sake (Aldington), **Supp. I Part 1:** 256

Life Full of Holes, A (Layachi), **Supp. IV Part 1:** 92

"Lifeguard" (Updike), **IV:** 226; **Retro. Supp. I:** 325

"Lifeguard, The" (Dickey), **Supp. IV Part 1:** 179–180

Life in the Clearings (Shields), **Supp. VII:** 313

"Life in the Country: A City Friend Asks, 'Is It Boring?'" (Paley), **Supp. VI:** 231

Life in the Forest (Levertov), **Supp. III Part 1:** 282–283

Life in the Iron Mills (Davis), **Supp. XIII:** 292, 295, 299, 305

Life in the Theatre, A (Mamet), **Supp. XIV:** 241, 255

Life Is a Miracle: An Essay Against Modern Superstition (Berry), **Supp. X:** 35

"Life Is Fine" (Hughes), **Supp. I Part 1:** 334, 338

"Life Is Motion" (Stevens), **IV:** 74

Life of Albert Gallatin, The (Adams), **I:** 6, 14

Life of Dryden (Johnson), **Retro. Supp. II:** 223

Life of Emily Dickinson, The (Sewall), **Retro. Supp. I:** 25

Life of Forms, The (Focillon), **IV:** 90

Life of Franklin Pierce (Hawthorne), **Retro. Supp. I:** 163

Life of George Cabot Lodge, The (Adams), **I:** 21

Life of George Washington (Irving), **II:** 314, 315–316

Life of Henry James (Edel), **Retro. Supp. I:** 224

"Life of Irony, The" (Bourne), **I:** 219

"Life of Lincoln West, The" (Brooks), **Supp. III Part 1:** 86

Life of Michelangelo (Grimm), **II:** 17

"Life of Nancy, The" (Jewett), **Retro. Supp. II:** 133, 144

Life of Oliver Goldsmith, The, with Selections from His Writings (Irving), **II:** 315

Life of Phips (Mather), **Supp. II Part 2:** 451, 452, 459

Life of Poetry, The (Rukeyser), **Supp. VI:** 271, 273, 275–276, 282, 283, 286

Life of Samuel Johnson (Boswell), **Supp. I Part 2:** 656

Life of Savage (Johnson), **Supp. I Part 2:** 523

Life of the Drama, The (Bentley), **IV:** 396

Life of the Right Reverend Joseph P. Machebeuf, The (Howlett), **Retro. Supp. I:** 17

Life of Thomas Paine, author of Rights of Men, With a Defence of his Writings (Chalmers), **Supp. I Part 2:** 514

Life of Thomas Paine, The (Cobbett), **Supp. I Part 2:** 517

"Life of Towne, The" (Carson), **Supp. XII:** 102

"Life on Beekman Place, A" (Naylor), **Supp. VIII:** 214

Life on the Hyphen: The Cuban-American Way (Firmat), **Supp. VIII:** 76; **Supp. XI:** 184

Life on the Mississippi (Twain), **I:** 209; **IV:** 198, 199; **Supp. I Part 2:** 440

"Life on the Rocks: The Galápagos" (Dillard), **Supp. VI:** 32

Life Story (Baker), **II:** 259

Life Studies (Lowell), **I:** 400; **II:** 384, 386, 543, 546–550, 551, 555; **Retro. Supp. II:** 180, 185, 186, 188, 189, 191; **Supp. I Part 2:** 543; **Supp. XI:** 240, 244, 250, 317; **Supp. XII:** 255; **Supp. XIV:** 15

"Life Studies" (Lowell), **Retro. Supp. II:** 188

"Life Styles in the Golden Land" (Didion), **Supp. IV Part 1:** 200

"Life That Is, The" (Bryant), **Supp. I Part 1:** 169

"Life Work" (Stafford), **Supp. XI:** 329–330

"Life You Save May Be Your Own, The" (O'Connor), **III:** 344, 350, 354; **Retro. Supp. II:** 229, 230, 233

"Lifting, The" (Olds), **Supp. X:** 210

"Ligeia" (Poe), **III:** 412, 414; **Retro. Supp. II:** 261, 270, 271, 275

Liggett, Walter W., **Supp. XIII:** 168

Light, James F., **IV:** 290; **Retro. Supp. II:** 325

Light around the Body, The (Bly), **Supp. IV Part 1:** 61–62, 62

"Light Comes Brighter, The" (Roethke), **III:** 529–530

"Light from Above" (Eberhart), **I:** 541

Light in August (Faulkner), **II:** 63–64, 65, 74; **IV:** 207; **Retro. Supp. I:** 82, 84, 85, 86, 89, 92; **Supp. XIV:** 12

"Light Man, A" (James), **II:** 322; **Retro. Supp. I:** 219

"Lightning" (Barthelme), **Supp. IV Part 1:** 53

"Lightning" (Oliver), **Supp. VII:** 235

"Lightning, The" (Swenson), **Supp. IV Part 2:** 645

"Lightning Rod Man, The" (Melville), **III:** 90

"Light of the World, The" (Hemingway), **II:** 249

"Lights in the Windows" (Nye), **Supp. XIII:** 280

Light Years (Salter), **Supp. IX:** 257–259

"LIKE, THIS IS WHAT I MEANT!" (Baraka), **Supp. II Part 1:** 59

"Like All the Other Nations" (Paley), **Supp. VI:** 220

"Like Decorations in a Nigger Cemetery" (Stevens), **IV:** 74, 79; **Retro. Supp. I:** 305

Like Ghosts of Eagles (Francis), **Supp. IX:** 86

"Like Life" (Moore), **Supp. X:** 163, 165, 172–173

Like Life: Stories (Moore), **Supp. X:** 163, 171–175, 177, 178

"Like Talk" (Mills), **Supp. XI:** 311

"Like the New Moon I Will Live My Life" (Bly), **Supp. IV Part 1:** 71

Li'l Abner (Capp), **IV:** 198

"Lilacs" (Lowell), **II:** 527

"Lilacs, The" (Wilbur), **Supp. III Part 2:** 557–558

"Lilacs for Ginsberg" (Stern), **Supp. IX:** 299

Lilith's Brood (O. Butler), **Supp. XIII:** 63

Lillabulero Press, **Supp. V:** 4, 5

Lillian Hellman (Adler), **Supp. I Part 1:** 297
Lillian Hellman (Falk), **Supp. I Part 1:** 297
Lillian Hellman: Playwright (Moody), **Supp. I Part 1:** 280
Lillo, George, **II:** 111, 112
"Lily Daw and the Three Ladies" (Welty), **IV:** 262
Lima, Agnes de, **I:** 231, 232
"Limbo: Altered States" (Karr), **Supp. XI:** 249–250
Lime Orchard Woman, The (Ríos), **Supp. IV Part 2:** 538, 547–550, 553
"Lime Orchard Woman, The" (Ríos), **Supp. IV Part 2:** 548
"Limits" (Emerson), **II:** 19
Lincoln, Abraham, **I:** 1, 4, 30; **II:** 8, 13, 135, 273, 555, 576; **III:** 576, 577, 580, 584, 587–590, 591; **IV:** 192, 195, 298, 347, 350, 444; **Supp. I Part 1:** 2, 8, 26, 309, 321; **Supp. I Part 2:** 379, 380, 382, 385, 390, 397, 399, 418, 424, 454, 456, 471, 472, 473, 474, 483, 579, 687; **Supp. VIII:** 108; **Supp. IX:** 15; **Supp. XIV:** 73
Lincoln: A Novel (Vidal), **Supp. IV Part 2:** 677, 684, 685, 688, 689–690, 691, 692
Lincoln, Kenneth, **Supp. IV Part 1:** 329; **Supp. IV Part 2:** 507
Lincoln, Mrs. Thomas (Nancy Hanks), **III:** 587
Lincoln: The Man (Masters), **Supp. I Part 2:** 471, 473–474
Lincoln, Thomas, **III:** 587
"Lincoln Relics, The" (Kunitz), **Supp. III Part 1:** 269
Lindbergh, Charles A., **I:** 482
"Linden Branch, The" (MacLeish), **III:** 19, 20
Linden Hills (Naylor), **Supp. VIII:** 214, 218, **219–223**
Linderman, Lawrence, **Supp. IV Part 2:** 579, 583, 585, 589
Lindsay, Howard, **III:** 284
Lindsay, John, **Supp. I Part 2:** 374
Lindsay, Mrs. Vachel (Elizabeth Connors), **Supp. I Part 2:** 398, 399, 473
Lindsay, Mrs. Vachel Thomas (Esther Catherine Frazee), **Supp. I Part 2:** 374, 375, 384–385, 398
Lindsay, Olive, **Supp. I Part 2:** 374, 375, 392
Lindsay, Vachel, **I:** 384; **II:** 263, 276, 530; **III:** 5, 505; **Retro. Supp. I:** 133; **Supp. I Part 1:** 324; **Supp. I Part 2: 374–403**, 454, 473, 474;

Supp. III Part 1: 63, 71
Lindsay, Vachel Thomas, **Supp. I Part 2:** 374, 375
Lindsey, David, **Supp. XIV:** 26
"Line, The" (Olds), **Supp. X:** 206
Lineage of Ragpickers, Songpluckers, Elegiasts, and Jewelers, A (Goldbarth), **Supp. XII:** 191
"Line of Least Resistance, The" (Wharton), **Retro. Supp. I:** 366
Line Out for a Walk, A: Familiar Essays (Epstein), **Supp. XIV:107**
"Liner Notes for the Poetically Unhep" (Hughes), **Retro. Supp. I:** 210
"Lines After Rereading T. S. Eliot" (Wright), **Supp. V:** 343
"Lines Composed a Few Miles Above Tintern Abbey" (Wordsworth), **Supp. III Part 1:** 12
"Lines for an Interment" (MacLeish), **III:** 15
"Lines for My Father" (Cullen), **Supp. IV Part 1:** 167
"Lines from Israel" (Lowell), **II:** 554
"Lines on Revisiting the Country" (Bryant), **Supp. I Part 1:** 164
"Lines Suggested by a Tennessee Song" (Agee), **I:** 28
"Line-Storm Song, A" (Frost), **Retro. Supp. I:** 127
"Lines Written at Port Royal" (Freneau), **Supp. II Part 1:** 264
Lingeman, Richard, **Supp. X:** 82
Linn, Elizabeth. *See* Brown, Mrs. Charles Brockden (Elizabeth Linn)
Linn, John Blair, **Supp. I Part 1:** 145
Linnaeus, Carolus, **II:** 6; **Supp. I Part 1:** 245
"Linnets" (Levis), **Supp. XI:** 260, 261
"Linoleum Roses" (Cisneros), **Supp. VII:** 63, 66
Linotte: 1914–1920 (Nin), **Supp. X:** 193, 196, 197
Linschoten, Hans, **II:** 362, 363, 364
"Lion and Honeycomb" (Nemerov), **III:** 275, 278, 280
Lion and the Archer, The (Hayden), **Supp. II Part 1:** 366, 367
Lion and the Honeycomb, The (Blackmur), **Supp. II Part 1:** 91
Lion Country (Buechner), **Supp. XII:** 52, 53
Lionel Lincoln (Cooper), **I:** 339, 342
"Lion for Real, The" (Ginsberg), **Supp. II Part 1:** 320
Lionhearted, The: A Story about the Jews of Medieval England (Reznikoff), **Supp. XIV:** 280, 289
Lion in the Garden (Meriweather and Millgate), **Retro. Supp. I:** 91

"Lionizing" (Poe), **III:** 411, 425
"Lions, Harts, and Leaping Does" (Powers), **III:** 356
Lions and Shadows: An Education in the Twenties (Isherwood), **Supp. XIV:** 158, 159, 160, 162
"Lions in Sweden" (Stevens), **IV:** 79–80
Lipman, William R., **Supp. XIII:** 170
Li Po, **Supp. XI:** 241; **Supp. XII:** 218
Lippmann, Walter, **I:** 48, 222–223, 225; **III:** 291, 600; **IV:** 429; **Supp. I Part 2:** 609, 643; **Supp. VIII:** 104
Lips Together, Teeth Apart (McNally), **Supp. XIII: 201–202**, 208, 209
Lipton, James, **Supp. IV Part 2:** 576, 577, 579, 583, 586, 588
Lipton, Lawrence, **Supp. IX:** 3
Lisbon Traviata, The (McNally), **Supp. XIII:** 198, **199–200**, 201, 204, 208
Lisicky, Paul, **Supp. XI:** 120, 131, 135
"Lisp, The" (Olds), **Supp. X:** 211
"Listeners and Readers: The Unforgetting of Vachel Lindsay" (Trombly), **Supp. I Part 2:** 403
"Listening" (Paley), **Supp. VI:** 218, 231, 232
"Listening" (Stafford), **Supp. XI:** 321, 322
"Listening to the Desert" (Henderson), **Supp. XIII:** 221–222
"Listening to the Mockingbird" (Woodard), **Supp. VIII:** 128
Listening to Your Life: Daily Meditations with Frederick Buechner (Buechner), **Supp. XII:** 53
Listen to the Desert/Oye al desierto (Mora), **Supp. XIII:** 221
"Listen to the People" (Benét), **Supp. XI:** 51–52
Liston, Sonny, **III:** 38, 42
Li T'ai-po, **II:** 526
"Litany" (Ashbery), **Supp. III Part 1:** 21–22, 25, 26
"Litany" (Sandburg), **III:** 593
"Litany for Dictatorships" (Benét), **Supp. XI:** 46, 58
"Litany for Survival, A" (Lorde), **Supp. XII:** 220
"Litany of the Dark People, The" (Cullen), **Supp. IV Part 1:** 170, 171
"Litany of the Heroes" (Lindsay), **Supp. I Part 2:** 397
"Litany of Washington Street, The" (Lindsay), **Supp. I Part 2:** 376, 398–399
Literary Anthropology (Trumpener and Nyce), **Retro. Supp. I:** 380
"Literary Blacks and Jews" (Ozick), **Supp. V:** 272

Literary Criticism: A Short History (Brooks and Wimsatt), **Supp. XIV:** 12

"Literary Criticism of Georg Lukács, The" (Sontag), **Supp. III Part 2:** 453

Literary Essays of Thomas Merton, The, **Supp. VIII:** 207

Literary Friends and Acquaintance (Howells), **Supp. I Part 1:** 318

"Literary Heritage of Tennyson, The" (Locke), **Supp. XIV:** 197

Literary History of the United States (Spiller et al., ed.), **Supp. I Part 1:** 104; **Supp. II Part 1:** 95

"Literary Importation" (Freneau), **Supp. II Part 1:** 264

"Literary Life of America, The" (Brooks), **I:** 245

Literary Outlaw: The Life and Times of William S. Burroughs (Morgan), **Supp. XIV:** 141

Literary Situation, The (Cowley), **Supp. II Part 1:** 135, 140, 144, 146, 147, 148

"Literary Worker's Polonius, The" (Wilson), **IV:** 431, 432

"Literature" (Emerson), **II:** 6

Literature and American Life (Boynton), **Supp. I Part 2:** 415

Literature and Life (Howells), **Supp. XIV:** 45–46

Literature and Morality (Farrell), **II:** 49

"Literature and Place: Varieties of Regional Experience" (Erisman), **Supp. VIII:** 126

"Literature as a Symptom" (Warren), **IV:** 237

"Literature of Exhaustion, The" (Barth), **Supp. IV Part 1:** 48

"Lithuanian Nocturne" (Brodsky), **Supp. VIII:** 29

"Lit Instructor" (Stafford), **Supp. XI:** 321

Littauer, Kenneth, **Retro. Supp. I:** 114

Little Big Man (Berger), **Supp. XII:** 171

Little Big Man (film), **Supp. X:** 124

Littlebird, Harold, **Supp. IV Part 2:** 499

Littlebird, Larry, **Supp. IV Part 2:** 499, 505

Little Birds: Erotica (Nin), **Supp. X:** 192, 195

"Little Brown Baby" (Dunbar), **Supp. II Part 1:** 206

"Little Brown Jug" (Baraka), **Supp. II Part 1:** 51

"Little Clown, My Heart" (Cisneros),

Supp. VII: 71

"Little Cosmic Dust Poem" (Haines), **Supp. XII:** 209–210

"Little Country Girl, A" (Chopin), **Retro. Supp. II:** 71

"Little Curtis" (Parker), **Supp. IX:** 193

Little Disturbances of Man, The (Paley), **Supp. VI:** 218

"Little Dog" (Hughes), **Supp. I Part 1:** 329

Little Dorrit (Dickens), **Supp. I Part 1:** 35

"Little Edward" (Stowe), **Supp. I Part 2:** 587

Little Essays Drawn from the Writings of George Santayana (L. P. Smith), **Supp. XIV:** 342

"Little Expressionless Animals" (Wallace), **Supp. X:** 305

"Little Fable" (Hay), **Supp. XIV:** 131

Littlefield, Catherine, **Supp. IX:** 58

Little Foxes, The (Hellman), **Supp. I Part 1:** 276, 278–279, 281, 283, 297

"Little Fred, the Canal Boy" (Stowe), **Supp. I Part 2:** 587

"Little French Mary" (Jewett), **II:** 400

Little Friend, Little Friend (Jarrell), **II:** 367, 372, 375–376

"Little Gidding" (Eliot), **I:** 582, 588; **II:** 539; **Retro. Supp. I:** 66

"Little Girl, My Stringbean, My Lovely Woman" (Sexton), **Supp. II Part 2:** 686

"Little Girl, The" (Paley), **Supp. VI:** 222, **228–229**

"Little Girl Tells a Story to a Lady, A" (Barnes), **Supp. III Part 1:** 36

"Little Goose Girl, The" (Grimm), **IV:** 266

Little Ham (Hughes), **Retro. Supp. I:** 203; **Supp. I Part 1:** 328, 339

Little Lady of the Big House, The (London), **II:** 481–482

"Little Lion Face" (Swenson), **Supp. IV Part 2:** 651

"Little Lobelia's Song" (Bogan), **Supp. III Part 1:** 66

"Little Local Color, A" (Henry), **Supp. II Part 1:** 399

Little Lord Fauntleroy (Burnett), **Retro. Supp. I:** 188

"Little Lyric" (Hughes), **Supp. I Part 1:** 334

Little Man, Little Man (Baldwin), **Supp. I Part 1:** 67

"Little Man at Chehaw Station, The" (Ellison), **Retro. Supp. II:** 123

Little Me (musical), **Supp. IV Part 2:** 575

Little Men (Alcott), **Supp. I Part 1:**

32, 39, 40

"Little Morning Music, A" (Schwartz), **Supp. II Part 2:** 662–663

Little Ocean (Shepard), **Supp. III Part 2:** 447

"Little Old Girl, A" (Larcom), **Supp. XIII:** 144

"Little Old Spy" (Hughes), **Supp. I Part 1:** 329

"Little Owl Who Lives in the Orchard" (Oliver), **Supp. VII:** 239

"Little Peasant, The" (Sexton), **Supp. II Part 2:** 690

"Little Rapids, The" (Swenson), **Supp. IV Part 2:** 645

Little Regiment and Other Episodes of the American Civil War, The (Crane), **I:** 408

Little River: New and Selected Poems (McCarriston), **Supp. XIV:269–272**

"Little Road not made of Man , A" (Dickinson), **Retro. Supp. I:** 44

Little Sister, The (Chandler), **Supp. IV Part 1:** 122, 130, 131–132

"Little Sleep's-Head Sprouting Hair in the Moonlight" (Kinnell), **Supp. III Part 1:** 247

"Little Snow White" (Grimm), **IV:** 266

"Little Testament of Bernard Martin, Aet. 30" (Mumford), **Supp. II Part 2:** 472, 473, 474

"Little Things" (Olds), **Supp. X:** 208

Little Tour in France (James), **II:** 337

Little Women (Alcott), **Supp. I Part 1:** 28, 29, 32, 35, 37, 38, 39–40, 41, 43, 44; **Supp. IX:** 128

Little Yellow Dog, A (Mosley), **Supp. XIII:** 237, 241

"Liturgy and Spiritual Personalism" (Merton), **Supp. VIII:** 199

Litz, A. Walton, **Retro. Supp. I:** 306

"Liu Ch'e" (Pound), **III:** 466

"Live" (Sexton), **Supp. II Part 2:** 684, 686

Live from Baghdad (screenplay, Shanley), **Supp. XIV:** 316

Live from Golgotha (Vidal), **Supp. IV Part 2:** 677, 682, 691, 692

Live Now and Pay Later (Garrett), **Supp. VII:** 111

"Live-Oak with Moss" (Whitman), **Retro. Supp. I:** 403

Live or Die (Sexton), **Supp. II Part 2:** 670, 683–687

Liveright, Horace, **Retro. Supp. I:** 80, 81, 83; **Supp. I Part 2:** 464

Lives (Plutarch), **II:** 5, 104

Lives of a Cell, The (L. Thomas), **Retro. Supp. I:** 322, 323

Lives of Distinguished American Naval

Officers (Cooper), **I:** 347

"Lives of Gulls and Children, The" (Nemerov), **III:** 271, 272

Lives of the Artists (Vasari), **Supp. I Part 2:** 450

Lives of the Poets (Doctorow), **Supp. IV Part 1:** 234

"Lives of the Poets" (Doctorow), **Supp. IV Part 1:** 234

"Lives of the—Wha'?, The" (Goldbarth), **Supp. XII:** 191

Living, The (Dillard), **Supp. VI:** 23

"Living at Home" (Gordon), **Supp. IV Part 1:** 311

Living by Fiction (Dillard), **Supp. VI:** 23, 31, **32,** 33

Living by the Word (Walker), **Supp. III Part 2:** 521, 522, 526, 527, 535

Living End, The (Elkin), **Supp. VI: 54,** 58

"Living Like Weasels" (Dillard), **Supp. VI:** 26, 33

Living Novel, The (Hicks), **III:** 342

Living of Charlotte Perkins Gilman, The (Gilman), **Supp. XI:** 193, 209

Living off the Country: Essays on Poetry and Place (Haines), **Supp. XII:** 199, 203, 207

Living Reed, The (Buck), **Supp. II Part 1:** 129–130

Living Theater, **Retro. Supp. I:** 424

"Living There" (Dickey), **Supp. IV Part 1:** 182–183

Living the Spirit: A Gay American Indian Anthology (Roscoe, ed.), **Supp. IV Part 1:** 330

"Living with a Peacock" (O'Connor), **III:** 350

"Livvie" (Welty), **IV:** 265; **Retro. Supp. I:** 348–349

"Livvie Is Back" (Welty), **Retro. Supp. I:** 351

Livy, **II:** 8

Lizzie (film), **Supp. IX:** 125

"Llantos de La Llorona: Warnings from the Wailer" (Mora), **Supp. XIII:** 217, 224

"L'Lapse" (Barthelme), **Supp. IV Part 1:** 45–47, 48

Lloyd, Henry Demarest, **Supp. I Part 1:** 5

Lloyd George, Harold, **I:** 490

"LMFBR" (Snyder), **Supp. VIII:** 302

"Loam" (Sandburg), **III:** 584–585

"Loan, The" (Malamud), **Supp. I Part 2:** 427, 428, 431, 437

"Local" (McCarriston), **Supp. XIV:** 270

Local Color (Capote), **Supp. III Part 1:** 120

"Local Color" (London), **II:** 475

Local Girls (Hoffman), **Supp. X:** 77, **90–91,** 92

"Local Girls" (Hoffman), **Supp. X:** 90

Local Time (Dunn), **Supp. XI:** 143, **148–149**

Lock, Helen, **Supp. XIII:** 233, 237–238

Lock, Robert H., **IV:** 319; **Retro. Supp. I:** 375

Locke, Alain, **Retro. Supp. II:** 115; **Supp. I Part 1:** 323, 325, 341; **Supp. II Part 1:** 53, 176, 182, 228, 247; **Supp. IV Part 1:** 170; **Supp. IX:** 306, 309; **Supp. X:** 134, 137, 139; **Supp. XIV:195–219**

Locke, Duane, **Supp. IX:** 273

Locke, John, **I:** 554–555, 557; **II:** 15–16, 113–114, 348–349, 480; **III:** 294–295; **IV:** 149; **Supp. I Part 1:** 130, 229, 230; **Supp. I Part 2:** 523

Locke, Sondra, **II:** 588

"Locked House, A" (Snodgrass), **Supp. VI:** 323

Locked Room, The (Auster), **Supp. XII:** 22, 24, **27–28**

Locket, The (Masters), **Supp. I Part 2:** 460

"Locksley Hall" (Tennyson), **Supp. IX:** 19

Lockwood Concern, The (O'Hara), **III:** 362, 364, 377–382

"Locus" (Ammons), **Supp. VII:** 28

"Locus" (Hayden), **Supp. II Part 1:** 361–362, 381

Loden, Barbara, **III:** 163

Lodge, Henry Cabot, **I:** 11–12, 21

Lodge, Mrs. Henry Cabot, **I:** 11–12, 19

Lodge, Thomas, **IV:** 370

Loeb, Gerald, **Supp. IV Part 2:** 523

Loeb, Jacques, **I:** 513; **Retro. Supp. II:** 104; **Supp. I Part 2:** 641

Loeffler, Jack, **Supp. XIII:** 1, 3, 12, 14, 16

"Log" (Merrlll), **Supp. III Part 1:** 328

Logan, Rayford W., **Supp. II Part 1:** 171, 194; **Supp. XIV:** 73

Logan, William, **Supp. X:** 201, 213; **Supp. XI:** 131, 132; **Supp. XII:** 98, 107, 113, 184

Log Book of "The Loved One," The, **Supp. XI:** 306

"Logging and Pimping and 'Your Pal, Jim' " (Maclean), **Supp. XIV:** 229

Logue, Christopher, **Supp. XIV:** 82

Lohengrin (Wagner), **I:** 216

Lohrfinck, Rosalind, **III:** 107, 117

Lolita (Nabokov), **III:** 246, 247, 255, 258–261; **Retro. Supp. I:** 263, 264, 265, 266, 269, 270, **272–274,** 275; **Supp. V:** 127, 252; **Supp. VIII:** 133

"Lolita" (Parker), **Supp. IX:** 193

Lombardi, Marilyn May, **Retro. Supp. II:** 40

London, Eliza, **II:** 465

London, Jack, **I:** 209; **II:** 264, 440, 444, 451, **462–485;** **III:** 314, 580; **Supp. IV Part 1:** 236; **Supp. V:** 281; **Supp. IX:** 1, 14; **Supp. XIII:** 312; **Supp. XIV:** 227

London, John, **II:** 464, 465

London, Mrs. Jack (Bessie Maddern), **II:** 465, 466, 473, 478

London, Mrs. Jack (Charmian Kittredge), **II:** 466, 468, 473, 476, 478, 481

London, Scott, **Supp. XIV:** 301, 307, 311

London Embassy, The (Theroux), **Supp. VIII:** 323

London Fields (Amis), **Retro. Supp. I:** 278

London Magazine (Plath), **Supp. I Part 2:** 541

London Snow: A Christmas Story (Theroux), **Supp. VIII:** 322

London Suite (Simon), **Supp. IV Part 2:** 576, 581, 582, 588

Lonely Are the Brave (film), **Supp. XIII:** 6

"Lonely Coast, A" (Proulx), **Supp. VII:** 264

Lonely for the Future (Farrell), **II:** 46, 47

Lonely Impulse of Delight, A (Shanley), **Supp. XIV:** 317–318

"Lonely Street, The" (W. C. Williams), **IV:** 413

"Lonely Worker, A" (Jewett), **Retro. Supp. II:** 132

Lonergan, Wayne, **Supp. I Part 1:** 51

Lonesome Dove (McMurtry), **Supp. V:** 226–228, 231, 232, 233

Lonesome Traveler (Kerouac), **Supp. III Part 1:** 219, 225

"Lone Striker, A" (Frost), **Retro. Supp. I:** 136, 137

Long, Ada, **Supp. V:** 178

Long, Huey, **I:** 489; **II:** 454; **IV:** 249; **Supp. IV Part 2:** 679; **Supp. XIV:** 14

Long, Ray, **II:** 430; **III:** 54

Long after Midnight (Bradbury), **Supp. IV Part 1:** 102

Long and Happy Life, A (Price), **Supp. VI:** 258, **259–260,** 262, 264, 265

Long Approach, The (Kumin), **Supp. IV Part 2:** 452–453, 453

Long Christmas Dinner, The (Wilder),

IV: 357, 365; **Supp. V:** 105
Long Christmas Dinner and Other Plays (Wilder), **IV:** 365–366
Long Day's Dying, A (Buechner), **Supp. XII: 45–47**
Long Day's Journey into Night (O'Neill), **III:** 385, 401, 403–404; **Supp. IV Part 1:** 359; **Supp. XIV:** 327
Long Desire, A (Connell), **Supp. XIV:** 79, 80, 97
"Long Distance" (Stafford), **Supp. XI:** 329
"Long-Distance Runner, The" (Paley), **Supp. VI:** 221–222, 228, 230
Long Dream, The (Wright), **IV:** 478, 488, 494
"Long Embrace, The" (Levine), **Supp. V:** 187
"Long Enough" (Rukeyser), **Supp. VI:** 274
"Longest Night of My Life, The " (Nichols), **Supp. XIII:** 269
Longfellow, Henry Wadsworth, **I:** 458, 471; **II:** 274, 277, 295–296, 310, 313, 402, **486–510; III:** 269, 412, 421, 422, 577; **IV:** 309, 371; **Retro. Supp. I:** 54, 123, 150, 155, 362; **Retro. Supp. II: 153–174; Supp. I Part 1:** 158, 299, 306, 317, 362, 368; **Supp. I Part 2:** 405, 406, 408, 409, 414, 416, 420, 586, 587, 602, 699, 704; **Supp. II Part 1:** 291, 353; **Supp. III Part 2:** 609; **Supp. IV Part 1:** 165; **Supp. IV Part 2:** 503; **Supp. XII:** 260; **Supp. XIII:** 141; **Supp. XIV:** 120
"Long Fourth, A" (Taylor), **Supp. V:** 313
Long Fourth and Other Stories, A (Taylor), **Supp. V:** 318–319
Long Gay Book, A (Stein), **IV:** 42
Long Goodbye, The (Chandler), **Supp. IV Part 1:** 120, 122, 132–134, 135
Long Goodbye, The (T. Williams), **IV:** 381
"Long Hair" (Snyder), **Supp. VIII:** 300
Longing for Home, The: Recollections and Reflections (Buechner), **Supp. XII:** 53
Longinus, Dionysius Cassius, **I:** 279
"Long-Legged House, The" (Berry), **Supp. X:** 21, 24–25, 27, 31
Long Live Man (Corso), **Supp. XII:** 129–130, 132
Long Love, The (Sedges), **Supp. II Part 1:** 125
Long Made Short (Dixon), **Supp. XII:** 152

Long March, The (Styron), **IV:** 97, 99, 104–107, 111, 113, 117
"Long Night, The" (Bambara), **Supp. XI:** 9
"Long Novel, A" (Ashbery), **Supp. III Part 1:** 6
Long Patrol, The (Mailer), **III:** 46
"Long Point Light" (Doty), **Supp. XI:** 127
Long Road of Woman's Memory, The (Addams), **Supp. I Part 1:** 17–18
"Long Run, The" (Wharton), **IV:** 314
Long Season, The (Brosnan), **II:** 424, 425
"Long Shadow of Lincoln, The: A Litany" (Sandburg), **III:** 591, 593
Longshot O'Leary (McGrath), **Supp. X:** 117
"Long Shower, The" (Francis), **Supp. IX:** 90
Longstreet, Augustus B., **II:** 70, 313; **Supp. I Part 1:** 352; **Supp. V:** 44; **Supp. X:** 227
"Long Summer" (Lowell), **II:** 553–554
"Long Term" (Dunn), **Supp. XI:** 149
Longtime Companion (film), **Supp. X:** 146, 152
Long Valley, The (Steinbeck), **IV:** 51
Long Voyage Home, The (O'Neill), **III:** 388
"Long Wail, A" (Crews), **Supp. XI:** 101
"Long Walk, The" (Bogan), **Supp. III Part 1:** 61
Long Walks and Intimate Talks (Paley), **Supp. VI:** 221
Long Way from Home, A (McKay), **Supp. X:** 132, 140
Lönnrot, Elias, **Retro. Supp. II:** 159
Looby, Christopher, **Supp. XIII:** 96
Look, Stranger! (Auden), **Supp. II Part 1:** 11
"Look, The" (Olds), **Supp. X:** 210
Look at the Harlequins (Nabokov), **Retro. Supp. I:** 266, 270
"Look for My White Self" (Ammons), **Supp. VII:** 25
Look Homeward, Angel (Wolfe), **II:** 457; **IV:** 450, 452, 453, 454, 455–456, 461, 462, 463, 464, 468, 471; **Supp. XI:** 216
"Looking a Mad Dog Dead in the Eyes" (Komunyakaa), **Supp. XIII:** 114
"Looking at Each Other" (Rukeyser), **Supp. VI:** 280, 285–286
"Looking at Kafka" (Roth), **Supp. III Part 2:** 402
"Looking Back" (Harjo), **Supp. XII:** 218

"Looking Back" (Merwin), **Supp. III Part 1:** 352
"Looking Back at Girlhood" (Jewett), **Retro. Supp. II:** 131, 133
Looking Backward (Bellamy), **II:** 276; **Supp. I Part 2:** 641; **Supp. XI:** 200
"Looking for a Ship" (McPhee), **Supp. III Part 1:** 312–313
"Looking for Dragon Smoke" (Bly), **Supp. IV Part 1:** 60
Looking for Holes in the Ceiling (Dunn), **Supp. XI:** 139, **143–145**
Looking for Langston (Julien; film), **Supp. XI:** 19, 20
Looking for Luck (Kumin), **Supp. IV Part 2:** 453, 454–455
"Looking for Mr. Green" (Bellow), **Retro. Supp. II:** 27
"Looking for the Buckhead Boys" (Dickey), **Supp. IV Part 1:** 182, 183
"Looking Forward to Age" (Harrison), **Supp. VIII:** 49
"Looking from Inside My Body" (Bly), **Supp. IV Part 1:** 71
"Looking Glass, The" (Wharton), **Retro. Supp. I:** 382
"Lookout's Journal" (Snyder), **Supp. VIII:** 291
"Looks Like They'll Never Learn" (McCoy), **Supp. XIII:** 166
"Look to Thy Heart . . ." (Hay), **Supp. XIV:** 130
Loon Lake (Doctorow), **Supp. IV Part 1:** 219, 222, 224–227, 230, 231, 232, 233
"Loon Point" (O'Brien), **Supp. V:** 237
Loosestrife (Dunn), **Supp. XI: 152– 154**
"Loosestrife" (Dunn), **Supp. XI:** 154
Loose Woman: Poems (Cisneros), **Supp. VII:** 58, 71–72
Lopate, Philip, **Supp. XII:** 184; **Supp. XIII:** 280–281
Lopatnikoff, Nikolai, **Supp. XIV:** 123
Lopez, Barry, **Supp. IV Part 1:** 416; **Supp. V:** 211; **Supp. X:** 29, 31; **Supp. XIII:** 16; **Supp. XIV:** 227
Lopez, Rafael, **Supp. IV Part 2:** 602
Lorca, Federico García, **IV:** 380; **Supp. I Part 1:** 345; **Supp. IV Part 1:** 83; **Supp. VIII:** 38, 39; **Supp. XIII:** 315, 323, 324
Lord, Judge Otis P., **I:** 454, 457, 458, 470
Lorde, Audre, **Supp. I Part 2:** 550, 571; **Supp. IV Part 1:** 325; **Supp. XI:** 20; **Supp. XII:** 217, 220; **Supp. XIII:** 295
Lord Jim (Conrad), **I:** 422; **II:** 26;

Retro. Supp. **II**: 292; **Supp. I Part 2**: 623; **Supp. IV Part 2**: 680; **Supp. V**: 251

"Lord of Hosts" (Pinsky), **Supp. VI**: 244

Lord of the Rings (Tolkien), **Supp. V**: 140

Lords of the Housetops (Van Vechten), **Supp. II Part 2**: 736

Lord's Prayer, **I**: 579

Lord Timothy Dexter of Newburyport, Mass. (Marquand), **III**: 55

Lord Weary's Castle (Lowell), **II**: 538, 542–551; **Retro. Supp. II**: 178, **186–187,** 188

"Lorelei" (Plath), **Retro. Supp. II**: 246; **Supp. I Part 2**: 538

Lorimer, George Horace, **II**: 430; **Retro. Supp. I**: 101, 113

Lorre, Peter, **Supp. IV Part 1**: 356

"Los Alamos" (Momaday), **Supp. IV Part 2**: 482

"Los Angeles, 1980" (Gunn Allen), **Supp. IV Part 1**: 325

"Los Angeles Days" (Didion), **Supp. IV Part 1**: 211

Losey, Joseph, **IV**: 383

"Losing a Language" (Merwin), **Supp. III Part 1**: 356

Losing Battles (Welty), **IV**: 261, 281–282; **Retro. Supp. I**: 341, 352, **353–354**

"Losing the Marbles" (Merrill), **Supp. III Part 1**: 337

"Losing Track of Language" (Clampitt), **Supp. IX**: 38, 40

Losses (Jarrell), **II**: 367, 372, 373–375, 376, 377, 380 381

"Losses" (Jarrell), **II**: 375–376

Lossky, N. O., **Supp. IV Part 2**: 519

"Loss of Breath" (Poe), **III**: 425–426

"Loss of My Arms and Legs, The" (Kingsolver), **Supp. VII**: 208

"Loss of the Creature, The" (Percy), **Supp. III Part 1**: 387

"Lost" (Wagoner), **Supp. IX**: 328

"Lost, The/Los Perdidos" (Kingsolver), **Supp. VII**: 208

"Lost and Found" (Levine), **Supp. V**: 188

"Lost Bodies" (Wright), **Supp. V**: 342

"Lost Boy, The" (Wolfe), **IV**: 451, 460, 466–467

"Lost Decade, The" (Fitzgerald), **II**: 98

Lost Galleon and Other Tales, The (Harte), **Supp. II Part 1**: 344

Lost Get-Back Boogie, The (Burke), **Supp. XIV**: 22, 25

"Lost Girls, The" (Hogan), **Supp. IV Part 1**: 406–407

Lost Highway (film), **Supp. X**: 314

Lost Illusions (Balzac), **I**: 500

Lost in the Bonewheel Factory (Komunyakaa), **Supp. XIII**: **114–115,** 116

Lost in the Cosmos: The Last Self-Help Book (Percy), **Supp. III Part 1**: 397

Lost in the Funhouse (Barth), **I**: 122, 135, 139; **Supp. X**: 307

"Lost in the Whichy Thicket" (Wolfe), **Supp. III Part 2**: 573, 574

"Lost in Translation" (Hass), **Supp. VIII**: 28

"Lost in Translation" (Merrill), **Supp. III Part 1**: 324, 329–330

Lost in Yonkers (film), **Supp. IV Part 2**: 588

Lost in Yonkers (Simon), **Supp. IV Part 2**: 576, 577, 584, 587–588, 590–591

Lost Lady, A (Cather), **I**: 323–325, 327; **Retro. Supp. I**: **15–16,** 20, 21, 382

"Lost Lover, A" (Jewett), **II**: 400–401, 402; **Retro. Supp. II**: 137

"Lost Loves" (Kinnell), **Supp. III Part 1**: 237, 245

Lost Man's River (Matthiessen), **Supp. V**: 212, 213, 214, 215

"Lost on September Trail, 1967" (Ríos), **Supp. IV Part 2**: 540

Lost Puritan (Mariani), **Retro. Supp. II**: 189

"Lost Sailor, The" (Freneau), **Supp. II Part 1**: 264

Lost Son, The (Roethke), **III**: 529, 530–532, 533

"Lost Son, The" (Roethke), **III**: 536, 537–539, 542

"Lost Sons" (Salter), **Supp. IX**: 260

Lost Souls (Singer). *See* Meshugah (Singer)

Lost Weekend, The (Jackson), **Supp. XIII**: 262

"Lost World, A" (Ashbery), **Supp. III Part 1**: 9

"Lost World, The" (Chabon), **Supp. XI**: 72–73

Lost World, The (Jarrell), **II**: 367, 368, 371, 379–380, 386, 387

"Lost World, The" cycle (Chabon), **Supp. XI**: **71–73**

"Lost World of Richard Yates, The: How the Great Writer of the Age of Anxiety Disappeared from Print" (O'Nan), **Supp. XI**: 348

"Lost Young Intellectual, The" (Howe), **Supp. VI**: 113, **115–116**

Lost Zoo, The: (A Rhyme for the Young, But Not Too Young) (Cullen), **Supp.**

IV Part 1: 173

Loti, Pierre, **II**: 311, 325; **Supp. IV Part 1**: 81

"Lot of People Bathing in a Stream, A" (Stevens), **IV**: 93

Lotringer, Sylvère, **Supp. XII**: 4

"Lot's Wife" (Nemerov), **III**: 270

"Lottery, The" (Jackson), **Supp. IX**: 113, 114, 118, 120, **122–123**

Lottery, The; or, The Adventures of James Harris (Jackson), **Supp. IX**: 113, 115, 116, 124, 125

Lotze, Hermann, **III**: 600

"Louie, His Cousin & His Other Cousin" (Cisneros), **Supp. VII**: 60

Louis, Joe, **II**: 589; **Supp. IV Part 1**: 360

Louis, Pierre Charles Alexandre, **Supp. I Part 1**: 302, 303

"Louisa, Please Come Home" (Jackson), **Supp. IX**: 122

Louis Lambert (Balzac), **I**: 499

"Louis Simpson and Walt Whitman: Destroying the Teacher" (Lazer), **Supp. IX**: 265

"Louis Zukofsky: *All: The Collected Short Poems, 1923–1958*" (Creeley), **Supp. IV Part 1**: 154

"Lounge" (Francis), **Supp. IX**: 83

Lounsbury, Thomas R., **I**: 335

Louter, Jan, **Supp. XI**: 173

"Love" (Olson), **Supp. II Part 2**: 571

"Love" (Paley), **Supp. VI**: 219, 222, 230

Love, Deborah, **Supp. V**: 208, 210

Love Alone: 18 Elegies for Rog (Monette), **Supp. X**: 146, 154

Love Always (Beattie), **Supp. V**: 29, 30, 35

Love among the Cannibals (Morris), **III**: 228, 230–231

"Love Among the Ruins" (Mosley), **Supp. XIII**: 247

Love and Death in the American Novel (Fiedler), **Supp. XIII**: 93, 96, **99–101,** 104

Love and Exile (Singer), **Retro. Supp. II**: **302–304,** 315

Love and Fame (Berryman), **I**: 170

Love and Friendship (Bloom), **Retro. Supp. II**: 31, 33–34

"Love and How to Cure It" (Wilder), **IV**: 365

"Love and the Hate, The" (Jeffers), **Supp. II Part 2**: 434–435

Love and Will (Dixon), **Supp. XII**: 148, 149

Love and Work (Price), **Supp. VI**: 261

"Love Calls Us to the Things of This World" (Wilbur), **Supp. III Part 2**:

544, 552–553

Love Course, The (Gurney), **Supp. V:** 98

Loved One, The (film), **Supp. XI: 305–306,** 307

Loved One, The (Waugh), **Supp. XI:** 305

Love Feast (Buechner), **Supp. XII:** 52

"Love Fossil" (Olds), **Supp. X:** 203

Love in Buffalo (Gurney), **Supp. V:** 96

"Love—In Other Words" (Lee), **Supp. VIII:** 113

"Love in the Morning" (Dubus), **Supp. VII:** 91

Love in the Ruins: The Adventures of a Bad Catholic at a Time near the End of the World (Percy), **Supp. III Part 1:** 385, 387, 393–394, 397–398

Love in the Western World (de Rougemont), **Retro. Supp. I:** 328

"Love Is a Deep and a Dark and a Lonely" (Sandburg), **III:** 595

Lovejoy, Elijah P., **Supp. I Part 2:** 588

Lovejoy, Owen R., **Supp. I Part 1:** 8

Lovejoy, Thomas, **Supp. X:** 108

Lovelace, Richard, **II:** 590

Love Letters (film), **Supp. IV Part 2:** 524

Love Letters (Gurney), **Supp. V:** 105, 108–109

Love Letters, The (Massie), **Supp. IV Part 2:** 524

Love Letters and Two Other Plays: The Golden Age and *What I Did Last Summer* (Gurney), **Supp. V:** 100

"Love Lies Sleeping" (Bishop), **Retro. Supp. II:** 42

Love Life (Mason), **Supp. VIII:** 145–146

"Love Life" (Mason), **Supp. VIII: 145–146**

Lovely Lady, The (Lawrence), **Retro. Supp. I:** 203

"Lovely Lady, The" (Lawrence), **Supp. I Part 1:** 329

Love Medicine (Erdrich), **Supp. IV Part 1:** 259, 260, 261, 263, 265, 266, 267–268, 270, 271, 274–275; **Supp. X:** 290

Love Medicine (expanded version) (Erdrich), **Supp. IV Part 1:** 263, 273, 274, 275

"Love Nest, The" (Lardner), **II:** 427, 429

Love Nest, The, and Other Stories (Lardner), **II:** 430–431, 436

Lovenheim, Barbara, **Supp. X:** 169

"Love of Elsie Barton: A Chronicle, The" (Warren), **IV:** 253

Love of Landry, The (Dunbar), **Supp.**

II Part 1: 212

"Love of Morning, The" (Levertov), **Supp. III Part 1:** 284

Love of the Last Tycoon, The: A Western. See Last Tycoon, The

"Love on the Bon Dieu" (Chopin), **Supp. I Part 1:** 213

Love Poems (Sexton), **Supp. II Part 2:** 687–689

Love Poems of May Swenson, The (Swenson), **Supp. IV Part 2:** 652, 653

"Love Poet" (Agee), **I:** 28

"Love Ritual" (Mora), **Supp. XIII:** 215

Loveroot (Jong), **Supp. V:** 115, 130

"Lovers, The" (Berryman), **I:** 174

"Lovers, The" (Buck), **Supp. II Part 1:** 128

"Lover's Garden, A" (Ginsberg), **Supp. II Part 1:** 311

"Lovers of the Poor, The" (Brooks), **Supp. III Part 1:** 81, 85

Lovers Should Marry (Martin), **Supp. IV Part 1:** 351

"Lover's Song" (Yeats), **Supp. I Part 1:** 80

"Love Rushes By" (Salinas), **Supp. XIII:** 326–327

Lovesick (Stern), **Supp. IX: 295–296**

Love's Labour's Lost (Shakespeare), **III:** 263

Love's Old Sweet Song (Saroyan), **Supp. IV Part 1:** 83

"Love Song of J. Alfred Prufrock, The" (Eliot), **I:** 52, 66, 569–570; **III:** 460; **Retro. Supp. I:** 55, 56, 57, 60; **Supp. II Part 1:** 5; **Supp. XIII:** 346

"Love Song of St. Sebastian" (Eliot), **Retro. Supp. I:** 57

Love's Pilgrimage (Sinclair), **Supp. V:** 286

"Love the Wild Swan" (Jeffers), **Supp. VIII:** 33

Love to Mamá: A Tribute to Mothers (Mora, ed.), **Supp. XIII:** 221

Lovett, Robert Morss, **II:** 43

"Love-Unknown" (Herbert), **Supp. I Part 1:** 80

Love! Valor! Compassion! (film), **Supp. XIII:** 206

Love! Valour! Compassion! (McNally), **Supp. XIII:** 199, **203–204,** 208, 209

"Love *versus* Law" (Stowe), **Supp. I Part 2:** 585–586

Love with a Few Hairs (Mrabet), **Supp. IV Part 1:** 92

Loving a Woman in Two Worlds (Bly), **Supp. IV Part 1:** 66, 67, 68–69, 71, 72

"Loving Shepherdess, The" (Jeffers),

Supp. II Part 2: 432

"Loving the Killer" (Sexton), **Supp. II Part 2:** 688

Lovin' Molly (film), **Supp. V:** 223, 226

Lowe, John, **Supp. XIII:** 238

Lowe, Pardee, **Supp. X:** 291

Lowell, Abbott Lawrence, **I:** 487; **II:** 513; **Supp. I Part 2:** 483

Lowell, Amy, **I:** 231, 384, 405, 475, 487; **II:** 174, **511–533,** 534; **III:** 465, 581, 586; **Retro. Supp. I:** 131, 133, 288; **Retro. Supp. II:** 46, 175; **Supp. I Part 1:** 257–259, 261–263, 265, 266; **Supp. I Part 2:** 465, 466, 707, 714, 729; **Supp. XIV:** 128

Lowell, Blanche, **Supp. I Part 2:** 409

Lowell, Harriet, **II:** 553, 554

Lowell, James Russell, **I:** 216, 458; **II:** 273, 274, 289, 302, 320, 402, 529, 530, 532, 534, 551; **III:** 409; **IV:** 129, 171, 175, 180, 182–183, 186; **Retro. Supp. I:** 228; **Retro. Supp. II:** 155, 175, 326; **Supp. I Part 1:** 168, 299, 300, 303, 306, 311, 312, 317, 318, 362; **Supp. I Part 2: 404–426; Supp. II Part 1:** 197, 291, 352

Lowell, Mrs. James Russell (Maria White), **Supp. I Part 2:** 405, 406, 414, 424

Lowell, Percival, **II:** 513, 525, 534

Lowell, Robert, **I:** 172, 381, 382, 400, 442, 521, 544–545, 550; **II:** 371, 376, 377, 384, 386–387, 532, **534–557; III:** 39, 44, 142, 508, 527, 528–529, 606; **IV:** 120, 138, 402, 430; **Retro. Supp. I:** 67, 140, 411; **Retro. Supp. II:** 27, 40, 44, 46, 48, 50, **175–193,** 221, 228–229, 235, 245; **Supp. I Part 1:** 89; **Supp. I Part 2:** 538, 543, 554; **Supp. III Part 1:** 6, 64, 84, 138, 147, 193, 194, 197–202, 205–208; **Supp. III Part 2:** 541, 543, 555, 561, 599; **Supp. IV Part 2:** 439, 620, 637; **Supp. V:** 81, 179, 180, 315–316, 337, 344; **Supp. VIII:** 27, 100, 271; **Supp. IX:** 325; **Supp. X:** 53, 58; **Supp. XI:** 146, 240, 244, 250, 317; **Supp. XII:** 253–254, 255; **Supp. XIII:** 76; **Supp. XIV:** 15, 126, 269

Lowell, Rose, **Supp. I Part 2:** 409

"Lowell in the Classroom" (Vendler), **Retro. Supp. II:** 191

Lowenthal, Michael, **Supp. XII:** 82

Lower Depths, The (Gorki), **III:** 402

"Lower the Standard" (Shapiro), **Supp. II Part 2:** 715

Lowes, John Livingston, **II:** 512, 516, 532; **IV:** 453, 455

Lowin, Joseph, **Supp. V:** 273

"Low-Lands" (Pynchon), **Supp. II Part 2:** 620, 624

Lowle, Percival, **Supp. I Part 2:** 404

Lownsbrough, John, **Supp. IV Part 1:** 209, 211

Lowth, Richard, **II:** 8

Loy, Mina, **III:** 194

Loy, Myrna, **Supp. IV Part 1:** 355

"Loyal Woman's No, A" (Larcom), **Supp. XIII:** 142, 143–144

"Luani of the Jungle" (Hughes), **Supp. I Part 1:** 328

Lubbock, Percy, **I:** 504; **II:** 337; **IV:** 308, 314, 319, 322; **Retro. Supp. I:** 366, 367, 373; **Supp. VIII:** 165

Lubin, Isidor, **Supp. I Part 2:** 632

Lubow, Arthur, **Supp. VIII:** 310

Lucas, Victoria (pseudonym). *See* Plath, Sylvia

Luce, Dianne C., **Supp. VIII:** 189

Lucid, Robert F., **Retro. Supp. II:** 195, 204

"Lucid Eye in Silver Town, The" (Updike), **IV:** 218

"Lucinda Matlock" (Masters), **Supp. I Part 2:** 461, 465

"Luck" (Dunn), **Supp. XI:** 149

Luck of Barry Lyndon, The (Thackeray), **II:** 290

"Luck of Roaring Camp, The" (Harte), **Supp. II Part 1:** 335, 344, 345–347

"Luck of the Bogans, The" (Jewett), **Retro. Supp. II:** 142

Lucky Life (Stern), **Supp. IX: 290–291**

Lucretius, **I:** 59; **II:** 162, 163; **III:** 600, 610–611, 612; **Supp. I Part 1:** 363

Lucy (Kincaid), **Supp. VII:** 180, 185, 186, 187–188, 194

Lucy, Saint, **II:** 211

Lucy Gayheart (Cather), **I:** 331; **Retro. Supp. I:** 19

Ludvigson, Susan, **Supp. IV Part 2:** 442, 446, 447, 448, 451

Luhan, Mabel Dodge, **Retro. Supp. I:** 7

Lu Ji, **Supp. VIII:** 303

Luke (biblical book), **III:** 606

"Luke Havergal" (Robinson), **III:** 524

Luks, George, **IV:** 411; **Retro. Supp. II:** 103

"Lullaby" (Auden), **Supp. II Part 1:** 9

"Lullaby" (Bishop), **Supp. I Part 1:** 85

"Lullaby" (Silko), **Supp. IV Part 2:** 560, 568–569

Lullaby: The Comforting of Cock Robin (Snodgrass), **Supp. VI:** 324

"Lullaby of Cape Cod" (Brodsky), **Supp. VIII:** 27–28

Lullaby Raft (Nye), **Supp. XIII:** 278

Lullaby Raft (Nye, album), **Supp. XIII:** 274

"Lulls" (Walker), **Supp. III Part 2:** 525

"Lulu" (Wedekind), **Supp. XII:** 14

Lulu on the Bridge (film), **Supp. XII:** 21

Lulu's Library (Alcott), **Supp. I Part 1:** 43

"Lumber" (Baker), **Supp. XIII:** 55, 56

"Lumens, The" (Olds), **Supp. X:** 209

Lume Spento, A (Pound), **III:** 470

Lumet, Sidney, **Supp. IV Part 1:** 236; **Supp. IX:** 253

"Lumumba's Grave" (Hughes), **Supp. I Part 1:** 344

"Luna, Luna" (Mora), **Supp. XIII:** 217

Lupercal (Hughes), **Retro. Supp. II:** 245; **Supp. I Part 2:** 540

Lupton, Mary Jane, **Supp. IV Part 1:** 7

Luria, Isaac, **IV:** 7

Lurie, Alison, **Supp. X:** 166

Lust and Other Stories (Minot), **Supp. VI:** 205

Lustgarten, Edith, **III:** 107

Lustra (Pound), **Retro. Supp. I:** 289, 290

Luther, Martin, **II:** 11–12, 506; **III:** 306, 607; **IV:** 490

"Luther on Sweet Auburn" (Bambara), **Supp. XI:** 16–17

Lux, Thomas, **Supp. XI:** 270

Luxury Girl, The (McCoy), **Supp. XIII:** 163

Lyall, Sarah, **Supp. XIII:** 247

Lycidas (Milton), **II:** 540; **IV:** 347; **Retro. Supp. I:** 60; **Retro. Supp. II:** 186; **Supp. I Part 1:** 370; **Supp. IX:** 41

Lydon, Susan, **Supp. XII:** 170

Lyell, Charles, **Supp. IX:** 180

Lyell, Frank H., **Supp. VIII:** 125

Lyford, Harry, **Supp. I Part 2:** 679

"Lying" (Wilbur), **Supp. III Part 2:** 547, 562

"Lying and Looking" (Swenson), **Supp. IV Part 2:** 652

"Lying in a Hammock at William Duffy's Farm in Pine Island, Minnesota" (Wright), **Supp. III Part 2:** 589, 599, 600

Lyles, Lois F., **Supp. XI:** 7, 8

Lyly, John, **III:** 536; **Supp. I Part 1:** 369

"Lynched Man, The" (Karr), **Supp. XI:** 241

Lynchers, The (Wideman), **Supp. X:** 320

"Lynching, The" (McKay), **Supp. I Part 1:** 63

"Lynching of Jube Benson, The" (Dunbar), **Supp. II Part 1:** 214

"Lynching Song" (Hughes), **Supp. I Part 1:** 331

Lynd, Staughton, **Supp. VIII:** 240

Lynn, Kenneth, **Supp. XIII:** 96–97

Lynn, Kenneth S., **Supp. XIV:** 103

Lynn, Vera, **Supp. XI:** 304

Lyon, Kate, **I:** 409; **II:** 138, 143, 144

Lyon, Thomas, **Supp. IX:** 175

"Lyonnesse" (Plath), **Supp. I Part 2:** 541

Lyons, Bonnie, **Supp. V:** 58; **Supp. VIII:** 138

Lyotard, Jean-François, **Supp. IV Part 1:** 54

Lyrical Ballads (Wordsworth), **III:** 583; **IV:** 120; **Supp. IX:** 274; **Supp. XI:** 243

Lyrics of Love and Laughter (Dunbar), **Supp. II Part 1:** 207

Lyrics of Lowly Life (Dunbar), **Supp. II Part 1:** 197, 199, 200, 207

Lyrics of the Hearthside (Dunbar), **Supp. II Part 1:** 206

Lytal, Tammy, **Supp. XI:** 102

Lytle, Andrew, **IV:** 125; **Retro. Supp. II:** 220, 221, 235; **Supp. II Part 1:** 139; **Supp. X:** 1, 25; **Supp. XI:** 101

Lytton of Knebworth. *See* Bulwer-Lytton, Edward George

"M. Degas Teaches Art & Science at Durfee Intermediate School, Detroit, 1942" (Levine), **Supp. V:** 181, 193

McAlexander, Hubert H., **Supp. V:** 314, 319, 320, 323

McAlmon, Mrs. Robert (Winifred Ellerman), **III:** 194. *See also* Ellerman, Winifred

McAlmon, Robert, **IV:** 404; **Retro. Supp. I:** 418, 419, 420; **Retro. Supp. II:** 328; **Supp. I Part 1:** 259; **Supp. III Part 2:** 614

McAninch, Jerry, **Supp. XI:** 297, 298

Macaulay, Catherine, **Supp. I Part 2:** 522

Macaulay, Rose, **Supp. XII:** 88; **Supp. XIV:** 348

Macaulay, Thomas, **II:** 15–16; **III:** 113, 591–592

Macauley, Robie, **Retro. Supp. II:** 228; **Supp. X:** 56

Macbeth (Shakespeare), **I:** 271; **IV:** 227; **Retro. Supp. I:** 131; **Supp. I Part 1:** 67; **Supp. I Part 2:** 457; **Supp. IV Part 1:** 87; **Supp. XIV:** 8

MacBeth, George, **Retro. Supp. II:** 250

McCaffery, Larry, **Supp. IV Part 1:**

217, 227, 234; **Supp. V:** 53, 238; **Supp. VIII:** 13, 14; **Supp. X:** 260, 268, 301, 303, 307

McCarriston, Linda, **Supp. X:** 204; **Supp. XIV:259–275**

McCarthy, Charles Joseph, Jr. *See* McCarthy, Cormac

McCarthy, Cormac, **Supp. VIII:** 175–192; **Supp. XII:** 310

McCarthy, Eugene, **Retro. Supp. II:** 182

McCarthy, Joseph, **I:** 31, 492; **II:** 562, 568; **Supp. I Part 1:** 294, 295; **Supp. I Part 2:** 444, 611, 612, 620

McCarthy, Mary, **II:** 558–584; **Supp. I Part 1:** 84; **Supp. IV Part 1:** 209, 297, 310; **Supp. VIII:** 96, 99, 100; **Supp. X:** 177; **Supp. XI:** 246; **Supp. XIV:** 3

McCay, Maura, **Supp. XII:** 271, 276

McClanahan, Ed, **Supp. X:** 24

McClanahan, Thomas, **Supp. XII:** 125–126

McClatchy, J. D., **Supp. XII:** 253–270

McClellan, John L., **I:** 493

McClung, Isabelle, **Retro. Supp. I:** 5

McClure, John, **Retro. Supp. I:** 80

McClure, Michael, **Supp. II Part 1:** 32; **Supp. VIII:** 289

McClure, S. S., **I:** 313; **II:** 465; **III:** 327; **Retro. Supp. I:** 5, 6, 9

McCombs, Judith, **Supp. XIII:** 33

McConnell, Frank, **Supp. X:** 260, 274

McCorkle, Jill, **Supp. X:** 6

McCourt, Frank, **Supp. XII:** 271–287

McCoy, Horace, **Supp. XIII:** 159–177

McCracken, Elizabeth, **Supp. X:** 86; **Supp. XII:** 310, 315–316, 321

McCullers, Carson, **I:** 113, 190, 211; **II:** 585–608; **IV:** 282, 384, 385, 386; **Retro. Supp. II:** 324; **Supp. II Part 1:** 17; **Supp. IV Part 1:** 31, 84; **Supp. IV Part 2:** 502; **Supp. VIII:** 124; **Supp. XII:** 309; **Supp. XIV:** 120

McCullers, Reeves, **III:** 585, 586, 587

McDavid, Raven I., **III:** 120; **Supp. XIV:** 14

McDermott, Alice, **Supp. XII:** 311

McDermott, John J., **II:** 364

MacDiarmid, Hugh, **Supp. X:** 112

Macdonald, Dwight, **I:** 233, 372, 379; **III:** 39; **Supp. V:** 265; **Supp. XIV:** 340

McDonald, E. J., **Supp. I Part 2:** 670

Macdonald, George, **Supp. XIII:** 75

MacDonald, Jeanette, **II:** 589

Macdonald, Ross, **Supp. IV Part 1:** 116, 136; **Supp. IV Part 2:** 459–477; **Supp. XIII:** 233

MacDowell, Edward, **I:** 228; **III:** 504, 508, 524

McDowell, Frederick P. W., **II:** 194

McDowell, Mary, **Supp. I Part 1:** 5

McDowell, Robert, **Supp. IX:** 266, 270, 276, 279

MacDowell, Robert, **Supp. XI:** 249

McElrath, Joseph, **Supp. XIV:** 62

McElroy, Joseph, **Supp. IV Part 1:** 279, 285

McEuen, Kathryn, **II:** 20

McEwen, Arthur, **I:** 206

McFarland, Ron, **Supp. IX:** 323, 327, 328, 333

McGann, Jerome, **Retro. Supp. I:** 47

McGovern, Edythe M., **Supp. IV Part 2:** 573, 582, 585

McGovern, George, **III:** 46

MacGowan, Christopher, **Retro. Supp. I:** 430

MacGowan, Kenneth, **III:** 387, 391

McGrath, Joseph, **Supp. XI:** 307, 309

McGrath, Patrick, **Supp. IX:** 113

McGrath, Thomas, **Supp. X:** 111–130

"McGrath on McGrath" (McGrath), **Supp. X:** 119, 120

McGuane, Thomas, **Supp. V:** 53, 220; **Supp. VIII:** 39, 40, 42, 43

MacGuffin, The (Elkin), **Supp. VI:** 55–56

Machado y Ruiz, Antonio, **Supp. XIII:** 315, 323

Machan, Tibor, **Supp. IV Part 2:** 528

Machen, Arthur, **IV:** 286

Machiavelli, Niccolò, **I:** 485

"Machine-Gun, The" (Jarrell), **II:** 371

"Machine Song" (Anderson), **I:** 114

McInerney, Jay, **Supp. X:** 7, 166; **Supp. XI:** 65; **Supp. XII:** 81

"Mac in Love" (Dixon), **Supp. XII:** 142

McIntire, Holly, **Supp. V:** 338

McIntosh, Maria, **Retro. Supp. I:** 246

Mack, Maynard, **Supp. XIV:** 12

Mackail, John William, **Supp. I Part 1:** 268; **Supp. I Part 2:** 461

McKay, Claude, **Supp. I Part 1:** 63; **Supp. III Part 1:** 75, 76; **Supp. IV Part 1:** 3, 79, 164; **Supp. IX:** 306; **Supp. X:** 131–144; **Supp. XI:** 91

McKay, Donald, **Supp. I Part 2:** 482

McKee, Elizabeth, **Retro. Supp. II:** 221, 222

McKee, Ellen, **Retro. Supp. II:** 67

McKenney, Eileen, **IV:** 288; **Retro. Supp. II:** 321, 330

McKenney, Ruth, **IV:** 288; **Retro. Supp. II:** 321

MacKenzie, Agnes, **I:** 199

Mackenzie, Captain Alexander, **III:** 94

Mackenzie, Compton, **II:** 82; **Retro. Supp. I:** 100, 102

McKenzie, Geraldine, **Supp. XII:** 107

MacKenzie, Margaret, **I:** 199

McKinley, William, **I:** 474; **III:** 506; **Supp. I Part 2:** 395–396, 707

MacKinnon, Catharine, **Supp. XII:** 6

MacLachlan, Suzanne L., **Supp. XII:** 300,**Supp. XII:** 299

McLaverty, Michael, **Supp. X:** 67

McLay, Catherine, **Supp. XIII:** 21

Maclean, Alasdair, **Supp. V:** 244

Maclean, Norman, **Supp. XIV:221–237**

MacLeish, Archibald, **I:** 283, 293, 429; **II:** 165, 228; **III:** 1–25, 427; **Supp. I Part 1:** 261; **Supp. I Part 2:** 654; **Supp. IV Part 1:** 359; **Supp. IV Part 2:** 586; **Supp. X:** 120; **Supp. XIV:** 11

MacLeish, Kenneth, **III:** 1

MacLeish, Mrs. Archibald (Ada Hitchcock), **III:** 1

McLennan, Gordon Lawson, **Supp. IX:** 89

McLeod, A. W., **Supp. I Part 1:** 257

McLuhan, Marshall, **Supp. IV Part 2:** 474

McLure, Michael, **Supp. XIV:** 150

Macmahon, Arthur, **I:** 226

McMahon, Helen, **Supp. IV Part 2:** 579

McMichael, George, **Supp. VIII:** 124

McMichael, Morton, **Supp. I Part 2:** 707

McMichaels, James, **Supp. XIII:** 114

McMillan, James B., **Supp. VIII:** 124

McMillan, Terry, **Supp. XIII:** 179–193

McMullan, Jim, **Supp. XIV:** 124

McMurtry, Josephine, **Supp. V:** 220

McMurtry, Larry, **Supp. V:** 219–235; **Supp. X:** 24; **Supp. XI:** 172

McNally, Terrence, **Supp. XIII:** 195–211

McNamer, Deirdre, **Supp. XI:** 190

McNeese, Gretchen, **Supp. V:** 123

MacNeice, Louis, **II:** 586; **III:** 527; **Supp. II Part 1:** 17, 24; **Supp. IV Part 2:** 440; **Supp. X:** 116; **Supp. XIII:** 347

McNeil, Claudia, **Supp. IV Part 1:** 360, 362

McPhee, John, **Supp. III Part 1:** 289–316; **Supp. X:** 29, 30

MacPherson, Aimee Semple, **Supp. V:** 278

McPherson, Dolly, **Supp. IV Part 1:** 2, 3, 4, 6, 8, 11, 12

McPherson, James Allen, **Retro. Supp. II:** 126

Macpherson, Jay, **Supp. XIII:** 19

MacPherson, Kenneth, **Supp. I Part 1:** 259

McQuade, Molly, **Supp. VIII:** 277, 281; **Supp. IX:** 151, 163

McQueen, Steve, **Supp. XI:** 306

Macrae, John, **I:** 252–253

McRobbie, Angela, **Supp. IV Part 2:** 691

MacShane, Frank, **Supp. IV Part 2:** 557; **Supp. XI:** 214, 216

"MacSwiggen" (Freneau), **Supp. II Part 1:** 259

McTaggart, John, **I:** 59

McTeague (Norris), **III:** 314, 315, 316–320, 322, 325, 327–328, 330, 331, 333, 335; **Retro. Supp. II:** 96; **Supp. IX:** 332

McWilliams, Carey, **Supp. XI:** 169

Madama Butterfly (Puccini), **III:** 139

"Madam and the Minister" (Hughes), **Supp. I Part 1:** 335

"Madam and the Wrong Visitor" (Hughes), **Supp. I Part 1:** 335

"Madame and Ahmad" (Bowles), **Supp. IV Part 1:** 93

"Madame Bai and the Taking of Stone Mountain" (Bambara), **Supp. XI:** 14–15

Madame Bovary (Flaubert), **II:** 185; **Retro. Supp. I:** 225; **Retro. Supp. II:** 70; **Supp. XI:** 334

"Madame Célestin's Divorce" (Chopin), **Supp. I Part 1:** 213

Madame Curie (film), **Retro. Supp. I:** 113

"Madame de Mauves" (James), **II:** 327; **Retro. Supp. I:** 218, 220

Madame de Treymes (Wharton), **IV:** 314, 323; **Retro. Supp. I:** 376

"Madam's Calling Cards" (Hughes), **Retro. Supp. I:** 206

Madden, David, **Supp. IV Part 1:** 285

Maddern, Bessie. *See* London, Mrs. Jack (Bessie Maddern)

Mad Dog Black Lady (Coleman), **Supp. XI:** 85–89, 90

Mad Dog Blues (Shepard), **Supp. III Part 2:** 437, 438, 441

Maddox, Lucy, **Supp. IV Part 1:** 323, 325

Mademoiselle Coeur-Brisé (Sibon, trans.), **IV:** 288

Mademoiselle de Maupin (Gautier), **Supp. I Part 1:** 277

"Mad Farmer, Flying the Flag of Rough Branch, Secedes from the Union, The" (Berry), **Supp. X:** 35

"Mad Farmer Manifesto, The: The First Amendment" (Berry), **Supp. X:** 35

"Mad Farmer's Love Song, The" (Berry), **Supp. X:** 35

Madheart (Baraka), **Supp. II Part 1:** 47

Madhouse, The (Farrell), **II:** 41

Madhubuti, Haki R. (Don L. Lee), **Supp. II Part 1:** 34, 247; **Supp. IV Part 1:** 244

Madison, Dolley, **II:** 303

Madison, James, **I:** 1, 2, 6–9; **II:** 301; **Supp. I Part 2:** 509, 524

"Madison Smartt Bell: *The Year of Silence*" (Garrett), **Supp. X:** 7

"Madman, A" (Updike), **Retro. Supp. I:** 320

"Madman's Song" (Wylie), **Supp. I Part 2:** 711, 729

"Madonna" (Lowell), **II:** 535–536

"Madonna of the Evening Flowers" (Lowell), **II:** 524

"Madonna of the Future, The" (James), **Retro. Supp. I:** 219

Madwoman in the Attic, The (Gilbert and Gubar), **Retro. Supp. I:** 42; **Supp. IX:** 66

"Maelzel's Chess-Player" (Poe), **III:** 419, 420

"Maestria" (Nemerov), **III:** 275, 278–279

Maeterlinck, Maurice, **I:** 91, 220

"Magazine-Writing Peter Snook" (Poe), **III:** 421

Magdeburg Centuries (Flacius), **IV:** 163

Magellan, Ferdinand, **Supp. I Part 2:** 497

Maggie: A Girl of the Streets (S. Crane), **I:** 407, 408, 410–411, 416; **IV:** 208; **Retro. Supp. II:** 97, 107

Maggie Cassidy (Kerouac), **Supp. III Part 1:** 220–221, 225, 227, 229, 232

"Maggie of the Green Bottles" (Bambara), **Supp. XI:** 2–3

"Magi" (Plath), **Supp. I Part 2:** 544–545

"Magi, The" (Garrett), **Supp. VII:** 97

"Magic" (Porter), **III:** 434, 435

Magic Barrel, The (Malamud), **Supp. I Part 2:** 427, 428, 430–434

"Magic Barrel, The" (Malamud), **Supp. I Part 2:** 427, 428, 431, 432–433

Magic Christian, The (film), **Supp. XI:** 309

Magic Christian, The (Southern), **Supp. XI:** 297, 299–301, 309

Magic City (Komunyakaa), **Supp. XIII:** 125–127, 128, 131

"Magic Flute, The" (Epstein), **Supp. XII:** 165

Magic Flute, The (Mozart), **III:** 164

Magician of Lublin, The (Singer), **IV:** 6, 9–10; **Retro. Supp. II:** 308–309

Magician's Assistant, The (Patchett), **Supp. XII:** 307, 310, 317–320, 322

"Magician's Wife, The" (Gordon), **Supp. IV Part 1:** 306

Magic Journey, The (Nichols), **Supp. XIII:** 266–267

Magic Kingdom, The (Elkin), **Supp. VI:** 42, 54–55, 56, 58

"Magic Mirror, The: A Study of the Double in Two of Doestoevsky's Novels" (Plath), **Supp. I Part 2:** 536

Magic Mountain, The (Mann), **III:** 281–282; **Supp. IV Part 2:** 522; **Supp. XII:** 321

Magic Tower, The (Willams), **IV:** 380

Magnalia Christi Americana (Mather), **II:** 302; **Supp. I Part 1:** 102; **Supp. I Part 2:** 584; **Supp. II Part 2:** 441, 442, 452–455, 460, 467, 468; **Supp. IV Part 2:** 434

"Magnificent Little Gift" (Salinas), **Supp. XIII:** 318

"Magnifying Mirror" (Karr), **Supp. XI:** 240

Magpie, The (Baldwin, ed.), **Supp. I Part 1:** 49

Magpie's Shadow, The (Winters), **Supp. II Part 2:** 786, 788

"Magpie's Song" (Snyder), **Supp. VIII:** 302

Magritte, René, **Supp. IV Part 2:** 623

Mahan, Albert Thayer, **Supp. I Part 2:** 491

Mahomet and His Successors (Irving), **II:** 314

Mahoney, Jeremiah, **IV:** 285

"Maiden in a Tower" (Stegner), **Supp. IV Part 2:** 613

"Maiden Without Hands" (Sexton), **Supp. II Part 2:** 691

"Maid of St. Philippe, The" (Chopin), **Retro. Supp. II:** 63

"Maid's Shoes, The" (Malamud), **Supp. I Part 2:** 437

Mailer, Fanny, **III:** 28

Mailer, Isaac, **III:** 28

Mailer, Norman, **I:** 261, 292, 477; **III:** 26–49, 174; **IV:** 98, 216; **Retro. Supp. II:** 182, 195–217, 279; **Supp. I Part 1:** 291, 294; **Supp. III Part 1:** 302; **Supp. IV Part 1:** 90, 198, 207, 236, 284, 381; **Supp. IV Part 2:** 689; **Supp. VIII:** 236; **Supp. XI:** 104, 218, 222, 229; **Supp. XIV:** 49, 53, 54, 111, 162

"Maimed Man, The" (Tate), **IV:** 136

Main Currents in American Thought:

The Colonial Mind, 1625–1800 (Parrington), **I:** 517; **Supp. I Part 2:** 484

"Maine Roustabout, A" (Eberhart), **I:** 539

"Maine Speech" (White), **Supp. I Part 2:** 669–670

Maine Woods, The (Thoreau), **IV:** 188

Main Street (Lewis), **I:** 362; **II:** 271, 440, 441–442, 447, 449, 453; **III:** 394

"Majorat, Das" (Hoffman), **III:** 415

Major Barbara (Shaw), **III:** 69

"Major Chord, The" (Bourne), **I:** 221

Majors and Minors (Dunbar), **Supp. II Part 1:** 197, 198

"Major's Tale, The" (Bierce), **I:** 205

Make-Believe Town: Essays and Remembrances (Mamet), **Supp. XIV:** 240, 251

Make It New (Pound), **III:** 470

Makers and Finders (Brooks), **I:** 253, 254, 255, 257, 258

"Making a Change" (Gilman), **Supp. XI:** 207

"Making a Living" (Sexton), **Supp. II Part 2:** 695

"Making Do" (Hogan), **Supp. IV Part 1:** 406

Making Face, Making Soul: Haciendo Caras, Creative and Critical Perspectives by Feminists of Color (Anzaldúa, ed.), **Supp. IV Part 1:** 330

Making It (Podhoretz), **Supp. VIII:** 231, 232, 233, **237–238,** 239, 244

"Making of a Marginal Farm, The" (Berry), **Supp. X:** 22

Making of Americans, The (Stein), **IV:** 35, 37, 40–42, 45, 46; **Supp. III Part 1:** 37

"Making of Ashenden, The" (Elkin), **Supp. VI:** 49, 50

"Making of a Soldier USA, The" (Simpson), **Supp. IX:** 270

"Making of Paths, The" (Stegner), **Supp. IV Part 2:** 614

"Making of Poems, The" (W. J. Smith), **Supp. XIII:** 348

Making of the Modern Mind (Randall), **III:** 605

Making the Light Come: The Poetry of Gerald Stern (Somerville), **Supp. IX:** 296–297

"Making Up Stories" (Didion), **Supp. IV Part 1:** 196, 203, 205

Malady of the Ideal, The: Oberman, Maurice de Guérin, and Amiel (Brooks), **I:** 240, 241, 242

Malamud, Bernard, **I:** 144, 375; **II:**

424, 425; **III:** 40, 272; **IV:** 216; **Retro. Supp. II:** 22, 279, 281; **Supp. I Part 2: 427–453; Supp. IV Part 1:** 297, 382; **Supp. V:** 257, 266; **Supp. IX:** 114, 227; **Supp. XIII:** 106, 264, 265, 294

Malamud, Mrs. Bernard (Ann de Chiara), **Supp. I Part 2:** 451

Malanga, Gerard, **Supp. III Part 2:** 629

Malaquais, Jean, **Retro. Supp. II:** 199

Malatesta, Sigismondo de, **III:** 472, 473

Malcolm (Purdy), **Supp. VII:** 270–273, 277

"Malcolm Cowley and the American Writer" (Simpson), **Supp. II Part 1:** 147

"MALCOLM REMEMBERED (FEB. 77)" (Baraka), **Supp. II Part 1:** 60

Malcolm X, **Retro. Supp. II:** 12, 13; **Supp. I Part 1:** 52, 63, 65, 66; **Supp. IV Part 1:** 2, 10; **Supp. VIII:** 330, 345; **Supp. X:** 240; **Supp. XIV:** 306

Malcolm X (film), **Retro. Supp. II:** 12

"Maldrove" (Jeffers), **Supp. II Part 2:** 418

Male, Roy, **II:** 239

Male Animal, The (Thurber), **Supp. I Part 2:** 605, 606, 610–611

"Malediction upon Myself" (Wylie), **Supp. I Part 2:** 722

Malefactors, The (Gordon), **II:** 186, 199, 213–216; **IV:** 139

"Malest Cornifici Tuo Catullo" (Ginsberg), **Supp. II Part 1:** 315

Malick, Terrence, **Supp. XI:** 234

Malin, Irving, **I:** 147

"Malinche's Tips: Pique from Mexico's Mother" (Mora), **Supp. XIII:** 223

Mallarmé, Stéphane, **I:** 66, 569; **II:** 529, 543; **III:** 8, 409, 428; **IV:** 80, 86; **Retro. Supp. I:** 56; **Supp. I Part 1:** 261; **Supp. II Part 1:** 1; **Supp. III Part 1:** 319–320; **Supp. III Part 2:** 630; **Supp. XIII:** 114

Mallia, Joseph, **Supp. XII:** 26, 29, 37

Mallon, Thomas, **Supp. IV Part 1:** 200, 209

Maloff, Saul, **Supp. VIII:** 238

Malory, Thomas, **II:** 302; **III:** 486; **IV:** 50, 61; **Supp. IV Part 1:** 47

"Mal Paso Bridge" (Jeffers), **Supp. II Part 2:** 415, 420

Malraux, André, **I:** 33–34, 127, 509; **II:** 57, 376; **III:** 35, 310; **IV:** 236, 247, 434; **Retro. Supp. I:** 73; **Retro. Supp. II:** 115–116, 119; **Supp. II Part 1:** 221, 232

Maltese Falcon, The (film), **Supp. IV Part 1:** 342, 353, 355

Maltese Falcon, The (Hammett), **IV:** 286; **Supp. IV Part 1:** 345, 348–351

Mama (McMillan), **Supp. XIII:** 182, **187–188**

"Mama and Daughter" (Hughes), **Supp. I Part 1:** 334

Mama Day (Naylor), **Supp. VIII: 223–226,** 230

Mama Poc: An Ecologist's Account of the Extinction of a Species (LaBastille), **Supp. X:** 99, **104–105,** 106

"Mama Still Loves You" (Naylor), **Supp. VIII:** 214

Mambo Hips and Make Believe (Coleman), **Supp. XI: 94–96**

Mambo Kings, The (film), **Supp. VIII:** 73, 74

Mambo Kings Play Songs of Love, The (Hijuelos), **Supp. VIII:** 73–74, **79–82**

"Ma'me Pélagie" (Chopin), **Retro. Supp. II:** 64

Mamet, David, **Supp. XIV:239–258,** 315

"Mamie" (Sandburg), **III:** 582

Mammedaty, Novarro Scott. *See* Momaday, N. Scott

"Mammon and the Archer" (O. Henry), **Supp. II Part 1:** 394, 408

Mammonart (Sinclair), **Supp. V:** 276–277

"Mamouche" (Chopin), **Retro. Supp. II:** 66

"Man" (Corso), **Supp. XII:** 130

"Man" (Herbert), **II:** 12

"Man Against the Sky, The" (Robinson), **III:** 509, 523

"Man and a Woman Sit Near Each Other, A" (Bly), **Supp. IV Part 1:** 71

Man and Boy (Morris), **III:** 223, 224, 225

"Man and the Snake, The" (Bierce), **I:** 203

"Man and Woman" (Caldwell), **I:** 310

Manassas (Sinclair), **Supp. V:** 280, 281, 285

"Man Bring This Up Road" (T. Williams), **IV:** 383–384

"Man Carrying Thing" (Stevens), **IV:** 90

Manchester, William, **III:** 103

"Man Child, The" (Baldwin), **Supp. I Part 1:** 63

Man Could Stand Up, A (Ford), **I:** 423

"Mandarin's Jade" (Chandler), **Supp.**

IV Part 1: 125

Mandelbaum, Maurice, I: 61

Mandelstam, Osip, **Retro. Supp. I:** 278; **Supp. III Part 1:** 268; **Supp. VIII:** 21, 22, 23, 27; **Supp. XIII:** 77

"Mandelstam: The Poem as Event" (Dobyns), **Supp. XIII:** 78

"Mandolin" (Dove), **Supp. IV Part 1:** 247

"Mandoline" (Verlaine), **IV:** 79

"Man Eating" (Kenyon), **Supp. VII:** 173

"Man Feeding Pigeons" (Clampitt), **Supp. IX: 49–50,** 52

Manfred, Frederick, **Supp. X:** 126

"Mango Says Goodbye Sometimes" (Cisneros), **Supp. VII:** 64

Manhattan (film), **Supp. IV Part 1:** 205

"Manhattan: Luminism" (Doty), **Supp. XI:** 135

"Manhattan Dawn" (Justice), **Supp. VII:** 117

Manhattan Transfer (Dos Passos), **I:** 26, 475, 478, 479, 480, 481, 482–484, 487; **II:** 286; **Supp. I Part 1:** 57

"Mania" (Lowell), **II:** 554

"Manic in the Moon, The" (Thurber), **Supp. I Part 2:** 620

"Man in Black" (Plath), **Supp. I Part 2:** 538

Man in Prehistory (Chard), **Supp. XII:** 177–178

Man in the Black Coat Turns, The (Bly), **Supp. IV Part 1:** 66–68, 71, 73

"Man in the Brooks Brothers Shirt, The" (McCarthy), **II:** 563–564

"Man in the Drawer, The" (Malamud), **Supp. I Part 2:** 437

Man in the Gray Flannel Suit, The (Wilson), **Supp. IV Part 1:** 387

Man in the Middle, The (Wagoner), **Supp. IX:** 324, **332–333**

Mankiewicz, Joseph, **Retro. Supp. I:** 113

Mankowitz, Wolf, **Supp. XI:** 307

"Man Made of Words, The" (Momaday), **Supp. IV Part 2:** 481, 484–485, 486, 487, 488

Man-Made World, The (Gilman), **Supp. XI:** 207

"Man-Moth, The" (Bishop), **Retro. Supp. II:** 42; **Supp. I Part 1:** 85–87, 88

Mann, Charles, **Retro. Supp. II:** 40

Mann, Erika, **Supp. II Part 1:** 11

Mann, Seymour (Samuel Weisman),

Supp. V: 113

Mann, Thomas, **I:** 271, 490; **II:** 42, 539; **III:** 231, 281–282, 283; **IV:** 70, 73, 85; **Supp. IV Part 1:** 392; **Supp. IV Part 2:** 522; **Supp. V:** 51; **Supp. IX:** 21; **Supp. XI:** 275; **Supp. XII:** 173, 310, 321; **Supp. XIV:** 87

Mannerhouse (Wolfe), **IV:** 460

Manner Music, The (Reznikoff), **Supp. XIV:293–295**

"Manners" (Bishop), **Supp. I Part 1:** 73

"Manners" (Emerson), **II:** 4, 6

"Manners, Morals, and the Novel" (Trilling), **Supp. III Part 2:** 502, 503

Mannheim, Karl, **I:** 279; **Supp. I Part 2:** 644

Manning, Frederic, **III:** 459

Manning, Robert, **Supp. IX:** 236

Mannix, Daniel P., **Supp. II Part 1:** 140

Man Nobody Knows, The (B. Barton), **Retro. Supp. I:** 179

"Man of Letters as a Man of Business, The" (Howells), **Supp. XIV:** 45–46

"Man of No Account, The" (Harte), **Supp. II Part 1:** 339

"Man of the Crowd, The" (Poe), **III:** 412, 417; **Retro. Supp. I:** 154

Man on Spikes (Asinof), **II:** 424

Man on Stage (Dixon), **Supp. XII:** 141, **154–155**

"Man on the Dump, The" (Stevens), **IV:** 74; **Retro. Supp. I:** 306

"Man on the Train, The" (Percy), **Supp. III Part 1:** 387

Manor, The (Singer), **IV:** 6, 17–19

Manrique, Jorge, **Retro. Supp. II:** 154

Mansart Builds a School (Du Bois), **Supp. II Part 1:** 185–186

Man's Fate (Malraux), **I:** 127; **Retro. Supp. II:** 121

"Man's Fate A Film Treatment of the Malraux Novel" (Agee), **I:** 33–34

Mansfield, June, **Supp. X:** 183, 194

Mansfield, Katherine, **III:** 362, 453

Mansfield, Stephanie, **Supp. IV Part 1:** 227

Man's Hope (Malraux), **IV:** 247

Mansion, The (Faulkner), **II:** 73; **Retro. Supp. I:** 74, 82

Man's Nature and His Communities (Niebuhr), **III:** 308

Manson, Charles, **Supp. IV Part 1:** 205

"Man Splitting Wood in the Daybreak, The" (Kinnell), **Supp. III Part 1:** 254

"Man's Pride" (Jeffers), **Supp. II Part 2:** 417

"Man's Story, The" (Anderson), **I:** 114

Man's Woman, A (Norris), **III:** 314, 322, 328, 329, 330, 332, 333

Man That Corrupted Hadleyburg, The (Twain), **I:** 204; **IV:** 208

"Man That Was Used Up, The" (Poe), **III:** 412, 425

"Mantis" (Zukofsky), **Supp. III Part 2:** 617

"'Mantis': An Interpretation" (Zukofsky), **Supp. III Part 2:** 617–618

Man to Send Rain Clouds, The (Rosen, ed.), **Supp. IV Part 2:** 499, 505, 513

"Man to Send Rain Clouds, The" (Silko), **Supp. IV Part 2:** 559

Mantrap (Lewis), **II:** 447

Manuductio Ad Ministerium (Mather), **Supp. II Part 2:** 465–467

"Manuelzinho" (Bishop), **Retro. Supp. II:** 47–48

Manuscript Books of Emily Dickinson, The (Franklin, ed.), **Retro. Supp. I:** 29, 41

"Man Waiting for It to Stop, A" (Dunn), **Supp. XI:** 144

"Man Who Became a Woman, The" (Anderson), **I:** 114

"Man Who Carries the Desert Around Inside Himself, The: For Wally" (Komunyakaa), **Supp. XIII:** 125

"Man Who Closed Shop, The" (Dunn), **Supp. XI:** 149

Man Who Gave Up His Name, The (Harrison), **Supp. VIII:** 45, 52

Man Who Had All the Luck, The (A. Miller), **III:** 148, 149, 164, 166

"Man Who Knew Belle Star, The" (Bausch), **Supp. VII:** 46

"Man Who Knew Coolidge, The" (Lewis), **II:** 449

Man Who Knew Coolidge, The: Being the Soul of Lowell Schmaltz, Constructive and Nordic Citizen (Lewis), **II:** 450

Man Who Lived Underground, The (Wright), **Supp. II Part 1:** 40

"Man Who Lived Underground, The" (Wright), **IV:** 479, 485–487, 492; **Retro. Supp. II:** 121

"Man Who Makes Brooms, The" (Nye), **Supp. XIII:** 276

"Man Who Studied Yoga, The" (Mailer), **III:** 35–36; **Retro. Supp. II:** 200

"Man Who Wanted to Win, The" (McCoy), **Supp. XIII:** 161

Man Who Was There, The (Morris), **III:** 220–221

"Man Who Writes Ants, The" (Merwin), **Supp. III Part 1:** 348

"Man with a Family" (Humphrey), **Supp. IX:** 94

Man without a Country, The (Hale), **I:** 488

"Man with the Blue Guitar, The" (Stevens), **I:** 266; **IV:** 85–87; **Retro. Supp. I: 303–305,** 306, 307, 309

Man with the Blue Guitar and Other Poems, The (Stevens), **IV:** 76; **Retro. Supp. I:** 303, 422

Man with the Golden Arm, The (Algren), **Supp. V:** 4; **Supp. IX:** 1, 3, **9–11,** 14, 15

Man with the Golden Arm, The (film), **Supp. IX:** 3

"Man with the Golden Beef, The" (Podhoretz), **Supp. IX:** 3

Manyan Letters (Olson), **Supp. II Part 2:** 571

Many Circles (Goldbarth), **Supp. XII:** 193

"Many Handles" (Sandburg), **III:** 594

"Many Happy Returns" (Auden), **Supp. II Part 1:** 15

Many Loves (W. C. Williams), **Retro. Supp. I:** 424

"Many Mansions" (H. Roth), **Supp. IX:** 233, 234

Many Marriages (Anderson), **I:** 104, 111, 113

"Many of Our Waters: Variations on a Poem by a Black Child" (Wright), **Supp. III Part 2:** 602

"Many Swans" (Lowell), **II:** 526

"Many Thousands Gone" (Baldwin), **Retro. Supp. II:** 4; **Supp. I Part 1:** 51

"Many Wagons Ago" (Ashbery), **Supp. III Part 1:** 22

"Many-Windowed House, A" (Cowley), **Supp. II Part 1:** 137

Many-Windowed House, A (Cowley), **Supp. II Part 1:** 141, 143

Mao II (DeLillo), **Supp. VI:** 2, 4, **5,** 6, **7,** 8, 9, 14, 16

"Map, The" (Bishop), **Retro. Supp. II:** 41; **Supp. I Part 1:** 72, 82, 85–88, 93

"Map, The" (Strand), **Supp. IV Part 2:** 623–624

"Maple Leaf, The" (Joplin), **Supp. IV Part 1:** 223

"Map of Montana in Italy, A" (Hugo), **Supp. VI:** 139

"Maps" (Hass), **Supp. VI:** 103–104

Mapson, Jo-Ann, **Supp. IV Part 2:** 440, 454

Map to the Next World, A: Poems and Tales (Harjo), **Supp. XII: 228–230**

"Mara" (Jeffers), **Supp. II Part 2:** 434

Ma Rainey's Black Bottom (Wilson), **Supp. VIII:** 331, **332–334,** 346, 349, 350

Marat, Jean Paul, **IV:** 117; **Supp. I Part 2:** 514, 515, 521

"Marathon" (Glück), **Supp. V:** 85

Marble Faun, The (Faulkner), **II:** 55, 56; **Retro. Supp. I:** 79

Marble Faun, The; or, The Romance of Monte Beni (Hawthorne), **II:** 225, 239, 242–243, 290, 324; **IV:** 167; **Retro. Supp. I:** 63, 149, 163, **164– 165; Supp. I Part 1:** 38; **Supp. I Part 2:** 421, 596; **Supp. XIII:** 102

Marbles (Brodsky), **Supp. VIII:** 26–27

"March" (W. C. Williams), **Retro. Supp. I:** 418

March, Fredric, **III:** 154, 403; **IV:** 357; **Supp. X:** 220

Marchalonis, Shirley, **Supp. XIII:** 138, 140, 141, 143, 147–148

"Marché aux Oiseaux" (Wilbur), **Supp. III Part 2:** 550

"Märchen, The" (Jarrell), **II:** 378–379

March Hares (Frederic), **II:** 143–144

Marching Men (Anderson), **I:** 99, 101, 103–105, 111

"Marching Music" (Simic), **Supp. VIII:** 281

Marco Millions (O'Neill), **III:** 391, 395

Marcosson, Isaac, **III:** 322

Marcus, Steven, **Retro. Supp. II:** 196, 200

Marcus Aurelius, **II:** 1; **III:** 566

Marcuse, Herbert, **Supp. I Part 2:** 645; **Supp. VIII:** 196; **Supp. XII:** 2

Mardi and a Voyage Thither (Melville), **I:** 384; **II:** 281; **III:** 77–79, 84, 87, 89; **Retro. Supp. I:** 247, 254, 256

Margaret (Judd), **II:** 290

"Margaret Fuller, 1847" (Clampitt), **Supp. IX:** 43

"Marginalia" (Wilbur), **Supp. III Part 2:** 544

Margin of Hope, A: An Intellectual Autobiography (Howe), **Supp. VI:** 113–114, 117, 125, 128

"Margins of Maycomb, The: A Rereading of *To Kill a Mockingbird*" (Phelps), **Supp. VIII:** 128

Margoshes, Samuel, **Supp. X:** 70

"Margrave" (Jeffers), **Supp. II Part 2:** 426

"Maria Concepción" (Porter), **III:** 434–435, 451

Mariani, Paul L., **Retro. Supp. I:** 412, 419; **Retro. Supp. II:** 189

Marianne Moore Reader, (Moore), **III:** 199

Marie Antoinette (film), **Retro. Supp. I:** 113

Mariella Gable, Sister, **III:** 339, 355

"Marijuana Notation" (Ginsberg), **Supp. II Part 1:** 313

Marilyn: A Biography (Mailer), **Retro. Supp. II:** 208

"Marin" (Cisneros), **Supp. VII:** 60, 61

Marin, Jay, **Retro. Supp. II:** 325

"Marina" (Eliot), **I:** 584, 585; **Retro. Supp. I:** 64

"Marine Surface, Low Overcast" (Clampitt), **Supp. IX: 47–48**

Marinetti, Tommaso, **Retro. Supp. I:** 59

Marionettes, The (Faulkner), **Retro. Supp. I:** 79

Maritain, Jacques, **I:** 402

Maritime Compact (Paine), **Supp. I Part 2:** 519

Maritime History of Massachusetts, 1783–1860, The (Morison), **Supp. I Part 2:** 481–483

Marjolin, Jean-Nicolas, **Supp. I Part 1:** 302

Marjorie Kinnan Rawlings: Sojourner at Cross Creek (Silverthorne), **Supp. X:** 220, 234

"Mark, The" (Bogan), **Supp. III Part 1:** 52

Marker, Chris, **Supp. IV Part 2:** 434, 436

"Market" (Hayden), **Supp. II Part 1:** 368, 369

Marketplace, The (Frederic), **II:** 145–146

Markham, Edwin, **I:** 199, 207

Markings (Hammarskjold), **Supp. II Part 1:** 26

Markopoulos, Gregory, **Supp. XII:** 2

Markowick-Olczakova, Hanna, **Supp. X:** 70

Marks, Alison, **Supp. I Part 2:** 660

Marks, Barry A., **I:** 435, 438, 442, 446

Mark Twain in Eruption (Twain), **IV:** 209

Mark Twain's America (De Voto), **I:** 248

Mark Twain's Autobiography (Twain), **IV:** 209

Marley, Bob, **Supp. IX:** 152

Marlowe, Christopher, **I:** 68, 368, 384; **II:** 590; **III:** 259, 491; **Retro. Supp. I:** 127; **Retro. Supp. II:** 76; **Supp.**

I **Part 2:** 422

"Marlowe Takes on the Syndicate" (Chandler), **Supp. IV Part 1:** 135

Marne, The (Wharton), **IV:** 319, 320; **Retro. Supp. I:** 378

Marquand, J. P., **I:** 362, 375; **II:** 459, 482–483; **III: 50–73,** 383; **Supp. I Part 1:** 196; **Supp. IV Part 1:** 31; **Supp. V:** 95

Marquand, John, **Supp. XI:** 301

Marquand, Mrs. John P. (Adelaide Hooker), **III:** 57, 61

Marquand, Mrs. John P. (Christina Sedgwick), **III:** 54, 57

Marquand, Philip, **III:** 52

Marquis, Don, **Supp. I Part 2:** 668

"Marriage" (Corso), **Supp. XII:** 117, 124, **127–128**

Marriage (Moore), **III:** 194

"Marriage" (Moore), **III:** 198–199, 213

Marriage A-la-Mode (Dryden), **Supp. IX:** 68

Marriage and Other Science Fiction (Goldbarth), **Supp. XII:** 189, 190

"Marriage in the Sixties, A" (Rich), **Supp. I Part 2:** 554

"Marriage of Heaven and Hell, The" (Blake), **III:** 544–545; **Supp. VIII:** 99

"Marriage of Phaedra, The" (Cather), **Retro. Supp. I:** 5

Marrow of Tradition, The (Chesnutt), **Supp. XIV:** 63, **71–75,** 76

Marryat, Captain Frederick, **III:** 423

"Marrying Absurd" (Didion), **Supp. IV Part 1:** 200

"Marrying Iseult?" (Updike), **Retro. Supp. I:** 329

Marrying Man (Simon), **Supp. IV Part 2:** 588

"Marrying the Hangman" (Atwood), **Supp. XIII:** 34

Marry Me: A Romance (Updike), **Retro. Supp. I:** 329, 330, 332

"Mars and Hymen" (Freneau), **Supp. II Part 1:** 258

Marsden, Dora, **III:** 471; **Retro. Supp. I:** 416

Marsena (Frederic), **II:** 135, 136–137

Marsh, Edward, **Supp. I Part 1:** 257, 263

Marsh, Fred T., **Supp. IX:** 232

Marsh, Mae, **Supp. I Part 2:** 391

Marshall, George, **III:** 3

Marshall, John, **Supp. I Part 2:** 455

Marshall, Paule, **Supp. IV Part 1:** 8, 14, 369; **Supp. XI:** 18, **275–292;** **Supp. XIII:** 295

"Marshall Carpenter" (Masters), **Supp. I Part 2:** 463

"Marshes of Glynn, The" (Lanier), **Supp. I Part 1:** 364, 365–368, 370, 373

"'Marshes of Glynn, The': A Study in Symbolic Obscurity" (Ross), **Supp. I Part 1:** 373

Marsh Island, A (Jewett), **II:** 405; **Retro. Supp. II:** 134

"Marshland Elegy" (Leopold), **Supp. XIV:** 187, 189

"Mars Is Heaven!" (Bradbury), **Supp. IV Part 1:** 103, 106

Marsman, Henrik, **Supp. IV Part 1:** 183

Marston, Ed, **Supp. IV Part 2:** 492

Marta y Maria (Valdes), **II:** 290

"Martha's Lady" (Jewett), **Retro. Supp. II:** 140, 143

Marthe, Saint, **II:** 213

Martial, **II:** 1, 169; **Supp. IX:** 152

Martian Chronicles, The (Bradbury), **Supp. IV Part 1:** 102, 103, 106–107

Martin, Benjamin, **Supp. I Part 2:** 503

Martin, Dick, **Supp. XII:** 44

Martin, Jay, **I:** 55, 58, 60, 61, 67; **III:** 307; **Retro. Supp. II:** 326, 327, 329; **Supp. XI:** 162

Martin, John, **Supp. XI:** 172

Martin, Judith, **Supp. V:** 128

Martin, Nell, **Supp. IV Part 1:** 351, 353

Martin, Reginald, **Supp. X:** 247, 249

Martin, Stephen-Paul, **Supp. IV Part 2:** 430

Martin, Tom, **Supp. X:** 79

Martin du Gard, Roger, **Supp. I Part 1:** 51

Martineau, Harriet, **Supp. II Part 1:** 282, 288, 294

Martin Eden (London), **II:** 466, 477–481

Martinelli, Sheri, **Supp. IV Part 1:** 280

Martínez, Guillermo, **Supp. XIII:** 313

Mart'nez, Rafael, **Retro. Supp. I:** 423

Martone, John, **Supp. V:** 179

"Martyr, The" (Porter), **III:** 454

Martz, Louis L., **IV:** 151, 156, 165; **Supp. I Part 1:** 107; **Supp. XIV:** 12

Marvell, Andrew, **IV:** 135, 151, 156, 161, 253; **Retro. Supp. I:** 62, 127; **Retro. Supp. II:** 186, 189; **Supp. I Part 1:** 80; **Supp. XII:** 159; **Supp. XIV:** 10

"Marvella, for Borrowing" (Ríos), **Supp. IV Part 2:** 551

Marx, Karl, **I:** 60, 267, 279, 283, 588; **II:** 376, 462, 463, 483, 577; **IV:** 429, 436, 443–444, 469; **Retro. Supp. I:** 254; **Supp. I Part 2:** 518, 628, 632, 633, 634, 635, 639, 643, 645, 646; **Supp. III Part 2:** 619; **Supp. IV Part 1:** 355; **Supp. VIII:** 196; **Supp. IX:** 133; **Supp. X:** 119, 134; **Supp. XIII:** 75

Marx, Leo, **Supp. I Part 1:** 233

"Marxism and Monastic Perpectives" (Merton), **Supp. VIII:** 196

Mary (Nabokov), **Retro. Supp. I: 267–268,** 270, 277

"Mary Karr, Mary Karr, Mary Karr, Mary Karr" (Harmon), **Supp. XI:** 248

Maryles, Daisy, **Supp. XII:** 271

Mary Magdalene, **I:** 303

"Mary O'Reilly" (Anderson), **II:** 44

"Mary Osaka , I Love You" (Fante), **Supp. XI:** 169

"Mary's Song" (Plath), **Supp. I Part 2:** 541

"Mary Winslow" (Lowell), **Retro. Supp. II:** 187

Masefield, John, **II:** 552; **III:** 523

Mask for Janus, A (Merwin), **Supp. III Part 1:** 339, 341, 342

Maslow, Abraham, **Supp. I Part 2:** 540

Mason, Bobbie Ann, **Supp. VIII: 133–149; Supp. XI:** 26; **Supp. XII:** 294, 298, 311

Mason, Charlotte, **Supp. XIV:** 201

Mason, David, **Supp. V:** 344

Mason, Lowell, **I:** 458

Mason, Marsha, **Supp. IV Part 2:** 575, 586

Mason, Otis Tufton, **Supp. I Part 1:** 18

"Mason Jars by the Window" (Ríos), **Supp. IV Part 2:** 548

Masque of Mercy, A (Frost), **II:** 155, 165, 167–168; **Retro. Supp. I:** 131, 140

"Masque of Mummers, The" (MacLeish), **III:** 18

"Masque of Pandora, The" (Longfellow), **Retro. Supp. II:** 167

Masque of Pandora, The, and Other Poems (Longfellow), **II:** 490, 494, 506; **Retro. Supp. II:** 169

Masque of Poets, A (Lathrop, ed.), **Retro. Supp. I:** 31; **Supp. I Part 1:** 365, 368

Masque of Reason, A (Frost), **II:** 155, 162, 165–167; **Retro. Supp. I:** 131, 140; **Retro. Supp. II:** 42

"Masque of the Red Death, The" (Poe), **III:** 412, 419, 424; **Retro. Supp. II:** 262, 268–269

"Masquerade" (Banks), **Supp. V:** 7

"Massachusetts 1932" (Bowles), **Supp. IV Part 1:** 94

Massachusetts, Its Historians and Its History (Adams), **Supp. I Part 2:** 484

"Massachusetts to Virginia" (Whittier), **Supp. I Part 2:** 688–689

"Massacre and the Mastermind, The" (Bausch), **Supp. VII:** 49

"Massacre at Scio, The" (Bryant), **Supp. I Part 1:** 168

"Massacre of the Innocents, The" (Simic), **Supp. VIII:** 282

Masses and Man (Toller), **I:** 479

"Masseur de Ma Soeur, Le" (Hecht), **Supp. X:** 58

Massey, Raymond, **Supp. IV Part 2:** 524

"Mass Eye and Ear: The Ward" (Karr), **Supp. XI:** 244

"Mass for the Day of St. Thomas Didymus" (Levertov), **Supp. III Part 1:** 283

Massie, Chris, **Supp. IV Part 2:** 524

Massing, Michael, **Supp. IV Part 1:** 208

Massinger, Philip, **Supp. I Part 2:** 422

Master Builder, The (Ibsen), **Supp. IV Part 2:** 522

Master Class (McNally), **Supp. XIII:** 204–205, 208

"Masterful" (Matthews), **Supp. IX:** 161–162

"Master Misery" (Capote), **Supp. III Part 1:** 117

Master of Dreams: A Memoir of Isaac Bashevis Singer (Telushkin), **Retro. Supp. II:** 317

"Master of Secret Revenges, The" (Gass), **Supp. VI:** 93

Master of the Crossroads (Bell), **Supp. X:** 16–17

"'Masterpiece of Filth, A': Portrait of Knoxville Forgets to Be Fair" (Howards), **Supp. VIII:** 178

Masterpieces of American Fiction, **Supp. XI:** 198

"Master Player, The" (Dunbar), **Supp. II Part 1:** 200

Masters, Edgar Lee, **I:** 106, 384, 475, 480, 518; **II:** 276, 529; **III:** 505, 576, 579; **IV:** 352; **Retro. Supp. I:** 131; **Supp. I Part 2:** 378, 386, 387, **454–478; Supp. III Part 1:** 63, 71, 73, 75; **Supp. IV Part 2:** 502; **Supp. IX:** 308; **Supp. XIV:** 282–283

Masters, Hardin W., **Supp. I Part 2:** 468

Masters, Hilary, **Supp. IX:** 96

Masters of Sociological Thought (Coser), **Supp. I Part 2:** 650

Masters of the Dew (Roumain), **Supp. IV Part 1:** 367

Matchmaker, The (Wilder), **IV:** 357, 369, 370, 374

Mate of the Daylight, The, and Friends Ashore (Jewett), **II:** 404; **Retro. Supp. II:** 146–147

Materassi, Mario, **Supp. IX:** 233

Mather, Cotton, **II:** 10, 104, 302, 506, 536; **III:** 442; **IV:** 144, 152–153, 157; **Supp. I Part 1:** 102, 117, 174, 271; **Supp. I Part 2:** 584, 599, 698; **Supp. II Part 2: 441–470; Supp. IV Part 2:** 430, 434

Mather, Increase, **II:** 10; **IV:** 147, 157; **Supp. I Part 1:** 100

Mathews, Cornelius, **III:** 81; **Supp. I Part 1:** 317

Mathews, Shailer, **III:** 293

"Matinees" (Merrill), **Supp. III Part 1:** 319, 327

"Matins" (Glück), **Supp. V:** 88

"Matisse: Blue Interior with Two Girls–1947" (Hecht), **Supp. X: 73–74**

Matisse, Henri, **III:** 180; **IV:** 90, 407; **Supp. I Part 2:** 619; **Supp. VIII:** 168; **Supp. IX:** 66; **Supp. X:** 73, 74

"Matisse: The Red Studio" (Snodgrass), **Supp. VI:** 316–317

Matlock, Lucinda, **Supp. I Part 2:** 462

Matson, Harold, **Supp. XIII:** 164, 166, 167, 169, 172

Matson, Peter, **Supp. IV Part 1:** 299

Matson, Suzanne, **Supp. VIII:** 281

Matters of Fact and Fiction: Essays 1973–1976 (Vidal), **Supp. IV Part 2:** 687

Matthew (biblical book), **IV:** 164

Matthew Arnold (Trilling), **Supp. III Part 2:** 500–501

Matthews, T. S., **II:** 430

Matthews, William, **Supp. V:** 4, 5; **Supp. IX: 151–170; Supp. XIII:** 112

Matthiessen, F. O., **I:** 254, 259–260, 517; **II:** 41, 554; **III:** 310, 453; **IV:** 181; **Retro. Supp. I:** 40, 217; **Retro. Supp. II:** 137; **Supp. IV Part 2:** 422; **Supp. XIII:** 93; **Supp. XIV:** 3

Matthiessen, Peter, **Supp. V: 199–217,** 332; **Supp. XI:** 231, 294; **Supp. XIV:** 82

Mattingly, Garrett, **Supp. IV Part 2:** 601

"Maud Island" (Caldwell), **I:** 310

Maud Martha (Brooks), **Supp. III Part 1:** 74, 78–79, 87; **Supp. XI:** 278

"Maud Muller" (Whittier), **Supp. I Part 2:** 698

Maugham, W. Somerset, **III:** 57, 64; **Supp. IV Part 1:** 209; **Supp. X:** 58; **Supp. XIV:** 161

Maule's Curse: Seven Studies in the History of American Obscurantism (Winters), **Supp. II Part 2:** 807–808, 812

"Mau-mauing the Flak Catchers" (Wolfe), **Supp. III Part 2:** 577

Maupassant, Guy de, **I:** 309, 421; **II:** 191–192, 291, 325, 591; **IV:** 17; **Retro. Supp. II:** 65, 66, 67, 299; **Supp. I Part 1:** 207, 217, 223, 320; **Supp. XIV:** 336

"Maurice Barrès and the Youth of France" (Bourne), **I:** 228

Maurier, George du, **II:** 338

Maurras, Charles, **Retro. Supp. I:** 55

Mauve Gloves & Madmen, Clutter & Vine (Wolfe), **Supp. III Part 2:** 581

Maverick in Mauve (Auchincloss), **Supp. IV Part 1:** 26

"Mavericks, The" (play) (Auchincloss), **Supp. IV Part 1:** 34

"Mavericks, The" (story) (Auchincloss), **Supp. IV Part 1:** 32

"Max" (H. Miller), **III:** 183

Max and the White Phagocytes (H. Miller), **III:** 178, 183–184

Maximilian (emperor of Mexico), **Supp. I Part 2:** 457–458

Maximilian: A Play in Five Acts (Masters), **Supp. I Part 2:** 456, 457–458

"Maximus, to Gloucester" (Olson), **Supp. II Part 2:** 574

"Maximus, to himself" (Olson), **Supp. II Part 2:** 565, 566, 567, 569, 570, 572

Maximus Poems, The (Olson), **Retro. Supp. I:** 209; **Supp. II Part 2:** 555, 556, 563, 564–580, 584; **Supp. VIII:** 305

Maximus Poems 1–10, The (Olson), **Supp. II Part 2:** 571

Maximus Poems IV, V, VI (Olson), **Supp. II Part 2:** 555, 580, 582–584

Maximus Poems Volume Three, The (Olson), **Supp. II Part 2:** 555, 582, 584–585

"Maximus to Gloucester, Letter 19 (A Pastoral Letter)" (Olson), **Supp. II Part 2:** 567

"Maximus to Gloucester, Sunday July 19" (Olson), **Supp. II Part 2:** 580

"Maximus to himself June 1964" (Olson), **Supp. II Part 2:** 584

Maxwell, William, **Supp. I Part 1:** 175; **Supp. III Part 1:** 62; **Supp. VIII: 151–174**

"May 1968" (Olds), **Supp. X:** 211–212
May, Abigail (Abba). *See* Alcott, Mrs. Amos Bronson (Abigail May)
May, Jill, **Supp. VIII:** 126
"May 24, 1980" (Brodsky), **Supp. VIII:** 28
"Mayan Warning" (Mora), **Supp. XIII:** 214
Maybe (Hellman), **Supp. IV Part 1:** 12
"Maybe" (Oliver), **Supp. VII:** 239
"Maybe, Someday" (Ritsos), **Supp. XIII:** 78
"Mayday" (Faulkner), **Retro. Supp. I:** 80
"May Day" (Fitzgerald), **II:** 88–89; **Retro. Supp. I:** 103
"May Day Dancing, The" (Nemerov), **III:** 275
"May Day Sermon to the Women of Gilmer County, Georgia, by a Woman Preacher Leaving the Baptist Church" (Dickey), **Supp. IV Part 1:** 182
Mayer, Elizabeth, **Supp. II Part 1:** 16; **Supp. III Part 1:** 63
Mayer, John, **Retro. Supp. I:** 58
Mayer, Louis B., **Supp. XII:** 160
Mayes, Wendell, **Supp. IX:** 250
Mayfield, Sara, **Supp. IX:** 65
Mayflower, The (Stowe), **Supp. I Part 2:** 585, 586
Maynard, Joyce, **Supp. V:** 23
Maynard, Tony, **Supp. I Part 1:** 65
Mayo, Robert, **III:** 478
Mayorga, Margaret, **IV:** 381
"Maypole of Merrymount, The" (Hawthorne), **II:** 229
May Sarton: Selected Letters 1916–1954, **Supp. VIII:** 265
"May Sun Sheds an Amber Light, The" (Bryant), **Supp. I Part 1:** 170
"May Swenson: The Art of Perceiving" (Stanford), **Supp. IV Part 2:** 637
"Maze" (Eberhart), **I:** 523, 525–526, 527
Mazurkiewicz, Margaret, **Supp. XI:** 2
Mazzini, Giuseppe, **Supp. I Part 1:** 2, 8; **Supp. II Part 1:** 299
M Butterfly (Hwang), **Supp. X:** 292
Mc. Names starting with Mc are alphabetized as if spelled Mac.
"Me, Boy Scout" (Lardner), **II:** 433
Me, Vashya! (T. Williams), **IV:** 381
Mead, Elinor. *See* Howells, Mrs. William Dean (Elinor Mead)
Mead, George Herbert, **II:** 27, 34; **Supp. I Part 1:** 5; **Supp. I Part 2:** 641

Mead, Margaret, **Supp. I Part 1:** 49, 52, 66; **Supp. IX:** 229
Meade, Frank, **Retro. Supp. II:** 114
Meade, Marion, **Supp. IX:** 191, 193, 194, 195
Meadow, Lynne, **Supp. XIII:** 198
Meadowlands (Glück), **Supp. V:** 88–90
"Mean, Mrs." (Gass), **Supp. VI:** 83
"Me and the Mule" (Hughes), **Supp. I Part 1:** 334
"Meaningless Institution, A" (Ginsberg), **Supp. II Part 1:** 313
"Meaning of a Literary Idea, The" (Trilling), **Supp. III Part 2:** 498
"Meaning of Birds, The" (C. Smith), **Supp. X:** 177
"Meaning of Death, The, An After Dinner Speech" (Tate), **IV:** 128, 129
"Meaning of Life, The" (Tate), **IV:** 137
"Meaning of Simplicity, The" (Ritsos), **Supp. XIII:** 78
Mean Spirit (Hogan), **Supp. IV Part 1:** 397, 404, 407–410, 415, 416–417
Mearns, Hughes, **III:** 220
"Measure" (Hass), **Supp. VI:** 99–100, 101
"Measuring My Blood" (Vizenor), **Supp. IV Part 1:** 262
Meatyard, Gene, **Supp. X:** 30
"Mechanism" (Ammons), **Supp. VII:** 28
"Mechanism in Thought and Morals" (Holmes), **Supp. I Part 1:** 314
Mecom, Mrs. Jane, **II:** 122
"Meddlesome Jack" (Caldwell), **I:** 309
Medea (Jeffers), **Supp. II Part 2:** 435
Medea and Some Poems, The (Cullen), **Supp. IV Part 1:** 169, 173
"Me Decade and the Third Great Awakening, The" (Wolfe), **Supp. III Part 2:** 581
"Médecin Malgré Lui, Le" (W. C. Williams), **IV:** 407–408
"Medfield" (Bryant), **Supp. I Part 1:** 157
Medical History of Contraception, A (Himes), **Supp. V:** 128
"Medicine Song" (Gunn Allen), **Supp. IV Part 1:** 326
Médicis, Marie de, **II:** 548
Medina (McCarthy), **II:** 579
"Meditation 1.6" (Taylor), **IV:** 165
"Meditation 1.20" (Taylor), **IV:** 165
"Meditation 2.102" (Taylor), **IV:** 150
"Meditation 2.112" (Taylor), **IV:** 165
"Meditation 20" (Taylor), **IV:** 154–155
"Meditation 40" (Second Series) (Taylor), **IV:** 147
"Meditation, A" (Eberhart), **I:** 533–535
"Meditation 2.68A" (Taylor), **IV:** 165

"Meditation at Lagunitas" (Hass), **Supp. VI:** 104–105
"Meditation at Oyster River" (Roethke), **III:** 537, 549
Meditations (Descartes), **III:** 618
"Meditations for a Savage Child" (Rich), **Supp. I Part 2:** 564–565
Meditations from a Movable Chair (Dubus), **Supp. VII:** 91
"Meditations in a Swine Yard" (Komunyakaa), **Supp. XIII:** 131
"Meditations of an Old Woman" (Roethke), **III:** 529, 540, 542, 543, 545–547, 548
Meditations on the Insatiable Soul (Bly), **Supp. IV Part 1:** 72–73
Meditative Poems, The (Martz), **IV:** 151
"Mediterranean, The" (Tate), **IV:** 129
"Medium of Fiction, The" (Gass), **Supp. VI:** 85–86
"Medley" (Bambara), **Supp. XI:** 9
"Medusa" (Bogan), **Supp. III Part 1:** 50, 51
Meehan, Thomas, **Supp. IV Part 2:** 577–578, 586, 590
Meek, Martha, **Supp. IV Part 2:** 439, 440, 441, 442, 445, 447, 448
Meeker, Richard K., **II:** 190
Meese, Elizabeth, **Supp. XIII:** 297
"Meeting and Greeting Area, The" (Cameron), **Supp. XII:** 84–85
Meeting by the River, A (Isherwood), **Supp. XIV:** 164, 170–171, 172
"Meeting-House Hill" (Lowell), **II:** 522, 527
"Meeting South, A" (Anderson), **I:** 115
"Meeting the Mountains" (Snyder), **Supp. VIII:** 300
Meet Me at the Morgue (Macdonald), **Supp. IV Part 2:** 472
Mehta, Sonny, **Supp. XI:** 178
Meine, Curt, **Supp. XIV:** 179
Meiners, R. K., **IV:** 136, 137, 138, 140
Meinong, Alexius, **Supp. XIV:** 198, 199
Meisner, Sanford, **Supp. XIV:** 240, 242
Meister, Charles W., **II:** 112
"Melancholia" (Dunbar), **Supp. II Part 1:** 194
"Melanctha" (Stein), **IV:** 30, 34, 35, 37, 38–40, 45
"Melancthon" (Moore), **III:** 212, 215
Meliboeus Hipponax (Lowell). *See Bigelow Papers, The* (Lowell)
Mellaart, James, **Supp. I Part 2:** 567
Mellard, James, **Supp. IV Part 1:** 387
Mellon, Andrew, **III:** 14
Melnick, Jeffrey, **Supp. X:** 252

Melnyczuk, Askold, **Supp. IV Part 1:** 70

Melodrama Play (Shepard), **Supp. III Part 2:** 440–441, 443, 445

Melodramatists, The (Nemerov), **III:** 268, 281–283, 284

Melting-Pot, The (Zangwill), **I:** 229

Melville, Allan, **III:** 74, 77

Melville, Gansevoort, **III:** 76

Melville, Herman, **I:** 104, 106, 211, 288, 340, 343, 348, 354, 355, 561–562; **II:** 27, 74, 224–225, 228, 230, 232, 236, 255, 259, 271, 272, 277, 281, 295, 307, 311, 319, 320, 321, 418, 477, 497, 539–540, 545; **III:** 29, 45, 70, **74–98,** 359, 438, 453, 454, 507, 562–563, 572, 576; **IV:** 57, 105, 194, 199, 202, 250, 309, 333, 345, 350, 380, 444, 453; **Retro. Supp. I:** 54, 91, 160, 215, 220, **243–262; Retro. Supp. II:** 76; **Supp. I Part 1:** 147, 238, 242, 249, 309, 317, 372; **Supp. I Part 2:** 383, 495, 579, 580, 582, 602; **Supp. IV Part 2:** 463, 613; **Supp. V:** 279, 281, 298, 308; **Supp. VIII:** 48, 103, 104, 105, 106, 108, 156, 175, 181, 188; **Supp. XI:** 83; **Supp. XII:** 282; **Supp. XIII:** 294, 305; **Supp. XIV:** 48, 227

Melville, Maria Gansevoort, **III:** 74, 77, 85

Melville, Mrs. Herman (Elizabeth Shaw), **III:** 77, 91, 92

Melville, Thomas, **III:** 77, 79, 92; **Supp. I Part 1:** 309

Melville, Whyte, **IV:** 309

Melville Goodwin, USA (Marquand), **III:** 60, 65–66

Melville's Marginalia (Cowen), **Supp. IV Part 2:** 435

"Melville's Marginalia" (Howe), **Supp. IV Part 2:** 435

Member of the Wedding, The (McCullers), **II:** 587, 592, 600–604, 605, 606; **Supp. VIII:** 124

"Meme Ortiz" (Cisneros), **Supp. VII:** 60

Memmon (song cycle) (Bowles), **Supp. IV Part 1:** 82

Memnoch the Devil (Rice), **Supp. VII:** 289, 290, 294, 296–299

"Memoir" (Untermeyer), **II:** 516–517

"Memoirist's Apology, A" (Karr), **Supp. XI:** 245, 246

Memoir of Mary Ann, A (O'Connor), **III:** 357

Memoir of Thomas McGrath, A (Beeching), **Supp. X:** 114, 118

Memoirs of Arii Taimai (Adams), **I:** 2–3

"Memoirs of Carwin, the Biloquist" (Brown), **Supp. I Part 1:** 132

Memoirs of Hecate County (Wilson), **IV:** 429

Memoirs of Margaret Fuller Ossoli (Fuller), **Supp. II Part 1:** 280, 283, 285

"Memoirs of Stephen Calvert" (Brown), **Supp. I Part 1:** 133, 144

Memorabilia (Xenophon), **II:** 105

Memorable Providences (Mather), **Supp. II Part 2:** 458

Memorial, The: Portrait of a Family (Isherwood), **Supp. XIV:** 156, 159, 160–161

"Memorial Day" (Cameron), **Supp. XII:** 80, **82–83**

"Memorial for the City" (Auden), **Supp. II Part 1:** 20

"Memorial Rain" (MacLeish), **III:** 15

"Memorial to Ed Bland" (Brooks), **Supp. III Part 1:** 77

"Memorial Tribute" (Wilbur), **Supp. IV Part 2:** 642

"Memories" (Whittier), **Supp. I Part 2:** 699

Memories of a Catholic Girlhood (McCarthy), **II:** 560–561, 566; **Supp. XI:** 246

"Memories of East Texas" (Karr), **Supp. XI:** 239

"Memories of Uncle Neddy" (Bishop), **Retro. Supp. II:** 38; **Supp. I Part 1:** 73, 93

"Memories of West Street and Lepke" (Lowell), **II:** 550

"Memory" (Epstein), **Supp. XII:** 163

"Memory, A" (Welty), **IV:** 261–262; **Retro. Supp. I:** 344–345

Memory Gardens (Creeley), **Supp. IV Part 1:** 141, 157

Memory of Murder, A (Bradbury), **Supp. IV Part 1:** 103

Memory of Old Jack, The (Berry), **Supp. X:** 34

Memory of Two Mondays, A (A. Miller), **III:** 153, 156, 158–159, 160, 166

"Memo to Non-White Peoples" (Hughes), **Retro. Supp. I:** 209

Men, Women and Ghosts (Lowell), **II:** 523–524

Menaker, Daniel, **Supp. VIII:** 151

Menand, Louis, **Supp. XIV:** 40, 197

Men and Angels (Gordon), **Supp. IV Part 1:** 304–305, 306, 308

Men and Brethen (Cozzens), **I:** 363–365, 368, 375, 378, 379

"Men and Women" (Bly), **Supp. IV Part 1:** 72

"Men at Forty" (Justice), **Supp. VII:** 126–127

Mencius (Meng-tzu), **IV:** 183

Mencken, August, **III:** 100, 108

Mencken, August, Jr., **III:** 99, 109, 118–119

Mencken, Burkhardt, **III:** 100, 108

Mencken, Charles, **III:** 99

Mencken, Gertrude, **III:** 99

Mencken, H. L., **I:** 199, 210, 212, 235, 245, 261, 405, 514, 515, 517; **II:** 25, 27, 42, 89, 90, 91, 271, 289, 430, 443, 449; **III: 99–121,** 394, 482; **IV:** 76, 432, 440, 475, 482; **Retro. Supp. I:** 1, 101; **Retro. Supp. II:** 97, 98, 102, 265; **Supp. I Part 2:** 484, 629–630, 631, 647, 651, 653, 659, 673; **Supp. II Part 1:** 136; **Supp. IV Part 1:** 201, 314, 343; **Supp. IV Part 2:** 521, 692, 693; **Supp. XI:** 163–164, 166; **Supp. XIII:** 161; **Supp. XIV:** 111

Mencken, Mrs. August (Anna Abhau), **III:** 100, 109

Mencken, Mrs. H. L. (Sara Haardt), **III:** 109, 111

"Men Deified Because of Their Cruelty" (Simic), **Supp. VIII:** 282

Mendelbaum, Paul, **Supp. V:** 159

Mendele, **IV:** 3, 10

Mendelief, Dmitri Ivanovich, **IV:** 421

Mendelsohn, Daniel, **Supp. X:** 153, 154

"Mending Wall" (Frost), **II:** 153–154; **Retro. Supp. I:** 128, 130; **Supp. X:** 64

Men in the Off Hours (Carson), **Supp. XII: 111–113**

"Men in the Storm, The" (Crane), **I:** 411

"Men Loved Wholly Beyond Wisdom" (Bogan), **Supp. III Part 1:** 50

"Men Made Out of Words" (Stevens), **IV:** 88

Men Must Act (Mumford), **Supp. II Part 2:** 479

Mennes, John, **II:** 111

Mennoti, Gian Carlo, **Supp. IV Part 1:** 84

Men of Brewster Place, The (Naylor), **Supp. VIII:** 213, **228–230**

"Men of Color, to Arms!" (Douglass), **Supp. III Part 1:** 171

Men of Good Hope: A Story of American Progressives (Aaron), **Supp. I Part 2:** 650

"Menstruation at Forty" (Sexton), **Supp. II Part 2:** 686

"Mental Hospital Garden, The" (W. C. Williams), **Retro. Supp. I:** 428

Mental Radio (Sinclair), **Supp. V:** 289

Men Who Made the Nation, The (Dos Passos), **I:** 485

Men Without Women (Hemingway), **II:** 249; **Retro. Supp. I:** 170, 176; **Supp. IX:** 202

"Merced" (Rich), **Supp. I Part 2:** 563

"Mercedes Hospital" (Bishop), **Retro. Supp. II:** 51

"Mercenary, A" (Ozick), **Supp. V:** 267

Merchant of Venice, The (Shakespeare), **IV:** 227; **Supp. XIV:** 325

Mercury Theatre, **Retro. Supp. I:** 65

Mercy, Pity, Peace, and Love (Ozick), **Supp. V:** 257, 258

Mercy, The (Levine), **Supp. V:** 194–195

Mercy of a Rude Stream (H. Roth), **Supp. IX:** 231, 234, **235–242**

Mercy Philbrick's Choice (Jackson), **Retro. Supp. I:** 26, 27, 33

Mercy Street (Sexton), **Supp. II Part 2:** 683, 689

Meredith, George, **II:** 175, 186; **Supp. IV Part 1:** 300

Meredith, Mary. *See* Webb, Mary

Meredith, William, **II:** 545; **Retro. Supp. II:** 181

"Merely to Know" (Rich), **Supp. I Part 2:** 554

"Mère Pochette" (Jewett), **II:** 400

"Merger II, The" (Auchincloss), **Supp. IV Part 1:** 34

"Mericans" (Cisneros), **Supp. VII:** 69

"Merida, 1969" (Matthews), **Supp. IX:** 151

"Meridian" (Clampitt), **Supp. IX: 48–49**

Meridian (Walker), **Supp. III Part 2:** 520, 524, 527, 528, 531–537

Mérimée, Prosper, **II:** 322

Meriweather, James B., **Retro. Supp. I:** 77, 91

Meriwether, James B., **Retro Supp. I:** 77, 91

"Meriwether Connection, The" (Cowley), **Supp. II Part 1:** 142

Merker, K. K., **Supp. XI:** 261

"Merlin" (Emerson), **II:** 19, 20

Merlin (Robinson), **III:** 522

"Merlin Enthralled" (Wilbur), **Supp. III Part 2:** 544, 554

Merrill, Christopher, **Supp. XI:** 329

Merrill, James, **Retro. Supp. I:** 296; **Retro. Supp. II:** 53; **Supp. III Part 1: 317–338; Supp. III Part 2:** 541, 561; **Supp. IX:** 40, 42, 48, 52; **Supp. X:** 73; **Supp. XI:** 123, 131,

249; **Supp. XII:** 44, 254, 255, 256, 261–262, 269–270; **Supp. XIII:** 76, 85

Merrill, Robert, **Retro. Supp. II:** 201

Merrill, Ronald, **Supp. IV Part 2:** 521

Merritt, Theresa, **Supp. VIII:** 332

"Merry-Go-Round" (Hughes), **Retro. Supp. I:** 194, 205; **Supp. I Part 1:** 333

Merry-Go-Round, The (Van Vechten), **Supp. II Part 2:** 734, 735

Merry Month of May, The (Jones), **Supp. XI: 227–228**

Merry Widow, The (Lehar), **III:** 183

Merton, Thomas, **III:** 357; **Supp. VIII: 193–212**

Merwin, W. S., **Supp. III Part 1: 339–360; Supp. III Part 2:** 541; **Supp. IV Part 2:** 620, 623, 626; **Supp. V:** 332; **Supp. IX:** 152, 155, 290; **Supp. XIII:** 274, 277

Meryman, Richard, **Supp. IV Part 2:** 579, 583

Meshugah (Singer), **Retro. Supp. II: 315–316**

Mesic, Michael, **Supp. IV Part 1:** 175

Mesic, Penelope, **Supp. X:** 15

Message in the Bottle, The (Percy), **Supp. III Part 1:** 387–388, 393, 397

"Message in the Bottle, The" (Percy), **Supp. III Part 1:** 388

"Message of Flowers and Fire and Flowers, The" (Brooks), **Supp. III Part 1:** 69

Messengers Will Come No More, The (Fiedler), **Supp. XIII:** 103

Messiah (Vidal), **Supp. IV Part 2:** 677, 680, 681–682, 685, 691, 692

Messiah of Stockholm, The (Ozick), **Supp. V:** 270–271

Metamorphic Tradition in Modern Poetry (Quinn), **IV:** 421

Metamorphoses (Ovid), **II:** 542–543; **III:** 467, 468

Metamorphoses (Pound, trans.), **III:** 468–469

Metamorphosis, The (Kafka), **IV:** 438; **Retro. Supp. II:** 287–288; **Supp. VIII:** 3

"Metamorphosis and Survival" (Woodcock), **Supp. XIII:** 33

"Metaphor as Mistake" (Percy), **Supp. III Part 1:** 387–388

Metaphor & Memory: Essays (Ozick), **Supp. V:** 272

"Metaphors of a Magnifico" (Stevens), **IV:** 92

Metaphysical Club, The (Menand), **Supp. XIV:** 40, 197

"Metaphysical Poets, The" (Eliot), **I:** 527, 586

"Metaphysics" (Ginsberg), **Supp. II Part 1:** 313

Metcalf, Paul, **Supp. XIV:** 96

"Meteor, The" (Bradbury), **Supp. IV Part 1:** 102

Metress, Christopher P., **Supp. V:** 314

Metrical History of Christianity, The (Taylor), **IV:** 163

Metropolis, The (Sinclair), **Supp. V:** 285

"Metzengerstein" (Poe), **III:** 411, 417

Mew, Charlotte, **Retro. Supp. II:** 247

Mewshaw, Michael, **Supp. V:** 57; **Supp. X:** 82

"Mexico" (Lowell), **II:** 553, 554

"Mexico, Age Four" (Salinas), **Supp. XIII:** 315

Mexico City Blues (Kerouac), **Supp. III Part 1:** 225, 229

"Mexico Is a Foreign Country: Five Studies in Naturalism" (Warren), **IV:** 241, 252

"Mexico's Children" (Rodriguez), **Supp. XIV:** 302

Meyer, Donald B., **III:** 298

Meyer, Ellen Hope, **Supp. V:** 123

Meyers, Jeffrey, **Retro. Supp. I:** 124, 138; **Retro. Supp. II:** 191

Meynell, Alice, **Supp. I Part 1:** 220

Mezey, Robert, **Supp. IV Part 1:** 60; **Supp. V:** 180; **Supp. XIII:** 312

Mezzanine, The (Baker), **Supp. XIII: 41–43,** 44, 45, 48, 55

"Mezzo Cammin" (Longfellow), **II:** 490

"Mi Abuelo" (Ríos), **Supp. IV Part 2:** 541

Miami (Didion), **Supp. IV Part 1:** 199, 210

Miami and the Siege of Chicago (Mailer), **Retro. Supp. II:** 206

"Michael" (Wordsworth), **III:** 523

Michael, Magali Cornier, **Supp. XIII:** 32

"Michael Angelo: A Fragment" (Longfellow), **II:** 490, 494, 495, 506; **Retro. Supp. II:** 167

"Michael Egerton" (Price), **Supp. VI:** 257–258, 260

Michael Kohlhaas (Kleist), **Supp. IV Part 1:** 224

Michaels, Walter Benn, **Retro. Supp. I:** 115, 369, 379

Michael Scarlett (Cozens), **I:** 358–359, 378

Michelangelo, **I:** 18; **II:** 11–12; **III:** 124; **Supp. I Part 1:** 363

Michel-Michot, Paulette, **Supp. XI:** 224–225

Michelson, Albert, **IV:** 27

Mickelsson's Ghosts (Gardner), **Supp. VI:** 63, **73–74**

Mickiewicz, Adam, **Supp. II Part 1:** 299

Mid-American Chants (Anderson), **I:** 109, 114

"Midas" (Winters), **Supp. II Part 2:** 801

"Mid-August at Sourdough Mountain Lookout" (Snyder), **Supp. VIII:** 292–293

Midcentury (Dos Passos), **I:** 474, 475, 478, 490, 492–494; **Supp. I Part 2:** 646

Mid-Century American Poets, **III:** 532

"Mid-Day" (Doolittle), **Supp. I Part 1:** 266–267

"Middle Age" (Lowell), **II:** 550

"Middleaged Man, The" (Simpson), **Supp. IX:** 274–275

Middle Ages, The (Gurney), **Supp. V:** 96, 105, 108

Middlebrook, Diane Wood, **Supp. IV Part 2:** 444, 451

"Middle Daughter, The" (Kingsolver), **Supp. VII:** 209

Middlemarch (Eliot), **I:** 457, 459; **II:** 290, 291; **Retro. Supp. I:** 225; **Supp. I Part 1:** 174; **Supp. IX:** 43; **Supp. XI:** 68; **Supp. XII:** 335

Middle of My Tether, The: Familiar Essays (Epstein), **Supp. XIV:106–107**

"Middle of Nowhere, The" (Wagoner), **Supp. IX:** 327–328

Middle of the Journey, The (Trilling), **Supp. III Part 2:** 495, 504–506

"Middle of the Way" (Kinnell), **Supp. III Part 1:** 242

"Middle Passage" (Hayden), **Supp. II Part 1:** 363, 375–376

Middle Passage (Johnson), **Supp. VI: 194–196,** 198, 199; **Supp. XIII:** 182

"Middle Toe of the Right Foot, The" (Bierce), **I:** 203

Middleton, Thomas, **Retro. Supp. I:** 62

Middle Years, The (James), **II:** 337–338; **Retro. Supp. I:** 235

"Middle Years, The" (James), **Retro. Supp. I:** 228, 272

"Midnight" (Dunn), **Supp. XI:** 147

"Midnight Consultations, The" (Freneau), **Supp. II Part 1:** 257

Midnight Cry, A (Mather), **Supp. II Part 2:** 460

"Midnight Gladness" (Levertov), **Supp. III Part 1:** 284–285

"Midnight Magic" (Mason), **Supp. VIII:** 146

Midnight Magic: Selected Stories of Bobbie Ann Mason (Mason), **Supp. VIII:** 148

Midnight Mass (Bowles), **Supp. IV Part 1:** 93

"Midnight Show" (Shapiro), **Supp. II Part 2:** 705

"Midpoint" (Updike), **Retro. Supp. I:** 321, 323, 327, 330, 335

Midpoint and Other Poems (Updike), **IV:** 214

"Midrash on Happiness" (Paley), **Supp. VI:** 217

"Midsummer in the Blueberry Barrens" (Clampitt), **Supp. IX:** 40–41

Midsummer Night's Dream, A (Shakespeare), **Supp. I Part 1:** 369–370; **Supp. X:** 69

"Midwest" (Stafford), **Supp. XI:** 317

Mieder, Wolfgang, **Supp. XIV:** 126

Mies van der Rohe, Ludwig, **Supp. IV Part 1:** 40

"Mighty Fortress, A" (Leopold), **Supp. XIV:** 185

"Migration, The" (Tate), **IV:** 130

Mihailovitch, Bata, **Supp. VIII:** 272

Miklitsch, Robert, **Supp. IV Part 2:** 628, 629

Mila 18 (Uris), **Supp. IV Part 1:** 379

Milagro Beanfield War, The (film), **Supp. XIII:** 267

Milagro Beanfield War, The (Nichols), **Supp. XIII:** 253, **265–266**

Milburn, Michael, **Supp. XI:** 239, 242

Milch, David, **Supp. XI:** 348

Miles, Barry, **Supp. XII:** 123

Miles, Jack, **Supp. VIII:** 86

Miles, Josephine, **Supp. XIII:** 275

Miles, Julie, **I:** 199

Miles, Kitty, **I:** 199

Milestone, Lewis, **Supp. I Part 1:** 281

Miles Wallingford (Cooper). *See Afloat and Ashore* (Cooper)

Milford, Nancy, **II:** 83; **Supp. IX:** 60

Milhaud, Darius, **Supp. IV Part 1:** 81

Miligate, Michael, **IV:** 123, 130, 132

"Militant Nudes" (Hardwick), **Supp. III Part 1:** 210–211

"Milk Bottles" (Anderson), **I:** 114

Milk Train Doesn't Stop Here Anymore, The (T. Williams), **IV:** 382, 383, 384, 386, 390, 391, 392, 393, 394, 395, 398

Mill, James, **II:** 357

Mill, John Stuart, **III:** 294–295; **Supp. XI:** 196; **Supp. XIV:** 22

Millar, Kenneth. *See* Macdonald, Ross

Millar, Margaret (Margaret Sturm), **Supp. IV Part 2:** 464, 465

Millay, Cora, **III:** 123, 133–134, 135–136

Millay, Edna St. Vincent, **I:** 482; **II:** 530; **III: 122–144; IV:** 433, 436; **Retro. Supp. II:** 48; **Supp. I Part 2:** 707, 714, 726; **Supp. IV Part 1:** 168; **Supp. IV Part 2:** 607; **Supp. V:** 113; **Supp. IX:** 20; **Supp. XIV:** 120, 121, 122, 127

Millennium Approaches (Kushner), **Supp. IX:** 141, 142, 145

Miller, Arthur, **I:** 81, 94; **III: 145–169; Supp. IV Part 1:** 359; **Supp. IV Part 2:** 574; **Supp. VIII:** 334; **Supp. XIII:** 127; **Supp. XIV:** 102, 239

Miller, Brown, **Supp. IV Part 1:** 67

Miller, Carol, **Supp. IV Part 1:** 400, 405, 409, 410, 411

Miller, Henry, **I:** 97, 157; **III:** 40, **170–192; IV:** 138; **Retro. Supp. II:** 327; **Supp. I Part 2:** 546; **Supp. V:** 119, 131; **Supp. X:** 183, 185, 187, 194, 195; **Supp. XIII:** 1, 17

Miller, Herman, **Supp. I Part 2:** 614, 617

Miller, J. Hillis, **Supp. IV Part 1:** 387

Miller, James E., Jr., **IV:** 352

Miller, Jeffrey, **Supp. IV Part 1:** 95

Miller, Joaquin, **I:** 193, 195, 459; **Supp. II Part 1:** 351

Miller, John Duncan, **Supp. I Part 2:** 604

Miller, Jonathan, **Retro. Supp. II:** 181

Miller, Laura, **Supp. XIII:** 48

Miller, Mrs. Arthur (Ingeborg Morath), **III:** 162–163

Miller, Mrs. Arthur (Marilyn Monroe), **III:** 161, 162–163

Miller, Mrs. Arthur (Mary Grace Slattery), **III:** 146, 161

Miller, Orilla, **Supp. I Part 1:** 48

Miller, Perry, **I:** 546, 547, 549, 550, 560; **IV:** 186; **Supp. I Part 1:** 31, 104; **Supp. I Part 2:** 484; **Supp. IV Part 2:** 422; **Supp. VIII:** 101

Miller, R. Baxter, **Retro. Supp. I:** 195, 207

Miller, Robert Ellis, **II:** 588

Miller, Ruth, **Supp. X:** 324

Miller, Sue, **Supp. X:** 77, 85; **Supp. XI:** 190; **Supp. XII: 289–305**

Miller of Old Church, The (Glasgow), **II:** 175, 181

"Miller's Tale" (Chaucer), **III:** 283

Millett, Kate, **Supp. X:** 193, 196

Millgate, Michael, **Retro. Supp. I:** 91

Mill Hand's Lunch Bucket (Bearden), **Supp. VIII:** 337

Millier, Brett C., **Retro. Supp. II:** 39

Milligan, Bryce, **Supp. XIII:** 274, 275, 277

Millions of Strange Shadows (Hecht), **Supp. X:** 57, **62–65**

"Million Young Workmen, 1915, A" (Sandburg), **III:** 585

Millroy the Magician (Theroux), **Supp. VIII:** 325

Mills, Alice, **Supp. XIII:** 233

Mills, Benjamin Fay, **III:** 176

Mills, C. Wright, **Supp. I Part 2:** 648, 650

Mills, Florence, **Supp. I Part 1:** 322

Mills, Ralph J., Jr., **III:** 530; **Supp. IV Part 1:** 64; **Supp. XI:** 311

Mills of the Kavanaughs, The (Lowell), **II:** 542–543, 546, 550; **III:** 508; **Retro. Supp. II:** 178, 179, 188

"Mills of the Kavanaughs, The" (Lowell), **II:** 542–543

Milne, A. A., **Supp. IX:** 189

Milne, A. J. M., **I:** 278

Milosz, Czeslaw, **Supp. III Part 2:** 630; **Supp. VIII:** 20, 22; **Supp. XI:** 267, 312

Miltner, Robert, **Supp. XI:** 142

Milton, Edith, **Supp. VIII:** 79; **Supp. X:** 82

Milton, John, **I:** 6, 138, 273, 587–588; **II:** 11, 15, 113, 130, 411, 540, 542; **III:** 40, 124, 201, 225, 274, 468, 471, 486, 487, 503, 511; **IV:** 50, 82, 126, 137, 155, 157, 241, 279, 347, 422, 461, 494; **Retro. Supp. I:** 60, 67, 127, 360; **Retro. Supp. II:** 161, 295; **Supp. I Part 1:** 124, 150, 370; **Supp. I Part 2:** 412, 422, 491, 501, 522, 622, 722, 724; **Supp. IV Part 2:** 430, 634; **Supp. VIII:** 294; **Supp. X:** 22, 23, 36; **Supp. XII:** 180; **Supp. XIV:** 5, 7

Milton, John R., **Supp. IV Part 2:** 503

Milton and His Modern Critics (L. P. Smith), **Supp. XIV:** 347

"Milton by Firelight" (Snyder), **Supp. II Part 1:** 314; **Supp. VIII:** 294

"Miltonic Sonnet, A" (Wilbur), **Supp. III Part 2:** 558

Mimesis (Auerbach), **III:** 453

"Mimnermos and the Motions of Hedonism" (Carson), **Supp. XII: 99–100**

"Mimnermos Interviews, The" (Carson), **Supp. XII: 100–101**

Mims, Edwin, **Supp. I Part 1:** 362, 364, 365, 371

"Mind" (Wilbur), **Supp. III Part 2:** 554

"Mind, The" (Kinnell), **Supp. III Part 1:** 245

Mind Breaths: Poems 1972–1977 (Ginsberg), **Supp. II Part 1:** 326

Mindfield: New and Selected Poems (Corso), **Supp. XII: 136**

"Mind in the Modern World" (Trilling), **Supp. III Part 2:** 512

"Mind Is Shapely, Art Is Shapely" (Ginsberg), **Supp. II Part 1:** 327

Mindlin, Henrique, **Supp. I Part 1:** 92

Mind of My Mind (O. Butler), **Supp. XIII:** 62, 63

Mind of Primitive Man, The (Boas), **Supp. XIV:** 209

"Mind-Reader, The" (Wilbur), **Supp. III Part 2:** 561–562

Mind-Reader, The (Wilbur), **Supp. III Part 2:** 560–562

Mindwheel (Pinsky), **Supp. VI:** 235

"Mined Country" (Wilbur), **Supp. III Part 2:** 546–548

"Mine Own John Berryman" (Levine), **Supp. V:** 179–180

Miner, Bob, **Supp. V:** 23

Miner, Earl, **III:** 466, 479

Miner, Madonne, **Supp. XIII:** 29

"Minerva Writes Poems" (Cisneros), **Supp. VII:** 63–64, 66

Mingus, Charles, **Supp. IX:** 152

"Mingus in Diaspora" (Matthews), **Supp. IX:** 166

"Mingus in Shadow" (Matthews), **Supp. IX:** 168–169

Ming Yellow (Marquand), **III:** 56

"Minimal, The" (Roethke), **III:** 531–532

"Mini-novela: *Rosa y sus espinas*" (Mora), **Supp. XIII:** 218

"Minions of Midas, The" (London), **II:** 474–475

Minister's Charge, The, or The Apprenticeship of Lemuel Barber (Howells), **II:** 285–286, 287

"Minister's Wooing, The" (Stowe), **Supp. I Part 2:** 592–595

Minister's Wooing, The (Stowe), **II:** 541

"Ministration of Our Departed Friends, The" (Stowe), **Supp. I Part 2:** 586–587

"Minneapolis Poem, The" (Wright), **Supp. III Part 2:** 601–602

"Minnesota Transcendentalist" (Peseroff), **Supp. IV Part 1:** 71

Minnie, Temple, **II:** 344

Minority Report: H. L. Mencken's Notebooks (Mencken), **III:** 112

Minor Pleasures of Life, The (Macaulay), **Supp. XIV:** 348

"Minor Poems" (Eliot), **I:** 579

"Minor Poet" (Hay), **Supp. XIV:** 127

"Minor Topics" (Howells), **II:** 274

Minot, Susan, **Supp. VI: 203–215**

"Minotaur Loves His Labyrinth, The" (Simic), **Supp. VIII:** 270, 279, 281

"Minstrel Man" (Hughes), **Supp. I Part 1:** 325

Mint (Nye), **Supp. XIII:** 277

"Minting Time" (Sarton), **Supp. VIII:** 259

Mint Snowball (Nye), **Supp. XIII:** 277–278, **284–285**

"Mint Snowball" (Nye), **Supp. XIII:** 278, 284

"Mint Snowball II" (Nye), **Supp. XIII:** 284, 285

Minutes to Go (Corso, Gysin, Beiles and Burroughs), **Supp. XII:** 129

Mirabell: Books of Number (Merrill), **Supp. III Part 1:** 332–334

"Miracle" (Carver), **Supp. III Part 1:** 139–140

"Miracle for Breakfast, A" (Bishop), **Retro. Supp. II:** 43

"Miracle of Lava Canyon, The" (Henry), **Supp. II Part 1:** 389, 390

Miracle of Mindfulness, The: A Manual on Meditation (Thich Nhat Hanh), **Supp. V:** 199–200

Mirage (Masters), **Supp. I Part 2:** 459, 470, 471

"Mirages, The" (Hayden), **Supp. II Part 1:** 373

"Miranda" (Buck), **Supp. II Part 1:** 128

Miranda, Carmen, **Supp. XII:** 165

Miranda, Francisco de, **Supp. I Part 2:** 522

"Miranda Over the Valley" (Dubus), **Supp. VII:** 81–83

"Miriam" (Capote), **Supp. III Part 1:** 117, 120, 122

"Miriam" (Whittier), **Supp. I Part 2:** 691, 703

"Miriam Tazewell" (Ransom), **Supp. X:** 58

"Mirror" (Merrill), **Supp. III Part 1:** 322

"Mirror" (Plath), **Retro. Supp. II:** 248–249, 257

"Mirror, The" (Glück), **Supp. V:** 83

"Mirroring Evil: Nazi Images/Recent Art" (Epstein), **Supp. XII:** 166

Mirrors (Creeley), **Supp. IV Part 1:** 156

Mirrors and Windows (Nemerov), **III:** 269, 275–277

"Mirrors of Chartres Street" (Faulkner), **II:** 56

Misanthrope, The (Molière; Wilbur, trans.), **Supp. III Part 2:** 552, 560

Miscellaneous Works of Mr. Philip Freneau, Containing His Essays and Additional Poems (Freneau), **Supp. II Part 1:** 263, 264, 266

Misery (King), **Supp. V:** 140, 141, 142, 147–148, 151, 152

Mises, Ludwig von, **Supp. IV Part 2:** 524

Misfits, The (A. Miller), **III:** 147, 149, 156, 161–162, 163

"Misogamist, The" (Dubus), **Supp. VII:** 86–87

Misrepresentations Corrected, and Truth Vindicated, in a Reply to the Rev. Mr. Solomon Williams's Book (Edwards), **I:** 549

"Miss Ella" (Z. Fitzgerald), **Supp. IX:** 57, 59, **71–72**

"Miss Emily and the Bibliographer" (Tate), **Supp. II Part 1:** 103

"Miss Furr and Miss Skeene" (Stein), **IV:** 29–30

"Missing Child" (Simic), **Supp. VIII:** 282

"Missing in Action" (Komunyakaa), **Supp. XIII:** 123, 124

Missing/Kissing: Missing Marisa, Kissing Christine (Shanley), **Supp. XIV:** 316

"Mission of Jane, The" (Wharton), **Retro. Supp. I:** 367

"Missions, The" (Rodriguez), **Supp. XIV:** 303

Mission to Moscow (film), **Supp. I Part 1:** 281

"Mississippi" (Faulkner), **Retro. Supp. I:** 77

"Mississippi" (Simpson), **Supp. IX:** 271

"Miss Kate in H-1" (Twain), **IV:** 193

Miss Leonora When Last Seen (Taylor), **Supp. V:** 323

Miss Lonelyhearts (West), **I:** 107; **II:** 436; **III:** 357; **IV:** 287, 288, 290–297, 300, 301, 305, 306; **Retro. Supp. II:** 321, 322, 325, 328, **332–335**

Miss Mamma Aimee (Caldwell), **I:** 308, 309, 310

"Miss Mary Pask" (Wharton), **IV:** 316; **Retro. Supp. I:** 382

"Miss McEnders" (Chopin), **Retro. Supp. II:** 67

"Missoula Softball Tournament" (Hugo), **Supp. VI:** 132

Miss Ravenel's Conversion from Secession to Loyalty (De Forest), **IV:** 350

"Miss Tempy's Watchers" (Jewett), **II:** 401; **Retro. Supp. II:** 139

"Miss Terriberry to Wed in Suburbs"

(Updike), **Retro. Supp. I:** 335

"Mist, The" (King), **Supp. V:** 144

"Mistaken Charity, A" (Freeman), **Retro. Supp. II:** 138

"Mister Toussan" (Ellison), **Retro. Supp. II:** 124–125; **Supp. II Part 1:** 238

"Mistress of Sydenham Plantation, The" (Jewett), **Retro. Supp. II:** 141

Mitchell, Burroughs, **Supp. XI:** 218, 222, 227

Mitchell, Dr. S. Weir, **IV:** 310

Mitchell, Margaret, **II:** 177

Mitchell, Roger, **Supp. IV Part 1:** 70

Mitchell, Tennessee. *See* Anderson, Mrs. Sherwood (Tennessee Mitchell)

Mitchell, Wesley C., **Supp. I Part 2:** 632, 643

Mitch Miller (Masters), **Supp. I Part 2:** 456, 466, 469–471, 474, 475, 476

Mitchum, Robert, **Supp. IX:** 95, 250

Mitgang, Herbert, **Supp. IV Part 1:** 220, 226, 307; **Supp. VIII:** 124

"Mixed Sequence" (Roethke), **III:** 547

Miyazawa Kenji, **Supp. VIII:** 292

Mizener, Arthur, **II:** 77, 81, 84, 94; **IV:** 132

Mladenoff, Nancy, **Supp. X:** 176

"M'liss: An Idyl of Red Mountain" (Harte), **Supp. II Part 1:** 339

"Mnemonic Devices" (Goldbarth), **Supp. XII:** 183

"Mobile in Back of the Smithsonian, The" (Swenson), **Supp. IV Part 2:** 646

Mobilio, Albert, **Supp. VIII:** 3

Moby Dick (film), **Supp. IV Part 1:** 102, 116

Moby Dick; or, The Whale (Melville), **I:** 106, 354; **II:** 33, 224–225, 236, 539–540; **III:** 28–29, 74, 75, 77, 81, 82, 83–86, 87, 89, 90, 91, 93, 94, 95, 359, 453, 556; **IV:** 57, 199, 201, 202; **Retro. Supp. I:** 160, 220, 243, 244, 248, **249–253**, 254, 256, 257, 335; **Retro. Supp. II:** 121, 186, 275; **Supp. I Part 1:** 249; **Supp. I Part 2:** 579; **Supp. IV Part 2:** 613; **Supp. V:** 281; **Supp. VIII:** 106, 188, 198

Mock, John, **Supp. XIII:** 174

"Mocking-Bird, The" (Bierce), **I:** 202

"Mock Orange" (Glück), **Supp. V:** 84–85

Modarressi, Mitra, **Supp. IV Part 2:** 657

Models of Misrepresentation: On the Fiction of E. L. Doctorow (Morris), **Supp. IV Part 1:** 231

Model World and Other Stories, A

(Chabon), **Supp. XI:** 66

Modern Brazilian Architecture (Bishop, trans.), **Supp. I Part 1:** 92

Modern Fiction Studies, **Supp. V:** 238

Modern Instance a Novel, A (Howells), **II:** 275, 279, 282–283, 285

Modern Library, The, **Retro. Supp. I:** 112, 113

Modern Mephistopheles, A (Alcott), **Supp. I Part 1:** 37–38

Modern Poetic Sequence, The (Rosenthal), **Supp. V:** 333

"Modern Poetry" (Crane), **I:** 390

Modern Poetry and the Tradition (Brooks), **Supp. XIV:5–7**

"Modern Race Creeds and Their Fallacies" (Locke), **Supp. XIV:** 210

Modern Rhetoric, with Readings (Brooks and Warren), **Supp. XIV:** 11

"Modern Sorcery" (Simic), **Supp. VIII:** 283

"Modern Times" (Zukofsky), **Supp. III Part 2:** 624

Modern Writer, The (Anderson), **I:** 117

Modersohn, Mrs. Otto (Paula Becker), **Supp. I Part 2:** 573–574

Modersohn, Otto, **Supp. I Part 2:** 573

"Modes of Being" (Levertov), **Supp. III Part 1:** 282

Modest Enquiry into the Nature and Necessity of a Paper-Currency, A (Franklin), **II:** 108–109

"Modest Proposal, A" (Swift), **I:** 295; **Retro. Supp. II:** 287

"Modest Self-Tribute, A" (Wilson), **IV:** 431, 432

Moeller, Philip, **III:** 398, 399

"Moench von Berchtesgaden, Der" (Voss), **I:** 199–200

Moers, Ellen, **Retro. Supp. II:** 99

Moe's Villa and Other Stories (Purdy), **Supp. VII:** 270, 280

Mogen, David, **Supp. IV Part 1:** 106

Mohammed, **I:** 480; **II:** 1

Mohawk (Russo), **Supp. XII: 326–328**

Moir, William Wilmerding, **Supp. V:** 279

"Moles" (Oliver), **Supp. VII:** 235

Molesworth, Charles, **Supp. IV Part 1:** 39; **Supp. VIII:** 292, 306

Molière (Jean-Baptiste Poquelin), **III:** 113; **Supp. I Part 2:** 406; **Supp. III Part 2:** 552, 560; **Supp. IV Part 2:** 585; **Supp. V:** 101

"Molino Rojo, El" (Ríos), **Supp. IV Part 2:** 544

Moll Flanders (Defoe), **Supp. V:** 127; **Supp. XIII:** 43

"Molloch in State Street" (Whittier),

Supp. I Part 2: 687

"Moll Pitcher" (Whittier), **Supp. I Part 2:** 684

"Molly Brant, Iroquois Matron" (Gunn Allen), **Supp. IV Part 1:** 331

"Moloch" (H. Miller), **III:** 177

Momaday, N. Scott, **Supp. IV Part 1:** 274, 323, 324, 404; **Supp. IV Part 2: 479–496,** 504, 557, 562; **Supp. XII:** 209

Moments of the Italian Summer (Wright), **Supp. III Part 2:** 602

"Momus" (Robinson), **III:** 508

Monaghan, Pat, **Supp. XI:** 121

"Mon Ami" (Bourne), **I:** 227

Monet, Claude, **Retro. Supp. I:** 378

"Monet's 'Waterlilies'" (Hayden), **Supp. II Part 1:** 361–362

Monette, Paul, **Supp. X: 145–161**

Money (Amis), **Retro. Supp. I:** 278

"Money" (Matthews), **Supp. IX:** 166

"Money" (Nemerov), **III:** 287

Money, Money, Money (Wagoner), **Supp. IX:** 324, **333–334**

Moneychangers, The (Sinclair), **Supp. V:** 285

Money Writes! (Sinclair), **Supp. V:** 277

Monica, Saint, **IV:** 140

Monikins, The (Cooper), **I:** 348, 354

Monk and the Hangman's Daughter, The (Bierce), **I:** 199–200, 209

"Monkey Garden, The" (Cisneros), **Supp. VII:** 63

"Monkey Puzzle, The" (Moore), **III:** 194, 207, 211

Monkeys (Minot), **Supp. VI:** 203–205, **206–210**

"Monkeys, The" (Moore), **III:** 201, 202

Monkey Wrench Gang, The (Abbey), **Supp. VIII:** 42; **Supp. XIII: 9–11,** 16

"Monk of Casal-Maggiore, The" (Longfellow), **II:** 505

"Monocle de Mon Oncle, Le" (Stevens), **IV:** 78, 84; **Retro. Supp. I:** 301; **Supp. III Part 1:** 20; **Supp. X:** 58

Monro, Harold, **III:** 465; **Retro. Supp. I:** 127

Monroe, Harriet, **I:** 235, 384, 390, 393; **III:** 458, 581, 586; **IV:** 74; **Retro. Supp. I:** 58, 131; **Retro. Supp. II:** 82, 83; **Supp. I Part 1:** 256, 257, 258, 262, 263, 267; **Supp. I Part 2:** 374, 387, 388, 464, 610, 611, 613, 614, 615, 616; **Supp. XIV:** 286

Monroe, James, **Supp. I Part 2:** 515, 517

Monroe, Lucy, **Retro. Supp. II:** 70

Monroe, Marilyn, **III:** 161, 162–163

Monroe's Embassy; or, the Conduct of the Government in Relation to Our Claims to the Navigation of the Mississippi (Brown), **Supp. I Part 1:** 146

"Monsoon Season" (Komunyakaa), **Supp. XIII:** 122

"Monster, The" (Crane), **I:** 418

Monster, The, and Other Stories (Crane), **I:** 409

Montage of a Dream Deferred (Hughes), **Retro. Supp. I:** 194, **208–209; Supp. I Part 1:** 333, 339–341

Montagu, Ashley, **Supp. I Part 1:** 314

"Montaigne" (Emerson), **II:** 6

Montaigne, Michel de, **II:** 1, 5, 6, 8, 14–15, 16, 535; **III:** 600; **Retro. Supp. I:** 247; **Supp. XIV:** 105

Montale, Eugenio, **Supp. III Part 1:** 320; **Supp. V:** 337–338; **Supp. VIII:** 30

"Montana; or the End of Jean-Jacques Rousseau" (Fiedler), **Supp. XIII: 97–98**

"Montana Memory" (Maclean), **Supp. XIV:** 221

"Montana Ranch Abandoned" (Hugo), **Supp. VI:** 139

"Mont Blanc" (Shelley), **Supp. IX:** 52

Montcalm, Louis Joseph de, **Supp. I Part 2:** 498

Montcalm and Wolfe (Parkman), **Supp. II Part 2:** 596, 609, 610, 611–613

Montgomery, Benilde, **Supp. XIII:** 202

Montgomery, Robert, **Supp. I Part 2:** 611; **Supp. IV Part 1:** 130

Month of Sundays, A (Updike), **Retro. Supp. I:** 325, 327, 329, 330, 331, 333, 335

Monti, Luigi, **II:** 504

Montoya, José, **Supp. IV Part 2:** 545

"Montrachet-le-Jardin" (Stevens), **IV:** 82

Mont-Saint-Michel and Chartres (Adams), **I:** 1, 9, 12–14, 18, 19, 21; **Supp. I Part 2:** 417

Montserrat (Hellman), **Supp. I Part 1:** 283–285

Montserrat (Robles), **Supp. I Part 1:** 283–285

"Monument, The" (Bishop), **Supp. I Part 1:** 89

Monument, The (Strand), **Supp. IV Part 2:** 629, 630

"Monument Mountain" (Bryant), **Supp. I Part 1:** 156, 162

"Monument to After-Thought Un-

veiled, A" (Frost), **Retro. Supp. I:** 124

Moo (Smiley), **Supp. VI:** 292, **303–305**

Moods (Alcott), **Supp. I Part 1:** 33, 34–35, 43

Moody, Anne, **Supp. IV Part 1:** 11

Moody, Mrs. William Vaughn, **I:** 384; **Supp. I Part 2:** 394

Moody, Richard, **Supp. I Part 1:** 280

Moody, William Vaughn, **III:** 507; **IV:** 26

"Moon and the Night and the Men, The" (Berryman), **I:** 172

"Moon Deluxe" (F. Barthelme), **Supp. XI:** 26, 27, 33, 36

Mooney, Tom, **I:** 505

"Moon-Face" (London), **II:** 475

Moon-Face and Other Stories (London), **II:** 483

"Moon Flock" (Dickey), **Supp. IV Part 1:** 186

Moon for the Misbegotten, A (O'Neill), **III:** 385, 401, 403, 404

Moon Is a Gong, The (Dos Passos). *See Garbage Man, The* (Dos Passos)

Moon Is Down, The (Steinbeck), **IV:** 51

Moon Lady, The (Tan), **Supp. X:** 289

"Moonlight Alert" (Winters), **Supp. II Part 2:** 801, 811, 815

"Moonlit Night" (Reznikoff), **Supp. XIV:** 285–286

Moon of the Caribbees, The (O'Neill), **III:** 388

Moon Palace (Auster), **Supp. XII:** 22, 27, **30–32**

"Moonshine" (Komunyakaa), **Supp. XIII:** 127, 128

"Moon Solo" (Laforgue), **Supp. XIII:** 346

Moonstruck (screenplay, Shanley), **Supp. XIV:** 315, 316, **321–324**

"Moon upon her fluent Route, The" (Dickinson), **I:** 471

Moony's Kid Don't Cry (T. Williams), **IV:** 381

Moore, Arthur, **Supp. I Part 1:** 49

Moore, Dr. Merrill, **III:** 506

Moore, George, **I:** 103

Moore, John Milton, **III:** 193

Moore, Lorrie, **Supp. VIII:** 145; **Supp. X: 163–180**

Moore, Marianne, **I:** 58, 285, 401, 428; **III: 193–217,** 514, 592–593; **IV:** 74, 75, 76, 91, 402; **Retro. Supp. I:** 416, 417; **Retro. Supp. II:** 39, 44, 48, 50, 82, 178, 179, 243, 244; **Supp. I Part 1:** 84, 89, 255, 257; **Supp. I Part 2:** 707; **Supp. II Part**

1: 21; **Supp. III Part 1:** 58, 60, 63; **Supp. III Part 2:** 612, 626, 627; **Supp. IV Part 1:** 242, 246, 257; **Supp. IV Part 2:** 454, 640, 641; **Supp. XIV:** 124, 130

Moore, Marie Lorena. *See* Moore, Lorrie

Moore, Mary Tyler, **Supp. V:** 107

Moore, Mary Warner, **III:** 193

Moore, Steven, **Supp. IV Part 1:** 279, 283, 284, 285, 287; **Supp. XII:** 151

Moore, Sturge, **III:** 459

Moore, Thomas, **II:** 296, 299, 303; **Supp. IX:** 104; **Supp. X:** 114

Moorehead, Caroline, **Supp. XIV:** 337

Moos, Malcolm, **III:** 116, 119

"Moose, The" (Bishop), **Retro. Supp. II:** 50; **Supp. I Part 1:** 73, 93, 94, 95; **Supp. IX:** 45, 46

"Moose Wallow, The" (Hayden), **Supp. II Part 1:** 367

Mora, Pat, **Supp. XIII: 213–232**

"Moral Bully, The" (Holmes), **Supp. I Part 1:** 302

"Moral Character, the Practice of Law, and Legal Education" (Hall), **Supp. VIII:** 127

"Moral Equivalent for Military Service, A" (Bourne), **I:** 230

"Moral Equivalent of War, The" (James), **II:** 361; **Supp. I Part 1:** 20

"Moral Imperatives for World Order" (Locke), **Supp. XIV:** 207, 213

Moralités Légendaires (Laforgue), **I:** 573

"Morality and Mercy in Vienna" (Pynchon), **Supp. II Part 2:** 620, 624

"Morality of Indian Hating, The" (Momaday), **Supp. IV Part 2:** 484

"Morality of Poetry, The" (Wright), **Supp. III Part 2:** 596–597, 599

Moral Man and Immoral Society (Niebuhr), **III:** 292, 295–297

"Morals Is Her Middle Name" (Hughes), **Supp. I Part 1:** 338

"Morals of Chess, The" (Franklin), **II:** 121

"Moral Substitute for War, A" (Addams), **Supp. I Part 1:** 20

"Moral Theology of Atticus Finch, The" (Shaffer), **Supp. VIII:** 127

"Moral Thought, A" (Freneau), **Supp. II Part 1:** 262

Moran, Thomas, **Supp. IV Part 2:** 603–604

Moran of the Lady Letty (Norris), **II:** 264; **III:** 314, 322, 327, 328, 329, 330, 331, 332, 333

Morath, Ingeborg. *See* Miller, Mrs. Arthur (Ingeborg Morath)

Moravia, Alberto, **I:** 301

Moré, Gonzalo, **Supp. X:** 185

More, Henry, **I:** 132

More, Paul Elmer, **I:** 223–224, 247; **Supp. I Part 2:** 423

Moreau, Gustave, **I:** 66

More Conversations with Eudora Welty (Prenshaw, ed.), **Retro. Supp. I:** 340, 341, 342, 343, 344, 352, 353, 354

More Die of Heartbreak (Bellow), **Retro. Supp. II:** 31, 33, 34

"More Girl Than Boy" (Komunyakaa), **Supp. XIII:** 117

"More Light! More Light!" (Hecht), **Supp. X:** 60

"Morella" (Poe), **III:** 412; **Retro. Supp. II:** 270

"More Love in the Western World" (Updike), **Retro. Supp. I:** 327–328, 329

"Morels" (W. J. Smith), **Supp. XIII: 336–339**

"More of a Corpse Than a Woman" (Rukeyser), **Supp. VI:** 280

"More Pleasant Adventures" (Ashbery), **Supp. III Part 1:** 1

More Poems to Solve (Swenson), **Supp. IV Part 2:** 640, 642, 648

More Stately Mansions (O'Neill), **III:** 385, 401, 404–405

"More Than Human" (Chabon), **Supp. XI:** 71–72

More Triva (L. P. Smith), **Supp. XIV:** 339

Morgan, Edmund S., **IV:** 149; **Supp. I Part 1:** 101, 102; **Supp. I Part 2:** 484

Morgan, Edwin, **Supp. IV Part 2:** 688

Morgan, Henry, **II:** 432; **IV:** 63

Morgan, J. P., **I:** 494; **III:** 14, 15

Morgan, Jack, **Retro. Supp. II:** 142

Morgan, Robert, **Supp. V:** 5

Morgan, Robin, **Supp. I Part 2:** 569

Morgan, Ted, **Supp. XIV:** 141

Morgan's Passing (Tyler), **Supp. IV Part 2:** 666–667, 668, 669

Morgenthau, Hans, **III:** 291, 309

Moricand, Conrad, **III:** 190

Morison, Mrs. Samuel Eliot (Elizabeth Shaw Greene), **Supp. I Part 2:** 483

Morison, Mrs. Samuel Eliot (Priscilla Barton), **Supp. I Part 2:** 493, 496, 497

Morison, Samuel Eliot, **Supp. I Part 2: 479–500**

"Morituri Salutamus" (Longfellow), **II:** 499, 500; **Retro. Supp. II:** 169;

Supp. I Part 2: 416

"Moriturus" (Millay), **III:** 126, 131–132

Morley, Christopher, **III:** 481, 483, 484; **Supp. I Part 2:** 653; **Supp. IX:** 124

Morley, Edward, **IV:** 27

Morley, Lord John, **I:** 7

Mormon Country (Stegner), **Supp. IV Part 2:** 598, 601–602

"Morning, The" (Updike), **Retro. Supp. I:** 329

"Morning after My Death, The" (Levis), **Supp. XI:** 260, 263–264

Morning for Flamingos, A (Burke), **Supp. XIV:** 30, 31, 32

"Morning Glory" (Merrill), **Supp. III Part 1:** 337

Morning Glory, The (Bly), **Supp. IV Part 1:** 63–65, 66, 71

"Morning Imagination of Russia, A" (W. C. Williams), **Retro. Supp. I:** 428

Morning in Antibes (Knowles), **Supp. XII:** 249

Morning in the Burned House (Atwood), **Supp. XIII:** 20, 35

Morning Is Near Us, The (Glaspell), **Supp. III Part 1:** 184–185

Morning Noon and Night (Cozzens), **I:** 374, 375, 376, 377, 379, 380

"Morning of the Day They Did It, The" (White), **Supp. I Part 2:** 663

"Morning Prayers" (Harjo), **Supp. XII:** 231

"Morning Roll Call" (Anderson), **I:** 116

"Mornings in a New House" (Merrill), **Supp. III Part 1:** 327

Mornings Like This (Dillard), **Supp. VI:** 23, 34

"Morning Song" (Plath), **Retro. Supp. II:** 252

Morning Watch, The (Agee), **I:** 25, 39–42

"Morning with Broken Window" (Hogan), **Supp. IV Part 1:** 405

Morrell, Ottoline, **Retro. Supp. I:** 60

Morris, Christopher D., **Supp. IV Part 1:** 231, 236

Morris, George Sylvester, **Supp. I Part 2:** 640

Morris, Gouverneur, **Supp. I Part 2:** 512, 517, 518

Morris, Lloyd, **III:** 458

Morris, Robert, **Supp. I Part 2:** 510

Morris, Timothy, **Retro. Supp. I:** 40

Morris, William, **II:** 323, 338, 523; **IV:** 349; **Supp. I Part 1:** 260, 356; **Supp. XI:** 202

Morris, Willie, **Supp. XI:** 216, 231, 234
Morris, Wright, **I:** 305; **III: 218–243,** 558, 572; **IV:** 211
Morrison, Charles Clayton, **III:** 297
Morrison, Jim, **Supp. IV Part 1:** 206
Morrison, Toni, **Retro. Supp. II:** 15, 118; **Supp. III Part 1: 361–381; Supp. IV Part 1:** 2, 13, 14, 250, 253, 257; **Supp. V:** 169, 259; **Supp. VIII:** 213, 214; **Supp. X:** 85, 239, 250, 325; **Supp. XI:** 4, 14, 20, 91; **Supp. XII:** 289, 310; **Supp. XIII:** 60, 185
"Morro Bay" (Jeffers), **Supp. II Part 2:** 422
Morrow, W. C., **I:** 199
Morse, Robert, **Supp. XI:** 305
Morse, Samuel F. B., **Supp. I Part 1:** 156
Mortal Acts, Mortal Words (Kinnell), **Supp. III Part 1:** 235, 236, 237, 249–254
Mortal Antipathy, A (Holmes), **Supp. I Part 1:** 315–316
"Mortal Enemies" (Humphrey), **Supp. IX:** 109
"Mortal Eternal" (Olds), **Supp. X:** 214
Mortal No, The (Hoffman), **IV:** 113
Morte D'Arthur, Le (Malory), **Supp. IV Part 1:** 47
Mortmere Stories, The (Isherwood and Upward), **Supp. XIV:** 159
Morton, David, **Supp. IX:** 76
Morton, Jelly Roll, **Supp. X:** 242
"Mosaic of the Nativity: Serbia, Winter 1993" (Kenyon), **Supp. VII:** 173
Mosby's Memoirs and Other Stories (Bellow), **Retro. Supp. II:** 27
Moscow under Fire (Caldwell), **I:** 296
Moser, Barry, **Supp. XIV:** 223
Moses, Man of the Mountain (Hurston), **Supp. VI:** 149, 158, 160
Mosle, Sara, **Supp. XI:** 254
Mosley, Walter, **Supp. XIII: 233–252**
Mosquito Coast, The (film), **Supp. VIII:** 323
Mosquito Coast, The (Theroux), **Supp. VIII:** 321, **322–323**
Mosquitos (Faulkner), **II:** 56; **Retro. Supp. I:** 79, 81
Moss, Howard, **III:** 452; **Supp. IV Part 2:** 642; **Supp. IX:** 39; **Supp. XIII:** 114
Moss, Stanley, **Supp. XI:** 321
Moss, Thylias, **Supp. XI:** 248
Mosses from an Old Manse (Hawthorne), **I:** 562; **II:** 224; **III:** 82, 83; **Retro. Supp. I:** 157, 248
"Moss of His Skin" (Sexton), **Supp. II**

Part 2: 676
"Most Extraordinary Case, A" (James), **II:** 322; **Retro. Supp. I:** 218
Most Likely to Succeed (Dos Passos), **I:** 491
"Most of It, The" (Frost), **Retro. Supp. I:** 121, 125, 129, 139
Motel Chronicles (Shepard), **Supp. III Part 2:** 445
"Mother" (Paley), **Supp. VI: 222–223**
"Mother" (Snyder), **Supp. VIII:** 298
Mother (Whistler), **IV:** 369
Mother, The (Buck), **Supp. II Part 1:** 118–119
"Mother and Jack and the Rain" (Sexton), **Supp. II Part 2:** 686
"Mother and Son" (Tate), **IV:** 128, 137–138
Mother Courage and Her Children (Brecht), **III:** 160; **Supp. IX:** 140; **Supp. XII:** 249
"Mother Earth: Her Whales" (Snyder), **Supp. VIII:** 302
"Motherhood" (Swenson), **Supp. IV Part 2:** 645
Mother Hubbard (Reed), **Supp. X:** 241
Mother Love (Dove), **Supp. IV Part 1:** 250–251, 254
"Mother Marie Therese" (Lowell), **Retro. Supp. II:** 188
Mother Night (Vonnegut), **Supp. II Part 2:** 757, 758, 767, 770, 771
"Mother Rosarine" (Kumin), **Supp. IV Part 2:** 442
Mother's Recompense, The (Wharton), **IV:** 321, 324; **Retro. Supp. I:** 382
"Mother's Tale, A" (Agee), **I:** 29–30
"Mother's Things" (Creeley), **Supp. IV Part 1:** 141
"Mother's Voice" (Creeley), **Supp. IV Part 1:** 156
Mother to Daughter, Daughter to Mother (Olsen, ed.), **Supp. XIII:** 295
"Mother Tongue" (Simic), **Supp. VIII:** 283
"Mother to Son" (Hughes), **Retro. Supp. I:** 199, 203; **Supp. I Part 1:** 321–322, 323
"Mother Writes to the Murderer, The: A Letter" (Nye), **Supp. XIII:** 276
"Motion, The" (Olson), **Supp. II Part 2:** 571
Motion of History, The (Baraka), **Supp. II Part 1:** 55, 56
"Motive for Metaphor, The" (Stevens), **IV:** 89; **Retro. Supp. I:** 310
Motiveless Malignity (Auchincloss), **Supp. IV Part 1:** 31
Motley, John Lothrop, **Supp. I Part 1:**

299; **Supp. I Part 2:** 479
"Motor Car, The" (White), **Supp. I Part 2:** 661
Motor-Flight Through France (Wharton), **I:** 12; **Retro. Supp. I:** 372
Mott, Michael, **Supp. VIII:** 204, 208
"Mountain, The" (Frost), **Retro. Supp. I:** 121
"Mountain Hermitage, The: Pages from a Japanese Notebook" (Passin), **Supp. XIII:** 337
Mountain Interval (Frost), **II:** 154; **Retro. Supp. I:** 131, 132, 133
"Mountain Lion" (Hogan), **Supp. IV Part 1:** 412
Mountainous Journey, A (Tuqan), **Supp. XIII:** 278
Mountains, The (Wolfe), **IV:** 461
Mountains and Rivers without End (Snyder), **Supp. VIII:** 295, **305–306**
"Mountains grow unnoticed, The" (Dickinson), **Retro. Supp. I:** 46
Mountains of California, The (Muir), **Supp. IX:** 183
"Mountain Whippoorwill, The" (Benét), **Supp. XI:** 44–45, 46, 47
"Mount-Joy: or Some Passages Out of the Life of a Castle-Builder" (Irving), **II:** 314
"Mourners, The" (Malamud), **Supp. I Part 2:** 431, 435, 436–437
Mourners Below (Purdy), **Supp. VII:** 274, 280
"Mourning and Melancholia" (Freud), **Supp. IV Part 2:** 450
Mourning Becomes Electra (O'Neill), **III:** 391, 394, 398–400
"Mourning Poem for the Queen of Sunday" (Hayden), **Supp. II Part 1:** 379–380
"Mouse Elegy" (Olds), **Supp. X:** 209
"Mouth of Brass" (Humphrey), **Supp. IX:** 101
Moveable Feast, A (Hemingway), **II:** 257; **Retro. Supp. I:** 108, 171, **186–187**
Movement, The: Documentary of a Struggle for Equality (Student Non-violent Coordinating Committee), **Supp. IV Part 1:** 369
"Move over Macho, Here Comes Feminismo" (Robbins), **Supp. X:** 272
"Move to California, The" (Stafford), **Supp. XI:** 318, 321
"Movie" (Shapiro), **Supp. II Part 2:** 707
Movie at the End of the World, The (McGrath), **Supp. X:** 127
Moviegoer, The (Percy), **Supp. III**

Part 1: 383–385, 387, 389–392, 394, 397

"Movie Magazine, The: A Low 'Slick'" (Percy), **Supp. III Part 1:** 385

Movies (Dixon), **Supp. XII:** 147

"Moving Around" (Matthews), **Supp. IX:** 155

"Moving Finger, The" (Wharton), **Retro. Supp. I:** 365

Moving On (McMurtry), **Supp. V:** 223–224

Moving Target, The (Macdonald), **Supp. IV Part 2:** 462, 463, 467, 470, 471, 473, 474

Moving Target, The (Merwin), **Supp. III Part 1:** 346, 347–348, 352, 357

"Mowbray Family, The" (Farrell and Alden), **II:** 45

"Mowing" (Frost), **II:** 169–170; **Retro. Supp. I:** 127, 128

"Moxan's Master" (Bierce), **I:** 206

Moyers, Bill, **Supp. IV Part 1:** 267; **Supp. VIII:** 331; **Supp. XI:** 126, 132; **Supp. XII:** 217; **Supp. XIII:** 274, 276

Moynihan, Daniel Patrick, **Retro. Supp. II:** 123; **Supp. VIII:** 241

Mozart, Wolfgang Amadeus, **I:** 479, 588; **IV:** 74, 358; **Supp. IV Part 1:** 284

"Mozart and the Gray Steward" (Wilder), **IV:** 358

Mr. and Mrs. Baby and Other Stories (Strand), **Supp. IV Part 2:** 631

"Mr. and Mrs. Fix-It" (Lardner), **II:** 431

Mr. Arcularis (Aiken), **I:** 54, 56

Mr. Bridge (Connell), **Supp. XIV:** 80, 82, 93

"Mr. Bruce" (Jewett), **II:** 397; **Retro. Supp. II:** 134, 143

"Mr. Burnshaw and the Statue" (Stevens), **Retro. Supp. I:** 298, 303

"Mr. Carson Death on His Nights Out" (McGrath), **Supp. X:** 118

Mr. Clemens and Mark Twain (Kaplan), **I:** 247–248

"Mr. Coffee and Mr. Fixit" (Carver), **Supp. III Part 1:** 145

"Mr. Cornelius Johnson, Office-Seeker" (Dunbar), **Supp. II Part 1:** 211, 213

"Mr. Costyve Duditch" (Toomer), **Supp. III Part 2:** 486

"Mr. Dajani, Calling from Jericho" (Nye), **Supp. XIII:** 286–287

"Mr. Edwards and the Spider" (Lowell), **I:** 544; **II:** 550; **Retro. Supp. II:** 187

Mr. Field's Daughter (Bausch), **Supp. VII:** 47–48, 51–52

"Mr. Flood's Party" (Robinson), **III:** 512

"Mr. Forster's Pageant" (Maxwell), **Supp. VIII:** 172

"Mr. Frost's Chickens" (Oliver), **Supp. VII:** 232–233

Mr. Hodge and Mr. Hazard (Wylie), **Supp. I Part 2:** 708, 709, 714, 721–724

"Mr. Hueffer and the Prose Tradition" (Pound), **III:** 465

Mr. Ives' Christmas (Hijuelos), **Supp. VIII:** 85–86

"Mr. Longfellow and His Boy" (Sandburg), **III:** 591

"Mr. Luna and History" (Ríos), **Supp. IV Part 2:** 551

Mr. Moto Is So Sorry (Marquand), **III:** 57, 58

Mr. Norris Changes Trains (Isherwood), **Supp. XIV:** 161

"Mr. Preble Gets Rid of His Wife" (Thurber), **Supp. I Part 2:** 615

"Mr. Rolfe" (Wilson), **IV:** 436

Mr. Sammler's Planet (Bellow), **I:** 144, 147, 150, 151, 152, 158; **Retro. Supp. II:** 19, 28, 30

"Mr. Shelley Speaking" (Wylie), **Supp. I Part 2:** 719

Mr. Spaceman (R. O. Butler), **Supp. XII:** 62, **74–75**

"Mr. Thompson's Prodigal" (Harte), **Supp. II Part 1:** 354

Mr. Vertigo (Auster), **Supp. XII: 34–35,** 36

"Mr. Whittier" (Scott), **Supp. I Part 2:** 705

Mr. Wilson's War (Dos Passos), **I:** 485

Mrabet, Mohammed, **Supp. IV Part 1:** 92, 93

Mrs. Albert Grundy: Observations in Philistia (Frederic), **II:** 138–139

"Mrs. Bilingsby's Wine" (Taylor), **Supp. V:** 323

Mrs. Bridge: A Novel (Connell), **Supp. XIV:** 79, 80, 81, 82, **89–94,** 95

"Mrs. Cassidy's Last Year" (Gordon), **Supp. IV Part 1:** 306

Mrs. Dalloway (Woolf), **Supp. IV Part 1:** 299; **Supp. VIII:** 5

"Mrs. Jellison" (Hay), **Supp. XIV:** 123

"Mrs. Krikorian" (Olds), **Supp. X:** 211

"Mrs. Maecenas" (Burke), **I:** 271

"Mrs. Mandrill" (Nemerov), **III:** 278

"Mrs. Manstey's View" (Wharton), **Retro. Supp. I:** 362, 363

"Mrs. Mobry's Reason" (Chopin), **Retro. Supp. II:** 61

Mrs. Reynolds (Stein), **IV:** 43

Mrs. Stevens Hears the Mermaids Sing-
ing (Sarton), **Supp. VIII:** 252–253, **256–257**

Mrs. Ted Bliss (Elkin), **Supp. VI: 56,** 58

"Mrs. Turner Cutting the Grass" (Shields), **Supp. VII:** 319–320

"Mrs. Walpurga" (Rukeyser), **Supp. VI:** 273

"MS. Found in a Bottle" (Poe), **III:** 411, 416; **Retro. Supp. II:** 274

"Ms. Lot" (Rukeyser), **Supp. VI:** 281

Ms. Magazine, **Supp. V:** 259

Mttron-Hirsch, Sidney, **III:** 484–485

"Muchas Gracias Por Todo" (Nye), **Supp. XIII:** 282–283

"Much Madness is divinest Sense" (Dickinson), **Retro. Supp. I:** 37–38

"Muck-A-Muck" (Harte), **Supp. II Part 1:** 342

"Mud Below, The" (Proulx), **Supp. VII:** 262

Mudge, Alden, **Supp. XIV:** 35

Mudrick, Marvin, **Retro. Supp. II:** 289

"Mud Season" (Kenyon), **Supp. VII:** 167–168

Mueller, Lisel, **Supp. I Part 1:** 83, 88; **Supp. XIV:** 268

Muggli, Mark, **Supp. IV Part 1:** 207

Muhammad, Elijah, **Supp. I Part 1:** 60

Muir, Edwin, **I:** 527; **II:** 368; **III:** 20

Muir, John, **Supp. VIII:** 296; **Supp. IX:** 33, **171–188**; **Supp. X:** 29; **Supp. XIV:** 177, 178, 181

Mujica, Barbara, **Supp. VIII:** 89

Mulatto (Hughes), **Retro. Supp. I:** 197, 203; **Supp. I Part 1:** 328, 339

Mulching of America, The (Crews), **Supp. XI:** 107

Muldoon, William, **I:** 500–501

Mule Bone (Hughes and Hurston), **Retro. Supp. I:** 194, 203; **Supp. VI:** 154

Mules and Men (Hurston), **Supp. VI:** 149, 153, 154, 160

Mulford, Prentice, **I:** 193

Mulligan, Robert, **Supp. VIII:** 128, 129

Mulligan Stew (Sorrentino), **Supp. XII:** 139

Mullins, Eustace, **III:** 479

Mullins, Priscilla, **II:** 502–503

Multitudes, Multitudes (Clampitt), **Supp. IX:** 39

Mumbo Jumbo (Reed), **Supp. X:** 240, 242, **245–248,** 251

Mumford, Lewis, **I:** 245, 250, 251, 252, 259, 261; **II:** 271, 473–474; **Supp. I Part 2:** 632, 638; **Supp. II Part 2:** 471–501

Mumford, Sophia Wittenberg (Mrs. Lewis Mumford), **Supp. II Part 2:** 474, 475

Mummy, The (film), **Supp. IV Part 1:** 104

"Mundus et Infans" (Auden), **Supp. II Part 1:** 15

"Munich, 1938" (Lowell), **II:** 554

"Munich Mannequins, The" (Plath), **Retro. Supp. II:** 256

"Municipal Report, A" (Henry), **Supp. II Part 1:** 406–407

Munro, Alice, **Supp. IX:** 212; **Supp. X:** 290; **Supp. XII:** 289–290, 310

Munsey, Frank, **I:** 501

Munson, Gorham, **I:** 252, 388, 432; **Retro. Supp. II:** 77, 78, 79, 82, 83; **Supp. I Part 2:** 454

Münsterberg, Hugo, **Supp. XIV:** 197

"Murano" (Doty), **Supp. XI:** 131

Murasaki, Lady, **II:** 577

Muray, Nicholas, **Supp. I Part 2:** 708

Murder, My Sweet (film), **Supp. IV Part 1:** 130

"Murderer Guest, The" (Gordon), **Supp. IV Part 1:** 306

Murder in Mount Holly (Theroux), **Supp. VIII:** 315–316

Murder in the Cathedral (Eliot), **I:** 571, 573, 580, 581; **II:** 20; **Retro. Supp. I:** 65; **Retro. Supp. II:** 222

Murder of Lidice, The (Millay), **III:** 140

"Murders in the Rue Morgue, The" (Poe), **III:** 412, 416, 419–420; **Retro. Supp. II:** 271, 272

Murdoch, Iris, **Supp. VIII:** 167

Murphy, Jacqueline Shea, **Retro. Supp. II:** 143

Murphy, Patrick, **Supp. XIII:** 214

Murphy, Richard, **Retro. Supp. II:** 250

Murray, Albert, **Retro. Supp. II:** 119, 120

Murray, Edward, **I:** 229

Murray, G. E., **Supp. X:** 201; **Supp. XI:** 143, 155

Murray, Gilbert, **III:** 468–469

Murray, Jan, **Supp. IV Part 2:** 574

Murray, John, **II:** 304; **III:** 76, 79; **Retro. Supp. I:** 246

Murray, Margaret A., **Supp. V:** 128

Murrell, John A., **IV:** 265

Mursell, James L., **Supp. I Part 2:** 608

"Muse" (Ammons), **Supp. VII:** 29

"Muse, Postmodern and Homeless, The" (Ozick), **Supp. V:** 272

"Musée des Beaux Arts" (Auden), **Retro. Supp. I:** 430; **Supp. II Part 1:** 14

Muses Are Heard, The (Capote), **Supp. III Part 1:** 126

"Muses of Terrence McNally, The" (Zinman), **Supp. XIII:** 207–208

"Muse's Tragedy, The" (Wharton), **Retro. Supp. I:** 364

Museum (Dove), **Supp. IV Part 1:** 245–247, 248

"Museum" (Hass), **Supp. VI:** 107

Museums and Women (Updike), **Retro. Supp. I:** 321

"Museum Vase" (Francis), **Supp. IX:** 83

"Mushrooms" (Plath), **Retro. Supp. II:** 246; **Supp. I Part 2:** 539

"Music" (Oliver), **Supp. VII:** 236

Music After the Great War (Van Vechten), **Supp. II Part 2:** 732

Music and Bad Manners (Van Vechten), **Supp. II Part 2:** 733

"Music for a Farce" (Bowles), **Supp. IV Part 1:** 83

Music for Chameleons (Capote), **Supp. III Part 1:** 120, 125–127, 131, 132

"Music for Museums?" (Van Vechten), **Supp. II Part 2:** 732

"Music for the Movies" (Van Vechten), **Supp. II Part 2:** 733

"Music from Spain" (Welty), **IV:** 272

Music of Chance, The (Auster), **Supp. XII:** 21, 23, **32–33**

"Music of Prose, The" (Gass), **Supp. VI:** 92

Music of Spain, The (Van Vechten), **Supp. II Part 2:** 734, 735

"Music of the Spheres" (Epstein), **Supp. XII:** 165

Music School, The (Updike), **IV:** 214, 215, 219, 226, 227; **Retro. Supp. I:** 320, 328, 329, 330

"Music School, The" (Updike), **Retro. Supp. I:** 326, 329, 335

"Music Swims Back to Me" (Sexton), **Supp. II Part 2:** 673

Muske, Carol, **Supp. IV Part 2:** 453–454

"Mussel Hunter at Rock Harbor" (Plath), **Supp. I Part 2:** 529, 537

Musset, Alfred de, **I:** 474; **II:** 543

Mussolini, Benito, **III:** 115, 473, 608; **IV:** 372, 373; **Supp. I Part 1:** 281, 282; **Supp. I Part 2:** 618; **Supp. V:** 290

"Must the Novelist Crusade?" (Welty), **IV:** 280

"Mutability of Literature, The" (Irving), **II:** 308

"Mutation of the Spirit" (Corso), **Supp. XII:** 132, 133

Mute, The (McCullers), **II:** 586

Mutilated, The (T. Williams), **IV:** 382, 386, 393

Mutiny of the Elsinore, The (London), **II:** 467

"My Adventures as a Social Poet" (Hughes), **Retro. Supp. I:** 194, 207

"My Alba" (Ginsberg), **Supp. II Part 1:** 320, 321

My Alexandria (Doty), **Supp. XI:** 119, 120, 121, **123–125,** 130

My Ántonia (Cather), **I:** 321–322; **Retro. Supp. I:** 1, 3, 4, **11–13,** 14, 17, 18, 22; **Supp. IV Part 2:** 608

"My Appearance" (Wallace), **Supp. X:** 306–307

My Argument with the Gestapo: A Macaronic Journal (Merton), **Supp. VIII:** 207

"My Arkansas" (Angelou), **Supp. IV Part 1:** 15

"My Aunt" (Holmes), **Supp. I Part 1:** 302, 310

"My Beginnings" (Simpson), **Supp. IX:** 273

My Bondage and My Freedom (Douglass), **Supp. III Part 1:** 155, 173

My Brother (Kincaid), **Supp. VII:** 191–193

"My Brother Paul" (Dreiser), **Retro. Supp. II:** 94

"My Brothers the Silent" (Merwin), **Supp. III Part 1:** 349–350

"My Brother's Work" (Dunn), **Supp. XI:** 147

"My Butterfly" (Frost), **II:** 151; **Retro. Supp. I:** 124

"My Children, and a Prayer for Us" (Ortiz), **Supp. IV Part 2:** 507

"My Confession" (McCarthy), **II:** 562

My Country and My People (Yutang), **Supp. X:** 291

"My Country 'Tis of Thee" (Reznikoff), **Supp. III Part 2:** 616

My Days of Anger (Farrell), **II:** 34, 35–36, 43

My Death My Life by Pier Paolo Pasolini (Acker), **Supp. XII:** 7

My Dog Stupid (Fante), **Supp. XI:** 160, **170–171**

My Emily Dickinson (Howe), **Retro. Supp. I:** 33, 43; **Supp. IV Part 2:** 430–431

"My English" (Alvarez), **Supp. VII:** 2

Myers, Linda A., **Supp. IV Part 1:** 10

"My Extended Family" (Theroux), **Supp. VIII:** 311

"My Father" (Sterne), **IV:** 466

"My Father: October 1942" (Stafford), **Supp. XI:** 323

"My Father at Eighty-Five" (Bly), **Supp. IV Part 1:** 73

"My Father Is a Simple Man" (Salinas), **Supp. XIII:** 324

"My Fathers Came From Kentucky" (Lindsay), **Supp. I Part 2:** 395

"My Father's Friends" (Maxwell), **Supp. VIII:** 171

"My Father's Ghost" (Wagoner), **Supp. IX:** 330

"My Father's God" (Fante), **Supp. XI:** 160, 174

"My Father's Love Letters" (Komunyakaa), **Supp. XIII:** 127

"My Father Speaks to me from the Dead" (Olds), **Supp. X:** 210

"My Father's Telescope" (Dove), **Supp. IV Part 1:** 246, 248

"My Father with Cigarette Twelve Years Before the Nazis Could Break His Heart" (Levine), **Supp. V:** 194

"My Favorite Murder" (Bierce), **I:** 205

My Favorite Plant: Writers and Gardeners on the Plants They Love (Kincaid), **Supp. VII:** 193–194

"My Fifty-Plus Years Celebrate Spring" (Salinas), **Supp. XIII:** 327

"My First Book" (Harte), **Supp. II Part 1:** 343

My First Summer in the Sierra (Muir), **Supp. IX:** 172, 173, **178–181**, 183, 185; **Supp. XIV:** 177

"My Fountain Pen" (McClatchy), **Supp. XII:** 254, 260

My Friend, Henry Miller (Perlès), **III:** 189

My Friend, Julia Lathrop (Addams), **Supp. I Part 1:** 25

"My Friend, Walt Whitman" (Oliver), **Supp. VII:** 245

"My Garden Acquaintance" (Lowell), **Supp. I Part 2:** 420

My Garden [Book]: (Kincaid), **Supp. VII:** 193–194

"My Grandfather" (Lowell), **II:** 554

"My Grandmother's Love Letters" (H. Crane), **Retro. Supp. II:** 78

"My Grandson, Home at Last" (Angelou), **Supp. IV Part 1:** 13

My Green Hills of Jamaica (McKay), **Supp. X:** 132, 142

My Guru and His Disciple (Isherwood), **Supp. XIV:** 157, 164, 172

My Heart's in the Highlands (Saroyan), **Supp. IV Part 1:** 83

"My High School Reunion" (Kingston), **Supp. V:** 169

"My Kinsman, Major Molineux" (Hawthorne), **II:** 228, 229, 237–239, 243; **Retro. Supp. I:** 153–154, 158, 160, 161; **Retro. Supp. II:** 181, 187

My Kinsman, Major Molineux (Lowell), **II:** 545–546

"My Last Afternoon with Uncle Devereux Winslow" (Lowell), **II:** 547–548; **Retro. Supp. II:** 189

"My Last Drive" (Hardy), **Supp. VIII:** 32

"My Life" (Strand), **Supp. IV Part 2:** 627

My Life, Starring Dara Falcon (Beattie), **Supp. V:** 31, 34–35

My Life a Loaded Gun: Dickinson, Plath, Rich, and Female Creativity (Bennett), **Retro. Supp. I:** 29

My Life and Hard Times (Thurber), **Supp. I Part 2:** 607, 609

My Life as a Man (Roth), **Retro. Supp. II:** 281, 286, 289; **Supp. III Part 2:** 401, 404, 405, 417–418

"My Life as a P.I.G., or the True Adventures of Smokey the Cop" (Abbey), **Supp. XIII:** 3

"My life closed twice before its close" (Dickinson), **Retro. Supp. I:** 38

"My Life had stood a Loaded Gun" (Dickinson), **Retro. Supp. I:** 42, 43, 45, 46; **Supp. IV Part 2:** 430

"My Life with Medicine" (Nye), **Supp. XIII:** 282

"My Life with R. H. Macy" (Jackson), **Supp. IX:** 118

"My Little Utopia" (Simic), **Supp. VIII:** 283

My Lives and How I Lost Them (Cullen), **Supp. IV Part 1:** 173

"My Lost City" (Fitzgerald), **Retro. Supp. I:** 102

"My Lost Youth" (Longfellow), **II:** 487, 499; **Retro. Supp. II:** 168

My Love Affair with America: The Cautionary Tale of a Cheerful Conservative (Podhoretz), **Supp. VIII:** 232, 233, 237, **244–246**

"My Lover Has Dirty Fingernails" (Updike), **Retro. Supp. I:** 332, 333

"My Lucy Friend Who Smells Like Corn" (Cisneros), **Supp. VII:** 68–69

"My Mammogram" (McClatchy), **Supp. XII:** 263–264

"My Man Bovanne" (Bambara), **Supp. XI:** 2

"My Mariner" (Larcom), **Supp. XIII:** 147

My Mark Twain (Howells), **II:** 276

"My Metamorphosis" (Harte), **Supp. II Part 1:** 339

"My Moby Dick" (Humphrey), **Supp. IX:** 95

My Mortal Enemy (Cather), **I:** 327–328; **Retro. Supp. I:** 16–17; **Supp. I Part 2:** 719

My Mother: Demonology (Acker), **Supp. XII:** 6

My Mother, My Father and Me (Hellman), **Supp. I Part 1:** 290–291

"My Mother and My Sisters" (Ortiz), **Supp. IV Part 2:** 499

"My Mother Is Speaking from the Desert" (Gordon), **Supp. IV Part 1:** 309, 314

"My Mother's Goofy Song" (Fante), **Supp. XI:** 164

"My Mother's Memoirs, My Father's Lie, and Other True Stories" (Banks), **Supp. V:** 15

"My Mother's Nipples" (Hass), **Supp. VI:** 109

"My Mother's Story" (Kunitz), **Supp. III Part 1:** 259

"My Mother with Purse the Summer They Murdered the Spanish Poet" (Levine), **Supp. V:** 194

My Movie Business: A Memoir (Irving), **Supp. VI:** 164

"My Name" (Cisneros), **Supp. VII:** 60

"My Negro Problem—And Ours" (Podhoretz), **Supp. VIII: 234–236**

"My New Diet" (Karr), **Supp. XI:** 241

"My Old Man" (Hemingway), **II:** 263

My Other Life (Theroux), **Supp. VIII:** 310, 324

My Own True Name: New and Selected Poems for Young Adults, 1984–1999 (Mora), **Supp. XIII:** 222

"My Passion for Ferries" (Whitman), **IV:** 350

"My People" (Hughes), **Retro. Supp. I:** 197; **Supp. I Part 1:** 321–322, 323

"My Playmate" (Whittier), **Supp. I Part 2:** 699–700

"My Priests" (Monette), **Supp. X:** 159

Myra Breckinridge (Vidal), **Supp. IV Part 2:** 677, 685–686, 689, 691

"My Recollections of S. B. Fairchild" (Jackson), **Supp. IX:** 118–119

"My Religion" (Carson), **Supp. XII: 105–106**

"My Road to Hell Was Paved" (Patchett), **Supp. XII:** 310–311

Myron (Vidal), **Supp. IV Part 2:** 677, 685, 686, 691

"My Roomy" (Lardner), **II:** 420, 421, 428, 430

"My Sad Self" (Ginsberg), **Supp. II Part 1:** 320

My Secret History (Theroux), **Supp. VIII:** 310, 324

"My Shoes" (Simic), **Supp. VIII:** 275

"My Side of the Matter" (Capote), **Supp. III Part 1:** 114, 115

My Silk Purse and Yours: The Publishing Scene and American Literary Art (Garrett), **Supp. VII:** 111; **Supp. X:** 7

My Sister Eileen (McKenney), **IV:** 288; **Retro. Supp. II:** 321

My Sister's Hand in Mine: The Collected Works of Jane Bowles, **Supp. IV Part 1:** 82–83

"My Son" (Strand), **Supp. IV Part 2:** 629

My Son, John (film), **Supp. I Part 1:** 67

"My Son, the Murderer" (Malamud), **Supp. I Part 2:** 437

"My Son the Man" (Olds), **Supp. X:** 212

"Mysteries of Caesar, The" (Hecht), **Supp. X:** 73

"Mysteries of Eleusis, The" (Hardwick), **Supp. III Part 1:** 195

Mysteries of Pittsburgh, The (Chabon), **Supp. XI:** 65, 68, **69–71**

Mysterious Stranger, The (Twain), **IV:** 190–191, 210

Mystery, A (Shields). *See Swann* (Shields)

"Mystery, The" (Dunbar), **Supp. II Part 1:** 199, 210

"Mystery, The" (Glück), **Supp. V:** 91

Mystery and Manners (O'Connor), **Retro. Supp. II:** 230

"'Mystery Boy' Looks for Kin in Nashville" (Hayden), **Supp. II Part 1:** 366, 372

"Mystery of Heroism, A" (Crane), **I:** 414

"Mystery of Marie Rogêt, The" (Poe), **III:** 413, 419; **Retro. Supp. II:** 271

"Mystic" (Plath), **Retro. Supp. II:** 257; **Supp. I Part 2:** 539, 541

"Mystical Poet, A" (Bogan), **Retro. Supp. I:** 36

"Mystic of Sex, The—A First Look at D. H. Lawrence" (Nin), **Supp. X:** 188

"Mystic Vision in 'The Marshes of Glynn'" (Warfel), **Supp. I Part 1:** 366, 373

"Mystification" (Poe), **III:** 425

My Study Windows (Lowell), **Supp. I Part 2:** 407

"Myth" (Rukeyser), **Supp. VI:** 281–282

Myth of Sisyphus, The (Camus), **I:** 294; **Supp. XIII:** 165

"Myth of the Isolated Artist, The" (Oates), **Supp. II Part 2:** 520

Myth of the Machine, The (Mumford), **Supp. II Part 2:** 476, 478, 482, 483, 493, 497

Mythology and the Romantic Tradition in English Poetry (Bush), **Supp. I Part 1:** 268

Myths and Texts (Snyder), **Supp. VIII: 295–296**

"My *Tocaya*" (Cisneros), **Supp. VII:** 69

My Uncle Dudley (Morris), **I:** 305; **III:** 219–220

"My Uncle's Favorite Coffee Shop" (Nye), **Supp. XIII:** 283

"My Weariness of Epic Proportions" (Simic), **Supp. VIII:** 276

My Wicked Wicked Ways (Cisneros), **Supp. VII:** 58, 64–68, 71

"My Wicked Wicked Ways" (Cisneros), **Supp. VII:** 58, 64–66

"My Word-house" (Mora), **Supp. XIII:** 219, 225

My Works and Days (Mumford), **Supp. II Part 2:** 475, 477, 481

My World and Welcome to It (Thurber), **Supp. I Part 2:** 610

Nabokov, Peter, **Supp. IV Part 2:** 490

Nabokov, Véra, **Retro. Supp. I:** 266, 270

Nabokov, Vladimir, **I:** 135; **III: 244–266,** 283, 286; **Retro. Supp. I: 263–281,** 317, 335; **Supp. I Part 1:** 196; **Supp. II Part 1:** 2; **Supp. IV Part 1:** 135; **Supp. V:** 127, 237, 251, 252, 253; **Supp. VIII:** 105, 133, 138; **Supp. IX:** 152, 212, 261; **Supp. X:** 283; **Supp. XI:** 66; **Supp. XII:** 310; **Supp. XIII:** 46, 52

Nabokov's Dozen (Nabokov), **Retro. Supp. I:** 266

Nabokov's Garden: A Guide to Ada (Mason), **Supp. VIII:** 138

Naca, Kristin, **Supp. XIII:** 133

Nadeau, Robert, **Supp. X:** 261, 270

Nadel, Alan, **Supp. IV Part 1:** 209

Naipaul, V. S., **Supp. IV Part 1:** 297; **Supp. VIII:** 314; **Supp. X:** 131; **Supp. XIV:** 111

Naked and the Dead, The (Mailer), **I:** 477; **III:** 26, 27, 28–30, 31, 33, 35, 36, 44; **Retro. Supp. II: 197–199;** **Supp. IV Part 1:** 381; **Supp. XI:** 218

Naked in Garden Hills (Crews), **Supp. XI:** 102, **110**

Naked Lunch (Burroughs), **Supp. III Part 1:** 92–95, 97–105; **Supp. IV Part 1:** 90

"Naked Nude" (Malamud), **Supp. I Part 2:** 450

Naked Poetry (Berg and Mezey, eds.), **Supp. IV Part 1:** 60

Naked Poetry (Levine), **Supp. V:** 180

Namedropping: Mostly Literary Memoirs (Coover), **Supp. V:** 40

"Name in the Papers" (Hughes), **Supp. I Part 1:** 330

Name Is Archer, The (Macdonald, under Millar), **Supp. IV Part 2:** 466

"Name Is Burroughs, The" (Burroughs), **Supp. III Part 1:** 93

Name Is Fogarty, The: Private Papers on Public Matters (Farrell), **II:** 49

Names, The (DeLillo), **Supp. VI:** 3, 10, 13, 14

Names, The (Momaday), **Supp. IV Part 2:** 479, 480, 483, 486, 487, 488, 489

Names and Faces of Heroes, The (Price), **Supp. VI:** 258, 260

Names of the Lost, The (Levine), **Supp. V:** 177–178, 179, 187–188

"Naming Myself" (Kingsolver), **Supp. VII:** 208

Naming of the Beasts, The (Stern). *See Rejoicings: Selected Poems, 1966–1972* (Stern)

Nana (Zola), **III:** 321

"Nancy Culpepper" (Mason), **Supp. VIII:** 141

Nancy Drew stories, **Supp. VIII:** 133, 135, 137, 142

"Nancy Knapp" (Masters), **Supp. I Part 2:** 461

"Naomi Shihab Nye: U.S. Mideast-History a Harbinger of 9-11?" (Nye), **Supp. XIII:** 286

"Nap, The" (Banks), **Supp. V:** 7

"Napoleon" (Emerson), **II:** 6

Napoleon I, **I:** 6, 7, 8, 474; **II:** 5, 309, 315, 321, 523; **Supp. I Part 1:** 153; **Supp. I Part 2:** 518, 519

Narcissa and Other Fables (Auchincloss), **Supp. IV Part 1:** 21, 34

"Narcissus as Narcissus" (Tate), **IV:** 124

"Narcissus Leaves the Pool" (Epstein), **Supp. XIV:** 110

Narcissus Leaves the Pool: Familiar Essays (Epstein), **Supp. XIV:** 110

Nardal, Paulette, **Supp. X:** 139

Nardi, Marcia, **Retro. Supp. I:** 426, 427

Narration (Stein), **IV:** 27, 30, 32, 33, 36

Narrative of a Four Months' Residence among the Natives of a Valley of the Marquesas Islands (Melville), **III:** 76

Narrative of Arthur Gordon Pym, The (Poe), **III:** 412, 416; **Retro. Supp. II:** 265, **273–275**; **Supp. XI:** 293

Narrative of the Life of Frederick Douglass, an American Slave, Written by Himself (Douglass), **Supp. III Part 1:** 154–159, 162, 165; **Supp. IV Part 1:** 13; **Supp. VIII:** 202

Narrenschiff, Das (Brant), **III:** 447

"Narrow Fellow in the Grass, A" (Dickinson), **Retro. Supp. I:** 30, 37

Narrow Heart, A: Portrait of a Woman (Gordon), **II:** 197, 217

Narrow Rooms (Purdy), **Supp. VII:** 274

Nash, Roderick, **Supp. IX:** 185; **Supp. XIV:** 191–192

Nash, Thomas, **Supp. III Part 1:** 387–388

Nashe, Thomas, **I:** 358

Nashville (film), **Supp. IX:** 143

Nasser, Gamal Abdel, **IV:** 490

Natalie Mann (Toomer), **Supp. III Part 2:** 484–486

Nathan, George Jean, **II:** 91; **III:** 103, 104, 106, 107; **IV:** 432; **Supp. IV Part 1:** 343; **Supp. IX:** 56–57; **Supp. XIII:** 161

"Nathanael West" (Herbst), **Retro. Supp. II:** 325

Nathanael West: The Art of His Life (Martin), **Retro. Supp. II:** 325

Nathan Coulter (Berry), **Supp. X:** 24, 33

"Nationalist, The" (Anderson), **I:** 115

"Nation Is Like Ourselves, The" (Baraka), **Supp. II Part 1:** 53

"Native, The" (Olds), **Supp. X:** 215

"Native American Attitudes to the Environment" (Momaday), **Supp. IV Part 2:** 481, 491

Native American Renaissance (Lincoln), **Supp. IV Part 2:** 507

Native American Testimony (Nabokov, ed.), **Supp. IV Part 2:** 490

"Native Hill, A" (Berry), **Supp. X:** 21

Native in a Strange Land: Trials & Tremors (Coleman), **Supp. XI:** 84–85, 87

Native of Winby and Other Tales, A (Jewett), **II:** 396; **Retro. Supp. II:** 138

Native Son (Wright), **IV:** 476, 477, 478, 479, 481, 482–484, 485, 487, 488, 491, 495; **Retro. Supp. II:** 107, 116; **Supp. I Part 1:** 51, 64, 67, 337; **Supp. II Part 1:** 170, 235–236; **Supp. IX:** 306; **Supp. XIV:** 73

"Native Trees" (Merwin), **Supp. III Part 1:** 355

Natorp, Paul, **Supp. XIV:** 198

Natural, The (Malamud), **II:** 424, 425; **Retro. Supp. II:** 288; **Supp. I Part 2:** 438–441, 443

"*Natural, The:* Malamud's World Ceres" (Wasserman), **Supp. I Part 2:** 439

"Natural History" (Olds), **Supp. X:** 210

"Natural History Note" (Hay), **Supp. XIV:** 124, 130

"Natural History of Some Poems, A" (Harrison), **Supp. VIII:** 53

"Natural History of the Dead" (Hemingway), **II:** 206; **Retro. Supp. I:** 176

"Naturally Superior School, A" (Knowles), **Supp. XII:** 235, 240–241

"Natural Method of Mental Philosophy" (Emerson), **II:** 14

"Natural Resources" (Rich), **Supp. I Part 2:** 575

Natural Selection (F. Barthelme), **Supp. XI:** 2, 28, 32, 33

Nature (Emerson), **I:** 463; **II:** 1, 8, 12, 16; **IV:** 171, 172–173

"Nature" (Emerson), **Retro. Supp. I:** 250; **Supp. I Part 2:** 383; **Supp. III Part 1:** 387; **Supp. IX:** 178

"Nature, Inc." (Lewis), **II:** 441

Nature: Poems Old and New (Swenson), **Supp. IV Part 2:** 652

Nature and Destiny of Man, The (Niebuhr), **III:** 292, 303–306, 310

"Nature and Life" (Emerson), **II:** 19

"Nature and Nurture: When It Comes to Twins, Sometimes It's Hard to Tell the Two Apart" (Bausch), **Supp. VII:** 40

"Nature-Metaphors" (Lanier), **Supp. I Part 1:** 352

Nature Morte (Brodsky), **Supp. VIII:** 25

Nature of Evil, The (James), **II:** 343

Nature of Peace, The (Veblen), **Supp. I Part 2:** 642

Nature of True Virtue, The (Edwards), **I:** 549, 557–558, 559

Nature's Economy: A History of Ecological Ideas (Worster), **Supp. IX:** 19

Nausea (Sartre), **Supp. VIII:** 7

"Navajo Blanket, A" (Swenson), **Supp. IV Part 2:** 649

Navarette, Don Martín de, **II:** 310

Navarro, Ramon, **Supp. IV Part 1:** 206

Navigator, The (film), **I:** 31

Naylor, Gloria, **Supp. VIII: 213–230**

Naylor, Paul Kenneth, **Supp. IV Part 2:** 420

Nazimova, **III:** 399

Neal, Larry, **Retro. Supp. II:** 112, 128; **Supp. X:** 324, 328

Neal, Lawrence P., **Supp. II Part 1:** 53

Neal, Patricia, **Supp. I Part 1:** 286; **Supp. IV Part 2:** 524; **Supp. V:** 223

Neale, Walter, **I:** 192, 208

Nearer the Moon: From "A Journal of Love," the Unexpurgated Diary of Anaïs Nin, 1937–1939, **Supp. X:** 184, 185

Near-Johannesburg Boy and Other Poems, The (Brooks), **Supp. III Part 1:** 86

Near Klamath (Carver), **Supp. III Part 1:** 137

"Near Perigord" (Pound), **Retro. Supp. I:** 289, 290

Near the Ocean (Lowell), **II:** 543, 550, 551–553, 554, 555; **Retro. Supp. II:** 182, 186, 189–190

"Near View of the High Sierra, A" (Muir), **Supp. IX:** 183

Nebeker, Helen, **Supp. IX:** 122

Necessary Angel, The (Stevens), **IV:** 76, 79, 89, 90

Necessities of Life: Poems, 1962–1965 (Rich), **Supp. I Part 2:** 553, 555

"Necrological" (Ransom), **III:** 486–489, 490, 492

Ned Christie's War (Conley), **Supp. V:** 232

"Need for a Cultural Base to Civil Rites & Bpower Mooments, The" (Baraka), **Supp. II Part 1:** 48

"Need for Christian Preaching, The" (Buechner), **Supp. XII:** 49

Needful Things (King), **Supp. V:** 139, 146

"Needle" (Simic), **Supp. VIII:** 275

"Needle Trade" (Reznikoff), **Supp. XIV:** 277, 289

"Need of Being Versed in Country Things, The" (Frost), **II:** 154; **Retro. Supp. I:** 133, 135

Neel, Philippe, **Supp. XIV:** 338

"Negative Capability" (Komunyakaa), **Supp. XIII:** 131

Negligible Tales (Bierce), **I:** 209

"Negotiating the Darkness, Fortified by Poets' Strength" (Karr), **Supp. XI:** 254; **Supp. XIII:** 285

Negotiating with the Dead (Atwood), **Supp. XIII:** 20, 35

Negritude movement, **Supp. X:** 131, 139

"Negro" (Hughes), **Supp. I Part 1:** 321–322

Negro, The (Du Bois), **Supp. II Part 1:** 178, 179, 185

Negro, The: The Southerner's Problem (Page), **Supp. II Part 1:** 168

Negro and His Music, The (Locke), **Supp. XIV:** 202

Negro Art: Past and Present (Locke), **Supp. XIV:** 202

"Negro Artisan, The" (Du Bois), **Supp. II Part 1:** 166

"Negro Artist and the Racial Mountain, The" (Hughes), **Retro. Supp. I:** 200, 207; **Supp. I Part 1:** 323, 325; **Supp. IV Part 1:** 169

"Negro Assays the Negro Mood, A" (Baldwin), **Supp. I Part 1:** 52

"Negro Citizen, The" (Du Bois), **Supp. II Part 1:** 179

"Negro Dancers" (Hughes), **Retro. Supp. I:** 199; **Supp. I Part 1:** 324

Negroes in America, The (McKay), **Supp. X:** 132, 136

"Negroes of Farmville, Virginia, The: A Social Study" (Du Bois), **Supp. II Part 1:** 166

Negro Family, The: The Case for National Action (Moynihan), **Retro. Supp. II:** 123

"Negro Farmer, The" (Du Bois), **Supp. II Part 1:** 167

"Negro Ghetto" (Hughes), **Supp. I Part 1:** 331

Negro in America, The (Locke), **Supp. XIV:** 208

Negro in American Civilization, The (Du Bois), **Supp. II Part 1:** 179

Negro in American Culture, The (Locke and Butcher), **Supp. XIV:** 202–203

Negro in Art, The: A Pictorial Record of the Negro Artist and of the Negro Theme in Art (Locke), **Supp. XIV:** 202

"Negro in Large Cities, The" (Du Bois), **Supp. II Part 1:** 169

"Negro in Literature and Art, The" (Du Bois), **Supp. II Part 1:** 174

Negro in New York, The (Ellison), **Supp. II Part 1:** 230

"Negro in the Black Belt, The: Some Social Sketches" (Du Bois), **Supp. II Part 1:** 166

"Negro in the Three Americas, The" (Locke), **Supp. XIV:** 211

"Negro in the Well, The" (Caldwell), **I:** 309

"Negro Love Song, A" (Dunbar), **Supp. II Part 1:** 204

Negro Mother, The (Hughes), **Supp. I Part 1:** 328

Negro Mother and Other Dramatic Recitations, The (Hughes), **Retro. Supp. I:** 203

Negro Novel in America, The (Bone), **Supp. IX:** 318–319

Negro Publication Society of America, **Retro. Supp. I:** 205

"Negro Renaissance, The: Jean Toomer and the Harlem of the 1920s" (Bontemps), **Supp. IX:** 306

"Negro Schoolmaster in the New South, A" (Du Bois), **Supp. II Part 1:** 168

"Negro's Contribution to American Culture, The" (Locke), **Supp. XIV:** 210, 211

"Negro Sermon, A: Simon Legree" (Lindsay), **Supp. I Part 2:** 393

"Negro Sings of Rivers, The" (Hughes), **Supp. IV Part 1:** 16

"Negro Speaks of Rivers, The" (Hughes), **Retro. Supp. I:** 199; **Supp. I Part 1:** 321

"Negro Spirituals, The (Locke), **Supp. XIV:** 201

"Negro Takes Stock, The" (Du Bois), **Supp. II Part 1:** 180

"Negro Theatre, The" (Van Vechten), **Supp. II Part 2:** 735

"Negro Voter Sizes Up Taft, A" (Hurston), **Supp. VI:** 160

"Negro Writer and His Roots, The: Toward a New Romanticism" (Hansberry), **Supp. IV Part 1:** 364

"Negro Youth Speaks" (Locke), **Supp. XIV:** 201

"Nehemias Americanus" (Mather), **Supp. II Part 2:** 453

Nehru, Jawaharlal, **IV:** 490

"Neighbor" (Hugo), **Supp. VI:** 135–136

"Neighbors" (Carver), **Supp. III Part 1:** 135, 139, 141; **Supp. XI:** 153

"Neighbors" (Hogan), **Supp. IV Part 1:** 405

"Neighbors, The" (Hay), **Supp. XIV:** 126

"Neighbour Rosicky" (Cather), **I:** 331–332

Neil Simon (Johnson), **Supp. IV Part 2:** 573

"Neil Simon: Toward Act III?" (Walden), **Supp. IV Part 2:** 591

"Neil Simon's Jewish-Style Comedies" (Walden), **Supp. IV Part 2:** 584, 591

Neilson, Heather, **Supp. IV Part 2:** 681

"Neither Out Far Nor In Deep" (Frost), **I:** 303; **Retro. Supp. I:** 121, 138

"Nellie Clark" (Masters), **Supp. I Part 2:** 461

Nelson, Ernest, **I:** 388

Nelson, Howard, **Supp. IV Part 1:** 66, 68

Nelson, Lord Horatio, **II:** 524

Nelson, Shirley, **Supp. XII:** 293

Nelson Algren (Cox and Chatterton), **Supp. IX:** 11–12

Nelson Algren: A Life on the Wild Side (Drew), **Supp. IX:** 2

Nemerov, David, **II:** 268

Nemerov, Howard, **III: 267–289; IV:** 137, 140; **Supp. III Part 2:** 541; **Supp. IV Part 2:** 455, 650; **Supp. IX:** 114

Nemiroff, Robert Barron, **Supp. IV Part 1:** 360, 361, 365, 369, 370, 374

Neoconservative Criticism: Norman Podhoretz, Kenneth S. Lynn, and Joseph Epstein (Winchell), **Supp. VIII:** 241; **Supp. XIV:** 103

"Neo-Hoodoo Manifesto, The" (Reed), **Supp. X:** 242

Neon Rain, The (Burke), **Supp. XIV:** 22, 24, 26–27, 28–29, 30

Neon Vernacular (Komunyakaa), **Supp. XIII:** 121, **127–128,** 131

Neon Wilderness, The (Algren), **Supp. IX:** 3, 4

Neo-Slave Narratives (Rushdy), **Supp. X:** 250

Nepantla: Essays from the Land in the Middle (Mora), **Supp. XIII:** 213, **219–221,** 227

Nephew, The (Purdy), **Supp. VII:** 271, 273, 282

"Nereids of Seriphos, The" (Clampitt), **Supp. IX:** 41

Nericcio, William, **Supp. XIV:** 304–305

Neruda, Pablo, **Supp. I Part 1:** 89; **Supp. IV Part 2:** 537; **Supp. V:** 332; **Supp. VIII:** 272, 274; **Supp. IX:** 157, 271; **Supp. X:** 112; **Supp. XI:** 191; **Supp. XII:** 217; **Supp. XIII:** 114, 315, 323

Nesbit, Edith, **Supp. VIII:** 171

Nesbitt, Robin, **Supp. VIII:** 89

Nesting Ground, The (Wagoner), **Supp. IX:** 324, **325–326**

Nest of Ninnies, A (Ashbery and Schuyler), **Supp. III Part 1:** 3

Nets to Catch the Wind (Wylie), **Supp. I Part 2:** 709, 710–712, 714

Nettleton, Asahel, **I:** 458

"Net to Snare the Moonlight, A" (Lindsay), **Supp. I Part 2:** 387

Neubauer, Carol E., **Supp. IV Part 1:** 9

Neugroschel, Joachim, **Supp. IX:** 138

Neuhaus, Richard John, **Supp. VIII:** 245

Neumann, Erich, **Supp. I Part 2:** 567; **Supp. IV Part 1:** 68, 69

Neuromancer (Gibson), **Supp. XII:** 15

"Neurotic America and the Sex Impulse" (Dreiser), **Retro. Supp. II:** 105

"Never Bet the Devil Your Head" (Poe), **III:** 425; **Retro. Supp. II:** 273

Never Come Morning (Algren), **Supp. IX:** 3, **7–9**

Never in a Hurry: Essays on People and Places (Nye), **Supp. XIII:** 273, **280–282**, 286

"Never Marry a Mexican" (Cisneros), **Supp. VII:** 70

"Never Room with a Couple" (Hughes), **Supp. I Part 1:** 330

"Nevertheless" (Moore), **III:** 214

Nevins, Allan, **I:** 253; **Supp. I Part 2:** 486, 493

"Nevsky Prospekt" (Olds), **Supp. X:** 205

"New Age of the Rhetoricians, The" (Cowley), **Supp. II Part 1:** 135

New American Literature, The (Pattee), **II:** 456

New American Novel of Manners, The (Klinkowitz), **Supp. XI:** 347

New American Poetry, 1945–1960 (Allen, ed.), **Supp. XIII:** 112

New American Poetry, The (Allen, ed.), **Supp. VIII:** 291, 292

"New American Writer, A" (W. C. Williams), **Retro. Supp. II:** 335

New and Collected Poems (Reed), **Supp. X:** 241

New and Collected Poems (Wilbur), **Supp. III Part 2:** 562–564

New and Selected Poems (Nemerov), **III:** 269, 275, 277–279

New and Selected Poems (Oliver), **Supp. VII:** 240–241, 245

New and Selected Poems (Wagoner), **Supp. IX: 326–327**

New and Selected Poems (W. J. Smith), **Supp. XIII:** 332

New and Selected Poems: 1974–1994 (Dunn), **Supp. XI: 151–152**

New and Selected Things Taking Place (Swenson), **Supp. IV Part 2:** 648–650, 651

"New Art Gallery Society, The" (Wolfe), **Supp. III Part 2:** 580

Newcomb, Ralph, **Supp. XIII:** 12

Newcomb, Robert, **II:** 111

New Conscience and an Ancient Evil, A (Addams), **Supp. I Part 1:** 14–15, 16

"New Conservatives, The: Intellectuals in Retreat" (Epstein), **Supp. XIV:** 103

New Criticism, The (Ransom), **III:** 497–498, 499, 501

"New Day, A" (Levine), **Supp. V:** 182

Newdick, Robert Spangler, **Retro. Supp. I:** 138

Newdick's Season of Frost (Newdick), **Retro. Supp. I:** 138

New Dictionary of Quotations, A (Mencken), **III:** 111

"New Directions in Poetry" (D. Locke), **Supp. IX:** 273

Newell, Henry, **IV:** 193

"New England" (Lowell), **II:** 536

"New England" (Robinson), **III:** 510, 524

New England: Indian Summer (Brooks), **I:** 253, 256

"New England Bachelor, A" (Eberhart), **I:** 539

"New Englander, The" (Anderson), **I:** 114

New England Girlhood, A (Larcom), **Supp. XIII:** 137, 142, 143, 144, **147–154**

New England Local Color Literature (Donovan), **Retro. Supp. II:** 138

"New England Sabbath-Day Chace, The" (Freneau), **Supp. II Part 1:** 273

New-England Tale, A (Sedgwick), **I:** 341

New England Tragedies, The (Longfellow), **II:** 490, 505, 506; **Retro. Supp. II:** 165, 167

Newer Ideals of Peace (Addams), **Supp. I Part 1:** 11–12, 15, 16–17, 19, 20–21

New Feminist Criticism, The: Essays on Women, Literature, and Theory (Showalter), **Supp. X:** 97

"New Folsom Prison" (Matthews), **Supp. IX:** 165

New Found Land: Fourteen Poems (MacLeish), **III:** 12–13

New Hampshire: A Poem with Notes and Grace Notes (Frost), **II:** 154–155; **Retro. Supp. I:** 132, 133, 135

"New Hampshire, February" (Eberhart), **I:** 536

New Hard-Boiled Writers (Panek), **Supp. XIV:** 27

New Industrial State, The (Galbraith), **Supp. I Part 2:** 648

"New Journalism, The" (Wolfe), **Supp. III Part 2:** 571

New Journalism, The (Wolfe and Johnson, eds.), **Supp. III Part 2:** 570, 579–581, 583, 586

New Left, The: The Anti-Industrial Revolution (Rand), **Supp. IV Part 2:** 527

"New Letters from Thomas Jefferson" (Stafford), **Supp. XI:** 324

New Letters on the Air: Contemporary Writers on Radio, **Supp. X:** 165, 169, 173

"New Life" (Glück), **Supp. V:** 90

New Life, A (Malamud), **Supp. I Part 2:** 429–466

"New Life at Kyerefaso" (Sutherland), **Supp. IV Part 1:** 9

"New Light on Veblen" (Dorfman), **Supp. I Part 2:** 650

Newman, Charles, **Supp. I Part 2:** 527, 546–548

Newman, Edwin, **Supp. IV Part 2:** 526

Newman, Judie, **Supp. IV Part 1:** 304, 305

Newman, Paul, **Supp. IV Part 2:** 473, 474

New Man, The (Merton), **Supp. VIII:** 208

"New Medea, The" (Howells), **II:** 282

New Mexico trilogy (Nichols), **Supp. XIII:** 269

"New Mother" (Olds), **Supp. X:** 206

"New Mothers, The" (Shields), **Supp. VII:** 310

New Music (Price), **Supp. VI:** 264, 265

"New Mutants, The" (Fiedler), **Supp. XIII:** 104

"New Name for Some Old Ways of Thinking, A" (James), **II:** 353

New Native American Novel, The: Works in Progress (Bartlett), **Supp. IV Part 1:** 335

"New Natural History, A" (Thurber), **Supp. I Part 2:** 619

"New Negro, The" (Locke), **Supp. XIV:** 201

New Negro, The (Locke, ed.), **Supp. II Part 1:** 176; **Supp. IX:** 309; **Supp. X:** 137

New Negro, The: An Interpretation (Locke, ed.), **Retro. Supp. I:** 199; **Supp. IV Part 1:** 170; **Supp. XIV:** 195, 201–202

New Negro for a New Century, A (Washington, Wood, and Williams), **Supp. XIV:** 201

New Orleans Sketches (Faulkner), **Retro. Supp. I:** 80

New Path to the Waterfall, A (Carver), **Supp. III Part 1:** 138–140, 147, 149

"New Poem, The" (Wright), **Supp. V:** 339, 340

"New Poems" (MacLeish), **III:** 19

"New Poems" (Oliver), **Supp. VII:** 240

New Poems: 1980–88 (Haines), **Supp. XII: 209–210**

New Poetry, The (Monroe and Henderson, eds.), **Supp. I Part 2:** 387

"New Poetry Handbook, The" (Strand), **Supp. IV Part 2:** 626

New Poetry of Mexico (Strand, trans.), **Supp. IV Part 2:** 630

New Poets of England and America (Hall, Pack, and Simpson, eds.), **Supp. IV Part 2:** 621

"Newport of Anchuria" (Henry), **Supp. II Part 1:** 409

"*New Republic* Moves Uptown, The" (Cowley), **Supp. II Part 1:** 142

"News, The" (McClatchy), **Supp. XII:** 269

"New Season" (Levine), **Supp. V:** 188

New Seeds of Contemplation (Merton), **Supp. VIII:** 200, 208

News from the Glacier: Selected Poems 1960–1980 (Haines), **Supp. XII:** 207, 208–209

"News Item" (Parker), **Supp. IX:** 190

New Song, A (Hughes), **Retro. Supp. I:** 202; **Supp. I Part 1:** 328, 331–332

"New South, The" (Lanier), **Supp. I Part 1:** 352, 354, 370

Newspaper Days, 1899–1906 (Mencken), **III:** 100, 102, 120

"New Spirit, The" (Ashbery), **Supp. III Part 1:** 14, 15

New Spoon River, The (Masters), **Supp. I Part 2:** 461–465, 473

New Star Chamber and Other Essays, The (Masters), **Supp. I Part 2:** 455–456, 459

New Tales of the Vampires (Rice), **Supp. VII:** 290

New Testament, **I:** 303, 457, 458; **II:** 167; **III:** 305; **IV:** 114, 134, 152; **Retro. Supp. I:** 58, 140, 360; **Supp. I Part 1:** 104, 106; **Supp. I Part 2:** 516. *See also* names of New Testament books

New Testament, A (Anderson), **I:** 101, 114

"New Theory of Thorstein Veblen, A" (Galbraith), **Supp. I Part 2:** 650

Newton, Benjamin Franklin, **I:** 454

Newton, Huey P., **Supp. I Part 1:** 66;

Supp. IV Part 1: 206

Newton, Isaac, **I:** 132, 557; **II:** 6, 103, 348–349; **III:** 428; **IV:** 18, 149

"New-Wave Format, A" (Mason), **Supp. VIII:** 141, 143, 147

New West of Edward Abbey, The (Ronald), **Supp. XIII:** 4

New Woman's Survival Sourcebook, The (Rennie and Grimstead, eds.), **Supp. I Part 2:** 569

New World, The: Tales (Banks), **Supp. V:** 8, 9, 10

New World Naked, A (Mariani), **Retro. Supp. I:** 419

New Worlds of Literature (Beaty and Hunter, eds.), **Supp. IV Part 1:** 331

New World Writing (Updike), **IV:** 217

New Year Letter (Auden), **Supp. II Part 1:** 14, 16

"New Year's Day" (Wharton), **Retro. Supp. I:** 381

"New Year's Eve" (Schwartz), **Supp. II Part 2:** 640, 656–657

New Year's Eve/1929 (Farrell), **II:** 43

"New Year's Eve 1968" (Lowell), **II:** 554

"New Year's Gift, The" (Stowe), **Supp. I Part 2:** 587

"New York" (Capote), **Supp. III Part 1:** 122

"New York" (Moore), **III:** 196, 198, 202, 206

"New York 1965" (Bowles), **Supp. IV Part 1:** 94

New York City Arts Project, **Supp. III Part 2:** 618

"New York City in 1979"(Acker), **Supp. XII:** 5

New York Edition, **Retro. Supp. I:** 235

"New York Edition" (James), **II:** 336, 337

"New York Gold Conspiracy, The" (Adams), **I:** 4

New York Intellectuals, **Supp. VIII:** 93

"New York Intellectuals, The" (Howe), **Supp. VI:** 120

New York Jew (Kazin), **Supp. VIII:** 95, **97–100**

New York Trilogy, The (Auster), **Supp. XII:** 21, **24–28**

Next (McNally), **Supp. XIII:** 197

"Next in Line, The" (Bradbury), **Supp. IV Part 1:** 102

Next Room of the Dream, The (Nemerov), **III:** 269, 275, 278, 279–280, 284

Next-to-Last Things: New Poems and Essays (Kunitz), **Supp. III Part 1:** 257–259, 261, 262, 265, 266, 268

"'Next to Reading Matter'" (Henry), **Supp. II Part 1:** 399

Nexus (H. Miller), **III:** 170, 187, 188, 189

Niatum, Duane, **Supp. IV Part 1:** 331; **Supp. IV Part 2:** 505

Nice and Noir (Schwartz), **Supp. XIV:** 23

Nice Jewish Boy, The (Roth), **Supp. III Part 2:** 412

Nicholas II, Tsar, **Supp. I Part 2:** 447

Nichols, Charles, **Retro. Supp. I:** 194

Nichols, John Treadwell, **Supp. XIII: 253–272**

Nichols, Luther, **Supp. X:** 265

Nichols, Mike, **Supp. IV Part 1:** 234; **Supp. IV Part 2:** 577

Nicholson, Colin, **Supp. VIII:** 129

Nicholson, Harold, **Supp. XIV:** 163

Nicholson, Jack, **Supp. V:** 26; **Supp. VIII:** 45; **Supp. XI:** 308

Nick Adams Stories, The (Hemingway), **II:** 258; **Retro. Supp. I:** 174

"Nick and the Candlestick" (Plath), **Supp. I Part 2:** 544

Nickel Mountain: A Pastoral Novel (Gardner), **Supp. VI:** 63, 64, 68, **69**

Nicoll, Allardyce, **III:** 400

Nicoloff, Philip, **II:** 7

Niebuhr, Gustav, **III:** 292

Niebuhr, H. Richard, **I:** 494

Niebuhr, Lydia, **III:** 292

Niebuhr, Reinhold, **III: 290–313; Supp. I Part 2:** 654

Niedecker, Lorine, **Supp. III Part 2:** 616, 623; **Supp. XIV:** 287

Nielsen, Ed, **Supp. IX:** 254

Nielson, Dorothy, **Supp. I Part 2:** 659

Nietzsche, Friedrich Wilhelm, **I:** 227, 283, 383, 389, 396, 397, 402, 509; **II:** 7, 20, 27, 42, 90, 145, 262, 462, 463, 577, 583, 585; **III:** 102–103, 113, 156, 176; **IV:** 286, 491; **Supp. I Part 1:** 254, 299, 320; **Supp. I Part 2:** 646; **Supp. IV Part 1:** 104, 105–106, 107, 110, 284; **Supp. IV Part 2:** 519; **Supp. V:** 277, 280; **Supp. VIII:** 11, 181, 189; **Supp. X:** 48; **Supp. XII:** 98; **Supp. XIV:** 339

Niflis, N. Michael, **Supp. IV Part 1:** 175

Nigger Heaven (Van Vechten), **Supp. II Part 2:** 739, 744–746

"Nigger Jeff" (Dreiser), **Retro. Supp. II:** 97

Nigger of the "Narcissus," The (Conrad), **II:** 91; **Retro. Supp. I:** 106

"NIGGY THE HO" (Baraka), **Supp. II Part 1:** 54

"Night, Death, Mississippi" (Hayden), **Supp. II Part 1:** 369

'Night, Mother (Norman), **Supp. VIII:** 141

"Night above the Avenue" (Merwin), **Supp. III Part 1:** 355

"Night among the Horses, A" (Barnes), **Supp. III Part 1:** 33–34, 39, 44

Night at the Movies, A, or, You Must Remember This: Fictions (Coover), **Supp. V:** 50–51

"Night at the Opera, A" (Matthews), **Supp. IX:** 167

"Nightbird" (Komunyakaa), **Supp. XIII:** 132

"Night-Blooming Cereus, The" (Hayden), **Supp. II Part 1:** 367

Night-Blooming Cereus, The (Hayden), **Supp. II Part 1:** 367, 373

Night-Born, The (London), **II:** 467

"Nightbreak" (Rich), **Supp. I Part 2:** 556

Night Dance (Price), **Supp. VI:** 264

"Night Dances, The" (Plath), **Supp. I Part 2:** 544

"Night Dream, The" (MacLeish), **III:** 15

"Night Ferry" (Doty), **Supp. XI:** 124

Night in Acadie, A (Chopin), **Retro. Supp. II:** 66–67, 73; **Supp. I Part 1:** 200, 219, 220, 224

"Night in Acadie, A" (Chopin), **Retro. Supp. II:** 66

"Night in June, A" (W. C. Williams), **Retro. Supp. I:** 424

"Night in New Arabia, A" (Henry), **Supp. II Part 1:** 402

Night in Question, The: Stories (Wolff), **Supp. VII:** 342–344

"Night Journey" (Roethke), **Supp. III Part 1:** 260

Night Light (Justice), **Supp. VII:** 126–127

"Nightmare" (Kumin), **Supp. IV Part 2:** 442

Nightmare Factory, The (Kumin), **Supp. IV Part 2:** 444–447, 451

"Nightmare Factory, The" (Kumin), **Supp. IV Part 2:** 445, 453

Nightmare on Main Street (Poe), **Retro. Supp. II:** 262

"Nightmare" poems (Benét), **Supp. XI:** 46, 58

Night Music (Odets), **Supp. II Part 2:** 541, 543, 544

"Night of First Snow" (Bly), **Supp. IV Part 1:** 71

Night of January 16th (Rand), **Supp. IV Part 2:** 527

Night of the Iguana, The (T. Williams),

IV: 382, 383, 384, 385, 386, 387, 388, 391, 392, 393, 394, 395, 397, 398

"Night of the Iguana, The" (T. Williams), **IV:** 384

"Night of the Living Beanfield: How an Unsuccessful Cult Novel Became an Unsuccessful Cult Film in Only Fourteen Years, Eleven Nervous Breakdowns, and $20 Million" (Nichols), **Supp. XIII:** 267

Night Rider (Warren), **IV:** 243, 246–247

Nights (Doolittle), **Supp. I Part 1:** 270, 271

Nights and Days (Merrill), **Supp. III Part 1:** 319, 320, 322–325

"Nights and Days" (Rich), **Supp. I Part 2:** 574

"Night Shift" (Plath), **Supp. I Part 2:** 538

"Night-Side" (Oates), **Supp. II Part 2:** 523

Night-Side (Oates), **Supp. II Part 2:** 522

"Night Sketches: Beneath an Umbrella" (Hawthorne), **II:** 235–237, 238, 239, 242

"Night-Sweat" (Lowell), **II:** 554

"Night-Talk" (Ellison), **Retro. Supp. II:** 126; **Supp. II Part 1:** 248

Night Thoughts (Young), **III:** 415

Night Traveler, The (Oliver), **Supp. VII:** 233

"Night Watch, The" (Wright), **Supp. V:** 339

"Night We All Had Grippe, The" (Jackson), **Supp. IX:** 118

Nightwood (Barnes), **Supp. III Part 1:** 31, 32, 35–37, 39–43

"Nihilist as Hero, The" (Lowell), **II:** 554; **Retro. Supp. II:** 190

Nikolai Gogol (Nabokov), **Retro. Supp. I:** 266

Niles, Thomas, **Retro. Supp. I:** 35

Niles, Thomas, Jr., **Supp. I Part 1:** 39

Nilsson, Christine, **Supp. I Part 1:** 355

Nilsson, Harry, **Supp. XI:** 309

Nimitz, Chester, **Supp. I Part 2:** 491

"Nimram" (Gardner), **Supp. VI:** 73

Nims, John Frederick, **III:** 527

Nin, Anaïs, **III:** 182, 184, 190; **Supp. III Part 1:** 43; **Supp. IV Part 2:** 680; **Supp. X:** 181–200

"9" (Oliver), **Supp. VII:** 244

"Nine from Eight" (Lanier), **Supp. I Part 1:** 352–354

Nine Headed Dragon River: Zen Journals 1969–1982 (Matthiessen), **Supp. V:** 199

"Nine Nectarines" (Moore), **III:** 203, 209, 215

Nine Plays (Reznikoff), **Supp. XIV:** 288

"Nine Poems for the Unborn Child" (Rukeyser), **Supp. VI:** 280–281, 284

Nine Stories (Nabokov), **Retro. Supp. I:** 266

Nine Stories (Salinger), **III:** 552, 558–564

1984 (Orwell), **Supp. XIII:** 29

"1940" (Stafford), **Supp. XI:** 328–329

"1945–1985: Poem for the Anniversary" (Oliver), **Supp. VII:** 237

19 Necromancers from Now (Reed), **Supp. X:** 240

1919 (Dos Passos), **I:** 482, 485–486, 487, 489, 490, 492

"1975" (Wright), **Supp. V:** 341

"1910" (Mora), **Supp. XIII:** 215

"1938" (Komunyakaa), **Supp. XIII:** 114

"1939" (Taylor), **Supp. V:** 316

1933 (Levine), **Supp. V:** 185–187

"1933" (Levine), **Supp. V:** 188

"Nineteenth New York, The" (Doctorow), **Supp. IV Part 1:** 232

"1929" (Auden), **Supp. II Part 1:** 6

19 Varieties of Gazelle (Nye), **Supp. XIII:** 275, **286–288**

"19 Varieties of Gazelle" (Nye), **Supp. XIII:** 286

95 Poems (Cummings), **I:** 430, 433, 435, 439, 446, 447

"90 North" (Jarrell), **II:** 370, 371

"91 Revere Street" (Lowell), **II:** 547; **Retro. Supp. II:** 188; **Supp. XI:** 240

90 Trees (Zukofsky), **Supp. III Part 2:** 631

"Nine Years Later" (Brodsky), **Supp. VIII:** 32

"Nirvana" (Lanier), **Supp. I Part 1:** 352

Nirvana Blues, The (Nichols), **Supp. XIII:** 266, 267

Nishikigi (play), **III:** 466

Niven, David, **Supp. XI:** 307

Nixon (film), **Supp. XIV:** 48

Nixon, Richard M., **I:** 376; **III:** 38, 46; **Supp. I Part 1:** 294, 295; **Supp. V:** 45, 46, 51; **Supp. XII:** 14; **Supp. XIV:** 306

"NJ Transit" (Komunyakaa), **Supp. XIII:** 132

Nketia, J. H., **Supp. IV Part 1:** 10

Nketsia, Nana, **Supp. IV Part 1:** 2, 10

Nkize, Julius, **Supp. IV Part 1:** 361

Nkrumah, Kwame, **I:** 490, 494; **Supp.**

IV Part 1: 361; **Supp. X:** 135

Noailles, Anna de, **IV:** 328

Noa Noa (Gauguin), **I:** 34

Nobel Lecture (Singer), **Retro. Supp. II:** 300

"No Better Than a 'Withered Daffodil'" (Moore), **III:** 216

Noble, David W., **Supp. I Part 2:** 650

"Noble Rider and the Sound of Words, The" (Stevens), **Retro. Supp. I:** 299

Noble Savage, The (Coover), **Supp. V:** 40

"No Bobolink reverse His Singing" (Dickinson), **Retro. Supp. I:** 45

Nobodaddy (MacLeish), **III:** 5–6, 8, 10, 11, 18, 19, 20

"Nobody in Hollywood" (Bausch), **Supp. VII:** 54

Nobody Knows My Name (Baldwin), **Supp. XIII:** 111

"Nobody Knows My Name" (Baldwin), **Retro. Supp. II:** 8; **Supp. I Part 1:** 52

Nobody Knows My Name: More Notes of a Native Son (Baldwin), **Retro. Supp. II:** 6, 8; **Supp. I Part 1:** 47, 52, 55

"Nobody knows this little Rose" (Dickinson), **Retro. Supp. I:** 30

"Nobody Said Anything" (Carver), **Supp. III Part 1:** 141

Nobody's Fool (Russo), **Supp. XII:** 326, **331–335,** 340

"No Change of Place" (Auden), **Supp. II Part 1:** 5

"Noche Triste, La" (Frost), **Retro. Supp. I:** 123

Nock, Albert Jay, **I:** 245; **Supp. IV Part 2:** 521, 524

"No Coward Soul Is Mine" (Brontë), **I:** 458

"No Crime in the Mountains" (Chandler), **Supp. IV Part 1:** 129

"Nocturne" (Komunyakaa), **Supp. XIII:** 126

"Nocturne" (MacLeish), **III:** 8

"Nocturne in a Deserted Brickyard" (Sandburg), **III:** 586

Nocturne of Remembered Spring (Aiken), **I:** 50

No Door (Wolfe), **IV:** 451–452, 456

"No Door" (Wolfe), **IV:** 456

"No Epitaph" (Carson), **Supp. XII:** 111

No Exit (Sartre), **I:** 82, 130; **Supp. XIV:** 320

No Exit (Sartre; Bowles, trans.), **Supp. IV Part 1:** 84

No Gifts from Chance (Benstock), **Retro. Supp. I:** 361

"No-Good Blues" (Komunyakaa),

Supp. XIII: 130

No Hero (Marquand), **III:** 57

No! In Thunder (Fiedler), **Supp. XIII:** 101

"Noiseless Patient Spider" (Whitman), **III:** 555; **IV:** 348; **Supp. IV Part 1:** 325

Noises Off (Frayn), **Supp. IV Part 2:** 582

Noi vivi. See We the Living (film)

"No Lamp Has Ever Shown Us Where to Look" (MacLeish), **III:** 9

Nolan, Sidney, **Retro. Supp. II:** 189

No Laughing Matter (Heller and Vogel), **Supp. IV Part 1:** 384, 389

No Love Lost, a Romance of Travel (Howells), **II:** 277

No Man Is an Island (Merton), **Supp. VIII:** 207

No Name in the Street (Baldwin), **Retro. Supp. II:** 13, 14; **Supp. I Part 1:** 47, 48, 52, 65–66, 67

No Nature: New and Selected Poems (Snyder), **Supp. VIII: 305**

Nonconformist's Memorial, The (Howe), **Supp. IV Part 2:** 434, 435–436

Nonconformity (Algren), **Supp. IX:** 15

None but the Lonely Heart (film), **Supp. II Part 2:** 546

Nones (Auden), **Supp. II Part 1:** 21

"Nones" (Auden), **Supp. II Part 1:** 22–23

None Shall Look Back (Gordon), **II:** 205–207, 208

"Noon" (Bryant), **Supp. I Part 1:** 157

"No One Remembers" (Levine), **Supp. V:** 187

"Noon Walk on the Asylum Lawn" (Sexton), **Supp. II Part 2:** 673

"Noon Wine" (Porter), **III:** 436, 437–438, 442, 446

"No Pain Whatsoever" (Yates), **Supp. XI:** 341

"No Place for You, My Love" (Welty), **IV:** 278, 279; **Retro. Supp. I:** 353

No Plays of Japan, The (Waley), **III:** 466

No Pockets in a Shroud (McCoy), **Supp. XIII: 166–168,** 171, 172, 173, 174

"No Poem So Fine" (Francis), **Supp. IX:** 83

Norcross, Frances, **I:** 456, 462

Norcross, Louise, **I:** 456, 462

Nordyke, Lewis, **Supp. XIII:** 5

No Relief (Dixon), **Supp. XII:** 139, **142–143**

No Resting Place (Humphrey), **Supp. IX:** 94, **106–108**

Norma (Bellini), **IV:** 309

Norma Ashe (Glaspell), **Supp. III Part 1:** 175, 186–187

"Normal Motor Adjustments" (Stein and Solomons), **IV:** 26

Norman, Charles, **III:** 479

Norman, Gurney, **Supp. X:** 24

Norman, Marsha, **Supp. VIII:** 141

Norman Mailer (Poirier), **Retro. Supp. II:** 207–208

Norman Mailer: Modern Critical Views (Bloom), **Retro. Supp. II:** 205

Norman Mailer Revisited (Merrill), **Retro. Supp. II:** 201

Norna; or, The Witch's Curse (Alcott), **Supp. I Part 1:** 33

Norris, Charles, **III:** 320; **Retro. Supp. I:** 100

Norris, Frank, **I:** 211, 355, 500, 506, 517, 518, 519; **II:** 89, 264, 276, 289, 307; **III:** 227, **314–336,** 596; **IV:** 29; **Retro. Supp. I:** 100, 325; **Retro. Supp. II:** 96, 101; **Supp. III Part 2:** 412; **Supp. VIII:** 101, 102; **Supp. IX:** 14, 15

"North" (Hugo), **Supp. VI:** 135

North, Milou (pseudonym), **Supp. IV Part 1:** 260. *See also* Dorris, Michael; Erdrich, Louise

North, Sir Thomas, **IV:** 370

"North American Sequence" (Roethke), **I:** 171–172, 183; **III:** 529, 545, 547, 548

"North Beach" (Snyder), **Supp. VIII:** 289

"North Country Sketches" (McClatchy), **Supp. XII:** 256

"Northeast Playground" (Paley), **Supp. VI:** 226–227, 229

Northern Lights (O'Brien), **Supp. V:** 237, 239, 241–244, 250

"Northern Motive" (Levine), **Supp. V:** 195

Northfield Poems (Ammons), **Supp. VII:** 29

"Northhanger Ridge" (Wright), **Supp. V:** 335, 340

"North Haven" (Bishop), **Retro. Supp. II:** 50

"North Labrador" (Crane), **I:** 386

North of Boston (Frost), **II:** 152, 153–154, 527; **Retro. Supp. I:** 121, 125, 127, **128–130,** 131; **Supp. I Part 1:** 263; **Supp. XIII:** 146

North of Jamaica (Simpson), **Supp. IV Part 2:** 448; **Supp. IX:** 275, 276

North of the Danube (Caldwell), **I:** 288, 290, 293, 294, 309, 310

Northrup, Cyrus, **Supp. I Part 1:** 350

"North Sea Undertaker's Complaint,

The" (Lowell), **II:** 550

North & South (Bishop), **Retro. Supp. II: 41–43; Supp. I Part 1:** 72, 84, 85, 89

North Star, The (Hellman), **Supp. I Part 1:** 281

Northup, Solomon, **Supp. XIV:** 32

Norton, Charles Eliot, **I:** 223, 568; **II:** 279, 322–323, 338; **Retro. Supp. I:** 371; **Retro. Supp. II:** 135; **Supp. I Part 1:** 103; **Supp. I Part 2:** 406, 479

Norton, Jody, **Supp. VIII:** 297

Norton, John, **Supp. I Part 1:** 99, 110, 112, 114

Norton Anthology of African American Literature, The, **Supp. X:** 325

Norton Anthology of American Literature, **Supp. X:** 325

Norton Anthology of Modern Poetry, The, **Supp. XI:** 259

Norton Anthology of Short Fiction, The, **Supp. IX:** 4

Norton Book of Personal Essays, The, **Supp. XIV:** 105

Norton Lectures, **Retro. Supp. I:** 65

Norwood, Vera, **Supp. IX:** 24

No Safe Harbour (Porter), **III:** 447

"No Speak English" (Cisneros), **Supp. VII:** 63

"Nostalgia of the Lakefronts" (Justice), **Supp. VII:** 118, 119, 120

"Nostalgic Mood" (Farrell), **II:** 45

No Star Is Lost (Farrell), **II:** 34, 35, 44

Nostromo (Conrad), **II:** 600; **IV:** 245

"Nosty Fright, A" (Swenson), **Supp. IV Part 2:** 651

Not about Nightingales (T. Williams), **IV:** 381

Not Dancing (Dunn), **Supp. XI:** 143, **148**

"Note about *Iconographs,* A" (Swenson), **Supp. IV Part 2:** 646

Notebook (Lowell), **Retro. Supp. II:** 186, 190; **Supp. V:** 343

Notebook 1967–68 (Lowell), **II:** 553–555; **Retro. Supp. II:** 182, 186, 190

Notebook of Malte Laurids Brigge, The (Rilke), **III:** 571

Notebooks (Fitzgerald), **Retro. Supp. I:** 110

"Note on Abraham Lincoln" (Vidal), **Supp. IV Part 2:** 688

"Note on Commercial Theatre" (Hughes), **Retro. Supp. I:** 207

"Note on Ezra Pound, A" (Eliot), **Retro. Supp. I:** 290

"Note on Lanier's Music, A" (Graham), **Supp. I Part 1:** 373

Note on Literary Criticism, A (Farrell),

II: 26, 49

"Note on Poetry, A" (Doolittle), **Supp. I Part 1:** 254, 267–268

"Note on Realism, A" (Anderson), **I:** 110

"Note on the Limits of 'History' and the Limits of 'Criticism,' A" (Brooks), **Supp. XIV:** 11

"Notes" (Dove), **Supp. IV Part 1:** 246

"Notes for a Moving Picture: The House" (Agee), **I:** 33, 34

"Notes for an Autobiography" (Van Vechten), **Supp. II Part 2:** 749

"Notes for a Novel About the End of the World" (Percy), **Supp. III Part 1:** 393

"Notes for a Preface" (Sandburg), **III:** 591, 596–597

"NOTES FOR A SPEECH" (Baraka), **Supp. II Part 1:** 33

Notes for the Green Box (Duchamp), **Supp. IV Part 2:** 423

Notes from a Bottle Found on the Beach at Carmel (Connell), **Supp. XIV:** 80, 87, 96, 97

Notes from a Sea Diary: Hemingway All the Way (Algren), **Supp. IX:** 16

"Notes from the Childhood and Girlhood" (Brooks), **Supp. III Part 1:** 77

"Notes from the River" (Stern), **Supp. IX:** 285, 287, 294, 295

Notes from Underground (Dostoyevsky), **III:** 571; **IV:** 485; **Retro. Supp. II:** 121

"Notes of a Faculty Wife" (Jackson), **Supp. IX:** 126

"Notes of a Native Daughter" (Didion), **Supp. IV Part 1:** 196, 197, 200, 201

Notes of a Native Son (Baldwin), **Retro. Supp. II:** 1, 2, 3, 5, 6; **Supp. I Part 1:** 50, 52, 54; **Supp. IV Part 1:** 163

"Notes of a Native Son" (Baldwin), **Supp. I Part 1:** 50, 54

Notes of a Son and Brother (James), **II:** 337; **Retro. Supp. I:** 235

"Notes on a Departure" (Trilling), **Supp. III Part 2:** 498

"Notes on Babbitt and More" (Wilson), **IV:** 435

"Notes on Camp" (Sontag), **Supp. XIV:** 167

"Notes on 'Camp'" (Sontag), **Supp. III Part 2:** 455–456

Notes on Democracy (Mencken), **III:** 104, 107–108, 109, 116, 119

"Notes on Free Verse" (Dobyns), **Supp. XIII:** 77

"Notes on 'Layover'" (Hass), **Supp. VI:** 109

Notes on Novelists (James), **II:** 336, 337; **Retro. Supp. I:** 235

"Notes on Nukes, Nookie, and Neo-Romanticism" (Robbins), **Supp. X:** 272

"Notes on Poetry" (Eberhart), **I:** 524, 527–528, 529

"Notes on the Craft of Poetry" (Strand), **Supp. IV Part 2:** 626

"Notes on the Decline of Outrage" (Dickey), **Supp. IV Part 1:** 181

Notes on the State of Virginia (1781–1782) (Jefferson), **Supp. XIV:** 191

"Notes to Be Left in a Cornerstone" (Benét), **Supp. XI:** 46, 58

"Notes toward a Supreme Fiction" (Stevens), **IV:** 87–89; **Retro. Supp. I:** 300, 306, **306–309,** 311; **Supp. I Part 1:** 80

"Notes towards a Poem That Can Never Be Written" (Atwood), **Supp. XIII:** 34–35

No Thanks (Cummings), **I:** 430, 431, 432, 436, 437, 441, 443, 446

"Nothing Big" (Komunyakaa), **Supp. XIII:** 121

"Nothing Gold Can Stay" (Frost), **Retro. Supp. I:** 133

"Nothing Missing" (O'Hara), **III:** 369

Nothing Personal (Baldwin), **Supp. I Part 1:** 58, 60

"Nothing Song, The" (Snodgrass), **Supp. VI:** 326

"Nothing Stays Put" (Clampitt), **Supp. IX:** 42

"Nothing Will Yield" (Nemerov), **III:** 279

No Third Path (Kosinski), **Supp. VII:** 215

"Not Ideas About the Thing but the Thing Itself" (Stevens), **IV:** 87

Notions of the Americans: Picked up by a Travelling Bachelor (Cooper), **I:** 343–345, 346

"Not-Knowing" (Barthelme), **Supp. IV Part 1:** 48

"Not Leaving the House" (Snyder), **Supp. VIII:** 300

"'Not Marble nor the Gilded Monument'" (MacLeish), **III:** 12

"Not Quite Social" (Frost), **II:** 156

"Not Sappho, Sacco" (Rukeyser), **Supp. VI:** 277

"Not Sixteen" (Anderson), **I:** 114

"Not Slightly" (Stein), **IV:** 44

Not So Deep as a Well (Parker), **Supp. IX:** 192

"Not Somewhere Else, but Here"

(Rich), **Supp. I Part 2:** 552, 573

Not So Simple: The "Simple" Stories by Langston Hughes (Harper), **Retro. Supp. I:** 194, 209

Not-So-Simple Neil Simon (McGovern), **Supp. IV Part 2:** 573

"Not the Point" (Cameron), **Supp. XII: 83**

"Not They Who Soar" (Dunbar), **Supp. II Part 1:** 199

Not This Pig (Levine), **Supp. V:** 178, 181, 182–183

Not to Eat; Not for Love (Weller), **III:** 322

Not Without Laughter (Hughes), **Retro. Supp. I:** 197, 198, 201; **Supp. I Part 1:** 328, 332

Nova Express (Burroughs), **Supp. III Part 1:** 93, 103, 104

Novel, The (Bulwer), **Retro. Supp. II:** 58

"Novel as a Function of American Democracy, The" (Ellison), **Retro. Supp. II:** 124

"Novel Démeublé, The" (Cather), **Retro. Supp. I:** 15

Novel History: Historians and Novelists Confront America's Past (and Each Other) (Carnes), **Supp. X:** 14

Novella (Goethe; Bogan and Mayer, trans.), **Supp. III Part 1:** 63

Novellas and Other Writings (Wharton), **Retro. Supp. I:** 360

"Novel of the Thirties, A" (Trilling), **Supp. III Part 2:** 499

Novels and Other Writings (Bercovitch), **Retro. Supp. II:** 325

Novels and Tales of Henry James, The (James), **Retro. Supp. I:** 232

"Novel-Writing and Novel-Reading" (Howells), **II:** 276, 290

"November" (Larcom), **Supp. XIII:** 143

"November Cotton Flower" (Toomer), **Supp. IX:** 312

November Twenty Six Nineteen Sixty Three (Berry), **Supp. X:** 24

"Novices" (Moore), **III:** 200–201, 202, 213

"Novogodnee" ("New Year's Greetings") (Tsvetayeva), **Supp. VIII:** 30

"Novotny's Pain" (Roth), **Supp. III Part 2:** 403

"No Voyage" (Oliver), **Supp. VII:** 231

No Voyage and Other Poems (Oliver), **Supp. VII:** 230–231, 232

Now and Another Time (Hearon), **Supp. VIII:** 58, **61–62**

Now and Then (Buechner), **Supp. XII:** 49, 53

"Now and Then, America" (Mora), **Supp. XIII:** 217

Nowhere Is a Place: Travels in Patagonia (Theroux and Chatwin), **Supp. VIII:** 322

"Now I Am Married" (Gordon), **Supp. IV Part 1:** 299

"Now I Lay Me" (Hemingway), **II:** 249; **Retro. Supp. I:** 175

"Now I Lay Me" (Olds), **Supp. X:** 208

"Now Is the Air Made of Chiming Balls" (Eberhart), **I:** 523

"No Word" (Kunitz), **Supp. III Part 1:** 263

Now Sheba Sings the Song (Angelou), **Supp. IV Part 1:** 16

"Now That We Live" (Kenyon), **Supp. VII:** 165

"Now the Servant's Name Was Malchus" (Wilder), **IV:** 358

"Now We Know" (O'Hara), **III:** 368–369

NOW with Bill Moyers (television), **Supp. XIII:** 286

Noyes, Alfred, **IV:** 434

Nuamah, Grace, **Supp. IV Part 1:** 10

"Nuances of a Theme by Williams" (Stevens), **Retro. Supp. I:** 422

Nuclear Age, The (O'Brien), **Supp. V:** 238, 243, 244, 246–248, 249, 251

Nude Croquet (Fiedler), **Supp. XIII:** 103

"Nude Descending a Staircase" (Duchamp), **IV:** 408; **Retro. Supp. I:** 416

Nugent, Bruce, **Retro. Supp. I:** 200

Nugent, Elliot, **Supp. I Part 2:** 606, 611, 613

Nuggets and Dust (Bierce), **I:** 195

"Nullipara" (Olds), **Supp. X:** 209

Number One (Dos Passos), **I:** 489

"Numbers, Letters" (Baraka), **Supp. II Part 1:** 50

Nunc Dimittis (Brodsky), **Supp. VIII:** 25–26, 28

"Nun No More, A" (Fante), **Supp. XI:** 160

"Nun's Priest's Tale" (Chaucer), **III:** 492

Nunzio, Nanzia, **IV:** 89

Nuptial Flight, The (Masters), **Supp. I Part 2:** 460, 471

"Nuptials" (Tate), **IV:** 122

"Nurse Whitman" (Olds), **Supp. X:** 203

Nurture (Kumin), **Supp. IV Part 2:** 453–454, 455

Nussbaum, Emily, **Supp. XI:** 143

Nussbaum, Felicity A., **Supp. X:** 189

Nutcracker, The (Tchaikovsky), **Retro. Supp. I:** 196

"Nux Postcoenatica" (Holmes), **Supp. I Part 1:** 303

Nyce, James M., **Retro. Supp. I:** 380

Nye, Naomi Shihab, **Supp. XI:** 316; **Supp. XIII: 273–290**

Nyerere, Julius, **Supp. X:** 135

"Nympholepsy" (Faulkner), **Retro. Supp. I:** 81

"Ö" (Dove), **Supp. IV Part 1:** 245

O. Henry Biography (C. A. Smith), **Supp. II Part 1:** 395

Oak and Ivy (Dunbar), **Supp. II Part 1:** 98

Oak Openings, The (Cooper), **I:** 354, 355

Oandasan, Bill, **Supp. IV Part 2:** 499

Oasis, The (McCarthy), **II:** 566–568

Oates, Joyce Carol, **Supp. II Part 2: 503–527; Supp. IV Part 1:** 205; **Supp. IV Part 2:** 447, 689; **Supp. V:** 323; **Supp. XI:** 239; **Supp. XII:** 343; **Supp. XIII:** 306; **Supp. XIV:** 26, 109

"Oath, The" (Tate), **IV:** 127

Obbligati (Hecht), **Supp. X:** 57

Ober, Harold, **Retro. Supp. I:** 101, 103, 105, 110, 113

Oberndorf, Clarence P., **Supp. I Part 1:** 315

Obey, André, **IV:** 356, 375

"Obit" (Lowell), **II:** 554

"Objective Value of a Social Settlement, The" (Addams), **Supp. I Part 1:** 4

"Objective Woman, The" (Jong), **Supp. V:** 119

Objectivist Anthology, An, **Supp. XIV:** 287

"Objectivist Ethics, The" (Rand), **Supp. IV Part 2:** 530–532

"Objectivists" Anthology, An (Zukofsky), **Supp. III Part 2:** 613, 615

"Objects" (Wilbur), **Supp. III Part 2:** 545–547

Oblique Prayers (Levertov), **Supp. III Part 1:** 283

"Oblivion" (Justice), **Supp. VII:** 121

Oblivion Seekers, The (Eberhardt), **Supp. IV Part 1:** 92

"Oblong Box, The" (Poe), **III:** 416

Obregon, Maurice, **Supp. I Part 2:** 488

O'Briant, Don, **Supp. X:** 8

O'Brien, Edward J., **I:** 289; **III:** 56

O'Brien, Fitzjames, **I:** 211

O'Brien, Geoffrey, **Supp. IV Part 2:** 471, 473

O'Brien, John, **Supp. V:** 48, 49; **Supp. X:** 239, 244

O'Brien, Tim, **Supp. V: 237–255; Supp. XI:** 234

"Obscene Poem, An" (Creeley), **Supp. IV Part 1:** 150

Obscure Destinies (Cather), **I:** 331–332; **Retro. Supp. I:** 19

"Observation Relative to the Intentions of the Original Founders of the Academy in Philadelphia" (Franklin), **II:** 114

"Observations" (Dillard), **Supp. VI:** 34

Observations (Moore), **III:** 194, 195–196, 197, 199, 203, 205, 215

Observations: Photographs by Richard Avedon: Comments by Truman Capote, **Supp. III Part 1:** 125–126

O Canada: An American's Notes on Canadian Culture (Wilson), **IV:** 429–430

"O Carib Isle!" (Crane), **I:** 400–401

O'Casey, Sean, **III:** 145; **Supp. IV Part 1:** 359, 361, 364

"Occidentals" (Ford), **Supp. V:** 71–72

"Occultation of Orion, The" (Longfellow), **Retro. Supp. II:** 168

"Occurrence at Owl Creek Bridge, An" (Bierce), **I:** 200–201; **II:** 264

"Ocean 1212-W" (Plath), **Supp. I Part 2:** 528

O'Connell, Nicholas, **Supp. IX:** 323, 325, 334

O'Connor, Edward F., Jr., **III:** 337

O'Connor, Flannery, **I:** 113, 190, 211, 298; **II:** 606; **III: 337–360; IV:** 4, 217, 282; **Retro. Supp. II:** 179, **219–239,** 272, 324; **Supp. I Part 1:** 290; **Supp. III Part 1:** 146; **Supp. V:** 59, 337; **Supp. VIII:** 13, 14, 158; **Supp. X:** 1, 26, 69, 228, 290; **Supp. XI:** 104; **Supp. XIII:** 294; **Supp. XIV:** 93

O'Connor, Frank, **III:** 158; **Retro. Supp. II:** 242; **Supp. I Part 2:** 531; **Supp. VIII:** 151, 157, 165, 167, 171

O'Connor, Richard, **II:** 467

O'Connor, T. P., **II:** 129

O'Connor, William, **IV:** 346; **Retro. Supp. I:** 392, 407

O'Connor, William Van, **III:** 479; **Supp. I Part 1:** 195

"Octascope" (Beattie), **Supp. V:** 27, 28

"Octaves" (Robinson), **Supp. III Part 2:** 593

"Octet" (Wallace), **Supp. X:** 309

October (Isherwood), **Supp. XIV:** 157, 164

"October" (Oliver), **Supp. VII:** 241

"October" (Swenson), **Supp. IV Part 2:** 649

"October 1913" (McCarriston), **Supp. XIV:** 266

"October, 1866" (Bryant), **Supp. I Part 1:** 169

"October and November" (Lowell), **II:** 554

"October in the Railroad Earth" (Kerouac), **Supp. III Part 1:** 225, 227, 229

October Light (Gardner), **Supp. VI:** 63, **69–71,** 72

"October Maples, Portland" (Wilbur), **Supp. III Part 2:** 556

"Octopus, An" (Moore), **III:** 202, 207–208, 214

"Octopus, The" (Merrill), **Supp. III Part 1:** 321

Octopus, The (Norris), **I:** 518; **III:** 314, 316, 322–326, 327, 331–333, 334, 335

"O Daedalus, Fly Away Home" (Hayden), **Supp. II Part 1:** 377–378

"OD and Hepatitis Railroad or Bust, The" (Boyle), **Supp. VIII:** 1

Odd Couple, The (film), **Supp. IV Part 2:** 589

Odd Couple, The (Simon), **Supp. IV Part 2:** 575, 579–580, 585, 586

Odd Couple, The (1985 version, Simon), **Supp. IV Part 2:** 580

Odd Jobs (Updike), **Retro. Supp. I:** 334

Odd Mercy (Stern), **Supp. IX: 298–299**

"Odds, The" (Hecht), **Supp. X:** 64–65

"Odds, The" (Salinas), **Supp. XIII:** 321

"Ode" (Emerson), **II:** 13

"Ode (Intimations of Immortality)" (Matthews), **Supp. IX:** 162

"Ode: Intimations of Immortality" (Wordsworth), **Supp. I Part 2:** 729; **Supp. III Part 1:** 12; **Supp. XIV:** 8

"Ode: My 24th Year" (Ginsberg), **Supp. II Part 1:** 312

"Ode for Memorial Day" (Dunbar), **Supp. II Part 1:** 199

"Ode for the American Dead in Asia" (McGrath), **Supp. X:** 119

"Ode Inscribed to W. H. Channing" (Emerson), **Supp. XIV:** 46

"Ode on a Grecian Urn" (Keats), **I:** 284; **III:** 472; **Supp. XII:** 113; **Supp. XIV:** 8, 9–10

"Ode on Human Destinies" (Jeffers), **Supp. II Part 2:** 419

"Ode on Indolence" (Keats), **Supp. XII:** 113

"Ode on Melancholy" (Keats), **Retro. Supp. I:** 301

Ode Recited at the Harvard Commemoration (Lowell), **Supp. I Part 2:** 416–418, 424

"Ode Recited at the Harvard Commemoration" (Lowell), **II:** 551

"Ode Secrète" (Valéry), **III:** 609

"Odes to Natural Processes" (Updike), **Retro. Supp. I:** 323

"Ode to a Nightingale" (Keats), **II:** 368; **Retro. Supp. II:** 261; **Supp. IX:** 52

"Ode to Autumn" (Masters), **Supp. I Part 2:** 458

"Ode to Cervantes" (Salinas), **Supp. XIII:** 324

"Ode to Coit Tower" (Corso), **Supp. XII:** 122

"Ode to Ethiopia" (Dunbar), **Supp. II Part 1:** 199, 207, 208, 209

"Ode to Fear" (Tate), **IV:** 128

"Ode to Meaning" (Pinsky), **Supp. VI: 249–250,** 251

"Ode to Night" (Masters), **Supp. I Part 2:** 458

"Ode to Our Young Pro-Consuls of the Air" (Tate), **IV:** 135

"Ode to the Austrian Socialists" (Benét), **Supp. XI:** 46, 58

"Ode to the Confederate Dead" (Tate), **II:** 551; **IV:** 124, 133, 137; **Supp. X:** 52

"Ode to the Johns Hopkins University" (Lanier), **Supp. I Part 1:** 370

"Ode to the Maggot" (Komunyakaa), **Supp. XIII:** 130

"Ode to the Mexican Experience" (Salinas), **Supp. XIII:** 316–317

"Ode to the Virginian Voyage" (Drayton), **IV:** 135

"Ode to the West Wind" (Shelley), **Retro. Supp. I:** 308; **Supp. I Part 2:** 728; **Supp. IX:** 52; **Supp. XII:** 117; **Supp. XIV:** 271–272

"Ode to Walt Whitman" (Benét), **Supp. XI:** 52

Odets, Clifford, **Supp. I Part 1:** 277, 295; **Supp. I Part 2:** 679; **Supp. II Part 2: 529–554; Supp. IV Part 2:** 587; **Supp. V:** 109; **Supp. VIII:** 96

Odier, Daniel, **Supp. III Part 1:** 97

O'Donnell, George Marion, **II:** 67

O'Donnell, Thomas F., **II:** 131

"Odor of Verbena" (Faulkner), **II:** 66

O'Doul, Lefty, **II:** 425

"Odysseus to Telemachus" (Brodsky),

Supp. VIII: 25

Odyssey (Bryant, trans.), **Supp. I Part 1:** 158

Odyssey (Homer), **III:** 14, 470; **Retro. Supp. I:** 286, 290; **Retro. Supp. II:** 121; **Supp. I Part 1:** 185; **Supp. IV Part 2:** 631; **Supp. IX:** 211; **Supp. X:** 114; **Supp. XIV:** 191

"Odyssey of a Wop, The" (Fante), **Supp. XI:** 164, 165

Oedipus Rex (Sophocles), **I:** 137; **III:** 145, 151, 152, 332; **Supp. I Part 2:** 428

Oedipus Tyrannus (Sophocles), **II:** 203

Oehlschlaeger, Fritz, **Supp. IX:** 123

"Of Alexander Crummell" (Du Bois), **Supp. II Part 1:** 170

O'Faoláin, Seán, **Supp. II Part 1:** 101

Of a World That Is No More (Singer), **IV:** 16

"Of Booker T. Washington and Others" (Du Bois), **Supp. II Part 1:** 168

"Of Bright & Blue Birds & the Gala Sun" (Stevens), **IV:** 93

"Of Christian Heroism" (Ozick), **Supp. V:** 272

"Of Dying Beauty" (Zukofsky), **Supp. III Part 2:** 610

"Of 'Father and Son'" (Kunitz), **Supp. III Part 1:** 262

Offenbach, Jacques, **II:** 427

"Offering for Mr. Bluehart, An" (Wright), **Supp. III Part 2:** 596, 601

"Offerings" (Mason), **Supp. VIII:** 141

"Official Piety" (Whittier), **Supp. I Part 2:** 687

"Off-Shore Pirates, The" (Fitzgerald), **II:** 88

Off the Beaten Path (Proulx), **Supp. VII:** 261

"Off the Cuff" (Simpson), **Supp. IX:** 278

Off the Map (Levine), **Supp. V:** 178

O'Flaherty, George, **Supp. I Part 1:** 202, 205–206

O'Flaherty, Kate. *See* Chopin, Kate

O'Flaherty, Thomas, **Supp. I Part 1:** 202, 203–204, 205

O'Flaherty, Thomas, Jr., **Supp. I Part 1:** 202

"Of Maids and Other Muses" (Alvarez), **Supp. VII:** 11

"Of Margaret" (Ransom), **III:** 491

Of Mice and Men (Steinbeck), **IV:** 51, 57–58

"Of Modern Poetry" (Stevens), **IV:** 92

Of Plymouth Plantation (Bradford), **Retro. Supp. II:** 161, 162

Of Plymouth Plantation (Morison, ed.),

Supp. I Part 2: 494

"Ofrenda for Lobo" (Mora), **Supp. XIII:** 224

"Often" (Kenyon), **Supp. VII:** 171

"Often, in Dreams, He Moved through a City" (Dobyns), **Supp. XIII:** 90

"Of the Coming of John" (Du Bois), **Supp. II Part 1:** 170

"Of the Culture of White Folk" (Du Bois), **Supp. II Part 1:** 175

Of the Farm (Updike), **IV:** 214, 217, 223–225, 233; **Retro. Supp. I:** 318, 329, 332

"Of 'The Frill'" (McCarriston), **Supp. XIV:** 274

"Of the Passing of the First-Born" (Du Bois), **Supp. II Part 1:** 170

"Of the Sorrow Songs" (Du Bois), **Supp. II Part 1:** 170

"Of the Wings of Atlanta" (Du Bois), **Supp. II Part 1:** 170

Of This Time, Of This Place (Trilling), **Supp. III Part 2:** 498, 504

Of Time and the River (Wolfe), **IV:** 450, 451, 452, 455, 456, 457, 458, 459, 462, 464–465, 467, 468, 469

Of Woman Born: Motherhood as Experience and Institution (Rich), **Supp. I Part 2:** 554, 567–569

Of Women and Their Elegance (Mailer), **Retro. Supp. II:** 209

Ogden, Archie, **Supp. XIII:** 174

Ogden, Henry, **II:** 298

Ogden, Uzal, **Supp. I Part 2:** 516

"Oh, Fairest of the Rural Maids" (Bryant), **Supp. I Part 1:** 169

"Oh, Immobility, Death's Vast Associate" (Dobyns), **Supp. XIII:** 89

"Oh, Joseph, I'm So Tired" (Yates), **Supp. XI:** 348

"O'Halloran's Luck" (Benét), **Supp. XI:** 47

O'Hara, Frank, **Supp. XII:** 121

O'Hara, J. D., **Supp. IV Part 1:** 43; **Supp. V:** 22

O'Hara, John, **I:** 375, 495; **II:** 444, 459; **III:** 66, **361–384;** **IV:** 59; **Retro. Supp. I:** 99, 112; **Supp. I Part 1:** 196; **Supp. II Part 1:** 109; **Supp. IV Part 1:** 31, 383; **Supp. IV Part 2:** 678; **Supp. V:** 95; **Supp. VIII:** 151, 156; **Supp. IX:** 208

O'Hehir, Andrew, **Supp. XII:** 280

"Ohio Pagan, An" (Anderson), **I:** 112, 113

Oil! (Sinclair), **Supp. V:** 276, 277–279, 282, 288, 289

"Oil Painting of the Artist as the Artist" (MacLeish), **III:** 14

O'Keeffe, Georgia, **Supp. IX:** 62, 66

"Oklahoma" (Levis), **Supp. XI:** 267

"Old, Old, Old, Old Andrew Jackson" (Lindsay), **Supp. I Part 2:** 398

"Old Amusement Park, An" (Moore), **III:** 216

"Old Angel Midnight" (Kerouac), **Supp. III Part 1:** 229–230

"Old Apple Dealer, The" (Hawthorne), **II:** 227, 233–235, 237, 238

"Old Apple-Tree, The" (Dunbar), **Supp. II Part 1:** 198

"Old Army Game, The" (Garrett), **Supp. VII:** 100–101

"Old Aunt Peggy" (Chopin), **Retro. Supp. II:** 64

"Old Barn at the Bottom of the Fogs, The" (Frost), **Retro. Supp. I:** 138

Old Beauty and Others, The (Cather), **I:** 331

Old Bruin: Commodore Matthew C. Perry, 1794–1858 (Morison), **Supp. I Part 2:** 494–495

"Old Cracked Tune, An" (Kunitz), **Supp. III Part 1:** 264

Old Curiosity Shop, The (Dickens), **I:** 458; **Supp. I Part 2:** 409

"Old Farmer, The" (Jeffers), **Supp. II Part 2:** 418

Old-Fashioned Girl, An (Alcott), **Supp. I Part 1:** 29, 41, 42

"Old Father Morris" (Stowe), **Supp. I Part 2:** 586

"Old Flame, The" (Lowell), **II:** 550

"Old Florist" (Roethke), **III:** 531

"Old Folsom Prison" (Matthews), **Supp. IX:** 165

Old Forest, The (Taylor), **Supp. V:** 320, 321, 326, 327

"Old Forest, The" (Taylor), **Supp. V:** 313, 321, 323, 326

Old Forest and Other Stories (Taylor), **Supp. V:** 326

Old Friends and New (Jewett), **II:** 402; **Retro. Supp. II:** 137, 140

Old Glory, The (Lowell), **II:** 543, 545–546, 555; **Retro. Supp. II:** 188

"Old Homestead, The" (Dunbar), **Supp. II Part 1:** 198

"Old Iron" (Nye), **Supp. XIII:** 276

"Old Ironsides" (Holmes), **Supp. I Part 1:** 302

"Old Lady We Saw, An" (Shields), **Supp. VII:** 310–311

"Old Love" (Singer), **Retro. Supp. II:** 307

"Old McGrath Place, The" (McGrath), **Supp. X:** 114

"Old Maid, The" (Wharton), **Retro. Supp. I:** 381, 382

"Old Man" (Faulkner), **II:** 68, 69

Old Man and the Sea, The (Hemingway), **II:** 250, 256–257, 258, 265; **III:** 40; **Retro. Supp. I:** 180, **185,** 186

"Old Man Drunk" (Wright), **Supp. III Part 2:** 595

"Old Man Feeding Hens" (Francis), **Supp. IX:** 78

"Old Man on the Hospital Porch" (Ríos), **Supp. IV Part 2:** 546–547

Old Man Rubbing His Eyes (Bly), **Supp. IV Part 1:** 65

"Old Manse, The" (Hawthorne), **II:** 224

"Old Man's Winter Night, An" (Frost), **Retro. Supp. I:** 126, 131

"Old Meeting House, The" (Stowe), **Supp. I Part 2:** 586

"Old Memory, An" (Dunbar), **Supp. II Part 1:** 198

"Old Men, The" (McCarthy), **II:** 566

"Old Mortality" (Porter), **III:** 436, 438–441, 442, 445, 446

"Old Mrs. Harris" (Cather), **I:** 332; **Retro. Supp. I:** 19

Old Neighborhood, The (Mamet), **Supp. XIV:** 240, 241, 242, 249–250, 251, 252, 254

Old New York (Wharton), **IV:** 322; **Retro. Supp. I:** 381

"Ol' Doc Hyar" (Campbell), **Supp. II Part 1:** 202

Old One-Two, The (Gurney), **Supp. V:** 98

"Old Order, The" (Porter), **III:** 443, 444–445, 451

"Old Osawatomie" (Sandburg), **III:** 584

Old Patagonia Express, The: By Train through the Americas (Theroux), **Supp. VIII:** 322

"Old People, The" (Faulkner), **II:** 71–72

"Old Poet Moves to a New Apartment 14 Times, The" (Zukofsky), **Supp. III Part 2:** 628

Old Possum's Book of Practical Cats (Eliot), **Supp. XIII:** 228, 344

"Old Red" (Gordon), **II:** 199, 200, 203

Old Red and Other Stories (Gordon), **II:** 157

Old Régime in Canada, The (Parkman), **Supp. II Part 2:** 600, 607, 608–609, 612

Old Religion, The (Mamet), **Supp. XIV:** 253

Olds, Sharon, **Supp. X:** 201–217; **Supp. XI:** 139, 142, 244; **Supp. XII:** 229; **Supp. XIV:** 265

"Old Saws" (Garrett), **Supp. VII:** 96–97

Old Testament, **I:** 109, 181, 300, 328, 401, 410, 419, 431, 457, 458; **II:** 166, 167, 219; **III:** 270, 272, 348, 390, 396; **IV:** 41, 114, 152, 309; **Retro. Supp. I:** 122, 140, 249, 311, 360; **Retro. Supp. II:** 299; **Supp. I Part 1:** 60, 104, 106, 151; **Supp. I Part 2:** 427, 515, 516; **Supp. IX:** 14. *See also* names of Old Testament books

"Old Things, The" (James), **Retro. Supp. I:** 229

"Old Times on the Mississippi" (Twain), **IV:** 199

Oldtown Folks (Stowe), **Supp. I Part 2:** 587, 596–598

"Old Town of Berwick, The" (Jewett), **Retro. Supp. II:** 132

"Old Trails" (Robinson), **III:** 513, 517

"Old Tyrannies" (Bourne), **I:** 233

"Old West" (Bausch), **Supp. VII:** 48

"Old Whorehouse, An" (Oliver), **Supp. VII:** 235

"Old Woman" (Pinsky), **Supp. VI:** 238

"Old Word, The" (Simic), **Supp. VIII:** 282

Oldys, Francis. *See* Chalmers, George

Oleanna (Mamet), **Supp. XIV:** 239, 241, 245, 248, 250

Olendorf, Donna, **Supp. IV Part 1:** 196

"Olga Poems, The" (Levertov), **Supp. III Part 1:** 279–281

"Olive Groves of Thasos, The" (Clampitt), **Supp. IX:** 51–52

Oliver, Bill, **Supp. VIII:** 138

Oliver, Mary, **Supp. VII:** 229–248; **Supp. X:** 31

Oliver, Sydney, **I:** 409

Oliver Goldsmith: A Biography (Irving), **II:** 315

Oliver Twist (Dickens), **I:** 354; **Supp. IV Part 2:** 464

"Olivia" (Salinas), **Supp. XIII:** 316

Olivieri, David (pseudonym), **Retro. Supp. I:** 361. *See also* Wharton, Edith

Ollive, Samuel, **Supp. I Part 2:** 503

Olmsted, Frederick Law, **Supp. I Part 1:** 355

Olsen, Lance, **Supp. IV Part 1:** 54; **Supp. IV Part 2:** 623

Olsen, Tillie, **Supp. V:** 114, 220; **Supp. XIII:** 291–309

Olson, Charles, **Retro. Supp. I:** 209; **Supp. II Part 1:** 30, 328; **Supp. II Part 2:** 555–587; **Supp. III Part 1:** 9, 271; **Supp. III Part 2:** 542, 624; **Supp. IV Part 1:** 139, 144, 146, 153, 154, 322; **Supp. IV Part 2:** 420, 421, 423, 426; **Supp. VIII:** 290, 291; **Supp. XII:** 2, 198; **Supp. XIII:** 104; **Supp. XIV:** 96

"Ol' Tunes, The" (Dunbar), **Supp. II Part 1:** 197

"O Lull Me, Lull Me" (Roethke), **III:** 536–537

Omar Khayyam, **Supp. I Part 1:** 363

O'Meally, Robert, **Retro. Supp. II:** 112

"Omen" (Komunyakaa), **Supp. XIII:** 126, 127

Omensetter's Luck (Gass), **Supp. VI:** 80–82, 87

"Ominous Baby, An" (Crane), **I:** 411

Ommateum, with Doxology (Ammons), **Supp. VII:** 24–26, 27, 28, 36

"Omnibus Jaunts and Drivers" (Whitman), **IV:** 350

Omoo: A Narrative of Adventures in the South Seas (Melville), **III:** 76–77, 79, 84; **Retro. Supp. I:** 247

O My Land, My Friends (H. Crane), **Retro. Supp. II:** 76

"On a Certain Condescension in Foreigners" (Lowell), **Supp. I Part 2:** 419

"On Acquiring Riches" (Banks), **Supp. V:** 5

On a Darkling Plain (Stegner), **Supp. IV Part 2:** 598, 607

On a Fire on the Moon (Mailer), **Retro. Supp. II:** 206

"On a Hill Far Away" (Dillard), **Supp. VI:** 28

"On a Honey Bee, Drinking from a Glass and Drowned Therein" (Freneau), **Supp. II Part 1:** 273

"On a Monument to a Pigeon" (Leopold), **Supp. XIV:** 187–188

"On a Mountainside" (Wagoner), **Supp. IX:** 332

O'Nan, Stewart, **Supp. XI:** 348

"On an Old Photograph of My Son" (Carver), **Supp. III Part 1:** 140

"On a Proposed Trip South" (W. C. Williams), **Retro. Supp. I:** 413

"On a Tree Fallen across the Road" (Frost), **Retro. Supp. I:** 134

"On a View of Pasadena from the Hills" (Winters), **Supp. II Part 2:** 795, 796–799, 814

"On a Visit to a Halfway House after a Long Absence" (Salinas), **Supp. XIII:** 325

"On a Windy Night" (Dixon), **Supp. XII:** 155

On Becoming a Novelist (Gardner),

Supp. VI: 64
"On Being an American" (Toomer), **Supp. III Part 2:** 479
"On Being a Woman" (Parker), **Supp. IX:** 201
On Being Blue (Gass), **Supp. VI:** 77, 78, 86, 94; **Supp. XIV:** 305
"On Being Too Inhibited" (Hay), **Supp. XIV:** 130
"On Burroughs' Work" (Ginsberg), **Supp. II Part 1:** 320
Once (Walker), **Supp. III Part 2:** 519, 522, 530
Once at Antietam (Gaddis), **Supp. IV Part 1:** 285
"Once by the Pacific" (Frost), **II:** 155; **Retro. Supp. I:** 122, 137
"Once More, the Round" (Roethke), **III:** 529
Once More around the Block: Familiar Essays (Epstein), **Supp. XIV:**107
"Once More to the Lake" (White), **Supp. I Part 2:** 658, 668, 673–675
"On Certain Political Measures Proposed to Their Consideration" (Barlow), **Supp. II Part 1:** 82
"Once There Was Light" (Kenyon), **Supp. VII:** 171–172
Ondaatje, Michael, **Supp. IV Part 1:** 252
On Distant Ground (R. O. Butler), **Supp. XII:** 62, **66–68,** 69, 74
O'Neale, Sondra, **Supp. IV Part 1:** 2
"One Arm" (T. Williams), **IV:** 383
One Arm, and Other Stories (T. Williams), **IV:** 383
"One Art" (Bell), **Supp. X:** 2
One Art (Bishop), **Retro. Supp. II:** 51
"One Art" (Bishop), **Retro. Supp. II:** 50; **Supp. I Part 1:** 72, 73, 82, 93, 94–95, 96
"One Art: The Poetry of Elizabeth Bishop, 1971–1976" (Schwartz), **Supp. I Part 1:** 81
"One Blessing had I than the rest" (Dickinson), **Retro. Supp. I:** 45
"One Body" (Hass), **Supp. VI:** 106
One Boy's Boston, 1887–1901 (Morison), **Supp. I Part 2:** 494
"One Coat of Paint" (Ashbery), **Supp. III Part 1:** 26
"One Dash-Horses" (Crane), **I:** 416
One Day (Morris), **III:** 233–236
One Day, When I Was Lost (Baldwin), **Retro. Supp. II:** 13; **Supp. I Part 1:** 48, 66, 67
"One Dead Friend" (Kumin), **Supp. IV Part 2:** 441
One Flew Over the Cuckoo's Nest (Kesey), **III:** 558

One for the Rose (Levine), **Supp. V:** 178, 179, 181, 187, 189–191
"One for the Rose" (Levine), **Supp. V:** 181, 190
"One Friday Morning" (Hughes), **Supp. I Part 1:** 330
"One Holy Night" (Cisneros), **Supp. VII:** 69–70
"One Home" (Stafford), **Supp. XI:** 321
"$106,000 Blood Money" (Hammett), **Supp. IV Part 1:** 345, 346
$106,000 Blood Money (Hammett), **Supp. IV Part 1:** 345
One Hundred Days in Europe (Holmes), **Supp. I Part 1:** 317
100 Faces of Death, The, Part IV (Boyle), **Supp. VIII:** 16
158-Pound Marriage, The (Irving), **Supp. VI:** 163, 164, **167–170**
O'Neil, Elizabeth Murrie, **Retro. Supp. I:** 427
O'Neill, Brendan, **Supp. XII:** 286
O'Neill, Eugene, **I:** 66, 71, 81, 94, 393, 445; **II:** 278, 391, 427, 585; **III:** 151, 165, **385–408; IV:** 61, 383; **Retro. Supp. II:** 82, 104; **Supp. III Part 1:** 177–180, 189; **Supp. IV Part 1:** 359; **Supp. IV Part 2:** 587, 607; **Supp. V:** 277; **Supp. VIII:** 332, 334; **Supp. XIV:** 239, 320, 328
"One Is a Wanderer" (Thurber), **Supp. I Part 2:** 616
"1 January 1965" (Brodsky), **Supp. VIII:** 23–24
"One Last Look at the Adige: Verona in the Rain" (Wright), **Supp. III Part 2:** 603
One Life (Rukeyser), **Supp. VI:** 273, 281, 283
One Life at a Time, Please (Abbey), **Supp. XIII:** 13
One Man in His Time (Glasgow), **II:** 178, 184
"One Man's Fortunes" (Dunbar), **Supp. II Part 1:** 211, 212–213
One Man's Initiation (Dos Passos), **I:** 476–477, 479, 488
"One Man's Meat" (White), **Supp. I Part 2:** 655
One Man's Meat (White), **Supp. I Part 2:** 654, 669, 676
"One Moment on Top of the Earth" (Nye), **Supp. XIII:** 282
"One More Song" (Lindsay), **Supp. I Part 2:** 400–401
"One More Thing" (Carver), **Supp. III Part 1:** 138, 144
"One More Time" (Gordon), **II:** 200
One Nation (Stegner), **Supp. IV Part 2:** 599, 608

"ONE NIGHT STAND" (Baraka), **Supp. II Part 1:** 32
"One of Our Conquerors" (Bourne), **I:** 223
One of Ours (Cather), **I:** 322–323; **Retro. Supp. I:** 1, 3, **13–15,** 20
"One of the Missing" (Bierce), **I:** 201–202
"One of the Rooming Houses of Heaven" (Doty), **Supp. XI:** 131
"One of the Smallest" (Stern), **Supp. IX:** 299–300
"One of Us" (Fante), **Supp. XI:** 165
"One Out of Twelve: Writers Who Are Women in Our Century" (Olsen), **Supp. XIII:** 294
"One Part Humor, 2 Parts Whining" (Kakutani), **Supp. XI:** 38
"One Person" (Wylie), **Supp. I Part 2:** 709, 724–727
"One Sister have I in our house" (Dickinson), **Retro. Supp. I:** 34
"One Song, The" (Strand), **Supp. IV Part 2:** 619
"One Summer in Spain" (Coover), **Supp. V:** 40
One Time, One Place: Mississippi in the Depression, a Snapshot Album (Welty), **Retro. Supp. I:** 339, 343, 344
1 x 1 (One Times One) (Cummings), **I:** 430, 436, 438–439, 441, 446, 447, 448
"One Touch of Nature" (McCarthy), **II:** 580
"One Trip Abroad" (Fitzgerald), **II:** 95
"One Way" (Creeley), **Supp. IV Part 1:** 150–151
One Way or Another (Cameron), **Supp. XII:** 81
One-Way Ticket (Hughes), **Retro. Supp. I:** 206, 207, 208; **Supp. I Part 1:** 333–334
One Way to Heaven (Cullen), **Supp. IV Part 1:** 170, 172
One Way to Spell Man (Stegner), **Supp. IV Part 2:** 595, 598, 601, 609
"One Way to Spell Man" (Stegner), **Supp. IV Part 2:** 601
"One Who Skins Cats, The" (Gunn Allen), **Supp. IV Part 1:** 331
"One Who Went Forth to Feel Fear" (Grimms), **Supp. X:** 86
"One Winter I Devise a Plan of My Own" (Ríos), **Supp. IV Part 2:** 549
One Writer's Beginnings (Welty), **Retro. Supp. I:** 339, 340, 341, 343, 344, 355–356
"One Year" (Olds), **Supp. X:** 210
"On First Looking Out through Juan

de la Cosa's Eyes" (Olson), **Supp. II Part 2:** 565, 566, 570, 579

"On First Opening *The Lyric Year*" (W. C. Williams), **Retro. Supp. I:** 414

"On Freedom's Ground" (Wilbur), **Supp. III Part 2:** 562

On Glory's Course (Purdy), **Supp. VII:** 275–276, 279, 280

On Grief and Reason (Brodsky), **Supp. VIII: 31–32**

"On Hearing a Symphony of Beethoven" (Millay), **III:** 132–133

"On Hearing the Airlines Will Use a Psychological Profile to Catch Potential Skyjackers" (Dunn), **Supp. XI:** 144–145

On Human Finery (Bell), **Supp. I Part 2:** 636

On Liberty (Mill), **Supp. XI:** 196

"On Looking at a Copy of Alice Meynell's Poems, Given Me, Years Ago, by a Friend" (Lowell), **II:** 527–528

"On Lookout Mountain" (Hayden), **Supp. II Part 1:** 380

Only a Few of Us Left (Marquand), **III:** 55

"Only Bar in Dixon, The" (Hugo), **Supp. VI:** 140, 141

Only Dark Spot in the Sky, The (Dove), **Supp. IV Part 1:** 244

"Only Good Indian, The" (Humphrey), **Supp. IX:** 101

Only in America (Golden), **Supp. VIII:** 244

"Only in the Dream" (Eberhart), **I:** 523

"Only Path to Tomorrow, The" (Rand), **Supp. IV Part 2:** 524

"Only Rose, The" (Jewett), **II:** 408

"Only Son of the Doctor, The" (Gordon), **Supp. IV Part 1:** 305, 306

"Only the Cat Escapes," **Supp. XII:** 150–151

"Only the Dead Know Brooklyn" (Wolfe), **IV:** 451

Only When I Laugh (Simon), **Supp. IV Part 2:** 575

On Moral Fiction (Gardner), **Supp. VI:** 61, **71**, 72, 73

"On Morality" (Didion), **Supp. IV Part 1:** 196

"On My Own" (Levine), **Supp. V:** 181, 189–190

"On My Own Work" (Wilbur), **Supp. III Part 2:** 541–542

On Native Grounds: An Interpretation of Modern American Prose Literature (Kazin), **I:** 517; **Supp. I Part**

2: 650; **Supp. VIII:** 93, 96–97, 98, **100–102**

"On Not Being a Dove" (Updike), **Retro. Supp. I:** 323

"On Open Form" (Merwin), **Supp. III Part 1:** 347–348, 353

On Photography (Sontag), **Supp. III Part 2:** 451, 458, 462–465

"On Political Poetry" (Bly), **Supp. IV Part 1:** 61

On Politics: A Carnival of Buncombe (Moos, ed.), **III:** 116

"On Pretentiousness" (Kushner), **Supp. IX:** 131–132

"On Quitting a Little College" (Stafford), **Supp. XI:** 321

"On Reading Eckerman's Conversations with Goethe" (Masters), **Supp. I Part 2:** 458

On Reading Shakespeare (L. P. Smith), **Supp. XIV:** 345–346

"On Reading to Oneself" (Gass), **Supp. VI:** 88, 89

On Revolution (Arendt), **Retro. Supp. I:** 87

"On Seeing Red" (Walker), **Supp. III Part 2:** 527

"On Social Plays" (A. Miller), **III:** 147, 148, 159

"On Steinbeck's Story 'Flight'" (Stegner), **Supp. IV Part 2:** 596

"On Style" (Sontag), **Supp. III Part 2:** 456–459, 465–466

"On Suicide" (Hay), **Supp. XIV:** 130, 132

"On the Antler" (Proulx), **Supp. VII:** 252–253

"On the Banks of the Wabash" (Paul Dresser), **Retro. Supp. II:** 94

"On the Beach, at Night" (Whitman), **IV:** 348

On the Boundary (Tillich), **Retro. Supp. I:** 326

"On the Building of Springfield" (Lindsay), **Supp. I Part 2:** 381

"On the Coast of Maine" (Hayden), **Supp. II Part 1:** 381

On the Contrary: Articles of Belief (McCarthy), **II:** 559, 562

"On the Death of a Friend's Child" (Lowell), **Supp. I Part 2:** 409

"On the Death of Senator Thomas J. Walsh" (Winters), **Supp. II Part 2:** 802, 806

"On the Death of Yeats" (Bogan), **Supp. III Part 1:** 59

"On the Death of Zhukov" (Brodsky), **Supp. VIII:** 27

"On the Disadvantages of Central

Heating" (Clampitt), **Supp. IX:** 41, 47, 52

"On the Edge" (Levine), **Supp. V:** 181–182

On the Edge and Over (Levine), **Supp. V:** 178, 180–182, 186

On the Edge of the Great Rift: Three Novels of Africa (Theroux), **Supp. VIII:** 316

"On the Eve of the Feast of the Immaculate Conception, 1942" (Lowell), **II:** 538; **Retro. Supp. II:** 185

"On the Eyes of an SS Officer" (Wilbur), **Supp. III Part 2:** 548

"On the Fall of General Earl Cornwallis" (Freneau), **Supp. II Part 1:** 261

"On the Folly of Writing Poetry" (Freneau), **Supp. II Part 1:** 263

On the Frontier (Auden and Isherwood), **Supp. II Part 1:** 13; **Supp. XIV:** 163

"On the Island" (Stern), **Supp. IX:** 290

"On the Late Eclipse" (Bryant), **Supp. I Part 1:** 152

On the Laws of the Poetic Art (Hecht), **Supp. X:** 58

"On the Marginal Way" (Wilbur), **Supp. III Part 2:** 558, 559

On the Mesa (Nichols), **Supp. XIII:** 268

"On the Moon and Matriarchal Consciousness" (Neumann), **Supp. IV Part 1:** 68

"On the Morning after the Sixties" (Didion), **Supp. IV Part 1:** 205, 206

On the Motion and Immobility of Douve (Bonnefoy; Kinnell, trans.), **Supp. III Part 1:** 235

"On the Murder of Lieutenant José del Castillo by the Falangist Bravo Martinez, July 12, 1936" (Levine), **Supp. V:** 187

"On the Night of a Friend's Wedding" (Robinson), **III:** 524

"On the Occasion of a Poem: Richard Hugo" (Wright), **Supp. III Part 2:** 596

On the Occasion of My Last Afternoon (Gibbons), **Supp. X:** 46, **50–53**

On the Origin of Species (Darwin), **Supp. XIV:** 192

"On the Parapet" (Tanner), **Retro. Supp. II:** 205

"On the Platform" (Nemerov), **III:** 287

On the Poetry of Philip Levine: Stranger to Nothing (Levis), **Supp. XI:** 257

"On the Powers of the Human Understanding" (Freneau), **Supp. II Part 1:** 274

On the Prejudices, Predilections, and Firm Beliefs of William Faulkner (Brooks), **Supp. XIV:** 13

"On the Pulse of Morning" (Angelou), **Supp. IV Part 1:** 15–17

"On the Railway Platform" (Jarrell), **II:** 370

"On the Rainy River" (O'Brien), **Supp. V:** 250

On the Rebound: A Story and Nine Poems (Purdy), **Supp. VII:** 276–277

"On the Religion of Nature" (Freneau), **Supp. II Part 1:** 275

"On the River" (Dunbar), **Supp. II Part 1:** 193

"On the River" (Levine), **Supp. V:** 193

On the River Styx and Other Stories (Matthiessen), **Supp. V:** 212

On the Road (Kerouac), **Retro. Supp. I:** 102; **Supp. III Part 1:** 92, 218, 222–224, 226, 230–231; **Supp. V:** 336; **Supp. X:** 269; **Supp. XIII:** 275; **Supp. XIV:** 138, 150

"On the Road Home" (Stevens), **Retro. Supp. I:** 306

On the Road with the Archangel (Buechner), **Supp. XII:** 54

On These I Stand: An Anthology of the Best Poems of Countee Cullen (Cullen), **Supp. IV Part 1:** 173

"On the Skeleton of a Hound" (Wright), **Supp. III Part 2:** 593

"On the Street: Monument" (Gunn Allen), **Supp. IV Part 1:** 326

"On the Subway" (Olds), **Supp. X:** 207

"On the System of Policy Hitherto Pursued by Their Government" (Barlow), **Supp. II Part 1:** 82

"On the Teaching of Modern Literature" (Trilling), **Supp. III Part 2:** 509–510

"On the Uniformity and Perfection of Nature" (Freneau), **Supp. II Part 1:** 275

"On the Universality and Other Attributes of the God of Nature" (Freneau), **Supp. II Part 1:** 275

"On the Use of Trisyllabic Feet in Iambic Verse" (Bryant), **Supp. I Part 1:** 156

On the Way toward a Phenomenological Psychology: The Psychology of William James (Linschoten), **II:** 362

"On the Way to Work" (Dunn), **Supp. XI:** 149–150

"On the Wide Heath" (Millay), **III:** 130

"On the Writing of Novels" (Buck),

Supp. II Part 1: 121

On This Island (Auden), **Supp. II Part 1:** 11

"On Time" (O'Hara), **III:** 369–370

"Ontology of the Sentence, The" (Gass), **Supp. VI:** 77

"On Top" (Leopold), **Supp. XIV:** 188

"On Top" (Snyder), **Supp. VIII:** 304

"On Translating Akhmatova" (Kunitz), **Supp. III Part 1:** 268

On William Stafford: The Worth of Local Things (Andrews, ed.), **Supp. XI:** 311, 312, 317, 321, 324, 326

"On Writing" (Carver), **Supp. III Part 1:** 142–143

"On Writing" (Nin), **Supp. X:** 182

Opatoshu, Joseph, **IV:** 9

"Open Boat, The" (Crane), **I:** 408, 415, 416–417, 423; **Retro. Supp. I:** 325; **Supp. XIV:** 51

Open Boat and Other Stories (Crane), **I:** 408

Open House (Roethke), **III:** 529–530, 540

"Open House" (Roethke), **III:** 529

"Opening, An" (Swenson), **Supp. IV Part 2:** 639

Opening of the Field, The (Duncan), **Supp. III Part 2:** 625

Opening the Hand (Merwin), **Supp. III Part 1:** 341, 353, 355

"Open Letter" (Roethke), **III:** 532, 534

"Open Letter to Surrealists Everywhere, An" (H. Miller), **III:** 184

Open Meeting, The (Gurney), **Supp. V:** 98

"Open Road, The" (Dreiser), **II:** 44

Open Sea, The (Masters), **Supp. I Part 2:** 471

Open Season: Sporting Adventures (Humphrey), **Supp. IX:** 95

"Open the Gates" (Kunitz), **Supp. III Part 1:** 264–265, 267

"Opera Company, The" (Merrill), **Supp. III Part 1:** 326

"Operation, The" (Sexton), **Supp. II Part 2:** 675, 679

Operation Shylock: A Confession (Roth), **Retro. Supp. II:** 279, 280, 291

Operation Sidewinder (Shepard), **Supp. III Part 2:** 434–435, 439, 446–447

Operations in North African Waters (Morison), **Supp. I Part 2:** 490

Operation Wandering Soul (Powers), **Supp. IX:** 212, **217–219**

Opffer, Emil, **Retro. Supp. II:** 80

"Opinion" (Du Bois), **Supp. II Part 1:** 173

Opinionator, The (Bierce), **I:** 209

Opinions of Oliver Allston (Brooks), **I:** 254, 255, 256

O Pioneers! (Cather), **I:** 314, 317–319, 320; **Retro. Supp. I:** 1, 5, 6, **7–9**, 10, 13, 20; **Retro. Supp. II:** 136

Oppen, George, **IV:** 415; **Supp. III Part 2:** 614, 615, 616, 626, 628; **Supp. XIV:** 285, 286, 287

Oppenheim, James, **I:** 106, 109, 239, 245

Oppenheimer, J. Robert, **I:** 137, 492

Oppenheimer, Judy, **Supp. IX:** 115, 116, 118, 120, 126

"Opportunity for American Fiction, An" (Howells), **Supp. I Part 2:** 645–646

Opposing Self, The (Trilling), **Supp. III Part 2:** 506–507

"Opposition" (Lanier), **Supp. I Part 1:** 368, 373

Opticks: A Poem in Seven Sections (Goldbarth), **Supp. XII:** 177, **178**

"Optimist's Daughter, The" (Welty), **IV:** 280–281

Optimist's Daughter, The (Welty), **IV:** 261, 280; **Retro. Supp. I:** 339, 355

Options (O. Henry), **Supp. II Part 1:** 410

Opus Posthumous (Stevens), **IV:** 76, 78

Oracle at Stoneleigh Court, The (Taylor), **Supp. V:** 328

Orage, Alfred, **III:** 473

Orange, Max (pseudonym). *See* Heller, Joseph

Orange Fish, The (Shields), **Supp. VII:** 318, 320, 323, 328

Oranges (McPhee), **Supp. III Part 1:** 298–299, 301, 309

Oration Delivered at Washington, July Fourth, 1809 (Barlow), **Supp. II Part 1:** 80, 83

Orations and Addresses (Bryant), **Supp. I Part 1:** 158

Orators, The (Auden), **Supp. II Part 1:** 6, 7, 11, 18–19

Orb Weaver, The (Francis), **Supp. IX:** **81–82**

"Orchard" (Doolittle), **Supp. I Part 1:** 263–264, 265, 266

"Orchard" (Eberhart), **I:** 539

Orchard Keeper, The (McCarthy), **Supp. VIII:** **175–176**

Orchestra (Davies), **III:** 541

"Orchids" (Roethke), **III:** 530–531

"Or Consider Prometheus" (Clampitt), **Supp. IX:** 44

Ordeal of Mansart, The (Du Bois), **Supp. II Part 1:** 185–186

Ordeal of Mark Twain, The (Brooks), **I:** 240, 247, 248; **II:** 482

"Order of Insects" (Gass), **Supp. VI:** 83

Order Out of Chaos (McPherson), **Supp. IV Part 1:** 2, 12

"Ordinary Afternoon in Charlottesville, An" (Wright), **Supp. V:** 344

"Ordinary Days" (Dunn), **Supp. XI:** 151

"Ordinary Evening in New Haven, An" (Stevens), **IV:** 91–92; **Retro. Supp. I:** 297, 300, 311, 312

Ordinary Love (Smiley), **Supp. VI:** 292, **299–300**

Ordinary Love; and Good Will: Two Novellas (Smiley), **Supp. VI:** 292, **299–300**

Ordinary Miracles (Jong), **Supp. V:** 115, 130–131

"Ordinary Time: Virginia Woolf and Thucydides on War" (Carson), **Supp. XII: 111**

"Ordinary Women, The" (Stevens), **IV:** 81

Ordways, The (Humphrey), **Supp. IX:** 95, **98–100,** 109

"Oread" (Doolittle), **II:** 520–521; **Supp. I Part 1:** 265–266

Oregon Message, An (Stafford), **Supp. XI: 328–329**

Oregon Trail, The (Parkman), **II:** 312; **Supp. II Part 2:** 592, 595–596, 598, 606

Oresteia (Aeschylus), **Supp. IX:** 103

"Orestes at Tauris" (Jarrell), **II:** 376, 377

Orfalea, Gregory, **Supp. XIII:** 278

Orfeo ed Euridice (Gluck), **II:** 210, 211

Orff, Carl, **Supp. X:** 63

"Organizer's Wife, The" (Bambara), **Supp. XI:** 8–9

"Orgy" (Rukeyser), **Supp. VI:** 280

Orgy, The (Rukeyser), **Supp. VI:** 274, 283

"Orientation of Hope, The" (Locke), **Supp. XIV:** 212–213

Orient Express (Dos Passos), **I:** 480

"Orient Express, The" (Jarrell), **II:** 382, 383–384

Origen, Adamantius, **IV:** 153

"Origin" (Harjo), **Supp. XII:** 219

Original Child Bomb: Points for Meditation to Be Scratched on the Walls of a Cave (Merton), **Supp. VIII:** 203

Original Essays on the Poetry of Anne Sexton (George), **Supp. IV Part 2:** 450

"Original Follies Girl, The" (Z. Fitzgerald), **Supp. IX:** 71

Original Light (Goldbarth), **Supp. XII:** 181, **183–184,** 188

Original of Laura, The (Nabokov), **Retro. Supp. I:** 266

"Original Sin" (Jeffers), **Supp. II Part 2:** 426

"Original Sin" (Warren), **IV:** 245

"Origin of Extermination in the Imagination, The" (Gass), **Supp. VI:** 89

Origin of Species, The (Darwin), **II:** 173, 462

Origin of the Brunists, The (Coover), **Supp. V:** 39, 41, 52

"Origins and History of Consciousness" (Rich), **Supp. I Part 2:** 570

"Origins of a Poem" (Levertov), **Supp. III Part 1:** 273

"Origins of the Beat Generation, The" (Kerouac), **Supp. III Part 1:** 231

Origo, Iris, **IV:** 328

"Orion" (Rich), **Supp. I Part 2:** 557

O'Riordan, Conal Holmes O'Connell, **III:** 465

Orlando (Woolf), **Supp. I Part 2:** 718; **Supp. VIII:** 263; **Supp. XII:** 9

Orlovsky, Peter, **Supp. XII:** 121, 126; **Supp. XIV:** 150

Ormond; or, The Secret Witness (Brown), **Supp. I Part 1:** 133–137

Ormonde, Czenzi, **Supp. IV Part 1:** 132

Orne, Sarah. *See* Jewett, Sarah Orne

Ornitz, Samuel, **Supp. IX:** 227; **Supp. XIII:** 166

Orphan Angel, The (Wylie), **Supp. I Part 2:** 707, 709, 714, 717, 719–721, 722, 724

Orpheus (Rukeyser), **Supp. VI:** 273

"Orpheus" (Winters), **Supp. II Part 2:** 801

"Orpheus (1)" (Atwood), **Supp. XIII:** 35

"Orpheus (2)" (Atwood), **Supp. XIII:** 35

"Orpheus, Eurydice, Hermes" (Rilke), **Supp. VIII:** 31, 32

"Orpheus Alone" (Strand), **Supp. IV Part 2:** 632

Orpheus Descending (T. Williams), **IV:** 380, 381, 382, 385, 386, 387, 389, 391–392, 395, 396, 398

Orr, Peter, **Supp. I Part 2:** 538, 540, 543

Ortega y Gasset, José, **I:** 218, 222; **Supp. IV Part 2:** 521

Ortiz, Simon J., **Supp. IV Part 1:** 319, 404; **Supp. IV Part 2: 497–515,** 557; **Supp. XII:** 217, 218

O'Ruddy, The (Crane), **I:** 409, 424

Orwell, George, **I:** 489; **II:** 454, 580; **Supp. I Part 2:** 523, 620; **Supp. II Part 1:** 143; **Supp. IV Part 1:** 236; **Supp. V:** 250; **Supp. VIII:** 241; **Supp. XIV:** 112, 158

Osborn, Dwight, **III:** 218–219, 223

"Osborn Look, The" (Morris), **III:** 221

Osgood, J. R., **II:** 283

O'Shea, Kitty, **II:** 137

O'Shea, Milo, **Supp. XI:** 308

"Oshkikwe's Baby" (traditional Chippewa story), **Supp. IV Part 1:** 333

Oshogay, Delia, **Supp. IV Part 1:** 333

Ossana, Diana, **Supp. V:** 230–231, 232

Ossian, **Supp. I Part 2:** 491

Ossip, Kathleen, **Supp. X:** 201

Ostanovka v Pustyne (A halt in the wilderness) (Brodsky), **Supp. VIII:** 21

Ostriker, Alicia, **Supp. I Part 2:** 540; **Supp. IV Part 2:** 439, 447, 449; **Supp. X:** 207, 208; **Supp. XI:** 143

Ostrom, Hans, **Retro. Supp. I:** 195

Oswald, Lee Harvey, **III:** 234, 235

Oswald II (DeLillo), **Supp. VI:** 16

Oswald's Tale (Mailer), **Retro. Supp. II:** 212–213

O Taste and See (Levertov), **Supp. III Part 1:** 278–279, 281

Othello (Shakespeare), **I:** 284–285

"Other, The" (Sexton), **Supp. II Part 2:** 692

Other America, The (Harrington), **I:** 306

Other Destinies: Understanding the American Indian Novel (Owens), **Supp. IV Part 1:** 404

"Other Frost, The" (Jarrell), **Retro. Supp. I:** 121

Other Gods: An American Legend (Buck), **Supp. II Part 1:** 123, 130–131

Other House, The (James), **Retro. Supp. I:** 229

"Other League of Nations, The" (Ríos), **Supp. IV Part 2:** 552

"Other Margaret, The" (Trilling), **Supp. III Part 2:** 504–505

"Other Miller, The" (Wolff), **Supp. VII:** 343–344

"Other Mothers" (Paley), **Supp. VI:** 225

"Other Night at Columbia, The" (Trilling), **Supp. XII:** 126

"Other Robert Frost, The" (Jarrell), **Retro. Supp. I:** 135

Others (Shields), **Supp. VII:** 310

Other Side, The (Gordon), **Supp. IV Part 1:** 299, 306, 307–309, 310–311

Other Side, The/El Otro Lado (Alvarez), **Supp. VII:** 9–12

Other Side of the River, The (Wright), **Supp. V:** 332–333, 342

"Other Side of the River, The" (Wright), **Supp. V:** 335

"Other Tradition, The" (Ashbery), **Supp. III Part 1:** 15, 18

"Other Two, The" (Wharton), **Retro. Supp. I:** 367

Other Voices, Other Rooms (Capote), **Supp. III Part 1:** 113–118, 121, 123–124

"Other War, The" (Cowley), **Supp. II Part 1:** 144

"Otherwise" (Kenyon), **Supp. VII:** 172, 174

Otherwise: New and Selected Poems (Kenyon), **Supp. VII:** 167, 172–174

"Other Woman, The" (Anderson), **I:** 114

Otho the Great: A Tragedy in Five Acts (Keats), **Supp. XII:** 113

Otis, Harrison Gray, **Supp. I Part 2:** 479–481, 483, 486, 488

Otis, James, **III:** 577; **Supp. I Part 2:** 486

O to Be a Dragon (Moore), **III:** 215

"Ouija" (McClatchy), **Supp. XII:** 269–270

Oupensky, Peter, **Supp. XIV:** 188

Our America (Frank), **I:** 229; **Supp. IX:** 308

Our America (Michaels), **Retro. Supp. I:** 379

"Our Assistant's Column" (Twain), **IV:** 193

"Our Bourgeois Literature" (Sinclair), **Supp. V:** 281

Our Brains and What Ails Them (Gilman), **Supp. XI:** 207

Our Century (Wilder), **IV:** 374

Our Country (Strong), **Supp. XIV:** 64

"Our Countrymen in Chains!" (Whittier), **Supp. I Part 2:** 688

"Our Cultural Humility" (Bourne), **I:** 223, 228

Our Depleted Society (Seymour), **Supp. XIII:** 264

"Our Father Who Drowns the Birds" (Kingsolver), **Supp. VII:** 208–209

"Our First House" (Kingston), **Supp. V:** 169

Our Gang (Roth), **Retro. Supp. II:** 287; **Supp. III Part 2:** 414; **Supp. IV Part 1:** 388

"Our Good Day" (Cisneros), **Supp. VII:** 60

Our Ground Time Here Will Be Brief (Kumin), **Supp. IV Part 2:** 450–452

Our House in the Last World (Hijuelos), **Supp. VIII:** 73, 76–79, 87, 88

"*Our Lady of the Annunciation*/Nuestra Señora de Anunciación" (Mora), **Supp. XIII:** 217, 224, 228

"Our Lady of Troy" (MacLeish), **III:** 3, 20

"Our Limitations" (Holmes), **Supp. I Part 1:** 314

"Our Martyred Soldiers" (Dunbar), **Supp. II Part 1:** 193

"Our Master" (Whittier), **Supp. I Part 2:** 704

"Our Mother Pocahontas" (Lindsay), **Supp. I Part 2:** 393

Our Mr. Wrenn: The Romantic Adventures of a Gentle Man (Lewis), **II:** 441

Our National Parks (Muir), **Supp. IX:** 181, 184

Our New York: A Personal Vision in Words and Photographs (Kazin), **Supp. VIII:** 106–107

"Our Old Aunt Who Is Now in a Retirement Home" (Shields), **Supp. VII:** 310

Our Old Home: A Series of English Sketches (Hawthorne), **II:** 225; **Retro. Supp. I:** 163

"Our Own Movie Queen" (Z. Fitzgerald), **Supp. IX:** 71

Ourselves to Know (O'Hara), **III:** 362, 365

"Our Story Begins" (Wolff), **Supp. VII:** 345

Our Town (Wilder), **IV:** 357, 364, 365, 366, 368–369

"Our Unplanned Cities" (Bourne), **I:** 229, 230

Our Wonder World, **Retro. Supp. I:** 341

Ouspensky, P. D., **I:** 383

"Out" (Harjo), **Supp. XII:** 219

"'Out, Out'" (Frost), **Retro. Supp. I:** 131

"Outcast" (McKay), **Supp. X:** 135

"Outcasts of Poker Flats, The" (Harte), **Supp. II Part 1:** 345, 347–348

Outcroppings (Harte), **Supp. II Part 1:** 343

Out Cry (T. Williams), **IV:** 383, 393

Outcry, The (James), **Retro. Supp. I:** 235

"Outdoor Shower" (Olds), **Supp. X:** 214

Outerbridge Reach (Stone), **Supp. V:** 306–308

Outer Dark (McCarthy), **Supp. VIII:** 176–177

Outermost Dream, The: Essays and Reviews (Maxwell), **Supp. VIII:** 171–172

"Outing, The" (Baldwin), **Supp. I Part 1:** 63

"Out Like a Lamb" (Dubus), **Supp. VII:** 91

"Outline of an Autobiography" (Toomer), **Supp. III Part 2:** 478

Outlyer and Ghazals (Harrison), **Supp. VIII:** 41

"Out of Business" (Mora), **Supp. XIII:** 217

"Out of Nowhere into Nothing" (Anderson), **I:** 113

"Out of Season" (Hemingway), **II:** 263

"Out of the Cradle Endlessly Rocking" (Whitman), **IV:** 342, 343–345, 346, 351; **Retro. Supp. I:** 404, 406

"Out of the Hospital and Under the Bar" (Ellison), **Retro. Supp. II:** 118–119; **Supp. II Part 1:** 246

"Out of the Rainbow End" (Sandburg), **III:** 594–595

"Out of the Sea, Early" (Swenson), **Supp. IV Part 2:** 645

"Out of the Snow" (Dubus), **Supp. VII:** 91

Out of the Stars (Purdy), **Supp. VII:** 281–282

Outre-Mer: A Pilgrimage beyond the Sea (Longfellow), **II:** 313, 491; **Retro. Supp. II:** 155, 165

"Outside" (Stafford), **Supp. XI:** 318

Outside, The (Glaspell), **Supp. III Part 1:** 179, 187

Outsider, The (Wright), **IV:** 478, 481, 488, 491–494, 495

Out West (Shanley), **Supp. XIV:** 317

"Out with the Old" (Yates), **Supp. XI:** 342

"Ouzo for Robin" (Merrill), **Supp. III Part 1:** 326

"Oval Portrait, The" (Poe), **III:** 412, 415; **Retro. Supp. II:** 270

"Oven Bird, The" (Frost), **Retro. Supp. I:** 131; **Supp. XI:** 153

"Over by the River" (Maxwell), **Supp. VIII:** 169, 170

"Overgrown Pasture, The" (Lowell), **II:** 523

"Over 2,000 Illustrations and a Complete Concordance" (Bishop), **Retro. Supp. II:** 45; **Supp. I Part 1:** 90–91

"Over Kansas" (Ginsberg), **Supp. II Part 1:** 320

Overland to the Islands (Levertov), **Supp. III Part 1:** 275, 276

"Over-Soul, The" (Emerson), **II:** 7

"Over the Hill" (Dubus), **Supp. VII:**

76, 79–80

Overtime (Gurney), **Supp. V:** 104

"Overwhelming Question, An" (Taylor), **Supp. V:** 323

Ovid, **I:** 62; **II:** 542–543; **III:** 457, 467, 468, 470; **Retro. Supp. I:** 63; **Supp. IV Part 2:** 634; **Supp. XII:** 264

"Ovid's Farewell" (McClatchy), **Supp. XII:** 257–258

Owen, David, **II:** 34

Owen, Maureen, **Supp. IV Part 2:** 423

Owen, Wilfred, **II:** 367, 372; **III:** 524; **Supp. X:** 146

Owens, Hamilton, **III:** 99, 109

Owens, Louis, **Supp. IV Part 1:** 404

"O Where Are You Going?" (Auden), **Supp. X:** 116

Owl in the Attic, The (Thurber), **Supp. I Part 2:** 614

Owl in the Mask of the Dreamer, The: Collected Poems (Haines), **Supp. XII:** 211

"Owl in the Sarcophagus, The" (Stevens), **Retro. Supp. I:** 300

"Owl's Clover" (Stevens), **IV:** 75

Owl's Clover (Stevens), **Retro. Supp. I:** 298, **303–304**

Owl's Insomnia, Poems by Rafael Alberti, The (Strand, trans.), **Supp. IV Part 2:** 630

"Owl Who Was God, The" (Thurber), **Supp. I Part 2:** 610

Owning Jolene (Hearon), **Supp. VIII: 66–67**

Oxford Anthology of American Literature, The, **III:** 197; **Supp. I Part 1:** 254

Oxford Book of American Verse (Matthiessen, ed.), **Retro. Supp. I:** 40

Oxford Book of Children's Verse in America, The (Hall, ed.), **Supp. XIV:** 126

Oxford History of the American People, The (Morison), **Supp. I Part 2:** 495–496

Oxford History of the United States, 1783–1917, The (Morison), **Supp. I Part 2:** 483–484

Oxherding Tale (Johnson), **Supp. VI: 190–192,** 193, 194, 196

"O Yes" (Olsen), **Supp. XIII:** 294, 298, **299–300,** 301

"O Youth and Beauty!" (Cheever), **Retro. Supp. I:** 335

"Oysters" (Sexton), **Supp. II Part 2:** 692

Ozick, Cynthia, **Supp. V: 257–274; Supp. VIII:** 141; **Supp. X:** 192

O-Zone (Theroux), **Supp. VIII:** 323–324

P. D. Kimerakov (Epstein), **Supp. XII:** 160, **162**

Pace, Patricia, **Supp. XI:** 245

Pacernik, Gary, **Supp. IX:** 287, 291

"Pacific Distances" (Didion), **Supp. IV Part 1:** 211

Pack, Robert, **Supp. IV Part 2:** 621

"Packed Dirt, Churchgoing, a Dying Cat, a Traded Cat" (Updike), **IV:** 219

Padel, Ruth, **Supp. XII:** 107

Pafko at the Wall (DeLillo), **Supp. VI:** 4

"Pagan Prayer" (Cullen), **Supp. IV Part 1:** 170

"Pagan Rabbi, The" (Ozick), **Supp. V:** 262, 264, 265

Pagan Rabbi and Other Stories, The (Ozick), **Supp. V:** 260, 261, 263–265

Pagan Spain (Wright), **IV:** 478, 488, 495

Page, Kirby, **III:** 297

Page, Thomas Nelson, **II:** 174, 176, 194; **Supp. XIV:** 61

Page, Walter Hines, **II:** 174, 175; **Supp. I Part 1:** 370

"Pages from Cold Point" (Bowles), **Supp. IV Part 1:** 85, 86, 87

Paid on Both Sides: A Charade (Auden), **Supp. II Part 1:** 6, 18–19

Paige, Satchel, **Supp. I Part 1:** 234

Paige, T. D. D., **III:** 475

Pain, Joseph, **Supp. I Part 2:** 502

Paine, Albert Bigelow, **I:** 249

Paine, Thomas, **I:** 490; **II:** 117, 302; **III:** 17, 148, 219; **Retro. Supp. I:** 390; **Supp. I Part 1:** 231; **Supp. I Part 2: 501–525; Supp. XI:** 55

"Pain has an Element of Blank" (Dickinson), **Retro. Supp. I:** 44

"Paint and Powder" (Z. Fitzgerald), **Supp. IX:** 71

Painted Bird, The (Kosinski), **Supp. VII:** 215–217, 219–221, 222, 227

Painted Desert (F. Barthelme), **Supp. XI:** 28–29, 32

Painted Dresses (Hearon), **Supp. VIII: 63**

"Painted Head" (Ransom), **III:** 491, 494; **Supp. II Part 1:** 103, 314

Painted Word, The (Wolfe), **Supp. III Part 2:** 580–581, 584

"Painter, The" (Ashbery), **Supp. III Part 1:** 5–6, 13

Painter Dreaming in the Scholar's House, The (Nemerov), **III:** 269

"Painters" (Rukeyser), **Supp. VI:** 281

"Painting a Mountain Stream" (Nemerov), **III:** 275

"Pair a Spurs" (Proulx), **Supp. VII:** 263–264

"Pair of Bright Blue Eyes, A" (Taylor), **Supp. V:** 321

"Pajamas" (Olds), **Supp. X:** 206

Pakula, Alan, **Supp. XIII:** 264

Palace at 4 A.M. (Giacometti), **Supp. VIII:** 169

"Palantine, The" (Whittier), **Supp. I Part 2:** 694, 696

Palatella, John, **Retro. Supp. II:** 48

Pale Fire (Nabokov), **III:** 244, 246, 252, 263–265; **Retro. Supp. I:** 264, 265, 266, 270, 271, 272, 276, 278, 335; **Supp. V:** 251, 253

"Pale Horse, Pale Rider" (Porter), **III:** 436, 437, 441–442, 445, 446, 449

Pale Horse, Pale Rider: Three Short Novels (Porter), **III:** 433, 436–442; **Supp. VIII:** 157

"Pale Pink Roast, The" (Paley), **Supp. VI:** 217

Paley, Grace, **Supp. VI: 217–233; Supp. IX:** 212; **Supp. X:** 79, 164; **Supp. XII:** 309

Paley, William, **II:** 9

Palgrave, Francis Turner, **Retro. Supp. I:** 124; **Supp. XIV:** 340

Palgrave's Golden Treasury (Palgrave), **IV:** 405

Palimpsest (Doolittle), **Supp. I Part 1:** 259, 268, 269, 270–271

Palimpsest (Vidal), **Supp. X:** 186

"Palingenesis" (Longfellow), **II:** 498

Pal Joey (O'Hara), **III:** 361, 367–368

"Pal Joey" stories (O'Hara), **III:** 361

Pallbearers Envying the One Who Rides (Dobyns), **Supp. XIII:** 89

"Palm, The" (Merwin), **Supp. III Part 1:** 355

Palmer, Charles, **II:** 111

Palmer, Elihu, **Supp. I Part 2:** 520

Palmer, George Herbert, **Supp. XIV:** 197

Palmer, Michael, **Supp. IV Part 2:** 421

Palmerston, Lord, **I:** 15

"Palo Alto: The Marshes" (Hass), **Supp. VI:** 100

Palpable God, A: Thirty Stories Translated from the Bible with an Essay on the Origins and Life of Narrative (Price), **Supp. VI:** 262, 267

Palubinskas, Helen, **Supp. X:** 292

Pamela (Richardson), **Supp. V:** 127

Panache de bouquets (Komunyakaa; Cadieux, trans.), **Supp. XIII:** 127

Pan-African movement, **Supp. II Part 1:** 172, 175

Pandaemonium (Epstein), **Supp. XII:** 161, **172–173**

"Pandora" (Adams), **I:** 5

Pandora: New Tales of Vampires (Rice), **Supp. VII:** 295

Panek, LeRoy, **Supp. XIV:** 27

"Pangolin, The" (Moore), **III:** 210

Panic: A Play in Verse (MacLeish), **III:** 2, 20

Panic in Needle Park (film), **Supp. IV Part 1:** 198

Pantagruel (Rabelais), **II:** 112

"Pantaloon in Black" (Faulkner), **II:** 71

Panther and the Lash, The (Hughes), **Retro. Supp. I:** 204, 211; **Supp. I Part 1:** 342–344, 345–346

"Panthers, The" (Southern), **Supp. XI:** 295

"Pan *versus* Moses" (Ozick), **Supp. V:** 262

"Papa and Mama Dance, The" (Sexton), **Supp. II Part 2:** 688

"Papa Who Wakes Up Tired in the Dark" (Cisneros), **Supp. VII:** 62

Pape, Greg, **Supp. V:** 180; **Supp. XIII:** 312

"Paper Dolls Cut Out of a Newspaper" (Simic), **Supp. VIII:** 282

"Paper House, The" (Mailer), **III:** 42–43

Papers on Literature and Art (Fuller), **Supp. II Part 1:** 292, 299

Papp, Joseph, **Supp. IV Part 1:** 234

"Paprika Johnson" (Barnes), **Supp. III Part 1:** 33

"Par" (Bausch), **Supp. VII:** 54

"Parable in the Later Novels of Henry James" (Ozick), **Supp. V:** 257

"Parable of the Gift" (Glück), **Supp. V:** 89

"Parable of the Hostages" (Glück), **Supp. V:** 89

"Parable of the King" (Glück), **Supp. V:** 89

Parable of the Sower (O. Butler), **Supp. XIII: 66–67,** 69

Parable of the Talents (O. Butler), **Supp. XIII:** 61,**Supp. XIII:** 66, **67–69**

"Parable of the Trellis" (Glück), **Supp. V:** 89

Parachutes & Kisses (Jong), **Supp. V:** 115, 123, 125–126, 129

"Parade of Painters" (Swenson), **Supp. IV Part 2:** 645

"Paradigm, The" (Tate), **IV:** 128

Paradise (Barthelme), **Supp. IV Part 1:** 52

"Paradise" (Doty), **Supp. XI:** 123

Paradise Lost (Milton), **I:** 137; **II:** 168, 549; **IV:** 126; **Supp. XII:** 173, 297

Paradise Lost (Odets), **Supp. II Part 2:** 530, 531, 538–539, 550

"Paradise of Bachelors and the Tartarus of Maids, The" (Melville), **III:** 91

Paradise Poems (Stern), **Supp. IX: 293–294,** 295

Paradiso (Dante), **Supp. IX:** 50

"Paradoxes and Oxymorons" (Ashbery), **Supp. III Part 1:** 23–24

Paradox of Progressive Thought, The (Noble), **Supp. I Part 2:** 650

Paragon, The (Knowles), **Supp. XII:** 249

"Parameters" (Dunn), **Supp. XI:** 154

"Paraphrase" (Crane), **I:** 391–392, 393

"Pardon, The" (Wilbur), **Supp. III Part 2:** 544, 550

Paredes, Américo, **Supp. XIII:** 225

Paredes, Raymund A., **Supp. XIII:** 320, 321

"Parentage" (Stafford), **Supp. XI:** 321, 322

"Parents" (F. Barthelme), **Supp. XI:** 34

"Parents Taking Shape" (Karr), **Supp. XI:** 243

"Parents' Weekend: Camp Kenwood" (Kenyon), **Supp. VII:** 169

Pareto, Vilfredo, **II:** 577

Paretsky, Sara, **Supp. XIV:** 26

Paretsky, Sarah, **Supp. IV Part 2:** 462

Parini, Jay, **Supp. X:** 17

"Paris" (Stern), **Supp. IX:** 300

"Paris, 7 A.M." (Bishop), **Retro. Supp. II:** 41, 42; **Supp. I Part 1:** 85, 89

Paris France (Stein), **IV:** 45

Park, Robert, **IV:** 475

"Park Bench" (Hughes), **Supp. I Part 1:** 331–332

Park City (Beattie), **Supp. V:** 24, 35–36

"Park City" (Beattie), **Supp. V:** 35

Parker, Charlie, **Supp. I Part 1:** 59; **Supp. X:** 240, 242, 246; **Supp. XIII:** 129

Parker, Dorothy, **Retro. Supp. II:** 327; **Supp. IV Part 1:** 353; **Supp. IX:** 62, 114, **189–206; Supp. X:** 164; **Supp. XI:** 28

Parker, Idella, **Supp. X:** 232, 234–235

Parker, Muriel, **Supp. IX:** 232

Parker, Robert B., **Supp. IV Part 1:** 135, 136

Parker, Theodore, **Supp. I Part 1:** 38; **Supp. I Part 2:** 518

Parker, Thomas, **Supp. I Part 1:** 102

"Parker's Back" (O'Connor), **III:** 348, 352, 358

Parkes, Henry Bamford, **Supp. I Part 2:** 617

Park-Fuller, Linda, **Supp. XIII:** 297

Parkman, Francis, **II:** 278, 310, 312; **IV:** 179, 309; **Supp. I Part 2:** 420, 479, 481–482, 486, 487, 493, 498; **Supp. II Part 2: 589–616**

Parkman Reader, The (Morison, ed.), **Supp. I Part 2:** 494

Parks, Gordon, Sr., **Supp. XI:** 17

Parks, Larry, **Supp. I Part 1:** 295

Parks, Rosa, **Supp. I Part 1:** 342

"Park Street Cemetery, The" (Lowell), **II:** 537, 538

Par le Détroit (cantata) (Bowles), **Supp. IV Part 1:** 82

Parliament of Fowls, The (Chaucer), **III:** 492

Parmenides (Plato), **II:** 10

Parnassus (Emerson), **II:** 8, 18

Parnell, Charles Stewart, **II:** 129, 137

Parole (film), **Supp. XIII:** 166

Parole Fixer (film), **Supp. XIII:** 170

Parrington, Vernon Louis, **I:** 254, 517, 561; **III:** 335, 606; **IV:** 173; **Supp. I Part 2:** 484, 640

Parrish, Robert, **Supp. XI:** 307

"Parrot, The" (Merrill), **Supp. III Part 1:** 320

"Parsley" (Dove), **Supp. IV Part 1:** 245, 246

Parson, Annie, **Supp. I Part 2:** 655

Parsons, Elsie Clews, **I:** 231, 235

Parsons, Ian, **Supp. IX:** 95

Parsons, Louella, **Supp. XII:** 173

Parsons, Talcott, **Supp. I Part 2:** 648

Parsons, Theophilus, **II:** 396, 504; **Retro. Supp. II:** 134; **Supp. I Part 1:** 155

"Parthian Shot, The" (Hammett), **Supp. IV Part 1:** 343

Partial Payments: Essays on Writers and Their Lives (Epstein), **Supp. XIV:** 111

Partial Portraits (James), **II:** 336

Parties (Van Vechten), **Supp. II Part 2:** 739, 747–749

"Parting" (Kunitz), **Supp. III Part 1:** 263

"Parting Gift" (Wylie), **Supp. I Part 2:** 714

"Parting Glass, The" (Freneau), **Supp. II Part 1:** 273

"Partings" (Hogan), **Supp. IV Part 1:** 413

Partington, Blanche, **I:** 199

Partisans (Matthiessen), **Supp. V:** 201

"Partner, The" (Roethke), **III:** 541–542

Partners, The (Auchincloss), **Supp. IV Part 1:** 31, 34

"Part of a Letter" (Wilbur), **Supp. III Part 2:** 551
Part of Speech, A (Brodsky), **Supp. VIII:** 22
"Part of the Story" (Dobyns), **Supp. XIII:** 79
Parton, Sara, **Retro. Supp. I:** 246
Partridge, John, **II:** 110, 111
"Parts of a Journal" (Gordon), **Supp. IV Part 1:** 310
Parts of a World (Stevens), **Retro. Supp. I: 305–306,** 307, 309, 313
"Party, The" (Dunbar), **Supp. II Part 1:** 198, 205–206
"Party, The" (Taylor), **Supp. V:** 315
Party at Jack's, The (Wolfe), **IV:** 451–452, 469
"Party Down at the Square, A" (Ellison), **Retro. Supp. II:** 124
Pascal, Blaise, **II:** 8, 159; **III:** 292, 301, 304, 428; **Retro. Supp. I:** 326, 330
"Passage" (Crane), **I:** 391
"Passage in the Life of Mr. John Oakhurst, A" (Harte), **Supp. II Part 1:** 353–354
"Passages from a Relinquished Work" (Hawthorne), **Retro. Supp. I:** 150
Passages toward the Dark (McGrath), **Supp. X:** 126, 127
"Passage to India" (Whitman), **IV:** 348
Passage to India, A (Forster), **II:** 600
Passaro, Vince, **Supp. X:** 167, 302, 309, 310
"Passenger Pigeons" (Jeffers), **Supp. II Part 2:** 437
Passin, Herbert, **Supp. XIII:** 337
"Passing of Grandison, The" (Chesnutt), **Supp. XIV:** 62, **66–69**
"Passing of Sister Barsett, The" (Jewett), **Retro. Supp. II:** 138–139, 143
"Passing Show, The" (Bierce), **I:** 208
"Passing Through" (Kunitz), **Supp. III Part 1:** 265
"Passion, The" (Barnes), **Supp. III Part 1:** 36
"Passion, The" (Merwin), **Supp. III Part 1:** 343
Passionate Pilgrim, A (James), **II:** 324; **Retro. Supp. I:** 219
"Passionate Pilgrim, A" (James), **II:** 322, 323–324; **Retro. Supp. I:** 218
Passion Play (Kosinski), **Supp. VII:** 215, 225–226
Passions of Uxport, The (Kumin), **Supp. IV Part 2:** 444
"Passive Resistance" (McKay), **Supp. X:** 133
Passport to the War (Kunitz), **Supp.**

III Part 1: 261–264
Passwords (Stafford), **Supp. XI: 329–330**
"Past, The" (Bryant), **Supp. I Part 1:** 157, 170
Past, The (Kinnell), **Supp. III Part 1:** 235, 253–254
"Past, The" (Kinnell), **Supp. III Part 1:** 254
Past and Present (Carlyle), **Supp. I Part 2:** 410
Pasternak, Boris, **II:** 544
"Pastiches et Pistaches" (Van Vechten), **Supp. II Part 2:** 732
"Past Is the Present, The" (Moore), **III:** 199–200
"Pastoral" (Carver), **Supp. III Part 1:** 137, 146
"Pastoral" (Dove), **Supp. IV Part 1:** 249
"Pastoral Hat, A" (Stevens), **IV:** 91
"Pastor Dowe at Tacaté" (Bowles), **Supp. IV Part 1:** 87
Pastorela (ballet) (Kirstein), **Supp. IV Part 1:** 83
Pastorius, Francis Daniel, **Supp. I Part 2:** 700
"Pasture Poems" (Kumin), **Supp. IV Part 2:** 446
Pastures of Heaven, The (Steinbeck), **IV:** 51
Patchen, Kenneth, **Supp. III Part 2:** 625
Patchett, Ann, **Supp. XII: 307–324**
Pater, Walter, **I:** 51, 272, 476; **II:** 27, 338; **III:** 604; **IV:** 74; **Retro. Supp. I:** 56, 79; **Retro. Supp. II:** 326; **Supp. I Part 2:** 552; **Supp. IX:** 66
Paterna (Mather), **Supp. II Part 2:** 451
"Paterson" (Ginsberg), **Supp. II Part 1:** 314–315, 321, 329
Paterson (W. C. Williams), **I:** 62, 446; **IV:** 418–423; **Retro. Supp. I:** 209, 284, 413, 419, 421, **424–428,** 428, 429, 430; **Retro. Supp. II:** 321, 328; **Supp. II Part 2:** 557, 564, 625; **Supp. VIII:** 275, 305; **Supp. XIV:** 96
Paterson, Book Five (W. C. Williams), **IV:** 422–423
Paterson, Book One (W. C. Williams), **IV:** 421–422
Paterson, Isabel, **Supp. IV Part 2:** 524
Paterson, Part Three (W. C. Williams), **IV:** 420–421
"Path, The" (Bryant), **Supp. I Part 1:** 169
Pathfinder, The (Cooper), **I:** 349, 350, 355

Pat Hobby Stories, The (Fitzgerald), **Retro. Supp. I:** 114
"Patience of a Saint, The" (Humphrey), **Supp. IX:** 106
Patinkin, Mandy, **Supp. IV Part 1:** 236
Paton, Alan, **Supp. VIII:** 126
Patria Mia (Pound), **III:** 460–461; **Retro. Supp. I:** 284
"Patria Mia" (Pound), **Retro. Supp. I:** 284
"Patriarch, The" (Alvares), **Supp. V:** 11
Patrimony: A True Story (Roth), **Retro. Supp. II:** 279, 280, 291; **Supp. III Part 2:** 427
Patriot, The (Buck), **Supp. II Part 1:** 122–123
Patriot, The (Connell), **Supp. XIV:** 94–95
Patriotic Gore: Studies in the Literature of the American Civil War (Wilson), **III:** 588; **IV:** 430, 438, 443, 445–445, 446; **Supp. VIII:** 100
"Patriots, The/Los Patriotas" (Kingsolver), **Supp. VII:** 209
Patron Saint of Liars, The (Patchett), **Supp. XII:** 307, 310, **311–314,** 317
Pattee, Fred L., **II:** 456
Patten, Gilbert, **II:** 423
Patten, Simon, **Supp. I Part 2:** 640
Patternmaster (O. Butler), **Supp. XIII:** 61, 62, 63
Patternmaster Series (O. Butler), **Supp. XIII: 62–63**
"Patterns" (Lowell), **II:** 524
Patterson, Floyd, **III:** 38
Patterson, William M., **Supp. I Part 1:** 265
Patton, General George, **III:** 575; **Supp. I Part 2:** 664
Paul, Saint, **I:** 365; **II:** 15, 494; **IV:** 122, 154, 164, 335; **Retro. Supp. I:** 247; **Supp. I Part 1:** 188
Paul, Sherman, **I:** 244; **IV:** 179
"Paula Becker to Clara Westhoff" (Rich), **Supp. I Part 2:** 573–574
"Paula Gunn Allen" (Ruppert), **Supp. IV Part 1:** 321
Paul Bowles: Romantic Savage (Caponi), **Supp. IV Part 1:** 95
Paulding, James Kirke, **I:** 344; **II:** 298, 299, 303; **Supp. I Part 1:** 157
Paul Marchand, F.M.C. (Chesnutt), **Supp. XIV:** 76
"Paul Monette: The Brink of Summer's End" (film), **Supp. X:** 152
"Paul Revere" (Longfellow), **II:** 489, 501
"Paul Revere's Ride" (Longfellow), **Retro. Supp. II:** 163

"Paul's Case" (Cather), **I:** 314–315; **Retro. Supp. I:** 3, 5

Paulsen, Friedrich, **III:** 600

"Pauper Witch of Grafton, The" (Frost), **Retro. Supp. II:** 42

"Pause by the Water, A" (Merwin), **Supp. III Part 1:** 354

"Pavane for the Nursery, A" (W. J. Smith), **Supp. XIII:** 335

"Pavement, The" (Olson), **Supp. II Part 2:** 571

Pavilion of Women (Buck), **Supp. II Part 1:** 125–126

"Pawnbroker, The" (Kumin), **Supp. IV Part 2:** 442, 443–444, 451

Payne, Daniel, **Supp. V:** 202

Payne, John Howard, **II:** 309

Paz, Octavio, **Supp. III Part 2:** 630; **Supp. VIII:** 272; **Supp. XI:** 191; **Supp. XIII:** 223

Peabody, Elizabeth, **Retro. Supp. I:** 155–156, 225

Peabody, Francis G., **III:** 293; **Supp. I Part 1:** 5

Peabody, Josephine Preston, **III:** 507

Peace and Bread in Time of War (Addams), **Supp. I Part 1:** 21, 22–23

"Peace Between Black and White in the United States" (Locke), **Supp. XIV:** 205

Peace Breaks Out (Knowles), **Supp. XII:** 249

"Peace March, The" (Simpson), **Supp. IX:** 279

"Peace of Cities, The" (Wilbur), **Supp. III Part 2:** 545

"Peaches—Six in a Tin Box, Sarajevo" (Cisneros), **Supp. VII:** 67

Peacock, Doug, **Supp. VIII:** 38; **Supp. XIII:** 12

Peacock, Gibson, **Supp. I Part 1:** 360

"Peacock, The" (Merrill), **Supp. III Part 1:** 320

Peacock, Thomas Love, **Supp. I Part 1:** 307; **Supp. VIII:** 125

"Peacock Room, The" (Hayden), **Supp. II Part 1:** 374–375

Pearce, Richard, **Supp. IX:** 254

Pearce, Roy Harvey, **II:** 244; **Supp. I Part 1:** 111, 114; **Supp. I Part 2:** 475

Pearl, The (Steinbeck), **IV:** 51, 62–63

Pearlman, Daniel, **III:** 479

Pearlman, Mickey, **Supp. XIII:** 293, 306

Pearl of Orr's Island, The (Stowe), **Supp. I Part 2:** 592–593, 595

Pears, Peter, **II:** 586; **Supp. IV Part 1:** 84

Pearson, Drew, **Supp. XIV:** 126

Pearson, Norman Holmes, **Supp. I Part 1:** 259, 260, 273

"Peasants' Way O' Thinkin'" (McKay), **Supp. X:** 133

Pease, Donald E., **Supp. IV Part 2:** 687

Peck, Gregory, **Supp. VIII:** 128, 129; **Supp. XII:** 160, 173

Peckinpah, Sam, **Supp. XI:** 306

"Peck of Gold, A" (Frost), **II:** 155

Peculiar Treasures: A Biblical Who's Who (Buechner), **Supp. XII:** 53

"Pedal Point" (Francis), **Supp. IX:** 87

"Pedersen Kid, The" (Gass), **Supp. VI:** 83

"Pedigree, The" (Creeley), **Supp. IV Part 1:** 150

Peebles, Melvin Van, **Supp. XI:** 17

"Peed Onk" (Moore). *See* "People Like That Are the Only People Here: Canonical Babbling in Peed Onk" (Moore)

"Peeler, The" (O'Connor), **Retro. Supp. II:** 225

Peikoff, Leonard, **Supp. IV Part 2:** 520, 526, 529

Peirce, Charles Sanders, **II:** 20, 352–353; **III:** 599; **Supp. I Part 2:** 640; **Supp. III Part 2:** 626

Pelagius, **III:** 295

"Pelican, The" (Merrill), **Supp. III Part 1:** 320

"Pelican, The" (Wharton), **IV:** 310; **Retro. Supp. I:** 364

Pellacchia, Michael, **Supp. XIII:** 16

Peltier, Leonard, **Supp. V:** 212

"Pen and Paper and a Breath of Air" (Oliver), **Supp. VII:** 245

"Pencil, The" (Chandler), **Supp. IV Part 1:** 135

Pencillings by the Way (Willis), **II:** 313

"Pencils" (Sandburg), **III:** 592

"Pendulum" (Bradbury and Hasse), **Supp. IV Part 1:** 102

"Penelope's Song" (Glück), **Supp. V:** 89

Penhally (Gordon), **II:** 197, 199, 201–203, 204

"Penis" (McClatchy), **Supp. XII:** 266–267

Penitent, The (Singer), **Retro. Supp. II:** 309–310, 313

Penn, Robert, **I:** 489

Penn, Sean, **Supp. XI:** 107

Penn, Thomas, **II:** 118

Penn, William, **Supp. I Part 2:** 683

"Pennsylvania Pilgrim, The" (Whittier), **Supp. I Part 2:** 700

"Pennsylvania Planter, The" (Freneau),

Supp. II Part 1: 268

Penny, Rob, **Supp. VIII:** 330

Penrod (Tarkington), **III:** 223

"Penseroso, Il" (Milton), **Supp. XIV:** 8

Pentagon of Power, The (Mumford), **Supp. II Part 2:** 498

Pentimento (Hellman), **Supp. I Part 1:** 280, 292–294, 296; **Supp. IV Part 1:** 12; **Supp. VIII:** 243

"Peonies at Dusk" (Kenyon), **Supp. VII:** 171

People, The (Glaspell), **Supp. III Part 1:** 179

People, Yes, The (Sandburg), **III:** 575, 589, 590, 591

"PEOPLE BURNING, THE" (Baraka), **Supp. II Part 1:** 49

"People in Hell Just Want a Drink of Water" (Proulx), **Supp. VII:** 263

"People Like That Are the Only People Here: Canonical Babbling in Peed Onk" (Moore), **Supp. X:** 168, **178–179**

People Live Here: Selected Poems 1949–1983 (Simpson), **Supp. IX:** 269, 277

"People Next Door, The" (Simpson), **Supp. IX:** 279

People of the Abyss, The (London), **II:** 465–466

"People on the Roller Coaster, The" (Hardwick), **Supp. III Part 1:** 196

People Shall Continue, The (Ortiz), **Supp. IV Part 2:** 510

"People's Surroundings" (Moore), **III:** 201, 202, 203

"People v. Abe Lathan, Colored, The" (Caldwell), **I:** 309

"Peppermint Lounge Revisited, The" (Wolfe), **Supp. III Part 2:** 571

Pepys, Samuel, **Supp. I Part 2:** 653

"Perch'io non spero di tornar giammai" (Cavalcanti), **Supp. III Part 2:** 623

Percy, Thomas, **Supp. XIV:** 2

Percy, Walker, **Supp. III Part 1:** 383–400; **Supp. IV Part 1:** 297; **Supp. V:** 334; **Supp. X:** 42; **Supp. XIV:** 21

Percy, William, **Supp. V:** 334

Percy, William Alexander, **Retro. Supp. I:** 341

"Peregrine" (Wylie), **Supp. I Part 2:** 712–713, 714

Perelman, Bob, **Supp. XII:** 23

Perelman, S. J., **IV:** 286; **Retro. Supp. I:** 342; **Retro. Supp. II:** 321, 322, 325, 326, 327, 336; **Supp. IV Part 1:** 353; **Supp. XI:** 66

Perestroika (Kushner), **Supp. IX:** 141, 142, 145

Péret, Benjamin, **Supp. VIII:** 272

Peretz, Isaac Loeb, **IV:** 1, 3; **Retro. Supp. II:** 299

Pérez Galdós, Benito, **II:** 275

Perfect Analysis Given by a Parrot, A (T. Williams), **IV:** 395

"Perfect Day for Bananafish, A" (Salinger), **III:** 563–564, 571

Perfect Ganesh, A (McNally), **Supp. XIII: 202–203,** 208, 209

"Perfect Knight, The" (Chandler), **Supp. IV Part 1:** 120

Perfect Party, The (Gurney), **Supp. V:** 100, 105, 106–107

"Perfect Things" (F. Barthelme), **Supp. XI:** 30, 33–34

"Performance, The" (Dickey), **Supp. IV Part 1:** 178–179, 181

"Perfume" (Mora), **Supp. XIII:** 218

"Perhaps the World Ends Here" (Harjo), **Supp. XII:** 228, 231

Perhaps Women (Anderson), **I:** 114

Pericles (Shakespeare), **I:** 585; **Supp. III Part 2:** 624, 627, 629

Period of Adjustment (T. Williams), **IV:** 382, 386, 387, 388, 389, 390, 392, 393, 394, 397

"Period Pieces from the Mid-Thirties" (Agee), **I:** 28

"Periphery" (Ammons), **Supp. VII:** 28

Perkins, David, **Supp. I Part 2:** 459, 475

Perkins, Maxwell, **I:** 252, 289, 290; **II:** 87, 93, 95, 252; **IV:** 452, 455, 457, 458, 461, 462, 463, 469; **Retro. Supp. I:** 101, 105, 108, 109, 110, 113, 114, 178; **Supp. IX:** 57, 58, 60, 232; **Supp. X:** 219, 224, 225, 229, 230, 233; **Supp. XI:** 218, 227

Perlès, Alfred, **III:** 177, 183, 187, 189

Perloff, Marjorie, **Supp. I Part 2:** 539, 542; **Supp. IV Part 1:** 68; **Supp. IV Part 2:** 420, 424, 432

Permanence and Change (Burke), **I:** 274

Permanent Errors (Price), **Supp. VI:** 261

"Permanent Traits of the English National Genius" (Emerson), **II:** 18

Permit Me Voyage (Agee), **I:** 25, 27

Perrault, Charles, **IV:** 266; **Supp. I Part 2:** 622

Perry, Anne, **Supp. V:** 335

Perry, Bliss, **I:** 243

Perry, Donna, **Supp. IV Part 1:** 322, 327, 335

Perry, Dr. William, **II:** 395, 396

Perry, Edgar A., **III:** 410

Perry, Lincoln, **Supp. V:** 24, 33

Perry, Matthew C., **Supp. I Part 2:** 494–495

Perry, Patsy Brewington, **Supp. I Part 1:** 66

Perry, Ralph Barton, **I:** 224; **II:** 356, 362, 364; **Supp. XIV:** 197

Perse, St.-John, **III:** 12, 13, 14, 17; **Supp. III Part 1:** 14; **Supp. IV Part 1:** 82; **Supp. XIII:** 344

"Persephone in Hell" (Dove), **Supp. IV Part 1:** 250, 251

"Persistence of Desire, The" (Updike), **IV:** 222–223, 228

"Persistences" (Hecht), **Supp. X: 68–69**

Person, Place, and Thing (Shapiro), **Supp. II Part 2:** 702, 705

Personae: The Collected Poems (Pound), **Retro. Supp. I:** 285, 286; **Supp. I Part 1:** 255

Personae of Ezra Pound (Pound), **III:** 458

"Personal" (Stern), **Supp. IX:** 299

"Personal and Occasional Pieces" (Welty), **Retro. Supp. I:** 355

Personal Narrative (Edwards), **I:** 545, 552, 553, 561, 562; **Supp. I Part 2:** 700

Personal Recollection of Joan of Arc (Twain), **IV:** 208

"Personals" (Didion), **Supp. IV Part 1:** 200

Persons and Places (Santayana), **III:** 615

Persons in Hiding (film), **Supp. XIII:** 170

Persons in Hiding (Hoover), **Supp. XIII:** 170

Person Sitting in Darkness, A (Twain), **IV:** 208

"Perspective" (Francis), **Supp. IX:** 78

"Perspective: Anniversary D-Day" (Karr), **Supp. XI:** 241

"Perspectives: Is It Out of Control?" (Gleason), **Supp. IX:** 16

Perspectives by Incongruity (Burke), **I:** 284–285

Perspectives on Cormac McCarthy (Arnold and Luce, eds.), **Supp. VIII:** 189

Pertes et Fracas (McCoy), **Supp. XIII:** 175

"Peruvian Child" (Mora), **Supp. XIII:** 218

Peseroff, Joyce, **Supp. IV Part 1:** 71

"Peter" (Cather), **Retro. Supp. I:** 4

"Peter" (Moore), **III:** 210, 212

Peter, Saint, **III:** 341, 346; **IV:** 86, 294

Peterkin, Julia, **Supp. I Part 1:** 328

"Peter Klaus" (German tale), **II:** 306

"Peter Parley" works (Goodrich), **Supp. I Part 1:** 38

"Peter Pendulum" (Poe), **III:** 425

"Peter Quince at the Clavier" (Stevens), **IV:** 81, 82

Peter Rabbit tales, **Retro. Supp. I:** 335

Peters, Cora, **Supp. I Part 2:** 468

Peters, Jacqueline, **Supp. XII:** 225

Peters, Margot, **Supp. VIII:** 252

Peters, Robert, **Supp. XIII:** 114

Peters, S. H. (pseudonym). *See* Henry, O.

Peters, Timothy, **Supp. XI:** 39

"Peter's Avocado" (Rodriguez), **Supp. XIV:** 308–309

Petersen, David, **Supp. XIII:** 2

Petersen, Donald, **Supp. V:** 180

Peterson, Houston, **I:** 60

Peterson, Roger Tory, **Supp. V:** 202

Peterson, Virgilia, **Supp. IV Part 1:** 30

Peter Whiffle: His Life and Works (Van Vechten), **Supp. II Part 2:** 728–729, 731, 735, 738–741, 749

"Petey and Yotsee and Mario" (H. Roth), **Supp. IX:** 234

"Petition, A" (Winters), **Supp. II Part 2:** 785

"'Pet Negro' System, The" (Hurston), **Supp. VI:** 159

"Petra and Its Surroundings" (Frost), **Retro. Supp. I:** 124

Petrarch, **I:** 176; **II:** 590; **III:** 4

"Petrified Man" (Welty), **IV:** 262; **Retro. Supp. I:** 345, 351

"Petrified Man, The" (Twain), **IV:** 195

"Petrified Woman, The" (Gordon), **II:** 199

Petronius, **III:** 174, 179

Petry, Ann, **Supp. VIII:** 214; **Supp. XI:** 6, 85

Pet Sematary (King), **Supp. V:** 138, 143, 152

Pettengill, Richard, **Supp. VIII:** 341, 345, 348

Pettis, Joyce, **Supp. XI:** 276, 277, 278, 281

Pfaff, Timothy, **Supp. V:** 166

Pfeil, Fred, **Supp. XIV:** 36

Pfister, Karin, **IV:** 467, 475

Phaedo (Plato), **II:** 10

Phaedra (Lowell and Barzun, trans.), **II:** 543–544

"Phantasia for Elvira Shatayev" (Rich), **Supp. I Part 2:** 570

Phantasms of War (Lowell), **II:** 512

"Phantom of the Movie Palace, The" (Coover), **Supp. V:** 50–51

"Pharaoh, The" (Kenyon), **Supp. VII:** 172

Pharr, Mary, **Supp. V:** 147

"Phases" (Stevens), **Retro. Supp. I:** 299

Phases of an Inferior Planet (Glasgow), **II:** 174–175

"Pheasant, The" (Carver), **Supp. III Part 1:** 146

Pheloung, Grant, **Supp. XI:** 39

Phelps, Elizabeth Stuart, **Retro. Supp. II:** 146; **Supp. XIII:** 141

Phelps, Teresa Godwin, **Supp. VIII:** 128

"Phenomena and Laws of Race Contacts, The" (Locke), **Supp. XIV:** 210

"Phenomenology of Anger, The" (Rich), **Supp. I Part 2:** 562–563, 571

Phenomenology of Moral Experience, The (Mandelbaum), **I:** 61

"Phenomenology of *On Moral Fiction*" (Johnson), **Supp. VI:** 188

Phidias, **Supp. I Part 2:** 482

Philadelphia Fire (Wideman), **Supp. X:** 320, 334

Philadelphia Negro, The (Du Bois), **Supp. II Part 1:** 158, 163–164, 166

Philbrick, Thomas, **I:** 343

Philip, Jim, **Supp. XII:** 136

Philip, Prince, **Supp. X:** 108

"Philip of Pokanoket" (Irving), **II:** 303

Philippians (biblical book), **IV:** 154

"Philippine Conquest, The" (Masters), **Supp. I Part 2:** 456

"Philip Roth Reconsidered" (Howe), **Retro. Supp. II:** 286

"Philistinism and the Negro Writer" (Baraka), **Supp. II Part 1:** 39, 44

Phillips, Adam, **Supp. XII:** 97–98

Phillips, David Graham, **II:** 444; **Retro. Supp. II:** 101

Phillips, Gene D., **Supp. XI:** 306

Phillips, J. O. C., **Supp. I Part 1:** 19

Phillips, Jayne Anne, **Supp. XIV:** 21

Phillips, Robert, **Supp. XIII:** 335, 344

Phillips, Wendell, **Supp. I Part 1:** 103; **Supp. I Part 2:** 524

Phillips, Willard, **Supp. I Part 1:** 154, 155

Phillips, William, **Supp. VIII:** 156

Phillips, William L., **I:** 106

"Philosopher, The" (Farrell), **II:** 45

Philosopher of the Forest (pseudonym). *See* Freneau, Philip

Philosophes classiques, Les (Taine), **III:** 323

"Philosophical Concepts and Practical Results" (James), **II:** 352

"Philosophical Investigation of Metaphor, A" (Gass), **Supp. VI:** 79

Philosophical Transactions (Watson), **II:** 114

"Philosophy, Or Something Like That" (Roth), **Supp. III Part 2:** 403

Philosophy: Who Needs It (Rand), **Supp. IV Part 2:** 517, 518, 527, 533

"Philosophy and Its Critics" (James), **II:** 360

"Philosophy and the Form of Fiction" (Gass), **Supp. VI:** 85

"Philosophy for People" (Emerson), **II:** 14

"Philosophy in Warm Weather" (Kenyon), **Supp. VII:** 168

"Philosophy Lesson" (Levine), **Supp. V:** 195

Philosophy of Alain Locke, The: Harlem Renaissance and Beyond (Harris, ed.), **Supp. XIV:** 196, 211–212

"Philosophy of Composition, The" (Poe), **III:** 416, 421; **Retro. Supp. II:** 266, 267, 271

Philosophy of Friedrich Nietzsche, The (Mencken), **III:** 102–103

"Philosophy of Handicap, A" (Bourne), **I:** 216, 218

"Philosophy of History" (Emerson), **II:** 11–12

Philosophy of Literary Form, The (Burke), **I:** 275, 281, 283, 291

Philosophy of the Human Mind, The (Stewart), **II:** 8

Philoxenes, **Supp. VIII:** 201

"Phineas" (Knowles), **Supp. XII:** 238–240

Phineas: Six Stories (Knowles), **Supp. XII:** 249

"Phocion" (Lowell), **II:** 536

Phoenix and the Turtle, The (Shakespeare), **I:** 284

"Phoenix Lyrics" (Schwartz), **Supp. II Part 2:** 665

"Phony War Films" (Jones), **Supp. XI:** 217, 232

"Photograph: Migrant Worker, Parlier, California, 1967" (Levis), **Supp. XI:** 272

"Photograph of a Child on a Vermont Hillside" (Kenyon), **Supp. VII:** 168

"Photograph of the Girl" (Olds), **Supp. X:** 205

"Photograph of the Unmade Bed" (Rich), **Supp. I Part 2:** 558

Photographs (Welty), **Retro. Supp. I:** 343

"Photographs, The" (Barthelme), **Supp. IV Part 1:** 53

"Photography" (Levine), **Supp. V:** 194

Phyrrho, **Retro. Supp. I:** 247

"Physical Universe" (Simpson), **Supp. IX:** 278

"Physicist We Know, A" (Shields), **Supp. VII:** 310

"Physics and Cosmology in the Fiction of Tom Robbins" (Nadeau), **Supp. X:** 270

"Physiology of Versification, The: Harmonies of Organic and Animal Life" (Holmes), **Supp. I Part 1:** 311

Physique de l'Amour (Gourmont), **III:** 467–468

Piaf, Edith, **Supp. IV Part 2:** 549

Piaget, Jean, **Supp. XIII:** 75

"Piano Fingers" (Mason), **Supp. VIII:** 146

Piano Lesson, The (Bearden), **Supp. VIII:** 342

Piano Lesson, The (Wilson), **Supp. VIII: 342–345**

Piatt, James, **Supp. I Part 2:** 420

Piatt, John J., **II:** 273

Piazza, Ben, **Supp. XIII:** 163

Piazza, Paul, **Supp. XIV:** 157, 160, 171

"Piazza de Spagna, Early Morning" (Wilbur), **Supp. III Part 2:** 553

Piazza Tales (Melville), **III:** 91

Picabia, Francis, **Retro. Supp. I:** 416; **Retro. Supp. II:** 331

Picasso (Stein), **IV:** 28, 32, 45

Picasso, Pablo, **I:** 429, 432, 440, 442, 445; **II:** 602; **III:** 197, 201, 470; **IV:** 26, 31, 32, 46, 87, 407, 436; **Retro. Supp. I:** 55, 63; **Supp. IV Part 1:** 81; **Supp. IX:** 66

"Piccola Comedia" (Wilbur), **Supp. III Part 2:** 561

Pickard, Samuel T., **Supp. I Part 2:** 682

"Picked-Up Pieces" (Updike), **Retro. Supp. I:** 320, 322, 323, 335

Picker, Lauren, **Supp. VIII:** 78, 83

Picker, Tobias, **Supp. XII:** 253

Pickford, Mary, **Retro. Supp. I:** 325; **Supp. I Part 2:** 391

"Picking and Choosing" (Moore), **III:** 205

Picnic Cantata (music) (Bowles), **Supp. IV Part 1:** 89

"Picnic Remembered" (Warren), **IV:** 240

Pictorial History of the Negro in America, A (Hughes), **Supp. I Part 1:** 345

"Picture, The" (Olson), **Supp. II Part 2:** 574

Picture Bride (Son), **Supp. X:** 292

"Picture I Want, The" (Olds), **Supp. X:** 209

Picture of Dorian Gray, The (Wilde), **Supp. IX:** 105

"Picture of Little J. A. in a Prospect of Flowers, A" (Ashbery), **Supp. III Part 1:** 3

Picture Palace (Theroux), **Supp. VIII:** 322

"Pictures at an Extermination" (Epstein), **Supp. XII:** 161

"Pictures from an Expedition" (Duffy), **Supp. IV Part 1:** 207

Pictures from an Institution (Jarrell), **II:** 367, 385

Pictures from Brueghel (W. C. Williams), **Retro. Supp. I:** 429–431

"Pictures from Brueghel" (W. C. Williams), **Retro. Supp. I:** 419

"Pictures of Columbus, the Genoese, The" (Freneau), **Supp. II Part 1:** 258

Pictures of Fidelman: An Exhibition (Malamud), **Supp. I Part 2:** 450–451

"Pictures of the Artist" (Malamud), **Supp. I Part 2:** 450

Pictures of the Floating World (Lowell), **II:** 521, 524–525

Pictures of Travel (Heine), **II:** 281

"Picturesque: San Cristóbal de las Casas" (Mora), **Supp. XIII:** 218

Picturesque America; or, the Land We Live In (Bryant, ed.), **Supp. I Part 1:** 158

Picture This (Heller), **Supp. IV Part 1:** 386, 388, 390–391

Picturing Will (Beattie), **Supp. V:** 29, 31–32, 34

"Piece, A" (Creeley), **Supp. IV Part 1:** 155, 156

"Piece of Moon, A" (Hogan), **Supp. IV Part 1:** 407

Piece of My Heart, A (Ford), **Supp. V:** 57, 58–61, 62

Piece of My Mind, A: Reflections at Sixty (Wilson), **IV:** 426, 430, 438, 441

"Piece of News, A" (Welty), **IV:** 263; **Retro. Supp. I:** 345, 346

Pieces (Creeley), **Supp. IV Part 1:** 155

Pieces and Pontifications (Mailer), **Retro. Supp. II:** 209–210

Pieces of the Frame (McPhee), **Supp. III Part 1:** 293

Pierce, Franklin, **II:** 225, 226, 227; **III:** 88; **Retro. Supp. I:** 150, 163, 164, 165

Pierce, Frederick, **Retro. Supp. I:** 136

Piercy, Josephine K., **Supp. I Part 1:** 103

Pierpont, Claudia Roth, **Supp. X:** 192, 193, 196

Pierre: or The Ambiguities (Melville), **III:** 86–88, 89; **IV:** 194; **Retro. Supp. I:** 249, 253–254, 256; **Supp. I Part 2:** 579

Pierre et Jean (Maupassant), **I:** 421

Pierrepont, Sarah. *See* Edwards, Sarah

Pierrot Qui Pleure et Pierrot Qui Rit (Rostand), **II:** 515

Pig Cookies (Ríos), **Supp. IV Part 2:** 537, 550, 552–554

Pigeon Feathers (Updike), **IV:** 214, 218, 219, 221–223, 226

"Pigeon Feathers" (Updike), **Retro. Supp. I:** 318, 322, 323

"Pigeons" (Rilke), **II:** 544

"Pigeon Woman" (Swenson), **Supp. IV Part 2:** 644

Pigs in Heaven (Kingsolver), **Supp. VII:** 197, 199, 209–210

Pike County Ballads, The (Hay), **Supp. I Part 1:** 352

Piket, Vincent, **Supp. IV Part 1:** 24

Pilar San-Mallafre, Maria del, **Supp. V:** 40

"Pilgrim" (Freneau), **Supp. I Part 1:** 125

"Pilgrimage" (Sontag), **Supp. III Part 2:** 454–455

"Pilgrimage, The" (Maxwell), **Supp. VIII:** 169, 171

Pilgrimage of Festus, The (Aiken), **I:** 50, 55, 57

Pilgrimage of Henry James, The (Brooks), **I:** 240, 248, 250; **IV:** 433

Pilgrim at Tinker Creek (Dillard), **Supp. VI:** 22, **23–26,** 28, 29, **30–31,** 34

"Pilgrim Makers" (Lowell), **II:** 541

Pilgrim's Progress (Bunyan), **I:** 92; **II:** 15, 168, 572; **Supp. I Part 1:** 32, 38; **Supp. I Part 2:** 599

Pili's Wall (Levine), **Supp. V:** 178, 183–184

"Pillar of Fire" (Bradbury), **Supp. IV Part 1:** 113–114

Pillars of Hercules, The: A Grand Tour of the Mediterranean (Theroux), **Supp. VIII:** 325

Pilot, The (Cooper), **I:** 335, 337, 339, 342–343, 350

"Pilot from the Carrier, A" (Jarrell), **II:** 374

"Pilots, Man Your Planes" (Jarrell), **II:** 374–375

"Pilots, The" (Levertov), **Supp. III Part 1:** 282

"Pimp's Revenge, A" (Malamud), **Supp. I Part 2:** 435, 450, 451

Pinball (Kosinski), **Supp. VII:** 215, 226

Pinchot, Gifford, **Supp. IX:** 184; **Supp. XIV:** 178

Pindar, **I:** 381; **II:** 543; **III:** 610

"Pine" (Dickey), **Supp. IV Part 1:** 183

Pine Barrens, The (McPhee), **Supp. III Part 1:** 298–301, 309

"Pineys, The" (Stern), **Supp. IX:** 288, 296

Pinget, Robert, **Supp. V:** 39

"Pink Dog" (Bishop), **Retro. Supp. II:** 48

Pinker, James B., **I:** 409; **Retro. Supp. I:** 231

Pinkerton, Jan, **Supp. V:** 323–324

"Pink Moon—The Pond" (Oliver), **Supp. VII:** 234

Pinocchio in Venice (Coover), **Supp. V:** 40, 51

Pinsker, Sanford, **Retro. Supp. II:** 23; **Supp. V:** 272; **Supp. IX:** 293, 327; **Supp. XI:** 251, 254, 317

Pinsky, Robert, **Retro. Supp. II:** 50; **Supp. VI: 235–251; Supp. IX:** 155, 158; **Supp. XIII:** 277, 285

Pinter, Harold, **I:** 71; **Supp. XIII:** 20, 196; **Supp. XIV:** 239

Pinto and Sons (Epstein), **Supp. XII:** 170, **171–172**

Pioneers, The (Cooper), **I:** 336, 337, 339, 340–341, 342, 348; **II:** 313

Pioneers of France in the New World (Parkman), **Supp. III Part 2:** 599, 602

"Pioneers! O Pioneers!" (Whitman), **Retro. Supp. I:** 8

"Pioneer's Vision, The" (Larcom), **Supp. XIII:** 140

Pious and Secular America (Niebuhr), **III:** 308

Pipe Night (O'Hara), **III:** 361, 368

Piper, Dan, **Supp. IX:** 65

"Piper's Rocks" (Olson), **Supp. IV Part 1:** 153

Pipkin, Charles W., **Supp. XIV:** 3

Pippa Passes (Browning), **IV:** 128

Piquion, René, **Supp. I Part 1:** 346

Pirandello, Luigi, **Supp. IV Part 2:** 576, 588

Pirate, The (Robbins), **Supp. XII:** 6

Pirate, The (Scott), **I:** 339

Pirates of Penzance, The (Gilbert and Sullivan), **IV:** 386

Pisan Cantos, The (Pound), **III:** 476; **Retro. Supp. I:** 140, 283, 285, 293; **Supp. III Part 1:** 63; **Supp. V:** 331, 337; **Supp. XIV:** 11

Piscator, Erwin, **IV:** 394

Pissarro, Camille, **I:** 478

"Pissing off the Back of the Boat into the Nevernais Canal" (Matthews), **Supp. IX:** 160–161

Pistol, The (Jones), **Supp. XI:** 219, **223–224**, 227, 234

Pit, The (Norris), **III:** 314, 322, 326–327, 333, 334

"Pit, The" (Roethke), **III:** 538

"Pit and the Pendulum, The" (Poe), **III:** 413, 416; **Retro. Supp. II:** 264, 269–270, 273

"Pitcher" (Francis), **Supp. IX:** 82

"Pitcher, The" (Dubus), **Supp. VII:** 87

Pitchford, Nicola, **Supp. XII:** 13

"Pits, The" (Graham), **Supp. XI:** 252, 254

Pitt, William, **Supp. I Part 2:** 510, 518

"Pity Me" (Wylie), **Supp. I Part 2:** 729

Pity the Monsters (Williamson), **Retro. Supp. II:** 185

Pius II, Pope, **III:** 472

Pius IX, Pope, **II:** 79

"Piute Creek" (Snyder), **Supp. VIII:** 293

Pixley, Frank, **I:** 196

Pizer, Donald, **III:** 321; **Retro. Supp. II:** 100, 199

"Place at the Outskirts" (Simic), **Supp. VIII:** 282

Place Called Estherville, A (Caldwell), **I:** 297, 307

"Place in Fiction" (Welty), **IV:** 260, 279

Place of Dead Roads, The (Burroughs), **Supp. III Part 1:** 196

Place of Love, The (Shapiro), **Supp. II Part 2:** 702, 706

"Place of Poetry, The" (Stevens), **Retro. Supp. I:** 304

Place of Science in Modern Civilization and Other Essays, The (Veblen), **Supp. I Part 2:** 629, 642

Place on Earth, A (Berry), **Supp. X:** 33–34, 36

Places Left Unfinished at the Time of Creation (Santos), **Supp. XIII:** 274

"Places to Look for Your Mind" (Moore), **Supp. X:** 174–175

"Place to Live, A" (Levertov), **Supp. III Part 1:** 281

"Place to Stand, A" (Price), **Supp. VI:** 258

Place to Stand, A (Wagoner), **Supp. IX:** 324

"Place (Any Place) to Transcend All Places, A" (W. C. Williams), **Retro. Supp. I:** 422

Placi, Carlo, **IV:** 328

"Plagiarist, The" (Singer), **IV:** 19

"Plain Language from Truthful James" (Harte). *See* "Heathen Chinee, The"

"Plain Sense of Things, The" (Stevens), **Retro. Supp. I:** 298, 299, 307, 312

Plain Song (Harrison), **Supp. VIII: 38–39**

"Plain Song for Comadre, A" (Wilbur), **Supp. III Part 2:** 554

"Plain Talk." *See Common Sense* (Paine)

Plaint of a Rose, The (Sandburg), **III:** 579

Plain Truth: Or, Serious Considerations on the Present State of the City of Philadelphia, and Province of Pennsylvania (Franklin), **II:** 117–119

Plainwater: Essays and Poetry (Carson), **Supp. XII:** 97, **99–104**

"Planchette" (London), **II:** 475–476

"Planetarium" (Rich), **Supp. I Part 2:** 557

Planet News: 1961–1967 (Ginsberg), **Supp. II Part 1:** 321

"Plantation a beginning, a" (Olson), **Supp. II Part 2:** 573

Plant Dreaming Deep (Sarton), **Supp. VIII:** 250, 263

Plante, David, **Supp. IV Part 1:** 310

Plarr, Victor, **III:** 459, 477

Plath, James, **Retro. Supp. I:** 334

Plath, Sylvia, **Retro. Supp. II:** 181, **241–260**; **Supp. I Part 2: 526–549**, 554, 571; **Supp. III Part 2:** 543, 561; **Supp. IV Part 2:** 439; **Supp. V:** 79, 81, 113, 117, 118, 119, 344; **Supp. X:** 201, 202, **203**, 215; **Supp. XI:** 146, 240, 241, 317; **Supp. XII:** 217, 308; **Supp. XIII:** 35, 76, 312; **Supp. XIV:** 269

Plath, Warren, **Supp. I Part 2:** 528

Plato, **I:** 224, 279, 383, 389, 485, 523; **II:** 5, 8, 10, 15, 233, 346, 391–392, 591; **III:** 115, 480, 600, 606, 609, 619–620; **IV:** 74, 140, 333, 363, 364; **Retro. Supp. I:** 247; **Retro. Supp. II:** 31; **Supp. I Part 2:** 595, 631; **Supp. IV Part 1:** 391; **Supp. IV Part 2:** 526; **Supp. X:** 78

"Plato" (Emerson), **II:** 6

"Platonic Relationship, A" (Beattie), **Supp. V:** 22

Platonic Scripts (Justice), **Supp. VII:** 115

Platonov, Dmitri, **Supp. VIII:** 30

Platt, Anthony M., **Supp. I Part 1:** 13–14

Plausible Prejudices: Essays on American Writing (Epstein), **Supp. XIV:** 111

Plautus, Titus Maccius, **IV:** 155; **Supp. III Part 2:** 630

Play and Other Stories, The (Dixon), **Supp. XII:** 148, 149

Playback (Chandler), **Supp. IV Part 1:** 134–135

Playback (script) (Chandler), **Supp. IV Part 1:** 131

"Play Ball!" (Francis), **Supp. IX:** 89

Playboy of the Western World, The (Synge), **Supp. III Part 1:** 34

Play Days (Jewett), **Retro. Supp. II:** 135

Play Days: A Book of Stories for Children (Jewett), **II:** 401–402

Player Piano (Vonnegut), **Supp. II Part 2:** 756, 757, 760–765

Players (DeLillo), **Supp. VI:** 3, 6, 8, 14

"Players, The" (W. J. Smith), **Supp. XIII:** 340, 343

"Playground, The" (Bradbury), **Supp. IV Part 1:** 104

Playing in the Dark (Morrison), **Retro. Supp. II:** 118; **Supp. XIII:** 185–186

"Playin with Punjab" (Bambara), **Supp. XI:** 6

Play It as It Lays (Didion), **Supp. IV Part 1:** 198, 201–203, 203, 211

Play It as It Lays (film), **Supp. IV Part 1:** 198

Plays: Winesburg and Others (Anderson), **I:** 113

"Plays and Operas Too" (Whitman), **IV:** 350

Plays of Negro Life: A Source-Book of Native American Drama (Locke and Gregory), **Supp. XIV:** 202

"Playthings" (Komunyakaa), **Supp. XIII:** 126

Playwright's Voice, The (Savran), **Supp. XIII:** 209

Plaza Suite (Simon), **Supp. IV Part 2:** 575, 581–582, 583, 589

"Plea for Captain Brown, A" (Thoreau), **IV:** 185

"Please" (Komunyakaa), **Supp. XIII:** 122

"Please Don't Kill Anything" (A. Miller), **III:** 161

Pleasure Dome (Frankenberg), **I:** 436

Pleasure Dome (Komunyakaa), **Supp. XIII:** 113, 121, **131–133**

Pleasure of Hope, The (Emerson), **II:** 8

"Pleasure of Ruins, The" (McClatchy), **Supp. XII:** 256

"Pleasures of Formal Poetry, The"

(Bogan), **Supp. III Part 1:** 51

"Plea to the Protestant Churches, A" (Brooks), **Supp. XIV:** 4

Plimpton, George, **Supp. IV Part 1:** 386; **Supp. V:** 201; **Supp. VIII:** 82, 157; **Supp. IX:** 256; **Supp. XI:** 294; **Supp. XIV:** 82

Pliny the Younger, **II:** 113

"Plot against the Giant, The" (Stevens), **IV:** 81

Plough and the Stars, The (O'Casey), **III:** 159

"Ploughing on Sunday" (Stevens), **IV:** 74

Plowing the Dark (Powers), **Supp. IX:** 212–213, **221–224**

"Plumet Basilisk, The" (Moore), **III:** 203, 208, 215

Plumly, Stanley, **Supp. IV Part 2:** 625

Plummer, Amanda, **Supp. IV Part 1:** 236

Plunder (serial movie), **Supp. IV Part 2:** 464

"Plunkville Patriot" (O'Henry), **Supp. II Part 1:** 389

"Pluralism and Ideological Peace" (Locke), **Supp. XIV:** 202, 212

"Pluralism and Intellectual Democracy" (Locke), **Supp. XIV:** 202, 208, 212

Pluralistic Universe, A (James), **II:** 342, 348, 357–358

Plutarch, **II:** 5, 8, 16, 555; **Retro. Supp. I:** 360

Plymell, Charles, **Supp. XIV:** 149

Plymell, Pam, **Supp. XIV:** 149

Pnin (Nabokov), **III:** 246; **Retro. Supp. I:** 263, 265, 266, 275, 335

"Po' Boy Blues" (Hughes), **Supp. I Part 1:** 327

Pocahontas, **I:** 4; **II:** 296; **III:** 584

"Pocahontas to Her English Husband, John Rolfe" (Gunn Allen), **Supp. IV Part 1:** 331

Podhoretz, Norman, **IV:** 441; **Retro. Supp. II:** 323; **Supp. IV Part 1:** 382; **Supp. VIII:** 93, **231–247;** **Supp. IX:** 3; **Supp. XIV:** 103

Podnieks, Elizabeth, **Supp. X:** 189, 190, 191, 192

"Pod of the Milkweed" (Frost), **Retro. Supp. I:** 141

Poe, Edgar Allan, **I:** 48, 53, 103, 190, 194, 200, 210, 211, 261, 340, 459; **II:** 74, 77, 194, 255, 273, 295, 308, 311, 313, 421, 475, 482, 530, 595; **III:** 259, **409–432,** 485, 507, 593; **IV:** 123, 129, 133, 141, 187, 261, 345, 350, 432, 438, 439, 453; **Retro. Supp. I:** 41, 273, 365, 421; **Retro.**

Supp. II: 102, 104, 160, 164, 220, **261–277,** 322; **Supp. I Part 1:** 36, 309; **Supp. I Part 2:** 376, 384, 385, 388, 393, 405, 413, 421, 474, 682; **Supp. II Part 1:** 385, 410; **Supp. III Part 2:** 544, 549–550; **Supp. IV Part 1:** 80, 81, 101, 128, 341, 349; **Supp. IV Part 2:** 464, 469; **Supp. VIII:** 105; **Supp. IX:** 115; **Supp. X:** 42, 78; **Supp. XI:** 85, 293; **Supp. XIII:** 100, 111

Poe Abroad: Influence, Reputation, Affinities (Vines), **Retro. Supp. II:** 261

"Poem" (Bishop), **Retro. Supp. II:** 40; **Supp. I Part 1:** 73, 76–79, 82, 95

"Poem" (Harrison), **Supp. VIII:** 38

"Poem" (Justice), **Supp. VII:** 125

"Poem" (Kunitz), **Supp. III Part 1:** 263

"Poem" (Wright), **Supp. III Part 2:** 590

"Poem About George Doty in the Death House, A" (Wright), **Supp. III Part 2:** 594–595, 597–598

"Poem about People" (Pinsky), **Supp. VI: 240–241,** 244, 248

"Poem as Mask, The" (Rukeyser), **Supp. VI:** 281, 285

"Poem Beginning 'The'" (Zukofsky), **Supp. III Part 2:** 610, 611, 614

"Poem for a Birthday" (Plath), **Supp. I Part 2:** 539

"POEM FOR ANNA RUSS AND FANNY JONES, A" (Baraka), **Supp. II Part 1:** 58

"Poem for Black Hearts, A" (Baraka), **Supp. II Part 1:** 50

"Poem for D. H. Lawrence" (Creeley), **Supp. IV Part 1:** 141

"POEM FOR DEEP THINKERS, A" (Baraka), **Supp. II Part 1:** 55

"Poem for Dorothy, A" (Merwin), **Supp. III Part 1:** 342

"Poem for Hemingway and W. C. Williams" (Carver), **Supp. III Part 1:** 147

"Poem for my Son" (Kumin), **Supp. IV Part 2:** 442

"Poem for People Who Are Understandably Too Busy to Read Poetry" (Dunn), **Supp. XI:** 147

"Poem for Someone Killed in Spain, A" (Jarrell), **II:** 371

"Poem for the Blue Heron, A" (Oliver), **Supp. VII:** 235–236

"Poem For Willie Best, A" (Baraka), **Supp. II Part 1:** 36

"Poem in Prose" (Bogan), **Supp. III Part 1:** 58

"Poem in Which I Refuse Contemplation" (Dove), **Supp. IV Part 1:** 249

"Poem Is a Walk, A" (Ammons), **Supp. VII:** 36

"Poem Like a Grenade, A" (Haines), **Supp. XII:** 204

"Poem of Flight, The" (Levine), **Supp. V:** 189

"Poem of Liberation, The" (Stern), **Supp. IX:** 292

Poem of the Cid (Merwin, trans.), **Supp. III Part 1:** 347

"Poem of the Forgotten" (Haines), **Supp. XII:** 202–203

"Poem on the Memorable Victory Obtained by the Gallant Captain Paul Jones" (Freneau), **Supp. II Part 1:** 261

"Poem out of Childhood" (Rukeyser), **Supp. VI:** 272, 277

"Poem Read at the Dinner Given to the Author by the Medical Profession" (Holmes), **Supp. I Part 1:** 310–311

Poems (Auden), **Supp. II Part 1:** 6

Poems (Berryman), **I:** 170

Poems (Bryant), **II:** 311; **Supp. I Part 1:** 155, 157

Poems (Cummings), **I:** 430, 447

Poems (Eliot), **I:** 580, 588; **IV:** 122; **Retro. Supp. I:** 59, 291

Poems (Emerson), **II:** 7, 8, 12–13, 17

Poems (Holmes), **Supp. I Part 1:** 303

Poems (Lowell), **Supp. I Part 2:** 405

Poems (Moore), **III:** 194, 205, 215

Poems (Poe), **III:** 411

Poems (Reznikoff), **Supp. XIV:** 282, 283, 284, 285

Poems (Tate), **IV:** 121

Poems (Winters), **Supp. II Part 2:** 809, 810

Poems (Wordsworth), **I:** 468

Poems (W. C. Williams), **Retro. Supp. I:** 412–413, 416, 424

Poems (W. J. Smith), **Supp. XIII:** 332

Poems 1940–1953 (Shapiro), **Supp. II Part 2:** 703, 711

Poems 1957–1967 (Dickey), **Supp. IV Part 1:** 178, 181

Poems, 1909–1925 (Eliot), **Retro. Supp. I:** 64

Poems, 1924–1933 (MacLeish), **III:** 7, 15

Poems, 1943–1956 (Wilbur), **Supp. III Part 2:** 554

Poems: 1947–1957 (W. J. Smith), **Supp. XIII:** 333

Poems: North & South–A Cold Spring, (Bishop), **Supp. I Part 1:** 83, 89

Poems, The (Freneau), **Supp. II Part 1:** 263

Poems 1918–1975 : The Complete Poems of Charles Reznikoff (Cooney, ed.), **Supp. XIV:** 289

Poems about God (Ransom), **III:** 484, 486, 491; **IV:** 121

"Poems about Painting" (Snodgrass), **Supp. VI:** 316

Poems and Essays (Ransom), **III:** 486, 490, 492

Poems and New Poems (Bogan), **Supp. III Part 1:** 60–62

"Poems and Places" (Haines), **Supp. XII:** 203

Poems and Poetry of Europe, The (Longfellow, ed.), **Retro. Supp. II:** 155

Poems by Emily Dickinson (Todd and Higginson, eds.), **I:** 469, 470; **Retro. Supp. I:** 35, 39

Poems by Emily Dickinson, Second Series (Todd and Higginson, eds.), **I:** 454; **Retro. Supp. I:** 35

Poems by Emily Dickinson, The (Bianchi and Hampson, eds.), **Retro. Supp. I:** 35

Poems by Emily Dickinson, Third Series (Todd, ed.), **Retro. Supp. I:** 35

Poems by James Russell Lowell, Second Series (Lowell), **Supp. I Part 2:** 406, 409

Poems by Sidney Lanier, (Lanier), **Supp. I Part 1:** 364

Poems from Black Africa (Hughes, ed.), **Supp. I Part 1:** 344

"Poems I Have Lost, The" (Ortiz), **Supp. IV Part 2:** 507

Poems of a Jew (Shapiro), **Supp. II Part 2:** 703, 712–713

Poems of Anna Akhmatova, The (Kunitz and Hayward, trans.), **Supp. III Part 1:** 269

Poems of Emily Dickinson, The (Bianchi and Hampson, eds.), **Retro. Supp. I:** 35

Poems of Emily Dickinson, The (Johnson, ed.), **I:** 470

Poems of François Villon (Kinnell, trans.), **Supp. III Part 1:** 235, 243, 249

"Poems of Our Climate, The" (Stevens), **Retro. Supp. I:** 313

Poems of Philip Freneau, Written Chiefly during the Late War (Freneau), **Supp. II Part 1:** 261

Poems of Places (Longfellow, ed.), **II:** 490; **Retro. Supp. II:** 155; **Supp. I Part 1:** 368

Poems of Stanley Kunitz, The (Kunitz),

Supp. III Part 1: 258, 263, 264, 266, 268

"Poems of These States" (Ginsberg), **Supp. II Part 1:** 323, 325

Poems of Two Friends (Howells and Piatt), **II:** 273, 277

"POEM SOME PEOPLE WILL HAVE TO UNDERSTAND, A" (Baraka), **Supp. II Part 1:** 49

Poems on Slavery (Longfellow), **II:** 489; **Retro. Supp. II:** 157, 168; **Supp. I Part 2:** 406

Poem Spoken at the Public Commencement at Yale College, in New Haven; September 1, 1781, A (Barlow), **Supp. II Part 1:** 67–68, 74, 75

Poems to Solve (Swenson), **Supp. IV Part 2:** 642

Poems Written and Published during the American Revolutionary War (Freneau), **Supp. II Part 1:** 273, 274

Poems Written between the Years 1768 and 1794 (Freneau), **Supp. II Part 1:** 269

"Poem That Took the Place of a Mountain" (Olson), **Supp. II Part 2:** 582

"Poem to My First Lover" (Olds), **Supp. X:** 206

"Poem to the Reader" (Olds), **Supp. X:** 213

"Poem with No Ending, A" (Levine), **Supp. V:** 186, 190

"Poem You Asked For, The" (Levis), **Supp. XI:** 259–260

Poe Poe Poe Poe Poe Poe Poe (Hoffman), **Retro. Supp. II:** 265

Poésies 1917–1920 (Cocteau), **Retro. Supp. I:** 82

"Poet, The" (Dunbar), **Supp. II Part 1:** 207, 209–210

"Poet, The" (Emerson), **II:** 13, 19, 20, 170

"Poet, The" (Ortiz), **Supp. IV Part 2:** 505

"Poet and His Book, The" (Millay), **III:** 126, 138

"Poet and His Public, The" (Jarrell), **Supp. I Part 1:** 96

"Poet and His Song, The" (Dunbar), **Supp. II Part 1:** 199

"Poet and the Person, The" (Kinard), **Supp. XIV:** 127

"Poet and the World, The" (Cowley), **Supp. II Part 1:** 145

"Poet as Anti-Specialist, The" (Swenson), **Supp. IV Part 2:** 638, 643

"Poet as *Curandera*" (Mora), **Supp. XIII:** 214, 220

"Poet as Hero, The: Keats in His Letters" (Trilling), **Supp. III Part 2:** 506–507

"Poet as Religious Moralist, The" (Larson), **Supp. XI:** 328

"Poet at Seven, The" (Rimbaud), **II:** 545

Poet at the Breakfast-Table, The (Holmes), **Supp. I Part 1:** 313–314

"Poète contumace, Le" (Corbiere), **II:** 384–385

"Poet for President, A" (Mora), **Supp. XIII:** 220–221

Poetic Achievement of Ezra Pound, The (Alexander), **Retro. Supp. I:** 293

Poetic Diction: A Study in Meaning (Barfield), **III:** 274, 279

"Poetic Principle, The" (Poe), **III:** 421, 426; **Retro. Supp. II:** 266

"Poetics" (Ammons), **Supp. VII:** 29–30

Poetics (Aristotle), **III:** 422; **Supp. XI:** 249; **Supp. XIII:** 75; **Supp. XIV:** 243

Poetics of Space, The (Bachelard), **Supp. XIII:** 225

"Poetics of the Periphery: Literary Experimentalism in Kathy Acker's *In Memoriam to Identity*" (Acker), **Supp. XII:** 17

"Poetics of the Physical World, The" (Kinnell), **Supp. III Part 1:** 239

Poet in the World, The (Levertov), **Supp. III Part 1:** 271, 273, 278, 282

"Poet or the Growth of a Lit'ry Figure" (White), **Supp. I Part 2:** 676

Poetry (Barber), **Supp. IV Part 2:** 550

"Poetry" (Moore), **III:** 204–205, 215

"Poetry" (Nye), **Supp. XIII:** 282

"Poetry: A Metrical Essay" (Holmes), **Supp. I Part 1:** 310

"Poetry, Community and Climax" (Snyder), **Supp. VIII:** 290

"Poetry and Belief in Thomas Hardy" (Schwartz), **Supp. II Part 2:** 666

Poetry and Criticism (Nemerov, ed.), **III:** 269

"Poetry and Drama" (Eliot), **I:** 588

Poetry and Fiction: Essays (Nemerov), **III:** 269, 281

"Poetry and Place" (Berry), **Supp. X:** 22, 28, 31, 32

Poetry and Poets (Lowell), **II:** 512

Poetry and the Age (Jarrell), **IV:** 352; **Retro. Supp. I:** 121; **Supp. II Part 1:** 135

"Poetry and the Primitive: Notes on Poetry as an Ecological Survival Technique" (Snyder), **Supp. VIII:**

291, 292, 299, 300
"Poetry and the Public World" (MacLeish), **III:** 11
Poetry and the World (Pinsky), **Supp. VI:** 236, 239, 244, 247
Poetry and Truth (Olson), **Supp. II Part 2:** 583
"Poetry As a Way of Life" (Bishop interview), **Retro. Supp. II:** 53
"Poetry as Survival" (Harrison), **Supp. VIII:** 45
"Poetry for the Advanced" (Baraka), **Supp. II Part 1:** 58
Poetry Handbook, A (Oliver), **Supp. VII:** 229, 245
"Poetry of Barbarism, The" (Santayana), **IV:** 353
Poetry of Chaucer, The (Gardner), **Supp. VI: 63**
Poetry of Meditation, The (Martz), **IV:** 151; **Supp. I Part 1:** 107
Poetry of Mourning: The Modern Elegy from Hardy to Heaney (Ramazani), **Supp. IV Part 2:** 450
Poetry of Stephen Crane, The (Hoffman), **I:** 405
Poetry of the Negro 1746–1949, The (Hughes, ed.), **Supp. I Part 1:** 345
Poetry Reading against the Vietnam War, A (Bly and Ray, eds.), **Supp. IV Part 1:** 61, 63
"Poetry Wreck, The" (Shapiro), **Supp. II Part 2:** 717
Poetry Wreck, The: Selected Essays (Shapiro), **Supp. II Part 2:** 703, 704, 717
Poet's Alphabet, A: Reflections on the Literary Art and Vocation (Bogan), **Supp. III Part 1:** 55, 64
Poet's Choice (Engle and Langland, eds.), **III:** 277, 542
Poets of the Old Testament, The (Gordon), **III:** 199
Poets of Today (Wheelock, ed.), **Supp. IV Part 2:** 639
Poets on Poetry (Nemerov, ed.), **III:** 269
"Poet's View, A" (Levertov), **Supp. III Part 1:** 284
"Poet's Voice, The" (Oliver), **Supp. VII:** 245
"Poet Turns on Himself, The" (Dickey), **Supp. IV Part 1:** 177, 181, 185
Poganuc People (Stowe), **Supp. I Part 2:** 581, 596, 599–600
Pogo (comic strip), **Supp. XI:** 105
Poincaré, Raymond, **IV:** 320
"Point, The" (Hayden), **Supp. II Part 1:** 373

"Point at Issue!, A" (Chopin), **Retro. Supp. II:** 61; **Supp. I Part 1:** 208
"Point of Age, A" (Berryman), **I:** 173
Point of No Return (Marquand), **III:** 56, 59–60, 65, 67, 69
Point Reyes Poems (Bly), **Supp. IV Part 1:** 71
Points for a Compass Rose (Connell), **Supp. XIV:** 79, 80, 96
"Point Shirley" (Plath), **Supp. I Part 2:** 529, 538
Points in Time (Bowles), **Supp. IV Part 1:** 93
"Points West" (column), **Supp. IV Part 1:** 198
Poirier, Richard, **I:** 136, 239; **III:** 34; **Retro. Supp. I:** 134; **Retro. Supp. II:** 207–208; **Supp. I Part 2:** 660, 665; **Supp. IV Part 2:** 690
Poison Pen (Garrett), **Supp. VII:** 111
Poisonwood Bible, The (Kingsolver), **Supp. VII:** 197–198, 202, 210–213
Poitier, Sidney, **Supp. IV Part 1:** 360, 362
"Polar Bear" (Heller), **Supp. IV Part 1:** 383
Pole, Rupert, **Supp. X:** 185
"Pole Star" (MacLeish), **III:** 16
Po Li, **Supp. I Part 1:** 262
Police (Baraka), **Supp. II Part 1:** 47
"Police" (Corso), **Supp. XII:** 117, 127
"Police Dreams" (Bausch), **Supp. VII:** 47
Politian (Poe), **III:** 412
"Political and Practical Conceptions of Race, The" (Locke), **Supp. XIV:** 209–210
Political Essays (Lowell), **Supp. I Part 2:** 407
Political Fable, A (Coover), **Supp. V:** 44, 46, 47, 49, 51
"Political Fables" (Mather), **Supp. II Part 2:** 450
"Political Interests" (Stevens), **Retro. Supp. I:** 295
"Political Litany, A" (Freneau), **Supp. II Part 1:** 257
"Political Pastoral" (Frost), **Retro. Supp. I:** 139
"Political Poem" (Baraka), **Supp. II Part 1:** 36
Politics (Acker), **Supp. XII:** 3, 4
Politics (Macdonald), **I:** 233–234
"Politics" (Paley), **Supp. VI:** 217
"Politics, Structure, and Poetic Development" (McCombs), **Supp. XIII:** 33
"Politics and the English Language" (Orwell), **Retro. Supp. II:** 287; **Supp. I Part 2:** 620

Politics and the Novel (Howe), **Supp. VI:** 113
"Politics of Silence, The" (Monette), **Supp. X:** 148
Politt, Katha, **Supp. XII:** 159
Polk, James, **Supp. XIII:** 20
Polk, James K., **I:** 17; **II:** 433–434
Pollack, Sydney, **Supp. XIII:** 159
"Pollen" (Nye), **Supp. XIII:** 284
Pollitt, Katha, **Supp. X:** 186, 191, 193
Pollock, Jackson, **IV:** 411, 420
"Polly" (Chopin), **Retro. Supp. II:** 72
Polo, Marco, **III:** 395
Polybius, **Supp. I Part 2:** 491
"Polydore" (Chopin), **Retro. Supp. II:** 66
"Pomegranate" (Glück), **Supp. V:** 82
"Pomegranate Seed" (Wharton), **IV:** 316; **Retro. Supp. I:** 382
Ponce de Leon, Luis, **III:** 391
"Pond, The" (Nemerov), **III:** 272
"Pond at Dusk, The" (Kenyon), **Supp. VII:** 168
Ponder Heart, The (Welty), **IV:** 261, 274–275, 281; **Retro. Supp. I:** 351–352
"Ponderosa Pine" (Huncke), **Supp. XIV:** 146
Poodle Springs (Parker and Chandler), **Supp. IV Part 1:** 135
Poodle Springs Story, The (Chandler), **Supp. IV Part 1:** 135
"Pool, The" (Doolittle), **Supp. I Part 1:** 264–265
Poole, Ernest, **II:** 444
"Pool Lights" (F. Barthelme), **Supp. XI:** 25, 26–27, 36
"Pool Room in the Lions Club" (Merwin), **Supp. III Part 1:** 346
"Poor Black Fellow" (Hughes), **Retro. Supp. I:** 204
"Poor Bustard, The" (Corso), **Supp. XII:** 134
"Poor but Happy" (Mamet), **Supp. XIV:** 252, 253
Poore, Charles, **III:** 364
Poor Fool (Caldwell), **I:** 291, 292, 308
Poorhouse Fair, The (Updike), **IV:** 214, 228–229, 232; **Retro. Supp. I:** 317, 320
"Poor Joanna" (Jewett), **II:** 394
"Poor Man's Pudding and Rich Man's Crumbs" (Melville), **III:** 89–90
"Poor Richard" (James), **II:** 322
Poor Richard's Almanac (undated) (Franklin), **II:** 112
Poor Richard's Almanac for 1733 (Franklin), **II:** 108, 110
Poor Richard's Almanac for 1739 (Franklin), **II:** 112

Poor Richard's Almanac for 1758 (Franklin), **II:** 101

Poor White (Anderson), **I:** 110–111

"Poor Working Girl" (Z. Fitzgerald), **Supp. IX:** 71

Popa, Vasko, **Supp. VIII:** 272

Pope, Alexander, **I:** 198, 204; **II:** 17, 114; **III:** 263, 267, 288, 517; **IV:** 145; **Retro. Supp. I:** 335; **Supp. I Part 1:** 150, 152, 310; **Supp. I Part 2:** 407, 422, 516, 714; **Supp. II Part 1:** 70, 71; **Supp. X:** 32, 36; **Supp. XII:** 260

Pope-Hennessy, James, **Supp. XIV:** 348

"Pope's Penis, The" (Olds), **Supp. X:** 207

"Poplar, Sycamore" (Wilbur), **Supp. III Part 2:** 549

Popo and Fifina (Hughes and Bontemps), **Retro. Supp. I:** 203

"Poppies" (Oliver), **Supp. VII:** 240

"Poppies in July" (Plath), **Supp. I Part 2:** 544

"Poppies in October" (Plath), **Supp. I Part 2:** 544

"Poppycock" (Francis), **Supp. IX:** 87

"Poppy Seed" (Lowell), **II:** 523

Popular Culture (Goldbarth), **Supp. XII: 186**

Popular History of the United States (Gay), **Supp. I Part 1:** 158

"Popular Songs" (Ashbery), **Supp. III Part 1:** 6

"Populist Manifesto" (Ferlinghetti), **Supp. VIII:** 290

"Porcelain Bowl" (Glück), **Supp. V:** 83

Porcher, Frances, **Retro. Supp. II:** 71

"Porcupine, The" (Kinnell), **Supp. III Part 1:** 244

Porcupine's Kiss, The (Dobyns), **Supp. XIII: 89–90**

Porgy and Bess (film), **Supp. I Part 1:** 66

Porgy and Bess (play), **Supp. IV Part 1:** 6

"Porphyria's Lover" (Browning), **II:** 522

Portable Beat Reader, The (Charters, ed.), **Supp. XIV:** 152

Portable Blake, The (Kazin, ed.), **Supp. VIII:** 103

Portable Faulkner, The (Cowley, ed.), **II:** 57, 59; **Retro. Supp. I:** 73

Portable Paul and Jane Bowles, The (Dillon), **Supp. IV Part 1:** 95

Portable Veblen, The (Veblen), **Supp. I Part 2:** 630, 650

"Porte-Cochere" (Taylor), **Supp. V:** 320

"Porter" (Hughes), **Supp. I Part 1:** 327

Porter, Bern, **III:** 171

Porter, Cole, **Supp. IX:** 189

Porter, Eliot, **Supp. IV Part 2:** 599

Porter, Herman W., **Supp. I Part 1:** 49

Porter, Horace, **Retro. Supp. II:** 4, 127

Porter, Jacob, **Supp. I Part 1:** 153

Porter, Katherine Anne, **I:** 97, 385; **II:** 194, 606; **III: 433–455,** 482; **IV:** 26, 138, 246, 261, 279, 280, 282; **Retro. Supp. I:** 354; **Retro. Supp. II:** 233, 235; **Supp. IV Part 1:** 31, 310; **Supp. V:** 225; **Supp. VIII:** 156, 157; **Supp. IX:** 93, 94, 95, 98, 128; **Supp. X:** 50; **Supp. XIII:** 294; **Supp. XIV:** 3

Porter, Noah, **Supp. I Part 2:** 640

Porter, William Sydney. *See* Henry, O.

Porteus, Beilby, **Supp. I Part 1:** 150

"Portland Going Out, The" (Merwin), **Supp. III Part 1:** 345

Portnoy's Complaint (Roth), **Retro. Supp. II: 282–286,** 291; **Supp. III Part 2:** 401, 404, 405, 407, 412–414, 426; **Supp. V:** 119, 122; **Supp. XI:** 140

Port of Saints (Burroughs), **Supp. III Part 1:** 106

"Portrait" (Dixon), **Supp. XII:** 154

"Portrait, A" (Parker), **Supp. IX:** 192–193

"Portrait, The" (Kunitz), **Supp. III Part 1:** 263

"Portrait, The" (Wharton), **Retro. Supp. I:** 364

"Portrait d'une Femme" (Pound), **Retro. Supp. I:** 288

Portrait in Brownstone (Auchincloss), **Supp. IV Part 1:** 21, 23, 27, 31

"Portrait in Georgia" (Toomer), **Supp. IX:** 314

"Portrait in Greys, A" (W. C. Williams), **Retro. Supp. I:** 416

"Portrait of a Girl in Glass" (T. Williams), **IV:** 383

"Portrait of a Lady" (Eliot), **I:** 569, 570, 571, 584; **III:** 4; **Retro. Supp. I:** 55, 56, 62

Portrait of a Lady, The (James), **I:** 10, 258, 461–462, 464; **II:** 323, 325, 327, 328–329, 334; **Retro. Supp. I:** 215, 216, 217, 219, 220, 223, **224–225,** 232, 233, 381

"Portrait of an Artist" (Roth), **Supp. III Part 2:** 412

Portrait of an Eye: Three Novels (Acker), **Supp. XII:** 6, **7–9**

"Portrait of an Invisible Man" (Auster), **Supp. XII:** 21

Portrait of Bascom Hawkes, A (Wolfe), **IV:** 451–452, 456

Portrait of Edith Wharton (Lubbock), **Retro. Supp. I:** 366

Portrait of Logan Pearsall Smith, Drawn from His Letters and Diaries, A (Russell, ed.), **Supp. XIV:** 349

Portrait of Picasso as a Young Man (Mailer), **Retro. Supp. II:** 213

"Portrait of the Artist as an Old Man, A" (Humphrey), **Supp. IX:** 109

Portrait of the Artist as a Young Man, A (Joyce), **I:** 475–476; **III:** 471, 561; **Retro. Supp. I:** 127; **Retro. Supp. II:** 4, 331; **Supp. IX:** 236; **Supp. XIII:** 53, 95

"Portrait of the Artist with Hart Crane" (Wright), **Supp. V:** 342

"Portrait of the Intellectual as a Yale Man" (McCarthy), **II:** 563, 564–565

"Port Town" (Hughes), **Retro. Supp. I:** 199

Portuguese Voyages to America in the Fifteenth Century (Morison), **Supp. I Part 2:** 488

"Po' Sandy" (Chesnutt), **Supp. XIV:** 60

Poseidon Adventure, The (film), **Supp. XII:** 321

"Poseidon and Company" (Carver), **Supp. III Part 1:** 137

"Positive Obsession" (O. Butler), **Supp. XIII:** 70

Poss, Stanley, **Supp. XIV:** 166

"Possessions" (H. Crane), **I:** 392–393; **Retro. Supp. II:** 78

Postal Inspector (film), **Supp. XIII:** 166

Postcards (Proulx), **Supp. VII:** 249, 256–258, 262

"Postcolonial Tale, A" (Harjo), **Supp. XII:** 227

"Posthumous Letter to Gilbert White" (Auden), **Supp. II Part 1:** 26

"Post-Larkin Triste" (Karr), **Supp. XI:** 242–243

Postlethwaite, Diana, **Supp. XII:** 317–318

"Postlude" (W. C. Williams), **Retro. Supp. I:** 415

Postman, Neil, **Supp. XI:** 275

Postman Always Rings Twice, The (Cain), **Supp. XIII:** 165–166

Postman Always Rings Twice, The (film), **Supp. XIV:** 241

"Postmortem Guide, A" (Dunn), **Supp. XI:** 155

Postrel, Virginia, **Supp. XIV:** 298, 311

"Postscript" (Du Bois), **Supp. II Part 1:** 173

"Postscript" (Nye), **Supp. XIII:** 287

"Potato" (Wilbur), **Supp. III Part 2:** 545

"Potatoes' Dance, The" (Lindsay), **Supp. I Part 2:** 394

Pot of Earth, The (MacLeish), **III:** 5, 6–8, 10, 12, 18

"Pot Roast" (Strand), **Supp. IV Part 2:** 629

Pot Shots at Poetry (Francis), **Supp. IX:** 83–84

Potter, Beatrix, **Supp. I Part 2:** 656

Potter, Stephen, **IV:** 430

Potter's House, The (Stegner), **Supp. IV Part 2:** 598, 606

Poulenc, Francis, **Supp. IV Part 1:** 81

Poulin, Al, Jr., **Supp. IX:** 272; **Supp. XI:** 259

Pound, Ezra, **I:** 49, 58, 60, 66, 68, 69, 105, 236, 243, 256, 384, 403, 428, 429, 475, 476, 482, 487, 521, 578; **II:** 26, 55, 168, 263, 316, 371, 376, 513, 517, 520, 526, 528, 529, 530; **III:** 2, 5, 8, 9, 13–14, 17, 174, 194, 196, 278, 430, 453, **456–479,** 492, 504, 511, 523, 524, 527, 575–576, 586, 590; **IV:** 27, 28, 407, 415, 416, 433, 446; **Retro. Supp. I:** 51, 52, 55, 58, 59, 63, 82, 89, 127, 140, 171, 177, 178, 198, 216, **283–294,** 298, 299, 359, 411, 412, 413, 414, 417, 418, 419, 420, 423, 426, 427, 430, 431; **Retro. Supp. II:** 178, 183, 189, 326; **Supp. I Part 1:** 253, 255–258, 261–268, 272, 274; **Supp. I Part 2:** 387, 721; **Supp. II Part 1:** 1, 8, 20, 30, 91, 136; **Supp. III Part 1:** 48, 63, 64, 73, 105, 146, 225, 271; **Supp. III Part 2:** 542, **609–617,** 619, 620, 622, 625, 626, 628, 631; **Supp. IV Part 1:** 153, 314; **Supp. V:** 331, 338, 340, 343, 345; **Supp. VIII:** 39, 105, 195, 205, 271, 290, 291, 292, 303; **Supp. IX:** 291; **Supp. X:** 24, 36, 112, 120, 122; **Supp. XII:** 97; **Supp. XIV:** 11, 55, 83, 272, 284, 286, 287, 347

Pound, Louise, **Retro. Supp. I:** 4

Pound, T. S., **I:** 428

"Pound Reweighed" (Cowley), **Supp. II Part 1:** 143

Powell, Betty, **Retro. Supp. II:** 140

Powell, Dawn, **Supp. IV Part 2:** 678, 682

Powell, Dick, **Supp. IX:** 250

Powell, John Wesley, **Supp. IV Part 2:** 598, 604, 611

Powell, Lawrence Clark, **III:** 189

Powell, William, **Supp. IV Part 1:** 355

"Power" (Corso), **Supp. XII:** 117, 126, 127, **128**

"Power" (Emerson), **II:** 2, 3

"Power" (Rich), **Supp. I Part 2:** 569

"Power and Light" (Dickey), **Supp. IV Part 1:** 182

Power and the Glory, The (Greene), **III:** 556

"Powerhouse" (Welty), **Retro. Supp. I:** 343, 346

"Power Never Dominion" (Rukeyser), **Supp. VI:** 281

"Power of Fancy, The" (Freneau), **Supp. II Part 1:** 255

Power of Myth, The (Campbell), **Supp. IX:** 245

"Power of Prayer, The" (Lanier), **Supp. I Part 1:** 357

"Power of Suggestion" (Auchincloss), **Supp. IV Part 1:** 33

Power of Sympathy, The (Brown), **Supp. II Part 1:** 74

Power Politics (Atwood), **Supp. XIII:** 20, 33–34, 35

Powers, J. F., **Supp. V:** 319

Powers, Kim, **Supp. VIII:** 329, 340

Powers, Richard, **Supp. IX: 207–225**

Powers of Attorney (Auchincloss), **Supp. IV Part 1:** 31, 32, 33

"Powers of Darkness" (Wharton), **Retro. Supp. I:** 379

Powys, John Cowper, **Supp. I Part 2:** 454, 476; **Supp. IX:** 135

Poynton, Jerome, **Supp. XIV:** 147, 150

Practical Agitation (Chapman), **Supp. XIV:** 41

Practical Criticism: A Study of Literary Judgment (Richards), **Supp. XIV:** 3, 16

Practical Magic (film), **Supp. X:** 80

Practical Magic (Hoffman), **Supp. X:** 78, 82, **88–89**

"Practical Methods of Meditation, The" (Dawson), **IV:** 151

Practical Navigator, The (Bowditch), **Supp. I Part 2:** 482

Practice of Perspective, The (Dubreuil), **Supp. IV Part 2:** 425

Practice of Reading, The (Donoghue), **Supp. VIII:** 189

Pragmatism: A New Name for Some Old Ways of Thinking (James), **II:** 352

"Pragmatism's Conception of Truth" (James), **Supp. XIV:** 40

Prague Orgy, The (Roth), **Retro. Supp. II:** 280

"Praire, The" (Clampitt), **Supp. IX:** 42

"Prairie" (Sandburg), **III:** 583, 584

Prairie, The (Cooper), **I:** 339, 342

"Prairie Birthday" (Leopold), **Supp. XIV:** 185

Prairie Home Companion, A (Keillor, radio program), **Supp. XIII:** 274

"Prairie Life, A Citizen Speaks" (Dunn), **Supp. XI:** 145

"Prairies, The" (Bryant), **Supp. I Part 1:** 157, 162, 163, 166

Praise (Hass), **Supp. VI:** 104–105, 106

"Praise for an Urn" (Crane), **I:** 388

"Praise for Sick Women" (Snyder), **Supp. VIII:** 294

"Praise in Summer" (Wilbur), **Supp. III Part 2:** 546–548, 560, 562

"Praise of a Palmtree" (Levertov), **Supp. III Part 1:** 284

"Praise of the Committee" (Rukeyser), **Supp. VI:** 278

"Praises, The" (Goldbarth), **Supp. XII:** 185

"Praises, The" (Olson), **Supp. II Part 2:** 558, 560, 563, 564

Praises and Dispraises (Des Pres), **Supp. X:** 120

Praisesong for the Widow (Marshall), **Supp. IV Part 1:** 14; **Supp. XI:** 18, 276, 278, **284–286,** 287

"Praise to the End!" (Roethke), **III:** 529, 532, 539

Prajadhipok, King of Siam, **I:** 522

Prater Violet (Isherwood), **Supp. XIV:164–166,** 169–170, 171

Pratt, Anna (Anna Alcott), **Supp. I Part 1:** 33

Pratt, Louis H., **Retro. Supp. II:** 6

Pratt, Mary Louise, **Retro. Supp. II:** 48

Pratt, Parley, **Supp. IV Part 2:** 603

"Prattler" (newspaper column), **I:** 207

"Prattler, The" (Bierce), **I:** 196

"Prayer" (Olds), **Supp. X:** 204

"Prayer" (Toomer), **Supp. IX:** 318

"Prayer, A" (Kushner), **Supp. IX: 134**

"Prayer for Columbus" (Whitman), **IV:** 348

"Prayer for My Daughter" (Yeats), **II:** 598

"Prayer for My Grandfather to Our Lady, A" (Lowell), **II:** 541–542

Prayer for Owen Meany, A (Irving), **Supp. VI:** 164, 165, 166, **175–176**

"PRAYER FOR SAVING" (Baraka), **Supp. II Part 1:** 52–53

"Prayer in Spring, A" (Frost), **II:** 153, 164

"Prayer on All Saint's Day" (Cowley), **Supp. II Part 1:** 138, 153

Prayers for Dark People (Du Bois), **Supp. II Part 1:** 186

"Prayer to Hermes" (Creeley), **Supp. IV Part 1:** 156, 157

"Prayer to Masks" (Senghor), **Supp. IV Part 1:** 16

"Prayer to the Child of Prague" (Salinas), **Supp. XIII:** 327

"Prayer to the Good Poet" (Wright), **Supp. III Part 2:** 603

"Prayer to the Pacific" (Silko), **Supp. IV Part 2:** 560

"Pray without Ceasing" (Emerson), **II:** 9–10

Praz, Mario, **IV:** 430

"Preacher, The" (Whittier), **Supp. I Part 2:** 698–699

Preacher and the Slave, The (Stegner), **Supp. IV Part 2:** 599, 608, 609

Precaution (Cooper), **I:** 337, 339

"Preconceptions of Economic Science, The" (Veblen), **Supp. I Part 2:** 634

Predecessors, Et Cetera (Clampitt), **Supp. IX:** 37

"Predicament, A" (Poe), **Retro. Supp. II:** 273

Predilections (Moore), **III:** 194

Prefaces and Prejudices (Mencken), **III:** 99, 104, 106, 119

Preface to a Twenty Volume Suicide Note. . . . (Baraka), **Supp. II Part 1:** 31, 33–34, 51, 61

"Preference" (Wylie), **Supp. I Part 2:** 713

"Prejudice against the Past, The" (Moore), **IV:** 91

Prejudices (Mencken), **Supp. I Part 2:** 630

Prejudices: A Selection (Farrell, ed.), **III:** 116

Prejudices: First Series (Mencken), **III:** 105

Prelude, A: Landscapes, Characters and Conversations from the Earlier Years of My Life (Wilson), **IV:** 426, 427, 430, 434, 445

Prelude, The (Wordsworth), **III:** 528; **IV:** 331, 343; **Supp. I Part 2:** 416, 676; **Supp. XI:** 248

Prelude and Liebestod (McNally), **Supp. XIII:** 201

"Preludes" (Eliot), **I:** 573, 576, 577; **Retro. Supp. I:** 55; **Supp. IV Part 2:** 436

Preludes for Memnon (Aiken), **I:** 59, 65

Preludes from Memnon (Aiken), **Supp. X:** 50

"Prelude to an Evening" (Ransom), **III:** 491, 492–493

Prelude to Darkness (Salinas), **Supp. XIII:** 311, **318–319,** 320

"Prelude to the Present" (Mumford), **Supp. II Part 2:** 471

"Premature Burial, The" (Poe), **III:** 415, 416, 418; **Retro. Supp. II:** 270

Preminger, Otto, **Supp. IX:** 3, 9

"Premonition" (Hay), **Supp. XIV:** 122

"Premonitions of the Bread Line" (Komunyakaa), **Supp. XIII:** 114, 115

Prenshaw, Peggy Whitman, **Supp. X:** 229

"Preparations" (Silko), **Supp. IV Part 2:** 560

Preparatory Meditations (Taylor), **IV:** 145, 148, 149, 150, 152, 153, 154–155, 164, 165

Prepositions: The Collected Critical Essays of Louis Zukofsky (Zukofsky), **Supp. III Part 2:** 630

Prescott, Anne, **Supp. IV Part 1:** 299

Prescott, Orville, **Supp. IV Part 2:** 680; **Supp. XI:** 340

Prescott, Peter, **Supp. X:** 83

Prescott, William, **Retro. Supp. I:** 123

Prescott, William Hickling, **II:** 9, 310, 313–314; **IV:** 309; **Supp. I Part 2:** 414, 479, 493, 494

"Prescription of Painful Ends" (Jeffers), **Supp. II Part 2:** 424

"Presence, The" (Gordon), **II:** 199, 200

"Presence, The" (Kumin), **Supp. IV Part 2:** 445, 455

"Presence of Others, The" (Kenyon), **Supp. VII:** 164

Presences (Taylor), **Supp. V:** 325

"Present Age, The" (Emerson), **II:** 11–12

Present Danger, The: Do We Have the Will to Reverse the Decline of American Power? (Podhoretz), **Supp. VIII:** 241

"Present Hour" (Sandburg), **III:** 593–594

Present Philosophical Tendencies (Perry), **I:** 224

"Present State of Ethical Philosophy, The" (Emerson), **II:** 9

"Present State of Poetry, The" (Schwartz), **Supp. II Part 2:** 666

"Preservation of Innocence" (Baldwin), **Supp. I Part 1:** 51

"Preserving Wildness" (Berry), **Supp. X:** 28, 29, 32

"President and Other Intellectuals, The" (Kazin), **Supp. VIII:** 104

Presidential Papers, The (Mailer), **III:** 35, 37–38, 42, 45; **Retro. Supp. II:** 203, 204, 206

"Presidents" (Merwin), **Supp. III Part 1:** 351

Presnell, Robert, Sr., **Supp. XIII:** 166

"PRES SPOKE IN A LANGUAGE" (Baraka), **Supp. II Part 1:** 60

"Pretext, The" (Wharton), **Retro. Supp. I:** 371

Pretty Boy Floyd (McMurtry), **Supp. V:** 231

"Pretty Girl, The" (Dubus), **Supp. VII:** 87–88

"Pretty Mouth and Green My Eyes" (Salinger), **III:** 560

"Previous Condition" (Baldwin), **Supp. I Part 1:** 51, 55, 63

"Previous Tenant, The" (Simpson), **Supp. IX:** 278–279

Priaulx, Allan, **Supp. XI:** 228

Price, Alan, **Retro. Supp. I:** 377

Price, Reynolds, **Supp. VI: 253–270;** **Supp. IX:** 256, 257

Price, Richard, **II:** 9; **Supp. I Part 2:** 522

Price, The (A. Miller), **III:** 165–166

"Price of the Harness, The" (Crane), **I:** 414

Pricksongs & Descants; Fictions (Coover), **Supp. V:** 39, 42, 43, 49, 50

"Pride" (Hughes), **Supp. I Part 1:** 331

Pride and Prejudice (Austen), **II:** 290

Prideaux, Tom, **Supp. IV Part 2:** 574, 590

"Priesthood, The" (Winters), **Supp. II Part 2:** 786

Priestly, Joseph, **Supp. I Part 2:** 522

Primary Colors, The (A. Theroux), **Supp. VIII:** 312

"Primary Ground, A" (Rich), **Supp. I Part 2:** 563

"Prime" (Auden), **Supp. II Part 1:** 22

"Primer Class" (Bishop), **Retro. Supp. II:** 38, 51

Primer for Blacks (Brooks), **Supp. III Part 1:** 85

"Primer for the Nuclear Age" (Dove), **Supp. IV Part 1:** 246

Primer of Ignorance, A (Blackmur), **Supp. II Part 1:** 91

"Primitive Black Man, The" (Du Bois), **Supp. II Part 1:** 176

"Primitive Like an Orb, A" (Stevens), **IV:** 89; **Retro. Supp. I:** 309

"Primitive Singing" (Lindsay), **Supp. I Part 2:** 389–390

Primitivism and Decadence (Winters), **Supp. II Part 2:** 786, 803–807, 812

Prince, Richard, **Supp. XII:** 4

"Prince, The" (Jarrell), **II:** 379

"Prince, The" (Winters), **Supp. II Part 2:** 802

Prince and the Pauper, The (Twain),

IV: 200–201, 206

Prince Hagen (Sinclair), **Supp. V:** 280

Prince of a Fellow, A (Hearon), **Supp. VIII:** 58, **62–63**

Princess, The (Tennyson), **Supp. I Part 2:** 410

Princess and the Goblins, The (Macdonald), **Supp. XIII:** 75

Princess Casamassima, The (James), **II:** 276, 291; **IV:** 202; **Retro. Supp. I:** 216, 221, 222, 225, **226–227**

"Princess Casamassima, The" (Trilling), **Supp. III Part 2:** 502, 503

Princess of Arcady, A (Henry), **Retro. Supp. II:** 97

"Principles" (Du Bois), **Supp. II Part 1:** 172

Principles of Literary Criticism (Richards), **I:** 274; **Supp. I Part 1:** 264; **Supp. XIV:** 3

Principles of Psychology, The (James), **II:** 321, 350–352, 353, 354, 357, 362, 363–364; **IV:** 28, 29, 32, 37

Principles of Zoölogy (Agassiz), **Supp. I Part 1:** 312

Prior, Matthew, **II:** 111; **III:** 521

Prior, Sir James, **II:** 315

"Prison, The" (Malamud), **Supp. I Part 2:** 431, 437

Prisoner of Second Avenue, The (Simon), **Supp. IV Part 2:** 583, 584

Prisoner of Sex, The (Mailer), **III:** 46; **Retro. Supp. II:** 206

Prisoner of Zenda, The (film), **Supp. I Part 2:** 615

Prisoner's Dilemma (Powers), **Supp. IX:** 212, **214–216,** 221

Pritchard, William H., **Retro. Supp. I:** 131, 141; **Supp. IV Part 1:** 285; **Supp. IV Part 2:** 642; **Supp. XI:** 326

Pritchett, V. S., **II:** 587; **Supp. II Part 1:** 143; **Supp. VIII:** 171; **Supp. XIII:** 168

"Privatation and Publication" (Cowley), **Supp. II Part 1:** 149

Private Contentment (Price), **Supp. VI:** 263

"Private History of a Campaign That Failed" (Twain), **IV:** 195

Private Life of Axie Reed, The (Knowles), **Supp. XII:** 249

"Private Man Confronts His Vulgarities at Dawn, A" (Dunn), **Supp. XI:** 146

Private Memoirs and Confessions of a Justified Sinner, The (Hogg), **Supp. IX:** 276

"Private Property and the Common

Wealth" (Berry), **Supp. X:** 25

"Private Theatricals" (Howells), **II:** 280

Privilege, The (Kumin), **Supp. IV Part 2:** 442–444, 451

"Probing the Dark" (Komunyakaa), **Supp. XIII:** 131

"Problem from Milton, A" (Wilbur), **Supp. III Part 2:** 550

"Problem of Being, The" (James), **II:** 360

Problem of Classification in the Theory of Value, The (Locke), **Supp. XIV:** 199

"Problem of Housing the Negro, The" (Du Bois), **Supp. II Part 1:** 168

"Problem of the Religious Novel, The" (Isherwood), **Supp. XIV:** 172

Problems and Other Stories (Updike), **Retro. Supp. I:** 322, 329

"Problem Solving" (Goldbarth), **Supp. XII:** 185

Procedures for Underground (Atwood), **Supp. XIII:** 33

"Procedures for Underground" (Atwood), **Supp. XIII:** 33

Processional (Lawson), **I:** 479

"Procession at Candlemas, A" (Clampitt), **Supp. IX:** 41

Proclus, **Retro. Supp. I:** 247

"Prodigal" (Ammons), **Supp. VII:** 29

"Prodigal, The" (Bishop), **Supp. I Part 1:** 90, 92

Prodigal Parents, The (Lewis), **II:** 454–455

"Prodigy" (Simic), **Supp. VIII:** 278

"Proem" (Crane), **I:** 397

"Proem, The: By the Carpenter" (O. Henry), **Supp. II Part 1:** 409

"Professions for Women" (Woolf), **Supp. XIII:** 305

"Professor" (Hughes), **Supp. I Part 1:** 330

"Professor, The" (Bourne), **I:** 223

Professor at the Breakfast Table, The (Holmes), **Supp. I Part 1:** 313, 316

"Professor Clark's Economics" (Veblen), **Supp. I Part 2:** 634

Professor of Desire, The (Roth), **Retro. Supp. II:** 288; **Supp. III Part 2:** 403, 418–420

Professor's House, The (Cather), **I:** 325–336; **Retro. Supp. I:** 16

"Professor Veblen" (Mencken), **Supp. I Part 2:** 630

Proffer, Carl R., **Supp. VIII:** 22

Profits of Religion, The (Sinclair), **Supp. V:** 276

"Prognosis" (Warren), **IV:** 245

"Progress Report" (Simic), **Supp. VIII:** 278

"Project for a Trip to China" (Sontag), **Supp. II Part 2:** 454, 469

"Project for *The Ambassadors*" (James), **Retro. Supp. I:** 229

"Projection" (Nemerov), **III:** 275

"Projective Verse" (Olson), **Supp. III Part 1:** 30; **Supp. III Part 2:** 555, 556, 557, 624; **Supp. IV Part 1:** 139, 153; **Supp. VIII:** 290

"Projector, The" (Baker), **Supp. XIII:** 53, 55

Prokofiev, Sergey Sergeyevich, **Supp. IV Part 1:** 81

"Prolegomena, Section 1" (Pound), **Supp. III Part 2:** 615–616

"Prolegomena, Section 2" (Pound), **Supp. III Part 2:** 616

"Prolegomenon to a Biography of Mailer" (Lucid), **Retro. Supp. II:** 195

Proletarian Literature in the United States (Hicks), **Supp. I Part 2: 609–610**

"Prologue" (MacLeish), **III:** 8, 14

"Prologue to Our Time" (Mumford), **Supp. III Part 2:** 473

"Prometheus" (Longfellow), **II:** 494

Prometheus Bound (Lowell), **II:** 543, 544, 545, 555

Promise, The (Buck), **Supp. II Part 1:** 124

"Promise, The" (Olds), **Supp. X:** 213

Promised Land, The (Antin), **Supp. IX:** 227

Promised Land, The (Porter), **III:** 447

Promised Lands (Sontag), **Supp. III Part 2:** 452

Promise of American Life, The (Croly), **I:** 229

"Promise of Blue Horses, The" (Harjo), **Supp. XII:** 228

Promise of Rest, The (Price), **Supp. VI:** 262, 266

Promises (Warren), **Supp. XIV:** 15

Promises: Poems 1954–1956 (Warren), **IV:** 244–245, 249, 252

Promises, Promises (musical), **Supp. IV Part 2:** 575

"Promise This When You Be Dying" (Dickinson), **Retro. Supp. I:** 44, 46

Proof, The (Winters), **Supp. II Part 2:** 786, 791, 792–794

Proofs and Theories: Essays on Poetry (Glück), **Supp. V:** 77, 79, 92; **Supp. XIV:** 269

"Propaganda of History, The" (Du Bois), **Supp. II Part 1:** 182

Propertius, Sextus, **III:** 467; **Retro.**

Supp. II: 187; Supp. XII: 2

Property Of: A Novel (Hoffman), Supp. X: 77, 79, **80–82**

"Prophecy of Samuel Sewall, The" (Whittier), Supp. I Part 2: 699

"Prophetic Pictures, The" (Hawthorne), II: 227

"Proportion" (Lowell), II: 525

"Proposal" (Carver), Supp. III Part 1: 149

Proposals Relating to the Education of Youth in Pensilvania (Franklin), II: 113

"Proposed New Version of the Bible" (Franklin), II: 110

Prose, Francine, Supp. XII: 333

"Prose for Departure" (Merrill), Supp. III Part 1: 336

"Prose Poem as an Evolving Form, The" (Bly), Supp. IV Part 1: 64

"Proserpina and the Devil" (Wilder), IV: 358

"Prosody" (Shapiro), Supp. II Part 2: 710

Prospect before Us, The (Dos Passos), I: 491

"Prospective Immigrants Please Note" (Rich), Supp. I Part 2: 555

Prospect of Peace, The (Barlow), Supp. II Part 1: 67, 68, 75

Prospects of Literature, The (L. P. Smith), Supp. XIV: 343

Prospects on the Rubicon (Paine), Supp. I Part 2: 510–511

Prospectus of a National Institution, to Be Established in the United States (Barlow), Supp. II Part 1: 80, 82

Prospice (Browning), IV: 366

"Protestant Easter" (Sexton), Supp. II Part 2: 684

"Prothalamion" (Schwartz), Supp. II Part 2: 649, 652

"Prothalamion" (Spenser), Retro. Supp. I: 62

Proud, Robert, Supp. I Part 1: 125

"Proud Farmer, The" (Lindsay), Supp. I Part 2: 381

Proud Flesh (Humphrey), Supp. IX: 94, 95, 96, **102–103**, 104, 105, 109

"Proud Flesh" (Warren), IV: 243

"Proud Lady" (Wylie), Supp. I Part 2: 711–712

Proulx, Annie, Supp. VII: **249–267**

Proust, Marcel, I: 89, 319, 327, 377, 461; II: 377, 514, 606; III: 174, 181, 184, 244–245, 259, 471; IV: 32, 201, 237, 301, 312, 328, 359, 428, 431, 434, 439, 443, 466, 467; Retro. Supp. I: 75, 89, 169, 335; Supp. III Part 1: 10, 12, 14, 15;

Supp. IV Part 2: 600; Supp. VIII: 103; Supp. IX: 211; Supp. X: 193, 194; Supp. XII: 289; Supp. XIV: 24, 83, 95

Proverbs, Supp. X: 45

"Providence" (Komunyakaa), Supp. XIII: 132

"Provincia deserta" (Pound), Retro. Supp. I: 289

Pruette, Lorine, Supp. IV Part 2: 522

Prufrock and Other Observations (Eliot), I: 569–570, 571, 573, 574, 576–577, 583, 584, 585; Retro. Supp. I: 59, 62

"Prufrock's Perivigilium" (Eliot), Retro. Supp. I: 57

Pryor, Richard, Supp. XIII: 343

Pryse, Marjorie, Retro. Supp. II: 139, 146

"Psalm" (Ginsberg), Supp. II Part 1: 312

"Psalm" (Simic), Supp. VIII: 282

"Psalm: Our Fathers" (Merwin), Supp. III Part 1: 350

"Psalm and Lament" (Justice), Supp. VII: 116, 117–118, 120–122, 124

"Psalm of Life, A" (Longfellow), II: 489, 496; Retro. Supp. II: 164, 168, 169; Supp. I Part 2: 409

"Psalm of the West" (Lanier), Supp. I Part 1: 362, 364

Psalms (biblical book), I: 83; II: 168, 232; Retro. Supp. I: 62; Supp. I Part 1: 125

Psalms, Hymns, and Spiritual Songs of the Rev. Isaac Watts, The (Worcester, ed.), I: 458

Psychiatric Novels of Oliver Wendell Holmes, The (Oberndorf), Supp. I Part 1: 315

Psychology: Briefer Course (James), II: 351–352

"Psychology and Form" (Burke), I: 270

Psychology of Art (Malraux), IV: 434

Psychology of Insanity, The (Hart), I: 241–242, 248–250

Psychopathia Sexualis (Shanley), Supp. XIV: 316, **329**

Psychophysiks (Fechner), II: 358

"Publication is the Auction" (Dickinson), Retro. Supp. I: 31

"Public Bath, The" (Snyder), Supp. VIII: 298

Public Burning, The (Coover), Supp. IV Part 1: 388; Supp. V: 44, 45, 46–47, 48, 51, 52

"Public Burning of Julius and Ethel Rosenberg, The: An Historical Romance" (Coover), Supp. V: 44

"Public Figure" (Hay), Supp. XIV: 124

"Public Garden, The" (Lowell), II: 550

Public Good (Paine), Supp. I Part 2: 509–510

Public Poetry of Robert Lowell, The (Cosgrave), Retro. Supp. II: 185

Public Speech: Poems (MacLeish), III: 15–16

Public Spirit (Savage), II: 111

"Puck" (Monette), Supp. X: 157–158

Pudd'nhead Wilson (Twain), I: 197

"Pudd'nhead Wilson's Calendar" (Twain), I: 197

"Pueblo Revolt, The" (Sando), Supp. IV Part 2: 510

Puella (Dickey), Supp. IV Part 1: 178, 185

Pulitzer, Alfred, Retro. Supp. I: 257

Pull Down Vanity (Fiedler), Supp. XIII: 103

Pullman, George, Supp. I Part 1: 9

"Pullman Car Hiawatha" (Wilder), IV: 365–366

Pull My Daisy (film), Supp. XII: 126–127

"Pulpit and the Pew, The" (Holmes), Supp. I Part 1: 302

"Pulse-Beats and Pen-Strokes" (Sandburg), III: 579

"Pump, The" (Humphrey), Supp. IX: 101

Pump House Gang, The (Wolfe), Supp. III Part 2: 575, 578, 580, 581

Punch, Brothers, Punch and Other Sketches (Twain), IV: 200

Punch: The Immortal Liar, Documents in His History (Aiken), I: 57, 61

Punishment Without Vengeance (Vega; Merwin, trans.), Supp. III Part 1: 341, 347

"Pupil" (F. Barthelme), Supp. XI: 26

"Pupil, The" (James), II: 331; Retro. Supp. I: 217, 219, 228

"Purchase" (Banks), Supp. V: 6

"Purchase of Some Golf Clubs, A" (O'Hara), III: 369

"Purdah" (Plath), Supp. I Part 2: 602

Purdy, Charles, Supp. VIII: 330

Purdy, James, Supp. VII: **269–285**

Purdy, Theodore, Supp. VIII: 153

"Pure and the Good, The: On Baseball and Backpaking" (Maclean), Supp. XIV: 222

"Pure Good of Theory, The" (Stevens), Retro. Supp. I: 310

Purgatorio (Dante), III: 182

Puritan Family (Morgan), Supp. I Part 1: 101

"Puritanical Pleasures" (Hardwick), Supp. III Part 1: 213–214

Puritan Origins of the American Self, The (Bercovitch), **Supp. I Part 1:** 99

Puritan Pronaos, The: Studies in the Intellectual Life of New England in the Seventeenth Century (Morison), **Supp. I Part 2:** 485

Puritans, The (P. Miller), **Supp. VIII:** 101

"Puritan's Ballad, The" (Wylie), **Supp. I Part 2:** 723

"Purloined Letter, The" (Poe), **Retro. Supp. II:** 271, 272

Purple Cane Road (Burke), **Supp. XIV:** 32, 33

Purple Decades, The (Wolfe), **Supp. III Part 2:** 584

"Purple Hat, The" (Welty), **IV:** 264

Purser, John T., **Supp. XIV:** 4

"Pursuit of Happiness" (Simpson), **Supp. IX:** 279

"Pursuit of Happiness, The" (Ashbery), **Supp. III Part 1:** 23

Pursuit of the Prodigal, The (Auchincloss), **Supp. IV Part 1:** 25

Pushcart at the Curb, A (Dos Passos), **I:** 478, 479

"Pushcart Man" (Hughes), **Supp. I Part 1:** 330

Pushcart Prize, XIII, The (Ford), **Supp. V:** 58

"Pushing 100" (Mora), **Supp. XIII:** 215

Pushkin, Aleksander, **III:** 246, 261, 262; **Retro. Supp. I:** 266, 269

Pussy, King of the Pirates (Acker), **Supp. XII:** 6–7

"Pussycat and the Expert Plumber Who Was a Man, The" (A. Miller), **III:** 146–147

Pussycat Fever (Acker), **Supp. XII:** 6

Putnam, George P., **II:** 314

Putnam, Phelps, **I:** 288

Putnam, Samuel, **II:** 26; **III:** 479; **Supp. III Part 2:** 615

"Put Off the Wedding Five Times and Nobody Comes to It" (Sandburg), **III:** 586–587

Puttenham, George, **Supp. I Part 1:** 113

Puttermesser Papers, The (Ozick), **Supp. V:** 269

"Putting on *Visit to a Small Planet*" (Vidal), **Supp. IV Part 2:** 683

Put Yourself in My Shoes (Carver), **Supp. III Part 1:** 139

"Put Yourself in My Shoes" (Carver), **Supp. III Part 1:** 139, 141

Puzo, Mario, **Supp. IV Part 1:** 390

"Puzzle of Modern Society, The" (Kazin), **Supp. VIII:** 103

Pygmalion (Shaw), **Supp. XII:** 14

Pyle, Ernie, **III:** 148; **Supp. V:** 240

Pylon (Faulkner), **II:** 64–65, 73; **Retro. Supp. I:** 84, 85

Pynchon, Thomas, **III:** 258; **Retro. Supp. I:** 278; **Retro. Supp. II:** 279, 324; **Supp. II Part 2:** 557, 617–638; **Supp. III Part 1:** 217; **Supp. IV Part 1:** 53, 279; **Supp. IV Part 2:** 570; **Supp. V:** 40, 44, 52; **Supp. VIII:** 14; **Supp. IX:** 207, 208, 212; **Supp. X:** 260, 301, 302; **Supp. XI:** 103; **Supp. XII:** 289; **Supp. XIV:** 49, 53, 54, 96

Pyrah, Gill, **Supp. V:** 126

"Pyramid Club, The" (Doctorow), **Supp. IV Part 1:** 234

"Pyrography" (Ashbery), **Supp. III Part 1:** 18

Pythagoras, **I:** 332

Pythagorean Silence (Howe), **Supp. IV Part 2:** 426, 428–429

"Qebehseneuf" (Goldbarth), **Supp. XII:** 186

"Quai d'Orléans" (Bishop), **Supp. I Part 1:** 89

"Quail for Mr. Forester" (Humphrey), **Supp. IX:** 94

"Quail in Autumn" (W. J. Smith), **Supp. XIII:** 334–335, 339

"Quaker Graveyard in Nantucket, The" (Lowell), **II:** 54, 550; **Retro. Supp. II:** 178, 186–187

"Quake Theory" (Olds), **Supp. X:** 203

Qualey, Carlton C., **Supp. I Part 2:** 650

"Quality Time" (Kingsolver), **Supp. VII:** 203

Quang-Ngau-chè, **III:** 473

Quarles, Francis, **I:** 178, 179

Quarry, The (Chesnutt), **Supp. XIV:** 76

"Quarry, The" (Nemerov), **III:** 272

Quarry, The: New Poems (Eberhart), **I:** 532, 539

Quartermain, Peter, **Supp. IV Part 2:** 423, 434

"Quaternions, The" (Bradstreet), **Supp. I Part 1:** 104–106, 114, 122

"Quatrains for Ishi" (Komunyakaa), **Supp. XIII:** 129

"Queen of the Blues" (Brooks), **Supp. III Part 1:** 75

Queen of the Damned, The (Rice), **Supp. VII:** 290, 292–293, 297, 299

Queen of the Mob (film), **Supp. XIII:** 170

"Queens of France" (Wilder), **IV:** 365

"Queen's Twin, The" (Jewett), **Retro. Supp. II:** 138

Queen's Twin, The, and Other Stories (Jewett), **Retro. Supp. II:** 140

Queen Victoria (Strachey), **Supp. I Part 2:** 485, 494; **Supp. XIV:** 342

Queer (Burroughs), **Supp. III Part 1:** 93–102

"Queer Beer" (Hansberry), **Supp. IV Part 1:** 374

"Quelques considérations sur la méthode subjective" (James), **II:** 345–346

"Question" (Swenson), **Supp. IV Part 2:** 640

"Question and Answer" (Hughes), **Retro. Supp. I:** 211

"Questioning Faces" (Frost), **Retro. Supp. I:** 141

"Question Mark in the Circle, The" (Stegner), **Supp. IV Part 2:** 597

"Questionnaire, The" (Snodgrass), **Supp. VI:** 318

"Question of Fidelity, A" (Beauvoir), **Supp. IX:** 4

"Question of Our Speech, The" (Ozick), **Supp. V:** 272

"Question of Simone de Beauvoir, The" (Algren), **Supp. IX:** 4

"Questions of Geography" (Hollander), **Supp. I Part 1:** 96

Questions of Travel (Bishop), **Retro. Supp. II: 46–48; Supp. I Part 1:** 72, 83, 92, 94

"Questions of Travel" (Bishop), **Retro. Supp. II:** 47

"Questions to Tourists Stopped by a Pineapple Field" (Merwin), **Supp. III Part 1:** 355

"Questions without Answers" (T. Williams), **IV:** 384

"Quest of the Purple-Fringed, The" (Frost), **Retro. Supp. I:** 139

Quest of the Silver Fleece, The (Du Bois), **Supp. II Part 1:** 176–178

Quevedo y Villegas, Francisco Gómez, **Retro. Supp. I:** 423

Quickly: A Column for Slow Readers (Mailer), **Retro. Supp. II:** 202

"Quies," (Pound), **Retro. Supp. I:** 413

Quiet Days in Clichy (H. Miller), **III:** 170, 178, 183–184, 187

"Quiet Desperation" (Simpson), **Supp. IX:** 277–278

"Quiet of the Mind" (Nye), **Supp. XIII:** 284

Quinlan, Kathleen, **Supp. X:** 80

Quinn, John, **III:** 471

Quinn, Paul, **Supp. V:** 71

Quinn, Sister M. Bernetta, **III:** 479; **IV:** 421

Quinn, Vincent, **I:** 386, 401, 402; **Supp. I Part 1:** 270

"Quinnapoxet" (Kunitz), **Supp. III Part 1:** 263

Quinn's Book (Kennedy), **Supp. VII:** 133, 148–150, 153

Quintero, José, **III:** 403

Quintilian, **IV:** 123

Quinzaine for This Yule, A (Pound), **Retro. Supp. I:** 285

Quite Contrary: The Mary and Newt Story (Dixon), **Supp. XII: 144,** 153

Quod Erat Demonstrandum (Stein), **IV:** 34

Quo Vadis? (Sienkiewicz), **Supp. IV Part 2:** 518

Raab, Max, **Supp. XI:** 309

"Rabbi, The" (Hayden), **Supp. II Part 1:** 363, 369

Rabbit, Run (Updike), **IV:** 214, 223, 230–234; **Retro. Supp. I:** 320, 325, 326, 327, 331, 333, 335; **Supp. XI:** 140; **Supp. XII:** 298

"Rabbit, The" (Barnes), **Supp. III Part 1:** 34

Rabbit at Rest (Updike), **Retro. Supp. I:** 334

Rabbit Is Rich (Updike), **Retro. Supp. I:** 334

Rabbit novels (Updike), **Supp. V:** 269

Rabbit Redux (Updike), **IV:** 214; **Retro. Supp. I:** 332, 333

"Rabbits Who Caused All the Trouble, The" (Thurber), **Supp. I Part 2:** 610

Rabelais, and His World (Bakhtin), **Retro. Supp. II:** 273

Rabelais, François, **I:** 130; **II:** 111, 112, 302, 535; **III:** 77, 78, 174, 182; **IV:** 68; **Supp. I Part 2:** 461

Rabelais and His World (Bakhtin), **Supp. X:** 120

Rabinbach, Anson, **Supp. XII:** 166

Rabinowitz, Paula, **Supp. V:** 161

"Race" (Emerson), **II:** 6

"Race Contacts and Inter-Racial Relations" (Locke), **Supp. XIV:** 211

"Race Contacts and Inter-Racial Relations: A Study in the Theory and Practice of Race" (lectures, Locke), **Supp. XIV:** 199, 209

Race Contacts and Interracial Relations: Lectures on the Theory and Practice of Race (Locke, Stewart, ed.), **Supp. XIV:** 196, **209–210**

"'RACE LINE' IS A PRODUCT OF CAPITALISM, THE" (Baraka), **Supp. II Part 1:** 61

"Race of Life, The" (Thurber), **Supp. I Part 2:** 614

"Race Problems and Modern Society"

(Toomer), **Supp. III Part 2:** 486

Race Questions, Provincialism, and Other American Problems (Royce), **Supp. XIV:** 199

"Race Riot, Tulsa, 1921" (Olds), **Supp. X:** 205

Race Rock (Matthiessen), **Supp. V:** 201

"Races, The" (Lowell), **II:** 554

Rachel Carson: Witness for Nature (Lear), **Supp. IX:** 19

"Racial Progress and Race Adjustment" (Locke), **Supp. XIV:** 210

Racine, Jean Baptiste, **II:** 543, 573; **III:** 145, 151, 152, 160; **IV:** 317, 368, 370; **Supp. I Part 2:** 716

"Radical" (Moore), **III:** 211

"Radical Chic" (Wolfe), **Supp. III Part 2:** 577–578, 584, 585

Radical Chic & Mau-mauing the Flak Catchers (Wolfe), **Supp. III Part 2:** 577–578

Radical Empiricism of William James, The (Wild), **II:** 362, 363–364

Radicalism in America, The (Lasch), **I:** 259

"Radical Jewish Humanism: The Vision of E. L. Doctorow" (Clayton), **Supp. IV Part 1:** 238

"Radically Condensed History of Postindustrial Life, A" (Wallace), **Supp. X:** 309

"Radio" (O'Hara), **III:** 369

"Radio Pope" (Goldbarth), **Supp. XII:** 188, 192

Raditzer (Matthiessen), **Supp. V:** 201

Radkin, Paul, **Supp. I Part 2:** 539

"Rafaela Who Drinks Coconut & Papaya Juice on Tuesdays" (Cisneros), **Supp. VII:** 63

Rafelson, Bob, **Supp. XIV:** 241

Raffalovich, Marc-André, **Supp. XIV:** 335

"Raft, The" (Lindsay), **Supp. I Part 2:** 393

Rag and Bone Shop of the Heart, The: Poems for Men (Bly, Hillman, and Meade, eds.), **Supp. IV Part 1:** 67

Rage to Live, A (O'Hara), **III:** 361

Raglan, Lord, **I:** 135

Rago, Henry, **Supp. III Part 2:** 624, 628, 629

Ragtime (Doctorow), **Retro. Supp. II:** 108; **Supp. IV Part 1:** 217, 222–224, 231, 232, 233, 234, 237, 238; **Supp. V:** 45

"Ragtime" (Doctorow), **Supp. IV Part 1:** 234

Ragtime (film), **Supp. IV Part 1:** 236

Ragtime (musical, McNally), **Supp. XIII:** 207

Rahv, Philip, **Retro. Supp. I:** 112; **Supp. II Part 1:** 136; **Supp. VIII:** 96; **Supp. IX:** 8; **Supp. XIV:** 3

"Raid" (Hughes), **Retro. Supp. I:** 208

Raids on the Unspeakable (Merton), **Supp. VIII:** 201, 208

Rail, DeWayne, **Supp. XIII:** 312

"Rain and the Rhinoceros" (Merton), **Supp. VIII:** 201

Rainbow, The (Lawrence), **III:** 27

"Rainbows" (Marquand), **III:** 56

Rainbow Tulip, The (Mora), **Supp. XIII:** 221

"Rain Country" (Haines), **Supp. XII:** 210

"Rain-Dream, A" (Bryant), **Supp. I Part 1:** 164

Raine, Kathleen, **I:** 522, 527

"Rain Falling Now, The" (Dunn), **Supp. XI:** 147

"Rain in the Heart" (Taylor), **Supp. V:** 317, 319

Rain in the Trees, The (Merwin), **Supp. III Part 1:** 340, 342, 345, 349, 354–356

"Rainmaker, The" (Humphrey), **Supp. IX:** 101

Rainwater, Catherine, **Supp. V:** 272

"Rainy Day" (Longfellow), **II:** 498

"Rainy Day, The" (Buck), **Supp. II Part 1:** 127

"Rainy Mountain Cemetery" (Momaday), **Supp. IV Part 2:** 486

Rainy Mountain Christmas Doll (painting) (Momaday), **Supp. IV Part 2:** 493

"Rainy Season: Sub-Tropics" (Bishop), **Supp. I Part 1:** 93

"Raise High the Roof Beam, Carpenters" (Salinger), **III:** 567–569, 571

Raise High the Roof Beam, Carpenters; and Seymour: An Introduction (Salinger), **III:** 552, 567–571, 572

Raise Race Rays Raze: Essays Since 1965 (Baraka), **Supp. II Part 1:** 47, 52, 55

Raisin (musical), **Supp. IV Part 1:** 374

Raising Demons (Jackson), **Supp. IX: 125–126**

Raisin in the Sun, A (film: Columbia Pictures), **Supp. IV Part 1:** 360, 367

Raisin in the Sun, A (Hansberry), **Supp. IV Part 1:** 359, 360, 361, 362–364; **Supp. VIII:** 343

Raisin in the Sun, A (television film: American Playhouse), **Supp. IV Part 1:** 367, 374

Raisin in the Sun, A (unproduced screenplay) (Hansberry), **Supp. IV**

Part 1: 360

Rajan, R., **I:** 390

"Rake, The" (Mamet), **Supp. XIV:** 240

Rake's Progress, The (opera), **Supp. II Part 1:** 24

Rakosi, Carl, **Supp. III Part 2:** 614, 615, 616, 617, 618, 621, 629; **Supp. XIV:** 286, 287

Ralegh, Sir Walter, **Supp. I Part 1:** 98

Raleigh, John Henry, **IV:** 366

Ramakrishna, Sri, **III:** 567

Ramakrishna and His Disciples (Isherwood), **Supp. XIV:** 164

Ramazani, Jahan, **Supp. IV Part 2:** 450

"Ramble of Aphasia, A" (O. Henry), **Supp. II Part 1:** 410

Ramey, Phillip, **Supp. IV Part 1:** 94

Rampersad, Arnold, **Retro. Supp. I:** 196, 200, 201, 204; **Supp. IV Part 1:** 244, 250

Rampling, Anne, **Supp. VII:** 201. *See also* Rice, Anne

Rampling, Charlotte, **Supp. IX:** 253

Ramsey, Priscilla R., **Supp. IV Part 1:** 15

Ramus, Petrus, **Supp. I Part 1:** 104

Rand, Ayn, **Supp. I Part 1:** 294; **Supp. IV Part 2: 517–535**

Randall, Jarrell, 1914–1965 (Lowell, Taylor, and Warren, eds.), **II:** 368, 385

Randall, John H., **III:** 605

Randolph, John, **I:** 5–6

"Range-Finding" (Frost), **Retro. Supp. I:** 131

Rangoon (F. Barthelme), **Supp. XI:** 25

Rank, Otto, **I:** 135; **Supp. IX:** 105; **Supp. X:** 183, 185, 193

Ranke, Leopold von, **Supp. I Part 2:** 492

Rankin, Daniel, **Retro. Supp. II:** 57, 72; **Supp. I Part 1:** 200, 203, 225

Ransohoff, Martin, **Supp. XI:** 305, 306

Ransom, John Crowe, **I:** 265, 301; **II:** 34, 367, 385, 389, 536–537, 542; **III:** 454, **480–502,** 549; **IV:** 121, 122, 123, 124, 125, 127, 134, 140, 141, 236, 237, 433; **Retro. Supp. I:** 90; **Retro. Supp. II:** 176, 177, 178, 183, 220, 228, 246; **Supp. I Part 1:** 80, 361; **Supp. I Part 2:** 423; **Supp. II Part 1:** 90, 91, 136, 137, 139, 318; **Supp. II Part 2:** 639; **Supp. III Part 1:** 318; **Supp. III Part 2:** 542, 591; **Supp. IV Part 1:** 217; **Supp. V:** 315, 331, 337; **Supp. X:** 25, 56, 58; **Supp. XIV:** 1

"Rape" (Coleman), **Supp. XI:** 89–90

"Rape, The" (Baraka), **Supp. II Part 1:** 40

Rape of Bunny Stuntz, The (Gurney), **Supp. V:** 109

"Rape of Philomel, The" (Shapiro), **Supp. II Part 2:** 720

"Rape of the Lock, The" (Pope), **Supp. XIV:** 8

Raphael, **I:** 15; **III:** 505, 521, 524; **Supp. I Part 1:** 363

"Rapist" (Dunn), **Supp. XI:** 144

Rap on Race, A (Baldwin and Mead), **Supp. I Part 1:** 66

"Rappaccini's Daughter" (Hawthorne), **II:** 229

"Rapunzel" (Sexton), **Supp. II Part 2:** 691

Rare & Endangered Species: A Novella & Short Stories (Bausch), **Supp. VII:** 51, 54

"Raree Show" (MacLeish), **III:** 9

Rascoe, Burton, **III:** 106, 115

"Raskolnikov" (Simic), **Supp. VIII:** 282

Rasmussen, Douglas, **Supp. IV Part 2:** 528, 530

Rasselas (Johnson), **Supp. XI:** 209

"Ration" (Baraka), **Supp. II Part 1:** 50

"Rationale of Verse, The" (Poe), **III:** 427–428; **Retro. Supp. II:** 266

Ratner's Star (DeLillo), **Supp. VI:** 1, 2, 3, 4, 10, 12, 14

"Rat of Faith, The" (Levine), **Supp. V:** 192

Rattigan, Terence, **III:** 152

Raugh, Joseph, **Supp. I Part 1:** 286

Rauschenbusch, Walter, **III:** 293; **Supp. I Part 1:** 7

Ravelstein (Bellow), **Retro. Supp. II:** 19, 33–34

Raven, Simon, **Supp. XII:** 241

"Raven, The" (Poe), **III:** 413, 421–422, 426; **Retro. Supp. II:** 265, 266–267

Raven, The, and Other Poems (Poe), **III:** 413

Ravenal, Shannon, **Supp. IV Part 1:** 93

"Raven Days, The" (Lanier), **Supp. I Part 1:** 351

Ravenna, Michael. *See* Welty, Eudora

Raven's Road (Gunn Allen), **Supp. IV Part 1:** 330, 335

Rawlings, Marjorie Kinnan, **Supp. X: 219–237**

Ray, David, **Supp. IV Part 1:** 61

Ray, Jeanne Wilkinson, **Supp. XII:** 308, 310

Ray, John, **II:** 111, 112

Ray, Man, **IV:** 404; **Retro. Supp. I:** 416; **Supp. XII:** 124

Ray Bradbury Theatre, The (television show), **Supp. IV Part 1:** 103

Reactionary Essays on Poetry and Ideas (Tate), **Supp. II Part 1:** 106, 146

Read, Deborah, **II:** 122

Read, Forrest, **III:** 478

Read, Herbert, **I:** 523; **II:** 372–373, 377–378; **Retro. Supp. I:** 54; **Supp. III Part 1:** 273; **Supp. III Part 2:** 624, 626

Read, William A., **Supp. XIV:** 4

Reade, Charles, **Supp. I Part 2:** 580

Reader, Constant. *See* Parker, Dorothy

Reader, Dennis J., **Supp. I Part 2:** 454

Reader's Encyclopedia, The: An Encyclopedia of World Literature and the Arts (W. Benét), **Supp. XI:** 44

Reader's Guide to William Gaddis's The Recognitions, A (Moore), **Supp. IV Part 1:** 283

"Reader's Tale, A" (Doty), **Supp. XI:** 119, 120, 128, 129

"Reading" (Auden), **Supp. VIII:** 155

"Reading Group Guide," **Supp. XI:** 244–245

"Reading Lao Tzu Again in the New Year" (Wright), **Supp. V:** 343

"Reading Late of the Death of Keats" (Kenyon), **Supp. VII:** 169

"Reading Myself" (Lowell), **II:** 555

Reading Myself and Others (Roth), **Retro. Supp. II:** 282; **Supp. V:** 45

"Reading *Ode to the West Wind* 25 Years Later" (McCarriston), **Supp. XIV:** 271–272

"Reading of the Psalm, The" (Francis), **Supp. IX:** 79

"Reading Philosophy at Night" (Simic), **Supp. VIII:** 272

Reading Rilke: Reflections on the Problems of Translation (Gass), **Supp. VI:** 92, **93–94**

"Reading Rorty and Paul Celan One Morning in Early June" (Wright), **Supp. V:** 343

"Readings of History" (Rich), **Supp. I Part 2:** 554

"Reading the Signs, Empowering the Eye" (Bambara), **Supp. XI:** 17–18

Reading the Spirit (Eberhart), **I:** 525, 527, 530

"Ready Or Not" (Baraka), **Supp. II Part 1:** 50

Reagan, Ronald, **Supp. IV Part 1:** 224–225

"Real Class" (Vidal), **Supp. IV Part 1:** 35

Real Dope, The (Lardner), **II:** 422–423

"Real Estate" (Moore), **Supp. X:** 178

"Real Gone Guy, A" (McGrath), **Supp. X:** 117

"Real Horatio Alger Story, The" (Cowley), **Supp. II Part 1:** 143

"Realities" (MacLeish), **III:** 4

"Reality in America" (Trilling), **Supp. III Part 2:** 495, 502

"Reality! Reality! What Is It?" (Eberhart), **I:** 536

Reality Sandwiches, 1953–60 (Ginsberg), **Supp. II Part 1:** 315, 320

Real Life of Sebastian Knight, The (Nabokov), **III:** 246; **Retro. Supp. I:** 266, 269, 270, 274

"Really Good Jazz Piano, A" (Yates), **Supp. XI:** 342

Real Presence: A Novel (Bausch), **Supp. VII:** 42–43, 50

"Real Revolution Is Love, The" (Harjo), **Supp. XII:** 224, 225–226

"Real Thing, The" (H. James), **Retro. Supp. I:** 228; **Retro. Supp. II:** 223

"Real Two-Party System" (Vidal), **Supp. IV Part 2:** 679

Real West Marginal Way, The (Hugo), **Supp. VI:** 132, 134

"Real World around Us, The" (Carson), **Supp. IX:** 21

Reaper Essays, The (Jarman and McDowell), **Supp. IX:** 270

"Reapers" (Toomer), **Supp. III Part 2:** 481; **Supp. IX:** 312

"Reason and Race: A Review of the Literature of the Negro for 1946" (Locke), **Supp. XIV:** 206

"Reason for Moving, A" (Strand), **Supp. IV Part 2:** 624

"Reason for Stories, The: Toward a Moral Fiction" (Stone), **Supp. V:** 298, 300

Reasons for Moving (Strand), **Supp. IV Part 2:** 624–626, 626

"Reasons for Music" (MacLeish), **III:** 19

"Rebellion" (Lowell), **Retro. Supp. II:** 187

Rebel Powers (Bausch), **Supp. VII:** 41, 45–46, 49–51

Rebel without a Cause (film), **Supp. XII:** 9

"Rebirth of God and the Death of Man, The " (Fiedler), **Supp. XIII:** 108

Rebolledo, Tey Diana, **Supp. XIII:** 214

Recapitulation (Stegner), **Supp. IV Part 2:** 598, 600, 612–613

"Recapitulation, The" (Eberhart), **I:** 522

"Recapitulations" (Shapiro), **Supp. II Part 2:** 701, 702, 708, 710–711

"Recencies in Poetry" (Zukofsky), **Supp. III Part 2:** 615

Recent Killing, A (Baraka), **Supp. II Part 1:** 55

"Recent Negro Fiction" (Ellison), **Supp. II Part 1:** 233, 235

"Recital, The" (Ashbery), **Supp. III Part 1:** 14

"Recitative" (H. Crane), **I:** 390; **Retro. Supp. II:** 78

Reckless Eyeballing (Reed), **Supp. X:** 241

Recognitions, The (Gaddis), **Supp. IV Part 1:** 279, 280–285, 286, 287, 288, 289, 291, 292, 294

Recollections of Logan Pearsall Smith: The Story of a Friendship (Gathorne-Hardy), **Supp. XIV:** 344

"Reconciliation" (Whitman), **IV:** 347

"Reconstructed but Unregenerate" (Ransom), **III:** 496

"Reconstruction and Its Benefits" (Du Bois), **Supp. II Part 1:** 171

Recovering (Sarton), **Supp. VIII:** 264

Recovering the U.S. Hispanic Literary Heritage (Paredes), **Supp. XIII:** 320

"Recovery" (Dove), **Supp. IV Part 1:** 248

Rector of Justin, The (Auchincloss), **Supp. IV Part 1:** 21, 23, 27–30, 36

"RED AUTUMN" (Baraka), **Supp. II Part 1:** 55

Red Badge of Courage, The (Crane), **I:** 201, 207, 212, 405, 406, 407, 408, 412–416, 419, 421, 422, 423, 477, 506; **II:** 264; **III:** 317; **IV:** 350; **Retro. Supp. II:** 108; **Supp. IV Part 1:** 380; **Supp. XIV:** 51

"Redbreast in Tampa" (Lanier), **Supp. I Part 1:** 364

"Red Brocade" (Nye), **Supp. XIII:** 288

Redburn: His First Voyage (Melville), **III:** 79–80, 84; **Retro. Supp. I:** 245, 247–248, 249

"Red Carpet for Shelley, A" (Wylie), **Supp. I Part 2:** 724

"Red Clowns" (Cisneros), **Supp. VII:** 63

Red Coal, The (Stern), **Supp. IX:** 291–292

Red Coat, The (Shanley), **Supp. XIV:** 316–317

"Red Cross" (Hughes), **Retro. Supp. I:** 205

Red Cross (Shepard), **Supp. III Part 2:** 440, 446

Red Death, A (Mosley), **Supp. XIII:** 237, 239, 240

Redding, Saunders, **Supp. I Part 1:** 332, 333

Reddings, J. Saunders, **Supp. IV Part 1:** 164

Red Dust (Levine), **Supp. V:** 178, 183–184, 188

"Red Dust" (Levine), **Supp. V:** 184

"Redemption" (Gardner), **Supp. VI:** 72

"Redeployment" (Nemerov), **III:** 267, 272

Redfield, Robert, **IV:** 475

Redford, Robert, **Supp. IX:** 253, 259; **Supp. XIII:** 267; **Supp. XIV:** 223

Redgrave, Lynn, **Supp. V:** 107

Red Harvest (Hammett), **Supp. IV Part 1:** 346–348, 348; **Supp. IV Part 2:** 468

Red-headed Woman (film), **Retro. Supp. I:** 110

"Red Horse Wind over Albuquerque" (Harjo), **Supp. XII:** 219

Red Hot Vacuum, The (Solotaroff), **Retro. Supp. II:** 281

"Red Leaves" (Faulkner), **II:** 72

"Red Meat: What Difference Did Stesichoros Make?" (Carson), **Supp. XII:** 107

"Red Pawn" (Rand), **Supp. IV Part 2:** 520

Red Pony, The (Steinbeck), **IV:** 50, 51, 58, 70

Redrawing the Boundaries (Fisher), **Retro. Supp. I:** 39

Red Roses for Bronze (Doolittle), **Supp. I Part 1:** 253, 268, 271

Red Rover, The (Cooper), **I:** 342–343, 355

"Red Silk Stockings" (Hughes), **Retro. Supp. I:** 200

Redskins, The (Cooper), **I:** 351, 353

Red Suitcase (Nye), **Supp. XIII:** 277, 278, 287

"Red Wheelbarrow, The" (W. C. Williams), **IV:** 411–412; **Retro. Supp. I:** 419, 430

"Red Wind" (Chandler), **Supp. IV Part 1:** 122

"Redwings" (Wright), **Supp. III Part 2:** 603

Reed, Ishmael, **Retro. Supp. II:** 111, 324–325; **Supp. II Part 1:** 34; **Supp. X:** 239–257, 331; **Supp. XIII:** 181, 182

Reed, John, **I:** 48, 476, 483; **Supp. X:** 136

Reed, Lou, **Retro. Supp. II:** 266

"Reedbeds of the Hackensack, The" (Clampitt), **Supp. IX:** 41

"Reed of Pan, A" (McCullers), **II:** 585

Reedy, Billy, **Retro. Supp. II:** 65, 67, 71, 73

Reedy, William Marion, **Supp. I Part 2:** 456, 461, 465

Reef, The (Wharton), **IV:** 317–318, 322; **Retro. Supp. I:** 372, **373–374**

Reena and Other Stories (Marshall), **Supp. XI:** 275, 277, 278

Reeve's Tale (Chaucer), **I:** 131

"Reflections" (Komunyakaa), **Supp. XIII:** 117

Reflections: Thinking Part I (Arendt), **Supp. I Part 2:** 570

Reflections at Fifty and Other Essays (Farrell), **II:** 49

"Reflections by a Fire" (Sarton), **Supp. VIII:** 259

Reflections in a Golden Eye (McCullers), **II:** 586, 588, 593–596, 604; **IV:** 384, 396

Reflections of a Jacobite (Auchincloss), **Supp. IV Part 1:** 31

Reflections on a Gift of Watermelon Pickle (Dunning), **Supp. XIV:** 126

Reflections on Poetry and Poetics (Nemerov), **III:** 269

"Reflections on the Constitution of Nature" (Freneau), **Supp. II Part 1:** 274

"Reflections on the Death of the Reader" (Morris), **III:** 237

Reflections on the End of an Era (Niebuhr), **III:** 297–298

"Reflections on the Life and Death of Lord Clive" (Paine), **Supp. I Part 2:** 505

Reflections on the Revolution in France (Burke), **Supp. I Part 2:** 511, 512

"Reflex Action and Theism" (James), **II:** 345, 363

"Refrains/Remains/Reminders" (Goldbarth), **Supp. XII:** 180–181, 181

"Refuge" (Kingsolver), **Supp. VII:** 208

"Refuge, A" (Goldbarth), **Supp. XII:** 190

Refugee Children: Theory, Research, and Services (Ahearn and Athey, eds.), **Supp. XI:** 184

"Refugees, The" (Jarrell), **II:** 371

Regarding Wave (Snyder), **Supp. VIII: 299–300**

Regina (Epstein), **Supp. XII: 170–171**

"Regional Literature of the South" (Rawlings), **Supp. X:** 228

"Regional Writer, The" (O'Connor), **Retro. Supp. II:** 223, 225

Régnier, Henri de, **II:** 528–529

Regulators, The (King), **Supp. V:** 141

Rehder, Robert, **Supp. IV Part 1:** 69

Reichel, Hans, **III:** 183

Reichl, Ruth, **Supp. X:** 79, 85

Reid, B. L., **II:** 41, 47

Reid, Thomas, **II:** 9; **Supp. I Part 1:** 151

Reign of Wonder, The (Tanner), **I:** 260

Rein, Yevgeny, **Supp. VIII:** 22

"Reincarnation" (Dickey), **Supp. IV Part 1:** 181–182

Reiner, Carl, **Supp. IV Part 2:** 591

Reinfeld, Linda, **Supp. IV Part 2:** 421

Reinventing the Enemy's Language: Contemporary Native Women's Writing of North America (Bird and Harjo, eds.), **Supp. XII:** 216, 217

Reisman, Jerry, **Supp. III Part 2:** 618

Reitlinger, Gerald, **Supp. XII:** 161

Reivers, The: A Reminiscence (Faulkner), **I:** 305; **II:** 57, 73; **Retro. Supp. I:** 74, 82, 91

"Rejoicings" (Stern), **Supp. IX:** 289–290

Rejoicings: Selected Poems, 1966–1972 (Stern), **Supp. IX: 289–290**

Relation of My Imprisonment, The (Banks), **Supp. V:** 8, 12–13

"Relations between Poetry and Painting, The" (Stevens), **Retro. Supp. I:** 312

Relations of the Alabama-Georgia Dialect to the Provincial Dialects of Great Britain, The (Brooks), **Supp. XIV:** 3

"Relativity of Beauty, The" (Rawlings), **Supp. X:** 226

Relearning the Alphabet (Levertov), **Supp. III Part 1:** 280, 281

"Release, The" (MacLeish), **III:** 16

Reles, Abe ("Kid Twist"), **Supp. IV Part 1:** 382

"Relevance of an Impossible Ethical Ideal, The" (Niebuhr), **III:** 298

"Religion" (Dunbar), **Supp. II Part 1:** 199

"Religion" (Emerson), **II:** 6

Religion of Nature Delineated, The (Wollaston), **II:** 108

Religious Rebel, A: The Letters of "H. W. S." (Mrs. Pearsall Smith) (L. P. Smith), **Supp. XIV:** 349

"Reluctance" (Frost), **II:** 153

Remains (Snodgrass), **Supp. VI:** 311, **313–314**

"Remains, The" (Strand), **Supp. IV Part 2:** 627

"Remarks on Spencer's *Definition of Mind as Correspondence*" (James), **II:** 345

Remarque, Erich Maria, **Retro. Supp. I:** 113; **Supp. IV Part 1:** 380

Rembrandt, **II:** 536; **IV:** 310; **Supp. IV Part 1:** 390, 391

"Rembrandt, The" (Wharton), **IV:** 310

"Rembrandt's Hat" (Malamud), **Supp. I Part 2:** 435, 437

Rembrandt Takes a Walk (Strand), **Supp. IV Part 2:** 631

"Rembrandt to Rembrandt" (Robinson), **III:** 521–522

Remembered Earth, The: An Anthology of Contemporary Native American Literature (Hobson, ed.), **Supp. IV Part 1:** 321

Remembered Yesterdays (Johnson), **Supp. IX:** 184

"Remembering" (Angelou), **Supp. IV Part 1:** 15

"Remembering Allen Tate" (Cowley), **Supp. II Part 1:** 153

"Remembering Barthes" (Sontag), **Supp. III Part 2:** 451, 471

"Remembering Guston" (Kunitz), **Supp. III Part 1:** 257

"Remembering James Laughlin" (Karr), **Supp. XI:** 242

Remembering Laughter (Stegner), **Supp. IV Part 2:** 598, 606, 607, 608, 611, 614

"Remembering Lobo" (Mora), **Supp. XIII:** 220, 227

"Remembering My Father" (Berry), **Supp. X:** 23

"Remembering that Island" (McGrath), **Supp. X:** 116

"Remembering the Children of Auschwitz" (McGrath), **Supp. X:** 127

"Remembering the Lost World" (Jarrell), **II:** 388

"Remembering the Sixties" (Simpson), **Supp. IX:** 279

Remember Me to Tom (T. Williams), **IV:** 379–380

"Remember the Moon Survives" (Kingsolver), **Supp. VII:** 209

Remember to Remember (H. Miller), **III:** 186

Remembrance of Things Past (Proust), **Supp. IV Part 2:** 600; **Supp. XII:** 9; **Supp. XIII:** 44

Remembrance Rock (Sandburg), **III:** 590

Reminiscence, A (Ashbery), **Supp. III Part 1:** 2

"Remora" (Merrill), **Supp. III Part 1:** 326

"Removal" (White), **Supp. I Part 2:** 664–665

"Removal, The" (Merwin), **Supp. III Part 1:** 350, 351

Removed from Time (Matthews and

Feeney), **Supp. IX:** 154

Remsen, Ira, **Supp. I Part 1:** 369

"Rémy de Gourmont, A Distinction" (Pound), **III:** 467

Renaissance in the South (Bradbury), **I:** 288–289

"Renaming the Kings" (Levine), **Supp. V:** 184

Renan, Joseph Ernest, **II:** 86; **IV:** 440, 444

Renard, Jules, **IV:** 79

"Renascence" (Millay), **III:** 123, 125–126, 128

Renault, Mary, **Supp. IV Part 2:** 685

"Rendezvous, The" (Kumin), **Supp. IV Part 2:** 455

René, Norman, **Supp. X:** 146, 152

"Renegade, The" (Jackson), **Supp. IX:** 120

Renewal of Life series (Mumford), **Supp. II Part 2:** 476, 479, 481, 482, 485, 495, 497

Renoir, Jean, **Supp. XII:** 259

Renouvrier, Charles, **II:** 344–345, 346

"Renunciation" (Banks), **Supp. V:** 10

Renza, Louis A., **Retro. Supp. II:** 142

Repent in Haste (Marquand), **III:** 59

Reperusals and Re-Collections (L. P. Smith), **Supp. XIV:** 346–347

"Repetitive Heart, The: Eleven Poems in Imitation of the Fugue Form" (Schwartz), **Supp. II Part 2:** 645–646

"Replacing Regionalism" (Murphy), **Retro. Supp. II:** 143

Replansky, Naomi, **Supp. X:** 119

"Reply to Mr. Wordsworth" (MacLeish), **III:** 19

"Report from a Forest Logged by the Weyhaeuser Company" (Wagoner), **Supp. IX:** 328

"Report from North Vietnam" (Paley), **Supp. VI:** 227

Report from Part One (Brooks), **Supp. III Part 1:** 70, 72, 80, 82–85

Report from Part Two (Brooks), **Supp. III Part 1:** 87

Report on a Game Survey of the North Central States (Leopold), **Supp. XIV:** 182

"Report on the Barnhouse Effect" (Vonnegut), **Supp. II Part 2:** 756

"Report to Crazy Horse" (Stafford), **Supp. XI:** 324–325

"Repose of Rivers" (H. Crane), **I:** 393; **Retro. Supp. II:** 78, 81

"Representation and the War for Reality" (Gass), **Supp. VI:** 88

Representative Men (Emerson), **II:** 1, 5–6, 8

"Representing Far Places" (Stafford), **Supp. XI:** 321

"REPRISE OF ONE OF A. G.'S BEST POEMS" (Baraka), **Supp. II Part 1:** 59

Republic (Plato), **I:** 485

"Republican Manifesto, A" (Paine), **Supp. I Part 2:** 511

Republic of Love, The (Shields), **Supp. VII:** 323–324, 326, 327

"Requa" (Olsen), **Supp. XIII:** 294, **302–303**, 304

Requa, Kenneth A., **Supp. I Part 1:** 107

"Requa I" (Olsen). See "Requa" (Olsen)

"Request for Offering" (Eberhart), **I:** 526

"Requiem" (Akhmatova), **Supp. VIII:** 20

"Requiem" (LaBastille), **Supp. X:** 105

Requiem for a Nun (Faulkner), **II:** 57, 72–73

Requiem for Harlem (H. Roth), **Supp. IX:** 235, 236, **240–242**

"Rescue, The" (Updike), **IV:** 214

Rescued Year, The (Stafford), **Supp. XI: 321–322**

"Rescued Year, The" (Stafford), **Supp. XI:** 322, 323

"Rescue with Yul Brynner" (Moore), **III:** 215

"Resemblance" (Bishop), **Supp. I Part 1:** 86

"Resemblance between a Violin Case and a Coffin, A" (T. Williams), **IV:** 378–379

"Reservations" (Taylor), **Supp. V:** 323

"Reserved Memorials" (Mather), **Supp. II Part 2:** 446, 449

"Resistance to Civil Government" (Thoreau), **Supp. X:** 27, 28

Resist Much, Obey Little (Berry), **Supp. XIII:** 2

Resources of Hope (R. Williams), **Supp. IX:** 146

"Respectable Place, A" (O'Hara), **III:** 369

"Respectable Woman, A" (Chopin), **Retro. Supp. II:** 66

Responses (Wilbur), **Supp. III Part 2:** 541

"Response to a Rumor that the Oldest Whorehouse in Wheeling, West Virginia, Has Been Condemned" (Wright), **Supp. III Part 2:** 602

Restif de La Bretonne, Nicolas, **III:** 175

"Rest of Life, The" (Gordon), **Supp. IV Part 1:** 311

Rest of Life, The: Three Novellas (Gordon), **Supp. IV Part 1:** 310–312

Rest of the Way, The (McClatchy), **Supp. XII:** 255, **258–259**

Restoration comedy, **Supp. I Part 2:** 617

"Restraint" (F. Barthelme), **Supp. XI:** 26

"Result" (Emerson), **II:** 6

"Résumé" (Parker), **Supp. IX:** 189

"Resurrection" (Harjo), **Supp. XII:** 224

Resurrection, The (Gardner), **Supp. VI:** 61, 63, **64–65**, 68, 69, 73, 74

"Retort" (Hay), **Supp. XIV:** 133

Retrieval System, The (Kumin), **Supp. IV Part 2:** 449, 451, 452

"Retrievers in Translation" (Doty), **Supp. XI:** 132

"Retroduction to American History" (Tate), **IV:** 129

"Retrospects and Prospects" (Lanier), **Supp. I Part 1:** 352

"Return" (Corso), **Supp. XII:** 135

"Return" (Creeley), **Supp. IV Part 1:** 141, 145

"Return" (MacLeish), **III:** 12

"Return: An Elegy, The" (Warren), **IV:** 239

"Return: Buffalo" (Hogan), **Supp. IV Part 1:** 411

"Return, The" (Pound), **Retro. Supp. I:** 288

"Return, The" (Roethke), **III:** 533

"Return, The: Orihuela, 1965" (Levine), **Supp. V:** 194

"Returning" (Komunyakaa), **Supp. XIII:** 122

"Returning a Lost Child" (Glück), **Supp. V:** 81

"Returning from the Enemy" (Harjo), **Supp. XII:** 229–230

"Returning the Borrowed Road" (Komunyakaa), **Supp. XIII:** 113, 133

"Return of Alcibiade, The" (Chopin), **Retro. Supp. II:** 58, 64

Return of Ansel Gibbs, The (Buechner), **III:** 310; **Supp. XII: 48**

"Return of Spring" (Winters), **Supp. II Part 2:** 791

Return of the Native, The (Hardy), **II:** 184–185, 186

Return of the Vanishing American, The (Fiedler), **Supp. XIII:** 103

Return to a Place Lit by a Glass of Milk (Simic), **Supp. VIII:** 274, 276, 283

"Return to Lavinia" (Caldwell), **I:** 310

Reuben (Wideman), **Supp. X:** 320

Reunion (Mamet), **Supp. XIV:** 240, 247, 254
"Reunion in Brooklyn" (H. Miller), **III:** 175, 184
Reuther brothers, **I:** 493
"Rev. Freemont Deadman" (Masters), **Supp. I Part 2:** 463
"Reveille" (Kingsolver), **Supp. VII:** 208
"Reveille, The" (Harte), **Supp. II Part 1:** 342–343
Revelation (biblical book), **II:** 541; **IV:** 104, 153, 154; **Supp. I Part 1:** 105, 273
"Revelation" (O'Connor), **III:** 349, 353–354; **Retro. Supp. II:** 237
"Revelation" (Warren), **III:** 490
Revenge (Harrison), **Supp. VIII:** 39, 45
"Revenge of Hamish, The" (Lanier), **Supp. I Part 1:** 365
"Revenge of Hannah Kemhuff, The" (Walker), **Supp. III Part 2:** 521
"Revenge of Rain-in-the-Face, The" (Longfellow), **Retro. Supp. II:** 170
Reverberator, The (James), **Retro. Supp. I:** 227
"Reverdure" (Berry), **Supp. X:** 22
"Reverend Father Gilhooley" (Farrell), **II:** 45
Reverse Transcription (Kushner), **Supp. IX:** 138
Reviewer's ABC, A (Aiken), **I:** 58
"Revolt, against the Crepuscular Spirit in Modern Poetry" (Pound), **Retro. Supp. I:** 286
Revolutionary Petunias (Walker), **Supp. III Part 2:** 520, 522, 530
Revolutionary Road (Yates), **Supp. XI:** 334, **335–340**
"Revolutionary Symbolism in America" (Burke), **I:** 272
"Revolutionary Theatre, The" (Baraka), **Supp. II Part 1:** 42
Revolution in Taste, A: Studies of Dylan Thomas, Allen Ginsberg, Sylvia Plath, and Robert Lowell (Simpson), **Supp. IX:** 276
"Revolution in the Revolution in the Revolution" (Snyder), **Supp. VIII:** 300
Revon, Marcel, **II:** 525
"Rewaking, The" (W. C. Williams), **Retro. Supp. I:** 430
"Rewrite" (Dunn), **Supp. XI:** 147
Rexroth, Kenneth, **II:** 526; **Supp. II Part 1:** 307; **Supp. II Part 2:** 436; **Supp. III Part 2:** 625, 626; **Supp. IV Part 1:** 145–146; **Supp. VIII:**

289; **Supp. XIII:** 75; **Supp. XIV:** 287
Reynolds, Clay, **Supp. XI:** 254
Reynolds, Quentin, **IV:** 286
Reynolds, Sir Joshua, **Supp. I Part 2:** 716
Reznikoff, Charles, **IV:** 415; **Retro. Supp. I:** 422; **Supp. III Part 2:** 615, 616, 617, 628; **Supp. XIV:277–296**
"Rhapsodist, The" (Brown), **Supp. I Part 1:** 125–126
"Rhapsody on a Windy Night" (Eliot), **Retro. Supp. I:** 55
Rhetoric of Motives, A (Burke), **I:** 272, 275, 278, 279
Rhetoric of Religion, The (Burke), **I:** 275, 279
"Rhobert" (Toomer), **Supp. IX:** 316–317
"Rhododendrons" (Levis), **Supp. XI:** 260, 263
"Rhyme of Sir Christopher, The" (Longfellow), **II:** 501
Rhymes to Be Traded for Bread (Lindsay), **Supp. I Part 2:** 380, 381–382
Rhys, Ernest, **III:** 458
Rhys, Jean, **Supp. III Part 1:** 42, 43
"Rhythm & Blues" (Baraka), **Supp. II Part 1:** 37–38
Rhythms (Reznikoff), **Supp. XIV:** 279, 282, 283
Rhythms II (Reznikoff), **Supp. XIV:** 282, 283, 284
Ribalow, Harold, **Supp. IX:** 236
Ribbentrop, Joachim von, **IV:** 249
Ribicoff, Abraham, **Supp. IX:** 33
Ricardo, David, **Supp. I Part 2:** 628, 634
Rice, Allen Thorndike, **Retro. Supp. I:** 362
Rice, Anne, **Supp. VII: 287–306**
Rice, Elmer, **I:** 479; **III:** 145, 160–161
Rice, Mrs. Grantland, **II:** 435
Rice, Philip Blair, **IV:** 141
Rice, Stan, **Supp. XII:** 2
Rice, Tom, **Supp. XIV:** 125
Rich, Adrienne, **Retro. Supp. I:** 8, 36, 42, 47, 404; **Retro. Supp. II:** 43, 191, 245; **Supp. I Part 2:** 546–547, **550–578; Supp. III Part 1:** 84, 354; **Supp. III Part 2:** 541, 599; **Supp. IV Part 1:** 257, 325; **Supp. V:** 82; **Supp. VIII:** 272; **Supp. XII:** 217, 229, 255; **Supp. XIII:** 294; **Supp. XIV:** 126, 129
Rich, Arnold, **Supp. I Part 2:** 552
Rich, Frank, **Supp. IV Part 2:** 585, 586; **Supp. V:** 106

Richard Cory (Gurney), **Supp. V:** 99–100, 105
"Richard Hunt's 'Arachne'" (Hayden), **Supp. II Part 1:** 374
Richard III (Shakespeare), **Supp. I Part 2:** 422
Richards, David, **Supp. IV Part 2:** 576
Richards, Grant, **I:** 515
Richards, I. A., **I:** 26, 273–274, 279, 522; **III:** 498; **IV:** 92; **Supp. I Part 1:** 264, 265; **Supp. I Part 2:** 647
Richards, Ivor Armonstrong, **Supp. XIV:** 2–3, 16
Richards, Laura E., **II:** 396; **III:** 505–506, 507
Richards, Leonard, **Supp. XIV:** 48
Richards, Lloyd, **Supp. IV Part 1:** 362; **Supp. VIII:** 331
Richards, Rosalind, **III:** 506
Richardson, Alan, **III:** 295
Richardson, Dorothy, **I:** 53; **II:** 320; **Supp. III Part 1:** 65
Richardson, Helen Patges, **Retro. Supp. II:** 95
Richardson, Henry Hobson, **I:** 3, 10
Richardson, Maurice, **Supp. XII:** 241
Richardson, Samuel, **I:** 134; **II:** 104, 111, 322; **Supp. V:** 127; **Supp. IX:** 128
Richardson, Tony, **Supp. XI:** 305, 306
"Richard Wright and Recent Negro Fiction" (Ellison), **Retro. Supp. II:** 116
"Richard Wright's Blues" (Ellison), **Retro. Supp. II:** 117, 124
"Richard Yates: A Requiem" (Lawrence), **Supp. XI:** 335
"Rich Boy, The" (Fitzgerald), **II:** 94; **Retro. Supp. I:** 98, 108
"Riches" (Bausch), **Supp. VII:** 54
Richler, Mordecai, **Supp. XI:** 294, 297
Richman, Robert, **Supp. XI:** 249
Richmond (Masters), **Supp. I Part 2:** 471
Richter, Conrad, **Supp. X:** 103
Richter, Jean Paul, **II:** 489, 492
Rickman, Clio, **Supp. I Part 2:** 519
Ricks, Christopher, **Retro. Supp. I:** 56
Riddel, Joseph N., **IV:** 95
"Riddle, The" (Hay), **Supp. XIV:** 130
"Riders to the Blood-Red Wrath" (Brooks), **Supp. III Part 1:** 82–83
Riders to the Sea (Synge), **III:** 157
Ridge, Lola, **Supp. IX:** 308
Riding, Laura, **I:** 437
"Riding Out at Evening" (McCarriston), **Supp. XIV:** 262–263
Riding the Iron Rooster: By Train through China (Theroux), **Supp. VIII:** 324

Riesenberg, Felix, **I:** 360, 361
Riesman, David, **Supp. I Part 2:** 649, 650
"Rif, to Music, The" (Bowles), **Supp. IV Part 1:** 89
Riffs & Reciprocities (Dunn), **Supp. XI: 154–155**
Riggs, Marlon, **Supp. XI:** 19
Right Madness on Skye, The (Hugo), **Supp. VI:** 145–147
Rights of Man (Paine), **Supp. I Part 2:** 508, 511, 512–514, 516, 519, 523
"Rights of Women, The" (Brown). *See Alcuin: A Dialogue* (Brown)
Right Stuff, The (Wolfe), **Supp. III Part 2:** 581–584
Right Thoughts in Sad Hours (Mather), **IV:** 144
Rigney, Barbara Hill, **Supp. VIII:** 215
"Rigorists" (Moore), **III:** 198
Riis, Jacob A., **I:** 293; **Supp. I Part 1:** 13
Riley, James Whitcomb, **I:** 205; **Supp. II Part 1:** 192, 193, 196, 197
Rilke, Rainer Maria, **I:** 445, 523; **II:** 367, 381, 382–383, 389, 543, 544; **III:** 552, 558, 563, 571, 572; **IV:** 380, 443; **Retro. Supp. II:** 20, 187; **Supp. I Part 1:** 264; **Supp. I Part 2:** 573; **Supp. III Part 1:** 239, 242, 246, 283, 319–320; **Supp. IV Part 1:** 284; **Supp. V:** 208, 343; **Supp. VIII:** 30, 40; **Supp. X:** 164; **Supp. XI:** 126; **Supp. XIII:** 74, 88
Rilke on Love and Other Difficulties (Rilke), **Supp. X:** 164
"Rilke's Growth as a Poet" (Dobyns), **Supp. XIII:** 77
"Rimbaud" (Kerouac), **Supp. III Part 1:** 232
Rimbaud, Arthur, **I:** 381, 383, 389, 391, 526; **II:** 528, 543, 545; **III:** 23, 174, 189; **IV:** 286, 380, 443; **Retro. Supp. I:** 56; **Retro. Supp. II:** 187, 326; **Supp. III Part 1:** 14, 195; **Supp. IV Part 2:** 624; **Supp. VIII:** 39, 40; **Supp. XII:** 1, 16, 128, 255; **Supp. XIII:** 284; **Supp. XIV:** 338
Rinehart, Stanley, **III:** 36
Ring, Frances Kroll, **Supp. IX:** 63, 64
Ring and the Book, The (Browning), **Supp. I Part 2:** 416, 468
Ring cycle (Wagner), **Supp. IV Part 1:** 392
Ringe, Donald, **I:** 339, 343; **Retro. Supp. II:** 270
"Ringing the Bells" (Sexton), **Supp. II Part 2:** 672, 687
Ringle, Ken, **Supp. X:** 15
Ring of Heaven: Poems (Hongo),

Supp. X: 292
Rink, The (musical, McNally), **Supp. XIII:** 207
Ríos, Alberto Alvaro, **Supp. IV Part 2:** 537–556
"Riot" (Brooks), **Supp. III Part 1:** 71, 84–85
Ripley, Ezra, **II:** 8; **IV:** 172
Rip-off Red, Girl Detective (Acker), **Supp. XII:** 3–4
Ripostes (Pound), **Retro. Supp. I:** 287–288, 413
Ripostes of Ezra Pound, The, Whereunto Are Appended the Complete Poetical Works of T. E. Hulme, with Prefatory Note (Pound), **III:** 458, 464, 465
Riprap (Snyder), **Supp. VIII: 292–294,** 295
"Riprap" (Snyder), **Supp. VIII:** 293–294
"Rip Van Winkle" (Irving), **II:** 304–306; **Supp. I Part 1:** 185
Risco-Lozado, Eliezar, **Supp. XIII:** 313
Rise of David Levinsky, The (Cahan), **Supp. IX:** 227; **Supp. XIII:** 106
Rise of Silas Lapham, The (Howells), **II:** 275, 279, 283–285; **IV:** 202; **Retro. Supp. II:** 93, 101
"Rise of the Middle Class" (Banks), **Supp. V:** 10
Rising and Falling (Matthews), **Supp. IX:** 154, **160**
"Rising Daughter, The" (Olds), **Supp. X:** 204
Rising from the Plains (McPhee), **Supp. III Part 1:** 309–310
Rising Glory of America, The (Brackenridge and Freneau), **Supp. I Part 1:** 124; **Supp. II Part 1:** 67, 253, 256, 263
"Rising of the Storm, The" (Dunbar), **Supp. II Part 1:** 199
Rising Sun in the Pacific, The (Morison), **Supp. I Part 2:** 490
Risk Pool, The (Russo), **Supp. XII: 328–331**
Ristovic, Aleksandar, **Supp. VIII:** 272
"Rita Dove: Identity Markers" (Vendler), **Supp. IV Part 1:** 247, 257
Ritchey, John, **Supp. XIV:** 122
"Rite of Passage" (Olds), **Supp. X:** 206
"Rites and Ceremonies" (Hecht), **Supp. X:** 61
"Rites of Spring, The" (Morris), **III:** 223
Ritschl, Albrecht, **III:** 309, 604
Ritsos, Yannis, **Supp. X:** 112

"Ritsos and the Metaphysical Moment" (Dobyns), **Supp. XIII:** 78
Rittenhouse, David, **Supp. I Part 2:** 507
"Ritual and Renewal: Keres Traditions in the Short Fiction of Leslie Silko" (Ruoff), **Supp. IV Part 2:** 559
Ritz, The (film), **Supp. XIII:** 206
Ritz, The (McNally), **Supp. XIII:** 198
"Rival, The" (Plath), **Retro. Supp. II:** 254
Riven Rock (Boyle), **Supp. VIII:** 5–6
"River" (Ammons), **Supp. VII:** 28
"River, The" (O'Connor), **III:** 344, 352, 353, 354, 356; **Retro. Supp. II:** 229, 231–232
Rivera, Tomás, **Supp. XIII:** 216, 221
Riverbed (Wagoner), **Supp. IX: 327–328**
"River Driftwood" (Jewett), **Retro. Supp. II:** 132, 133, 147
"River Jordan, The" (DeLillo), **Supp. VI:** 3, 4
River King, The (Hoffman), **Supp. X:** 78, 85, 90, **91–92**
"River Merchant's Wife: A Letter, The" (Pound), **III:** 463
"River Now, The" (Hugo), **Supp. VI:** 144
"River of Rivers in Connecticut, The" (Stevens), **Retro. Supp. I:** 313
River of the Mother of God and Other Essays by Aldo Leopold, The (Leopold), **Supp. XIV:** 180
"River Profile" (Auden), **Supp. II Part 1:** 26
"River Road" (Kunitz), **Supp. III Part 1:** 260
"River Runs Through It, A" (Maclean), **Supp. XIV:** 222–223, **223–229,** 233, 234, 235
River Runs Through It and Other Stories, A (Maclean), **Supp. XIV:** 221, 223
Rivers, Larry, **Supp. III Part 1:** 3
Rivers and Mountains (Ashbery), **Supp. III Part 1:** 10, 26
Riverside Drive (Simpson), **Supp. IX: 275–276**
River Styx, Ohio, and Other Poems, The (Oliver), **Supp. VII:** 231, 232
"River That Is East, The" (Kinnell), **Supp. III Part 1:** 241–242
"River Towns" (Masters), **Supp. I Part 2:** 473
Rives, Amélie, **II:** 194
Rivière, Jacques, **Retro. Supp. I:** 63
"Rivington's Last Will and Testament" (Freneau), **Supp. II Part 1:** 261
"Rivulet, The" (Bryant), **Supp. I Part**

1: 155, 162

Rix, Alice, **I:** 199

RL's Dream (Mosley), **Supp. XIII:** 234, **244–245,** 249

Roach, Max, **Supp. X:** 239

Road Between, The (Farrell), **II:** 29, 38, 39–40

"Road Between Here and There, The" (Kinnell), **Supp. III Part 1:** 254

"Road Home, The" (Hammett), **Supp. IV Part 1:** 343

Road Home, The (Harrison), **Supp. VIII:** 37, 45, 48, **49–50,** 53

"Road Not Taken, The" (Frost), **II:** 154; **Retro. Supp. I:** 131; **Supp. XI:** 150

Roadside Poems for Summer Travellers (Larcom, ed.), **Supp. XIII:** 142

Roads of Destiny (O. Henry), **Supp. II Part 1:** 410

Road through the Wall, The (Jackson), **Supp. IX:** 115, 118, 120, 123–124

"Road to Avignon, The" (Lowell), **II:** 516

"Road to Hell, The" (Fante), **Supp. XI:** 160

Road to Los Angeles, The (Fante), **Supp. XI:** 160, 166, 167, **168,** 172

Road to Many a Wonder, The (Wagoner), **Supp. IX:** 327, **336**

Road to the Temple, The (Glaspell), **Supp. III Part 1:** 175, 182, 186

Road to Wellville, The (Boyle), **Supp. VIII:** 6–8

Road to Xanadu, The (Lowes), **IV:** 453

"Roan Stallion" (Jeffers), **Supp. II Part 2:** 428–429

"Roast-beef" (Stein), **IV:** 43

"Roast Possum" (Dove), **Supp. IV Part 1:** 247, 248

Robards, Jason, Jr., **III:** 163, 403

Robbe-Grillet, Alain, **I:** 123; **IV:** 95; **Supp. IV Part 1:** 42; **Supp. V:** 47, 48

Robber Bride, The (Atwood), **Supp. XIII:** 30–31

Robber Bridegroom, The (Welty), **IV:** 261, 266–268, 271, 274; **Retro. Supp. I:** 347

Robbins, Harold, **Supp. XII:** 6

Robbins, Henry, **Supp. IV Part 1:** 198, 201, 210, 211

Robbins, Katherine Robinson, **Supp. X:** 264

Robbins, Tom, **Supp. IV Part 1:** 227; **Supp. VIII:** 14; **Supp. X: 259–288; Supp. XIII:** 11

"Robe, The" (Douglas), **IV:** 434

"Robert Bly" (Davis), **Supp. IV Part 1:** 70

Robert Bly (Sugg), **Supp. IV Part 1:** 68

Robert Bly: An Introduction to the Poetry (Nelson), **Supp. IV Part 1:** 66

Robert Bly: The Poet and His Critics (Davis), **Supp. IV Part 1:** 63

"Robert Bly and the Trouble with America" (Mitchell), **Supp. IV Part 1:** 70

Robert Coover: The Universal Fiction-making Process (Gordon), **Supp. V:** 46

Robert Creeley (Ford), **Supp. IV Part 1:** 140

Robert Creeley and the Genius of the American Common Place (Clark), **Supp. IV Part 1:** 140

Robert Creeley's Poetry: A Critical Introduction (Edelberg), **Supp. IV Part 1:** 155

Robert Frost (Meyers), **Retro. Supp. I:** 138

Robert Lowell (Meyers), **Retro. Supp. II:** 191

Robert Lowell: The First Twenty years (Staples), **Retro. Supp. II:** 187

Robert Lowell and the Sublime (Hart), **Retro. Supp. II:** 187

Robert Lowell's Shifting Colors (Doreski), **Retro. Supp. II:** 185

Roberts, Diane, **Supp. X:** 15

Roberts, J. M., **IV:** 454

Roberts, Leo, **II:** 449

Roberts, Margaret, **II:** 449; **IV:** 453, 454

Roberts, Matthew, **Retro. Supp. II:** 324

Roberts, Meade, **IV:** 383

Roberts, Michael, **I:** 527, 536

Roberts, Richard, **III:** 297

Roberts, Wally, **Supp. XI:** 119, 120, 126

Roberts, William, **Supp. XI:** 343

Roberts Brothers, **Retro. Supp. I:** 31, 35

Robertson, D. B., **III:** 311

Robertson, David, **Supp. VIII:** 305

Robertson, Nan, **Supp. IV Part 1:** 300

Robertson, William, **II:** 8

Robert the Devil (Merwin, trans.), **Supp. III Part 1:** 341, 346

Robeson, Paul, **III:** 392; **Supp. IV Part 1:** 360, 361; **Supp. X:** 137

Robespierre, Maximilien, **Supp. I Part 2:** 514, 515, 517

Robinson, Christopher L., **Supp. XII:** 13, 14

Robinson, Dean, **III:** 506

Robinson, Edward, **III:** 505

Robinson, Edward G., **Supp. XI:** 306

Robinson, Edwin Arlington, **I:** 480; **II:** 388, 391, 529, 542; **III:** 5, **503–526,** 576; **Supp. I Part 2:** 699; **Supp. II Part 1:** 191; **Supp. III Part 1:** 63, 75; **Supp. III Part 2:** 592, 593; **Supp. IX:** 77, 266, 276, 308

Robinson, Forrest G., **Supp. IV Part 2:** 597, 601, 604

Robinson, H. M., **IV:** 369, 370

Robinson, Herman, **III:** 506–507

Robinson, Jackie, **Supp. I Part 1:** 338

Robinson, James Harvey, **I:** 214; **Supp. I Part 2:** 492

Robinson, James K., **Supp. IX:** 328

Robinson, Margaret G., **Supp. IV Part 2:** 597, 601, 604

Robinson, Mary, **Supp. XI:** 26

Robinson, Sugar Ray, **Supp. IV Part 1:** 167

Robinson, Ted, **Supp. XIII:** 166

Robinson Crusoe (Defoe), **II:** 159; **III:** 113, 423; **IV:** 369; **Retro. Supp. II:** 274; **Supp. I Part 2:** 714; **Supp. IV Part 2:** 502

Robison, Mary, **Supp. V:** 22

Roblès, Emmanuel, **Supp. I Part 1:** 283

"Robstown" (Salinas), **Supp. XIII:** 315

Rochefoucauld, Louis Alexandre, **Supp. I Part 2:** 510

"Rock" (Nye), **Supp. XIII:** 287

Rock (Wagoner), **Supp. IX:** 324, **334,** 335

Rock, Catherine, **Supp. XII:** 17

Rock, The (Eliot), **Retro. Supp. I:** 65

Rock, The (Stevens), **Retro. Supp. I:** 309, 312

"Rock, The" (Stevens), **Retro. Supp. I:** 312

Rockaway (Shanley), **Supp. XIV:** 315

"Rock Climbers, The" (Francis), **Supp. IX:** 82

Rock-Drill (Pound), **Retro. Supp. I:** 293

Rockefeller, John D., **I:** 273; **III:** 580; **Supp. I Part 2:** 486; **Supp. V:** 286

Rockefeller, Nelson, **III:** 14, 15

Rocket to the Moon (Odets), **Supp. II Part 2:** 541–543, 544

Rock Garden, The (Shepard), **Supp. III Part 2:** 432, 447

"Rocking Horse Winner, The" (Lawrence), **Supp. I Part 1:** 329

Rocking the Boat (Vidal), **Supp. IV Part 2:** 683

"Rockpile, The" (Baldwin), **Supp. I Part 1:** 63

Rock Springs (Ford), **Supp. V:** 57, 58–59, 68–69

Rocky Mountains, The: or, Scenes, Incidents, and Adventures in the Far West; Digested from the Journal of Captain E. L. E Bonneville, of the Army of the United States, and Illustrated from Various Other Sources (Irving), **II:** 312

Roderick Hudson (James), **II:** 284, 290, 324, 326, 328; **Retro. Supp. I:** 219, **220–221**, 221, 226; **Supp. IX:** 142

Rodgers, Richard, **III:** 361

Rodgers, Ronald, **Supp. IV Part 2:** 503

Rodker, John, **III:** 470

Rodman, Selden, **Supp. I Part 1:** 83; **Supp. X:** 115

"Rodrigo Returns to the Land and Linen Celebrates" (Cisneros), **Supp. VII:** 68

Rodriguez, Randy A., **Supp. XIV:** 312

Rodriguez, Richard, **Supp. XIV:297–313**

Roethke, Charles, **III:** 531

Roethke, Theodore, **I:** 167, 171–172, 183, 254, 285, 521; **III:** 273, **527–550;** **IV:** 138, 402; **Retro. Supp. II:** 178, 181, 246; **Supp. I Part 2:** 539; **Supp. III Part 1:** 47, 54, 56, 239, 253, 260–261, 350; **Supp. IV Part 2:** 626; **Supp. IX:** 323

"Roger Malvin's Burial" (Hawthorne), **II:** 243; **Retro. Supp. I:** 153

Rogers, Michael, **Supp. X:** 265, 266

Rogers, Samuel, **II:** 303; **Supp. I Part 1:** 157

Rogers, Will, **I:** 261; **IV:** 388

Roger's Version (Updike), **Retro. Supp. I:** 325, 327, 330

Roget, Peter Mark, **Supp. I Part 1:** 312

"Rogue River Jet-Board Trip, Gold Beach, Oregon, July 4, 1977" (Carver), **Supp. III Part 1:** 140

"Rogue's Gallery" (McCarthy), **II:** 563

Roland de La Platière, Jean Marie, **II:** 554

Rôle du Nègre dans la culture des Amériques, La (Locke), **Supp. XIV:** 202

"Role of Society in the Artist, The" (Ammons), **Supp. VII:** 34

Rolfe, Alfred, **IV:** 427

"Roll, Jordan, Roll" (spiritual), **Supp. IV Part 1:** 16

"Roll Call" (Komunyakaa), **Supp. XIII:** 123

Rolle, Esther, **Supp. IV Part 1:** 367

Rollin, Charles, **II:** 113

Rolling Stones (O. Henry), **Supp. II Part 1:** 410

Rolling Thunder Logbook (Shepard), **Supp. III Part 2:** 433

"Rolling Up" (Simpson), **Supp. IX:** 265, 274, 280

Rollins, Howard E., Jr., **Supp. IV Part 1:** 236

Rollins, Hyder E., **Supp. IV Part 1:** 168

Rollins, Sonny, **Supp. V:** 195

"Rollo" tales (Abbott), **Supp. I Part 1:** 38

"Roma I" (Wright), **Supp. V:** 338

"Roma II" (Wright), **Supp. V:** 338

Romains, Jules, **I:** 227

Román, David, **Supp. XIII:** 208

"Romance and a Reading List" (Fitzgerald), **Retro. Supp. I:** 101

Romance of a Plain Man, The (Glasgow), **II:** 175, 180–181

"Romance of Certain Old Clothes, The" (James), **II:** 322; **Retro. Supp. I:** 218

"Roman Elegies" (Brodsky), **Supp. VIII:** 29

"Roman Fever" (Wharton), **Retro. Supp. I:** 382

"Roman Fountain" (Bogan), **Supp. III Part 1:** 56

"*Romanitas* of Gore Vidal, The" (Tatum), **Supp. IV Part 2:** 684

"Roman Sarcophagus, A" (Lowell), **II:** 544

Roman Spring of Mrs. Stone, The (T. Williams), **IV:** 383, 385

"Romantic, The" (Bogan), **Supp. III Part 1:** 50

Romantic Comedians, The (Glasgow), **II:** 175, 186, 190, 194

Romantic Egoists, The (Auchincloss), **Supp. IV Part 1:** 25

Romantic Egotist, The (Fitzgerald), **II:** 82

"Romantic Egotist, The" (Fitzgerald), **Retro. Supp. I:** 100

"Romanticism and Classicism" (Hulme), **III:** 196

"Romanticism Comes Home" (Shapiro), **Supp. II Part 2:** 713

Romantic Manifesto, The: A Philosophy of Literature (Rand), **Supp. IV Part 2:** 521, 523, 527, 529–530

"Romantic Regionalism of Harper Lee, The" (Erisman), **Supp. VIII:** 126

"Rome" (W. C. Williams), **Retro. Supp. I:** 420

Rome Brothers, **Retro. Supp. I:** 393

Romeo and Juliet (Shakespeare), **Supp. V:** 252; **Supp. VIII:** 223

Romola (Eliot), **II:** 291; **IV:** 311

Romulus: A New Comedy (Vidal), **Supp. IV Part 2:** 683

Romulus der Grosse (Dürrenmatt), **Supp. IV Part 2:** 683

Ronald, Ann, **Supp. XIII:** 4, 5, 6, 7, 9, 11

"Rondel for a September Day" (White), **Supp. I Part 2:** 676

"Ron Narrative Reconstructions, The" (Coleman), **Supp. XI:** 83

Ronsard, Pierre de, **Supp. X:** 65

Rood, John, **IV:** 261

"Roof, the Steeple, and the People, The" (Ellison), **Retro. Supp. II:** 118, 126; **Supp. II Part 1:** 248

"Room" (Levertov), **Supp. III Part 1:** 282

"Room at the Heart of Things, A" (Merrill), **Supp. III Part 1:** 337

Room Called Remember, A: Uncollected Pieces (Buechner), **Supp. XII:** 53

"Roomful of Hovings, A" (McPhee), **Supp. III Part 1:** 291, 294

Room of One's Own, A (Woolf), **Supp. V:** 127; **Supp. IX:** 19; **Supp. XIII:** 305

Room Temperature (Baker), **Supp. XIII:** 41, **43–45**, 48, 50

Roosevelt, Eleanor, **IV:** 371; **Supp. IV Part 2:** 679

Roosevelt, Franklin, **Supp. V:** 290

Roosevelt, Franklin Delano, **I:** 482, 485, 490; **II:** 553, 575; **III:** 2, 18, 69, 110, 297, 321, 376, 476, 580, 581; **Supp. I Part 2:** 488, 489, 490, 491, 645, 654, 655

Roosevelt, Kermit, **III:** 508

Roosevelt, Theodore, **I:** 14, 62; **II:** 130; **III:** 508; **IV:** 321; **Retro. Supp. I:** 377; **Supp. I Part 1:** 1, 21; **Supp. I Part 2:** 455, 456, 502, 707; **Supp. V:** 280, 282; **Supp. IX:** 184

Roosevelt After Inauguration And Other Atrocities (Burroughs), **Supp. III Part 1:** 98

"Roosters" (Bishop), **Retro. Supp. II:** 39, 43, 250; **Supp. I Part 1:** 89

Root, Abiah, **I:** 456

Root, Elihu, **Supp. IV Part 1:** 33

Root, Simeon, **I:** 548

Root, Timothy, **I:** 548

Rootabaga Stories (Sandburg), **III:** 583, 587

"Rootedness: The Ancestor as Foundation" (Morrison), **Supp. III Part 1:** 361

Roots in the Soil (film), **Supp. IV Part 1:** 83

"Rope" (Porter), **III:** 451

Rope, The (O'Neill), **III:** 388

Ropemakers of Plymouth, The (Morison), **Supp. I Part 2:** 494

"Ropes" (Nye), **Supp. XIII:** 276

"Rope's End, The" (Nemerov), **III:** 282

Roquelaure, A. N., **Supp. VII:** 301. *See also* Rice, Anne

Rorem, Ned, **Supp. IV Part 1:** 79, 84

"Rosa" (Ozick), **Supp. V:** 271

Rosa, Rodrigo Rey, **Supp. IV Part 1:** 92

Rosaldo, Renato, **Supp. IV Part 2:** 544

"Rosalia" (Simic), **Supp. VIII:** 278

Roscoe, Will, **Supp. IV Part 1:** 330

"Rose" (Dubus), **Supp. VII:** 88

Rose, Alice, Sister, **III:** 348

Rose, Philip, **Supp. IV Part 1:** 362

"Rose, The" (Roethke), **III:** 537

"Rose, The" (W. C. Williams), **Retro. Supp. I:** 419

"Rose for Emily, A" (Faulkner), **II:** 72; **Supp. IX:** 96

Rose in Bloom (Alcott), **Supp. I Part 1:** 42

"Rose-Johnny" (Kingsolver), **Supp. VII:** 203

Rose Madder (King), **Supp. V:** 141, 148, 150, 152

"Rose-Morals" (Lanier), **Supp. I Part 1:** 364

Rosen, Kenneth, **Supp. IV Part 2:** 499, 505, 513

Rosenbaum, Alissa Zinovievna. *See* Rand, Ayn

Rosenberg, Bernard, **Supp. I Part 2:** 650

Rosenberg, Julius and Ethel, **Supp. I Part 1:** 295; **Supp. I Part 2:** 532; **Supp. V:** 45

Rosenbloom, Joel, **Supp. IV Part 2:** 527

Rosenfeld, Alvin H., **Supp. I Part 1:** 120

Rosenfeld, Isaac, **Supp. XII:** 160

Rosenfeld, Paul, **I:** 116, 117, 231, 245

Rosenfelt, Deborah, **Supp. XIII:** 296, 304

Rosenfield, Isaac, **IV:** 3

Rosenthal, Ira, **Supp. XIV:** 146–147

Rosenthal, Lois, **Supp. VIII:** 258

Rosenthal, M. L., **II:** 550; **III:** 276, 479; **Supp. V:** 333

"Rose Pogonias" (Frost), **Retro. Supp. I:** 127

"Rose Red and Snow White" (Grimms), **Supp. X:** 82

"Roses" (Dove), **Supp. IV Part 1:** 246

"Roses and Skulls" (Goldbarth), **Supp. XII:** 192

"Roses for Lubbock" (Nye), **Supp. XIII:** 281

"Roses Only" (Moore), **III:** 195, 198, 200, 202, 215

Rose Tattoo, The (T. Williams), **IV:** 382, 383, 387, 388, 389, 392–393, 394, 397, 398

"Rosewood, Ohio" (Matthews), **Supp. IX:** 160

Rosinante to the Road Again (Dos Passos), **I:** 478

Rosmersholm (Ibsen), **III:** 152

Rosmond, Babette, **II:** 432

Ross, Eleanor. *See* Taylor, Eleanor Ross

Ross, Harold, **Supp. I Part 1:** 174; **Supp. I Part 2:** 607, 617, 653, 654, 655, 660; **Supp. VIII:** 151, 170; **Supp. IX:** 190

Ross, John F., **II:** 110

Ross, Lillilan, **Retro. Supp. II:** 198

Ross, Mitchell S., **Supp. IV Part 2:** 692; **Supp. X:** 260

Rossen, Robert, **Supp. XI:** 306

Rosset, Barney, **III:** 171

Rossetti, Christina, **Supp. XIV:** 128

Rossetti, Dante Gabriel, **I:** 433; **II:** 323; **Retro. Supp. I:** 128, 286; **Supp. I Part 2:** 552

Rossetti, William Michael, **Retro. Supp. I:** 407

Rosskam, Edwin, **IV:** 477

Ross Macdonald (Bruccoli), **Supp. IV Part 2:** 468, 470

Rostand, Edmond, **II:** 515; **Supp. IV Part 2:** 518

Rosy Crucifixion, The (H. Miller), **III:** 170, 187, 188–189, 190

Roth, Henry, **Supp. IV Part 1:** 314; **Supp. VIII:** 233; **Supp. IX:** 227–243; **Supp. XIII:** 106

Roth, Philip, **I:** 144, 161; **II:** 591; **Retro. Supp. II:** 22, **279–297;** **Supp. I Part 1:** 186, 192; **Supp. I Part 2:** 431, 441, 443; **Supp. II Part 1:** 99; **Supp. III Part 2: 401– 429;** **Supp. IV Part 1:** 236, 379, 388; **Supp. V:** 45, 119, 122, 257, 258; **Supp. VIII:** 88, 236, 245; **Supp. IX:** 227; **Supp. XI:** 64, 68, 99, 140; **Supp. XII:** 190, 310; **Supp. XIV:** 79, 93, 111, 112

Rothenberg, Jerome, **Supp. VIII:** 292; **Supp. XII:** 3

Rothermere, Lady Mary, **Retro. Supp. I:** 63

Rothstein, Mervyn, **Supp. VIII:** 142

"Rouge High" (Hughes), **Supp. I Part 1:** 330

Rougemont, Denis de, **II:** 586; **IV:** 216; **Retro. Supp. I:** 328, 329, 330, 331

Roughing It (Twain), **II:** 312; **IV:** 195, 197, 198

Roughing It in the Bush (Shields), **Supp. VII:** 313

"Rough Outline" (Simic), **Supp. VIII:** 276

Rougon-Macquart, Les (Zola), **II:** 175– 176

Roumain, Jacques, **Retro. Supp. I:** 202; **Supp. IV Part 1:** 360, 367

"Round, The" (Kunitz), **Supp. III Part 1:** 268

"Round Trip" (Dunn), **Supp. XI:** 148– 149

Round Up (Lardner), **II:** 426, 430, 431

Rourke, Constance, **I:** 258; **IV:** 339, 352

Rourke, Milton, **Retro. Supp. II:** 89

Rousseau, Jean-Jacques, **I:** 226; **II:** 8, 343; **III:** 170, 178, 259; **IV:** 80, 173, 440; **Supp. I Part 1:** 126; **Supp. I Part 2:** 637, 659; **Supp. IV Part 1:** 171; **Supp. XI:** 245

Roussel, Raymond, **Supp. III Part 1:** 6, 7, 10, 15, 16, 21

"Route Six" (Kunitz), **Supp. III Part 1:** 258

Route Two (Erdrich and Dorris), **Supp. IV Part 1:** 260

"Routine Things Around the House, The" (Dunn), **Supp. XI:** 148

Rover Boys (Winfield), **III:** 146

Rovit, Earl, **IV:** 102

Rowan, Carl T., **Supp. XIV:** 306

Rowe, Anne E., **Supp. X:** 223

Rowe, John Carlos, **Retro. Supp. I:** 216

"Rowing" (Sexton), **Supp. II Part 2:** 696

"Rowing Endeth, The" (Sexton), **Supp. II Part 2:** 696

Rowlandson, Mary, **Supp. IV Part 2:** 430, 431

"Rows of Cold Trees, The" (Winters), **Supp. II Part 2:** 790–791, 800

Rowson, Susanna, **Supp. I Part 1:** 128

Roxanna Slade (Price), **Supp. VI:** 267

"Royal Palm" (Crane), **I:** 401

Royce, Josiah, **I:** 443; **III:** 303, 600; **IV:** 26; **Retro. Supp. I:** 57; **Supp. XIV:** 197, 199

Royster, Sarah Elmira, **III:** 410, 429

Rózewicz, Tadeusz, **Supp. X:** 60

Ruas, Charles, **Supp. IV Part 1:** 383

Rubáiyát (Khayyám), **I:** 568

Rubaiyat of Omar Khayyam (Fitzgerald), **Supp. I Part 2:** 416; **Supp. III Part 2:** 610

Rubin, Louis, **Supp. I Part 2:** 672, 673, 679; **Supp. X:** 42

Rubin, Louis D., Jr., **IV:** 116, 462–463

Rubin, Stan, **Supp. XIV:** 307, 310

Rubin, Stan Sanvel, **Supp. IV Part 1:** 242, 245, 252

"Ruby Brown" (Hughes), **Supp. I Part 1:** 327

"Ruby Daggett" (Eberhart), **I:** 539

Rucker, Rudy, **Supp. X:** 302

Rudd, Hughes, **Supp. XII:** 141

"Rude Awakening, A" (Chopin), **Retro. Supp. II:** 64

Rudens (Plautus), **Supp. III Part 2:** 630

Ruderman, Judith, **Supp. IV Part 1:** 380

Rudge, Olga, **Supp. V:** 338

Rudikoff, Sonya, **Supp. XIV:** 113

Rueckert, William, **I:** 264

Rugby Chapel (Arnold), **Supp. I Part 2:** 416

"Rugby Road" (Garrett), **Supp. VII:** 100

Ruining the New Road (Matthews), **Supp. IX:** 154, **155–157**

"Ruins of Italica, The" (Bryant, trans.), **Supp. I Part 1:** 166

Rukeyser, Muriel, **Retro. Supp. II:** 48; **Supp. VI: 271–289**

"Rule of Phase Applied to History, The" (Adams), **I:** 19

Rule of the Bone (Banks), **Supp. V:** 16

"Rules by Which a Great Empire May Be Reduced to a Small One" (Franklin), **II:** 120

Rules For the Dance: A Handbook for Reading and Writing Metrical Verse (Oliver), **Supp. VII:** 229, 247

Rules of the Game, The (film), **Supp. XII:** 259

Rulfo, Juan, **Supp. IV Part 2:** 549

Rumbaut, Rubén, **Supp. XI:** 184

Rumens, Carol, **Supp. XI:** 14

Rumkowski, Chaim, **Supp. XII:** 168

Rummel, Mary Kay, **Supp. XIII:** 280

"Rumor and a Ladder" (Bowles), **Supp. IV Part 1:** 93

Rumors (Simon), **Supp. IV Part 2:** 582–583, 591

Rumpelstiltskin (Gardner), **Supp. VI:** 72

"Rumpelstiltskin" (Grimm), **IV:** 266

"Rumpelstiltskin" (Sexton), **Supp. II Part 2:** 690

"Runagate Runagate" (Hayden), **Supp. II Part 1:** 377

"Runes" (Nemerov), **III:** 267, 277–278

"Running" (Wilbur), **Supp. III Part 2:** 558–559

Running Dog (DeLillo), **Supp. VI:** 3, 6, 8, 14

"Run of Bad Luck, A" (Proulx), **Supp. VII:** 253–254

Run of Jacks, A (Hugo), **Supp. VI:** 131, 133, 134, 135, 136

Run River (Didion), **Supp. IV Part 1:** 197, 199–200, 201

Ruoff, A. LaVonne Brown, **Supp. IV Part 1:** 324, 327; **Supp. IV Part 2:** 559

Rupert, Jim, **Supp. XII:** 215

Ruppert, James, **Supp. IV Part 1:** 321

Rural Hours (Cooper), **Supp. XIII:** 152

"Rural Route" (Wright), **Supp. V:** 340

"Rural South, The" (Du Bois), **Supp. II Part 1:** 174

Rush, Benjamin, **Supp. I Part 2:** 505, 507

Rushdie, Salman, **Supp. IV Part 1:** 234, 297

Rushdy, Ashraf, **Supp. X:** 250

Rushing, Jimmy, **Retro. Supp. II:** 113

Rusk, Dean, **II:** 579

Ruskin, John, **II:** 323, 338; **IV:** 349; **Retro. Supp. I:** 56, 360; **Supp. I Part 1:** 2, 10, 87, 349; **Supp. I Part 2:** 410

Russell, Ada Dwyer, **II:** 513, 527

Russell, Bertrand, **II:** 27; **III:** 605, 606; **Retro. Supp. I:** 57, 58, 59, 60; **Supp. I Part 2:** 522; **Supp. V:** 290; **Supp. XII:** 45; **Supp. XIV:** 337

Russell, Diarmuid, **Retro. Supp. I:** 342, 345, 346–347, 349–350

Russell, George, **Retro. Supp. I:** 342

Russell, Herb, **Supp. I Part 2:** 465–466

Russell, John, **Supp. XIV:** 344, 347, 348

Russell, Peter, **III:** 479

Russell, Richard, **Supp. XI:** 102

Russell, Sue, **Supp. IV Part 2:** 653

Russert, Tim, **Supp. XII:** 272

Russia at War (Caldwell), **I:** 296

Russian Journal, A (Steinbeck), **IV:** 52, 63

Russo, Richard, **Supp. XI:** 349; **Supp. XII: 325–344**

"Rusty Autumn" (Swenson), **Supp. IV Part 2:** 640

Rutabaga-Roo: I've Got a Song and It's for You (Nye, album), **Supp. XIII:** 274

Ruth (biblical book), **Supp. I Part 2:** 516

Ruth, George Herman ("Babe"), **II:** 423; **Supp. I Part 2:** 438, 440

Ruth Hall (Fern), **Supp. V:** 122

Rutledge, Ann, **III:** 588; **Supp. I Part 2:** 471

Ruwe, Donelle R., **Supp. XII:** 215

Ryder (Barnes), **Supp. III Part 1:** 31, 36–38, 42, 43

"Ryder" (Rukeyser), **Supp. VI:** 273, 283

Rymer, Thomas, **IV:** 122

S-1 (Baraka), **Supp. II Part 1:** 55, 57

S. (Updike), **Retro. Supp. I:** 330, 331, 332, 333

Saadi, **II:** 19

"Sabbath, The" (Stowe), **Supp. I Part 2:** 587

"Sabbath Mom" (White), **Supp. I Part 2:** 671–672

Sabbaths (Berry), **Supp. X:** 31

Sabbath's Theater (Roth), **Retro. Supp. II:** 279, 288

Sabines, Jaime, **Supp. V:** 178

"Sabotage" (Baraka), **Supp. II Part 1:** 49, 53

Sacco, Nicola, **I:** 482, 486, 490, 494; **II:** 38–39, 426; **III:** 139–140; **Supp. I Part 2:** 446; **Supp. V:** 288–289; **Supp. IX:** 199

Sachs, Hanns, **Supp. I Part 1:** 259; **Supp. X:** 186

"Sacks" (Carver), **Supp. III Part 1:** 143–144

Sacks, Peter, **Supp. IV Part 2:** 450

Sackville-West, Vita, **Supp. VIII:** 263

"Sacrament of Divorce, The" (Patchett), **Supp. XII:** 309

"Sacraments" (Dubus), **Supp. VII:** 91

Sacred and Profane Memories (Van Vechten), **Supp. II Part 2:** 735, 749

"Sacred Chant for the Return of Black Spirit and Power" (Baraka), **Supp. II Part 1:** 51

"Sacred Factory, The" (Toomer), **Supp. IX:** 320

Sacred Fount, The (James), **II:** 332–333; **Retro. Supp. I:** 219, 228, 232

"Sacred Hoop, The: A Contemporary Perspective" (Gunn Allen), **Supp. IV Part 1:** 324

Sacred Hoop, The: Recovering the Feminine in American Indian Traditions (Gunn Allen), **Supp. IV Part 1:** 319, 320, 322, 324, 325, 328–330, 331, 333, 334

Sacred Journey, The (Buechner), **Supp. XII:** 42, 53

Sacred Wood, The (Eliot), **IV:** 431; **Retro. Supp. I:** 59, 60; **Supp. I Part 1:** 268; **Supp. II Part 1:** 136, 146

"Sacrifice, The" (Oates), **Supp. II Part 2:** 523

Sacrilege of Alan Kent, The (Caldwell), **I:** 291–292

"Sad Brazil" (Hardwick), **Supp. III Part 1:** 210

"Sad Dust Glories" (Ginsberg), **Supp. II Part 1:** 376

Sad Dust Glories: Poems Written Work Summer in Sierra Woods (Ginsberg), **Supp. II Part 1:** 326

Sade, Marquis de, **III:** 259; **IV:** 437, 442; **Supp. XII:** 1, 14–15

Sad Flower in the Sand, A (film), **Supp. XI:** 173

Sad Heart at the Supermarket, A (Jarrell), **II:** 386

"Sadie" (Matthiessen), **Supp. V:** 201

Sadness and Happiness (Pinsky), **Supp. VI:** 235, **237–241**

"Sadness of Brothers, The" (Kinnell), **Supp. III Part 1:** 237, 251

"Sadness of Days, The" (Salinas), **Supp. XIII:** 325

Sadness of Days, The: Selected and New Poems (Salinas), **Supp. XIII:** 311, **324–326**

"Sadness of Lemons, The" (Levine), **Supp. V:** 184

"Sad Rite" (Karr), **Supp. XI:** 243

"Sad Strains of a Gay Waltz" (Stevens), **Retro. Supp. I:** 302

"Safe" (Gordon), **Supp. IV Part 1:** 299, 306

"Safe in their Alabaster Chambers" (Dickinson), **Retro. Supp. I:** 30

"Safe Subjects" (Komunyakaa), **Supp. XIII:** 118

"Safeway" (F. Barthelme), **Supp. XI:** 26, 27, 36

Saffin, John, **Supp. I Part 1:** 115

Saffy, Edna, **Supp. X:** 227

"Saga of Arturo Bandini" (Fante), **Supp. XI:** 159, **166–169**

"Saga of King Olaf, The" (Longfellow), **II:** 489, 505; **Retro. Supp. II:** 154, 155, 164

"Sage of Stupidity and Wonder, The" (Goldbarth), **Supp. XII:** 191

Sahl, Mort, **II:** 435–436

"Said" (Dixon), **Supp. XII:** 149–150

"Sailing after Lunch" (Stevens), **IV:** 73

"Sailing Home from Rapallo" (Lowell), **Retro. Supp. II:** 189

Sailing through China (Theroux), **Supp. VIII:** 323

"Sailing to Byzantium" (Yeats), **III:** 263; **Supp. VIII:** 30; **Supp. X:** 74; **Supp. XI:** 281

"Sail Made of Rags, The" (Nye), **Supp. XIII:** 277

"Sailors Lost at Sea" (Shields), **Supp. VII:** 318

"St. Augustine and the Bullfights" (Porter), **III:** 454

St. Elmo (Wilson), **Retro. Supp. I:** 351–352

"St. Francis Einstein of the Daffodils" (W. C. Williams), **IV:** 409–411

"St. George, the Dragon, and the Virgin" (Bly), **Supp. IV Part 1:** 73

St. George and the Godfather (Mailer), **III:** 46; **Retro. Supp. II:** 206, 208

St. John, David, **Supp. V:** 180; **Supp. XI:** 270, 272; **Supp. XIII:** 312

St. John, Edward B., **Supp. IV Part 2:** 490

St. John, James Hector. *See* Crèvecoeur, Michel-Guillaume Jean de

St. Louis Woman (Bontemps and Cullen), **Supp. IV Part 1:** 170

St. Mawr (Lawrence), **II:** 595

St. Petersburg (Biely), **Supp. XII:** 13

"St. Roach" (Rukeyser), **Supp. VI:** 286

"St. Thomas Aquinas" (Simic), **Supp. VIII:** 281

"*St Anne*/Santa Ana" (Mora), **Supp. XIII:** 229

"*Saint Anthony of Padua*/San Antonio de Padua" (Mora), **Supp. XIII:** 228

Sainte-Beuve, Charles Augustin, **IV:** 432

Sainte Vierge, La (Picabia), **Retro. Supp. II:** 331

Saint-Exupéry, Antoine de, **Supp. IX:** 247

Saint-Gaudens, Augustus, **I:** 18, 228; **II:** 551

Saint Jack (Theroux), **Supp. VIII:** 319

"Saint John and the Back-Ache" (Stevens), **Retro. Supp. I:** 310

Saint Judas (Wright), **Supp. III Part 2:** **595–599**

"Saint Judas" (Wright), **Supp. III Part 2:** 598–599

Saint Maybe (Tyler), **Supp. IV Part 2:** 670–671

"Saint Nicholas" (Moore), **III:** 215

"Saint Robert" (Dacey), **Supp. IV Part 1:** 70

Saintsbury, George, **IV:** 440

Saints' Everlasting Rest, The (Baxter), **III:** 199; **IV:** 151, 153

Saint-Simon, Claude Henri, **Supp. I Part 2:** 648

Saks, Gene, **Supp. IV Part 2:** 577, 588

Salamun, Tomaz, **Supp. VIII:** 272

Salazar, Dixie, **Supp. V:** 180

Saldívar, José David, **Supp. IV Part 2:** 544, 545

Sale, Richard, **Supp. IV Part 1:** 379

Sale, Roger, **Supp. V:** 244

Saleh, Dennis, **Supp. V:** 182, 186

"Salem" (Lowell), **II:** 550

Salemi, Joseph, **Supp. IV Part 1:** 284

Salem's Lot (King), **Supp. V:** 139, 144, 146, 151

"Sale of the Hessians, The" (Franklin), **II: 120**

Salinas, Luis Omar, **Supp. IV Part 2:** 545; **Supp. V:** 180; **Supp. XIII:** **311–330**

"Salinas Is on His Way" (Salinas), **Supp. XIII:** 317

"Salinas Sends Messengers to the Stars" (Salinas), **Supp. XIII:** 317

"Salinas Summering at the Caspian and Thinking of Hamlet" (Salinas), **Supp. XIII:** 320

"Salinas Wakes Early and Goes to the Park to Lecture Sparrows" (Salinas), **Supp. XIII:** 320

Salinger, Doris, **III:** 551

Salinger, J. D., **II:** 255; **III:** **551–574;** **IV:** 190, 216, 217; **Retro. Supp. I:** 102, 116, 335; **Supp. IV Part 2:** 502; **Supp. V:** 23, 119; **Supp. VIII:** 151; **Supp. XI:** 2, 66; **Supp. XIV:** 93

Salisbury, Harrison, **Supp. I Part 2:** 664

Salle, David, **Supp. XII:** 4

Salley, Columbus, **Supp. XIV:** 195

"Sally" (Cisneros), **Supp. VII:** 63

Salmagundi; or, The Whim-Whams and Opinions of Launcelot Langstaff Esq., and Others (Irving), **II:** 299, 300, 304

Salome (Strauss), **IV:** 316

Salon (online magazine), **Supp. VIII:** 310; **Supp. X:** 202

Salt Eaters, The (Bambara), **Supp. XI:** 1, **12–14**

Salt Ecstasies, The (White), **Supp. XI:** 123

Salter, James, **Supp. IX:** **245–263**

Salter, Mary Jo, **Supp. IV Part 2:** 653; **Supp. IX:** 37, 292

Salt Garden, The (Nemerov), **III:** 269, 272–275, 277

"Salt Garden, The" (Nemerov), **III:** 267–268

Salting the Ocean (Nye, ed.), **Supp. XIII:** 280

"Salts and Oils" (Levine), **Supp. V:** 190

Saltzman, Arthur, **Supp. XIII:** 48

Saltzman, Harry, **Supp. XI:** 307

"Salut au Monde!" (Whitman), **Retro. Supp. I:** 387, 396, 400

"Salute" (MacLeish), **III:** 13

"Salute to Mister Yates, A" (Dubus), **Supp. XI:** 347, 349

Salvador (Didion), **Supp. IV Part 1:** 198, 207–208, 210

"Salvage" (Clampitt), **Supp. IX:** 41

Samain, Albert, **II:** 528

Same Door, The (Updike), **IV:** 214, 219, 226; **Retro. Supp. I:** 320

"Same in Blues" (Hughes), **Retro. Supp. I:** 208

Sam Lawson's Oldtown Fireside Stories (Stowe), **Supp. I Part 2:** 587, 596, 598–599

"Sa'm Pèdi" (Bell), **Supp. X:** 17

"Sampler, A" (MacLeish), **III:** 4

Sampoli, Maria, **Supp. V:** 338

Sampson, Edward, **Supp. I Part 2:** 664, 673

Sampson, Martin, **Supp. I Part 2:** 652

Samson Agonistes (Milton), **III:** 274

"Samson and Delilah" (Masters), **Supp. I Part 2:** 459

Samuel de Champlain: Father of New France (Morison), **Supp. I Part 2:** 496–497

Samuels, Charles Thomas, **Retro. Supp. I:** 334

"Samuel Sewall" (Hecht), **Supp. X:** 58

Sanborn, Franklin B., **IV:** 171, 172, 178

Sanborn, Kate, **Supp. XIII:** 152

Sanborn, Sara, **Supp. XIV:** 113

Sanchez, Carol Anne, **Supp. IV Part 1:** 335

Sanchez, Carol Lee, **Supp. IV Part 2:** 499, 557

Sanchez, Sonia, **Supp. II Part 1:** 34

Sanctified Church, The (Hurston), **Supp. VI:** 150

"Sanction of the Victims, The" (Rand), **Supp. IV Part 2:** 528

Sanctuary (Faulkner), **II:** 57, 61–63, 72, 73, 74, 174; **Retro. Supp. I:** 73, 84, 86–87, 87; **Supp. I Part 2:** 614; **Supp. XII:** 16

Sanctuary (Wharton), **IV:** 311

"Sanctuary" (Wylie), **Supp. I Part 2:** 711

"Sanctuary, The" (Nemerov), **III:** 272, 274

Sand, George, **II:** 322; **Retro. Supp. I:** 235, 372

"Sandalphon" (Longfellow), **II:** 498

Sandbox, The (Albee), **I:** 74–75, 89

Sandburg, Carl, **I:** 103, 109, 384, 421; **II:** 529; **III:** 3, 20, **575–598; Retro. Supp. I:** 133, 194; **Supp. I Part 1:** 257, 320; **Supp. I Part 2:** 387, 389, 454, 461, 653; **Supp. III Part 1:** 63, 71, 73, 75; **Supp. IV Part 1:**

169; **Supp. IV Part 2:** 502; **Supp. IX:** 1, 15, 308; **Supp. XIII:** 274, 277

Sandburg, Helga, **III:** 583

Sandburg, Janet, **III:** 583, 584

Sandburg, Margaret, **III:** 583, 584

Sandburg, Mrs. Carl (Lillian Steichen), **III:** 580

Sand County Almanac and Sketches Here and There, A (Leopold), **Supp. XIV:** 177, 178, **182–192**

"Sand Dabs" (Oliver), **Supp. VII:** 245

"Sand Dunes" (Frost), **Retro. Supp. I:** 137; **Retro. Supp. II:** 41

Sander, August, **Supp. IX:** 211

"Sandman, The" (Barthelme), **Supp. IV Part 1:** 47

Sando, Joe S., **Supp. IV Part 2:** 510

Sandoe, James, **Supp. IV Part 1:** 131; **Supp. IV Part 2:** 470

Sandperl, Ira, **Supp. VIII:** 200

"Sand-Quarry and Moving Figures" (Rukeyser), **Supp. VI:** 271, 278

Sand Rivers (Matthiessen), **Supp. V:** 203

"Sand Roses, The" (Hogan), **Supp. IV Part 1:** 401

Sands, Diana, **Supp. IV Part 1:** 362

Sands, Robert, **Supp. I Part 1:** 156, 157

"Sands at Seventy" (Whitman), **IV:** 348

"Sandstone Farmhouse, A" (Updike), **Retro. Supp. I:** 318

Sanford, John, **IV:** 286, 287

"San Francisco Blues" (Kerouac), **Supp. III Part 1:** 225

Sangamon County Peace Advocate, The (Lindsay), **Supp. I Part 2:** 379

Sanger, Margaret, **Supp. I Part 1:** 19

Sansom, William, **IV:** 279

Sans Soleil (film), **Supp. IV Part 2:** 436

"Santa" (Sexton), **Supp. II Part 2:** 693

Santa Claus: A Morality (Cummings), **I:** 430, 441

"Santa Fé Trail, The" (Lindsay), **Supp. I Part 2:** 389

"Santa Lucia" (Hass), **Supp. VI:** 105–106

"Santa Lucia II" (Hass), **Supp. VI:** 105–106

Santayana, George, **I:** 222, 224, 236, 243, 253, 460; **II:** 20, 542; **III:** 64, **599–622; IV:** 26, 339, 351, 353, 441; **Retro. Supp. I:** 55, 57, 67, 295; **Retro. Supp. II:** 179; **Supp. I Part 2:** 428; **Supp. II Part 1:** 107; **Supp. X:** 58; **Supp. XIV:** 199, 335, 340, 342

Santiago, Esmeralda, **Supp. XI:** 177

"Santorini: Stopping the Leak" (Merrill), **Supp. III Part 1:** 336

Santos, John Phillip, **Supp. XIII:** 274

Santos, Sherod, **Supp. VIII:** 270

Sapir, Edward, **Supp. VIII:** 295

Sapphira and the Slave Girl (Cather), **I:** 331; **Retro. Supp. I:** 2, **19–20**

Sappho, **II:** 544; **III:** 142; **Supp. I Part 1:** 261, 269; **Supp. I Part 2:** 458; **Supp. XII:** 98, 99

"Sappho" (Wright), **Supp. III Part 2:** 595, 604

"Sarah" (Schwartz), **Supp. II Part 2:** 663

"Saratoga" mysteries (Dobyns), **Supp. XIII:** 79–80

Sargent, John Singer, **II:** 337, 338

Saroyan, William, **III:** 146–147; **IV:** 393; **Supp. I Part 2:** 679; **Supp. IV Part 1:** 83; **Supp. IV Part 2:** 502; **Supp. XIII:** 280

Sarris, Greg, **Supp. IV Part 1:** 329, 330

Sarton, George, **Supp. VIII:** 249

Sarton, May, **Supp. III Part 1:** 62, 63; **Supp. VIII: 249–268; Supp. XIII:** 296

Sartoris (Faulkner), **II:** 55, 56–57, 58, 62; **Retro. Supp. I:** 77, 81, 82, 83, 88

Sartor Resartus (Carlyle), **II:** 26; **III:** 82

Sartre, Jean-Paul, **I:** 82, 494; **II:** 244; **III:** 51, 204; 292, 453, 619; **IV:** 6, 223, 236, 477, 487, 493; **Retro. Supp. I:** 73; **Supp. I Part 1:** 51; **Supp. IV Part 1:** 42, 84; **Supp. VIII:** 11; **Supp. IX:** 4; **Supp. XIII:** 74, 171; **Supp. XIV:** 24

Sassone, Ralph, **Supp. X:** 171

Sassoon, Siegfried, **II:** 367

Satan in Goray (Singer), **IV:** 1, 6–7, 12; **Retro. Supp. II:** 303, **304–305**

Satan Says (Olds), **Supp. X:** 201, 202, **202–204**, 215

"Satan Says" (Olds), **Supp. X:** 202

Satanstoe (Cooper), **I:** 351–352, 355

"Sather Gate Illumination" (Ginsberg), **Supp. II Part 1:** 329

"Satire as a Way of Seeing" (Dos Passos), **III:** 172

Satires of Persius, The (Merwin, trans.), **Supp. III Part 1:** 347

Satirical Rogue on Poetry, The (Francis). *See Pot Shots at Poetry* (Francis)

Satori in Paris (Kerouac), **Supp. III Part 1:** 231

"Saturday" (Salinas), **Supp. XIII:** 315

Saturday Night at the War (Shanley), **Supp. XIV:** 315

"Saturday Route, The" (Wolfe), **Supp. III Part 2:** 580

Satyagraha (Gandhi), **IV:** 185

Saunders, Richard, **II:** 110

Savage, Augusta, **Retro. Supp. II:** 115

Savage, James, **II:** 111

Savage Holiday (Wright), **IV:** 478, 488

Savage in Limbo: A Concert Play (Shanley), **Supp. XIV:** 315, **319–321,** 323, 324

Savage Love (Shepard and Chaikin), **Supp. III Part 2:** 433

Savage Wilds (Reed), **Supp. X:** 241

Save Me, Joe Louis (Bell), **Supp. X:** 7, 10, **11–12**

Save Me the Waltz (Z. Fitzgerald), **II:** 95; **Retro. Supp. I:** 110; **Supp. IX:** 58, 59, 65, **66–68**

Savers, Michael, **Supp. XI:** 307

Saving Lives (Goldbarth), **Supp. XII:** 192

Saving Private Ryan (film), **Supp. V:** 249; **Supp. XI:** 234

Savings (Hogan), **Supp. IV Part 1:** 397, 404, 405, 406, 410

Savo, Jimmy, **I:** 440

Savran, David, **Supp. IX:** 145; **Supp. XIII:** 209

Sawyer-Lauçanno, Christopher, **Supp. IV Part 1:** 95

Saxon, Lyle, **Retro. Supp. I:** 80

Saye and Sele, Lord, **Supp. I Part 1:** 98

Sayer, Mandy, **Supp. XIII:** 118

Sayers, Dorothy, **Supp. IV Part 1:** 341; **Supp. IV Part 2:** 464

Sayers, Valerie, **Supp. XI:** 253

"Sayings/For Luck" (Goldbarth), **Supp. XII:** 176

Say! Is This the U.S.A.? (Caldwell), **I:** 293, 294–295, 304, 309, 310

Saylor, Bruce, **Supp. XII:** 253

Sayre, Joel, **Supp. XIII:** 166

Sayre, Nora, **Supp. XII:** 119

Sayre, Zelda, **Retro. Supp. I:** 101, 102–103, 104, 105, 108, 109, 110, 113, 114. *See also* Fitzgerald, Zelda (Zelda Sayre)

"Say Yes" (Wolff), **Supp. VII:** 344

"Scales of the Eyes, The" (Nemerov), **III:** 272, 273, 277

Scalpel (McCoy), **Supp. XIII: 174–175**

Scalpel (screen treatment, McCoy), **Supp. XIII:** 174

Scandalabra (Zelda Fitzgerald), **Supp. IX:** 60, 61, 65, 67, **68–70**

"Scandal Detectives, The" (Fitzgerald),

II: 80–81; **Retro. Supp. I:** 99

Scarberry-García, Susan, **Supp. IV Part 2:** 486

"Scarecrow, The" (Farrell), **II:** 45

"Scarf, A" (Shields), **Supp. VII:** 328

Scarlet Letter, The (Hawthorne), **II:** 63, 223, 224, 231, 233, 239–240, 241, 243, 244, 255, 264, 286, 290, 291, 550; **Retro. Supp. I:** 63, 145, 147, 152, **157–159,** 160, 163, 165, 220, 248, 330, 335; **Retro. Supp. II:** 100; **Supp. I Part 1:** 38; **Supp. II Part 1:** 386; **Supp. VIII:** 108, 198; **Supp. XII:** 11

Scarlet Plague, The (London), **II:** 467

Scar Lover (Crews), **Supp. XI:** 103, 107, **114–115**

"Scarred Girl, The" (Dickey), **Supp. IV Part 1:** 180

Scates, Maxine, **Supp. XIV:** 264, 265, 274

"Scenario" (H. Miller), **III:** 184

"Scene" (Howells), **II:** 274

"Scene in Jerusalem, A" (Stowe), **Supp. I Part 2:** 587

"Scenes" (Shields), **Supp. VII:** 318

Scènes d'Anabase (chamber music) (Bowles), **Supp. IV Part 1:** 82

Scenes from American Life (Gurney), **Supp. V:** 95, 96, 105, 108

Scenes from Another Life (McClatchy), **Supp. XII: 255–256**

"Scenes of Childhood" (Merrill), **Supp. III Part 1:** 322, 323, 327

"Scented Herbage of My Breast" (Whitman), **IV:** 342–343

"Scent of Unbought Flowers, The" (Ríos), **Supp. IV Part 2:** 547

Scepticisms (Aiken), **I:** 58

Scève, Maurice, **Supp. III Part 1:** 11

Schad, Christian, **Supp. IV Part 1:** 247

Schafer, Benjamin G., **Supp. XIV:** 144

Schaller, George, **Supp. V:** 208, 210–211

Schapiro, Meyer, **II:** 30

Scharmann, Hermann Balthazar, **Supp. XII:** 41

Schary, Dore, **Supp. IV Part 1:** 365; **Supp. XIII:** 163

Schaumbergh, Count de, **II:** 120

Scheffauer, G. H., **I:** 199

"Scheherazade" (Ashbery), **Supp. III Part 1:** 18

Scheick, William, **Supp. V:** 272

Scheler, Max, **I:** 58

Schelling, Friedrich, **Supp. I Part 2:** 422

Schenk, Margaret, **I:** 199

Scheponik, Peter, **Supp. X:** 210

Scherer, Loline, **Supp. XIII:** 161

Schevill, James, **I:** 116

Schilder, Paul, **Supp. I Part 2:** 622

Schiller, Andrew, **II:** 20

Schiller, Frederick, **Supp. V:** 290

Schiller, Johann Christoph Friedrich von, **I:** 224; **Supp. IV Part 2:** 519

Schiller, Lawrence, **Retro. Supp. II:** 208, 212, 214

Schimmel, Harold, **Supp. V:** 336

Schlegel, Augustus Wilhelm, **III:** 422, 424

Schlegell, David von, **Supp. IV Part 2:** 423

Schleiermacher, Friedrich, **III:** 290–291, 309

Schlesinger, Arthur, Jr., **III:** 291, 297–298, 309

Schmidt, Jon Zlotnik, **Supp. IV Part 1:** 2

Schmidt, Kaspar. *See* Stirner, Max

Schmidt, Michael, **Supp. X:** 55

Schmitt, Carl, **I:** 386–387

Schmitz, Neil, **Supp. X:** 243

Schneider, Alan, **I:** 87

Schneider, Louis, **Supp. I Part 2:** 650

Schneider, Romy, **Supp. IV Part 2:** 549

Schneider, Steven, **Supp. IX:** 271, 274

Schnellock, Emil, **III:** 177

Schneour, Zalman, **IV:** 11

"Scholar Gypsy, The" (Arnold), **II:** 541

"Scholastic and Bedside Teaching" (Holmes), **Supp. I Part 1:** 305

Schöler, Bo, **Supp. IV Part 1:** 399, 400, 403, 407, 409; **Supp. IV Part 2:** 499

Scholes, Robert, **Supp. V:** 40, 42

Schomburg, Arthur, **Supp. X:** 134

Schoolcraft, Henry Rowe, **II:** 503; **Retro. Supp. II:** 160

"School Daze" (Bambara), **Supp. XI:** 19

School Daze (film), **Supp. XI:** 19, 20

"Schoolhouse" (Levis), **Supp. XI:** 258

"School of Giorgione, The" (Pater), **I:** 51

"School Play, The" (Merrill), **Supp. III Part 1:** 336

"Schooner Fairchild's Class" (Benét), **Supp. XI:** 55

Schopenhauer, Arthur, **III:** 600, 604; **IV:** 7; **Retro. Supp. I:** 256; **Retro. Supp. II:** 94; **Supp. I Part 1:** 320; **Supp. I Part 2:** 457; **Supp. X:** 187

Schorer, Mark, **II:** 28; **III:** 71; **Retro. Supp. I:** 115; **Supp. IV Part 1:** 197, 203, 211

Schott, Webster, **Supp. IX:** 257

Schotts, Jeffrey, **Supp. XII:** 193

Schrader, Mary von. *See* Jarrell, Mrs.

Randall (Mary von Schrader)

Schreiner, Olive, **I:** 419; **Supp. XI:** 203

Schroeder, Eric James, **Supp. V:** 238, 244

Schubert, Franz Peter, **Supp. I Part 1:** 363

Schubnell, Matthias, **Supp. IV Part 2:** 486

Schulberg, Budd, **II:** 98; **Retro. Supp. I:** 113; **Supp. XIII:** 170

Schulz, Bruno, **Supp. IV Part 2:** 623

Schuman, William, **Supp. XII:** 253

Schumann, Dr. Alanson Tucker, **III:** 505

Schuster, Edgar H., **Supp. VIII:** 126

Schuyler, George S., **III:** 110

Schuyler, William, **Supp. I Part 1:** 211

Schwartz, Delmore, **I:** 67, 168, 188, 288; **IV:** 128, 129, 437; **Retro. Supp. II:** 29, 178; **Supp. II Part 1:** 102, 109; **Supp. II Part 2: 639–668; Supp. VIII:** 98; **Supp. IX:** 299; **Supp. XIII:** 320; **Supp. XIV:** 3

Schwartz, Lloyd, **Supp. I Part 1:** 81

Schwartz, Marilyn, **Supp. XII:** 126, 128, 130, 132

Schwartz, Richard B., **Supp. XIV:** 23, 27

Schweitzer, Albert, **Supp. IV Part 1:** 373

Schweitzer, Harold, **Supp. X:** 210

Schwerdt, Lisa M., **Supp. XIV:** 155, 171

Schwitters, Kurt, **III:** 197; **Retro. Supp. II:** 322, 331, 336; **Supp. IV Part 1:** 79

"Science" (Jeffers), **Supp. II Part 2:** 426

Science and Health with Key to the Scriptures (Eddy), **I:** 383

"Science Favorable to Virtue" (Freneau), **Supp. II Part 1:** 274

Science of English Verse, The (Lanier), **Supp. I Part 1:** 368, 369

"Science of the Night, The" (Kunitz), **Supp. III Part 1:** 258, 265

Sciolino, Martina, **Supp. XII:** 9

Scopes, John T., **III:** 105, 495

"Scorched Face, The" (Hammett), **Supp. IV Part 1:** 344

"Scorpion, The" (Bowles), **Supp. IV Part 1:** 84, 86

Scorsese, Martin, **Supp. IV Part 1:** 356

Scott, A. O., **Supp. X:** 301, 302; **Supp. XII:** 343

Scott, Anne Firor, **Supp. I Part 1:** 19

Scott, Evelyn, **Retro. Supp. I:** 73

Scott, George C., **III:** 165–166; **Supp. XI:** 304

Scott, George Lewis, **Supp. I Part 2:** 503, 504

Scott, Herbert, **Supp. V:** 180

Scott, Howard, **Supp. I Part 2:** 645

Scott, Lizabeth, **Supp. IV Part 2:** 524

Scott, Lynn Orilla, **Retro. Supp. II:** 12

Scott, Mark, **Retro. Supp. I:** 127

Scott, Nathan A., Jr., **II:** 27

Scott, Paul, **Supp. IV Part 2:** 690

Scott, Ridley, **Supp. XIII:** 268

Scott, Sir Walter, **I:** 204, 339, 341, 343, 354; **II:** 8, 17, 18, 217, 296, 301, 303, 304, 308; **III:** 415, 482; **IV:** 204, 453; **Retro. Supp. I:** 99; **Supp. I Part 2:** 579, 580, 685, 692; **Supp. IV Part 2:** 690; **Supp. IX:** 175; **Supp. X:** 51, 114

Scott, Winfield Townley, **II:** 512; **Supp. I Part 2:** 705

Scottsboro boys, **I:** 505; **Supp. I Part 1:** 330

Scottsboro Limited (Hughes), **Retro. Supp. I:** 203; **Supp. I Part 1:** 328, 330–331, 332

Scoundrel Time (Hellman), **Supp. I Part 1:** 294–297; **Supp. IV Part 1:** 12; **Supp. VIII:** 243

Scratch (MacLeish), **III:** 22–23

"Scream, The" (Lowell), **II:** 550

"Screamer, The" (Coleman), **Supp. XI:** 92–93

"Screamers, The" (Baraka), **Supp. II Part 1:** 38

"Screen Guide for Americans" (Rand), **Supp. IV Part 2:** 524

"Screeno" (Schwartz), **Supp. II Part 2:** 660

Screens, The (Genet), **Supp. XII:** 12

Scripts for the Pageant (Merrill), **Supp. III Part 1:** 332, 333, 335

Scrolls from the Dead Sea, The (Wilson), **IV:** 429

Scruggs, Earl, **Supp. V:** 335

Scudder, Horace Elisha, **II:** 400, 401; **Retro. Supp. II:** 67; **Supp. I Part 1:** 220; **Supp. I Part 2:** 410, 414

Scully, James, **Supp. XII:** 131

"Sculpting the Whistle" (Ríos), **Supp. IV Part 2:** 549

"Sculptor" (Plath), **Supp. I Part 2:** 538

"Sculptor's Funeral, The" (Cather), **I:** 315–316; **Retro. Supp. I:** 5, 6

Scum (Singer), **Retro. Supp. II:** 316–317

Scupoli, Lorenzo, **IV:** 156

"Scythe Song" (Lang), **Retro. Supp. I:** 128

Sea and the Mirror, The: A Com-

mentary on Shakespeare's "The Tempest" (Auden), **Supp. II Part 1:** 2, 18

Sea around Us, The (Carson), **Supp. IX:** 19, **23–25**

Sea around Us, The (film), **Supp. IX:** 25

Sea Birds Are Still Alive, The (Bambara), **Supp. XI:** 1, 4, **7–12**

"Sea Birds Are Still Alive, The" (Bambara), **Supp. XI:** 8

"Sea-Blue and Blood-Red" (Lowell), **II:** 524

Seabrook, John, **Supp. VIII:** 157

"Sea Burial from the Cruiser Reve" (Eberhart), **I:** 532–533

Seabury, David, **Supp. I Part 2:** 608

"Sea Calm" (Hughes), **Retro. Supp. I:** 199

"Sea Chanty" (Corso), **Supp. XII:** 118

"Sea Dream, A" (Whitter), **Supp. I Part 2:** 699

"Seafarer, The" (Pound, trans.), **Retro. Supp. I:** 287

Seagall, Harry, **Supp. XIII:** 166

Sea Garden (Doolittle), **Supp. I Part 1:** 257, 259, 266, 269, 272

Seager, Allan, **IV:** 305

"Sea Lily" (Doolittle), **Supp. I Part 1:** 266

Sea Lions, The (Cooper), **I:** 354, 355

Sealts, Merton M., Jr., **Retro. Supp. I:** 257

Seaman, Donna, **Supp. VIII:** 86; **Supp. X:** 1, 4, 12, 16, 213

"Séance, The" (Singer), **IV:** 20

Séance and Other Stories, The (Singer), **IV:** 19–21

Sea of Cortez (Steinbeck), **IV:** 52, 54, 62, 69

"Sea Pieces" (Melville), **III:** 93

Searches and Seizures (Elkin), **Supp. VI:** 49

"Search for Southern Identity, The" (Woodward), **Retro. Supp. I:** 75

Search for the King, A: A Twelfth-Century Legend (Vidal), **Supp. IV Part 2:** 681

Searching for Caleb (Tyler), **Supp. IV Part 2:** 663–665, 671

"Searching for Poetry: Real *vs.* Fake" (B. Miller), **Supp. IV Part 1:** 67

Searching for Survivors (Banks), **Supp. V:** 7

"Searching for Survivors (I)" (Banks), **Supp. V:** 8

"Searching for Survivors (II)" (Banks), **Supp. V:** 7, 8

Searching for the Ox (Simpson), **Supp. IX:** 266, **274–275**

"Searching for the Ox" (Simpson), **Supp. IX:** 275, 280

"Searching in the Britannia Tavern" (Wagoner), **Supp. IX:** 327

Searching Wing, The, (Hellman), **Supp. I Part 1:** 277, 278, 281–282, 283, 292, 297

"Search Party, The" (Matthews), **Supp. IX: 156**

Searle, Ronald, **Supp. I Part 2:** 604, 605

Sea Road to the Indies (Hart), **Supp. XIV:** 97

"Seascape" (Bishop), **Retro. Supp. II:** 42–43

"Sea's Green Sameness, The" (Updike), **IV:** 217

Seaside and the Fireside, The (Longfellow), **II:** 489; **Retro. Supp. II:** 159, 168

Season in Hell, A (Rimbaud), **III:** 189

Seasons, The (Thomson), **II:** 304; **Supp. I Part 1:** 151

Seasons' Difference, The (Buechner), **Supp. XII: 47**

Seasons of Celebration (Merton), **Supp. VIII:** 199, 208

Seasons of the Heart: In Quest of Faith (Kinard, comp.), **Supp. XIV:** 127

"Seasons of the Soul" (Tate), **IV:** 136–140

"Sea Surface Full of Clouds" (Stevens), **IV:** 82

"Sea Unicorns and Land Unicorns" (Moore), **III:** 202–203

Seaver, Richard, **Supp. XI:** 301

"Seaweed" (Longfellow), **II:** 498

Sea-Wolf, The (London), **II:** 264, 466, 472–473

Sebald, W. G., **Supp. XIV:** 96

Seckler, David, **Supp. I Part 2:** 650

Second American Revolution and Other Essays (1976–1982), The (Vidal), **Supp. IV Part 2:** 679, 687, 688

Secondary Colors, The (A. Theroux), **Supp. VIII:** 312

Second Chance (Auchincloss), **Supp. IV Part 1:** 33

"Second Chances" (Hugo), **Supp. VI:** 144, 145

Second Coming, The (Percy), **Supp. III Part 1:** 383, 384, 387, 388, 396–397

"Second Coming, The" (Yeats), **III:** 294; **Retro. Supp. I:** 290, 311; **Supp. VIII:** 24

Second Decade, The. See Stephen King, The Second Decade: "Danse Macabre" to "The Dark Half" (Magistrale)

Second Dune, The (Hearon), **Supp. VIII:** 58, **59–60**

Second Flowering, A: Works and Days of the Lost Generation (Cowley), **Retro. Supp. II:** 77; **Supp. II Part 1:** 135, 141, 143, 144, 147, 149

Second Growth (Stegner), **Supp. IV Part 2:** 599, 608

Second Marriage (F. Barthelme), **Supp. XI:** 32, 33

"Second Marriage" (McCarriston), **Supp. XIV:** 262

Second Nature (Hoffman), **Supp. X:** 88, 89

"2nd Air Force" (Jarrell), **II:** 375

Second Set, The (Komunyakaa and Feinstein, eds.), **Supp. XIII:** 125

Second Sex, The (Beauvoir), **Supp. IV Part 1:** 360

Second Stone, The (Fiedler), **Supp. XIII:** 102

"Second Swimming, The" (Boyle), **Supp. VIII:** 13, 14

Second Tree from the Corner (White), **Supp. I Part 2:** 654

"Second Tree from the Corner" (White), **Supp. I Part 2:** 651

Second Twenty Years at Hull-House, The: September 1909 to September 1929, with a Record of a Growing World Consciousness (Addams), **Supp. I Part 1:** 24–25

Second Voyage of Columbus, The (Morison), **Supp. I Part 2:** 488

Second Words, (Atwood), **Supp. XIII:** 35

Second World, The (Blackmur), **Supp. II Part 1:** 91

"Secret, The" (Levine), **Supp. V:** 195

Secret Agent, The (Conrad), **Supp. IV Part 1:** 341

Secret Agent X-9 (Hammett), **Supp. IV Part 1:** 355

"Secret Courts of Men's Hearts, The: Code and Law in Harper Lee's *To Kill a Mockingbird*" (Johnson), **Supp. VIII:** 126

"Secret Dog, The" (Cameron), **Supp. XII: 83–84**

Secret Garden, The (Burnett), **Supp. I Part 1:** 44

Secret Historie (J. Smith), **I:** 131

Secret History of the Dividing Line (Howe), **Supp. IV Part 2:** 424, 425–426

"Secret Integration, The" (Pynchon), **Supp. II Part 2:** 624

"Secret Life of Walter Mitty, The" (Thurber), **Supp. I Part 2:** 623

"Secret Lion, The" (Ríos), **Supp. IV Part 2:** 543, 544

"Secret of the Russian Ballet, The" (Van Vechten), **Supp. II Part 2:** 732

"Secret Prune" (Ríos), **Supp. IV Part 2:** 549

Secret River, The (Rawlings), **Supp. X:** 233

Secrets and Surprises (Beattie), **Supp. V:** 23, 27, 29

Secrets from the Center of the World (Harjo), **Supp. XII: 223–224**

"Secret Sharer, The" (Conrad), **Supp. IX:** 105

"Secret Society, A" (Nemerov), **III:** 282

Secular Journal of Thomas Merton, The, **Supp. VIII:** 206

"Security" (Stafford), **Supp. XI:** 329

Sedges, John (pseudonym). *See* Buck, Pearl S.

Sedgwick, Catherine Maria, **I:** 341; **Supp. I Part 1:** 155, 157

Sedgwick, Christina. *See* Marquand, Mrs. John P. (Christina Sedgwick)

Sedgwick, Ellery, **I:** 217, 229, 231; **III:** 54–55

Sedgwick, Henry, **Supp. I Part 1:** 156

Sedgwick, Robert, **Supp. I Part 1:** 156

Sedore, Timothy, **Supp. XIV:** 312

"Seduction and Betrayal" (Hardwick), **Supp. III Part 1:** 207

Seduction and Betrayal: Women and Literature (Hardwick), **Supp. III Part 1:** 194, 204, 206–208, 212, 213; **Supp. XIV:** 89

Seed, David, **Supp. IV Part 1:** 391

"Seed Eaters, The" (Francis), **Supp. IX:** 82

"Seed Leaves" (Wilbur), **Supp. III Part 2:** 558

"Seeds" (Anderson), **I:** 106, 114

Seeds of Contemplation (Merton), **Supp. VIII:** 199, 200, 207, 208

Seeds of Destruction (Merton), **Supp. VIII:** 202, 203, 204, 208

Seeing through the Sun (Hogan), **Supp. IV Part 1:** 397, 400, 401–402, 402, 413

"See in the Midst of Fair Leaves" (Moore), **III:** 215

"Seekers, The" (McGrath), **Supp. X:** 117

"Seeking a Vision of Truth, Guided by a Higher Power" (Burke), **Supp. XIV:** 21, 23

"Seele im Raum" (Jarrell), **II:** 382–383

"Seele im Raum" (Rilke), **II:** 382–383

"See Naples and Die" (Hecht), **Supp. X:** 69, 70

"Seen from the 'L'" (Barnes), **Supp. III Part 1:** 33

"See the Moon?" (Barthelme), **Supp. IV Part 1:** 42, 49–50, 50

Segal, D. (pseudonym). *See* Singer, Isaac Bashevis

Segal, George, **Supp. XI:** 343

Segregation: The Inner Conflict in the South (Warren), **IV:** 237, 238, 246, 252

Seidel, Frederick, **I:** 185

Seize the Day (Bellow), **I:** 144, 147, 148, 150, 151, 152, 153, 155, 158, 162; **Retro. Supp. II:** 19, **23–24,** 27, 32, 34; **Supp. I Part 2:** 428

Selby, Hubert, **Supp. III Part 1:** 125

Selby, John, **Retro. Supp. II:** 221, 222

Selden, John, **Supp. XIV:** 344

Seldes, Gilbert, **II:** 437, 445; **Retro. Supp. I:** 108

Selected Criticism: Prose, Poetry (Bogan), **Supp. III Part 1:** 64

Selected Essays (Eliot), **I:** 572

Selected Letters (W. C. Williams), **Retro. Supp. I:** 430

Selected Letters, 1940–1956 (Kerouac), **Supp. XIV:** 137, 144

Selected Letters of Robert Frost (Thompson, ed.), **Retro. Supp. I:** 125

Selected Levis, The (Levis), **Supp. XI:** 257, 272

Selected Poems (Aiken), **I:** 69

Selected Poems (Ashbery), **Supp. III Part 1:** 25–26

Selected Poems (Bly), **Supp. IV Part 1:** 60, 62, 65, 66, 68, 69–71

Selected Poems (Brodsky), **Supp. VIII:** 22

Selected Poems (Brooks), **Supp. III Part 1:** 82–83

Selected Poems (Corso), **Supp. XII:** 129

Selected Poems (Dove), **Supp. IV Part 1:** 241, 243, 250

Selected Poems (Frost), **Retro. Supp. I:** 133, 136

Selected Poems (Guillevic; Levertov, trans.), **Supp. III Part 1:** 283

Selected Poems (Hayden), **Supp. II Part 1:** 363, 364, 367

Selected Poems (Hughes), **Retro. Supp. I:** 202; **Supp. I Part 1:** 341, 345, 346

Selected Poems (Hugo), **Supp. VI:** 143

Selected Poems (Jarrell), **II:** 367, 370, 371, 374, 377, 379, 380, 381, 382, 384

Selected Poems (Justice), **Supp. VII:** 115

Selected Poems (Kinnell), **Supp. III Part 1:** 235, 253

Selected Poems (Levine, 1984), **Supp. V:** 178, 179

Selected Poems (Lowell), **II:** 512, 516; **Retro. Supp. II:** 184, 186, 188, 190

Selected Poems (Merton), **Supp. VIII:** 207, 208

Selected Poems (Moore), **III:** 193, 194, 205–206, 208, 215

Selected Poems (Pound), **Retro. Supp. I:** 289, 291

Selected Poems (Ransom), **III:** 490, 492

Selected Poems (Reznikoff), **Supp. XIV:** 288

Selected Poems (Rukeyser), **Supp. VI:** 274

Selected Poems (Sexton), **Supp. IV Part 2:** 449

Selected Poems (Strand), **Supp. IV Part 2:** 630

Selected Poems 1936–1965 (Eberhart), **I:** 541

Selected Poems 1965–1975 (Atwood), **Supp. XIII: 32–34**

Selected Poems, 1923–1943 (Warren), **IV:** 241–242, 243

Selected Poems, 1928–1958 (Kunitz), **Supp. III Part 1:** 261, 263–265

Selected Poems, 1938–1988 (McGrath), **Supp. X:** 127

Selected Poems: 1957–1987 (Snodgrass), **Supp. VI:** 314–315, 323, 324

Selected Poems, 1963–1983 (Simic), **Supp. VIII:** 275

Selected Poems II: Poems Selected and New, 1976–1986 (Atwood), **Supp. XIII:** 20, **34–35**

Selected Poems of Ezra Pound (Pound), **Supp. V:** 336

Selected Poems of Gabriela Mistral (Hughes, trans.), **Supp. I Part 1:** 345

Selected Poetry of Amiri Baraka/LeRoi Jones (Baraka), **Supp. II Part 1:** 58

Selected Stories (Dubus), **Supp. VII:** 88–89

Selected Stories of Richard Bausch, The (Bausch), **Supp. VII:** 42

Selected Translations (Snodgrass), **Supp. VI:** 318, 324, **325–326**

Selected Works of Djuna Barnes, The (Barnes), **Supp. III Part 1:** 44

Selected Writings 1950–1990 (Howe), **Supp. VI:** 116–117, 118, 120

Selected Writings of John Jay Chapman, The (Barzun), **Supp. XIV:** 54

Select Epigrams from the Greek Anthology (Mackail), **Supp. I Part 2:** 461

"Selene Afterwards" (MacLeish), **III:** 8

"Self" (James), **II:** 351

Self and the Dramas of History, The (Niebuhr), **III:** 308

Self-Consciousness (Updike), **Retro. Supp. I:** 318, 319, 320, 322, 323, 324

Self-Help: Stories (Moore), **Supp. X:** 163, 166, **167–169,** 174, 175

Self-Interviews (Dickey), **Supp. IV Part 1:** 179

"Self-Made Man, A" (Crane), **I:** 420

"Self-Portrait" (Creeley), **Supp. IV Part 1:** 156

"Self-Portrait" (Mumford), **Supp. II Part 2:** 471

"Self-Portrait" (Wylie), **Supp. I Part 2:** 729

Self-Portrait: Ceaselessly into the Past (Millar, ed. Sipper), **Supp. IV Part 2:** 464, 469, 472, 475

"Self-Portrait in a Convex Mirror" (Ashbery), **Supp. III Part 1:** 5, 7, 9, 16–19, 22, 24, 26

"Self-Reliance" (Emerson), **II:** 7, 15, 17; **Retro. Supp. I:** 159; **Retro. Supp. II:** 155; **Supp. X:** 42, 45

Sélincourt, Ernest de, **Supp. I Part 2:** 676

Selinger, Eric Murphy, **Supp. XI:** 248

Sellers, Isaiah, **IV:** 194–195

Sellers, Peter, **Supp. XI:** 301, 304, 306, 307, 309

Sellers, William, **IV:** 208

Seltzer, Mark, **Retro. Supp. I:** 227

Selznick, David O., **Retro. Supp. I:** 105, 113; **Supp. IV Part 1:** 353

"Semi-Lunatics of Kilmuir, The" (Hugo), **Supp. VI:** 145

"Semiotics/The Doctor's Doll" (Goldbarth), **Supp. XII:** 183–184

Semmelweiss, Ignaz, **Supp. I Part 1:** 304

Senancour, Étienne Divert de, **I:** 241

Sendak, Maurice, **Supp. IX:** 207, 208, 213, 214

Seneca, **II:** 14–15; **III:** 77

Senghor, Leopold Sédar, **Supp. IV Part 1:** 16; **Supp. X:** 132, 139

Senier, Siobhan, **Supp. IV Part 1:** 330

"Senility" (Anderson), **I:** 114

"Senior Partner's Ethics, The" (Auchincloss), **Supp. IV Part 1:** 33

Senlin: A Biography (Aiken), **I:** 48, 49, 50, 52, 56, 57, 64

Sennett, Mack, **III:** 442

"Señora X No More" (Mora), **Supp. XIII:** 218

"Señor Ong and Señor Ha" (Bowles), **Supp. IV Part 1:** 87

Sense of Beauty, The (Santayana), **III:** 600

Sense of Life in the Modern Novel, The (Mizener), **IV:** 132

"Sense of Shelter, A" (Updike), **Retro. Supp. I:** 318

Sense of the Past, The (James), **II:** 337–338

"Sense of the Past, The" (Trilling), **Supp. III Part 2:** 503

"Sense of the Present, The" (Hardwick), **Supp. III Part 1:** 210

"Sense of the Sleight-of-Hand Man, The" (Stevens), **IV:** 93

"Sense of Where You Are, A" (McPhee), **Supp. III Part 1:** 291, 296–298

"Sensibility! O La!" (Roethke), **III:** 536

"Sensible Emptiness, A" (Kramer), **Supp. IV Part 1:** 61, 66

"Sensuality Plunging Barefoot Into Thorns" (Cisneros), **Supp. VII:** 68

"Sentence" (Barthelme), **Supp. IV Part 1:** 47

Sent for You Yesterday (Wideman), **Supp. X:** 320, 321

"Sentimental Education, A" (Banks), **Supp. V:** 10

"Sentimental Journey" (Oates), **Supp. II Part 2:** 522, 523

"Sentimental Journey, A" (Anderson), **I:** 114

Sentimental Journey, A (Sterne), **Supp. I Part 2:** 714

"Sentimental Journeys" (Didion), **Supp. IV Part 1:** 211

"Sentiment of Rationality, The" (James), **II:** 346–347

Separate Flights (Dubus), **Supp. VII:** 78–83

"Separate Flights" (Dubus), **Supp. VII:** 83

Separate Peace, A (Knowles), **Supp. IV Part 2:** 679; **Supp. XII:** 241–249

Separate Way (Reznikoff), **Supp. XIV:** 280

"Separating" (Updike), **Retro. Supp. I:** 321

"Separation, The" (Kunitz), **Supp. III Part 1:** 263

"Sepia High Stepper" (Hayden), **Supp. II Part 1:** 379

"September" (Komunyakaa), **Supp. XIII:** 130

"September 1, 1939" (Auden), **Supp. II Part 1:** 13; **Supp. IV Part 1:** 225; **Supp. VIII:** 30, 32

September 11, 2001: American Writers Respond (Heyen), **Supp. XIII:** 285

September Song (Humphrey), **Supp. IX:** 101, 102, **108–109**

"Sept Vieillards, Les" (Millay, trans.), **III:** 142

Sequel to Drum-Taps (Whitman), **Retro. Supp. I:** 406

"Sequence, Sometimes Metaphysical" (Roethke), **III:** 547, 548

Sequence of Seven Plays with a Drawing by Ron Slaughter, A (Nemerov), **III:** 269

Sequoya, Jana, **Supp. IV Part 1:** 334

Seraglio, The (Merrill), **Supp. III Part 1:** 331

Seraphita (Balzac), **I:** 499

Seraph on the Suwanee (Hurston), **Supp. VI:** 149, 159–160

Serenissima: A Novel of Venice (Jong). *See Shylock's Daughter: A Novel of Love in Venice (Serenissima)* (Jong)

Sergeant, Elizabeth Shepley, **I:** 231, 236, 312, 319, 323, 328

Sergeant Bilko (television show), **Supp. IV Part 2:** 575

"Serious Talk, A" (Carver), **Supp. III Part 1:** 138, 144

Serly, Tibor, **Supp. III Part 2:** 617, 619

"Sermon by Doctor Pep" (Bellow), **I:** 151

Sermones (Horace), **II:** 154

"Sermon for Our Maturity" (Baraka), **Supp. II Part 1:** 53

Sermons and Soda Water (O'Hara), **III:** 362, 364, 371–373, 382

"Sermons on the Warpland" (Brooks), **Supp. III Part 1:** 84

"Serpent in the Wilderness, The" (Masters), **Supp. I Part 2:** 458

Servant of the Bones (Rice), **Supp. VII:** 298, 302

"Servant to Servants, A" (Frost), **Retro. Supp. I:** 125, 128; **Supp. X:** 66

Seshachari, Neila, **Supp. V:** 22

"Session, The" (Adams), **I:** 5

"Sestina" (Bishop), **Supp. I Part 1:** 73, 88

Set-angya, **Supp. IV Part 2:** 493

Seth's Brother's Wife (Frederic), **II:** 131–132, 137, 144

Set This House on Fire (Styron), **IV:** 98, 99, 105, 107–113, 114, 115, 117

Setting Free the Bears (Irving), **Supp. VI:** 163, **166–167,** 169–170

Setting the Tone (Rorem), **Supp. IV Part 1:** 79

Settle, Mary Lee, **Supp. IX:** 96

Settlement Horizon, The: A National Estimate (Woods and Kennedy), **Supp. I Part 1:** 19

"Settling the Colonel's Hash" (McCarthy), **II:** 559, 562

Setzer, Helen, **Supp. IV Part 1:** 217

"Seurat's Sunday Afternoon along the Seine" (Schwartz), **Supp. II Part 2:** 663–665

Seven against Thebes (Aeschylus; Bacon and Hecht, trans.), **Supp. X:** 57

Seven Ages of Man, The (Wilder), **IV:** 357, 374–375

Seven Deadly Sins, The (Wilder), **IV:** 357, 374–375

Seven Descents of Myrtle, The (T. Williams), **IV:** 382

Seven Guitars (Wilson), **Supp. VIII:** 331, **348–351**

Seven-League Crutches, The (Jarrell), **II:** 367, 372, 381, 382, 383–384, 389

Seven Mountains of Thomas Merton, The (Mott), **Supp. VIII:** 208

Seven-Ounce Man, The (Harrison), **Supp. VIII:** 51

"Seven Places of the Mind" (Didion), **Supp. IV Part 1:** 200, 210

Seven Plays (Shepard), **Supp. III Part 2:** 434

"Seven Stanzas at Easter" (Updike), **IV:** 215

Seven Storey Mountain, The (Merton), **Supp. VIII:** 193, 195, 198, 200, 207, 208

Seventh Heaven (Hoffman), **Supp. X:** 87, 89

"Seventh of March" (Webster), **Supp. I Part 2:** 687

"7000 Romaine, Los Angeles 38" (Didion), **Supp. IV Part 1:** 200

"Seventh Street" (Toomer), **Supp. IX:** 316

Seven Types of Ambiguity (Empson), **II:** 536; **IV:** 431

77 Dream Songs (Berryman), **I:** 168, 169, 170, 171, 174, 175, 183–188

73 Poems (Cummings), **I:** 430, 431, 446, 447, 448

7 Years from Somehwere (Levine), **Supp. V:** 178, 181, 188–189

Sevier, Jack, **IV:** 378

Sévigné, Madame de, **IV:** 361

Sewall, Richard, **Retro. Supp. I:** 25

Sewall, Samuel, **IV:** 145, 146, 147, 149, 154, 164; **Supp. I Part 1:** 100, 110

Sewell, Elizabeth, **Supp. XIII:** 344

Sex, Economy, Freedom and Com-

munity (Berry), **Supp. X:** 30, 36
"Sex Camp" (Mamet), **Supp. XIV:** 240
Sex & Character (Weininger), **Retro. Supp. I:** 416
"Sext" (Auden), **Supp. II Part 1:** 22
Sexton, Anne, **Retro. Supp. II:** 245; **Supp. I Part 2:** 538, 543, 546; **Supp. II Part 2: 669–700; Supp. III Part 2:** 599; **Supp. IV Part 1:** 245; **Supp. IV Part 2:** 439, 440–441, 442, 444, 447, 449, 451, 620; **Supp. V:** 113, 118, 124; **Supp. X:** 201, 202, 213; **Supp. XI:** 146, 240, 317; **Supp. XII:** 217, 253, 254, 256, 260, 261; **Supp. XIII:** 35, 76, 294, 312; **Supp. XIV:** 125, 126, 132, 269
Sexual Behavior in the American Male (Kinsey), **Supp. XIII:** 96–97
Sexual Perversity in Chicago (Mamet), **Supp. XIV:** 239, 240, 246–247, 249
"Sexual Revolution, The" (Dunn), **Supp. XI:** 142
Sexus (H. Miller), **III:** 170, 171, 184, 187, 188
"Sex Without Love" (Olds), **Supp. X:** 206
Seyersted, Per E., **Retro. Supp. II:** 65; **Supp. I Part 1:** 201, 204, 211, 216, 225; **Supp. IV Part 2:** 558
Seyfried, Robin, **Supp. IX:** 324
"Seymour: An Introduction" (Salinger), **III:** 569–571, 572
Seymour, Miranda, **Supp. VIII:** 167
Shacochis, Bob, **Supp. VIII:** 80
"Shadow" (Creeley), **Supp. IV Part 1:** 158
"Shadow, The" (Lowell), **II:** 522
Shadow and Act (Ellison), **Retro. Supp. II:** 119; **Supp. II Part 1:** 245–246
"Shadow and Shade" (Tate), **IV:** 128
"Shadow and the Flesh, The" (London), **II:** 475
"Shadow A Parable" (Poe), **III:** 417–418
Shadow Country (Gunn Allen), **Supp. IV Part 1:** 322, 324, 325–326
Shadow Man, The (Gordon), **Supp. IV Part 1:** 297, 298, 299, 312–314, 315
Shadow of a Dream, The, a Story (Howells), **II:** 285, 286, 290
"Shadow of the Crime, The: A Word from the Author" (Mailer), **Retro. Supp. II:** 214
Shadow on the Dial, The (Bierce), **I:** 208, 209
"Shadow Passing" (Merwin), **Supp. III Part 1:** 355
Shadows (Gardner), **Supp. VI:** 74

Shadows by the Hudson (Singer), **IV:** 1
Shadows of Africa (Matthiessen), **Supp. V:** 203
Shadows on the Hudson (Singer), **Retro. Supp. II: 311–313**
Shadows on the Rock (Cather), **I:** 314, 330–331, 332; **Retro. Supp. I:** 18
Shadow Train (Ashbery), **Supp. III Part 1:** 23–24, 26
"Shad-Time" (Wilbur), **Supp. III Part 2:** 563
Shaffer, Thomas L., **Supp. VIII:** 127, 128
Shaft (Parks; film), **Supp. XI:** 17
Shaftesbury, Earl of, **I:** 559
Shahn, Ben, **Supp. X:** 24
Shakelford, Dean, **Supp. VIII:** 129
Shaker, Why Don't You Sing? (Angelou), **Supp. IV Part 1:** 16
Shakespear, Mrs. Olivia, **III:** 457; **Supp. I Part 1:** 257
"Shakespeare" (Emerson), **II:** 6
Shakespeare, William, **I:** 103, 271, 272, 284–285, 358, 378, 433, 441, 458, 461, 573, 585, 586; **II:** 5, 8, 11, 18, 72, 273, 297, 302, 309, 320, 411, 494, 577, 590; **III:** 3, 11, 12, 82, 83, 91, 124, 130, 134, 145, 153, 159, 183, 210, 263, 286, 468, 473, 492, 503, 511, 567, 575–576, 577, 610, 612, 613, 615; **IV:** 11, 50, 66, 127, 132, 156, 309, 313, 362, 368, 370, 373, 453; **Retro. Supp. I:** 43, 64, 91, 248; **Retro. Supp. II:** 114, 299; **Supp. I Part 1:** 79, 150, 262, 310, 356, 363, 365, 368, 369, 370; **Supp. I Part 2:** 397, 421, 422, 470, 494, 622, 716, 720; **Supp. II Part 2:** 624, 626; **Supp. IV Part 1:** 31, 83, 87, 243; **Supp. IV Part 2:** 430, 463, 519, 688; **Supp. V:** 252, 280, 303; **Supp. VIII:** 160, 164; **Supp. IX:** 14, 133; **Supp. X:** 42, 62, 65, 78; **Supp. XII:** 54–57, 277, 281; **Supp. XIII:** 111, 115, 233; **Supp. XIV:** 97, 120, 225, 245, 306
Shakespeare and His Forerunners (Lanier), **Supp. I Part 1:** 369
Shakespeare in Harlem (Hughes), **Retro. Supp. I:** 194, 202, 205, 206, 207, 208; **Supp. I Part 1:** 333, 334, 345
Shalit, Gene, **Supp. VIII:** 73
Shall We Gather at the River (Wright), **Supp. III Part 2:** 601–602
"Shame" (Oates), **Supp. II Part 2:** 520
"Shame" (Wilbur), **Supp. III Part 2:** 556
"Shameful Affair, A" (Chopin), **Retro.**

Supp. II: 61
Shamela (Fielding), **Supp. V:** 127
"Shampoo, The" (Bishop), **Retro. Supp. II:** 46; **Supp. I Part 1:** 92
Shange, Ntozake, **Supp. VIII:** 214
Shank, Randy, **Supp. X:** 252
Shankaracharya, **III:** 567
Shanley, John Patrick, **Supp. XIV:315–332**
Shannon, Sandra, **Supp. VIII:** 333, 348
"Shape of Flesh and Bone, The" (MacLeish), **III:** 18–19
Shape of the Journey, The (Harrison), **Supp. VIII:** 53
Shapes of Clay (Bierce), **I:** 208, 209
Shaping Joy, A: Studies in the Writer's Craft (Brooks), **Supp. XIV:** 13
Shapiro, David, **Supp. XII:** 175, 185
Shapiro, Dorothy, **IV:** 380
Shapiro, Karl, **I:** 430, 521; **II:** 350; **III:** 527; **Supp. II Part 2: 701–724; Supp. III Part 2:** 623; **Supp. IV Part 2:** 645; **Supp. X:** 116; **Supp. XI:** 315
Shapiro, Laura, **Supp. IX:** 120
Sharif, Omar, **Supp. IX:** 253
"Shark Meat" (Snyder), **Supp. VIII:** 300
Shatayev, Elvira, **Supp. I Part 2:** 570
Shaviro, Steven, **Supp. VIII:** 189
Shaw, Colonel Robert Gould, **II:** 551
Shaw, Elizabeth. *See* Melville, Mrs. Herman (Elizabeth Shaw)
Shaw, George Bernard, **I:** 226; **II:** 82, 271, 276, 581; **III:** 69, 102, 113, 145, 155, 161, 162, 163, 373, 409; **IV:** 27, 64, 397, 432, 440; **Retro. Supp. I:** 100, 228; **Supp. IV Part 1:** 36; **Supp. IV Part 2:** 585, 683; **Supp. V:** 243–244, 290; **Supp. IX:** 68, 308; **Supp. XI:** 202; **Supp. XII:** 94; **Supp. XIV:** 343
Shaw, Irwin, **IV:** 381; **Supp. IV Part 1:** 383; **Supp. IX:** 251; **Supp. XI:** 221, 229, 231
Shaw, Joseph Thompson ("Cap"), **Supp. IV Part 1:** 121, 345, 351; **Supp. XIII:** 161
Shaw, Judge Lemuel, **III:** 77, 88, 91
Shaw, Sarah Bryant, **Supp. I Part 1:** 169
Shaw, Wilbur, Jr., **Supp. XIII:** 162
Shawl, The (Mamet), **Supp. XIV:** 245
Shawl, The (Ozick), **Supp. V:** 257, 260, 271
"Shawl, The" (Ozick), **Supp. V:** 271–272
Shawl and Prarie du Chien, The: Two

Plays (Mamet), **Supp. XIV:** 243–244

Shawn, William, **Supp. VIII:** 151, 170

"Shawshank Redemption, The" (King), **Supp. V:** 148

She (Haggard), **III:** 189

Shearer, Flora, **I:** 199

"Sheaves, The" (Robinson), **III:** 510, 524

"She Came and Went" (Lowell), **Supp. I Part 2:** 409

Sheed, Wilfrid, **IV:** 230; **Supp. XI:** 233

Sheeler, Charles, **IV:** 409; **Retro. Supp. I:** 430

Sheeper (Rosenthal), **Supp. XIV:** 147

Sheffer, Jonathan, **Supp. IV Part 1:** 95

She Had Some Horses (Harjo), **Supp. XII:** 220–223, 231

"She Had Some Horses" (Harjo), **Supp. XII:** 215, 222

"Shell, The" (Humphrey), **Supp. IX:** 94

Shelley, Percy Bysshe, **I:** 18, 68, 381, 476, 522, 577; **II:** 331, 516, 535, 540; **III:** 412, 426, 469; **IV:** 139; **Retro. Supp. I:** 308, 360; **Supp. I Part 1:** 79, 311, 349; **Supp. I Part 2:** 709, 718, 719, 720, 721, 722, 724, 728; **Supp. IV Part 1:** 235; **Supp. V:** 258, 280; **Supp. IX:** 51; **Supp. XII:** 117, 132, 136–137, 263; **Supp. XIV:** 271–272

Shellow, Sadie Myers, **Supp. I Part 2:** 608

"Shelter" (Doty), **Supp. XI:** 132

Sheltered Life, The (Glasgow), **II:** 174, 175, 179, 186, 187–188

Sheltering Sky, The (Bowles), **Supp. IV Part 1:** 82, 84, 85–86, 87

Sheltering Sky, The (film), **Supp. IV Part 1:** 94, 95

Shelton, Frank, **Supp. IV Part 2:** 658

Shelton, Mrs. Sarah. *See* Royster, Sarah Elmira

Shelton, Richard, **Supp. XI:** 133; **Supp. XIII:** 7

Shenandoah (Schwartz), **Supp. II Part 2:** 640, 651–652

"Shenandoah" (Shapiro), **Supp. II Part 2:** 704

Shepard, Alice, **IV:** 287

Shepard, Odell, **II:** 508; **Supp. I Part 2:** 418

Shepard, Sam, **Supp. III Part 2:** 431–450

Shepard, Thomas, **I:** 554; **IV:** 158

Sheppard Lee (Bird), **III:** 423

"She Remembers the Future" (Harjo), **Supp. XII:** 222

Sheridan, Richard Brinsley, **Retro.**

Supp. I: 127

Sherlock, William, **IV:** 152

Sherman, Sarah Way, **Retro. Supp. II:** 145

Sherman, Stuart Pratt, **I:** 222, 246–247; **Supp. I Part 2:** 423

Sherman, Susan, **Supp. VIII:** 265

Sherman, Tom, **IV:** 446

Sherman, William T., **IV:** 445, 446

Sherwood, Robert, **II:** 435; **Supp. IX:** 190

Sherwood Anderson & Other Famous Creoles (Faulkner), **I:** 117; **II:** 56

Sherwood Anderson Reader, The (Anderson), **I:** 114, 116

Sherwood Anderson's Memoirs (Anderson), **I:** 98, 101, 102, 103, 108, 112, 116

Sherwood Anderson's Notebook (Anderson), **I:** 108, 115, 117

She Stoops to Conquer (Goldsmith), **II:** 514

Shestov, Lev, **Supp. VIII:** 20, 24

Shetley, Vernon, **Supp. IX:** 292; **Supp. XI:** 123

"She Wept, She Railed" (Kunitz), **Supp. III Part 1:** 265

"Shiddah and Kuziba" (Singer), **IV:** 13, 15

Shield of Achilles, The (Auden), **Supp. II Part 1:** 21

"Shield of Achilles, The" (Auden), **Supp. II Part 1:** 21, 25

Shields, Carol, **Supp. VII:** 307–330

Shifting Landscape: A Composite, 1925–1987 (H. Roth), **Supp. IX:** 233–235

Shifts of Being (Eberhart), **I:** 525

Shigematsu, Soiko, **Supp. III Part 1:** 353

Shihab, Aziz, **Supp. XIII:** 273

Shih-hsiang Chen, **Supp. VIII:** 303

"Shiloh" (Mason), **Supp. VIII:** 140

Shiloh and Other Stories (Mason), **Supp. VIII:** 133, **139–141,** 143, 145

Shilts, Randy, **Supp. X:** 145

Shining, The (King), **Supp. V:** 139, 140, 141, 143–144, 146, 149, 151, 152

Shinn, Everett, **Retro. Supp. II:** 103

"Ship of Death" (Lawrence), **Supp. I Part 2:** 728

Ship of Fools (Porter), **III:** 433, 447, 453, 454; **IV:** 138

Shipping News, The (Proulx), **Supp. VII:** 249, 258–259

"Ships" (O. Henry), **Supp. II Part 1:** 409

Ships Going into the Blue: Essays and

Notes on Poetry (Simpson), **Supp. IX:** 275

Ship to America, A (Singer), **IV:** 1

"Shipwreck, The" (Merwin), **Supp. III Part 1:** 346

"Shirt" (Pinsky), **Supp. VI: 236–237,** 239, 240, 241, 245, 247

"Shirt Poem, The" (Stern), **Supp. IX:** 292

"Shiva and Parvati Hiding in the Rain" (Pinsky), **Supp. VI:** 244

Shively, Charley, **Retro. Supp. I:** 391; **Supp. XII:** 181, 182

Shock of Recognition, The (Wilson), **II:** 530

Shock of the New, The (Hughes), **Supp. X:** 73

Shoe Bird, The (Welty), **IV:** 261; **Retro. Supp. I:** 353

"Shoes" (O. Henry), **Supp. II Part 1:** 409

"Shoes of Wandering, The" (Kinnell), **Supp. III Part 1:** 248

"Shooters, Inc." (Didion), **Supp. IV Part 1:** 207, 211

"Shooting, The" (Dubus), **Supp. VII:** 84, 85

"Shooting Niagara; and After?" (Carlyle), **Retro. Supp. I:** 408

"Shooting Script" (Rich), **Supp. I Part 2:** 558; **Supp. IV Part 1:** 257

Shooting Star, A (Stegner), **Supp. IV Part 2:** 599, 608–609

"Shooting Whales" (Strand), **Supp. IV Part 2:** 630

"Shopgirls" (F. Barthelme), **Supp. XI:** 26, 27, 33, 36

Shop Talk (Roth), **Retro. Supp. II:** 282

Shoptaw, John, **Supp. IV Part 1:** 247

Shore Acres (Herne), **Supp. II Part 1:** 198

Shorebirds of North America, The (Matthiessen), **Supp. V:** 204

"Shore House, The" (Jewett), **II:** 397

Shore Leave (Wakeman), **Supp. IX:** 247

"Shoreline Horses" (Ríos), **Supp. IV Part 2:** 553

Shores of Light, The: A Literary Chronicle of the Twenties and Thirties (Wilson), **IV:** 432, 433

Shorey, Paul, **III:** 606

Short Cuts (film), **Supp. IX:** 143

"Short End, The" (Hecht), **Supp. X:** 65

Short Fiction of Norman Mailer, The (Mailer), **Retro. Supp. II:** 205

Short Friday and Other Stories (Singer), **IV:** 14–16

"Short Happy Life of Francis Macomber, The" (Hemingway), **II:** 250, 263–264; **Retro. Supp. I:** 182; **Supp. IV Part 1:** 48; **Supp. IX:** 106

Short Novels of Thomas Wolfe, The (Wolfe), **IV:** 456

Short Poems (Berryman), **I:** 170

"SHORT SPEECH TO MY FRIENDS" (Baraka), **Supp. II Part 1:** 35

Short Stories (Rawlings), **Supp. X:** 224

"Short Story, The" (Welty), **IV:** 279

Short Story Masterpieces, **Supp. IX:** 4

Short Studies of American Authors (Higginson), **I:** 455

"Short-timer's Calendar" (Komunyakaa), **Supp. XIII:** 125

Shosha (Singer), **Retro. Supp. II:** 313–314

Shostakovich, Dimitri, **IV:** 75; **Supp. VIII:** 21

"Shots" (Ozick), **Supp. V:** 268

"Should Wizard Hit Mommy?" (Updike), **IV:** 221, 222, 224; **Retro. Supp. I:** 335

"Shovel Man, The" (Sandburg), **III:** 553

Showalter, Elaine, **Retro. Supp. I:** 368; **Supp. IV Part 2:** 440, 441, 444; **Supp. X:** 97

"Shower of Gold" (Welty), **IV:** 271–272

"Shrike and the Chipmunks, The" (Thurber), **Supp. I Part 2:** 617

Shrimp Girl (Hogarth), **Supp. XII:** 44

"Shrouded Stranger, The" (Ginsberg), **Supp. II Part 1:** 312

"Shroud of Color, The" (Cullen), **Supp. IV Part 1:** 166, 168, 170, 171

Shuffle Along (musical), **Supp. I Part 1:** 322; **Supp. X:** 136

Shultz, George, **Supp. IV Part 1:** 234

Shurr, William, **Retro. Supp. I:** 43

Shuster, Joel, **Supp. XI:** 67

Shusterman, Richard, **Retro. Supp. I:** 53

"Shut a Final Door" (Capote), **Supp. III Part 1:** 117, 120, 124

Shut Up, He Explained (Lardner), **II:** 432

Shylock's Daughter: A Novel of Love in Venice (Serenissima) (Jong), **Supp. V:** 115, 127, 128–129

Siberian Village, The (Dove), **Supp. IV Part 1:** 255, 256

Sibley, Mulford Q., **Supp. I Part 2:** 524

"Sibling Mysteries" (Rich), **Supp. I Part 2:** 574

Sibon, Marcelle, **IV:** 288

"Sicilian Emigrant's Song" (W. C. Williams), **Retro. Supp. I:** 413

"Sick Wife, The" (Kenyon), **Supp. VII:** 173, 174

"'Sic transit gloria mundi'" (Dickinson), **Retro. Supp. I:** 30

Sid Caesar Show (television show), **Supp. IV Part 2:** 575

Siddons, Sarah, **II:** 298

Side of Paradise, This (Fitgerald), **Supp. IX:** 56

Sidnee Poet Heroical, The (Baraka), **Supp. II Part 1:** 55

Sidney, Algernon, **II:** 114

Sidney, Mary, **Supp. I Part 1:** 98

Sidney, Philip, **II:** 470; **Supp. I Part 1:** 98, 111, 117–118, 122; **Supp. I Part 2:** 658; **Supp. II Part 1:** 104–105; **Supp. V:** 250; **Supp. XII:** 264; **Supp. XIV:** 128

Sidney, Sylvia, **Supp. I Part 1:** 67

Sidney Lanier: A Bibliographical and Critical Study (Starke), **Supp. I Part 1:** 371

Sidney Lanier: A Biographical and Critical Study (Starke), **Supp. I Part 1:** 371

Siegel, Barry, **Supp. XIV:** 82

Siegel, Catherine, **Supp. XII:** 126

Siegel, Jerry, **Supp. XI:** 67

"Siege of London, The" (James), **Retro. Supp. I:** 227

Siegle, Robert, **Supp. XII:** 8

Sienkiewicz, Henryk, **Supp. IV Part 2:** 518

"Sierra Kid" (Levine), **Supp. V:** 180–181

Sigg, Eric, **Retro. Supp. I:** 53

"Sight" (Merwin), **Supp. III Part 1:** 356

"Sight in Camp in the Daybreak Gray and Dim, A" (Whitman), **II:** 373

Sights and Spectacles (McCarthy), **II:** 562

"Sights from a Steeple" (Hawthorne), **Retro. Supp. I:** 62

Sights Unseen (Gibbons), **Supp. X:** 49–50

"Signals" (Carver), **Supp. III Part 1:** 143

"Signature for Tempo" (MacLeish), **III:** 8–9

"Signed Confession of Crimes against the State" (Merton), **Supp. VIII:** 201

Signifying Monkey, The (Gates), **Supp. X:** 243

Signifying Monkey, The (Hughes), **Retro. Supp. I:** 195

"Signing, The (Dixon), **Supp. XII: 146**

Sign in Sidney Brustein's Window, The (Hansberry), **Supp. IV Part 1:** 359, 365, 369, 370–372

Sign of Jonas, The (Merton), **Supp. VIII:** 194–195, 195, 197, 200, 206, 207

"Sign of Saturn, The" (Olds), **Supp. X:** 206

Sigourney, Lydia, **Supp. I Part 2:** 684

Sikora, Malgorzata, **Retro. Supp. II:** 324

Silas Marner (Eliot), **II:** 26

"Silence" (Moore), **III:** 212

"Silence" (Poe), **III:** 416

"Silence, A" (Clampitt), **Supp. IX:** 53

"Silence—A Fable" (Poe), **III:** 416

"Silence Before Harvest, The" (Merwin), **Supp. III Part 1:** 352

Silence Dogood Papers, The (Franklin), **II:** 106–107

Silence in the Snowy Fields (Bly), **Supp. IV Part 1:** 60–61, 62, 63, 65, 66, 72

Silence of History, The (Farrell), **II:** 46–47

Silence Opens, A (Clampitt), **Supp. IX: 53**

Silences (Olsen), **Supp. XIII:** 293, 294, 295, 296, **304–306**

"Silences: When Writers Don't Write" (Olsen), **Supp. XIII:** 294

Silencing the Past: Power and the Production of History (Trouillot), **Supp. X:** 14

"Silent in America" (Levine), **Supp. V:** 183

Silent Life, The (Merton), **Supp. VIII:** 208

Silent Partner, The (Odets), **Supp. II Part 2:** 539

"Silent Poem" (Francis), **Supp. IX:** 86

"Silent Slain, The" (MacLeish), **III:** 9

"Silent Snow, Secret Snow" (Aiken), **I:** 52

Silent Spring (Carson), **Supp. V:** 202; **Supp. IX:** 19, 24, **31–34;** **Supp. XIV:** 177

"Silken Tent, The" (Frost), **Retro. Supp. I:** 138–139; **Supp. IV Part 2:** 448

Silko, Leslie Marmon, **Supp. IV Part 1:** 274, 319, 325, 333–334, 335, 404; **Supp. IV Part 2:** 499, 505, **557–572;** **Supp. V:** 169; **Supp. XI:** 18; **Supp. XII:** 217

Silliman, Ron, **Supp. IV Part 2:** 426

Silman, Roberta, **Supp. X:** 6

"Silver Crown, The" (Malamud), **Supp. I Part 2:** 434–435, 437; **Supp. V:** 266

"Silver Dish, The" (Bellow), **Retro. Supp. II:** 30

"Silver Filigree" (Wylie), **Supp. I Part 2:** 707

Silvers, Phil, **Supp. IV Part 2:** 574

Silverthorne, Elizabeth, **Supp. X:** 220, 221, 222, 226, 234

"Silver To Have and to Hurl" (Didion), **Supp. IV Part 1:** 197

Simic, Charles, **Supp. V:** 5, 332; **Supp. VIII:** 39, **269–287; Supp. XI:** 317

"Similar Cases" (Gilman), **Supp. XI:** 200, 202

Similitudes, from the Ocean and Prairie (Larcom), **Supp. XIII:** 141

Simmel, Georg, **Supp. I Part 2:** 644

Simmons, Charles, **Supp. XI:** 230

Simmons, Maggie, **Retro. Supp. II:** 21

Simms, Michael, **Supp. XII:** 184

Simms, William Gilmore, **I:** 211

Simon, John, **Supp. IV Part 2:** 691

Simon, Neil, **Supp. IV Part 2: 573–594**

"Simon Gerty" (Wylie), **Supp. I Part 2:** 713

Simonides, **Supp. XII:** 110–111

"Simon Ortiz" (Gingerich), **Supp. IV Part 2:** 510

Simon Ortiz (Wiget), **Supp. IV Part 2:** 509

Simonson, Lee, **III:** 396

"Simple Art of Murder, The" (Chandler), **Supp. IV Part 1:** 121, 341

"Simple Autumnal" (Bogan), **Supp. III Part 1:** 52–53

Simple Heart (Flaubert), **I:** 504

Simple Speaks his Mind (Hughes), **Retro. Supp. I:** 209; **Supp. I Part 1:** 337

Simple Stakes a Claim (Hughes), **Retro. Supp. I:** 209; **Supp. I Part 1:** 337

Simple's Uncle Sam (Hughes), **Retro. Supp. I:** 209; **Supp. I Part 1:** 337

Simple Takes a Wife (Hughes), **Retro. Supp. I:** 209; **Supp. I Part 1:** 337

Simple Truth, The (Hardwick), **Supp. III Part 1:** 199, 200, 208

Simple Truth, The (Levine), **Supp. V:** 178, 179, 193–194

Simply Heavenly (Hughes), **Retro. Supp. I:** 209; **Supp. I Part 1:** 338, 339

Simpson, Louis, **Supp. III Part 2:** 541; **Supp. IV Part 2:** 448, 621; **Supp. VIII:** 39, 279; **Supp. IX: 265–283,** 290; **Supp. XI:** 317; **Supp. XII:** 130; **Supp. XIII:** 337

Sinatra, Frank, **Supp. IX:** 3; **Supp. X:** 119; **Supp. XI:** 213

Sincere Convert, The (Shepard), **IV:** 158

Sincerely, Willis Wayde (Marquand), **III:** 61, 63, 66, 67–68, 69

Sincerity and Authenticity (Trilling), **Supp. III Part 2:** 510–512

"Sincerity and Objectification: With Special Reference to the Work of Charles Reznikoff" (Zukofsky), **Supp. XIV:** 286

Sinclair, Mary Craig (Mary Craig Kimbrough), **Supp. V:** 275, 286, 287

Sinclair, Upton, **II:** 34, 440, 444, 451; **III:** 580; **Retro. Supp. II:** 95; **Supp. V: 275–293; Supp. VIII:** 11

Sinclair Lewis: An American Life (Schorer), **II:** 459

"Singapore" (Oliver), **Supp. VII:** 239, 240

Singer, Bennett L., **Supp. IV Part 1:** 330

Singer, Beth, **Supp. XIV:** 203

Singer, Isaac Bashevis, **I:** 144; **IV: 1–24; Retro. Supp. II:** 22, **299–320; Supp. IX:** 114

Singer, Israel Joshua, **IV:** 2, 16, 17; **Retro. Supp. II:** 302

Singer, Joshua, **IV:** 4

Singer, Rabbi Pinchos Menachem, **IV:** 16

Singin' and Swingin' and Gettin' Merry Like Christmas (Angelou), **Supp. IV Part 1:** 2, 5, 6–7, 9, 13, 14

"Singing & Doubling Together" (Ammons), **Supp. VII:** 34–35

Singing Jailbirds (Sinclair), **Supp. V:** 277

"Singing the Black Mother" (Lupton), **Supp. IV Part 1:** 7

Single Hound, The (Sarton), **Supp. VIII:** 251, 265

Single Hound, The: Poems of a Lifetime (Dickinson; Bianchi, ed.), **Retro. Supp. I:** 35

Single Man, A (Isherwood), **Supp. XIV:** 157, 164, **169–170,** 171

"Single Sonnet" (Bogan), **Supp. III Part 1:** 56–58

Singley, Carol, **Retro. Supp. I:** 373

Singular Family, A: Rosacoke and Her Kin (Price), **Supp. VI: 258–259,** 260

Singularities (Howe), **Supp. IV Part 2:** 431

"Sinister Adolescents, The" (Dos Passos), **I:** 493

Sinister Street (Mackenzie), **II:** 82

Sinners in the Hands of an Angry God (Edwards), **I:** 546, 552–553, 559, 562

Sinning with Annie, and Other Stories (Theroux), **Supp. VIII:** 318

"Sins of Kalamazoo, The" (Sandburg), **III:** 586

Sintram and His Companions (La Motte-Fouqué), **III:** 78

"Siope" (Poe), **III:** 411

"Sipapu: A Cultural Perspective" (Gunn Allen), **Supp. IV Part 1:** 323

Sipchen, Bob, **Supp. X:** 145

Sipper, Ralph B., **Supp. IV Part 2:** 475

"Sire" (Cisneros), **Supp. VII:** 62–63, 64

"Siren and Signal" (Zukofsky), **Supp. III Part 2:** 611, 612

Sirens of Titan, The (Vonnegut), **Supp. II Part 2:** 757, 758, 760, 765–767

"Sir Galahad" (Tennyson), **Supp. I Part 2:** 410

Sirin, V. (pseudonym), **Retro. Supp. I:** 266. *see also* Nabokov, Vladimir

Sir Vadia's Shadow: A Friendship across Five Continents (Theroux), **Supp. VIII:** 309, 314, 321, 325

"Sis" (F. Barthelme), **Supp. XI:** 26

Sisley, Alfred, **I:** 478

Sissman, L. E., **Supp. X:** 69

"Sister" (Hughes), **Retro. Supp. I:** 208

Sister Carrie (Dreiser), **I:** 482, 497, 499, 500, 501–502, 503–504, 505, 506, 515, 519; **III:** 327; **IV:** 208; **Retro. Supp. I:** 376; **Retro. Supp. II:** 93, **96–99**

"Sister of the Minotaur" (Stevens), **IV:** 89; **Supp. IX:** 332

"Sisters, The" (Whittier), **Supp. I Part 2:** 696

Sister's Choice (Showalter), **Retro. Supp. I:** 368

"Sisyphus" (Kumin), **Supp. IV Part 2:** 443, 444, 451

"Sitalkas" (Doolittle), **Supp. I Part 1:** 266

Sitney, P. Adams, **Supp. XII:** 2

Sitting Bull, **Supp. IV Part 2:** 492

"Sitting in a Rocking Chair Going Blind" (Komunyakaa), **Supp. XIII:** 114

Sitti's Secrets (Nye), **Supp. XIII:** 278

Situation Normal (A. Miller), **III:** 148, 149, 156, 164

Situation of Poetry, The: Contemporary Poetry and Its Traditions (Pinsky), **Supp. VI: 237–238,** 239, 241, 242

Sitwell, Edith, **IV:** 77; **Supp. I Part 1:** 271

"Six Brothers" (Cisneros), **Supp. VII:** 67

Six Characters in Search of an Author (Pirandello), **Supp. IV Part 2:** 576

"Six Days: Some Rememberings" (Paley), **Supp. VI:** 226

"65290" (Leopold), **Supp. XIV:** 184–185

Six French Poets (Lowell), **II:** 528–529

"Six Persons" (Baraka), **Supp. II Part 1:** 53

Six Sections from Mountains and Rivers without End (Snyder), **Supp. VIII:** 305

"Sixteen Months" (Sandburg), **III:** 584

1601, or Conversation as It Was by the Fireside in the Time of the Tudors (Twain), **IV:** 201

"Sixth-Month Song in the Foothills" (Snyder), **Supp. VIII:** 297

Sixties, The (magazine) (Bly), **Supp. IV Part 1:** 60; **Supp. IX:** 271

"Sixty" (Dunn), **Supp. XI:** 155

"Sixty Acres" (Carver), **Supp. III Part 1:** 141

Sixty Stories (Barthelme), **Supp. IV Part 1:** 41, 42, 44, 47, 49, 50

63: Dream Palace (Purdy), **Supp. VII:** 270–271

"Six Variations" (Levertov), **Supp. III Part 1:** 277–278

"Six-Year-Old Boy" (Olds), **Supp. X:** 206

"Six Years Later" (Brodsky), **Supp. VIII:** 26, 28

"Size and Sheer Will" (Olds), **Supp. X:** 206

Size of Thoughts, The: Essays and Other Lumber (Baker), **Supp. XIII: 52–53,** 55, 56

Sizwe Bansi Is Dead (Fugard), **Supp. VIII:** 330

"Skagway" (Haines), **Supp. XII:** 206

"Skaters, The" (Ashbery), **Supp. III Part 1:** 10, 12, 13, 18, 25

"Skaters, The" (Jarrell), **II:** 368–369

Skau, Michael, **Supp. XII:** 129, 130, 132, 134

Skeeters Kirby (Masters), **Supp. I Part 2:** 459, 470, 471

Skeleton Crew (King), **Supp. V:** 144

"Skeleton in Armor, The" (Longfellow), **Retro. Supp. II:** 168

"Skeleton's Cave, The" (Bryant), **Supp. I Part 1:** 157

Skelton, John, **III:** 521

Sketch Book of Geoffrey Crayon, Gent., The (Irving), **II:** 295, 303, 304–308, 309, 311, 491; **Supp. I Part 1:** 155

Sketches of Art (Jameson), **Retro. Supp. II:** 58

Sketches of Eighteenth Century America (Crèvecoeur), **Supp. I Part 1:** 233, 240–241, 250, 251

Sketches of Switzerland (Cooper), **I:** 346

Sketches Old and New (Twain), **IV:** 198

"Sketch for a Job-Application Blank" (Harrison), **Supp. VIII:** 38

Sketch of Old England, by a New England Man (Paulding), **I:** 344

"Skier and the Mountain, The" (Eberhart), **I:** 528–529

Skinker, Mary Scott, **Supp. IX:** 20

Skinny Island (Auchincloss), **Supp. IV Part 1:** 33

Skinny Legs and All (Robbins), **Supp. X:** 267, 273, **276–279**

Skin of Our Teeth, The (Wilder), **IV:** 357, 358, 369–372; **Supp. IV Part 2:** 586

"Skins" (Wright), **Supp. V:** 340

Skins and Bones: Poems 1979–1987 (Gunn Allen), **Supp. IV Part 1:** 321, 331

"Skipper Ireson's Ride" (Whittier), **Supp. I Part 2:** 691, 693–694

"Skirmish at Sartoris" (Faulkner), **II:** 67

Skow, John, **Supp. V:** 213

"Skunk Cabbage" (Oliver), **Supp. VII:** 235, 236

"Skunk Hour" (Lowell), **II:** 548–550; **Retro. Supp. II:** 188, 189; **Supp. XIV:** 269

"Sky Dance" (Leopold), **Supp. XIV:** 186

"Sky Line" (Taylor), **Supp. V:** 316

"Sky Line, The" (Mumford), **Supp. II Part 2:** 475

"Skyscraper" (Sandburg), **III:** 581–582

Sky's the Limit, The: A Defense of the Earth (Nichols), **Supp. XIII:** 268

"Sky Valley Rider" (Wright), **Supp. V:** 335, 340

Sky-Walk; or the Man Unknown to Himself (Brown), **Supp. I Part 1:** 127–128

"Slang in America" (Whitman), **IV:** 348

Slapstick (Vonnegut), **Supp. II Part 2:** 753, 754, 778

Slapstick Tragedy (T. Williams), **IV:** 382, 393

Slate, Lane, **Supp. IX:** 251, 253

Slattery, Mary Grace. See Miller, Mrs. Arthur (Mary Grace Slattery)

"Slaughterer, The" (Singer), **IV:** 19

Slaughterhouse-Five (Vonnegut), **Supp. II Part 2:** 755, 758–759, 760, 770, 772–776; **Supp. V:** 41, 244

Slave, The (Baraka), **Supp. II Part 1:** 42, 44, 56

Slave, The: A Novel (Singer), **IV:** 13; **Retro. Supp. II: 305–307**

"Slave Coffle" (Angelou), **Supp. IV Part 1:** 16

"Slave on the Block" (Hughes), **Supp. I Part 1:** 329

Slave Power, The: The Free North and Southern Domination, 1780–1860 (Richards), **Supp. XIV:** 48

"Slave Quarters" (Dickey), **Supp. IV Part 1:** 181

"Slave's Dream, The" (Longfellow), **Supp. I Part 2:** 409

Slave Ship: A Historical Pageant (Baraka), **Supp. II Part 1:** 47–49, 53, 56–57

"Slave-Ships, The" (Whittier), **Supp. I Part 2:** 687–688

Slavs! Thinking about the Longstanding Problems of Virtue and Happiness (Kushner), **Supp. IX: 146**

Sledge, Eugene, **Supp. V:** 250

Sleek for the Long Flight (Matthews), **Supp. IX:** 154, 155, **157–158**

Sleep (Dixon), **Supp. XII:** 154

"Sleep, The" (Strand), **Supp. IV Part 2:** 627

"Sleeper, The" (Poe), **III:** 411

"Sleeper 1, The" (Hay), **Supp. XIV:** 132–133

"Sleeper 2, The" (Hay), **Supp. XIV:** 132–133

"Sleepers, The" (Whitman), **IV:** 336

"Sleepers in Jaipur" (Kenyon), **Supp. VII:** 172

Sleepers in Moon-Crowned Valleys (Purdy), **Supp. VII:** 274, 275

"Sleepers Joining Hands" (Bly), **Supp. IV Part 1:** 63, 73

Sleeping Beauty (Macdonald), **Supp. IV Part 2:** 474, 475

Sleeping Fury, The (Bogan), **Supp. III Part 1:** 58

Sleeping Fury, The: Poems (Bogan), **Supp. III Part 1:** 55–58

Sleeping Gypsy and Other Poems, The (Garrett), **Supp. VII:** 96–98

Sleeping in the Forest (Oliver), **Supp. VII:** 233

"Sleeping in the Forest" (Oliver), **Supp. VII:** 233–234

Sleeping in the Woods (Wagoner), **Supp. IX: 328**

Sleeping on Fists (Ríos), **Supp. IV Part 2:** 540

"Sleeping Standing Up" (Bishop), **Supp. I Part 1:** 85, 89, 93

"Sleeping with Animals" (Kumin), **Supp. IV Part 2:** 454

Sleeping with One Eye Open (Strand), **Supp. IV Part 2:** 621–624, 623, 628

"Sleepless at Crown Point" (Wilbur), **Supp. III Part 2:** 561

Sleepless Nights (Hardwick), **Supp. III Part 1:** 193, 208–211

Sleight, Ken, **Supp. XIII:** 12

Slick, Sam (pseudonym). *See* Haliburton, Thomas Chandler

"Slick Gonna Learn" (Ellison), **Retro. Supp. II:** 116; **Supp. II Part 1:** 237–238

"Slight Rebellion off Madison" (Salinger), **III:** 553

"Slight Sound at Evening, A" (White), **Supp. I Part 2:** 672

"Slim Greer" series (Hayden), **Supp. II Part 1:** 369

"Slim in Hell" (Hayden), **Supp. II Part 1:** 369

"Slim Man Canyon" (Silko), **Supp. IV Part 2:** 560

"Slippery Fingers" (Hammett), **Supp. IV Part 1:** 343

Slipping-Down Life, A (Tyler), **Supp. IV Part 2:** 660–661

Sloan, Jacob, **IV:** 3, 6

Sloan, John, **I:** 254; **IV:** 411; **Retro. Supp. II:** 103

"Slob" (Farrell), **II:** 25, 28, 31

Slocum, Joshua, **Supp. I Part 2:** 497

Slonim, Véra. *See* Nabokov, Véra

Slouching towards Bethlehem (Didion), **Supp. IV Part 1:** 196, 197, 200–201, 202, 206, 210

"Slow Child with a Book of Birds" (Levis), **Supp. XI:** 268

"Slow Down for Poetry" (Strand), **Supp. IV Part 2:** 620

"Slow Pacific Swell, The" (Winters), **Supp. II Part 2:** 790, 793, 795, 796, 799

"Slumgullions" (Olsen), **Supp. IV Part 1:** 54

Slumgullion Stew: An Edward Abbey Reader (Abbey), **Supp. XIII:** 4

"S & M" (Komunyakaa), **Supp. XIII:** 114

Small, Albion, **Supp. I Part 1:** 5

"Small, Good Thing, A" (Carver), **Supp. III Part 1:** 145, 147

Small, Miriam Rossiter, **Supp. I Part 1:** 319

Small Boy and Others, A (James), **II:** 337, 547; **Retro. Supp. I:** 235

"Small but Urgent Request to the Unknowable" (Karr), **Supp. XI:** 243

Small Ceremonies (Shields), **Supp. VII:** 312–315, 320

Small Craft Warnings (T. Williams), **IV:** 382, 383, 384, 385, 386, 387, 392, 393, 396, 398

Small Place, A (Kincaid), **Supp. VII:** 186–187, 188, 191

"Small Rain, The" (Pynchon), **Supp. II Part 2:** 620

Small Room, The (Sarton), **Supp. VIII:** 252, **255–256**

Smalls, Bob, **II:** 128

Small Town, A (Hearon), **Supp. VIII:** **65–66**

"Small Vases from Hebron, The" (Nye), **Supp. XIII:** 283

"Small Vision, The" (Goldbarth), **Supp. XII:** 180

"Small Wire" (Sexton), **Supp. II Part 2:** 696

Smart, Christopher, **III:** 534; **Supp. I Part 2:** 539; **Supp. IV Part 2:** 626

Smart, Joyce H., **Supp. XI:** 169

"Smart Cookie, A" (Cisneros), **Supp. VII:** 64

"Smashup" (Thurber), **Supp. I Part 2:** 616

Smedly, Agnes, **Supp. XIII:** 295

"Smelt Fishing" (Hayden), **Supp. II Part 1:** 367

"Smiles" (Dunn), **Supp. XI:** 151

Smiles, Samuel, **Supp. X:** 167

Smiley, Jane, **Supp. VI:** **291–309;** **Supp. XII:** 73, 297; **Supp. XIII:** 127

Smith, Adam, **II:** 9; **Supp. I Part 2:** 633, 634, 639

Smith, Annick, **Supp. XIV:** 223

Smith, Benjamin, **IV:** 148

Smith, Bernard, **I:** 260

Smith, Bessie, **Retro. Supp. I:** 343; **Supp. VIII:** 330

Smith, Charlie, **Supp. X:** 177

Smith, Dave, **Supp. V:** 333; **Supp. XI:** 152; **Supp. XII:** 178, 198

Smith, David, **Supp. XIII:** 246, 247

Smith, David Nichol, **Supp. XIV:** 2

Smith, Dinitia, **Supp. VIII:** 74, 82, 83

Smith, Elihu Hubbard, **Supp. I Part 1:** 126, 127, 130

Smith, George Adam, **III:** 199

Smith, Hannah Whitall, **Supp. XIV:** 333, 334, 338

Smith, Harrison, **II:** 61

Smith, Henry Nash, **IV:** 210; **Supp. I Part 1:** 233

Smith, Herbert F., **Supp. I Part 2:** 423

Smith, James, **II:** 111

Smith, Jedediah Strong, **Supp. IV Part 2:** 602

Smith, Jerome, **Supp. IV Part 1:** 369

Smith, Joe, **Supp. IV Part 2:** 584

Smith, John, **I:** 4, 131; **II:** 296

Smith, John Allyn, **I:** 168

Smith, Johnston (pseudonym). *See* Crane, Stephen

Smith, Kellogg, **Supp. I Part 2:** 660

Smith, Lamar, **II:** 585

Smith, Lee, **Supp. XII:** 311

Smith, Logan Pearsall, **Supp. XIV:333–351**

Smith, Lula Carson. *See* McCullers, Carson

Smith, Martha Nell, **Retro. Supp. I:** 33, 43, 46, 47

Smith, Mary Rozet, **Supp. I Part 1:** 5, 22

Smith, Mrs. Lamar (Marguerite Walters), **II:** 585, 587

Smith, Oliver, **II:** 586

Smith, Patricia Clark, **Supp. IV Part 1:** 397, 398, 402, 406, 408, 410; **Supp. IV Part 2:** 509; **Supp. XII:** 218

Smith, Patrick, **Supp. VIII:** 40, 41

Smith, Patti, **Supp. XII:** 136; **Supp. XIV:** 151

Smith, Porter, **III:** 572

Smith, Red, **II:** 417, 424

Smith, Robert Pearsall, **Supp. XIV:** 333

Smith, Seba, **Supp. I Part 2:** 411

Smith, Sidonie Ann, **Supp. IV Part 1:** 11

Smith, Stevie, **Supp. V:** 84

Smith, Sydney, **II:** 295; **Supp. XIV:** 112

Smith, Thorne, **Supp. IX:** 194

Smith, Wendy, **Supp. XII:** 330, 335

Smith, Wilford Bascom "Pitchfork," **Supp. XIII:** 168

Smith, William, **II:** 114

Smith, William Jay, **Supp. XIII:** **331–350**

Smoke (film), **Supp. XII:** 21

Smoke and Steel (Sandburg), **III:** 585–587, 592

"Smokers" (Wolff), **Supp. VII:** 340–341

"Smoking My Prayers" (Ortiz), **Supp. IV Part 2:** 503

"Smoking Room, The" (Jackson), **Supp. IX:** 116

"Smoky Gold" (Leopold), **Supp. XIV:** 186

Smollett, Tobias G., **I:** 134, 339, 343; **II:** 304–305; **III:** 61

Smuggler's Bible, A (McElroy), **Supp.**

IV Part 1: 285

Smuggler's Handbook, The (Goldbarth), **Supp. XII:** 181, 183

Smugglers of Lost Soul's Rock, The (Gardner), **Supp. VI: 70**

Smyth, Albert Henry, **II:** 123

"Snail, The" (Hay), **Supp. XIV:** 124

"Snake, The" (Berry), **Supp. X:** 31

"Snake, The" (Crane), **I:** 420

"Snakecharmer" (Plath), **Supp. I Part 2:** 538

"Snakes, Mongooses" (Moore), **III:** 207

"Snakes of September, The" (Kunitz), **Supp. III Part 1:** 258

"Snapshot of 15th S.W., A" (Hugo), **Supp. VI:** 141

"Snapshots of a Daughter-in-Law" (Rich), **Supp. I Part 2:** 553–554

Snapshots of a Daughter-in-Law: Poems, 1954–1962 (Rich), **Supp. I Part 2:** 550–551, 553–554; **Supp. XII:** 255

"Sneeze, The" (Chekhov), **Supp. IV Part 2:** 585

Snell, Ebenezer, **Supp. I Part 1:** 151

Snell, Thomas, **Supp. I Part 1:** 153

"Snob, The" (Shapiro), **Supp. II Part 2:** 705

Snobbery: The America Version (Epstein), **Supp. XIV:** 102, 114–115

Snodgrass, W. D., **I:** 400; **Retro. Supp. II:** 179; **Supp. III Part 2:** 541; **Supp. V:** 337; **Supp. VI: 311–328**; **Supp. XI:** 141, 315; **Supp. XIII:** 312

"Snow" (Frost), **Retro. Supp. I:** 133

"Snow" (Haines), **Supp. XII:** 212

"Snow" (Sexton), **Supp. II Part 2:** 696

Snow, C. P., **Supp. I Part 2:** 536

Snow, Hank, **Supp. V:** 335

Snow: Meditations of a Cautious Man in Winter (Banks), **Supp. V:** 6

Snow Ball, The (Gurney), **Supp. V:** 99

"Snow-Bound" (Whittier), **Supp. I Part 2:** 700–703

"Snow Bound at Eagle's" (Harte), **Supp. II Part 1:** 356

"Snowflakes" (Longfellow), **II:** 498

Snow-Image and Other Twice Told Tales, The (Hawthorne), **II:** 237; **Retro. Supp. I:** 160

"Snowing in Greenwich Village" (Updike), **IV:** 226; **Retro. Supp. I:** 321

"Snow in New York" (Swenson), **Supp. IV Part 2:** 644

Snow Leopard, The (Matthiessen), **Supp. V:** 199, 207–211

"Snow Man, The" (Stevens), **IV:** 82–83; **Retro. Supp. I:** 299, 300, 302, 306, 307, 312

"Snowmass Cycle, The" (Dunn), **Supp. XI:** 152

Snow Poems, The (Ammons), **Supp. VII:** 32–34

"Snows of Kilimanjaro, The" (Hemingway), **II:** 78, 257, 263, 264; **Retro. Supp. I:** 98, 182; **Supp. XII:** 249

"Snow Songs" (Snodgrass), **Supp. VI:** 324

"Snowstorm, The" (Oates), **Supp. II Part 2:** 523

"Snowstorm as It Affects the American Farmer, A" (Crèvecoeur), **Supp. I Part 1:** 251

Snow White (Barthelme), **Supp. IV Part 1:** 40, 47, 48–49, 50, 52; **Supp. V:** 39

"Snowy Mountain Song, A" (Ortiz), **Supp. IV Part 2:** 506

Snyder, Gary, **Supp. III Part 1:** 350; **Supp. IV Part 2:** 502; **Supp. V:** 168–169; **Supp. VIII:** 39, **289–307**

Snyder, Mike, **Supp. XIV:** 36

"So-and-So Reclining on Her Couch" (Stevens), **IV:** 90

"Soapland" (Thurber), **Supp. I Part 2:** 619

Soares, Lota de Macedo, **Retro. Supp. II:** 44; **Supp. I Part 1:** 89, 94

"Sobbin' Women, The" (Benét), **Supp. XI:** 47

Social Ethics (Gilman), **Supp. XI:** 207

"Socialism and the Negro" (McKay), **Supp. X:** 135

Socialism of the Skin, A (Liberation, Honey!)" (Kushner), **Supp. IX:** 135

Social Thought in America: The Revolt against Formalism (White), **Supp. I Part 2:** 648, 650

"Society, Morality, and the Novel" (Ellison), **Retro. Supp. II:** 118, 123–124

"Sociological Habit Patterns in Linguistic Transmogrification" (Cowley), **Supp. II Part 1:** 143

"Sociological Poet, A" (Bourne), **I:** 228

Socrates, **I:** 136, 265; **II:** 8–9, 105, 106; **III:** 281, 419, 606; **Supp. I Part 2:** 458; **Supp. XII:** 98

Socrates Fortlow stories (Mosley), **Supp. XIII: 242–243**

So Forth (Brodsky), **Supp. VIII:** 32–33

"So Forth" (Brodsky), **Supp. VIII:** 33

Soft Machine, The (Burroughs), **Supp. III Part 1:** 93, 103, 104

"Soft Mask" (Karr), **Supp. XI:** 243

Soft Side, The (James), **II:** 335; **Retro. Supp. I:** 229

"Soft Spring Night in Shillington, A" (Updike), **Retro. Supp. I:** 318, 319

"Soft Wood" (Lowell), **II:** 550–551

"So Help Me" (Algren), **Supp. IX:** 2

"Soirée in Hollywood" (H. Miller), **III:** 186

Sojourner, The (Rawlings), **Supp. X:** 233–234

"Sojourn in a Whale" (Moore), **III:** 211, 213

"Sojourns" (Didion), **Supp. IV Part 1:** 205

Solar Storms (Hogan), **Supp. IV Part 1:** 397, 410, 414–415

"Soldier, The" (Frost), **II:** 155

Soldier Blue (film), **Supp. X:** 124

"Soldier's Home" (Hemingway), **Retro. Supp. I:** 189

Soldier's Joy (Bell), **Supp. X:** 7, **7–8**, 10, 11

Soldiers of the Storm (film), **Supp. XIII:** 163

Soldiers' Pay (Faulkner), **I:** 117; **II:** 56, 68; **Retro. Supp. I:** 80, 81

"Soldier's Testament, The" (Mumford), **Supp. II Part 2:** 473

"Soliloquy: Man Talking to a Mirror" (Komunyakaa), **Supp. XIII:** 116–117

"Solitary Pond, The" (Updike), **Retro. Supp. I:** 323

So Little Time (Marquand), **III:** 55, 59, 65, 67, 69

"Solitude" (Maupassant), **Supp. I Part 1:** 223

Solo Faces (Salter), **Supp. IX: 259–260**

Solomon, Andy, **Supp. X:** 11

Solomon, Carl, **Supp. XIV:** 143, 150

Solomon, Charles, **Supp. VIII:** 82

Solomon, Henry, Jr., **Supp. I Part 2:** 490

Solomons, Leon, **IV:** 26

So Long, See You Tomorrow (Maxwell), **Supp. VIII:** 156, 160, 162, **167–169**

"So Long Ago" (Bausch), **Supp. VII:** 41–42

Solotaroff, Robert, **Retro. Supp. II:** 203

Solotaroff, Theodore, **III:** 452–453; **Retro. Supp. II:** 281; **Supp. I Part 2:** 440, 445; **Supp. X:** 79; **Supp. XI:** 340; **Supp. XII:** 291

"Solstice" (Jeffers), **Supp. II Part 2:** 433, 435

"Solstice, The" (Merwin), **Supp. III Part 1:** 356

"Solus Rex" (Nabokov), **Retro. Supp. I:** 274

"Solutions" (McCarthy), **II:** 578

"Solving the Puzzle" (Dunn), **Supp. XI:** 152

Solzhenitsyn, Alexandr, **Retro. Supp. I:** 278; **Supp. VIII:** 241

"Some Afternoon" (Creeley), **Supp. IV Part 1:** 150–151

Some American People (Caldwell), **I:** 292, 294, 295, 296, 304, 309

"Some Ashes Drifting above Piedra, California" (Levis), **Supp. XI:** 264–265

"Some Aspects of the Grotesque in Southern Fiction" (O'Connor), **Retro. Supp. II:** 223, 224

"Somebody Always Grabs the Purple" (H. Roth), **Supp. IX:** 234

Somebody in Boots (Algren), **Supp. IX:** 3, **5–7,** 12

Somebody's Darling (McMurtry), **Supp. V:** 225

Some Came Running (film), **Supp. XI:** 213

Some Came Running (Jones), **Supp. XI:** 214, 215, 220, **222–223,** 226, 227, 232

Some Can Whistle (McMurtry), **Supp. V:** 229

"Some Children of the Goddess" (Mailer), **Retro. Supp. II:** 204

Someday, Maybe (Stafford), **Supp. XI:** **323–325; Supp. XIII:** 281

"Some Dreamers of the Golden Dream" (Didion), **Supp. IV Part 1:** 200

"Some Foreign Letters" (Sexton), **Supp. II Part 2:** 674

"Some Good News" (Olson), **Supp. II Part 2:** 575, 576, 577

"Some Grass along a Ditch Bank" (Levis), **Supp. XI:** 266

"Some Greek Writings" (Corso), **Supp. XII:** 130

Some Honorable Men: Political Conventions, 1960–1972 (Mailer), **Retro. Supp. II:** 208

Some Imagist Poets (Lowell), **III:** 511, 518, 520; **Supp. I Part 1:** 257, 261

"Some keep the Sabbath going to Church" (Dickinson), **Retro. Supp. I:** 30

"Some Like Indians Endure" (Gunn Allen), **Supp. IV Part 1:** 330

"Some Like Them Cold" (Lardner), **II:** 427–428, 430, 431; **Supp. IX:** 202

"Some Lines from Whitman" (Jarrell), **IV:** 352

"Some Negatives: X. at the Chateau" (Merrill), **Supp. III Part 1:** 322

"Some Neglected Points in the Theory of Socialism" (Veblen), **Supp. I Part 2:** 635

"Some Notes for an Autobiographical Lecture" (Trilling), **Supp. III Part 2:** 493, 497, 500

"Some Notes on French Poetry" (Bly), **Supp. IV Part 1:** 61

"Some Notes on Miss L." (West), **IV:** 290–291, 295; **Retro. Supp. II:** 322

"Some Notes on Organic Form" (Levertov), **Supp. III Part 1:** 272, 279

"Some Notes on Teaching: Probably Spoken" (Paley), **Supp. VI:** 225

"Some Notes on the Gazer Within" (Levis), **Supp. XI:** 270

"Some Notes on Violence" (West), **IV:** 304; **Retro. Supp. II:** 322, 323

Some of the Dharma (Kerouac), **Supp. III Part 1:** 225

"Someone Is Buried" (Salinas), **Supp. XIII:** 324

"Someone Puts a Pineapple Together" (Stevens), **IV:** 90–91

"Someone's Blood" (Dove), **Supp. IV Part 1:** 245

"Someone Talking" (Harjo), **Supp. XII:** 219–220

"Someone Talking to Himself" (Wilbur), **Supp. III Part 2:** 557

"Someone to Watch Over Me" (Stern), **Supp. IX:** 300

Someone to Watch Over Me: Stories (Bausch), **Supp. VII:** 53

Some People, Places, & Things That Will Not Appear in My Next Novel (Cheever), **Supp. I Part 1:** 184–185

Some Problems of Philosophy: A Beginning of an Introduction to Philosophy (James), **II:** 360–361

"Some Questions You Might Ask" (Oliver), **Supp. VII:** 238–239

"Some Remarks on Humor" (White), **Supp. I Part 2:** 672

"Some Remarks on Rhythm" (Roethke), **III:** 548–549

Somers, Fred, **I:** 196

Somerville, Jane, **Supp. IX:** 289, 296–297

"Some Secrets" (Stern), **Supp. IX:** 286, 287, 288, 289, 295

Some Sort of Epic Grandeur (Bruccoli), **Retro. Supp. I:** 115, 359

"Something" (Oliver), **Supp. VII:** 236

Something Happened (Heller), **Supp. IV Part 1:** 383, 386–388, 389, 392

"*Something Happened:* The Imaginary, the Symbolic, and the Discourse of the Family" (Mellard), **Supp. IV Part 1:** 387

Something in Common (Hughes), **Supp. I Part 1:** 329–330

Something Inside: Conversations with Gay Fiction Writers (Gambone), **Supp. XII:** 81

"Something New" (Stern), **Supp. IX:** 290

"Something Spurious from the Mindinao Deep" (Stegner), **Supp. IV Part 2:** 605

Something to Declare (Alvarez), **Supp. VII:** 1, 2, 11, 17–19

Something to Remember Me By (Bellow), **Retro. Supp. II:** 32

"Something to Remember Me By" (Bellow), **Retro. Supp. II:** 32

Something Wicked This Way Comes (Bradbury), **Supp. IV Part 1:** 101, 110–111

"Something Wild . . ." (T. Williams), **IV:** 381

"Some Thoughts" (McNally), **Supp. XIII:** 207

"Some Thoughts on the Line" (Oliver), **Supp. VII:** 238

"Sometimes, Reading" (Stafford), **Supp. XI:** 314

"Sometimes I Wonder" (Hughes), **Supp. I Part 1:** 337

Sometimes Mysteriously (Salinas), **Supp. XIII:** 311, **326–328**

"Sometimes Mysteriously" (Salinas), **Supp. XIII:** 328

Some Trees (Ashbery), **Supp. III Part 1:** 3–7, 12

"Some Trees" (Ashbery), **Supp. III Part 1:** 2

"Some Views on the Reading and Writing of Short Stories" (Welty), **Retro. Supp. I:** 351

"Somewhere" (Nemerov), **III:** 279–280

"Somewhere Else" (Paley), **Supp. VI:** 227

"Somewhere in Africa" (Sexton), **Supp. II Part 2:** 684–685

"Somewhere Is Such a Kingdom" (Ransom), **III:** 492

"Somewhere near Phu Bai" (Komunyakaa), **Supp. XIII:** 123–124

"Some Words with a Mummy" (Poe), **III:** 425

"Some Yips and Barks in the Dark" (Snyder), **Supp. VIII:** 291

Sommers, Michael, **Supp. IV Part 2:** 581

Sommers, William, **I:** 387, 388

"Somnambulisma" (Stevens), **Retro. Supp. I:** 310

"So Much Summer" (Dickinson), **Retro. Supp. I:** 26, 44, 45

"So Much the Worse for Boston" (Lindsay), **Supp. I Part 2:** 398

"So Much Water So Close to Home" (Carver), **Supp. III Part 1:** 143, 146

Son, Cathy, **Supp. X:** 292

"Son, The" (Dove), **Supp. IV Part 1:** 245

"Sonata for the Invisible" (Harjo), **Supp. XII:** 228

Sonata for Two Pianos (Bowles), **Supp. IV Part 1:** 83

Son at the Front, A (Wharton), **II:** 183; **IV:** 320; **Retro. Supp. I:** 378

Sondheim, Stephen, **Supp. XII:** 260

Son Excellence Eugène Rougon (Zola), **III:** 322

"Song" (Bogan), **Supp. III Part 1:** 57

"Song" (Bryant). *See* "Hunter of the West, The"

"Song" (Dunbar), **Supp. II Part 1:** 199

"Song" (Ginsberg), **Supp. II Part 1:** 317

"Song" (Kenyon), **Supp. VII:** 169

"Song" (Rich), **Supp. I Part 2:** 560

"Song" (Wylie), **Supp. I Part 2:** 729

"Song, A" (Creeley), **Supp. IV Part 1:** 145

"Song: Love in Whose Rich Honor" (Rukeyser), **Supp. VI:** 285

"Song: 'Rough Winds Do Shake the Darling Buds of May'" (Simpson), **Supp. IX:** 268

Song and Idea (Eberhart), **I:** 526, 529, 533, 539

"Song for Myself and the Deer to Return On" (Harjo), **Supp. XII:** 225

"Song for Occupations, A" (Whitman), **Retro. Supp. I:** 394

"Song for Simeon, A" (Eliot), **Retro. Supp. I:** 64

"Song for the Coming of Smallpox" (Wagoner), **Supp. IX:** 329, 330

"Song for the First People" (Wagoner), **Supp. IX:** 328

"Song for the Last Act" (Bogan), **Supp. III Part 1:** 64

"Song for the Middle of the Night, A" (Wright), **Supp. III Part 2:** 594

"Song for the Rainy Season" (Bishop), **Supp. I Part 1:** 93–94, 96

"Song for the Romeos, A" (Stern), **Supp. IX:** 296

"Songline of Dawn" (Harjo), **Supp. XII:** 229

"Song of Advent, A" (Winters), **Supp. II Part 2:** 789

"Song of a Man Who Rushed at the Enemy" (Wagoner), **Supp. IX:** 329, 330

"Song of Courage, A" (Masters), **Supp. I Part 2:** 458

Song of God, The: Bhagavad-Gita (Isherwood and Prabhavananda, trans.), **Supp. XIV:** 156, 157, 164

Song of Hiawatha, The (Longfellow), **II:** 501, 503–504; **Retro. Supp. II:** 155, **159–161,** 162, 163

"Song of Innocence, A" (Ellison), **Retro. Supp. II:** 126; **Supp. II Part 1:** 248

"Song of My Fiftieth Birthday, The" (Lindsay), **Supp. I Part 2:** 399

"Song of Myself" (Whitman), **II:** 544; **III:** 572, 584, 595; **IV:** 333, 334, 337–339, 340, 341, 342, 344, 348, 349, 351, 405; **Retro. Supp. I:** 388, 389, 395–399, 400; **Supp. V:** 122; **Supp. IX:** 131, 136, 143, 328, 331; **Supp. XIV:** 139

Song of Russia (film), **Supp. I Part 1:** 281, 294

"Song of Self" (Huncke), **Supp. XIV:** 138–139, 145

Song of Solomon (biblical book), **III:** 118; **IV:** 150

Song of Solomon (Morrison), **Supp. III Part 1:** 364, 368, 369, 372, 379

Song of Songs (biblical book), **II:** 538; **IV:** 153–154

"Song of the Answerer" (Whitman), **Retro. Supp. I:** 393, 399

"Song of the Chattahoochee, The" (Lanier), **Supp. I Part 1:** 365, 368

"Song of the Degrees, A" (Pound), **III:** 466

"Song of the Exposition" (Whitman), **IV:** 332

"Song of the Gavilan" (Leopold), **Supp. XIV:** 189

"Song of the Greek Amazon" (Bryant), **Supp. I Part 1:** 168

Song of the Lark, The (Cather), **I:** 312, 319–321, 323; **Retro. Supp. I:** 1, 3, 7, **9–11,** 13, 19, 20

"Song of the Open Road" (McGrath), **Supp. X:** 127

"Song of the Open Road" (Whitman), **IV:** 340–341; **Retro. Supp. I:** 400; **Supp. IX:** 265

"Song of the Redwood Tree" (Whitman), **IV:** 348

"Song of the Scullery" (McCarriston), **Supp. XIV:** 272

"Song of the Sky Loom" (traditional Tewa poem), **Supp. IV Part 1:** 325

"Song of the Son" (Toomer), **Supp. III Part 2:** 482–483; **Supp. IX:** 313

"Song of the Sower, The" (Bryant), **Supp. I Part 1:** 169

"Song of the Stars" (Bryant), **Supp. I Part 1:** 163

"Song of the Swamp-Robin, The" (Frederic), **II:** 138

"Song of the Vermonters, The" (Whittier), **Supp. I Part 2:** 692

"Song of Three Smiles" (Merwin), **Supp. III Part 1:** 344

"Song of Wandering Aengus, The" (Yeats), **IV:** 271; **Retro. Supp. I:** 342, 350

"Song of Welcome" (Brodsky), **Supp. VIII:** 32

"Song on Captain Barney's Victory" (Freneau), **Supp. II Part 1:** 261

"Song/Poetry and Language-Expression and Perception" (Ortiz), **Supp. IV Part 2:** 500, 508

Songs and Satires (Masters), **Supp. I Part 2:** 465–466

Songs and Sonnets (L. P. Smith), **Supp. XIV:** 341

Songs and Sonnets (Masters), **Supp. I Part 2:** 455, 459, 461, 466

"Songs for a Colored Singer" (Bishop), **Supp. I Part 1:** 80, 85

Songs for a Summer's Day (A Sonnet Cycle) (MacLeish), **III:** 3

Songs for Eve (MacLeish), **III:** 3, 19

"Songs for Eve" (MacLeish), **III:** 19

"Songs for My Father" (Komunyakaa), **Supp. XIII:** 128

Songs from This Earth on Turtle's Back: Contemporary American Indian Poetry (Bruchac, ed.), **Supp. IV Part 1:** 320, 328

"Songs of a Housewife" (Rawlings), **Supp. X:** 221–222

"Songs of Billy Bathgate, The" (Doctorow), **Supp. IV Part 1:** 230

Songs of Innocence (Blake), **Supp. I Part 2:** 708

Songs of Jamaica (McKay), **Supp. X:** 131, 133

"Songs of Maximus, The" (Olson), **Supp. II Part 2:** 567

"Songs of Parting" (Whitman), **IV:** 348

Songs of the Sierras (J. Miller), **I:** 459

Songs of Three Centuries (Whittier and Larcom, eds.), **Supp. XIII:** 142

"Song to David" (Smart), **III:** 534

"Song to No Music, A" (Brodsky), **Supp. VIII:** 26

Sonneschein, Rosa, **Retro. Supp. II:** 65

"Sonnet" (Rukeyser), **Supp. VI:** 284

"Sonnets at Christmas" (Tate), **IV:** 135

"Sonnet-To Zante" (Poe), **III:** 421

"Sonny's Blues" (Baldwin), **Retro. Supp. II:** 7, 8, 10, 14; **Supp. I Part 1:** 58–59, 63, 67; **Supp. XI:** 288

Son of Laughter, The: A Novel (Buechner), **Supp. XII:** 54

Son of Perdition, The (Cozzens), **I:** 359–360, 377, 378, 379

Son of the Circus, A (Irving), **Supp. VI:** 165, 166, **176–179**

"Son of the Gods, A" (Bierce), **I:** 202

Son of the Morning (Oates), **Supp. II Part 2:** 518, 519, 520–522

Son of the Morning Star: Custer and the Little Bighorn (Connell), **Supp. XIV:** 80, 82, 97

"Son of the Romanovs, A" (Simpson), **Supp. IX:** 273–274

Son of the Wolf, The (London), **II:** 465, 469

"Son of the Wolfman" (Chabon), **Supp. XI:** 76

"Sonrisas" (Mora), **Supp. XIII:** 216, 219

Sons (Buck), **Supp. II Part 1:** 117–118

Sons and Lovers (Lawrence), **III:** 27

Sontag, Susan, **IV:** 13, 14; **Retro. Supp. II:** 279; **Supp. I Part 2:** 423; **Supp. III Part 2: 451–473; Supp. VIII:** 75; **Supp. XIV:** 14, 15, 95–96, 167

"Soonest Mended" (Ashbery), **Supp. III Part 1:** 1, 13

"Sootfall and Fallout" (White), **Supp. I Part 2:** 671

Sophocles, **I:** 274; **II:** 291, 385, 577; **III:** 145, 151, 152, 153, 159, 398, 476, 478, 609, 613; **IV:** 291, 363, 368, 370; **Supp. I Part 1:** 153, 284; **Supp. I Part 2:** 491; **Supp. V:** 97; **Supp. VIII:** 332

"Sophronsiba" (Bourne), **I:** 221

Sorcerer's Apprentice, The: Tales and Conjurations (Johnson), **Supp. VI: 192–193,** 194

"Sorcerer's Eye, The" (Nemerov), **III:** 283

Sordello (Browning), **III:** 467, 469, 470

"Sordid? Good God!" (Williams), **Retro. Supp. II:** 334

"Sorghum" (Mason), **Supp. VIII:** 146

Sorokin, Pitirim, **Supp. I Part 2:** 679

Sorrentino, Gilbert, **Retro. Supp. I:** 426; **Supp. IV Part 1:** 286; **Supp. XII:** 139

"Sorrow" (Komunyakaa), **Supp. XIII:** 119

Sorrow Dance, The (Levertov), **Supp. III Part 1:** 279–280, 283

"Sorrowful Guest, A" (Jewett), **Retro. Supp. II:** 137

Sorrows of Fat City, The: A Selection of Literary Essays and Reviews (Garrett), **Supp. VII:** 111

Sorrows of Young Werther, The (Goethe), **Supp. XI:** 169

Sorrows of Young Werther, The (Goethe; Bogan and Mayer, trans.), **Supp. III Part 1:** 63

"Sorting Facts; or, Nineteen Ways of Looking at Marker" (Howe), **Supp. IV Part 2:** 434, 436

"S O S" (Baraka), **Supp. II Part 1:** 50

"So Sassafras" (Olson), **Supp. II Part 2:** 574

"So There" (Creeley), **Supp. IV Part 1:** 157

Sotirov, Vasil, **Supp. IX:** 152

Soto, Gary, **Supp. IV Part 2:** 545; **Supp. V:** 180; **Supp. XI:** 270; **Supp. XIII:** 313, 315, 316, 320, 323

"Soto Thinking of the Ocean" (Salinas), **Supp. XIII:** 321

"Sotto Voce" (Kunitz), **Supp. III Part 1:** 265

Sot-Weed Factor, The (Barth), **I:** 122, 123, 125, 129, 130, 131–134, 135

Soul, The (Brooks), **I:** 244

Soul and Body of John Brown, The (Rukeyser), **Supp. VI:** 273

Soul Clap Hands and Sing (Marshall), **Supp. XI:** 276, 278, **280–282**

Soul Expeditions (Singer). *See* Shosha (Singer)

Soul Gone Home (Hughes), **Retro. Supp. I:** 203; **Supp. I Part 1:** 328

"Soul inside the Sentence, The" (Gass), **Supp. VI:** 88

Soul Is Here for Its Own Joy, The (Bly, ed.), **Supp. IV Part 1:** 74

Soul of Man under Socialism, The (Wilde), **Supp. IX:** 134–135

Soul of the Far East, The (Lowell), **II:** 513

Soul on Ice (Cleaver), **Retro. Supp. II:** 12, 13

"Souls Belated" (Wharton), **Retro. Supp. I:** 364

"Soul selects her own Society, The" (Dickinson), **Retro. Supp. I:** 37

Souls of Black Folk, The (Du Bois), **Supp. II Part 1:** 33, 40, 160, 168–170, 176, 183; **Supp. IV Part 1:** 164; **Supp. IX:** 305, 306; **Supp. X:** 133; **Supp. XIII:** 185, 238, 243

"Sound, The" (Olds), **Supp. X:** 214

"Sound and Fury" (O. Henry), **Supp. II Part 1:** 402

Sound and the Fury, The (Faulkner), **I:** 480; **II:** 55, 57, 58–60, 73; **III:** 237; **IV:** 100, 101, 104; **Retro. Supp. I:** 73, 75, 77, 82, **83–84,** 86, 88, 89, 90, 91, 92; **Supp. VIII:** 215; **Supp. IX:** 103; **Supp. X:** 44; **Supp. XII:** 33; **Supp. XIV:** 12

"Sound Bites" (Alvarez), **Supp. VII:** 11

Sound I Listened For, The (Francis), **Supp. IX: 78–79,** 87

"Sound Mind, Sound Body" (Lowell), **II:** 554

"Sound of Distant Thunder, A" (Elkin), **Supp. VI: 42–43,** 44

"Sound of Light, The" (Merwin), **Supp. III Part 1:** 356

Sound of Mountain Water, The (Stegner), **Supp. IV Part 2:** 595, 596, 598, 600, 608

"Sound of Talking" (Purdy), **Supp. VII:** 270

Sounds of Poetry, The (Pinsky), **Supp. VI:** 236, 247, 248

Soupault, Philippe, **IV:** 288, 404; **Retro. Supp. II:** 85, 321, 324

Source (Doty), **Supp. XI:** 121, **134–137**

"Source" (Doty), **Supp. XI:** 136

"Source, The" (Olds), **Supp. X:** 211

"Source, The" (Porter), **III:** 443

Source of Light, The (Price), **Supp. VI: 262,** 266

"Sources of Soviet Conduct, The" (Kennan), **Supp. VIII:** 241

Sour Grapes (W. C. Williams), **Retro. Supp. I:** 418

"South" (Levis), **Supp. XI:** 266

"South, The" (Hughes), **Supp. I Part 1:** 321

"Southbound on the Freeway" (Swenson), **Supp. IV Part 2:** 643

Southern, Terry, **Supp. IV Part 1:** 379; **Supp. V:** 40, 201; **Supp. XI: 293–310**

Southern Cross, The (Wright), **Supp. V:** 332, 342

"Southern Cross, The" (Wright), **Supp. V:** 338

"Southerner's Problem, The" (Du Bois), **Supp. II Part 1:** 168

"Southern Girl" (Zelda Fitzgerald), **Supp. IX:** 71

"Southern Mode of the Imagination, A" (Tate), **IV:** 120

"Southern Romantic, A" (Tate), **Supp. I Part 1:** 373

Southern Terry, **Supp. XIV:** 82

Southey, Robert, **II:** 304, 502; **Supp. I Part 1:** 154

South Moon Under (Rawlings), **Supp. X:** 225–226, 229, 233

Southpaw, The (Harris), **II:** 424–425

"South Sangamon" (Cisneros), **Supp. VII:** 66

Southwell, Robert, **IV:** 151

Southwick, Marcia, **Supp. XI:** 259

Southworth, E. D. E. N, **Retro. Supp. I:** 246

Souvenir of the Ancient World, Selected Poems of Carlos Drummond de Andrade (Strand, trans.), **Supp. IV Part 2:** 630

"Sow" (Plath), **Supp. I Part 2:** 537

Space between Our Footsteps, The: Poems and Paintings from the Middle East (Nye, ed.), **Supp. XIII:** 280

"Space Quale, The" (James), **II:** 349

"Spaces Between, The" (Kingsolver), **Supp. VII:** 209

"Spain" (Auden), **Supp. II Part 1:** 12–13, 14

"Spain in Fifty-Ninth Street" (White), **Supp. I Part 2:** 677

"Spanish-American War Play" (Crane), **I:** 422

Spanish Ballads (Merwin, trans.), **Supp. III Part 1:** 347

Spanish Bayonet (Benét), **Supp. XI:** 45, 47

Spanish Earth, The (film), **Retro. Supp. I:** 184

Spanish Papers and Other Miscellanies (Irving), **II:** 314

"Spanish Revolution, The" (Bryant), **Supp. I Part 1:** 153, 168

Spanish Student, The (Longfellow), **II:** 489, 506; **Retro. Supp. II:** 165

Spanking the Maid (Coover), **Supp. V:** 47, 48, 49, 52

Spargo, John, **Supp. I Part 1:** 13

"Spark, The" (Wharton), **Retro. Supp. I:** 381

"Sparkles from the Wheel" (Whitman), **IV:** 348

Sparks, Debra, **Supp. X:** 177

Sparks, Jared, **Supp. I Part 1:** 156

"Sparrow" (Berry), **Supp. X:** 31

Sparrow, Henry, **III:** 587

Sparrow, Mrs. Henry, **III:** 587

"Spawning Run, The" (Humphrey), **Supp. IX:** 95

"Speak, Gay Memory" (Kirp), **Supp. XI:** 129

Speak, Memory (Nabokov), **III:** 247–250, 252; **Retro. Supp. I:** 264, 265, 266, 267, 268, 277

Speaking and Language (Shapiro), **Supp. II Part 2:** 721

Speaking for Nature: How Literary Naturalists from Henry Thoreau to Rachel Carson Have Shaped America (Brooks), **Supp. IX:** 31

Speaking for Ourselves: American Ethnic Writing (Faderman and Bradshaw, eds.), **Supp. XIII:** 313

"Speaking of Counterweights" (White), **Supp. I Part 2:** 669

Speaking of Literature and Society (Trilling), **Supp. III Part 2:** 494, 496, 499

Speaking on Stage (Kolin and Kullman, eds.), **Supp. IX:** 145

Speak What We Feel (Not What We Ought to Say): Reflections on Literature and Faith (Buechner), **Supp. XII:** 57

Spear, Roberta, **Supp. V:** 180

"Special Kind of Fantasy, A: James Dickey on the Razor's Edge" (Niflis), **Supp. IV Part 1:** 175

"Special Pleading" (Lanier), **Supp. I Part 1:** 364

"Special Problems in Teaching Leslie Marmon Silko's *Ceremony*" (Gunn Allen), **Supp. IV Part 1:** 333

Special Providence, A (Yates), **Supp. XI:** 342, **344–345**

"Special Time, a Special School, A" (Knowles), **Supp. XII:** 236

Special View of History, The (Olson), **Supp. II Part 2:** 566, 569, 572

Specimen Days (Whitman), **IV:** 338, 347, 348, 350; **Retro. Supp. I:** 408

Specimens of the American Poets, **Supp. I Part 1:** 155

"Spectacles, The" (Poe), **III:** 425

Spectator Bird, The (Stegner), **Supp. IV Part 2:** 599, 604, 606, 611–612

Spector, Robert, **Supp. XIII:** 87

"Spectre Bridegroom, The" (Irving), **II:** 304

"Spectre Pig, The" (Holmes), **Supp. I Part 1:** 302

"Speech Sounds" (O. Butler), **Supp. XIII:** 61, **70**

"Speech to a Crowd" (MacLeish), **III:** 16

"Speech to the Detractors" (MacLeish), **III:** 16

"Speech to the Young" (Brooks), **Supp. III Part 1:** 79, 86

"Speech to Those Who Say Comrade" (MacLeish), **III:** 16

Speedboat (Adler), **Supp. X:** 171

Speed of Darkness, The (Rukeyser), **Supp. VI:** 274, 281

Speed-the-Plow (Mamet), **Supp. XIV:** 241, 246, 249, 250, 251

Speilberg, Steven, **Supp. XI:** 234

"Spell" (Francis), **Supp. IX:** 87

Spence, Thomas, **Supp. I Part 2:** 518

Spence + Lila (Mason), **Supp. VIII:** 133, **143–145**

Spencer, Edward, **Supp. I Part 1:** 357, 360

Spencer, Herbert, **I:** 515; **II:** 345, 462–463, 480, 483, 536; **III:** 102, 315; **IV:** 135; **Retro. Supp. II:** 60, 65, 93, 98; **Supp. I Part 1:** 368; **Supp. I Part 2:** 635

Spencer, Sharon, **Supp. X:** 185, 186, 195, 196

Spencer, Theodore, **I:** 433; **Supp. III Part 1:** 2

Spender, Natasha, **Supp. IV Part 1:** 119, 127, 134

Spender, Stephen, **II:** 371; **III:** 504, 527; **Retro. Supp. I:** 216; **Retro. Supp. II:** 243, 244; **Supp. I Part 2:** 536; **Supp. II Part 1:** 11; **Supp. IV Part 1:** 82, 134; **Supp. IV Part 2:** 440; **Supp. X:** 116

Spengler, Oswald, **I:** 255, 270; **II:** 7, 577; **III:** 172, 176; **Retro. Supp. II:** 324; **Supp. I Part 2:** 647

Spens, Sir Patrick, **Supp. I Part 2:** 404

Spenser, Edmund, **I:** 62; **III:** 77, 78, 89; **IV:** 155, 453; **Retro. Supp. I:** 62; **Supp. I Part 1:** 98, 152, 369; **Supp. I Part 2:** 422, 719

"Spenser's Ireland" (Moore), **III:** 211, 212

Sperry, Margaret, **Supp. IV Part 1:** 169

Sphere: The Form of a Motion (Ammons), **Supp. VII:** 24, 32, 33, 35, 36

"Sphinx" (Hayden), **Supp. II Part 1:** 373

"Spiced Plums" (Ríos), **Supp. IV Part 2:** 553

"Spider and the Ghost of the Fly, The" (Lindsay), **Supp. I Part 2:** 375

Spider Bay (Van Vechten), **Supp. II Part 2:** 746

"Spiders" (Schwartz), **Supp. II Part 2:** 665

Spider's House, The (Bowles), **Supp. IV Part 1:** 87–89, 90, 91

Spider Woman's Granddaughters: Traditional Tales and Contemporary Writing by Native American Women (Gunn Allen, ed.), **Supp. IV Part 1:** 320, 326, 332–333; **Supp. IV Part 2:** 567

Spiegelman, Willard, **Supp. XI:** 126

Spillane, Mickey, **Supp. IV Part 2:** 469, 472

Spiller, Robert E., **I:** 241; **Supp. I Part 1:** 104

Spillway (Barnes), **Supp. III Part 1:** 44

Spingarn, Amy, **Supp. I Part 1:** 325, 326

Spingarn, Joel, **I:** 266; **Supp. I Part 1:** 325

Spinoza, Baruch, **I:** 493; **II:** 590, 593; **III:** 600; **IV:** 5, 7, 11, 12, 17; **Retro. Supp. II:** 300; **Supp. I Part 1:** 274; **Supp. I Part 2:** 643

"Spinoza of Market Street, The" (Singer), **IV:** 12–13; **Retro. Supp. II:** 307

"Spinster" (Plath), **Supp. I Part 2:** 536

"Spinster's Tale, A" (Taylor), **Supp. V:** 314–315, 316–317, 319, 323

Spiral of Memory, The: Interviews (Coltelli, ed.), **Supp. XII:** 215

Spires, Elizabeth, **Supp. X:** 8

"Spire Song" (Bowles), **Supp. IV Part 1:** 80

Spirit and the Flesh, The: Sexual Diversity in American Indian Culture (W. L. Williams), **Supp. IV Part 1:** 330

"Spirit Birth" (Cullen), **Supp. IV Part 1:** 168

Spirit in Man, The (Jung), **Supp. IV Part 1:** 68

Spirit of Culver (West), **IV:** 287

Spirit of Romance, The (Pound), **III:** 470; **Retro. Supp. I:** 286

Spirit of Youth and the City Streets, The (Addams), **Supp. I Part 1:** 6–7, 12–13, 16, 17, 19

"Spirits" (Bausch), **Supp. VII:** 46–47

Spirits, and Other Stories (Bausch), **Supp. VII:** 46–47, 54

"Spirit Says, You Are Nothing, The" (Levis), **Supp. XI:** 265–266

Spiritual Conflict, The (Scupoli), **IV:** 156

Spiritual Exercises, The (Loyola), **IV:** 151; **Supp. XI:** 162

"Spiritual Manifestation, A" (Whittier), **Supp. I Part 2:** 699

"Spirituals and Neo-Spirituals" (Hurston), **Supp. VI:** 152–153

Spits, Ellen Handler, **Supp. XII:** 166

"Spitzbergen Tales" (Crane), **I:** 409, 415, 423

Spitzer, Philip, **Supp. XIV:** 21

"Spleen" (Eliot), **I:** 569, 573–574

Spleen de Paris, Le (Baudelaire), **Supp. XIV:** 337

Splendid Drunken Twenties, The (Van Vechten), **Supp. II Part 2:** 739–744

"Splittings" (Rich), **Supp. I Part 2:** 570–571

"Splitting Wood at Six Above" (Kumin), **Supp. IV Part 2:** 449

Spofford, Harriet Prescott, **Supp. XIII:** 143

Spoils of Poynton, The (James), **I:** 463; **Retro. Supp. I:** 229–230

Spoken Page, The (Nye), **Supp. XIII:** 274

"Spokes" (Auster), **Supp. XII:** 23

Spokesmen (Whipple), **II:** 456

Spook Sonata, The (Strindberg), **III:** 387, 392

Spooky Art, The: A Book about Writing (Mailer), **Retro. Supp. II:** 214

"Spoon, The" (Simic), **Supp. VIII:** 275

Spoon River Anthology (Masters), **I:** 106; **III:** 579; **Supp. I Part 2:** 454, 455, 456, 460–465, 466, 467, 471, 472, 473, 476; **Supp. IX:** 306; **Supp. XIV:** 282–283

Sport and a Pastime, A (Salter), **Supp. IX:** 254–257

Sporting Club, The (McGuane), **Supp. VIII:** 43

Sport of the Gods, The (Dunbar), **Supp. II Part 1:** 193, 200, 207, 214–217

Sportsman's Sketches, A (Turgenev), **I:** 106; **IV:** 277

Sportswriter, The (Ford), **Supp. V:** 57, 58, 62–67

"Spotted Horses" (Faulkner), **IV:** 260

Sprague, Morteza, **Retro. Supp. II:** 115

Spratling, William, **II:** 56; **Retro. Supp. I:** 80

"Spray Paint King, The" (Dove), **Supp. IV Part 1:** 252–253

Spreading Fires (Knowles), **Supp. XII:** 249

Sprigge, Elizabeth, **IV:** 31

"Spring" (Millay), **III:** 126

"Spring" (Mora), **Supp. XIII:** 217

Spring and All (W. C. Williams), **Retro. Supp. I:** 412, 418, **418–420**, 427, 430, 431

"Spring and All" (W. C. Williams), **Retro. Supp. I:** 419

"Spring Evening" (Farrell), **II:** 45

"Spring Evening" (Kenyon), **Supp. VII:** 173

"Springfield Magical" (Lindsay), **Supp. I Part 2:** 379

Spring in New Hampshire and Other Poems (McKay), **Supp. X:** 131, 135

"Spring Pastoral" (Wylie), **Supp. I Part 2:** 707

"Spring Pools" (Frost), **II:** 155; **Retro. Supp. I:** 137

"Spring Snow" (Matthews), **Supp. IX:** 160

"SPRING SONG" (Baraka), **Supp. II Part 1:** 60

Springsteen, Bruce, **Supp. VIII:** 143

"Spring Strains" (W. C. Williams), **Retro. Supp. I:** 416

Spring Tides (Morison), **Supp. I Part 2:** 494

Springtime and Harvest (Sinclair), **Supp. V:** 280

Spruance, Raymond, **Supp. I Part 2:** 479, 491

"Spruce Has No Taproot, The" (Clampitt), **Supp. IX:** 41–42

"Spunk" (Hurston), **Supp. VI:** 150, 151–152

Spunk: The Selected Stories (Hurston), **Supp. VI:** 150

Spy, The (Cooper), **I:** 335, 336, 337, 339, 340; **Supp. I Part 1:** 155

"Spy, The" (Francis), **Supp. IX:** 81

Spy, The (Freneau), **Supp. II Part 1:** 260

Spy in the House of Love, A (Nin), **Supp. X:** 186

Squanto, **Supp. I Part 2:** 486

"Square Business" (Baraka), **Supp. II Part 1:** 49

Square Root of Wonderful, The (McCullers), **II:** 587–588

"Squash in Blossom" (Francis), **Supp. IX:** 81

"Squatter on Company Land, The" (Hugo), **Supp. VI:** 133

"Squatter's Children" (Bishop), **Retro. Supp. II:** 47

Squeeze Play (Auster), **Supp. XII:** 21

Squires, Radcliffe, **IV:** 127

Squirrels (Mamet), **Supp. XIV:** 240

S.S. Gliencairn (O'Neill), **III:** 387, 388, 405

S.S. San Pedro (Cozzens), **I:** 360–362, 370, 378, 379

"Ssshh" (Olds), **Supp. X:** 215

"Stacking the Straw" (Clampitt), **Supp. IX:** 41

Stade, George, **Supp. IV Part 1:** 286

Staël, Madame de, **II:** 298

"Staff of Life, The" (H. Miller), **III:** 187

Stafford, Jean, **II:** 537; **Retro. Supp. II:** 177; **Supp. V:** 316

Stafford, William, **Supp. IV Part 1:** 72; **Supp. IV Part 2:** 642; **Supp. IX:** 273; **Supp. XI: 311–332; Supp. XIII:** 76, 274, 276, 277, 281, 283; **Supp. XIV:** 119, 123

"Stage All Blood, The" (MacLeish), **III:** 18

"Staggerlee Wonders" (Baldwin), **Retro. Supp. II:** 15

Stained White Radiance, A (Burke), **Supp. XIV:** 28, 31

Stalin, Joseph, **I:** 261, 490; **II:** 39, 40, 49, 564; **III:** 30, 298; **IV:** 372; **Supp. V:** 290

"Stalking the Billion-Footed Beast: A Literary Manifesto for the New Social Novel" (Wolfe), **Supp. III Part 2:** 586

Stallman, R. W., **I:** 405

Stamberg, Susan, **Supp. IV Part 1:** 201; **Supp. XII:** 193

Stamford, Anne Marie, **Supp. XII:** 162

Stanard, Mrs. Jane, **III:** 410, 413

Stand, The (King), **Supp. V:** 139, 140–141, 144–146, 148, 152

"Standard of Living, The" (Parker), **Supp. IX: 198–199**

Stander, Lionel, **Supp. I Part 1:** 289

Standing by Words (Berry), **Supp. X:** 22, 27, 28, 31, 32, 33, 35

"Standing Halfway Home" (Wagoner), **Supp. IX:** 324

Stand in the Mountains, A (Taylor), **Supp. V:** 324

Standish, Burt L. (pseudonym). *See* Patten, Gilbert

Standish, Miles, **I:** 471; **II:** 502–503

Standley, Fred L., **Retro. Supp. II:** 6

Stand Still Like the Hummingbird (H. Miller), **III:** 184

"Stand Up" (Salinas), **Supp. XIII:** 315

Stand with Me Here (Francis), **Supp. IX:** 76

Stanford, Ann, **Retro. Supp. I:** 41; **Supp. I Part 1:** 99, 100, 102, 103, 106, 108, 109, 113, 117; **Supp. IV Part 2:** 637

Stanford, Donald E., **II:** 217

Stanford, Leland, **I:** 196, 198

Stanislavsky, Konstantin, **Supp. XIV:** 240, 243

"Stanley Kunitz" (Oliver), **Supp. VII:** 237

Stanton, Frank L., **Supp. II Part 1:** 192

Stanton, Robert J., **Supp. IV Part 2:** 681

"Stanzas from the Grande Chartreuse" (Arnold), **Supp. I Part 2:** 417

Stanzas in Meditation (Stein), **Supp. III Part 1:** 13

Staples, Hugh, **Retro. Supp. II:** 187

Star, Alexander, **Supp. X:** 310

Starbuck, George, **Retro. Supp. II:** 53, 245; **Supp. I Part 2:** 538; **Supp. IV Part 2:** 440; **Supp. XIII:** 76

Star Child (Gunn Allen), **Supp. IV Part 1:** 324

"Stare, The" (Updike), **Retro. Supp. I:** 329

"Starfish, The" (Bly), **Supp. IV Part 1:** 72

"Staring at the Sea on the Day of the Death of Another" (Swenson), **Supp. IV Part 2:** 652

Star Is Born, A (film), **Supp. IV Part 1:** 198; **Supp. IX:** 198

Stark, David, **Supp. XII:** 202

"Stark Boughs on the Family Tree" (Oliver), **Supp. VII:** 232

Starke, Aubrey Harrison, **Supp. I Part 1:** 350, 352, 356, 360, 362, 365, 370, 371

Starkey, David, **Supp. XII:** 180, 181

"Starlight" (Levine), **Supp. V:** 188

"Starlight Scope Myopia" (Komunyakaa), **Supp. XIII:** 123, 124

"Star of the Nativity" (Brodsky), **Supp. VIII:** 33

Starr, Ellen Gates, **Supp. I Part 1:** 4, 5, 11

Starr, Ringo, **Supp. XI:** 309

Star Rover, The (London), **II:** 467

"Starry Night, The" (Sexton), **Supp. II Part 2:** 681

"Stars" (Frost), **II:** 153

Stars, the Snow, the Fire, The: Twenty-five Years in the Northern Wilderness (Haines), **Supp. XII: 199–201,** 206, 209

Star Shines over Mt. Morris Park, A (H. Roth), **Supp. IX:** 227, 236, **236–237**

"Stars of the Summer Night" (Longfellow), **II:** 493

"Stars over Harlem" (Hughes), **Retro. Supp. I:** 207

"Star-Spangled" (García), **Supp. XI:** 177, 178

Star-Spangled Girl, The (Simon), **Supp. IV Part 2:** 579

"Star-Splitter, The" (Frost), **Retro. Supp. I:** 123, 133

Stars Principal (McClatchy), **Supp. XII: 256–258**

"Starting from Paumanok" (Whitman), **IV:** 333

Starting Out in the Thirties (Kazin), **Supp. VIII: 95–97**

"Starved Lovers" (MacLeish), **III:** 19

Starved Rock (Masters), **Supp. I Part 2:** 465

"Starving Again" (Moore), **Supp. X:** 163, 172, 175

"State, The" (Bourne), **I:** 233

State and Main (Mamet), **Supp. XIV:** 241

"Statement: Phillipa Allen" (Rukeyser), **Supp. VI:** 283–284

"Statement of Principles" (Ransom), **III:** 496

"Statements on Poetics" (Snyder), **Supp. VIII:** 291, 292

"State of the Art, The" (Elkin), **Supp. VI:** 52

State of the Nation (Dos Passos), **I:** 489

"State of the Union" (Vidal), **Supp. IV Part 2:** 678

"Statue, The" (Berryman), **I:** 173

"Statue and Birds" (Bogan), **Supp. III Part 1:** 50

"Statues, The" (Schwartz), **Supp. II Part 2:** 654, 659

"Status Rerum" (Pound), **Supp. I Part 1:** 257

Stavans, Ilan, **Supp. XI:** 190

"Staying Alive" (Levertov), **Supp. III Part 1:** 281

Staying Alive (Wagoner), **Supp. IX:** 324, **326**

"Staying at Ed's Place" (Swenson), **Supp. IV Part 2:** 648

Stayton, Richard, **Supp. IX:** 133

Steadman, Goodman, **IV:** 147

"Steak" (Snyder), **Supp. VIII:** 301

Stealing Beauty (Minot), **Supp. VI:** 205

Stealing Glimpses (McQuade), **Supp. IX:** 151

"Stealing the Thunder: Future Visions for American Indian Women, Tribes, and Literary Studies" (Gunn Allen), **Supp. IV Part 1:** 331

"Steam Shovel Cut" (Masters), **Supp. I Part 2:** 468

Stearns, Harold, **I:** 245

Stedman, Edmund Clarence, **Supp. I Part 1:** 372; **Supp. II Part 1:** 192

Steele, Max, **Supp. XIV:** 82

Steele, Sir Richard, **I:** 378; **II:** 105, 107, 300; **III:** 430

Steenburgen, Mary, **Supp. IV Part 1:** 236

Steeple Bush (Frost), **II:** 155; **Retro. Supp. I:** 140; **Retro. Supp. II:** 42

"Steeple-Jack, The" (Moore), **III:** 212, 213, 215

"Steerage" (Goldbarth), **Supp. XII:** 187

Steers, Nina, **Retro. Supp. II:** 25

Steffens, Lincoln, **II:** 577; **III:** 580; **Retro. Supp. I:** 202; **Retro. Supp. II:** 101; **Supp. I Part 1:** 7

Stegner, Page, **IV:** 114, 116; **Supp. IV**

Part 2: 599

Stegner, Wallace, **Supp. IV Part 2: 595–618; Supp. V:** 220, 224, 296; **Supp. X:** 23, 24; **Supp. XIV:** 82, 193, 230, 233

"Stegner's Short Fiction" (Ahearn), **Supp. IV Part 2:** 604

Steichen, Edward, **III:** 580, 594–595

Steichen, Lillian. *See* Sandburg, Mrs. Carl (Lillian Steichen)

Steier, Rod, **Supp. VIII:** 269

Steiger, Rod, **Supp. XI:** 305

Stein, Gertrude, **I:** 103, 105, 476; **II:** 56, 251, 252, 257, 260, 262–263, 264, 289; **III:** 71, 454, 471–472, 600; **IV: 24–48,** 368, 375, 404, 415, 443, 477; **Retro. Supp. I:** 108, 170, 176, 177, 186, 418, 422; **Retro. Supp. II:** 85, 207, 326, 331; **Supp. I Part 1:** 292; **Supp. III Part 1:** 13, 37, 225, 226; **Supp. III Part 2:** 626; **Supp. IV Part 1:** 11, 79, 80, 81, 322; **Supp. IV Part 2:** 468; **Supp. V:** 53; **Supp. IX:** 55, 57, 62, 66; **Supp. XII:** 1, 139; **Supp. XIV:** 336

Stein, Karen F., **Supp. XIII:** 29, 30

Stein, Leo, **IV:** 26; **Supp. XIV:** 336

Stein, Lorin, **Supp. XII:** 254

Steinbeck, John, **I:** 107, 288, 301, 378, 495, 519; **II:** 272; **III:** 382, 453, 454, 589; **IV: 49–72; Retro. Supp. II:** 19, 196; **Supp. IV Part 1:** 102, 225; **Supp. IV Part 2:** 502; **Supp. V:** 290, 291; **Supp. VIII:** 10; **Supp. IX:** 33, 171; **Supp. XI:** 169; **Supp. XIII:** 1, 17; **Supp. XIV:** 21, 181

Steinbeck, Olive Hamilton, **IV:** 51

Steinberg, Saul, **Supp. VIII:** 272

Steinem, Gloria, **Supp. IV Part 1:** 203

Steiner, George, **Retro. Supp. I:** 327; **Supp. IV Part 1:** 286

Steiner, Nancy, **Supp. I Part 2:** 529

Steiner, Stan, **Supp. IV Part 2:** 505

Steinman, Michael, **Supp. VIII:** 172

Steinmetz, Charles Proteus, **I:** 483

Steinway Quintet Plus Four, The (Epstein), **Supp. XII:** 159, **162–166**

Stekel, Wilhelm, **III:** 554

Stella (Goethe), **Supp. IX:** 133, 138

Stella (Kushner), **Supp. IX:** 133

Stella, Joseph, **I:** 387

"Stellaria" (Francis), **Supp. IX:** 83

Stelligery and Other Essays (Wendell), **Supp. I Part 2:** 414

Stendhal, **I:** 316; **III:** 465, 467; **Supp. I Part 1:** 293; **Supp. I Part 2:** 445

Stepanchev, Stephen, **Supp. XI:** 312

Stephen, Leslie, **IV:** 440

Stephen, Saint, **II:** 539; **IV:** 228

Stephen, Sir Leslie, **IV:** 440; **Supp. I Part 1:** 306

Stephen Crane (Berryman), **I:** 169–170, 405

Stephen King: The Art of Darkness (Winter), **Supp. V:** 144

Stephen King, The Second Decade: "Danse Macabre" to "The Dark Half" (Magistrale), **Supp. V:** 138, 146, 151

Stephens, Jack, **Supp. X:** 11, 14, 15, 17

Stephenson, Gregory, **Supp. XII:** 120, 123

"Stepping Out" (Dunn), **Supp. XI:** 140, 141

Steps (Kosinski), **Supp. VII:** 215, 221–222, 225

"Steps" (Nye), **Supp. XIII:** 288

Steps to the Temple (Crashaw), **IV:** 145

"Steps Toward Poverty and Death" (Bly), **Supp. IV Part 1:** 60

Stepto, Robert B., **Retro. Supp. II:** 116, 120, 123

Sterile Cuckoo, The (Nichols), **Supp. XIII:** 258, **259–263,** 264

Sterling, George, **I:** 199, 207, 208, 209; **II:** 440; **Supp. V:** 286

Stern, Bernhard J., **Supp. XIV:** 202, 213

Stern, Daniel, **Supp. VIII:** 238

Stern, Frederick C., **Supp. X:** 114, 115, 117

Stern, Gerald, **Supp. IX: 285–303; Supp. XI:** 139, 267

Stern, Madeleine B., **Supp. I Part 1:** 35

Stern, Maurice, **IV:** 285

Stern, Philip Van Doren, **Supp. XIII:** 164

Stern, Richard, **Retro. Supp. II:** 291

Stern, Richard G., **Retro. Supp. II:** 204

"Sterne" (Schwartz), **Supp. II Part 2:** 663

Sterne, Laurence, **II:** 302, 304–305, 308; **III:** 454; **IV:** 68, 211, 465; **Supp. I Part 2:** 714; **Supp. IV Part 1:** 299; **Supp. V:** 127; **Supp. X:** 324

Sterritt, David, **Supp. IV Part 2:** 574

Stetson, Caleb, **IV:** 178

Stetson, Charles Walter, **Supp. XI:** 195, 196, 197, 202, 204, 209

Stevens, Mrs. Wallace (Elsie Kachel), **IV:** 75

Stevens, Wallace, **I:** 60, 61, 266, 273, 462, 521, 528, 540–541; **II:** 56, 57, 530, 552, 556; **III:** 19, 23, 194, 216, 270–271, 272, 278, 279, 281, 453, 463, 493, 509, 521, 523, 600, 605, 613, 614; **IV: 73–96,** 140, 141, 332, 402, 415; **Retro. Supp. I:** 67, 89, 193, 284, 288, **295–315,** 335, 403, 411, 416, 417, 422; **Retro. Supp. II:** 40, 44, 326; **Supp. I Part 1:** 80, 82, 257; **Supp. II Part 1:** 9, 18; **Supp. III Part 1:** 2, 3, 12, 20, 48, 239, 318, 319, 344; **Supp. III Part 2:** 611; **Supp. IV Part 1:** 72, 393; **Supp. IV Part 2:** 619, 620, 621, 634; **Supp. V:** 337; **Supp. VIII:** 21, 102, 195, 271, 292; **Supp. IX:** 41; **Supp. X:** 58; **Supp. XI:** 123, 191, 312; **Supp. XIII:** 44, 45

"Stevens and the Idea of the Hero" (Bromwich), **Retro. Supp. I:** 305

Stevenson, Adlai, **II:** 49; **III:** 581

Stevenson, Burton E., **Supp. XIV:** 120

Stevenson, David, **Supp. XI:** 230

Stevenson, Robert Louis, **I:** 2, 53; **II:** 283, 290, 311, 338; **III:** 328; **IV:** 183–184, 186, 187; **Retro. Supp. I:** 224, 228; **Supp. I Part 1:** 49; **Supp. II Part 1:** 404–405; **Supp. IV Part 1:** 298, 314; **Supp. VIII:** 125; **Supp. XIII:** 75; **Supp. XIV:** 40

Stevick, Robert D., **III:** 509

Stewart, Dugald, **II:** 8, 9; **Supp. I Part 1:** 151, 159; **Supp. I Part 2:** 422

Stewart, Jeffrey C., **Supp. XIV:** 196, 209, 210

Stewart, Randall, **II:** 244

Stewart, Robert E., **Supp. XI:** 216

Stickeen (Muir), **Supp. IX:** 182

Sticks and Stones (Mumford), **Supp. II Part 2:** 475, 483, 487–488

Sticks & Stones (Matthews), **Supp. IX:** 154, 155, 157, 158

Stieglitz, Alfred, **Retro. Supp. I:** 416; **Retro. Supp. II:** 103; **Supp. VIII:** 98

"Stigmata" (Oates), **Supp. II Part 2:** 520

Stiles, Ezra, **II:** 108, 122; **IV:** 144, 146, 148

Still, William Grant, **Retro. Supp. I:** 203

"Stillborn" (Plath), **Supp. I Part 2:** 544

"Still Here" (Hughes), **Retro. Supp. I:** 211

"Still Just Writing" (Tyler), **Supp. IV Part 2:** 658

"Still Life" (Hecht), **Supp. X:** 68

"Still Life" (Malamud), **Supp. I Part 2:** 450

"Still Life" (Sandburg), **III:** 584

"Still Life: Moonlight Striking up on a Chess-Board" (Lowell), **II:** 528

"Still Life Or" (Creeley), **Supp. IV Part 1:** 141, 150, 158

Still Life with Oysters and Lemon (Doty), **Supp. XI:** 119, 121, **133–134**

Still Life with Woodpecker (Robbins), **Supp. X:** 260, **271–274,** 282

"Still Moment, A" (Welty), **IV:** 265; **Retro. Supp. I:** 347

Stillness (Gardner), **Supp. VI:** 74

"Still Small Voices, The" (Fante), **Supp. XI:** 164

Still Such (Salter), **Supp. IX:** 246

"Still the Place Where Creation Does Some Work on Itself" (Davis), **Supp. IV Part 1:** 68

Stimpson, Catharine R., **Supp. IV Part 2:** 686

Stimson, Eleanor Kenyon. *See* Brooks, Mrs. Van Wyck

"Stings" (Plath), **Retro. Supp. II:** 255; **Supp. I Part 2:** 541

"Stirling Street September" (Baraka), **Supp. II Part 1:** 51

Stirner, Max, **II:** 27

"Stirrup-Cup, The" (Lanier), **Supp. I Part 1:** 364

Stitt, Peter, **Supp. IV Part 1:** 68; **Supp. IV Part 2:** 628; **Supp. IX:** 152, 163, 291, 299; **Supp. XI:** 311, 317; **Supp. XIII:** 87

Stivers, Valerie, **Supp. X:** 311

Stock, Noel, **III:** 479

Stockton, Frank R., **I:** 201

Stoddard, Charles Warren, **I:** 193, 195, 196; **Supp. II Part 1:** 192, 341, 351

Stoddard, Elizabeth, **II:** 275

Stoddard, Richard, **Supp. I Part 1:** 372

Stoddard, Solomon, **I:** 545, 548; **IV:** 145, 148

Stoic, The (Dreiser), **I:** 497, 502, 508, 516; **Retro. Supp. II:** 95, 96, 101, 108

"Stolen Calf, The" (Dunbar), **Supp. II Part 1:** 196

Stolen Past, A (Knowles), **Supp. XII:** 249

Stone, Edward, **III:** 479

Stone, I. F., **Supp. XIV:** 3

Stone, Irving, **II:** 463, 466, 467

Stone, Oliver, **Supp. XIV:** 48, 316

Stone, Phil, **II:** 55

Stone, Richard, **Supp. XIV:** 54

Stone, Robert, **Supp. V:** 295–312; **Supp. X:** 1

Stone, Wilmer, **Supp. I Part 1:** 49

Stone and the Shell, The (Hay), **Supp. XIV:** 122, 123, 127, 130

"Stone Bear, The" (Haines), **Supp. XII:** 206–207, 212

"Stone City" (Proulx), **Supp. VII:** 251–253

Stone Diaries, The (Shields), **Supp. VII:** 307, 315, 324–326, 327

"Stone Dreams" (Kingsolver), **Supp. VII:** 203

Stone Harp, The (Haines), **Supp. XII:** **204,** 205, 206, 207

Stonemason, The (McCarthy), **Supp. VIII:** 175, 187

"Stones" (Kumin), **Supp. IV Part 2:** 447

"Stones, The" (Plath), **Supp. I Part 2:** 535, 539

"Stones in My Passway, Hellhounds on My Trail" (Boyle), **Supp. VIII:** 15

Stones of Florence, The (McCarthy), **II:** 562

"Stone Walls" (Sarton), **Supp. VIII:** 259

"Stop" (Wilbur), **Supp. III Part 2:** 556

"Stop Me If You've Heard This One" (Lardner), **II:** 433

Stopover: Tokyo (Marquand), **III:** 53, 57, 61, 70

Stoppard, Tom, **Retro. Supp. I:** 189

"Stopping by Woods" (Frost), **II:** 154

"Stopping by Woods on a Snowy Evening" (Frost), **Retro. Supp. I:** 129, 133, 134, 135, 139

Stopping Westward (Richards), **II:** 396

"Stop Player. Joke No. 4" (Gaddis), **Supp. IV Part 1:** 280

Store, The (Stribling), **Supp. VIII:** 126

"*Store* and *Mockingbird:* Two Pulitzer Novels about Alabama" (Going), **Supp. VIII:** 126

Storer, Edward, **Supp. I Part 1:** 261, 262

Stories, Fables and Other Diversions (Nemerov), **III:** 268–269, 285

Stories for the Sixties (Yates, ed.), **Supp. XI:** 343

Stories from the Old Testament Retold (L. P. Smith), **Supp. XIV:** 342

Stories from World Literature, **Supp. IX:** 4

"Stories in the Snow" (Leopold), **Supp. XIV:** 183

Stories of F. Scott Fitzgerald, The (Cowley, ed.), **Retro. Supp. I:** 115

Stories of F. Scott Fitzgerald, The (Fitzgerald), **II:** 94

Stories of Modern America, **Supp. IX:** 4

Stories of Stephen Dixon, The (Dixon), **Supp. XII:** 152

Stories of the Spanish Civil War (Hemingway), **II:** 258

Stories Revived (James), **II:** 322

Stories that Could Be True (Stafford),

Supp. XI: 325–327

Storm, The (Buechner), **Supp. XII:** **54–57**

"Storm, The" (Chopin), **Retro. Supp. II:** 60, 68; **Supp. I Part 1:** 218, 224

"Storm Fear" (Frost), **II:** 153; **Retro. Supp. I:** 127

"Storm Ship, The" (Irving), **II:** 309

"Storm Warnings" (Kingsolver), **Supp. VII:** 207–208

"Stormy Weather" (Ellison), **Supp. II Part 1:** 233

"Story, A" (Jarrell), **II:** 371

Story, Richard David, **Supp. IV Part 2:** 575, 588

"Story about Chicken Soup, A" (Simpson), **Supp. IX:** 272–273

"Story about the Anteater, The" (Benét), **Supp. XI:** 53

"Story About the Body, A" (Hass), **Supp. VI:** **107–108**

"Story Hearer, The" (Paley), **Supp. VI:** 230, 231

"Story Hour" (Hay), **Supp. XIV:** 124

Story Hour: A Second Look at Cinderella, Bluebeard, and Company (Hay), **Supp. XIV:** 119, 124, 125, 132, 133

Story of a Country Town, The (Howe), **I:** 106

"Story of an Hour, The" (Chopin), **Retro. Supp. II:** 72; **Supp. I Part 1:** 212–213, 216

Story of a Novel, The (Wolfe), **IV:** 456, 458

"Story of a Proverb, The" (Lanier), **Supp. I Part 1:** 365

"Story of a Proverb, The: A Fairy Tale for Grown People" (Lanier), **Supp. I Part 1:** 365

Story of a Story and Other Stories, The: A Novel (Dixon), **Supp. XII:** 155

Story of a Wonder Man, The (Lardner), **II:** 433–434

"Story of a Year, The" (James), **Retro. Supp. I:** 218

"Story of Gus, The" (A. Miller), **III:** 147–148

"Story of How a Wall Stands, A" (Ortiz), **Supp. IV Part 2:** 499, 507

Story of Mount Desert Island, Maine, The (Morison), **Supp. I Part 2:** 494

Story of My Boyhood and Youth, The (Muir), **Supp. IX:** **172–174,** 176

Story of My Father, The: A Memoir (Miller), **Supp. XII:** 301

Story of O, The (Réage), **Supp. XII:** 9, 10

Story of Our Lives, The (Strand), **Supp.**

IV Part 2: 620, 628–629, 629
Story of the Normans, The, Told Chiefly in Relation to Their Conquest of England (Jewett), II: 406
"Story of Toby, The" (Melville), III: 76
Story of Utopias, The (Mumford), Supp. II Part 2: 475, 483–486, 495
Story on Page One, The (Odets), Supp. II Part 2: 546
Storyteller (Silko), Supp. IV Part 2: 558, 559, 560, 561, 566–570
"Storyteller" (Silko), Supp. IV Part 2: 569
"*Storyteller:* Grandmother Spider's Web" (Danielson), Supp. IV Part 2: 569
"Storyteller's Notebook, A" (Carver), Supp. III Part 1: 142–143
Story Teller's Story, A: The Tale of an American Writer's Journey through His Own Imaginative World and through the World of Facts . . . (Anderson), I: 98, 101, 114, 117
"Story That Could Be True, A" (Stafford), Supp. XI: 326
"Stout Gentleman, The" (Irving), II: 309
Stover at Yale (Johnson), III: 321
Stowe, Calvin, IV: 445; Supp. I Part 2: 587, 588, 590, 596, 597
Stowe, Charles, Supp. I Part 2: 581, 582
Stowe, Eliza, Supp. I Part 2: 587
Stowe, Harriet Beecher, II: 274, 399, 403, 541; Retro. Supp. I: 34, 246; Retro. Supp. II: 4, 138, 156; Supp. I Part 1: 30, 206, 301; Supp. I Part 2: 579–601; Supp. III Part 1: 154, 168, 171; Supp. IX: 33; Supp. X: 223, 246, 249, 250; Supp. XI: 193; Supp. XIII: 141, 295
Stowe, Samuel Charles, Supp. I Part 2: 587
Stowe, William, Supp. IV Part 1: 129
Strachey, Lytton, I: 5; IV: 436; Retro. Supp. I: 59; Supp. I Part 2: 485, 494; Supp. XIV: 342
Straight Cut (Bell), Supp. X: 5, 6–7, 10
Straight Man (Russo), Supp. XII: 335–339, 340
Strand, Mark, Supp. IV Part 2: 619–636; Supp. V: 92, 332, 337, 338, 343; Supp. IX: 155; Supp. XI: 139, 145; Supp. XII: 254; Supp. XIII: 76
Strand, Paul, Supp. VIII: 272
Strandberg, Victor, Supp. V: 273
Strange Case of Dr. Jekyll and Mr.

Hyde, The (Stevenson), II: 290
Strange Children, The (Gordon), II: 196, 197, 199, 211–213
"Strange Fruit" (Harjo), Supp. XII: 224, 225
"Strange Fruit" (song), Supp. I Part 1: 80
Strange Interlude (O'Neill), III: 391, 397–398; IV: 61
Stranger, The (Camus), I: 53, 292; Supp. VIII: 11
"Stranger, The" (Rich), Supp. I Part 2: 555, 560
"Stranger, The" (Salinger), III: 552–553
"Stranger in My Own Life, A: Alienation in American Indian Poetry and Prose" (Gunn Allen), Supp. IV Part 1: 322
"Stranger in the Village" (Baldwin), Retro. Supp. II: 3; Supp. I Part 1: 54; Supp. IV Part 1: 10
"Stranger in Town" (Hughes), Supp. I Part 1: 334
"Strangers" (Howe), Supp. VI: 120
Strangers and Wayfarers (Jewett), Retro. Supp. II: 138
"Strangers from the Horizon" (Merwin), Supp. III Part 1: 356
Strangers on a Train (Highsmith), Supp. IV Part 1: 132
"Strange Story, A" (Taylor), Supp. V: 323
"Strange Story, A" (Wylie), Supp. I Part 2: 723
Strange Things (Atwood), Supp. XIII: 35
"Strato in Plaster" (Merrill), Supp. III Part 1: 328
Straus, Ralph, Supp. XIII: 168
Straus, Roger, Supp. VIII: 82
Strauss, Johann, I: 66
Strauss, Richard, IV: 316
Strauss, Robert, Supp. XI: 141, 142
Stravinsky (De Schloezer), III: 474
Stravinsky, Igor, Retro. Supp. I: 378; Supp. IV Part 1: 81; Supp. XI: 133
"Stravinsky's Three Pieces 'Grotesques,' for String Quartet" (Lowell), II: 523
Straw, The (O'Neill), III: 390
"Stray Document, A" (Pound), II: 517
Streaks of the Tulip, The: Selected Criticism (W. J. Smith), Supp. XIII: 333, 334, 344, 347–348
Streamline Your Mind (Mursell), Supp. I Part 2: 608
"Street, Cloud" (Ríos), Supp. IV Part 2: 549
Streetcar Named Desire, A (T.

Williams), IV: 382, 383, 385, 386, 387, 389–390, 395, 398; Supp. IV Part 1: 359
Street in Bronzeville, A (Brooks), Retro. Supp. I: 208; Supp. III Part 1: 74–78
"Street Musicians" (Ashbery), Supp. III Part 1: 18
"Street off Sunset, A" (Jarrell), II: 387
"Streets" (Dixon), Supp. XII: 145–146
Streets in the Moon (MacLeish), III: 5, 8–11, 15, 19
Streets of Laredo (McMurtry), Supp. V: 230
"Streets of Laredo" (screenplay) (McMurtry and Ossana), Supp. V: 226, 230
Streets of Night (Dos Passos), I: 478, 479–480, 481, 488
Streitfeld, David, Supp. XIII: 234
Strength of Fields, The (Dickey), Supp. IV Part 1: 178
"Strength of Fields, The" (Dickey), Supp. IV Part 1: 176, 184–185
"Strength of Gideon, The" (Dunbar), Supp. II Part 1: 212
Strength of Gideon and Other Stories, The (Dunbar), Supp. II Part 1: 211, 212
Strether, Lambert, II: 313
Stribling, T. S., Supp. VIII: 126
Strickland, Joe (pseudonym). *See* Arnold, George W.
"Strictly Bucolic" (Simic), Supp. VIII: 278
Strictly Business (O. Henry), Supp. II Part 1: 410
"Strike, The" (Olsen), Supp. XIII: 292, 297
Strindberg, August, I: 78; III: 145, 165, 387, 390, 391, 392, 393; IV: 17
"String, The" (Dickey), Supp. IV Part 1: 179
"Strivings of the Negro People" (Du Bois), Supp. II Part 1: 167
Stroby, W. C., Supp. XIV: 26
Strohbach, Hermann, Supp. XI: 242
"Stroke of Good Fortune, A" (O'Connor), III: 344; Retro. Supp. II: 229, 232
Strom, Stephen, Supp. XII: 223
Strong, George Templeton, IV: 321
Strong, Josiah, Supp. XIV: 64
"Strong Draughts of Their Refreshing Minds" (Dickinson), Retro. Supp. I: 46
Strong Opinions (Nabokov), Retro. Supp. I: 263, 266, 270, 276

"Strong Women" (Dorman), **Supp. XI:** 240

Strout, Elizabeth, **Supp. X:** 86

Structure of Nations and Empires, The (Niebuhr), **III:** 292, 308

"Strumpet Song" (Plath), **Retro. Supp. II:** 246; **Supp. I Part 2:** 536

Strunk, William, **Supp. I Part 2:** 652, 662, 670, 671, 672

Strunsky, Anna, **II:** 465

"Strut for Roethke, A" (Berryman), **I:** 188

Stuart, Gilbert, **I:** 16

Stuart, J. E. B., **III:** 56

Stuart Little (White), **Supp. I Part 2:** 655–658

"Student, The" (Moore), **III:** 212, 215

"Student of Salmanaca, The" (Irving), **II:** 309

"Student's Wife, The" (Carver), **Supp. III Part 1:** 141

Studies in American Indian Literature: Critical Essays and Course Designs (Gunn Allen), **Supp. IV Part 1:** 324, 333

Studies in Classic American Literature (Lawrence), **II:** 102; **III:** 33; **IV:** 333; **Retro. Supp. I:** 421

"Studs" (Farrell), **II:** 25, 28, 31

Studs Lonigan: A Trilogy (Farrell), **II:** 25, 26, 27, 31–34, 37, 38, 41–42

"Study of Images" (Stevens), **IV:** 79

"Study of Lanier's Poems, A" (Kent), **Supp. I Part 1:** 373

Study of Milton's Prosody (Bridges), **II:** 537

"Study of the Negro Problems, The" (Du Bois), **Supp. II Part 1:** 165

Stuewe, Paul, **Supp. IV Part 1:** 68

Stuhlmann, Gunther, **Supp. X:** 182, 184, 185, 187

Stultifera Navis (Brant), **III:** 447

Sturak, John Thomas, **Supp. XIII:** 162, 163, 165, 168

Sturgis, George, **III:** 600

Sturgis, Howard, **IV:** 319; **Retro. Supp. I:** 367, 373

Sturgis, Susan, **III:** 600

Sturm, Margaret. *See* Millar, Margaret

Stuttaford, Genevieve, **Supp. IX:** 279

Stuyvesant, Peter, **II:** 301

"Style" (Nemerov), **III:** 275

Styles of Radical Will (Sontag), **Supp. III Part 2:** 451, 459, 460–463

Styron, William, **III:** 40; **IV:** 4, **97–119,** 216; **Supp. V:** 201; **Supp. IX:** 208; **Supp. X:** 15–16, 250; **Supp. XI:** 229, 231, 343; **Supp. XIV:** 82

Suares, J. C., **Supp. IV Part 1:** 234

Suarez, Ernest, **Supp. IV Part 1:** 175;

Supp. V: 180

"Sub, The" (Dixon), **Supp. XII:** 146

Subjection of Women, The (Mill), **Supp. XI:** 196, 203

"Subjective Necessity for Social Settlements" (Addams), **Supp. I Part 1:** 4

"Subject of Childhood, A" (Paley), **Supp. VI:** 221

"Submarginalia" (Howe), **Supp. IV Part 2:** 422

Substance and Shadow (James), **II:** 344

Subterraneans, The (Kerouac), **Supp. III Part 1:** 225, 227–231

Subtreasury of American Humor, A (White and White), **Supp. I Part 2:** 668

"Suburban Culture, Imaginative Wonder: The Fiction of Frederick Barthelme" (Brinkmeyer), **Supp. XI:** 38

Suburban Sketches (Howells), **II:** 274, 277

"Subverted Flower, The" (Frost), **Retro. Supp. I:** 139

"Subway, The" (Tate), **IV:** 128

"Subway Singer, The" (Clampitt), **Supp. IX:** 45

"Success" (Mora), **Supp. XIII:** 217

Successful Love and Other Stories (Schwartz), **Supp. II Part 2:** 661, 665

Succession, The: A Novel of Elizabeth and James (Garrett), **Supp. VII:** 104–107, 108

"Success is counted sweetest" (Dickinson), **Retro. Supp. I:** 30, 31–32, 38

Success Stories (Banks), **Supp. V:** 14–15

"Success Story" (Banks), **Supp. V:** 15

"Such Counsels You Gave to Me" (Jeffers), **Supp. II Part 2:** 433

Such Silence (Milburn), **Supp. XI:** 242

"Such Things Happen Only in Books" (Wilder), **IV:** 365

Suddenly, Last Summer (film) (Vidal), **Supp. IV Part 2:** 683

Suddenly Last Summer (T. Williams), **I:** 73; **IV:** 382, 383, 385, 386, 387, 389, 390, 391, 392, 395–396, 397, 398

Sudermann, Hermann, **I:** 66

Sugg, Richard P., **Supp. IV Part 1:** 68

"Suggestion from a Friend" (Kenyon), **Supp. VII:** 171

"Suicide" (Barnes), **Supp. III Part 1:** 33

"Suicide off Egg Rock" (Plath), **Supp.**

I Part 2: 529, 538

"Suicide's Note" (Hughes), **Retro. Supp. I:** 199

"Suitable Surroundings, The" (Bierce), **I:** 203

"Suitcase, The" (Ozick), **Supp. V:** 262, 264

"Suite for Augustus, A" (Dove), **Supp. IV Part 1:** 245

"Suite for Lord Timothy Dexter" (Rukeyser), **Supp. VI:** 283, 285

"Suite from the Firebird" (Stravinsky), **Supp. XI:** 133

"Suitor, The" (Kenyon), **Supp. VII:** 164–165

Sukarno, **IV:** 490

Sukenick, Ronald, **Supp. V:** 39, 44, 46; **Supp. XII:** 139

Sula (Morrison), **Supp. III Part 1:** 362, 364, 367, 368, 379; **Supp. VIII:** 219

Sullivan, Andrew, **Supp. IX:** 135

Sullivan, Frank, **Supp. IX:** 201

Sullivan, Harry Stack, **I:** 59

Sullivan, Jack, **Supp. X:** 86; **Supp. XII:** 331

Sullivan, Noel, **Retro. Supp. I:** 202; **Supp. I Part 1:** 329, 333

Sullivan, Richard, **Supp. VIII:** 124

Sullivan, Walter, **Supp. VIII:** 168

"Sullivan County Sketches" (Crane), **I:** 407, 421

"Sumach and Goldenrod: An American Idyll" (Mumford), **Supp. II Part 2:** 475

Suma Genji (Play), **III:** 466

Sumerian Vistas (Ammons), **Supp. VII:** 34, 35

"Summer" (Emerson), **II:** 10

"Summer" (Lowell), **II:** 554

Summer (Wharton), **IV:** 317; **Retro. Supp. I:** 360, 367, 374, **378–379,** 382

Summer, Bob, **Supp. X:** 1, 5, 6, 42

"Summer: West Side" (Updike), **Retro. Supp. I:** 320

Summer and Smoke (T. Williams), **IV:** 382, 384, 385, 386, 387, 395, 397, 398; **Supp. IV Part 1:** 84

Summer Anniversaries, The (Justice), **Supp. VII:** 115, 117

"Summer Commentary, A" (Winters), **Supp. II Part 2:** 808

"Summer Day" (O'Hara), **III:** 369

"Summer Days, The" (Oliver), **Supp. VII:** 239

"Summer Night" (Hughes), **Supp. I Part 1:** 325

"Summer Night, A" (Auden), **Supp. II Part 1:** 8

"Summer Noon: 1941" (Winters), **Supp. II Part 2:** 811

"Summer of '82" (Merwin), **Supp. III Part 1:** 355–356

Summer on the Lakes in 1843 (Fuller), **Supp. II Part 1:** 279, 295–296

"Summer People" (Hemingway), **II:** 258–259

"Summer People, The" (Jackson), **Supp. IX:** 120

"Summer People, The" (Merrill), **Supp. III Part 1:** 325–326

"Summer Ramble, A" (Bryant), **Supp. I Part 1:** 162, 164

Summers, Claude J., **Supp. IV Part 2:** 680–681; **Supp. XIV:** 161, 169

Summers, Robert, **Supp. IX:** 289

"Summer Solstice, New York City" (Olds), **Supp. X:** 207

"Summer's Reading, A" (Malamud), **Supp. I Part 2:** 430–431, 442

"Summer Storm" (Simpson), **Supp. IX:** 268

"'Summertime and the Living . . .'" (Hayden), **Supp. II Part 1:** 363, 366

Summertime Island (Caldwell), **I:** 307–308

"Summit Beach, 1921" (Dove), **Supp. IV Part 1:** 249

Summoning of Stones, A (Hecht), **Supp. X:** 57, 58, **58–59**

Summons to Memphis, A (Taylor), **Supp. V:** 313, 314, 327

Summons to the Free, A (Benét), **Supp. XI:** 47

Sumner, Charles, **I:** 3, 15; **Supp. I Part 2:** 685, 687

Sumner, John, **Retro. Supp. II:** 95

Sumner, John B., **I:** 511

Sumner, William Graham, **III:** 102, 108; **Supp. I Part 2:** 640

"Sumptuous Destination" (Wilbur), **Supp. III Part 2:** 553

"Sun" (Moore), **III:** 215

"Sun" (Swenson), **Supp. IV Part 2:** 640

"Sun, Sea, and Sand" (Marquand), **III:** 60

Sun Also Rises, The (Hemingway), **I:** 107; **II:** 68, 90, 249, 251–252, 260, 600; **III:** 36; **IV:** 35, 297; **Retro. Supp. I:** 171, **177–180**, 181, 189; **Supp. I Part 2:** 614; **Supp. XIII:** 263

"Sun and Moon" (Kenyon), **Supp. VII:** 168

"Sun and the Still-born Stars, The" (Southern), **Supp. XI:** 295

Sun at Midnight (Soseki; Merwin and Shigematsu, trans.), **Supp. III Part 1:** 353

"Sun Crosses Heaven from West to East Bringing Samson Back to the Womb, The" (Bly), **Supp. IV Part 1:** 73

"Sun Dance Shield" (Momaday), **Supp. IV Part 2:** 491

Sunday, Billy, **II:** 449

"Sunday Afternoons" (Komunyakaa), **Supp. XIII:** 127

Sunday after the War (H. Miller), **III:** 184

"Sunday at Home" (Hawthorne), **II:** 231–232

"Sunday Morning" (Stevens), **II:** 552; **III:** 278, 463, 509; **IV:** 92–93; **Retro. Supp. I:** 296, 300, 301, 304, 307, 313

"Sunday Morning Apples" (Crane), **I:** 387

"Sunday Morning Prophecy" (Hughes), **Supp. I Part 1:** 334

"Sundays" (Salter), **Supp. IX:** 257

"Sundays, They Sleep Late" (Rukeyser), **Supp. VI:** 278

"Sundays of Satin-Legs Smith, The" (Brooks), **Supp. III Part 1:** 74, 75

"Sundays Visiting" (Ríos), **Supp. IV Part 2:** 541

Sundial, The (Jackson), **Supp. IX:** **126–127**

Sundog (Harrison), **Supp. VIII: 46–48**

Sun Dogs (R. O. Butler), **Supp. XII: 64–65**

Sun Do Move, The (Hughes), **Supp. I Part 1:** 339

Sundquist, Eric, **Supp. XIV:** 66, 71

"Sunflower Sutra" (Ginsberg), **Supp. II Part 1:** 317, 321

Sunlight Dialogues, The (Gardner), **Supp. VI:** 63, **68,** 69, 70

"Sunlight Is Imagination" (Wilbur), **Supp. III Part 2:** 549

"Sunrise" (Lanier), **Supp. I Part 1:** 370

"Sunrise runs for Both, The" (Dickinson), **Retro. Supp. I:** 45

Sunrise with Seamonsters: Travels and Discoveries, 1964–1984 (Theroux), **Supp. VIII:** 311, 313, 323, 325

"Sun Rising" (Donne), **Supp. VIII:** 164

"Sunset" (Ransom), **III:** 484

"Sunset from Omaha Hotel Window" (Sandburg), **III:** 584

Sunset Gun (Parker), **Supp. IX:** 192

Sunset Limited (Burke), **Supp. XIV:** 32, 33

Sunset Limited (Harrison), **Supp. VIII:** 51

"Sunset Maker, The" (Justice), **Supp. VII:** 123

Sunset Maker, The: Poems, Stories, a Memoir (Justice), **Supp. VII:** 116, 118, 119, 123–124

Sunshine Boys, The (film), **Supp. IV Part 2:** 589

Sunshine Boys, The (Simon), **Supp. IV Part 2:** 575, 584–585

"Sunthin' in the Pastoral Line" (Lowell), **Supp. I Part 2:** 415–416

Sun to Sun (Hurston), **Supp. VI:** 154

Sun Tracks (Ortiz), **Supp. IV Part 2:** 499, 500

Sun Under Wood (Hass), **Supp. VI:** 103, 108–109

"Superb Lily, The" (Pinsky), **Supp. VI:** 250

"Superman Comes to the Supermarket" (Mailer), **Retro. Supp. II:** 204

"Supermarket in California, A" (Ginsberg), **Supp. XI:** 135

"Supper After the Last, The" (Kinnell), **Supp. III Part 1:** 239

"Supposedly Fun Thing I'll Never Do Again, A" (Wallace), **Supp. X:** 315

Supposedly Fun Thing I'll Never Do Again, A: Essays and Arguments (Wallace), **Supp. X: 314–316**

Suppressed Desires (Glaspell), **Supp. III Part 1:** 178

Suppression of the African Slave Trade to the United States of America, 1638–1870 (Du Bois), **Supp. II Part 1:** 157, 162

Sure Hand of God, The (Caldwell), **I:** 297, 302

"Surety and Fidelity Claims" (Stevens), **Retro. Supp. I:** 296, 309

Surface of Earth, The (Price), **Supp. VI:** 261–262

"Surfaces" (Ammons), **Supp. VII:** 36

Surfacing (Atwood), **Supp. XIII:** 20, 21, **22–23**, 24, 33, 35

"Surgeon at 2 A.M." (Plath), **Supp. I Part 2:** 545

Surmmer Knowledge (Schwartz), **Supp. II Part 2:** 662, 665

"Surprise" (Kenyon), **Supp. VII:** 173

Surprised by Sin: The Reader in Paradise Lost (Fish), **Supp. XIV:** 15

"Surround, The Imagining Herself as the Environment,/She Speaks to James Wright at Sundow" (Dickey), **Supp. IV Part 1:** 185

"Survey of Literature" (Ransom), **III:** 480

"Surveyor, The" (H. Roth), **Supp. IX:** 233, 234

Survival (Atwood), **Supp. XIII:** 20, 22, 35

Survival of the Bark Canoe, The (McPhee), **Supp. III Part 1:** 301, 302, 308, 313

Survival This Way: Interviews with American Indian Poets (Bruchac), **Supp. IV Part 2:** 506

"Surviving Love" (Berryman), **I:** 173

Survivor (O. Butler), **Supp. XIII:** 62, 63

Susanna Moodie: Voice and Vision (Shields), **Supp. VII:** 313

Suspect in Poetry, The (Dickey), **Supp. IV Part 1:** 177

"Sustained by Fiction" (Hoffman), **Supp. X:** 90, 92

"Susto" (Ríos), **Supp. IV Part 2:** 553

Sutherland, Donald, **IV:** 38, 44; **Supp. IX:** 254

Sutherland, Efua, **Supp. IV Part 1:** 9, 16

Sutherland-Smith, James, **Supp. X:** 211, 212

Sut Lovingood's Yarns (Harris), **II:** 70

Sutton, Roger, **Supp. X:** 266

Sutton, Walter, **III:** 479

Suttree (McCarthy), **Supp. VIII: 178–180,** 189

Suvero, Mark di, **Supp. IX:** 251

Svevo, Italo, **Supp. XIV:** 112

Swados, Harvey, **Supp. XI:** 222

Swallow, Alan, **Supp. X:** 112, 115, 116, 120, 123

Swallow Barn (Kennedy), **II:** 313

Swan, Barbara, **Supp. IV Part 2:** 447

Swan, Jon, **Supp. IV Part 1:** 176

Swan Lake (Tchaikovsky), **Supp. IX:** 51

"Swan Legs" (Stern), **Supp. IX:** 299

Swann (Shields), **Supp. VII:** 315, 318–323, 326

Swann, Brian, **Supp. IV Part 2:** 500

Swanson, Gloria, **II:** 429

Swanson, Stevenson, **Supp. XIV:** 111

Swanton, John Reed, **Supp. VIII:** 295

"Swarm, The" (Plath), **Retro. Supp. II:** 255

"Sway" (Simpson), **Supp. IX:** 276

Sweat (Hurston), **Supp. VI:** 152

Swedenborg, Emanuel, **II:** 5, 10, 321, 342, 343–344, 396

Sweeney Agonistes (Eliot), **I:** 580; **Retro. Supp. I:** 64, 65; **Retro. Supp. II:** 247

"Sweeney Among the Nightingales" (Eliot), **III:** 4

Sweet, Blanche, **Supp. I Part 2:** 391

Sweet, Timothy, **Supp. IV Part 1:** 330

Sweet and Sour (O'Hara), **III:** 361

Sweet Bird of Youth (T. Williams), **IV:** 382, 383, 385, 386, 387, 388, 389, 390, 391, 392, 395, 396, 398; **Supp. IV Part 1:** 84, 89

Sweet Charity (musical), **Supp. IV Part 2:** 575

Sweet Flypaper of Life, The (Hughes), **Supp. I Part 1:** 335–336

"Sweetheart of the Song Tra Bong, The" (O'Brien), **Supp. V:** 243, 249

"Sweethearts" (Ford), **Supp. V:** 69

Sweet Hereafter, The (Banks), **Supp. V:** 15–16

Sweet Machine (Doty), **Supp. XI:** 121, **131–132,** 135

Sweet Sue (Gurney), **Supp. V:** 105, 107–108

Sweet Sweetback's Baadasss Song (Peebles; film), **Supp. XI:** 17

Sweet Thursday (Steinbeck), **IV:** 50, 52, 64–65

Sweet Will (Levine), **Supp. V:** 178, 187, 189, 190

"Sweet Will" (Levine), **Supp. V:** 190

"Sweet Words on Race" (Hughes), **Retro. Supp. I:** 211

Sweezy, Paul, **Supp. I Part 2:** 645

"Swell-Looking Girl, A" (Caldwell), **I:** 310

Swenson, May, **Retro. Supp. II:** 44; **Supp. IV Part 2: 637–655**

"Swift" (Schwartz), **Supp. II Part 2:** 663

Swift, Jonathan, **I:** 125, 194, 209, 441; **II:** 110, 302, 304–305, 577; **III:** 113; **IV:** 68; **Retro. Supp. I:** 66; **Supp. I Part 2:** 406, 523, 603, 656, 665, 708, 714; **Supp. IV Part 1:** 51; **Supp. IV Part 2:** 692; **Supp. XI:** 105, 209; **Supp. XII:** 276

"Swimmer" (Francis), **Supp. IX:** 82

"Swimmer, The" (Cheever), **Supp. I Part 1:** 185, 187

"Swimmer, The" (Glück), **Supp. V:** 82

"Swimmers, The" (Fitzgerald), **Retro. Supp. I:** 110, 111

"Swimmers, The" (Tate), **IV:** 136

"Swimming" (Harjo), **Supp. XII:** 218

Swinburne, Algernon C., **I:** 50, 384, 568; **II:** 3, 4, 129, 400, 524; **IV:** 135; **Retro. Supp. I:** 100; **Supp. I Part 1:** 79; **Supp. I Part 2:** 422, 552; **Supp. XIV:** 120, 344

"Swinburne as Poet" (Eliot), **I:** 576

Swinger of Birches, A: A Portrait of Robert Frost (Cox), **Retro. Supp. I:** 132

"Swinging on a Birch-Tree" (Larcom),

Supp. XIII: 147

Switch, The (Dixon), **Supp. XII:** 141

Swope, D. B., **Supp. IX:** 95

Sword Blades and Poppy Seed (Lowell), **II:** 518, 520, 522, 532

Sybil (Auchincloss), **Supp. IV Part 1:** 25

"Sycamore" (Stern), **Supp. IX:** 294

"Sycamore, The" (Moore), **III:** 216

"Sycamores, The" (Whittier), **Supp. I Part 2:** 699

Sylvester, Johnny, **Supp. I Part 2:** 438

Sylvester, Joshua, **I:** 178, 179; **II:** 18; **III:** 157; **Supp. I Part 1:** 98, 104, 114, 116

Sylvia (Gurney), **Supp. V:** 105

"Sylvia" (Larcom), **Supp. XIII:** 144

"Sylvia" (Stern), **Supp. IX:** 297

Sylvia Plath: Method and Madness (Butscher), **Supp. I Part 2:** 526

Sylvia Plath: Poetry and Existence (Holbrook), **Supp. I Part 2:** 526–527

"Sylvia's Death" (Sexton), **Supp. II Part 2:** 671, 684, 685

"Symbol and Image in the Shorter Poems of Herman Melville" (Dickey), **Supp. IV Part 1:** 176

Symbolist Movement in Literature, The (Symons), **I:** 50, 569; **Retro. Supp. I:** 55

Symonds, John Addington, **I:** 241, 242, 251, 259; **IV:** 334; **Supp. XIV:** 329, 335

Symons, Arthur, **I:** 50, 569; **Retro. Supp. I:** 55

Symons, Julian, **Supp. IV Part 1:** 343, 351

"Sympathy" (Dunbar), **Supp. IV Part 1:** 15

Sympathy of Souls, A (Goldbarth), **Supp. XII:** 175, 176, **186–187**

"Symphony, The" (Lanier), **Supp. I Part 1:** 352, 360–361, 364; **Supp. I Part 2:** 416

Symposium (Plato), **Retro. Supp. II:** 31; **Supp. IV Part 1:** 391

Symposium: To Kill a Mockingbird (Alabama Law Review), **Supp. VIII:** 127, 128

Symptoms of Being 35 (Lardner), **II:** 434

Synge, John Millington, **I:** 434; **III:** 591–592; **Supp. III Part 1:** 34; **Supp. VIII:** 155

Synthetic Philosophy (Spencer), **II:** 462–463

"Syringa" (Ashbery), **Supp. III Part 1:** 19–21, 25

"Syrinx" (Clampitt), **Supp. IX:** 53

"Syrinx" (Merrill), **Supp. III Part 1:** 328

Syrkin, Marie, **Supp. XIV:** 279, 288, 291

"System, The" (Ashbery), **Supp. III Part 1:** 14, 15, 18, 21–22

System of Dante's Hell, The (Baraka), **Supp. II Part 1:** 39–41, 55

"System of Dante's Inferno, The" (Baraka), **Supp. II Part 1:** 40

"System of Doctor Tarr and Professor Fether, The" (Poe), **III:** 419, 425

System of General Geography, A (Brown), **Supp. I Part 1:** 146

Sze, Mai-mai, **Supp. X:** 291

Szentgyorgyi, Tom, **Supp. IX:** 135, 136, 140, 141–142

Szymborka, Wislawa, **Supp. XI:** 267

T. S. Eliot and American Philosophy (Jain), **Retro. Supp. I:** 58

T. S. Eliot's Silent Voices (Mayer), **Retro. Supp. I:** 58

"Table of Delectable Contents, The" (Simic), **Supp. VIII:** 276

Tabloid Dreams (R. O. Butler), **Supp. XII: 70–72,** 74

Tacitus, Cornelius, **I:** 485; **II:** 113

Tadic, Novica, **Supp. VIII:** 272

Taft (Patchett), **Supp. XII:** 307, 312, **314–317**

"Tag" (Hughes), **Supp. I Part 1:** 341

Taggard, Genevieve, **IV:** 436

Taggart, John, **Supp. IV Part 2:** 421

Tagore, Rabindranath, **I:** 383

"Taibele and Her Demon" (Singer), **Retro. Supp. II:** 307

"Tailor Shop, The" (H. Miller), **III:** 175

"Tails" (Dixon), **Supp. XII:** 154

Taine, Hippolyte, **I:** 503; **II:** 271; **III:** 323; **IV:** 440, 444

"Tain't So" (Hughes), **Supp. I Part 1:** 330

Takasago (play), **III:** 466

Take Me Back: A Novel (Bausch), **Supp. VII:** 41, 43–45, 46, 49

"Take My Saddle from the Wall: A Valediction" (McMurtry), **Supp. V:** 219

"'Take No for an Answer'" (Didion), **Supp. IV Part 1:** 203

"Take Pity" (Malamud), **Supp. I Part 2:** 427, 428, 435, 436, 437

"Takers, The" (Olds), **Supp. X:** 205

"Take the I Out" (Olds), **Supp. X:** 213

"Taking Away the Name of a Nephew" (Ríos), **Supp. IV Part 2:** 545–546

Taking Care of Mrs. Carroll (Monette), **Supp. X:** 153

"Taking of Captain Ball, The" (Jewett),

Retro. Supp. II: 134

"Taking Out the Lawn Chairs" (Karr), **Supp. XI:** 241

"Taking the Bypass" (Epstein), **Supp. XIV:** 110

"Taking the Forest" (Howe), **Supp. IV Part 2:** 433

"Taking the Lambs to Market" (Kumin), **Supp. IV Part 2:** 455

"Tale, A" (Bogan), **Supp. III Part 1:** 50, 51

Taleb-Khyar, Mohamed, **Supp. IV Part 1:** 242, 243, 244, 247, 257

"Tale of Jerusalem, A" (Poe), **III:** 411

Tale of Possessors Self-Dispossessed, A (O'Neill), **III:** 404

Tale of the Body Thief, The (Rice), **Supp. VII:** 290, 293–294, 297

Tale of Two Cities, A (film), **Supp. I Part 1:** 67

"Tale of Two Liars, A" (Singer), **IV:** 12

Tales (Baraka), **Supp. II Part 1:** 39, 55

Tales (Poe), **III:** 413

Tales and Stories for Black Folks (Bambara, ed.), **Supp. XI:** 1

Tales before Midnight (Benét), **Supp. XI:** 46, 53, 57

Tales of a Traveller (Irving), **II:** 309–310

Tales of a Wayside Inn (Longfellow), **II:** 489, 490, 501, 502, 504–505; **Retro. Supp. II:** 154, **162–165**

Tales of Glauber-Spa (Bryant, ed.), **Supp. I Part 1:** 157

Tales of Manhattan (Auchincloss), **Supp. IV Part 1:** 23

Tales of Men and Ghosts (Wharton), **IV:** 315; **Retro. Supp. I:** 372

Tales of Rhoda, The (Rice), **Supp. VII:** 288

Tales of Soldiers and Civilians (Bierce), **I:** 200–203, 204, 206, 208, 212

Tales of the Argonauts (Harte), **Supp. II Part 1:** 337, 348, 351

Tales of the Fish Patrol (London), **II:** 465

Tales of the Grotesque and Arabesque (Poe), **II:** 273; **III:** 412, 415; **Retro. Supp. II:** 270

Tales of the Jazz Age (Fitzgerald), **II:** 88; **Retro. Supp. I:** 105; **Supp. IX:** 57

"Talisman, A" (Moore), **III:** 195–196

Talisman, The (King), **Supp. V:** 140, 144, 152

"Talkin Bout Sonny" (Bambara), **Supp. XI:** 6–7

"Talking" (Merwin), **Supp. III Part 1:** 354

Talking All Morning (Bly), **Supp. IV Part 1:** 59, 60, 61, 62, 64, 65

Talking Dirty to the Gods (Komunyakaa), **Supp. XIII: 130–131**

"Talking Horse" (Malamud), **Supp. I Part 2:** 435

Talking Soft Dutch (McCarriston), **Supp. XIV:260–263,** 266, 270, 271

"Talking to Barr Creek" (Wagoner), **Supp. IX:** 328

"Talking to Sheep" (Sexton), **Supp. II Part 2:** 695

"Talk of the Town" (*The New Yorker* column), **IV:** 215; **Supp. IV Part 1:** 53, 54

"Talk with the Yellow Kid, A" (Bellow), **I:** 151

Tallent, Elizabeth, **Supp. IV Part 2:** 570

Tallman, Warren, **Supp. IV Part 1:** 154

TallMountain, Mary, **Supp. IV Part 1:** 324–325

Talma, Louise, **IV:** 357

Talmey, Allene, **Supp. IV Part 1:** 197; **Supp. XIII:** 172

Talmud, **IV:** 8, 17

Taltos: Lives of the Mayfair Witches (Rice), **Supp. VII:** 299–300

"Tamar" (Jeffers), **Supp. II Part 2:** 427–428, 436

Tamar and Other Poems (Jeffers), **Supp. II Part 2:** 416, 419

Tambourines to Glory (Hughes), **Supp. I Part 1:** 338–339

"Tame Indians" (Jewett), **Retro. Supp. II:** 141

"Tamerlane" (Poe), **III:** 426

Tamerlane and Other Poems (Poe), **III:** 410

"Tam O'Shanter" (Burns), **II:** 306

Tan, Amy, **Supp. X: 289–300**

Tangential Views (Bierce), **I:** 209

"Tangier 1975" (Bowles), **Supp. IV Part 1:** 94

"Tankas" (McClatchy), **Supp. XII:** 266

Tanner, Laura E., **Supp. X:** 209

Tanner, Tony, **I:** 260, 261; **Retro. Supp. II:** 205; **Supp. IV Part 1:** 285

Tannhäuser (Wagner), **I:** 315

"Tan Ta Ra, Cries Mars...," (Wagoner), **Supp. IX:** 325

Tao of Physics, The (Capra), **Supp. X:** 261

Tapahonso, Luci, **Supp. IV Part 1:** 404; **Supp. IV Part 2:** 499, 508

Tape for the Turn of the Year (Ammons), **Supp. VII:** 31–33, 35

"Tapestry" (Ashbery), **Supp. III Part 1:** 22–23

"Tapiama" (Bowles), **Supp. IV Part 1:** 89–90

"Tapiola" (W. C. Williams), **Retro. Supp. I:** 429

Tappan, Arthur, **Supp. I Part 2:** 588

Taps at Reveille (Fitzgerald), **II:** 94, 96; **Retro. Supp. I:** 113

Tar: A Midwest Childhood (Anderson), **I:** 98, 115; **II:** 27

Tarantino, Quentin, **Supp. IV Part 1:** 356

Tar Baby (Morrison), **Supp. III Part 1:** 364, 369–372, 379; **Supp. IV Part 1:** 13

Tarbell, Ida, **III:** 322, 580; **Retro. Supp. II:** 101

"Target Study" (Baraka), **Supp. II Part 1:** 49–50, 54

Tarkington, Booth, **II:** 444; **III:** 70; **Retro. Supp. I:** 100

Tarpon (film), **Supp. VIII:** 42

Tarr, Rodger L., **Supp. X:** 222, 224, 226

Tartuffe (Molière; Wilbur, trans.), **Supp. III Part 2:** 560

Tarumba, Selected Poems of Jaime Sabines (Levine and Trejo, trans.), **Supp. V:** 178

"Tarzan Is an Expatriate" (Theroux), **Supp. VIII:** 313

Task, The (Cowper), **II:** 304

Tasso, Torquato, **I:** 276

Taste of Palestine, A: Menus and Memories (Shihab), **Supp. XIII:** 273

Tate, Allen, **I:** 48, 49, 50, 67, 69, 381, 382, 386, 390, 396, 397, 399, 402, 441, 468; **II:** 197–198, 367, 536, 537, 542, 551, 554; **III:** 424, 428, 454, 482, 483, 485, 493, 495, 496, 497, 499, 500, 517; **IV: 120–143,** 236, 237, 433; **Retro. Supp. I:** 37, 41, 90; **Retro. Supp. II:** 77, 79, 82, 83, 89, 176, 178, 179; **Supp. I Part 1:** 364, 371; **Supp. I Part 2:** 423; **Supp. II Part 1:** 90–91, 96, 98, 103–104, 136, 139, 144, 150, 151, 318; **Supp. II Part 2:** 643; **Supp. III Part 2:** 542; **Supp. V:** 315, 331; **Supp. X:** 1, 52; **Supp. XIV:** 2

Tate, Benjamin Lewis Bogan, **IV:** 127

Tate, Greg, **Supp. XIII:** 233, 237

Tate, James, **Supp. V:** 92, 338; **Supp. VIII:** 39, 279

Tate, John Allen, **IV:** 127

Tate, Michael Paul, **IV:** 127

Tate, Mrs. Allen (Caroline Gordon). *See* Gordon, Caroline

Tate, Mrs. Allen (Helen Heinz), **IV:** 127

Tate, Mrs. Allen (Isabella Gardner), **IV:** 127

Tate, Nancy, **II:** 197

Tattooed Countess, The (Van Vechten), **I:** 295; **Supp. II Part 2:** 726–728, 738, 742

Tattooed Feet (Nye), **Supp. XIII:** 274

"Tattoos" (McClatchy), **Supp. XII:** 266–267, 268

"Tattoos" (Wright), **Supp. V:** 335, 340

Tatum, Anna, **I:** 516

Tatum, James, **Supp. IV Part 2:** 684

Taupin, René, **II:** 528, 529; **Supp. III Part 2:** 614, 615, 617, 621

Tawney, Richard Henry, **Supp. I Part 2:** 481

Taylor, Bayard, **II:** 275; **Supp. I Part 1:** 350, 361, 362, 365, 366, 372

Taylor, Cora. *See* Howarth, Cora

Taylor, Deems, **III:** 138

Taylor, Edward, **III:** 493; **IV: 144–166;** **Supp. I Part 1:** 98; **Supp. I Part 2:** 375, 386, 546

Taylor, Eleanor Ross, **Supp. V:** 317, 318

Taylor, Elizabeth, **II:** 588

Taylor, Frank, **III:** 81

Taylor, Frederick Winslow, **Supp. I Part 2:** 644

Taylor, Graham, **Supp. I Part 1:** 5

Taylor, Henry, **Retro. Supp. I:** 212; **Supp. XI:** 317; **Supp. XIII:** 333

Taylor, Henry W., **IV:** 144

Taylor, Jeremy, **II:** 11; **III:** 487; **Supp. I Part 1:** 349; **Supp. XII:** 45; **Supp. XIV:** 344, 345

Taylor, John, **IV:** 149

Taylor, Katherine, **Supp. VIII:** 251

Taylor, Kezia, **IV:** 148

Taylor, Mrs. Edward (Elizabeth Fitch), **IV:** 147, 165

Taylor, Mrs. Edward (Ruth Wyllys), **IV:** 148

Taylor, Nathaniel W., **Supp. I Part 2:** 580

Taylor, Paul, **I:** 293

Taylor, Peter, **Retro. Supp. II:** 179; **Supp. V: 313–329; Supp. XIV:** 3

Taylor, Richard, **IV:** 146

Taylor, Robert, **Supp. I Part 1:** 294

Taylor, Thomas, **II:** 10

Taylor, William, **IV:** 145–146

Taylor, Zachary, **I:** 3; **II:** 433–434

Tchelitchew, Peter, **II:** 586

Tea and Sympathy (Anderson), **Supp. I Part 1:** 277; **Supp. V:** 108

"Tea at the Palaz of Hoon" (Stevens), **Retro. Supp. I:** 300, 302, 306

"Teacher's Pet" (Thurber), **Supp. I Part 2:** 605–606

"Teaching and Story Telling" (Maclean), **Supp. XIV:** 234

Teaching a Stone to Talk: Expeditions and Encounters (Dillard), **Supp. VI:** 23, 26, 28, 32, 33, 34–35

Teachings of Don B., The (Barthelme), **Supp. IV Part 1:** 53

Teale, Edwin Way, **Supp. XIII:** 7

Teall, Dorothy, **I:** 221

Team Team Team (film), **Supp. IX:** 251

"Tea on the Mountain" (Bowles), **Supp. IV Part 1:** 90

"Tea Party, The" (MacLeish), **III:** 11

"Tears, Idle Tears" (Lord Tennyson), **Supp. XIV:** 8

"Tears of the Pilgrims, The" (McClatchy), **Supp. XII:** 256

Teasdale, Sara, **Retro. Supp. I:** 133; **Supp. I Part 2:** 393, 707; **Supp. XIV:** 127

Tebeaux, Elizabeth, **Supp. IX:** 109

Technics and Civilization (Mumford), **Supp. I Part 2:** 638; **Supp. II Part 2:** 479, 493, 497

Technics and Human Development (Mumford), **Supp. I Part 2:** 638; **Supp. II Part 2:** 497

"Teddy" (Salinger), **III:** 561–563, 571

"Te Deum" (Reznikoff), **Supp. XIV:** 281

Tedlock, Dennis, **Supp. IV Part 2:** 509

"Teeth Mother Naked at Last, The" (Bly), **Supp. IV Part 1:** 63, 68, 73

Teggart, Richard, **Supp. I Part 2:** 650

Tegnér, Esaias, **Retro. Supp. II:** 155

Teilhard de Chardin, Pierre, **Supp. I Part 1:** 314

Telephone, The (film), **Supp. XI:** 309

"Telephone Call, A" (Parker), **Supp. IX: 202–203**

"Telephone Number of the Muse, The" (Justice), **Supp. VII:** 124–125

Telephone Poles and Other Poems (Updike), **IV:** 214, 215

"Television" (Beattie), **Supp. V:** 33

Teller, Edward, **I:** 137

"Telling" (Ortiz), **Supp. IV Part 2:** 509

"Telling It in Black and White: The Importance of the Africanist Presence in *To Kill a Mockingbird*" (Baecker), **Supp. VIII:** 128

Telling Secrets (Buechner), **Supp. XII:** 53–54

Telling Stories (Didion), **Supp. IV Part 1:** 197

"Telling Stories" (Didion), **Supp. IV Part 1:** 197

"Telling the Bees" (Whittier), **Supp. I Part 2:** 694–695

Telling the Truth: The Gospel as Tragedy, Comedy, and Fairy Tale (Buechner), **Supp. XII:** 53

"Tell Me" (Hughes), **Supp. VIII:** 213

Tell Me, Tell Me (Moore), **III:** 215

Tell Me a Riddle (film), **Supp. XIII:** 295

Tell Me a Riddle (Olsen), **Supp. XIII:** 294, 296, **298–302,** 303, 305

"Tell Me a Riddle" (Olsen), **Supp. XIII:** 294, 297, 298, **300–302,** 305

Tell Me How Long the Train's Been Gone (Baldwin), **Retro. Supp. II:** 9, **11–12,** 14; **Supp. I Part 1:** 48, 52, 63–65, 67

"Tell Me My Fortune" (Epstein), **Supp. XII:** 163

Tell Me Your Answer True (Sexton), **Supp. II Part 2:** 683

Tell My Horse (Hurston), **Supp. VI:** 149, 156, 158

"Tell-Tale Heart, The" (Poe), **III:** 413, 414–415, 416; **Retro. Supp. II:** 267, 269, 270

"Tell the Women We're Going" (Carver), **Supp. III Part 1:** 138, 144

"Telluride Blues—A Hatchet Job" (Abbey), **Supp. XIII:** 10

Telushkin, Dvorah, **Retro. Supp. II:** 317

Temblor (Howe), **Supp. IV Part 2:** 431

"Temper of Steel, The" (Jones), **Supp. XI:** 218

Tempers, The (W. C. Williams), **Retro. Supp. I: 413–414,** 415, 416, 424

Tempest, The (Shakespeare), **I:** 394; **II:** 12; **III:** 40, 61, 263; **Retro. Supp. I:** 61; **Supp. IV Part 2:** 463; **Supp. V:** 302–303; **Supp. XII:** 54–57

Temple, Minnie, **II:** 323

Temple, The (Herbert), **IV:** 145, 153

Temple, William, **III:** 303

Temple of My Familiar, The (Walker), **Supp. III Part 2:** 521, 527, 529, 535, 537; **Supp. IV Part 1:** 14

"Temple of the Holy Ghost, A" (O'Connor), **III:** 344, 352; **Retro. Supp. II:** 232

Templin, Charlotte, **Supp. V:** 116

Temporary Shelter (Gordon), **Supp. IV Part 1:** 299, 305–307

"Temporary Shelter" (Gordon), **Supp. IV Part 1:** 306

Temptation Game, The (Gardner), **Supp. VI:** 72

"Temptation of St. Anthony, The" (Barthelme), **Supp. IV Part 1:** 47

Temptations, The, **Supp. X:** 242

"Tenancy, A" (Merrill), **Supp. III Part 1:** 322, 323

Tenants, The (Malamud), **Supp. I Part 2:** 448–450

Ten Commandments (McClatchy), **Supp. XII: 262–265**

Ten Days That Shook the World (Reed), **II:** 577; **Supp. X:** 136

Tendencies in Modern American Poetry (Lowell), **II:** 529

Tender Buttons (Stein), **I:** 103, 105; **IV:** 27, 42–43; **Retro. Supp. II:** 331

"Tenderfoot" (Haines), **Supp. XII:** 209

Tender Is the Night (Fitzgerald), **I:** 375; **II:** 79, 84, 91, 95–96, 97, 98, 420; **Retro. Supp. I:** 105, 108, 109, **110–112,** 114; **Supp. IX:** 59, 60, 61

"Tenderloin" (Crane), **I:** 408

"Tenderly" (Dobyns), **Supp. XIII:** 86–87

'Tender Man, A" (Bambara), **Supp. XI:** 9–10

"Tenderness" (Dunn), **Supp. XI:** 149, 150

"Tender Offer, The" (Auchincloss), **Supp. IV Part 1:** 34

"Tenebrae" (Komunyakaa), **Supp. XIII:** 132

"Ten Forty-Four" (Kingsolver), **Supp. VII:** 208

Ten Indians (Bell), **Supp. X:** 7, **12**

"Ten Neglected American Writers Who Deserve to Be Better Known" (Cantor), **Supp. IV Part 1:** 285

Tennent, Gilbert, **I:** 546

Tennessee Day in St. Louis (Taylor), **Supp. V:** 324

"Tennessee's Partner" (Harte), **Supp. II Part 1:** 345, 348–350

"Tennis" (Pinsky), **Supp. VI:** 241, 242

Tennis Court Oath, The (Ashbery), **Supp. III Part 1:** 7, 9, 12, 14, 26

Ten North Frederick (O'Hara), **III:** 361

Tennyson, Alfred, Lord, **I:** 587–588; **II:** 18, 82, 273, 338, 404, 439, 604; **III:** 5, 409, 469, 485, 511, 521, 523; **Retro. Supp. I:** 100, 325; **Retro. Supp. II:** 135; **Supp. I Part 1:** 349, 356; **Supp. I Part 2:** 410, 416, 552; **Supp. IX:** 19; **Supp. X:** 157; **Supp. XIII:** 111; **Supp. XIV:** 40, 120

"Ten O'Clock News" (Ortiz), **Supp. IV Part 2:** 503–504

Ten Poems (Dove), **Supp. IV Part 1:** 244

Ten Poems of Francis Ponge Translated by Robert Bly and Ten Poems of Robert Bly Inspired by the Poems by Francis Ponge (Bly), **Supp. IV Part 1:** 71

"Tension in Poetry" (Tate), **IV:** 128, 129, 135

Tenth Muse, The (Bradstreet), **Supp. I Part 1:** 102, 103, 114

"Tent on the Beach, The" (Whittier), **Supp. I Part 2:** 703

"Teodoro Luna Confesses after Years to His Brother, Anselmo the Priest, Who Is Required to Understand, But Who Understands Anyway, More Than People Think" (Ríos), **Supp. IV Part 2:** 552

Teodoro Luna's Two Kisses (Ríos), **Supp. IV Part 2:** 550–552, 553

"Tepeyac" (Cisneros), **Supp. VII:** 69

"Terce" (Auden), **Supp. II Part 1:** 22

Terence, **IV:** 155, 363; **Supp. I Part 2:** 405

Terkel, Studs, **Supp. IV Part 1:** 364

"Term" (Merwin), **Supp. III Part 1:** 356–357

"Terminal Days at Beverly Farms" (Lowell), **Retro. Supp. II:** 189

Terminating, or Sonnet LXXV, or "Lass Meine Schmerzen nicht verloren sein, or Ambivalence" (Kushner), **Supp. IX:** 132

Terminations (James), **Retro. Supp. I:** 229

"Terminus" (Emerson), **II:** 13, 19

"Terminus" (Wharton), **Retro. Supp. I:** 371

"Terms in Which I Think of Reality, The" (Ginsberg), **Supp. II Part 1:** 311

Terms of Endearment (film), **Supp. V:** 226

Terms of Endearment (McMurtry), **Supp. V:** 224–225

"Terrace, The" (Wilbur), **Supp. III Part 2:** 550

"Terrence McNally" (Bryer), **Supp. XIII:** 200

"Terrence McNally" (Di Gaetani), **Supp. XIII:** 200

Terrence McNally: A Casebook (Zinman), **Supp. XIII:** 209

"Terrible Peacock, The" (Barnes), **Supp. III Part 1:** 33

Terrible Threes, The (Reed), **Supp. X:** 241, 253

Terrible Twos, The (Reed), **Supp. X:** 241, **252–253**

"Terrific Mother" (Moore), **Supp. X:** 178

Territory Ahead, The (Morris), **III:** 228–229, 236

Terry, Edward A., **II:** 128, 129

Terry, Rose, **Supp. I Part 2:** 420

Tertium Organum (Ouspensky), **I:** 383

Tess of the d'Ubervilles (Hardy), **II:** 181; **Retro. Supp. II:** 100

"Testament" (Berry), **Supp. X:** 36

"Testament (Or, Homage to Walt Whitman)" (Jong), **Supp. V:** 130

"Testament of Flood" (Warren), **IV:** 253

Testament of François Villon, The (Pound, opera), **Retro. Supp. I:** 287

"Testimonia on the Question of Stesichoros' Blinding by Helen" (Carson), **Supp. XII:** 107

"Testimony" (Komunyakaa), **Supp. XIII:** 129

Testimony: The United States (1885–1890): Recitative (Reznikoff), **Supp. XIV:** 279, 280, 281, 285, **289–291**

Testimony: The United States (1891–1900): Recitative (Reznikoff), **Supp. XIV:** 291

"Testing-Tree, The" (Kunitz), **Supp. III Part 1:** 269

Testing-Tree, The (Kunitz), **Supp. III Part 1:** 260, 263, 264, 267, 268

Test of Poetry, A (Zukofsky), **Supp. III Part 2:** 618, 622

"Texas Moon, and Elsewhere, The" (McMurtry), **Supp. V:** 225

Texas Poets in Concert: A Quartet (Gwynn, ed.), **Supp. XIII:** 277

Texas Summer (Southern), **Supp. XI:** 309

Texasville (McMurtry), **Supp. V:** 228, 233

Thacher, Molly Day, **IV:** 381

Thackeray, William Makepeace, **I:** 194, 354; **II:** 182, 271, 282, 288, 316, 321, 322; **III:** 64, 70; **IV:** 326; **Retro. Supp. I:** 218; **Supp. I Part 1:** 307; **Supp. I Part 2:** 421, 495, 579; **Supp. IV Part 1:** 297; **Supp. IX:** 200; **Supp. XI:** 277; **Supp. XIV:** 306

Thaddeus, Janice Farrar, **Supp. IV Part 1:** 299

"Thailand" (Barthelme), **Supp. IV Part 1:** 41

Thalberg, Irving, **Retro. Supp. I:** 109, 110, 114

Thales, **I:** 480–481

Thalia Trilogy (McMurtry), **Supp. V:** 220–223, 234

Tham, Claire, **Supp. VIII:** 79

"Thanatopsis" (Bryant), **Supp. I Part 1:** 150, 154, 155, 170

Thanatos Syndrome, The (Percy), **Supp. III Part 1:** 385, 397–399

"Thanksgiving" (Glück), **Supp. V:** 83

"Thanksgiving, A" (Auden), **Supp. II Part 1:** 26

"Thanksgiving for a Habitat" (Auden), **Supp. II Part 1:** 24

"Thanksgiving Spirit" (Farrell), **II:** 45

Thanksgiving Visitor, The (Capote), **Supp. III Part 1:** 116, 118, 119

Thank You, Fog (Auden), **Supp. II Part 1:** 24

"Thank You, Lord" (Angelou), **Supp. IV Part 1:** 15

Thank You, Mr. Moto (Marquand), **III:** 57, 58

"Thank You in Arabic" (Nye), **Supp. XIII:** 273, 281

"Thar's More in the Man Than Thar Is in the Land" (Lanier), **Supp. I Part 1:** 352–353, 359–360

"That Evening Sun" (Faulkner), **II:** 72; **Retro. Supp. I:** 75, 83

That Horse (Hogan), **Supp. IV Part 1:** 397, 404, 405

"That I Had the Wings" (Ellison), **Supp. II Part 1:** 238

"That's the Place Indians Talk About" (Ortiz), **Supp. IV Part 2:** 511

"That the Soul May Wax Plump" (Swenson), **Supp. IV Part 2:** 650

"That Tree" (Porter), **III:** 434–435, 446, 451

That Was the Week That Was (television program), **Supp. XIV:** 125

"That Year" (Olds), **Supp. X:** 203

Thaxter, Celia, **Retro. Supp. II:** 136, 147; **Supp. XIII:** 143, 153

Thayer, Abbott, **I:** 231

Thayer, Scofield, **I:** 231; **Retro. Supp. I:** 58

Thayer and Eldridge, **Retro. Supp. I:** 403

"Theater" (Toomer), **Supp. IX:** 309, 317–318

"Theater Chronicle" (McCarthy), **II:** 562

Theatricals (James), **Retro. Supp. I:** 228

"Theft" (Porter), **III:** 434, 435

Theft, A (Bellow), **Retro. Supp. II:** 31–32, 34

Their Eyes Were Watching God (Hurston), **Supp. VI:** 149, 152, 156–157

Their Heads Are Green and Their Hands Are Blue: Scenes from the Non-Christian World (Bowles), **Supp. IV Part 1:** 89

"Their Losses" (Taylor), **Supp. V:** 320

Their Wedding Journey (Howells), **II:** 277–278; **Retro. Supp. I:** 334

them (Oates), **Supp. II Part 2:** 503, 511–514

Theme Is Freedom, The (Dos Passos), **I:** 488–489, 492, 494

"Theme with Variations" (Agee), **I:** 27

"Then" (Barthelme), **Supp. IV Part 1:** 48

"Then It All Came Down" (Capote), **Supp. III Part 1:** 125, 131

Theocritus, **II:** 169; **Retro. Supp. I:** 286

"Theodore the Poet" (Masters), **Supp. I Part 2:** 461

Theological Position, A (Coover), **Supp. V:** 44

Theophrastus, **I:** 58

"Theoretical and Scientific Conceptions of Race, The" (Locke), **Supp. XIV:** 209

Theory and Practice of Rivers and Other Poems, The (Harrison), **Supp. VIII:** 47, 49

Theory of Business Enterprise, The (Veblen), **Supp. I Part 2:** 638, 641, 644

Theory of Flight (Rukeyser), **Supp. VI:** 272, 275, **277–278**, 284

"Theory of Flight" (Rukeyser), **Supp. VI:** 277–278

Theory of Moral Sentiments, The (A. Smith), **Supp. I Part 2:** 634

Theory of the Leisure Class, The (Veblen), **I:** 475–476; **Supp. I Part 2:** 629, 633, 641, 645; **Supp. IV Part 1:** 22

"There" (Taylor), **Supp. V:** 323

"There Are No Such Trees in Alpine California" (Haines), **Supp. XII:** 207

"There Goes (Varoom! Varoom!) That Kandy-Kolored Tangerine-Flake Streamline Baby" (Wolfe), **Supp. III Part 2:** 569–571

"There Is a Lesson" (Olsen), **Supp. XIII:** 292, 297

"There Is Only One of Everything" (Atwood), **Supp. XIII:** 34

There Is Something Out There (McNally). *See And Things That Go Bump in the Night* (McNally)

"There's a certain Slant of light" (Dickinson), **Retro. Supp. I:** 38

Thérèse de Lisieux, Saint, **Supp. VIII:** 195

"There She Is She Is Taking Her Bath" (Anderson), **I:** 113, 114

"There Was a Child Went Forth" (Whitman), **IV:** 348

"There Was a Man, There Was a Woman" (Cisneros), **Supp. VII:** 70

"There Was an Old Woman She Had So Many Children She Didn't Know What to Do" (Cisneros), **Supp. VII:** 60

"There Was a Youth Whose Name Was Thomas Granger" (Olson), **Supp. II Part 2:** 558, 560, 563

There Were Giants in the Land (Benét), **Supp. XI:** 50

There You Are (Simpson), **Supp. IX: 279–280**

"There You Are" (Simpson), **Supp. IX:** 279

"Thermopylae" (Clampitt), **Supp. IX:** 43

Theroux, Alexander, **Supp. VIII:** 312

Theroux, Marcel, **Supp. VIII:** 325

Theroux, Paul, **Supp. V:** 122; **Supp. VIII: 309–327**

"These Are My People" (Hayden), **Supp. II Part 1:** 365

"These are the days when Birds come back" (Dickinson), **Retro. Supp. I:** 30

"These Days" (Olds), **Supp. X:** 215

"These Flames and Generosities of the Heart: Emily Dickinson and the Illogic of Sumptuary Values" (Howe), **Supp. IV Part 2:** 431

"These saw Visions" (Dickinson), **Retro. Supp. I:** 46

These Thirteen (Faulkner), **II:** 72

These Three (film), **Supp. I Part 1:** 281

"Thessalonica: A Roman Story" (Brown), **Supp. I Part 1:** 133

Thew, Harvey, **Supp. XIII:** 166

"They Ain't the Men They Used To Be" (Farrell), **II:** 45

"They Burned the Books" (Benét), **Supp. XI:** 46

They Came Like Swallows (Maxwell), **Supp. VIII: 155–159,** 168, 169

"They Can't Turn Back" (Baldwin), **Supp. I Part 1:** 52

They Feed They Lion (Levine), **Supp. V:** 178, 179, 181, 184–185, 186

"They Feed They Lion" (Levine), **Supp. V:** 188

"They Lion Grow" (Levine), **Supp. V:** 184–185

"They're Not Your Husband" (Carver), **Supp. III Part 1:** 141, 143

They're Playing Our Song (musical), **Supp. IV Part 2:** 589

They Shall Inherit the Laughter (Jones), **Supp. XI:** 217, 218, 232

They Shoot Horses (film), **Supp. XIII:** 159

They Shoot Horses, Don't They? (McCoy), **Supp. XIII:** 159, **164–166,** 168, 171, 172, 174

"They Sing, They Sing" (Roethke), **III:** 544

They Stooped to Folly (Glasgow), **II:** 175, 186–187

They Whisper (R. O. Butler), **Supp. XII: 72–73**

"Thieves" (Yates), **Supp. XI:** 349

Thieves of Paradise (Komunyakaa), **Supp. XIII:** 113, **128–130,** 132

"Thimble, The" (Kenyon), **Supp. VII:** 164

"Thing and Its Relations, The" (James), **II:** 357

"Things" (Haines), **Supp. XII:** 207

"Things" (Kenyon), **Supp. VII:** 169

"Things, The" (Kinnell), **Supp. III Part 1:** 246

Things As They Are (Stein), **IV:** 34, 37, 40

"Things Don't Stop" (Nye), **Supp. XIII:** 287

Things Gone and Things Still Here (Bowles), **Supp. IV Part 1:** 91

"Things of August" (Stevens), **Retro. Supp. I:** 309

Things of This World (Wilbur), **Supp. III Part 2:** 552–555

Things Themselves: Essays and Scenes (Price), **Supp. VI:** 261

Things They Carried, The (O'Brien), **Supp. V:** 238, 239, 240, 243, 248–250

"Thing That Killed My Father Off, The" (Carver), **Supp. III Part 1:** 143

Think Back on Us . . . (Cowley), **Supp. II Part 1:** 139, 140, 142

Think Fast, Mr. Moto (Marquand), **III:** 57, 58

"Thinking about Barbara Deming" (Paley), **Supp. VI:** 227

"Thinking about Being Called Simple by a Critic" (Stafford), **Supp. XI:** 328

Thinking about the Longstanding Problems of Virtue and Happiness: Essays, a Play, Two Poems, and a Prayer (Kushner), **Supp. IX:** 131, 134, 135

"Thinking about the Past" (Justice), **Supp. VII:** 123–124

"Thinking about Western Thinking" (Didion), **Supp. IV Part 1:** 204, 206

"'Thinking against Oneself': Reflections on Cioran" (Sontag), **Supp. III Part 2:** 459–460

"Thinking Back Through Our Mothers: Traditions in Canadian Women's Writing" (Shields), **Supp. VII:** 307–308

"Thinking for Berky" (Stafford), **Supp. XI:** 320

"Thinking like a Mountain" (Leopold), **Supp. XIV:** 188, 189

"Thinking of the Lost World" (Jarrell), **II:** 338–389

Thin Man, The (film), **Supp. IV Part 1:** 342, 355

Thin Man, The (Hammett), **Supp. IV Part 1:** 354–355

"Thinnest Shadow, The" (Ashbery), **Supp. III Part 1:** 5

"Thin People, The" (Plath), **Supp. I Part 2:** 538, 547

Thin Red Line, The (film), **Supp. V:** 249

Thin Red Line, The (Jones), **Supp. XI:** 219, **224–225,** 229, 231, 232, 233, 234

"Thin Strips" (Sandburg), **III:** 587

"Third Avenue in Sunlight" (Hecht), **Supp. X:** 61

"Third Body, A" (Bly), **Supp. IV Part 1:** 71

Third Circle, The (Norris), **III:** 327

"Third Expedition, The" (Bradbury), **Supp. IV Part 1:** 103, 106

Third Life of Grange Copeland, The (Walker), **Supp. III Part 2:** 520, 527–536

Third Mind, The (Burroughs), **Supp. XII:** 3

Third Rose, The (Brinnin), **IV:** 26

"Third Sermon on the Warpland, The" (Brooks), **Supp. III Part 1:** 85

"Third Thing That Killed My Father Off, The" (Carver), **Supp. III Part 1:** 144

Third Violet, The (Crane), **I:** 408, 417–418

Thirlwall, John C., **Retro. Supp. I:** 430

"Thirst: Introduction to Kinds of Water" (Carson), **Supp. XII: 103**

13 by Shanley (Shanley), **Supp. XIV:** 316

Thirteen Hands: A Play in Two Acts (Shields), **Supp. VII:** 322–323

Thirteen O'Clock (Benét), **Supp. XI:** 46

Thirteen Other Stories (Purdy), **Supp. VII:** 278

"Thirteenth and Pennsylvania" (Stafford), **Supp. XI:** 324

"Thirteen Ways of Looking at a Blackbird" (Stevens), **IV:** 94; **Supp. IX:** 47

"30. Meditation. 2. Cor. 5.17. He Is a New Creature" (Taylor), **IV:** 144

30: Pieces of a Novel (Dixon), **Supp. XII:** 152, **153–154**

30/6 (poetry chapbook), **Supp. V:** 5, 6

"Thirty Bob a Week" (Davidson), **Retro. Supp. I:** 55

"Thirty Delft Tiles" (Doty), **Supp. XI:** 131

"35/10" (Olds), **Supp. X:** 206

"35,000 Feet—The Lanterns" (Goldbarth), **Supp. XII:** 182

31 Letters and 13 Dreams (Hugo), **Supp. VI:** 141–144

Thirty Poems (Bryant), **Supp. I Part 1:** 157, 158

Thirty-Six Poems (Warren), **IV:** 236, 239, 240

"33" (Alvarez), **Supp. VII:** 4

"3275" (Monette), **Supp. X:** 148, 159

Thirty Years (Marquand), **III:** 56, 60–61

Thirty Years of Treason (Bentley), **Supp. I Part 1:** 297

This, My Letter (Hay), **Supp. XIV:** 121, 122, 129, 131

"This, That & the Other" (Nemerov), **III:** 269

This Body Is Made of Camphor and Gopherwood (Bly), **Supp. IV Part 1:** 63–65, 66, 71

This Boy's Life: A Memoir (T. Wolff), **Supp. VII:** 334–339, 340, 343; **Supp. XI:** 246, 247

"This Bright Dream" (Benét), **Supp. XI:** 55

This Coffin Has No Handles (McGrath), **Supp. X:** 117

"This Configuration" (Ashbery), **Supp. III Part 1:** 22

"This Corruptible" (Wylie), **Supp. I Part 2:** 727, 729

"This Crutch That I Love" (Nye), **Supp. XIII:** 288

"This Gentile World" (H. Miller), **III:** 177

"This Hand" (Wylie), **Supp. I Part 2:** 713

"This Hour" (Olds), **Supp. X:** 212

"This House I Cannot Leave" (Kingsolver), **Supp. VII:** 208

This Hunger (Nin), **Supp. X:** 185

"This Is a Photograph of Me" (Atwood), **Supp. XIII:** 33

"This Is It" (Stern), **Supp. IX:** 290

"This Is Just to Say" (W. C. Williams), **Supp. XI:** 328

"This Is My Heart" (Harjo), **Supp. XII:** 230

"This Is Not Who We Are" (Nye), **Supp. XIII:** 285, 286

"This Is What I Said" (Salinas), **Supp. XIII:** 322

This Journey (Wright), **Supp. III Part 2:** 605–606

This Man and This Woman (Farrell), **II:** 42

"This Morning" (Kenyon), **Supp. VII:** 164

"This Morning, This Evening, So Soon" (Baldwin), **Supp. I Part 1:** 63

"This Morning Again It Was in the Dusty Pines" (Oliver), **Supp. VII:** 240

This Music Crept by Me upon the Waters (MacLeish), **III:** 21

This People Israel: The Meaning of Jewish Existence (Baeck), **Supp. V:** 260

"This Personal Maze Is Not the Prize" (Selinger), **Supp. XI:** 248

"This Place in the Ways" (Rukeyser), **Supp. VI:** 273–274

This Property Is Condemned (T. Williams), **IV:** 378

This Proud Heart (Buck), **Supp. II Part 1:** 119–120

This Same Sky: A Collection of Poems from around the World (Nye, ed.), **Supp. XIII:** 280

"This Sandwich Has No Mayonnaise" (Salinger), **III:** 552–553

This Side of Paradise (Fitzgerald), **I:** 358; **II:** 77, 80, 81, 82–83, 84, 85–87, 88; **Retro. Supp. I:** 99–100, **101–102**, 103, 105, 106, 110, 111

This Stubborn Self: Texas Autobiographies (Almon), **Supp. XIII:** 288

This Thing Don't Lead to Heaven (Crews), **Supp. XI:** **112**

This Time: New and Selected Poems (Stern), **Supp. IX:** 290–291, **299**

"Thistle Seed in the Wind" (Francis), **Supp. IX:** 81

"Thistles in Sweden, The" (Maxwell), **Supp. VIII:** 169

"This Tokyo" (Snyder), **Supp. VIII:** 298

This Tree Will Be Here for a Thousand Years (Bly), **Supp. IV Part 1:** 65–66, 71, 72

This Tree Will Be Here for a Thousand Years (revised edition) (Bly), **Supp. IV Part 1:** 66

This Very Earth (Caldwell), **I:** 297, 302

Thoens, Karen, **Supp. V:** 147

Thomas, Brandon, **II:** 138

Thomas, D. M., **Supp. VIII:** 5

Thomas, Debra, **Supp. XIII:** 114

Thomas, Dylan, **I:** 49, 64, 382, 432, 526, 533; **III:** 21, 521, 528, 532, 534; **IV:** 89, 93, 136; **Supp. I Part 1:** 263; **Supp. III Part 1:** 42, 47; **Supp. V:** 344; **Supp. VIII:** 21; **Supp. IX:** 114; **Supp. X:** 115

Thomas, Edward, **II:** 154; **Retro. Supp. I:** 127, 131, 132; **Supp. I Part 1:** 263; **Supp. II Part 1:** 4

Thomas, J. Parnell, **Supp. I Part 1:** 286

Thomas, Lewis, **Retro. Supp. I:** 323

Thomas, William I., **Supp. I Part 2:** 641

Thomas-a-Kempis, **Retro. Supp. I:** 247

Thomas and Beulah (Dove), **Supp. IV Part 1:** 242, 247–248, 249

Thomas Aquinas (Saint), **I:** 13, 14, 265, 267; **III:** 270; **Retro. Supp. II:** 222; **Supp. IV Part 2:** 526

"Thomas at the Wheel" (Dove), **Supp. IV Part 1:** 248

"Thomas McGrath: Words for a Vanished Age" (Vinz), **Supp. X:** 117

Thomas Merton on Peace, **Supp. VIII:** 208

Thomas Merton Studies Center, The, **Supp. VIII:** 208

Thompson, Barbara, **Supp. V:** 322

Thompson, Cy, **I:** 538

Thompson, Dorothy, **II:** 449–450, 451, 453

Thompson, E. P., **Supp. X:** 112, 117

Thompson, Francis, **Retro. Supp. I:** 55

Thompson, Frank, **II:** 20

Thompson, George, **Supp. I Part 2:** 686

Thompson, Hunter S., **Supp. VIII:** 42; **Supp. XI:** 105; **Supp. XIII:** 1, 17

Thompson, James R., **Supp. IV Part 1:** 217

Thompson, John, **Supp. V:** 323

Thompson, Lawrance, **II:** 508

Thompson, Lawrance Roger, **Retro. Supp. I:** 138, 141

Thompson, Morton, **Supp. XIII:** 170

Thompson, Theresa, **Supp. V:** 141

Thompson, William T., **Supp. I Part 2:** 411

Thomson, James, **II:** 304; **Supp. I Part 1:** 150, 151

Thomson, Virgil, **IV:** 45; **Supp. IV Part 1:** 81, 83, 84, 173

"Thoreau" (Lowell), **Supp. I Part 2:** 420, 422

Thoreau, Henry David, **I:** 98, 104, 228, 236, 257, 258, 261, 305, 433; **II:** 7, 8, 13, 17, 101, 159, 224, 273–274, 295, 312–313, 321, 457–458, 540, 546–547; **III:** 171, 174, 186–187,

189, 208, 214–215, 453, 454, 507, 577; **IV: 167–189**, 191, 341; **Retro. Supp. I:** 51, 62, 122; **Retro. Supp. II:** 13, 96, 142, 158; **Supp. I Part 1:** 29, 34, 116, 188, 299, 358; **Supp. I Part 2:** 383, 400, 420, 421, 507, 540, 579, 580, 655, 659, 660, 664, 678; **Supp. III Part 1:** 340, 353; **Supp. IV Part 1:** 236, 392, 416; **Supp. IV Part 2:** 420, 430, 433, 439, 447; **Supp. V:** 200, 208; **Supp. VIII:** 40, 42, 103, 105, 198, 201, 204, 205, 292, 303; **Supp. IX:** 25, 90, 171; **Supp. X:** 21, 27, 28–29, 101, 102; **Supp. XI:** 155; **Supp. XIII:** 1, 17; **Supp. XIV:** 40, 54, 106, 177, 181

Thoreau, John, **IV:** 171, 182

Thoreau, Mrs. John, **IV:** 172

"Thorn, The" (Gordon), **Supp. IV Part 1:** 314

Thorne, Francis, **Supp. XII:** 253

"Thorn Merchant, The" (Komunyakaa), **Supp. XIII:** 119–120

Thornton, Billy Bob, **Supp. VIII:** 175

Thornton, Lionel, **III:** 291

"Thorofare" (Minot), **Supp. VI: 209–210**

"Thorow" (Howe), **Supp. IV Part 2:** 419, 420, 421, 431, 433–434

Thorp, Willard, **Supp. XIII:** 101

Thorslev, Peter L., Jr., **I:** 524

Thorstein Veblen (Dowd), **Supp. I Part 2:** 650

Thorstein Veblen (Qualey, ed.), **Supp. I Part 2:** 650

Thorstein Veblen: A Chapter in American Economic Thought (Teggart), **Supp. I Part 2:** 650

Thorstein Veblen: A Critical Interpretation (Riesman), **Supp. I Part 2:** 649, 650

Thorstein Veblen: A Critical Reappraisal (Dowd, ed.), **Supp. I Part 2:** 650

Thorstein Veblen and His America (Dorfman), **Supp. I Part 2:** 631, 650

Thorstein Veblen and the Institutionalists: A Study in the Social Philosophy of Economics (Seckler), **Supp. I Part 2:** 650

"Those before Us" (Lowell), **II:** 550

"Those Being Eaten by America" (Bly), **Supp. IV Part 1:** 62

Those Bones Are Not My Child (Bambara), **Supp. XI:** 1, 14, **20–22**

Those Extraordinary Twins (Twain), **IV:** 205–206

"Those Graves in Rome" (Levis),

Supp. XI: 266

"Those of Us Who Think We Know" (Dunn), **Supp. XI:** 146

"Those Times . . ." (Sexton), **Supp. II Part 2:** 670, 684

"Those Various Scalpels" (Moore), **III:** 202

"Those Were the Days" (Levine), **Supp. V:** 190

"Those Who Don't" (Cisneros), **Supp. VII:** 60

"Those Who Thunder" (Hogan), **Supp. IV Part 1:** 406

"Thought, A" (Sarton), **Supp. VIII:** 262

Thought and Character of William James (Perry), **II:** 362

Thoughtbook of Francis Scott Key Fitzgerald (Fitzgerald), **Retro. Supp. I:** 99

"Thoughtful Roisterer Declines the Gambit, The" (Hecht), **Supp. X:** 63

"Thought of Heaven, The" (Stern), **Supp. IX:** 297

"Thoughts after Lambeth" (Eliot), **I:** 587; **Retro. Supp. I:** 324

Thoughts and Reflections (Lord Halifax), **II:** 111

Thoughts in Solitude (Merton), **Supp. VIII:** 207

"Thoughts on Being Bibliographed" (Wilson), **IV:** 435

"Thoughts on the Establishment of a Mint in the United States" (Paine), **Supp. I Part 2:** 512

"Thoughts on the Gifts of Art" (Kenyon), **Supp. VII:** 167

Thousand Acres, A (Smiley), **Supp. VI:** 292, **301–303**

"Thousand and Second Night, The" (Merrill), **Supp. III Part 1:** 324

"Thousand Dollar Vagrant, The" (Olsen), **Supp. XIII:** 292, 297

"Thousand Faces of Danny Torrance, The" (Figliola), **Supp. V:** 143

"Thousand Genuflections, A" (McCarriston), **Supp. XIV:** 266

Thousand-Mile Walk to the Gulf, A (Muir), **Supp. IX: 177–178**

"Thou Shalt Not Steal" (McClatchy), **Supp. XII:** 264

"Thread, The" (Merwin), **Supp. III Part 1:** 351

Three (film), **Supp. IX:** 253

3-3-8 (Marquand), **III:** 58

"Three Academic Pieces" (Stevens), **IV:** 90

"Three Agee Wards, The" (Morris), **III:** 220–221

"Three American Singers" (Cather),

Retro. Supp. I: 10

"Three Around the Old Gentleman" (Berryman), **I:** 188

"Three Avilas, The" (Jeffers), **Supp. II Part 2:** 418

Three Books of Song (Longfellow), **II:** 490

"Three Bushes" (Yeats), **Supp. I Part 1:** 80

Three Cantos (Pound), **Retro. Supp. I:** 290

Three Centuries of Harvard (Morison), **Supp. I Part 2:** 485

Three Comrades (Remarque), **Retro. Supp. I:** 113

"Three Corollaries of Cultural Relativism" (Locke), **Supp. XIV:** 202

"Three-Day Blow, The" (Hemingway), **II:** 248

Three Essays on America (Brooks), **I:** 246

Three Farmers on Their Way to a Dance (Powers), **Supp. IX:** 211–212, **213–214**, 222

"Three Fates, The" (Benét), **Supp. XI:** 48–49, 50

Three Gospels (Price), **Supp. VI:** 267

"Three Kings, The: Hemingway, Faulkner, and Fitzgerald" (Ford), **Supp. V:** 59

Three Lives (Auchincloss), **Supp. IV Part 1:** 25

Three Lives (Stein), **I:** 103; **IV:** 26, 27, 31, 35, 37–41, 42, 45, 46; **Supp. IX:** 306

"THREE MOVEMENTS AND A CODA" (Baraka), **Supp. II Part 1:** 50

Three on the Tower: The Lives and Works of Ezra Pound, T. S. Eliot, and William Carlos Williams (Simpson), **Supp. IX:** 276

Three Papers on Fiction (Welty), **IV:** 261

Three-Penny Opera (Brecht), **I:** 301; **Supp. XIV:** 162

Three Philosophical Poets (Santayana), **III:** 610–612

"Three Players of a Summer Game" (T. Williams), **IV:** 383

Three Poems (Ashbery), **Supp. III Part 1:** 2, 3, 14, 15, 18, 24–26

"Three Pokes of a Thistle" (Nye), **Supp. XIII:** 281

Three Roads, The (Macdonald, under Millar), **Supp. IV Part 2:** 466, 467

"Three Silences of Molinos, The" (Longfellow), **Retro. Supp. II:** 169

"Three Sisters, The" (Cisneros), **Supp. VII:** 64

Three Soldiers (Dos Passos), **I:** 477–478, 480, 482, 488, 493–494

"Three Songs at the End of Summer" (Kenyon), **Supp. VII:** 169–170

"Three Steps to the Graveyard" (Wright), **Supp. III Part 2:** 593, 596

Three Stories and Ten Poems (Hemingway), **II:** 68, 263

Three Taverns, The (Robinson), **III:** 510

"Three Taverns, The" (Robinson), **III:** 521, 522

Three Tenant Families (Agee), **I:** 37–38

"Three Types of Poetry" (Tate), **IV:** 131

"Three Vagabonds of Trinidad" (Harte), **Supp. II Part 1:** 338

"Three Waterfalls, The" (Lanier), **Supp. I Part 1:** 350

"Three-Way Mirror" (Brooks), **Supp. III Part 1:** 69–70

"Three Women" (Plath), **Supp. I Part 2:** 539, 541, 544, 545, 546

Three Young Poets (Swallow, ed.), **Supp. X:** 116

Threnody (Emerson), **Supp. I Part 2:** 416

"Threnody" (Emerson), **II:** 7

"Threnody for a Brown Girl" (Cullen), **Supp. IV Part 1:** 166

"Threshing-Floor, The" (Baldwin), **Supp. I Part 1:** 50

Threshold (film), **Supp. IX:** 254

"Threshold" (Goldbarth), **Supp. XII:** 175

Threshold (Jackson), **Supp. IX:** 117

"Throat" (Goldbarth), **Supp. XII:** 177–178

Thrones (Pound), **Retro. Supp. I:** 293

Through Dooms of Love (Kumin), **Supp. IV Part 2:** 444

"Through the Black Curtain" (Kingston), **Supp. V:** 169

Through the Forest: New and Selected Poems, 1977–1987 (Wagoner), **Supp. IX:** 330–331

"Through the Hills of Spain" (Salinas), **Supp. XIII:** 315

"Through the Hole in the Mundane Millstone" (West), **Retro. Supp. II:** 321, 322

Through the Ivory Gate (Dove), **Supp. IV Part 1:** 242, 243, 251, 252, 253–254, 254

"Through the Kitchen Window, Chiapas" (Nye), **Supp. XIII:** 277

"Through the Smoke Hole" (Snyder), **Supp. VIII:** 299

Thucydides, **II:** 418; **IV:** 50; **Supp. I**

Part 2: 488, 489, 492; **Supp. IV Part 1:** 391; **Supp. XIII:** 233

Thunderbolt and Lightfoot (film), **Supp. X:** 126

"Thunderhead" (MacLeish), **III:** 19

Thurber, James, **I:** 487; **II:** 432; **IV:** 396; **Supp. I Part 2: 602–627,** 653, 654, 668, 672, 673, 679; **Supp. II Part 1:** 143; **Supp. IV Part 1:** 349; **Supp. IX:** 118; **Supp. XIV:** 104

Thurber, Mrs. James (Althea Adams), **Supp. I Part 2:** 613, 615, 617

Thurber, Mrs. James (Helen Muriel Wismer), **Supp. I Part 2:** 613, 617, 618

Thurber, Robert, **Supp. I Part 2:** 613, 617

Thurber, Rosemary, **Supp. I Part 2:** 616

Thurber, William, **Supp. I Part 2:** 602

Thurber Album, The (Thurber), **Supp. I Part 2:** 611, 619

Thurber Carnival, The (Thurber), **Supp. I Part 2:** 620; **Supp. XIV:** 104

Thurman, Judith, **Supp. IV Part 1:** 309

Thurman, Wallace, **Retro. Supp. I:** 200; **Supp. I Part 1:** 325, 326, 328, 332; **Supp. IV Part 1:** 164; **Supp. X:** 136, 139

"Thursday" (Millay), **III:** 129

"Thurso's Landing" (Jeffers), **Supp. II Part 2:** 433

Thus Spake Zarathustra (Nietzsche), **II:** 463; **Supp. IV Part 1:** 110; **Supp. IV Part 2:** 519

Thwaite, Lady Alicia. *See* Rawlings, Marjorie Kinnan

"Tiara" (Doty), **Supp. XI:** 122

Ticket for a Seamstitch, A (Harris), **II:** 424–425

Tickets for a Prayer Wheel (Dillard), **Supp. VI:** 22, 34

Ticket That Exploded, The (Burroughs), **Supp. III Part 1:** 93, 103, 104

Tickless Time (Glaspell), **Supp. III Part 1:** 179

Ticknor, George, **II:** 488; **Supp. I Part 1:** 313

"Ti Démon" (Chopin), **Supp. I Part 1:** 225

Tide of Time, The (Masters), **Supp. I Part 2:** 471

"Tide Rises, the Tide Falls, The" (Longfellow), **I:** 498

Tidyman, Ernest, **Supp. V:** 226

"Tiger" (Blake), **Supp. I Part 1:** 80; **Supp. VIII:** 26

"Tiger, The" (Buechner), **Supp. XII:** 48

Tiger in the House, The (Van Vechten), **Supp. II Part 2:** 736

Tiger Joy (Benét), **Supp. XI:** 45

Tiger-Lilies (Lanier), **Supp. I Part 1:** 350–351, 357, 360, 371

Tiger Who Wore White Gloves, The: or, What You Are, You Are (Brooks), **Supp. III Part 1:** 86

Till, Emmett, **Supp. I Part 1:** 61

Tillich, Paul, **II:** 244; **III:** 291, 292, 303, 309; **IV:** 226; **Retro. Supp. I:** 325, 326, 327; **Supp. V:** 267; **Supp. XIII:** 74, 91

Tillie Olsen: A Study of the Short Fiction (Frye), **Supp. XIII:** 292, 296, 298, 299, 302

Tillman, Lynne, **Supp. XII:** 4

Tillotson, John, **II:** 114

Tillstrom, Burr, **Supp. XIV:** 125

Till the Day I Die (Odets), **Supp. II Part 2:** 530, 533–536, 552

Tilton, Eleanor, **Supp. I Part 1:** 317

Timaeus (Plato), **II:** 10; **III:** 609

Timber (Jonson), **II:** 16

Timbuktu (Auster), **Supp. XII:** 34, **35–36**

"Time" (Matthews), **Supp. IX:** 165–**166**

"Time" (Merrill), **Supp. III Part 1:** 325

Time and a Place, A (Humphrey), **Supp. IX:** 95, 98, **100–102**

"Time and the Garden" (Winters), **Supp. II Part 2:** 801, 809

"Time and the Liturgy" (Merton), **Supp. VIII:** 199

Time in the Rock (Aiken), **I:** 65

Time Is Noon, The (Buck), **Supp. II Part 1:** 129, 130–131

Time & Money (Matthews), **Supp. IX:** 155, **165–167**

"Time of Friendship, The" (Bowles), **Supp. IV Part 1:** 90–91

"Time of Her Time, The" (Mailer), **III:** 37, 45; **Retro. Supp. II:** 200

Time of Our Time, The (Mailer), **Retro. Supp. II:** 213–214

Time of the Assassins, The: A Study of Rimbaud (H. Miller), **III:** 189

"Time Past" (Morris), **III:** 232

"Time Present" (Morris), **III:** 232

"Times" (Beattie), **Supp. V:** 31

"Times, The" (Emerson), **II:** 11–12

Times Are Never So Bad, The (Dubus), **Supp. VII:** 87–88

Time's Arrow (Amis), **Retro. Supp. I:** 278

"Time Shall Not Die" (Chandler), **Supp. IV Part 1:** 120

Times of Melville and Whitman, The

(Brooks), **I:** 257

"Timesweep" (Sandburg), **III:** 595–596

Time to Act, A (MacLeish), **III:** 3

Time to Go (Dixon), **Supp. XII:** 147

Time to Kill (film), **Supp. IV Part 1:** 130

Time to Speak, A (MacLeish), **III:** 3

Time Will Darken It (Maxwell), **Supp. VIII:** 159, **162–164,** 169

"Timing of Sin, The" (Dubus), **Supp. VII:** 91

Tim O'Brien (Herzog), **Supp. V:** 239

Timoleon (Melville), **III:** 93; **Retro. Supp. I:** 257

Timothy Dexter Revisited (Marquand), **III:** 55, 62, 63

Tin Can, The (W. J. Smith), **Supp. XIII:** 334, **Supp. XIII:** 336, 337

"Tin Can, The" (W. J. Smith), **Supp. XIII: 337–339**

Tin Can Tree, The (Tyler), **Supp. IV Part 2:** 659–660

Tinker, Chauncey Brewster, **Supp. XIV:** 12

Tintern Abbey (Wordsworth), **Supp. I Part 2:** 673, 675

Tiny Alice (Albee), **I:** 81–86, 87, 88, 94

"Tiny Mummies! The True Story of the Ruler of 43rd Street's Land of the Walking Dead" (Wolfe), **Supp. III Part 2:** 573, 574

"Tired" (Hughes), **Supp. I Part 1:** 331

"Tired and Unhappy, You Think of Houses" (Schwartz), **Supp. II Part 2:** 649

"Tiresias" (Garrett), **Supp. VII:** 96–97

'Tis (McCourt), **Supp. XII:** 271, **279–286**

Tisch (Dixon), **Supp. XII:** 141, **155–156**

Titan, The (Dreiser), **I:** 497, 501, 507–508, 509, 510; **Retro. Supp. II:** 94, 101, 102

Titian, **Supp. I Part 2:** 397, 714

"Tito's Goodbye" (García), **Supp. XI:** 190

To a Blossoming Pear Tree (Wright), **Supp. III Part 2:** 602–605

"To a Blossoming Pear Tree" (Wright), **Supp. III Part 2:** 604

"To Abolish Children" (Shapiro), **Supp. II Part 2:** 717

To Abolish Children and Other Essays (Shapiro), **Supp. II Part 2:** 703

"To a Caty-Did, the Precursor of Winter" (Freneau), **Supp. II Part 1:** 274–275

"To a Chameleon" (Moore), **III:** 195, 196, 215

"To a Conscript of 1940" (Read), **II:** 372–373, 377–378

"To a Contemporary Bunk Shooter" (Sandburg), **III:** 582

"To a Cough in the Street at Midnight" (Wylie), **Supp. I Part 2:** 727, 729–730

"To a Defeated Savior" (Wright), **Supp. III Part 2:** 593–594, 596

"To a Face in the Crowd" (Warren), **IV:** 239

"To a Fish Head Found on the Beach near Malaga" (Levine), **Supp. V:** 185

"To a Friend" (Nemerov), **III:** 272

"To a Friend Whose Work Has Come to Triumph" (Sexton), **Supp. II Part 2:** 683

To a God Unknown (Steinbeck), **I:** 107; **IV:** 51, 59–60, 67

"To a Greek Marble" (Aldington), **Supp. I Part 1:** 257

"To a Locomotive in Winter" (Whitman), **IV:** 348

"To a Military Rifle" (Winters), **Supp. II Part 2:** 810, 811, 815

"To a Mouse" (Burns), **Supp. IX:** 173

"To a Negro Jazz Band in a Parisian Cabaret" (Hughes), **Supp. I Part 1:** 325

"To an Old Philosopher in Rome" (Stevens), **III:** 605; **Retro. Supp. I:** 312

"To an Old Poet in Peru" (Ginsberg), **Supp. II Part 1:** 322

"To Any Would-Be Terrorists" (Nye), **Supp. XIII:** 285, 286

"To a Poet" (Rich), **Supp. I Part 2:** 571

"To a Prize Bird" (Moore), **III:** 215

"To a Republican, with Mr. Paine's Rights of Man" (Freneau), **Supp. II Part 1:** 267

"To a Shade" (Yeats), **III:** 18

"To a Skylark" (Shelley), **Supp. I Part 2:** 720; **Supp. X:** 31

"Toast to Harlem, A" (Hughes), **Supp. I Part 1:** 338

"To Aunt Rose" (Ginsberg), **Supp. II Part 1:** 320

"To Autumn" (Keats), **Supp. IX:** 50

"To a Waterfowl" (Bryant), **Supp. I Part 1:** 154, 155, 162, 171

"To a Young Writer" (Stegner), **Supp. X:** 24

Tobacco Road (Caldwell), **I:** 288, 289, 290, 295–296, 297, 298, 302, 307, 309, 310; **IV:** 198

"To Be a Monstrous Clever Fellow" (Fante), **Supp. XI:** 167

To Bedlam and Part Way Back (Sexton), **Retro. Supp. II:** 245; **Supp. II Part 2:** 672–678; **Supp. IV Part 2:** 441; **Supp. XI:** 317

"To Beethoven" (Lanier), **Supp. I Part 1:** 364

Tobey, Mark, **Supp. X:** 264

To Be Young, Gifted, and Black: Lorraine Hansberry in Her Own Words (Nemiroff), **Supp. IV Part 1:** 372, 374

"To Big Mary from an Ex-Catholic" (Mora), **Supp. XIII:** 217, 224, 228

"Tobin's Palm" (O. Henry), **Supp. II Part 1:** 408

Tobit (apocryphal book), **I:** 89

"To Build a Fire" (London), **II:** 468

Toby Tyler: or, Ten Weeks with a Circus (Otis), **III:** 577

"To Change in a Good Way" (Ortiz), **Supp. IV Part 2:** 511

"To Charlotte Cushman" (Lanier), **Supp. I Part 1:** 364

"To Cole, the Painter, Departing for Europe" (Bryant), **Supp. I Part 1:** 157, 161

Tocqueville, Alexis de, **III:** 261; **IV:** 349; **Retro. Supp. I:** 235; **Supp. I Part 1:** 137; **Supp. I Part 2:** 659, 660; **Supp. II Part 1:** 281, 282, 284; **Supp. XIV:** 306, 312

"To Crispin O'Conner" (Freneau), **Supp. II Part 1:** 268

"To Da-Duh, In Memoriam" (Marshall), **Supp. XI:** 276

"TODAY" (Baraka), **Supp. II Part 1:** 55

"Today" (Ginsberg), **Supp. II Part 1:** 328

"Today Is a Good Day To Die" (Bell), **Supp. X:** 7

Todd, Mabel Loomis, **I:** 454, 470; **Retro. Supp. I:** 33, 34, 35, 39, 47

"To Death" (Levertov), **Supp. III Part 1:** 274

"To Delmore Schwartz" (Lowell), **II:** 547; **Retro. Supp. II:** 188

"to disembark" (Brooks), **Supp. III Part 1:** 86

"To Dr. Thomas Shearer" (Lanier), **Supp. I Part 1:** 370

"To E. T." (Frost), **Retro. Supp. I:** 132

"To Earthward" (Frost), **II:** 154

"To Edwin V. McKenzie" (Winters), **Supp. II Part 2:** 801

"To Eleonora Duse" (Lowell), **II:** 528

"To Elizabeth Ward Perkins" (Lowell), **II:** 516

"To Elsie" (W. C. Williams), **Retro. Supp. I:** 419

"To Emily Dickinson" (H. Crane), **Retro. Supp. II:** 76

Toffler, Alvin, **Supp. IV Part 2:** 517

"To Fill" (Moore), **Supp. X:** 168, 169

"To Gabriela, a Young Writer" (Mora), **Supp. XIII:** 220

To Have and Have Not (Hemingway), **I:** 31; **II:** 253–254, 264; **Retro. Supp. I:** 182, **183,** 187

"To Helen" (Poe), **III:** 410, 411, 427; **Retro. Supp. II:** 102

"To Hell With Dying" (Walker), **Supp. III Part 2:** 523

"To His Father" (Jeffers), **Supp. II Part 2:** 415

Toilet, The (Baraka), **Supp. II Part 1:** 37, 40–42

"To James Russell Lowell" (Holmes), **Supp. I Part 1:** 311

To Jerusalem and Back (Bellow), **Retro. Supp. II:** 29

"To Jesus on His Birthday" (Millay), **III:** 136–137

"To John Keats" (Lowell), **II:** 516

"To Judge Faolain, Dead Long Enough: A Summons" (McCarriston), **Supp. XIV:** 264–265

"To Justify My Singing" (Wright), **Supp. III Part 2:** 590

To Kill a Mockingbird (film), **Supp. VIII:** 128–129

To Kill a Mockingbird (Lee), **Supp. VIII: 113–129**

"*To Kill a Mockingbird:* Harper Lee's Tragic Vision" (Dave), **Supp. VIII:** 126

To Kill a Mockingbird: Threatening Boundaries (Johnson), **Supp. VIII:** 126

Toklas, Alice B., **IV:** 27; **Supp. IV Part 1:** 81, 91

"To Light" (Hogan), **Supp. IV Part 1:** 402

Tolkien, J. R. R., **Supp. V:** 140

Tolkin, Michael, **Supp. XI:** 160

Toller, Ernst, **I:** 479

"To Lose the Earth" (Sexton), **Supp. II Part 2:** 684, 685

Tolson, Melvin, **Retro. Supp. I:** 208, 209, 210

Tolstoy, Leo, **I:** 6, 7, 58, 103, 312, 376; **II:** 191–192, 205, 271, 272, 275, 276, 281, 285, 286, 320, 407, 542, 559, 570, 579, 606; **III:** 37, 45, 61, 323, 467, 572; **IV:** 17, 21, 170, 285; **Retro. Supp. I:** 91, 225; **Retro. Supp. II:** 299; **Supp. I Part 1:** 2, 3, 6, 20; **Supp. IV Part 1:** 392; **Supp. V:** 277, 323; **Supp. IX:** 246; **Supp. XI:** 68; **Supp. XII:** 310, 322; **Supp.**

XIV: 87, 97, 98

"To Lu Chi" (Nemerov), **III:** 275

Tom (Cummings), **I:** 430

"Tom" (Oliver), **Supp. VII:** 232

"Tom, Tom, the Piper's Son" (Ransom), **Supp. X:** 58

"To M, with a Rose" (Lanier), **Supp. I Part 1:** 364

To Make a Prairie (Kumin), **Supp. IV Part 2:** 440, 441

"To Make Words Disappear" (Simpson), **Supp. IX:** 265–266

Tomás and the Library Lady (Mora), **Supp. XIII:** 216, 221

"Tomatoes" (Francis), **Supp. IX:** 82

"Tom Brown at Fisk" (Du Bois), **Supp. II Part 1:** 160

Tom Brown's School Days (Hughes), **Supp. I Part 2:** 406

"Tomb Stone" (Dickey), **Supp. IV Part 1:** 185

Tomcat in Love (O'Brien), **Supp. V:** 238, 240, 243, 252–254

"Tom Fool at Jamaica" (Moore), **III:** 215

To Mix with Time (Swenson), **Supp. IV Part 2:** 637, 643–645, 645

Tom Jones (Fielding), **I:** 131; **Supp. V:** 127

Tommy Gallagher's Crusade (Farrell), **II:** 44

Tommyknockers, The (King), **Supp. V:** 139, 144

"Tommy's Burglar" (Henry), **Supp. II Part 1:** 399, 401

Tomo Cheeki (pseudonym). *See* Freneau, Philip

"Tomorrow the Moon" (Dos Passos), **I:** 493

"Tom Outland's Story" (Cather), **I:** 325–326

Tompson, Benjamin, **Supp. I Part 1:** 110, 111

Tom Sawyer (musical) (Gurney), **Supp. V:** 96

Tom Sawyer (Twain). *See Adventures of Tom Sawyer, The* (Twain)

Tom Sawyer Abroad (Twain), **II:** 482; **IV:** 19, 204

Tom Sawyer Detective (Twain), **IV:** 204

"Tom's Husband" (Jewett), **Retro. Supp. II:** 132, 141

Tom Swift (Stratemeyer), **III:** 146

"Tom Wolfe's Guide to Etiquette" (Wolfe), **Supp. III Part 2:** 578

"To My Brother Killed: Haumont Wood: October, 1918" (Bogan), **Supp. III Part 1:** 58

"To My Class, on Certain Fruits and Flowers Sent Me in Sickness"

(Lanier), **Supp. I Part 1:** 370

"To My Ghost Reflected in the Auxvasse River" (Levis), **Supp. XI:** 265

"To My Greek" (Merrill), **Supp. III Part 1:** 326

"To My Mother" (Berry), **Supp. X:** 23

"To My Small Son, at the Photographer's" (Hay), **Supp. XIV:** 121

"To My Small Son, on Certain Occasions" (Hay), **Supp. XIV:** 121

"To Name is to Possess" (Kincaid), **Supp. VII:** 194

Tone, Aileen, **I:** 21–22

"Tongue Is, The" (Komunyakaa), **Supp. XIII:** 113

Tongues (Shepard and Chaikin), **Supp. III Part 2:** 433

Tongues of Angels, The (Price), **Supp. VI:** 265

Tongues Untied (Riggs; film), **Supp. XI:** 19, 20

"Tonight" (Lowell), **II:** 538

Tony Kushner in Conversation (Vorlicky, ed.), **Supp. IX:** 132

"Too Anxious for Rivers" (Frost), **II:** 162

"Too Blue" (Hughes), **Retro. Supp. I:** 207

"Too Early" (Leopold), **Supp. XIV:** 186

"Too Early Spring" (Benét), **Supp. XI:** 53

"Too Far from Home" (Bowles), **Supp. IV Part 1:** 94–95

Too Far from Home: Selected Writings of Paul Bowles (Halpern, ed.), **Supp. IV Part 1:** 94, 95

Too Far to Go: The Maples Stories (Updike), **Retro. Supp. I:** 321

"Too Good To Be True": The Life and Art of Leslie Fiedler (Winchell), **Supp. XIII:** 94, 98, 99, 101

Toohey, John Peter, **Supp. IX:** 190

Toolan, David, **Supp. IV Part 1:** 308

Too Late (Dixon), **Supp. XII: 143–144**

"Too-Late Born, The" (Hemingway), **III:** 9

Toole, John Kennedy, **Supp. XIV:** 21

Toomer, Jean, **Retro. Supp. II:** 79; **Supp. I Part 1:** 325, 332; **Supp. III Part 2: 475–491; Supp. IV Part 1:** 16, 164, 168; **Supp. IX: 305–322; Supp. XIII:** 305

Toomer, Nathan Eugene Pinchback. *See* Toomer, Jean

Too Much Johnson (film), **Supp. IV Part 1:** 83

"To One Who Said Me Nay" (Cullen), **Supp. IV Part 1:** 166

"Tooth, The" (Jackson), **Supp. IX:** 122

Tooth of Crime, The (Shepard); **Supp. III Part 2:** 432, 441–445, 447

"Too Young" (O'Hara), **III:** 369

"To P. L., 1916–1937" (Levine), **Supp. V:** 185

"Top Israeli Official Hints at 'Shared' Jerusalem" (Nye), **Supp. XIII:** 287

"To Please a Shadow" (Brodsky), **Supp. VIII:** 30

"Top of the Hill" (Jewett), **II:** 406

"Topography" (Olds), **Supp. X:** 208

Topper (T. Smith), **Supp. IX:** 194

Torah, **IV:** 19

"Torquemada" (Longfellow), **II:** 505; **Retro. Supp. II:** 164

Torrence, Ridgely, **III:** 507

Torrent and the Night Before, The (Robinson), **III:** 504

Torrents of Spring, The (Hemingway), **I:** 117; **II:** 250–251

Torres, Héctor A., **Supp. XIII:** 225

Torres, Louis, **Supp. IV Part 2:** 529, 530

Torsney, Cheryl, **Retro. Supp. I:** 224

Tortilla Curtain, The (Boyle), **Supp. VIII:** 9–10

Tortilla Flat (Steinbeck), **IV:** 50, 51, 61, 64

Tory Lover, The (Jewett), **II:** 406; **Retro. Supp. II:** 144–145

"Toscana" (Dixon), **Supp. XII:** 154

"To Sir Toby" (Freneau), **Supp. II Part 1:** 269

"To Sophy, Expectant" (Mumford), **Supp. II Part 2:** 475

"To Speak of Woe That Is in Marriage" (Lowell), **II:** 550

"To Statecraft Embalmed" (Moore), **III:** 197

To Stay Alive (Levertov), **Supp. III Part 1:** 280–282

"Total Eclipse" (Dillard), **Supp. VI:** 28

Toth, Emily, **Retro. Supp. II:** 71

Toth, Susan Allan, **Retro. Supp. II:** 138

"To the Americans of the United States" (Freneau), **Supp. II Part 1:** 271

"To the Apennines" (Bryant), **Supp. I Part 1:** 157, 164

"To the Bleeding Hearts Association of American Novelists" (Nemerov), **III:** 281

"To the Botequim & Back" (Bishop), **Retro. Supp. II:** 51

To the Bright and Shining Sun (Burke), **Supp. XIV:** 22, 25

"To the Citizens of the United States" (Paine), **Supp. I Part 2:** 519–520

"To the Dandelion" (Lowell), **Supp. I Part 2:** 424

"To the End" (Haines), **Supp. XII:** 212–213

To the Ends of the Earth: The Selected Travels of Paul Theroux, **Supp. VIII:** 324

To the Finland Station: A Study in the Writing and Acting of History (Wilson), **IV:** 429, 436, 443–444, 446

"To the Governor & Legislature of Massachusetts" (Nemerov), **III:** 287

To the Holy Spirit (Winters), **Supp. II Part 2:** 810

"To the Keeper of the King's Water Works" (Freneau), **Supp. II Part 1:** 269

"To the Lacedemonians" (Tate), **IV:** 134

"To the Laodiceans" (Jarrell), **Retro. Supp. I:** 121, 140

To the Lighthouse (Woolf), **I:** 309; **II:** 600; **Retro. Supp. II:** 337; **Supp. VIII:** 155

"To the Man on Trail" (London), **II:** 466

"To the Memory of the Brave Americans Under General Greene" (Freneau), **Supp. II Part 1:** 262, 274

"To the Muse" (Wright), **Supp. III Part 2:** 601

"To the Nazi Leaders" (Hay), **Supp. XIV:** 121

"To the New World" (Jarrell), **II:** 371

"To the One of Fictive Music" (Stevens), **IV:** 89; **Retro. Supp. I:** 297, 300

"To the One Upstairs" (Simic), **Supp. VIII:** 283

"To the Peoples of the World" (Du Bois), **Supp. II Part 1:** 172

"To the Pliocene Skull" (Harte), **Supp. II Part 1:** 343–344

"To the Reader" (Baudelaire), **II:** 544–545

"To the Reader" (Levertov), **Supp. III Part 1:** 277

"To the River Arve" (Bryant), **Supp. I Part 1:** 163

"To the Snake" (Levertov), **Supp. III Part 1:** 277

"To the Stone-Cutters" (Jeffers), **Supp. II Part 2:** 420

"To the Unseeable Animal" (Berry), **Supp. X:** 31

"To the Western World" (Simpson), **Supp. IX:** 269, 270

To the White Sea (Dickey), **Supp. IV Part 1:** 186, 190–191

"To the Young Who Want to Die" (Brooks), **Supp. III Part 1:** 85–86

"To Train a Writer" (Bierce), **I:** 199

"Touch, The" (Sexton), **Supp. II Part 2:** 687

"Touching the Tree" (Merwin), **Supp. III Part 1:** 355

Touching the World (Eakin), **Supp. VIII:** 167

Touch of Danger, A (Jones), **Supp. XI:** 226, **228–229**

Touch of the Poet, A (O'Neill), **III:** 385, 401, 404

Touchstone, The (Wharton), **Retro. Supp. I:** 365

"Touch-up Man" (Komunyakaa), **Supp. XIII:** 119

Tough Guys Don't Dance (Mailer), **Retro. Supp. II:** 211

Toulet, Paul Jean, **IV:** 79

Tour (McNally), **Supp. XIII:** 197

"Tour 5" (Hayden), **Supp. II Part 1:** 381

To Urania (Brodsky), **Supp. VIII:** 22, 28–29

Tourgée, Albion W., **Supp. XIV:** 63

"Tour Guide" (Komunyakaa), **Supp. XIII:** 114

"Tourist Death" (MacLeish), **III:** 12

Tour of Duty (Dos Passos), **I:** 489

Touron the Prairies, A (Irving), **II:** 312–313

Tovey, Donald Francis, **Supp. XIV:** 336

To Walk a Crooked Mile (McGrath), **Supp. X:** 117

Toward a New Synthesis (Begiebing), **Retro. Supp. II:** 210

"Toward Nightfall" (Simic), **Supp. VIII:** 277

Towards a Better Life (Burke), **I:** 270

"Towards a Chicano Poetics: The Making of the Chicano Subject, 1969–1982" (Saldívar), **Supp. IV Part 2:** 544

Towards an Enduring Peace (Bourne), **I:** 232

Toward the Gulf (Masters), **Supp. I Part 2:** 465–466

"Toward the Solstice" (Rich), **Supp. I Part 2:** 575–576

Toward Wholeness in Paule Marshall's Fiction (Pettis), **Supp. XI:** 276

"Tower" (Merwin), **Supp. III Part 1:** 343

"Tower Beyond Tragedy, The" (Jeffers), **Supp. II Part 2:** 429–430

Tower of Ivory (MacLeish), **III:** 3–4

Towers, Robert, **Supp. IX:** 259

"To Whistler, American" (Pound), **III:** 465–466

"To Wine" (Bogan), **Supp. III Part 1:** 57, 58

Town, The (Faulkner), **II:** 57, 73; **Retro. Supp. I:** 74, 82

Town and the City, The (Kerouac), **Supp. III Part 1:** 222–224; **Supp. XIV:** 143

"Town Crier" (Bierce), **I:** 193, 194, 195, 196

"Town Crier Exclusive, Confessions of a Princess Manqué: 'How Royals Found Me "Unsuitable" to Marry Their Larry'" (Elkin), **Supp. VI:** 56

Town Down the River, The (Robinson), **III:** 508

"Town Dump, The" (Nemerov), **III:** 272, 275, 281

Towne, Robert, **Supp. XI:** 159, 172, 174

"Townhouse Interior with Cat" (Clampitt), **Supp. IX:** 40

"Townies" (Dubus), **Supp. VII:** 86

"Town of the Sound of a Twig Breaking" (Carson), **Supp. XII:** 102

"Town Poor, The" (Jewett), **Retro. Supp. II:** 138, 139, 143

Townsend, Alison, **Supp. XIII:** 222

Townsend, Ann, **Supp. V:** 77

"Towns in Colour" (Lowell), **II:** 523–524

Townsman, The (Sedges), **Supp. II Part 1:** 124–125

Toys in a Field (Komunyakaa), **Supp. XIII: 121–122**

"Toys in a Field" (Komunyakaa), **Supp. XIII:** 122

Toys in the Attic (Hellman), **Supp. I Part 1:** 289–290

Tracer (F. Barthelme), **Supp. XI:** 31–32, 33

Traces of Thomas Hariot, The (Rukeyser), **Supp. VI:** 273, 274, 283

"Tracing Life with a Finger" (Caldwell), **I:** 291

Tracker (Wagoner), **Supp. IX:** 329, **336–337**

"Tracking" (Wagoner), **Supp. IX:** 329

"Track Meet, The" (Schwartz), **Supp. II Part 2:** 665

Tracks (Erdrich), **Supp. IV Part 1:** 259, 262–263, 269, 272, 273–274, 274, 275

"Tract" (W. C. Williams), **Retro. Supp. I:** 414

"Tract against Communism, A" (Twelve Southerners), **IV:** 125, 237

Tracy, Lee, **IV:** 287, 288

Tracy, Steven, **Retro. Supp. I:** 195

"Trade, The" (Levine), **Supp. V:** 193

Trading Twelves (Callahan and Murray, eds.), **Retro. Supp. II:** 119

"Tradition and Industrialization" (Wright), **IV:** 489–490

"Tradition and Mythology: Signatures of Landscape in Chicana Poetry" (Rebolledo), **Supp. XIII:** 214

"Tradition and the Individual Talent" (Eliot), **I:** 441, 574, 585; **Retro. Supp. I:** 59, 286

Tragedies, Life and Letters of James Gates Percival (Swinburne), **Supp. I Part 2:** 422

Tragedy of Don Ippolito, The (Howells), **II:** 279

"Tragedy of Error, A" (James), **II:** 322; **Retro. Supp. I:** 218

Tragedy of Pudd'nhead Wilson, The (Twain), **IV:** 206–207

Tragic America (Dreiser), **Retro. Supp. II:** 95

"Tragic Dialogue" (Wylie), **Supp. I Part 2:** 724

Tragic Ground (Caldwell), **I:** 297, 306

Tragic Muse, The (James), **Retro. Supp. I:** 227

Traherne, Thomas, **IV:** 151; **Supp. III Part 1:** 14; **Supp. V:** 208

"Trail, The" (W. J. Smith), **Supp. XIII:** 342

Trailerpark (Banks), **Supp. V:** 12

"Trailing Arbutus, The" (Whittier), **Supp. I Part 2:** 691

Trail of the Lonesome Pine, The (Fox), **Supp. XIII:** 166

"Train, The" (O'Connor), **Retro. Supp. II:** 225

"Train Rising Out of the Sea" (Ashbery), **Supp. III Part 1:** 22

"Trains" (Banks), **Supp. V:** 8

"Train Tune" (Bogan), **Supp. III Part 1:** 64

"Traits of Indian Character" (Irving), **II:** 303

Tramp Abroad, A (Twain), **IV:** 200

Tramping With a Poet in the Rockies (Graham), **Supp. I Part 2:** 397

Tramp's Excuse, The (Lindsay), **Supp. I Part 2:** 379, 380, 382

"Transatlantic" (Toomer), **Supp. III Part 2:** 486

Transatlantic Sketches (James), **II:** 324; **Retro. Supp. I:** 219

"Transcendental Etude" (Rich), **Supp. I Part 2:** 576

"Transcontinental Highway" (Cowley), **Supp. II Part 1:** 141

"Transducer" (Ammons), **Supp. VII:** 28

"Transfigured Bird" (Merrill), **Supp. III Part 1:** 320–321

"Transformations" (Harjo), **Supp. XII:** 226

Transformations (Sexton), **Supp. II Part 2:** 689–691; **Supp. IV Part 2:** 447; **Supp. XIV:** 125

Transit to Narcissus, A (Mailer), **Retro. Supp. II:** 196

"Translation and Transposition" (Carne-Ross), **Supp. I Part 1:** 268–269

"Translation of a Fragment of Simonides" (Bryant), **Supp. I Part 1:** 153, 155

"Translations" (Rich), **Supp. I Part 2:** 563

Translations of Ezra Pound, The (Kenner, ed.), **III:** 463

"Trans-National America" (Bourne), **I:** 229, 230

Transparent Man, The (Hecht), **Supp. X:** 57, **69–71**

"Transparent Man, The" (Hecht), **Supp. X:** **69–70**

Transparent Things (Nabokov), **Retro. Supp. I:** 266, 270, 277

"Transport" (Simic), **Supp. VIII:** 282

Transport to Summer (Stevens), **IV:** 76, 93; **Retro. Supp. I:** 309–312

Tranströmer, Thomas, **Supp. IV Part 2:** 648

"Traps for the Unwary" (Bourne), **I:** 235

Trash Trilogy (McMurtry), **Supp. V:** 225–226, 231

Traubel, Horace, **IV:** 350

"Travel: After a Death" (Kenyon), **Supp. VII:** 169

Travel Alarm (Nye), **Supp. XIII:** 277

"Traveler, The" (Haines), **Supp. XII:** 203–204, 210

"Traveler, The" (Stegner), **Supp. IV Part 2:** 605

Traveler at Forty, A (Dreiser), **I:** 515

Traveler from Altruria, a Romance A, (Howells), **II:** 285, 287

Traveler's Tree, The: New and Selected Poems (W. J. Smith), **Supp. XIII:** 332, 347

"Traveling" (Paley), **Supp. VI:** 230

"Traveling Light" (Wagoner), **Supp. IX:** 329

"Traveling Onion, The" (Nye), **Supp. XIII:** 276

Traveling through the Dark (Stafford), **Supp. XI:** 311, 316, **318–321**

"Traveling through the Dark"

(Stafford), **Supp. XI:** 318–320, 321, 323, 329

Travelling in Amherst: A Poet's Journal, 1931–1954, **Supp. IX: 88–89**

Travels in Alaska (Muir), **Supp. IX:** 182, 185–186

"Travels in Georgia" (McPhee), **Supp. III Part 1:** 293–294

Travels in the Congo (Gide), **III:** 210

"Travels in the South" (Ortiz), **Supp. IV Part 2:** 506

Travels with Charley (Steinbeck), **IV:** 52

"Travel Writing: Why I Bother" (Theroux), **Supp. VIII:** 310

Travis, Merle, **Supp. V:** 335

Travisano, Thomas, **Retro. Supp. II:** 40

Treasure Hunt (Buechner), **Supp. XII:** 52

Treasure Island (Stevenson), **Supp. X:** 230

"Treasure of the Redwoods, A" (Harte), **Supp. II Part 1:** 337

Treasury of Art Masterpieces, A: From the Renaissance to the Present Day (Craven), **Supp. XII:** 44

Treasury of English Aphorisms, A (L. P. Smith), **Supp. XIV:** 344

Treasury of English Prose, A (L. P. Smith, ed.), **Supp. XIV:** 341

Treasury of the Theatre, A (Gassner), **Supp. I Part 1:** 292

Treasury of Yiddish Stories, A (Howe and Greenberg, eds.), **Supp. I Part 2:** 432

Treat 'Em Rough (Lardner), **II:** 422–423

Treatise Concerning Religious Affections (Edwards), **I:** 547, 552, 554, 555, 557, 558, 560, 562

Treatise Concerning the Lord's Supper (Doolittle), **IV:** 150

"Treatise on Poetry" (Milosz), **Supp. VIII:** 20

Treatise on Right and Wrong, A (Mencken), **III:** 110, 119

"Treatise on Tales of Horror, A" (Wilson), **IV:** 438

Treatise on the Gods, A (Mencken), **III:** 108–109, 119

Tre Croce (Tozzi), **Supp. III Part 2:** 616

"Tree, a Rock, a Cloud, A" (McCullers), **II:** 587

"Tree, The" (Pound), **Retro. Supp. I:** 286; **Supp. I Part 1:** 255

"Tree, the Bird, The" (Roethke), **III:** 548

"Tree at My Window" (Frost), **II:** 155

"Tree House at Night, The" (Dickey), **Supp. IV Part 1:** 179

Tree Is Older Than You Are, The (Nye, ed.), **Supp. XIII:** 280

"Tree of Laughing Bells, The" (Lindsay), **Supp. I Part 2:** 376

"Tree of Night, A" (Capote), **Supp. III Part 1:** 114, 120

Tree of Night and Other Stories, A (Capote), **Supp. III Part 1:** 114

"Trees, The" (Rich), **Supp. I Part 2:** 555

"Trees Listening to Bach" (Merrill), **Supp. III Part 1:** 336

Tree Where Man Was Born, The (Matthiessen), **Supp. V:** 199, 203, 204

Trejo, Ernesto, **Supp. V:** 178, 180; **Supp. XIII:** 313, 316

Trelawny, Edward John, **Supp. I Part 2:** 721

"Trellis for R., A" (Swenson), **Supp. IV Part 2:** 647

Tremblay, Bill, **Supp. XIII:** 112

"Trespass" (Frost), **Retro. Supp. I:** 139

"Tretitoli, Where the Bomb Group Was" (Hugo), **Supp. VI:** 138

Trevelyan, Robert C., **Supp. XIV:** 334

Trevor-Roper, Hugh, **Supp. XIV:** 348

Trial, The (Kafka), **IV:** 113; **Retro. Supp. II:** 20

"Trial, The" (Rukeyser), **Supp. VI:** 278

"Trial by Existence, The" (Frost), **II:** 166

Trial of a Poet, The (Shapiro), **Supp. II Part 2:** 710

Trial of the Hawk, The: A Comedy of the Seriousness of Life (Lewis), **II:** 441

Tribal Secrets: Recovering American Indian Intellectual Traditions (Warrior), **Supp. IV Part 1:** 329

"Tribute (To My Mother)" (Cullen), **Supp. IV Part 1:** 166

"Tribute, A" (Easton), **Supp. IV Part 2:** 461

"Tribute, The" (Doolittle), **Supp. I Part 1:** 267

Tribute to Freud (Doolittle), **Supp. I Part 1:** 253, 254, 258, 259, 260, 268

Tribute to the Angels (Doolittle), **Supp. I Part 1:** 272

"Trick on the World, A" (Ríos), **Supp. IV Part 2:** 553

"Tricks" (Olds), **Supp. X:** 203–204

"Trick Scenery" (F. Barthelme), **Supp. XI:** 26

Trifler, The (Masters), **Supp. I Part 2:** 459–460

Trifles (Glaspell), **Supp. III Part 1:** 175, 178, 179, 182, 186, 187; **Supp. X:** 46

Trifonov, Iurii V., **Retro. Supp. I:** 278

Triggering Town, The: Lectures and Essays on Poetry and Writing (Hugo), **Supp. VI:** 133, 140

Trilling, Diana, **II:** 587, 600; **Supp. I Part 1:** 297; **Supp. XII:** 126

Trilling, Lionel, **I:** 48; **II:** 579; **III:** 308, 310, 319, 327; **IV:** 201, 211; **Retro. Supp. I:** 19, 97, 121, 216, 227; **Supp. III Part 2: 493–515;** **Supp. V:** 259; **Supp. VIII:** 93, 98, 190, 231, 236, 243; **Supp. IX:** 266, 287; **Supp. XIII:** 100–101; **Supp. XIV:** 280, 288–289

Trilogy (Doolittle), **Supp. I Part 1:** 271, 272

Trilogy of Desire (Dreiser), **I:** 497, 508; **Retro. Supp. II:** 94, 96, **101–102**

Trimmed Lamp, The (O. Henry), **Supp. II Part 1:** 410

"Trinc" (McGrath), **Supp. X:** 127

Trio (Baker), **Supp. I Part 1:** 277

"Trip" (F. Barthelme), **Supp. XI:** 26

Triple Thinkers, The: Ten Essays on Literature (Wilson), **IV:** 428, 431; **Supp. II Part 1:** 146

"Triplex" (Doolittle), **Supp. I Part 1:** 271

Tripmaster Monkey: His Fake Book (Kingston), **Supp. V:** 157, 158, 169, 170–173

"Trip to Hanoi" (Sontag), **Supp. III Part 2:** 460–462

"Triptych" (Eberhart), **I:** 522, 539

Tristan and Iseult, **Retro. Supp. I:** 328, 329, 330, 331

Tristessa (Kerouac), **Supp. III Part 1:** 225, 227, 229

Tristram (Robinson), **III:** 521, 522, 523

Tristram Shandy (Sterne), **I:** 299; **IV:** 465–466; **Supp. V:** 127

"Triumphal March" (Eliot), **I:** 580; **III:** 17; **Retro. Supp. I:** 64

Triumph of Achilles, The (Glück), **Supp. V:** 79, 84–86, 92

"Triumph of a Modern, The, or, Send for the Lawyer" (Anderson), **I:** 113, 114

"Triumph of the Egg, The" (Anderson), **I:** 113

Triumph of the Egg, The: A Book of Impressions from American Life in

Tales and Poems (Anderson), **I:** 112, 114

Triumph of the Spider Monkey, The (Oates), **Supp. II Part 2:** 522

Triumphs of the Reformed Religion in America (Mather), **Supp. II Part 2:** 453

Trivia; or, the Art of Walking the Streets of London (Gay), **Supp. XIV:** 337

Trivia: Printed from the Papers of Anthony Woodhouse, Esq. (L. P. Smith), **Supp. XIV:** 336, **337–340**

Trivial Breath (Wylie), **Supp. I Part 2:** 709, 722–724

Trocchi, Alexander, **Supp. XI:** 294, 295, 301

Troilus and Criseyde (Chaucer), **Retro. Supp. I:** 426

Trois contes (Flaubert), **IV:** 31, 37

Trojan Horse, The: A Play (MacLeish), **III:** 21

"Trojan Women, The" (Maxwell), **Supp. VIII:** 169

Troll Garden, The (Cather), **I:** 313, 314–316, 322; **Retro. Supp. I:** 5, 6, 8, 14

"Trolling for Blues" (Wilbur), **Supp. III Part 2:** 563–564

Trollope, Anthony, **I:** 10, 375; **II:** 192, 237; **III:** 51, 70, 281, 382; **Retro. Supp. I:** 361

Trombly, Albert Edmund, **Supp. I Part 2:** 403

"Troop Train" (Shapiro), **Supp. II Part 2:** 707

"Tropes of the Text" (Gass), **Supp. VI:** 88

Tropic of Cancer (H. Miller), **III:** 170, 171, 174, 177, 178–180, 181, 182, 183, 187, 190; **Supp. V:** 119; **Supp. X:** 187

Tropic of Capricorn (H. Miller), **III:** 170, 176–177, 178, 182, 183, 184, 187, 188–189, 190

Trotsky, Leon, **I:** 366; **II:** 562, 564; **IV:** 429

Trotter, W., **I:** 249

Troubled Island (opera; Hughes and Still), **Retro. Supp. I:** 203

Troubled Lovers in History (Goldbarth), **Supp. XII:** 176, **192–193**

Trouble Follows Me (Macdonald, under Millar), **Supp. IV Part 2:** 466

Trouble in July (Caldwell), **I:** 297, 304–305, 306, 309

Trouble Island (Hughes), **Supp. I Part 1:** 328

"Trouble of Marcie Flint, The" (Cheever), **Supp. I Part 1:** 186

Trouble with Francis, The: An Autobiography (Francis), **Supp. IX:** 76, 77, 82, **84–85**

Trouble with God, The (Francis), **Supp. IX:** 88

"Trouble with the Stars and Stripes" (Nye), **Supp. XIII:** 277

Trouillot, Michel-Rolphe, **Supp. X:** 14–15

Troupe, Quincy, **Retro. Supp. II:** 15, 111; **Supp. X:** 242

"Trout" (Hugo), **Supp. VI:** 135

Trout Fishing in America (Brautigan), **Supp. VIII:** 43

"Trouvée" (Bishop), **Retro. Supp. II:** 49

"Truce of the Bishop, The" (Frederic), **II:** 139–140

"Truck Stop: Minnesota" (Dunn), **Supp. XI:** 145–146

True and False: Heresy and Common Sense for the Actor (Mamet), **Supp. XIV:** 241, 243

Trueblood, Valerie, **Supp. XIII:** 306

True Confessions (Dunne), **Supp. IV Part 1:** 198

True Confessions (film), **Supp. IV Part 1:** 198

True History of the Conquest of New Spain, The (Castillo), **III:** 13

True Intellectual System of the Universe, The (Cuddleworth), **II:** 10

"True Love" (Olds), **Supp. X:** 212

Trueman, Matthew (pseudonym). *See* Lowell, James Russell

"True Morality" (Bell), **Supp. X:** 13

True Stories (Atwood), **Supp. XIII:** 34–35

"True Stories" (Atwood), **Supp. XIII:** 34

"True Stories of Bitches" (Mamet), **Supp. XIV:** 246, 252

"Truest Sport, The: Jousting with Sam and Charlie" (Wolfe), **Supp. III Part 2:** 581–582

"True Vine" (Wylie), **Supp. I Part 2:** 723

True West (Shepard), **Supp. III Part 2:** 433, 441, 445, 447, 448

Truman, Harry, **III:** 3

Trumbo, Dalton, **Supp. I Part 1:** 295; **Supp. XIII:** 6

Trumbull, John, **Supp. II Part 1:** 65, 69, 70, 268

Trump, Donald, **Supp. IV Part 1:** 393

Trumpener, Katie, **Retro. Supp. I:** 380

"Trumpet Player" (Hughes), **Supp. I Part 1:** 333

Trumpet Shall Sound, The (Wilder), **IV:** 356

"Truro Bear, The" (Oliver), **Supp. VII:** 234

Truscott, Lucian K., **Supp. IV Part 2:** 683

Trust (Ozick), **Supp. V:** 257–258, 259, 260–263, 270, 272

Trust Me (Updike), **Retro. Supp. I:** 322

"Trust Yourself" (Emerson), **II:** 10

"Truth" (Emerson), **II:** 6

"Truth, The" (Jarrell), **II:** 381–382

"Truth about God, The" (Carson), **Supp. XII:** **105–106**

"Truthful James" (Harte), **IV:** 196

"Truth Is, The" (Hogan), **Supp. IV Part 1:** 401–402

"Truth Is Forced, The" (Swenson), **Supp. IV Part 2:** 652

"Truth of the Matter, The" (Nemerov), **III:** 270

Truth Serum (Cooper), **Supp. XI:** 129

"Truth the Dead Know, The" (Sexton), **Supp. II Part 2:** 681

Trying to Save Piggy Sneed (Irving), **Supp. VI:** **19–165**

"Trying to Talk with a Man" (Rich), **Supp. I Part 2:** 559

"Tryptich I" (Bell), **Supp. X:** 7

"Tryst, The" (Wharton), **Retro. Supp. I:** 378

"Try the Girl" (Chandler), **Supp. IV Part 1:** 125

"Ts'ai Chih" (Pound), **III:** 466

Tsvetayeva, Marina, **Supp. VIII:** 30

"T-2 Tanker Blues" (Snyder), **Supp. VIII:** 294

Tuckerman, Frederick Goddard, **IV:** 144

"Tuesday, November 5th, 1940" (Benét), **Supp. XI:** 46, 52

"Tuesday April 25th 1966" (Olson), **Supp. II Part 2:** 585

"Tuesday Night at the Savoy Ballroom" (Komunyakaa), **Supp. XIII:** 132

"Tuft of Flowers, The" (Frost), **II:** 153; **Retro. Supp. I:** 126, 127

Tufts, James Hayden, **Supp. I Part 2:** 632

Tu Fu, **II:** 526

Tu Fu (Ayscough), **II:** 527

Tugwell, Rexford Guy, **Supp. I Part 2:** 645

"Tulip" (Hammett), **Supp. IV Part 1:** 356

"Tulip Man, The" (McCarriston), **Supp. XIV:** 261

"Tulips" (Nye), **Supp. XIII:** 281

"Tulips" (Plath), **Retro. Supp. II:** 252–

253; **Supp. I Part 2:** 540, 542, 544

"Tulips" (Snodgrass), **Supp. VI:** 325

Tulips and Chimneys (Cummings), **I:** 436, 437, 440, 445, 447

Tully, Jim, **III:** 103, 109

Tumble Tower (Modarressi and Tyler), **Supp. IV Part 2:** 657

"Tuned in Late One Night" (Stafford), **Supp. XI:** 327–328

Tunnel, The (Gass), **Supp. V:** 44; **Supp. VI: 89–91,** 94

"Tunnel, The" (Strand), **Supp. IV Part 2:** 622

"Tunnels" (Komunyakaa), **Supp. XIII:** 123

Tuqan, Fadwa, **Supp. XIII:** 278

Tura, Cosimo, **III:** 474–475

Turandot and Other Poems (Ashbery), **Supp. III Part 1:** 3

Turgenev, Ivan Sergeevich, **I:** 106; **II:** 263, 271, 275, 280, 281, 288, 319, 320, 324–325, 338, 407; **III:** 461; **IV:** 17, 277; **Retro. Supp. I:** 215, 222; **Supp. VIII:** 167

Turgot, Anne Robert Jacques, **II:** 103; **Supp. I Part 1:** 250

"Turkey and Bones and Eating and We Liked It" (Stein), **IV:** 44

Turman, Glynn, **Supp. IV Part 1:** 362

Turnbull, Dr. George, **II:** 113

Turnbull, Lawrence, **Supp. I Part 1:** 352

"Turned" (Gilman), **Supp. XI:** 207

Turner, Addie, **IV:** 123

Turner, Darwin, **Supp. I Part 1:** 339; **Supp. IV Part 1:** 165

Turner, Frederick Jackson, **Supp. I Part 2:** 480, 481, 632, 640; **Supp. IV Part 2:** 596

Turner, Nat, **IV:** 113–114, 115, 116, 117

Turner, Patricia, **Supp. XIII:** 237

Turner, Victor, **Supp. IV Part 1:** 304

"Turning Away Variations on Estrangement" (Dickey), **Supp. IV Part 1:** 183

Turning Point, The (McCoy), **Supp. XIII:** 175

"Turning Thirty, I Contemplate Students Bicycling Home" (Dove), **Supp. IV Part 1:** 250

Turning Wind, A (Rukeyser), **Supp. VI:** 272–273, 279–280

Turn of the Screw, The (James), **Retro. Supp. I:** 219, 231; **Supp. IV Part 2:** 682

"Turn of the Screw, The" (James), **II:** 331–332; **Retro. Supp. I:** 228, 229, 231, 232

Turns and Movies and Other Tales in

Verse (Aiken), **I:** 65

"Turn with the Sun, A" (Knowles), **Supp. XII:** 237–238

Turow, Scott, **Supp. V:** 220

Turrinus, Lucius Mamilius, **IV:** 373

"Turtle" (Hogan), **Supp. IV Part 1:** 401

Turtle, Swan (Doty), **Supp. XI: 121–122**

"Turtle, Swan" (Doty), **Supp. XI:** 121–122

Turtle Island (Snyder), **Supp. VIII: 300–303**

Turtle Moon (Hoffman), **Supp. X:** 77, **87–88,** 89

"Turtle Shrine near Chittagong, The" (Nye), **Supp. XIII:** 277

Turturro, John, **Supp. XI:** 174

Tuscan Cities (Howells), **II:** 280

Tuskegee movement, **Supp. II Part 1:** 169, 172

Tuten, Frederic, **Supp. VIII:** 75, 76; **Supp. XIII:** 237, 249

Tuthill, Louisa Cavolne, **Supp. I Part 2:** 684

"Tutored Child, The" (Kunitz), **Supp. III Part 1:** 264

Tuttleton, James W., **Supp. IV Part 1:** 166, 168

"T.V.A." (Agee), **I:** 35

Tvedten, Brother Benet, **Supp. IV Part 2:** 505

"TV Men" (Carson), **Supp. XII: 105, 112**

Twain, Mark, **I:** 57, 103, 107, 109, 190, 192, 193, 195, 197, 203, 209, 245, 246, 247–250, 255, 256, 257, 260, 261, 292, 342, 418, 469, 485; **II:** 70, 140, 259, 262, 266–268, 271, 272, 274–275, 276, 277, 280, 285–286, 287, 288, 289, 301, 304, 306, 307, 312, 415, 432, 434, 436, 446, 457, 467, 475, 476, 482; **III:** 65, 101, 102, 112–113, 114, 220, 347, 357, 409, 453, 454, 504, 507, 554, 558, 572, 575, 576; **IV: 190–213,** 333, 349, 451; **Retro. Supp. I:** 169, 194, 195; **Retro. Supp. II:** 123; **Supp. I Part 1:** 37, 39, 44, 247, 251, 313, 317; **Supp. I Part 2:** 377, 385, 393, 410, 455, 456, 457, 473, 475, 579, 602, 604, 618, 629, 651, 660; **Supp. II Part 1:** 193, 344, 354, 385; **Supp. IV Part 1:** 386, 388; **Supp. IV Part 2:** 463, 468, 603, 607, 693; **Supp. V:** 44, 113, 131; **Supp. VIII:** 40, 189; **Supp. IX:** 14, 171; **Supp. X:** 51, 227; **Supp. XII:** 343; **Supp. XIII:** 1, 17

"Twa Sisters, The" (ballad), **Supp. I**

Part 2: 696

Twelfth Night (Shakespeare), **Supp. IV Part 1:** 83; **Supp. IX:** 14

Twelve Men (Dreiser), **Retro. Supp. II:** 94, 104

Twelve Moons (Oliver), **Supp. VII:** 231, 233–236, 238, 240

"12 O'Clock News" (Bishop), **Retro. Supp. II:** 48

Twelve Southerners, **IV:** 125; **Supp. X:** 25

Twelve Years a Slave (Northup), **Supp. XIV:** 32

Twentieth Century Authors, **I:** 376, 527

"Twentieth Century Fiction and the Black Mask of Humanity" (Ellison), **Retro. Supp. II:** 118

Twentieth Century Pleasures (Hass), **Supp. VI:** 103, 106, 109

"28" (Levine), **Supp. V:** 187, 191

"Twenty-Four Poems" (Schwartz), **Supp. II Part 2:** 646, 649

"2433 Agnes, First Home, Last House in Missoula" (Hugo), **Supp. VI:** 139–140

"Twenty Hill Hollow" (Muir), **Supp. IX:** 178

"Twenty Minutes" (Salter), **Supp. IX:** 260

"Twenty-One Love Poems" (Rich), **Supp. I Part 2:** 572–573

"Twenty-One Poems" (MacLeish), **III:** 19

Twenty Poems (Haines), **Supp. XII:** 204, **205–206**

Twenty Poems of Anna Akhmatova (Kenyon), **Supp. VII:** 165–166

Twenty Questions: (Posed by Poems) (McClatchy), **Supp. XII:** 254, **259–262**

27 Wagons Full of Cotton and Other One-Act Plays (T. Williams), **IV:** 381, 383

Twenty Thousand Leagues under the Sea (Verne), **I:** 480; **Supp. XI:** 63

"Twenty Years Ago" (Lindsay), **Supp. I Part 2:** 384, 399

Twenty Years at Hull-House (Addams), **Supp. I Part 1:** 3, 4, 11, 16

Twice-Told Tales (Hawthorne), **I:** 354; **II:** 224; **III:** 412, 421; **Retro. Supp. I:** 154–155, 160

Twichell, Chase, **Supp. V:** 16

Twilight (Frost), **II:** 151

"Twilight's Last Gleaming" (Burroughs and Elvins), **Supp. III Part 1:** 93, 94, 101

Twilight Sleep (Wharton), **IV:** 320–322, 324–325, 327, 328; **Retro. Supp. I:** 381

"Twin, The" (Olds), **Supp. X:** 207

"Twin Beds in Rome" (Updike), **Retro. Supp. I:** 332

"Twins of Table Mountain, The" (Harte), **Supp. II Part 1:** 355

"Twist, The" (Olson), **Supp. II Part 2:** 570

Two: Gertrude Stein and Her Brother (Stein), **IV:** 43

Two Admirals, The (Cooper), **I:** 350

Two against One (F. Barthelme), **Supp. XI:** 32, 33, 36

"Two Boys" (Moore), **Supp. X:** 173

"Two Brothers, The" (Jewett), **Retro. Supp. II:** 132

Two-Character Play, The (T. Williams), **IV:** 382, 386, 393, 398

Two Citizens (Wright), **Supp. III Part 2:** 602–604

"Two Domains, The" (Goldbarth), **Supp. XII:** 192

"Two Environments, The" (Trilling), **Supp. III Part 2:** 510

"Two-Fisted Self Pity" (Broyard), **Supp. XI:** 348

Two for Texas (Burke), **Supp. XIV:** 25, 34

"Two Friends" (Cather), **I:** 332

"Two Gardens in Linndale" (Robinson), **III:** 508

Two Gentlemen in Bonds (Ransom), **III:** 491–492

"Two Ghosts" (Francis), **Supp. IX:** 87

"Two Hangovers" (Wright), **Supp. III Part 2:** 596

Two-Headed Poems (Atwood), **Supp. XIII:** 34

Two Hours to Doom (Bryant), **Supp. XI:** 302

"Two Ladies in Retirement" (Taylor), **Supp. V:** 320

Two Letters to the Citizens of the United States, and One to General Washington (Barlow), **Supp. II Part 1:** 80

"Two Lives, The" (Hogan), **Supp. IV Part 1:** 400, 402, 403, 406, 411

Two Long Poems (Stern), **Supp. IX:** 296

"Two Lovers and a Beachcomber by the Real Sea" (Plath), **Supp. I Part 2:** 536

"Two Men" (McClatchy)", **Supp. XII:** 269

Two Men of Sandy Bar (Harte), **Supp. II Part 1:** 354

"Two Moods of Love" (Cullen), **Supp. IV Part 1:** 166

"Two Morning Monologues" (Bellow), **I:** 150; **Retro. Supp. II:** 20

Two-Ocean War, The (Morison), **Supp. I Part 2:** 491

"Two of Hearts" (Hogan), **Supp. IV Part 1:** 410

"Two on a Party" (T. Williams), **IV:** 388

"Two Pendants: For the Ears" (W. C. Williams), **Retro. Supp. I:** 423

"Two Poems of Going Home" (Dickey), **Supp. IV Part 1:** 182–183

"Two Portraits" (Chopin), **Supp. I Part 1:** 218

"Two Presences, The" (Bly), **Supp. IV Part 1:** 65

"Two Rivers" (Stegner), **Supp. IV Part 2:** 605

Tworkov, Jack, **Supp. XII:** 198

"Two Scenes" (Ashbery), **Supp. III Part 1:** 4

Two Serious Ladies (Jane Bowles), **Supp. IV Part 1:** 82

"Two Sisters" (Farrell), **II:** 45

Two Sisters: A Memoir in the Form of a Novel (Vidal), **Supp. IV Part 2:** 679

"Two Sisters of Persephone" (Plath), **Retro. Supp. II:** 246

"Two Songs on the Economy of Abundance" (Agee), **I:** 28

"Two Temples, The" (Melville), **III:** 89–90

Two Thousand Seasons (Armah), **Supp. IV Part 1:** 373

Two Trains Running (Wilson), **Supp. VIII: 345–348**

"Two Tramps in Mudtime" (Frost), **II:** 164; **Retro. Supp. I:** 137; **Supp. IX:** 261

"Two Views of a Cadaver Room" (Plath), **Supp. I Part 2:** 538

"Two Villages" (Paley), **Supp. VI:** 227

"Two Voices in a Meadow" (Wilbur), **Supp. III Part 2:** 555

"Two Witches" (Frost), **Retro. Supp. I:** 135

"Two Words" (Francis), **Supp. IX:** 81

Two Years before the Mast (Dana), **I:** 351

Tyler, Anne, **Supp. IV Part 2: 657–675; Supp. V:** 227, 326; **Supp. VIII:** 141; **Supp. X:** 1, 77, 83, 85; **Supp. XII:** 307

Tyler, Royall, **I:** 344; **Retro. Supp. I:** 377

Tymms, Ralph, **Supp. IX:** 105

Tyndale, William, **II:** 15

Tyndall, John, **Retro. Supp. II:** 93

Typee: A Peep at Polynesian Life (Melville), **III:** 75–77, 79, 84;

Retro. Supp. I: 245–246, 249, 252, 256

Typewriter Town (W. J. Smith), **Supp. XIII:** 332

"Typhus" (Simpson), **Supp. IX:** 277

Tyranny of the Normal (Fiedler), **Supp. XIII: 107–108**

"Tyranny of the Normal" (Fiedler), **Supp. XIII:** 107–108

"Tyrant of Syracuse" (MacLeish), **III:** 20

"Tyrian Businesses" (Olson), **Supp. II Part 2:** 567, 568, 569

Tytell, John, **Supp. XIV:** 140

Tzara, Tristan, **Supp. III Part 1:** 104, 105

U and I (Baker), **Supp. XIII: 45–47,** 48, 52, 55

Überdie Seelenfrage (Fechner), **II:** 358

"Ulalume" (Poe), **III:** 427; **Retro. Supp. II:** 264, 266

Ulin, David, **Supp. XIII:** 244

Ullman, Leslie, **Supp. IV Part 2:** 550

Ultimate Good Luck, The (Ford), **Supp. V:** 57, 61–62

Ultima Thule (Longfellow), **II:** 490; **Retro. Supp. II:** 169

"Ultima Thule" (Nabokov), **Retro. Supp. I:** 274

Ultramarine (Carver), **Supp. III Part 1:** 137, 138, 147, 148

Ulysses (Joyce), **I:** 395, 475–476, 478, 479, 481; **II:** 42, 264, 542; **III:** 170, 398; **IV:** 103, 418, 428, 455; **Retro. Supp. I:** 59, 63, 290, 291; **Retro. Supp. II:** 121; **Supp. I Part 1:** 57; **Supp. III Part 2:** 618, 619; **Supp. IV Part 1:** 285; **Supp. IV Part 2:** 424; **Supp. V:** 261; **Supp. IX:** 102; **Supp. X:** 114; **Supp. XIII:** 43, 191

"*Ulysses,* Order and Myth" (Eliot), **Retro. Supp. I:** 63

Unaccountable Worth of the World, The (Price), **Supp. VI:** 267

Unamuno y Jugo, Miguel de, **III:** 310

"Unattached Smile, The" (Crews), **Supp. XI:** 101

"Unbeliever, The" (Bishop), **Retro. Supp. II:** 43

"Unborn Song" (Rukeyser), **Supp. VI:** 274

Unbought Spirit: A John Jay Chapman Reader (Stone, ed.), **Supp. XIV:** 54

Uncalled, The (Dunbar), **Supp. II Part 1:** 200, 211, 212

Uncertain Certainty, The: Interviews, Essays, and Notes on Poetry (Simic), **Supp. VIII:** 270, 273, 274

Uncertainty and Plenitude: Five Con-

temporary Poets (Stitt), **Supp. IX:** 299

"Uncle" (Levine), **Supp. V:** 186

"Uncle Christmas" (Ríos), **Supp. IV Part 2:** 552

"Uncle Jim's Baptist Revival Hymn" (Lanier and Lanier), **Supp. I Part 1:** 353

"Uncle Lot" (Stowe), **Supp. I Part 2:** 585–586

Uncle Remus Tales (Harris), **Supp. II Part 1:** 201

Uncle Tom's Cabin (Stowe), **II:** 291; **Supp. I Part 1:** 49; **Supp. I Part 2:** 410, 579, 582, 589–592; **Supp. II Part 1:** 170; **Supp. III Part 1:** 154, 171; **Supp. IX:** 19; **Supp. X:** 246, 249, 250; **Supp. XIII:** 95

Uncle Tom's Children (Wright), **IV:** 476, 478, 488; **Supp. II Part 1:** 228, 235

"Uncle Wiggily in Connecticut" (Salinger), **III:** 559–560, 563

"Unclouded Day, The" (Proulx), **Supp. VII:** 254–255

"Uncommon Visage" (Brodsky), **Supp. VIII:** 31

Uncompromising Fictions of Cynthia Ozick (Pinsker), **Supp. V:** 272

"Unconscious Came a Beauty" (Swenson), **Supp. IV Part 2:** 646

"Uncreation, The" (Pinsky), **Supp. VI:** 245

"Undead, The" (Wilbur), **Supp. III Part 2:** 556

"Undefeated, The" (Hemingway), **II:** 250; **Retro. Supp. I:** 180

Under a Glass Bell (Nin), **Supp. X:** 186

"Under Ben Bulben" (Yeats), **Supp. V:** 220

Undercliff: Poems 1946–1953 (Eberhart), **I:** 528, 536–537

Under Cover (Goldbarth), **Supp. XII:** 177, 180, 193

Undercover Doctor (film), **Supp. XIII:** 170

"Under Cygnus" (Wilbur), **Supp. III Part 2:** 558

"Under Forty" (Trilling), **Supp. III Part 2:** 494

Underground Man, The (film), **Supp. IV Part 2:** 474

Underground Man, The (Macdonald), **Supp. IV Part 2:** 474, 475

"Under Libra: Weights and Measures" (Merrill), **Supp. III Part 1:** 328

Under Milk Wood (D. Thomas), **III:** 21

"Undersea" (Carson), **Supp. IX:** 21

Understanding Cynthia Ozick (Friedman), **Supp. V:** 273

Understanding Drama (Brooks and Heilman), **Supp. XIV:** 12

Understanding E. L. Doctorow (Fowler), **Supp. IV Part 1:** 226

Understanding Fiction (Brooks and Warren), **IV:** 279; **Supp. XIV:** 11

Understanding Flannery O'Connor (Whitt), **Retro. Supp. II:** 226

Understanding Nicholson Baker (Saltzman), **Supp. XIII:** 48

Understanding Poetry: An Anthology for College Students (Brooks and Warren), **IV:** 236; **Retro. Supp. I:** 40, 41; **Supp. XIV:** 4–5

Understanding Tim O'Brien (Kaplan), **Supp. V:** 241

Understanding To Kill a Mockingbird: A Student Casebook to Issues, Sources, and Documents (Johnson), **Supp. VIII:** 127

Undertaker's Garland, The (Wilson and Bishop), **IV:** 427

"Under the Cedarcroft Chestnut" (Lanier), **Supp. I Part 1:** 364

"Under the Harbour Bridge" (Komunyakaa), **Supp. XIII:** 125

Under the Lilacs (Alcott), **Supp. I Part 1:** 42–43, 44

"Under the Maud Moon" (Kinnell), **Supp. III Part 1:** 246–247

Under the Mountain Wall: A Chronicle of Two Seasons in the Stone Age (Matthiessen), **Supp. V:** 202

"Under the Rose" (Pynchon), **Supp. II Part 2:** 620

Under the Sea-Wind: A Naturalist's Picture of Ocean Life (Carson), **Supp. IX:** 19, **22–23**

Under the Sign of Saturn (Sontag), **Supp. III Part 2:** 451, 452, 458, 470–471

"Under the Sign of Saturn" (Sontag), **Supp. III Part 2:** 470

"Under the Sky" (Bowles), **Supp. IV Part 1:** 87

"Under the Willows" (Lowell), **Supp. I Part 2:** 416

Under the Willows and Other Poems (Lowell), **Supp. I Part 2:** 424

Underwood, Wilbur, **Retro. Supp. II:** 79

Underworld (DeLillo), **Supp. VI:** 2, 4–5, 6–7, 8, 9, 10, 11, **13–15; Supp. XI:** 68

Undine (La Motte-Fouqué), **II:** 212; **III:** 78

Undiscovered Country, The (Howells), **II:** 282

Uneasy Chair, The (Stegner), **Supp. IV Part 2:** 599

"Unemployed, Disabled, and Insane, The" (Haines), **Supp. XII:** 211–212

Unending Blues (Simic), **Supp. VIII: 278–279**

"Unexpressed" (Dunbar), **Supp. II Part 1:** 199

"Unfinished Bronx, The" (Paley), **Supp. VI:** 228

"Unfinished Poems" (Eliot), **I:** 579

Unfinished Woman, An (Hellman), **Supp. I Part 1:** 292, 293, 294; **Supp. IV Part 1:** 12, 353–354; **Supp. IX:** 196, 200–201

Unforeseen Wilderness, The: An Essay on Kentucky's Red River Gorge (Berry), **Supp. X:** 28, 29, 30, 36

Unforgotten Years (L. P. Smith), **Supp. XIV:** 333, 334, 335, 336, 347

"Unfortunate Coincidence" (Parker), **Supp. IX:** 190

Unframed Originals (Merwin), **Supp. III Part 1:** 341

Ungar, Sanford, **Supp. XI:** 228

Ungaretti, Giuseppe, **Supp. V:** 337

Unguided Tour (Sontag), **Supp. III Part 2:** 452

"Unidentified Flying Object" (Hayden), **Supp. II Part 1:** 368

"Unifying Principle, The" (Ammons), **Supp. VII:** 28

"Union" (Hughes), **Supp. I Part 1:** 331

"Union Street: San Francisco, Summer 1975" (Carver), **Supp. III Part 1:** 138

United States Army in World War II (Morison), **Supp. I Part 2:** 490

United States Constitution, **I:** 6, 283

United States Essays, 1951–1991 (Vidal), **Supp. IV Part 2:** 678, 687

United States of Poetry, The (television series), **Supp. XIII:** 274

"Unity through Diversity" (Locke), **Supp. XIV:** 212, 213

Universal Baseball Asociation, Inc., J. Henry Waugh, Prop., The (Coover), **Supp. V:** 39, 41–42, 44, 46

Universal Passion (Young), **III:** 111

"Universe of Death, The" (H. Miller), **III:** 184

Universe of Time, A (Anderson), **II:** 27, 28, 45, 46, 48, 49

"Universities" (Emerson), **II:** 6

"Universities: A Mirage? " (Mora), **Supp. XIII:** 219

"University" (Shapiro), **Supp. II Part 2:** 704–705, 717

"University Avenue" (Mora), **Supp.**

XIII: 216
"University Days" (Thurber), **Supp. I Part 2:** 605
"University Hospital, Boston" (Oliver), **Supp. VII:** 235
"Unknowable, The" (Levine), **Supp. V:** 195
"Unknown Girl in the Maternity Ward" (Sexton), **Supp. II Part 2:** 676
"Unknown Love, The" (Chandler), **Supp. IV Part 1:** 120
"Unknown War, The" (Sandburg), **III:** 594
Unleashed (anthology), **Supp. XI:** 132
"Unlighted Lamps" (Anderson), **I:** 112
Unloved Wife, The (Alcott), **Supp. I Part 1:** 33
Unmarried Woman, An (film), **Supp. IV Part 1:** 303
"Unnatural Mother, The" (Gilman), **Supp. XI:** 207
"Unnatural State of the Unicorn" (Komunyakaa), **Supp. XIII:** 119
"Unparalleled Adventure of One Hans Pfaall, The" (Poe), **III:** 424
Unprecedented Era, The (Goebbels), **III:** 560
"Unprofitable Servant, The" (O. Henry), **Supp. II Part 1:** 403
Unpublished Poems of Emily Dickinson (Bianchi and Hampson, ed.), **Retro. Supp. I:** 35
Unpunished (Gilman), **Supp. XI:** 208
"Unseen, The" (Pinsky), **Supp. VI:** 243–244
"Unseen, The" (Singer), **Retro. Supp. II:** 307
Unseen Hand, The (Shepard), **Supp. III Part 2:** 439, 445–446
Unselected Poems (Levine), **Supp. V:** 179
Unsettling of America, The: Culture and Agriculture (Berry), **Supp. X:** 22, 26, 29, 32, 33, 35; **Supp. XIV:** 177, 179
Unspeakable Gentleman, The (Marquand), **III:** 53–54, 60, 63
Unspeakable Practices, Unnatural Acts (Barthelme), **Supp. IV Part 1:** 39
"Unspeakable Things Unspoken: The Afro-American Presence in American Literature" (Morrison), **Supp. III Part 1:** 375, 377–379
"Untelling, The" (Strand), **Supp. IV Part 2:** 629
Unterecker, John, **I:** 386
Untermeyer, Jean, **II:** 530
Untermeyer, Louis, **II:** 516–517, 530, 532; **III:** 268; **Retro. Supp. I:** 124, 133, 136; **Supp. III Part 1:** 2; **Supp.**

IX: 76; **Supp. XIV:** 119, 123
Untimely Papers (Bourne), **I:** 218, 233
"Untitled Blues" (Komunyakaa), **Supp. XIII:** 117
"Untrustworthy Speaker, The" (Glück), **Supp. V:** 86
"Unused" (Anderson), **I:** 112, 113
Unvanquished, The (Faulkner), **II:** 55, 67–68, 71; **Retro. Supp. I:** 84; **Supp. I Part 2:** 450
"Unvexed Isles, The" (Warren), **IV:** 253
"Unwedded" (Larcom), **Supp. XIII:** 144
"Unweepables, The" (Karr), **Supp. XI:** 243
Unwelcome Words (Bowles), **Supp. IV Part 1:** 93, 94
"Unwelcome Words" (Bowles), **Supp. IV Part 1:** 94, 95
Unwin, T. Fisher, **Supp. XI:** 202
"Unwithered Garland, The" (Kunitz), **Supp. III Part 1:** 265
Unwobbling Pivot, The (Pound, trans.), **III:** 472
"Unwritten, The" (Merwin), **Supp. III Part 1:** 352
"Unwritten Law" (Glück), **Supp. V:** 91
Up (Sukenick), **Supp. V:** 39
Up Above the World (Bowles), **Supp. IV Part 1:** 82, 91, 92
"Up and Down" (Merrill), **Supp. III Part 1:** 328
Upanishads, **IV:** 183
Up Country: Poems of New England (Kumin), **Supp. IV Part 2:** 446, 447–448, 453
"Update" (Dunn), **Supp. XI:** 150–151
Updike, John, **I:** 54; **III:** 572; **IV: 214–235; Retro. Supp. I:** 116, **317–338; Retro. Supp. II:** 213, 279, 280; **Supp. I Part 1:** 186, 196; **Supp. IV Part 2:** 657; **Supp. V:** 23, 43, 95, 119; **Supp. VIII:** 151, 167, 236; **Supp. IX:** 208; **Supp. XI:** 65, 66, 99, 140; **Supp. XII:** 140, 296, 298, 310; **Supp. XIII:** 45–46, 47, 52; **Supp. XIV:** 79, 93, 111
Updike, Mrs. Wesley, **IV:** 218, 220
Up from Slavery (Washington), **Supp. II Part 1:** 169; **Supp. IX:** 19
Upham, Thomas Goggswell, **II:** 487
"Upholsterers, The" (Lardner), **II:** 435
"Up in Michigan" (Hemingway), **II:** 263
Upjohn, Richard, **IV:** 312
"Upon a Spider Catching a Fly" (Taylor), **IV:** 161
"Upon a Wasp Child with Cold" (Taylor), **IV:** 161

"Upon Meeting Don L. Lee, in a Dream" (Dove), **Supp. IV Part 1:** 244
"Upon My Dear and Loving Husband His Going into England, Jan. 16, 1661" (Bradstreet), **Supp. I Part 1:** 110
"Upon Returning to the Country Road" (Lindsay), **Supp. I Part 2:** 382
"Upon the Burning of Our House, July 10th, 1666" (Bradstreet), **Supp. I Part 1:** 107–108, 122
"Upon the Sweeping Flood" (Taylor), **IV:** 161
"Upon Wedlock, and Death of Children" (Taylor), **IV:** 144, 147, 161
"Upset, An" (Merrill), **Supp. III Part 1:** 336
Upstairs and Downstairs (Vonnegut), **Supp. II Part 2:** 757
Upstate (Wilson), **IV:** 447
Upton, Lee, **Supp. X:** 209
"Upturned Face" (Crane), **I:** 423
Upward, Allen, **Supp. I Part 1:** 262
Upward, Edward, **Supp. XIV:** 159, 160
"Upward Moon and the Downward Moon, The" (Bly), **Supp. IV Part 1:** 71
Urania: A Rhymed Lesson (Holmes), **Supp. I Part 1:** 300
"Urban Convalescence, An" (Merrill), **Supp. III Part 1:** 322–324
"Urban Renewal" (Komunyakaa), **Supp. XIII:** 113
Urial Accosta: A Play (Reznikoff), **Supp. XIV:** 282, 288
Urich, Robert, **Supp. V:** 228
"Uriel" (Emerson), **II:** 19
Uris, Leon, **Supp. IV Part 1:** 285, 379
Uroff, Margaret D., **Supp. I Part 2:** 542
"Us" (Sexton), **Supp. II Part 2:** 687
U.S. 1 (Rukeyser), **Supp. VI:** 272, 278, 283, 285
"U.S. Commercial Orchid, The" (Agee), **I:** 35
U.S.A. (Dos Passos), **I:** 379, 475, 478, 482–488, 489, 490, 491, 492, 493, 494, 495; **Retro. Supp. II:** 197; **Supp. I Part 2:** 646; **Supp. III Part 1:** 104, 105; **Supp. XIV:** 24
"U.S.A. School of Writing, The" (Bishop), **Retro. Supp. II:** 43
"Used-Boy Raisers, The" (Paley), **Supp. VI:** 218, 228
"Used Cars on Oahu" (Nye), **Supp. XIII:** 282
"Used Side of the Sofa, The" (Ríos), **Supp. IV Part 2:** 551
Use of Fire, The (Price), **Supp. VI:** 265

"Use of Force, The" (W. C. Williams), **Retro. Supp. I:** 424

Use of Poetry and the Use of Criticism, The (Eliot), **Retro. Supp. I:** 65

Uses of Enchantment, The: The Meaning and Importance of Fairy Tales (Bettelheim), **Supp. XIV:** 126

Uses of Enchantment, The: The Meaning and Importance of Fairy Tales (Bettleheim), **Supp. X:** 77

Uses of Literacy, The (Hoggart), **Supp. XIV:** 299

"Uses of Poetry, The" (W. C. Williams), **Retro. Supp. I:** 412

"Uses of the Blues, The" (Baldwin), **Retro. Supp. II:** 8

"USFS 1919: The Ranger, the Cook, and a Hole in the Sky" (Maclean), **Supp. XIV:** 230, 234

Ushant: An Essay (Aiken), **I:** 49, 54, 55, 56, 57

"Usher 11" (Bradbury), **Supp. I Part 2:** 622

"Using Parrots to Kill Mockingbirds: Yet Another Racial Prosecution and Wrongful Conviction in Maycomb" (Fair), **Supp. VIII:** 128

Usual Star, The (Doolittle), **Supp. I Part 1:** 270

"Usurpation (Other People's Stories)" (Ozick), **Supp. V:** 268, 271

Utopia 14 (Vonnegut), **Supp. II Part 2:** 757

V. (Pynchon), **Supp. II Part 2:** 618, 620–622, 627–630; **Supp. IV Part 1:** 279

V. S. Naipaul: An Introduction to His Work (Theroux), **Supp. VIII:** 314, 318

"V. S. Pritchett's Apprenticeship" (Maxwell), **Supp. VIII:** 172

"V. V." (Alcott), **Supp. I Part 1:** 37

"Vacation" (Stafford), **Supp. XI:** 321, 322

"Vacation Trip" (Stafford), **Supp. XI:** 322

Vachel Lindsay: A Poet in America (Masters), **Supp. I Part 2:** 473, 474

"Vachel Lindsay: The Midwest as Utopia" (Whitney), **Supp. I Part 2:** 403

"Vachel Lindsay Writes to Floyd Dell" (Tanselle), **Supp. I Part 2:** 403

Vadim, Roger, **Supp. XI:** 293, 307

"Vag" (Dos Passos), **I:** 487–488

Valentine, Jean, **Supp. V:** 92

Valentine, Saint, **IV:** 396

Valentino, Rudolph, **I:** 483

Valéry, Paul, **II:** 543, 544; **III:** 279, 409, 428, 609; **IV:** 79, 91, 92, 428,

443; **Retro. Supp. II:** 187

"Valhalla" (Francis), **Supp. IX:** 77

Valhalla and Other Poems (Francis), **Supp. IX:** 76

Validity in Interpretation (Hirsch), **Supp. XIV:** 15

Valitsky, Ken, **Supp. XII:** 7

Vallejo, César, **Supp. V:** 332; **Supp. IX:** 271; **Supp. XIII:** 114, 315, 323

"Valley Between, The" (Marshall), **Supp. XI:** 278

Valley of Decision, The (Wharton), **IV:** 311, 315; **Retro. Supp. I:** 365–367

Valley of the Moon, The (London), **II:** 467, 481

"Valley of Unrest, The" (Poe), **III:** 411

Valli, Alida, **Supp. IV Part 2:** 520

"Valor" (Bausch), **Supp. VII:** 54

"Values and Fictions" (Toomer), **Supp. III Part 2:** 485–486

"Values and Imperatives" (Locke), **Supp. XIV:** 199, 202, 212

Values of Veblen, The: A Critical Appraisal (Rosenberg), **Supp. I Part 2:** 650

"Vampire" (Karr), **Supp. XI:** 241

Vampire Armand, The (Rice), **Supp. VII:** 290, 294–295

Vampire Chronicles, The (Rice), **Supp. VII:** 290

Vampire Lestat, The (Rice), **Supp. VII:** 290–292, 298, 299

Van Buren, Martin, **II:** 134, 312; **III:** 473

Vande Kieft, Ruth M., **IV:** 260

Vanderbilt, Cornelius, **III:** 14

Van Dine, S. S., **Supp. IV Part 1:** 341

Van Doren, Carl, **I:** 252–253, 423; **II:** 103, 111, 112; **Supp. I Part 2:** 474, 486, 707, 709, 717, 718, 727; **Supp. II Part 1:** 395; **Supp. VIII:** 96–97

Van Doren, Mark, **I:** 168; **III:** 4, 23, 589; **Supp. I Part 2:** 604; **Supp. III Part 2:** 626; **Supp. VIII:** 231; **Supp. IX:** 266, 268

Vandover and the Brute (Norris), **III:** 314, 315, 316, 320–322, 328, 333, 334

Van Duyn, Mona, **Supp. IX:** 269

Van Dyke, Annette, **Supp. IV Part 1:** 327

Van Dyke, Henry, **I:** 223; **II:** 456

Van Gogh, Vincent, **I:** 27; **IV:** 290; **Supp. I Part 2:** 451; **Supp. IV Part 1:** 284

Van Gogh's Room at Arles (Elkin), **Supp. VI:** 56

"Vanisher, The" (Whittier), **Supp. I Part 2:** 691

"Vanishing Red, The" (Frost), **Retro. Supp. II:** 47

"Vanity" (B. Diop), **Supp. IV Part 1:** 16

Vanity Fair (Thackeray), **I:** 354; **II:** 91; **III:** 70; **Supp. IX:** 200

"Vanity of All Wordly Things, The" (Bradstreet), **Supp. I Part 1:** 102, 119

Vanity of Duluoz (Kerouac), **Supp. III Part 1:** 221, 222

"Vanity of Existence, The" (Freneau), **Supp. II Part 1:** 262

Van Matre, Lynn, **Supp. V:** 126

Vanquished, The (Faulkner), **I:** 205

Van Rensselaer, Stephen, **I:** 351

Van Vechten, Carl, **I:** 295; **IV:** 76; **Supp. I Part 1:** 324, 327, 332; **Supp. I Part 2:** 715; **Supp. II Part 2: 725–751; Supp. X:** 247

Vanzetti, Bartolomeo, **I:** 482, 486, 490, 494; **II:** 38–39, 426; **III:** 139–140; **Supp. I Part 2:** 446, 610, 611; **Supp. V:** 288–289; **Supp. IX:** 199

"Vapor Trail Reflected in the Frog Pond" (Kinnell), **Supp. III Part 1:** 242–243

"Vapor Trails" (Snyder), **Supp. VIII:** 298

"Variation: Ode to Fear" (Warren), **IV:** 241

"Variation on a Sentence" (Bogan), **Supp. III Part 1:** 60

"Variation on Gaining a Son" (Dove), **Supp. IV Part 1:** 248

"Variation on Pain" (Dove), **Supp. IV Part 1:** 248

"Variations: The air is sweetest that a thistle guards" (Merrill), **Supp. III Part 1:** 321

"Variations: White Stag, Black Bear" (Merrill), **Supp. III Part 1:** 321

"Varick Street" (Bishop), **Supp. I Part 1:** 90, 92

Varieties of Metaphysical Poetry, The (Eliot), **Retro. Supp. I:** 65

Varieties of Religious Experience, The (William James), **II:** 344, 353, 354, 359–360, 362; **IV:** 28, 291; **Supp. IX:** 19

Variety (film), **Supp. XII:** 7

Variorum (Whitman), **Retro. Supp. I:** 406

Various Miracles (Shields), **Supp. VII:** 318–320, 323, 324

"Various Miracles" (Shields), **Supp. VII:** 318–319, 324

"Various Tourists" (Connell), **Supp. XIV:** 79

"Varmint Question, The" (Leopold),

Supp. XIV: 180–181
Vasari, Giorgio, Supp. I Part 2: 450; Supp. III Part 1: 5
Vasquez, Robert, Supp. V: 180
Vassall Morton (Parkman), Supp. II Part 2: 595, 597–598
Vasse, W. W., III: 478
Vaudeville for a Princess (Schwartz), Supp. II Part 2: 661–662
Vaughan, Henry, IV: 151
Vaughn, Robert, Supp. XI: 343
"Vaunting Oak" (Ransom), III: 490
Vazirani, Reetika, Supp. XIII: 133
Veblen (Hobson), Supp. I Part 2: 650
Veblen, Andrew, Supp. I Part 2: 640
Veblen, Mrs. Thorstein (Ellen Rolfe), Supp. I Part 2: 641
Veblen, Oswald, Supp. I Part 2: 640
Veblen, Thorstein, I: 104, 283, 475–476, 483, 498, 511; II: 27, 272, 276, 287; Supp. I Part 2: 628–650; Supp. IV Part 1: 22
Veblenism: A New Critique (Dobriansky), Supp. I Part 2: 648, 650
"Veblen's Attack on Culture" (Adorno), Supp. I Part 2: 650
Vechten, Carl Van, Retro. Supp. I: 199
Vedanta for Modern Man (Isherwood, ed.), Supp. XIV: 164
Vedanta for the Western World (Isherwood, ed.), Supp. XIV: 164
Vedas, IV: 183
Vega, Janine Pommy, Supp. XIV: 148
Vega, Lope de, Retro. Supp. I: 285; Supp. III Part 1: 341, 347
Vegetable, The (Fitzgerald), Retro. Supp. I: 105; Supp. IX: 57
Vegetable, The, or From President to Postman (Fitzgerald), II: 91
Veinberg, Jon, Supp. V: 180; Supp. XIII: 313
Vein of Iron (Glasgow), II: 175, 186, 188–189, 191, 192, 194
Vein of Riches, A (Knowles), Supp. XII: 249
Velie, Alan R., Supp. IV Part 2: 486
Velocities: New and Selected Poems, 1966–1992 (Dobyns), Supp. XIII: 86–87, 87, 88
"Velorio" (Cisneros), Supp. VII: 66
"Velvet Shoes" (Wylie), Supp. I Part 2: 711, 714
Venant, Elizabeth, Supp. XI: 343
Vencloca, Thomas, Supp. VIII: 29
Vendler, Helen H., Retro. Supp. I: 297; Retro. Supp. II: 184, 191; Supp. I Part 1: 77, 78, 92, 95; Supp. I Part 2: 565; Supp. IV Part 1: 245, 247, 249, 254, 257; Supp.

IV Part 2: 448; Supp. V: 78, 82, 189, 343; Supp. XII: 187, 189
"Venetian Blind, The" (Jarrell), II: 382–383
Venetian Glass Nephew, The (Wylie), Supp. I Part 2: 707, 709, 714, 717–719, 721, 724
Venetian Life (Howells), II: 274, 277, 279
Venetian Vespers, The (Hecht), Supp. X: 57, 65–69
"Venetian Vespers, The" (Hecht), Supp. X: 65, 66–67
Venice Observed (McCarthy), II: 562
Ventadorn, Bernard de, Supp. IV Part 1: 146
"Ventriloquists' Conversations" (Gentry), Supp. IV Part 1: 236
"Venus, Cupid, Folly and Time" (Taylor), Supp. V: 322–323
Venus and Adonis (film), Supp. IV Part 1: 82
Venus in Sparta (Auchincloss), Supp. IV Part 1: 25
"Venus's-flytraps" (Komunyakaa), Supp. XIII: 126, 127
"Veracruz" (Hayden), Supp. II Part 1: 371, 373
Verga, Giovanni, II: 271, 275
Verghese, Abraham, Supp. X: 160
Verhaeren, Emile, I: 476; II: 528, 529
Verlaine, Paul, II: 529, 543; III: 466; IV: 79, 80, 86, 286; Retro. Supp. I: 56, 62; Retro. Supp. II: 326
"Vermeer" (Nemerov), III: 275, 278, 280
Vermeer, Jan, Retro. Supp. I: 335
Vermont Notebook, The (Ashbery), Supp. III Part 1: 1
"Vernal Ague, The" (Freneau), Supp. II Part 1: 258
Verne, Jules, I: 480; Retro. Supp. I: 270; Supp. XI: 63
Vernon, John, Supp. X: 15
Verplanck, Gulian C., Supp. I Part 1: 155, 156, 157, 158
Verrazano, Giovanni da, Supp. I Part 2: 496, 497
Verse (Zawacki), Supp. VIII: 272
"Verse for Urania" (Merrill), Supp. III Part 1: 329, 330
Verses (Wharton), Retro. Supp. I: 362
Verses, Printed for Her Friends (Jewett), II: 406
"Verses for Children" (Lowell), II: 516
"Verses Made at Sea in a Heavy Gale" (Freneau), Supp. II Part 1: 262
"Verses on the Death of T. S. Eliot" (Brodsky), Supp. VIII: 19
"Version of a Fragment of Simonides"

(Bryant), Supp. I Part 1: 153, 155
Verulam, Baron. *See* Bacon, Francis
Very, Jones, III: 507
"Very Hot Sun in Bermuda, The" (Jackson), Supp. IX: 126
Very Old Bones (Kennedy), Supp. VII: 133, 148, 150–153
"Very Proper Gander, The" (Thurber), Supp. I Part 2: 610
"Very Short Story, A" (Hemingway), II: 252; Retro. Supp. I: 173
"Vesalius in Zante" (Wharton), Retro. Supp. I: 372
Vesey, Denmark, Supp. I Part 2: 592
Vesey, Desmond, Supp. XIV: 162
"Vespers" (Auden), Supp. II Part 1: 23
"Vespers" (Glück), Supp. V: 88
Vestal Lady on Brattle, The (Corso), Supp. XII: 119, 120–121, 134
Vested Interests and the Common Man, The (Veblen), Supp. I Part 2: 642
"Vesuvius at Home" (Rich), Retro. Supp. I: 42
"Veteran, The" (Crane), I: 413
"Veteran Sirens" (Robinson), III: 512, 524
"Vetiver" (Ashbery), Supp. III Part 1: 26
"Via Dieppe-Newhaven" (H. Miller), III: 183
"Via Negativa" (Salter), Supp. IX: 257
Vicar of Wakefeld, The (Goldsmith), I: 216
"Vicissitudes of the Avant-Garde, The" (Gass), Supp. VI: 91
Victim, The (Bellow), I: 144, 145, 147, 149, 150, 151, 152, 153, 155, 156, 158, 159, 164; IV: 19; Retro. Supp. II: 21, 22, 34
"Victor" (Mumford), Supp. II Part 2: 476
"Victory at Sea" (television series), Supp. I Part 2: 490
"Victory comes late" (Dickinson), Retro. Supp. I: 45
"Victory of the Moon, The" (Crane), I: 420
Vidal, Gore, II: 587; IV: 383; Supp. IV Part 1: 22, 35, 92, 95, 198; Supp. IV Part 2: 677–696; Supp. IX: 96; Supp. X: 186, 195; Supp. XIV: 156, 170, 338
Viebahn, Fred, Supp. IV Part 1: 248
Viera, Joseph M., Supp. XI: 178, 186
Viereck, Peter, Supp. I Part 2: 403
Viertel, Berthold, Supp. XIV: 165
Viet Journal (Jones), Supp. XI: 230–231
Vietnam (McCarthy), II: 578–579

"Vietnam in Me, The" (O'Brien), **Supp. V:** 241, 252

Vie unanime, La (Romains), **I:** 227

"View, The" (Roussel), **Supp. III Part 1:** 15, 16, 21

View from 80, The (Cowley), **Supp. II Part 1:** 141, 144, 153

View from the Bridge, A (A. Miller), **III:** 147, 148, 156, 158, 159–160

View of My Own, A: Essays in Literature and Society (Hardwick), **Supp. III Part 1:** 194, 200

"View of the Capital from the Library of Congress" (Bishop), **Retro. Supp. II:** 45

View of the Soil and Climate of the United States, A (Brown, trans.), **Supp. I Part 1:** 146

"View of the Woods, A" (O'Connor), **III:** 349, 351, 358; **Retro. Supp. II:** 237

"Views of the Mysterious Hill: The Appearance of Parnassus in American Poetry" (Strand), **Supp. IV Part 2:** 631

"Vigil" (Karr), **Supp. XI:** 241

"Vigil, The" (Dante), **III:** 542

Vigny, Alfred Victor de, **II:** 543

Vile Bodies (Waugh), **Supp. I Part 2:** 607

Villa, Pancho, **I:** 210; **III:** 584

"Village Blacksmith, The" (Longfellow), **Retro. Supp. II:** 167, 168; **Supp. I Part 2:** 409

Village Hymns, a Supplement to Dr. Watts's Psalms and Hymns (Nettleton), **I:** 458

"Village Improvement Parade, The" (Lindsay), **Supp. I Part 2:** 388, 389

Village Magazine, The (Lindsay), **Supp. I Part 2:** 379–380, 382

Village Virus, The (Lewis), **II:** 440

"Villanelle at Sundown" (Justice), **Supp. VII:** 119, 122–123

"Villanelle of Change" (Robinson), **III:** 524

Villard, Oswald, **Supp. I Part 1:** 332

"Villa Selene" (Simpson), **Supp. IX:** 279

Villon, François, **II:** 544; **III:** 9, 174, 592; **Retro. Supp. I:** 286; **Supp. I Part 1:** 261; **Supp. III Part 1:** 235, 243, 249, 253; **Supp. III Part 2:** 560; **Supp. IX:** 116

"Villonaud for This Yule" (Pound), **Retro. Supp. I:** 286

Vindication of the Rights of Woman (Wollstonecraft), **Supp. I Part 1:** 126; **Supp. XI:** 203

Vines, Lois Davis, **Retro. Supp. II:** 261

"Vintage Thunderbird, A" (Beattie), **Supp. V:** 27

Vinz, Mark, **Supp. X:** 117

Violence (Bausch), **Supp. VII:** 48–49, 54

Violent Bear It Away, The (O'Connor), **III:** 339, 345–348, 350, 351, 354, 355, 356, 357; **Retro. Supp. II:** 233, **234–236**

"Violent Vet, The" (O'Brien), **Supp. V:** 238

Violin (Rice), **Supp. VII:** 302

Viorst, Judith, **Supp. X:** 153

Viper Run (Karr), **Supp. XI: 248–251**

Virgil, **I:** 312, 322, 587; **II:** 133, 542; **IV:** 137, 359; **Retro. Supp. I:** 135; **Supp. I Part 1:** 153; **Supp. I Part 2:** 494; **Supp. IV Part 2:** 631

"Virgin and the Dynamo" (Adams), **III:** 396

"Virgin Carrying a Lantern, The" (Stevens), **IV:** 80

Virginia (Glasgow), **II:** 175, 178, 181–182, 193, 194

"Virginia" (Lindsay), **Supp. I Part 2:** 398

"Virginia Britannia" (Moore), **III:** 198, 208–209

"Virginians Are Coming Again, The" (Lindsay), **Supp. I Part 2:** 399

"Virgin Violeta" (Porter), **III:** 454

"Virility" (Ozick), **Supp. V:** 262, 265

Virtue of Selfishness, The: A New Concept of Egoism (Rand), **Supp. IV Part 2:** 527, 530–532

"Virtuoso" (Francis), **Supp. IX:** 82

Virtuous Woman, A (Gibbons), **Supp. X: 44–45,** 46, 50

Visconti, Luchino, **Supp. V:** 51

Visible Saints: The History of a Puritan Idea (Morgan), **IV:** 149

"Vision, A" (Olds), **Supp. X:** 214

"Vision, A" (Winters), **Supp. II Part 2:** 785, 795

"Vision and Prayer" (D. Thomas), **I:** 432

"Visionary, The" (Poe), **III:** 411

Visionary Farms, The (Eberhart), **I:** 537–539

Visioning, The (Glaspell), **Supp. III Part 1:** 175–177, 180, 187, 188

Vision in Spring (Faulkner), **Retro. Supp. I:** 79

Vision of Columbus (Barlow), **Supp. I Part 1:** 124; **Supp. II Part 1:** 67, 68, 70–75, 77, 79

Vision of Sir Launfal, The (Lowell), **Supp. I Part 1:** 311; **Supp. I Part 2:** 406, 409, 410

"Vision of the World, A" (Cheever), **Supp. I Part 1:** 182, 192

Visions of Cody (Kerouac), **Supp. III Part 1:** 225–227

Visions of Gerard (Kerouac), **Supp. III Part 1:** 219–222, 225, 227, 229

"Visions of the Daughters of Albion" (Blake), **III:** 540

"Visit" (Ammons), **Supp. VII:** 28–29

"Visit, The" (Kenyon), **Supp. VII:** 169

"Visitant, The" (Dunn), **Supp. XI:** 147

"*Visitation, The*/La Visitación" (Mora), **Supp. XIII:** 217, 224, 228

"Visit Home, A" (Stafford), **Supp. XI:** 318

Visit in 2001, The (musical, McNally), **Supp. XIII:** 207

"Visiting My Own House in Iowa City" (Stern), **Supp. IX:** 300

"Visit of Charity, A" (Welty), **IV:** 262

"Visitors" (Salinas), **Supp. XIII:** 318

"Visitors, The/Los Visitantes" (Kingsolver), **Supp. VII:** 208

"Visits to St. Elizabeths" (Bishop), **Retro. Supp. II:** 47

"Visit to a Small Planet" (teleplay) (Vidal), **Supp. IV Part 2:** 682

Visit to a Small Planet: A Comedy Akin to Vaudeville (Vidal), **Supp. IV Part 2:** 682–683

"Visit to Avoyelles, A" (Chopin), **Supp. I Part 1:** 213

"Vissi d'Arte" (Moore), **Supp. X: 173–174**

Vistas of History (Morison), **Supp. I Part 2:** 492

"Vita" (Stafford), **Supp. XI:** 330

Vital Provisions (Price), **Supp. VI:** 262–263

"Vitamins" (Carver), **Supp. III Part 1:** 138

Vita Nova (Glück), **Supp. V:** 90–92

Vittorio, the Vampire (Rice), **Supp. VII:** 295–296

Viudas (Dorfman), **Supp. IX:** 138

Vizenor, Gerald, **Supp. IV Part 1:** 260, 262, 329, 404; **Supp. IV Part 2:** 502

Vladimir Nabokov: The American Years (Nabokov), **Retro. Supp. I:** 275

"Vlemk, the Box Painter" (Gardner), **Supp. VI:** 73

"V-Letter" (Shapiro), **Supp. II Part 2:** 707

V-Letter and Other Poems (Shapiro), **Supp. II Part 2:** 702, 706

"Vocabulary of Dearness" (Nye), **Supp. XIII:** 284

"Vocation" (Stafford), **Supp. XI:** 312, 321

Vocation and a Voice, A (Chopin), **Retro. Supp. II:** 67, 72

"Vocation and a Voice, A" (Chopin), **Retro. Supp. II:** 72; **Supp. I Part 1:** 200, 220, 224, 225

Vogel, Speed, **Supp. IV Part 1:** 390

"Voice, The" (Dunn), **Supp. XI:** 152

Voiced Connections of James Dickey, The (Dickey), **Supp. IV Part 1:** 177

"Voice from the Woods, A" (Humphrey), **Supp. IX:** 101

"Voice from Under the Table, A" (Wilbur), **Supp. III Part 2:** 553, 554

Voice of Reason, The: Essays in Objectivist Thought (Rand), **Supp. IV Part 2:** 527, 528, 532

"Voice of Rock, The" (Ginsberg), **Supp. II Part 1:** 313

Voice of the Butterfly, The (Nichols), **Supp. XIII:** 270

Voice of the City, The (O. Henry), **Supp. II Part 1:** 410

"Voice of the Mountain, The" (Crane), **I:** 420

Voice of the Negro (Barber), **Supp. II Part 1:** 168

Voice of the People, The (Glasgow), **II:** 175, 176

Voice of the Turtle: American Indian Literature 1900–1970 (Gunn Allen, ed.), **Supp. IV Part 1:** 332, 334

Voices from the Moon (Dubus), **Supp. VII:** 88–89

"Voices from the Other World" (Merrill), **Supp. III Part 1:** 331

Voices in the House (Sedges), **Supp. II Part 1:** 125

Voices of the Night (Longfellow), **II:** 489, 493; **Retro. Supp. II:** 154, 157, 168

"Voices of Village Square, The" (Wolfe), **Supp. III Part 2:** 571–572

Voice That Is Great within Us, The (Caruth, ed.), **Supp. XIII:** 112

Voigt, Ellen Bryan, **Supp. XIII:** 76

Volkening, Henry, **Retro. Supp. II:** 117

Vollmann, William T., **Supp. XIV:** 96

Volney, Constantin François de Chasseboeuf, **Supp. I Part 1:** 146

Voltaire, **I:** 194; **II:** 86, 103, 449; **III:** 420; **IV:** 18; **Retro. Supp. II:** 94; **Supp. I Part 1:** 288–289; **Supp. I Part 2:** 669, 717

Vonnegut, Kurt, **Retro. Supp. I:** 170; **Supp. II Part 2:** 557, 689, **753–784; Supp. IV Part 1:** 227, 392;

Supp. V: 40, 42, 237, 244, 296; **Supp. X:** 260; **Supp. XI:** 104; **Supp. XII:** 139, 141

"Voracities and Verities" (Moore), **III:** 214

Vore, Nellie, **I:** 199

Vorlicky, Robert, **Supp. IX:** 132, 135, 136, 141, 144, 147

"Vorticism" (Pound), **Retro. Supp. I:** 288

Voss, Richard, **I:** 199–200

"Vow, The" (Hecht), **Supp. X:** 64

"Vowels 2" (Baraka), **Supp. II Part 1:** 51

Vow of Conversation, A: Journal, 1964–1965 (Merton), **Supp. VIII:** 206

Vox (Baker), **Supp. XIII:** **47–49,** 50, 52, 53

"Voyage" (MacLeish), **III:** 15

"Voyage, The" (Irving), **II:** 304

Voyage, The, and Other Versions of Poems by Baudelaire (Lowell), **Retro. Supp. II:** 187

Voyage dans la Haute Pennsylvanie et dans l'état de New-York (Crèvecoeur), **Supp. I Part 1:** 250–251

Voyage of the Beagle (Darwin), **Supp. IX:** 211

"Voyages" (H. Crane), **I:** 393–395; **Retro. Supp. II:** 78, 80, 81

"Voyages" (Levine), **Supp. V:** 190

Voyages and Discoveries of the Companions of Columbus (Irving), **II:** 310

Voyage to Pagany, A (W. C. Williams), **IV:** 404; **Retro. Supp. I:** 418–419, **420–421,** 423

Voznesensky, Andrei, **II:** 553; **Supp. III Part 1:** 268; **Supp. III Part 2:** 560

Vrbovska, Anca, **Supp. IV Part 2:** 639

"Vulgarity in Literature" (Huxley), **III:** 429–430

"Vultures" (Oliver), **Supp. VII:** 235

W (Viva) (Cummings), **I:** 429, 433, 434, 436, 443, 444, 447

"W. D. Sees Himself Animated" (Snodgrass), **Supp. VI:** 327

"W. D. Sits in Kafka's Chair and Is Interrogated Concerning the Assumed Death of Cock Robin" (Snodgrass), **Supp. VI:** 319

"W. D. Tries to Warn Cock Robin" (Snodgrass), **Supp. VI:** 319

Wabash (R. O. Butler), **Supp. XII:** 61, **68–69**

Wade, Grace, **I:** 216

"Wading at Wellfleet" (Bishop), **Retro.**

Supp. II: 42, 43; **Supp. I Part 1:** 80, 85, 86

Wadsworth, Charles, **I:** 454, 470; **Retro. Supp. I:** 32, 33

Wagenknecht, Edward, **II:** 508; **Supp. I Part 2:** 408, 584; **Supp. IV Part 2:** 681

Wagner, Jean, **Supp. I Part 1:** 341, 346; **Supp. IV Part 1:** 165, 167, 171

Wagner, Richard, **I:** 284, 395; **II:** 425; **III:** 396, 507; **Supp. IV Part 1:** 392

Wagner, Robert, **Supp. IX:** 250

"Wagnerians, The" (Auchincloss), **Supp. IV Part 1:** 23

"Wagner Matinee, A" (Cather), **I:** 315–316; **Retro. Supp. I:** 5, 8

Wagoner, David, **Supp. IX:** **323–340; Supp. XII:** 178

Waid, Candace, **Retro. Supp. I:** 360, 372, 373

Waif, The (Longfellow, ed.), **Retro. Supp. II:** 155

"Waif of the Plains, A" (Harte), **Supp. II Part 1:** 354

Wain, John, **Supp. XIV:** 166

"Wait" (Kinnell), **Supp. III Part 1:** 250

"Waiting" (Dubus), **Supp. VII:** 87

"Waiting" (W. C. Williams), **Retro. Supp. I:** 418

"Waiting, The" (Olds), **Supp. X:** 209

"Waiting between the Trees" (Tan), **Supp. X:** 290

"Waiting by the Gate" (Bryant), **Supp. I Part 1:** 171

Waiting for God (Weil), **I:** 298

Waiting for Godot (Beckett), **I:** 78, 91, 298; **Supp. IV Part 1:** 368–369

Waiting for Lefty (Odets), **Supp. I Part 1:** 277; **Supp. II Part 2:** 529, 530–533, 540; **Supp. V:** 109

Waiting for the End of the World (Bell), **Supp. X:** **4–5,** 11

"Waiting in a Rain Forest" (Wagoner), **Supp. IX:** 329

Waiting to Exhale (McMillan), **Supp. XIII:** 184, 185, **189–190,** 191

"Waiting to Freeze" (Banks), **Supp. V:** 5, 6

Waiting to Freeze: Poems (Banks), **Supp. V:** 6, 8

Waits, Tom, **Supp. VIII:** 12

Wait until Spring, Bandini (Fante), **Supp. XI:** 160, 161, 164, 165, **166–167**

Wait until Spring, Bandini (film), **Supp. XI:** 173

"Wake, The" (Dove), **Supp. IV Part 1:** 250

"Wakefield" (Hawthorne), **Retro. Supp. I:** 154, 159
Wakefield, Dan, **Supp. VIII:** 43
Wakefield, Richard, **Supp. IX:** 323
"Wake Island" (Rukeyser), **Supp. VI:** 273
Wakeman, Frederic, **Supp. IX:** 247
Wake Up and Live! (Brande), **Supp. I Part 2:** 608
Waking, The (Roethke), **III:** 541
"Waking Early Sunday Morning" (Lowell), **II:** 552; **Retro. Supp. II:** 190
"Waking in the Blue" (Lowell), **II:** 547; **Retro. Supp. II:** 180
"Waking in the Dark" (Rich), **Supp. I Part 2:** 559
"Waking Up the Rake" (Hogan), **Supp. IV Part 1:** 415–416, 416
Wakoski, Diane, **Supp. V:** 79; **Supp. XII:** 184
Walcott, Charles C., **II:** 49
Walcott, Derek, **Supp. VIII:** 28; **Supp. X:** 122, 131
Walcott, Jersey Joe, **Supp. V:** 182
Wald, Lillian, **Supp. I Part 1:** 12
Walden (Thoreau), **Supp. XIV:** 177, 227
Walden, Daniel, **Supp. IV Part 2:** 584, 591; **Supp. V:** 272
Walden; or, Life in the Woods (Thoreau), **I:** 219, 305; **II:** 8, 142, 159, 312–313, 458; **IV:** 168, 169, 170, 176, 177–178, 179–182, 183, 187; **Retro. Supp. I:** 62; **Supp. I Part 2:** 579, 655, 664, 672; **Supp. VIII:** 296; **Supp. X:** 27, 101; **Supp. XIII:** 152
Waldman, Anne, **Supp. XIV:** 150
Waldmeir, Joseph, **III:** 45
Waldmeir, Joseph J., **Supp. I Part 2:** 476
Waldo (Theroux), **Supp. VIII:** 313, 314, **314–315**
Waley, Arthur, **II:** 526; **III:** 466; **Supp. V:** 340
"Walk, A" (Snyder), **Supp. VIII:** 297
"Walk at Sunset, A" (Bryant), **Supp. I Part 1:** 155
"Walk before Mass, A" (Agee), **I:** 28–29
Walker, Alice, **Retro. Supp. I:** 215; **Supp. I Part 2:** 550; **Supp. III Part 2:** 488, **517–540; Supp. IV Part 1:** 14; **Supp. VIII:** 141, 214; **Supp. IX:** 306, 311; **Supp. X:** 85, 228, 252, 325, 330; **Supp. XIII:** 179, 185, 291, 295
Walker, Cheryl, **Supp. XI:** 145
Walker, David, **Supp. V:** 189

Walker, Franklin D., **III:** 321
Walker, Gue, **Supp. XII:** 207
Walker, Marianne, **Supp. VIII:** 139
Walker, Obadiah, **II:** 113
Walker in the City, A (Kazin), **Supp. VIII: 93–95,** 99
"Walking" (Hogan), **Supp. IV Part 1:** 416
"Walking" (Thoreau), **Supp. IV Part 1:** 416; **Supp. IX:** 178
"Walking Along in Winter" (Kenyon), **Supp. VII:** 167
"Walking around the Block with a Three-Year-Old" (Wagoner), **Supp. IX:** 331–332
"Walking Backwards into the Future" (R. Williams), **Supp. IX:** 146
Walking Down the Stairs: Selections from Interviews (Kinnell), **Supp. III Part 1:** 235, 249
"Walking Home at Night" (Ginsberg), **Supp. II Part 1:** 313
Walking Light (Dunn), **Supp. XI:** 140, 141, 153
"Walking Man of Rodin, The" (Sandburg), **III:** 583
"Walking Sticks and Paperweights and Water Marks" (Moore), **III:** 215
Walking Tall (Dunn), **Supp. XI:** 140
Walking the Black Cat (Simic), **Supp. VIII:** 280, **282–284**
Walking to Sleep (Wilbur), **Supp. III Part 2:** 557–560
"Walking to Sleep" (Wilbur), **Supp. III Part 2:** 544, 557, 559, 561, 562
Walkin' the Dog (Mosley), **Supp. XIII:** 242
"Walk in the Moonlight, A" (Anderson), **I:** 114
Walk on the Wild Side, A (Algren), **Supp. V:** 4; **Supp. IX:** 3, **12–13,** 14
"Walks in Rome" (Merrill), **Supp. III Part 1:** 337
Walk with Tom Jefferson, A (Levine), **Supp. V:** 179, 187, 190–191
"Wall, The" (Brooks), **Supp. III Part 1:** 70, 71, 84
Wall, The (Hersey), **IV:** 4
"Wall, The" (Roethke), **III:** 544
"Wall, The" (Sexton), **Supp. II Part 2:** 696
Wallace, David Foster, **Retro. Supp. II:** 279; **Supp. X:** 301–318
Wallace, Henry, **I:** 489; **III:** 111, 475; **Supp. I Part 1:** 286; **Supp. I Part 2:** 645
Wallace, Mike, **Supp. IV Part 1:** 364; **Supp. IV Part 2:** 526
Wallace Stevens (Kermode), **Retro. Supp. I:** 301

Wallace Stevens: The Poems of our Climate (Bloom), **Retro. Supp. I:** 299
Wallace Stevens: Words Chosen out of Desire (Stevens), **Retro. Supp. I:** 297
Wallach, Eli, **III:** 161
Wallas, Graham, **Supp. I Part 2:** 643
"Walled City" (Oates), **Supp. II Part 2:** 524
Wallenstein, Anna. *See* Weinstein, Mrs. Max (Anna Wallenstein)
Waller, Edmund, **III:** 463
Waller, Fats, **IV:** 263
Walling, William English, **Supp. I Part 2:** 645
Walls Do Not Fall, The (Doolittle), **Supp. I Part 1:** 271, 272
"Wall Songs" (Hogan), **Supp. IV Part 1:** 413
Wall Writing (Auster), **Supp. XII:** 23–24
Walpole, Horace, **I:** 203; **Supp. I Part 2:** 410, 714
Walpole, Hugh, **Retro. Supp. I:** 231
Walpole, Robert, **IV:** 145
Walsh, Ed, **II:** 424
Walsh, George, **Supp. IV Part 2:** 528
Walsh, Raoul, **Supp. XIII:** 174
Walsh, Richard J., **Supp. II Part 1:** 119, 130
Walsh, William, **Supp. IV Part 1:** 242, 243, 246, 248, 252, 254, 257
Walter Benjamin at the Dairy Queen: Reflections at Sixty and Beyond (McMurtry), **Supp. V:** 232
Walters, Barbara, **Supp. XIV:** 125
Walters, Marguerite. *See* Smith, Mrs. Lamar (Marguerite Walters)
"Walter T. Carriman" (O'Hara), **III:** 368
Walton, Izaak, **Supp. I Part 2:** 422
"Walt Whitman" (Masters), **Supp. I Part 2:** 458
"Walt Whitman at Bear Mountain" (Simpson), **Supp. IX:** 265
Walt Whitman Bathing (Wagoner), **Supp. IX: 331–332**
Walt Whitman Handbook (Allen), **IV:** 352
Walt Whitman Reconsidered (Chase), **IV:** 352
"Waltz, The" (Parker), **Supp. IX:** 204
"Waltzer in the House, The" (Kunitz), **Supp. III Part 1:** 258
Walzer, Kevin, **Supp. XII:** 202
Wambaugh, Joseph, **Supp. X:** 5
Wampeters, Foma, & Granfalloons (Vonnegut), **Supp. II Part 2:** 758, 759–760, 776, 779

Wand, David Hsin-fu, **Supp. X:** 292

"Wanderer, The" (W. C. Williams), **Retro. Supp. I:** 414, 421

"Wanderers, The" (Welty), **IV:** 273–274

"Wandering Jew, The" (Robinson), **III:** 505, 516–517

Wanderings of Oisin (Yeats), **Supp. I Part 1:** 79

Wang, Dorothy, **Supp. X:** 289

Waniek, Marilyn Nelson, **Supp. IV Part 1:** 244

"Wan Lee, the Pagan" (Harte), **Supp. II Part 1:** 351

"Want, The" (Olds), **Supp. X:** 210

Want Bone, The (Pinsky), **Supp. VI:** 236–237, 244–245, 247

"Wanted: An Ontological Critic" (Ransom), **III:** 498

"Wanting to Die" (Sexton), **Supp. II Part 2:** 684, 686; **Supp. XIV:** 132

"Wants" (Paley), **Supp. VI:** 219

Waples, Dorothy, **I:** 348

Wapshot Chronicle, The (Cheever), **Supp. I Part 1:** 174, 177–180, 181, 196

Wapshot Scandal, The (Cheever), **Supp. I Part 1:** 180–184, 187, 191, 196

"War" (Kingston), **Supp. V:** 169

"War" (Simic), **Supp. VIII:** 282

"War, Response, and Contradiction" (Burke), **I:** 283

War and Peace (Tolstoy), **I:** 6, 7; **II:** 191, 205, 291; **IV:** 446; **Supp. V:** 277; **Supp. XI:** 68; **Supp. XIV:** 97

War and War (F. Barthelme), **Supp. XI:** 25

"War Between Men and Women, The" (Thurber), **Supp. I Part 2:** 615

War Bulletins (Lindsay), **Supp. I Part 2:** 378–379

Ward, Aileen, **II:** 531

Ward, Artemus (pseudonym). *See* Browne, Charles Farrar

Ward, Douglas Turner, **Supp. IV Part 1:** 362

Ward, Henry, **Supp. I Part 2:** 588

Ward, Leo R., **Supp. VIII:** 124

Ward, Lester F., **Supp. I Part 2:** 640; **Supp. XI:** 202, 203

Ward, Lynn, **I:** 31

Ward, Mrs. Humphry, **II:** 338

Ward, Nathaniel, **Supp. I Part 1:** 99, 102, 111, 116

Ward, Theodora, **I:** 470; **Retro. Supp. I:** 28

Ward, William Hayes, **Supp. I Part 1:** 371

"War Debt, A" (Jewett), **Retro. Supp.**

II: 138, 141

"War Diary, A" (Bourne), **I:** 229

War Dispatches of Stephen Crane, The (Crane), **I:** 422

"Ward Line, The" (Morris), **III:** 220

Warfel, Harry R., **Supp. I Part 1:** 366

War Games (Morris), **III:** 238

War in Heaven, The (Shepard and Chaikin), **Supp. III Part 2:** 433

War Is Kind (Crane), **I:** 409; **III:** 585

"War Is Kind" (Crane), **I:** 419

Warlock (Harrison), **Supp. VIII:** 45, **46**

Warner, Charles Dudley, **II:** 405; **IV:** 198

Warner, Jack, **Supp. XII:** 160–161

Warner, John R., **III:** 193

Warner, Oliver, **I:** 548

Warner, Susan, **Retro. Supp. I:** 246

Warner, Sylvia Townsend, **Supp. VIII:** 151, 155, 164, 171

Warner, W. Lloyd, **III:** 60

"Warning" (Hughes), **Supp. I Part 1:** 343

"Warning" (Pound), **III:** 474

"Warning, The" (Creeley), **Supp. IV Part 1:** 150

"Warning, The" (Longfellow), **II:** 498

Warning Hill (Marquand), **III:** 55–56, 60, 68

"War of Eyes, A" (Coleman), **Supp. XI:** 93–94

War of Eyes and Other Stories, A (Coleman), **Supp. XI:** **91–92**

War of the Classes (London), **II:** 466

"War of the Wall, The" (Bambara), **Supp. XI:** 15–16

"War Poems" (Sandburg), **III:** 581

Warren, Austin, **I:** 265, 268, 271; **Supp. I Part 2:** 423

Warren, Earl, **III:** 581

Warren, Gabriel, **IV:** 244

Warren, Mrs. Robert Penn (Eleanor Clark), **IV:** 244

Warren, Robert Penn, **I:** 190, 211, 517; **II:** 57, 217, 228, 253; **III:** 134, 310, 382–383, 454, 482, 485, 490, 496, 497; **IV:** 121, 122, 123, 125, 126, **236–259,** 261, 262, 279, 340–341, 458; **Retro. Supp. I:** 40, 41, 73, 90; **Retro. Supp. II:** 220, 235; **Supp. I Part 1:** 359, 371; **Supp. I Part 2:** 386, 423; **Supp. II Part 1:** 139; **Supp. III Part 2:** 542; **Supp. V:** 261, 316, 318, 319, 333; **Supp. VIII:** 126, 176; **Supp. IX:** 257; **Supp. X:** 1, 25, 26; **Supp. XI:** 315; **Supp. XII:** 254, 255; **Supp. XIV:** 1, 2, 3, 4, 11, 14, 15

Warren, Rosanna, **IV:** 244

Warrington Poems, The (Ríos), **Supp. IV Part 2:** 540

Warrior, Robert Allen, **Supp. IV Part 1:** 329

"Warrior, The" (Gunn Allen), **Supp. IV Part 1:** 326

"Warrior: 5th Grade" (Olds), **Supp. X:** 214

"Warrior Road" (Harjo), **Supp. XII:** 217

Warshavsky, Isaac (pseudonym). *See* Singer, Isaac Bashevis

Warshow, Robert, **Supp. I Part 1:** 51

Wars I Have Seen (Stein), **IV:** 27, 36, 477

Wartime (Fussell), **Supp. V:** 241

"War Widow, The" (Frederic), **II:** 135–136

"Was" (Creeley), **Supp. IV Part 1:** 155

"Was" (Faulkner), **II:** 71

"Wash" (Faulkner), **II:** 72

Wash, Richard, **Supp. XII:** 14

"Washed in the Rain" (Fante), **Supp. XI:** 165

Washington, Booker T., **Supp. I Part 2:** 393; **Supp. II Part 1:** 157, 160, 167, 168, 171, 225; **Supp. XIV:** 198, 199, 201

Washington, D.C. (Vidal), **Supp. IV Part 2:** 677, 684, 686–687, 690

Washington, George, **I:** 453; **II:** 313–314; **Supp. I Part 2:** 399, 485, 508, 509, 511, 513, 517, 518, 520, 599

Washington Post Book World (Lesser), **Supp. IV Part 2:** 453; **Supp. VIII:** 80, 84, 241; **Supp. X:** 282

Washington Square (James), **II:** 327, 328; **Retro. Supp. I:** 215, 220, **222–223**

"Washington Square, 1946" (Ozick), **Supp. V:** 272

Washington Square Ensemble, The (Bell), **Supp. X:** 1, **3–4**

"Was Lowell an Historical Critic?" (Altick), **Supp. I Part 2:** 423

Wasserman, Earl R., **Supp. I Part 2:** 439, 440

Wasserman, Jakob, **Supp. I Part 2:** 669

Wasserstein, Wendy, **Supp. IV Part 1:** 309

Wasson, Ben, **Retro. Supp. I:** 79, 83

"Waste Carpet, The" (Matthews), **Supp. IX:** 158–159

Waste Land, The (Eliot), **I:** 107, 266, 298, 395, 396, 482, 570–571, 572, 574–575, 577–578, 580, 581, 584, 585, 586, 587; **III:** 6–8, 12, 196, 277–278, 453, 471, 492, 586; **IV:** 122, 123, 124, 140, 418, 419, 420;

Retro. Supp. I: 51, 60, **60–62**, 63, 64, 66, 210, 290, 291, 299, 311, 420, 427; **Retro. Supp. II:** 85, 121, 190; **Supp. I Part 1:** 272; **Supp. I Part 2:** 439, 455, 614; **Supp. II Part 1:** 4, 5, 11, 96; **Supp. III Part 1:** 9, 10, 41, 63, 105; **Supp. IV Part 1:** 47, 284; **Supp. V:** 338; **Supp. IX:** 158, 305; **Supp. X:** 125; **Supp. XIII:** 341–342, 344, 346; **Supp. XIV:** 6, 284

"Waste Land, The": A Facsimile and Transcript of the Original Drafts Including the Annotations of Ezra Pound (Eliot, ed.), **Retro. Supp. I:** 58

Watch and Ward (James), **II:** 323; **Retro. Supp. I:** 218, **219,** 220

"Watcher, The" (Bly), **Supp. IV Part 1:** 71

"Watcher by the Dead, A" (Bierce), **I:** 203

Watchfires (Auchincloss), **Supp. IV Part 1:** 23

"Watching Crow, Looking toward the Manzano Mountains" (Harjo), **Supp. XII:** 219

"Watching the Sunset" (Coleman), **Supp. XI:** 92

Watch on the Rhine (Hellman), **Supp. I Part 1:** 276, 278, 279–281, 283–284; **Supp. IV Part 1:** 83

"Water" (Emerson), **II:** 19

"Water" (Komunyakaa), **Supp. XIII:** 132

"Water" (Lowell), **II:** 550

"Waterbird" (Swenson), **Supp. IV Part 2:** 651

"Water Borders" (Dillard), **Supp. VI:** 27

"Water Buffalo" (Komunyakaa), **Supp. XIII:** 122

"Watercolor of Grantchester Meadows" (Plath), **Supp. I Part 2:** 537

"Waterfall, The" (Clampitt), **Supp. IX:** 44

Waterhouse, Keith, **Supp. VIII:** 124

"Waterlily Fire" (Rukeyser), **Supp. VI:** 285, 286

Waterlily Fire: Poems 1935–1962 (Rukeyser), **Supp. VI:** 274, 283, 285

Watermark (Brodsky), **Supp. VIII:** 29

Water-Method Man, The (Irving), **Supp. VI:** 163, **167–179,** 180

Water Music (Boyle), **Supp. VIII:** 1, 3–5, 8, 14

"Water Music for the Progress of Love in a Life-Raft Down the Sammamish Slough" (Wagoner), **Supp. IX:** 326

"Water People" (Burke), **Supp. XIV:** 21

"Water Picture" (Swenson), **Supp. IV Part 2:** 641

"Water Rising" (Hogan), **Supp. IV Part 1:** 400

Waters, Ethel, **II:** 587

Waters, Frank, **Supp. X:** 124

Waters, Muddy, **Supp. VIII:** 345

"Watershed" (Kingsolver), **Supp. VII:** 208

"Watershed" (Warren), **IV:** 239

"Watershed, The" (Auden), **Supp. II Part 1:** 5

Waters of Siloe, The (Merton), **Supp. VIII:** 196, 208

Waterston, Sam, **Supp. IX:** 253

Water Street (Merrill), **Supp. III Part 1:** 321–323

"Water Walker" (Wilbur), **Supp. III Part 2:** 548, 560

Water-Witch, The (Cooper), **I:** 342–343

Waterworks, The (Doctorow), **Supp. IV Part 1:** 218, 222, 223, 231–233, 234

"Water Works, The" (Doctorow), **Supp. IV Part 1:** 234

Watkin, E. I., **Retro. Supp. II:** 187

Watkins, Floyd C., **IV:** 452

Watkins, James T., **I:** 193, 194

Watkins, Mel, **Supp. X:** 330; **Supp. XIII:** 246

Watrous, Peter, **Supp. VIII:** 79

Watson, J. B., **II:** 361

Watson, James Sibley, Jr., **I:** 261

Watson, Richard, **Supp. I Part 2:** 516, 517

Watson, William, **II:** 114

Watt, Ian, **Supp. VIII:** 4

Watteau, Jean Antoine, **III:** 275; **IV:** 79

Watts, Emily Stipes, **Supp. I Part 1:** 115

Waugh, Evelyn, **I:** 480; **III:** 281; **Supp. I Part 2:** 607; **Supp. IV Part 2:** 688; **Supp. XI:** 305, 306

"Wave" (Snyder), **Supp. VIII:** 299

Wave, A (Ashbery), **Supp. III Part 1:** 1, 4, 24–26

"Wave, A" (Ashbery), **Supp. III Part 1:** 9, 19, 24–25

"Wave, The" (MacLeish), **III:** 19

"Waxwings" (Francis), **Supp. IX:** 82

Way, The (Steiner and Witt, eds.), **Supp. IV Part 2:** 505

"Way Down, The" (Kunitz), **Supp. III Part 1:** 263

"Way It Is, The" (Ellison), **Supp. II Part 1:** 245

"Way It Is, The" (Jones), **Supp. XI:** 229

Way It Is, The (Stafford), **Supp. XIII:** 274

"Way It Is, The" (Strand), **Supp. IV Part 2:** 627

Wayne, John, **Supp. IV Part 1:** 200

Way of Chuang-Tzu, The (Merton), **Supp. VIII:** 208

"Way of Exchange in James Dickey's Poetry, The" (Weatherby), **Supp. IV Part 1:** 175

Way Out, A (Frost), **Retro. Supp. I:** 133

Wayside Motor Inn, The (Gurney), **Supp. V:** 96, 105, 109

Ways of the Hour, The (Cooper), **I:** 354

Ways of White Folks, The (Hughes), **Retro. Supp. I:** 203, 204; **Supp. I Part 1:** 329, 330, 332

Way Some People Die, The (Macdonald), **Supp. IV Part 2:** 470, 471, 472, 474

Way Some People Live, The (Cheever), **Supp. I Part 1:** 175

"Way the Cards Fall, The" (Komunyakaa), **Supp. XIII:** 117

Way to Rainy Mountain, The (Momaday), **Supp. IV Part 2:** 485–486, 487–489, 491, 493

Way to Wealth, The (Franklin), **II:** 101–102, 110

Wayward and the Seeking, The: A Collection of Writings by Jean Toomer (Toomer), **Supp. III Part 2:** 478–481, 484, 487

Wayward Bus, The (Steinbeck), **IV:** 51, 64–65

"Way We Live Now, The" (Sontag), **Supp. III Part 2:** 467–468

"Way You'll Never Be, A" (Hemingway), **II:** 249

Weaks, Mary Louise, **Supp. X:** 5

Weales, Gerald, **II:** 602

"Wealth," from *Conduct of Life, The* (Emerson), **II:** 2, 3–4

"Wealth," from *English Traits* (Emerson), **II:** 6

Wealth of Nations, The (A. Smith), **II:** 109

"We Are Looking at You, Agnes" (Caldwell), **I:** 309

"We Are the Crazy Lady and Other Feisty Feminist Fables" (Ozick), **Supp. V:** 259

Weary Blues, The (Hughes), **Retro. Supp. I:** 195, 197, 198, 199, 200, 203, 205; **Supp. I Part 1:** 325

"Weary Blues, The" (Hughes), **Retro.**

Supp. I: 198, 199; **Supp. I Part 1:** 324, 325

"Weary Kingdom" (Irving), **Supp. VI:** 163

Weasels and Wisemen: Ethics and Ethnicity in the Work of David Mamet (Kane), **Supp. XIV:** 250

Weatherby, H. L., **Supp. IV Part 1:** 175

"Weathering Out" (Dove), **Supp. IV Part 1:** 248

Weaver, Harriet, **III:** 471

Weaver, Mike, **Retro. Supp. I:** 430

"Weaving" (Larcom), **Supp. XIII:** 142, **Supp. XIII:** 144–145, 150, 151

"Web" (Oliver), **Supp. VII:** 236

Web and the Rock, The (Wolfe), **IV:** 451, 455, 457, 459–460, 462, 464, 467, 468

Webb, Beatrice, **Supp. I Part 1:** 5

Webb, Mary, **I:** 226

Webb, Sidney, **Supp. I Part 1:** 5

Webb, W. P., **Supp. V:** 225

Weber, Brom, **I:** 383, 386

Weber, Carl, **Supp. IX:** 133, 138, 141

Weber, Max, **I:** 498; **Supp. I Part 2:** 637, 648

Weber, Sarah, **Supp. I Part 1:** 2

Web of Earth, The (Wolfe), **IV:** 451–452, 456, 458, 464, 465

"Web of Life, The" (Nemerov), **III:** 282

Webster, Daniel, **II:** 5, 9; **Supp. I Part 2:** 659, 687, 689, 690

Webster, John, **I:** 384; **Supp. I Part 2:** 422

Webster, Noah, **Supp. I Part 2:** 660; **Supp. II Part 1:** 77

Wector, Dixon, **II:** 103

"Wedding Cake" (Nye), **Supp. XIII:** 283

"Wedding in Brownsville, A" (Singer), **IV:** 15

Wedding in Hell, A (Simic), **Supp. VIII:** 280, **282**

"Wedding of the Rose and Lotus, The" (Lindsay), **Supp. I Part 2:** 387

"Wedding Toast, A" (Wilbur), **Supp. III Part 2:** 561

Wedekind, Frank, **III:** 398

Wedge, The (W. C. Williams), **Retro. Supp. I:** 424

"Wednesday at the Waldorf" (Swenson), **Supp. IV Part 2:** 647

"We Don't Live Here Anymore" (Dubus), **Supp. VII:** 78–79, 85

"Weed" (McCarriston), **Supp. XIV:** 259, 273

"Weed, The" (Bishop), **Supp. I Part 1:** 80, 88–89

"Weeds, The" (McCarthy), **II:** 566

"Weekend" (Beattie), **Supp. V:** 27

Weekend, The (Cameron), **Supp. XII:** 80, 81, **86–88**

"Weekend at Ellerslie, A" (Wilson), **IV:** 431

Weekend Edition (National Public Radio), **Supp. IX:** 299

Week on the Concord and Merrimack Rivers, A (Thoreau), **IV:** 168, 169, 177, 182–183; **Supp. I Part 2:** 420; **Supp. XIV:** 227

Weeks, Edward, **III:** 64

Weeks, Jerome, **Supp. VIII:** 76

"Weeping Burgher" (Stevens), **IV:** 77

"Weeping Women" (Levertov), **Supp. III Part 1:** 282

We Fly Away (Francis), **Supp. IX: 79– 80,** 84

We Have Always Lived in the Castle (Jackson), **Supp. IX:** 121, 126, **127– 128**

"We Have Our Arts So We Won't Die of Truth" (Bradbury), **Supp. IV Part 1:** 105

Weich, Dave, **Supp. XII:** 321

"Weight" (Wideman), **Supp. X:** 321

Weigl, Bruce, **Supp. VIII:** 269, 274

Weil, Robert, **Supp. IX:** 236

Weil, Simone, **I:** 298

Weiland (C. B. Brown), **Supp. XIII:** 100

Weinberger, Eliot, **Supp. IV Part 1:** 66; **Supp. VIII:** 290, 292

Weininger, Otto, **Retro. Supp. I:** 416

Weinreb, Mindy, **Supp. X:** 24

Weinreich, Regina, **Supp. XIV:** 22

Weinstein, Hinda, **IV:** 285

Weinstein, Max, **IV:** 285

Weinstein, Mrs. Max (Anna Wallenstein), **IV:** 285, 287

Weinstein, Nathan. *See* West, Nathanael

Weisheit, Rabbi, **IV:** 76

Weismuller, Johnny, **Supp. X:** 264

Weiss, Peter, **IV:** 117

Weiss, Theodore, **Supp. IV Part 2:** 440; **Supp. IX:** 96

Weist, Dianne, **Supp. X:** 80

Weithas, Art, **Supp. XI:** 231

Welch, James, **Supp. IV Part 1:** 404; **Supp. IV Part 2:** 503, 513, 557, 562

Welch, Lew, **Supp. V:** 170; **Supp. VIII:** 303

"Welcome from War" (Rukeyser), **Supp. VI:** 286

"Welcome Morning" (Sexton), **Supp. II Part 2:** 696

"Welcome the Wrath" (Kunitz), **Supp.**

III Part 1: 261

Welcome to Hard Times (Doctorow), **Supp. IV Part 1:** 218, 219–220, 222, 224, 230, 238

Welcome to Hard Times (film), **Supp. IV Part 1:** 236

Welcome to Our City (Wolfe), **IV:** 461

Welcome to the Monkey House (Vonnegut), **Supp. II Part 2:** 758

Welcome to the Moon (Shanley), **Supp. XIV:** 318

Welcome to the Moon and Other Plays (Shanley), **Supp. XIV:** 315, **316– 319**

Weld, Theodore, **Supp. I Part 2:** 587, 588

Weld, Tuesday, **Supp. XI:** 306

Welded (O'Neill), **III:** 390

"Well, The" (Momaday), **Supp. IV Part 2:** 483

"Well Dressed Man with a Beard, The" (Stevens), **Retro. Supp. I:** 297

Wellek, René, **I:** 253, 261, 282; **II:** 320; **Supp. XIV:** 12, 14

Weller, George, **III:** 322

Welles, Gideon, **Supp. I Part 2:** 484

Welles, Orson, **IV:** 476; **Supp. I Part 1:** 67; **Supp. IV Part 1:** 82, 83; **Supp. V:** 251; **Supp. VIII:** 46; **Supp. XI:** 169, 307

"Wellfleet Whale, The" (Kunitz), **Supp. III Part 1:** 263, 269

Wellfleet Whale and Companion Poems, The (Kunitz), **Supp. III Part 1:** 263

Wellman, Flora, **II:** 463–464, 465

"Well Rising, The" (Stafford), **Supp. XI:** 318

Wells, H. G., **I:** 103, 226, 241, 243, 253, 405, 409, 415; **II:** 82, 144, 276, 337, 338, 458; **III:** 456; **IV:** 340, 455; **Retro. Supp. I:** 100, 228, 231

Wellspring, The (Olds), **Supp. X: 211– 212**

Well Wrought Urn, The: Studies in the Structure of Poetry (Brooks), **Supp. XIV:** 1, **8–9,** 14, 15, 16

Welsh, Mary. *See* Hemingway, Mrs. Ernest (Mary Welsh)

Welty, Eudora, **II:** 194, 217, 606; **IV: 260–284; Retro. Supp. I:** 339–358; **Retro. Supp. II:** 235; **Supp. IV Part 2:** 474; **Supp. V:** 59, 315, 336; **Supp. VIII:** 94, 151, 171; **Supp. X:** 42, 290; **Supp. XII:** 310, 322; **Supp. XIV:** 3

"We miss Her, not because We see—" (Dickinson), **Retro. Supp. I:** 46

We Must Dance My Darlings (Trilling), **Supp. I Part 1:** 297

Wendell, Barrett, **III:** 507; **Supp. I Part 2:** 414; **Supp. XIV:** 197

Wendell, Sarah. *See* Holmes, Mrs. Abiel (Sarah Wendell)

Wept of Wish-ton-Wish, The (Cooper), **I:** 339, 342, 350

Werbe, Peter, **Supp. XIII:** 236

"We Real Cool" (Brooks), **Supp. III Part 1:** 80

We're Back! A Dinosaur's Story (screenplay, Shanley), **Supp. XIV:** 316

"We're Friends Again" (O'Hara), **III:** 372–373

"Were the Whole Realm of Nature Mine" (Watts), **I:** 458

Werewolves in Their Youth (Chabon), **Supp. XI:** 66, **76–77**

Werlock, Abby, **Supp. XIII:** 293

Werthman, Michael, **Supp. V:** 115

"Wer-Trout, The" (Proulx), **Supp. VII:** 255–256

Wescott, Glenway, **I:** 288; **II:** 85; **III:** 448, 454; **Supp. VIII:** 156; **Supp. XIV:** 342

"We Shall All Be Born Again But We Shall Not All Be Saved" (Matthews), **Supp. IX:** 162

West, Anthony, **Supp. IV Part 1:** 284

West, Benjamin, **Supp. I Part 2:** 511

West, Dorothy, **Supp. XIII:** 295

West, James, **II:** 562

West, Nathanael, **I:** 97, 107, 190, 211, 298; **II:** 436; **III:** 357, 425; **IV:** **285–307**; **Retro. Supp. II: 321–341; Supp. IV Part 1:** 203; **Supp. VIII:** 97; **Supp. XI:** 85, 105, 159, 296; **Supp. XII:** 173, 310; **Supp. XIII:** 106, 170

West, Rebecca, **II:** 412, 445

Westall, Julia Elizabeth. *See* Wolfe, Mrs. William Oliver (Julia Elizabeth Westall)

"We Stand United" (Benét), **Supp. XI:** 46

"West Authentic, The: Willa Cather" (Stegner), **Supp. IV Part 2:** 608

"West Coast, The: Region with a View" (Stegner), **Supp. IV Part 2:** 608–609

Westcott, Edward N., **II:** 102

"Western Association of Writers" (Chopin), **Supp. I Part 1:** 217

"Western Ballad, A" (Ginsberg), **Supp. II Part 1:** 311

Western Borders, The (Howe), **Supp. IV Part 2:** 424–425

Western Canon: The Books and Schools of the Ages (Bloom), **Supp. IX:** 146

Western Lands, The (Burroughs), **Supp.**

III Part 1: 106

Western Star (Benét), **Supp. XI:** 46, 47, 57

"West Marginal Way" (Hugo), **Supp. VI:** 131, 135

West of Yesterday, East of Summer: New and Selected Poems, 1973–1993 (Monette), **Supp. X:** 159

West of Your City (Stafford), **Supp. XI:** 316, **317–318**, 321, 322

Weston, Jessie L., **II:** 540; **III:** 12; **Supp. I Part 2:** 438

"West Real" (Ríos), **Supp. IV Part 2:** 539, 540

"West-running Brook" (Frost), **II:** 150, 162–164

West-running Brook (Frost), **II:** 155; **Retro. Supp. I:** 136, 137

"West Wall" (Merwin), **Supp. III Part 1:** 355

"Westward Beach, A" (Jeffers), **Supp. II Part 2:** 418

Westward Ho (Harrison), **Supp. VIII:** 51, **52**

Westward the Course of Empire (Leutze), **Supp. X:** 307

"Westward the Course of Empire Takes Its Way" (Wallace), **Supp. X: 307–308**

"West Wind" (Oliver), **Supp. VII:** 246

West Wind: Poems and Prose Poems (Oliver), **Supp. VII:** 243, 246–248

"West Wind, The" (Bryant), **Supp. I Part 1:** 155

"Wet Casements" (Ashbery), **Supp. III Part 1:** 18–20

We the Living (film), **Supp. IV Part 2:** 520

We the Living (Rand), **Supp. IV Part 2:** 520–521

Wet Parade (Sinclair), **Supp. V:** 289

"We've Adjusted Too Well" (O'Brien), **Supp. V:** 247

Wevill, David, **Retro. Supp. II:** 247, 249

"We Wear the Mask" (Dunbar), **Supp. II Part 1:** 199, 207, 209–210

Weybright, Victor, **Supp. XIII:** 172

Weyden, Rogier van der, **Supp. IV Part 1:** 284

Whalen, Marcella, **Supp. I Part 1:** 49

Whalen, Philip, **Supp. VIII:** 289

Whalen-Bridge, John, **Retro. Supp. II:** 211–212

Wharton, Edith, **I:** 12, 375; **II:** 96, 180, 183, 186, 189–190, 193, 283, 338, 444, 451; **III:** 69, 175, 576; **IV:** 8, 53, 58, **308–330; Retro. Supp. I:** 108, 232, **359–385; Supp. IV Part 1:** 23, 31, 35, 36, 80, 81, 310; **Supp.**

IX: 57; **Supp. XII:** 308; **Supp. XIV:** 337, 347

Wharton, Edward Robbins, **IV:** 310, 313–314, 319

"What" (Dunn), **Supp. XI:** 144

What a Kingdom It Was (Kinnell), **Supp. III Part 1:** 235, 238, 239

"What America Would Be Like without Blacks" (Ellison), **Retro. Supp. II:** 123

What Are Masterpieces (Stein), **IV:** 30–31

What Are Years (Moore), **III:** 208–209, 210, 215

"What Are Years?" (Moore), **III:** 211, 213

What a Way to Go (Morris), **III:** 230–232

"What Became of the Flappers?" (Zelda Fitzgerald), **Supp. IX:** 71

"What Can I Tell My Bones?" (Roethke), **III:** 546, 549

"What Do We Have Here" (Carson), **Supp. XII: 101**

"What Do We See" (Rukeyser), **Supp. VI:** 282

What Do Women Want? Bread Roses Sex Power (Jong), **Supp. V:** 115, 117, 129, 130

"What Do You Do in San Francisco?" (Carver), **Supp. III Part 1:** 143

Whatever Happened to Gloomy Gus of the Chicago Bears? (Coover), **Supp. V:** 51, 52

Whatever Happened to Jacy Farrow? (Cleveland), **Supp. V:** 222

"What Every Boy Should Know" (Maxwell), **Supp. VIII:** 169

"What Feels Like the World" (Bausch), **Supp. VII:** 46

"What God Is Like to Him I Serve" (Bradstreet), **Supp. I Part 1:** 106–107

"What Happened Here Before" (Snyder), **Supp. VIII:** 302

What Have I Ever Lost by Dying? (Bly), **Supp. IV Part 1:** 71–72

What Have You Lost? (Nye, ed.), **Supp. XIII:** 280

"What I Believe" (Mumford), **Supp. II Part 2:** 479

"What I Call What They Call Onanism" (Goldbarth), **Supp. XII:** 175

What I Did Last Summer (Gurney), **Supp. V:** 96, 100, 107, 108

"What if God" (Olds), **Supp. X:** 208

"What I Have to Defend, What I Can't Bear Losing" (Stern), **Supp. IX:** 286, 287, 288, 298

"What I Know about Being a Playwright" (McNally), **Supp. XIII:** 195, 207

"What I Mean" (Ortiz), **Supp. IV Part 2:** 497

"What Is an Emotion" (James), **II:** 350

What Is Art? (Tolstoy), **I:** 58

"What Is Civilization? Africa's Answer" (Du Bois), **Supp. II Part 1:** 176

"What Is College For?" (Bourne), **I:** 216

"What Is Exploitation?" (Bourne), **I:** 216

"What Is It?" (Carver), **Supp. III Part 1:** 139

What Is Man? (Twain), **II:** 434; **IV:** 209

"What Is Poetry" (Ashbery), **Supp. III Part 1:** 19

"What Is Seized" (Moore), **Supp. X:** 164, 168, 169, 172, 175

"What Is the Earth?" (Olds), **Supp. X:** 213

"What Is This Poet" (Stern), **Supp. IX:** 295

"What I Think" (Hogan), **Supp. IV Part 1:** 406

What Maisie Knew (James), **II:** 332; **Retro. Supp. I:** 229, **230**

What Makes Sammy Run? (Schulberg), **Supp. XIII:** 170

What Moon Drove Me to This? (Harjo), **Supp. XII: 218–220**

"What Must" (MacLeish), **III:** 18

"What Sally Said" (Cisneros), **Supp. VII:** 63

"What's Happening in America" (Sontag), **Supp. III Part 2:** 460–461

"What's in Alaska?" (Carver), **Supp. III Part 1:** 141, 143

What's New, Pussycat? (Allen; film), **Supp. XI:** 307

"What's New in American and Canadian Poetry" (Bly), **Supp. IV Part 1:** 67

What's O'Clock (Lowell), **II:** 511, 527, 528

"What the Arts Need Now" (Baraka), **Supp. II Part 1:** 47

"What the Brand New Freeway Won't Go By" (Hugo), **Supp. VI:** 132–133

"What the Gypsies Told My Grandmother While She Was Still a Young Girl" (Simic), **Supp. VIII:** 283

"What the Prose Poem Carries with It" (Bly), **Supp. IV Part 1:** 64

"What They Wanted" (Dunn), **Supp. XI:** 151

What Thou Lovest Well (Hugo), **Supp.**

VI: 140, 141

"What Thou Lovest Well Remains American" (Hugo), **Supp. VI:** 140, 141

What Time Collects (Farrell), **II:** 46, 47–48

What to Do? (Chernyshevsky), **Retro. Supp. I:** 269

What Use Are Flowers? (Hansberry), **Supp. IV Part 1:** 359, 368–369, 374

What Was Literature? (Fiedler), **Supp. XIII:** 96–97, **105–106**

What Was Mine (Beattie), **Supp. V:** 33, 35

What Was the Relationship of the Lone Ranger to the Means of Production? (Baraka), **Supp. II Part 1:** 58

"What We Came Through" (Goldbarth), **Supp. XII:** 179–180

What We Talk About When We Talk About Love (Carver), **Supp. III Part 1:** 142–146

What We Talk about When We Talk about Love (Carver), **Supp. XII:** 139

"What Why When How Who" (Pinsky), **Supp. VI:** 244

What Will Suffice: Contemporary American Poets on the Art of Poetry (Buckley and Young, eds.), **Supp. XIII:** 313

What Work Is (Levine), **Supp. V:** 181, 187, 192–193

"What You Hear from 'Em" (Taylor), **Supp. V:** 314, 320, 324

"What You Want" (O. Henry), **Supp. II Part 1:** 402

Wheatly, Phyllis, **Supp. XIII:** 111

Wheeler, John, **II:** 433

Wheelock, John Hall, **IV:** 461; **Supp. IX:** 268; **Supp. XIV:** 120

Wheel of Life, The (Glasgow), **II:** 176, 178, 179, 183

"When" (Olds), **Supp. X:** 207

When Boyhood Dreams Come True (Farrell), **II:** 45

"When Death Came April Twelve 1945" (Sandburg), **III:** 591, 593

"When Death Comes" (Oliver), **Supp. VII:** 241

"When De Co'n Pone's Hot" (Dunbar), **Supp. II Part 1:** 202–203

"When Grandma Died—1942" (Shields), **Supp. VII:** 311

"When I Buy Pictures" (Moore), **III:** 205

"When I Came from Colchis" (Merwin), **Supp. III Part 1:** 343

"When I Left Business for Literature" (Anderson), **I:** 101

"When in Rome—Apologia" (Komunyakaa), **Supp. XIII:** 120

"When It Comes" (Olds), **Supp. X:** 213

"When I Was Seventeen" (Kincaid), **Supp. VII:** 181

When Knighthood Was in Flower (Major), **III:** 320

"[When] Let by rain" (Taylor), **IV:** 160–161

"When Lilacs Last in the Dooryard Bloom'd" (Whitman), **IV:** 347–348, 351; **Retro. Supp. I:** 406; **Supp. IV Part 1:** 16

"When Malindy Sings" (Dunbar), **Supp. II Part 1:** 200, 204–205

When Peoples Meet: A Study of Race and Culture (Locke and Stern), **Supp. XIV:** 202, 213

When She Was Good (Roth), **Retro. Supp. II:** 282, 283, 284; **Supp. III Part 2:** 403, 405, 410–413

"When Sue Wears Red" (Hughes), **Retro. Supp. I:** 195, 204

"When the Dead Ask My Father about Me" (Olds), **Supp. X:** 210

"When the Frost Is on the Punkin" (Riley), **Supp. II Part 1:** 202

When the Jack Hollers (Hughes), **Retro. Supp. I:** 203; **Supp. I Part 1:** 328

"When the Light Gets Green" (Warren), **IV:** 252

"When the Peace Corps Was Young" (Theroux), **Supp. VIII:** 314

"When the World Ended as We Knew It" (Harjo), **Supp. XII:** 231

When Time Was Born (Farrell), **II:** 46, 47

"When We Dead Awaken: Writing as Re-Vision" (Rich), **Supp. I Part 2:** 552–553, 560

"When We Gonna Rise" (Baraka), **Supp. II Part 1:** 48

"When We Have To" (Salinas), **Supp. XIII:** 322–323

"WHEN WE'LL WORSHIP JESUS" (Baraka), **Supp. II Part 1:** 54

"When Women Throw Down Bundles: Strong Women Make Strong Nations" (Gunn Allen), **Supp. IV Part 1:** 328

"'When You Finally See Them': The Unconquered Eye in *To Kill a Mockingbird*" (Champion), **Supp. VIII:** 128

"When You Lie Down, the Sea Stands Up" (Swenson), **Supp. IV Part 2:** 643

Where Does One Go When There's No

Place Left to Go? (Crews), **Supp. XI:** 103

"Where I Come from Is Like This" (Gunn Allen), **Supp. IV Part 1:** 319

"Where I'm Calling From" (Carver), **Supp. III Part 1:** 145

Where I'm Calling From: New and Selected Stories (Carver), **Supp. III Part 1:** 138, 148

"Where I Ought to Be" (Erdrich), **Supp. IV Part 1:** 265

Where Is My Wandering Boy Tonight? (Wagoner), **Supp. IX:** 335–336

"Where Is the Island?" (Francis), **Supp. IX:** 78

"Where Is the Voice Coming From?" (Welty), **IV:** 280; **Retro. Supp. I:** 355

Where Joy Resides (Isherwood), **Supp. XIV:** 156

"Where Knock Is Open Wide" (Roethke), **III:** 533–535

"Where My Sympathy Lies" (H. Roth), **Supp. IX:** 234

Where's My Money? (Shanley), **Supp. XIV:** 316, 328, **330–331**

Where the Bluebird Sings to the Lemonade Springs (Stegner), **Supp. IV Part 2:** 596, 597, 598, 600, 604, 606, 613

Where the Cross Is Made (O'Neill), **III:** 388, 391

"Where the Soft Air Lives" (Nye), **Supp. XIII:** 275

Where the Twilight Never Ends (Haines), **Supp. XII:** 211

Where the Wild Things Are (Sendak), **Supp. IX:** 207

"Wherever Home Is" (Wright), **Supp. III Part 2:** 605, 606

Where Water Comes Together With Other Water (Carver), **Supp. III Part 1:** 147, 148

"Where We Crashed" (Hugo), **Supp. VI:** 138

"Where You Are" (Doty), **Supp. XI:** 131

Where You'll Find Me, and Other Stories (Beattie), **Supp. V:** 30–31

Whicher, Stephen, **II:** 20

"Which Is More Than I Can Say for Some People" (Moore), **Supp. X:** 177, 178

Which Ones Are the Enemy? (Garrett), **Supp. VII:** 98

"Which Theatre Is the Absurd One?" (Albee), **I:** 71

"Which Way to the Future?" (Rehder), **Supp. IV Part 1:** 69

While I Was Gone (Miller), **Supp. XII:** 290, **301–303**

"While Seated in a Plane" (Swenson), **Supp. IV Part 2:** 645

Whilomville Stories (Crane), **I:** 414

"Whip, The" (Robinson), **III:** 513

Whipple, Thomas K., **II:** 456, 458; **IV:** 427

"Whippoorwill, The" (Francis), **Supp. IX:** 90

"Whip-poor-will, The" (Thurber), **Supp. I Part 2:** 616

"Whispering Gallery, The" (Komunyakaa), **Supp. XIII:** 132

"Whispering Leaves" (Glasgow), **II:** 190

Whispering to Fool the Wind (Ríos), **Supp. IV Part 2:** 540–541, 544, 545

"Whispers in the Next Room" (Simic), **Supp. VIII:** 278

"Whispers of Heavenly Death" (Whitman), **IV:** 348

"Whispers of Immortality" (Eliot), **Supp. XI:** 242

Whistle (Jones), **Supp. XI:** 219, 224, **231–234**

"Whistle, The" (Franklin), **II:** 121

"Whistle, The" (Komunyakaa), **Supp. XIII:** 111, 126

"Whistle, The" (Welty), **IV:** 262

Whistler, James, **I:** 484; **III:** 461, 465, 466; **IV:** 77, 369

Whistler, James Abbott McNeill, **Supp. XIV:** 335–336

"Whistling Dick's Christmas Stocking" (O. Henry), **Supp. II Part 1:** 390, 392

Whistling in the Dark (Garrett), **Supp. VII:** 111

Whistling in the Dark: True Stories and Other Fables (Garrett), **Supp. VII:** 95

Whitcher, Frances Miriam Berry, **Supp. XIII:** 152

"White" (Simic), **Supp. VIII: 275–276**

White, Barbara, **Retro. Supp. I:** 379

White, E. B., **Retro. Supp. I:** 335; **Supp. I Part 2:** 602, 607, 608, 612, 619, 620, **651–681; Supp. II Part 1:** 143; **Supp. VIII:** 171; **Supp. IX:** 20, 32

White, Elizabeth Wade, **Supp. I Part 1:** 100, 103, 111

White, Henry Kirke, **Supp. I Part 1:** 150

White, James L., **Supp. XI:** 123

White, Joel, **Supp. I Part 2:** 654, 678

White, Katharine. (Katharine Sergeant Angell), **Supp. I Part 2:** 610, 653, 655, 656, 669; **Supp. VIII:** 151, 171

White, Lillian, **Supp. I Part 2:** 651

White, Lucia, **I:** 258

White, Maria. *See* Lowell, Mrs. James Russell (Maria White)

White, Morton, **I:** 258; **Supp. I Part 2:** 647, 648, 650

White, Roberta, **Supp. XII:** 293

White, Stanford, **Supp. IV Part 1:** 223

White, Stanley, **Supp. I Part 2:** 651, 655

White, T. H., **III:** 522

White, T. W., **III:** 411, 415

White, Walter, **Supp. I Part 1:** 345

White, William, **Retro. Supp. II:** 326

White, William A., **I:** 252

White Album, The (Didion), **Supp. IV Part 1:** 198, 202, 205–207, 210

"White Album, The" (Didion), **Supp. IV Part 1:** 205, 206

White Buildings (H. Crane), **I:** 385, 386, 390–395, 400; **Retro. Supp. II:** 77–78, **80–81,** 82, 83, 85

White Butterfly (Mosley), **Supp. XIII:** 237, 238, 240

White Center (Hugo), **Supp. VI:** 144–145

"White Center" (Hugo), **Supp. VI:** 144, 146

Whited, Stephen, **Supp. XI:** 135

White Deer, The (Thurber), **Supp. I Part 2:** 606

White Doves at Morning (Burke), **Supp. XIV:** 22–23, 32, 35–36

"White Eagle, The" (Chopin), **Retro. Supp. II:** 72

White Fang (London), **II:** 471–472, 481

Whitefield, George, **I:** 546

White-Footed Deer and Other Poems (Bryant), **Supp. I Part 1:** 157

White Goddess, The (Graves), **Supp. IV Part 1:** 280

White-Haired Lover (Shapiro), **Supp. II Part 2:** 703, 717

Whitehead, Alfred North, **III:** 605, 619, 620; **IV:** 88; **Supp. I Part 2:** 554, 647

Whitehead, Colson, **Supp. XIII:** 233, 241

Whitehead, Margaret, **IV:** 114, 115, 116

Whitehead, Mrs. Catherine, **IV:** 116

White Heat (Walsh), **Supp. XIII:** 174

"White Heron, A" (Jewett), **II:** 409; **Retro. Supp. II:** 17

White Heron and Other Stories, A (Jewett), **II:** 396

White Horses (Hoffman), **Supp. X: 83–85,** 90, 92

White House Diary, A (Lady Bird Johnson), **Supp. IV Part 1:** 22

White Jacket; or, The World in a Man-of-War (Melville), **III:** 80, 81, 84, 94; **Retro Supp. I:** 248, 249, 254

White Lantern, The (Connell), **Supp. XIV:** 97

"White Lights, The" (Robinson), **III:** 524

"White Lilies, The" (Glück), **Supp. V:** 88

White Man, Listen! (Wright), **IV:** 478, 488, 489, 494

"White Mulberry Tree, The" (Cather), **I:** 319; **Retro. Supp. I:** 7, 9, 17

White Mule (W. C. Williams), **Retro. Supp. I:** 423

"White Negro, The" (Mailer), **III:** 36–37; **Retro. Supp. II:** 202

"Whiteness of the Whale, The" (Melville), **III:** 84, 86

"White Night" (Oliver), **Supp. VII:** 236

"White Nights" (Auster), **Supp. XII:** 23–24

White Noise (DeLillo), **Supp. VI:** 1, 3–4, 5–7, 10, 11–12, 16

White Oxen and Other Stories, The (Burke), **I:** 269, 271

White Paper on Contemporary American Poetry (McClatchy), **Supp. XII:** 253, **259–260**

"White Pine" (Oliver), **Supp. VII:** 244

White Pine: Poems and Prose Poems (Oliver), **Supp. VII:** 243–246

"White Silence, The" (London), **II:** 468

"White Silk" (Nye), **Supp. XIII:** 275

"White Snake, The" (Sexton), **Supp. II Part 2:** 691

"White Spot" (Anderson), **I:** 116

"White-Tailed Hornet, The" (Frost), **Retro. Supp. I:** 138

Whitfield, Raoul, **Supp. IV Part 1:** 345

Whitlock, Brand, **II:** 276

Whitman (Masters), **Supp. I Part 2:** 473, 475, 476

Whitman, George, **IV:** 346, 350

Whitman, Sarah Wyman, **Retro. Supp. II:** 136

"Whitman: The Poet and the Mask" (Cowley), **Supp. II Part 1:** 143

Whitman, Walt, **I:** 61, 68, 98, 103, 104, 109, 219, 220, 227, 228, 242, 246, 250, 251, 260, 261, 285, 381, 384, 386, 396, 397, 398, 402, 419, 430, 459, 460, 483, 485, 486, 577; **II:** 7, 8, 18, 127, 140, 273–274, 275, 289, 295, 301, 320, 321, 373, 445, 446, 451, 457, 494, 529, 530, 552; **III:** 171, 175, 177, 181–182, 189, 203, 234, 260, 426, 430, 453, 454, 461, 505, 507–508, 511, 528, 548, 552, 555, 559, 567, 572, 576, 577, 579, 584, 585, 595, 606, 609; **IV:** 74, 169, 191, 192, 202, **331–354**, 405, 409, 416, 444, 450–451, 457, 463, 464, 469, 470, 471; **Retro. Supp. I:** 8, 52, 194, 254, 283, 284, 333, **387–410**, 412, 417, 427; **Retro. Supp. II:** 40, 76, 93, 99, 155, 156, 158, 170, 262; **Supp. I Part 1:** 6, 79, 167, 311, 314, 325, 365, 368, 372; **Supp. I Part 2:** 374, 384, 385, 387, 389, 391, 393, 399, 416, 436, 455, 456, 458, 473, 474, 475, 525, 540, 579, 580, 582, 682, 691; **Supp. III Part 1:** 6, 20, 156, 239–241, 253, 340; **Supp. III Part 2:** 596; **Supp. IV Part 1:** 16, 169, 325; **Supp. IV Part 2:** 597, 625; **Supp. V:** 113, 118, 122, 130, 170, 178, 183, 277, 279, 332; **Supp. VIII:** 42, 95, 105, 126, 198, 202, 269; **Supp. IX:** 8, 9, 15, 38, 41, 44, 48, 53, 131, 292, 298, 299, 308, 320; **Supp. X:** 36, 112, 203, 204; **Supp. XI:** 83, 123, 132, 135, 203, 321; **Supp. XII:** 132, 185, 190, 256; **Supp. XIII:** 1, 77, 115, 153, 221, 304, 335; **Supp. XIV:** 89, 312, 334, 335, 338

Whitmarsh, Jason, **Supp. VIII:** 283

Whitmer, Peter, **Supp. X:** 264, 265

Whitney, Blair, **Supp. I Part 2:** 403

Whitney, Josiah, **Supp. IX:** 180, 181

Whitt, Margaret Earley, **Retro. Supp. II:** 226

Whittemore, Reed, **III:** 268; **Supp. XI:** 315

Whittier, Elizabeth, **Supp. I Part 2:** 700, 701, 703; **Supp. XIII:** 141, 142

Whittier, John Greenleaf, **I:** 216; **II:** 275; **III:** 52; **Retro. Supp. I:** 54; **Retro. Supp. II:** 155, 163, 169; **Supp. I Part 1:** 168, 299, 313, 317, 372; **Supp. I Part 2:** 420, 602, **682–707**; **Supp. VIII:** 202, 204; **Supp. XI:** 50; **Supp. XIII:** 140, 145

Whittier, Mary, **Supp. I Part 2:** 683

"Whittier Birthday Speech" (Twain), **Supp. I Part 1:** 313

"Who" (Kenyon), **Supp. VII:** 174

"Who Am I—Who I Am" (Corso), **Supp. XII:** 134

"Who Be Kind To" (Ginsberg), **Supp. II Part 1:** 323

"Whoever Was Using This Bed" (Carver), **Supp. III Part 1:** 148

"Whoever You Are Holding Me Now in Hand" (Whitman), **IV:** 342; **Retro. Supp. I:** 52

Who Gathered and Whispered behind Me (Goldbarth), **Supp. XII:** 181, 182

"Who in One Lifetime" (Rukeyser), **Supp. VI:** 276, 279

"Who Is Your Mother? Red Roots of White Feminism" (Gunn Allen), **Supp. IV Part 1:** 329

Whole Hog (Wagoner), **Supp. IX:** 337–338

"Whole Mess...Almost, The" (Corso), **Supp. XII:** 135

"Whole Moisty Night, The" (Bly), **Supp. IV Part 1:** 69

Whole New Life, A (Price), **Supp. VI:** 265, **266**, 267

"Whole Self, The" (Nye), **Supp. XIII:** 275

"Whole Soul, The" (Levine), **Supp. V:** 192

"Whole Story, The" (Strand), **Supp. IV Part 2:** 622

"Whole World Knows, The" (Welty), **IV:** 272; **Retro. Supp. I:** 343

Who'll Stop the Rain (film), **Supp. V:** 301

Who Lost an American? (Algren), **Supp. IX: 15–16**

Who Owns America? (symposium), **Supp. XIV:** 4

"Who Puts Together" (Hogan), **Supp. IV Part 1:** 403, 405, 412–413

Who's Afraid of Virginia Woolf? (Albee), **I:** 71, 77–81, 83, 85, 86, 87, 94; **IV:** 230

Who Shall Be the Sun? Poems Based on the Lore, Legends, and Myths of the Northwest Coast and Plateau Indians (Wagoner), **Supp. IX:** 328, **329–330**, 337

"Whosis Kid, The" (Hammett), **Supp. IV Part 1:** 344

"Who's Passing for Who?" (Hughes), **Supp. I Part 1:** 330

Who Will Run the Frog Hospital?: A Novel (Moore), **Supp. X:** 163, 165, 169, **175–177**

Why Are We in Vietnam? (Mailer), **III:** 27, 29, 30, 33, 34–35, 39, 42, 44; **Retro. Supp. II:** 205–206

"Why Did the Balinese Chicken Cross the Road?" (Walker), **Supp. III Part 2:** 527

"Why Do the Heathens Rage?" (O'Connor), **III:** 351

"Why Do You Write About Russia?" (Simpson), **Supp. IX:** 277

"Why I Am a Danger to the Public" (Kingsolver), **Supp. VII:** 204

Why I Am Not a Christian (Russell),

Supp. I Part 2: 522

"Why I Entered the Gurdjieff Work" (Toomer), **Supp. III Part 2:** 481

"Why I Like Laurel" (Patchett), **Supp. XII:** 309

"Why I Live at the P.O." (Welty), **IV:** 262; **Retro. Supp. I:** 345

"Why Is Economics Not an Evolutionary Science?" (Veblen), **Supp. I Part 2:** 634

"Why I Write" (Didion), **Supp. IV Part 1:** 201, 203

"Why Negro Women Leave Home" (Brooks), **Supp. III Part 1:** 75

"Why the Little Frenchman Wears His Hand in a Sling" (Poe), **III:** 425

Why We Behave Like Microbe Hunters (Thurber), **Supp. I Part 2:** 606

Why We Were in Vietnam (Podhoretz), **Supp. VIII:** 241

"Why Write?" (Updike), **Retro. Supp. I:** 317

"Wichita Vortex Sutra" (Ginsberg), **Supp. II Part 1:** 319, 321, 323–325, 327

Wickes, George, **Supp. XIV:** 165

Wickford Point (Marquand), **III:** 50, 58, 64–65, 69

Wicks, Robert Russell, **Supp. XII:** 49

"Wide Empty Landscape with a Death in the Foreground" (Momaday), **Supp. IV Part 2:** 492

Wideman, John Edgar, **Retro. Supp. II:** 123; **Supp. X:** 239, 250, **319–336**; **Supp. XI:** 245; **Supp. XIII:** 247

"Wide Net, The" (Welty), **IV:** 266

Wide Net and Other Stories, The (Welty), **IV:** 261, 264–266, 271; **Retro. Supp. I: 347–349,** 352, 355

Widening Spell of the Leaves, The (Levis), **Supp. XI:** 258, 259, 261, **268–269,** 271

"Wide Prospect, The" (Jarrell), **II:** 376–377

Widow for One Year, A (Irving), **Supp. VI:** 165, **179–181**

Widows of Thornton, The (Taylor), **Supp. V:** 320, 321

Wieland; or, The Transformation. An American Tale (Brown), **Supp. I Part 1:** 128–132, 133, 137, 140

Wiene, Robert, **Retro. Supp. I:** 268

Wiener, John, **Supp. IV Part 1:** 153

Wieners, John, **Supp. II Part 1:** 32

"Wife, Forty-five, Remembers Love, A" (Shields), **Supp. VII:** 310

"Wifebeater, The" (Sexton), **Supp. II Part 2:** 693

"Wife for Dino Rossi, A" (Fante),

Supp. XI: 165

"Wife of His Youth, The" (Chesnutt), **Supp. XIV:63–66**

Wife of His Youth and Other Stories of the Color Line, The (Chesnutt), **Supp. XIV:** 62, 63

"Wife of Jesus Speaks, The" (Karr), **Supp. XI:** 250–251

"Wife of Nashville, A" (Taylor), **Supp. V:** 320

Wife's Story, The (Shields), **Supp. VII:** 316. *See also* Happenstance

"Wife-Wooing" (Updike), **IV:** 226

Wigan, Gareth, **Supp. XI:** 306

Wiget, Andrew, **Supp. IV Part 2:** 509

Wigglesworth, Michael, **IV:** 147, 156; **Supp. I Part 1:** 110, 111

Wilbur, Richard, **III:** 527; **Retro. Supp. II:** 50; **Supp. III Part 1:** 64; **Supp. III Part 2: 541–565; Supp. IV Part 2:** 626, 634, 642; **Supp. V:** 337; **Supp. VIII:** 28; **Supp. X:** 58, 120; **Supp. XII:** 258; **Supp. XIII:** 76, 336

Wilcocks, Alexander, **Supp. I Part 1:** 125

Wilcox, Ella Wheeler, **Supp. II Part 1:** 197

Wild 90 (film) (Mailer), **Retro. Supp. II:** 205

Wild, John, **II:** 362, 363–364

Wild, Peter, **Supp. V:** 5

Wild, Robert, **IV:** 155

"Wild, The" (Berry), **Supp. X:** 30

Wild Boy of Aveyron, The (Itard). *See* De l'éducation d'un homme sauvage

Wild Boys, The: A Book of the Dead (Burroughs), **Supp. III Part 1:** 106–107

Wilde, Oscar, **I:** 50, 66, 381, 384; **II:** 515; **IV:** 77, 350; **Retro. Supp. I:** 56, 102, 227; **Retro. Supp. II:** 76, 326; **Supp. IV Part 2:** 578, 679, 683; **Supp. V:** 106, 283; **Supp. IX:** 65, 66, 68, 189, 192; **Supp. X:** 148, 151, 188–189; **Supp. XIV:** 324, 334

Wilder, Amos Parker, **IV:** 356

Wilder, Billy, **Supp. IV Part 1:** 130; **Supp. XI:** 307

Wilder, Isabel, **IV:** 357, 366, 375

Wilder, Mrs. Amos Parker (Isabella Thornton Niven), **IV:** 356

Wilder, Thornton, **I:** 360, 482; **IV: 355–377,** 431; **Retro. Supp. I:** 109, 359; **Supp. I Part 2:** 609; **Supp. IV Part 2:** 586; **Supp. V:** 105; **Supp. IX:** 140; **Supp. XII:** 236–237

"Wilderness" (Leopold), **Supp. XIV:** 190

"Wilderness" (Sandburg), **III:** 584, 595

Wilderness (Warren), **IV:** 256

"Wilderness, The" (Merwin), **Supp. III Part 1:** 340, 345

"Wilderness, The" (Robinson), **III:** 524

Wilderness of Vision, The: On the Poetry of John Haines (Bezner and Walzer, eds.), **Supp. XII:** 202

Wilderness World of Anne LaBastille, The (LaBastille), **Supp. X: 105,** 106

Wild Flag, The (White), **Supp. I Part 2:** 654

"Wildflower, The" (W. C. Williams), **Retro. Supp. I:** 420

"Wild Flowers" (Caldwell), **I:** 310

"Wildflowers" (Minot), **Supp. VI:** 208

"Wild Geese" (Oliver), **Supp. VII:** 237

"Wild Honey Suckle, The" (Freneau), **Supp. II Part 1:** 253, 264, 266

Wild in the Country (Odets), **Supp. II Part 2:** 546

Wild Iris, The (Glück), **Supp. V:** 79, 87–89, 91

Wildlife (Ford), **Supp. V:** 57, 69–71

Wildlife in America (Matthiessen), **Supp. V:** 199, 201, 204

"Wildlife in American Culture" (Leopold), **Supp. XIV:** 190, 191

Wild Old Wicked Man, The (MacLeish), **III:** 3, 20

Wild Palms, The (Faulkner), **II:** 68–69; **Retro. Supp. I:** 85

"Wild Palms, The" (Faulkner), **II:** 68

"Wild Peaches" (Wylie), **Supp. I Part 2:** 707, 712

Wild Roses of Cape Ann and Other Poems (Larcom), **Supp. XIII:** 142, 147

Wild Seed (O. Butler), **Supp. XIII:** 62, 63

"Wildwest" (MacLeish), **III:** 14

Wiley, Craig, **Supp. VIII:** 313

Wilhelm Meister (Goethe), **II:** 291

Wilkes, John, **Supp. I Part 2:** 503, 519, 522

Wilkie, Curtis, **Supp. V:** 11

Wilkins, Roy, **Supp. I Part 1:** 345

Wilkinson, Alec, **Supp. VIII:** 164, 168, 171

Wilkinson, Max, **Supp. IX:** 251

Willard, Samuel, **IV:** 150

Willard Gibbs (Rukeyser), **Supp. VI:** 273, 283, 284

Willett, Ralph, **Supp. XIV:** 27

Willey, Basil, **Retro. Supp. II:** 243

William Carlos Williams (Koch), **Retro. Supp. I:** 428

William Carlos Williams: An American Artist (Breslin), **Retro. Supp. I:** 430

William Carlos Williams: The American Background (Weaver), **Retro.**

Supp. I: 430

William Carlos Williams and Alterity (Ahearn), **Retro. Supp. I:** 415

William Carlos Williams and the Meanings of Measure (Cushman), **Retro. Supp. I:** 430

William Faulkner: A Critical Study (Howe), **Supp. VI:** 119–120, 125

William Faulkner: Early Prose and Poetry (Faulkner), **Retro. Supp. I:** 80

William Faulkner: First Encounters (Brooks), **Supp. XIV:** 13

"William Faulkner: The Stillness of *Light in August*" (Kazin), **Supp. VIII:** 104

William Faulkner: The Yoknapatawpha Country (Brooks), **Supp. XIV:** 12–13, 16

William Faulkner: Toward Yoknapatawpha and Beyond (Brooks), **Supp. XIV:** 13

"William Faulkner's Legend of the South" (Cowley), **Supp. II Part 1:** 143

"William Humphrey, 73, Writer of Novels about Rural Texas" (Gussow), **Supp. IX:** 93

William Humphrey. Boise State University Western Writers Series (Winchell), **Supp. IX:** 109

William Humphrey, Destroyer of Myths (Almon), **Supp. IX:** 93

William Humphrey. Southwestern Series (Lee), **Supp. IX:** 109

"William Humphrey Remembered" (Masters), **Supp. IX:** 96

"William Ireland's Confession" (A. Miller), **III:** 147–148

William James and Phenomenology: A Study of the "Principles of Psychology" (Wilshire), **II:** 362

William Lloyd Garrison (Chapman), **Supp. XIV:** 46–51, 52, 53, 55

Williams, Annie Laurie, **Supp. IX:** 93

Williams, C. K., **Supp. XIII:** 114

Williams, Cecil, **II:** 508

Williams, Charles, **Supp. II Part 1:** 15, 16

Williams, Dakin, **IV:** 379

Williams, David Reichard /?/, **Supp. XIII:** 162

Williams, Edward, **IV:** 404

Williams, Edwina Dakin, **IV:** 379

Williams, Esther, **Supp. XII:** 165

Williams, Fannie Barrier, **Supp. XIV:** 201

Williams, George, **Supp. V:** 220

Williams, Horace, **IV:** 453

Williams, Joan, **Supp. IX:** 95

Williams, John Sharp, **IV:** 378

Williams, Lyle, **Supp. XIV:** 22

Williams, Michael, **Supp. V:** 286

Williams, Miller, **Supp. XIV:** 126

Williams, Mrs. William Carlos (Florence Herman), **IV:** 404

Williams, Paul, **IV:** 404

Williams, Raymond, **Supp. IX:** 146

Williams, Roger, **Supp. I Part 2:** 699

Williams, Rose, **IV:** 379

Williams, Sherley Anne, **Supp. V:** 180

Williams, Solomon, **I:** 549

Williams, Stanley T., **II:** 301, 316; **Supp. I Part 1:** 251

Williams, Stephen, **IV:** 148

Williams, Ted, **IV:** 216; **Supp. IX:** 162

Williams, Tennessee, **I:** 73, 81, 113, 211; **II:** 190, 194; **III:** 145, 147; **IV:** 4, 378–401; **Supp. I Part 1:** 290, 291; **Supp. IV Part 1:** 79, 83, 84, 359; **Supp. IV Part 2:** 574, 682; **Supp. IX:** 133; **Supp. XI:** 103; **Supp. XIII:** 331; **Supp. XIV:** 250, 315

Williams, Terry Tempest, **Supp. XIII:** 16

Williams, Walter L., **Supp. IV Part 1:** 330, 331

Williams, William, **IV:** 404, 405

Williams, William Carlos, **I:** 61, 62, 229, 255, 256, 261, 285, 428, 438, 446, 539; **II:** 133, 536, 542, 543, 544, 545; **III:** 194, 196, 198, 214, 269, 409, 453, 457, 458, 464, 465, 591; **IV:** 30, 74, 75, 76, 94, 95, 286, 287, 402–425; **Retro. Supp. I:** 51, 52, 62, 209, 284, 285, 288, 296, 298, 411–433; **Retro. Supp. II:** 178, 181, 189, 250, 321, 322, 326, 327, 328, 334, 335; **Supp. I Part 1:** 254, 255, 259, 266; **Supp. II Part 1:** 9, 30, 308, 318; **Supp. II Part 2:** 421, 443; **Supp. III Part 1:** 9, 147, 239, 271, 275, 276, 278, 350; **Supp. III Part 2:** 542, 610, 613, 614, 615, 616, 617, 621, 622, 626, 628; **Supp. IV Part 1:** 151, 153, 246, 325; **Supp. V:** 180, 337; **Supp. VIII:** 195, 269, 272, 277, 292; **Supp. IX:** 38, 268, 291; **Supp. X:** 112, 120, 204; **Supp. XI:** 311, 328; **Supp. XII:** 198; **Supp. XIII:** 77, 90, 335; **Supp. XIV:** 280, 284, 285, 293

Williams, Wirt, **Supp. XIV:** 24

Williamson, Alan, **Retro. Supp. II:** 185

William Styron's Nat Turner: Ten Black Writers Respond (Clarke, ed.), **IV:** 115

Williams-Walsh, Mary Ellen, **Supp. IV Part 2:** 611

William the Conqueror, **Supp. I Part 2:** 507

William Wetmore Story and His Friends (James), **Retro. Supp. I:** 235

William Wilson (Gardner), **Supp. VI:** 72

"William Wilson" (Poe), **II:** 475; **III:** 410, 412; **Retro. Supp. II:** 269; **Supp. IX:** 105

"Willie" (Angelou), **Supp. IV Part 1:** 15

Willie Masters' Lonesome Wife (Gass), **Supp. VI:** 77, **84–85, 86–87**

"Willing" (Moore), **Supp. X:** 178

Willis, Bruce, **Supp. IV Part 1:** 236

Willis, Mary Hard, **Supp. V:** 290–291

Willis, Nathaniel Parker, **II:** 313; **Supp. I Part 2:** 405

Williwaw (Vidal), **Supp. IV Part 2:** 677, 680, 681

"Willow Woman" (Francis), **Supp. IX:** 78

Wills, Garry, **Supp. I Part 1:** 294; **Supp. IV Part 1:** 355

Wills, Ridley, **IV:** 122

Wills, Ross B., **Supp. XI:** 169

"Will to Believe, The" (James), **II:** 352; **Supp. XIV:** 50

Will to Believe, The, and Other Essays in Popular Philosophy (James), **II:** 356; **IV:** 28

Will to Change, The: Poems, 1968–1970 (Rich), **Supp. I Part 2:** 551, 557–559

"Will You Please Be Quiet, Please?" (Carver), **Supp. III Part 1:** 137, 141

Will You Please Be Quiet, Please? (Carver), **Supp. III Part 1:** 138, 140, 144

"Will You Tell Me?" (Barthelme), **Supp. IV Part 1:** 42, 47

Wilshire, Bruce, **II:** 362, 364

Wilshire, Gaylord, **Supp. V:** 280

Wilson, Angus, **IV:** 430, 435

Wilson, August, **Supp. VIII:** 329–353

Wilson, Augusta Jane Evans, **Retro. Supp. I:** 351

Wilson, E. O., **Supp. X:** 35

Wilson, Earl, **Supp. X:** 264

Wilson, Edmund, **I:** 67, 185, 236, 247, 260, 434, 482; **II:** 79, 80, 81, 86, 87, 91, 97, 98, 146, 276, 430, 530, 562, 587; **III:** 588; **IV:** 308, 310, 426–449; **Retro. Supp. I:** 1, 97, 100, 101, 103, 104, 105, 115, 274; **Retro. Supp. II:** 321, 327, 329; **Supp. I Part 1:** 372; **Supp. I Part 2:** 407, 646, 678, 709; **Supp. II Part 1:** 19, 90, 106, 136, 137, 143; **Supp. III Part 2:** 612; **Supp. IV Part 2:**

693; **Supp. VIII:** 93, 95, 96, 97, 98–99, 100, 101, 103, 105, 162; **Supp. IX:** 55, 65, 190; **Supp. X:** 186; **Supp. XI:** 160; **Supp. XIII:** 170; **Supp. XIV:** 338

Wilson, Edmund (father), **IV:** 441

Wilson, Henry, **Supp. XIV:** 48

Wilson, Reuel, **II:** 562

Wilson, Robert, **Supp. XI:** 144

Wilson, Sloan, **Supp. IV Part 1:** 387

Wilson, Thomas, **IV:** 153

Wilson, Victoria, **Supp. X:** 166

Wilson, Woodrow, **I:** 245, 246, 490; **II:** 183, 253; **III:** 105, 581; **Supp. I Part 1:** 21; **Supp. I Part 2:** 474, 643; **Supp. V:** 288

Wilton, David, **IV:** 147

Wimsatt, William K., **Supp. XIV:** 12

Winchell, Mark, **Supp. VIII:** 176, 189

Winchell, Mark Royden, **Supp. VIII:** 241; **Supp. IX:** 97, 98, 109; **Supp. XIII:** 94, 98, 99, 101; **Supp. XIV:** 103, 106, 111

Winckelmann, Johann Joachim, **Supp. XII:** 178

Wind, Sand, and Stars (Saint-Exupéry), **Supp. IX:** 247

Windham, Donald, **IV:** 382

"Windhover" (Hopkins), **I:** 397; **II:** 539; **Supp. IX:** 43

"Winding Street, The" (Petry), **Supp. XI:** 6

"Window" (Pinsky), **Supp. VI:** 237, 247

Windows (Creeley), **Supp. IV Part 1:** 157, 158

"Windows" (Jarrell), **II:** 388, 389

"Window Seat, A" (Goldbarth), **Supp. XII:** 185

Wind Remains, The (opera) (Bowles), **Supp. IV Part 1:** 83

"Winds, The" (Welty), **IV:** 265; **Retro. Supp. I:** 348, 350

"Wind up Sushi" (Goldbarth), **Supp. XII:** 186–187

"Windy Day at the Reservoir, A" (Beattie), **Supp. V:** 33

Windy McPherson's Son (Anderson), **I:** 101, 102–103, 105, 111

"Wine" (Carver), **Supp. III Part 1:** 138

"Wine Menagerie, The" (H. Crane), **I:** 389, 391; **Retro. Supp. II:** 82

Wine of the Puritans, The: A Study of Present-Day America (Brooks), **I:** 240

"Wine of Wizardry, A" (Sterling), **I:** 208

Winer, Linda, **Supp. IV Part 2:** 580

Winesburg, Ohio: A Group of Tales of

Ohio Small Town Life (Anderson), **I:** 97, 102, 103, 104, 105–108; **III:** 112, 113, 114, 116, 224, 579; **Supp. V:** 12; **Supp. IX:** 306, 308; **Supp. XI:** 164

Wing-and-Wing, The (Cooper), **I:** 350, 355

Winged Words: American Indian Writers Speak (Coltelli), **Supp. IV Part 2:** 493, 497

"Wingfield" (Wolff), **Supp. VII:** 341–342

"Wings, The" (Doty), **Supp. XI:** 124

Wings of the Dove, The (James), **I:** 436; **II:** 320, 323, 333, 334–335; **Retro. Supp. I:** 215, 216, 217, 232, **233–234**; **Supp. II Part 1:** 94–95; **Supp. IV Part 1:** 349

Winner Take Nothing (Hemingway), **II:** 249; **Retro. Supp. I:** 170, 175, 176, 181

"Winnie" (Brooks), **Supp. III Part 1:** 86

Winokur, Maxine. *See* Kumin, Maxine

Winslow, Devereux, **II:** 547

Winslow, Harriet, **II:** 552–553

Winslow, Ola Elizabeth, **I:** 547

Winslow, Warren, **II:** 540

Winston, Andrew, **Supp. XII:** 189

Winston, Michael R., **Supp. XIV:** 197

Winter, Douglas, **Supp. V:** 144

Winter, Johnny and Edgar, **Supp. V:** 334

Winter, Kate, **Supp. X:** 104

"Winter Branch, A" (Irving), **Supp. VI:** 163

"Winter Burial, A" (Clampitt), **Supp. IX:** 48

Winter Carnival (film), **Retro. Supp. I:** 113

"Winter Daybreak at Vence, A" (Wright), **Supp. III Part 1:** 249–250

Winter Diary, A (Van Doren), **I:** 168

"Winter Dreams" (Fitzgerald), **II:** 80, 94; **Retro. Supp. I:** 108

"Winter Drive, A" (Jewett), **Retro. Supp. II:** 147

"Winter Eden, A" (Frost), **Retro. Supp. I:** 137

"Winter Father, The" (Dubus), **Supp. VII:** 83, 87

Winter Hours: Prose, Prose Poems, and Poems (Oliver), **Supp. VII:** 230, 247

"Winter in Dunbarton" (Lowell), **II:** 547; **Retro. Supp. II:** 187

"Wintering" (Plath), **Retro. Supp. II:** 255

Winter Insomnia (Carver), **Supp. III**

Part 1: 138

Winter in the Blood (Welch), **Supp. IV Part 2:** 562

"Winter Landscape" (Berryman), **I:** 174; **Retro. Supp. I:** 430

Winter Lightning (Nemerov), **III:** 269

Winter News (Haines), **Supp. XII:** 199, **201–204**, 207–208, 208

Winternitz, Mary. *See* Cheever, Mrs. John (Mary Winternitz)

Winter of Our Discontent, The (Steinbeck), **IV:** 52, 65–66, 68

"Winter on Earth" (Toomer), **Supp. III Part 2:** 486

"Winter Piece, A" (Bryant), **Supp. I Part 1:** 150, 155

"Winter Rains, Cataluña" (Levine), **Supp. V:** 182

"Winter Remembered" (Ransom), **III:** 492–493

Winterrowd, Prudence, **I:** 217, 224

Winters, Jonathan, **Supp. XI:** 305

Winters, Yvor, **I:** 59, 63, 386, 393, 397, 398, 402, 471; **III:** 194, 498; **IV:** 153; **Retro. Supp. II:** 76, 77, 78, 82, 83, 85, 89; **Supp. I Part 1:** 268; **Supp. II Part 2:** 416, 666, **785–816**; **Supp. IV Part 2:** 480; **Supp. V:** 180, 191–192; **Supp. XIV:** 287

"Winter Scenes" (Bryant). *See* "Winter Piece, A"

Winterset (Anderson), **III:** 159

"Winter Sleep" (Wylie), **Supp. I Part 2:** 711, 729

Winter's Tale, The (Shakespeare), **Supp. XIII:** 219

Winter Stars (Levis), **Supp. XI:** 259, **266–268**

"Winter Stars" (Levis), **Supp. XI:** 267–268

"Winter Swan" (Bogan), **Supp. III Part 1:** 52

Winter Trees (Plath), **Retro. Supp. II:** 257; **Supp. I Part 2:** 526, 539, 541

"Winter Weather Advisory" (Ashbery), **Supp. III Part 1:** 26

"Winter Words" (Levine), **Supp. V:** 192

Winthrop, John, **Supp. I Part 1:** 99, 100, 101, 102, 105; **Supp. I Part 2:** 484, 485

Winthrop Covenant, The (Auchincloss), **Supp. IV Part 1:** 23

Wirt, William, **I:** 232

Wirth, Louis, **IV:** 475

"Wisdom Cometh with the Years" (Cullen), **Supp. IV Part 1:** 166

Wisdom of the Desert, The: Sayings from the Desert Fathers of the Fourth Century (Merton), **Supp.**

VIII: 201

Wisdom of the Heart, The (H. Miller), **III:** 178, 184

Wise Blood (O'Connor), **III:** 337, 338, 339–343, 344, 345, 346, 350, 354, 356, 357; **Retro. Supp. II:** 219, 221, 222, 223, **225–228**

Wise Men, The (Price), **Supp. VI:** 254

"Wiser Than a God" (Chopin), **Retro. Supp. II:** 61; **Supp. I Part 1:** 208

"Wish for a Young Wife" (Roethke), **III:** 548

Wishful Thinking: A Theological ABC (Buechner), **Supp. XII:** 53

Wishing Tree, The: Christopher Isherwood on Mystical Religion (Adjemian, ed.), **Supp. XIV:** 164, 173

Wismer, Helen Muriel. *See* Thurber, Mrs. James (Helen Muriel Wismer)

Wisse, Ruth, **Supp. XII:** 167, 168

Wister, Owen, **I:** 62; **Retro. Supp. II:** 72; **Supp. XIV:** 39

"Witchbird" (Bambara), **Supp. XI:** 11

"Witch Burning" (Plath), **Supp. I Part 2:** 539

Witchcraft of Salem Village, The (Jackson), **Supp. IX:** 121

"Witch Doctor" (Hayden), **Supp. II Part 1:** 368, 380

Witches of Eastwick, The (Updike), **Retro. Supp. I:** 330, 331

Witching Hour, The (Rice), **Supp. VII:** 299–300

"Witch of Coös, The" (Frost), **II:** 154–155; **Retro. Supp. I:** 135; **Retro. Supp. II:** 42

"Witch of Owl Mountain Springs, The: An Account of Her Remarkable Powers" (Taylor), **Supp. V:** 328

"Witch of Wenham, The" (Whittier), **Supp. I Part 2:** 694, 696

"With a Little Help from My Friends" (Kushner), **Supp. IX:** 131

"With Che at Kitty Hawk" (Banks), **Supp. V:** 6

"With Che at the Plaza" (Banks), **Supp. V:** 7

"With Che in New Hampshire" (Banks), **Supp. V:** 6

"Withdrawal Symptoms" (Mora), **Supp. XIII:** 216

"Withered Skins of Berries" (Toomer), **Supp. III Part 2:** 485; **Supp. IX:** 320

Withers, Harry Clay, **Supp. XIII:** 161

Witherspoon, John, **Supp. I Part 2:** 504

With Eyes at the Back of Our Heads

(Levertov), **Supp. III Part 1:** 276–277

With Her in Ourland (Gilman), **Supp. XI:** 208–209

With His Pistol in His Hand (Paredes), **Supp. XIII:** 225

"Within the Words: An Apprenticeship" (Haines), **Supp. XII:** 197

"With Kit, Age 7, at the Beach" (Stafford), **Supp. XI:** 323

"With Mercy for the Greedy" (Sexton), **Supp. II Part 2:** 680

With My Trousers Rolled (Epstein), **Supp. XIV:** 101, 105

Without a Hero (Boyle), **Supp. VIII:** 16

Without Stopping (Bowles), **Supp. IV Part 1:** 79, 81, 85, 90, 91, 92

"Without Tradition and within Reason: Judge Horton and Atticus Finch in Court" (Johnson), **Supp. VIII:** 127

With Shuddering Fall (Oates), **Supp. II Part 2:** 504–506

"With the Dog at Sunrise" (Kenyon), **Supp. VII:** 170

With the Empress Dowager of China (Carl), **III:** 475

"With the Horse in the Winter Pasture" (McCarriston), **Supp. XIV:** 262

With the Old Breed: At Peleliu and Okinawa (Sledge), **Supp. V:** 249–250

"With the Violin" (Chopin), **Retro. Supp. II:** 61

"Witness" (Clampitt), **Supp. IX:** 42–43, 45, 46

"Witness" (Dubus), **Supp. VII:** 89

"Witness" (Harjo), **Supp. XII:** 227–228

Witness (McNally), **Supp. XIII:** 197

"Witness, The" (Porter), **III:** 443–444

"Witness for Poetry, A" (Stafford), **Supp. XI:** 324

"Witness for the Defense" (Hay), **Supp. XIV:** 124

"Witnessing My Father's Will" (Karr), **Supp. XI:** 241

Witness to the Times! (McGrath), **Supp. X:** 118

Witness Tree, A (Frost), **II:** 155; **Retro. Supp. I:** 122, 137, 139

Wit's End: Days and Nights of the Algonquin Round Table (Gaines), **Supp. IX:** 190

Wits Recreations (Mennes and Smith), **II:** 111

Witt, Shirley Hill, **Supp. IV Part 2:** 505

Wittenberg, Judith Bryant, **Retro. Supp. II:** 146

Wittgenstein, Ludwig, **Retro. Supp. I:** 53; **Supp. III Part 2:** 626–627; **Supp. X:** 304; **Supp. XII:** 21

Wittliff, William, **Supp. V:** 227

"Witty War, A" (Simpson), **Supp. IX:** 268

"Wives and Mistresses" (Hardwick), **Supp. III Part 1:** 211–212

Wizard of Loneliness, The (Nichols), **Supp. XIII:** 259, 263, 264

Wizard of Oz, The (Baum), **Supp. IV Part 1:** 113

Wizard of Oz, The (film), **Supp. X:** 172, 214

Wizard's Tide, The: A Story (Buechner), **Supp. XII:** 54

Wodehouse, P. G., **Supp. IX:** 195

Woiwode, Larry, **Supp. VIII:** 151

Wojahn, David, **Supp. IX:** 161, 292, 293

Wolcott, James, **Supp. IX:** 259

Wolf: A False Memoir (Harrison), **Supp. VIII:** 40, **41–42**, 45

Wolf, Christa, **Supp. IV Part 1:** 310, 314

Wolf, Daniel, **Retro. Supp. II:** 202

Wolfe, Ben, **IV:** 454

Wolfe, Gregory, **Supp. XIV:** 307

Wolfe, James, **Supp. I Part 2:** 498

Wolfe, Linnie, **Supp. IX:** 176

Wolfe, Mabel, **IV:** 454

Wolfe, Mrs. William Oliver (Julia Elizabeth Westall), **IV:** 454

Wolfe, Thomas, **I:** 288, 289, 374, 478, 495; **II:** 457; **III:** 40, 108, 278, 334, 482; **IV:** 52, 97, 357, **450–473**; **Retro. Supp. I:** 382; **Supp. I Part 1:** 29; **Supp. IV Part 1:** 101; **Supp. IX:** 229; **Supp. X:** 225; **Supp. XI:** 213, 216, 217, 218; **Supp. XIII:** 17; **Supp. XIV:** 122

Wolfe, Tom, **Supp. III Part 2: 567–588; Supp. IV Part 1:** 35, 198; **Supp. V:** 296; **Supp. X:** 264; **Supp. XI:** 239

Wolfe, William Oliver, **IV:** 454

"Wolfe Homo Scribens" (Cowley), **Supp. II Part 1:** 144

Wolfert's Roost (Irving), **II:** 314

Wolff, Cynthia Griffin, **Retro. Supp. I:** 379; **Supp. IV Part 1:** 203

Wolff, Donald, **Supp. XIII:** 316, 317, 326

Wolff, Geoffrey, **Supp. II Part 1:** 97; **Supp. XI:** 239, 245, 246

Wolff, Tobias, **Retro. Supp. I:** 190; **Supp. V:** 22; **Supp. VII: 331–346; Supp. X:** 1; **Supp. XI:** 26, 239, 245, 246, 247

Wolfson, P. J., **Supp. XIII:** 172

"Wolf Town" (Carson), **Supp. XII: 102**

Wolf Willow: A History, a Story, and a Memory of the Last Plains Frontier (Stegner), **Supp. IV Part 2:** 595, 596, 597, 598, 599, 600, 601, 604, 606, 611, 613, 614

Wollaston, William, **II:** 108

Wollstonecraft, Mary, **Supp. I Part 1:** 126; **Supp. I Part 2:** 512, 554

"Woman" (Bogan), **Supp. X:** 102

"Woman, I Got the Blues" (Komunyakaa), **Supp. XIII: 117**

"Woman, Why Are You Weeping?" (Kenyon), **Supp. VII:** 174–175

"Woman, Young and Old, A" (Paley), **Supp. VI:** 222, 225

Woman at the Washington Zoo, The (Jarrell), **II:** 367, 386, 387, 389

"Woman Dead in Her Forties, A" (Rich), **Supp. I Part 2:** 574–575

"Woman Hanging from the Thirteenth Floor Window, The" (Harjo), **Supp. XII:** 216, 221

"Woman Hollering Creek" (Cisneros), **Supp. VII:** 70

Woman Hollering Creek and Other Stories (Cisneros), **Supp. VII:** 58, 68–70

"Womanhood" (Brooks), **Supp. III Part 1:** 77

Woman in the Dark (Hammett), **Supp. IV Part 1:** 343

"Woman in the House, A" (Caldwell), **I:** 310

Woman in the Nineteenth Century (Fuller), **Retro. Supp. I:** 156; **Supp. II Part 1:** 279, 292, 294–296; **Supp. XI:** 197, 203

Woman in White, The (Collins), **Supp. I Part 1:** 35, 36

"Womanizer, The" (Ford), **Supp. V:** 71, 72

Woman Lit by Fireflies, The (Harrison), **Supp. VIII: 50–51**

"Woman Loses Cookie Bake-Off, Sets Self on Fire" (R. O. Butler), **Supp. XII:** 72

Woman of Andros, The (Wilder), **IV:** 356, 363–364, 367, 368, 374

Woman of Means, A (Taylor), **Supp. V:** 319–320

Woman on the Edge of Time (Piercy), **Supp. XIII:** 29

Woman on the Porch, The (Gordon), **II:** 199, 209–211

"Woman on the Stair, The" (MacLeish), **III:** 15–16

"Woman's Heartlessness" (Thaxter), **Retro. Supp. II:** 147

Woman's Honor (Glaspell), **Supp. III Part 1:** 179

"Woman Singing" (Ortiz), **Supp. IV Part 2:** 513

Woman's Share in Primitive Culture (Mason), **Supp. I Part 1:** 18

"Woman Struck by Car Turns into Nymphomaniac" (R. O. Butler), **Supp. XII:** 72

"Woman's Work" (Alvarez), **Supp. VII:** 4

"Woman Uses Glass Eye to Spy on Philandering Husband" (R. O. Butler), **Supp. XII:** 70, 72

Woman Warrior (Kingston), **Supp. IV Part 1:** 12; **Supp. V:** 157, 158, 159, 160–164, 166, 169; **Supp. X:** 291–292; **Supp. XIV:** 162

Woman Who Fell from the Sky, The (Harjo), **Supp. XII: 226–228**

"Woman Who Fell From the Sky, The" (Iroquois creation story), **Supp. IV Part 1:** 327

Woman Who Owned the Shadows, The (Gunn Allen), **Supp. IV Part 1:** 320, 322, 326, 327–328

Woman Within, The (Glasgow), **II:** 183, 190–191

"Womanwork" (Gunn Allen), **Supp. IV Part 1:** 326

Women (Bukowski), **Supp. XI:** 172

"Women" (Didion), **Supp. IV Part 1:** 205

"Women" (Swenson), **Supp. IV Part 2:** 647

Women, The (film), **Retro. Supp. I:** 113

Women and Economics (Gilman), **Supp. I Part 2:** 637; **Supp. V:** 284; **Supp. XI:** 200, **203–204,** 206

Women and Thomas Harrow (Marquand), **III:** 50, 61, 62, 66, 68, 69–70, 71

Women and Wilderness (LaBastille), **Supp. X:** 97, **102–104**

Women at Point Sur, The (Jeffers), **Supp. II Part 2:** 430–431

Women in Love (Lawrence), **III:** 27, 34

Women of Brewster Place, The: A Novel in Seven Stories (Naylor), **Supp. VIII:** 213, **214–218**

Women of Manhattan: An Upper West Side Story (Shanley), **Supp. XIV:** 315, **326–327**

"Women of My Color" (Coleman), **Supp. XI:** 88–89

Women of Trachis (Pound, trans.), **III:** 476

Women on the Wall, The (Stegner), **Supp. IV Part 2:** 599, 605, 606

Women Poets in English (Stanford, ed.), **Retro. Supp. I:** 41

"Women Reformers and American Culture, 1870–1930" (Conway), **Supp. I Part 1:** 19

"Women's Movement, The" (Didion), **Supp. IV Part 1:** 206

"Women Waiting" (Shields), **Supp. VII:** 320

"Women We Love Whom We Never See Again" (Bly), **Supp. IV Part 1:** 66

"Women We Never See Again" (Bly), **Supp. IV Part 1:** 66

Women with Men (Ford), **Supp. V:** 57, 71–72

"Wonder" (Olds), **Supp. X:** 210

Wonder Boys (Chabon), **Supp. XI:** 67, **73–75,Supp. XI:** 78

Wonder Boys (film), **Supp. XI:** 67

Wonderful O, The (Thurber), **Supp. I Part 2:** 612

"Wonderful Old Gentleman, The" (Parker), **Supp. IX:** 197

"Wonderful Pen, The" (Swenson), **Supp. IV Part 2:** 650

Wonderful Words, Silent Truth: Essays on Poetry and a Memoir (Simic), **Supp. VIII:** 270

Wonderland (Oates), **Supp. II Part 2:** 511, 512, 514–515

Wonders of the Invisible World, The (Mather), **Supp. II Part 2:** 456–459, 460, 467

Wonder-Working Providence (Johnson), **IV:** 157

Wong, Hertha, **Supp. IV Part 1:** 275

Wong, Jade Snow, **Supp. X:** 291

"Wood" (Nye), **Supp. XIII:** 276

Wood, Audrey, **IV:** 381

Wood, Clement Biddle, **Supp. XI:** 307

Wood, James, **Supp. XIV:** 95–96

Wood, Mabel, **I:** 199

Wood, Michael, **Supp. IV Part 2:** 691

Wood, Mrs. Henry, **Supp. I Part 1:** 35

Wood, Norman Barton, **Supp. XIV:** 201

Woodard, Calvin, **Supp. VIII:** 128

Woodard, Charles L., **Supp. IV Part 2:** 484, 493

Woodard, Deborah, **Supp. XIII:** 114

Woodberry, George Edward, **III:** 508

Woodbridge, Frederick, **I:** 217, 224

Woodbridge, John, **Supp. I Part 1:** 101, 102, 114

"Wood-Choppers, The" (Chopin), **Retro. Supp. II:** 72

Woodcock, George, **Supp. XIII:** 33

"Wood Dove at Sandy Spring, The" (MacLeish), **III:** 19

"Wooden Spring" (Rukeyser), **Supp. VI:** 285

"Wooden Umbrella, The" (Porter), **IV:** 26

"Woodnotes" (Emerson), **II:** 7, 19

"Wood-Pile, The" (Frost), **Retro. Supp. I:** 128; **Supp. IV Part 2:** 445

Woodrow, James, **Supp. I Part 1:** 349, 366

"Woods, Books, and Truant Officers, The" (Maclean), **Supp. XIV:** 221, 225

Woods, Robert A., **Supp. I Part 1:** 19

Woods, The (Mamet), **Supp. XIV:** 241, 254–255

Woodswoman (LaBastille), **Supp. X:** 95, **96–99,** 108

Woodswoman III: Book Three of the Woodswoman's Adventures (LaBastille), **Supp. X:** 95, **106–107**

"Wood Thrush" (Kenyon), **Supp. VII:** 172

Woodward, C. Vann, **IV:** 114, 470–471; **Retro. Supp. I:** 75, 76

"Wooing the Inanimate" (Brodsky), **Supp. VIII:** 32

Woolcott, Alexander, **Supp. IX:** 197

Wooley, Bryan, **Supp. V:** 225

Woolf, Leonard, **Supp. IX:** 95

Woolf, Virginia, **I:** 53, 79, 112, 309; **II:** 320, 415; **IV:** 59; **Retro. Supp. I:** 59, 75, 170, 215, 291, 359; **Supp. I Part 2:** 553, 714, 718; **Supp. IV Part 1:** 299; **Supp. V:** 127; **Supp. VIII:** 5, 155, 251, 252, 263, 265; **Supp. IX:** 66, 109; **Supp. XI:** 134, 193; **Supp. XII:** 81, 98, 289; **Supp. XIII:** 305; **Supp. XIV:** 341–342, 342, 343, 346, 348

Woollcott, Alexander, **IV:** 432; **Retro. Supp. II:** 327; **Supp. I Part 2:** 664; **Supp. IX:** 190, 194

Woolman, John, **Supp. VIII:** 202, 204, 205

Woolson, Constance Fenimore, **Retro. Supp. I:** 224, 228

Worcester, Samuel, **I:** 458

Word and Idioms: Studies in the English Language (L. P. Smith), **Supp. XIV:** 343

Word of God and the Word of Man, The (Barth), **Retro. Supp. I:** 327

"Word out of the Sea, A" (Whitman), **IV:** 344

Words (Creeley), **Supp. IV Part 1:** 139, 150–153, 154, 155, 158

"Words" (Creeley), **Supp. IV Part 1:** 152

"Words" (Merwin), **Supp. III Part 1:** 352

"Words" (Plath), **Supp. I Part 2:** 547

"Words" (Shields), **Supp. VII:** 323

"Words, The" (Wagoner), **Supp. IX:** 326

"Words above a Narrow Entrance" (Wagoner), **Supp. IX:** 325

"Words for a Bike-Racing, Osprey-Chasing Wine-Drunk Squaw Man" (Gunn Allen), **Supp. IV Part 1:** 325

Words for Dr. Y (Sexton), **Supp. II Part 2:** 698

"Words for Hart Crane" (Lowell), **I:** 381; **II:** 547; **Retro. Supp. II:** 188

"Words for Maria" (Merrill), **Supp. III Part 1:** 327

"Words for the Unknown Makers" (Kunitz), **Supp. III Part 1:** 264

Words for the Wind (Roethke), **III:** 529, 533, 541, 543, 545

"Words for the Wind" (Roethke), **III:** 542–543

Words in the Mourning Time (Hayden), **Supp. II Part 1:** 361, 366, 367

"Words in the Mourning Time" (Hayden), **Supp. II Part 1:** 370–371

"Words into Fiction" (Welty), **IV:** 279

"Words Like Freedom" (Hughes), **Retro. Supp. I:** 207

"Words of a Young Girl" (Lowell), **II:** 554

Words under the Words: Selected Poems (Nye), **Supp. XIII:** 277

Wordsworth, Dorothy, **Supp. IX:** 38

Wordsworth, William, **I:** 283, 522, 524, 525, 588; **II:** 7, 11, 17, 18, 97, 169, 273, 303, 304, 532, 549, 552; **III:** 219, 263, 277, 278, 511, 521, 523, 528, 583; **IV:** 120, 331, 343, 453, 465; **Retro. Supp. I:** 121, 196; **Supp. I Part 1:** 150, 151, 154, 161, 163, 312, 313, 349, 365; **Supp. I Part 2:** 375, 409, 416, 422, 607, 621, 622, 673, 674, 675, 676, 677, 710–711, 729; **Supp. II Part 1:** 4; **Supp. III Part 1:** 12, 15, 73, 279; **Supp. IV Part 2:** 597, 601; **Supp. V:** 258; **Supp. VIII:** 273; **Supp. IX:** 38, 41, 265, 274; **Supp. X:** 22, 23, 65, 120; **Supp. XI:** 248, 251, 312; **Supp. XIII:** 214; **Supp. XIV:** 184

Work (Alcott), **Supp. I Part 1:** 32–33, 42

Work (Dixon), **Supp. XII:** 141, **143**

"Work" (Oliver), **Supp. VII:** 243

Work and Love (Dunn), **Supp. XI:** **147–148**

"Worker" (Coleman), **Supp. XI:** 89

"Working the Landscape" (Dunn), **Supp. XI:** 151

Workin' on the Chain Gang: Shaking Off the Dead Hand of History (Mosley), **Supp. XIII:** 247, 248

"Work Notes '66" (Baraka), **Supp. II Part 1:** 47

Work of Art (Lewis), **II:** 453–454

"Work of Shading, The" (Simic), **Supp. VIII:** 277–278

Work of Stephen Crane, The (Follett, ed.), **I:** 405

"Work on Red Mountain, The" (Harte), **Supp. II Part 1:** 339

Works of Love, The (Morris), **III:** 223–224, 225, 233

"World, The" (Simic), **Supp. VIII:** 282

World According to Garp, The (Irving), **Supp. VI:** 163, 164, **170–173,** 181

World and Africa, The: An Inquiry into the Part Which Africa Has Played in World History (Du Bois), **Supp. II Part 1:** 184–185

"World and All Its Teeth, The" (Nye), **Supp. XIII:** 282

"World and the Door, The" (O. Henry), **Supp. II Part 1:** 402

"World and the Jug, The" (Ellison), **Retro. Supp. II:** 112, 119, 123

World Authors 1950–1970, **Supp. XIII:** 102

World Below, The (Miller), **Supp. XII:** **303–304**

World Below the Window, The: Poems 1937–1997 (W. J. Smith), **Supp. XIII:** 332, 340, 345

World Doesn't End, The (Simic), **Supp. VIII:** 272, **279–280**

World Elsewhere, A: The Place of Style in American Literature (Poirier), **I:** 239

"World Ends Here, The" (Harjo), **Supp. XII:** 227–228

World Enough and Time (Warren), **IV:** 243, 253–254

"World I Live In, The" (T. Williams), **IV:** 388

World I Never Made, A (Farrell), **II:** 34, 35, 424

World in the Attic, The (Morris), **III:** 222–223, 224

World in the Evening, The (Isherwood), **Supp. XIV:** 157, 164, 165, **166–167,** 170

World Is a Wedding, The (Schwartz), **Supp. II Part 2:** 643, 654–660

"World Is a Wedding, The" (Schwartz), **Supp. II Part 2:** 655–656, 657

"World Is Too Much with Us, The" (Wordsworth), **Supp. I Part 1:** 312

Worldly Hopes (Ammons), **Supp. VII:** 34

Worldly Philosophers, The

(Heilbroner), **Supp. I Part 2:** 644, 650

World of Apples, The (Cheever), **Supp. I Part 1:** 191, 193

World of David Wagoner, The (McFarland), **Supp. IX:** 323

"World of Easy Rawlins, The" (Mosley), **Supp. XIII:** 234, 236

World of Gwendolyn Brooks, The (Brooks), **Supp. III Part 1:** 83, 84

World of H. G. Wells, The (Brooks), **I:** 240, 241, 242

World of Light, A: Portraits and Celebrations (Sarton), **Supp. III Part 1:** 62; **Supp. VIII:** 249, 253, 262

World of Our Fathers: The Journey of the Eastern European Jews to America and the Life They Found and Made (Howe), **Supp. VI:** 113, 114, 116, 118, 119, **120–125; Supp. XIV:** 104

"World of Pure Experience, A" (James), **II:** 356–357

World of Raymond Chandler, The (Spender), **Supp. IV Part 1:** 119

World of Sex, The (H. Miller), **III:** 170, 178, 187

"World of the Perfect Tear, The" (McGrath), **Supp. X:** 116, 118

World of the Ten Thousand Things, The: Selected Poems (Wright), **Supp. V:** 333

"World of Tomorrow, The" (White), **Supp. I Part 2:** 663

World of Washington Irving, The (Brooks), **I:** 256–257

World Over, The (Wharton), **Retro. Supp. I:** 382

"Worlds" (Goldbarth), **Supp. XII:** 183, 189

World's Body, The (Ransom), **III:** 497, 499; **Supp. II Part 1:** 146

World's End (Boyle), **Supp. VIII:** **11–12**

World's End and Other Stories (Theroux), **Supp. VIII:** 322

"World's Fair" (Berryman), **I:** 173

World's Fair (Doctorow), **Supp. IV Part 1:** 217, 224, 227–229, 234, 236–237

World's Fair, The (Fitzgerald), **II:** 93

Worlds of Color (Du Bois), **Supp. II Part 1:** 185–186

"Worlds of Color" (Du Bois), **Supp. II Part 1:** 175

World So Wide (Lewis), **II:** 456

"World-Telegram" (Berryman), **I:** 173

World View on Race and Democracy: A Study Guide in Human Group Re-

lations (Locke), **Supp. XIV:** 205, 206

World within the Word, The (Gass), **Supp. VI:** 77

"World Without Objects Is a Sensible Place, A" (Wilbur), **Supp. III Part 2:** 550

"World Without Rodrigo, The" (Cisneros), **Supp. VII:** 68

"Worm Moon" (Oliver), **Supp. VII:** 234

"Worn Path, A" (Welty), **IV:** 262; **Retro. Supp. I:** 345–346

"Worsening Situation" (Ashbery), **Supp. III Part 1:** 17–18

"Worship" (Emerson), **II:** 2, 4–5

"Worship and Church Bells" (Paine), **Supp. I Part 2:** 521

Worster, Donald, **Supp. IX:** 19

Worthington, Marjorie, **Supp. XII:** 13

Wouldn't Take Nothing for My Journey Now (Angelou), **Supp. IV Part 1:** 10, 12, 14, 15, 16

Wound and the Bow, The: Seven Studies in Literature (Wilson), **IV:** 429

Wounds in the Rain (Crane), **I:** 409, 414, 423

Woven Stone (Ortiz), **Supp. IV Part 2:** 501, 514

Woven Stories (Ortiz), **Supp. IV Part 2:** 503

"Wraith, The" (Roethke), **III:** 542

"Wrath of God, The" (Fante), **Supp. XI:** 160, 164

"Wreath for a Bridal" (Plath), **Supp. I Part 2:** 537

Wreath for Garibaldi and Other Stories, A (Garrett), **Supp. VII:** 99–101

"Wreath of Women" (Rukeyser), **Supp. VI:** 280

Wreckage of Agathon, The (Gardner), **Supp. VI:** 63, **65–66**

Wrecking Crew (Levis), **Supp. XI:** **259–260**

"Wreck of Rivermouth, The" (Whittier), **Supp. I Part 2:** 694, 696–697

"Wreck of the Deutschland" (Hopkins), **Supp. X:** 61

"Wreck of the Hesperus, The" (Longfellow), **Retro. Supp. II:** 168, 169

Wrestler's Cruel Study, The (Dobyns), **Supp. XIII: 82–83**

"Wrestler with Sharks, A" (Yates), **Supp. XI:** 341

Wright, Bernie, **I:** 191, 193

Wright, Charles, **Supp. V:** 92, **331–346; Supp. VIII:** 272; **Supp. XIII:** 114

Wright, Chauncey, **II:** 344

Wright, Frank Lloyd, **I:** 104, 483

Wright, George, **III:** 479

Wright, Harold Bell, **II:** 467–468

Wright, Holly, **Supp. VIII:** 272

Wright, James, **I:** 291; **Supp. III Part 1:** 249; **Supp. III Part 2:** 541, **589–607; Supp. IV Part 1:** 60, 72; **Supp. IV Part 2:** 557, 558, 561, 566, 571, 623; **Supp. V:** 332; **Supp. IX:** 152, 155, 159, 265, 271, 290, 293, 296; **Supp. X:** 69, 127; **Supp. XI:** 150; **Supp. XII:** 217; **Supp. XIII:** 76

Wright, Mrs. Richard (Ellen Poplar), **IV:** 476

Wright, Nathalia, **IV:** 155

Wright, Philip Green, **III:** 578, 579, 580

Wright, Richard, **II:** 586; **IV:** 40, **474–497; Retro. Supp. II:** 4, 111, 116, 120; **Supp. I Part 1:** 51, 52, 64, 332, 337; **Supp. II Part 1:** 17, 40, 221, 228, 235, 250; **Supp. IV Part 1:** 1, 11, 84, 374; **Supp. VIII:** 88; **Supp. IX:** 316; **Supp. X:** 131, 245, 254; **Supp. XI:** 85; **Supp. XII:** 316; **Supp. XIII:** 46, 233; **Supp. XIV:** 73

Wright, Sarah, **Supp. IV Part 1:** 8; **Supp. XIII:** 295

Wright, William, **Retro. Supp. II:** 76, 77

"Writer, The" (Wilbur), **Supp. III Part 2:** 561, 562

"Writer as Alaskan, The" (Haines), **Supp. XII:** 199

Writer in America, The (Brooks), **I:** 253, 254, 257

Writer in America, The (Stegner), **Supp. IV Part 2:** 597, 599, 607

"Writers" (Lowell), **II:** 554

Writer's Almanac, The (Keillor, radio program), **Supp. XIII:** 274

Writer's America, A: Landscape in Literature (Kazin), **Supp. VIII:** 106

Writer's Capital, A (Auchincloss), **Supp. IV Part 1:** 21, 23, 24, 31

"Writer's Credo, A" (Abbey), **Supp. XIII:** 1, 17

Writer's Eye, A: Collected Book Reviews (Welty), **Retro. Supp. I:** 339, 354, 356

Writers in Revolt (Southern, Seaver, and Trocchi, eds.), **Supp. XI:** 301

Writer's Notebook, A (Maugham), **Supp. X:** 58

Writers on America (U.S. Department of State, ed.), **Supp. XIII:** 288

Writers on the Left (Aaron), **IV:** 429; **Supp. II Part 1:** 137

"Writer's Prologue to a Play in Verse" (W. C. Williams), **Retro. Supp. I:** 424

"Writer's Quest for a Parnassus, A" (T. Williams), **IV:** 392

Writers' Workshop (University of Iowa), **Supp. V:** 42

"Writing" (Nemerov), **III:** 275

"Writing About the Universe" (Mosley), **Supp. XIII:** 247

"Writing American Fiction" (Roth), **Retro. Supp. II:** 279; **Supp. I Part 1:** 192; **Supp. I Part 2:** 431; **Supp. III Part 2:** 414, 420, 421; **Supp. V:** 45

"Writing and a Life Lived Well" (Patchett), **Supp. XII:** 308

Writing a Woman's Life (Heilbrun), **Supp. IX:** 66

Writing Chicago: Modernism, Ethnography, and the Novel (Cappetti), **Supp. IX:** 4, 8

"Writing from the Inside Out: Style Is Not the Frosting; It's the Cake" (Robbins), **Supp. X:** 266

"Writing here last autumn of my hopes of seeing a hoopoe" (Updike), **Retro. Supp. I:** 335

Writing in Restaurants (Mamet), **Supp. XIV:** 246

"Writing Lesson, The" (Gordon), **Supp. IV Part 1:** 306

Writing Life, The (Dillard), **Supp. VI:** 23, 31

"Writing of Apollinaire, The" (Zukofsky), **Supp. III Part 2:** 616, 617

"Writing of *Fearless Jones*, The" (Mosley), **Supp. XIII:** 242

Writing on the Wall, The, and Literary Essays (McCarthy), **II:** 579

Writings to an Unfinished Accompaniment (Merwin), **Supp. III Part 1:** 352

Writing the World (Stafford), **Supp. XI:** 314

"Writing to Save Our Lives" (Milligan), **Supp. XIII:** 274

Writin' Is Fightin' (Reed), **Supp. X:** 241

"Writ on the Eve of My 32nd Birthday" (Corso), **Supp. XII:** 129–130

"Written History as an Act of Faith" (Beard), **Supp. I Part 2:** 492

"Wrought Figure" (McCarriston), **Supp. XIV:** 272

"Wunderkind" (McCullers), **II:** 585

Wunderlich, Mark, **Supp. XI:** 119, 132

Wundt, Wilhelm, **II:** 345

Wurster, William Wilson, **Supp. IV Part 1:** 197

WUSA (film), **Supp. V:** 301

Wuthering Heights (E. Brontë), **Supp. V:** 305; **Supp. X:** 89

WWII (Jones), **Supp. XI:** 219, 231

Wyandotté (Cooper), **I:** 350, 355

Wyatt, Robert B., **Supp. V:** 14

Wyatt, Thomas, **Supp. I Part 1:** 369

Wycherly Woman, The (Macdonald), **Supp. IV Part 2:** 473

Wylie, Elinor, **IV:** 436; **Supp. I Part 2:** 707–730; **Supp. III Part 1:** 2, 63, 318–319; **Supp. XI:** 44; **Supp. XIV:** 127

Wylie, Horace, **Supp. I Part 2:** 708, 709

Wylie, Philip, **III:** 223

Wyllys, Ruth. *See* Taylor, Mrs. Edward (Ruth Wyllys)

"Wyoming Valley Tales" (Crane), **I:** 409

Wyzewa, Théodore de, **Supp. XIV:** 336

Xaipe (Cummings), **I:** 430, 432–433, 447

Xenogenesis trilogy (O. Butler), **Supp. XIII:** 63–66, 69

Xenophon, **II:** 105

Xingu and Other Stories (Wharton), **IV:** 314, 320; **Retro. Supp. I:** 378

Xionia (Wright), **Supp. V:** 333

XLI Poems (Cummings), **I:** 429, 432, 440, 443

Yacoubi, Ahmed, **Supp. IV Part 1:** 88, 92, 93

Yage Letters, The (Burroughs), **Supp. III Part 1:** 94, 98, 100

Yagoda, Ben, **Supp. VIII:** 151

Yamamoto, Isoroku, **Supp. I Part 2:** 491

Yankee City (Warner), **III:** 60

Yankee Clipper (ballet) (Kirstein), **Supp. IV Part 1:** 82

Yankee in Canada, A (Thoreau), **IV:** 188

Yankey in London (Tyler), **I:** 344

"Yánnina" (Merrill), **Supp. III Part 1:** 329

"Yanosz Korczak's Last Walk" (Markowick-Olczakova), **Supp. X:** 70

Yarboro, Chelsea Quinn, **Supp. V:** 147

Yardley, Jonathan, **Supp. V:** 326; **Supp. XI:** 67

"Yard Sale" (Kenyon), **Supp. VII:** 169

Yates, Richard, **Supp. XI:** 333–350

"Year, The" (Sandburg), **III:** 584

Yearling, The (Rawlings), **Supp. X:** 219, 230–231, 233, 234

Year of Happy, A (Goldbarth), **Supp. XII:** 180

"Year of Mourning, The" (Jeffers), **Supp. II Part 2:** 415

Year of Silence, The (Bell), **Supp. X:** 1, 5–6, 7

"Year of the Double Spring, The" (Swenson), **Supp. IV Part 2:** 647

Year's Life, A (Lowell), **Supp. I Part 2:** 405

"Years of Birth" (Cowley), **Supp. II Part 1:** 149

Years of My Youth (Howells), **II:** 276

"Years of Wonder" (White), **Supp. I Part 2:** 652, 653

Years With Ross, The (Thurber), **Supp. I Part 2:** 619

Yeats, John Butler, **III:** 458

Yeats, William Butler, **I:** 69, 172, 384, 389, 403, 434, 478, 494, 532; **II:** 168–169, 566, 598; **III:** 4, 5, 8, 18, 19, 20, 23, 29, 40, 205, 249, 269, 270–271, 272, 278, 279, 294, 347, 409, 457, 458–460, 472, 473, 476–477, 521, 523, 524, 527, 528, 533, 540, 541, 542, 543–544, 591–592; **IV:** 89, 93, 121, 126, 136, 140, 271, 394, 404; **Retro. Supp. I:** 59, 66, 127, 141, 270, 283, 285, 286, 288, 290, 311, 342, 350, 378, 413; **Retro. Supp. II:** 185, 331; **Supp. I Part 1:** 79, 80, 254, 257, 262; **Supp. I Part 2:** 388, 389; **Supp. II Part 1:** 1, 4, 9, 20, 26, 361; **Supp. III Part 1:** 59, 63, 236, 238, 253; **Supp. IV Part 1:** 81; **Supp. IV Part 2:** 634; **Supp. V:** 220; **Supp. VIII:** 19, 21, 30, 155, 156, 190, 239, 262, 292; **Supp. IX:** 43, 119; **Supp. X:** 35, 58, 119, 120; **Supp. XI:** 140; **Supp. XII:** 132, 198, 217, 266; **Supp. XIII:** 77, **Supp. XIII:** 87; **Supp. XIV:** 7

Yellow Back Radio Broke-Down (Reed), **Supp. X:** 240, 242, 243–245

"Yellow Dog Café" (Komunyakaa), **Supp. XIII:** 126

"Yellow Girl" (Caldwell), **I:** 310

Yellow Glove (Nye), **Supp. XIII:** 275, 276–277

"Yellow Glove" (Nye), **Supp. XIII:** 276

"Yellow Gown, The" (Anderson), **I:** 114

Yellow House on the Corner, The (Dove), **Supp. IV Part 1:** 244, 245, 246, 254

"Yellow Raft, The" (Connell), **Supp. XIV:85–86**

"Yellow River" (Tate), **IV:** 141

"Yellow Violet, The" (Bryant), **Supp. I Part 1:** 154, 155

"Yellow Wallpaper, The" (Gilman), **Supp. XI: 198–199,** 207

"Yellow Woman" (Keres stories), **Supp. IV Part 1:** 327

"Yellow Woman" (Silko), **Supp. IV Part 2:** 567–568

Yelverton, Theresa, **Supp. IX:** 181

Yenser, Stephen, **Supp. X:** 207, 208

"Yentl the Yeshiva Boy" (Singer), **IV:** 15, 20

Yerkes, Charles E., **I:** 507, 512

Yerma (opera) (Bowles), **Supp. IV Part 1:** 89

"Yes" (Stafford), **Supp. XI:** 329

Yes, Mrs. Williams (W. C. Williams), **Retro. Supp. I:** 423

Yes, Yes, No, No (Kushner), **Supp. IX:** 133

"Yes and It's Hopeless" (Ginsberg), **Supp. II Part 1:** 326

Yesenin, Sergey, **Supp. VIII:** 40

"Yes! No!" (Oliver), **Supp. VII:** 243–244

"Yet Another Example of the Porousness of Certain Borders" (Wallace), **Supp. X:** 309

"Yet Do I Marvel" (Cullen), **Supp. IV Part 1:** 165, 169

Yet Other Waters (Farrell), **II:** 29, 38, 39, 40

Yevtushenko, Yevgeny, **Supp. III Part 1:** 268

Yezzi, David, **Supp. XII:** 193

Y no se lo trago la tierra (And the Earth Did Not Cover Him) (Rivera), **Supp. XIII:** 216

¡Yo! (Alvarez), **Supp. VII:** 1, 15–17

Yohannan, J. D., **II:** 20

Yonge, Charlotte, **II:** 174

"Yonnondio" (Whitman), **Supp. XIII:** 304

Yonnondio: From the Thirties (Olsen), **Supp. XIII:** 295, 295, **Supp. XIII:** 292, 296, **303–304,** 305

"Yore" (Nemerov), **III:** 283

"York Beach" (Toomer), **Supp. III Part 2:** 486

Yorke, Dorothy, **Supp. I Part 1:** 258

Yorke, Henry Vincent. *See* Green, Henry

"York Garrison, 1640" (Jewett), **Retro. Supp. II:** 141

Yosemite, The (Muir), **Supp. IX:** 185

"Yosemite Glaciers: Ice Streams of the Great Valley" (Muir), **Supp. IX:** 181

Yoshe Kalb (Singer), **IV:** 2

"You, Andrew Marvell" (MacLeish), **III:** 12–13

"You, Dr. Martin" (Sexton), **Supp. II Part 2:** 673

You, Emperors, and Others: Poems 1957–1960 (Warren), **IV:** 245

"You, Genoese Mariner" (Merwin), **Supp. III Part 1:** 343

"You All Know the Story of the Other Woman" (Sexton), **Supp. II Part 2:** 688

You Are Happy (Atwood), **Supp. XIII:** 34

"You Are Happy" (Atwood), **Supp. XIII:** 34

"You Are in Bear Country" (Kumin), **Supp. IV Part 2:** 453, 455

"You Are Not I" (Bowles), **Supp. IV Part 1:** 87

"You Begin" (Atwood), **Supp. XIII:** 34

"You Bring Out the Mexican in Me" (Cisneros), **Supp. VII:** 71

You Came Along (film), **Supp. IV Part 2:** 524

"You *Can* Go Home Again" (TallMountain), **Supp. IV Part 1:** 324–325

"You Can Have It" (Levine), **Supp. V:** 188–189

You Can't Go Home Again (Wolfe), **IV:** 450, 451, 454, 456, 460, 462, 468, 469, 470

You Can't Keep a Good Woman Down (Walker), **Supp. III Part 2:** 520, 525, 531

You Can't Take It with You (Kaufman and Hart), **Supp. XIV:** 327

"You Can't Tell a Man by the Song He Sings" (Roth), **Supp. III Part 2:** 406

"You Don't Know What Love Is" (Carver), **Supp. III Part 1:** 147

"You Have Left Your Lotus Pods on the Bus" (Bowles), **Supp. IV Part 1:** 91

You Have Seen Their Faces (Caldwell), **I:** 290, 293–294, 295, 304, 309

You Know Me Al (comic strip), **II:** 423

You Know Me Al (Lardner), **II:** 26, 415, 419, 422, 431

"You Know What" (Beattie), **Supp. V:** 33

"You Know Who You Are" (Nye), **Supp. XIII:** 275

You Might As Well Live: The Life and Times of Dorothy Parker (Keats), **Supp. IX:** 190

You Must Revise Your Life (Stafford), **Supp. XI:** 312–313, 313–314, 315

"Young" (Sexton), **Supp. II Part 2:** 680

Young, Al, **Supp. X:** 240

Young, Art, **IV:** 436

Young, Brigham, **Supp. IV Part 2:** 603

Young, Edward, **II:** 111; **III:** 415, 503

Young, Mary, **Supp. XIII:** 236, 238, 239, 240

Young, Philip, **II:** 306; **Retro. Supp. I:** 172

Young Adventure (Benét), **Supp. XI:** 44

"Young Child and His Pregnant Mother, A" (Schwartz), **Supp. II Part 2:** 650

Young Christian, The (Abbott), **Supp. I Part 1:** 38

"Young Dr. Gosse" (Chopin), **Supp. I Part 1:** 211, 216

"Young Folks, The" (Salinger), **III:** 551

Young Folk's Cyclopaedia of Persons and Places (Champlin), **III:** 577

"Young Goodman Brown" (Hawthorne), **II:** 229; **Retro. Supp. I:** 151–152, 153, 154; **Supp. XI:** 51; **Supp. XIV:** 48, 50

Young Hearts Crying (Yates), **Supp. XI:** 348

"Young Housewife, The" (W. C. Williams), **Retro. Supp. I:** 415

Young Immigrants, The (Lardner), **II:** 426

Young Lonigan: A Boyhood in Chicago Streets (Farrell), **II:** 31, 41

Young Manhood of Studs Lonigan, The (Farrell), **II:** 31, 34

Young Men and Fire (Maclean), **Supp. XIV:** 221, **231–233**

Young People's Pride (Benét), **Supp. XI:** 44

Young Poet's Primer (Brooks), **Supp. III Part 1:** 86

"Young Sammy's First Wild Oats" (Santayana), **III:** 607, 615

"Young Sor Juana, The" (Mora), **Supp. XIII:** 218

"Your Death" (Dove), **Supp. IV Part 1:** 250

"You're Ugly, Too" (Moore), **Supp. X:** 171

"Your Face on the Dog's Neck" (Sexton), **Supp. II Part 2:** 686

"Your Life" (Stafford), **Supp. XI:** 329

"Your Mother's Eyes" (Kingsolver), **Supp. VII:** 209

"You Take a Train through a Foreign Country" (Dobyns), **Supp. XIII:** 90

"Youth" (Hughes), **Supp. I Part 1:** 321

"Youth" (Huncke), **Supp. XIV:** 145

Youth and Life (Bourne), **I:** 217–222, 232

Youth and the Bright Medusa (Cather),

I: 322; **Retro. Supp. I:** 14

"Youthful Religious Experiences" (Corso), **Supp. XII:** 117

Youth of Parnassus, and Other Stories, The (L. P. Smith), **Supp. XIV:** 336

You Touched Me! (Williams and Windham), **IV:** 382, 385, 387, 390, 392–393

Yurka, Blanche, **Supp. I Part 1:** 67

Yutang, Adet, **Supp. X:** 291

Yutang, Anor, **Supp. X:** 291

Yutang, Lin, **Supp. X:** 291

Yutang, Mei-mei, **Supp. X:** 291

Yvernelle: A Legend of Feudal France (Norris), **III:** 314

Y & X (Olson), **Supp. II Part 2:** 556

Zabel, Morton Dauwen, **II:** 431; **III:** 194, 215; **Supp. I Part 2:** 721

Zagarell, Sandra A., **Retro. Supp. II:** 140, 143

"Zagrowsky Tells" (Paley), **Supp. VI:** 229

Zakrzewska, Marie, **Retro. Supp. II:** 146

Zaleski, Jeff, **Supp. XI:** 143

Zall, Paul, **Supp. XIV:** 156

Zaltzberg, Charlotte, **Supp. IV Part 1:** 374

"Zambesi and Ranee" (Swenson), **Supp. IV Part 2:** 647

Zamir, Israel, **Retro. Supp. II:** 303, 317

Zamora, Bernice, **Supp. IV Part 2:** 545

Zangwill, Israel, **I:** 229

Zanita: A Tale of the Yosemite (Yelverton), **Supp. IX:** 181

Zanuck, Darryl F., **Supp. XI:** 170; **Supp. XII:** 165

Zapata, Emiliano, **Supp. XIII:** 324

"Zapatos" (Boyle), **Supp. VIII:** 15

Zarathustra, **III:** 602

Zawacki, Andrew, **Supp. VIII:** 272

"Zaydee" (Levine), **Supp. V:** 186

Zebra-Striped Hearse, The (Macdonald), **Supp. IV Part 2:** 473

Zechariah (biblical book), **IV:** 152

Zeidner, Lisa, **Supp. IV Part 2:** 453

"Zeitl and Rickel" (Singer), **IV:** 20

Zeke and Ned (McMurtry and Ossana), **Supp. V:** 232

Zeke Proctor, Cherokee Outlaw (Conley), **Supp. V:** 232

Zelda: A Biography (Milford), **Supp. IX:** 60

"Zelda and Scott: The Beautiful and Damned" (National Portrait Gallery exhibit), **Supp. IX:** 65

Zen and the Birds of Appetite (Merton), **Supp. VIII:** 205–206, 208

Zend-Avesta (Fechner), **II:** 358

Zeno, **Retro. Supp. I:** 247

Zero db and Other Stories (Bell), **Supp. X:** 1, 5, 6

"Zeus over Redeye" (Hayden), **Supp. II Part 1:** 380

Zevi, Sabbatai, **IV:** 6

Ziegfeld, Florenz, **II:** 427–428

Zigrosser, Carl, **I:** 226, 228, 231

Zimmerman, Paul D., **Supp. IV Part 2:** 583, 589, 590

Zinman, Toby Silverman, **Supp. XIII:** 207–208, 209

Zinn, Howard, **Supp. V:** 289

Zinsser, Hans, **I:** 251, 385

Zipes, Jack, **Supp. XIV:** 126

"Zizi's Lament" (Corso), **Supp. XII:** 123

Zodiac, The (Dickey), **Supp. IV Part 1:** 178, 183–184, 185

Zola, Émile, **I:** 211, 411, 474, 500, 502, 518; **II:** 174, 175–176, 182, 194, 275, 276, 281, 282, 319, 325, 337, 338; **III:** 315, 316, 317–318, 319–320, 321, 322, 323, 393, 511, 583; **IV:** 326; **Retro. Supp. I:** 226, 235; **Retro. Supp. II:** 93; **Supp. I Part 1:** 207; **Supp. II Part 1:** 117

Zolotow, Maurice, **III:** 161

"Zone" (Bogan), **Supp. III Part 1:** 60–61

Zone Journals (Wright), **Supp. V:** 332–333, 342–343

"Zooey" (Salinger), **III:** 564–565, 566, 567, 569, 572

"Zoo Revisited" (White), **Supp. I Part 2:** 654

Zoo Story, The (Albee), **I:** 71, 72–74, 75, 77, 84, 93, 94; **III:** 281

Zorach, William, **I:** 260

Zuckerman Bound: A Trilogy and Epilogue (Roth), **Supp. III Part 2:** 423

Zuckerman Unbound (Roth), **Retro. Supp. II:** 283; **Supp. III Part 2:** 421–422

Zueblin, Charles, **Supp. I Part 1:** 5

Zuger, Abigail, **Supp. X:** 160

Zukofsky, Celia (Mrs. Louis), **Supp. III Part 2:** 619–621, 623, 625, 626–629, 631

Zukofsky, Louis, **IV:** 415; **Retro. Supp. I:** 422; **Supp. III Part 2:** 619–636; **Supp. IV Part 1:** 154; **Supp. XIV:** 279, 282, 285, 286–287

Zukofsky, Paul, **Supp. III Part 2:** 622, 623–626, 627, 628

Zuleika Dobson (Beerbohm), **Supp. I Part 2:** 714

Zverev, Aleksei, **Retro. Supp. I:** 278

Zwinger, Ann, **Supp. X:** 29

Zyda, Joan, **Retro. Supp. II:** 52

A Complete Listing of Authors in
American Writers

Abbey, Edward   Supp. XIII
Acker, Kathy   Supp. XII
Adams, Henry   Vol. I
Addams, Jane   Supp. I
Agee, James   Vol. I
Aiken, Conrad   Vol. I
Albee, Edward   Vol. I
Alcott, Louisa May   Supp. I
Algren, Nelson   Supp. IX
Alvarez, Julia   Supp. VII
Ammons, A. R.   Supp. VII
Anderson, Sherwood   Vol. I
Angelou, Maya   Supp. IV
Ashbery, John   Supp. III
Atwood, Margaret   Supp. XIII
Auchincloss, Louis   Supp. IV
Auden, W. H.   Supp. II
Auster, Paul   Supp. XII
Baker, Nicholson   Supp. XIII
Baldwin, James   Supp. I
Baldwin, James   Retro. Supp. II
Bambara, Toni Cade   Supp. XI
Banks, Russell   Supp. V
Baraka, Amiri   Supp. II
Barlow, Joel   Supp. II
Barnes, Djuna   Supp. III
Barth, John   Vol. I
Barthelme, Donald   Supp. IV
Barthelme, Frederick   Supp. XI
Bausch, Richard   Supp. VII
Beattie, Ann   Supp. V
Bell, Madison Smartt   Supp. X
Bellow, Saul   Vol. I
Bellow, Saul   Retro. Supp. II
Benét, Stephen Vincent   Supp. XI
Berry, Wendell   Supp. X

Berryman, John   Vol. I
Bierce, Ambrose   Vol. I
Bishop, Elizabeth   Supp. I
Bishop, Elizabeth   Retro. Supp. II
Blackmur, R. P.   Supp. II
Bly, Robert   Supp. IV
Bogan, Louise   Supp. III
Bourne, Randolph   Vol. I
Bowles, Paul   Supp. IV
Boyle, T. C.   Supp. VIII
Bradbury, Ray   Supp. IV
Bradstreet, Anne   Supp. I
Brodsky, Joseph   Supp. VIII
Brooks, Cleanth   Supp. XIV
Brooks, Gwendolyn   Supp. III
Brooks, Van Wyck   Vol. I
Brown, Charles Brockden   Supp. I
Bryant, William Cullen   Supp. I
Buck, Pearl S.   Supp. II
Buechner, Frederick   Supp. XII
Burke, James Lee   Supp. XIV
Burke, Kenneth   Vol. I
Burroughs, William S.   Supp. III
Butler, Octavia   Supp. XIII
Butler, Robert Olen   Supp. XII
Caldwell, Erskine   Vol. I
Cameron, Peter   Supp. XII
Capote, Truman   Supp. III
Carson, Anne   Supp. XII
Carson, Rachel   Supp. IX
Carver, Raymond   Supp. III
Cather, Willa   Vol. I
Cather, Willa   Retro. Supp. I
Chabon, Michael   Supp. XI
Chandler, Raymond   Supp. IV
Chapman, John Jay   Supp. XIV
Cheever, John   Supp. I

Chesnutt, Charles W.   Supp. XIV
Chopin, Kate   Supp. I
Chopin, Kate   Retro. Supp. II
Cisneros, Sandra   Supp. VII
Clampitt, Amy   Supp. IX
Coleman, Wanda   Supp. XI
Connell, Evan S.   Supp. XIV
Cooper, James Fenimore   Vol. I
Coover, Robert   Supp. V
Corso, Gregory   Supp. XII
Cowley, Malcolm   Supp. II
Cozzens, James Gould   Vol. I
Crane, Hart   Vol. I
Crane, Hart   Retro. Supp. II
Crane, Stephen   Vol. I
Creeley, Robert   Supp. IV
Crèvecoeur, Michel-Guillaume Jean de
    Supp. I
Crews, Harry   Supp. XI
Cullen, Countee   Supp. IV
Cummings, E. E.   Vol. I
DeLillo, Don   Supp. VI
Dickey, James   Supp. IV
Dickinson, Emily   Vol. I
Dickinson, Emily   Retro. Supp. I
Didion, Joan   Supp. IV
Dillard, Annie   Supp. VI
Dixon, Stephen   Supp. XII
Dobyns, Stephen   Supp. XIII
Doctorow, E. L.   Supp. IV
Doolittle, Hilda (H.D.)   Supp. I
Dos Passos, John   Vol. I
Doty, Mark   Supp. XI
Douglass, Frederick   Supp. III
Dove, Rita   Supp. IV
Dreiser, Theodore   Vol. I
Dreiser, Theodore   Retro. Supp. II
Du Bois, W. E. B.   Supp. II
Dubus, Andre   Supp. VII
Dunbar, Paul Laurence   Supp. II
Dunn, Stephen   Supp. XI
Eberhart, Richard   Vol. I
Edwards, Jonathan   Vol. I
Eliot, T. S.   Vol. I

Eliot, T. S.   Retro. Supp. I
Elkin, Stanley   Supp. VI
Ellison, Ralph   Supp. II
Ellison, Ralph   Retro. Supp. II
Emerson, Ralph Waldo   Vol. II
Epstein, Joseph   Supp. XIV
Epstein, Leslie   Supp. XII
Erdrich, Louise   Supp. IV
Fante, John   Supp. XI
Farrell, James T.   Vol. II
Faulkner, William   Vol. II
Faulkner, William   Retro. Supp. I
Fiedler, Leslie   Supp. XIII
Fitzgerald, F. Scott   Vol. II
Fitzgerald, F. Scott   Retro. Supp. I
Fitzgerald, Zelda   Supp. IX
Ford, Richard   Supp. V
Francis, Robert   Supp. IX
Franklin, Benjamin   Vol. II
Frederic, Harold   Vol. II
Freneau, Philip   Supp. II
Frost, Robert   Vol. II
Frost, Robert   Retro. Supp. I
Fuller, Margaret   Supp. II
Gaddis, William   Supp. IV
García, Cristina   Supp. XI
Gardner, John   Supp. VI
Garrett, George   Supp. VII
Gass, William   Supp. VI
Gibbons, Kaye   Supp. X
Gilman, Charlotte Perkins   Supp. XI
Ginsberg, Allen   Supp. II
Glasgow, Ellen   Vol. II
Glaspell, Susan   Supp. III
Goldbarth, Albert   Supp. XII
Glück, Louise   Supp. V
Gordon, Caroline   Vol. II
Gordon, Mary   Supp. IV
Gunn Allen, Paula   Supp. IV
Gurney, A. R.   Supp. V
Haines, John   Supp. XII
Hammett, Dashiell   Supp. IV
Hansberry, Lorraine   Supp. IV
Hardwick, Elizabeth   Supp. III

Harjo, Joy   Supp. XII
Harrison, Jim   Supp. VIII
Harte, Bret   Supp. II
Hass, Robert   Supp. VI
Hawthorne, Nathaniel   Vol. II
Hawthorne, Nathaniel   Retro. Supp. I
Hay, Sara Henderson   Supp. XIV
Hayden, Robert   Supp. II
Hearon, Shelby   Supp. VIII
Hecht, Anthony   Supp. X
Heller, Joseph   Supp. IV
Hellman, Lillian   Supp. I
Hemingway, Ernest   Vol. II
Hemingway, Ernest   Retro. Supp. I
Henry, O.   Supp. II
Hijuelos, Oscar   Supp. VIII
Hoffman, Alice   Supp. X
Hogan, Linda   Supp. IV
Holmes, Oliver Wendell   Supp. I
Howe, Irving   Supp. VI
Howe, Susan   Supp. IV
Howells, William Dean   Vol. II
Hughes, Langston   Supp. I
Hughes, Langston   Retro. Supp. I
Hugo, Richard   Supp. VI
Humphrey, William   Supp. IX
Huncke, Herbert   Supp. XIV
Hurston, Zora Neale   Supp. VI
Irving, John   Supp. VI
Irving, Washington   Vol. II
Isherwood, Christopher   Supp. XIV
Jackson, Shirley   Supp. IX
James, Henry   Vol. II
James, Henry   Retro. Supp. I
James, William   Vol. II
Jarrell, Randall   Vol. II
Jeffers, Robinson   Supp. II
Jewett, Sarah Orne   Vol. II
Jewett, Sarah Orne   Retro. Supp. II
Johnson, Charles   Supp. VI
Jones, James   Supp. XI
Jong, Erica   Supp. V
Justice, Donald   Supp. VII
Karr, Mary   Supp. XI

Kazin, Alfred   Supp. VIII
Kennedy, William   Supp. VII
Kenyon, Jane   Supp. VII
Kerouac, Jack   Supp. III
Kincaid, Jamaica   Supp. VII
King, Stephen   Supp. V
Kingsolver, Barbara   Supp. VII
Kingston, Maxine Hong   Supp. V
Kinnell, Galway   Supp. III
Knowles, John   Supp. XII
Komunyakaa, Yusef   Supp. XIII
Kosinski, Jerzy   Supp. VII
Kumin, Maxine   Supp. IV
Kunitz, Stanley   Supp. III
Kushner, Tony   Supp. IX
LaBastille, Anne   Supp. X
Lanier, Sidney   Supp. I
Larcom, Lucy   Supp. XIII
Lardner, Ring   Vol. II
Lee, Harper   Supp. VIII
Leopold, Aldo   Supp. XIV
Levertov, Denise   Supp. III
Levine, Philip   Supp. V
Levis, Larry   Supp. XI
Lewis, Sinclair   Vol. II
Lindsay, Vachel   Supp. I
Locke, Alain   Supp. XIV
London, Jack   Vol. II
Longfellow, Henry Wadsworth   Vol. II
Longfellow, Henry Wadsworth   Retro. Supp. II
Lowell, Amy   Vol. II
Lowell, James Russell   Supp. I
Lowell, Robert   Vol. II
Lowell, Robert   Retro. Supp. II
McCarriston, Linda   Supp. XIV
McCarthy, Cormac   Supp. VIII
McCarthy, Mary   Vol. II
McClatchy, J. D.   Supp. XII
McCourt, Frank   Supp. XII
McCoy, Horace   Supp. XIII
McCullers, Carson   Vol. II
Macdonald, Ross   Supp. IV
McGrath, Thomas   Supp. X

McKay, Claude   Supp. X
Maclean, Norman   Supp. XIV
MacLeish, Archibald   Vol. III
McMillan, Terry   Supp. XIII
McMurty, Larry   Supp. V
McNally, Terrence   Supp. XIII
McPhee, John   Supp. III
Mailer, Norman   Vol. III
Mailer, Norman   Retro. Supp. II
Malamud, Bernard   Supp. I
Mamet, David   Supp. XIV
Marquand, John P.   Vol. III
Marshall, Paule   Supp. XI
Mason, Bobbie Ann   Supp. VIII
Masters, Edgar Lee   Supp. I
Mather, Cotton   Supp. II
Matthews, William   Supp. IX
Matthiessen, Peter   Supp. V
Maxwell, William   Supp. VIII
Melville, Herman   Vol. III
Melville, Herman   Retro. Supp. I
Mencken, H. L.   Vol. III
Merrill, James   Supp. III
Merton, Thomas   Supp. VIII
Merwin, W. S.   Supp. III
Millay, Edna St. Vincent   Vol. III
Miller, Arthur   Vol. III
Miller, Henry   Vol. III
Miller, Sue   Supp. XII
Minot, Susan   Supp. VI
Momaday, N. Scott   Supp. IV
Monette, Paul   Supp. X
Moore, Lorrie   Supp. X
Moore, Marianne   Vol. III
Mora, Pat   Supp. XIII
Morison, Samuel Eliot   Supp. I
Morris, Wright   Vol. III
Morrison, Toni   Supp. III
Mosley, Walter   Supp. XIII
Muir, John   Supp. IX
Mumford, Lewis   Supp. III
Nabokov, Vladimir   Vol. III
Nabokov, Vladimir   Retro. Supp. I
Naylor, Gloria   Supp. VIII

Nemerov, Howard   Vol. III
Nichols, John   Supp. XIII
Niebuhr, Reinhold   Vol. III
Nin, Anaïs   Supp. X
Norris, Frank   Vol. III
Nye, Naomi Shihab   Supp. XIII
Oates, Joyce Carol   Supp. II
O'Brien, Tim   Supp. V
O'Connor, Flannery   Vol. III
O'Connor, Flannery   Retro. Supp. II
Odets, Clifford   Supp. II
O'Hara, John   Vol. III
Olds, Sharon   Supp. X
Oliver, Mary   Supp. VII
Olsen, Tillie   Supp. XIII
Olson, Charles   Supp. II
O'Neill, Eugene   Vol. III
Ortiz, Simon J.   Supp. IV
Ozick, Cynthia   Supp. V
Paine, Thomas   Supp. I
Paley, Grace   Supp. VI
Parker, Dorothy   Supp. IX
Parkman, Francis   Supp. II
Patchett, Ann   Supp. XII
Percy, Walker   Supp. III
Pinsky, Robert   Supp. VI
Plath, Sylvia   Supp. I
Plath, Sylvia   Retro. Supp. II
Podhoretz, Norman   Supp. VIII
Poe, Edgar Allan   Vol. III
Poe, Edgar Allan   Retro. Supp. II
Porter, Katherine Anne   Vol. III
Pound, Ezra   Vol. III
Pound, Ezra   Retro. Supp. I
Powers, Richard   Supp. IX
Price, Reynolds   Supp. VI
Proulx, Annie   Supp. VII
Purdy, James   Supp. VII
Pynchon, Thomas   Supp. II
Rand, Ayn   Supp. IV
Ransom, John Crowe   Vol. III
Rawlings, Marjorie Kinnan   Supp. X
Reed, Ishmael   Supp. X
Reznikoff, Charles   Supp. XIV

Rice, Anne   Supp. VII
Rich, Adrienne   Supp. I
Rich, Adrienne   Retro. Supp. II
Ríos, Alberto Álvaro   Supp. IV
Robbins, Tom   Supp. X
Robinson, Edwin Arlington   Vol. III
Rodriguez, Richard   Supp. XIV
Roethke, Theodore   Vol. III
Roth, Henry   Supp. IX
Roth, Philip   Supp. III
Roth, Philip   Retro. Supp. II
Rukeyser, Muriel   Supp. VI
Russo, Richard   Supp. XII
Salinas, Luis Omar   Supp. XIII
Salinger, J. D.   Vol. III
Salter, James   Supp. IX
Sandburg, Carl   Vol. III
Santayana, George   Vol. III
Sarton, May   Supp. VIII
Schwartz, Delmore   Supp. II
Sexton, Anne   Supp. II
Shanley, John Patrick   Supp. XIV
Shapiro, Karl   Supp. II
Shepard, Sam   Supp. III
Shields, Carol   Supp. VII
Silko, Leslie Marmon   Supp. IV
Simic, Charles   Supp. VIII
Simon, Neil   Supp. IV
Simpson, Louis   Supp. IX
Sinclair, Upton   Supp. V
Singer, Isaac Bashevis   Vol. IV
Singer, Isaac Bashevis   Retro. Supp. II
Smiley, Jane   Supp. VI
Smith, Logan Pearsall   Supp. XIV
Smith, William Jay   Supp. XIII
Snodgrass, W. D.   Supp. VI
Snyder, Gary   Supp. VIII
Sontag, Susan   Supp. III
Southern, Terry   Supp. XI
Stafford, William   Supp. XI
Stegner, Wallace   Supp. IV
Stein, Gertrude   Vol. IV
Steinbeck, John   Vol. IV
Stern, Gerald   Supp. IX

Stevens, Wallace   Vol. IV
Stevens, Wallace   Retro. Supp. I
Stone, Robert   Supp. V
Stowe, Harriet Beecher   Supp. I
Strand, Mark   Supp. IV
Styron, William   Vol. IV
Swenson, May   Supp. IV
Tan, Amy   Supp. X
Tate, Allen   Vol. IV
Taylor, Edward   Vol. IV
Taylor, Peter   Supp. V
Theroux, Paul   Supp. VIII
Thoreau, Henry David   Vol. IV
Thurber, James   Supp. I
Toomer, Jean   Supp. IX
Trilling, Lionel   Supp. III
Twain, Mark   Vol. IV
Tyler, Anne   Supp. IV
Updike, John   Vol. IV
Updike, John   Retro. Supp. I
Van Vechten, Carl   Supp. II
Veblen, Thorstein   Supp. I
Vidal, Gore   Supp. IV
Vonnegut, Kurt   Supp. II
Wagoner, David   Supp. IX
Walker, Alice   Supp. III
Wallace, David Foster   Supp. X
Warren, Robert Penn   Vol. IV
Welty, Eudora   Vol. IV
Welty, Eudora   Retro. Supp. I
West, Nathanael   Vol. IV
West, Nathanael   Retro. Supp. II
Wharton, Edith   Vol. IV
Wharton, Edith   Retro. Supp. I
White, E. B.   Supp. I
Whitman, Walt   Vol. IV
Whitman, Walt   Retro. Supp. I
Whittier, John Greenleaf   Supp. I
Wilbur, Richard   Supp. III
Wideman, John Edgar   Supp. X
Wilder, Thornton   Vol. IV
Williams, Tennessee   Vol. IV
Williams, William Carlos   Vol. IV
Williams, William Carlos   Retro. Supp. I

Wilson, August   Supp. VIII

Wilson, Edmund   Vol. IV

Winters, Yvor   Supp. II

Wolfe, Thomas   Vol. IV

Wolfe, Tom   Supp. III

Wolff, Tobias   Supp. VII

Wright, Charles   Supp. V

Wright, James   Supp. III

Wright, Richard   Vol. IV

Wylie, Elinor   Supp. I

Yates, Richard   Supp. XI

Zukofsky, Louis   Supp. III

ISBN 0-684-31234-4

90000

ADX - 9208

9/28/0

50

138-

PS
129
A55
———
supp. 14

ADX - 9208